Complete CompTIA A+ Guide to IT Hardware and Software

SEVENTH EDITION

CHERYL A. SCHMIDT

FLORIDA STATE COLLEGE AT JACKSONVILLE

PEARSON IT
CERTIFICATION

800 EAST 96TH STREET
INDIANAPOLIS, INDIANA 466240

Complete CompTIA A+ Guide to IT Hardware and Software, Seventh Edition

Copyright © 2016 by Pearson Education, Inc.

All rights reserved. No part of this book shall be reproduced, stored in a retrieval system, or transmitted by any means, electronic, mechanical, photocopying, recording, or otherwise, without written permission from the publisher. No patent liability is assumed with respect to the use of the information contained herein. Although every precaution has been taken in the preparation of this book, the publisher and author assume no responsibility for errors or omissions. Nor is any liability assumed for damages resulting from the use of the information contained herein.

ISBN-13: 978-0-7897-5645-9
ISBN-10: 0-7897-5645-5

Library of Congress Control Number: 2016938552

Printed in the United States of America

1 16

Trademarks

All terms mentioned in this book that are known to be trademarks or service marks have been appropriately capitalized. Pearson IT Certification cannot attest to the accuracy of this information. Use of a term in this book should not be regarded as affecting the validity of any trademark or service mark.

Warning and Disclaimer

Every effort has been made to make this book as complete and as accurate as possible, but no warranty or fitness is implied. The information provided is on an "as is" basis. The author and the publisher shall have neither liability nor responsibility to any person or entity with respect to any loss or damages arising from the information contained in this book.

Special Sales

For information about buying this title in bulk quantities, or for special sales opportunities (which may include electronic versions; custom cover designs; and content particular to your business, training goals, marketing focus, or branding interests), please contact our corporate sales department at corpsales@pearsoned.com or (800) 382-3419.

For government sales inquiries, please contact governmentsales@pearsoned.com.

For questions about sales outside the U.S., please contact intlcs@pearson.com.

Editor-in-Chief
Mark Taub

Executive Editor
Mary Beth Ray

Development Editor
Ginny Munroe

Managing Editor
Sandra Schroeder

Project Editor
Mandie Frank

Copy Editor
Deadline Driven
Publishing

Indexer
WordWise Publishing
Services

Proofreader
Chuck Hutchinson

**Technical Editor and
Contributors**
Chris Crayton
Jeff Burns
Melodie Schmidt
Karl Schmidt

Publishing Coordinator
Vanessa Evans

Cover Designer
Chuti Prasertsith

Compositor
Tricia Bronkella

Art Production
Justin Ache
Katherine Martin
Marc Durrence
Amanda McIntosh
KC Frick
Vived Graphics

Photographers
Raina Durrence
George Nichols

Contents at a Glance

Contents

Part II CompTIA 220-902 Exam Focus

About the Author

Cheryl Schmidt is a professor of Network Engineering Technology at Florida State College at Jacksonville. Prior to joining the faculty ranks, she oversaw the LAN and PC support for the college and other organizations. She started her career as an electronics technician in the U.S. Navy. She teaches computer repair and various networking topics, including CCNA, CCNP, VoIP, QoS, and wireless technologies. She has published other works with Pearson, including *IP Telephony Using CallManager Express* and *Routing and Switching in the Enterprise Lab Guide*.

Cheryl has won awards for teaching and technology, including Outstanding Faculty of the Year, Innovative Teacher of the Year, Cisco Networking Academy Instructor Excellence Award, and Cisco Networking Academy Stand Out Instructor. She has presented at U.S. and international conferences. Cheryl keeps busy maintaining her technical certifications and teaching, but also loves to travel, hike, do all types of puzzles, and read.

Dedication

A Note to Instructors:

I was a teacher long before I had the title professor. Sharing what I know has always been as natural as walking to me, but sitting still to write what I know is not as natural, so composing this text has always been one of my greatest challenges. Thank you so much for choosing this text. I thank you for sharing your knowledge and experience with your students. Your dedication to education is what makes the student experience so valuable.

A Note to Students:

Writing a textbook is really different from teaching class. I have said for years that my students are like my children, except that I don't have to pay to send them through college. I am happy to claim any of you who have this text. I wish that I could be in each classroom with you as you start your IT career. How exciting!

Another thing that I tell my students is that I am not an expert. IT support is an ever-changing field and I have been in it since PCs started being used. You have to be excited about the never-ending changes to be good in this field. You can never stop learning or you will not be very good any more. I offer one important piece of advice:

> Consistent, high-quality service boils down to two equally important things: caring and competence.
> —Chip R. Bell and Ron Zemke

I dedicate this book to you. I can help you with the competence piece, but you are going to have to work on the caring part. Do not ever forget that there are people behind those machines that you love to repair. Taking care of people is as important as taking care of the computers.

Acknowledgments

I am so thankful for the support of my family during the production of this book. My husband Karl and daughters Raina and Karalina were such a source of inspiration and encouragement. Thanks to my colleagues, adjuncts, and students at my college who offered numerous valuable suggestions for improvement and testing the new material. I am especially grateful for the help and edits provided by my sister-in-law, Melodie, and my husband, Karl. I couldn't have done this book without them. My mother, Barbara Cansler, a retired English teacher and my brother, Jeff Cansler, were a wonderful form of encouragement and entertainment. Last, I want to thank my personal technical team of Justin Ache, Raina Durrence, Marc Durrence, and Jeff Burns.

Many thanks are also due the folks at Pearson. The professionalism and support given during this edition was stellar. Thank you so much Pearson team and especially Drew Cupp, Mary Beth Ray, Ginny Munroe, Mandie Frank, and my favorite technical reviewer/hatchet man, Chris Crayton. A special thanks to Mary Beth Ray, my executive editor, who created an advisory committee for this book. I hope all of you can see the results of your contributions. I thank the whole team so much for your conscientious efforts.

Finally, thank you to the students who have taken the time to share their recommendations for improvement. You are the reason I write this book each time. Please send me any ideas and comments you may have. I love hearing from you and of your successes. I may be reached at cheryl.schmidt@fscj.edu.

Fotolia Image Credits

Chapter 1: vivat, Tatjana Brila, Hellen Sergeyeva, Bondarau, norikko, alexlmx, Oleksiy Mark, Bondarau, Petr Malyshev, vadymg, Hellen Sergeyeva

Chapter 2: robootb, ctpaep, Gudellaphoto, Ruslan Kudrin, Shawn Hempel, 100pk, Gudellaphoto, Hellen Sergeyeva

Chapter 3: Aleksei Lazukov, Oleksandr Delyk, Timur Anikin, Y. L. Photographies, Denis Dryashkin, Auran, Graham Kidd Zenith, markd800, Denis Dryashkin, markd800, Hellen Sergeyeva, Bondarau, algre, iQoncept

Chapter 4: maxhalanski, Bondarau, our_lucky_photo, stokkete

Chapter 5: yauhenka, StockPhotosArt, Dmitriy Melnikov, likasiri, Gudellaphoto, LoloStock, cristi180884, thodonal, WavebreakmediaMicro, anake, chokmoso, RZ, thodonal, unclepodger, Popova Olga, cristi180884, Stepan Popov, yauhenka, Style-Photography, Winai Tepsuttinun, magraphics.eu, vetkit, Andriy Brazhnykov, House @ Brasil, cristi180884, cristi180884

Chapter 6: Oleksiy Mark, arudolf, Joseph Scott, pongpatpic, Kataieva, Andres Rodriguez

Chapter 7: photka, leksiy Mark, Aleksandr Lazarev , orcea david, mbongo, Oliver Sved, vetkit, dcwsco, Denis Ponkratov, Sergejs Katkovskis, Vladimir Kolesnikov, Artyom Rudenko, Murat BAYSAN, Chris leachman, witthaya, lipowski, CyberVam, PVMil, Igor Groshev, Oleksiy Mark, Cake78 (3D & photo), concept w, design56, primzrider, Dmitry, Amy Walters, Giovanni Cancemi

Chapter 8: studio306fotolia, Huseyin Bas, Xuejun li, Denis Dryashkin, Olexandr, Tommroch, averz, DDRockstar, kevma20, pathdoc, magraphics.eu, Bacho Foto, kenrey.de, Oleksiy Mark, Thomas Siepmann, olya6105, schamie, Hardheadmonster, nikkytok, Piotr Pawinski, Coprid, gustavofrazao

Chapter 9: Africa Studio, violetkaipa, bloomua, Artur Marciniec, Nikolai Sorokin, Tsiumpa, Vladislav Kochelaevs, ©vetkit, Oleksiy Mark, ksena32, vetkit, JcJg Photography, chesky, putilov_denis, vetkit, vetkit, slyudmila, jiaking1, jiaking1, Calado, Yury Zap

Chapter 10: TheVectorminator, Kamiya Ichiro, burnel11, doomu, Sinisa Botas, manaemedia, mik_cz, vetkit, Dario Sabljak, lexey111, lovegtr35, science photo, Robert Szczepanek, baloon111, Thor Jorgen Udvang, Michael Pettigrew, manaemedia

Chapter 11: Welf Aaron, Syda Productions, payamona, diego cervo, goir, forest71, Alexey Rotanov, iccardomojana, 3dmavr, Renars2014, Oleksiy Mark, Yulia Mladich, grgroup, photosaint, serjiunea, Alex Ishchenko, Popova Olga, Oleksandr Kovalchuk, weerapat1003, Popova Olga, Laurentiu Iordache, ras-slava, alexlmx, quaddplusq, Denys Prykhodov, Natalia Merzlyakova, Coprid, highwaystarz, sahua d, Tyler Olson, Dmitry, venimo, mast3r, Christos Georghiou, Mathias Rosenthal, kilroy79, artisticco, fserega, ratmaner, ussatlantis, jipen, denis_romash, mickyso, Joggie Botma, yauhenka, vrihu, jipen, jipen, blue_moon_images, ras-slava, tab62, ayutaroupapa, mindscanner, kulyk, Ruslan Olinchuk, poko42, Yomka, mckaphoto, naruedom, rfvectors.com, scusi, Grafvision, cocooo, Yomka

Chapter 12: corepics, Micko1986, Stocked House Studio, Kittichai, fkdkondmi, Tyler Olson, Devyatkin, amorphis, Galyna Andrushko, cartoonresource, Sashkin, pathdoc

Chapter 13: fuyi, sutichak, rocketclips, airborne77, ChiccoDodiFC, Roman Pyshchyk, Jovan Nikolic, hywards, carlos_bcn

Chapter 14: Dmitry, Georgios Alexandris, Callum Bennetts, zhekos, SV Art, SV Art, Fotofermer, ludodesign, nengredeye, mdcracker, plus69, yurdakul, Alexey Rotanov, Karl Yamashita, airborne77, pairoj, alehdats, hoboton, eugenesergeev, Scruggelgreen, angelus_liam, hxdyl, plus69, Don_Pomidor, Oleksiy Mark, amophoto.net, Denis Dryashkin, RealVector, Denis Dryashkin, ultramcu, Oleksandr Delyk, luna2631, arrow, samsonovs, angelus_liam, Amy Walters, Oleksiy Mark, jackykids, callmerobin

Chapter 15: Oleksandr Dibrova, dizain, Carolyn Franks

Chapter 16: adrian_ilie825, ribkhan, mnovelo, Oleksiy Mark, jijomathai, anyaberkut, Thomas Jansa, mageconcept_de, antimartina

Chapter 17: Africa Studio, McCarony, Marek

Chapter 18: Jürgen Fälchle, patrimonio designs, JonikFoto.pl, qingwa, John Tomaselli, dzimin, PhotographyByMK, buchachon, Alexandr Mitiuc, Focus Pocus LTD, cartoonresource, BirDiGoL, carlos_bcn, Sean Gladwell, Elemiyan01, kasezo, baurka, AKS, Grasko, Dmitry, Cake78 (3D & photo), rommma, iQoncept

Chapter 19: bdstudio, peefay, WavebreakmediaMicro, srki66, Stillfx, ninun, petovarga, Givaga, Sherry Young, Sherry Young, weerapat1003, enterphoto, evilratalex, improvize, SimFan, yaaqov Tshuva, YOR, cartoonresource, Séa, beatpavel, noppyviva, iQoncept, iQoncept, cartoonresource, Rawpixel.com, PrettyVectors, studiostoks, dizain, Jane, cartoonresource, Seraphim Vector, JanMika, Jane Kelly

We Want to Hear from You!

As the reader of this book, *you* are our most important critic and commentator. We value your opinion and want to know what we're doing right, what we could do better, what areas you'd like to see us publish in, and any other words of wisdom you're willing to pass our way.

We welcome your comments. You can email or write to let us know what you did or didn't like about this book—as well as what we can do to make our books better.

Please note that we cannot help you with technical problems related to the topic of this book.

When you write, please be sure to include this book's title and author as well as your name and email address. We will carefully review your comments and share them with the author and editors who worked on the book.

Email: feedback@pearsonitcertification.com

Mail: Pearson IT Certification
          800 East 96th Street
          Indianapolis, IN 46240 USA

Introduction

Complete CompTIA A+ Guide to IT Hardware and Software, Seventh Edition, is an all-in-one textbook-lab manual intended for one or more courses geared toward CompTIA A+ Certification and Computer Repair. It covers all the material needed for the CompTIA A+ 220-901 and 220-902 exams. The book is written so that it is easy to read and understand, with concepts presented in building-block fashion. The book focuses on hardware, software, mobile devices, virtualization, basic networking, and security.

Some of the best features of the book include the coverage of difficult subjects in a step-by-step manner, carefully developed graphics that illustrate concepts, photographs that demonstrate various technologies, reinforcement questions, critical thinking skills, soft skills, and hands-on exercises at the end of each chapter. Also, this book is written by a teacher who understands the value of a textbook from someone who has been in IT her entire career.

What's New in the Seventh Edition?

This update has been revised to include coverage of Windows 8, Windows 10, Linux, and Mac OS X. This edition differs from the Sixth Edition Update book in the following ways:

> It conforms with the latest CompTIA A+ Exam requirements, including the CompTIA A+ 220-901 exam, as well as the CompTIA A+ 220-902 exam.
> The other peripherals chapter has been split into two chapters—Video Technologies and Printers.
> The logical troubleshooting chapter has been combined with the computer design chapter and a troubleshooting review provided.
> A new first chapter introducing the world of IT is provided. The chapter includes Internet search tips, how to use Notepad, and how to take screen shots in an effort to (1) provide useful skills for the classroom and work that may be done outside the classroom, and (2) provide tools that are useful when documenting problems in the workforce.
> Mobile devices have been expanded to include Windows Mobile, mobile accessories, and other mobile devices.
> A new chapter on OS X and Linux operating systems has great screen shots and tables in case you do not have Mac computers.
> A new chapter on operational procedures includes some of the prior safety information contained in the old disassembly and power chapter as well as the six steps of logical troubleshooting that were in the old logical troubleshooting chapter. Even though every chapter has a small amount of soft skills information, this new chapter has all of the certification-related material in one place.
> The pages on subnetting in the network chapter have been moved to an appendix.
> Chapters 1 through 10 focus on hardware. Chapters 11 covers mobile devices. Chapter 12 is on computer design and serves as a troubleshooting review. Chapters 13 and 14 cover Internet/networking concepts. Chapters 15 through 17 cover operating systems. Chapter 18 handles security concepts. Finally, Chapter 19 contains operational procedures.
> The book has always been filled with graphics and photos, but even more have been added to target those naturally drawn to the IT field. This edition is full color.
> The number of questions at the end of each chapter was reduced, but more questions are available in the test bank available from the Pearson Instructor Resource Center.

Organization of the Text

The text is organized to allow thorough coverage of all topics and also to be a flexible teaching tool. It is not necessary to cover all the chapters, nor do the chapters have to be covered in order.

> **Chapter 1** covers an introduction to IT and careers that need the information in this book. It also has computer part identification. Chapter 1 does not have a specific soft skills section as do the other chapters. Instead, it focuses on common technician qualities that are explored in greater detail in the soft skills sections of later chapters. Finally, Chapter 1 has a great introduction to using Notepad, the Windows Snipping Tool, and Internet search techniques.

> **Chapter 2** is about connecting things to the computer and port identification. Details are provided on video ports, USB and IEEE 1394 FireWire ports, and sound ports. The soft skills section is on using appropriate titles.

> **Chapter 3** details components, features, and concepts related to motherboards, including processors, cache, expansion slots, and chipsets. Active listening skills are the focus for the soft skills section.

> **Chapter 4** deals with system configuration basics. BIOS options, UEFI BIOS, and system resources are key topics. The soft skills section covers how one thing at a time should be done when replacing components.

> **Chapter 5** steps the student through how to disassemble and reassemble a computer. Tools, ESD, EMI, and preventive maintenance are discussed. Subsequent chapters also include preventive maintenance topics. Basic electronics and computer power concepts are also included in this chapter. The soft skills section involves written communication.

> **Chapter 6** covers memory installation, preparation, and troubleshooting. The importance of teamwork is emphasized as the soft skill.

> **Chapter 7** deals with storage devices including IDE PATA/SATA and SSDs (even though PATA is not on the certification exam). RAID is also covered. Phone communication skills make up the target area for soft skills in this chapter.

> **Chapter 8** covers multimedia devices, including optical drives, sound cards, cameras, scanners, and speakers. The chapter ends with a section on having a positive, proactive attitude.

> **Chapter 9** deals with video technologies that include displays, ports, and projectors. The soft skills section tries to get the student to look at a problem from the user's prospective and be more empathetic.

> **Chapter 10** provides details on printers. A discussion of work ethics finishes the chapter.

> **Chapter 11** is the new mobile device chapter. Within the chapter are details on mobile device operating systems, configuration, backup, security, and troubleshooting. A brief foray into professional appearance is in the soft skills section.

> **Chapter 12** contains a one-of-a-kind prospective on computer design. Not only are the specialized computers and components needed within those types of systems covered, but computer subsystem design is also included. Because design and troubleshooting are high on the academic learning progression, the chapter also includes a review of troubleshooting, the logic of it, error codes, and an introduction to using troubleshooting flow charts. The soft skills section targets recommendations for dealing with irate customers.

> **Chapter 13** handles Internet connectivity. Analog and digital modems, cable modems, DSL modems, and mobile connectivity including wireless, WiMax, and broadband cellular are all discussed. Internet browser configuration is covered along with the soft skill of mentoring.

> **Chapter 14** introduces networking. Basic concepts, terminology, and exercises make this chapter a favorite. The introduction to subnetting has been moved to an appendix. The focus of the soft skills section is being proactive instead of reactive.

> **Chapter 15** introduces the Windows operating system including common desktop or home icons, how to manage files and folders, the registry, what to do when the operating system fails, and how to function from a command prompt. The soft skills section includes tips on how to stay current in this fast-paced field.

> **Chapter 16** covers Windows Vista, 7, 8, and 10. Details include how to install, configure, and troubleshoot the environment. Avoiding burnout is the soft skill discussed in this chapter.

> **Chapter 17** is an exciting new chapter on Mac OS X and Linux. It is just an introduction to these two environments so that a technician is familiar with the environment and a few tools. The soft skills section talks about being humble.

> **Chapter 18** describes computer, mobile device, and network security. The exercises include file and folder security, event monitoring, and local policy creation. The soft skills section is on building customer trust.

> **Chapter 19** guides the student through operational procedures such as workplace safety, recycling, disposal, a review of power protection, a review of the six troubleshooting steps, and brief coverage of the soft skills that are on the CompTIA 220-902 A+ certification exam.

Features of This Book

The following key features of the book are designed to enable a better learning experience.

> **OBJECTIVES**   Each chapter begins with *both* chapter objectives and the CompTIA A+ exam objectives.

In this chapter you will learn:

> To recognize and identify important motherboard parts

> To explain the basics of how a processor works

> Issues to consider when upgrading or replacing the motherboard or processor

> Information regarding GPUs

> How to add cards to computers

> The differences between PCI, PCI-X, AGP, and PCIe adapters and slots

> Motherboard technologies such as HyperTransport, HyperThreading, and multi-core

> The benefits of active listening

CompTIA Exam Objectives:

What CompTIA A+ exam objectives are covered in this chapter?

✓ **901-1.2**   Explain the importance of motherboard components, their purpose, and properties.

✓ **901-1.4**   Install and configure PC expansion cards.

✓ **901-1.6**   Install and configure various types of CPUs and apply the appropriate cooling method.

✓ **901-4.1**   Given a scenario, troubleshoot common problems related to motherboards, RAM, CPU, and power with appropriate tools.

✓ **902-5.4**   Demonstrate proper communication techniques and professionalism.

> **GRAPHICS AND PHOTOGRAPHS**   Many more full-color images and all-new graphics have been added to better illustrate the concepts.

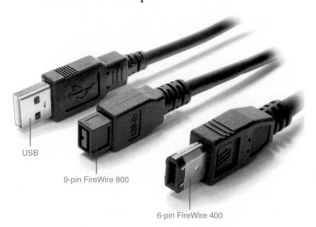

USB

9-pin FireWire 800

6-pin FireWire 400

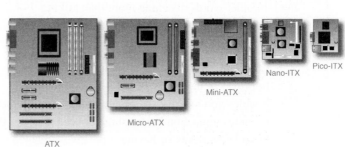

ATX

Micro-ATX

Mini-ATX

Nano-ITX

Pico-ITX

> **TECH TIPS** The chapters are filled with Tech Tips that highlight technical issues and certification exam topics.

TECH TIP

What if I don't have the right IEEE 1394 cable?

FireWire devices can have three types of connectors—4-, 6-, and 9-pin connectors. A 4-pin cable does not provide for voltage over the IEEE 1394 bus. Placing a 6-pin connection on a FireWire 800 cable reduces connection speeds to a maximum of 400Mb/s. Converters can be purchased to convert 4- to 6-pin or 6- to 9-pin connectors.

> **KEY TERMS IN CONTEXT** As you read the chapter, terms that appear in blue are considered key terms and are defined in the glossary.

Motherboards come in different sizes, known as **form factors**. The most common motherboard form factor is **ATX**. The different types of ATX are known as **micro-ATX** (sometimes shown as µATX, **mini-ATX**, FlexATX, EATX, WATX, nano-ATX, pico-ATX, and mobileATX). A smaller form factor is **ITX**, which comes in **mini-ITX**, nano-ITX, and pico-ITX sizes. Some motherboards, such as the NLX and LPX form factors, had a riser board that attached to the smaller motherboard. Adapters go into the slots on the riser board instead of into motherboard slots. Figure 3.39 shows some of the motherboard form factors.

> **KEY TERMS LIST** At the end of the chapter, all key terms are listed with page references to which to refer for context.

Key Terms

adapters 15	hard drive 13	optical drive...................13
BIOS 11	hardware.....................10	optical mouse 17
bit 19	keyboards 18	output device.................11
byte...........................19	kilobyte 20	PC.................................9
device driver................10	KVM switch...................12	power supply 12
display.......................11	megabyte......................20	RAM 14
expansion slot..............15	memory 14	software........................10
firmware 11	motherboard.................14	terabyte........................21
gigabyte.....................21	operating system 10	

> **SOFT SKILLS** Technology is not the only thing you must learn and practice; each chapter offers advice, activities, and examples of how to be a good tech, an ethical tech, a good work mate, a good communicator, and so on.

SOFT SKILLS—ACTIVE LISTENING

Active listening is participating in a conversation where you focus on what the customer is saying—in other words, listening more than talking. For a technician, active listening has the following benefits:

> Enables you to gather data and symptoms quickly
> Enables you to build customer rapport
> Improves your understanding of the problem
> Enables you to solve the problem more quickly because you understand the problem better
> Provides mutual understanding between you and the customer
> Provides a means of having a positive, engaged conversation rather than having a negative, confrontational encounter

> CHAPTER SUMMARY   Recap the key concepts of the chapter, and use this for review to ensure you've mastered the chapter's learning objectives.

Chapter Summary

> Easily identify various ports to determine which device attaches to them: VGA, DVI, HDMI, DisplayPort, Thunderbolt, USB, IEEE 1394, 3.5mm sound jack, TOSLINK, RCA jack, PS/2, RJ-45, eSATA, and RJ-11.

> The most popular method for adding devices to desktops, laptops, and tablets is to use a USB port.

> USB 3.0/3.1 will accept 3.0/3.1 and older devices and provide more power. You can add additional ports by connecting a USB hub.

> Up to five USB hubs can be daisy-chained to one port. Upstream ports connect to the computer or another USB port. Devices connect to downstream ports.

> USB hubs can be self-powered or bus powered.

> IEEE 1394 devices do not have to have a computer port and can be cabled to each other; otherwise, an IEEE 1394 device can be cabled to a port or a hub.

> Certification Exam Tips   Read through these tips on the CompTIA A+ exams so you aren't caught off guard when you sit for the exam.

A+ CERTIFICATION EXAM TIPS

✓ A lot of questions from both exams can come from this chapter, especially in the troubleshooting areas. Review the troubleshooting bullets. Research issues on the Internet and read people's postings. Their stories and frustration (and successes) will stick in your mind and help you with the exam.

✓ Go to at least one computer and go through the BIOS/UEFI menus. Review what types of things can be configured through BIOS/UEFI. Review Table 4.1 blue-colored options.

✓ Review the many differences between a BIOS and a UEFI BIOS.

✓ Review different sections of Device Manager. Device Manager is a critical tool for troubleshooting computer issues. Know how to determine what driver is installed. Practice finding drivers on Internet sites.

✓ Know reasons you would upgrade the BIOS.

✓ Review the key terms in Table 4.1 and what each of those settings control.

> **REVIEW QUESTIONS**   Hundreds of review questions, including true/false, multiple choice, matching, fill-in-the-blank, and open-ended questions, assess your knowledge of the topics taught in each chapter.

Review Questions

1. Match the part to the description.
    _____ motherboard   a. Converts AC to DC
    _____ RAM   b. Holds the most data
    _____ optical drive   c. Has the most electronics
    _____ hard drive   d. Fits in an expansion slot
    _____ adapter   e. Contents disappear when power is off
    _____ power supply   f. Holds a disc

2. Which career choice(s) would probably *not* need the information in this book? (Select all that apply.)
    [PC repair technician | database administrator | programmer | helpdesk support | office manager | network cable installer | PC power supply reseller]

3. Which of the following are important suggested Internet search tips? (Choose two.)

    A. Try another search engine when the first one does not provide satisfactory results.

    B. Use as many common words as possible like the, in, at, or for.

    C. Put quotations around two or more words that might be found consecutively in output.

    D. Use as few words as possible.

    E. Avoid using the name of the equipment manufacturer.

4. Which type of memory is commonly found on a motherboard? _____

5. When lifting a heavy computer, you should squat, bend at the knees, and use your legs to lift. [T | F]

> **APPLYING YOUR KNOWLEDGE**   There are hundreds of Exercises, Activities, and Labs by which to put into practice what you are learning. For example:

> **EXERCISES**   Sometimes called "paper labs," these need no lab devices to complete in the classroom or for homework.

Exercises

Exercise 2.1 Computer Port Identification

Objective: To identify various computer ports correctly

Procedure: Identify each computer port in Figure 2.42.

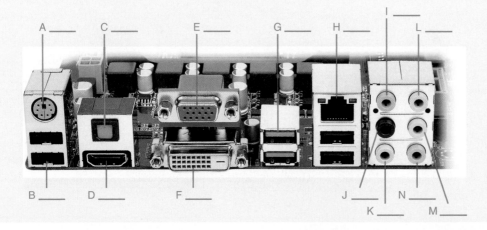

> **ACTIVITIES**   Extensive practice with Internet Discovery, Soft Skills, and Critical Thinking Skills round out your technical knowledge so that you can be prepared for IT work. These can be used to "Flip the Classroom"; instead of lectures, instruction is interactive and in the hands of the students.

Activities

Internet Discovery

Objective: To obtain specific information from the Internet regarding a computer or its associated parts

Parts: Computer with Internet access

Procedure: Complete the following procedure and answer the accompanying questions.

Questions: For Questions 1–4: Obtain technical information about a particular computer (maybe your own model or a model number given by the instructor). Answer the following questions based on the information. You may need to obtain more documents or you may need to select a different computer model to answer questions. Please use only one computer model.

Soft Skills

Objective: To enhance and fine-tune a future technician's ability to listen, communicate in both written and oral forms, and support people who use computers in a professional manner

Procedure:

1.   In teams of two, one student writes a professional note that contains Internet acronyms that are commonly used for texting. The other student tries to then guess what the acronyms mean. Together, rewrite the note so it is more professional.

2.   Draft an email to a pretend computer customer that you just met yesterday for the first time. You did not have the part needed to repair the computer, but now the part has come in. Be sure you use professionalism in your email.

Critical Thinking Skills

Objective: To analyze and evaluate information as well as apply learned information to new or different situations

Procedure:

1.   Find an advertisement for a computer in a local computer flyer, in a newspaper, in a magazine, in a book, or on the Internet. List which ports you know in one column and the ports you do not know in the other column. Select one port you do not know and research that component. Write the new information and share with at least one other person.

_____

2.   Work in groups of three. As a group, do you think future computers will only have wireless connections or continue to have both wired and wireless connectivity? Why or why not? What might be some hindrances that would prevent this from happening?

_____

_____

_____

_____

_____

3.   Provide five tips that might help someone identify the different computer ports. If possible, each person in the class should state a tip without duplicating someone else's tip.

> **LAB EXERCISES**   More than 140 labs enable you to link theory to practical experience

Labs

Lab 3.1 Using Windows to Discover Processor Information

Objective: To identify various computer features such as the type of processor being used, processor socket, and additional expansion ports

Parts: Computer with Windows Vista, 7, 8, or 10

Procedure: Complete the following procedure and answer the accompanying questions.

Note: If you do not remember how to locate an application, please refer to Lab 1.1 for Windows 7, Lab 1.2 for Windows 8, or Lab 1.3 for Windows 10.

1. Boot the computer and log in.

    In Windows Vista or 7, access *Windows Explorer* through *All Programs, Search programs and files.*

    In Windows 8, access *File Explorer* using the *Search* function or a desktop tile.

    In Windows 10, access *File Explorer* using the *Search the web and Windows* search textbox or through the Start button.

2. Right-click on the computer in the far left panel. This is commonly shown as Computer or This PC. Select *Properties*. Use the information displayed to answer the questions.

    Which processor is used?

    _____

    How much RAM is installed?

    _____

3. Click on the *Device Manager* link in the left panel. From the top menu, select *View > Devices by type*.

4. If only one line displays in the *Computer* category, expand the information by clicking on the icon to the left of the computer name. Is the computer a 32- or 64-bit computer?

    _____

5. Expand the *Processors* category.

    How many CPUs are listed?

    _____

6. Expand the *System devices* category.

    List any expansion slot types shown.

    _____

    _____

7. Close all windows.

Companion Website

Register this book to get access to videos and other study materials plus additional bonus content to help you succeed with this course and the certification exam. Check this site regularly for any updates or errata that might become available for this book. Be sure to check the box that you would like to hear from us to receive news of updates and exclusive discounts on related products.

To access this companion website, follow the steps below:

1. Go to www.pearsonITcertification.com/register and log in or create a new account.
2. Enter the ISBN: 978-0-7897-5645-9
3. Answer the challenge question as proof of purchase.
4. Click the "Access Bonus Content" link in the Registered Products section of your account page, to be taken to the page where your downloadable content is available.

Please note that many of our companion content files can be very large, especially image and video files.

If you are unable to locate the files for this title by following the steps above, please visit www.pearsonITcertification.com/contact and select the "Site Problems/Comments" option. Our customer service representatives will assist you.

CompTIA A+ Exam Objectives

To get CompTIA A+ certified, you must pass both the 220-901 and 220-902 certification exams.

Tables I-1 and I-2 summarize the domain content for each exam.

TABLE I-1 CompTIA A+ 220-901 exam

Domain	Percentage of Examination
1.0 Hardware	34%
2.0 Networking	21%
3.0 Mobile Devices	17%
4.0 Hardware & Network Troubleshooting	28%
Total	100%

TABLE I-2 CompTIA A+ 220-902 Exam

Domain	Percentage of Examination
1.0 Windows Operating Systems	29%
2.0 Other Operating Systems & Technologies	12%
3.0 Security	22%
4.0 Software Troubleshooting	24%
5.0 Operational Procedures	13%
Total	100%

Table I-3 shows a summary of the exam domains by chapter. Each chapter will list the certification objectives it covers in the chapter opener. See Appendix B on the companion website for a detailed table that identifies where you can find all the CompTIA A+ exam objectives covered in this book.

TABLE I-3 Summary of Exam Domains by Chapter

Table of Contents	220-901 Domains	220-902 Domains
Chapter 1: Intro to the World of IT	1	5
Chapter 2: Connectivity	1	5
Chapter 3: On the Motherboard	1, 4	5
Chapter 4: Introduction to Configuration	1, 4	
Chapter 5: Disassembly and Power	1, 4	1, 4, 5
Chapter 6: Memory	1, 4	1
Chapter 7: Storage Devices	1, 4	1, 4, 5
Chapter 8: Multimedia Devices	1	1, 5
Chapter 9: Video Technologies	1, 4	1
Chapter 10: Printers	1, 4	1, 5
Chapter 11: Mobile Devices	1, 3, 4	2, 3, 4
Chapter 12: Computer Design and Troubleshooting Review	1, 4	5
Chapter 13: Internet Connectivity	1, 2	1, 3, 4
Chapter 14: Networking	1, 2, 4	1, 2, 3, 5
Chapter 15: Basic Windows		1, 2
Chapter 16: Windows Vista, 7, 8, and 10		1, 2, 4
Chapter 17: OS X and Linux Operating Systems		2, 4
Chapter 18: Computer and Network Security	1	1, 2, 3, 4, 5
Chapter 19: Operational Procedures		5

CompTIA.

Becoming a CompTIA Certified IT Professional is Easy

It's also the best way to reach greater professional opportunities and rewards.

Why Get CompTIA Certified?

Growing Demand

Labor estimates predict some technology fields will experience growth of over 20% by the year 2020.* CompTIA certification qualifies the skills required to join this workforce.

Higher Salaries

IT professionals with certifications on their resume command better jobs, earn higher salaries and have more doors open to new multi-industry opportunities.

Verified Strengths

91% of hiring managers indicate CompTIA certifications are valuable in validating IT expertise, making certification the best way to demonstrate your competency and knowledge to employers.**

Universal Skills

CompTIA certifications are vendor neutral—which means that certified professionals can proficiently work with an extensive variety of hardware and software found in most organizations.

 Learn >  Certify > Work

Learn more about what the exam covers by reviewing the following:

- Exam objectives for key study points.

- Sample questions for a general overview of what to expect on the exam and examples of question format.

- Visit online forums, like LinkedIn, to see what other IT professionals say about CompTIA exams.

Purchase a voucher at a Pearson VUE testing center or at CompTIAstore.com.

- Register for your exam at a Pearson VUE testing center:

- Visit pearsonvue.com/CompTIA to find the closest testing center to you.

- Schedule the exam online. You will be required to enter your voucher number or provide payment information at registration.

- Take your certification exam.

Congratulations on your CompTIA certification!

- Make sure to add your certification to your resume.

- Check out the CompTIA Certification Roadmap to plan your next career move.

Learn more: **Certification.CompTIA.org/aplus**

* Source: CompTIA 9th Annual Information Security Trends study: 500 U.S. IT and Business Executives Responsible for Security
** Source: CompTIA Employer Perceptions of IT Training and Certification

1 Intro to the World of IT

In this chapter you will learn:

> Qualities a technician should have

> Basic skills needed to function in the Windows environment and in the technical world

> Important computer parts

> Basic computer terms

CompTIA Exam Objectives:

What CompTIA A+ exam objectives are covered in this chapter?

✓ 901-1.12 Install and configure common peripheral devices.

✓ 902-5.1 Given a scenario, use appropriate safety procedures

✓ 902-5.4 Demonstrate proper communication techniques and professionalism.

Who Needs This Book?

More types of people than you would first think need this book. People who obviously need this information are those who will fix computers or work on a help desk or support desk. However, there are other types of users who might not be so obvious. Many folks who break into the information technology (IT) world do so through jobs that require the A+ certification. Consider medical electronics technicians who repair common equipment used in hospitals. These technicians need this course because so many of their devices connect to a PC or have the PC-based software that controls the medical device. Further, the medical devices commonly attach to the wired and wireless network.

Another related field that must get A+ certified includes programmers. Programmers are expected to be able to install and remove software and hardware as part of their job. Similarly, database administrators might need to upgrade a server. Web developers might want to build their own machines. Look at Figure 1.1 to see the types of jobs of people who need the information in this book. It might also give you ideas about something you might like to do for a career.

FIGURE 1.1   IT roles

Technician Qualities

Each chapter includes a small bit of space on qualities a technician should possess or strive toward. Spending a little brain power on improving what many call your "soft skills" will pay off in promotions and divergence into other IT-related fields. Three of the most important qualities that a technician can have are active listening skills, a good attitude, and logic. Active listening means that you truly listen to what a person (especially one who is having a problem) is saying. Active listening skills involve good eye contact, nodding your head every now and then to show that you are following the conversation, taking notes on important details, and avoiding distractions such as incoming cell phone calls or text messages. Clarify customer statements by asking pertinent questions and avoid interrupting. Allow customers to complete their sentences. Many technicians jump into a problem the moment they hear the first symptom described by the user. Listen to the entire problem. Do not act superior because you know terms and things that they do not. Ask open-ended questions—questions that allow the user to expand on the answer rather than answer with a single word, such as *yes* or *no*. Figure 1.2 illustrates this point.

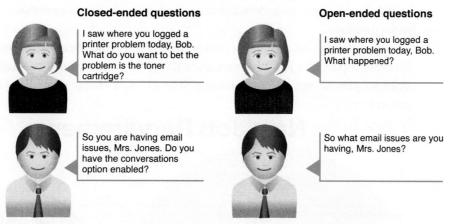

Closed-ended questions

I saw where you logged a printer problem today, Bob. What do you want to bet the problem is the toner cartridge?

So you are having email issues, Mrs. Jones. Do you have the conversations option enabled?

Open-ended questions

I saw where you logged a printer problem today, Bob. What happened?

So what email issues are you having, Mrs. Jones?

Allow the users to state the problem without leading them toward a solution. Restate the problem to ensure understanding and ask questions for clarity and to narrow your understanding.

FIGURE 1.2   Asking technical questions

A positive attitude is probably the best quality a technician can possess. Many technicians treat customers abruptly, not taking the time to listen to their problems or to find the best solutions. A good attitude is helpful when a user is upset because a computer or an attached device is not working properly. A technician with a positive attitude does not diminish the customer's problem; every problem is equally important to the computer user. A positive attitude is critical for being successful in the computer service industry. Figure 1.3 shows how negative attitudes affect your success.

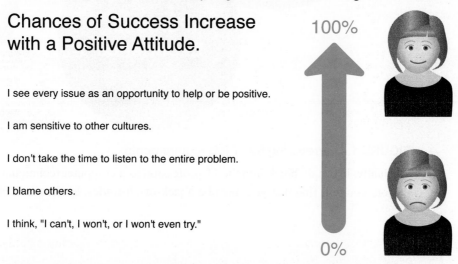

Chances of Success Increase with a Positive Attitude.

100%

I see every issue as an opportunity to help or be positive.

I am sensitive to other cultures.

I don't take the time to listen to the entire problem.

I blame others.

I think, "I can't, I won't, or I won't even try."

0%

FIGURE 1.3   Have a positive attitude

A technician must be familiar with and thoroughly understand computer terminology to (1) use logic to solve problems; (2) speak intelligently to other technical support staff in clear, concise, and direct statements; (3) explain the problem to the user; and (4) be proficient in the field. Changes occur so frequently that technicians must constantly update their skills. Develop a passion for learning the latest information and searching for information that helps you solve problems. Do not develop tunnel vision in that you think the answer can be only one thing. Step back and look at the problem so that all possible issues can be evaluated. Be logical in your assessment and methods used to troubleshoot and repair. This book will help you with all of this by explaining computer terminology in easy-to-understand terms and providing analogies that can be used when dealing with customers.

Before delving into computer topics, you should remember that a class can't fully prepare you for every aspect of a job. You must learn things on your own and constantly strive to update your skills so you do not become obsolete. The IT field changes rapidly. Figure 1.4 illustrates this concept.

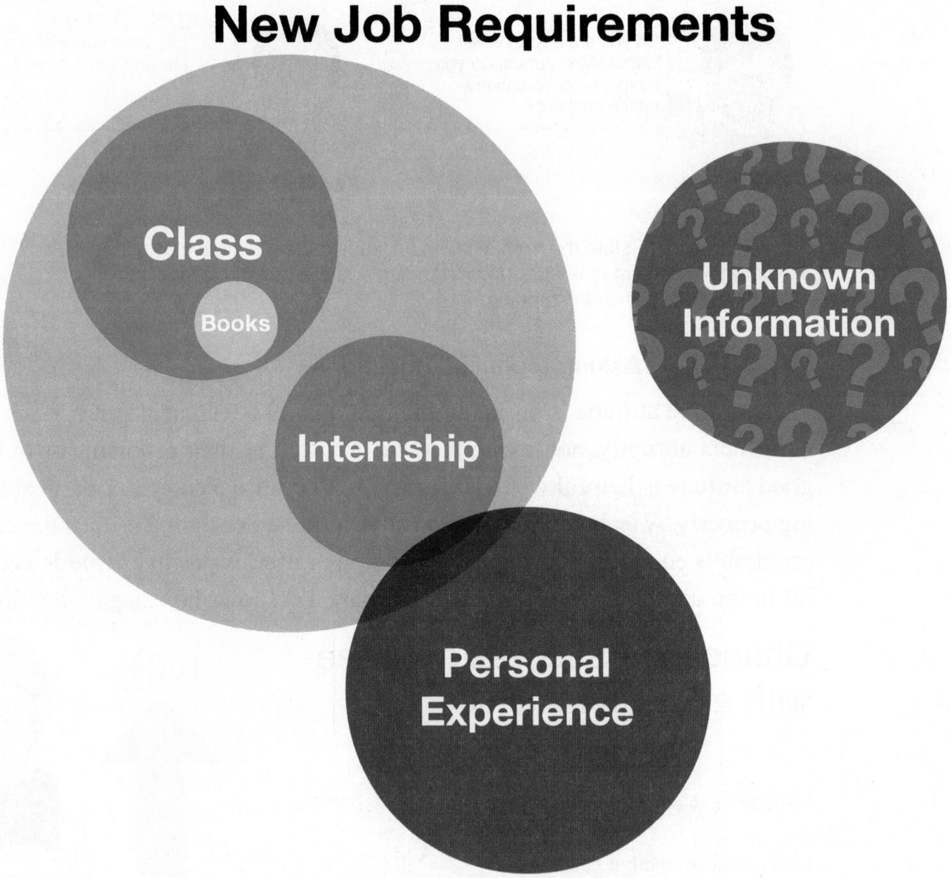

New Job Requirements

FIGURE 1.4   Preparing for IT job requirements

Finally, if you do break into the IT profession as a computer technician or as a helpdesk support person, you will find that you must be a jack-of-all-trades, as shown in Figure 1.5.

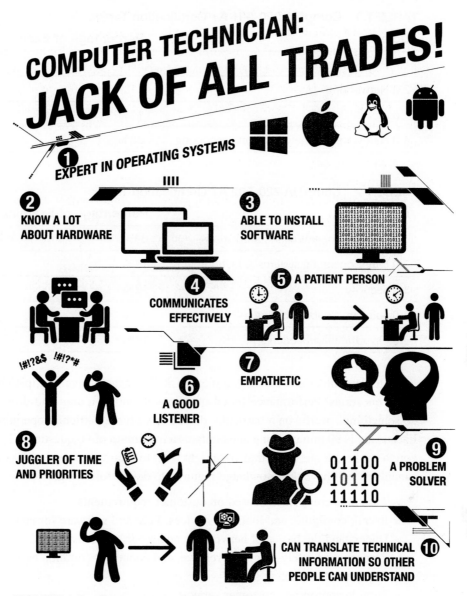

FIGURE 1.5 Computer technician skills

Breaking into IT with the CompTIA A+ Certification

Many information technology (IT) jobs require the A+ certification. Even if not required, the certification shows that you have a good understanding of how computers work. This certification does not guarantee you a job, but it does open doors in that a company may interview you in the absence of IT experience.

A+ certification requires that you take two exams (220-901 and 220-902). You do not have to take both of the exams on the same day. You do not have to take the 220-901 exam before you take the 220-902 exam. Each exam covers specific material. Table 1.1 shows the major categories for the 220-901 exam and how they map to information in this book. Table 1.2 is for the 220-902 exam.

TABLE 1.1   CompTIA 220-901 A+ Certification Topics

Domain	Percentage of Examination	Chapter(s)
1.0 Hardware	34%	1–10, 12
2.0 Networking	21%	13–14
3.0 Mobile devices	17%	11
4.0 Hardware and network troubleshooting	28%	1–14

TABLE 1.2   CompTIA 220-902 A+ Certification Topics

Domain	Percentage of Examination	Chapter(s)
1.0 Windows operating systems	29%	15–16
2.0 Other operating systems & technologies	12%	17
3.0 Security	22%	18
4.0 Software troubleshooting	24%	15–18
5.0 Operational procedures	13%	19

"What are the exams like?" you might ask. The exams have multiple choice and performance-based questions. Performance-based questions might be a drag-and-drop scenario or ask you to do something specific on a particular device or within a particular operating system environment. Each exam is 90 minutes long and contains a maximum of 90 questions. The testing system allows you to bookmark questions that you might want to return to at the end if you have time. Successful candidates will have the knowledge required to do the following:

> Assemble components based on customer requirements.
> Install, configure, and maintain devices, PCs, and software for end users.
> Understand the basics of networking and security/forensics.
> Properly and safely diagnose, resolve, and document common hardware and software issues.
> Apply troubleshooting skills.
> Provide appropriate customer support.
> Understand the basics of virtualization, desktop imaging, and deployment.

More information can be found on the CompTIA website (www.comptia.org).

At the beginning of each chapter, you will see a listing of which of the CompTIA A+ exam objectives are covered in that chapter. At the end of each chapter, I've provided some A+ Certification Exam Tips—tips to definitely pay attention to if you plan on taking the A+ exam. By the end of this course, you will have learned all the topics covered on the certification exam; however, before you actually take the exam, I recommend that you dedicate some time to review the chapters in this book thoroughly, study the objectives, and take some practice exams. Pearson IT Certification, the publisher of this book, develops many different certification exam prep resources that will suit your study style. See the back of this book for more information or go to http://pearsonitcertification. com/aplus to browse the options.

Basic Skills for This Course

In order to repair a computer, you need a few basic skills that include being familiar with the keyboard and inputting information, searching for information on the Internet, and capturing information. Just because you may not be a good typist does not mean that you will not be good in an IT-related field.

Searching for Information on the Internet

IT people need to use all available resources including online resources. As noted, you need to be capable of searching for information online. Figure 1.6 illustrates various online resources that IT people search all the time.

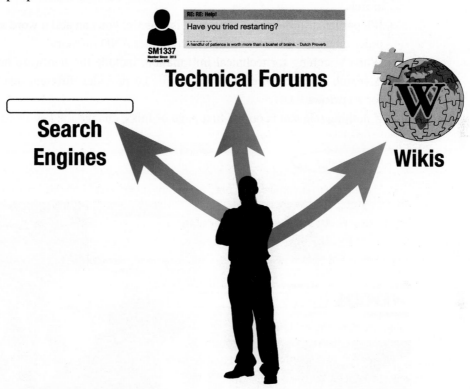

FIGURE 1.6 Search skills

Each chapter in the book has an activity at the end of it that enables you to practice searching the Internet for information relevant to the chapter. Tips for searching include the following:

> Search engines use different algorithms, so if one does not work, try another one. Examples of search engines are Google, Bing, Yahoo, AOL, Ask, and Lycos. To access a search engine, open a web browser and type one of the search engine names followed by ".com." Figure 1.7 shows www.Lycos.com entered in the address bar.

> Use descriptive key words.

> Do not include common words like *the*, *in*, *at*, or *for* because search engines tend to skip these words anyway. If you do want to use them, put a plus sign (⊞) in front of the word.

> Avoid using the plural or past tense of a word to avoid elimination of pages that are relevant. For example, to search for how to install a Bluetooth headset, avoid using the word *installation*, *installed*, or *installing* in the search window. Simply include the word "*install*."

> If there are several words used together (an exact phrase) such as Windows 10, put quotations around the phrase—"*Windows 10*".
> Use as many distinguishing words as possible.
> If two words mean the same and are commonly used, use the word "or" in the search. For example, if you were searching for generic information on a dot matrix printer, which is sometimes called an impact printer, the search would be as follows: `"dot matrix" or impact printer`. Note that the vertical bar (I), which is the key above the [←Enter] key, can be used instead of the word "or."
> If a particular term can have two meanings such as the word *memory* relating to something inside a computer or else relating to a brain function, then you can use the minus sign in order to keep that information from being displayed. Memory –brain is an example of such a search.
> If a particular term such as memory is generic, you can add a word and use the word *AND* in order to clarify the search, such as computer AND memory.
> When searching for technical information, include the hardware or software manufacturer. A search for `Microsoft Windows 10` provides different results than simply a search for `Windows 10`.
> If nothing relevant is on the first page of links, change the key words used in your search.

FIGURE 1.7   Lycos search engine

Take the situation of a keyboard that intermittently works on a Microsoft Surface computer. The keyboard does not come standard as part of a Surface purchase. You do not own a Surface yourself and are unfamiliar with the tablet, but must support it. An example of what might be typed into a search engine is `Microsoft Surface intermittent keyboard`. A lab at the end of the chapter demonstrates search techniques.

Capturing Files

Sometimes, part of technical documentation is being able to capture what is on the screen. Windows Vista (any version but Home Basic) and higher comes with a great tool for doing just that. The Snipping Tool makes documenting problems easy. It is also easy to copy what you capture into other applications. No matter what IT job you may have when you enter the workforce, documentation is a part of all IT jobs. A lab at the end of the chapter shows how you might use this tool.

Creating a Text File

Another part of documentation might involve creating or using a text file known as a .txt file. You might need to send it as an attachment or you might need to create a text file as part of the documentation process or as part of the job. Sometimes a text file is the easiest way to create a file, especially on a mobile device. Text files can be created using a word processor and the *Save As* process, or can be created using specific text software or an app. Text files are popular because they can be opened by so many applications or other mobile apps. Text files commonly include only text, but not multiple fonts or graphics. Windows ships with a basic application called Notepad that can be used to create or open text files. A lab at the end of the chapter helps with this skill.

Types of Computers

The simplest place to start to learn about computer technical support is with the devices themselves. Computer devices come in many shapes and sizes. The **PC**, or personal computer, comes in desktop, tower, and all-in-one models, as well as mobile models such as a laptops, tablets, and ultrabooks. Figure 1.8 shows some of the computing devices technical staff are expected to support.

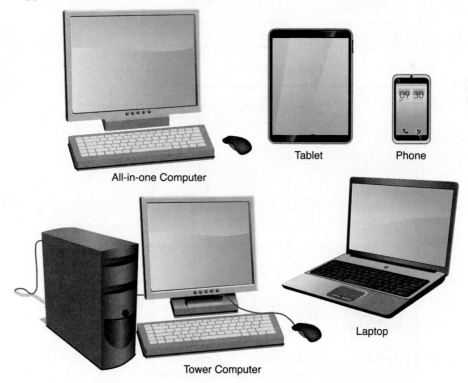

FIGURE 1.8   Types of computers

Basic Computer Parts

Computer systems include hardware, software, and firmware. **Hardware** is something you can touch and feel—the physical computer and the parts inside the computer are examples of hardware. The monitor, keyboard, and mouse are hardware components. **Software** interacts with the hardware. Windows, Linux, OS X, Microsoft Office, Solitaire, Google Chrome, Adobe Acrobat Reader, and WordPerfect are examples of software.

Without software that directs the hardware to accomplish something, a computer is no more than a doorstop. Every computer needs an important piece of software called an **operating system**, which coordinates the interaction between hardware and software applications. The operating system also handles the interaction between a user and the computer. Examples of operating systems include Windows 7, 8, 8.1, and 10, OS X, and various Linux systems, such as Red Hat and Ubuntu.

A **device driver** is a special piece of software designed to enable a hardware component. The device driver enables the operating system to recognize, control, and use the hardware component. Device drivers are hardware and operating system specific. For example, a printer requires a specific device driver when connected to a computer loaded with Windows 7. The same printer will most likely require a different device driver when using Windows 8 or 10. Each piece of installed hardware requires a device driver for the operating system being used. Figure 1.9 shows how hardware and software must work together.

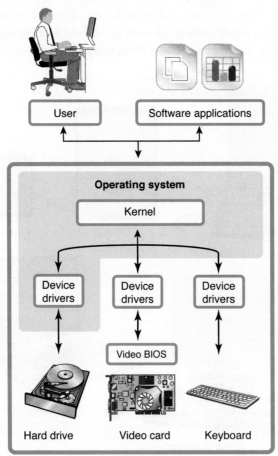

FIGURE 1.9 Hardware and software

Notice in Figure 1.9 the operating system kernel. The kernel is the central part of an operating system. The kernel is the connection between hardware and the applications being used.

Software applications are normally loaded onto the hard drive. When a user selects an application, the operating system controls the loading of the application. The operating system also controls any hardware devices (such as the mouse, keyboard, monitor through the video adapter, and printer) used with the application.

Firmware is a combination of hardware and software such as when electronic chips contain software inside them. The chip is physical, which is hardware, and it has software built into the chip. An example of firmware is the basic input/output system (**BIOS**) chip. The BIOS always has startup software inside it that must be present for a computer to operate. This startup software locates and loads the operating system. The BIOS also contains software instructions for communication with input/output devices, as well as important hardware parameters that determine to some extent what hardware can be installed. For example, the system BIOS has the ability to allow other BIOS chips that are located on adapters (such as the video card) to load software that is loaded in the card's BIOS.

A PC typically consists of a case (chassis), a keyboard that allows users to provide input into the computer, a monitor that outputs or displays information, and a mouse that allows data input or is used to select menus and options. An input device is used to put data into the computer. A microphone, keyboard, mouse, and your finger (when used with a touchscreen or touch-enabled device) are great examples. Also, biometric devices can be input devices. Common biometric devices are a finger swipe reader and an integrated camera that can be used for facial recognition to gain access to a device.

An **output device** such as a display accepts data from the computer. A **display** is the monitor screen. Figure 1.10 shows a computer display that could be called a flat panel, monitor, display, or screen.

FIGURE 1.10   Computer display

Some devices can be both input and output devices, such as a smart TV, set-top box (the box used to connect a TV to a cable or satellite system), musical instrument digital interface- (MIDI) enabled devices (which are electronic musical devices), touch screen, or printer. In the case of a printer, data is sent from your computer to the printer, and the printer can send data (information), such as an out-of-ink message, back to the computer. Figure 1.11 contains common input and output devices.

Input Devices

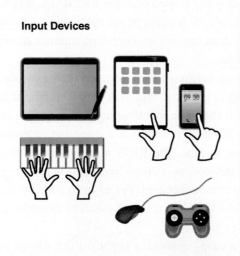

Output Devices

Mouse, Keyboard, Digital Pen, Digital Tablet, Finger, Signature, Pad, Touch Screen, Track Pad, Touch Pad, Trackball, Track Stick, Stylus, Barcode Reader, Digitizer, Game Pad/Console, Joystick, Scanner, Camera

Printer, Speakers, Display Devices

FIGURE 1.11   Input and output devices

A device that can be both an input device and an output device is a **KVM switch**. KVM stands for keyboard, video, mouse. A KVM switch allows connectivity of multiple devices so they can be shared between computers. For example, one keyboard, one mouse, and one display could connect to a KVM switch. A KVM switch has cables that allow it to connect or output to two or more computers. Figure 1.12 shows the back side of a KVM switch.

FIGURE 1.12   KVM switch

Once the computer cover or side is opened or removed, the parts inside can be identified. The easiest part to identify is the **power supply**, which is the metal box normally located in a back corner of the case. A power cord connects the power supply to a wall outlet or surge strip. One purpose of the power supply is to convert the outlet AC voltage to DC voltage used in the PC. The power supply distributes this DC voltage using power cables that connect to the various internal computer parts. A fan located inside the power supply keeps the computer cool, which avoids damage to the components.

A personal computer usually has a device to store software applications and files. Two examples of storage devices are the hard drive and optical drive. The **hard drive**, sometimes called hard disk, is a rectangular box normally inside the computer's case that is sealed to keep out dust and dirt. An **optical drive** holds discs (compact discs, or CDs), digital versatile discs (DVDs), or Blu-ray discs (BDs) that have data, music, video, or software applications on them. Figure 1.13 shows the major components of a tower computer. Figure 1.14 shows a hard drive as it would look before you install it. Figure 1.15 shows an optical drive. Figure 1.16 shows a power supply. Figure 1.17 shows a tower computer case.

FIGURE 1.13   Tower computer

FIGURE 1.14   Hard drive

FIGURE 1.15   Optical drive

FIGURE 1.16   Power supply

FIGURE 1.17   Tower case

The **motherboard** is the main circuit board located inside a PC and contains the most electronics. It is normally located on the bottom of a desktop or laptop computer and mounted on the side of a tower computer. Other names for the motherboard include mainboard, planar, or system board. The motherboard is the largest electronic circuit board in the computer. The keyboard and mouse frequently connect directly to the back of the motherboard. Figure 1.18 shows a motherboard when it is not installed inside a computer.

The motherboard holds memory modules. **Memory** is an important part of any computing device. Memory modules hold applications, part of the operating system, and user documents. Random access memory (**RAM**) is the most common type of memory and is volatile—that is, the data inside the module is lost when power is removed. When a user types a document in a word processing program, both the word processing application and the document are in RAM. If the user turns the computer off without saving the document to removable media or the hard drive, the document is lost because the information does not stay in RAM. (Note that some applications have the ability to periodically save a document, but this is not a guarantee that it has the latest information.) Figure 1.19 shows some memory modules when they are not installed into the motherboard memory slots. Look back to Figure 1.18 to see the memory modules installed in the motherboard. Memory is covered in great detail in Chapter 7.

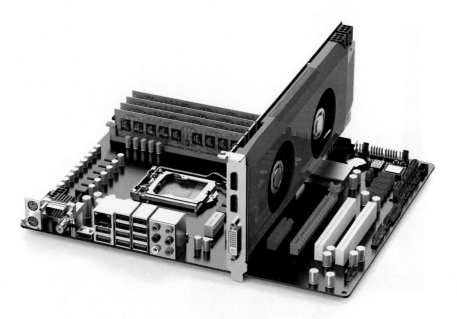

FIGURE 1.18   Computer motherboard

FIGURE 1.19   Memory modules

A device may have a cable that connects the device to the motherboard. Other devices require an adapter. **Adapters** are electronic circuit cards that normally plug into an **expansion slot** on the motherboard. Other names for an adapter are controller, card, controller card, circuit card, circuit board, and adapter board. Adapters allow someone to add a functionality that is not provided through the ports on the motherboard. An example is someone who wants better sound or video graphics, or additional ports of some type in order to connect external devices. Figure 1.20 shows an adapter. Notice how the contacts at the bottom are a particular shape. Chapter 3 goes into more detail about the types of expansion slots and adapters. You can also look back to Figure 1.18 to see a video adapter installed into a motherboard expansion slot.

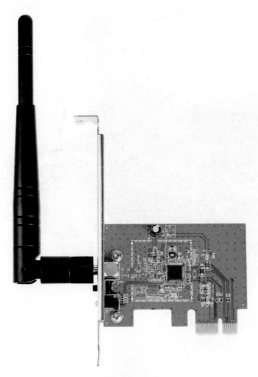

FIGURE 1.20 **Adapter**

How to identify an adapter's function

Tracing the cable(s) attached to an adapter or looking at a device connected to an adapter can usually help with identifying an adapter's function. For example, typically a monitor has a cable going between it and a video adapter or motherboard.

The following are the generic steps for installing adapters:

Step 1. Always follow the manufacturer's installation directions. Use an anti-static wrist strap when handling adapters. Electrostatic discharge (ESD) can damage electronic parts. (See Chapter 5 for more details on ESD.)

Step 2. Be sure the computer is powered off and unplugged.

Step 3. Remove any brackets from the case or plastic covers from the rear of the computer that may prevent adapter installation. Install the adapter in a free expansion slot and reattach any securing hardware.

Step 4. Attach any internal device cables that connect to the adapter, as well as any cables that go to an external port on the adapter, if necessary.

Step 5. Attach any internal or external devices to the opposite ends of the cable, if necessary.

Step 6. Power on any external devices connected to the adapter, if applicable.

Step 7. Reattach the computer power cord and power on the computer.

Step 8. Load any application software or device drivers needed for the devices attached to the adapter.

Step 9. Test the device(s) connected to the adapter.

See Figure 1.21 for an illustration of a motherboard, expansion slots, memory, and an adapter in an expansion slot.

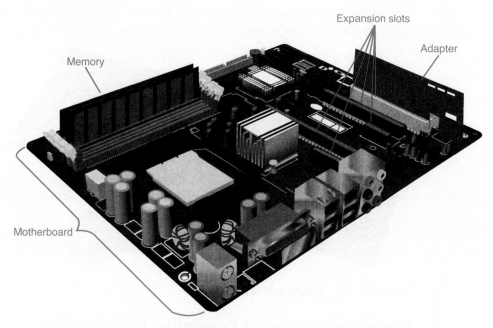

FIGURE 1.21   Motherboard with expansion slots and an adapter

Mice and Keyboards

Input devices, such as the mouse and keyboard, attach to the motherboard. The most common type of mouse is an **optical mouse**, which has optical sensors that detect the direction in which the mouse moves. It uses reflections from light-emitting diodes (LED) from almost any surface to detect the mouse location. Mice commonly can be adjusted for sensitivity—how far you have to move the mouse for how far it moves on the screen. Mice are rated in dots per inch (DPI). The higher the number, the more sensitive the mouse is. Mouse sensitivity can range from 500 to 3500 DPI. Figure 1.22 shows a photo of the bottom of an optical mouse.

FIGURE 1.22   Optical mouse

Keyboards are input devices that connect to a port on the motherboard or attach wirelessly. Features users look for in a keyboard include a separate numeric keypad for those that have to input a great deal of numbers, adjustable tilt legs, and spill-resistance. Figure 1.23 shows a keyboard and mouse that are commonly used with a tower, desktop, or all-in-one computer.

FIGURE 1.23   Keyboard and mouse

Mouse and Keyboard Preventive Maintenance

Mouse cleaning kits are available in computer stores, but normal household supplies also work. Use the following procedures to clean an optical mouse:

> Wipe the bottom with a damp, lint-free cloth.
> Use compressed air to clean the optical sensors.

Keyboards also need periodic cleaning. Figure 1.24 shows keyboard-cleaning techniques.

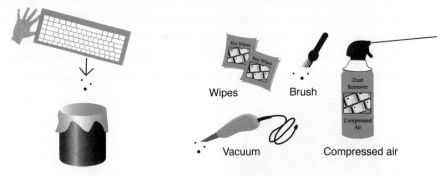

1. Turn keyboard upside down and gently shake out debris

2. Clean the keyboard (several options shown)

FIGURE 1.24   Keyboard cleaning techniques

Keyboard/Mouse Troubleshooting

One of the easiest ways to determine whether a keyboard is working is to press the [Caps Lock] or [Num Lock] key and watch to see if the keyboard light illuminates. Sometimes an application setting may be causing what appears to be a keyboard problem. Use another application to see if the keyboard is the problem. Keyboards can have LED lights that indicate a particular function. Table 1.3 contains the most common ones. Note that different vendors can label the lights in various ways.

TABLE 1.3 Common keyboard lights

Associated toggle key	Keyboard light	Description
Num Lock	Number lock (NUM LOCK)	Toggles the 10-key pad between digits 0 through 9 and various functions such as HOME, PG UP, PG DOWN, END, and various arrow keys.
Caps Lock	Capital letters lock (CAPS LOCK)	Toggles between all uppercase and lowercase letters.
Scroll Lock	Scroll lock	A rarely used key used to prevent scrolling and use the arrow keys to progress through information displayed.

TECH TIP

One key doesn't work

If a particular key is not working properly, remove the key cap. The chip-removal tool included with a PC tool kit is great for this. A tweaker (small, flat-tipped) screwdriver also does a good job. After removing the key cap, use compressed air around the sticky or malfunctioning key.

If coffee or another liquid spills into the keyboard, all is not lost. Many people have cleaned their PC keyboard by disconnecting it and soaking it in a bathtub or a flat pan of water. Distilled or boiled water cooled to room temperature works best. Afterward, the keyboard can be disassembled and/or scrubbed with lint-free swabs or cloths. PC keyboards and mice are normally considered throw-away technology. The customer's cost to pay a technician to keep cleaning a keyboard over and over again would pay for a new keyboard. Keep this in mind when troubleshooting such inexpensive devices.

1s and 0s

Computers are digital devices. That means they understand 1s and 0s. One 1 or one 0 is known as a **bit**. In actuality, a "1" is simply a voltage level to the computer. So, when we type characters into a word processing application, for example, those letters get translated by the keyboard into voltage levels. Figure 1.25 shows this concept. Notice that each letter is represented by a combination of eight 1s and 0s. Each 1 will be a voltage level sent to the motherboard (and components on it). Each 0 is simply the absence of a voltage level.

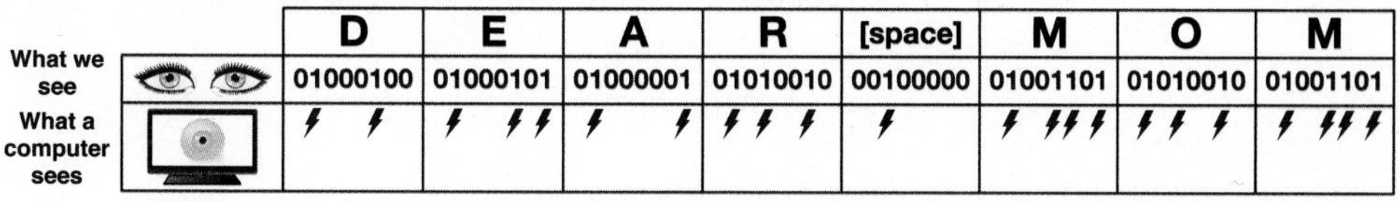

		D	E	A	R	[space]	M	O	M
What we see	👁👁	01000100	01000101	01000001	01010010	00100000	01001101	01010010	01001101
What a computer sees	💻	ϟ ϟ	ϟ ϟϟ	ϟ	ϟ ϟϟϟ	ϟ	ϟ ϟϟϟ	ϟϟ ϟ	ϟ ϟϟϟ

FIGURE 1.25 Binary bits

Technicians need to be able to describe capacities such as hard drive capacities or available drive space. Eight bits grouped together are a **byte**. See Figure 1.26 to see how the hot dog is divided into eight sections (eight sections make a big old "byte").

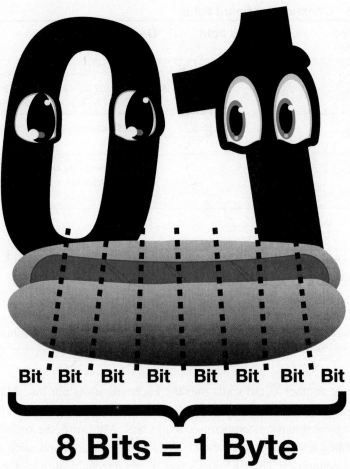

FIGURE 1.26   A byte

Approximately 1,000 bytes is a **kilobyte** (kB) as seen in Figure 1.27. 1kB is 1,024 bytes to be exact, but industry folks simply round off the number to the nearest thousand for ease of calculation.

Approximately 1 million bytes is a **megabyte** (MB), but a true megabyte is 1,048,576 bytes. 540 megabytes is shown as 540MB, or 540M. Notice in Figure 1.28 how a megabyte is a lot more storage of 1s and 0s than a kilobyte.

FIGURE 1.27   A kilobyte

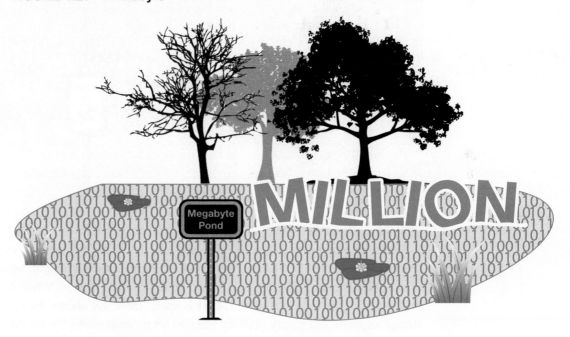

FIGURE 1.28   A megabyte

Approximately 1 billion bytes (1,073,741,824 bytes) is a **gigabyte** (GB) and is shown as 1GB or 1G. Approximately 1 trillion bytes (1,099,511,627,776 bytes) is a **terabyte** shown as 1TB or 1T. Figures 1.29 and 1.30 show how storage capacities get larger.

FIGURE 1.29   A gigabyte

FIGURE 1.30   A terabyte

When information needs to be expressed exactly, binary prefixes are used. For example, when describing a value of 2^{10} (1,024), instead of saying that it is 1 kilobyte, which people tend to think of as approximately 1,000 bytes, the term kibibyte (KiB) is used. When describing a value of 2^{20}, or 1,048,576, the term mebibyte (MiB) is used. Table 1.4 shows the terms used with computer storage capacity and binary prefixes when exact measurements are needed.

TABLE 1.4   Storage terms and binary prefixes

Term	Abbreviation	Description
Kilobyte/kibibyte	kB/KiB	~1 thousand bytes/2^{10} bytes
Megabyte/mebibyte	MB/MiB	~1 million bytes/2^{20} bytes
Gigabyte/gibibyte	GB/GiB	~1 billion bytes/2^{30} bytes
Terabyte/tebibyte	TB/TiB	~1 trillion bytes/2^{40} bytes
Petabyte/pibibyte	PB/PiB	~1,000 trillion bytes/2^{50} bytes
Exabyte/exbibyte	EB/EiB	~1 quintillion bytes/2^{60} bytes

Term	Abbreviation	Description
Zetabyte/zebibyte	ZB/ZiB	~1,000 exabytes/2^{70} bytes
Yottabyte/yobibyte	YB/YiB	~1 million exabytes/2^{80} bytes

Frequencies are also important measurements in computers because everybody wants to know how fast their computer, processor, memory, and other parts are operating. Frequencies are shown in similar measurements, but instead of bits (b) or bytes (B), speeds are shown in Hertz (Hz). A hertz is a measurement of cycles per second. Something that operates at approximately one million cycles per second is known as 1 megahertz (1 MHz). For one billion cycles per second, 1 gigahertz or 1 GHz is seen. Transfer speeds are commonly shown in bits per second such as gigabits per second or Gb/s or bytes per second such as in megabytes per second or MB/s. Notice the capital letter B when bytes are used compared to the lowercase b when bits are used. These measurements are used in a lot of IT-related hardware and software.

Safety Notes

As a parting note into your journey into computer hardware and software, let's take a moment to just mention safety. Safety is covered in each chapter, especially in Chapter 5, but no book on computer repair can begin without stating that both the technician and the computer can be harmed by poor safety habits. Before beginning any PC service, remove jewelry. To protect yourself and the computer, make sure to power off the computer and remove the power cord when disassembling, installing, or removing hardware, or doing preventive maintenance (cleaning).

> **TECH TIP**
>
> **Some things should be left alone**
>
> Never take an older CRT monitor or power supply apart unless you have been specifically trained on these components.

Technicians can also be harmed in doing menial tasks such as lifting a computer or heavy laser printer. Lifting is a common requirement listed in IT job advertisements or explained during interviews. Technical jobs frequently specify a maximum lifting requirement of 40 to 50 pounds. Use proper safety precautions, such as those shown in Figure 1.31. The type of equipment you need and things that you can do to prevent harm to the computer are covered more explicitly in Chapter 5, on power and disassembly.

Remove jewelry
before working
inside of a computer

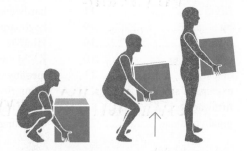

• Bend at the knees
• Use your legs to lift
• Use lifting aids when possible
• Ask for assistance when possible

FIGURE 1.31   Safety tips

Chapter Summary

> Many IT roles require detailed knowledge of PC hardware and software.
> Computer technicians should actively listen, have a positive attitude, and use logic when solving problems.
> The CompTIA A+ certification requires two exams: 220-901 and 220-902. Many people break into the IT field with this certification.
> IT staff must be proficient at searching for information on the Internet, capturing files, and documenting technical information.
> Computers consist of hardware (the physical parts), software (the operating system and applications), and firmware (hardware that contains software).
> Identify important computer parts installed in a computer and as standalone parts: case, keyboard, mouse, motherboard, monitor, power supply, hard drive, optical drive, adapter, riser board, and memory.
> Input devices provide data into the computer. The computer sends data to output devices. Some devices can be both an input and an output device.
> Mice, keyboards, and touch screens are important input devices. Mice and keyboards can be wired or wireless.
> Safety is important when working on a computer. Power it down and remove the power cord before working inside it.
> Use proper lifting techniques when servicing equipment.

A+ CERTIFICATION EXAM TIPS

✓ Get a good night's rest the night before the exam.

✓ Ensure that you are knowledgeable and proficient with all of the terms and technologies listed in the official CompTIA A+ exam objectives.

✓ Ensure that you can identify the basic parts of the computer and explain the purpose of each one. Ensure that you know the following parts: hard drive, optical drive, power supply, motherboard, and RAM.

✓ The following communication and professionalism skills are part of the 220-902 exam: (1) use proper language; (2) maintain a positive attitude/project confidence; (3) actively listen (take notes) and do not interrupt the customer; (4) be culturally sensitive.

Key Terms

Review Questions

1. Match the part to the description.

   __c__ motherboard   a. Converts AC to DC

   __e__ RAM   b. Holds the most data

   __f__ optical drive   c. Has the most electronics

   __b__ hard drive   d. Fits in an expansion slot

   __d__ adapter   e. Contents disappear when power is off

   __a__ power supply   f. Holds a disc

2. Which career choice(s) would probably *not* need the information in this book? (Select all that apply.)
   [PC repair technician | database administrator | programmer | helpdesk support | office manager | network cable installer | PC power supply reseller]

3. Which of the following are important suggested Internet search tips? (Choose two.)

   a. Try another search engine when the first one does not provide satisfactory results.

   b. Use as many common words as possible like the, in, at, or for.

   c. Put quotations around two or more words that might be found consecutively in output.

   d. Use as few words as possible.

   e. Avoid using the name of the equipment manufacturer.

4. Which type of memory is commonly found on a motherboard? __RAM__

5. When lifting a heavy computer, you should squat, bend at the knees, and use your legs to lift. [T | F]

6. How many tests must a person take in order to be A+ certified? [0 | 1 | 2 | 3 | 4]

7. Is the following question open-ended or closed-ended? You say your computer has been running slow since Monday. Which applications have you installed this week?
   [open-ended | closed-ended]

8. List one example of having a positive attitude. __listening to others problems and just always thinking of better ways and more efficent ways to solve issues__

9. Which of the following devices are commonly output devices? Select all that apply.
   [digital piano | speakers | display | stylus | track stick | barcode reader | printer]

10. People who work with computers might be expected to lift up to how many pounds? __40-50__

11. Which Microsoft Windows application could be used to create a text file?
    [Textpad | Notepad | WriteIt | NoteIt]

12. Which Windows tool can be used to capture the screen?
    [Notepad | Bluetooth | Internet Explorer | Snipping Tool]

13. Rewrite the following conversation into an open-ended question.

    Technician: Good morning. I have a service log that states you are getting an error message whenever you access a PDF file. Have you done your Acrobat updates lately?

    __what else is going on or what have you noticed__

14. List one procedure you would do to help an erratic optical mouse.

clean the lens

15. Match the capacity to the description.

_b_	bit	a. 8 bits
_c_	kilobyte	b. a 1 or a 0
_d_	megabyte	c. approximately 1,000 bytes
_a_	byte	d. approximately 1 million bytes
_f_	gigabyte	e. approximately 1 trillion bytes
_e_	terabyte	f. approximately 1 billion bytes

Exercises

Exercise 1.1   Identifying Tower Computer Parts

Objective: To identify various computer parts correctly

Procedure: Identify each computer part in Figure 1.32.

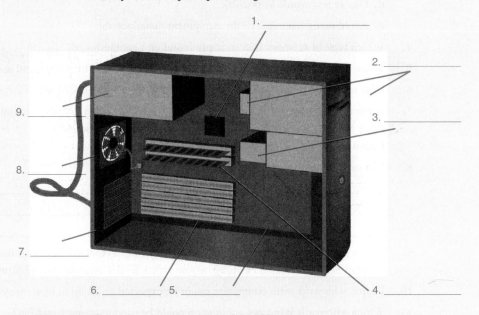

FIGURE 1.32   Tower computer parts identification

1. _Processor_
2. _____
3. _____
4. _RAM_
5. _Motherboard_
6. _expansion slots/adaptors_
7. _____
8. _Fan_
9. _power supply_

Exercise 1.2 Identifying Computer Parts

Objective: To identify various computer parts correctly

Procedure: Identify each computer part in Figure 1.33.

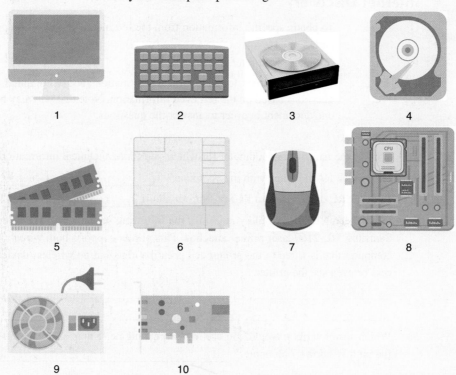

FIGURE 1.33   Computer parts identification

1. monitor
2. keyboard
3. disk drive
4. Hard drive
5. Ram
6. case
7. mouse
8. motherboard
9. power supply
10. adapter
    sound card?

Activities

Internet Discovery

Objective: To obtain specific information from the Internet regarding a computer or its associated parts

Parts: Computer with Internet access

Procedure: Using the Internet, locate technical information about a computer. Answer the following questions based on the retrieved information. Note that you may need to open more than one document in order to answer the questions.

Questions:

1.   What is the name of the computer for which you found technical information? _____

2.   How much RAM comes with the computer? _____

3.   Which URL did you use to find this information? _____

4.   Which search term(s) would you use for the following scenario? An HP Windows 7 computer has a Samsung ML-2160 laser printer attached. This printer supports both wired and wireless printing. The computer that is wired to the printer can print just fine, but no wireless devices in the house can access or even see the printer.

    _____

    _____

5.   Which search term(s) would you use in a search engine to help a friend who has accidently deleted a file on a Windows 7 computer? _____

    _____

6.   Which search terms would you use to find a video that shows you how to add an application to a Windows 8.1 desktop? _____

    _____

Soft Skills

Objective: To enhance and fine-tune a future technician's ability to listen, communicate in both written and oral forms, and support people who use computers in a professional manner

Procedure:

1.   In a team environment, list three qualities that are important in a computer technician. Create scenarios that demonstrate these qualities. Share these findings in a clear and concise way with the class.

2.   In a team environment, list three qualities that are not good practices for computer technicians. Create scenarios that demonstrate these qualities. Share these findings in a clear and concise way with the class.

Critical Thinking Skills

Objective: To analyze and evaluate information as well as apply learned information to new or different situations

Procedure:

1.   Find an advertisement for a computer in a local computer flyer, in a newspaper, in a magazine, in a book, or on the Internet. List which components you know in one column and the components you do not know in the other column. Select one component you do not know and research that component. On a separate piece of paper, write a description of the component based on your research, and then share it with at least one other person. Write the name of the person with whom you shared.

2. Why do you think that many computer components are considered "throw-away" technology? List your reasoning. In groups of three or four, share your thoughts. Nominate a spokesperson to share your group reaction in two sentences or less.

3. One device touts a transfer speed of 100Mb/s, whereas another device advertises 50MB/s. Compare the two devices' transfer speeds and indicate which one is faster. Locate a component you have or would like to have. Compare products paying particular attention to the transfer speed. Document your findings.

Labs

Lab 1.1 Getting Started in Windows 7

Objective: To be able to use Windows 7 to locate and launch applications.

Parts: Windows 7 computer

Procedure: Complete the following procedure and answer the accompanying questions.

1. Power on the computer and log in. You may need to contact an instructor or student assistant for the userid and password.

2. Click the *Start* button in the bottom left corner of the screen. The Start button is used to launch applications and utilities, search for files and other computers, obtain help, and add/remove hardware and software. The Start button menu is configurable, as shown in a later lab. Figure 1.34 shows a sample Windows 7 Start button menu.

Start button

FIGURE 1.34   Windows 7 Start button

3. The left panel of the Start button window contains a list of commonly used applications. Items that have arrows to the right of the name have a submenu that contains recently used application files that can be accessed by holding the pointer over the right arrow and clicking on the file name in the right panel. A recently used file does not have to be used. You can simply click the name of the application and it will open.

List one application found in the left panel of the Start button menu.

4. There are several other ways to access applications from the Start button menu especially if it is not shown in the left panel. Explore one way by clicking on the *All programs* link at the bottom. The All Programs Start button option contains applications and folders that contain other applications. Notice the scrollbar on the right (see Figure 1.35) that enables you to scroll through the installed applications.

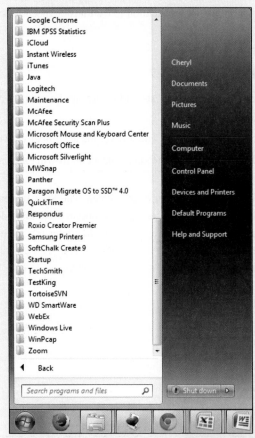

FIGURE 1.35   Windows 7 All Programs menu

What is the name of the last All Programs application or folder shown on your computer?

_____

5. Examine the available applications located throughout the list.

Which application do you think you might use the most?

_____

6. To access an application within a folder, you must first click on the folder, then click on the application. Locate and select the *Accessories* folder.

List three applications found in the Accessories folder.

_____

_____

7. Another way of accessing applications is through the *Search programs and files* textbox accessed from the Start button. Click on the *Start* button. Right above the Start button is this textbox. Click once inside the textbox and start typing the word **note**. Notice how at the top of the screen a couple of programs that have the word "note" in them appear.

List one application found using the keyword "note."

_____

8. Click on the *Notepad* application at the top of the list. The Notepad application opens.

9. Notice the three buttons in the top right corner. These three buttons are common in a window and shown in Figure 1.36. Table 1.5 details the purpose of these buttons.

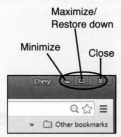

FIGURE 1.36   Windows 7 window buttons

TABLE 1.5   Windows top right window buttons

Button	Purpose
Minimize (straight line)	Keeps the program running, but removes it from being active on the screen. Use the $\boxed{Alt}$ + $\boxed{Tab}$ buttons to re-access the app.
Maximize/Restore Down (rectangle)	Used to make the window that holds the app full screen (maximize) or, if you size the window, restore it to its default size.
Close (X)	Used to close an app.

10. Click on the far right close button to close Notepad.

11. Use the *Search programs and files* textbox to locate and launch the *Calculator* application.

    Which three menu items are available with the Calculator application?

    _____

12. Whenever you use an application, the open application icon appears on the Windows 7 taskbar at the bottom of the screen. The taskbar is customizable and this skill is taught later in the book. Notice how a small calculator icon appears on the taskbar. Click on an icon and that application appears on the desktop.

13. Minimize the Calculator application by clicking on the *Minimize* button (straight line) in the top right corner. Notice how the calculator is still loaded as indicated by the icon on the taskbar.

14. Use the *All Programs* Start button item to locate the *Sticky Notes* application accessory. Remember you must first access the Accessories folder to locate the applications within that folder. Notice how the Sticky Notes application icon is on the taskbar.

15. An easy way to move between applications is by using the ⌐Alt⌐ + ⌐Tab⌐ keys. Hold down the ⌐Alt⌐ key. While keeping that key held down, tap once on the ⌐Tab⌐ key. A window with all open applications appears. While keeping the ⌐Alt⌐ key depressed and tapping the ⌐Tab⌐ key once, the cursor cycles through the open applications. When it highlights the application you want to re-access, let the ⌐Alt⌐ and ⌐Tab⌐ keys go. Use the ⌐Alt⌐ and ⌐Tab⌐ key to re-access the Calculator application.

Instructor initials: _____

16. Close the Calculator application by using the *Close* button.

17. Click on the *Sticky Notes* application icon on the taskbar. Close the Sticky Notes application by using the *Close* button.

18. Easily access the Windows 7 Start button menu at any time by pressing the ▮ key.

Lab 1.2 Getting Started in Windows 8

Objective: To be able to use Windows 8 to locate and launch applications and locate control panels used in future labs.

Parts: Windows 8 computer

Procedure: Complete the following procedure and answer the accompanying questions.

1. Power on the computer. Windows 8 was designed for mobile (touch) devices so the Windows 8 desktop is different from previous Windows versions. However, some people bought computers and laptops that did not have touch monitors. The method used to unlock a Windows desktop depends on the type of computer you have.

    • Touch screen—Press your finger on the screen and move upward.

    • Desktop computer—Press any key and release, click the mouse anywhere, click the mouse near the bottom of the screen, or hold the mouse button down while moving the cursor upward.

    • Laptop—Press any key and release, click the mouse anywhere, hold down the left track pad section or button, or move the cursor upward.

2. Type the password. Contact the instructor or lab assistant if the password is unknown.

    Note: Anywhere in this lab when the direction is to "click" something, if a touch screen is available, you can tap with your finger instead.

3. The Windows Start screen appears. Figure 1.37 shows a sample Windows Start screen. You can press the Windows key (▮) at any time to bring up the Start screen. You can also point at the bottom left corner of the screen until a small Start screen display appears so you can click on it.

Point here to access charms

FIGURE 1.37   Windows 8 Start screen

4.   The Start screen has the user listed in the upper-right corner. This icon can lock the computer and sign out of the user account.

   What user account is being used to do this lab?

   _____

5.   The Start screen also contains tiles. Tiles are used to access apps, such as the current news, weather, or traditional applications such as a web browser or word processing software. Tiles are rectangular or square and fill the Start screen. Use the scrollbar at the bottom of the screen to access the tiles to the right.

   What is the name of the last app shown on the right?

   _____

6.   Examine the available tiles.

   Which app do you think you might use the most frequently?

   _____

7.   Parts of the Start screen that are not immediately evident are the charms. Charms are little icons that are used to quickly access apps. The charms that will appear depend on the manufacturer and are software-dependent. The charms seen from the Start screen commonly include charms to perform a search and access some common Windows settings. Figure 1.38 shows a sample of Windows 8 Start screen charms.

FIGURE 1.38   Windows 8 Start screen charms

8.   Access the Start screen charms by pointing to the bottom right corner of the screen. Click the *Search* charm. Figure 1.39 shows an example of the menu that appears.

FIGURE 1.39   Windows 8 Search Apps window

9.   The options below the Search text window are selectable items to designate where you want to search. When learning to configure, maintain, and repair Windows, you will commonly use the default selection of Apps. In the Search textbox, type **notepad** and *do not* press ⏎Enter. Notice how the Notepad application appears to the left.

10. Click once on the *Notepad* app. The Notepad app opens.

11. Notice the three buttons in the top right corner. These three buttons are common in a window. Look back to Figure 1.36 in Lab 1.1 to see them. Table 1.5 (also in Lab 1.1) details the purpose of these buttons.

12. Click on the far right *Close* button to close Notepad.

13. Sometimes the application you need is not one you remember. When you click on the Search charm, all apps display in the left panel and you can use the scrollbar at the bottom of the screen to search through them. Once found, click the app to open.

14. Access the *Search* charm. Do not type in the Search charm textbox. Instead, access it by clicking one time in the panel to the left where all apps display. Locate the Sticky Notes app by scrolling through the apps. Open the *Sticky Notes* app.

    Which symbol is in the top left corner of the Sticky Notes app?

    _____

15. Close the Sticky Notes app by using the *Close* button.

16. There are several ways to access the traditional Windows desktop. One way is to access the Desktop tile from the Start screen. Use one of the methods described to access the Desktop tile from the Start screen.

    What happened when you clicked or tapped the Desktop tile from the Start screen?

    _____

Instructor initials: _____

17. Re-access the Windows 8 Start screen by pressing the ■ key, clicking the *Windows* icon in the bottom left corner, if available, or pointing the mouse to the bottom left corner of the screen and clicking on the small *Start* screen that appears.

Lab 1.3 Getting Started in Windows 10

Objective: To be able to use Windows 10 to locate and launch applications and locate control panels used in future labs.

Parts: Windows 10 computer

Procedure: Complete the following procedure and answer the accompanying questions.

1. Power on the computer. The method used to unlock a Windows desktop depends on the type of computer you have.

    - Touchscreen—Press your finger on the screen and move upward.

    - Desktop computer—Press any key and release, click the mouse anywhere, click the mouse near the bottom of the screen, or hold the mouse button down while moving the cursor upward.

    - Laptop—Press any key and release, click the mouse anywhere, hold down the left track pad section or button, or move the cursor upward.

2. Type the password. Contact the instructor or lab assistant if the password is unknown.

    Note: Anywhere in this lab when the direction is to "click" something, if a touch screen is available, you can tap with your finger instead.

3.   Windows 10 was designed for both traditional desktop and mobile (touch) devices. The Windows 10 desktop is different from previous Windows versions and it is a mixture of Windows 7 and Windows 8, as shown in Figure 1.40. You can press the ▦ key on the keyboard at any time to bring up the desktop.

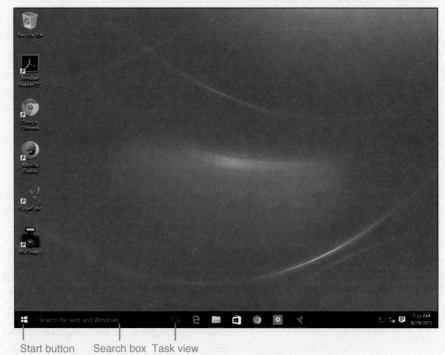

Start button   Search box   Task view

FIGURE 1.40   Windows 10 desktop

4.   Notice the *Start* button in the right corner. Click on the *Start* button to access the tiled apps similar to the Windows 8 Start screen, as shown in Figure 1.41.

FIGURE 1.41   Windows 10 Start button

5. Click the *Windows* icon again in the lower-left corner to return to the desktop. The desktop has a new look to it along the bottom. The Start button is different. The text area to the immediate right of the Start button used to be in the Start button menu or part of charms in Windows 8. There is an area for the icons of the most commonly used applications. To the far right is the notification area.

    List one icon of a commonly used application that is on your desktop.

    _____

6. Click the *Start* button. Locate and select the *All apps* option. Scroll through the options. Notice the list contains both applications and folders.

7. Locate and select the *Windows Accessories* folder to expand it. Locate and select the *Notepad* app to launch it.

    What is the name of the last menu item shown on the far right inside the Notepad app?

    _____

8. Notice the three buttons in the top right corner in the Notepad window. These three buttons are common in a window. Look back to Figure 1.36 in Lab 1.1 to see them. Table 1.5 (also in Lab 1.1) details the purpose of these buttons. Use the Minimize button (straight line). Notice how the application icon displays at the bottom of the screen in the taskbar as a small blue spiral notebook.

9. Click on the *Notepad* application icon at the bottom of the screen. The Notepad application opens on the screen. Use the *Close* button (X) to close the application.

10. Another way to locate and launch an app is by using the *Search the web and Windows* textbox. Click once inside this textbox and type the word **note**, but do not press [←Enter]. Notice that at the top of the screen the Notepad desktop app is listed. The Sticky Notes app also shows.

    List one other app that is shown that has the letters "note" in its name.

    _____

    _____

    Note: When you have two or more applications open in Windows 10, you can hold the [Alt] key down and press the [Tab] key to cycle through any open applications. Windows 10 has a Task View icon on the taskbar that serves the same purpose. Refer back to Figure 1.40 to see that useful icon.

11. Select and launch the *Sticky Notes* app. The Sticky Notes app opens.

    What symbol is in the top left corner of the Sticky Notes app?

    _____

12. Close the *Sticky Notes* app.

13. Click on the *Start* button in the bottom left corner. Click in the tiled apps area. Launch one of the apps by clicking on a tile.

    Which app did you choose?

    _____

Instructor initials: _____

14. Close the application using the *Close* button.

Lab 1.4 Using a Search Engine

Objective: To use Google to effectively search for information

Parts: Windows 7, 8, or 10 computer with Internet access

Procedure: Complete the following procedure and answer the accompanying questions.

1.   Power on the computer. Log in or unlock the screen.

2.   Windows 7 users, click on the icon (*Start* button) in the bottom left corner, select *All Programs*, and then select a web browser.

   Windows 8.1 users—Access and launch a browser app such as Windows Explorer, Google Chrome, or Mozilla Firefox from the Windows start screen. If one is not readily visible, click on the Windows icon in the bottom left corner to get a customized view of the applications. (On a mobile device this may be a Windows symbol you touch on the front side of the device to access these apps. You can then click the (⊕) that is inside the circle in the bottom left to view All Apps and pick a browser app from there.)

   Windows 10 users—Access and launch a browser app such as Microsoft Edge, Microsoft Internet Explorer, Google Chrome, or Mozilla Firefox from the Windows start screen. If one is not readily visible, click *All apps* and scroll through the list to locate a browser app. Click on the browser app name to launch it.

3.   In the browser window, type the following: `www.google.com`

   If a computer user has a Dell Windows 8.1 computer that the user complains is slow to boot, what search terms would you put in the browser window? List at least three.

   _____

4.   In the search textbox, type the following: `Windows 8 computer problems`

   Approximately how many results list at the top of the screen under the menu?

   _____

5.   Change the search criteria to `Windows 8 computer problem`.

   Approximately how many results list at the top of the screen under the menu?

   _____

6.   Go into the first three problems by clicking on the first title line. To return to the search results, click the Back arrow ((←)).

   Do any of the problems have anything to do with slow booting?

   _____

7.   In the search textbox, type the following: `Windows 8.1 slow boot`

   Access the first result by clicking on the title line.

   What was the resolution given in the resulting web link?

   _____

8.   Sometimes computer resolutions contain links to software that might not be free after so many days and may contain malware or a virus. Only click on a link or use software tools from trustworthy vendors. Return to the search criteria by clicking on the Back arrow or retyping `www.google.com` in the search textbox. Now change the search to the following: `Microsoft Windows 8.1 slow boot` and access the first result.

   Approximately how many results are available?

   _____

Which resolution was given?

_____

_____

_____

Do you think that this might be a good solution for the person who owns the Dell computer?
[Yes | No | I have no idea]

_____

9. Now add the word Dell into the search criteria. Make the search the following: `Microsoft Windows 8.1 Dell slow boot`

    Approximately how many results are available?

_____

10. Access the first result by clicking on the title line.

    What resolution was given?

_____

_____

_____

Lab 1.5 Screen Capture with Snipping Tool

Objective: To use the Microsoft Windows Snipping Tool to effectively capture information

Parts: Windows 7, 8, or 10 computer with the Snipping Tool application

Procedure: Complete the following procedure and answer the accompanying questions. If you are not familiar with launching an application, complete Lab 1.1, 1.2, or 1.3 before doing this lab.

1. Power on the computer. Log in or unlock the screen.

2. Access a web browser. Leave it on the screen.

3. Many times when you are solving a problem, performing a task, or simply helping someone else, a picture is worth a thousand words. Locate and launch the Snipping Tool. The Snipping Tool application starts as shown by a small window that opens (see Figure 1.42).

FIGURE 1.42   Snipping Tool application window

4. The Snipping Tool enables you to capture everything that shows on the screen (full-screen snip), a particular window that is open on the screen (window snip), a particular section of the screen that could be captured in a rectangle (rectangular snip), a particular part of the screen that is odd shaped, or when you simply want to capture an icon or symbol. Click the ▼ beside the _New_ menu option. The four options display. The default one has a ⊙ beside it.

5. Click on the _Options_ menu item. One particular option that you can select by clicking inside a box is the Ink color and Show selection ink after snips are captured option. This option automatically creates a box around whatever information is captured. Do not select it yet. Click _Cancel_.

6. Ensure the browser window is not taking up the entire desktop area. You can use the Maximize/Restore Down button located in the top right corner to size the window. Look at Figure 1.36 in Lab 1.1 to see them. Table 1.5 (also in Lab 1.1) details the purpose of these buttons.

7. In the Snipping Tool window, click the ⬇ beside the *New* menu option and select *Full-screen Snip*. The Snipping Tool application captures whatever is on the screen. If that is not what you want to capture and you only want to capture the search textbox, click *New* and the Snipping Tool reverts to the small window.

8. Click on the ⬇ beside *New* again and select *Window Snip*. With a window snip, you must do an additional step by clicking on the window that you want. Click anywhere in the browser window.

   What information is shown inside the Snipping Tool window?

   _____

9. Pretend this still is not what you wanted because it is so big and you want to just capture the search textbox. Click the *Minimize* button (the button to the left of the Maximize/Restore Down button you used before). The Minimize button is the icon in the top right that has a single line at the bottom of the icon. It is to the immediate left of the Maximize/Restore Down button.

10. Re-access the browser window by clicking anywhere on it. In the browser window, type **www.pearson.com** in the textbox at the top of the screen, but do not press the ⏎Enter key.

11. With the browser window open, re-access the Snipping Tool by clicking on the *Snipping Tool* icon located in the taskbar (scissors within a red circle icon) at the bottom of the screen. If the taskbar is not there, such as on a Window 8 computer, hold down the Alt key and while continuing to hold it down, press Tab. The currently running programs appear. Press the Tab key again until the Snipping tool is selected. Let go of both keys and the Snipping Tool application window appears on the screen. Ensure the Snipping Tool application window is on a part of the desktop by itself (not on top of the browser window). In order to move a window, you can click on the top part of the Snipping Tool window and while continuing to hold down the mouse or touchpad, drag the window to a different part of the screen.

12. Click the *New* menu option and select *Rectangular Snip*. The screen appears grayed out. This is normal. A crosshairs symbol (that looks like a plus symbol) appears on the screen. Move the screen cursor (which, in turn, moves the crosshairs symbol) to the top part of the browser window that contains the search textbox. Click and drag the crosshairs until it captures the part of the browser window that shows www.pearson.com.

   List one instance where you think an IT person might use the rectangular snip option.

   _____

13. After taking a screen capture, the Snipping Tool window has more menu options available. Click the *File* menu option.

   Which four menu options are available?

   _____

14. Click the *Edit* menu option. This option can be used to select *Copy* so you can simply paste into an email or word processing document. Select the *Tools* menu item. Point to the *Pen* option and select *Blue Pen* from the menu. Use the pen to circle the words *pearson.com*.

15. Access the *Tools* menu item again and select the *Highlighter* option. Highlight *www*.

   Instructor initials: _____

16. Close the Snipping Tool window by clicking on the *Close* button, which is located to the immediate right of the Maximize/Restore Down button. The Close button is in the top right of the Snipping Tool application window and has an X on the icon.

17. When asked if you want to save the snipped document, click *No*.

Lab 1.6 Creating a Text File

Objective: To use the various applications and apps to create a text file

Parts: Windows 7, 8, or 10 computer

Procedure: Complete the following procedure and answer the accompanying questions. If you are not familiar with launching an application, complete Lab 1.1, 1.2, or 1.3 before doing this lab.

1. Power on the computer. Log in or unlock the screen.

2. Locate and launch the *Notepad* application. The Notepad application starts, as shown in Figure 1.43.

FIGURE 1.43   Notepad application

Which five menu options are available?

_____

Which menu options do you think would be used to automatically insert the date and time?

_____

3. Notepad can be used to document problems on a computer that does not have word processing applications loaded or that has other issues. Both Microsoft Notepad and WordPad ship with the Windows operating system. Notepad does not have as many capabilities as WordPad. One of the things you can do with Notepad is insert the date and time into the document. Click the *Edit* menu item to see the full Edit menu, as shown in Figure 1.44.

FIGURE 1.44   Notepad Edit menu

4. Notice the words on the left and the corresponding keystrokes to the right. This means you can either use the mouse to access the Edit menu and then select *Time/Date* or you can simply press the [F5] key to do the same thing. Click away from the Edit menu so you can try the keyboard shortcut. Click inside the blank Notepad window. Now press the [F5] key.

5.   Click the *View > Status bar* menu option.

What did this option do?

_____

_____

6.   Click the *View > Status bar* menu option again and notice how there is a checkmark now by the Status bar option indicating that this option is enabled.

7.   Notepad allows a few font modifications. To bold the date and time, click the *Format > Font* menu option to see the options as shown in Figure 1.45.

FIGURE 1.45   Notepad Font menu

What is the default font (the font that is selected and highlighted by default)?

_____

What are the names of the first and last font types? Use your mouse and the control bar to see the fonts.

_____

8.   Click the *Bold* option in the Font style section. Click the *OK* button. You return to the Notepad window. Your date and time should have turned bold. Redo Steps 7 and 8 if the words are not darker (bolded).

On your own, add the following message to the Notepad document. Ensure that you use the Verdana Regular 12 font type and size:

`Replaced display and tested. User confirms that the problem is solved.`

9.   Click the *Help > View Help* menu option.

Which help topic would be of most interest to you?

_____

10.   Close the Help window by clicking on the *X* in the upper-right corner.

11. A header is a part of a document that might not appear on the screen, but when the document is printed, the information inside the header prints at the top of the page. A footer is at the bottom of the document. To insert a header and a footer in Notepad, click on the *File > Page Setup* option. Note that when you change the information in the header and footer, that information stays there for the current Notepad document and future documents as well.

    Use Help to determine what the &f, the default setting for the header, and Page &p, the default setting for the footer, mean. Document your findings.

    _____

    _____

12. Close the Help window.

    ____ Instructor's Initials

13. To save the document, click the *File > Save* option. A window with several options appears, as shown in Figure 1.46.

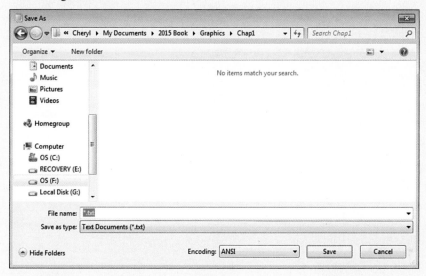

FIGURE 1.46   Notepad Save menu

14. When saving a file, you want to give it an appropriate name. That is entered in the File name textbox. Start typing **documentation** in the File name textbox. Notice how it automatically replaces the highlighted *.txt name. Do not press ⏎Enter yet.

15. The current location is shown at the top of the screen. To change this location and save it onto your flash drive, for example, you must first select your flash drive from the left window. Note that drive letters change depending on the system. In Figure 1.46, the flash drive is G:. Click the *Documents* option in the left window. If any folders are on the drive, they appear. Click the *Cancel* button.

16. From the Notepad window, click the *Close* button (the button with a red X in the top right corner). What message appears?

    _____

17. Click the *Don't Save* button.

2 Connectivity

In this chapter you will learn:

> The purpose of various computer ports

> What to do if you don't have a particular port

> What types of devices connect to specific ports

> Symbols and colors associated with particular ports

CompTIA Exam Objectives:

What CompTIA A+ exam objectives are covered in this chapter?

✓ 901-1.7 Compare and contrast various PC connection interfaces, their characteristics and purposes, including physical connections, wireless connections, and characteristics of each.

✓ 901-1.11 Identify common PC connector types and associated cables including display connector types, display cable types, device cables and connectors, adapters, and converters.

✓ 902-5.4 Demonstrate proper communication techniques and professionalism.

Introduction to Connectivity

Now that we know what the basic parts of a PC are, we dive into the technical details. This chapter explores wired and wireless connectivity—specifically, how to connect input and output devices to specific ports. This chapter also explores what to do when things go wrong. Some of the ports may be a challenge at first, but it is important that people going into the IT field know how to connect devices to PCs and mobile devices.

External Connectivity

A **port** is a connector on a motherboard or on a separate adapter that allows a device to connect to a computer. Sometimes a motherboard has ports built directly into the motherboard. A technician must be able to identify these ports readily to ensure that (1) the correct cable plugs into a port and (2) the technician can troubleshoot problems in the right area. All IT professionals should be able to recognize and identify the common ports used today.

Many port connections are either male or female. Male ports have metal pins that protrude from the connector. A male port requires a cable with a female connector. Female ports have holes in the connector into which the male cable pins are inserted.

Some connectors on integrated motherboards are either D-shell connectors or DIN connectors. A **D-shell connector** (sometimes called a D-sub) has more pins or holes on top than on the bottom, so a cable connected to the D-shell connector can be inserted in only one direction and cannot be accidentally flipped upside down. Many documents represent a D-shell connector by using the letters DB, a hyphen, and the number of pins—for example, DB-9, DB-15, or DB-25.

A **mini-DIN-6 connector** is round with small holes and is normally keyed. When a connector is **keyed**, the cable can be inserted only one way. Keyboard and mouse connectors, commonly called PS/2 ports, are examples of mini-DIN connectors. Today, a keyboard and mouse most often connect to USB ports (shown later). Figure 2.1 shows the back of a computer with a motherboard and some of the ports (DVI and VGA) covered later in this chapter. You can see a DIN and two D-shell connectors on the motherboard.

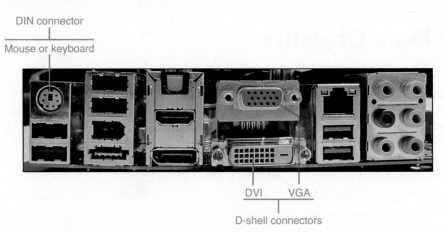

FIGURE 2.1   Mini-DIN and D-shell connectors

Mouse and Keyboard Ports

Mouse and **keyboard ports** have traditionally been 6-pin mini-DIN ports that are sometimes called **PS/2 ports**. Otherwise, USB ports are used for mouse and keyboard connectivity. Many manufacturers color code the PS/2 mouse port as green and the PS/2 keyboard port as purple or they may put a small diagram of a keyboard or a mouse by each connector. Figure 2.2 shows mouse and keyboard connectivity options.

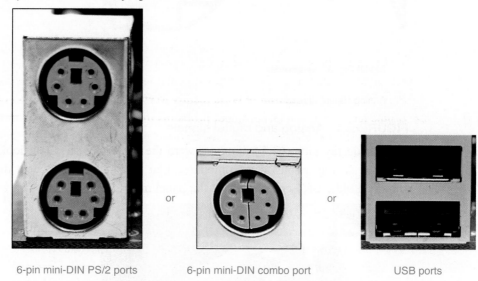

6-pin mini-DIN PS/2 ports   or   6-pin mini-DIN combo port   or   USB ports

FIGURE 2.2   Mouse and keyboard ports

TECH TIP

Don't confuse the mouse and keyboard ports

On motherboards that have two PS/2 ports, the mouse and keyboard ports are not interchangeable, even if they use the same pin configuration (unless, of course, you have that 6-pin mini-DIN combo port).

Video Ports

A video port is used to connect a display. Video output can be the older method of **analog signal** (varying levels, such as seen with an audio signal) or the newer output method of **digital signal** (1s and 0s). Because the computer uses all digital signals, sending 1s and 0s is more efficient than having to convert the 1s and 0s to an analog signal. This is relevant because there are still video ports around that are designed for analog signals. Figure 2.3 shows the difference between analog and digital signals.

Analog Versus Digital Signal

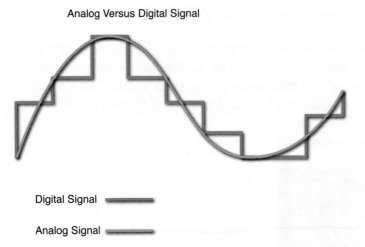

Digital Signal ━━━━

Analog Signal ━━━━

FIGURE 2.3   Analog and digital signals

Cathode ray tube (CRT) monitors were the big bulky ones that looked like old TV sets that accepted analog output from computers. Flat panel monitors accept digital signals. Figure 2.4 shows an older CRT compared to a flat panel monitor.

FIGURE 2.4   CRT monitor and flat-panel monitor

Video Graphics Array (VGA)

The video graphics array **(VGA) port** was designed for analog output to a CRT monitor. VGA ports are easy to identify because they have three rows of holes. The female port is sometimes advertised as an **HD-15** or **DE-15** port. The VGA cable has a **DB-15** male end that attaches to the DE-15 port.

Digital Visual Interface (DVI)

A newer port is a Digital Visual Interface (**DVI**) **port**, and it has three rows of square holes. DVI ports are used to connect flat panel digital displays. Some flat panel monitors can also use the older VGA port. Some video adapters also enable you to connect a video device (such as a television) that has an **S-Video port**. Figure 2.5 shows a video adapter with all three ports. The left port is the DVI connector, the center port is for S-Video, and the right port is a VGA port.

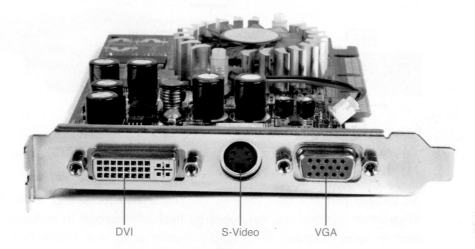

DVI   S-Video   VGA

FIGURE 2.5   DVI, S-Video, and VGA ports

There are several types of DVI connectors. The one used depends on the type of monitor attached. Two terms used with these DVI connectors are single link and dual link. A **single link** connection allows video resolutions up to 1920×1080. With a **dual link** connection, more pins are available to send more signals, thus allowing higher resolutions. The two major types of connectors are DVI-D and DVI-I. **DVI-D** is used for digital video connectivity only. **DVI-I** can be used for both digital and analog monitors, and it is the most common. A less common type is **DVI-A**, which is used for analog connectivity and not shown in Figure 2.6 with the other DVI connector types.

Single link DVI-I   Dual link DVI-I   Single link DVI-D   Dual link DVI-D

FIGURE 2.6   DVI connectors

TECH TIP

Match a monitor to the DVI port type

Be careful when installing a monitor. Ensure that the video port matches the DVI connection type for the monitor. Converters can be purchased to adapt to a monitor with a VGA port.

DisplayPort

The **DisplayPort** developed by VESA (Video Electronics Standards Association) can send and receive video, audio, or both types of signals simultaneously. The port is designed to primarily output to display devices, such as computer monitors, televisions, and home theaters. A passive converter can be used to convert to a single-link DVI or HDMI port (covered next). You use an active converter to convert to a dual-link DVI.

To understand why an active converter is needed, you must understand the difference between active and passive cables. A **passive cable** is one that does not contain a chip like active cables. **Active cables** have a chip that boosts the signals, thus allowing cables to be thinner and to support sending signals further and faster than passive cables. Active and passive cables are found in computer networks and video systems.

A mini DisplayPort is also available on mobile devices. Figure 2.7 shows the DisplayPort and a cable that would connect to this port.

FIGURE 2.7   DisplayPort

Thunderbolt

An updated port that uses some of the DisplayPort technology is the **Thunderbolt port**. The Thunderbolt interface was developed by Intel with support from Apple. The Thunderbolt port used on Apple computers is the same connector as the mini DisplayPort. Thunderbolt 3 will use the USB Type-C connector shown in the USB section that follows. In addition to carrying video signals, a Thunderbolt cable can also be used to carry audio signals and data to external storage devices. Figure 2.8 shows the current Thunderbolt port and cable.

FIGURE 2.8   Thunderbolt cable and port

High-Definition Multimedia Interface (HDMI)

Another upgrade to DVI is High-Definition Multimedia Interface (**HDMI**), a digital interface that can carry audio and video over the same cable. HDMI is found on cable TV boxes, televisions, video adapters, laptops, desktops, and tablets. **MiniHDMI,** or microHDMI connectors, are used with devices such as cameras, tablets, and smartphones. Table 2.1 describes the different HDMI ports.

TABLE 2.1   HDMI ports

HDMI connector type	Description
A	19-pin port found on a TV or PC that can have a Category 1 (standard) or Category 2 (high-speed) cable attached
B	29-pin port used with very high-resolution displays
C	19-pin mini port (2.42mm × 10.42mm) found on mobile devices
D	19-pin micro port (2.8mm × 6.4mm) found on mobile devices

Figure 2.9 shows a video card that would be used in a gaming computer (one the user plays video games on). On top is a dual-link DVI-D port. On the bottom from left to right are a DisplayPort, HDMI port, and a dual-link DVI-I port. Table 2.2 summarizes important PC video ports for the 901 certification exam.

DisplayPort
HDMI
DVI-I
DVI-D

FIGURE 2.9   Video ports, including a DisplayPort, HDMI port, and two DVI ports

TABLE 2.2   Video port summary

Port type	Analog (A), Digital (D), or both (B)	Transfer speeds	Carries audio	Max cable lengths
VGA	A	N/A	N	Depends on resolution
DVI	B	Dual-link 7.92Gb/s	N	Up to 15′ for display resolutions up to 1280 × 1024
HDMI	D	18Gb/s	Y	Up to 16′ for standard cable Up to 49′ for high speed with quality cable and connectors
DisplayPort	D	25.92Gb/s	Y	9.8′ (passive) 108′ (active)
Thunderbolt 20Gb/s (v2) 30Gb/s (v3)	D	10Gb/s 200′ optical	Y	9.8′ copper (passive)

High-Bandwidth Digital Content (HDCP)

In an effort to prevent piracy, some vendors implement the high-bandwidth digital content protection (**HDCP**) feature on the DVI, DisplayPort, or HDMI port. HDCP is part of Intel's digital rights management (**DRM**) specification, which is designed to protect copyrighted material. What this means is if you are on an Apple MacBook that has this feature, you cannot externally display a legally purchased movie unless the external display is HDCP-capable.

Bayonet Neill-Concelman (BNC)

The last type of connector you might see associated with video, but more likely with cable TV, is a Bayonet Neill-Concelman (BNC) connector. A **BNC connector** is used with **coaxial** cable that is found in video networks such as a school where multiple TVs connect to the same distribution center or in a home that obtains TV channels through a cable provider. A BNC connector has a center conductor that pushes onto the receptacle. Then the metal outside is twisted to snap the connector into place. Figure 2.10 shows a BNC connector.

FIGURE 2.10   BNC connector

Video Adapters and Converters

Converters can be purchased for video ports. For example, a **DVI-to-HDMI converter** is shown in Figure 2.11. The figure shows both ends of the same converter. Figure 2.12 shows a VGA-to-DVI converter. Figure 2.13 shows the opposite, the ends of a **DVI-to-VGA converter**. An **HDMI-to-VGA converter** would look like a combination of the left port in Figure 2.11 and the right port in 2.13. Figure 2.14 shows a **Thunderbolt-to-DVI converter**. Finally, Figure 2.15 shows a Thunderbolt-to-VGA converter.

HDMI   DVI

FIGURE 2.11   DVI-to-HDMI converter

VGA   DVI

FIGURE 2.12   VGA-to-DVI converter

DVI   VGA

FIGURE 2.13   DVI-to-VGA converter

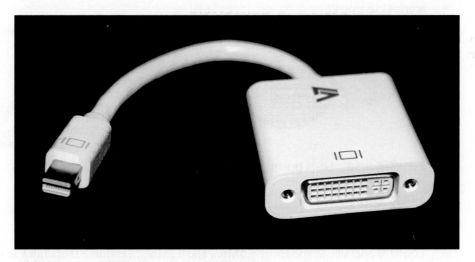

FIGURE 2.14   Thunderbolt-to-DVI converter

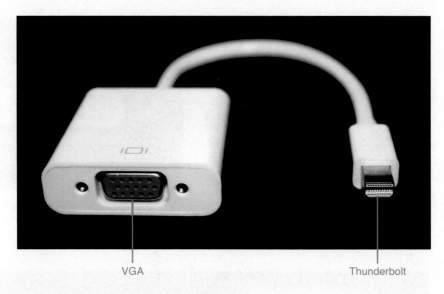

VGA   Thunderbolt

FIGURE 2.15   Thunderbolt-to-VGA converter

An exercise at the end of the chapter provides an opportunity to practice port identification.

USB Ports

USB stands for Universal Serial Bus. A **USB port** allows up to 127 connected devices to transmit at speeds up to 10Gb/s (10 billion bits per second). Devices that can connect to a USB port include printers, scanners, mice, keyboards, joysticks, optical drives, tape drives, game pads, cameras, modems, speakers, telephones, video phones, data gloves, and digitizers. Additional ports can sometimes be found on the front of a PC case or on the side of a mobile device. Figure 2.16 shows some USB ports.

FIGURE 2.16   USB ports

USB Versions

USB ports and devices come in three versions: 1.0/1.1, 2.0 (Hi-Speed), and 3.0 (SuperSpeed). USB 1.0 operates at speeds of 1.5Mb/s and 12Mb/s; version 2.0 operates at speeds up to 480Mb/s. Version 3.0 transmits data up to 5Gb/s. The 3.0 USB port, which still accepts older devices and cables, is colored blue. Version 3.1 increases the speed to 10Gb/s, is backward compatible with prior versions, can deliver more power, and ports are colored teal.

To achieve USB 3.0/1 speeds, however, a 3.0/1 device, 3.0/1 port, and 3.0/1 cable must be used. The version 1 and 2 cables used 4 wires. Version 3 cables use 9 wires. Figure 2.17 shows the different version and speed symbols. Note that the port is not required to be labeled, and sometimes looking at the technical specifications for the computer or motherboard is the only way to determine port speed.

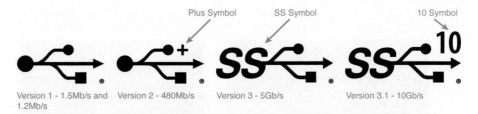

Plus Symbol   SS Symbol   10 Symbol

Version 1 - 1.5Mb/s and   Version 2 - 480Mb/s   Version 3 - 5Gb/s   Version 3.1 - 10Gb/s
1.2Mb/s

FIGURE 2.17   USB versions, speeds, and symbols

USB Cables

Each USB standard has a maximum cable length:

> Version 1.0/1.1: 9.8 feet, or 3 meters
> Version 2.0: 16.4 feet, or 5 meters
> Version 3.x: 9.8 feet, or 3 meters

USB cables can be longer than these specifications, but the standards are provided to ensure that devices function properly. Sometimes a USB extender cable is needed. Figure 2.18 shows a cable used to extend the length of a standard USB cable.

FIGURE 2.18   USB extension cable

USB Connectors

USB ports are known as upstream ports and downstream ports. An **upstream port** is used to connect to a computer or another hub. A USB device connects to a **downstream port**. Downstream ports are commonly known as **USB Type-A** and **USB Type-B**. A standard USB cable has a Type-A male connector on one end and a Type-B male connector on the other end. The port on the computer is a Type-A port. The Type-A connector inserts into the Type-A port. The Type-B connector attaches to the Type-B port on the USB device. Figure 2.19 shows Type-A and Type-B connectors.

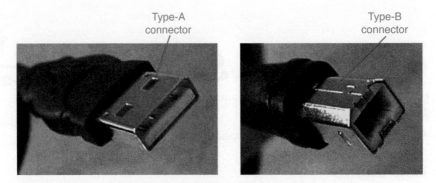

FIGURE 2.19   USB Type-A and Type-B connectors

The USB Type-C connector is the latest connector that will eventually replace the Type-A and Type-B connectors. Older devices use an adapter and the older cables in order to attach to a Type-C connector. Many USB 3.x ports are Type-C connectors, but they do not have to be. Figure 2.20 shows the USB Type-C connector and cable.

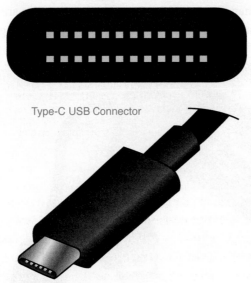

Type-C USB Connector

FIGURE 2.20   USB Type-C connector and cable

USB Hubs

A USB port can have more than one device attached to the port through the use of a USB hub. Many hubs can operate in two power modes—self-powered and bus-powered—and a hub may have a switch control that must be set to the appropriate mode. A **self-powered hub** has an external power supply attached. A **bus-powered hub** has no external power supply connected to it. Once USB devices attached to a hub are tested, the hub's power supply can be removed and the devices can be retested. If all attached devices work properly, the hub power supply can be left disconnected. Figure 2.21 shows USB hub connectivity, and Figure 2.22 shows USB cabling rules.

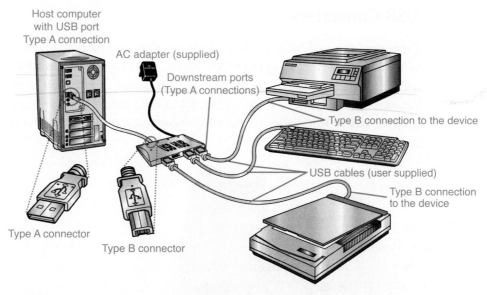

Host computer
with USB port
Type A connection

AC adapter (supplied)

Downstream ports
(Type A connections)

Type B connection to the device

USB cables (user supplied)

Type B connection
to the device

Type A connector

Type B connector

FIGURE 2.21   USB hub connectivity

USB cabling rules

• 5 hubs maximum (total max range of 88.5 feet or 27 meters)
• 127 devices maximum connected to up to 5 hubs
• Maximum distance between 2 USB hubs
         high-speed devices – 16.4 feet or 5 meters
         low-speed devices – 9.8 feet or 3 meters

FIGURE 2.22   USB cabling rules

USB ports have always been able to provide power to unpowered devices, such as flash drives. A **charging USB port** is a port designed to be able to provide power- and charge-attached devices. Note that not all USB devices can be powered on while charging. A **sleep-and-charge USB port** is one in which the port still provides power to the device (power to charge the device), even when the computer is powered off. See the computing device's specifications to see if a USB port supports this feature. Table 2.3 summarizes USB speeds, port colors, and alternate names.

TECH TIP

Safely remove USB devices

To remove a USB device, do not simply unplug it from the port. Instead, click on the *Safely Remove Hardware* icon from the notification area and select the USB device to remove. The operating system prompts when it is safe to unplug the device.

TABLE 2.3   USB port summary

Port type	Speed	Port color	Alternate name
USB 1.x	1.5 and 12Mb/s	Usually white	Low speed and full speed
USB 2.0	480Mb/s	Black	High speed
USB 3.0	5Gb/s	Blue	SuperSpeed
USB 3.1 Gen 1	5Gb/s	Blue	SuperSpeed
USB 3.1 Gen 2	10Gb/s	Teal	SuperSpeed+
USB sleep-and-charge	N/A	Yellow, orange, or red	N/A

USB Converters

Converters are available to convert a USB port to a different type of connector (or vice versa), such as PS/2 mouse/keyboard, or mini-DIN. Figure 2.23 shows a **PS/2-to-USB converter** that inserts into a PS/2 mini-DIN connector and allows a USB mouse or keyboard to be connected if the device supports USB. Figure 2.24 shows a USB-to-PS/2 mouse and keyboard connector. Figure 2.25 shows a **USB-to-Ethernet converter** used to connect a device, such as a tablet that has a USB port to a wired network.

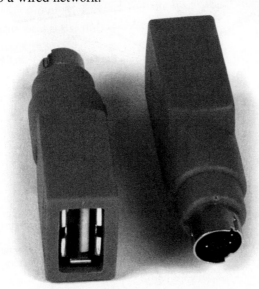

FIGURE 2.23   Mini-DIN-to-USB converter

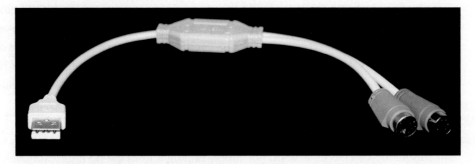

FIGURE 2.24   USB-to-PS/2 mouse and keyboard converter

A smaller USB port used on small devices such as USB hubs, digital cameras, and phones is known as a mini-USB port. There are several types of smaller USB ports: mini-A, mini-AB, micro-B, and micro-AB. The mini-/micro-AB ports accept either a mini-/micro-A or a mini-/micro-B cable end. Figure 2.26 shows the standard Type-A USB port found on a PC compared to the mini-B and micro-B ports found on mobile devices. The micro-USB ports are now a standard interface for smartphones. Figure 2.27 shows a USB 3.0 micro-B connector and port. Figure 2.28 shows a set of USB connectors that can be purchased as a set including a **USB A-to-USB B converter**.

FIGURE 2.25   USB-to-Ethernet converter

Standard Type-A
USB

Mini-
USB

Micro-
USB

FIGURE 2.26   USB Type-A, mini, and micro ports

FIGURE 2.27   USB micro-B 3.0 port and cable

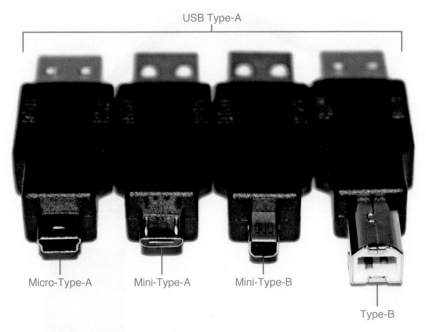

FIGURE 2.28   USB converter kit

Other USB Types

USB has expanded into other fields. **USB OTG** (on-the-go) is a supplement to the USB 2.0 specification and is included in the specification for USB 3.0. Normally with USB, a device that does not have too much intelligence built into it attaches to a host—specifically, a PC. USB OTG allows a USB device, such as an audio player or a mobile phone, to act as the host device. This allows two USB devices to communicate without the use of a PC or a hub. The supplement still allows the USB OTG device to attach to a PC because USB OTG is backward compatible with the USB 2.0 standard.

Certified W-USB (wireless USB) supports high-speed, secure wireless connectivity between a USB device and a PC, at speeds comparable to Hi-Speed USB. Certified Wireless USB is not a networking technology; it is just another way that you can connect your favorite USB devices to a host. You just don't have to plug a cable into a USB port. Wireless USB supports speeds of 480Mb/s at a range up to 3 meters (~10 feet) or 110Mb/s up to 10 meters (~30 feet). Wireless USB uses ultra-wideband low-power radio over a range of 3.1 to 10.5GHz. Figure 2.29 shows the various USB logos that might be found on devices.

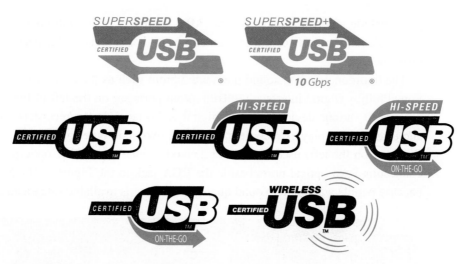

FIGURE 2.29   USB logos

Installing Extra USB Ports

Sometimes people want more USB ports and do not want to add another hub or a hub with more ports. Many motherboards support adding two or more USB ports by using a cable that attaches to motherboard pins, which is also known as a USB header. The ports mount in an expansion slot space, but they do not take an expansion slot. Even if the motherboard has such pins, the ports and cable assembly might have to be purchased separately. Figure 2.30 shows sample USB ports that attach to a motherboard.

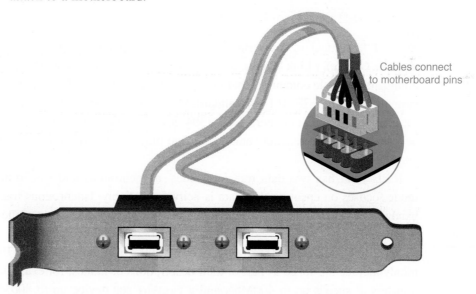

FIGURE 2.30   Installing extra USB ports

Audio Ports

A **sound card** converts digital computer signals to sound and sound to digital computer signals. A sound card is sometimes called an audio card. Sound ports are commonly integrated into the motherboard, but some people want better sound and so they add a card. The most common sound ports include a port for a microphone, MP3 player, or other audio device and one or more ports for speakers. The ports can accept analog or digital signals. Refer back to Figure 2.3 to see the difference.

The traditional analog sound ports are 3.5mm such as those shown in Figure 2.31. The newer Sony/Phillips Digital interface (**S/PDIF**) in/out ports are on the left in Figure 2.31 and are used to connect to various devices, such as digital audio tape players/recorders, DVD players/recorders, and external disc players/recorders. There are two main types of S/PDIF connectors: an **RCA** jack (last port on the left) used to connect a coaxial cable and a fiber-optic port for a **TOSLINK** cable connection (two optical ports beside the RCA jack in the Figure 2.31). Sound cards are popular because people want better sound quality than what is available integrated into a motherboard.

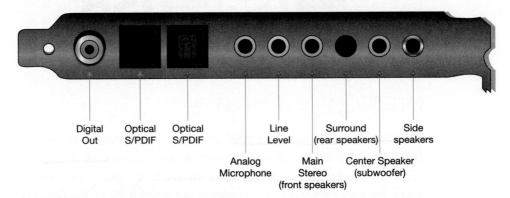

FIGURE 2.31   Sound card ports

IEEE 1394 (FireWire) Ports

The **IEEE 1394** standard is a serial technology developed by Apple Inc. Sometimes it is known as **FireWire** (Apple), i.Link (Sony), or Lynx (Texas Instruments). **IEEE 1394 ports** have been more predominant on Apple computers, but they are also seen on some PCs. Windows and Apple operating systems support the IEEE 1394 standard. Many digital products have an integrated IEEE 1394 port for connecting to a computer. IEEE 1394 devices include camcorders, cameras, printers, storage devices, video conferencing cameras, optical players and drives, tape drives, film readers, speakers, and scanners.

IEEE 1394 has two data transfer modes: asynchronous and isochronous. The asynchronous mode focuses on ensuring that data is delivered reliably. Isochronous transfers allow guaranteed bandwidth (which is needed for audio/video transfers) but do not provide for error correction or retransmission.

Speeds supported are 100, 200, 400, 800, 1200, 1600, and 3200Mb/s. IEEE 1394 devices commonly include the speed as part of their descriptions or names; for example, a **FireWire 400** device transfers at speeds up to 400Mb/s and a **FireWire 800** device up to 800Mb/s. With FireWire, as many as 63 devices (using cable lengths up to 14 feet) can be connected (daisy-chained). The IEEE 1394 standard supports hot swapping, plug-and-play, and powering of low-power devices.

An IEEE 1394 cable has 4, 6, or 9 pins. A 4-pin cable/connector does not provide power, so the device must have its own power source. The 6- and 9-pin connectors do provide power. A 6-pin connector is used on desktop computers and can provide power to the attached IEEE 1394 device. A 9-pin connector is used to connect to 800Mb/s devices that are also known as IEEE 1394b devices. Figure 2.32 shows an IEEE 1394 port found on PCs, a mini port found on mobile devices, and a 9-pin port found on 800Mb/s IEEE 1394 devices. Figure 2.33 shows three IEEE 1394 ports on an adapter.

6-pin FireWire 400   Mobile device   9-pin FireWire 800
                            4-pin IEEE
                            1394 port

FIGURE 2.32   FireWire ports

FIGURE 2.33   IEEE 1394 ports on an adapter

An IEEE 1394 device can connect to a port built into the motherboard, an IEEE 1394 port on an adapter, another IEEE 1394 device, or a hub. A motherboard might have pins to connect additional IEEE 1394 ports. IEEE 1394 does not require a PC to operate; two IEEE 1394 devices can communicate via a cable. The IEEE 1394 bus is actually a peer-to-peer standard, meaning that a computer is not needed. Two IEEE 1394–compliant devices can be connected (for example, a hard drive and a digital camera), and data transfer can occur across the bus.

IEEE 1394c devices transmit at 800Mb/s, but instead of using a 9-pin connector, they have an RJ-45 connector, such as an Ethernet port (shown later in this chapter, in the "Network Ports" section). The IEEE 1394d standard uses a fiber connection. Table 2.4 provides a summary of the different IEEE 1394 standards.

TABLE 2.4   IEEE 1394 standards

Standard	Other names	Description	Cable
IEEE 1394	S100, S200, S400, and FireWire 400	Speeds of 100, 200, or 400Mb/s half-duplex (one transmission direction at a time); 6-pin connector (later named the Alpha connector)*	~15 feet (4.5 meters) on a single cable; up to 60 feet (18 meters) with extra cables and a repeater
IEEE 1394a	S100, S200, S400, and FireWire 400	Added a 4-pin nonpowered connector	See IEEE 1394

Standard	Other names	Description	Cable
IEEE 1394b	S800, S1600, S3200, and FireWire 800	Speeds up to 3200Mb/s; added a 9-pin (Beta) connector and CAT5e or better UTP (unshielded twisted pair) cable*	~15 feet (4.5 meters) on a single cable; 330 feet (100 meters) with CAT5e or better or optical cable
IEEE 1394c	S800T	Up to 800Mb/s over CAT5e or better UTP cable*	See IEEE 1394b
IEEE 1394d	N/A	Added support for single-mode fiber	N/A

*See Chapter 18 for more information on half-duplex and CAT UTP cabling.

Figure 2.34 shows a USB and two IEEE 1394 connectors. The leftmost connector is the Type-A USB connector. The center connector is the 9-pin FireWire 800 connector. The right connector is a 6-pin FireWire 400 cable.

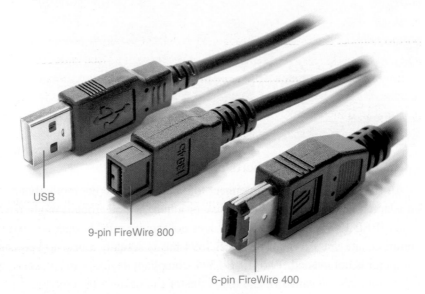

USB

9-pin FireWire 800

6-pin FireWire 400

FIGURE 2.34   USB and IEEE 1394 cables

TECH TIP

What if I don't have the right IEEE 1394 cable?

FireWire devices can have three types of connectors—4-, 6-, and 9-pin connectors. A 4-pin cable does not provide for voltage over the IEEE 1394 bus. Placing a 6-pin connection on a FireWire 800 cable reduces connection speeds to a maximum of 400Mb/s. Converters can be purchased to convert 4- to 6-pin or 6- to 9-pin connectors.

eSATA Ports

SATA (serial AT attachment) is used for connecting storage devices such as hard drives or optical drives. eSATA can transfer data at 600MB/s. A 7-pin nonpowered external SATA (**eSATA**) port is used to connect external storage devices to computers at a maximum of approximately 6.6 feet or 2 meters. An eSATA port is commonly found on laptops to provide additional storage. If the internal hard drive has crashed, an external drive connected to an eSATA or USB port could be used to boot and troubleshoot the system.

A variation of the eSATA port is the **eSATAp port**, which is also known as eSATA/USB or power over eSATA. This variation can accept eSATA or USB cables and provides power when necessary. Figure 2.35 shows a standard eSATA port and an eSATAp (eSATA/USB combination) port.

FIGURE 2.35   eSATA and eSATAp ports

Network Ports

Network ports are used to connect a computer to other computers, including a network server. The most common type of network port is an **Ethernet port**. A network cable inserts into the Ethernet port to connect the computing device to the wired network. A network port or an adapter that has a network port is commonly called a **NIC** (network interface card/controller).

Ethernet adapters commonly contain an **RJ-45** port that looks like an **RJ-11** phone jack, as shown in the next section, but the RJ-45 connector has 8 conductors instead of 4. UTP (unshielded twisted pair) cable connects to the RJ-45 port so the computing device can be connected to a wired network. An RJ-45 Ethernet port can also be found on external storage devices. A storage device could be cabled to the wired network in the same fashion as the PC. Figure 2.36 shows an Ethernet NIC with an RJ-45 port.

FIGURE 2.36   An RJ-45 Ethernet port

TECH TIP

Ethernet port symbols

Ethernet ports may not have any symbol above the port or one of the following:

Modem Ports

A **modem** connects a computer to a phone line. A modem can be internal or external. An internal modem is an adapter that has one or two RJ-11 phone jack connectors. An external modem is a separate device that sits outside the computer and connects to a 9-pin serial port or a USB port. The external modem can also have one or two RJ-11 connectors. The RJ-11 connectors look like typical phone jacks. With two RJ-11 connectors, one can be used for a telephone and the other has a cable that connects to the wall jack. The RJ-11 connector labeled *Line* is for the connection to the wall jack. The RJ-11 connector labeled *Phone* is for the connection to the phone. An internal modem with only one RJ-11 connector connects to the wall jack. Figure 2.37 shows an internal modem with two ports.

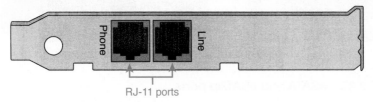

FIGURE 2.37   An internal modem with two RJ-11 ports

Integrated Motherboard Ports

An integrated motherboard provides expandability because ports are built in and do not require separate adapters. If a motherboard includes the USB, network, sound, keyboard, mouse, and video ports, there is more space available for other adapters. The number of available expansion slots in a system depends on the motherboard manufacturer. Figure 2.38 shows integrated motherboard ports.

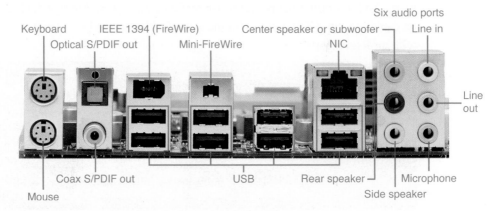

FIGURE 2.38   Integrated motherboard ports

Ports built into a motherboard are faster than those on an expansion board. All adapters in expansion slots run slower than the motherboard components. Computers with integrated motherboards are easier to set up because you do not have to install an adapter or configure the ports. Normally, systems with integrated motherboards are easier to troubleshoot because the components are on one board. The drawback is that when one port goes bad, you have to add an adapter that has the same type of port as the one that went bad. Furthermore, ports found on an adapter might be of higher quality or have more capabilities than an integrated port. See Figure 2.39.

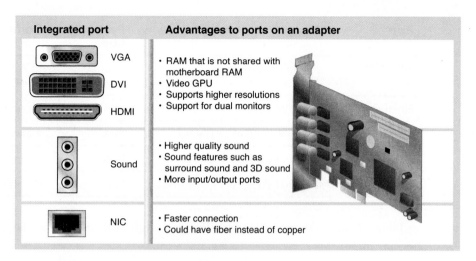

Integrated port	Advantages to ports on an adapter
VGA DVI HDMI	• RAM that is not shared with motherboard RAM • Video GPU • Supports higher resolutions • Support for dual monitors
Sound	• Higher quality sound • Sound features such as surround sound and 3D sound • More input/output ports
NIC	• Faster connection • Could have fiber instead of copper

FIGURE 2.39   Advantages of adapters

Getting to Know Ports

Being able to identify ports quickly and accurately is a critical skill in computer repair. Table 2.5 lists the most common computer ports.

TABLE 2.5   Common ports

Port	Usage	Port color code	Common connector
PS/2 mouse	Mouse	Green	6-pin mini-DIN
PS/2 keyboard	Keyboard	Purple	6-pin mini-DIN
IEEE 1394	Camcorder, video recorder, camera, printer, optical drive, scanner, speaker, hard drive	Gray	4-, 6-, or 9-pin IEEE 1394
USB	Printer, mouse, keyboard, camera, scanner, digitizer, external hard drive, optical drive	Black or blue	USB Type-A , Type-B, Type-C, mini-USB, micro-USB
Video	Analog monitor (VGA or higher)	Blue	3-row 15-pin female D-shell or mini-VGA port
Video	DVI digital or analog monitor	White	3-row 18- or 24-pin female DVI , mini-DVI, or micro-DVI
Video	HDMI digital audio and video monitor	N/A	19- or 29-pin HDMI, mini-HDMI, or micro-HDMI
Video	DisplayPort digital audio and video monitor	N/A	20-pin DisplayPort or mini-DisplayPort
Video	Thunderbolt	N/A	20-pin DisplayPort or mini-DisplayPort
Audio	Analog audio input	Light pink	1/8-inch (3.5mm) jack
Audio	Analog line level audio input	Light blue	1/8-inch (3.5mm) jack
Audio	Analog line level audio output from main stereo signal	Lime green	1/8-inch (3.5mm) jack
Audio	Analog line level audio for right-to-left speaker	Brown	1/8-inch (3.5mm) jack

Port	Usage	Port color code	Common connector
S/PDIF	Audio input/output	Orange	RCA jack (coax) or TOSLINK (fiber)
Ethernet	UTP network	N/A	8-conductor RJ-45
Modem	Internal modem or phone	N/A	4-conductor RJ-11
eSATA	External storage devices	N/A	7-pin eSATA port
eSATAp	External devices	N/A	Combination eSATA/USB port

Table 2.6 has older computer ports that you might still see, but they are not on the A+ certification any more.

TABLE 2.6   Older ports

Port	Usage	Port color code	Common connector
Parallel	Printer, tape backup	Burgundy (dark pink)	25-pin female D-shell
Serial	External modem, digitizer	Teal or turquoise	9-pin male D-shell
S-Video	Composite video device	Yellow	7-pin mini-DIN
Game port/MIDI	Joystick or MIDI device	Gold	15-pin female D-shell

Wireless Connectivity for Input Devices

Many input devices, such as keyboards, mice, game pads, touch pads, and headphones, have wireless connectivity. Technologies used to connect without a cord include infrared, radio, Bluetooth, and near field communication (NFC). Many computing devices, especially smartphones and other mobile devices, have cordless connectivity integrated into the device; otherwise, a transceiver is connected to a USB port to allow connectivity to the computing device. Figure 2.40 shows a wireless presenter used with a computing device and a projector.

FIGURE 2.40   Wireless presenter

Table 2.7 summarizes the various wireless technologies used with **input and output** devices.

TABLE 2.7 Wireless input/output technologies

Technology	Description
Infrared (**IR**)	Used for very short distances. Cheaper than other technologies.
Radio	Works in the 27 or 900MHz, or 2.4, 5, or 60GHz radio frequency range. Longer distances are supported than with infrared.
Bluetooth	Includes 128-bit security and works in the 2.4GHz range. There are three classes of devices, with ranges up to 3 feet (1 meter), 33 feet (10 meters), and 328 feet (100 meters). Up to eight devices can be connected in a master-slave relationship, with only one device being the master.
Near Field Communication (**NFC**)	Used to print from a phone or a camera or to transfer data between two smartphones that are positioned very close to one another (less than 6 inches). Works in the 13.56MHz range at transfer speeds up to 424kb/s.

SOFT SKILLS—USE APPROPRIATE TITLES

The Internet and mobile devices have brought us new methods of communication. In today's social media world, communication tends to be more casual with people using colloquialisms, slang, and other language habits that aren't necessarily professional. In addition, acronyms, such as HAGD, LOL, BTW, NRN, TYVM, and YMMD are examples of what some people use regularly to communicate, and it bleeds over into emails, notes, text messages, and memos.

Many places of business are returning to the basics when it comes to customer service, and these businesses expect you as an IT professional to use professional communication methods. People expect the IT department to up its game by using more professional communication skills. This has translated into improved soft skills that are emphasized during the hiring process. For example, the expectation is that IT personnel use appropriate titles such as Dr., Mr., Professor, and Ms. when talking to non-IT personnel, including external vendors. In the work environment, you should use a person's title, sir, or ma'am until the person you are addressing tells you otherwise. Figure 2.41 shows a couple of examples.

FIGURE 2.41   At work, use appropriate salutations

Chapter Summary

> Easily identify various ports to determine which device attaches to them: VGA, DVI, HDMI, DisplayPort, Thunderbolt, USB, IEEE 1394, 3.5mm sound jack, TOSLINK, RCA jack, PS/2, RJ-45, eSATA, and RJ-11.
> The most popular method for adding devices to desktops, laptops, and tablets is to use a USB port.
> USB 3.0/3.1 will accept 3.0/3.1 and older devices and provide more power. You can add additional ports by connecting a USB hub.
> Up to five USB hubs can be daisy-chained to one port. Upstream ports connect to the computer or another USB port. Devices connect to downstream ports.
> USB hubs can be self-powered or bus powered.
> IEEE 1394 devices do not have to have a computer port and can be cabled to each other; otherwise, an IEEE 1394 device can be cabled to a port or a hub.
> Converters are available for display ports, such as DVI to VGA.
> Converters are available for USB ports, such as USB Type A to mini-Type-A.

> Audio ports can be analog or digital. S/PDIF ports are digital. There are two types of S/PDIF ports: TOSLINK and fiber.

> Input devices can connect to the computer using four wireless technologies: IR, radio, Bluetooth, or NFC.

> When speaking with others, use appropriate professional titles when appropriate.

> Some vendors implement the **HDCP** feature on the video port. HDCP protects copyrighted material.

A+ CERTIFICATION EXAM TIPS

✓ Know what port(s) a device can use. Particular ports to know include HDMI, VGA, DVI, DisplayPort, Thunderbolt, USB, IEEE 1394, eSATA, eSATAp, PS/2, RJ-45, RJ-11, and Ethernet. (On 3×5 cards, write the names of ports you have a hard time remembering. Put a picture of the port on one side and the term on the other. Take the cards with you wherever you go the week before the exam and practice with them.)

✓ The following communication and professionalism skills are part of the 220-902 exam: Be culturally sensitive and use appropriate professional titles when applicable.

Key Terms

Review Questions

1. Match the port to the description.

    _____ DVI   a. Ethernet

    _____ VGA   b. TOSLINK

    _____ PS/2   c. up to 127 devices

    _____ USB   d. mouse/keyboard

    _____ NIC   e. CRT

    _____ S/PDIF   f. flat panel monitor

2. What is one visual indication that a USB port can be used to charge a mobile device?

    _____

3. What is a visual indication that a port is USB version 3.0?

    _____

4. What is another name for IEEE 1394?

    _____

5. How is an eSATAp port different from an eSATA port?

    _____

6. When considering VGA, HDMI, DVI, DisplayPort, and Thunderbolt, which video port can output both digital audio and video signals and is the most technologically advanced?

    _____

7. What is the most common DVI port?

    _____

8. Which has the faster transfer time when connected externally to a computer, USB 3.0, or FireWire 800?

    _____

9. What are the two ports most commonly used to attach a keyboard?

    _____

10. Describe the physical difference between an analog sound port and a digital one.

    _____

    _____

    _____

11. List two titles that might be used in the workplace that are not sir or ma'am.

    _____

12. You see a port on a computer that you have never seen before. There are no markings. How will you determine the purpose of the port?

    _____

13. What type of port uses an RJ-45 connector? [Ethernet | modem | display | keyboard]

    _____

14. List one reason why using professional titles is important to an IT person.

    _____

15. Which adapter would be used to convert from an analog signal to a digital one? [VGA to DVI-D | DVI-I to HDMI | Thunderbolt-to-DVI-I | S-Video to VGA]?

    _____

16. Which USB port type is commonly found on a PC?

_____

17. In addition to carrying video signals, which cable can also carry audio and be used to connect external storage devices? [HDMI | DVI-I | Thunderbolt | DIN]

_____

18. In which of the following situations would Bluetooth most likely be used?

   a. To connect to a corporate wireless network

   b. To attach a keyboard to a PC

   c. To connect a PC to a phone line

   d. To connect a flash drive to a camera

19. List one advantage of having an adapter rather than an integrated motherboard port. Answers will vary, but normally it is because the user wants better quality than offered by the port integrated into the motherboard. Common ports added are sound, video, and network card.

20. Draw one symbol you might see above an Ethernet port.

_____

Exercises

Exercise 2.1 Computer Port Identification

Objective: To identify various computer ports correctly

Procedure: Identify each computer port in Figure 2.42.

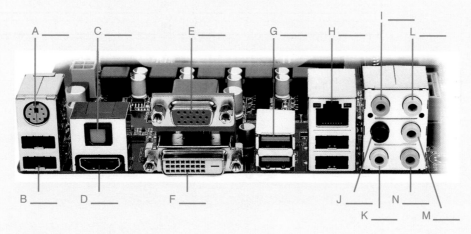

FIGURE 2.42   Identify Motherboard Ports

A._____   H._____

B._____   I._____

C._____   J._____

D._____   K._____

E._____   L._____

F._____   M._____

G._____   N._____

Exercise 2.2   More Computer Port Identification

Objective: To identify various computer port using graphics

Procedure: Identify each computer port in Figure 2.43.

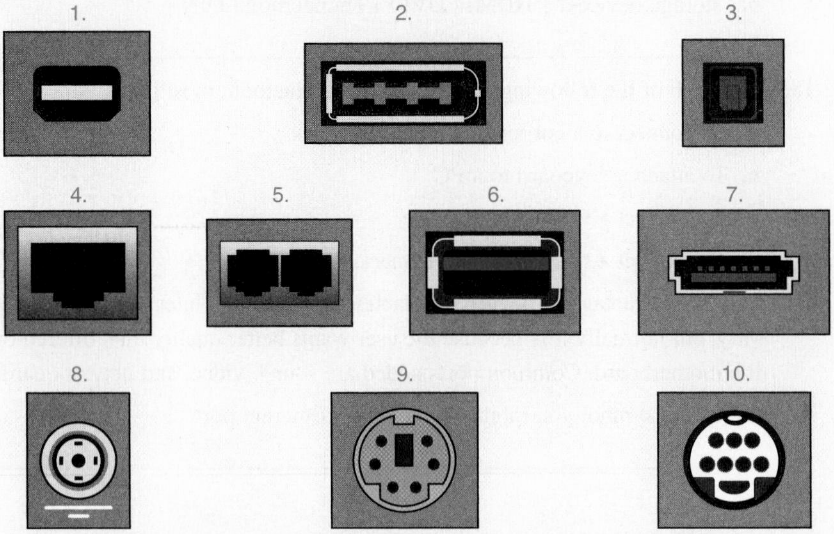

FIGURE 2.43   Identify computer port graphics

1._____   6._____

2._____   7._____

3._____   8._____

4._____   9._____

5._____   10._____

Exercise 2.3   Display Port Identification

Objective: To identify various display ports correctly

Procedure: Identify each display port in Figure 2.44.

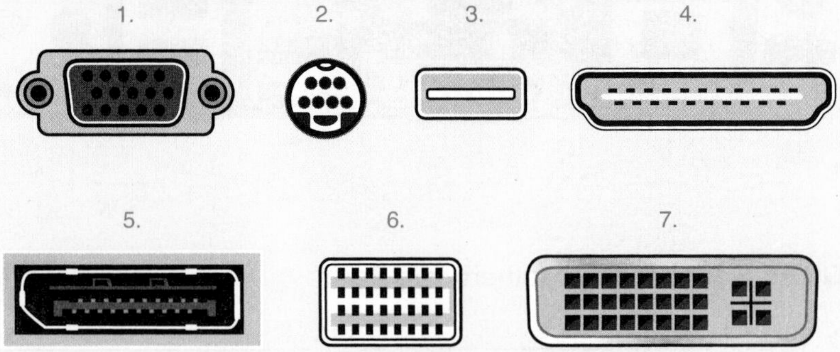

FIGURE 2.44   Identify video port graphics

1._____

2._____

3._____

4._____

5._____

6._____

7._____

Activities

Internet Discovery

Objective: To obtain specific information from the Internet regarding a computer or its associated parts

Parts: Computer with Internet access

Procedure: Complete the following procedure and answer the accompanying questions.

Questions: For Questions 1–4: Obtain technical information about a particular computer (maybe your own model or a model number given by the instructor). Answer the following questions based on the information. You may need to obtain more documents or you may need to select a different computer model to answer questions. Please use only one computer model.

1. Which ports are available on the front of the computer?

_____

2. Which ports are available on the back of the computer?

_____

3. How many drive bays are available to install devices such as hard drives, optical drives, tape drives, and so on?

_____

4. Were the photos in the documentation clear enough to differentiate between the different ports? If not, explain what is wrong.

_____

5. List ten Internet acronyms and what they stand for that would be appropriate in a text message to a family member, but inappropriate to use when communicating (even texting) with an employee from a non-IT department that is not a close friend but a professional acquaintance. Also, provide the URL(s) where this information is found.

_____
_____
_____
_____
_____
_____
_____
_____
_____
_____
_____
_____

6. Using the Internet, list one fact about NFC that was not in the chapter and the URL where you found this information.

_____
_____
_____
_____

Soft Skills

Objective: To enhance and fine-tune a future technician's ability to listen, communicate in both written and oral forms, and support people who use computers in a professional manner

Procedure:

1.   In teams of two, one student writes a professional note that contains Internet acronyms that are commonly used for texting. The other student tries to then guess what the acronyms mean. Together, rewrite the note so it is more professional.

2.   Draft an email to a pretend computer customer that you just met yesterday for the first time. You did not have the part needed to repair the computer, but now the part has come in. Be sure you use professionalism in your email.

Critical Thinking Skills

Objective: To analyze and evaluate information as well as apply learned information to new or different situations

Procedure:

1.   Find an advertisement for a computer in a local computer flyer, in a newspaper, in a magazine, in a book, or on the Internet. List which ports you know in one column and the ports you do not know in the other column. Select one port you do not know and research that component. Write the new information and share with at least one other person.

2.   Work in groups of three. As a group, do you think future computers will only have wireless connections or continue to have both wired and wireless connectivity? Why or why not? What might be some hindrances that would prevent this from happening?

_____

_____

_____

_____

_____

_____

3.   Provide five tips that might help someone identify the different computer ports. If possible, each person in the class should state a tip without duplicating someone else's tip.

_____

_____

_____

_____

_____

_____

_____

_____

Labs

Lab 2.1 Port Identification

Objective: To identify various computer ports correctly

Parts: Computer ports, either built into a specific computer or as separate adapters

Procedure:

1. Contact your instructor for a computer on which to work or to obtain adapters.

2. Identify the computer port(s) given to you by the instructor. In Table 2.8, fill in the connector type, number of pins, and port type. Note you may have to refer to information in the book or on the Internet.

TABLE 2.8   Connector identification

Connector type (D-shell, DIN, etc.)	Number of pins	Port purpose (video, USB, NIC, etc.)
1. _____	_____	_____
2. _____	_____	_____
3. _____	_____	_____
4. _____	_____	_____
5. _____	_____	_____
6. _____	_____	_____
7. _____	_____	_____
8. _____	_____	_____
9. _____	_____	_____
10. _____	_____	_____

Lab 2.2 Device/Port Identification

Objective: To identify various computer ports correctly based on the type of connected device

Parts: Computer that has devices connected

Procedure:

1. Contact your instructor for a computer on which to work.

2. Ensure the computer is powered off.

3. Each device connected to the computer will go through the same three (3) step process: (1) Identify one item attached to the computer. Trace its cable to a port. In Table 2.9, write the name of the device in the first line. (2) On the same line in the second column, identify all ports that the device could possibly use to attach to the computer. (3) Disconnect the device from the port. On the same line in the third column, identify the port to which the device actually attaches. Do the same for all devices connected to the computer.

   Note: You may have to refer to information in the book or on the Internet.

TABLE 2.9   Port Identification

Device attached	Ports that possibly could have this device attached	Remove device and identify the port the device actually connects to. Reattach device when finished.
1. _____	_____	_____
2. _____	_____	_____
3. _____	_____	_____
4. _____	_____	_____

3 On the Motherboard

In this chapter you will learn:

> To recognize and identify important motherboard parts

> To explain the basics of how a processor works

> Issues to consider when upgrading or replacing the motherboard or processor

> Information regarding GPUs

> How to add cards to computers

> The differences between PCI, PCI-X, AGP, and PCIe adapters and slots

> Motherboard technologies such as HyperTransport, Hyper-Threading, and multi-core

> The benefits of active listening

CompTIA Exam Objectives:

What CompTIA A+ exam objectives are covered in this chapter?

✓ 901-1.2   Explain the importance of motherboard components, their purpose, and properties.

✓ 901-1.4   Install and configure PC expansion cards.

✓ 901-1.6   Install and configure various types of CPUs and apply the appropriate cooling method.

✓ 901-4.1   Given a scenario, troubleshoot common problems related to motherboards, RAM, CPU, and power with appropriate tools.

✓ 902-5.4   Demonstrate proper communication techniques and professionalism.

On the Motherboard Overview

Chapter 1 introduced you to the motherboard, which holds the majority of the electronics in the computer. Chapter 2 focused on connecting devices to a motherboard port or through an adapter port. Some parts of the motherboard are of specific interest to IT staff and that is what this chapter delves into. Key parts of the motherboard include the processor and processor socket, memory or RAM slots, and the various types of expansion slots. Figure 3.1 points out these key motherboard components.

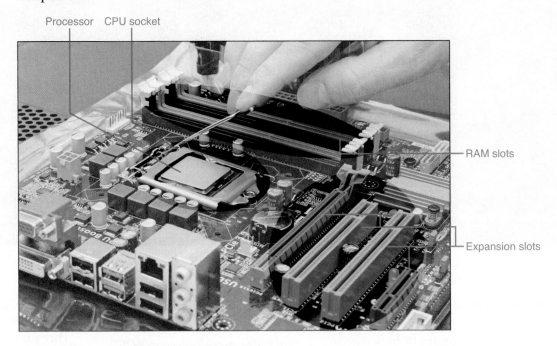

FIGURE 3.1 **Key motherboard components**

Processor Overview

At the heart of every computer is a special motherboard chip called the **processor**, which determines, to a great extent, the power of the computer. The processor is also called the central processing unit (**CPU**) or microprocessor. The processor executes instructions, performs calculations, and coordinates input/output operations. Each motherboard has electronic chips that work with the CPU and are designed to exact specifications. Whether these other electronic components can keep up with the processor depends on the individual component's specifications. The major processor manufacturers today are Intel, Motorola, VIA, Samsung, NVIDIA, Apple Inc., Qualcomm, and AMD (Advanced Micro Devices, Inc.). Intel and AMD are the predominant manufacturers for desktop and laptop processors, and the other manufacturers target the mobile/smartphone markets. Figure 3.2 shows a processor.

FIGURE 3.2   Intel processor

Processor Basics

Processors come in a variety of speeds, measured in **gigahertz** (GHz). Hertz is a measurement of cycles per second. One hertz equals one cycle per second. One gigahertz is 1 billion cycles per second, or 1GHz. The original PC CPU, the 8088 microprocessor, ran at 4.77MHz. Today's processors run at speeds near 5GHz.

The number of bits processed at one time is the processor's register size (word size). Intel's 8086 processor's register size is 16 bits, or 2 bytes. Today's CPUs have register sizes of 64 or 128 bits.

Buses

Processors operate on 1s and 0s. Processors operate on 1s and 0s. The 1s and 0s must travel from one place to another inside the processor, as well as outside to other chips. To move the 1s and 0s around, electronic lines called a **bus** are used. The electronic lines inside the CPU are known as the **internal data bus** or system bus. In the 8086, the internal data bus comprises 16 separate lines, with each line carrying one 1 or one 0. The word size and the number of lines for the internal data bus are equal. The 8086, for example, has a 16-bit word size, and 16 lines carry 16 bits on the internal data bus. In today's processors, 64 or 128 internal data bus lines operate concurrently.

For a CPU to communicate with devices in the outside world, such as a printer, the 1s and 0s travel on the **external data bus**. The external data bus connects the processor to adapters, the keyboard, the mouse, the hard drive, and other devices. An external data bus is also known as an external data path. You can see the external data lines by looking between the expansion slots on the motherboard. Some solder lines between the expansion slots are used to send data out along the external data bus to the expansion slots. Today's processors have 64- and 128-bit external data paths. Figure 3.3 shows the internal and external data buses.

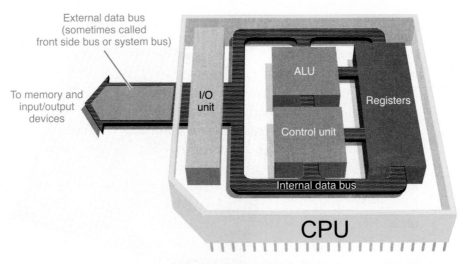

FIGURE 3.3   Internal and external data buses

ALUs

A processor has a special component called the arithmetic logic unit (ALU), which does all the calculations and comparison logic that the computer needs. Figure 3.3 shows the basic concept of how the ALU connects to the registers, control unit, and internal bus. The control unit coordinates activities inside the processor. The I/O unit manages data entering and leaving the processor. The registers in the CPU make up a high-speed storage area for 1s and 0s before the bits are processed.

To make sense of all of this, take a look at a letter typed on a computer that starts out *DEAR MOM*. To the computer, each letter of the alphabet is a different combination of eight 1s and 0s. For example, the letter *D* is 01000100, and the letter *E* is 01000101. Figure 3.4 demonstrates that the size of the bus greatly increases performance on a computer similar to the way that increasing the number of lanes of a highway decreases congestion.

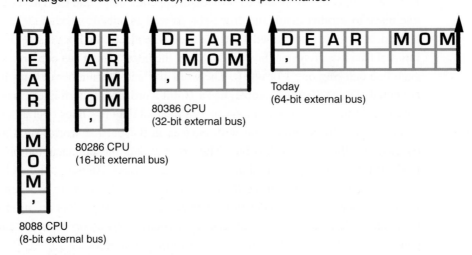

FIGURE 3.4   Bus performance

Pipelines

Processors have multiple pipelines (separate internal buses) that operate simultaneously. To understand pipelining, take the example of a fast-food restaurant. In the restaurant, assume that there are five steps (and one employee per step) involved in making a burger and giving it to the customer. First, (1) take the order and input it into the computer system; (2) brown the buns and cook the burgers; (3) add the condiments to the buns and burgers; (4) wrap the burgers, add fries, and insert them into the bag; and then (5) take the customer's money and give the bag to the customer. Keep in mind that the person taking the customer's order and inputting the order can serve another customer once he or she has completed this task for the first customer. The same is true for each person along the line. To make this burger process go faster, you could (maybe) do one of the things shown in Figure 3.5. (1) Make your employees work faster; (2) break the tasks into smaller tasks (such as seven steps instead of five and have seven people); or, (3) have more lines of people doing exactly the same process tasks.

FIGURE 3.5   **Ways to get faster processes**

To relate this to processors, making the employees work faster is the same as increasing the CPU clock speed. Breaking the tasks into smaller tasks is the same as changing the structure of the CPU pipeline. Instead of performing the standard 5 tasks, the CPU might perform 6, 7, 14, 20, or even more steps. This allows each step to be acted upon more quickly, the task to be smaller, and production to be faster. Having more lines of people doing the same complete process is like having multiple pipelines.

A 32- or 64-bit CPU can have separate paths, each of which handles 32 or 64 bits. For example, if a processor has two pipelines, the Dear Mom letter can be in one pipeline, while a photo upload using a different application can be in the other pipeline.

A processor might have 12 pipelines for integers and 17 pipelines for floating-point numbers. (A floating-point number is a number that can include a decimal point.) Other processors contain anywhere from 20- to 31-stage pipelines. Debate continues about whether a longer pipeline improves performance.

Speeding Up Processor Operations Overview

You can determine the speed of a processor by looking at the model number on the chip, but processors frequently have devices attached to them for cooling, which makes it difficult to see the writing on the chip. A processor commonly does not use its maximum speed all the time in order to save power or stay cool. Also, a processor is not always functioning at its maximum potential for a lot of reasons including coding used within an application, the user switching from application to application, inadequate bus width, or the amount of RAM installed. The processor can also operate beyond its rated specifications. Intel Turbo Boost allows the processor to operate faster than it is rated in order to handle periods of increased workload.

TECH TIP

Locating your processor speed

An easy way to tell processor speed with Windows is to right-click *Computer (Vista/7) or This PC (8/10)* from within Windows Explorer/File Explorer > *Properties*.

We have already taken a look at how increasing the CPU pipeline can, to some extent, improve processor operations, but other technologies also exist. We will start by defining some of the terms that relate to this area and associating those terms with concepts and the various technologies used. Table 3.1 list some terms related to speed.

TABLE 3.1   Motherboard speed terms

Term	Explanation
clock or **clock speed**	The speed of the processor's internal clock, measured in gigahertz.
bus speed	The speed at which data is delivered when a particular bus on the motherboard is being used.
front side bus (FSB)	The speed between the CPU and some of the motherboard components. This is what most people would term the motherboard speed. Sometimes the speed is listed in megatransfers per second, or MT/s. With MT/s, not only is the speed of the FSB considered, but also how many processor transfers occur each clock cycle. A 266MHz FSB that can do four transfers per second could list as 1064MT/s. The FSB is being upgraded with technologies such as AMD's HyperTransport and Intel's QPI (QuickPath Interconnect) and DMI (Direct Media Interface).
back side bus	The speed between the CPU and the L2 cache located outside the main CPU but on the same chip.
PCI bus speed	The speed at which data is delivered when the PCI bus is being used. Common speeds for the PCI bus are 33 and 66MHz, allowing bandwidths up to 533MB/s.
PCIe bus speed	The speed at which data is delivered when the PCIe bus is being used. This bus is the main bus used on the motherboard and is used for PCIe adapters. Common speeds for the PCIe bus v2.x are from 500MB/s (x1) to 8GB/s (x16), v3.x are from 985MB/s (x1) to 15.75GB/s (x16), and 4.x are from 1969 MB/s (x1) to 31.51GB/s (x16).

Term	Explanation
AGP bus speed	The speed at which data is delivered when the AGP bus is being used. The AGP bus is an older standard used for video cards.
CPU speed	The speed at which the CPU operates; it can be changed on some motherboards.
CPU throttling	Reducing the clock frequency to slow the CPU in order to reduce power consumption and heat. This is especially useful in mobile devices.

Cache

An important concept related to processor speed is keeping data flowing into the processor. Registers are a type of high-speed memory storage inside the processor. They are used to temporarily hold calculations, data, or instructions. The data or instruction the CPU needs to operate on is usually found in one of three places: cache memory, the motherboard memory (main memory), or the hard drive.

Cache memory is a very fast type of memory designed to increase the speed of processor operations. CPU efficiency is increased when data continuously flows into the CPU. Cache provides the fastest access. If the information is not in cache, the processor looks for the data in motherboard RAM. If the information is not there, it is retrieved from the hard drive and placed into the motherboard memory or the cache. Hard drive access is the slowest of the three. Table 3.2 lists the types of cache.

TABLE 3.2   Types of cache

Type	Explanation
L1 cache	Cache memory integrated into the processor
L2 cache	Cache in the processor packaging, but not part of the CPU; also called on-die cache
L3 cache	Usually found in the more powerful processors and can be located in the CPU housing (on-die) or on the motherboard

An analogy best explains this. Consider a glass of cold lemonade, a pitcher of lemonade, and a can of frozen lemonade concentrate. If you were thirsty, you would drink from the glass because it is the fastest and most easily accessible. If the glass were empty, you would pour lemonade from the pitcher to refill the glass. If the pitcher were empty, you would go to the freezer to get the frozen concentrate to make more lemonade. Figure 3.6 shows this concept.

Usually, the more cache memory a system has, the better that system performs, but this is not always true. System performance also depends on the efficiency of the cache controller (the chip that manages the cache memory), the system design, the amount of available hard drive space, and the speed of the processor. When determining memory requirements, you must consider the operating system used, applications used, and hardware installed. The Windows XP operating system takes a lot less memory than Windows 10. High-end games and desktop publishing take more RAM than word processing. Free hard drive space and video memory are often as important as RAM in improving a computer's performance. Memory is only one piece of the puzzle. All of the computer's parts must work together to provide efficient system performance. Figure 3.7 shows this hierarchy of data access for the CPU.

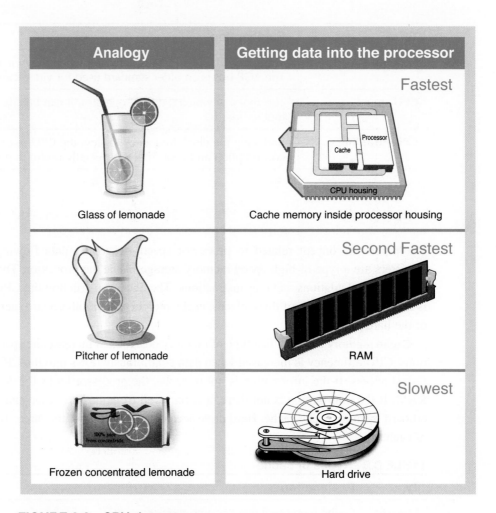

Analogy	Getting data into the processor
Glass of lemonade	Fastest Cache memory inside processor housing
Pitcher of lemonade	Second Fastest RAM
Frozen concentrated lemonade	Slowest Hard drive

FIGURE 3.6   CPU data sources

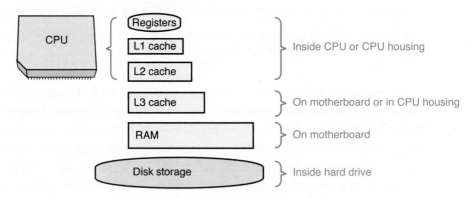

FIGURE 3.7   Data access hierarchy

Clocking

The motherboard generates a clock signal that is used to control the transfer of 1s and 0s to and from the processor. A clock signal can be illustrated as a sine wave. One clock cycle is from one point on the sine wave to the next point that is located on the same point on the sine wave later in time, as shown in Figure 3.8.

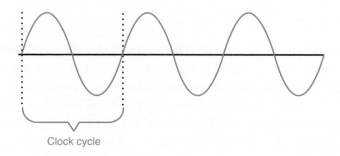

Clock cycle

FIGURE 3.8   Clock cycle

In older computers, data was sent to the CPU only once during a clock cycle. Then, newer memory technologies evolved that allow data to be sent twice during every clock cycle. Today, data is sent four times during a single clock cycle, as shown in Figure 3.9.

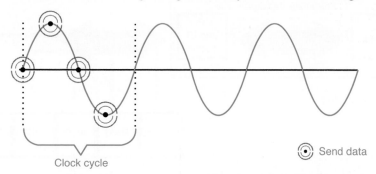

Clock cycle

⊙ Send data

FIGURE 3.9   Clock cycle that clocks data four times per cycle

Threading Technology

Several threading techniques are used to speed up processor efficiency: multithreading and HT (Hyper-Threading Technology). A **thread** is a small piece of an application process that can be handled by an operating system. An operating system such as Windows schedules and assigns resources to a thread. Each thread can share resources (such as the processor or cache memory) with other threads. A thread in the pipeline might have a delay due to waiting on data to be retrieved or access to a port or another hardware component. Multithreading keeps the line moving by letting another thread execute some code. This is like a grocery cashier taking another customer while someone goes for a forgotten loaf of bread. Figure 3.10 shows this concept.

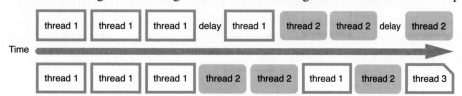

FIGURE 3.10   Multithreading

Intel's HTT (**Hyper-Threading** HT or HT Technology) allows a single processor to handle two separate sets of instructions simultaneously. To the operating system, HT makes the system appear as if it has multiple processors. Intel claims that the system can have up to a 30 percent increase in performance, but studies have shown that the increase is application dependent. If the application being used cannot take advantage of the multithreading, then HT can be disabled in the system BIOS/unified extensible firmware interface (UEFI) (covered in Chapter 4).

Connecting to the Processor

We have considered various ways to speed up processor operations, including having more stages in the processor, increasing the speed of the clock, and sending more data in the same amount of time. Accessing L2 cache and motherboard components was a bottleneck in older systems because the CPU used the same bus to communicate with RAM and other motherboard components as it did with L2 and motherboard cache. The solution is DIB (dual independent bus). With DIB, two buses are used: a back side bus and a front side bus. The back side bus connects the CPU to the L2 cache. The FSB (front side bus) connects the CPU to the motherboard components. The FSB is considered the speed of the motherboard. Figure 3.11 illustrates the concept of a front side bus. Remember that the front side bus is more detailed than what is shown; the figure simply illustrates the difference between the back side bus and the front side bus.

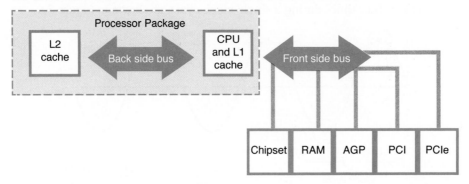

FIGURE 3.11   Front and back side bus

Many people think that the higher the CPU speed, the faster the computer. This is seldom true. Several factors contribute to computer speed. One factor is bus speed. Bus speed describes how fast the CPU can communicate with motherboard components, such as memory, the chipset, or the PCI/PCIe bus. The first Pentium CPUs ran at the same speed as the bus (60MHz); in time, CPUs got faster and buses stayed the same. Advances in technology have not reached the rest of the motherboard components (and it would cost too much to try to have them keep pace).

Intel and AMD have technologies to replace the front side bus in some parts. AMD's solution is Direct Connect. Direct Connect allows each of the processor cores to connect directly to memory, to the other motherboard components such as the expansion slots, and to other processor cores using a high-speed bus called **HyperTransport**. Figure 3.13, later in this chapter, shows HyperTransport connectivity. Intel has QuickPath Interconnect (QPI), Serial Peripheral Interface (SPI), and Direct Media Interface (DMI), which are full-duplex (that is, traffic can flow in both directions simultaneously) point-to-point connections between the processor and one or more motherboard components. This type of connectivity used with Intel-based processors and chipsets is shown later in Figure 3.38.

Multi-Core Processors

In the past, when two processors were installed, software had to be specifically written to support having multiple processors. That is no longer true. A **dual-core** processor combines two CPUs in a single unit. A tri-core processor has three processors in a single unit. Both Intel and AMD have **quad-core** CPU technologies, which is either two dual-core CPUs installed on the same motherboard, two dual-core CPUs installed in a single socket, or today's model of all four cores installed in one unit. Now there are also **hexa-core** (six cores) and **octa-core** (eight cores) processors. IT professionals in the field find it easiest to just say *multi-core* to describe the multiple cores contained in the same processor housing.

Single-core processors and early dual-core processors accessed memory through a memory controller, as shown in Figure 3.12. Today, the processor cores have their own memory controller built into the processor. Figure 3.13 shows how an AMD quad-core processor has an integrated controller and interfaces with the rest of the motherboard using a high-speed bus called HyperTransport. HyperTransport is a feature of AMD's Direct Connect architecture. With Direct Connect, there are no front side buses. Instead, the memory controller and input/output functions directly connect to the CPU.

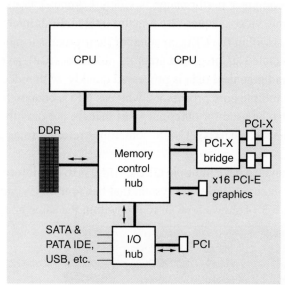

FIGURE 3.12   Older method of processors interfacing with memory

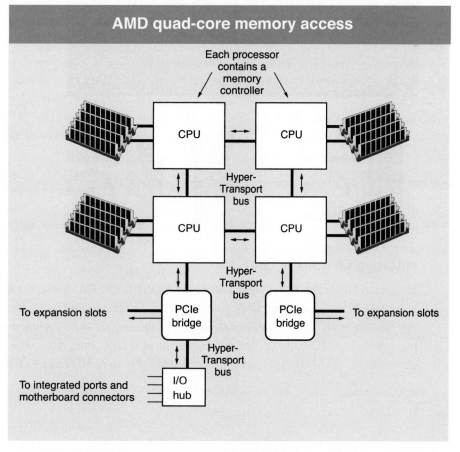

FIGURE 3.13   AMD quad-core memory access

All applications can take advantage of the multi-core technology and the background processes that are associated with the operating system and applications. This improves operations when multitasking or when running powerful applications that require many instructions to be executed, such as drawing applications and games.

Graphics Processing Unit (GPU)

Another bottleneck for computer performance is video. Computer users who want better video performance buy a separate video adapter that contains a GPU. Both Intel and AMD have a graphics processing unit (**GPU**) within the CPU on some of their processor models. With an integrated GPU (**iGPU**), sometimes called an integrated graphics processor (**IGP**), an external video card with a GPU is not required, and graphical data is processed quickly, with reduced power consumption. Today's CPUs contain multiple core processors, whereas GPUs contain hundreds of smaller core processors. GPUs can also be used for other purposes that are not directly related to graphics that increase system performance. These GPUs are sometimes referred to as a general-purpose GPU (GPGPU).

A computer system can also have multiple GPUs. AMD provides information about the number of "compute cores." For example, an AMD system that has four CPUs and two GPUs would have six compute cores. Figure 3.14 shows how an IGP is within the same housing as the CPU cores.

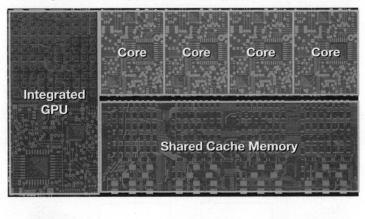

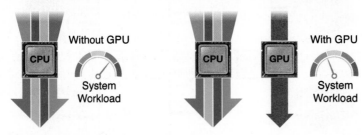

FIGURE 3.14   CPU vs. GPU

Integrated GPUs can either share part of the motherboard RAM with the rest of the system or have a separate block of memory dedicated for video. Integrated GPUs can have their own cache memory or share with the CPU. IGPs can be part of the chipset or be included as part of the CPU housing (on-die). AMD calls its processors that have a GPU integrated with the CPU an accelerated processing unit (**APU**). Intel calls its integrated GPU Intel HD Graphics and Intel Iris Graphics.

Virtualization

One advantage of having multiple processor cores is that home and business computers can take advantage of virtualization. **Virtualization** is having one or two virtual machines on the same computer. Virtualization software, such as VMware Workstation, Oracle VM VirtualBox, or Microsoft Hyper-V, enables one computer to act as if it were two or more computers. The computer can have two or more operating systems installed through the use of the virtualization software. Each operating system would have no knowledge of the other operating system.

Windows 7 has Virtual PC and Windows 8 has Hyper-V, which allow an application to run in a virtual environment as if an older operating system had been installed. The concept of virtualization is of interest to businesses so that legacy software can be put on a newer machine but kept separate from the main operating system or another virtualized machine on the same computer. Reduced costs and physical space are benefits of virtualization. Home computer users can install multiple operating systems in separate VMs (virtual machines) within the same physical box, with each VM being seen as a separate computer. This would be important for those of you taking the CompTIA A+ certification. You could install Windows Visa, Windows 7, Windows 8, and Linux in order to better prepare for the exam.

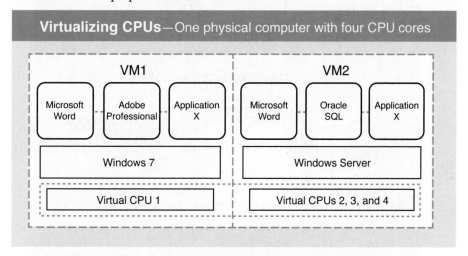

FIGURE 3.15   The concept of virtualization

Selecting a motherboard and processor is important when in a virtual environment. Not all processors were designed for virtualization. Refer to the virtualization software documentation to determine whether the CPU used is allowed to be used in a virtual environment. Another issue regarding processors and virtualization is licensing. For virtualization software that must be purchased (that is, is not freeware), the software manufacturer can charge on a per-processor or per-socket license basis or a per-core basis. If a CPU has four cores, then pricing might play into what virtualization software is purchased.

Intel Processors

Traditionally, Intel has rated its processors by GHz and people have compared processors based on speed alone. Now, Intel arranges its products by family numbers. In a family of processors, you can compare attributes such as speed and the amount of cache memory and other technologies. Table 3.3 shows Intel's processor families. Figure 3.16 shows a close-up of a processor installed into the motherboard.

TABLE 3.3   Intel processor families

Processor family*	Comments
Core i7	Multi-core with cache memory shared between cores and on-board memory controller. Good for virtualization, graphic/multimedia design and creation, and gaming.
Core i5	Midrange dual- and quad-core processor. Used for video, photos, and email, and Internet access.
Core i3	Low-end desktop and mobile processor used for common tasks such as word processing and Internet access.
Pentium	Single- or dual-core desktop/laptop processor for general computing.
Celeron	Entry-level desktop or mobile device processor for general computing.
Atom	Mobile Internet device processor.

*Intel is constantly upgrading processors. For more information, visit www.intel.com.

— Processor

FIGURE 3.16   Installed processor

CPU Sockets

A processor inserts into a socket or slot, depending on the model. Most processors today insert into a socket. There are different types of sockets: pin grid array (PGA), which has even rows of holes around a square socket; staggered pin grid array (SPGA), which has staggered holes so more pins can be inserted; plastic pin grid array (PPGA); micro pin grid array (µPGA); flip chip ball grid array (FCBGA); and land grid array (LGA) are all used with either AMD and/or Intel processors. Figure 3.17 shows a CPU socket.

AMD Processors

AMD is Intel's largest rival in computer processors. Anyone buying a processor should research all models and vendors. Table 3.4 lists the AMD processor families.

TABLE 3.4   AMD processor families

Processor family	Comments
FX	Multi-core (4-, 6-, or 8-core) high-performance desktop processor.
Phenom II	Multi-core (2, 3, 4, or 6 cores in a single package) high-end desktop for HD support, multimedia creation and editing, gaming, and virtualization. Supports 32- and 64-bit computing, 3DNow!, SSE, SSE2, SSE3, SSE4a, HyperTransport, and Direct Connect technologies.
Athlon II/Mobile/ and Athlon APU	Multi-core (2-, 3-, or 4-core) desktop/mobile processor for productivity, photos, and music.
Sempron APU/Mobile	Lower-cost, low noise, low heat desktop/notebook processor for basic productivity, email, and web browsing or in a home theater computer.
A-series APU/Mobile	Multi-core (2-, 3-, or 4-core) high-performance processor with integrated GPU.
Turion II	Single- or dual-core notebook processor.

FIGURE 3.17   CPU socket

Processor sockets are also called zero insertion force (**ZIF**) **sockets**; they come in different sizes. A processor socket accepts one or more specific processor models. The socket has a small lever to the side that, when lifted, brings the processor slightly up and out of the socket holes. When installing a processor, the CPU is aligned over the holes and the lever is depressed to bring the processor pins into the slot with equal force on all the pins. In Figure 3.17, notice the lever beside the socket that is used to lift the metal cover so the CPU can be installed into the socket. Table 3.5 lists the commonly used Intel and AMD CPU sockets and is a good study table for the A+ certification.

TECH TIP

Buying the right CPU

If you buy a motherboard and processor separately, it is important to ensure that the motherboard CPU socket is the correct type for the processor.

TABLE 3.5   Desktop CPU sockets

Socket	Description
LGA 775	775-pin for Intel Pentium 4s, Celerons, Core 2 Duo, Core 2 Extreme, and Core 2 Quads
LGA 1150	1150-pin for Intel Core Haswell, Broadwell
LGA 1155	1155-pin for Intel Core i7, i5, i3
LGA 1156	1156-pin for Intel Core i7, i5, i3
LGA 1366	1366-pin for Intel Core i7, Xeon, and Celeron
LGA 2011	2011-pin for Intel Core i7 and Xeon
AM3	940-pin for AMD Phenom II X3, X4, and Athlon II
AM3+	942-pin for AMD FX, Phenom II, Athlon II, Sempron
FM1	905-pin for AMD Athlon II, Llano
FM2	904-pin for AMD APUs, Trinity
FM2+	906-pin for AMD APUs, Kaveri, Godavari, and A8/A10 series

Processor Cooling

Keeping the CPU cool is critical. Both Intel and AMD have technologies that reduce processor energy consumption (and heat) by turning off unused parts of the processor or slowing down the processor when it starts to overheat. But these measures alone are not enough. Today's systems use one or more of the methods listed in Table 3.6. Figure 3.18 shows a heat sink and a fan.

TABLE 3.6   Processor cooling methods

Method	Description
heat sink	A block of metal (usually aluminum or copper), metal bars, or metal fins that attach to the top of the processor or other motherboard components. Heat from the processor is transferred to the heat sink and then blown away by the air flow throughout the computer case.
fan	Fans can be attached to the processor, beside the processor, and in the case.
thermal paste or thermal pad	Thermal paste, compound, or grease is applied to the top of the processor before a heat sink is attached. Some heat sinks and fans come pre-applied. A thermal pad provides uniform heat dispersion and lies between the processor and the heat sink.
liquid cooling	Liquid is circulated through the system, including through a heat sink that is mounted on the CPU. Heat from the processor is transferred to the cooler liquid. The now-hot liquid is transported to the back of the system, converted to heat, and released outside the case. CPU temperature remains constant, no matter the usage. Some systems require the liquid to be periodically refilled.
phase-change cooling (vapor cooling)	Expensive option that uses a technique similar to a refrigerator: A gas is converted to a liquid that is converted back to gas.
heat pipe	A metal tube used to transfer heat away from an electronic component.
passive cooling	Passive cooling involves no fans, so a heat sink that does not have a fan attached is known as a passive heat sink.

Heat sink   Fan

FIGURE 3.18   Heat sink and fan

The largest chip on the motherboard with a fan or a heat sink attached is easily recognized as the processor. Figure 3.19 shows an Intel Core i7 that has a fan and a heat sink installed. Notice the heat pipes that are used as part of the heat sink.

FIGURE 3.19   CPU with heat sink and fan attached

Additional motherboard components can also have heat sinks attached. These are normally the chipset and/or the I/O (input/output) controller chips. Figure 3.20 shows a motherboard with these cooling elements.

CHAPTER 3

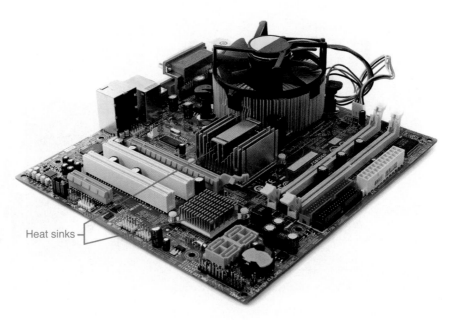

Heat sinks

FIGURE 3.20   Motherboard heat sinks

> **TECH TIP**
>
> **When thermal paste acts like glue**
>
> Over time, thermal paste can act like glue, making the processor hard to separate from the heat sink. You can use a thermal paste cleaner, acetone, or denatured alcohol to separate the two parts. Do not pry!

Installing a Processor

Processors are sold with installation instructions. Also, motherboard manuals (documentation) include the steps to upgrade or install the CPU. The following are the general steps for installing a processor:

Parts: Proper processor for the motherboard (refer to motherboard documentation)
Anti-static materials

Step 1. Ensure that power to the computer is off and the computer is unplugged.

Step 2. Place an anti-static wrist strap around your wrist and attach the other end to a ground or unpainted metal part of the computer. Otherwise, use an anti-static glove.

Step 3. Push the retention lever down and outward to release the CPU retention plate. Move the handle backward until the retention plate is fully open. Do not touch the CPU socket.

Step 4. Remove the processor from packaging, taking care to hold it by the edges and never touch the bottom metal portion of the processor. Remember that a CPU fits only one way into the socket. Look at the processor and the socket before inserting the chip to ensure proper alignment. A socket and CPU normally have a triangle marking or circular dot that indicates pin 1 as shown in Figure 3.21. The processor also has notches on each side that align with the socket. Do not force! Insert the CPU into the socket by aligning it with the socket and lowering it until it is flush with the socket as shown in Figure 3.22.

FIGURE 3.21   Pin 1 and notch on a processor

FIGURE 3.22   Installing a CPU

TECH TIP

Handling the CPU

Always hold the CPU by the edges to avoid bending or touching the pins underneath. Do not touch the CPU until it is ready to be installed in the socket.

TECH TIP

Cool the CPU

Do not apply power to the computer until the CPU and the heat sink, fan, and/or cooling unit are installed. Running the CPU without installing appropriate cooling mechanisms will overheat the CPU and destroy or weaken it.

Upgrading Processors

Two common questions asked of technicians are "Can a computer be upgraded to a higher or faster processor?" and "Should a computer be upgraded to a higher or faster processor?" Whether or not a computer can be upgraded to a higher or faster processor depends on the capability of the motherboard. When a customer asks if a processor should be upgraded, the technician should ask, "What operating system and applications are you using?" The newer the operating system, the more advanced a processor should be. Some games and applications that must perform calculations, as well as graphic-oriented applications, require a faster, more advanced processor. The motherboard's documentation is very important when considering a CPU upgrade. Read the documentation to determine whether the motherboard can accept a faster processor.

TECH TIP

Upgrading your CPU

Do not upgrade a processor unless the documentation or manufacturer states that the motherboard supports a newer or faster processor.

Throttle management is the ability to control the CPU speed by slowing it down when it is not being used heavily or when it is hot. Usually this feature is controlled by a system BIOS//UEFI setting and the Windows *Power Options* Control Panel. Some users may not want to use CPU throttling so that performance is at a maximum. Others, such as laptop users, may want to conserve power whenever possible to extend the time the laptop can be used on battery power.

Upgrading components other than the processor can also increase speed in a computer. Installing more memory, a faster hard drive, or a motherboard with a faster front side bus sometimes may improve a computer's performance more than installing a new processor. All devices and electronic components must work together to transfer the 1s and 0s efficiently. The processor is only one piece of the puzzle. Many people do not realize that upgrading only one computer component does not always make a computer faster or better.

Overclocking Processors

Overclocking is changing the front side bus speed and/or multiplier to boost CPU and system speed. Overclocking has some issues:

> CPU speed ratings are conservative.
> The processor, motherboard, memory, and other components can be damaged by overclocking.
> Applications may crash, the operating system may not boot, and/or the system may hang (lock up) when overclocking.
> The warranty may be void on some CPUs if you overclock.

> When you increase the speed of the CPU, the processor's heat increases. Extra cooling, using fans and larger heat sinks, is essential.
> Input/output devices may not react well to overclocking.
> The memory chips may need to be upgraded to be able to keep up with the faster processing.
> You need to know how to reset the system BIOS/UEFI in case the computer will not boot properly after you make changes. This process is covered in Chapter 4.

TECH TIP

Be ready to cool

The primary problem with overclocking is insufficient cooling. Make sure you purchase a larger heat sink and/or extra fans before starting the overclocking process.

Many motherboard manufacturers do not allow changes to the CPU, multiplier, and clock settings. The changes to the motherboard are most often made through BIOS/UEFI Setup. However, CPU manufacturers may provide tuning tools in the form of applications installed on the computer for overclocking configuration. Keep in mind that overclocking is a trial-and-error situation. There are websites geared toward documenting specific motherboards and overclocked CPUs.

Installing CPU Thermal Solutions

Some CPUs come with a thermal solution such as a heat sink and/or fan. The thermal solution commonly comes with a preapplied thermal paste or attached thermal pad. Heat sinks and fans attach to the processor using different methods. The most common methods are screws, thermal compound, and clips. Clips can use retaining screws, pressure release (where you press down on them, and they release), or a retaining slot. Small screwdrivers can be used to release the clips that attach using the retaining slot. Clips for fans or heat sinks can be difficult to install. The type of heat sink and/or fan installed must fit the processor and case. Additional hardware may have to be installed on the motherboard to be able to attach the CPU thermal solution. Figure 3.23 shows a CPU cooler being installed.

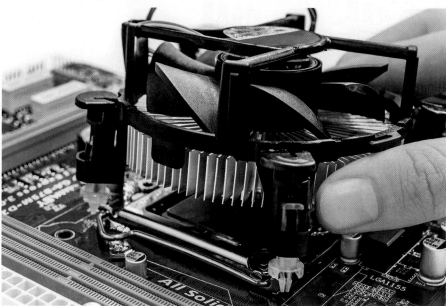

FIGURE 3.23 CPU heat sink/fan installation

Take a pic of the CPU

Before attaching a heat sink and/or fan to the CPU, take a picture of the markings on top. These could be used if you ever need technical support and need the exact specifications. Techs often take pictures to document motherboard replacements and wiring.

If a used thermal solution is being installed, then the thermal pad or old thermal paste should be removed and new thermal paste applied. Do not scratch the surface of the heat sink. Use a plastic scribe or tool to remove a thermal pad or old paste. A thermal paste cleaner, acetone, or denatured alcohol with a lint-free cloth can be used to remove residual paste.

When installing thermal paste, you should apply the prescribed amount in the center of the processor. Spread the compound evenly in a fine layer over the portion of the center of the CPU that comes in contact with the heat sink. When the heat sink is attached to the processor, the thermal compound will spread (hopefully not over the edges). Always follow the heat sink installation directions.

CPU fans frequently have a 3- or 4-pin cable that attaches to the motherboard. The motherboard might have a 3- or 4-pin connector. A 3-pin fan can be attached to a 4-pin motherboard connector, and a 4-pin fan cable can be connected to a 3-pin motherboard connector, as shown in Figure 3.24. Note that when a 3-pin cable attaches to 4-pin connector, the fan is always on and cannot be controlled, like a 4-pin cable to 4-pin connector can.

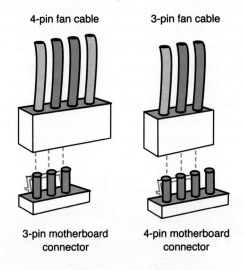

4-pin fan cable   3-pin fan cable

3-pin motherboard   4-pin motherboard
   connector   connector

FIGURE 3.24   CPU fan connectivity

Troubleshooting Processor Issues

Processor issues can appear in different ways, as illustrated in Figure 3.25.

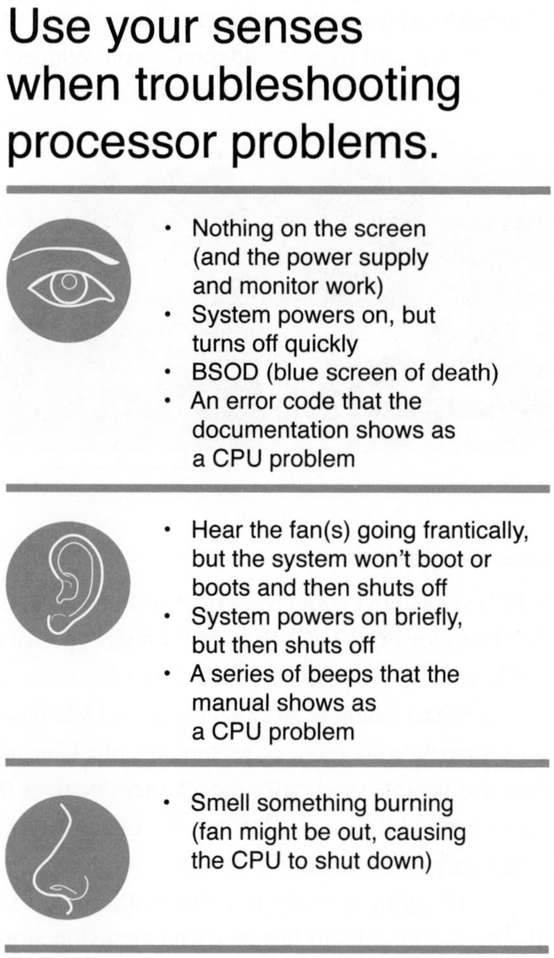

Use your senses when troubleshooting processor problems.

- Nothing on the screen (and the power supply and monitor work)
- System powers on, but turns off quickly
- BSOD (blue screen of death)
- An error code that the documentation shows as a CPU problem

- Hear the fan(s) going frantically, but the system won't boot or boots and then shuts off
- System powers on briefly, but then shuts off
- A series of beeps that the manual shows as a CPU problem

- Smell something burning (fan might be out, causing the CPU to shut down)

FIGURE 3.25　Detecting processor problems

The following measures can help you solve CPU issues:

> The number-one issue related to processor problems is heat. Ensure that the fans work. Fans are cheap devices compared to replacing a processor or motherboard. Ensure the computer has adequate circulation/cooling. Vacuum any dust from the motherboard/CPU. Cool the room more.

> Many BIOS/UEFI screens show the CPU temperature. (This is covered in more detail in Chapter 4.)

> Research any visual codes shown on the motherboard LEDs or listen for audio beeps as the computer beeps. Refer to the computer or motherboard manufacturer website.

Processor issues and determining whether an issue is a CPU or motherboard issue are some of the hardest things to troubleshoot. When your video port does not work, you can insert another video card to determine the problem. However, diagnosing processor and motherboard issues isn't so simple. If you have power to the system (that is, the power supply has power coming out of it), the hard drive works (try it in a different computer), and the monitor works (try it on a different computer), then the motherboard and/or CPU are prime suspects.

CHAPTER 3

Expansion Slots

If a computer is to be useful, the CPU must communicate with the outside world, including other motherboard components and adapters plugged into the motherboard. An expansion slot is used to add an adapter to the motherboard. It has rules that control how many bits can be transferred at a time to the adapter, what signals are sent over the adapter's gold connectors, and how the adapter is configured. Figure 3.26 shows expansion slots on a motherboard.

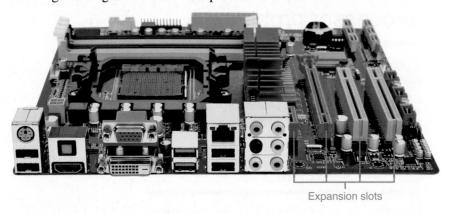

Expansion slots

FIGURE 3.26   Motherboard expansion slots

Expansion slots used in PCs are usually some form of PCI (Peripheral Component Interconnect), AGP (Accelerated Graphics Port), or PCIe (PCI Express). Other types of expansion slots that have been included with older PCs are ISA (Industry Standard Architecture), EISA (Extended Industry Standard Architecture), MCA (Micro Channel Architecture), and VL-bus (sometimes called VESA [video electronics standards association] bus). A technician must be able to distinguish among adapters and expansion slots and be able to identify the adapters/devices that use an expansion slot. A technician must also realize the abilities and limitations of each type of expansion slot when installing upgrades, replacing parts, and making recommendations.

An alternative to an adapter plugging directly into the motherboard is the use of a riser board. A riser board plugs into the motherboard and has its own expansion slots. Adapters can plug into these expansion slots instead of directly into the motherboard. Riser boards are used with rack-mounted servers and low-profile desktop computer models. The riser card is commonly inserted into a motherboard slot or attached using screws. Figure 3.27 shows how a riser board attaches to a motherboard.

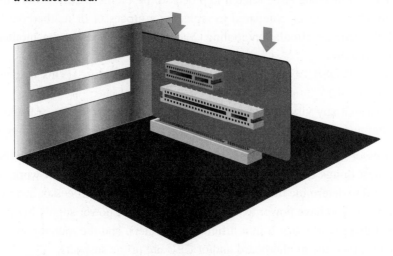

FIGURE 3.27   Installing a riser board

PCI (Peripheral Component Interconnect)

A previously popular expansion slot is Peripheral Component Interconnect (**PCI**). PCI comes in four varieties: 32-bit 33MHz, 32-bit 66MHz, 64-bit 33MHz, and 64-bit 66MHz. Figure 3.28 shows the most common type of PCI expansion slot.

FIGURE 3.28   PCI expansion slot

An upgrade to the PCI bus called **PCI-X** can operate at 66, 133, 266, 533, and 1066MHz. PCI-X allows faster speeds and is backward compatible with the previous versions of the bus. PCI-X expansion slots were commonly found in network servers (powerful computers used in the corporate environment). A chip called the PCI bridge controls the PCI devices and PCI bus. With the PCI-X bus, a separate bridge controller chip is added. Today's motherboards may have a limited number (or none) of PCI or PCI-X expansion slots because of a newer standard called PCI Express (PCIe), which is covered later in this chapter. Figure 3.29 shows how the PCI-X bus integrates into the system board. AGP and the north bridge are covered later in this chapter.

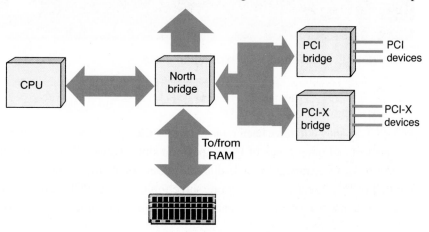

FIGURE 3.29   PCI-X block diagram

AGP (Accelerated Graphics Port)

AGP (Accelerated Graphics Port) is a bus interface for graphics adapters developed from the PCI bus. Intel provided the majority of the development for AGP, and the specification was originally designed around the Pentium II processor. AGP speeds up 3-D graphics, 3-D acceleration, and full-motion playback. Previous video adapters were limited by the bottleneck caused by going through an adapter and a bus shared with other devices. With AGP, the video subsystem is isolated from the rest of the computer. Figure 3.30 shows an illustration of an AGP slot compared with PCI expansion slots. All of these expansion slots have been replaced by PCIe (covered next).

FIGURE 3.30   AGP and PCI expansion slots

PCIe (Peripheral Component Interconnect Express)

PCI, PCI-X, and AGP have been replaced with **PCIe** (PCI Express), which is also seen as PCI-E. PCIe outperforms all other types of PCI expansion slots. Table 3.7 shows different PCIe versions.

The older PCI standard is half-duplex bidirectional, which means that data is sent to and from the PCI or PCI-X card using only one direction at a time. PCIe sends data full-duplex bidirectionally; in other words, it can send and receive at the same time. Figure 3.31 shows this concept.

TABLE 3.7   PCIe versions

PCIe version	Speed (per lane per direction)
1.0	2.5GT/s (gigatransfers per second) or 250MB/s
2.0	5GT/s or 500MB/s
3.0	8GT/s or 1GB/s
4.0	16GT/s or 2GB/s

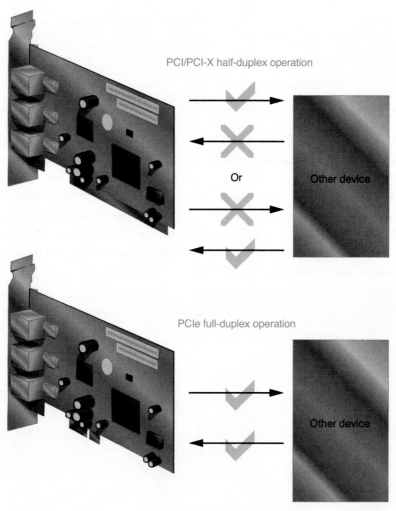

PCI/PCI-X half-duplex operation

Or

Other device

PCIe full-duplex operation

Other device

FIGURE 3.31   A comparison of PCI/PCI-X and PCIe transfers

TECH TIP

PCI cards in PCIe slots

Older PCI, PCI-X, and AGP adapters will not work in any type of PCIe slots.

The older PCI standards, including PCI-X, use a parallel bus where data is sent with multiple 1s and 0s simultaneously. PCIe is a serial bus, and data is sent one bit at a time. Table 3.8 shows a comparison of the PCI, PCI-X, AGP, and PCIe buses.

TABLE 3.8   Comparing bus bandwidth

Bus	Maximum bandwidth
PCI	133 or 266MB/s (depending on bus speed)
PCI-X	266–4,266MB/s (depending on bus speed)
AGP 2x	533MB/s
PCIe x1	250MB/s (in each direction)
PCIe x2	500MB/s (in each direction)
PCIe x4	1,000MB/s (in each direction)
PCIe x8	2,000MB/s (in each direction)
PCIe x16	4,000MB/s (in each direction)
PCIe x32	8,000MB/s (in each direction)

Another difference between PCI and PCIe is that PCIe slots come in different versions, depending on the maximum number of lanes that can be assigned to the card inserted into the slot. For example, an x1 slot can have only one transfer lane used by the x1 card inserted into the slot; x2, x4, x8, and x16 slots are also available. The standard supports an x32 slot, but these are rare because of the length. An x16 slot accepts up to 16 lanes, but fewer lanes can be assigned. Figure 3.32 shows the concepts of PCIe lanes. Notice how one lane has two unidirectional communication channels. Also note how only seven lanes are used. PCIe has the capability to use a reduced number of lanes if one lane has a failure or a performance issue.

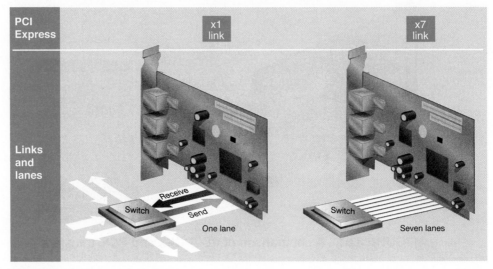

FIGURE 3.32   PCIe lanes

TECH TIP

Beware of the PCIe fine print

Some motherboard manufacturers offer a larger slot size (such as x8), but the slot runs at a slower speed (x4, for example). This keeps the cost down. The manual would show such a slot as x8 (x4 mode) in the PCIe slot description.

A PCIe x1 adapter can fit in an x1 or higher slot. A larger card, such as a PCIe x16, cannot fit in a lower-numbered (x8, x4, x2, or x1) slot. Figure 3.33 shows this concept.

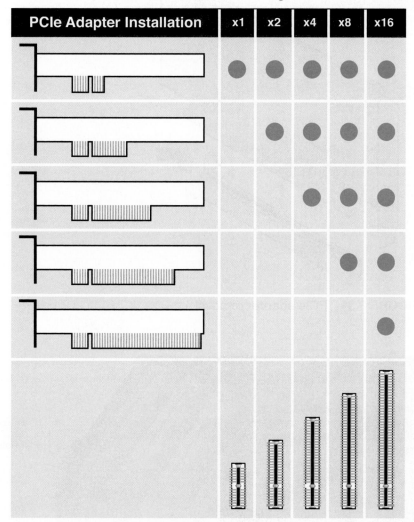

FIGURE 3.33   Correct slots for PCIe cards

Removing an adapter is normally just a matter of removing a retaining screw or plate and lifting the adapter out of the slot. Some AGP and PCIe expansion slots have retention levers. You move the retention lever to the side in order to lift the adapter from the expansion slot. Figure 3.34 shows an example of the PCIe adapter removal process. Figure 3.35 shows a motherboard with two x1 PCIe, two x16 PCIe, and three PCI expansion slots. Notice that the PCIe x16 slot has a retention lever.

TECH TIP

Removing PCIe adapters

PCIe x16 adapters commonly have a release lever. You must press the lever while pulling the adapter out of the expansion slot, or you may damage the board (and possibly the motherboard).

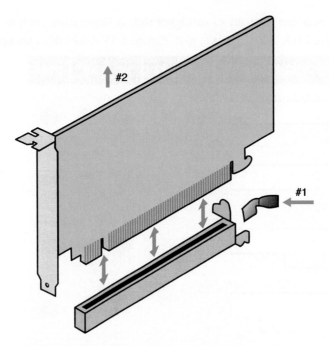

FIGURE 3.34   PCIe adapter removal

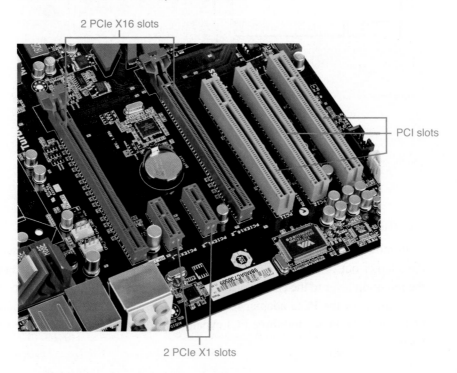

FIGURE 3.35   Motherboard with PCIe and PCI slots

PCI, PCI-X, AGP, and PCIe are important for connectivity in both workstation and portable computers. Traditional PCI connectivity will need to be supported for several more years in new machines for backward compatibility and in computers already in use. PCIe is the current bus for internal and external device connectivity.

Chipsets

The principal chips on the motherboard that work in conjunction with the processor are known collectively as a **chipset**. These allow certain features on the computer. For example, chipsets control the maximum amount of motherboard memory, the type of RAM chips, the motherboard's capacity for two or more CPUs, and whether the motherboard supports the latest version of PCIe. Common chipset manufacturers include Intel, VIA Technologies, ATI technologies (now owned by AMD), Silicon Integrated Systems (SiS), AMD, and NVIDIA Corporation.

The chipset is a square integrated circuit and looks similar to a processor. You normally can't see this because the chipset is soldered to the motherboard and commonly covered with a heat sink. Look for the chipset close to the processor as shown in Figure 3.36.

FIGURE 3.36   The Intel Z97 chipset

TECH TIP

Know your chipset

A technician must keep informed about chipsets on the market; customers often ask for recommendations about motherboard upgrades and new computer purchases. A technician should at least know where to find the information.

Usually, a chipset goes with a particular processor and determines which memory chips a motherboard can have. Chipsets determine a lot about what a motherboard can allow or support. The chipset coordinates traffic to and from motherboard components and the CPU. When buying a motherboard, pick a proper processor and a good chipset. Figure 3.37 shows the Intel 975X chipset.

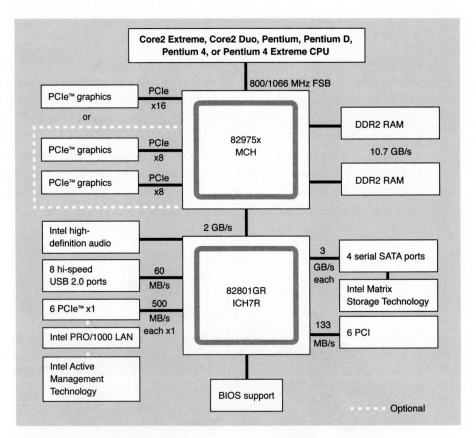

FIGURE 3.37 The Intel 975X chipset connectivity

Finding your chipset

To locate the chipset, which may be one or two chips, look in the motherboard documentation for a diagram that shows the location. If it's not shown, look in the documentation for the chipset manufacturer and then visually inspect the motherboard to locate the chip(s).

Notice in Figure 3.37 the **MCH** (memory controller hub). This important chip, sometimes called the **north bridge**, connects directly to an older Intel CPU. On a motherboard that has a newer AMD or Intel CPU, the MCH would be incorporated into the CPU. Also notice the iCH7R chip. The **ICH** (I/O controller hub), also known as the **south bridge**, is a chip that controls what features, ports, and interfaces the motherboard supports.

Figure 3.38 shows the Z170 chipset, which connects to one of Intel's Core processors that has an integrated GPU. Notice how the processor handles things that were previously handled by the MCH part of a chipset.

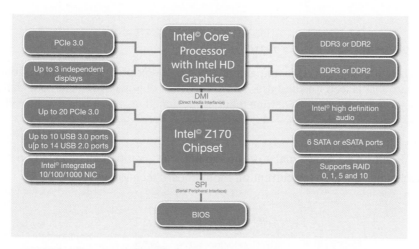

FIGURE 3.38   Intel Z170 chipset connectivity

Types of Motherboards

Motherboards come in different sizes, known as **form factors**. The most common motherboard form factor is **ATX**. The different types of ATX are known as **micro-ATX** (sometimes shown as µATX, **mini-ATX**, FlexATX, EATX, WATX, nano-ATX, pico-ATX, and mobileATX). A smaller form factor is **ITX**, which comes in **mini-ITX**, nano-ITX, and pico-ITX sizes. Some motherboards, such as the NLX and LPX form factors, had a riser board that attached to the smaller motherboard. Adapters go into the slots on the riser board instead of into motherboard slots. Figure 3.39 shows some of the motherboard form factors.

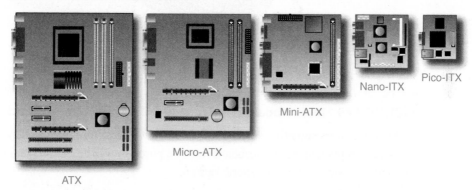

FIGURE 3.39   Motherboard form factors

TECH TIP

The motherboard form factor and case must match

The case used for a computer must match the motherboard form factor. Some cases can accommodate different form factors, but you should always check. When you are building a computer or replacing a motherboard, it is important to obtain the correct form factor.

The BTX form factor was intended to replace ATX. But further development of the BTX standard was canceled in favor of propriety form factors. Within the BTX family of form factors are the smaller versions called microBTX (sometimes shown as µBTX), nano-BTX, and pico-BTX. The WTX (for Workstation Technology Extended) is an older form factor that is larger than ATX or BTX and was used with high-end workstations, such as those with multiple processors and more drives.

TECH TIP

Go green with a motherboard or CPU

When upgrading or replacing a motherboard and/or processor, consider going green. Select a board that is lead free and uses a lower amount of power (wattage), one that uses a smaller form factor (such as micro-ATX), one that has integrated video, or one that has all these features.

Figure 3.40 shows many of the motherboard components labeled on an older motherboard. A technician should stay current on motherboard technologies.

FIGURE 3.40   Motherboard components on an older motherboard

Manufacturers sometimes design a case so that it requires a proprietary motherboard. With such a design, a replacement motherboard must be purchased from the original manufacturer and is usually more expensive than a generic option.

Upgrading and Replacing Motherboards

When upgrading a motherboard or processor, you must consider several issues. The following list guides you through making the decision (or helping a customer make the decision) whether to upgrade a motherboard:

> Why is the computer being upgraded? For example, does the computer need more memory? Are more expansion slots needed? Does the computer need a bigger/faster CPU to run certain operating systems or applications? Is more space wanted in the computer area? Sometimes upgrading the motherboard does not help unless the other computer components are

upgraded. The most expensive and fastest motherboard/CPU will not run applications well unless it has the proper amount of memory. Hard drives are another issue. If software access is slow, the solution might not be a new motherboard but a faster and larger hard drive or more RAM.

> Which type of expansion slot (PCI, AGP, or PCIe) and how many adapters of each type are needed from the old motherboard? Does the new motherboard have the required expansion slots?
> What type of chipsets does the new motherboard support? What features, if any, would this bring to the new motherboard?
> Will the new motherboard fit in the current computer case, or is a new one required?
> If upgrading the CPU, will the motherboard support the new type of CPU?
> Does the motherboard allow for future CPU upgrades?
> How much memory (RAM) does the motherboard allow? What memory chips are required on the new motherboard? Will the old memory chips work in the new motherboard or with the new CPU?

Before replacing a motherboard, it is important to do all the following:

> Remove the CPU and CPU fan.
> Remove adapters from expansion slots.
> Remove memory chips from expansion slots.
> Disconnect power connectors.
> Disconnect ribbon cables.
> Disconnect external devices such as mouse, keyboard, and monitor.

Replacement motherboards do not normally come with RAM, so the old modules are removed from the bad/older motherboard. A motherboard usually does not come with a CPU. Make note of the CPU orientation before removing it from the bad/older motherboard. Some retailers sell kits that include the computer case, power supply, motherboard, and CPU so that the components match, function together correctly, and are physically compatible.

TECH TIP

Use good anti-static measures when installing a motherboard

When replacing a motherboard or removing it from the case, place the motherboard on a nonconductive surface such as an anti-static mat or the anti-static bag that comes with the motherboard.

When upgrading any component or the entire computer, remember that the older part can be donated to a charity or educational institution. Something that one person considers outdated may be an upgrade to someone else. Educational institutions are always seeking components to use in classrooms. Many stores have recycling programs for computer parts.

Motherboard Troubleshooting

Common symptoms of motherboard issues are similar to CPU problems: The system does not display anything; an error code appears; one or more beeps occur; the system locks; the system reboots; a Windows BSOD (blue screen of death) appears; or one or more of the ports, expansion slots, or memory modules fails.

Motherboard problems and power problems are probably the most difficult issues to troubleshoot. Because various components are located on the motherboard, many things can cause errors. POST (power-on self-test) is one of the most beneficial aids for troubleshooting a motherboard. The meaning of any codes that appear on the screen should be researched. If multiple POST error codes appear, you should troubleshoot them in the order they are presented. The following list helps with motherboard troubleshooting:

> Is the motherboard receiving power? Check the power supply to see if the fan is turning. If the CPU or motherboard has a fan, see if it is turning. Check voltages going from the power supply to the motherboard. See Chapter 5 for directions.
> Check the BIOS/UEFI settings (covered in Chapter 4) for accuracy.
> Check for overheating. Power down the computer and allow the computer to cool. Power on the computer with the cover off.
> Check the motherboard for **distended capacitors**. These are small components that might appear to be bulging. If sighted, replace the motherboard as soon as possible.
> Reseat the CPU, adapters, and memory chips.
> Remove unnecessary adapters and devices and boot the computer.
> Plug the computer into a different power outlet and circuit, if possible.
> Check to determine whether the motherboard is shorting out on the frame.
> Check the CMOS battery (see Chapter 5 for how to take voltage readings).
> With a motherboard that has diagnostic LEDs, check the output for any error code. Refer to the motherboard documentation or online documentation for the problem and possible solution.

TECH TIP

These concepts relate to Apple computers, too

Even though this book focuses on PCs, concepts related to CPU, motherboards, expansion slots, cache, and chipsets also apply to Apple computers. Apple computers and PCs have similar CPU and memory requirements.

SOFT SKILLS—ACTIVE LISTENING

Active listening is participating in a conversation where you focus on what the customer is saying—in other words, listening more than talking. For a technician, active listening has the following benefits:

> Enables you to gather data and symptoms quickly
> Enables you to build customer rapport
> Improves your understanding of the problem
> Enables you to solve the problem more quickly because you understand the problem better
> Provides mutual understanding between you and the customer
> Provides a means of having a positive, engaged conversation rather than having a negative, confrontational encounter
> Focuses on the customer rather than the technician
> Provides an environment in which the customer might be more forthcoming with information related to the problem

Frequently, when a technician arrives onsite or contacts a customer who has a technical problem, the technician is (1) rushed; (2) thinking of other things, including the problems that need to be solved; (3) assuming that he or she knows exactly what the problem is, even though the user has not finished explaining the problem; or (4) is more interested in the technical problem than in the customer and the issues. Active listening changes the focus from the technician's problems to the customer's problems.

A common but ineffective service call involves a technician doing most of the talking and questioning, using technical jargon and acronyms and a flat or condescending tone. The customer who feels vulnerable experiences a heightened anxiety level. Active listening changes this scenario by helping you build a professional relationship with your customers. The following list outlines some measures that help you implement active listening. Figure 3.41 has a to-do list for you that is for your entire IT career.

FIGURE 3.41 Active listening

Have a positive, engaged professional attitude when talking and listening to customers:

> Leave your prejudices behind; be polite and aware of other cultures and customs; be open-minded and nonjudgmental.
> Have a warm and caring attitude.
> Do not fold your arms in front of your chest because doing so distances you from the problem and the customer.
> Do not blame others or talk badly about other technicians.
> Do not act as if the problem is not your responsibility.

Focus on what the customer is saying:

> Turn off or ignore electronic devices.
> Maintain eye contact; don't let your mind wander.
> Allow the customer to finish explaining the problem; do not interrupt; avoid arguing with the customer or being defensive.
> Stop all irrelevant behaviors and activities.
> Mentally review what the customer is saying.
> Refrain from talking to co-workers unnecessarily while interacting with customers.
> Avoid personal interruptions or distractions.

Participate in the conversation in a limited, but active manner:

> Maintain a professional demeanor (suspend negative emotions); do not minimize or diminish the customer's problem.
> Acknowledge that you are listening by occasionally nodding and making comments, such as "I see."
> Use positive body language such as leaning slightly forward or taking notes.
> Observe the customer's behavior to determine when it is appropriate to ask questions.

Briefly talk with the customer:

> Speak with a positive tone; use a tone that is empathetic and genuine, not condescending.
> Restate or summarize points made by the customer.
> Ask nonthreatening, probing questions related to the customer's statements or questions.
> Do not jump between topics.
> Do not use technical jargon.
> Clarify the meaning of the customer's situation.
> Identify clues to help solve the problem and reduce your troubleshooting time by listening carefully to what the customer says.
> Follow up with the person at a later date to ensure that the problem is solved and to verify satisfaction.
> Offer different repair or replacement options, if possible.

Chapter Summary

> Important motherboard parts include the following: processor, RAM slots, RAM, expansion slots (PCI, PCI-X, PCIe, and AGP), and cooling devices.
> Processors can be multi-core and contain very fast cache memory: L1 cache inside the processor and L2 cache outside the processor but inside the chip. Processors can also support L3 cache.

> Intel processors use Hyper-Threading to make efficient use of processor time by the processor executing separate sets of instructions simultaneously.

> Processors must be kept cool with fans and/or heat sinks. A thermal paste or pad is applied between a heat sink and a processor. Never turn the processor on without some type of thermal cooling.

> The clock speed refers to the processor's internal clock. This is not the same as the FSB or bus speed.

> CPU throttling slows down the processor to prevent overheating.

> PCI/PCI-X is a 32- and 64-bit parallel bus. PCI, PCI-X, and AGP have been replaced with the point-to-point serial PCIe bus.

> PCIe slots have a specific number of bidirectional lanes that are the maximum a card can use. A PCIe adapter can fit in a slot of the same number of lanes or a slot that has the ability to process a higher number of lanes.

> A chipset is one or more chips that coordinate communication between the processor and the rest of the motherboard. A chipset could have an MCH (north bridge) to coordinate between the CPU and some expansion slots as well as memory. The chipset can also have an ICH (south bridge) to coordinate between the CPU and the rest of the motherboard expansion slots and ports. The chipset dictates the maximum number and type of slots and ports on a motherboard. AMD and Intel have created technologies to address the slowness of the FSB: HyperTransport, QPI, and DMI.

> An integrated GPU is on-die with the CPU and processes graphics-related functions.

> When replacing a motherboard, ensure that the CPU socket and number/types of expansion slots are appropriate.

> Active listening is an important skill for a technician. Don't be distracted by people or technology, take notes, make good eye contact, and ask directed questions when appropriate.

CHAPTER 3

A+ CERTIFICATION EXAM TIPS

✓ Know where you might see a PCI, PCI-X, and PCIe expansion slot.

✓ Review diagrams for PCI, PCI-X, and PCIe expansion slots. Use the Internet to view motherboards to see if you can determine the type of expansion slot. The exam has graphics that are unlabeled. Do the same for other motherboard components, including the processor.

✓ Know the difference between the north bridge and the south bridge.

✓ Know when to use an integrated GPU.

✓ Review the types of CPU cooling methods.

✓ Be able to install a CPU and thermal cooling system. Know how and where to connect a CPU fan.

✓ Know the differences between and be able to identify ATX, micro-ATX, ITX, and mini-ITX motherboard form factors.

✓ Know what a distended capacitor is.

✓ Know what fanless/passive cooling means.

Key Terms

Review Questions

1. Which component can be located both on a video card and on a motherboard?

   [chipset | PS/2 port | PCI expansion slot | GPU]

2. Which expansion slot is *best* for a video card in a desktop computer?
   [PCI-X | PCIe | PCI | ExpressCard/54 | AGP]

3. A motherboard has a PCIe x16 expansion slot. Which PCIe adapter(s) will fit in this slot? (Select any that apply.) [x1 | x2 | x4 | x8 | x16 | x32]

4. Match the motherboard part with its associated description.

   ____ L1 cache   a. Mounted on top of the CPU

   ____ CPU   b. Memory found in the CPU

   ____ FSB   c. Executes software instructions

   ____ heat sink   d. Bus between the CPU and motherboard components

   ____ HT   e. Slowing of CPU to cool

   ____ throttle   f. Allows one processor to handle multiple instructions simultaneously

5. What is the front side bus?

   a. The internal data bus that connects the processor core to the L1 cache

   b. The internal data bus that connects the processor core to the L2 cache

   c. The external data bus that connects the processor to the motherboard components

   d. The external data bus that connects the processor to the L2 cache

6. A customer wants to upgrade the L2 cache. Which of the following does this definitely require?

   a. A motherboard purchase

   b. A CPU purchase

   c. A ROM module purchase

   d. A RAM module purchase

7. Match the expansion slot to its definition.

   ____ PCI-X   a. 32- or 64-bit parallel bus

   ____ AGP   b. Parallel bus with speeds over 4GB/s

   ____ PCI   c. Just for video cards

   ____ PCIe   d. Has a varying number of lanes

8. What is the difference between hyper-threading and HyperTransport?

   _____

   _____

   _____

9. Which of the following is a function of a chipset? (Select all that apply.)

   a. Process instructions obtained from RAM

   b. Setting the maximum number of USB 3.0 ports allowed on a motherboard

   c. Coordinating between the CPU and motherboard components

   d. Temporarily holding documents and instructions

   e. Providing permanent storage

   f. Prioritizing threads being queued for processing by the CPU

CHAPTER 3

10. Which of the following statements is true regarding PCIe?

    a. A PCIe slot will not accept a PCI card.

    b. PCIe is a parallel bus technology.

    c. PCIe is a 32- or 64-bit bus technology.

    d. PCIe is being replaced by PCI-X.

11. [T | F] An x8 PCIe adapter always transmits using eight lanes.

12. What is the significance of a motherboard specification that states the following: 1 PCIe x16 (x8 mode) slot?

    a. The slot accepts x8 or x16 cards.

    b. The slot can transmit traffic using 8 or 16 lanes.

    c. The slot can transmit in bursts of 8 or 16 bytes at a time.

    d. The slot accepts x16 cards but uses only 8 lanes.

13. What determines whether a motherboard can use a specific model of RAM, such as DDR3 or DDR4? [CPU | chipset | PCIe standard | processor speed]

14. A technician for a college is going to repair a problem in another building. A professor stops the technician to talk about her slow computer. The technician gives a little eye roll, but then stops and listens to the teacher. The teacher comments, "I can't get my email or even type my tests. The computer takes at least 20 minutes just to boot." As the technician looks around a little exasperated, he says "Uh huh." "I logged this problem over a week ago," continues the professor, "and no one has dropped by." "Uh huh," replies the technician again. "Do you know when you folks might get to that issue or have an idea about what might be the problem?" the professor asks. The technician looks at the professor and says, "It is probably a virus that has been going around. Jim was supposed to get to those. We will get to you as soon as we can." The technician's phone rings, and he walks away to get to the phone.

    List three active listening techniques and good customer support procedures that could improve this situation.

    _____

    _____

    _____

    _____

15. Explain how a technician might be culturally insensitive.

    _____

    _____

16. Which component deals with threads? [heat sink | CPU | expansion slot | chipset]

    _____

17. [T | F] When installing a CPU, orient pin 1 to pin 1 on the socket and align the other pins. Lower the ZIF socket lever and lock. Power on the computer to ensure that the CPU works. Power down the computer and install the heat sink and/or fan.

18. What is applied between a processor and a heat sink to increase heat dissipation?

    _____

19. What component is affected by the LGA 2011 specification?
    [RAM | chipset | processor | expansion slot]

20. Which method is *not* used to cool a processor?

    a. CPU fan

    b. Case fan

    c. Heat tube

    d. Thermal tank

    e. Heat sink

Exercises

Exercise 3.1 ATX Motherboard Parts Identification Exercise

Objective: To identify various motherboard parts

Parts: None

Procedure: Using Figure 3.42, label each of the ATX motherboard parts.

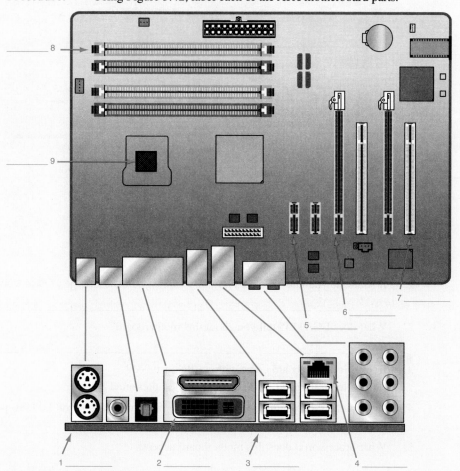

FIGURE 3.42   Motherboard ports, slots, and parts

1. _____

2. _____

3. _____

4. _____

5. _____

6. _____

7. _____

8. _____

9. _____

Exercise 3.2 Motherboard Analysis

Objective:	To identify various motherboard parts
Parts:	None
Procedure:	Using the information you learned in this chapter and related to the specifications found in Figure 3.43, answer the questions that follow.

XYZ Motherboard Specifications

Form factor	ATX		Expansion slots	
Power connector	24-pin		PCIe 3.0/2.0 x16	2 (single x16 or dual x8)
			PCIe 2.0 x16	1 (x4 mode)
CPU			PCIe 2.0 x1	2
CPU socket type	LGA1155		PCI	2
CPUs supported	Celeron, Pentium, Core i3, i5, i7			
Chipset	Intel Z77		**Onboard LAN**	
			Max LAN speed	10/100/1000Mb/s
Graphics			Wireless LAN	WiFi 802.11 b/g/n
Integrated GPU	Multi-VGA output support: HDMI/DVI/ RGB/DisplayPort ports		**Rear ports**	
			PS/2	1 x PS/2 keyboard/mouse port
Memory			Video	D-sub + DVI
Memory	4x240-pin		HDMI	1 x HDMI
Memory standard	DDR3 2600(O.C.), 2400(O.C.), 2200(O.C.), 2133(O.C.), 1866(O.C.), 1800(O.C.), 1600, 1333		DisplayPort	1 x DisplayPort
			USB 1.1/2.0	2 x USB 2.0
			USB 3.0	4 x USB 3.0
Maximum memory	32GB		S/PDIF out	1 x optical
Memory channel	Dual channel		Audio	6 ports

FIGURE 3.43   Motherboard advertisement

1. If someone you know were buying this motherboard, what type of case would you need to purchase?

    _____

2. What does LGA1155 tell you about this motherboard?

    _____

3. Does this motherboard come with a CPU installed?
    [Yes | No | Cannot tell from the information presented]

4. What motherboard component controls the maximum number of 3.0 USB ports this motherboard *could* have?

5. What processor(s) does this motherboard accept?

    _____

6. What do you think that the letters O.C. after some of the memory chips mean in relationship to this motherboard?

    _____

    _____

7. What is the most significant difference between a version 2.0 PCIe slot and a version 3.0 PCIe expansion slot?

    _____

    _____

8. What does the PCIe 3.0/2.0 x16 line that states "2 (single x16 or dual x8)" mean?

    a. The adapter that goes into this slot can use a single lane that goes at x16 speeds or two lanes that go at x8 speeds.

    b. One single x16 adapter and/or one single x8 adapter can go into the expansion slots.

    c. One x16 adapter can go into one of the version 3.0 slots and achieve 3.0 speeds or two x16 adapters can be installed, but they can transfer only eight lanes at a time at 3.0 speeds.

    d. A single x16 adapter can be installed in one of the version 3.0 slots or two x8 adapters can be installed in the two version 3.0 slots.

9. What device cable can insert into the PS/2 port? (Select the best answer.)
    [Speaker | Mouse or keyboard | Display | External storage]

10. Which type of video port is described as a D-sub in this documentation?

    _____

11. What is an advantage of having an integrated GPU in the CPU?

    _____

12. What is the most likely reason this motherboard manufacturer chose to include two PCI expansion slots?

    _____

    _____

    _____

Activities

Internet Discovery

Objective: To obtain specific information on the Internet regarding a computer or its associated parts

Parts: A computer with Internet access

Procedure: Locate documentation on the Internet for a GIGABYTE GA-Z170-HD3 motherboard in order to answer Questions 1–12. Continue your Internet search in order to answer Questions 13 and 14.

Questions:

1. Does the motherboard support an Intel or AMD processor?_____

2. Which chipset is used?_____

3. How many expansion slots are on the motherboard? _____

4. Which form factor does this motherboard use?_____

5. Which processors can be used on this motherboard? _____

    _____

6. Does the motherboard support having an integrated GPU in the CPU? How can you tell whether it does or not?

    _____

7. Which type of CPU socket does the motherboard have? _____

8. How many and of what type of PCIe slots does it have? _____

9. Is there any other type of expansion slot on this motherboard? If so, what is it?

_____

10. Does this motherboard have an integrated USB 3.1 10 Gb/s port?

11. What is the maximum number and type of USB ports available on the rear of the motherboard?

_____

12. Write the URL where you found the motherboard information.

_____

_____

13. Find a vendor for a motherboard that uses the A55 chipset that can support PCIe 3.0. Document the motherboard model and vendor.

_____

14. Find an Internet site that describes the dimensions of the extended ATX motherboard form factor. List the dimensions and the website. _____

_____

Soft Skills

Objective: To enhance and fine-tune a future technician's ability to listen, communicate in both written and oral form, and support people who use computers in a professional manner

Activities:

1. On a piece of paper or an index card, list three ways you can practice active listening at school. Share this information with your group. Consolidate ideas and present five of the best ideas to the class.

2. In a team environment, determine two situations in which team members have experienced a situation in which a support person (a PC support person, sales clerk, checkout clerk, person being asked directions, and so on) could have provided better service if he or she had been actively listening. Share your findings with the class.

3. In teams of two, have one person tell a story and the other person practice active listening skills. The person telling the story should critique the listener. The pair should then exchange roles.

Critical Thinking Skills

Objective: To analyze and evaluate information and to apply learned information to new or different situations

Activities:

1. Find an advertisement for a computer in a local computer flyer, newspaper, magazine, or book or on the Internet. Determine all the information about the motherboard and ports that you can from the ad. Write down any information you do not understand. Research this information and share your findings with a classmate.

2. Your parents want to give you a new computer as a present. The one they are considering has a GPU integrated into the CPU. List at least one argument you might use for getting a different computer model.

3. Why do you think a motherboard has different buses that operate at different speeds?

Labs

Lab 3.1 Using Windows to Discover Processor Information

Objective:	To identify various computer features such as the type of processor being used, processor socket, and additional expansion ports
Parts:	Computer with Windows Vista, 7, 8, or 10
Procedure:	Complete the following procedure and answer the accompanying questions.
Note:	If you do not remember how to locate an application, please refer to Lab 1.1 for Windows 7, Lab 1.2 for Windows 8, or Lab 1.3 for Windows 10.

1. Boot the computer and log in.

   In Windows Vista or 7, access *Windows Explorer* through *All Programs*, *Search programs and files*.

   In Windows 8, access *File Explorer* using the *Search* function or a desktop tile.

   In Windows 10, access *File Explorer* using the *Search the web and Windows* search textbox or through the Start button.

2. Right-click on the computer in the far left panel. This is commonly shown as Computer or This PC. Select *Properties*. Use the information displayed to answer the questions.

   Which processor is used?

   _____

   How much RAM is installed?

   _____

3. Click on the *Device Manager* link in the left panel. From the top menu, select *View > Devices by type*.

4. If only one line displays in the *Computer* category, expand the information by clicking on the icon to the left of the computer name. Is the computer a 32- or 64-bit computer?

   _____

5. Expand the *Processors* category.

   How many CPUs are listed?

   _____

6. Expand the *System devices* category.

   List any expansion slot types shown.

   _____

   _____

7. Close all windows.

Lab 3.2 Processor Speed, Processor Socket, and Ports

Objective: To identify various computer features such as the type of processor being used, processor socket, and additional expansion ports

Parts: Computer with Internet access

Procedure: Complete the following procedure and answer the accompanying questions.

1. Boot the computer.

2. Use Windows/File Explorer and the computer properties to determine the processor type and speed. Write down the processor type and speed.

   _____

3. Power off the computer. Open or remove the cover. Locate the processor. Which type of processor socket is on the motherboard? If you are unsure, use the Internet as a resource. Use some of the search skills used in Chapter 1. Write down the processor socket type.

   _____

4. Which model of processors can go into this type of socket?

   _____

5. List the type of cooling that is used for the processor.

   _____

   _____

6. Look at the back of the computer, where the ports are located. List every port located on the computer and one device that could connect to the port. Document your findings using Table 3.9. Add more lines as needed.

TABLE 3.9   Activity for computer ports

Port	No. of ports	Device that commonly connects to the port

7. Locate a picture of an IEEE 1394 port or connector on the Internet. Write down the URL for the site where you find this picture.

    _____

    _____

8. Using the Internet, locate one vendor that makes a motherboard that supports the Intel Z170 chipset. Provide the name/model of the motherboard and the URL where you found this information.

    _____

    _____

4 Introduction to Configuration

In this chapter you will learn:

> To make configuration changes to a computer

> The importance of BIOS and UEFI BIOS

> How to replace a motherboard battery

> What system resources are and how to view/change them

> Basics steps needed to install, configure, and verify common peripheral devices and USB/FireWire cards

> To troubleshoot configuration and device issues

CompTIA Exam Objectives:

What CompTIA A+ exam objectives are covered in this chapter?

✓ 901-1.1   Given a scenario, configure settings and use BIOS/UEFI tools on a PC.

✓ 901-1.2   Explain the importance of motherboard components, their purpose, and properties.

✓ 901-1.4   Install and configure PC expansion cards.

✓ 901.1.6 Install various types of CPUs and apply the appropriate cooling methods.

✓ 901-4.1   Given a scenario, troubleshoot common problems related to motherboards, RAM, CPU, and power with appropriate tools.

✓ 902-4.1 Given a scenario, troubleshoot PC operating system problems with appropriate tools.

Configuration Overview

Installing and configuring the motherboard, the processor, RAM, or other devices can involve using the system BIOS Setup program or the operating system. The system **Setup** program enables you to configure the motherboard, power, and devices. It also enables you to set performance options.

BIOS Overview

The basic input/output system (BIOS) is an important motherboard component that is commonly soldered to the motherboard, as seen in Figure 4.1. The BIOS has the following functions:

> Holds and executes power-on self-test (**POST**)—a program that identifies, tests, and initializes basic hardware components.
> Holds a basic routine called a bootstrap program that locates an operating system and launches it, allowing the operating system to then control the system.
> Holds Setup, which is a program that allows settings related to the display, date/time, processor, memory, and drives to be viewed and managed. Other names used for Setup include BIOS Setup, System Setup, and CMOS Setup.
> Turns control over to an adapter's onboard BIOS so that the card can initialize during the computer boot process.

FIGURE 4.1   Motherboard BIOS

POST performs basic tests of individual hardware components, such as the motherboard, RAM modules, keyboard, optical drive, and hard drive. When a computer is turned on with the power switch, BIOS executes POST. An indication that POST is running is that the lights on the keyboard momentarily flash on and then off, or you will see the hard drive or optical drive light momentarily flash. Turning the computer on with the power switch is known as a cold boot. Users perform a cold boot every time they power on their computer. A technician performs a cold boot when troubleshooting a computer and needs POST to execute. BIOS can be configured to reduce the time and number of devices checked by POST.

In contrast, a warm boot is when you restart the computer. Restart a Windows computer with a traditional desktop by clicking on the *Start* button > right arrow adjacent to the lock button and select *Restart* or press (Ctrl) + (Alt) + (Del), select the Up arrow in bottom right corner, and choose *Restart* from the menu. On Windows 8 you can press the ▦ + (I) to access Settings (or move the pointer to the far right corner) > *Power* > *Restart*. Warm booting causes any changes that have been made to take effect without putting as much strain on the computer as a cold boot does. A warm boot does not execute POST.

When assembling, troubleshooting, or repairing a computer, a technician must go into a Setup program to configure the system. The Setup program is held in BIOS, and through the Setup program, you can see and possibly configure such things as how much RAM is in the computer, the type and number of drives installed, where the computer looks for its boot files, the current date and time, and so on. An error message is displayed if the information in the Setup program fails to match the hardware or if a specific device does not work properly.

> **TECH TIP**
>
> **Using Setup to disable integrated ports and connectors**
>
> Motherboards include connectors for hard drives, optical drives, and so on. If any of these connectors fails, you can disable it through Setup and obtain a replacement adapter just as you would if an integrated port fails.

There are two main ways to configure your system or an adapter: through the Setup program held in system BIOS and through the operating system. Let's examine the Setup program first.

> **TECH TIP**
>
> **How to access Setup**
>
> The key or keys used to access Setup are normally displayed briefly during the boot process. Otherwise, look in the motherboard documentation for the proper keystroke(s) to use.

The Setup Program

Computers have Setup software built into the system BIOS chip on the motherboard that you can access with specific keystrokes determined by the BIOS manufacturer. During the boot process, most computers display a message stating which keystroke(s) will launch the Setup program. The message shown is usually in one of the four screen corners. See Figure 4.2. The keystroke can be one or more keys pressed during startup, such as the (Esc), (Insert), (Del), (F1), (F2), or (F10) keys. Another key combination is (Ctrl) + (Alt) + some other key.

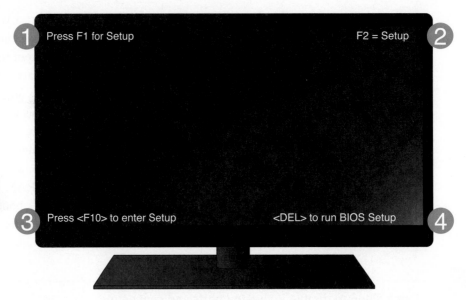

FIGURE 4.2   Setup keystrokes

Accessing BIOS Setup in Windows 8 and Windows 10

To access BIOS Setup through Windows 8, point to the upper-right corner of the screen, and then click > *Settings* > *Change PC Settings* > *Update and recovery* > *Recovery* > *Restart now* button under Advanced startup > *Troubleshoot* > *Advanced options* > *UEFI Firmware Settings* > *Restart* > *App Menu* > *Setup*. To access BIOS Setup in Windows 10, click *Notification Area* > *Action Center* > *All Settings* > *Update and Security* > *Recovery* > *Advanced startup* > *Restart now*.

Flash BIOS

Flash BIOS is the most common type of BIOS; it allows changing the BIOS without installing a new chip or chips. Common computer BIOS manufacturers include AMI (American Megatrends, Inc.), Phoenix, Byosoft (Nanjing Byosoft Co., Ltd), and Insyde Software. Many computer companies customize their own BIOS chips or subcontract with one of these companies to customize them.

To determine the current BIOS version, you can do one of the following:

> Watch the computer screen as it boots. Note that you might be able to press the Pause/Break key.
> Enter BIOS Setup using a particular keystroke during the boot process.
> From within Windows 8 or 10, access BIOS Setup. A lab at the end of the chapter demonstrates this process.

An upgrade of the BIOS normally involves removing all BIOS settings stored in CMOS and the BIOS software. Some manufacturers provide utilities that enable you to save the current CMOS settings before upgrading the BIOS. Two things should be done before upgrading the flash BIOS if possible: back up current CMOS settings and back up the current BIOS.

UEFI

Unified Extensible Firmware Interface (**UEFI**), and sometimes known as simply EFI, is the interface between the operating system and firmware, which can be the traditional BIOS, or UEFI can replace the BIOS. The traditional BIOS has roots in the original PC; the BIOS always checks for certain things, such as a keyboard, before allowing the system to boot. A traditional BIOS made configuring kiosks and other touch screen technologies difficult. UEFI fixed these issues.

With UEFI, you can boot into the environment (which includes configuration parameters), but unlike the original BIOS environment, you can use your mouse and possibly do some of the following (depending on the manufacturer): connect to the Internet, run applications, run a virus scan, have a GUI environment, execute utilities, or perform a backup or a restore—a lot more configuration options and in a much easier-to-use environment. Figure 4.3 shows an example of such an environment.

FIGURE 4.3 Sample UEFI main menu

Many manufacturers have moved to the UEFI type of BIOS for the following reasons:

> It is a graphical environment that provides mouse support.
> It enables you to have a virus-scanning utility that is not operating system-dependent.
> It offers more BIOS software that is not just configuration screens.
> It offers optional Internet access for troubleshooting or download capabilities.
> It offers better system support for cooling, voltage levels, performance, and security.
> It provides support for increased hard drive capacities and ability to divide the hard drive into sections that did not have the limitations found with the traditional BIOS.
> It commonly has monitoring data (temperature, voltage, CPU speed, bus speed, and fan speed) prominently displayed.
> It can have a boot manager instead of relying on a boot sector. See Chapter 7 for more information on a GUID partition table (GPT) and boot sector.

From the UEFI BIOS main menu, there might be icons you can use to access utilities or more advanced configurations. Figure 4.4 shows the type of menu options you might see if you had clicked on the Advanced button from the main menu. Other manufacturers might have these category icons available from the main menu.

FIGURE 4.4   Sample UEFI advanced menu

UEFI/BIOS Configuration Settings

UEFI/BIOS options vary according to manufacturer, but many options are similar. Table 4.1 shows some common settings and briefly explains each. Most Setup programs have help that can be accessed from within the Setup program to explain the purpose of each option. Note that the highlighted items are on the CompTIA A+ Certification.

TABLE 4.1   Common Setup options

Setup option	Description
System Information	Displays general information, such as the processor, processor speed, amount of RAM, type and number of hard drives and optical drives installed, BIOS manufacturer, and BIOS date.
General Optimization	Allows faster booting by disabling features such as memory checking, booting to the network, and booting from removable drives.
Date/Time	Manually configures the system date and time.
Boot Sequence, Boot Drive Order, or Boot Menu	Prioritizes devices in the order the computer looks for an operating system.
CPU Configuration or Advanced CPU Settings	Contains settings such as CPU TM function, which affects CPU throttle management (slows the CPU when overheated); clock speed, which may not be changeable; PECI (Platform Environment Control Interface), which affects how the thermal sensors report the core temperature of your CPU; Max CPUID, which is used to be compatible with older operating systems; CPU Ratio control, which sets the CPU multipliers; and Vanderpool Technology, which is used with Intel virtualization.
Fan control	Enables the configuration of case and/or CPU fans, including the ability to place the fans in silent mode or control fan speed.
Video Options	Enables configuration such as DVMT (dynamic video memory technology) to control video memory, aperture size (the amount of system RAM dedicated for the video adapter use), and which video controller is primary or secondary.
Onboard Device Configuration	Allows modification of devices built into the motherboard, such as audio, Bluetooth wireless, network, USB, or video ports.
Passwords, Power on Password, Password Options, Supervisor Password, or User Password	Allows protection of the BIOS menu options, specifically configuration of a password to enter the Setup program, to allow the computer to boot, or to distinguish between someone who can make minor changes such as boot options or date and time (user password), or someone who can view and change all Setup options (supervisor password). Other vendors might have the following levels: full access (all screens except supervisor password), limited access, view-only access, or no access.

Setup option	Description
Virus Protection	A small virus-scanning application located in BIOS. Some operating systems and software updates require disabling this option for the upgrade.
Numlock On/Off	Allows default setting (enabled or disabled) of the Num Lock key option after booting.
USB Configuration	Allows modification of parameters such as support for legacy devices, USB speed options, and the number of ports to enable.
HyperThreading	Allows enabling/disabling of Hyper-Threading technology.
Integrated Peripherals (**enabling/disabling devices & ports**)	Allows enabling/disabling and configuration of motherboard-controlled devices such as PATA/SATA ports and integrated ports including USB, audio, and network. Sets the amount of RAM dedicated for video use. If the computer has an ample amount of RAM, increasing this setting can increase performance, especially in applications (such as games) that use high-definition graphics.
HD Audio Controller	Enables/disables a high-definition audio controller.
Advanced BIOS Options	Allows configuration of options such as CPU and memory frequencies, CPU, front side bus, north bridge, south bridge, chipset, and memory voltage levels.
IDE Configuration	Allows manual configuration of IDE devices such as PATA, hard drives, and optical drives.
SATA Configuration	Allows viewing Serial ATA values assigned by BIOS and changing some of the related options, as well as RAID configuration.
PCI/PnP Configuration	Allows viewing and changing PCI slot configuration, including IRQ and DMA assignments.
PCIe Configuration	Allows manual configuration of the PCIe version.
Virtualization support, Virtualization Technology, or Secure Virtual Machine Mode	Enable/disable virtualization so the virtualization software can access additional hardware capabilities.
ACPI (advanced configuration and power interface)	Determines what happens if power is lost, power options if a call comes into a modem, and power options when directed by a PCI or PCIe device or by mouse/keyboard action.
Hardware Monitor	Allows viewing of CPU and motherboard **temperature monitoring** as well as the status of CPU, chassis, **voltages**, **clock speeds**, **fan speeds**, **bus speeds**, chassis intrusion detection/notification, and power supply fans.
Disable execute bit, Execute Disable, or No Execute	Can prevent executable code (viruses) from being executed from specific marked memory area.
Drive encryption	A secret key is used to encrypt the data on the hard drive. The computer will not boot without the correct password. The drive cannot be moved to another computer either unless the correct password is entered.
Trusted Platform Module (**TPM**)	Allows initialization and setting a password for the TPM motherboard chip that generates and stores cryptographic keys.
LoJack	Allows security settings to perform such tasks as locating the device, locking the device remotely, displaying an "if lost" message, or data to be deleted if stolen.
Intrusion Detection/Notification or Chassis Intrusion	Allows notification if the cover has been removed.

CHAPTER 4

Setup option	Description
Secure boot	Checks every driver before launching the drivers and the operating system. Prevents an unauthorized operating system or software from loading during the boot process.
iGPU	Configuration of how much memory is allocated for the integrated GPU
Built-in diagnostics	Used to access hardware components, the hard drive, memory, the battery, and other diagnostic tests.

TECH TIP

Boots from wrong device

If the computer tries or even boots from the wrong device, change the Boot Sequence setting in UEFI/BIOS. Examples of boot devices include USB, hard drive, optical, or PXE (network boot or image). You might have also left an optical disc in the drive or a non-bootable USB drive attached and that is the first boot option currently selected.

Figure 4.5 shows a sample UEFI BIOS screen where you can set the administrator or user BIOS password. Note that this is not a Windows or corporate network password.

FIGURE 4.5 Password security menu

You must save your changes whenever you make configuration changes. Incorrectly saving the changes is a common mistake. The options available when exiting BIOS depend on the model of BIOS being used. Table 4.2 lists sample BIOS exit options.

TABLE 4.2   Sample configuration change options

Option	Description
Save & Exit Setup	A commonly used option that saves all changes and leaves the Setup program.
Exit Without Saving	Used when changes have been made in error or more research is needed.

Option	Description
Load Fail-Safe Defaults	Sets the default settings programmed by the manufacturer. Used when getting unpredictable results after changing an option.
Load Optimized Defaults	An option programmed by the manufacturer. It has more aggressive settings than the *Load Fail-Safe Defaults* option.

TECH TIP

Settings for CPU installations

When installing a processor, two BIOS settings can be important: CPU bus frequency and bus frequency multiple. The CPU bus frequency setting allows the motherboard to run at a specific speed. This speed is the external rate at which data travels *outside* the processor. The bus frequency multiple enables the motherboard to recognize the *internal* processor speed.

CMOS Memory

Settings changed in system BIOS are recorded and stored in complementary metal-oxide semiconductor (**CMOS**) found in the motherboard chipset (south bridge or I/O controller hub). CMOS is memory that requires a small amount of power, provided by a small coin-sized lithium battery when the system is powered off. The memory holds the settings configured through BIOS. Part of the BIOS software routine checks CMOS for information about what components are supposed to be installed. These components are then tested as part of the POST routine. POST knows what hardware is *supposed* to be in the computer by obtaining the settings from CMOS. If the settings do not match, an error occurs.

When working on a computer with a POST error code, ensure that the user or another technician has not changed the configuration through the Setup program or removed or installed any hardware without changing the Setup program or updating the operating system. Correct system Setup information is crucial for proper PC operation.

TECH TIP

Incorrect Setup information causes POST errors

If you incorrectly input configuration information, POST error codes or error messages that would normally indicate a hardware problem appear.

The information inside CMOS memory can be kept there for several years, using a small coin-sized lithium battery known as the **CMOS battery**. When the battery dies, all configuration information in CMOS is lost and must be re-entered or relearned after the battery is replaced.

Motherboard Battery

The most common CMOS battery used today is a CR2032 lithium battery, which is about the size of a nickel. Figure 4.6 shows a photo of a lithium battery installed on a motherboard. If you cannot find the motherboard battery, refer to the motherboard or computer documentation for the exact location.

CHAPTER 4

FIGURE 4.6 Motherboard battery

Date and/or time loss

A first indication that a battery is failing is the loss of the date or time on the computer.

No battery lasts forever. High temperatures and powering devices that use batteries on and off shorten a battery's life span. Computer motherboard batteries last three to eight years. Today, batteries last longer, and people replace their computers more frequently; therefore, replacing batteries is not the issue it once was.

Using a battery recycling program

Many states have environmental regulations regarding battery disposal. Many companies also have battery recycling programs. The earth911.com website has information regarding recycling and disposing of batteries and computer components by zip code or city/state.

Flashing the BIOS

The flash BIOS can be upgraded. The term used for this process is "flashing the BIOS." A computer may need a BIOS upgrade for a variety of reasons, including the following:

> To provide support for new or upgraded hardware such as a processor or a faster USB port
> To provide support for a higher-capacity hard drive
> For increased virus protection
> For optional password protection
> To solve problems with the current version
> To provide a security patch
> To reduce the time a computer takes to boot

Viruses can infect the flash BIOS, so you should keep the BIOS write-protected until you need to update it. Refer to the computer or motherboard documentation to find the exact procedure for removing the write protection and updating the flash BIOS. The following procedure is one example of flashing the BIOS.

Step 1. After the system BIOS upgrade is downloaded from the Internet, execute the update.

Step 2. Follow the directions on the screen or from the manufacturer.

Step 3. Reboot the computer.

At times, you might need to reset the BIOS and might come across the need to change a jumper. A **jumper** is a small piece of plastic that fits over pins. A jumper can be used to enable or disable a particular feature, such as resetting the system Setup settings or write-protecting the BIOS. Figure 4.7 shows an enlarged jumper; the pins and jumper are much smaller in real life than what is shown.

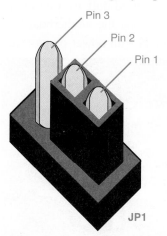

FIGURE 4.7   JP1 jumper block with pins 1 and 2 jumpered together

If flashing a laptop BIOS, ensure the laptop battery is fully charged or connect the laptop to AC power. If the BIOS is downloaded (and not saved locally), connect the laptop to a wired network to do the download to ensure connectivity during the download process. See Chapter 14 for how to connect a device to a wired network.

Table 4.3 contains some of the methods used to recover a BIOS. Keep in mind that not all vendors provide a method of recovering a BIOS if a flash update does not go well. A computer without an operational BIOS cannot boot and a new motherboard must be purchased. For this reason, you should have a good reason for flashing the BIOS and research the method the motherboard uses before flashing the BIOS.

TABLE 4.3   Flash BIOS recovery methods

Recovery Method	Description
Recovery utility	A software program that can be accessed from specific keystrokes or downloaded from the motherboard manufacturer website.
Recovery jumper, switch, or push button	The recovery jumper, switch, or push button is commonly located on the motherboard.
Backup BIOS	More expensive motherboards have a second BIOS
Read-only portion of the BIOS	Some vendors have a read-only portion of the BIOS that is never changed. That way if the BIOS update fails, the system can still boot to the menu.
Update to USB flash drive first	Download a program to a USB flash drive along with the BIOS update. The computer is booted from the USB drive to ensure that the BIOS update works.

Clearing CMOS

Sometimes BIOS Setup settings get all messed up and some folks would like to start over. Resetting all BIOS settings to factory default is clearing the CMOS, which can be done as a UEFI/BIOS menu option, a motherboard switch, a motherboard push button, or a back panel (where the ports are located) push button. Clearing the CMOS is not the same as flashing the BIOS.

One specific CMOS setting that is sometimes cleared is the power-on password. Look at the computer or motherboard documentation for the exact procedure to remove the power-on password. Some motherboards distinguish between supervisor and user passwords. Another possible security option is whether a password is needed every time the computer boots or only when someone tries to enter the Setup program. The options available in Setup and Advanced Setup are machine-dependent due to the different BIOS chips and the different chipsets installed on the motherboard. Figure 4.8 shows a jumper that is used only to reset the power-on password. If all else fails, you can try removing and then replacing the motherboard battery, but then all saved BIOS settings stored in CMOS would be reset. Not all power-on passwords can be reset this way.

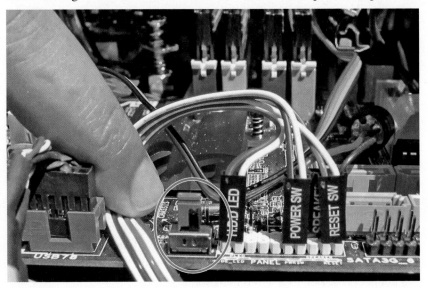

FIGURE 4.8   A CMOS password jumper

TECH TIP

Don't clear CMOS after a BIOS update

Do not clear the CMOS immediately after upgrading the BIOS. Power down the system and then power it back on before clearing CMOS data.

Other Configuration Parameters

Other possible parameters contained and set via the Setup program or operating system are interrupt requests (IRQs), input/output (I/O) addresses, direct memory access (DMA) channels, and memory addresses. These parameters are assigned to individual adapters and ports, such as disk controllers, and the USB, serial, parallel, and mouse ports. Sometimes these ports must be disabled through Setup in order for other devices or adapter ports to work. No matter how the parameters are assigned, collectively they are known as **system resources**. These are not the same system resources that we refer to when we discuss Windows operating systems. Let's take a look at three important system resources: IRQs, I/O addresses, and memory addresses. Table 4.4 lists brief descriptions of these.

TABLE 4.4 System resources

Type	Description
IRQ	A number assigned to an adapter, port, or device so orderly communication can occur between it and the processor. For example, when a key is pressed at the same time the mouse is moved, the keyboard has the highest priority because of its IRQ number.
I/O address	Unique addresses for the processor to distinguish among the devices with which it communicates. Allows an adapter, port, or device to exchange data with a processor.
Memory address	Unique addresses assign to memory chips installed anywhere in the system. Used by the CPU when it accesses information inside the memory chip.

IRQ

Imagine being in a room of 20 students when 4 students want the teacher's attention. If all 4 students talk at once, the teacher is overloaded and unable to respond to the 4 individuals' needs. Instead, the teacher needs an orderly process of acknowledging each request, prioritizing the requests (which student is first), and then answering each question. The same thing happens when multiple devices want the attention of the CPU. For example, which device gets to go first if a key on the PS/2 keyboard is pressed and the PS/2 mouse is moved simultaneously? The answer lies in what interrupt request numbers are assigned to the keyboard and the mouse. Every device requests permission to do something by interrupting the processor (which is similar to a student raising his hand). The CPU has a priority system to handle such situations.

TECH TIP

How IRQs are assigned to multiple-device ports

Ports such as USB and FireWire that support multiple devices require only one interrupt per port. For example, a single USB port can support up to 127 devices but needs only one IRQ.

PCI/PCIe Interrupts

When a PC first boots, the operating system discovers what AGP, PCI, and PCIe adapters and devices are present and the system resources each one needs. The operating system allocates resources such as an interrupt to the adapter/device. If the adapter or device has a ROM or flash BIOS chip installed that contains software that initializes and/or controls the device, the software is allowed to execute during the boot process.

PCI/PCIe devices use interrupts called INTA, INTB, INTC, INTD, and so on. These interrupts are commonly referred to as PCI interrupts. Some motherboard documentation uses the numbers 1, 2, 3, and 4 to replace the letters A, B, C, and D. Devices that use these interrupts are allowed to share them as necessary.

TECH TIP

What to do when a conflict occurs

If you suspect a resource conflict with a card, reboot the computer. The BIOS and operating system will try to work things out. This may take multiple reboots. If an adapter is installed, move it to another slot.

CHAPTER 4

PCI interrupts are normally assigned dynamically to the USB, PCI, PCIe, and SATA devices as the interrupts are needed. When an adapter needs an interrupt, the operating system finds an available interrupt (which may be currently used by another device that does not need it) and allows the requesting device to use it. During the boot process, the system BIOS configures adapters. Windows examines the resources assigned by the BIOS and uses those resources when communicating with a piece of hardware. Table 4.5 shows an example of how a motherboard might make PCI IRQ assignments.

Starting with PCI version 2.2 and continuing on with PCIe, an adapter can use a different type of interrupt method called MSI or MSI-X. Message signaled interrupt (**MSI**) allows an interrupt to be delivered to the CPU using software and memory space. **MSI-X** supports more interrupts. This method was optional with PCI, but PCIe cards are required to support MSI and MSI-X.

TABLE 4.5   Sample PCI/PCIe interrupt assignments

	A	B	C	D	E	F	G
PCI slot 1						used	
LAN		shared					
PCIe x16 1	shared						
PCIe x16 2	shared						
PCIe x1			shared				
USB 2.0 controller 1							shared
USB 2.0 controller 2		shared					
SATA controller 1		shared					
SATA controller 2				shared			

TECH TIP

How to get to a command prompt

To get to a command prompt in Windows, type command from the *Search* textbox. Review Labs 1.1, 1.2, or 1.3 for locating the Search textbox.

Interrupts for integrated ports and some devices can be set through a system's Setup program. Other adapter and device interrupts are set by using Device Manager in Windows or using various Control Panels. **Device Manager** is an important tool for a technician to know how to use because it shows the status of installed hardware. Figure 4.9 shows the various methods used to access Device Manager.

Figure 4.10 shows how IRQs appear in *Device Manager > View > Resources by type*. In Figure 4.10, notice that some interrupts have multiple entries. Multiple entries do not always indicate a resource conflict. They are allowed because devices may share IRQs. The next section goes into more detail on this issue.

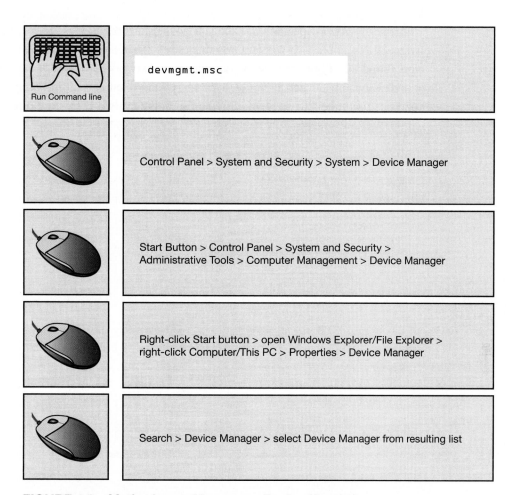

FIGURE 4.9   Methods used to access Device Manager

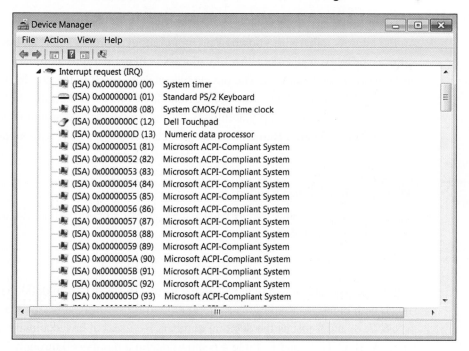

FIGURE 4.10   IRQs in Device Manager

In order to access specifics in Device Manager, use the *View > Devices by Type* option. Expand any specific section such as Network adapters. Right-click on a particular device or adapter and select Properties. Figure 4.11 shows an integrated network card's properties that cannot be changed through Device Manager as denoted by the Change Setting button being grayed out. (However, properties might be able to be modified through the system BIOS Setup program.)

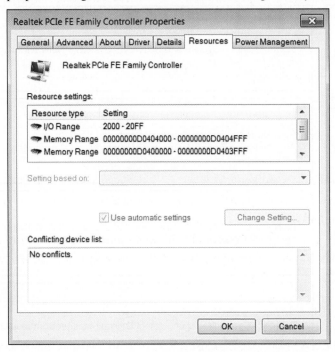

FIGURE 4.11   Resources tab in Device Manager

I/O (Input/Output) Addresses

An I/O address, otherwise known as an input/output address or port address, enables a device and a processor to exchange data. An I/O address is like a mailbox number; it must be unique, or the postal worker gets confused. The device places data (mail) in the box for the CPU to pick up. The processor delivers the data to the appropriate device through the same I/O address (mailbox number). I/O addresses are simply addresses for the processor to distinguish among the devices with which it communicates. Remember that you cannot deliver mail without an address.

TECH TIP

When is an I/O address needed?

Remember that every device must have a separate I/O address. Otherwise, the CPU cannot distinguish between installed devices.

I/O addresses are shown in hexadecimal format (base 16), from 0000 to FFFF. Some outputs are shown with eight positions, such as 00000000 to FFFFFFFF. Hexadecimal numbers are 0, 1, 2, 3, 4, 5, 6, 7, 8, and 9 just as the decimal numbers we use, but hexadecimal numbers also include the letters A, B, C, D, E, and F. Table 4.6 shows decimal numbers 0 through 15 and their hexadecimal and binary equivalents.

TABLE 4.6 Decimal, binary, and hexadecimal numbers

Decimal	Hexadecimal	Binary	Decimal	Hexadecimal	Binary
0	0	0000	8	8	1000
1	1	0001	9	9	1001
2	2	0010	10	A	1010
3	3	0011	11	B	1011
4	4	0100	12	C	1100
5	5	0101	13	D	1101
6	6	0110	14	E	1110
7	7	0111	15	F	1111

An example of an I/O address is 390h. Normally, devices need more than one hexadecimal address location. The number of extra addresses depends on the individual device and what business it does with the processor. In manuals or documentation for a device or an adapter, a technician might see just one I/O address listed. I/O addresses can be set for some devices and ports through the BIOS system Setup program, Device Manager, or through various Windows Control Panels.

Memory Addresses

A memory address is a unique address assigned to memory chips installed anywhere in the system. The memory address is used by the CPU when it accesses information inside the chip. Memory addresses are shown as a range of hexadecimal addresses in Device Manager, as seen in Figure 4.12. Exercises at the end of the chapter help to identify IRQs, I/O addresses, and memory addresses for various devices and operating systems.

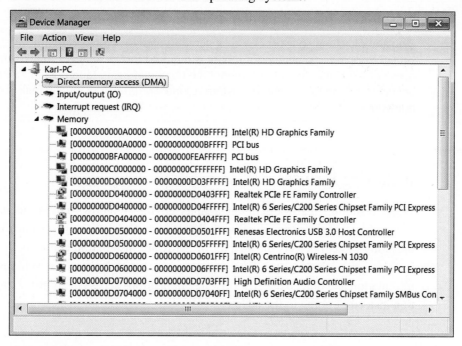

FIGURE 4.12 Memory addresses in Device Manager

TECH TIP

An IEEE 1394 port uses the same system resources to access any devices attached to the same port

If one or more FireWire devices connect to a FireWire port (integrated or on an adapter), the devices use the same system resources that are assigned to the port.

Hardware Configuration Overview

Configuration of adapters and other hardware is easy if you follow the documentation and know how to obtain device drivers. Documentation for installation is frequently available through the Internet, as are many device drivers. Device drivers are also provided as part of the Windows update process.

The system BIOS plays an important role as part of the startup routine. Not only does it check hardware for errors as part of POST, but it also detects installed adapters and devices. The BIOS, along with the operating system, determines what resources to assign to a device or adapter. This information is stored in a part of CMOS known as the Extended System Configuration Data (**ESCD**) area. After information is configured in the ESCD area, the information stays there and does not have to be recomputed unless another device is added.

After resources are allocated, the BIOS looks in the saved settings of CMOS to determine which device it should look to first for an operating system. This part of the BIOS routine is known as the bootstrap loader. If BIOS cannot locate an operating system in the first location specified in the saved settings, it tries the second device and continues on, looking to each device specified in the saved settings for an operating system. Keep in mind that once an operating system is found, the operating system loads.

TECH TIP

What to do if a new adapter is not recognized by the system

Plug and play (and sometimes a configuration utility supplied with a device) is used to configure system resources. Sometimes, a reboot is required for the changes to take effect. If the device does not work after the reboot, reboot the computer again (and possibly a third time) to allow the operating system to sort out the system resources. You can manually make changes if this does not work.

Installing Drivers

When installing hardware or an adapter in the Windows environment, a driver is required. Remember that a driver is software that allows the operating system to control hardware. The operating system detects the adapter or hardware installation and adds the device's configuration information to the registry. The **registry** is a central database in Windows that holds hardware information and other data. All software applications access the registry for configuration information instead of going to the adapter.

Windows comes with many drivers for common devices such as keyboards, mice, printers, and displays. Here are some processes used to install a driver:

> For a standard keyboard or mouse, Windows commonly includes the driver. When the device is attached, the driver loads and the device configuration is added to the registry.

> Windows updates include updated device drivers. To determine if the latest Windows Vista, 7, or 8 updates are installed, search for and open the *Windows Update* Control Panel. Select the link to check for updates. Windows 10 does not have such a link.

> You might be prompted to install or search for the driver as part of the installation process. You may have to designate where the driver is located such as on a CD that comes with the hardware. You might also be required to download it and designate where the downloaded file is located.

> Use Device Manager to install a driver. Open *Device Manager* > expand the relevant particular hardware category > locate the device and right-click on it > *Update Driver Software* as shown in Figure 4.13.

> Use Windows Explorer (Windows Vista or 7) or File Explorer (Windows 8 or 10) to locate an executable file that comes with the hardware. Double-click on the Setup file provided to install software and/or a driver.

> Use the *Add a device* (in Windows Vista, 7, or 8) or *Add devices* (in Windows 10) link.

> Use the Add Hardware Wizard by typing `hdwwiz` in the Windows Start Search (Vista), Search programs and files (7), Search (8), or Search the web and Windows (10) textbox.

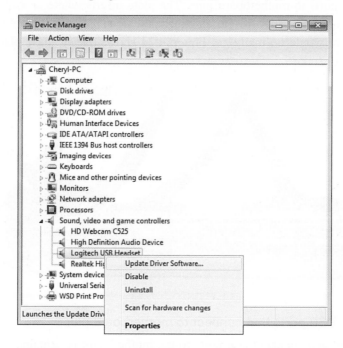

FIGURE 4.13 Update Driver Software option in Device Manager

Installing a USB Device

To install a USB device, perform the following steps:

Step 1. Power on the computer.

Step 2. Optionally, install the USB device's software. Note that some manufacturers require that software and/or device drivers be installed before the USB device is attached.

Step 3. Optionally, power on the device. Not all USB devices have external power adapters or a power button because they receive power from the USB bus.

Step 4. Locate a USB port on the rear or front of the computer or on a USB hub. Plug the USB device into a free port. The operating system normally detects the USB device and loads the device driver. You may have to browse to the driver.

Step 5. Verify installation in Device Manager. Refer back to Figure 4.13 and notice that the USB headset did not have any unusual symbols beside it in Device Manager (which would indicate no issues with the installation).

TECH TIP

Ignoring manufacturer's advice gets you in trouble

If the manufacturer recommends installing the device driver before attaching the USB device, follow the instructions! Failure to do so may require you to uninstall a driver and then reinstall using recommended procedures in order for the device to work properly.

Installing/Configuring USB Cards

Additional USB ports can be added by using a USB hub, or connecting a metal plate that has additional USB ports to motherboard pins. The plate inserts where an expansion card goes, but does not have connectors that fit into an expansion slots. The metal plate simply slides into the spot where a card would normally go. Figure 4.14 shows one of these plates that has two USB ports and an eSATA port.

FIGURE 4.14   USB ports that connect to motherboard pins

How to install and connect these ports to the motherboard is explained in Chapter 5. Keep in mind that if a motherboard does not have any pins, you can add more USB ports by purchasing a PCI or PCIe USB adapter with multiple ports. The adapter might not have the capability of providing power unless the adapter supports having a power cable from the power supply attached to the card.

Install a USB card to add additional USB ports to a computer. USB ports are powered; therefore, a USB card normally has a place to connect power. If the power supply does not have the appropriate power connector, a power adapter may have to be purchased. Always follow the manufacturer's instructions when installing an adapter to provide additional USB ports. Generic instructions follow:

Step 1. Power down the computer and remove the power cord.

Step 2. Remove the computer cover. Locate an empty expansion slot. You may have to remove a screw or raise a retaining bar to be able to use the expansion slot. See Figure 4.15.

Step 3. Using proper anti-static procedures (see Chapter 5), ground yourself, or use anti-static gloves.

Step 4. Optionally, attach a power connector to the adapter.

Step 5. Ensure the proper expansion slot is being used and insert the card firmly into the expansion slot. See Figure 4.16. Ensure the card is fully inserted by pressing firmly down on the adapter and visually inspecting it afterward. The card should be at a 90° angle from the PC. It should not tilt at either end. Ensure the card fits snuggly in the expansion slot.

Step 6. Lower the expansion bar or attach a screw.

Step 7. Reinstall the computer cover, reattach the power cord, and power on the computer. Install drivers as necessary.

Step 8. Test by attaching a USB device to each port.

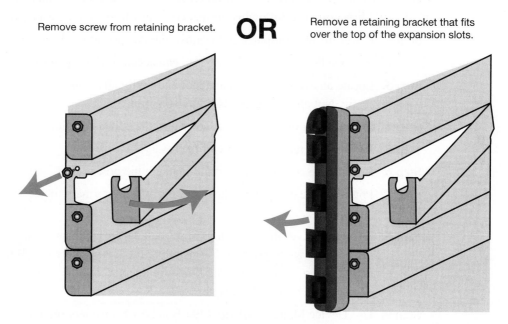

FIGURE 4.15   Adapter screw or retainer bar

FIGURE 4.16   Insert adapter directly into expansion slot

Installing/Configuring FireWire Cards

When connecting a FireWire device, always follow the manufacturer's instructions. Attach the device to an available port on the motherboard or an adapter, another IEEE 1394 device, or an IEEE 1394 hub port. The following are generic steps for installing a FireWire adapter:

Step 1.   Power off the computer and remove the AC power cord.

Step 2.   Remove the computer case so you can access the computer interior.

Step 3.   Locate an available expansion slot and optionally remove the slot cover and retaining screw. Not all computer cases have this now.

Step 4.   Firmly insert the FireWire adapter into the expansion slot.

Step 5.   Reinsert the retaining screw, if necessary.

Step 6.   Replace the computer cover and reattach the power cord.

Step 7.   Power on the computer. The operating system normally detects the newly installed hardware.

Step 8.   Insert the driver disc that ships with the adapter and browse to the location of the driver. Follow the prompts for installing the driver. Note that Windows normally detects the correct driver for the FireWire adapter, but the computer may have to be rebooted to recognize the adapter.

Step 9.   Use Device Manager (IEEE 1394 Bus host controllers section) to verify installation.

Troubleshooting Configurations

Indications of a resource conflict (including IRQ, DMA, I/O address, and memory address conflict) are as follows:

> The new device is installed and the new device or a previously installed device does not work.
> The computer locks up or restarts when performing a specific function, such as when playing or recording audio.
> The computer hangs during startup or shutdown.
> A device does not work properly or fails to work at all.

TECH TIP

Verifying hardware with Device Manager

A small down arrow on the device icon means disabled, and an exclamation point (!) on a yellow field usually indicates a resource conflict or driver problem. An "i" indicates that the Use Automatic Settings feature is not being used for the device, and resources were manually configured.

In Device Manager, if an exclamation point (!) appears, the hardware device is not working properly. Check for cabling issues, resource conflicts, and configuration issues. If a yellow question mark appears, Windows does not recognize the device. Try one of the following:

> See if there is a Windows update that might contain updated drivers.
> Manually update the driver: Right-click the device in *Device Manager > Properties > Driver* tab > *Update Driver*. You can download this driver from the device manufacturer website or let Windows try to find the driver.

TECH TIP

Use the General tab for troubleshooting

On the *General* tab of any adapter or port properties, check the *Device status* section for any error codes, including those for resource conflicts.

With any Device Manager issue, you can right-click the device and select *Properties*. On the General tab, notice whether there are error codes. Table 4.7 lists some Device Manager codes and descriptions. You can review all the codes at Microsoft's TechNet website.

TABLE 4.7   Device Manager error codes

Error	Description
Code 1	The device does not have a device driver or is configured improperly.
Code 3	Either the device driver is corrupted or the system is running low on system resources.
Code 10	The device did not start. Try updating the device driver or researching the problem on the vendor website.
Code 12	A system resource conflict has occurred. Reboot the computer multiple times to see if the operating system can work out the conflict. Look for manually assigned (conflicting) resources.
Code 14	The device requires a system restart.
Code 18	The device driver needs to be reinstalled.
Code 19	Registry configuration information is corrupt or damaged. Uninstall the device and reinstall.
Code 22	The device is disabled.
Code 28	The drivers for the device are not installed.
Code 37	Windows cannot start the device driver. Reboot the computer.
Code 47	The device has been prepared for safe removal, but has not been removed from the computer.

CHAPTER 4

Configuration problems can also be associated with specific BIOS/UEFI settings. Table 4.8 lists some problems and what might help.

TABLE 4.8   Troubleshooting UEFI/BIOS-related issues

Issue	Things to try
Message appears that the date and time are not set, the clock is not set, all saved UEFI/BIOS settings are lost, or unexpected issues occur in more than one application.	Check the date and time through the operating system. Check the date and time setting in UEFI/BIOS to see if it matches. Replace the motherboard CMOS battery.
Cannot configure a system for virtualization or XP mode.	Enable virtualization in BIOS.
Attached device does not work.	If the device connects to a motherboard port, ensure the port is not disabled in UEFI/BIOS. Ensure the device connects to the correct port including a possible port on an adapter instead of the motherboard. If the device connects to a port on an adapter that is the same type of port as one found on the motherboard, the integrated port may need to be disabled in UEFI/BIOS.
System locks up sporadically.	If overclocking, put the system back to its original settings.
System is slow to boot or boots from the wrong device.	Check the UEFI/BIOS boot order setting.

Troubleshooting USB

To troubleshoot USB device problems, check the obvious first: the cabling and power. Verify whether any USB device that plugs into a USB hub works. If no devices work, swap the hub or attach to a different USB port. If some hub ports work and some do not, attach an external power source to the hub, change its configuration if necessary, and retest the devices. Restart the computer and retest the USB device.

USB 3.1 ports can provide power at different levels: 2A at 5V (10W), 5A at 12V (60W), and 5A at 20V (100W). USB 3.0 ports can provide 900mA (4.5W) of 5V power—both 3.x versions provide more power than the previous USB versions (500mA/2.5W). Note that a 3.x port can go into low-power mode when the port isn't being used. You can verify how much power a USB device is using by examining the device in Windows Device Manager, following these steps:

Step 1. Open *Device Manager* using the following operating system–dependent Control Panel.

> **Windows Vista:** *System and Maintenance* Control Panel
>
> **Windows 7:** *System and Security* Control Panel
>
> **Windows 8:** *Hardware and Sound* Control Panel
>
> **Windows 10:** *Settings* > type `Device Manager` in the *Find a setting* textbox.

Step 2. Locate and select *Device Manager*.

Step 3. Expand the *Universal Serial Bus Hub Controllers* section.

Step 4. Right-click on each *Generic USB Hub* option and select *Properties*.

Step 5. Access the *Power* tab.

Step 6. Locate the USB device and note how much power is being requested of the USB port/hub, as shown in Figure 4.17.

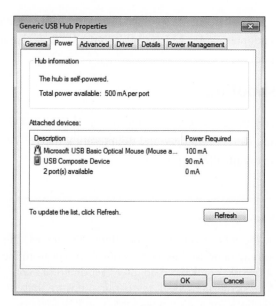

FIGURE 4.17 USB hub power requirements

A USB device could be drawing more power than is allowed. If this is the case, the computer can disable the port. The only way to re-enable the port is to restart the computer. If a device is using less than 50mA of power, the USB port never becomes active. Try plugging the USB device into a different USB port or verifying the device works on another computer.

A USB device requires a driver that may be loaded automatically. An incorrect or outdated driver could be loaded and causing problems. The following list can also help when troubleshooting USB devices:

> Use Device Manager to ensure that a hub is functioning properly.
> Ensure that the UEFI/BIOS firmware is up-to-date.
> Use Device Manager to ensure that no USB device has an IRQ assigned and shared with another non-USB device.
> USB devices sometimes do not work in safe mode and require hardware support configured through the UEFI/BIOS.
> Sometimes a USB device stops working on a hub that has an external power source. In such a case, remove the hub's external power source and retest.
> If a self-powered USB hub gets its power disconnected, the hub becomes a bus-powered hub and outputs only lower power on each port. Reattach the power cord or remove the hub and then reattach it.
> If a newly attached USB device reports that it is attached but does not work properly, upgrade the driver.
> Do not connect USB devices to a computer that is in standby mode or sleep mode. Doing so may prevent the computer from coming out of standby mode.
> For intermittent USB device problems, disable power management to see if this is causing the problem.
> Test a device connected to a USB hub by connecting it directly to a USB port that has nothing else attached. The problem may be caused by other USB devices or a USB hub.
> Remove the USB device's driver and reinstall. Sometimes you must reboot the computer to give the new drivers priority over the general-purpose drivers.
> If a USB device is running slowly, try attaching it to a different port that has fewer devices connected to the same port.

Verify that the USB port is enabled in BIOS if integrated into the motherboard or attached to the motherboard through an adapter cable. Always refer to the USB device manufacturer's website for specific troubleshooting details.

IEEE 1394 Troubleshooting

Use Device Manager to verify the correct installation for an IEEE 1394 device or port. To verify installation in Windows, open *Device Manager* and double-click the *1394 Bus Controller* option to verify that an IEEE 1394 host controller is present.

TECH TIP

What if IEEE 1394 is not working properly?

If a question mark appears by the IEEE 1394 host controller in Device Manager, remove or delete the driver and reinstall it. You may need to download a newer driver from the adapter manufacturer's website. If this does not work, change the adapter to a different expansion slot. If a yellow symbol appears by the FireWire controller, check the cabling, ensure that the device is not disabled, replace the driver, and check for a system resource conflict.

Like USB hubs, FireWire hubs can be self-powered or bus powered. A slide switch may be used to select the appropriate power mode. Most FireWire hub manufacturers recommend powering the hub only during installation. Once installed, test the FireWire devices, remove the hub power, and retest the devices. If all devices operate properly, leave the hub power adapter disconnected. With a cable that has a 6-pin connector at each end, connect the hub to the computer's FireWire port. Attach FireWire devices to the hub as needed.

SOFT SKILLS—A GOOD TECHNICIAN QUALITY: ONE THING AT A TIME

The least effective type of computer technician is a "gun slinger." The term *gun slinger* brings to mind images of Wild West ruffians who had shooting matches with other gangsters in the town's main street. Gun slingers drew their guns frequently and with little provocation. They did not put much thought into their method or consider other possible resolutions. You must strive *not* to be this type of technician.

A gun slinger technician changes multiple things simultaneously. For example, if there is no display on the output, the technician might swap out the monitor, disable the onboard video port, add a new video adapter, power on the computer, and, when output appears, call the problem "solved." If a computer problem is repaired using such a technique, the technician never knows exactly what solved the problem. A gun slinger technician might get frustrated easily because it is easy to forget what has been tried when multiple things have been tried simultaneously (see Figure 4.18).

FIGURE 4.18   A gun slinger technician in action

A good technician, on the other hand, makes a list of symptoms (even if it is simply a mental list) followed by a list of things to try. Then the technician tries the possible solutions, starting with the simplest one (the one that costs the least amount of time to the computer user). The technician documents each step. After each approach that does not fix the problem, the technician puts the system back to the original configuration before attempting the next possible solution. This method keeps the technician focused on what has been tested, and if another technician takes over, the steps do not have to be repeated. Best of all, when one of the possible solutions fixes the problem, the exact solution is known.

Gun slinger technicians do not learn as fast as other technicians because they do not determine the real causes of problems. Each time they are presented with a problem similar to one they have seen in the past, gun slinger technicians use the same haphazard troubleshooting method. These technicians are actually dangerous to an organization because they are not good at documenting what they have done and determining exactly what fixes a particular problem. A good computer technician should methodically troubleshoot a problem by making only one change at a time and reverting the change if the change did not solve the problem. Furthermore, the technician documents the issue and its resolution for future problems.

Chapter Summary

> The UEFI/system flash BIOS is used to enable/disable, configure, and troubleshoot motherboard components, expansion slots, and ports, and it sets power-on and BIOS passwords. When the computer is off, a motherboard battery holds saved settings in CMOS.

> An updated type of BIOS is UEFI BIOS, which allows the use of a mouse and a graphical environment. Security options, support for larger hard drives, antivirus software, remote management, and utilities may also be included.

> Each port and card uses system resources such as interrupts, I/O addresses, and memory addresses.

> System resources can be viewed and changed using Device Manager. Specific Device Manager codes and messages help in troubleshooting conflicts.

> A USB or IEEE 1394 FireWire adapter can be added to provide additional ports.

> Drivers can be installed/updated using Device Manager or by using the Add New Hardware wizard (`hdwwiz`).

> USB device drivers and/or software may have to be installed before installing a USB device. USB ports can provide power (2A at 5V [10W], 5A at 12V [60W] or 20V[100W] version 3.1; 900mA/4.5W version 3.0; and 500ma/2.5W for lower versions). Verify installation and power usage through Device Manager.

A+ CERTIFICATION EXAM TIPS

✓ A lot of questions from both exams can come from this chapter, especially in the troubleshooting areas. Review the troubleshooting bullets. Research issues on the Internet and read people's postings. Their stories and frustration (and successes) will stick in your mind and help you with the exam.

✓ Go to at least one computer and go through the BIOS/UEFI menus. Review what types of things can be configured through BIOS/UEFI. Review Table 4.1 blue-colored options.

✓ Review the many differences between a BIOS and a UEFI BIOS.

✓ Review different sections of Device Manager. Device Manager is a critical tool for troubleshooting computer issues. Know how to determine what driver is installed. Practice finding drivers on Internet sites.

✓ Know reasons you would upgrade the BIOS.

✓ Review the key terms in Table 4.1 and what each of those settings control.

Key Terms

boot sequence....................134	ESCD 146	passwords.........................134
built-in diagnostics...........136	fan speed 135	POST................................130
bus speed..........................135	flash BIOS.........................132	registry 146
clock speed.......................135	I/O address 141	secure boot 136
CMOS 137	intrusion detection/	Setup 130
CMOS battery 137	notification 135	system resources 140
date/time...........................134	IRQ....................................141	temperature monitoring....135
Device Manager................142	jumper 139	TPM 135
disable execute bit............135	LoJack 135	UEFI..................................132
drive encryption 135	memory address 141	virtualization support 135
enabling/disabling devices	MSI 142	voltages 135
& ports 135	MSI-X 142	

Review Questions

1. When would a technician flash a BIOS?

    a. When the date and time start to be incorrect

    b. When a port or motherboard component does not perform at its maximum potential

    c. When the driver for a motherboard port is out of date

    d. When the motherboard has an upgrade such as a new processor, extra RAM, or an additional adapter installed into an expansion slot

2. What is the effect of setting an administrator password in BIOS?

    a. It prevents the computer from having multiple devices that can boot the system.

    b. It prevents the BIOS from being infected with a virus.

    c. It prevents a user from accessing the computer operating system.

    d. It prevents a user from changing system Setup settings.

3. Which program is used to determine the driver version being used for a specific component?
    [BIOS | CMOS | Task Manager | Device Manager | system Setup]

4. Which program is commonly used to verify a new piece of hardware is recognized by the operating system, functions, and the system resources assigned?
    [BIOS | CMOS | manufacturer-provided application | Device Manager]

5. Where would a CR2032 lithium battery most likely be used in a computing device?

    a. As a laptop battery

    b. Inside the processor

    c. As a component on the motherboard

    d. In the CMOS

6. Which BIOS/UEFI option might need to be modified in order to boot a Windows computer from a flash drive that contains Ubuntu, a Linux-based operating system? [Lojack | Secure Boot | Virus Protection | USB Configuration | HyperThreading] _____

7. [T | F] If a power failure occurs during a BIOS update, the motherboard might have to be replaced.

8. What is the result of attaching a USB 2.0 device and a USB 3.0 device to a USB hub attached to a motherboard USB 3.0 port?

    a. The devices share system resources.

    b. The 3.0 device gets a higher-priority IRQ.

    c. If either of the devices is an externally powered device, that particular device gets a higher-priority IRQ. Otherwise, the two devices share an interrupt.

    d. The 3.0 device always has a higher-priority I/O address.

9. Which device properties tab has a *Device status* section that might contain helpful troubleshooting information or the status of the device?
    [General | Advanced | Driver | Details | Management]

10. A technician receives a complaint about a computer being slow to respond to typed keystrokes. The technician installs more memory and a new keyboard. The customer is happy. What, if anything, could have been done better?_____

    _____

    _____

    _____

11. What is the maximum wattage that can be provided by a USB3.1 port?
    [100 | 5 | 2.5 | 4.5]

Consider the following BIOS configuration menu options for answering Questions 12–15.

Main Menu	Onboard Devices	Boot Device Priority
BIOS Information	PCIE Training	1st Boot Device
BIOS Version	LAN1 Controller	2nd Boot Device
Build Date	USB 1.1 Controller	3rd Boot Device
EC F/W Version	USB 2.0 Controller	4th Boot Device
CPU Information	USB 3.0 Controller	
Memory Information	Audio	
System Information	OnChip PATA Controller	
System Language	OnChip SATA Controller	
System Date	SATA	
System Time	HDMI/DVI	

12. Which menu item would you use to determine whether the system should be flashed?

    a. Main Menu

    b. Onboard Devices

    c. Boot Device Priority

13. A computer is mounted inside a cabinet, and you want to know if an IEEE 1394 port is available. Which menu item would you use?

    a. Main menu

    b. Onboard Devices

    c. Boot Device Priority

14. [T | F] The system date and time must be configured through the system BIOS.

15. A technician wants to boot from an eSATA external hard drive. Which submenu item is used? [OnChip SATA controller | SATA | PCIE training | 1st Boot Device]

16. A technician keeps having to configure the date and time. What component is suspect? [CPU | BIOS | battery | chipset | CMOS]

17. What are three ways to get more USB ports? (Choose three.)

    a. Connect a USB hub to an existing USB port.

    b. Connect an IEEE 1394 hub to an existing USB port.

    c. Install a PCI or PCIe adapter that has USB ports.

    d. Install an AGP adapter that has USB ports.

    e. Install a USB plate that has USB ports and attaches to motherboard pins.

    f. Use a USB port multiplexer.

18. When would a technician use UEFI?

    a. When managing configuration through Device Manager

    b. When the date and/or time continues to be wrong

    c. When an adapter has just been installed

    d. When replacing a motherboard

19. A computer is being used in a medical office. For security reasons, the technician has been asked to reasonably ensure that no one attaches any external media. What would the technician probably do?

    a. Password protect the BIOS and disable unused ports.

    b. Swap out the motherboard for one that doesn't have extra ports.

    c. Assign user rights through user passwords on the computer.

    d. Encrypt the hard drive.

    e. Flash the chipset.

20. A technician for a small company set a BIOS password on every computer. The technician leaves the company, and the replacement technician needs to access the BIOS. What should the new technician do? _____

    _____

Activities

Internet Discovery

Objective: To obtain specific information on the Internet regarding a computer or its associated parts

Parts: Computer with Internet access

Procedure: Use the Internet to answer the following questions. Assume that the customer owns a Lenovo A740 all-in-one computer when answering Questions 1 and 2.

Questions:

1. A customer owns a Lenovo A740 all-in-one computer. Determine the procedure for accessing the computer's Setup program. Write the key(s) to press and the URL where you find this information.

    _____

    _____

2. What is the latest BIOS version for the Lenovo A740? _____

3. A Windows 8 HP computer owner just updated the BIOS, but after the upgrade, the following message appeared on the screen: Error: CMOS Checksum bad. What should the customer do next if the BIOS version is 7? Provide the URL where you found this information. _____

    _____

    _____

    _____

4. A customer owns a Tyan S7025 motherboard. How many and which type of PCIe slots does this motherboard have? Write the answer and the URL where you find the answer. _____

    _____

    _____

    _____

5. On the same Tyan S7025 motherboard, which motherboard jumper is used to clear CMOS? Write the answer and the URL where you find the information. _____

    _____

6. On the same Tyan S7025 motherboard, which BIOS menu option is used to configure the order in which the system looks for devices to boot the computer? Write the answer and the URL where you find the answer. _____

    _____

Soft Skills

Objective: To enhance and fine-tune a future technician's ability to listen, communicate in both written and oral form, and support people who use computers in a professional manner

Activities:

1. In teams, come up with a troubleshooting scenario that involves a computer technician who uses gun-slinging techniques and the same scenario involving a technician who is methodical. Explain what each technician type does and how they solve the problem. Also, detail how they treat the customer differently. Determine ways of how a gun-slinging technician might be harmful to a computer repair business. Either demonstrate or report on your findings.

2. After exploring the BIOS options, turn to a fellow student, pretend he or she is a customer over the phone, and walk the student through accessing Setup. Explain the purposes of at least five of the options. Reverse roles and cover five other options. Be sure to act like a typical computer user when playing the customer role.

3. Brainstorm a troubleshooting scenario in which you fix the problem that involves accessing the Setup program and/or an adapter. Document the problem using a word processing application. Create an invoice using either a word processing or spreadsheet application. Share your documents with others in the class.

Critical Thinking Skills

Objective: To analyze and evaluate information as well as apply learned information to new or different situations

Activities:

1. Why do you think so few computers today have very few PCI adapters or slots? _____
    _____
    _____

2. Compare and contrast a post office with IRQs, I/O addresses, and memory addresses shown in Device Manager. For example, how might something that happens in a post office relate to an IRQ in a PC (or I/O address or memory address)? _____
    _____
    _____
    _____
    _____
    _____
    _____
    _____
    _____
    _____
    _____

3. Your parents want to buy you a new computer, and they are doing research. They ask you to explain whether they should buy a PCIe 3.1 or 2.1 video adapter. Explain to them (either verbally or in writing) the differences between them and your recommendation. _____
    _____
    _____
    _____
    _____

Labs

Lab 4.1   Configuration Method Exercise and Review

Objective: To determine which configuration method a computer uses

Parts: A computer and Internet access

Procedure: Complete the following procedure and answer the accompanying questions.

1. Open the computer and look at the motherboard. Note that you may have to use the computer model number and the Internet to do research for parts of this lab or to answer some of the questions. Verify any information found on the Internet with what you see in the computer.

   Document (write down) the location, name, and purpose of all motherboard jumpers.

   _____

   _____

2. Locate the motherboard battery and document the battery type.

   What type of battery is installed?

   _____

   How can you tell the purpose of the jumper(s)?

   _____

   _____

   What is one of the first indications of a failing battery?

   _____

   _____

   What is the keystroke(s) required to access the Setup program?

   _____

Lab 4.2 Examining BIOS options

Objective: To examine BIOS features

Parts: A computer

Note: Internet access may be required.

Procedure: Complete the following procedure and answer the accompanying questions.

1. Power on the computer and watch the screen closely for directions for how to access the BIOS. Press the appropriate key before the operating system boots. Note that you may have to restart the computer, or power it down and then power it back on in order to access it. This may take several tries. You may also be required to research the computer brand and model on the Internet to determine which keystroke is required.

   Which keystroke is required to access BIOS?

   _____

CHAPTER 4

2. Examine the main menu.

List at least three main menu options.

_____

Which keystroke(s) allow(s) you to save settings and exit BIOS?

_____

3. Explore various menus in order to answer the following questions.

List the boot devices in the order that they are currently configured through BIOS.

1st boot device _____

2nd boot device _____

3rd boot device _____

On which menu screen can you set a power-on password?

_____

List the options you can set for any integrated motherboard port.

_____

The BIOS enables which type of monitoring? Select all that apply and add any that are not listed.
[power | fan | CPU | HDD (hard disk drive) | temperature]

_____

What diagnostics, if any, are available through BIOS?

_____

Which power save options, if any, are available through BIOS?

_____

Through which menu option is virtualization support enabled or disabled?

_____

Which tool would a technician use for troubleshooting?

_____

Which setting(s) would you choose to make the computer boot faster?

_____

What is the BIOS version?

_____

Which keystroke(s) allow(s) you to exit BIOS without saving any changes?

_____

4. Using whatever keystroke(s) you documented in the previous question of Step 3, exit BIOS without saving any changes.

Lab 4.3 Accessing BIOS/UEFI through Windows 8 or 10

Objective: To access BIOS/UEFI through the operating system

Parts: A working Windows 8 or 10 computer

Note: Refer to Labs 1.2 or 1.3 for directions on basic Windows 8 or 10 usage.

Procedure: Complete the following procedure and answer the accompanying questions.

1. Power on the computer and log in as required.

2. With newer devices that have fast-booting hard drives, accessing BIOS setup is a challenge. Windows 8 and 10 support accessing BIOS through Windows.

   Windows 8: Point to the upper-right corner of the screen or access *Settings > Change PC Settings* link > *Update and recovery > Recovery > Restart now* button under Advanced startup > *Troubleshoot > Advanced options > UEFI Firmware Settings > Restart* button

   Windows 10: Access *Settings > Update and security > Recovery > Restart now* button under Advanced startup > *Troubleshoot > Advanced options > UEFI Firmware Settings > Restart* button

   Describe a situation where you think a technician would use this technique?

   _____

   What BIOS options are available on the main screen?

   _____

   What option or keystroke(s) allow you to exit BIOS?

   _____

3. Using whatever keystroke(s) you documented in the last question of Step 2, exit BIOS without changing any settings.

Lab 4.4   System Resource Configuration through the Setup Program

Objective: To access the system resources through the Setup program

Parts: A computer

Procedure: Complete the following procedure and answer the accompanying questions.

1. Power on the computer.

2. Press the appropriate key(s) to enter the Setup program.

3. Go through the various menus or icons until you find an interrupt (IRQ) setting for a particular device or port.

   Write the device or port and the associated IRQ in the space below.

   IRQ   Device or Port

   _____   _____

   Why do different devices generally not have the same interrupt?

   _____

4. Go through the various menus or icons until you find an I/O address setting for a particular device or port.

   Write the device or port in the space provided, along with the associated I/O address.

   I/O Address   Device or Port

   _____   _____

   Why must each device and port have a separate and unique I/O address?

   _____

How do I/O addresses, interrupts, and memory addresses get assigned to an installed adapter?

_____

_____

What is the best source for viewing interrupts, I/O addresses, and memory addresses that have been assigned?

_____

5.   Exit the Setup program.

6.   Go to Device Manager and determine whether the information collected in Steps 3 and 4 is the same.

Instructor initials: _____

Lab 4.5 Examining System Resources by Using Windows

Objective: To be able to view and access system resources by using Windows

Parts: A computer with Windows loaded

Procedure: Complete the following procedure and answer the accompanying questions.

1.   Power on the computer and verify that Windows loads. Log on to the computer, using the user ID and password provided by the instructor or lab assistant.

2.   Locate and access *Device Manager*. If necessary, refer to Labs 1.1 (Windows 7), 1.2 (Windows 8), or 1.3 (Windows 10) for basic Windows usage.

3.   Click the *View* menu option and select *Resources by type*.

Which types of system resources are shown?

_____

4.   Click the *plus sign* (or arrow) or *Interrupt request* (IRQ) to expand the section.

Scroll through the list to determine whether there are any interrupts in use by multiple devices (the same number used by two things)? If so, list one.

_____

What device, if any, is using IRQ8?

_____

Is this the standard IRQ for this device?

_____

Instructor initials: _____

5.   Collapse the Interrupt request (IRQ section). Expand the *Input/output (IO)* section.

What is the first I/O address range listed for the first occurrence of the Direct Memory Access controller?

_____

6.   Collapse the *Input/output* section. Expand the *Direct memory access (DMA)* section.

Are any DMA channels being used? If so, list them.

_____

7.   Collapse the *DMA* section. Expand the *IRQ* section again. Click to select any device listed in the IRQ section. Move your mouse slowly over the icons at the top until you locate the *Update Driver Software* icon. When the mouse is moved slowly enough, a description of the icon appears.

In what position is the Update Driver Software Icon located?

[first | last | second | third from the right | answer not listed]

_____

_____

8. Move your mouse slowly over the icons at the top until you locate the *Uninstall* icon. *Do not click this icon.* Now locate the *Disable* icon. Both options can be used to troubleshoot problem devices.

    In what situation do you think a technician would use either option?

    _____

9. From the main menu, *View > Devices by type*. Expand any section and select a particular device. Select the *Action* menu item and select *Properties*. The *Properties* window opens. The General tab shows you the status of the device and whether it is working properly or not.

    What device was chosen?

    _____

    What is the status of the device?

    _____

10. Click the *Driver* tab. The Driver tab shows information about the device driver.

    What is the device driver version being used by the device chosen?

    _____

    What other important button is found on this tab that you think might be used if a device is not performing exactly as expected?

    _____

11. Click the *Resources* tab. The Resources tab shows what system resources a particular device is using. What resources are being used?

    _____

    What message displays in the conflicting *device list* section?

    _____

    Is the *Use automatic settings* checkbox enabled?

    _____

Instructor initials: _____

12. Click the *Cancel* button to return to Device Manager. Close the Device Manager window.

Lab 4.6 Device Drivers

Objective: To become familiar with finding driver, driver information, and current driver version

Parts: A computer with access to the Internet

Procedure: Use the Internet and a computer to answer the accompanying questions.

1. A customer is looking to upgrade to Windows 10. She has a Creative Labs Sound Blaster Z PCIe sound card installed.

    Is there a device driver for this card if the customer decides to upgrade? Provide the URL where you find the answer.

    _____

    _____

    What is the latest device driver version for a PNY NVIDIA GeForce GT610 video adapter for a Windows 7 64-bit computer? Also provide the URL where you find this information.

    _____

    _____

What are the device driver version and date for any USB Root Hub on the computer?

_____

Locate a USB Enhanced Host Controller in Device Manager. Use the Driver tab and update the driver if possible. Record your results.

_____
_____

What is the latest Windows driver revision for a StarTech PCIe 1000Mbps fiber network card that has the part number ST1000SPEX?

_____

5 Disassembly and Power

In this chapter you will learn:

> How to prevent static electricity, RFI, and EMI from harming or interfering with a computer

> The tools needed to work on computers

> How to take apart a computer and put it back together

> How to perform basic voltage and continuity checks

> How to upgrade or replace a power supply

> Tips for good written communication

CompTIA Exam Objectives:

What CompTIA A+ exam objectives are covered in this chapter?

✓ 901-1.2 Explain the importance of motherboard components, their purpose, and properties.

✓ 901-1.8 Install a power supply based on given specifications.

✓ 901-4.1 Given a scenario, troubleshoot common problems related to motherboards, RAM, CPU, and power with appropriate tools.

✓ 901-4.6 Given a scenario, troubleshoot printers with appropriate tools.

✓ 902-1.5 Given a scenario, use Windows Control Panel utilities.

✓ 902-4.1 Given a scenario, troubleshoot PC operating system problems with appropriate tools.

✓ 902-5.1 Given a scenario, use appropriate safety procedures.

✓ 902-5.2 Given a scenario with potential environmental impacts, apply the appropriate controls.

✓ 902-5.4 Demonstrate proper communication techniques and professionalism.

Disassembly Overview

It is seldom necessary to completely disassemble a computer. However, when a technician is first learning about PCs, disassembly can be both informative and fun. Technicians might disassemble a computer to perform preventive cleaning or to troubleshoot a problem. It might also be appropriate to disassemble a computer when it has a problem of undetermined cause. Sometimes, the only way to diagnose a problem is to disassemble the computer outside the case or remove components one by one. Disassembling a computer outside the case might help with grounding problems. A **grounding** problem occurs when the motherboard or adapter is not properly installed and a trace (a metal line on the motherboard or adapter) touches the computer frame, causing the adapter and possibly other components to stop working. Don't forget to remove jewelry and use proper lifting techniques, as described in Figure 1.31 (see Chapter 1) before disassembling a computer.

Electrostatic Discharge (ESD)

You must take precautions when disassembling a computer. The electronic circuits located on the motherboard and adapters are subject to ESD. Electrostatic discharge (**ESD**) is a difference of potential between two items that cause static electricity. Static electricity can damage electronic equipment without the technician's knowledge. The average person requires a static discharge of 3,000 volts before he or she feels it. An electronic component can be damaged with as little as 30 volts. Some electronic components might not be damaged the first time static electricity occurs. However, the effects of static electricity can be cumulative, weakening or eventually destroying a component. An ESD event is not recoverable—nothing can be done about the damage it induced. Electronic chips and memory modules are most susceptible to ESD strikes.

> **TECH TIP**
>
> **Atmospheric conditions affect static electricity**
>
> When humidity is low, the potential for ESD is greater than at any other time; however, too much humidity is bad for electronics. Keep humidity between 45 and 55 percent to reduce the threat of ESD.

A technician can prevent ESD by using a variety of methods. The most common tactic is to use an **anti-static wrist strap** also called an **ESD strap**. One end encircles the technician's wrist. At the other end, an alligator clip attaches to the computer. The clip attaches to a grounding post or a metal part such as the power supply. The electronic symbol for ground is ⏚.

An anti-static wrist strap allows the technician and the computer to be at the same voltage potential. As long as the technician and the computer or electronic part are at the same potential, static electricity does not occur. An exercise at the end of the chapter demonstrates how to attach an anti-static wrist strap and how to perform maintenance on it. Technicians should use an ESD wrist strap whenever possible.

A resistor inside an anti-static wrist strap protects the technician in case something accidentally touches the ground to which the strap attaches while he or she is working inside a computer. This resistor cannot protect the technician against the possible voltages inside a CRT monitor or power supply. See Figure 5.1 for an illustration of an anti-static wrist strap. Figure 5.2 shows a good location for attaching an anti-static wrist strap.

TECH TIP

When *not* to wear an anti-static wrist strap

Technicians should not wear an ESD wrist strap when working inside a CRT monitor or power supply because of the high voltages there. Of course, a technician should not be inside these devices unless properly trained in electronics.

FIGURE 5.1   Anti-static wrist strap

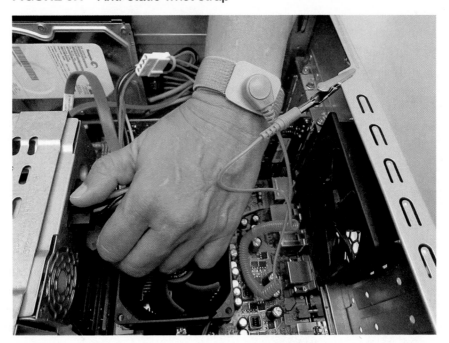

FIGURE 5.2   Attaching an anti-static wrist strap

Anti-static gloves can also be used instead of an anti-static wrist strap. Laptops frequently do not have good places to attach the wrist strap and the anti-static gloves work better. Figure 5.3 shows what these look like.

FIGURE 5.3   Anti-static gloves

Anti-static bags are good for storing spare adapters and motherboards when the parts are not in use. However, anti-static bags lose their effectiveness after a few years. **ESD mats** are available to place underneath a computer being repaired, which might have a snap for connecting the anti-static wrist strap. Anti-static heel straps are also available. Figure 5.4 shows an anti-static bag with an adapter inside it.

FIGURE 5.4   Anti-static bag

If an anti-static wrist strap is not available, you can still reduce the chance of ESD damage. After removing the computer case, stay attached to an unpainted metal computer part. One such part is the power supply. If you are right-handed, place your bare left arm on the power supply. Remove the computer parts one by one, always keeping your left elbow (or some other bare part of your arm) touching the power supply. If you are left-handed, place your right arm on the power supply. By placing your elbow on the power supply, both hands are free to remove computer parts. This **"self-grounding"** method is an effective way of keeping the technician and the computer at the same voltage potential, thus reducing the chance of ESD damage. It is not as safe as using an anti-static wrist strap. Also, removing the power cable from the back of the computer is a good idea.

A power supply provides a small amount of power to the motherboard even when the computer is powered off. Always unplug the computer and use an anti-static wrist strap when removing or replacing parts inside a computer!

TECH TIP

Good news about ESD

Because your body and clothing can store up to 2,500V of static electricity, you will be happy to note that electronic manufacturers are designing components that are less susceptible to ESD. However, still ground yourself using any means possible. Each zap weakens a component!

Electromagnetic Interference (EMI)

Electromagnetic interference (**EMI**, sometimes called EMR, for electromagnetic radiation) is noise caused by electrical devices. Many devices can cause EMI, such as a computer, a pencil sharpener, a motor, a vacuum cleaner, an air conditioner, and fluorescent lighting. The electrical devices around the computer case, including a CRT-type monitor and speakers, cause more problems than the computer.

TECH TIP

Replace empty slot covers

To help with EMI and RFI problems, replace slot covers for expansion slots that are no longer being used. Slot covers are shown in Figure 4.15 (see Chapter 4). Slot covers also keep out dust and improve the airflow within the case.

A specific type of electromagnetic interference that negatively affects computers is radio frequency interference (**RFI**). RFI is simply noises that occur in the radio frequency range. Anytime a computer has an intermittent problem, check the surrounding devices for the source of that problem. For example, if the computer goes down only when the pencil sharpener operates or when using the optical drive, EMI could be to blame. EMI problems are very hard to track to the source. Any electronic device, including computers and printers, can be a source of EMI or RFI. EMI/RFI can affect any electronic circuit. EMI can also come through power lines. Move the computer to a different wall outlet or to a totally different circuit to determine whether the power outlet is the problem source. EMI can also affect files on a hard drive.

Tools

No chapter on disassembly and reassembly is complete without mentioning tools. Tools can be divided into two categories: (1) those you should not leave the office without and (2) those that are nice to have in the office, at home, or in the car.

Many technicians do not go on a repair call with a full tool case. Ninety-five percent of all repairs are completed with the following basic tools:

> Small and medium flat-tipped screwdrivers
> #0, #1, and #2 Phillips screwdrivers
> 1/4- and 3/16-inch hex nut drivers
> Small diagonal cutters
> Needle-nose pliers

Screwdrivers take care of most disassemblies and reassemblies. Sometimes manufacturers place tie wraps on new parts, new cables, or the cables inside the computer case. The diagonal cutters are great for removing the tie wraps without cutting cables or damaging parts. Needle-nose pliers are good for straightening bent pins on cables or connectors, and doing a million other things. Small tweaker screwdrivers and needle-nose pliers are indispensable. Figure 5.5 shows the common basic tools.

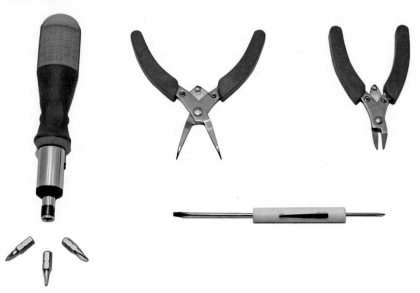

FIGURE 5.5   Basic PC technician tools

TECH TIP

Getting those wayward screws

Magnetic screwdrivers are handy to pick up dropped screws. If a screw rolls under the motherboard and cannot be reached, tilt the computer so that the screw rolls out. Sometimes the case must be tilted in different directions until the screw becomes dislodged.

Many technicians start with a basic $15 microcomputer repair kit and build from there. A bargain table 6-in-1 or 4-in-1 combination **screwdriver** that has two sizes of flat-tipped and two sizes of Phillips screwdrivers is a common tool among new technicians. A specialized Swiss army knife with screwdrivers is the favorite of some technicians. Other technicians prefer to carry an all-in-one tool in a pouch that connects to their belt.

There are tools that no one thinks of as tools but that should be taken on a service call every time. They include a pen or pencil with which to take notes and fill out the repair slip and a bootable disc containing the technician's favorite repair utilities. Usually a technician has several bootable discs for different operating systems and utilities. Often a flashlight comes in handy because some rooms and offices are dimly lit. Finally, do not forget to bring a smile and a sense of humor.

A **multimeter** is a tool used to take voltage readings from power supply connectors and electrical wall outlets. A multimeter can also measure current (amps) and resistance (ohms) as discussed later in the chapter. Figure 5.6 shows a multimeter, a #1 Phillips screwdriver, and a set of nut drivers. Tools that are nice to have but not used daily include a multimeter and other devices found in the list that follow.

> Multimeter
> Screw pick-up tool
> Screwdriver extension tool
> Soldering iron, solder, and flux
> Screw-starter tool
> Medium-size diagonal cutters
> Metric nut drivers
> Cable-making tools
> Cable tester
> Loopback plug
> Punch-down tool
> Toner generator and probe
> Wire/cable stripper
> Crimper
> Wi-Fi analyzer

> External enclosure
> AC circuit tester
> Right-angled, flat-tipped, and Phillips screwdrivers
> Hemostats
> Pliers
> Optical laser cleaning kit
> Nonstatic low airflow vacuum or toner vacuum
> Compressed air
> Disposable gloves
> Safety goggles
> Air filter/mask
> Small plastic scribe
> T8, 10, 15, 20, and 25 Torx (star) screwdriver

Multimeter   #1 Phillips screwdriver

Scribe

Nut driver set

FIGURE 5.6   Tools: Multimeter, #1 Phillips screwdriver, scribe, and nut driver set

You could get some nice muscle tone from carrying all these nice-to-have, but normally unnecessary, tools. When starting out in computer repair, get the basics. As your career path and skill level grow, so will your tool kit. Getting to a job site and not having the right tool can be a real hassle. However, because there are no standards or limitations on what manufacturers can use in their product lines, it is impossible to always have the right tool on hand.

Disassembly

Before a technician disassembles a computer, several steps should be performed or considered. The following disassembly tips are helpful:

> Do not remove the motherboard battery, or the configuration information in CMOS will be lost.
> Use proper grounding procedures to prevent ESD damage.
> Keep paper, a pen, a phone, and a digital camera nearby for note taking, diagramming, and photo taking. Even if you have taken apart computers for years, you might find something unique or different inside this one.

> Have ample flat and clean workspace.
> When removing adapters, do not stack the adapters on top of one another.
> If possible, place removed adapters inside a special ESD protective bag.
> Handle each adapter, motherboard, or processor on the side edges. Avoid touching the gold contacts on the bottom of adapters. Sweat, oil, and dirt cause problems.
> Remember that hard drives require careful handling. A very small jolt can cause damage to stored data.
> You can remove a power supply, but do not disassemble a CRT-style monitor or power supply without proper training and tools.
> Document screw and cable locations. Label them if possible.

Step 1. Remove Power and External Cables

Before disassembling the computer, you should always remove the power cord. A small amount of power is sent to the motherboard even when the computer is powered off. This is so the computer can be "woken up" in a corporate environment and updates applied. Make notes as to what cable attaches to a specific port. Figure 5.7 shows the back of the computer where this is done.

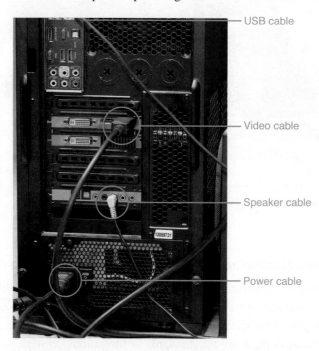

USB cable

Video cable

Speaker cable

Power cable

FIGURE 5.7   Remove power and external cables

Step 2. Open the Case

Opening or removing the case is sometimes the hardest part of disassembly. Some manufacturers have tabs or covers over the retaining screws, and others have retention levers or tabs that have to be depressed before the cover slides open or away. For some computers, you must press a tab on top of the computer downward while simultaneously pressing upward on a tab on the bottom of the computer. Once the tabs are pressed, the cover can be pried open. Sound like a two-person job? Sometimes it is.

Some cases have screws that loosen but do not have to be removed all the way to remove or open the case. For all computer screws, make diagrams and use an egg carton by labeling each section of the carton with where you got the screws. Remember to remove or loosen a screw, turn the screwdriver to the left. When possible, refer to the manufacturer's directions when opening a case. Most of the time, you can access inside the computer by simply removing the screws that hold down the side panel, as shown in Figure 5.8.

FIGURE 5.8   Remove case screws

Step 3. Remove Internal Cables and Connectors

Internal cables commonly connect from a device to the motherboard, the power supply to a device, the motherboard to the front panel buttons or ports, and/or from a card that occupies an expansion space to a device. Cables can be tricky. Inserting a cable backward into a device or adapter can damage the device, motherboard, or adapter. Most cables are keyed so the cable inserts only one way into the connector. However, some cables or connectors are *not* keyed.

Removing a cable for the first time requires some muscle. Many cables have a pull tab or plastic piece used to remove the cable from the connector and/or device. Use this if possible and do not yank on the cable. Some cables have connectors with locking tabs. Release the locking tab *before* disconnecting the cable; otherwise, damage can be done to the cable and/or connector.

Be careful with drive cables. Some of the narrow drive cables, such as the one shown in Figure 5.9, are not as sturdy and do not connect as firmly as some of the other computer cables. Also, with this particular cable type, it does not matter which cable end attaches to the device. A 90°-angled cable (see Figure 5.10) might attach to devices in a case that has a limited-space design and might have a release latch.

FIGURE 5.9   Both cable ends are the same

FIGURE 5.10   90°-angled cable with a latch

TECH TIP

Pin 1 is the cable edge that is colored

Pin 1 on a ribbon cable is easily identified by the colored stripe that runs down the edge of the cable.

Each cable has a certain number of pins, and all cables have a **pin 1**. Pin 1 on a cable connects to pin 1 on a connector. In the event that the pin 1 is *not* easily identified, both ends of the cable should be labeled with either a 1 or 2 on one side or a higher number on the other end. Pins 1 and 2 are always on the same end of a cable. If you find a higher number, pin 1 is on the opposite end. Also, the cable connector usually has an arrow etched into its molding showing the pin 1 connection. Figure 5.11 shows pin 1 on a ribbon cable.

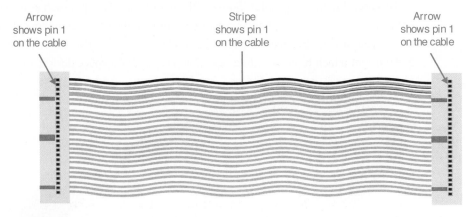

FIGURE 5.11   Pin 1 on a ribbon cable

TECH TIP

Snug connections

When connecting cables to a motherboard or internal components, ensure that each cable is connected tightly, evenly, and securely.

Motherboard connectors are usually notched so that the cable inserts only one way; however, not all cables are notched. Some motherboards have pin 1 (or the opposite pin) labeled. Always refer to the motherboard documentation for proper orientation of a cable into a motherboard connector. Figure 5.12 shows the motherboard connectors used for the cables shown in Figures 5.9 and 5.10. These connectors commonly have hard drives and optical drives attached. Figure 5.13 shows two other motherboard connectors—the top one for older drives and the bottom one for motherboard power. Notice how the top connector has a notch (opening). Notice how the bottom connector has certain connector openings that are different from the square ones to prevent inserting the cable in the wrong direction.

FIGURE 5.12   Motherboard drive connectors

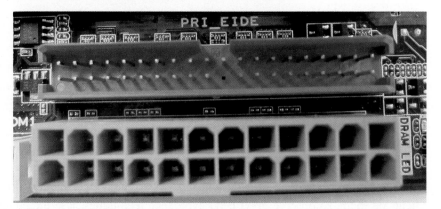

FIGURE 5.13   Two motherboard connectors (old driver and motherboard power)

Specific cables connect from the motherboard to lights, ports, or buttons on the front panel. These include the power button, a reset button, USB ports, IEEE 1394 ports, a microphone port, a headphone port, speakers, fans, the drive activity light, and the power light, to name a few. Be very careful when removing and reinstalling these cables. Usually, each one of these has a connector that must attach to the appropriate motherboard pins. Be sure to check all ports and buttons once you have reconnected these cables. Refer to the motherboard documentation if your diagramming or notes are inaccurate or if you have no diagrams or notes. Figure 5.14 shows the motherboard pins and the cables.

FIGURE 5.14 Motherboard front panel cables

Be careful when connecting front panel cables

Ensure you connect the front panel cables to the appropriate pins and in the correct direction. Some manufacturers label the cables. As shown in Figure 5.14, once you have one oriented correctly (such as the words appearing toward the outside of the motherboard), the others are commonly oriented in the same direction. Also notice how all the white cables orient in the same direction.

The motherboard also contains pins that are used to connect cables such as those that go to the CPU or case fans. Look back to Figure 3.24 to see how fans connect to pins on the motherboard. Note that the fan might be a 3- or 4-pin cable and the motherboard might have a 3- or 4-pin connector. Even if a 3-pin cable has to attach to a 4-pin connector or a 4-pin cable connects to a 3-pin motherboard connector, the fan still works.

Step 4. Remove Adapters

Adapters commonly have retaining screws or a bar that keeps the adapters firmly in the case. Refer back to Figure 4.15 for an illustration of these two methods. Adapters do have electronic components on them, so observe good ESD avoidance techniques. Use the edges of the adapter to pull it upward out of the expansion slot. Do not touch the gold contacts on the bottom of the adapter. Never pile adapters on top of one another. If an adapter will not be re-installed, insert an expansion slot blank cover in the empty expansion slot so proper airflow will be maintained within the case. Figure 5.15 shows an adapter being removed.

FIGURE 5.15   Adapter removal

Step 5. Remove Storage Devices

Hard drives must be handled with care when disassembling a computer. Inside traditional hard drives are hard platters with tiny read/write heads located just millimeters above the platters. If dropped, the read/write heads might touch the platter, causing damage to the platter and/or the read/write heads. The platter holds data and applications. Today's mechanical hard drives have self-parking heads that pull the heads away to a safe area when the computer is powered off or in a power-saving mode. Always be careful neither to jolt nor to jar the hard drive when removing it from the computer. Even with self-parking heads, improper handling can cause damage to the hard drive.

A solid-state drive (SSD) does not contain fragile heads. However, these drives are susceptible to ESD. Use proper anti-static handling procedures when removing/installing them. Store a solid-state drive in an anti-static bag when not in use.

Hard drives slide into a drive bay. Some cases require the hard drive to have hard drive rails that attach to the side of the drive and then the drive slides into a drive bay. Other cases require that the drive be screwed into the hard drive bay. Figure 5.16 shows a hard drive being removed. You can see that this particular case requires screws to secure drives inserted into the drive bays. The screws must be removed before the drive can be removed.

Figure 5.17 shows a hard drive that has a guide rail attached and a different set of guide rails below the drive. When replacing a drive, the drive rails would have to be removed from the old drive and attached to the replacement drive. When installing a new drive, drive rails might have to be purchased.

FIGURE 5.16   Removing a hard drive

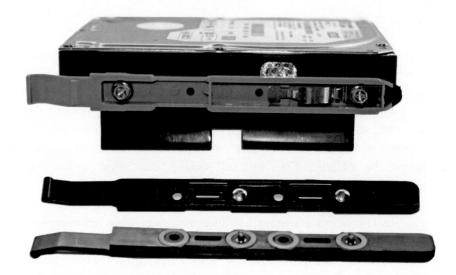

FIGURE 5.17   Hard drive rails

Step 6. Remove Motherboard

Chapter 3 covered motherboard replacement extensively, so here we discuss issues related to building a computer from scratch or disassembling a computer: I/O shield, standoffs, and retaining clips. Some cases include a standard I/O panel shield that might need to be removed to install the I/O shield that comes with some motherboards. The **I/O shield** is a part that allows for optimum airflow and grounding for the motherboard ports. The I/O shield helps ensure the motherboard is installed correctly and properly aligned with the case. Figure 5.18 shows a motherboard I/O shield.

Some computer cases have plastic or metal (commonly brass) **standoffs** that allow the motherboard to be screwed into the case without the motherboard solder joints touching and grounding to the computer case, causing the motherboard not to work. Some standoffs are plastic, and they slide into slots on the computer case. Do not remove these types of standoffs; just leave them attached and slide the motherboard out of the slots. The most common type of standoff is a metal standoff that screws into the case; this standoff has a threaded side that the motherboard sits on and a screw that attaches the motherboard to the standoff, as shown in Figure 5.19.

FIGURE 5.18 Motherboard I/O shield

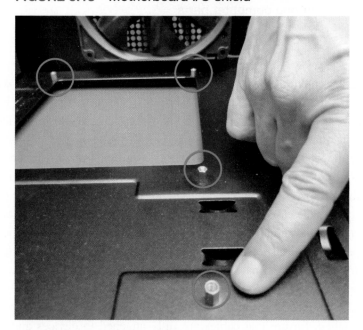

FIGURE 5.19 Motherboard standoff

Some motherboards not only have screws that attach them to the metal standoffs but one or more retaining clips. A retaining clip might need to be pressed down, lifted up, or bent upward in order to slide the motherboard out of the case. The case might contain one or more notches and require the motherboard to be slid in a particular direction (usually in the direction going away from the back I/O ports) before being lifted from the case.

All-in-One Computers

All-in-one computers have all of the components built in with the display. The same concepts apply regarding cabling, storage device removal, RAM removal, motherboard removal, and power. The difference is the space in which the devices are installed—the all-in-one computer has everything installed on the back of the display as shown in Figure 5.20.

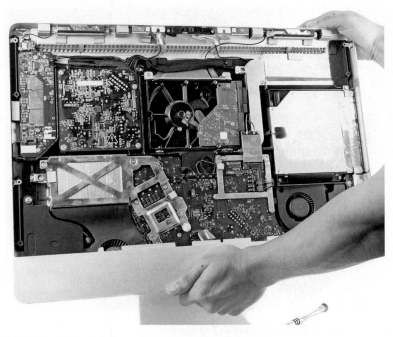

FIGURE 5.20   All-in-one computer parts

Reassembly

Reassembling a computer is easy if the technician is careful and properly diagrams the disassembly. Simple tasks such as inserting the optical drive in the correct drive bay become confusing after many parts have been removed. Writing reminders or taking photos takes less time than having to troubleshoot the computer because of poor reassembly. Reinsert all components into their proper place; be careful to replace all screws and parts. Install missing slot covers, if possible.

Three major reassembly components are motherboards, cables, and connectors. When reinstalling a motherboard, reverse the procedure used during disassembly. Ensure that the motherboard is securely seated into the case and that all retaining clips and/or screws are replaced. This procedure requires practice, but eventually a technician will be able to tell when a motherboard is seated into the case properly. Visual inspection can also help. Ensure that the ports extend fully from the case through the I/O shield. As a final step, ensure that the drives and cover are aligned properly when the case is reinstalled.

Cables and connectors are the most common source of reassembly problems once the motherboard is installed. Ensure that cables are fully attached to devices and the same motherboard connector. Ensure that power cables are securely attached. Matching pin 1 on the cable to pin 1 on the motherboard connector is critical for older ribbon cables. Attaching the correct device to the correct cable can be difficult if proper notes were not taken.

Preventive Maintenance

In the course of daily usage, computers get dirty, especially inside. Dust accumulates on top of electronic components, in air vents and fans, around ports and adapters, and between drives, thus creating insulation and increasing the amount of heat generated. Additional heat can cause electronic components to overheat and fail. Additional heat can cause the processor to consistently run at a lower speed. Dust is an enemy of computers. Look at Figure 5.21 to see how dust accumulates inside a computer.

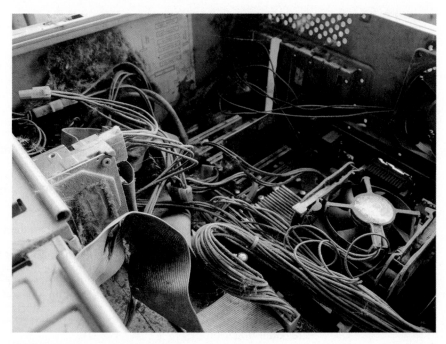

FIGURE 5.21   Dust inside a compartment

Preventive maintenance includes certain procedures performed to prolong the life of a computer. Some computer companies sell maintenance contracts that include preventive maintenance programs. A computer in a normal working environment should be cleaned at least once a year. Typical preventive measures include vacuuming the computer and cleaning the optical drive laser, keyboard keys, printers, and display screen. Be sure to power down the computer and remove the power cord for any computer, remove the battery and AC adapter for a laptop or other mobile device, and allow a laser printer to cool before accessing internal parts. Always ensure that the device has proper ventilation and vents are clear of any obstructions. Preventive measures for many individual devices are described in their respective chapters. For example, the steps detailing how to clean optical discs are included in Chapter 8. This section gives an overview of a preventive maintenance program and some general tips about cleaning solvents.

TECH TIP

Be careful when cleaning LCD monitors and laptop displays

Use one of the following to clean LCD monitors and laptop displays: (1) wipes specifically designed for LCDs or (2) a soft lint-free cloth dampened with either water or a mixture of isopropyl alcohol and water. Never put liquid directly on the display and ensure that the display is dry before closing the laptop.

When performing preventive maintenance, power on the computer to be certain it operates. Perform an audio and visual inspection of the computer as it boots. Ensure the room temperature is appropriate for the device. Electronic equipment like PCs and mobile devices are designed to operate at room temperature (~73°F). Anything above 80 °F should warrant additional cooling methods for the device.

It is a terrible feeling to perform preventive maintenance on a computer only to power it on and find it does not work. You will wonder if the cleaning you performed caused the problem or if the computer had a problem before the preventive maintenance. Be sure to document any parts removed.

Repair companies frequently provide a preventive **maintenance kit** for service calls. The kit normally includes the components listed and described in Table 5.1.

TABLE 5.1   Preventive maintenance items

Item	Description
Portable vacuum	Used to suck dirt from inside of the computer. Be sure to use nonmetallic attachments. Some vacuum cleaners have the ability to blow air. Vacuum first, and then set the vacuum cleaner to blow to get dust out of hard-to-reach places. Hold fan blades in place.
Toner vacuum	A special vacuum that can be used to clean computers and laser printers. Special vacuum bags are used so that the toner does not melt and damage the vacuum cleaner.
Special vacuum bags	Used for laser printers so that the toner does not melt on vacuum motor.
Compressed air	Used to remove dust in hard-to-reach places (preferably after vacuuming).
Urethane swabs	Used to clean between keys on a keyboard. If a key is sticking, disconnect the keyboard before spraying or using contact cleaner on it.
Monitor wipes	Used on the front of the display. Ones with an anti-static solution work best.
Lint-free cloths	Used to clean laptop touchpad and other components. Dampen to remove residual finger oil.
General-purpose cloths	Used to clean the outside of the case and to clean the desktop areas under and around the computer.
General-purpose cleanser	Never spray or pour liquid on any computer part. Liquid cleaners are used with soft lint-free cloths or lint-free swabs.
Denatured alcohol	Used on rubber rollers, such as those found inside printers.
Anti-static brush	Used to brush dirt from hard-to-reach places.
Optical drive cleaning kit	Can include a lens cleaner that removes dust and debris from an optical lens; a disc cleaner that removes dust, dirt, fingerprints, and oils from the disc; and a scratch repair kit used to resurface, clean, and polish CDs, DVDs, and BDs.
Gold contact cleaner	Used to clean adapter contacts as well as contacts on laptop batteries and the contacts where the battery inserts.
Safety goggles	Used in dusty environments or when dealing with chemicals in a poorly ventilated area. Indirect vented googles prevent a splash from coming into contact with eyes. Nonvented goggles protect from dust, splash, and chemical vapors.
Air filter/mask	Used for protection from airborne fumes, dust, and smoke. Two types of filters—vapors and particles. Filtering for vapors helps when using chemical cleaners and solvents. Filtering for particles help with things that make you sneeze like dust, pollen, and mold.

Many cleaning solution companies provide a material safety data sheet (**MSDS**) or safety data sheet (**SDS**) that contains information about a product, including its toxicity, storage, disposal, and health/safety concerns. Computer components have the potential to contain toxic substances. Larger companies have very specific rules about how electronic waste is handled, but in both large and small companies, an IT person that deals with hardware needs to be familiar with toxic waste handling. Each state commonly has specific disposal procedures for chemical solvents and toxic waste. Check with the company's safety coordinator for storage and disposal information, use the MSDS/SDS, and research handling and disposal guidelines according to local government regulations.

Know your state aerosol can disposal laws

Some states have special requirements for disposal of aerosol cans, especially those that are clogged and still contain some product.

To perform the preventive maintenance, power off the computer, remove the power cord, and vacuum the computer with a nonmetallic attachment. Do not start with compressed air or by blowing dust out of the computer because the dirt and dust will simply go into the air and eventually fall back into the computer and surrounding equipment. Figure 5.22 shows vacuuming inside a computer. Remember to hold your finger or a brush on the fan blade so it does not spin out of control and damage the fan. The technician should have removed the watch before performing this maintenance.

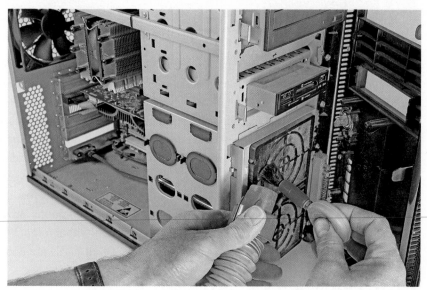

FIGURE 5.22   Preventive maintenance vacuuming

After vacuuming as much as possible, use compressed air to blow the dust out of hard-to-reach places, such as inside the power supply and under the motherboard. If you are performing maintenance on a laptop computer, remove as many modules as possible, such as the optical drive, battery, and hard drive, before vacuuming or using compressed air. Inform people in the immediate area that they might want to leave the area if they have allergies (see Figure 5.23). Use appropriate safety equipment including safety goggles and an air filter/mask when performing preventive maintenance.

If you remove an adapter from an expansion slot, replace it into the same slot. If the computer battery is on a riser board, it is best to leave the riser board connected to the motherboard so the system does not lose its configuration information. The same steps covered in the disassembly section of this chapter hold true when you are performing preventive maintenance.

TECH TIP

Use a preventive maintenance call as a time for updates

A preventive maintenance call is a good time to check for operating system, BIOS/UEFI, antivirus, and driver updates.

CHAPTER 5

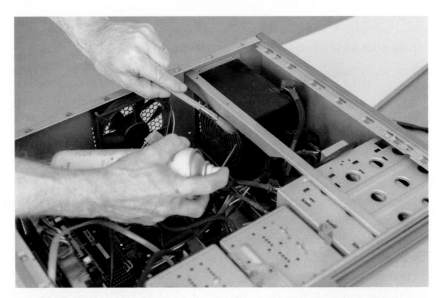

FIGURE 5.23   Preventive maintenance using compressed air

When you perform preventive maintenance, take inventory and document what is installed in the computer, such as the hard drive size, amount of RAM, available hard drive space, and so on. During the maintenance procedure, communicate with the user. Ask whether the computer has been giving anyone trouble lately or if it has been performing adequately. Computer users like to know that you care about their computing needs. Also, users frequently ask questions such as whether sunlight or cold weather harms the computer. Always respond with answers the user can understand. Users appreciate it when you explain things in terms they comprehend and that make sense.

A preventive maintenance call is the perfect opportunity to check that the computer is protected against viruses. Preventive maintenance measures help limit computer problems as well as provide a chance to interact with customers and help with a difficulty that might seem minuscule but could worsen. The call is also a good time to take inventory of all hardware and software installed.

Basic Electronics Overview

A technician needs to know a few basic electronic terms and concepts when testing components. The best place to start is with electricity. There are two types of electricity: AC and DC. The electricity provided by a wall outlet is alternating current (**AC**), and the type of electricity used by computer components is direct current (**DC**). Devices such as radios, TVs, and toasters use AC power. Low-voltage DC power is used for a computer's internal components and anything powered by batteries. A computer's power supply converts AC electricity from the wall outlet to DC for the internal components. Electricity involves electrons flowing through a conductor, similar to the way that water runs through a pipe. With AC, electrons flow alternately in both directions. With DC, electrons flow in one direction only.

Electronics: Terminology

Voltage, current, power, and resistance are terms commonly used in the computer industry. **Voltage**, which is a measure of the pressure pushing electrons through a circuit, is measured in **volts**. A power supply's output is measured in volts. Power supplies typically put out +3.3 volts, +5 volts, +12 volts, and −12 volts. You will commonly see these voltages shown in power supply documentation as +5V or +12V. Another designation is +5VSB. This is for the computer's **standby power**. This power is always provided, even when the computer is powered off. This supplied voltage is why you have to unplug a computer when working inside it.

Polarity is important only when measuring DC voltage

When a technician measures the voltage coming out of a power supply, the black meter lead (which is negative) connects to the black wire from the power supply (which is ground). The red meter lead connects to either the +5 or +12 volt wires from the power supply.

The term *volts* is also used to describe voltage from a wall outlet. Wall outlet voltage is normally 120VAC (120 volts AC). Exercises at the end of the chapter explain how to take both AC and DC voltage readings. Figure 5.24 shows a photograph of a multimeter being used to take a DC voltage reading on the power connectors coming from a power supply. When the meter leads are inserted correctly, the voltage level shown is of the correct polarity.

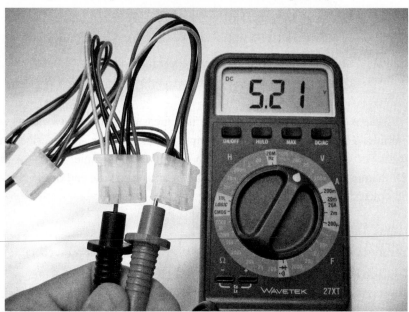

FIGURE 5.24   DC voltage reading

The reading on the meter could be the opposite of what it should be if the meter's leads are reversed. Because electrons flow from one area where there are many of them (negative polarity) to an area where there are few electrons (positive polarity), polarity shows which way an electric current will flow. Polarity is the condition of being positive or negative with respect to some reference point. Polarity is not important when measuring AC. Figure 5.25 shows rules to observe when working with meters.

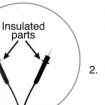

Insulated parts

Meter probes

1. Select AC or DC on the meter (some meters automatically select AC or DC).

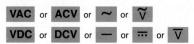

2. Select the appropriate voltage range (0-10V, 0-100V, etc). The meter can be damaged if you measure a high voltage in a low range (but not the reverse). Use the highest range for unknown voltages.

3. Touch only the insulated parts of the meter probes.

FIGURE 5.25   Meter rules

Monitors and power supplies can have dangerous voltage levels. Monitors can have up to 35,000 volts going to the back of the CRT. Flat-panel displays and mobile device displays also contain high voltage levels (but not at the voltage levels of CRTs). 120 volts AC is present inside the power supply. Power supplies and monitors have capacitors inside them. A **capacitor** is a component that holds a charge even after the computer is turned off. Capacitors inside a monitor can hold a charge for several hours after the monitor has been powered off.

Current is measured in **amps** (amperes), which is the number of electrons going through a circuit every second. In the water pipe analogy, voltage is the amount of pressure applied to force the water through the pipe, and current is the amount of water flowing. Every device needs a certain amount of current to operate. A power supply is rated for the amount of total current (in amps) it can supply at each voltage level. For example, a power supply could be rated at 20 amps for the 5-volt level and 8 amps for the 12-volt level.

TECH TIP

Do not work inside a CRT monitor unless you have special training

Monitors require high-voltage meters and special precautions.

Power is measured in **watts**, which is a measurement of how much work is being done. It is determined by multiplying volts by amps. Power supplies are described as providing a maximum number of watts. This is the sum of all outputs: for example, 5 volts × 20 amps (100 watts) plus 12V 8 amps (96 watts) equals 196 watts. An exercise at the end of the chapter explains how current and power relate to a technician's job.

TECH TIP

Current is what kills people when an electrical shock is received

Voltage determines how much current flows through the body. A high-current and low-voltage situation is the most dangerous.

Resistance is measured in **ohms**, which is the amount of opposition to current in an electronic circuit. The resistance range on a meter can be used to check continuity or check whether a fuse is good. A **continuity** check is used to determine whether a wire has a break in it. A conductor (wire) in a cable or a good fuse will have very low resistance to electricity (close to zero ohms). A broken wire or a bad fuse will have a very high resistance (millions of ohms, sometimes shown as infinite ohms, or OL). For example, a cable is normally made up of several wires that go from one connector to another. If you measure the continuity from one end of a wire to the other, it should show no resistance. If the wire has a break in it, the meter shows infinite resistance. Figure 5.26 shows examples of a good wire reading and a broken wire reading.

TECH TIP

Always unplug a computer before working inside it

The power supply provides power to the motherboard, even if the computer is powered off. Leaving the power cord attached can cause damage when replacing components such as the processor or RAM.

FIGURE 5.26   Sample resistance meter readings

Digital meters have different ways of displaying infinity. Always refer to the meter manual for this reading. When checking continuity, the meter is placed on the ohms setting, as shown in Figure 5.26. The ohms setting is usually illustrated by an omega symbol (Ω).

TECH TIP

Dealing with small connections and a meter

Some connectors have small pin connections. Use a thin meter probe or insert a thin wire, such as a paper clip, into the hole and touch the meter to the wire to take your reading.

Polarity is not important when performing a continuity check. Either meter lead (red or black) can be placed at either end of the wire. However, you do need a pin-out diagram (wiring list) for the cable before you can check continuity because pin 1 at one end could connect to a different pin number at the other end. An exercise at the end of the chapter steps through this process.

The same concept of continuity applies to fuses. A fuse has a tiny wire inside it that extends from end to end. The fuse is designed so that the wire melts (breaks) if too much current flows through it. The fuse keeps excessive current from damaging electronic circuits or starting a fire. A fuse is rated for a particular amount of current. For example, a 5-amp fuse protects a circuit if the amount of current exceeds 5 amps.

TECH TIP

Use the right fuse or lose

Never replace a fuse with one that has a higher amperage rating. You could destroy electronic circuits or cause a fire by allowing too much current to be passed by the fuse, defeating the fuse's purpose.

Take a fuse out of the circuit before testing it. A good fuse has a meter reading of 0 ohms (or close to that reading). A blown fuse shows a meter reading of infinite ohms. Refer to the section on resistance and Figure 5.26. An exercise at the end of this chapter demonstrates how to check a fuse.

A technician needs to be familiar with basic electronics terms and checks. Table 5.2 consolidates this information.

TABLE 5.2   Basic electronics terms

Term	Value	Usage
Voltage	Volts	Voltage is relevant when checking AC voltage from a wall outlet (typically 120VAC) and when checking the DC output voltage from a power supply (typically +/– 12, +3.3, and +/– 5 VDC).
Current	Amps (amperes)	Each device needs a certain amount of current to operate. A power supply is rated for total current in amps for each voltage level (such as 24 amps for 5-volt power and 50 amps for 12-volt power).
Resistance	Ohms	Resistance is the amount of opposition to electric current. Resistance is used to check continuity on cables and fuses. A cable that shows little or no resistance has no breaks in it. A good fuse shows no resistance. If a cable has a break in it or if a fuse is bad, the resistance is infinite.
Wattage (power)	Watts	Watts is a measure of power and is derived by multiplying amps by volts. Power supply output is measured in watts.
Apparent power	Volt-ampere	Volt-ampere is used with watts to describe how much power an uninterruptible power supply (UPS) can deliver. A UPS is used to provide power when AC power is lost and is covered later in the chapter.

Power Supply Overview

A power supply is an essential component within a computer; no internal computer device works without it. The power supply converts AC to DC, distributes lower-voltage DC power to components throughout the computer, and provides cooling through the use of a fan located inside the power supply. The AC voltage a power supply accepts is normally either 100 to 120 volts or 200 to 240 volts. Some **dual-voltage** power supplies can accept either. This type of power supply can have a selector switch on the back or can automatically detect the input voltage level. The power supply is sometimes a source of unusual problems. The effects of the problems can range from those not noticed by the user to those that shut down the system.

> **TECH TIP**
>
> **Powering on a power supply without anything attached could damage the power supply**
>
> Do not power on a power supply without connecting to the motherboard and possibly a device such as an optical drive or hard drive. An ATX power supply usually requires a motherboard connection at a minimum.

There are two basic types of power supplies: switching and linear. A computer uses a switching power supply. It provides efficient power to all the computer's internal components (and possibly to some external ones, such as USB devices). It also generates minimum heat, comes in small sizes, and is cheaper than linear power supplies. A switching power supply requires a load (something attached to it) in order to operate properly. With today's power supplies, a motherboard is usually a sufficient load, but a technician should always check the power supply specifications to be sure.

Power supplies are seldom opened, but look at Figure 5.27 to see inside one. Look closely to see how dirty the inside of the power supply can get.

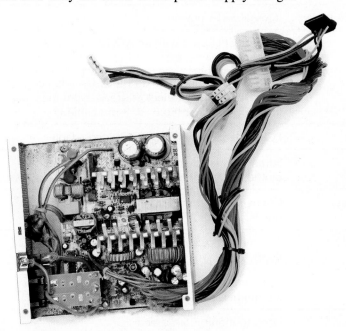

FIGURE 5.27 **Inside a power supply**

Power Supply Form Factors

Just as motherboards come in different shapes and sizes, so do power supplies. Today's power supply form factors are ATX, ATX12V v1.x, ATX12V v2.x, and micro-ATX. The **ATX power supply form factor** was the first type to allow a small amount of voltage to be provided to the motherboard so that both hardware and software could be used to "wake up" the device and/or lower voltage to conserve power. This was known as a soft switch. The ATX12V version 2 standard has a 24-pin motherboard connector instead of a 20-pin version 1 connector. This did away with the need for the extra 6-pin auxiliary connector. In addition, version 2 power supplies have a SATA power connector. Some 24-pin motherboard connectors accept the 20-pin power supply connector.

The **micro-ATX power supply form factor** is a smaller version than a full-sized ATX power supply to fit in smaller cases. (The ones highlighted are fair game for the A+ certification exam.) Other form factors include LFX12V (low profile), SFX12V (small form factor), EPS12V (used with server motherboards and has an extra 8-pin connector), CFX12V (compact form factor), SFX12V (small form factor), TFX12V (thin form factor), WTX12V (workstation form factor for high-end workstations and select servers), and FlexATX (smaller systems that have no more than three expansion slots).

Intel, AMD, and video card manufacturers certify specific power supplies that work with their processors and video cards. A computer manufacturer can also have a proprietary power supply form factor that is not compatible with different computer models or other vendors' machines. Laptop power supplies are commonly proprietary. Table 5.3 lists the possible ATX power supply connectors.

TABLE 5.3   ATX power supply connectors*

Connector	Notes	Voltage(s)
24-pin main power	Main ATX power connector to the motherboard	+3.3, +5, +12, −12
20-pin main power	Older main power connector to the motherboard	+3.3, +5, −5, +12, −12
15-pin SATA power	Internal SATA power connector	+3.3, +5, +12
8-pin 12V	12V for CPU used with an ATX12V v1 power supply	+12
8-pin PCIe	PCIe video; connects to a PCIe video adapter (Note that some connectors are 6+2-pin meaning they accept either the 6- or 8-pin cable.)	+12
6-pin PCIe	PCIe video; connects to PCIe video adapter	+12
6-pin	Sometimes labeled as AUX; connects to the motherboard if it has a connector	+3.3, +5
4-pin Molex	Connects to peripheral devices such as hard drives and CD/DVD drives	+5, +12
4-pin Berg	Connects to peripheral devices such as the floppy drive	+5, +12
4-pin 12V	Sometimes labeled as AUX or 12V; connects to the motherboard for CPU	+12
3-pin	Used to monitor fan speed	N/A

*Note that the terms in blue are testable on the CompTIA A+ Certification.

TECH TIP

The motherboard, case, and power supply must be size-compatible

The motherboard and case form factor and the power supply form factor must fit in the case and work together. For optimum performance, research what connectors and form factors are supported by both components.

Figure 5.28 shows a few ATX power supply connectors. Figure 5.29 shows more ATX power supply connectors.

4-pin CPU power connector   SATA power connector   6-pin PCIe power connector

FIGURE 5.28   Common power supply connectors

TECH TIP

Not all 24-pin motherboard connectors accept 20-pin power supply connectors

You can purchase a 24-pin to 20-pin power adapter. The site http://www.formfactors.org provides information regarding power supply form factors.

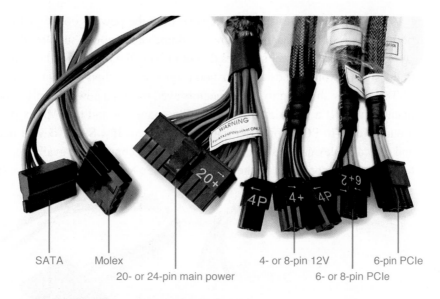

SATA   Molex   4- or 8-pin 12V   6-pin PCIe

20- or 24-pin main power   6- or 8-pin PCIe

FIGURE 5.29   ATX power supply connectors

Figure 5.30 illustrates the compatibility between the ATX 20- and 24-pin motherboard connector standards. Notice in Figure 5.30 that the power cable is only one connector, notched so the cable inserts into the connector one way only. Also, notice that a **power good signal** (labeled PWR_OK in Figure 5.30) goes to the motherboard. When the computer is turned on, part of POST is to allow the power supply to run a test on each of the voltage levels. The voltage levels must be correct before any other devices are tested and allowed to initialize. If the power is okay, a power good signal is sent to the motherboard. If the power good signal is not sent from the power supply, a timer chip on the motherboard resets the CPU. Once a power good signal is sent, the CPU begins executing software from the BIOS/UEFI. Figure 5.30 also shows the +5vsb connection to provide standby power for features such as Wake on LAN or Wake on Ring (covered later in this chapter).

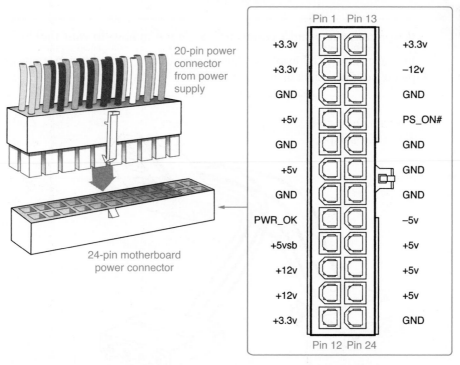

FIGURE 5.30   ATX 20- and 24-pin motherboard connectivity

A high-quality power supply delays sending the power good signal until all of the power supply's voltages have a chance to stabilize. Some cheap power supplies do not delay the power good signal. Other cheap power supplies do not provide the power good circuitry, but instead, tie 5 volts to the signal (which sends a power good signal even when it is not there).

The number and quantity of connectors available on a power supply depend on the power supply manufacturer. If a video card needs a PCIe connector and two Molex power connectors are free, a dual Molex-to-PCIe converter can be purchased. If a SATA device needs a power connection and only a Molex cable is free, a Molex-to-SATA converter is available. Figure 5.31 shows a dual Molex-to-PCIe converter on the left and a Molex-to-SATA converter on the right.

FIGURE 5.31   Dual Molex-to-PCIe and Molex-to-SATA converters

Power supply connectors can connect to any device; there is not a specific connector for the hard drive, the optical drive, and so on. If there are not enough connectors from the power supply for the number of devices installed in a computer, a Y power connector can be purchased at a computer or electronics store. The Y connector adapts a single Molex connector to two Molex connectors for two devices. Verify that the power supply can output enough power to handle the extra device being installed. Figure 5.32 shows a Y power connector.

TECH TIP

Power converters and Y connectors are good to have in your tool kit

In case a service call involves adding a new device, having various power converters available as part of your tool kit is smart.

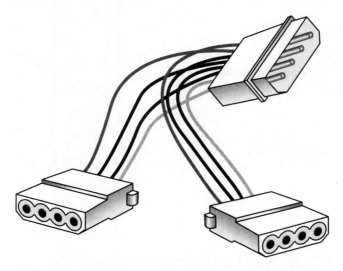

FIGURE 5.32   Molex connector

Purposes of a Power Supply

The power from a wall outlet is high-voltage AC. The type of power computers need is low-voltage DC. All computer parts (the electronic chips on the motherboard and adapters, the electronics on the drives, and the motors in the hard drive and optical drive) need DC power to operate. Power supplies in general come in two types: linear and switching. Computers use switching power supplies. The main functions of a power supply include the following:

> Convert AC to DC
> Provide DC voltage to the motherboard, adapters, and peripheral devices
> Provide cooling and facilitate airflow through the case

One purpose of a power supply is to convert AC to DC so the computer has proper power to run its components. With the ATX power supply, a connection from the front panel switch to the motherboard simply provides a 5-volt signal that allows the motherboard to tell the power supply to turn on. This 5-volt signal allows ATX power supplies to support ACPI, which is covered later in the chapter, and also lets the motherboard and operating system control the power supply. Figure 5.33 shows the front panel connections to the motherboard.

TECH TIP

On an ATX power supply that has an on/off switch, ensure that it is set to the *on* position

If an ATX power supply switch is present and in the off position, the motherboard and operating system cannot turn on the power supply. Some ATX power supplies do not have external on/off switches, and the computer can be powered down only via the operating system.

FIGURE 5.33   Front panel connections to a motherboard

Check input voltage selector

Some power supplies and laptops have input voltage selectors; others have the ability to accept input from 100 to 240 volts for use in various countries (dual-voltage). Ensure that the power supply accepts or is set to the proper input voltage.

Another purpose of a power supply is to distribute proper DC voltage to each component. Several cables with connectors come out of the power supply. With ATX motherboards, there is only a 20- or 24-pin connector used to connect power to the motherboard. The power connector inserts only one way into the motherboard connector. Figure 5.34 shows an ATX connector being inserted into a motherboard.

FIGURE 5.34   Installing an ATX power connector on a motherboard

Another purpose for a power supply is to provide cooling for the computer. The power supply's fan circulates air throughout the computer. Most computer cases have air vents on one side, on both sides, or in the rear of the computer. The ATX-style power supply blows air inside the case instead of out the back, which is reverse flow cooling. The air blows over the processor and memory to keep them cool. This type of power supply keeps the inside of the computer cleaner than older styles.

Don't block air vents

Whether a computer is a desktop model, a tower model, or a desktop model mounted in a stand on the floor, ensure that nothing blocks the air vents in the computer case.

Because heat sinks generate a lot of heat, it is important to have the proper amount of airflow in the right direction. Additional fans can be installed to provide additional cooling for the PC. Figure 5.35 shows an extra cooling fan mounted in the rear of a case (as well as over the processor). Notice how this computer needs preventive maintenance performed on it.

FIGURE 5.35   Computer case auxiliary fan

TECH TIP

Airflow and ventilation

Airflow should be through the computer and over the motherboard to provide cooling for the motherboard components.

If you install an additional fan to help with cooling, there are two likely places for fan placement: (1) near the power supply directly behind the CPU, and (2) on the lower front part of the case. Cases have different numbers of and locations of mounting spots for the case fan(s). Figure 5.36 shows two possible installation sites for an additional fan.

Electronic components generate a great deal of heat but are designed to withstand fairly high temperatures. Auxiliary fans can be purchased to help cool the internal components of a computer. Some cases have an extra mount and cutout for an auxiliary fan. Some auxiliary fans mount in adapter slots or drive bays.

TECH TIP

Be careful when installing an auxiliary fan

Place the fan so the outflow of air moves in the same direction as the flow of air generated by the power supply. If an auxiliary fan is installed inside a case in the wrong location, the auxiliary airflow could work against the power supply airflow, reducing the cooling effect.

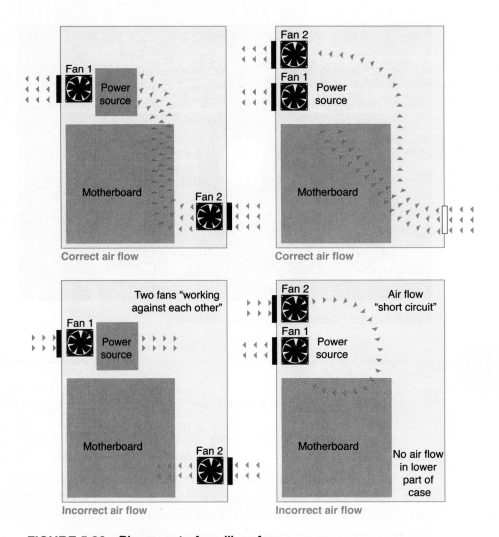

FIGURE 5.36   Placement of auxiliary fans

Advanced Configuration and Power Interface (ACPI)

Today's computer user needs to leave a computer on for extended periods of time in order to receive faxes, run computer maintenance tasks, automatically answer phone calls, and download software upgrades and patches. Network managers want control of computers so they can push out software upgrades, perform backups, download software upgrades and patches, and perform tests. Laptop users have always been plagued by power management problems, such as short battery life, inconsistent handling of screen blanking, and screen blanking in the middle of presentations. Such problems occurred because originally the BIOS/UEFI controlled power. Power management has changed.

Advanced Configuration and Power Interface (**ACPI**) gives the UEFI/BIOS and operating system control over various devices' power and modes of operation, as shown in Figure 5.37. With ACPI, the user can control how the power switch operates and when power to specific devices, such as the hard drive and monitor, is lowered. For example, the *Instant On/Off* UEFI/BIOS setting can control how long the power switch is held in before the power supply turns on or off. Case temperatures, CPU temperatures, and CPU fans can be monitored. The power supply can be adjusted for power requirements. The CPU clock can be throttled or slowed down to keep the temperature lower and prolong the life of the CPU and reduce power requirements especially in portable devices when activity is low or nonexistent. ACPI has various operating states, as shown in Table 5.4.

An act like this...   might bring to life the...

FIGURE 5.37   ACPI actions

TABLE 5.4   ACPI operating states

Global system state	Sleep state	Description
G0 Working	(S0)	The computer is fully functional. Software, such as the autosave function used with Microsoft products, can be optimized for performance or lower battery usage.
G1 Sleeping		Requires less power than the G0 state and has multiple sleep states: S1, S2, S3, and S4.
	(S1)	CPU is still powered, and unused devices are powered down. RAM is still being refreshed. Hard drives are not running.
	(S2)	CPU is not powered. RAM is still being refreshed. System is restored instantly upon user intervention.
	(S3)	Power supply output is reduced. RAM is still being refreshed. Some info in RAM is restored to CPU and cache.
	(S4)	Lowest-power sleep mode and takes the longest to come up. Info in RAM is saved to nonvolatile memory such as a hard drive or flash media. Some manufacturers call this the hibernate state.
G2 Soft off	(S5)	Power consumption is almost zero. Requires the operating system to reboot. No information is saved anywhere.
G3 Mechanical off		Also called off. This is the only state where the computer can be disassembled. You must power on the computer to use it again.

ACPI allows apps to work with the operating system to manage power, such as when an application is set to automatically save a document, but might not do so until the hard drive is being used for something else in order to conserve power in a laptop. In the Windows environment, the **sleep mode** (also known as **suspend mode**) uses one of the G1 sleeping ACPI states to allow the device to be awakened to continue working. The **hibernate mode** uses the G1 S4 mode and takes the longest to bring a device back to a working state.

> **TECH TIP**
>
> **Which power option should I select: standby or hibernate?**
>
> Most people would select the standby option if they want to quickly re-access the device. If this is the case, you want hibernate, which saves more energy.

Two common BIOS/UEFI and adapter features that take advantage of ACPI are Wake on LAN and Wake on Ring. The **Wake on LAN** feature allows a network administrator to control the power to a workstation remotely and directs the computer to come out of sleep mode. Software applications can also use the Wake on LAN feature to perform updates, upgrades, and maintenance tasks. The feature can also be used to bring up computers immediately before the business day starts. Wake on LAN can be used with Web or network cameras to start recording when motion is detected or to bring up a network printer so that it can be used when needed.

Wake on Ring allows a computer to come out of sleep mode when the telephone line has an incoming call. This lets the computer receive phone calls, faxes, and emails when the user is not present. Common BIOS/UEFI settings related to ACPI are listed in Table 5.5.

> **TECH TIP**
>
> **Why leave computers on at the office**
>
> In Windows, when a computer is shut down, it is put in soft off or S5 state. Wake on LAN is not officially supported from this state and for that reason, corporate environments request that users leave their computers turned on, but logged off on specific days or every day.

> **TECH TIP**
>
> **Windows power management**
>
> Use the *Power Options* Control Panel to configure power from within the Windows environment.

TABLE 5.5 Common BIOS/UEFI power settings

Setting	Description
Delay Prior to Thermal	Defines the number of minutes the system waits to shut down the system once an overheating situation occurs.
CPU Warning Temperatures	Specifies the CPU temperature at which a warning message is displayed on the screen.
ACPI Function	Enables or disables ACPI. This is the preferred method for disabling ACPI in the event of a problem.
Soft-off	Specifies the length of time a user must press the power button to turn off the computer.

Setting	Description
Deep S4/S5	Uses less power and only wakes from S4/S5 states with the power button or an RTC (real-time clock) alarm, such as waking the computer to complete a task.
Power on by Ring, Resume by Ring, or Wakeup	Allows the computer to wake when an adapter or an external device supports Wake on Ring.
Resume by Alarm	Allows a date and time to be set when the system is awakened from Suspend mode. Commonly used to update the system during nonpeak periods.
Wake Up on LAN	Allows the computer to wake when a Wake on LAN signal is received across the network.
CPU THRM Throttling	Allows a reduction in CPU speed when the system reaches a specific temperature.
Power on Function	Specifies which key (or key combination) will activate the system's power.
Hot Key Power On	Defines what keystrokes will reactivate system power.
Doze Mode	When the system is in a reduced activity state, the CPU clock is throttled (slowed down). All other devices operate at full speed.
After Power Failure	Sets power mode after a power loss.

Windows Vista, 7, 8, and 10 have three power plans available, and you can customize these power plans. You might want to customize a power plan such as when there is a problem with poor video quality when playing a movie. Use the *Change plan settings* link followed by the *Change advanced power settings* link to expand a section such as the *Multimedia settings* option. Additional plans might be available from the computer manufacturer. Table 5.6 shows the three main power plans you can just click and select.

TABLE 5.6   Windows Vista, 7, 8, and 10 power plans

Power plan	Description
Balanced	The most common plan because it provides full power when you need it and saves power when the computer is not being used.
Power saver	Saves power by running the CPU more slowly and reducing screen brightness.
High performance	Select the *Show additional plans* link to see this option. This provides the maximum performance possible.

Links on the left of the *Power Options* Control Panel provide access to advanced settings such as requiring a password to come out of sleep mode. The power options for a Windows 7 desktop are shown in Figure 5.38.

You can edit the power settings in order to configure passwords, standby power behavior, and other power-related settings. Figure 5.39 shows the types of modifications that can be made to a laptop.

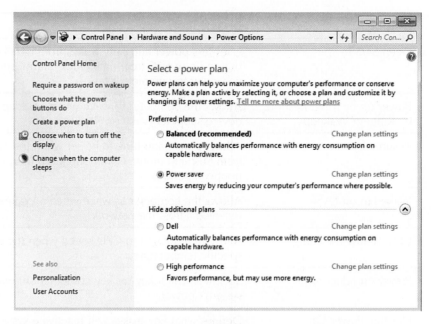

FIGURE 5.38   Windows 7 power plans

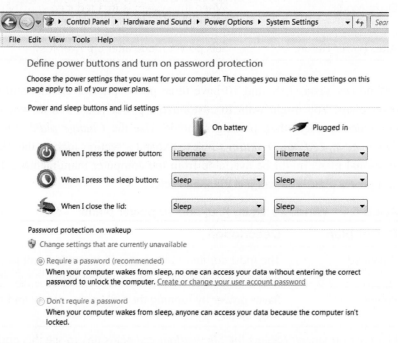

FIGURE 5.39   Windows 7 laptop power modifications

If the computer does not go into the sleep mode, check the following:

> Determine whether ACPI is enabled in BIOS/UEFI.
> Try disabling the antivirus program to see whether it is causing the problem.
> Set the screen saver to *None* to see if it is causing the problem.
> Determine whether all device drivers are ACPI compliant.
> Determine whether power management is enabled through the operating system (use the *Power Options* Control Panel).
> Disconnect USB devices to see whether they are causing problems.

Replacing or Upgrading a Power Supply

Power supplies are rated in watts. Today's typical computers have power supplies with ratings ranging from 250 to 500 watts, although powerful computers, such as network servers or higher-end gaming systems, can have power supplies rated 600 watts or higher. Each voltage level has a maximum number of amps (amperage). For example, the +5V part of the power supply might provide a maximum of 20 amps (which is equal to 100 watts of the total power supply wattage). Internal and external devices powered by a particular type of port such as USB are affected by the number of amps available from the +5 and +12V DC power supply output and the total amount of wattage available.

Each device inside a computer uses a certain amount of power, and the power supply must provide enough power to run all the devices. The power each device or adapter requires is usually defined in the documentation for the device or adapter or on the manufacturer's website. The computer uses the wattage needed, not the total capacity of a power supply.

TECH TIP

Watch the wattage

Many manufacturers overstate the wattage. The wattage advertised is *not* the wattage available at higher temperatures, such as when mounted inside a computer. Research a model before purchasing.

Some power supplies are listed as being dual or triple (or tri) rail. A **dual-rail power supply** has two +12V output lines that are monitored for an over current condition. A triple-rail power supply simply has three +12V output lines monitored. Keep in mind that most manufacturers do not have two or more independent 12V sources; they all derive from the same 12V source but have independent output lines. Figure 5.40 shows how the +12V rails might be used.

+12V

Look on top of the power supply for the various voltage levels and maximum current output in amps.

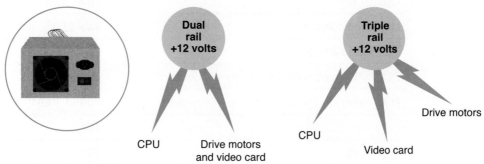

FIGURE 5.40   12V rails

The second thing to consider is watts. Power supplies are rated in watts. Today's typical computers have power supplies with ratings ranging from 250 to 500 watts, although powerful computers, such as network servers or higher-end gaming systems, can have power supplies rated 600 watts or higher. Each device inside a computer uses a certain amount of power, and the power supply must provide enough to run all the devices. The power each device or adapter requires is usually defined in the documentation for the device or adapter or on the manufacturer's website.

The computer uses the wattage needed, not the total capacity of a power supply. The efficiency (less AC is required to convert power to DC) is what changes the electricity bill.

Power supplies can be auto-switching or have a fixed input. An **auto-switching** power supply monitors the incoming voltage from the wall outlet and automatically switches itself accordingly. Auto-switching power supplies accept voltages from 100 to 240VAC at 50 to 60Hz. These power supplies are popular in mobile devices and are great for international travel. A power supply might also allow adjusting the input value by manually selecting the value through a voltage selector switch on the power supply. A fixed-input power supply is rated for a specific voltage and frequency for a country, such as 120VAC 60Hz for the United States.

Some people are interested in exactly how much power their system is consuming. Every device in a computer consumes power, and each device could use one or more different voltage levels (for example, +5V, −5V, +12V, −12V, and +3.3V). A power supply has a maximum amperage for each voltage level (for example, 30 amps at +5 volts and 41 amps at +12V). To determine the maximum power being used, in watts, multiply the amps and volts. If you add all the maximum power levels, the amount will be greater than the power supply's rating. This means that you cannot use the maximum power at every single voltage level (but because the −5V and −12V are not used very often, normally this is not a problem).

To determine the power being consumed, you must research every device to determine how much current it uses at a specific voltage level. Internet power calculators are available to help with this task. Table 5.7 lists sample computer components' power requirements.

TABLE 5.7 Sample computer component power requirements

Component	Power consumption
Motherboard (without processor)	5 to 150W
Processor	10 to 140W
Floppy drive	5W
PATA hard drive	3 to 30W
SATA hard drive	2 to 15W
Optical drive	10 to 30W
Nonvideo adapter	4 to 25W
AGP video adapter	20 to 50W
PCIe video card with one power connector	50 to 150W
PCIe video card with two power connectors	100 to 300W
Extra fan	3W
RAM stick	15W

Power management on both laptops and desktops is important. Most computer components are available as energy-efficient items. ENERGY STAR is a joint effort by the U.S. EPA (Environmental Protection Agency) and Department of Energy to provide device standards and ratings that easily identify products (including computer components) that are energy efficient. Settings such as power options, CPU throttling, and some advanced BIOS/UEFI settings affect power settings. A technician must be aware of all these options and be willing to offer advice such as turn the computer off when finished working on it; set the power management option to allow work to be performed at an affordable cost; disable options not being used, such as wireless capabilities when wired networking is functioning; be aware of monitor costs (CRT-type monitors take the most energy, followed by plasma displays and then LCD or flat-panel technology); and purchase energy-efficient parts and computers.

Choosing a Power Supply

When choosing a power supply, the first thing to consider is size and form factor because the power supply has to fit in the case. Different physical sizes of power supplies are available. The second thing to consider is wattage. Get equal to or more than the original power supply. Lastly, do not forget to check that the on/off switch on the new power supply is in a location that fits in the computer case.

TECH TIP

All power supplies are not created equal

A technician needs to replace a power supply with one that provides an equal or greater amount of power. Search the Internet for power supply reviews. A general rule of thumb is that if two power supplies are equal in wattage, the heavier one is better because it uses a bigger transformer, bigger heat sinks, and more quality components.

The 80 PLUS is a power supply efficiency rating system that has been incorporated into ENERGY STAR specifications. Efficiency is converting more AC to DC. The rating system consists of six levels of efficiency. Each level must provide a particular level of efficiency at a specific amount of load (number of components being used simultaneously that require power). Table 5.8 shows the levels and efficiency requirements of each level that relate to PCs.

TABLE 5.8   80 PLUS levels and energy efficiency requirements

Level	Efficiency		
	20% load	**50% load**	**100% load**
80 PLUS	80%	80%	80%
80 PLUS Bronze	82%	85%	82%
80 PLUS Silver	85%	88%	85%
80 PLUS Gold	87%	90%	87%
80 PLUS Platinum	90%	92%	89%

Just because a power supply is not certified as 80 PLUS does not mean that it is not an energy-efficient power supply, but these levels do give you an idea of the difference. When choosing a power supply, the most important things to consider are as follows:

> Size and form factor
> Wattage
> Number and type of connectors
> Energy efficiency
> Number of 12V rails monitored for an over current condition

Some people like extra features like colored lights inside the power supply, power supply fan, and/or ports. Some power supplies come with detachable cables (see Figure 5.41) so that cables that are not used are simply not attached to the power supply to aid in cable management.

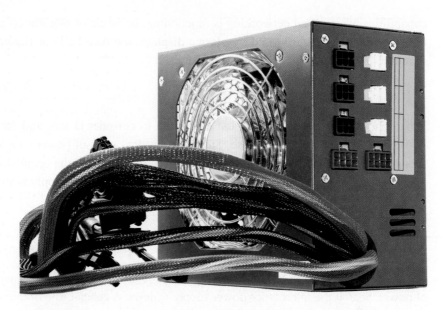

FIGURE 5.41   Power supply with detachable cable ports

Adverse Power Conditions

There are two adverse AC power conditions that can damage or adversely affect a computer: overvoltage and undervoltage. **Overvoltage** occurs when the output voltage from the wall outlet (the AC voltage) is over the rated amount. Normally, the output of a wall outlet is 110 to 130 volts AC. When the voltage rises above 130 volts, an overvoltage condition exists. The power supply takes the AC voltage and converts it to DC. An overvoltage condition is harmful to the components because too much DC voltage destroys electronic circuits. An overvoltage condition can be a surge or a spike.

When the voltage falls below 110 volts AC, an **undervoltage** condition exists. If the voltage is too low, a computer power supply cannot provide enough power to all the components. Under these conditions, the power supply draws too much current, causing it to overheat, weakening or damaging the components. An undervoltage condition is known as a brownout or sag. Table 5.9 explains these power terms.

TABLE 5.9   Adverse power conditions

Major type	Subtype	Explanation
Overvoltage	**spike**	A spike lasts 1 to 2 nanoseconds. A nanosecond is one-billionth of a second. A spike is harder to guard against than a surge because it has such short duration and high intensity.
	surge	A surge lasts longer (3 or more nanoseconds) than a spike. Also called transient voltage. Causes of surges include lightning, poorly regulated electricity, faulty wiring, and devices that turn on periodically, such as elevators, air conditioners, and refrigerators.

Major type	Subtype	Explanation
Undervoltage	**brownout**	In a brownout, power circuits become overloaded. Occasionally, an electric company intentionally causes a brownout to reduce the power drawn by customers during peak periods.
	sag	A sag occurs when the voltage from the wall outlet drops momentarily.
	blackout	A blackout is a total loss of power.

Electric companies offer surge protection for homes. Frequently, there are two choices. A basic package protects large appliances, such as refrigerators, air conditioners, washers, and dryers. It allows no more than 800 volts to enter the electrical system. A premium package protects more sensitive devices (TVs, stereos, and computers) and reduces the amount of voltage allowed to 323 volts or less. Some suppressors handle surges up to 20,000 volts. The exterior surge arrestor does not protect against voltage increases that originate inside the building, such as those caused by faulty wiring.

Adverse Power Protection

Power supplies have built-in protection against adverse power conditions. However, the best protection for a computer is to unplug it during a power outage or thunderstorm. Surge protectors and uninterruptible power supplies (UPS) are commonly used to protect against adverse power conditions. A line conditioner can also be used. Each device has a specific purpose and guards against certain conditions. A technician must be familiar with each device in order to make recommendations for customers.

Surge Protectors

A **surge suppressor**, also known as a surge strip or surge protector, is commonly a multi-outlet strip that offers built-in protection against overvoltage. Surge protectors do not protect against undervoltage; they protect against voltage increases. Figure 5.42 shows a picture of a Tripp Lite surge protector. The green "Power Save" outlets do not provide power to the attached device if it is not being used. The black "Always On" outlets provide continuous power to devices such as cable modems. Two RJ-45 outlets in the center protect power from going through the network cable to potentially damage a device.

Most surge protectors have an electronic component called a metal oxide varistor (**MOV**), which protects the computer or device that plugs into one of the outlets on the surge strip. An MOV is positioned between the AC coming in and the outlet into which devices are plugged. When a surge occurs, the MOV prevents the extra voltage from passing to the outlets. An MOV, however, has some drawbacks. If a large surge occurs, the MOV will take the hit and be destroyed, which is better than damaging the computer. However, with small overvoltages, each small surge weakens the MOV. A weakened MOV might not give the proper protection to the computer in the event of a bigger surge. Also, there is no simple check for an MOV's condition. Some MOVs have indicator lamps attached, but they indicate only when the MOV has been destroyed, not when it is weakened. Still, having an indicator lamp is better than nothing at all. Some surge protectors also have replaceable fuses and/or indicator lamps for the fuse. A fuse works only once and then is destroyed during a surge in order to protect devices plugged into surge protector outlets. Figure 5.43 shows a surge protector that has done its job.

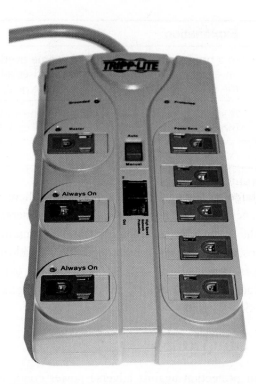

FIGURE 5.42 Tripp Lite surge protector

Do not create a trip hazard with a surge strip

When installing a surge protector, do not install it in such a manner that it causes a trip hazard because the cord lies in an area where people walk.

FIGURE 5.43 Blown surge protector

Several surge protector features deserve consideration. Table 5.10 outlines some of them.

TABLE 5.10   Surge protector features

Feature	Explanation
Clamping voltage	The level at which a surge protector starts protecting the computer. The lower the value, the better the protection.
Clamping speed	How much time elapses before protection begins. The lower the value, the better the protection. Surge protectors cannot normally protect against power spikes (overvoltages of short duration) because of their rated clamping speed.
Energy absorption/ dissipation	The greater the number of joules (a unit of energy) that can be dissipated, the more effective and durable a surge protector is. This feature is sometimes called energy absorption. A surge protector rating of 630 joules is more effective than a rating of 210 joules.
TVS (transient voltage suppressing) rating	This is also known as response time. The lower the rating, the better. For example, a 330 TVS-rated surge protector is better than a 400 TVS-rated one.
UL rating	UL (Underwriters Laboratories) developed the **UL 1449 VPR** (voltage protection rating) standard to measure the maximum amount of voltage a surge protector will let through to the attached devices. The UL 497A standard is for phone line protection, and the UL 1283 standard is for EMI/RFI.

The federal government designates surge suppressor grades—A, B, and C. Suppressors are evaluated on a basis of 1,000 surges at a specific number of volts and amps. A Class A rating is the best and indicates tolerance up to 6,000 volts and 3,000 amps.

TECH TIP

Which surge strip to buy?

When purchasing or recommending a surge protector, be sure it conforms to the UL 1449 standard and has an MOV status lamp. Also, check to see if the vendor offers to repair or replace the surge-protected equipment in the event that they are damaged during a surge.

Common surge suppressor criteria used when buying one include the following:

> Cable length
> Number of outlets
> Space to connect peripheral power connectors that may take additional space
> Diagnostic LED(s)
> Integrated circuit breaker
> Outlets that power off when not in use for nonessential electronics such as lamps, speakers, or printers
> Outlets that are always on for devices such as cordless phone handset cradles, modems, and external hard drives
> Insurance
> UL 1449-compliant

Surge protectors are not the best protection for a computer system because most provide very little protection against other adverse power conditions. Even the good ones protect only against overvoltage conditions. Those with the UL 1449 rating and an MOV status lamp are usually more expensive. Unfortunately, people tend to put their money into their computer parts, but not into the protection of those parts.

Line Conditioners

An alternative for computer protection is a line conditioner. **Line conditioners**, sometimes known as power conditioners, are more expensive than surge protectors, but they protect a computer from overvoltages, undervoltages, and adverse noise conditions over electrical lines. A line conditioner monitors AC electricity. If the voltage is too low, the line conditioner boosts voltage to the proper range. If the voltage level is too high, the line conditioner clamps down the voltage and sends the proper amount to the computer. Figure 5.44 shows a line conditioner.

TECH TIP

Be careful not to plug too many devices into a line conditioner

A line conditioner is rated for a certain amount of current. Some devices, such as laser printers, can draw a great deal of current (up to 15 amps). Some line conditioners are not rated to handle these devices. Because laser printers draw so much current, if a computer and a laser printer are on the same electrical circuit, that circuit should be wired to a 20-amp circuit breaker. Most outlets in today's buildings are on 20-amp breakers.

FIGURE 5.44   Line conditioner

Battery Backup

Battery backup provides AC power when power from the wall outlet fails. The power is provided by a battery within a unit. Two different types of battery backup are available for home and business computers and devices—an uninterruptible power supply (UPS) or a standby power supply (SPS). Let's see what the differences are between the two types.

UPSes

A **UPS**, sometimes called an online (or true) UPS or a line interactive UPS, provides power to a computer or other device for a limited amount of time when there is a power outage. A UPS provides enough time to save work and safely shut down the computer. Some operating systems do not operate properly if power abruptly cuts off and the computer is not brought to a logical stopping place. A network server, the main computer for a network, is a great candidate for a UPS. Network operating systems are particularly susceptible to problems during a power outage. Some UPSes have a connection for a cable and special software that automatically maintains voltages to the computer, quits all applications, and powers off the computer. Some UPS units have USB and/or network connections as well.

A UPS also provides power conditioning for the devices attached to it. The AC power is used to charge a battery inside the UPS. The battery inside the UPS supplies power to an inverter. The inverter makes AC for the computer. When AC power from the outlet fails, the battery inside the UPS continues to supply power to the computer. The battery inside the UPS outputs DC power, and the computer accepts (and expects) AC power. Therefore, the DC power from the battery must be converted to AC voltage. AC voltage looks like a sine wave when it is in its correct form, but cheaper UPSes produce a square wave (especially when power comes from the battery) that is not as effective. Some computer servers, systems, and peripherals do not work well on a 120VAC square wave, modified sine wave, simulated sine wave, or quasi-sine wave. Figure 5.45 illustrates a sine wave and a square wave.

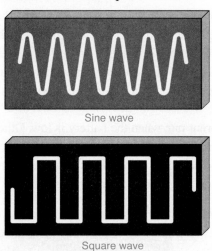

Sine wave

Square wave

FIGURE 5.45   Sine wave and square wave

TECH TIP

Do not plug a laser printer into a UPS unless it has a rating less than 1400VA

Most UPSes cannot handle the very high current requirements of a laser printer. Other devices to avoid attaching to the UPS include space heaters, vacuums, curling irons, paper shredders, and copiers.

A UPS can be the best protection against adverse power conditions because it protects against overvoltage and undervoltage conditions, and it provides power so a system can be shut down properly. When purchasing a UPS, be sure that (1) the amount of battery time is sufficient to protect all devices; (2) the amount of current the UPS produces is sufficient to protect all devices; and (3) the output waveform is a sine wave.

To install a UPS, perform the following steps:

Step 1.   Connect the UPS to a wall outlet and power it on. When a UPS is first plugged in, the battery is not charged. See the UPS manufacturer's installation manual for the specific time it will take to charge.

Step 2.   Power off the UPS.

Step 3. Attach device power cords, such as the PC, to the UPS. Ensure that the UPS is rated to supply power to the number and type of connected devices. Note that some UPS units have two sets of outlets. One set can provide battery-supplied power in the event of an outage. The other set provides surge protection, but no battery backup provided power.

Step 4. Power on the UPS.

A UPS has a battery inside that is similar to a car battery (except that the UPS battery is sealed). Because this battery contains acid, you should never drop a UPS or throw it in the trash. Research your state's requirements for recycling batteries. All batteries fail after some time, and most UPSes have replaceable batteries.

UPS troubleshooting is not difficult. In addition to following the manufacturer's recommendations for troubleshooting, try the following guidelines:

> If a UPS will not power on, check the on/off switch. Verify that the UPS is attached to an electrical outlet. Ensure that the outlet has power and that the circuit breaker for the outlet has not been tripped. Ensure that the battery is installed properly.
> Check whether the UPS unit has a self-test procedure and includes a self-test button.
> With some UPS units, a beep indicates that a power interruption has occurred. This is a normal function.
> Some UPS units beep at a different rate when the battery is low. Others have a light indicator to indicate that it's time to recharge or replace the battery.
> If a UPS is overloaded—that is, has too many devices attached—the UPS may shut off, trip a circuit breaker, beep, or turn on a light indication for this problem.

Figure 5.46 shows the front and back of a UPS.

FIGURE 5.46   Front and back of a UPS

Standby Power Supply (SPS)

A device similar to a UPS is a standby power supply (SPS). An SPS contains a battery like the UPS, but the battery provides power to the computer only when it loses AC power. It might not provide constant power, like the UPS. It might use a simulated sine wave. An SPS is not as effective as a UPS because the SPS must detect a power-out condition first and then switch over to the battery to supply power to the computer. As a result, SPS switching time is important. Any time under

5 milliseconds is fine for most systems. Figure 5.47 shows a CyberPower UPS that produces a simulated sine wave (which would be fine for a home system).

FIGURE 5.47 CyberPower UPS (simulated sine wave output)

Comparison of UPS and SPS

Sometimes it is difficult to discern between UPS and SPS products. When providing protection and battery backup for a home computer, an SPS or simulated sine wave output might be fine for the supplied power time and the reduced cost. Figures 5.48 and 5.49 show the differences between how some SPSs and UPSes work.

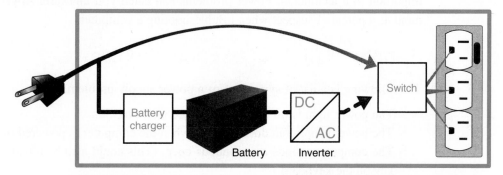

SPS/Line interactive UPS normal operation (solid line)
1. AC power is brought through the UPS.
2. The battery is charged simultaneously.
3. With some units, small over- or undervoltages are evened out before sending through the UPS.

SPS/Line interactive UPS abnormal power operation (dashed line)
1. When high voltage or large undervoltage for some units and with loss of power is present in all units, DC power from the battery is sent to the inverter for as long as the battery lasts.
2. The DC power is converted to AC and provided to the attached devices.

FIGURE 5.48 SPS/line interactive UPS operation

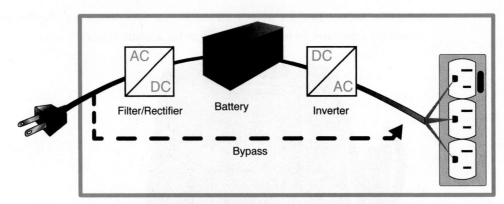

Online UPS normal operation (solid line)
1. AC power is brought into the UPS and cleaned up by the filter and converted to DC by the rectifier.
2. The battery is charged and outputs DC to the inverter.
3. The DC is converted to AC and provided to the attached devices.

Online UPS abnormal power operation (dashed line)
1. When the battery has died, the attached devices still receive power through the bypass circuit.

FIGURE 5.49   Online UPS operation

Phone Line Isolator

Just like AC power outlets, phone outlets can experience power fluctuations. A power surge can enter a computer through a modem, a device used to connect a computer to a phone line. Not only can a modem be damaged by a power surge on the phone line, but other electronics inside the computer, such as the motherboard, can be damaged. A **phone line isolator**, sometimes called a **modem isolator**, can be purchased at an electronics store. It provides protection against phone line surges. No computer connected to a phone line through a modem should be without one. Some surge protectors come with a modem isolator built into the strip.

Power supplies and associated protection equipment are not exciting topics, but they are very important to a technician. Power problems can catch you unaware. Always keep power in your mind as a potential suspect when troubleshooting a computer.

Symptoms of Power Supply Problems

The following is a list of symptoms of a power supply problem:

> The power light is off and/or the device won't turn on.
> The power supply fan does not turn when the computer is powered on.
> The computer sounds a continuous beep. (This could also be a bad motherboard or a stuck key on the keyboard.)
> When the computer powers on, it does not beep at all. (This could also be a bad motherboard.)
> When the computer powers on, it sounds repeating short beeps. (This could also be a bad motherboard.)
> During POST, a 02X or parity POST error code appears (where X is any number); one of the POST checks is a power good signal from the power supply; a 021, 022, . . . error message indicates that the power supply did not pass the POST test.
> The computer reboots or powers down without warning.
> The power supply fan is noisy.
> The power supply is too hot to touch.

> The computer emits a burning smell.
> The power supply fan spins, but there is no power to other devices.
> The monitor has a power light, but nothing appears on the monitor, and no PC power light illuminates.

Power Supply Voltages

Refer to Figure 5.30 and notice how +3.3, +5, −5, +12, and −12 volts are supplied to the motherboard. The motherboard and adapters use +3.3 and +5 volts. The −5 volts is seldom used. If the motherboard has integrated serial ports, they sometimes use +12V and −12V power. Hard drives and optical drives commonly use +5 and +12 volts. The +12 voltage is used to operate the device motors found in drives, the CPU, internal cooling fans, and the graphics card. Drives are now being made that use +5V motors. Chips use +5 volts and +3.3 volts. The +3.3 volts are also used for memory, AGP/PCI/PCIe adapters, and some laptop fans. The negative voltages are seldom used.

A technician must occasionally check voltages in a system. There are four basic checks for power supply situations: (1) wall outlet AC voltage, (2) DC voltages going to the motherboard, (3) DC voltages going to a device, and (4) ground or lack of voltage with an outlet tester. A **power supply tester** can be used to check DC power levels on the different power supply connectors. Figure 5.50 shows a PC power supply tester. The type of connectors vary among vendors, so make sure you can get one that can do Molex, SATA, and main system power as a minimum.

FIGURE 5.50   PC power supply tester

Solving Power Supply Problems

When you suspect that the power supply is causing a problem, swap the power supply, make the customer happy, and be on your way! Power problems are not usually difficult to detect or troubleshoot.

TECH TIP

Do not disassemble a power supply

Power supplies are not normally disassembled. Manufacturers often rivet them shut. Even when a power supply can be disassembled, you should not take it apart unless you have a background in electronics.

Do not overlook the most obvious power supply symptom. Start by checking the computer power light. If it is off, check the power supply's fan by placing your palm at the back of the computer. If the fan is turning, it means the wall outlet is providing power to the computer and you can assume that the wall outlet is functioning. Check the motherboard for LEDs and refer to the manual for their meaning. Test the power outlet with another device. Ensure that the power cord is inserted fully into the wall outlet and the computer. If you suspect that the wall outlet is faulty, use an **AC circuit tester** to verify that the wall outlet is wired properly.

The following troubleshooting questions can help you determine the location of a power problem:

> Did the power supply work before? If not, check the input voltage selector switch on the power supply and verify that it is on the proper setting.
> Is the power supply's fan turning? If yes, check voltages going to the motherboard. If they are good, maybe just the power supply fan is bad. If the power supply's fan is not turning, check the wall outlet for proper AC voltages.
> Is a surge strip used? If so, check to see whether the surge strip is powered on, and then try a different outlet in the surge strip, or replace the surge strip.
> Is the computer's power cord okay? Verify that the power cord plugs snugly into the outlet and into the back of the computer. Swap the power cord to verify that it is functioning.
> Is the front panel power button stuck?
> Are the voltages going to the motherboard at the proper levels? If they are low, something might be overloading the power supply. Disconnect the power cable to one device and recheck the voltages. Replace the power cable to the device. Remove the power cable from another device and recheck the motherboard voltages. Continue doing this until the power cord for each device has been disconnected and the motherboard voltages have been checked. A single device can short out the power supply and cause the system to malfunction. Replace any device that draws down the power supply's output voltage and draws too much current. If none of the devices is the cause of the problem, replace the power supply. If replacing the power supply does not solve the problem, replace the motherboard.

If a computer does not boot properly, but it does boot when you press Ctrl + Alt + Delete, the power good signal is likely the problem. Some motherboards are more sensitive to the power good signal than others. For example, say that a motherboard has been replaced and the system does not boot. At first glance, this might appear to be a bad replacement board, but the problem could be caused by a power supply failing to output a consistent power good signal.

TECH TIP

Check the power good (sometimes called power OK) signal

Check the power supply documentation to see whether the power supply outputs a power good signal (rather than the normal +5 volts). Turn on the computer. Check the power good signal on the main motherboard power connector (attached to the power supply). Do this before replacing the motherboard. A power supply with a power good signal below +3V needs to be replaced.

Sometimes, when a computer comes out of sleep mode, not all devices respond, and the computer's power or reset button has to be pressed to reboot the computer. The following situations can cause this to happen:

> A screen saver conflicts with ACPI.
> All adapters/devices are not ACPI compliant.

> An adapter/device has an outdated driver.

> The system BIOS/UEFI or an installed adapter BIOS needs to be updated.

To see whether the screen saver causes a problem, use the *Display* Control Panel and set the screen saver option to *None*. Identifying a problem adapter, device, or driver will take Internet research. Check each adapter, device, and driver one by one. Use the *Power Options* Control Panel to change the power scheme. Also check all devices for a *Power Management* tab on the *Properties* dialog box. Changes can be made there.

CHAPTER 5

SOFT SKILLS—WRITTEN COMMUNICATIONS SKILLS

When technicians are in school, they seldom think that the skills they should be learning involve writing. However, in the workplace, technicians use written communication skills when they document problems and use email (see Figure 5.51). Advisory committees across the country say that in addition to having technical knowledge, it is important that technicians be able to communicate effectively both written and orally, be comfortable working in a team environment, and possess critical thinking skills (that is, solve problems even though they have not been taught the specific problem).

FIGURE 5.51 Technicians must frequently provide written communication

Regardless of the size of a company, documentation is normally required. The documentation might be only the number of hours spent on a job and a basic description of what was done, but most companies require a bit more. Documentation should be written so others can read and understand it. Keep in mind that if another technician must handle another problem from the same customer, it saves time and money to have good documentation. The following list includes complaints from managers who hire technicians. You can use this list to improve and avoid making the same mistakes:

> Avoids doing documentation in a timely manner
> Does not provide adequate or accurate information on what was performed or tried
> Has poor spelling, grammar, capitalization, and punctuation skills
> Writes in short, choppy sentences, using technical jargon
> Does not provide updates on the status of a problem

Email is a common means of communication for technicians. However, most technicians do not take the time to communicate effectively using email. The following is a list of guidelines for effective email communication:

> Do not use email when a meeting or a phone call is more appropriate.
> Include a short description of the email topic in the subject line.
> Do not write or respond to an email when you are angry.
> Send email only to the appropriate people; do not copy others unnecessarily.
> Stick to the point; do not digress.
> Use a spelling and grammar checker; if one is not included in the email client, write the email in a word processing application, check it, and then paste the document into the email.

> Use proper grammar, punctuation, and capitalization; do not write in all uppercase or all lowercase letters.
> Smile when you are typing. Your good attitude will come across in your writing.
> Focus on the task at hand. Read your note over out loud if it is a critical one.
> Write each email as if you were putting the message on a billboard (see Figure 5.52); you never know how the content might be used or who might see it.

The number-one complaint about technical support staff is not their lack of technical skills but their lack of communication skills. Spend as much of your education practicing your communication skills as you do your technical skills.

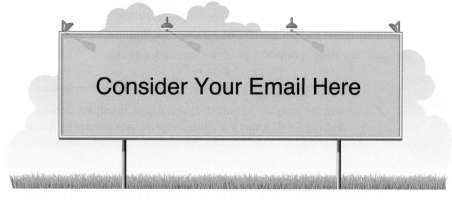

FIGURE 5.52   Consider what you write in written communications (it could be publicized)

Chapter Summary

> Wearing a wrist strap or staying in contact with unpainted metal keeps you and the computing device at the same electrical potential so you won't induce current into any part and weaken/ damage it.
> EMI and RFI cause issues. Move the computer or the offending device and replace all slot covers/openings.
> When removing parts, have the right tools, lighting, anti-static items, and ample workspace. Take notes. Don't use magnetized tools. Avoid jarring hard drives.
> Be careful installing an I/O shield and be aware of standoffs when dealing with the motherboard.
> Preventive maintenance procedures prolong the life of the computer. Vacuum before spraying compressed air.
> An MSDS/SDS describes disposal and storage procedures and contains information about toxicity and health concerns. Cities/states have specific disposal rules for chemicals, batteries, CRTs, electronics, and so on. Always know the disposal rules in the area where you work.
> AC power goes into the power supply or mobile device power brick. DC power is provided to all internal parts of the computing device. AC and DC voltage checks can be done and only with DC power does polarity matter. Use the highest meter setting possible with unknown voltage levels. Power is measured in watts.
> Continuity checks are done on cabling, and a good wire shows close to 0 ohms.
> A power supply converts AC to DC, distributes DC throughout a unit, and provides cooling. The power supply must be the correct form factor and able to supply the current amount of wattage for a particular voltage level such as +5V or +12V. Multiple "rails" are commonly available for +12V because the CPU commonly needs its own connection. The number and type of connectors vary, but converters can be purchased.

> Use ACPI to control power options through UEFI/BIOS and the operating system. Wake on LAN and Wake on Ring are power features that allow a device to be powered up from a lowered power condition for a specific purpose.
> The *Power Options* Control Panel is used to configure the power scheme within Windows.
> An AC circuit tester, multimeter, and power supply tester are tools used with power problems.
> Power issues include overvoltage conditions such as a surge or spike that can be helped with surge protectors, power conditioners, and UPSes. Power conditioners and UPSes help with undervoltage conditions such as a sag. A UPS is the only device that powers a computer when a blackout occurs.
> Ensure that a surge protector has a Class A rating and adheres to the UL 1449 standard.
> Two types of battery backup are UPS and SPS.
> In all communications and written documentation, be professional and effective. Use proper capitalization, grammar, punctuation, and spelling.

A+ CERTIFICATION EXAM TIPS

✓ Review the chapter summary. Quite a few questions are about preventive maintenance procedures. Don't forget that other chapters have preventive maintenance tips, too, including the chapters on storage devices, multimedia devices, and other peripherals chapters.

✓ Power down a computer, remove the power cord/power brick/battery, and allow a laser printer to cool before performing maintenance.

✓ Know all about static electricity, RFI, and EMI and how to prevent them. Be familiar with proper component handling and storage, including the use of self-grounding techniques, anti-static bags, ESD straps, and ESD mats.

✓ Know the purpose of MSDS.

✓ Know that both with safety issues and when dealing with chemicals and components that could have potential environmental impact, IT personnel must comply with local government regulations.

✓ Know what tools are commonly used: flat-tip/Phillips screwdrivers, and anti-static wrist strap (don't use in a CRT monitor or inside a power supply).

✓ Know the purpose of a toner vacuum and to use a vacuum and compressed air to deal with dust and debris.

✓ Know the purpose of and what is contained within a preventive maintenance kit.

✓ Know the power supply connector types and their voltages: SATA (+3.3, +5, +12V), Molex (+5 and +12V), 4/8 pin CPU (+12V), PCIe 6/8-pin (+12V), 20-pin, and 24-pin main motherboard (+3.3, +5, +12, −12V).

✓ Be familiar with common power problem symptoms, including the fan spins, but no power is provided to other devices, no power, noisy or inoperative fan, computer reboots or powers down without warning.

✓ Be familiar with motherboard connections to the top and front panels (USB, audio, power button, power light, drive activity lights, and reset button).

✓ Know information regarding power supply specifications including wattage, dual-rail, size, number of connectors, and ATX versus micro-ATX.

✓ Be familiar with all the power options that can be set in Windows.

✓ Be able to recommend specific products for power surges, brownouts, and blackouts.

✓ The following communication and professionalism skills are part of the 220-902 exam: Provide proper documentation on the services provided as well as document findings, actions, and outcomes.

Key Terms

Review Questions

1. What would happen if you removed the battery from the motherboard by accident?

   _____

2. List three tasks commonly performed during preventive maintenance.

   _____

   _____

   _____

3. Computers used in a grocery store warehouse for inventory control have a higher part failure rate than the other company computers. Which of the following is most likely to help in this situation?

   a. an anti-static wrist strap

   b. a preventive maintenance plan

   c. anti-static pads

   d. high wattage power supplies

4. Which of the following can prolong the life of a computer and conserve resources? (Select all that apply.)

   a. a preventive maintenance plan

   b. anti-static mats and pads

   c. upgraded power supply

   d. a power plan

   e. using a Li-ion battery as a replacement

   f. extra case fans

5. Which power component has a 24-pin connector?

   a. main motherboard connector

   b. power supply fan

   c. case fan

   d. AUX power for the CPU

6. An optical drive randomly becomes unavailable, and after replacing the drive, the technician now suspects a power issue. What could help in this situation?

   a. a UPS

   b. a surge protector

   c. anti-static wipes

   d. a preventive maintenance plan

   e. a multimeter

7. Where would you configure a computer so that it powered down the display after it was not used for 20 minutes?

   a. Device Manager

   b. Power Options Control Panel

   c. BIOS/UEFI

   d. CMOS

8. When disassembling a computer, which tool will help you remove the memory module?

   a. magnetic screwdriver

   b. needle-nose pliers

   c. #1 or #2 Phillips screwdriver

   d. anti-static wrist strap

9. A user had a motherboard problem last week and the technician fixed it. Now the same computer has a different problem. The user reports that the USB ports on the front do not work anymore. What is the first thing you should check?

   a. power supply

   b. power connection to the front panel

   c. motherboard connections to the front panel

   d. voltage output from the power supply to the USB connectors

10. Which part would be specialized when used with a laser printer?
    [surge strip | vacuum | multimeter | anti-static wrist strap]

11. Which two of the following would most likely cause a loud noise on a desktop computer? (Select two.) [motherboard | USB drive | power supply | case fan | memory | PCIe adapter]

12. A computer will not power on. Which of the following would be used to check the wall outlet?
    [power supply tester | UPS | multimeter | POST]

13. A computer will not power on. After checking the wall outlet and swapping the power cord, what would the technician use next?

    a. resistance

    b. power supply tester

    c. anti-static wrist strap

    d. magnetic screwdriver

    e. nonmagnetic screwdriver

14. Which of the following is affected by the power supply wattage rating?

    a. number of internal storage devices

    b. number of power supply connectors

    c. speed of the processor

    d. type of processor

    e. type of power supply connectors

15. Which of the following would help with computer heat?

    a. increased power supply wattage

    b. larger power supply form factor

    c. unplug unused power connectors

    d. install case fans

16. [T | F] Power supply disassembly is a common requirement of a PC technician.

17. Consider the following email.

> From: Cheryl a. Schmidt
> To: Network Engineering Technology Faculty
> Subj: [None]
> We have little time to get the PMS done on the PCs and N/W gear. What software do you want?

Reword this email to illustrate good written communication skills.

18. List three recommendations for good technical written communication.

19. A computer is doing weird things…shutting down unexpectedly or hanging. You suspect a power problem. You check the power good (power OK) signal on the power supply's main motherboard connector. The voltage reading shows you have power (+2.5 volts). What are you going to do next?

    a. Check the voltage coming out of a Molex or SATA connector.

    b. Check wall outlet voltage.

    c. Replace the power supply.

    d. Check the power supply cable for resistance.

20. What is the purpose of the I/O shield?

    a. prevents dust and dirt from coming in through the front computer ports

    b. provides grounding for motherboard ports

    c. prevents dust and dirt from coming into the power supply

    d. protects the technician from shocks

21. Which two items would help the technician maintain personal safety while working on PCs and printers in an extremely dusty warehouse? (Choose two.)

   [vacuum | toner vacuum | safety goggles | anti-static wrist strap | air filter/mask]

22. Which power protection is commonly used in corporate cubicles?

   [surge suppressor | UPS | phone line isolator | modem isolator]

23. For which adverse power condition can a UPS provide protection? (Select all that apply).
   [sag | surge | blackout | brownout | overvoltage]

24. Which UL rating and surge suppressor grade would be best when ordering new surge strips for a small business? (Choose two answers.)

   [UL 497 | UL 1283 | UL 1449 | Class A | Class B | Class C]

25. Inside the case is a two-conductor cable labeled Power SW. Where will this cable attach?
   [to the hard drive | to the motherboard | to the power supply | to the graphics adapter]

Exercises

Exercise 5.1 Identify power supply connectors

Objective: To be able to identify the purpose of common power supply connectors

Procedure: Use Figure 5.53 to document power supply connectors.

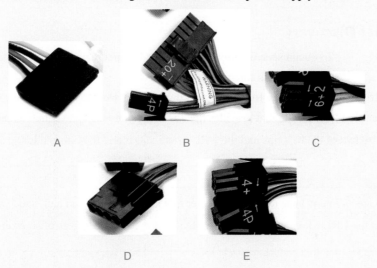

FIGURE 5.53   Identify power connectors

Match the power supply connector with its purpose.

_____   1. Molex for older optical drive

_____   2. SATA for hard drive

_____   3. PCIe video

_____   4. Main motherboard

_____   5. CPU

Exercise 5.2 Recognizing Computer Replacement Parts

Objective: To be able to recognize parts from a computer

Procedure: Use the following information to answer the questions.

The following parts were ordered by someone building his or her own computer:

1 - Intel Core i7 4.4GHz

2 - ASUS Rampage V Extreme X99 (does not include USB 3.1 headers)

3 - Triage 8GB

4 - Micro-ATX with two 3.5" internal and two 5.25" external drive bays

5 - EVA 450W

1.   What part is designated by the number 1? [memory I hard drive I optical drive I CPU]

2.   What part is designated by the number 2? [motherboard I processor I memory I hard drive]

3.   What part is designated by the number 3? [motherboard I optical drive I RAM I SATA hard drive I SSD]

4.   What part is designated by the number 4? [RAM I case I all storage devices I power supply]

5.   What part is designated by the number 5? [case I SSD I optical drive I power supply]

Activities

Internet Discovery

Objective: To obtain specific information on the Internet regarding a computer or its associated parts

Parts: Computer with Internet access

Procedure: Complete the following procedure and answer the accompanying questions.

1.   Locate an Internet site that provides tips for doing computer preventive maintenance.

Write two of the best tips and the URL where you found the information.

_____

_____

2.   Locate an Internet site to buy a computer tool kit that includes an anti-static wrist strap.

List the URL where you found the tool kit and at least three sizes of screwdrivers or bits provided.

_____

_____

_____

3.   Locate a power supply tester that includes a SATA connector.

List the manufacturer and model.

_____

_____

4.   Find a website on good netiquette.

Give the three recommendations and the name of the website (not the URL).

_____

_____

_____

_____

_____

5. You have just started working at a place that uses the HP Elite 800 G2 23-inch nontouch all-in-one computer.

   You have been sent to do power checks on the power supply of one of these units. How do you get the cover off? Give detailed explanations in complete sentences.

   _____

   _____

   _____

   _____

   What recommendation does HP give to clean the case for stubborn stains that might be found on the computers in the maintenance shop?

   _____

   According to the documentation, what is different about removing an AMD processor than a model that has an Intel processor?

   _____

   _____

   _____

Soft Skills

Objective: To enhance and fine-tune a future technician's ability to listen, communicate in both written and oral form, and support people who use computers in a professional manner

Activities:

1. Prepare a business proposal for a replacement power supply. Present your proposal to the class.

2. Write an informal report on the skills learned while taking a computer apart and reassembling it. Share your best practices with a small group.

3. Work in teams to decide the best way to inform a customer about the differences between a line conditioner and a UPS. Present your description to the class as if you were talking to the customer. Each team member must contribute. Each classmate votes for the best team explanation.

Critical Thinking Skills

Objective: To analyze and evaluate information as well as apply learned information to new or different situations

Activities:

1. Locate a computer on the Internet that lists each device that is installed and the type of motherboard, integrated ports, and so on. Then locate a power supply calculator. Find a replacement power supply, based on the calculations performed. Write the details of what you looked for in the replacement power supply, the power supply, vendor, number and type of connectors, and cost.

2. For one of the computers in the classroom, locate the documentation on how to disassemble it. Looking through the documentation, find at least three things that are good tips that you might not have thought of immediately if you were disassembling the computer. Then, find at least three safety tips. Place all of this information in an outline. An alternative is to be creative and put the tips graphically on one page or presentation slide.

CHAPTER 5

Labs

Lab 5.1 Performing Maintenance on an Anti-static Wrist Strap

Objective:	To understand how to care for and properly use an anti-static wrist strap
Parts:	Anti-static wrist strap
	Computer chassis
	Multimeter
Note:	Electrostatic discharge (ESD) has great potential to harm the electronic components inside a computer. Given this fact, it is vitally important that you practice proper ESD precautions when working inside a computer case. One tool you can use to prevent ESD is an anti-static wrist strap. This tool channels any static electricity from your body to the computer's chassis, where it is dissipated safely.
Procedure:	Complete the following procedure and answer the accompanying questions.

1. Examine the wrist strap for any obvious defects such as worn or broken straps, loose grounding lead attachments, dirt or grease buildup, and so on.

2. If necessary, remove any dirt or grease buildup from the wrist strap, paying close attention to the electrical contact points such as the wrist contact point, the ground lead attachment point, and the computer chassis attachment clip. Use denatured alcohol to clean these contact points.

3. If possible, use a multimeter to check continuity between the wrist contact point and the computer chassis attachment clip. A reading of zero ohms of resistance indicates a good electrical pathway.

   How many volts of static electricity does it take to harm a computer's electrical components?

   _____

4. Adjust the wrist strap so it fits snugly yet comfortably around your wrist. Ensure that the wrist contact is in direct contact with your skin, with no clothing, hair, and so on, being in the way.

5. Attach the ground lead to the wrist strap and ensure it snaps securely into place.

6. Attach the computer chassis attachment clip to a clean metal attachment point on the computer chassis.

7. Any static electricity generated or attracted by your body will now be channeled through the anti-static wrist strap to the computer chassis, where it will be safely dissipated.

   How many volts will an ESD be before you will feel anything?

   _____

   Should you use an anti-static wrist strap when working inside a CRT monitor or laser printer high voltage power supply? Why or why not?

   _____

   _____

   _____

Instructor initials: _____

Lab 5.2 Computer Disassembly/Reassembly

Objective:	To disassemble and reassemble a computer correctly
Parts:	A computer to disassemble
	A tool kit
	An anti-static wrist strap (if possible)
Note:	Observe proper ESD handling procedures when disassembling and reassembling a computer.
Procedure:	Complete the following procedure and answer the accompanying questions.

1. Gather the proper tools needed to disassemble the computer.

2. Clear as much workspace as possible around the computer.

3.   Power on the computer.

Why is it important to power on the computer before you begin?

_____

External Cables

4.   Turn off the computer and all peripherals. Remove the power cable from the wall outlet, and then remove the power cord from the computer.

5.   Note where the monitor cable plugs into the back of the computer. Disconnect the monitor including the power cord and move it to a safe place. Take appropriate notes.

6.   Remove all external cables from the back of the computer. Take notes on the location of each cable. Move the peripheral devices to a safe place.

Did the mouse cable connect to a PS/2 or USB port?

_____

Computer Case Side Access or Removal

7.   If possible, remove one or both sides of the case. This is usually the hardest step in disassembly if the computer is one that has not been seen before. Diagram the screw locations. Keep the cover screws separated from other screws. An egg carton or a container with small compartments makes an excellent screw holder. Label each compartment and reuse the container. Otherwise, open the case as directed by the manufacturer.

Adapter Placement

8.   Make notes or draw the placement of each adapter in the expansion slots.

9.   On your notes, draw the internal cable connections before removing any adapters or cables from the computer. Make notes regarding how and where the cable connects to the adapter. Do not forget to include cables that connect to the motherboard or to the computer case.

List some ways to determine the correct orientation for an adapter or cable.

_____

_____

_____

Internal Cable Removal

10.   Remove all internal cables. WARNING: Do not pull on a cable; use the pull tab, if available, or use the cable connector to pull out the cable. Some cables have connectors with locking tabs. Release the locking tabs before you disconnect the cable. Make appropriate notes regarding the cable connections. Some students find that labeling cables and the associated connectors makes reassembly easier, but good notes usually suffice.

Adapter Removal

11.   Start with the left side of the computer (facing the front of the computer) and locate the leftmost adapter.

12.   If applicable, remove the screw or retaining bracket that holds the adapter to the case. Place the screw in a separate, secure location away from the other screws already removed. Make notes about where the screw goes or any other notes that will help you when reassembling the computer.

13.   Remove the adapter from the computer.

Why must you be careful not to touch the gold contacts at the bottom of each adapter?

_____

_____

CHAPTER 5

14. Remove the remaining adapters in the system by repeating Steps 11–13. Take notes regarding screw locations, jumpers, switches, and so forth, for each adapter.

Drives

15. Remove all power connections to drives, such as hard drives, floppy drives, CD/DVD/BD drives, and so on. Note the placement of each drive and each cable, as well as any reminders needed for reassembly.

16. Remove any screws holding the drives in place. Make notes about where the screws go. Keep these screws separate from any previously removed screws.

17. Remove all drives.

Why must you be careful when handling a mechanical hard drive?

_____

_____

What would you do differently when handling an SSD than a SATA hard drive?

_____

_____

Power Supply

18. Before performing this step, ensure that the power cord is removed from the wall outlet and the computer. Remove the connectors that connect the power supply to the motherboard.

19. Take very good notes here so you will be able to insert the connectors correctly when reassembling.

20. Remove the power supply.

What is the purpose of the power supply?

_____

Motherboard

21. Make note of any motherboard switches or jumpers and indicate whether the switch position is on or off.

What is the importance of documenting switches and jumpers on the motherboard?

_____

22. Remove any remaining connectors. Take appropriate notes.

23. Remove any screws that hold the motherboard to the case. Place these screws in a different location from the other screws removed from the system. Write any notes pertaining to the motherboard screws. Look for retaining clips or tabs that hold the motherboard into the case.

24. Remove the motherboard. Make notes pertaining to the motherboard removal. The computer case should be empty after you complete this step.

Instructor initials: _____

Reassembly

25. Reassemble the computer by reversing the steps for disassembly. Pay particular attention to cable orientation when reinstalling cables. Before reconnecting a cable, ensure that the cable and the connectors are correctly oriented and aligned before pushing the cable firmly in place. Refer to your notes. The first step is to install the motherboard in the computer case and reconnect all motherboard connections and screws.

26. Install the power supply by attaching all screws that hold the power supply in the case. Reattach the power connectors to the motherboard. Refer to your notes.

27. Install all drives by attaching screws, cables, and power connectors. Refer to your notes. Attach any cables that connect the drive to the motherboard.

28. Install all adapters. Attach all cables from the adapter to the connecting device. Replace any retaining clips or screws that hold adapters in place. Refer to your previous notes and diagrams.

29. Connect any external connectors to the computer. Refer to previously made notes, when necessary.

30. Replace the computer cover. Ensure that slot covers are replaced and that the drives and the front cover are aligned properly. Ensure that all covers are installed properly.

31. Reinstall the computer power cable.

32. Once the computer is reassembled, power on all external peripherals and the computer. A chassis intrusion error message might appear. This is just an indication that the cover was removed. Did the computer power on with POST error codes? If so, recheck all diagrams, switches, and cabling. Also, check a similar computer model that still works to see whether you made a diagramming error. The most likely problem is with a cable connection or with a part not seated properly in its socket.

Instructor initials: _____

Lab 5.3 Amps and Wattage

Objective: To determine the correct capacity and wattage of a power supply

Parts: Power supply

               Internet access (as needed)

Procedure: Complete the following procedure and answer the accompanying questions.

1. Locate the documentation stenciled on the power supply, if possible.

2. Use the Internet to find the power supply's documentation on the manufacturer's website. Use the information you find on the power supply or the website to answer the following questions.

   How many amps is the power supply rated for at 5 volts?

   _____

   How many amps is the power supply rated for at 12 volts?

   _____

   How many +12V rails does the power supply have?

   _____

   What is the maximum rated output power of the power supply in watts?

   _____

Instructor initials: _____

Lab 5.4 Continuity Check

Objective: To perform a continuity check on a cable and find any broken wires

Parts: Multimeter

               Cable and pin-out diagram

Procedure: Complete the following procedure and answer the accompanying questions.

1. Obtain a meter, cable, and pin-out diagram from your instructor.

2. Set the meter to ohms.

3. Power on the meter.

4. Lay the cable horizontally in front of you. The connector on the left is referred to as Connector A. The connector on the right is referred to as Connector B.

5. Determine the number of pins on the cable connector. On a separate sheet of paper, write numbers vertically down the left side of the paper, similar to the numbering used in Lab 5.5. There should be a number for each connector pin. At the top of the numbers, write **Connector A** as the heading. Create a corresponding set of identical numbers vertically on the right side of the paper.

6. Check the continuity of each wire. Document your findings by placing a check mark beside each pin number that has a good continuity check.

   Which meter setting did you use to check continuity, and which meter symbol is used for this setting?

   _____

7. Power off the meter and return all supplies to the instructor.

Instructor initials: _____

Lab 5.5 Pin-Out Diagramming

Objective: To draw a pin-out diagram using a working cable

Parts: Multimeter

               Good cable

Procedure: Complete the following procedure and perform the accompanying activities.

1. Obtain a meter and a good cable from your instructor.

2. Set the meter to ohms.

Instructor initials: _____

3. Power on the meter.

4. Lay the cable horizontally in front of you. The connector on the left is referred to as Connector A. The connector on the right is referred to as Connector B.

5. Touch one meter lead to Connector A's pin 1. Touch the other meter lead to every Connector B pin. Notice when the meter shows zero resistance, indicating a connection.

   Using the table that follows, draw a line from Connector A's pin 1 to any Connector B pins that show zero resistance. Add more pin numbers as needed to the table or use a separate piece of paper. Remember that all pins do not have to be used in the connector. There are no review questions; however, there is a connector table that contains connection lines.

Connector A	Connector B
❏ 1	❏ 1
❏ 2	❏ 2
❏ 3	❏ 3
❏ 4	❏ 4
❏ 5	❏ 5
❏ 6	❏ 6
❏ 7	❏ 7
❏ 8	❏ 8
❏ 9	❏ 9
❏ 10	❏ 10
❏ 11	❏ 11
❏ 12	❏ 12
❏ 13	❏ 13
❏ 14	❏ 14
❏ 15	❏ 15
❏ 16	❏ 16
❏ 17	❏ 17
❏ 18	❏ 18
❏ 19	❏ 19
❏ 20	❏ 20

6. Power off the meter.

Instructor initials: _____

7. Return all supplies to the instructor.

Lab 5.6 Fuse Check

Objective: To determine whether a fuse is good

Parts: Multimeter

Fuse

Procedure: Complete the following procedure and answer the accompanying questions.

1. Obtain a meter and a fuse from your instructor.

2. Look at the fuse and determine its amp rating.

What is the amperage rating of the fuse?

_____

3. Set the meter to ohms.

Instructor initials: _____

4. Power on the meter.

5. Connect one meter lead to one end of the fuse. Connect the other meter lead to the opposite end.

6. Look at the resistance reading on the meter.

What is the resistance reading?

_____

Is the fuse good?

_____

7. Power off the meter.

Instructor initials: _____

8. Return all materials to the instructor.

Lab 5.7 Using a Multimeter

Objective: To check voltage and resistance levels using a multimeter

Parts: Multimeter

AA, AAA, C, D, or 9-volt battery

Extended paperclip or wire

Caution: Keep both hands behind the protective rings on the meter handles. See Figures 5.24 and 5.25.

Procedure: Complete the following procedure and perform the accompanying activities.

1. All voltage inside the computer is DC voltage (except for some parts inside the power supply, of course). Learning how to measure DC voltage is important for a technician. The best place to start is with a battery. Obtain a battery. Look carefully at the battery and determine where the positive end or connector is located (usually has a + [plus] symbol nearby) and where the negative end or connector is located.

Why is it important to locate positive and negative on a battery?

_____

2. Look carefully at the battery and determine the voltage rating.

Document your findings.

_____

_____

3. Place the battery on a flat surface. If the battery is an AA, AAA, C, or D battery, place the battery so that the positive side (the side with a nodule) points toward your right side. If the battery is a 9-volt battery, place the battery so that the connectors are facing you and the positive connector (the smaller connector) is on your right side.

4. If the meter has leads that attach, attach the black meter lead to the appropriate port colored as a black port or the labeling of COM. Attach the red meter lead to the positive or port marked with a plus sign (+).

5. Turn on the meter. Set the meter so that it is measuring VDC (DC voltage). This might involve manually rotating a dial and/or pushing a button. Note that some meters can autodetect the setting, but most involve configuration.

    Document what you did to configure the meter for VDC.

    _____

    What indication, if any, did the meter show in the meter window that VDC is being measured?

    _____

    _____

6. Hold the meter leads so that the black lead is in your left hand and the right lead is in your right hand. Ensure your hands are behind the protective ring on the meter handle. Refer to Figures 5.24 and 5.25 if you are unsure.

7. Place the black meter lead to the negative side (left side or left connector). Also touch the red meter lead to the positive side (right side or right connector) of the battery.

    Make a note of the meter reading.

    _____

    Based on your findings, is the battery good (usable in an electronic device)?

    _____

8. Now reverse the meter leads—place the black lead to the positive side and the red lead to the negative side.

    Record your findings.

    _____

    What was different from the original meter reading?

    _____

Instructor initials: _____

9. Perform this voltage check on any other batteries given to you by the instructor or lab assistant.

10. Straighten a paperclip or obtain a wire. Place the paperclip or wire on a flat surface.

11. Change the meter so that it reads ohms. This is normally shown by the omega symbol (Ω).

    While having the meter leads up in the air (not touching each other), what does the meter display?

    _____

12. Touch the meter leads together to make a complete circuit or path.

    What does the meter display now?

    _____

13. Touch one meter lead to one end of the paperclip or wire, and touch the other meter lead to the opposite paperclip or wire end. Sometimes it is easier to just lay the meter lead on top of the wire close to the end.

    What is the meter reading?

    _____

14. Some meters have the ability to make a sound when a wire is good. This is frequently shown on your meter as a sound wave $)$**)**. If your meter has this ability, configure the meter and redo the test. You can see how much easier this would be than trying to hold your meter leads straight and watch the meter.

Instructor initials: _____

15. Power off the meter. Disconnect the leads as necessary. Return all parts to the appropriate location.

Lab 5.8 Wall Outlet and Power Cord AC Voltage Check

Objective: To check the voltage from a wall outlet and through a power cord

Parts: Multimeter

                Computer power cord

Caution: Exercise extreme caution when working with AC voltages!

Procedure: Complete the following procedure and perform the accompanying activities.

1. Set the multimeter to AC VOLTAGE (refer to the meter's manual if you are unsure about this setting). Important: Using a current or resistance setting could destroy the meter.

2. Power on the multimeter. Locate an AC power outlet. Refer to Figure 5.54 for the power connections.

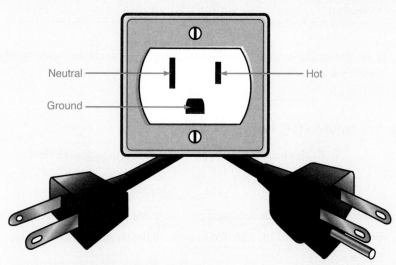

FIGURE 5.54   AC outlet

3. Insert the meter's black lead into the round (Ground) AC outlet plug.

4. Insert the meter's red lead into the smaller flat (Hot) AC outlet plug. The meter reading should be around 120 volts. Use Table 5.11 to record the reading.

5. Move the meter's red lead into the larger flat (Neutral) AC outlet plug. The meter reading should be 0 volts. Use Table 5.11 to record the reading.

TABLE 5.11 Wall outlet AC checks

Connections	Expected voltage	Actual voltage
GND to hot	120VAC	
GND to neutral	0VAC	
Hot to neutral	120VAC	

6. Remove both leads from the wall outlet.

7. Insert the meter's black lead into the smaller flat (hot) AC outlet plug.

8. Insert the meter's red lead into the larger flat (neutral) AC outlet plug. The meter reading should be around 120 volts. Use Table 5.11 to record the reading.

9. Plug the computer power cord into the AC wall outlet that was checked using Steps 3 through 8.

10. Verify the other end of the power cord is not plugged into the computer.

11. Perform the same checks you performed in Steps 3 through 8, except this time check the power cord end that plugs into the computer. Use Table 5.12 to record the reading.

TABLE 5.12 Power cord AC checks

Connections	Expected voltage	Actual voltage
GND to hot	120VAC	
GND to neutral	0VAC	
Hot to neutral	120VAC	

12. If the voltage through the power cord is correct, power off the meter. Notify the instructor of any incorrect voltages.

Instructor initials: _____

Lab 5.9 Device DC Voltage Check

Objective: To check the power supply voltages sent to various devices

Parts: Multimeter
                 Computer

Procedure: Complete the following procedure and perform the accompanying activities.

1. Set the multimeter to DC VOLTAGE (refer to the meter's manual if unsure about the setting).

2. Power on the multimeter.

3. Power off the computer.

4. Remove the computer case.

5. Locate a Molex or Berg power connector. If one is not available, disconnect a power connector from a device.

6. Power on the computer.

7. Check the +5 volt DC output from the power supply by placing the meter's *black* lead in (if the connector is a Molex) or on (if the connector is a Berg) one of the grounds* (a black wire). Place the meter's *red* lead on the +5 volt wire (normally a red wire) in or on the connector. Consult Figure 5.55 for the layout of the Molex and Berg power supply connections. Figure 5.55 also contains a table with the acceptable voltage levels.

    *Use and check both ground connections (black wires going into the connector); do not check all the voltages using only one ground connection.

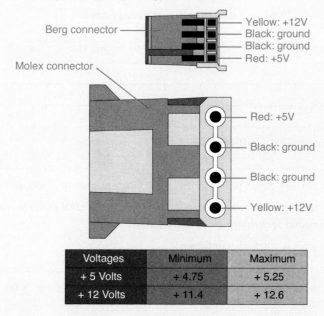

Voltages	Minimum	Maximum
+ 5 Volts	+ 4.75	+ 5.25
+ 12 Volts	+ 11.4	+ 12.6

FIGURE 5.55   Molex and Berg power connectors

Write the voltage level found for the +5 volt wire in Table 5.13.

TABLE 5.13   +5 volt check

Voltage being checked	Voltage found
+5 volts	

8. Check the +12 volt DC output by placing the meter's *black* lead in (if the connector is a Molex) or on (if the connector is a Berg) one of the grounds. Place the meter's *red* lead on the +12 volt wire in or on the connector. See Figure 5.55 for the layout of the Molex and Berg power supply connections. The figure also contains a table with acceptable voltage levels. Write the voltage level found or the +12 volt wire in Table 5.14.

TABLE 5.14   +12 volt check

Voltage being checked	Voltage found
+12 volts	

9. Notify the instructor of any voltages out of the acceptable range.

10. Power off the meter.

Instructor initials: _____

11. Power off the computer.

Lab 5.10 Windows Vista/7 Power Options

Objective: To be able to control power options via BIOS/UEFI and Windows Vista/7

Parts: Computer with Windows Vista or 7 loaded

Procedure: Complete the following procedure and answer the accompanying questions.

1. Power on the computer and ensure it boots properly before the exercise begins.

2. Reboot the computer and access BIOS Setup.

    List the BIOS/UEFI options related to power management.

    _____

    _____

    _____

    _____

    _____

    Can ACPI be disabled via BIOS/UEFI?

    _____

3. Exit the BIOS/UEFI Setup program without saving any settings. Boot to Windows Vista/7.

4. Access the current power settings by using the *Start > Control Panel > System and Maintenance* (Vista)/*System and Security (7) > Power Options*.

    What power plan is currently configured?

    _____

5. Select the *Create a power plan* link on the left. Type a unique name in the *Plan name* textbox. Click *Next*.

6. Use the *Turn off the display* drop-down menu to select a time. Use the *Put the computer to sleep* drop-down menu to select a time for the computer to go into reduced power mode. Note that on a laptop computer there will be two columns of choices: *On battery* and *Plugged in*.

    Which global ACPI state do you think this would assign? Look back through the chapter to review.

    _____

7. Click the *Create* button. Notice that your new plan appears in the list of preferred plans. Also notice that the *Show additional plans* reveal arrow might be in the center of the window on the right if someone has hidden the additional plans. Click *Show additional plans*, and other plans are revealed.

8. Click the *Change plan settings* link under or beside the plan you just created. Select the *Change advanced power settings* link.

    List at least three devices for which you can have power controlled through this Control Panel.

    _____

    _____

    _____

9. Expand the USB settings, if possible, and the *USB selective suspend* setting.

    What is the current setting?

    _____

10. Expand the *Processor power management* setting, if possible.

    What is the minimum processor state?

    _____

    What is the maximum processor state?

    _____

11. Expand the *Multimedia* settings, if possible.

   What setting(s) is configured with this option?

   _____

12. Click the *Cancel* button to return to the Change settings window. Click the *Cancel* button again. Show the instructor or lab assistant your settings.

Instructor initials: _____

13. To delete a power plan you created (the default ones cannot be deleted), select the radio button for the original power plan. Refer to Step 4, if necessary. Under the plan you created, select the *Change settings for the plan* link. Select the *Delete this plan* link and click *OK*. The plan should be removed from the power options list. Show the instructor or lab assistant that the plan has been deleted.

Instructor initials: _____

Lab 5.11 Windows 8/10 Power Options

Objective: To be able to control power options via BIOS/UEFI and Windows 8/10

Parts: Computer with Windows 8 or 10 loaded

Procedure: Complete the following procedure and answer the accompanying questions.

1. Power on the computer and ensure it boots properly before the exercise begins.

2. Reboot the computer and access BIOS Setup.

   List the BIOS/UEFI options related to power management.

   _____

   _____

   _____

   _____

   _____

   Can ACPI be disabled via BIOS/UEFI?

   _____

3. Exit the BIOS/UEFI Setup program without saving any settings. Boot to Windows.

4. Access the current power settings by using the *Power Options* Control Panel.

   Which power plan is currently configured?

   _____

5. Select the *Create a power plan* link on the left. Type a unique name in the *Plan name* textbox. Click *Next*.

6. Use the various options to select specific power plans. Not all platforms have all options, but document your settings in Table 5.15.

TABLE 5.15   Power plan options

Option	Minutes selected
Display	
Display brightness (mobile devices)	
Computer sleep	

7. When you are finished configuring, click the *Create* button. Notice that your new plan appears in the list of preferred plans. Also notice that the *Show additional plans* reveal arrow might be in the center of the window on the right if someone has hidden the additional plans. Click *Show additional plans*, and other plans are revealed.

    What global ACPI state do you think this would assign? Look back through the chapter to review.

    _____

    _____

8. Click the *Change plan settings* link under or beside the plan you just created. Select the *Change advanced power settings* link.

    List at least three devices for which you can have power controlled through this Control Panel.

    _____

    _____

    _____

Instructor initials: _____

9. If available and possible, expand the USB settings and the *USB selective suspend* setting.

    What is the current setting?

    _____

10. Expand the *Processor power management* setting, if possible.

    What is the minimum processor state?

    _____

11. Expand the *Desktop background settings > Slide show* setting, if possible.

    What setting(s) is configured with this option?

    _____

12. Click the *Cancel* button to return to the Change settings window. Click the *Cancel* button again.

13. To delete a power plan you created (the default ones cannot be deleted), select the radio button for the original power plan. Refer to Step 4, if necessary. Under the plan you created, select the *Change plan settings* link. Select the *Delete this plan* link and click *OK*. The plan should be removed from the power options list.

6 Memory

In this chapter you will learn:

> Different memory technologies
> How to plan for a memory installation or upgrade

> How to install and remove memory modules
> How to optimize memory for Windows platforms

> Best practices for troubleshooting memory problems
> The benefits of teamwork

CompTIA Exam Objectives:

What CompTIA A+ exam objectives are covered in this chapter?

✓ 901-1.1 Given a scenario, configure settings and use BIOS/UEFI tools on a PC.

✓ 901-1.2 Explain the importance of motherboard components, their purpose, and properties.

✓ 901-1.3 Compare and contrast various RAM types and their features.

✓ 901-4.1 Given a scenario, troubleshoot common problems related to motherboards, RAM, CPU, and power with appropriate tools.

✓ 902-1.4 Given a scenario, use appropriate Microsoft operating system features and tools.

Memory Overview

Computer systems need software to operate. The software must reside in computer memory. A technician must understand memory terminology, determine the optimum amount of memory for a system, install the memory, fine-tune it for the best performance, and troubleshoot and solve any memory problems.

The two main types of memory are random-access memory (**RAM**) and read-only memory (ROM), and the difference between them is shown in Figure 6.1.

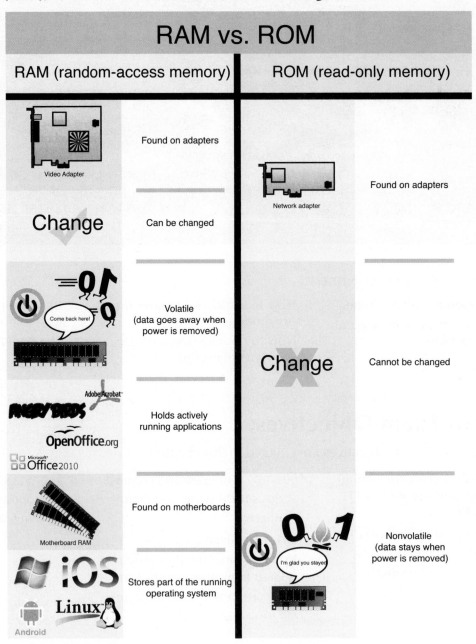

FIGURE 6.1   RAM versus ROM

RAM is divided into two major types: dynamic RAM (**DRAM**) and static RAM (**SRAM**). DRAM is less expensive but slower than SRAM. With DRAM, the 1s and 0s inside the chip must be refreshed. Over time, the charge, which represents information inside a DRAM chip, leaks out. The information, stored in 1s and 0s, is periodically rewritten to the memory chip through the

refresh process. The refreshing is accomplished inside the DRAM while other processing occurs. Refreshing is one reason DRAM chips are slower than SRAM.

Most memory on a motherboard is DRAM, but a small amount of SRAM can be found inside the processor, just outside the processor inside the processor housing, and sometimes on the motherboard. SRAM is also known as **cache memory**. Cache memory holds the most frequently used data so the CPU does not return to the slower DRAM chips to obtain the data. For example, on a motherboard with a bus speed of 233MHz, accessing DRAM could take as long as 90 nanoseconds. (A nanosecond [ns] is one-billionth of a second.) Accessing the same information in cache could take as little as 23 nanoseconds.

TECH TIP

The CPU should never have to wait to receive an instruction

Using pipelined burst cache speeds up processing for software applications.

The data or instruction that the processor needs is usually found in one of three places: cache, DRAM, or the hard drive. Cache gives the fastest access. If the information is not in cache, the processor looks for it in DRAM. If the information is not in DRAM, it is retrieved from the hard drive and placed into DRAM or the cache. Hard drive access is the slowest of the three. In a computer, it takes roughly a million times longer to access information from the hard drive than it does from DRAM or cache.

TECH TIP

Don't forget hard drive space and video memory

RAM is only one piece of the puzzle. All of a computer's parts including RAM, hard drive space, and video memory must work together to provide good (optimal) system performance.

As noted in Chapter 3, to determine a computer's memory requirements, you must consider the operating system, applications, and installed hardware. Memory is one of the most critical things on the motherboard that can easily be upgraded. Let's start with the physical memory module.

Memory Physical Packaging

A dual in-line package (DIP) chip has a row of legs running down each side. The oldest motherboards use DIP chips for the DRAM. Single in-line memory modules (SIMM) came along next. Sometimes you might see SIMMs as memory in laser printers. The memory chip used on motherboards today is a dual in-line memory module (**DIMM**), which has 168, 184, 240, or 288 pins. Memory can also be called a memory stick, or a technician might call one memory module a stick of memory, or simply RAM. Figure 6.2 shows the progression of memory packaging.

RIMMs are used in older Intel Pentium 4 computers. Figure 6.3 shows a RIMM. The RIMM has two notches in the center.

CHAPTER 6

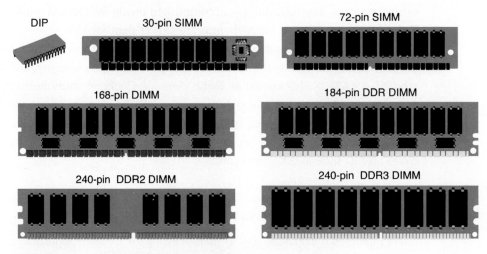

FIGURE 6.2   Memory chips/modules

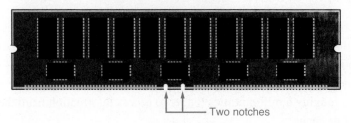

Two notches

FIGURE 6.3   184-pin RIMM

Planning the Memory Installation

Now that you know a little about memory types, let us look at the practical side—how to go about planning a memory installation. Some key points follow:

> Refer to the system or motherboard documentation to see what type of memory is supported.
> Determine what features are supported.
> Determine how much memory is needed.
> Determine how many of each memory module is needed.
> Research prices and purchase memory module(s).

Planning the Memory Installation—Memory Module Types

Technology has provided faster DRAM speeds without increasing the cost too greatly. Table 6.1 lists some of the memory modules available today.

TABLE 6.1   Memory module types

Technology	Explanation
Synchronous DRAM (**SDRAM**)	Performs very fast burst memory access. New memory addresses are placed on the address but before the prior memory address retrieval and execution is complete. SDRAM synchronizes its operation with the CPU clock signal to speed up memory access. Used with DIMMs.
Double data rate (**DDR**)	Sometimes called DDR SDRAM or DDR RAM and developed from SDRAM technology. DDR memory can send twice as much data as the older PC133 SDRAM because data is transmitted on both sides of the clock signal (rising and falling edges instead of just rising edge).

Technology	Explanation
DDR2	Sometimes called DDR2 RAM. DDR2 uses 240-pin DIMMs and is not compatible with DDR.
DDR3	An upgrade from DDR2 (8-bit prefetch buffer compared to 4 bit with DDR2). DDR3 uses 240-pin DIMMs and is not compatible with DDR2 or DDR. The technology better supports multi-core processor-based systems and more efficient power utilization.
DDR3L	A DDR3 module that runs at a lower voltage (1.35V) than the 1.5V or higher DDR/DDR2/DDR3 modules. Less voltage means less heat and less power consumed.
DDR4	Operates at a lower voltage and faster speeds than DDR3 modules. DDR4 uses 288-pin DIMMs and is not compatible with DDR, DDR2, or DDR3. Allows for storage up to 512GB on a single module.
DDR4L	Uses a lower voltage (1.05V) than a standard DDR4 module.
Rambus DRAM (RDRAM)	Developed by Rambus, Inc., and packaged in 184-pin RIMMs (which is a trademark of Rambus, Inc.). Must be installed in pairs with dual- and quad-channel motherboards. When RIMMs are used, all memory slots must be filled, even if a slot is not needed because the memory banks are tied together. Put a C-RIMM (continuity RIMM), which is a blank module, in any empty (unfilled) slot.

Whether or not a motherboard supports faster memory chips is determined by the chipset, which performs most functions in conjunction with the processor. A chipset is one to five electronic chips on the motherboard. The chipset contains the circuitry to control the local bus, memory, DMA, interrupts, and cache memory. The motherboard manufacturer determines which chipset to use.

TECH TIP

Use the right type of memory chips

The chipset and motherboard design are very specific about what type, speed, and features the memory chips can have. Refer to the motherboard documentation.

Most people cannot tell the difference among DDR, DDR2, DDR3, and DDR4 memory modules. Even though DDR uses 184 pins, DDR2 and DDR3 use 240 pins, and DDR4 has 288 pins, they are the same physical size. Even though both DDR2 and DDR3 modules have 240 pins, a DDR3 module does not fit in a DDR2 memory slot. Figure 6.4 shows DDR3 DIMMs.

Notice in Figure 6.4 the metal casing or **heat spreader** on the outside of the memory module. Aluminum or copper is commonly used on heat spreaders in order to dissipate heat away from the memory. Table 6.2 lists many of the DIMM models.

FIGURE 6.4   DDR3 DIMMs

TABLE 6.2   DIMMs

Memory type	Other name	Clock speed	Data rate (transfers per second)
PC2-8500	DDR2-1066	533MHz	1.07G
PC2-9200	DDR2-1150	575MHz	1.15G
PC2-9600	DDR2-1200	600MHz	1.2G
PC3-6400	DDR3-800	400MHz	800M
PC3-8500	DDR3-1066	533MHz	1.06G
PC3-10600	DDR3-1333	666MHz	1.33G
PC3-12800	DDR3-1600	800MHz	1.6G
PC3-16000	DDR3-2000	1000MHz	2G
PC3-17000	DDR3-2133	1066MHz	2.13G
PC4-12800	DDR4-1600	800MHz	1.6G
PC4-14900	DDR4-1866	933MHz	1.86G
PC4-19200	DDR4-2400	1200MHz	2.4G
PC4-21300	DDR4-2666	1333MHz	2.66G
PC4-25600	DDR4-3200	1600MHz	3.2G

Because a DIMM can be shown with either the PCX- or DDRX- designation, which type you buy can be confusing. A brief explanation might help. DDR3-800 is a type of DDR3 memory that can run on a 400MHz front side bus (the number after DDR3 divided in half). Another way of showing the same chip would be to use the designation PC3-6400, which is the theoretical bandwidth of the memory chip in MB/s.

Planning the Memory Installation—Memory Features

In addition to determining what type of memory chips are going to be used, you must determine what features the memory chip might have. The computer system or motherboard documentation is going to delineate what features are supported. Table 6.3 helps characterize memory features.

TABLE 6.3   Memory features

Feature	Explanation
parity	A method for checking data accuracy. (See tech tip.)
non-parity	Chips that do not use any error checking.
error correcting code (**ECC**)	An alternative to parity checking that uses a mathematical algorithm to verify data accuracy. ECC can detect up to 4-bit memory errors and correct 1-bit memory errors. ECC is used in higher-end computers and network servers. **Non-ECC** memory modules are simply modules that do not support ECC.
unbuffered memory	The opposite of registered memory, used in low- to medium-powered computers. Unbuffered memory is faster than registered or fully buffered memory.
buffered memory (registered memory)	Buffered memory modules have extra chips (registers) near the bottom of the chip that delay all data transfers by one clock tick to ensure accuracy. They are used in servers and high-end computers. If you install a registered memory module into a system that allows both registered and unbuffered memory, all memory must be registered modules. These modules are sometimes advertised as fully buffered DIMMs (FBDIMM).
serial presence detect (**SPD**)	The module has an extra EEPROM that holds information about the DIMM (capacity, voltage, refresh rates, and so on). The BIOS/UEFI reads and uses this data for best performance. Some modules have **thermal sensors** (sometimes listed as TS in an advertisement) used to monitor and report memory heat conditions.
single-sided memory	A memory module that has one "bank" of memory and 64 bits are transferred out of the memory module to the CPU. A better term for single-sided memory is single-banked memory. The module might or might not have all of its "chips" on one side.
double-sided memory	A single memory module developed in a special way that it actually contains two memory modules in one container (two banks). If the motherboard slot has been designed to accept this type of memory module, data is still sent to the CPU 64 bits at a time. This is a way for having more banks of memory on the motherboard without requiring more memory slots. These modules normally have memory chips on both sides, but all modules with chips on both sides are not double-sided memory.
dual-voltage memory	A module that can operate at a lower voltage level (thus less heat) if the motherboard supports this feature. Note that all installed modules must also support the lower voltage for the system to operate in this mode.
extreme memory profile (**XMP**)	A type of memory module that allows the BIOS to configure voltage and timing settings in order to overclock the memory.

CHAPTER 6

TECH TIP

How parity works

If a system uses even parity and the data bits 10000001 go into memory, the ninth bit, or parity bit, is a 0 because an even number of bits (2) are 1s. The parity changes to a 1 only when the number of bits in the data is an odd number of 1s. If the system uses even parity and the data bits 10000011 go into memory, the parity bit is a 1. There are only three 1s in the data bits. The parity bit adjusts the 1s to an even number. When checking data for accuracy, the parity method detects if one bit is incorrect. However, if 2 bits are in error, parity does not catch the error.

Keep in mind that some motherboards might support both non-parity and ECC (error correcting code) or might require a certain feature such as SPD. It is important that you research this *before* you look to purchase memory.

A memory module might use more than one of the categories listed in the two previous tables. For example, a DIMM could be a DDR3 module, be registered, and support ECC for error detection and correction. Most registered memory also uses the ECC technology. Memory modules can support either ECC or non-ECC and they can be registered or unbuffered memory.

Memory technology is moving quite quickly today. Chipsets also change constantly. Technicians are continually challenged to keep up with the features and abilities of the technology so that they can make recommendations to their customers. Trade magazines and the Internet are excellent resources for updates. Never forget to check the motherboard's documentation when dealing with memory. Information is a technician's best friend.

TECH TIP

If error correction isn't mentioned in the advertisement...

If error correction is not mentioned, the chip is a non-parity chip. Most memory modules today are non-parity because the memory controller circuitry provides error correction.

Planning for Memory—Amount of Memory to Install

When you want to improve the performance of a computer, adding memory is one of the easiest upgrades. The amount of memory needed depends on the operating system, applications, number of applications open at the same time, type of computer, and the maximum amount allowed by your motherboard.

The operating system you use determines to a great extent the starting point for the amount of memory to have. Generally, the older or less powerful your operating system is, the smaller amount of RAM you need. Table 6.4 is the starting point for calculating memory requirements. Remember that as you want to run more applications simultaneously and the higher the application function (such as gaming or photo/video/sound manipulation), the more memory you will need. Also note that the memory recommendations shown in Table 6.4 are not the minimum requirements listed by the operating system creators. Notice that Apple computers (OS X) have similar memory recommendations to PCs.

TABLE 6.4   Minimum operating system starting memory recommendations

Operating system	Minimum amount of RAM to start calculations
Windows Vista/Windows 7	1GB
Windows 8/10	1GB (32-bit)/2GB (64-bit)
Mac OS X Mountain Lion/ Mavericks/Yosemite/El Capitan	2GB
Linux	Depends on version (some as little as 64MB)

When upgrading memory, you need to know a couple of key pieces of information:

> How much memory are you starting with?
> How many motherboard RAM slots are currently being used and are there any slots free?
> What is the maximum amount of memory that your motherboard supports?

TECH TIP

Windows might have memory limitations

Even if the motherboard allows more memory, your operating system has limitations. Upgrade the operating system if this is the case. Table 6.5 shows the Windows memory limits.

TABLE 6.5   Windows Vista/7/8/10 memory limits

Operating system	32-bit version limit	64-bit version limit
Vista/7 Starter edition	1GB (Vista)/2GB (7)	N/A
Vista/7 Home Basic	4GB	8GB
Vista/7 Home Premium	4GB	16GB
Vista/7 Business/Professional/Enterprise/Ultimate	4GB	128GB (Vista)/192GB (7)
8 RT	4GB	N/A
8	4GB	128GB
8 Professional/Enterprise	4GB	512GB
10 Home	4GB	128GB
10 Pro/Enterprise	4GB	2TB

To determine how much memory, use Windows Explorer (Vista/7) or File Explorer (8/10). In Windows Vista/7 right-click *Computer > Properties*. In Windows 8/10 right-click (or tap and hold briefly) *This PC > Properties*. Or, in any version of Windows, access the *System Information* window from a command prompt by typing `msinfo32` and pressing (Enter). Scroll down to see the memory information. Figure 6.5 shows how a computer system currently has 24GB of RAM installed (24.0GB Total Physical Memory).

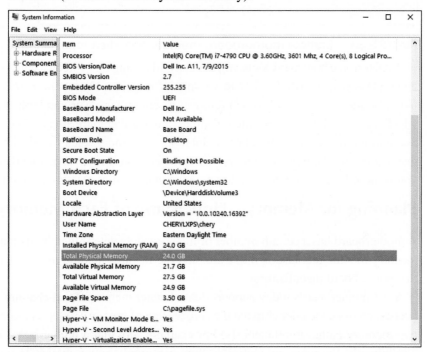

FIGURE 6.5   System Information window

CHAPTER 6

TECH TIP

Every motherboard has a maximum

Each motherboard supports a maximum amount of memory. You must check the computer or motherboard documentation to see how much this is. There is not a workaround for this limitation. If you want more memory than the motherboard allows, you must upgrade to a different motherboard.

Figure 6.6 shows a sample advertisement for a micro-ATX motherboard. The *Specifications* tab commonly shows the type of memory supported (sometimes it shows the exact speeds supported), the maximum amount of memory, and the number of memory slots.

Overview	Specifications	Warranty

Specifications

Motherboard Specifications	
Motherboard Type	Desktop
Processor Socket	Intel
Processor Interface	LGA1150
Form Factor	Micro ATX
Processors Supported	Intel® Core™ i3, i5, i7, Pentium, Celeron, Xeon
Chipset	
Northbridge	Intel H81 Express
Memory	
Memory Type	DDR3
Maximum Memory Supported	16GB
Number of Slots	2

FIGURE 6.6   Sample motherboard memory specifications

To determine how many slots you are currently using and whether you have any free, you need to either (1) access the BIOS/UEFI to see this information; (2) use the *Task Manager > Performance* tab in Windows 7, 8, or 10; or (3) remove the computer cover and look at the motherboard to see which memory slots have installed modules and whether there are any free slots. Some BIOS/UEFI Setup programs show the number of slots. Some memory sales websites have a software program that determines the type of memory you are using and makes recommendations. However, because you want to be a proficient technician, you can determine this for yourself.

Planning for Memory—How Many of Each Memory Type?

A motherboard has a certain number of memory slots determined by its manufacturer. The type of memory module that inserts into a slot and the features that the module has are all determined by the motherboard manufacturer.

Most motherboards today support dual-channel memory. **Dual-channel** means that the motherboard memory controller chip handles processing of memory requests more efficiently by handling two memory paths simultaneously. For example, say that a motherboard has four memory slots. Traditionally, the memory controller chip, commonly called the MCH (memory controller hub), had one channel through which all data from the four slots traveled. With dual-channeling, the four slots are divided into two channels with each channel having two slots each. Figure 6.7 shows this concept.

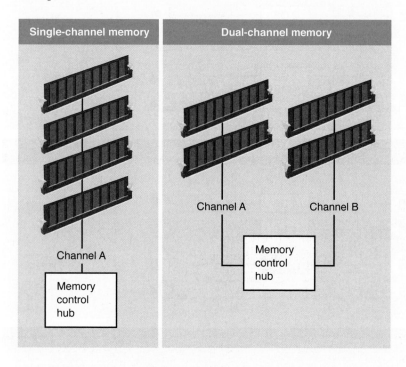

FIGURE 6.7   Dual-channel memory

Dual-channeling increases a system's performance. However, it speeds things up only if the memory modules match exactly—same memory type, same memory features, same speed, and same capacity. Note that on some motherboards, the memory modules on Channel A and Channel B do not have to have the same capacities, but the total capacity of the memory module in Channel A should match the total capacity of the memory modules installed in Channel B. Some motherboards require this. Figure 6.8 illustrates this concept.

TECH TIP

Dual-channel should use exact memory module pairs

Channel A and Channel B (sometimes labeled Channel 0 and Channel 1) should have matching memory modules. Buy a kit (a package of pre-tested memory modules that are guaranteed to work together) to ensure that the two modules are the same.

Notice in Figure 6.8 that in the first example, two identical memory modules are inserted. One memory module is in Channel A, and the other in Channel B. Motherboard manufacturers frequently require that the memory modules match in all respects—manufacturer, timing, and capacity—in order to support dual-channeling.

In the next section of Figure 6.8, three DIMMs are used. Some manufacturers support dual-channeling with three DIMMS, but you should always check the motherboard or system documentation to ensure that this is the case. Another example that is not shown in the figure is when an uneven amount of memory is installed in Channel A and Channel B. For example, Channel A has 2GB, and Channel B has a 1GB memory module. Some motherboards can dual-channel for the first 1GB. But only if the motherboard supports this can dual-channeling be achieved.

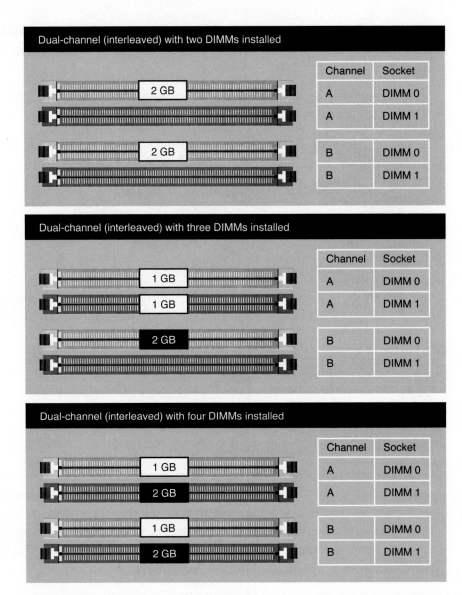

FIGURE 6.8 The total capacity of the memory module installed in Channel A should match the total capacity in Channel B

In the last section shown in Figure 6.8, all four DIMMs are installed. Notice how the Channel A total capacity matches the Channel B total capacity (3GB in both channels, for a total of 6GB). When dual-channeling, buy memory modules in pairs from a single source. Memory vendors sell them this way.

TECH TIP

Beware of RAM over 4GB

Do not install over 4GB on a computer with a 32-bit operating system such as 32-bit Windows. The operating system will not be able to recognize anything over 4GB. As a matter of fact, even when a system has 4GB installed, the 32-bit operating system shows the installed amount as slightly less than 4GB because some of that memory space is used for devices attached to the PCI/PCIe bus.

To plan for the correct amount of memory, you must refer to the motherboard documentation, and each motherboard is different. An example helps with this concept. Figure 6.9 shows a motherboard layout with four memory slots that has different labeling than shown in Figure 6.8. Remember that motherboard manufacturers can label their motherboards any way they want. This is part of why documentation is so important.

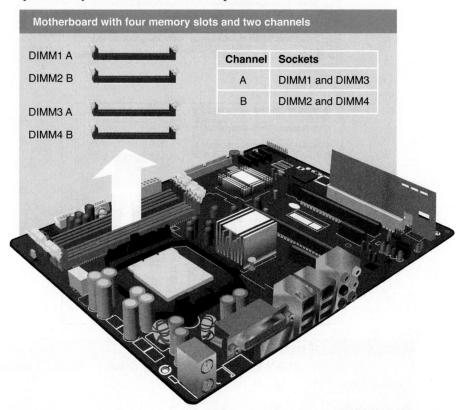

FIGURE 6.9   Motherboard with four memory slots and two channels

The motherboard in Figure 6.9 allows 512MB, 1GB, and 2GB unbuffered non-ECC DDR2-533 240-pin DIMMs, for a maximum of 8GB. Pretend the customer wants 2GB of RAM. What could you do? How many memory modules do you buy, and what capacities? Table 6.6 shows the possible solutions. The best solution is the second one because it has the largest-capacity chips taking advantage of dual-channeling, with slots left over for more upgrading.

TABLE 6.6   Possible solutions

Solution	Number and size of memory module(s) needed
1	Four 512MB DIMMs installed in DIMM1, DIMM2, DIMM3, and DIMM4 slots (dual-channeling)
2*	Two 1GB DIMMs installed in DIMM1 and DIMM2 slots (dual-channeling)
3	Two 1GB DIMMs installed in DIMM1 and DIMM3 slots (not dual-channeling)
4	One 2GB DIMM installed in DIMM1 (not dual-channeling)

*Best solution

Many newer motherboards and server motherboards support **triple-channel** memory, where three memory modules work together, or **quadruple-channel** memory, where four memory modules are accessed simultaneously. Figure 6.10 shows a motherboard that has six memory expansion slots and supports triple-channeling. Labs at the end of this chapter help you with these concepts.

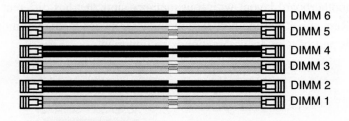

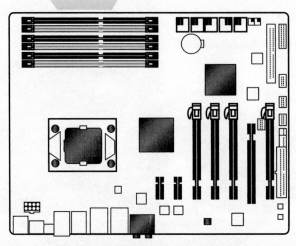

Dual-channel Configuration						
	DIMM 1	DIMM 2	DIMM 3	DIMM 4	DIMM 5	DIMM 6
Two modules	X		X			
Four modules	X	X	X	X		

Triple-channel Configuration						
	DIMM 1	DIMM 2	DIMM 3	DIMM 4	DIMM 5	DIMM 6
Three modules	X		X		X	
Six modules	X	X	X	X	X	X

FIGURE 6.10   Motherboard with six memory slots and three channels

Planning for Memory—Researching and Buying Memory

The researching and buying step of planning for a memory installation/upgrade is the step most likely to make your head spin. Different websites list memory differently. Some give you too much information and some too little. A few, such as Kingston Technology (http://www.kingston.com) and Crucial (http://www.crucial.com), specialize in memory and make it as painless as possible. Nevertheless, as a technician, you should be familiar with all aspects of memory and memory advertisements.

A confusing aspect of buying memory is memory speed. Memory speed can be represented as MHz or the PC rating. The higher the number, the faster the speed of the module.

To understand memory, it is best to look at some examples. Table 6.7 shows sample memory advertisements.

TABLE 6.7   Sample DIMM advertisements

Memory module	Advertisement
2GB	DDR3 PC3-10600 • CL=9 • UNBUFFERED • NON-ECC • DDR3-1333 • 1.35V • 256Meg×64
2GB	DDR3 PC3-12800E • CL=11 • REGISTERED • ECC • DDR3-1600 • 1.35V • 256Meg×72
2GB kit (1GB×2)	DDR3 PC3-10600 • CL=9 • REGISTERED • ECC • DDR3-1333 • 1.5V • 128Meg×72
2GB	DDR2 PC2-5300FB • CL=5 • FULLY BUFFERED • ECC • DDR2-667 • 1.8V • 256Meg×72

Notice in Table 6.7 (as in most memory advertisements) that the memory capacity is shown first. The third advertisement is a kit for a motherboard that has dual-channeling capabilities. It includes two 1GB memory modules, for a total of a 2GB memory gain. Also pay attention to the type of memory module being advertised. Notice in Table 6.7 that the first three memory modules are DDR3 and show the PC3 rating. Later, the advertisement also shows the effective data transfer rate of 1333MHz or 1600MHz. Some vendors add an E to the PC3 number to show an ECC module or an F or FB to the PC3 number to show that the module has the fully buffered feature.

Another listing in the memory advertisement shown in Table 6.7 is the **CL rating**. CL (column address strobe [CAS] latency) is the amount of time (clock cycles) that passes before the processor moves on to the next memory address. RAM is made up of cells where data is held. A cell is the intersection of a row and a column. Think of it as a spreadsheet application. The CAS signal picks which memory column to select, and a signal called RAS (row address strobe) picks which row to select. The intersection of the two is where the data is stored.

TECH TIP

CL ratings and a track race

The lower the CL rating, the faster the memory. Think of access time like a track race—the person with the lowest time wins the race and is considered to be the fastest. Chips with a lower CL rating are faster than those with higher numbers.

Motherboard manufacturers sometimes list a minimum CL or CAS latency value for memory modules. Motherboard documentation, memory magazine advertisements, and online memory retailers list the CL rating as a series of numbers, such as 3-1-1-1. The first number is the CL rating—a CL3, in this example. The 3-1-1-1 is more detailed in that for a 32-bit transfer, it takes three clock cycles to send the first byte (8 bits), but the next 3 bytes are sent using one clock cycle each. In other words, it takes six clock cycles to transfer the 32 bits. Note that DDR3 CL ratings are higher than the DDR2 advertisement. Sample DDR3 ratings are 9-9-9-24 or 11-11-11-28.

TECH TIP

Buy the fastest type of memory a motherboard allows

Buying memory that is faster than the motherboard allows does no good. This is like taking a race car on a one-lane unpaved road: The car has the ability to go faster, but it is not feasible with the type of road being used. Sometimes you must buy faster memory because the older memory is not sold. This is all right, as long as it is the correct type, such as DDR2, DDR3, or DDR4.

Also notice in Table 6.7 that memory features are listed—fully buffered, unbuffered, and registered. Be sure that the type of memory for which you planned is the type you are researching to buy. The voltage level for the memory module is shown (these are standard values), as is the capacity. With the capacity, if you see the number 64 at the end, the module is a non-parity one. If you see 72, the memory module uses ECC.

Usually, you can mix CL memory modules

Most systems allow mixing of CL modules; for example, a motherboard could have a memory module rated for CL8 and a different memory module rated for CL9. However, when mixing memory modules, the system will run at the slower memory speed (CL9).

Installing Memory Overview

Memory is an important part of computer performance. Installation includes planning (see Figure 6.11), installing, and possibly removing some older modules. Lack of planning can lead to less than optimal performance.

FIGURE 6.11   Plan the memory installation

The following is the best method to determine which memory chips to install in each bank:

Step 1. Determine which chip capacities can be used for the system. Look in the documentation included with the motherboard or computer for this information.

Step 2. Determine how much memory is needed. Ask the users which operating system is installed and which applications they are using (or look yourself). Refer to documentation for each application to determine the amount of RAM recommended. Plan for growth.

Step 3. Determine the capacity of the chips that go in each bank by drawing a diagram of the system, planning the memory population on paper, and referring to the documentation of the system or motherboard.

Depending on the type of motherboard, the number of banks available on the motherboard, whether the computer memory is being upgraded, and whether the memory is a new installation, some memory modules might need to be removed in order to put higher-capacity ones into the bank. Look at what is already installed in the system, refer to the documentation, and remove any existing modules as necessary to upgrade the memory.

TECH TIP

Memory safety reminder

Before installing a memory module, power off the computer, disconnect the power cord from the back of the computer, and use proper anti-static procedures. Memory modules are especially susceptible to ESD. If ESD damages a memory module, a problem might not appear immediately and could be intermittent and hard to diagnose.

Removing/Installing Memory

When removing a DIMM and using proper ESD-prevention techniques, push down on the retaining tabs that clasp over the DIMM. Be careful not to overextend the tabs when pushing on them. If a plastic tab breaks, the only solution is to replace the motherboard. The DIMM lifts slightly out of the socket. Always ensure you are grounded to prevent ESD by using an anti-static wrist strap or maintaining contact with metal with a bare part of your arm (self-grounding). Lift the module out of the socket once it is released. Figure 6.12 shows how to remove a DIMM.

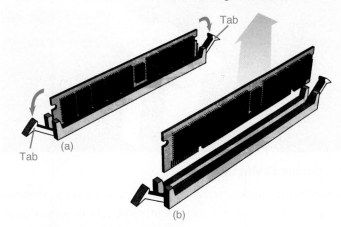

FIGURE 6.12   DIMM removal

A DIMM has one or more notches on the bottom where the gold or tin contacts are located. The DIMM inserts into the memory socket only one way. Verify that the notches on the bottom of the module align with the notches in the motherboard socket. The DIMM will not insert into the memory socket unless it is oriented properly.

A DIMM is inserted straight down into the socket, not at a tilt like a laptop module. Make sure the side tabs are pulled out before you insert the DIMM and close the tabs over the DIMM once it is firmly inserted into the socket. If the DIMM does not go into the slot easily, do not force it and check the notch or notches for correct alignment. However, once the DIMM is aligned correctly into the slot, push the DIMM firmly into the slot and the tabs should naturally close over the DIMM or on the sides of the DIMM. Figure 6.13 illustrates how to insert a DIMM. Figure 6.14 shows a close-up of how the tab needs to fit securely in the memory module notch.

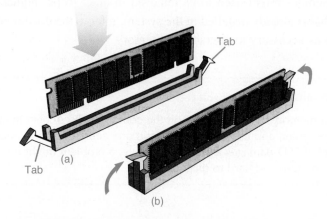

FIGURE 6.13   DIMM installation

FIGURE 6.14   Secure DIMM tab

Today's motherboards automatically recognize new memory; however, some advanced BIOS/UEFI options exist for tweaking memory performance. With some computers, the Setup program can be used to select parity, non-parity, or ECC options. Always refer to the motherboard or the computer system documentation.

> **TECH TIP**
>
> **POST error codes are normal after a memory installation/upgrade**
>
> Some computers show a POST error message or automatically go into the Setup program. This is normal. The important thing to notice during POST is that the memory shown in BIOS/UEFI should equal the amount of memory installed.

Adding More Cache/RAM

Most computers today have cache built into the processor. The motherboard manufacturer determines whether any cache can be installed. Check the documentation included with the motherboard or computer to determine the amount of cache (SRAM).

Adding more RAM can make a noticeable difference in computer performance (up to a point, of course). When a computer user is sitting in front of a computer waiting for a document to appear or waiting to go to a different location within a document, it might be time to install more RAM. If you have several opened applications on the taskbar, click one of them. If you have to wait several seconds before it appears, it might be a good idea to upgrade your RAM.

Windows Disk Caching

Virtual memory is a method of using hard drive space as if it were RAM. Virtual memory allows the operating system to run larger applications and manage multiple applications that are loaded simultaneously. The amount of hard drive space used is dynamic—it increases or decreases as needed. If the system begins to page frequently and is constantly swapping data from RAM to the hard drive, the cache size automatically shrinks.

> **TECH TIP**
>
> **Hard drive swap file tips**
>
> If multiple hard drives are available, a technician might want to move the swap file to a different drive. Always put the swap file on the fastest hard drive unless that hard drive lacks space. It is best to keep the swap file on a hard drive that does not contain the operating system. You can configure the computer to place the swap file on multiple hard drives. The amount of virtual memory is dynamically created by the operating system and does not normally need to be set manually. If manually set, the minimum amount should be equal to the amount of RAM installed.

A **swap file** is a block of hard drive space that applications use like RAM. Other names for the swap file include page file and paging file. Look back to Figure 6.5 and see in the System Information screen the data on Total Virtual Memory, Available Virtual Memory, and Page File Space. For optimum performance in any Windows operating system, set aside as much free hard drive space as possible to allow ample room for virtual memory and caching. Keep the hard drive cleaned of temporary files and outdated files/applications.

To adjust the virtual memory size, perform the following:

> In Vista/Windows 7, access the *System and Security* Control Panel > *System* > *Performance Information and Tools* link > *Advanced tools* > *Adjust the appearance and performance of Windows* link > *Continue* if a user account control (UAC) dialog box appears > *Advanced* tab > *Change* button. Change the parameters and click the *OK* button twice.

> In Windows 8, access the *System and Security* Control Panel > *System* > *Advanced system settings* link > *Advanced* tab. Locate and select the *Settings* button from within the *Performance* section > *Advanced* tab > *Change* button. Change the parameters and click the *OK* button twice.

> In Windows 10, access the *Start* button > *Settings* > in the *Find a setting* search textbox, type `performance` > select the *Adjust the appearance and performance of Windows* link > *Advanced* tab > *Change* button. Change the parameters and click the *OK* button twice.

32-bit Windows uses 32-bit demand-paged virtual memory, and each process gets 4GB of address space divided into two 2GB sections. One 2GB section is shared with the rest of the system, whereas the other 2GB section is reserved for one application. All the memory space is divided into 4KB blocks of memory called **pages**. The operating system allocates as much available RAM as possible to an application. Then the operating system swaps or pages the application to and from the temporary swap file as needed. The operating system determines the optimum setting for this swap file; however, the swap file size can be changed. Figure 6.15 illustrates how Windows uses virtual memory.

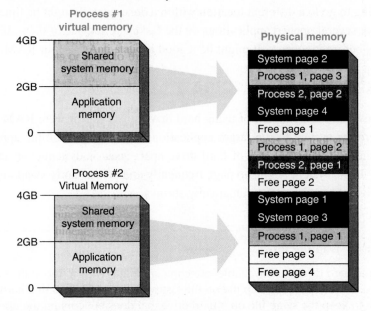

FIGURE 6.15   Windows virtual memory usage

In Figure 6.15, notice that each application has its own memory space. The Memory Pager maps the virtual memory addresses from the individual processes' address space to physical pages in the computer's memory chips. Figure 6.16 shows how all this relates to RAM and hard drive space.

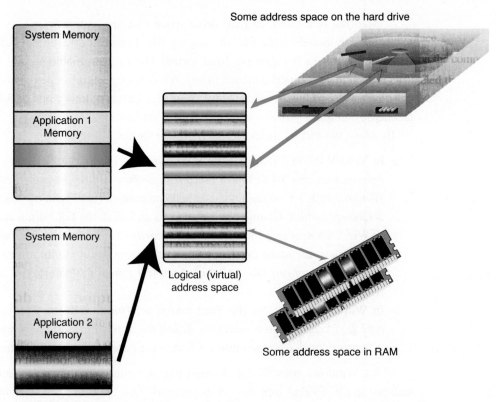

FIGURE 6.16   Virtual memory

32-bit Windows has a natural limitation of 4GB of physical memory. Physical address extension (PAE) is supported only on some motherboards and only relevant when 32-bit Windows operating systems are being used. PAE allows up to 64GB or 128GB of physical memory to be used. You can view whether a system supports PAE by viewing the computer's properties through Windows Explorer (Windows Vista/7) File Explorer (Windows 8/10).

Windows 64-bit processes are similar except Microsoft doesn't split virtual memory evenly between shared system memory and an application. Instead, on a desktop computer, the application portion is limited to 8TB of the 16EB theoretical maximum.

Monitoring Memory Usage under Windows

Windows has a **Performance utility** in Task Manager to monitor memory usage. To access Task Manager, press Ctrl+Alt+Delete. Select the *Performance* tab, which has graphs that visually demonstrate the CPU and memory usage. Figure 6.17 shows the Task Manager *Performance* tab, and Table 6.8 lists the Task Manager *Performance* tab fields.

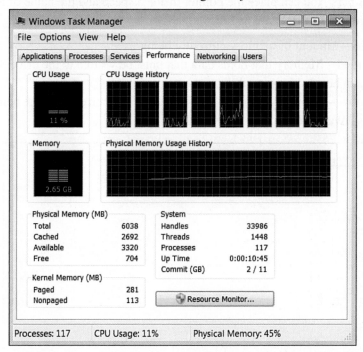

FIGURE 6.17   Windows 7 Task Manager Performance tab

TABLE 6.8   Windows 7 Task Manager Performance tab fields

Field	Description
Total Physical Memory	The amount of RAM installed.
Cached Physical Memory	Memory pages that could be written to disk and be made available.
Available Physical Memory	The amount of memory (physical and paged) for application use.
Free Physical Memory	The amount of available physical RAM.
Paged Kernel Memory	Memory that can be used by applications as needed that can be copied to the paging file (which frees up RAM).
Nonpaged Kernel Memory	Memory available only to the operating system and stays in RAM.
Handles	The number of resources the operating system is currently dealing with.
Threads	The number of objects contained within currently running processes that are executing program instructions.

CHAPTER 6

Field	Description
Processes	A running executable program, such as Notepad or a service that is currently running.
Up Time	How long the system has been up.
Commit	A snapshot of virtual memory requests—note that if the commit charge exceeds the total physical memory, the system is probably paging to the hard drive too much. Add more RAM.

Windows 8 and 10 have a redesigned Task Manager, as shown in Figure 6.18, and clarified in Table 6.9. Note that in order to see the memory-related data, you must click the memory option in the left pane. In the section titled "Memory composition," there are several sections separated by vertical bars. You can place the pointer inside a space and the name of the section appears. The sections from left to right are as follows:

> In use—Amount of memory currently being used
> Modified—Memory that holds data that must be written to the drive before the memory location can be used by something else
> Standby—Amount of memory that is cached and currently is not being used
> Free—Available memory to be used

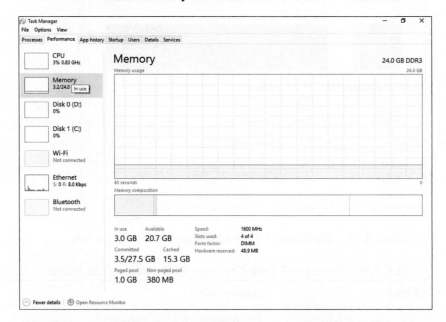

FIGURE 6.18   Windows 8/10 Task Manager Performance tab—Memory

TABLE 6.9   Windows 8/10 Task Manager Performance tab memory-related fields

Field	Description
In use	The amount of memory currently being used by applications, the operating system, drivers, and processes.
Available	The amount of physical memory for application/operating system use.
Committed	This is shown as two numbers. The first number is how much memory the operating system has identified that needs memory (and that might get removed or paged out of RAM if other, more important, processes need the space). The second number is the amount of physical and virtual memory available.

Field	Description
Cached	The memory space that includes data that needs to be written to disk before being available as well as cached data that is currently not being used.
Paged pool	Memory set aside for operating system functions or device drivers that could be written to disk if necessary.
Non-paged pool	Memory set aside for operating system functions or device drivers that must remain in physical memory (cannot be paged out).
Speed	Speed of the RAM chips.
Slots used	Number of memory slots used for memory modules and total number of slots.
Form factor	Type of memory module such as DIMM or small outline DIMM (SO-DIMM) used in laptops. Chapter 11 covers mobile devices and SO-DIMMs.
Hardware reserved	Memory reserved for device drivers or firmware that cannot be used by Windows for any other function.

Older Applications under Windows

Older applications are sometimes a challenge in the newer versions of Windows. Some dated applications do not operate in the newer Windows versions because these programs frequently make direct calls to hardware, which Vista, 7, 8, and 10 do not allow. These programs might also require that you change the color depth and resolution settings through the Display Control Panel.

For Windows Vista and higher, Microsoft states that some older software might not run properly and offers **Compatibility mode**. Right-click the application icon from the *Start* menu or right-click the program executable file and select *Properties*. Use the *Compatibility* tab to select the Windows version for which the application was written. If you do not know the version, you can select the *Run compatibility troubleshooter* button, and then select the *Try recommended settings* link. Figure 6.19 shows the Compatibility tab.

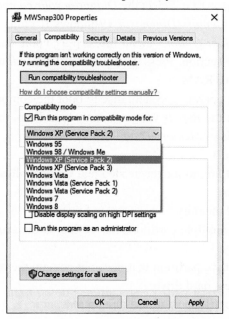

FIGURE 6.19   Windows Compatibility tab

You can also configure virtual machines using virtualization software such as Microsoft's Virtual PC, Hyper-V, Oracle VM VirtualBox, or VMware Workstation to run older operating systems as well as run older applications. A **virtual machine** (VM) allows you to reduce hardware costs by running multiple operating systems simultaneously on a single computer (without one interfering with the other). Virtualization used to be used only with servers, but many home computers and corporate desktops are virtualized today.

Troubleshooting Memory Problems

You can get "out of memory" errors, POST code errors, motherboard diagnostic lights or codes, system slowdowns, and application locking due to memory problems with any operating system. With any of these problems, no matter which operating system is being used, check the amount of available memory and free hard drive space. Sometimes you must close all applications, reboot the computer, and open only the application that was running when the out of memory error occurred because some applications do not release the memory space they hold. The following tips and troubleshooting steps help with memory management:

> Add more RAM. To see the amount of physical memory (RAM) currently installed, access *Windows Explorer* or *File Explorer*, right-click (or tap and hold briefly) *Computer* or *This PC*, and select *Properties*.
> If you just installed new memory and an error appears, this is normal. Enter *Setup* because the system BIOS/UEFI knows something has changed.
> If you just installed new memory and the computer will not boot, check your installation by carefully pushing harder on the memory module (after shutting down and removing power, of course) to ensure that the module is fully seated into the slot. Check for loosened cables near the memory module(s). Ensure that you are installing the right memory type. You might need to upgrade your BIOS/UEFI so that your motherboard recognizes the increased amount of RAM.
> Use the **Windows Memory Diagnostics Tool**, by using one of the following methods:
  > Use the *System and Maintenance* (Vista) or *System and Security* (7) Control Panel > *Administrative Tools* > *Windows Memory Diagnostic* link. In Windows 8 or 10, search using the words memory diagnostic. Select the *Diagnose your computer's memory problems* (Windows 8) or *Windows Memory Diagnostic* (Windows 10) link.
  > Boot into the *Advanced Boot Options* menu (press F8 upon startup). Press Esc. Press Tab to move to the *Tools* section. Press Enter to use the *Windows Memory Diagnostics Tool* to thoroughly test your RAM.
  > Use the original Windows operating system disc to boot the computer. Enter the language requirements and then use the *Repair your computer* link. From the *System Recovery Options* window, select *Windows Memory Diagnostic Tool*.
  > Use the command mdsched.
> Delete files/applications that are no longer needed and close applications that are not being used. Empty the Recycle Bin.
> Adjust the size of the virtual memory.
> Do not put the swap file on multiple partitions that reside on the same hard drive. Use multiple hard drives, if necessary.
> Put the swap file on a hard drive partition that does not contain the operating system.
> Put the swap file on the fastest hard drive.
> Remove the desktop wallpaper scheme or use a plain one.

> Adjust your Temporary Internet Files setting. From Internet Explorer (Windows Vista, 7, or 8), select the *Tools > Internet Options > Settings* button. Adjust how much drive space is set aside for caching Web pages. For Microsoft Edge in Windows 10, search for Internet Explorer (not Microsoft Edge) and use the same directions for prior Windows to adjust the drive space setting.

> Defragment the hard drive. See Chapter 7 for the steps.

TECH TIP

Upgrading memory is one of the easiest ways to help with performance issues

Keep in mind that sometimes there is nothing to do but buy more RAM—but try the previously mentioned tips first.

If you receive a message that SPD device data is missing or inconclusive, your motherboard is looking for SPD data that it cannot receive from the memory module. If this is a new module, ensure that it supports SPD. If it is an older module, you need to replace one of your memory modules.

POST usually detects a problem with a memory chip, and most systems show an error code or message. The motherboard might also contain diagnostic lights or a code. If either occurs, turn off the computer, remove the cover, and press down on any memory modules and reboot. Another option is to clean the memory module slots with compressed air and reinstall the module. The key to good memory chip troubleshooting is to divide and conquer. Narrow the problem to a suspected memory module and then swap banks, if possible. Keep in mind that most memory problems are not in the hardware but in the software applications and operating system.

TECH TIP

Adding more memory did not allow my application to load or run faster

Today's operating systems rely almost as much on hard drive space as they do on RAM because of multitasking. Lack of hard drive space is almost as bad as not having enough RAM.

Flash Memory

Flash memory is a type of nonvolatile, solid-state memory that holds data even when the computer power is off. PCs use flash memory as a replacement for the BIOS chip. Network devices, smartphones, and tablets use flash memory to store the operating system and instructions. Some tablets can use external flash media for storage. Digital cameras use flash memory to store pictures; scanners use flash memory to store images; printers use flash memory to store fonts. Flash memory does not have to be refreshed like DRAM, and it does not need constant power like SRAM. Figure 6.20 shows various flash memory.

USB flash drives (sometimes called thumb drives, memory bars, or memory sticks) allow storage up to 256GB, with higher capacities expected. Refer to Figure 6.20. The blue and lime green colored items are USB flash drives. Flash drives connect to a USB port and are normally recognized by the Windows operating system. After attaching the drive to a USB port, a drive letter is assigned and Windows Explorer or File Explorer can be used to copy files to the drive.

FIGURE 6.20 Flash memory

The number-one cause of flash drive failure is improper removal

When you are finished using a flash drive, double-click the *Remove Hardware* icon located in the notification area. The icon has a white check mark on a green field. You might have to click the left arrow or up arrow to see this icon. Click *Safely Remove Hardware and Eject Media*. Select the appropriate flash drive. When a message appears that you can safely remove the drive, remove the flash drive from the USB port.

Various models are available, including drives that fit on a neck chain, inside watches, and on a key ring. Security features that are available on flash drives include password protection to the drive and data encryption. Flash drives are a very good memory storage solution, and they are inexpensive and easy to use. Figure 6.21 shows the interior of a flash drive. Chapter 11 goes into more detail on the types of flash memory used with such devices.

FIGURE 6.21 Inside a USB flash drive

Memory is one of the most critical components of a computer, and it is important for a technician to be well versed in the different memory technologies. Because memory is one of the most common upgrades, becoming proficient and knowledgeable about populating memory is important. Lab exercises at the end of the chapter help prepare you for the workforce and installing/upgrading memory.

SOFT SKILLS—TEAMWORK

Technicians tend not to like working in teams as much as they like working on their own. Much of a technician's job is done alone. However, a technician normally has one or more peers, a supervisor, and a network of partners involved with the job such as suppliers, subcontractors, and part-time help. It is easy to have tunnel vision in a technical support job and lose sight of the mission of the business. Many technical jobs have the main purpose of generating revenue—solving people's computer and network problems for the purpose of making money. Other technicians have more of a back-office support role—planning, installing, configuring, maintaining, and troubleshooting technologies the business uses to make money.

Technicians must focus on solving the customer's problems and ensuring that the customer feels his or her problem has been solved professionally and efficiently. However, you cannot lose sight of the business-first mentality; remember that you play a support role whether you generate revenue or not. You are a figure on someone's balance sheet, and you need to keep your skills and attitudes finely tuned to be valuable to the company. No matter how good you are at your job, you are still better to a company if you are part of a team than if you're on your own. Being the person who is late, takes off early, chats too much with customers, blames others, and so on, is not being a team member. If you are going to be late for work or leave early, inform your supervisor and co-workers so they can take care of any issues that arise. If you are going to be late for a customer appointment, contact the customer and let him or her know you are running late.

Technicians need to be good team players and see themselves as a reflection of their company when on the job (see Figure 6.22). **Teamwork** is part of the skill set that employers seek as much as they want you to have technical skills. Think of ways that you can practice teamwork even as a student, and refine those skills when you join the workforce

FIGURE 6.22 Teamwork

Chapter Summary

> Memory on a motherboard is SDRAM, a type of RAM that is cheaper and slower than SRAM, the type of memory inside the CPU and processor housing.

> A DDR module fits in a DDR slot. A DDR2 module requires a DDR2 slot; a DDR3 module requires a DDR3 slot; a DDR4 module requires a DDR4 slot.

> Unbuffered memory is the memory normally installed in computers.

> ECC is used for error checking and is commonly found in high-end computers and servers. An older method of error checking was called parity.

> The CL rating or the timing sequence first number shows how fast the processor can access data in sequential memory locations. The lower the first number, the faster the access.

> SPD is a technology used so the memory module can communicate specifications to the BIOS/UEFI.

> Double-sided memory is one module that acts like two modules (not that it has chips on both sides even though it most likely does). A motherboard must support using double-sided modules.

> Before installing memory, plan your strategy: Read the manual to see the type of memory; determine the total amount of memory; determine whether any memory is to be removed; determine the memory to purchase; and be mindful of getting the most out of your memory by implementing dual-, triple-, or even quadruple-channeling.

> When implementing dual-, triple-, or quadruple-channeling, buy matching memory modules.

> Any 32-bit operating system is limited to 4GB of memory.

> Particular versions of Windows have memory limitations. For example, Windows 7 Starter edition is limited to 2GB, but any of the other Windows 7 versions can go to 4GB for the 32-bit versions. 64-bit versions allow much more memory to be installed and accessed.

> RAM is very susceptible to ESD events. Use proper anti-static-handling procedures, including using an anti-static wrist strap.

> Before removing or installing memory, disconnect the power cord and remove the battery on a mobile device.

> Having as much RAM in the system as possible is an important performance factor, and so is having free hard drive space because hard drive space is used as memory. This is called virtual memory, and the information stored temporarily on a hard drive is stored in an area known as a page file, paging file, or swap file. The swap file should be on the fastest drive that has the most free storage.

> Use Task Manager to monitor memory performance.

> Use POST, motherboard LED/display output codes, BIOS/UEFI diagnostics, and the Windows Memory Diagnostic Tool to diagnose memory problems.

> Flash media is used to provide memory or additional storage space for computing devices and includes USB flash drives.

> A technician is part of a business and should contribute to the team. A technician should professionally represent a company.

A+ CERTIFICATION EXAM TIPS

✓ Know how to calculate what memory is needed for an upgrade or a new install.

✓ Be able to identify memory slots on a motherboard.

✓ Know how to populate memory when dual- or triple-channeling is being implemented.

✓ The first thing to do when populating memory is to consult the motherboard documentation.

✓ Be able to describe the difference between buffered and unbuffered memory, parity and non-parity, ECC and non-ECC modules, as well as single-sided and double-sided modules.

✓ Know that memory chips are especially susceptible to ESD and how to prevent ESD damage when installing or removing memory.

✓ Remember that if any application is slow to respond, the computer may need more RAM.

✓ Review the troubleshooting symptoms and tips. Know that adding memory is one of the easiest ways to improve computer performance.

✓ Know when and how to use Compatibility mode and Windows Memory Diagnostics.

✓ Keep in mind that the following professionalism skills are part of the 220-902 exam: (1) maintain a positive attitude and (2) be on time (or, if late, contact the customer). Do not forget to review the professionalism skills.

Key Terms

CHAPTER 6

Review Questions

The following specifications for motherboard RAM are used for Questions 1–5:

Considering the features that are shown and the documentation provided, which memory features are needed for a desktop computer with the following specifications?

> Four 240-pin DDR3 SDRAM DIMM sockets arranged in two channels
> Support for DDR3 1600+MHz, DDR3 1333MHz, and DDR3 1066MHz DIMMs
> Support for non-ECC memory
> Support for up to 16GB of system memory

1. Of the given features, which one(s) would be applicable to this computer? (Select all that apply.) Note that all memory is unbuffered unless specified.

    [unbuffered | registered | 204-pin SO-DIMM | 240-pin DDR2 DIMM | 240-pin DDR3 DIMM | ECC]

2. Say that this computer has 4GB of memory and four memory slots. Write all combinations of memory population in the slots.

    _____

3. [T | F] The memory used in this system does not perform error checking.

    _____

4. What does the statement "four 240-pin DDR3 SDRAM DIMM sockets arranged in two channels" mean?

    _____

    _____

5. Would there be an issue if this motherboard contained 6GB of RAM and the computer had 32-bit Windows 7 installed? If so, explain the issue.

    _____

    _____

Consider the following memory advertisements for desktop memory used in Questions 6, 7, 8, and 9:
> a. 2GB (1GB x 2) 240-pin DIMM PC2-6400 memory module
> b. 2GB DDR3 1600 DIMM
> c. 2GB ECC registered DDR2 SDRAM DIMM
> d. 4GB : 2 x 2GB DIMM 240-pin DDR2 800 MHz/PC2-6400 CL6 1.9-2.0V
> e. 4GB 1333MHz DDR3L ECC CL9 DIMM SR x8 1.35V with TS desktop memory
> f. 4G FB DDR2 800 memory PC2-5300 5-5-5-18
> g. 8GB kit (2 x 4GB) DDR3 DIMM (240-pin) 1333Mhz PC3-10600/PC3-10666 9-9-9-25 1.5v
> h. 16GB kit (2 x 8GB) 1600MHz DDR3 non-ECC CL9 DIMM XMP
> i. 16GB kit (2 x 8GB) 1600MHz DDR3 CL10 DIMM

6. In these advertisements, which DDR2 option would hold the most data in a single memory module and be best suited for a desktop computer?

    _____

    _____

    _____

    _____

7. In option e, what does the L in DDR3L mean?

    _____

    _____

    _____

8. A customer wants to dual-channel 8GB of RAM on a desktop computer. Which memory module(s) would be best to buy, given the following documentation from the motherboard manual? (Memory module slots are in order from closest to the CPU: 1, 3, 2, and 4.)

   > Do not install ECC memory modules.

   > If you remove your original memory modules from the computer during an upgrade, keep the old ones separate from any new modules you might have. If possible, do not pair an original module with a new module. Otherwise, the computer might not start properly.

   The memory configurations are as follows:

   > A pair of matched modules in DIMM connectors 1 and 2

   > A pair of matched modules in DIMM connectors 1 and 2 and another pair in connectors 3 and 4

   If you install mixed pairs, the memory modules function at the speed of the slowest memory module installed.

   _____

9. When comparing options h and i and imagining that both modules cost the same, which one would be the better purchase? Explain your reasoning.

   _____

   _____

10. What type of memory feature will be needed if data accuracy is paramount for a new computer? ECC

11. What is the minimum amount of RAM recommended to install 32-bit Windows 8?

    [512MB | 1GB | 2GB | 4GB]

12. What method is most effective for preventing an ESD event when installing RAM?

    a. placing the computer on an anti-static mat

    b. wearing an anti-static wrist strap

    c. staying in contact with an unpainted metal part of the computer

    d. wearing rubber-soled shoes and using the buddy system by having another technician standing by

13. What would be the first sign that a user would see that would indicate to a technician that more RAM was needed?

    a. The computer is slow to respond.

    b. The computer makes a ticking noise.

    c. A POST error message appears.

    d. A recommendation to use the *Windows Memory Diagnostics Tool* appeared.

14. How would a technician adjust Internet Explorer (Windows Vista, 7, and 8) for how much drive space is configured for caching web pages?

    a. Right-click *Computer* from *Windows Explorer/File Explorer > Manage*

    b. *Settings > Safety*

    c. [F8] on startup > *Windows Memory Diagnostics Tool*

    d. *Tools > Internet Options*

15. List one easy way to tell how much RAM is installed in a computer.

    _____

16. [T | F] A DDR4 DIMM can fit in a DDR3 expansion slot.

17. You have just added two new memory modules to a computer, but now the system will not boot and is beeping multiple times. What will you check first?

    _____

    _____

CHAPTER 6

18. Give an example of how a technician might show teamwork while working on a help desk.

   _____

   _____

19. A system already has installed two 1333MHz memory modules when a technician adds two more modules that operate at 1600MHz. What will be the result of this action?

   a. The computer won't boot.

   b. The computer might freeze at times.

   c. The memory will operate at the 1333MHz speed.

   d. All memory will operate at the 1600MHz speed.

20. A technician has received a complaint that a computer is not performing as well as it used to. Which Windows 8 tool would the technician get the user to open to QUICKLY tell how much RAM is currently being used by the open applications?

   [Performance Monitor | Device Manager | System Information Tool | Task Manager]

Exercises

Exercise 6.1 Configuring Memory on Paper

Objective: To be able to determine the correct amount and type of memory to install on a motherboard

Parts: Internet access or access to magazines or ads that show memory prices

Procedure: Refer to Figure 6.23 and Table 6.10 to answer the questions. This motherboard supports 533/667/800MHz DDR2 memory modules. The capacities supported are 1GB and 2GB for a total of 8GB maximum. It is not recommended to use a three DIMM configuration with this board. Memory channel speed is determined by the slowest DIMM populated in the system.

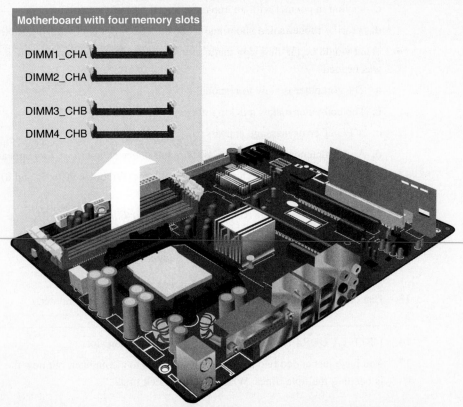

FIGURE 6.23   Motherboard with four memory slots and two channels

TABLE 6.10 Motherboard single-/dual-channel combinations

		Sockets			
Mode	**Scenario**	**DIMM1**	**DIMM2**	**DIMM3**	**DIMM4**
Single	1	Populated			
	2		Populated		
	3			Populated	
	4				Populated
Dual-channel	1	Populated		Populated	
	2		Populated		Populated
	3	Populated	Populated	Populated	Populated

Questions:

1. What memory modules are needed if the customer wants 3GB of RAM? What capacities and how many modules of each capacity are required?

_____

_____

_____

_____

2. Is triple-channeling supported by this motherboard?

_____

3. Using the Internet, a magazine, or a list of memory modules, determine the exact part numbers and quantities of memory modules that you would buy. List them with the location of where you obtained the information.

_____

_____

4. This motherboard already has 1GB of RAM installed in the DIMM1 slot. The customer would like to upgrade to 4GB total memory, use the existing module if possible, and use dual-channel. What memory modules are needed? What capacities and how many of each capacity are required?

_____

_____

_____

_____

5. What memory slots will be used to install the memory based on the information provided?

_____

_____

_____

6. What does the documentation mean when referencing DDR2 533/667/800MHz RAM?

_____

_____

CHAPTER 6

7.   How do you know which one of the 533, 667, or 800 types of modules to use?

_____

_____

_____

_____

_____

8.   Using the Internet, a magazine, or a provided list of memory modules, determine the exact part numbers and quantities of memory modules that you would buy. List them with the location of where you obtained the information.

_____

Exercise 6.2 Configuring Memory on Paper

Objective: To be able to determine the correct amount and type of memory to install on a motherboard

Parts: Internet access or access to magazines or ads that show memory prices

Procedure: Refer to Figure 6.24 and Table 6.11 to answer the questions. This motherboard supports the following memory configurations:

- Up to 2GB utilizing 256MB technology
- Up to 4GB utilizing 512MB or 1GB technology
- Up to 8GB utilizing 1GB technology

The desktop board supports either single- or dual-channel memory configurations. The board has four 240-pin DDR2 SDRAM DIMM connectors with gold-plated contacts. It provides support for unbuffered, non-registered single or double-sided DIMMs, non-ECC DDR2 533/667/800MHz memory, and Serial Presence Detect (SPD) memory only.

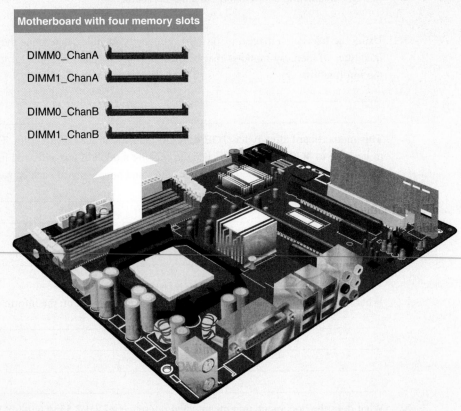

FIGURE 6.24   Motherboard with four memory slots and two channels

TABLE 6.11   Motherboard single-/dual-channel guidelines

Installed memory	Guidelines
2 DIMMs dual-channel	Install a matched pair of DIMMs equal in speed and size in DIMM0 of both Channel A and Channel B.
4 DIMMs dual-channel	Follow the directions for two DIMMs and add another matched pair of DIMMs in DIMM1 of both Channels A and B.
3 DIMMs dual-channel	Install a matched pair of DIMMs equal in speed and size in DIMM0 and DIMM1 of Channel A. Install a DIMM equal in speed and total size of the DIMMs installed in Channel A in either DIMM0 or DIMM1 of Channel B.
Single-channel	All other memory configurations result in single-channel memory operation.

Questions:

1.   How can this motherboard support 8GB of RAM with only four slots?

2.   What memory features, if any, are used? (Select all that apply.) [parity | non-parity | ECC | registered | fully buffered | unbuffered | SPD]

3.   What memory modules are needed if the customer wants 3GB of dual-channel RAM? (What capacities and how many of each capacity are required?)

4.   What memory slots will be used to install the memory based on the information provided?

5.   Using the Internet, a magazine, or a list of memory modules, determine the exact part numbers and quantities of memory modules that you would buy. List them with the location of where you obtained the information.

6.   Will it matter if the motherboard has tin contacts in the memory slots? Why or why not?

7.   Can DDR memory modules be used with this motherboard? How can you tell?

8.   If this motherboard already has 1GB of RAM installed in the DIMM0_ChanA slot and the customer would like to upgrade to 2GB of dual-channel RAM, what memory modules are needed? (What capacities and how many of each capacity are required?)

9.   What suggestions, if any, would you make to the customer before researching prices?

10. What memory slots will be used to install the memory, based on the information provided?

_____

_____

_____

11. Using the Internet, a magazine, or a list of memory modules, determine the exact part numbers and quantities of memory modules that you would buy. List them with the location of where you obtained the information.

_____

Exercise 6.3 Configuring Memory on Paper

Objective: To be able to determine the correct amount and type of memory to install on a motherboard

Parts: Internet access or access to magazines or ads that show memory prices

Procedure: Refer to Figure 6.25 to answer the questions. The motherboard supports the following memory configurations:

- 1GB, 2GB, 4GB unbuffered and non-ECC DDR3 DIMMs can be used in the DIMM slots (1, 2, 3, and 4) for a total of 32GB max using DDR3 1066/1333MHz modules.
- Recommended memory configurations are modules in DIMMs 1 and 3 or modules in DIMMs 1, 2, 3, and 4.
- Single- and dual-channel modes are supported.
- You may install different sizes in Channel A and B. The dual-channel configuration will be the total size of the lowest-sized channel. Any excess memory will operate in single-channel mode.
- >1.65V DIMMs are recommended.
- Use the same CAS latency and obtain from the same vendor, if possible.
- The default memory operation frequency is dependent on SPD.

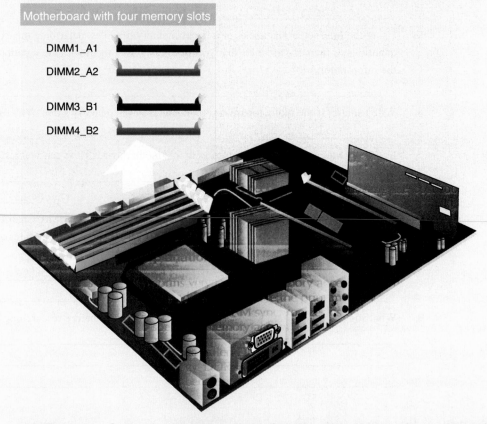

Motherboard with four memory slots

DIMM1_A1

DIMM2_A2

DIMM3_B1

DIMM4_B2

FIGURE 6.25   Second motherboard with four memory slots and two channels

Questions:

1. What memory features, if any, are used? (Select all that apply.) [parity | non-parity | ECC | registered | unbuffered | SPD]

2. The customer wants 4GB of RAM. What memory modules are needed? What capacities and how many of each capacity are required?

   _____

3. What memory slots will be used to install the memory suggested in Question 2?

   _____

   _____

4. Using the Internet, a magazine, or a list of memory modules provided by the instructor, determine the exact part numbers and quantities of memory modules that you would buy. List them with the location of where you obtained this information.

   _____

5. In what type of systems would ECC modules most likely be used? [student desktop | smartphones | tablets | servers | ultrabooks]

6. What is the purpose of ECC modules?

   _____

7. What is the purpose of SPD?

   _____

Exercise 6.4 Configuring Memory on Paper

Objective: To be able to determine the correct amount and type of memory to install on a motherboard

Parts: Internet access or access to magazines or ads that show memory prices

Procedure: Refer to Figure 6.26 to answer the questions. The motherboard supports the following memory configurations:

- Max memory supported: 16GB
- Memory types: DDR3-1600/1333/1066/800
- Memory channels: 3
- Number of DIMMs: 4
- ECC supported: Yes
- Connectors use gold-plated contacts
- Unbuffered, non-registered single- or double-sided SPD DIMMs with a voltage rating of 1.65V or less
- Optimal performance can be achieved by installing three matching DIMMs in the ChanA, ChanB, and ChanC memory slots.
- Dual-channel operation can be achieved by installing matching DIMMs in ChanB and ChanC or all four memory slots.

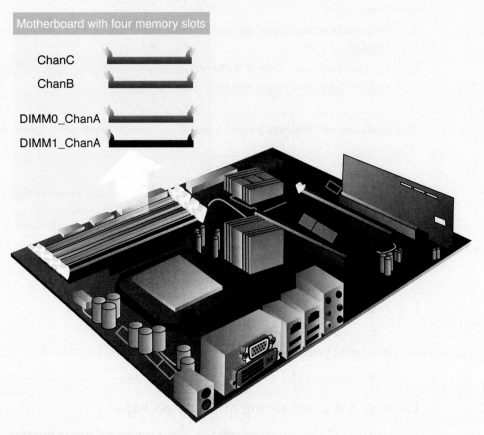

Motherboard with four memory slots

ChanC

ChanB

DIMM0_ChanA

DIMM1_ChanA

FIGURE 6.26   Triple-channel motherboard

Questions:

1.   What memory features, if any, are used? (Select all that apply.) [parity | non-parity | ECC | registered | unbuffered | SPD]

2.   The customer wants 8GB of RAM performing triple-channeling. Can this be done? Why or why not? [Yes | No]

   _____

   _____

3.   What memory modules are needed to put 8GB of memory on the motherboard? (What capacities and how many of each capacity are required?) Justify your choice.

   _____

   _____

   _____

4.   What memory slots will be used to install the memory suggested in Question 3?

   _____

5.   Using the Internet, a magazine, or a list of memory modules provided by the instructor, determine the exact part numbers and quantities of memory modules that you would buy. List them with the location of where you obtained this information.

   _____

6. The user has 32-bit Windows 7 installed on this computer. Will there be any issues with the 8GB of RAM? If so what might those issues be?

_____

_____

7. List one method a technician could use to ensure the 8GB are recognized by the system.

_____

_____

Activities

Internet Discovery

Objective:	To become familiar with researching memory chips using the Internet
Parts:	A computer with Internet access
Procedure:	Use the Internet to complete the following procedure.

- Power on the computer and start an Internet browser.
- Using any search engine, locate two vendors that sell memory chips.
- Create a table like the one below and fill in your findings for each of the memory sites.

	Site 1	Site 2
Internet URL		
Type of DIMM		
Largest-capacity DIMM		
Pros of website		
Cons of website		

Soft Skills

Objective:	To enhance and fine-tune a future technician's ability to listen, communicate in both written form and oral form, and support people who use computers in a professional manner

Activities:

1. On your own, use the Internet to find a utility that tests soft skills or your personality. Compare your scores with others in the class. Make a list of how you might improve in specific weak areas. Present your findings to a group and share your group findings with another group.

_____

_____

2. Note that this activity requires two computers. In groups of two, have one person describe in great detail to the other person how to upgrade the computer's memory by removing memory from one computer and adding it to the other. The person doing the physical installation can do nothing unless the partner describes how to do it. Reverse roles for removing the memory and re-installing back in the original computer. At the end of the exercise, the two participants describe to the teacher what they experienced.

3. In small groups, find a video that describes how to do something on the computer. Critique the video for how the speaker might do a better job communicating to people who are not technicians. Share the video with the class along with your recommendations for doing it better. As an option, script a short presentation for how to do something. Tape/record it if possible and have the class critique each group's presentation.

Critical Thinking Skills

Objective: To analyze and evaluate information as well as apply learned information to new or different situations

Activities:

1. Refer to Figure 6.9 and Table 6.7 in this chapter. Compare and contrast Solution 2 with Solution 3 as it relates to dual-channeling. Write a list of your findings and share them with the class.

_____

_____

_____

_____

2. Using Figure 6.9 in the chapter again, list the repercussions of discovering that the motherboard supports both single-side and double-sided memory modules. What would the memory population look like for 8GB (the maximum) of RAM?

_____

_____

_____

_____

3. Download a motherboard manual from the Internet or use one provided in the classroom. Find the memory section and make a list of any terms or directions that are given that you do not understand. In groups of four or five, share your lists and come up with as many solutions as possible. Share your group list with the class. Write any unsolved questions on the board and bring the answers to those questions back in a week.

Labs

Lab 6.1 Examining Memory Resources Using Device Manager in Windows 7/8

Objective: To be able to view memory resources currently being used by Windows 7 or 8

Parts: A computer with Windows 7 or 8 installed and rights to use Device Manager

Procedure: Complete the following procedure and answer the accompanying questions.

1. Power on the computer and verify that Windows loads. Log on to Windows using the known user ID and password or one provided by the instructor or lab assistant.

2. Access the *System and Security* Control Panel. Under the *System* section, select the *Device Manager* link.

3. Click the *View* menu option and select *Resources by type*. Expand the *Memory* section by clicking the arrow beside the option.

    Which memory addresses are used by the system board?

    _____

4. Right-click the first memory address shown. Select *Properties*.

What tabs are shown in the window?

_____

5. Select the *Resources* tab. All memory resources used by the first device or option are shown.

Can the motherboard memory resources be changed using the Resources tab options?

_____

6. Close the *Device Manager* window.

Lab 6.2 Examining Memory Resources Using Device Manager in Windows 10

Objective: To be able to view memory resources currently being used by Windows 10

Parts: A computer with Windows 10 installed and rights to use Device Manager

Procedure: Complete the following procedure and answer the accompanying questions.

1. Power on the computer and verify that Windows loads. Log on to Windows using the known user ID and password or one provided by the instructor or lab assistant.

2. From the *Start* button in the *Search the web and Windows* textbox, type **device** and click the *Device Manager* Control Panel link from the resulting list.

3. Click the *View* menu option and select *Resources by type*. Expand the *Memory* section by clicking the arrow beside the option.

Which memory addresses are used by the system board?

_____

4. Right-click the first memory address shown. Select *Properties*.

What tabs are shown in the window?

_____

5. Select the *Resources* tab. All memory resources used by the first device or option are shown.

Can the motherboard memory resources be changed using the Resources tab options?

_____

6. Close the *Device Manager* window.

Lab 6.3 Using the System Information Tool in Windows 7 to View Memory

Objective: To be able to view memory resources currently being used by Windows 7

Parts: A computer with Windows 7 installed and rights to use the System Information Tool

Procedure: Complete the following procedure and answer the accompanying questions.

1. Access the *System and Security* Control Panel. Select the *System* link.

2. On the bottom-left side, select the *Performance Information and Tools* link.

3. From the left panel, select the *Advanced tools* link.

4. Select the *View advanced system details in System Information* link. Note that an alternate way to do this is to type **msinfo32** in the *Search programs and files* textbox and press Enter.

How much physical RAM is installed?

_____

How much physical RAM is available?

_____

How much total virtual memory does the machine have?

_____

How much available virtual memory does the machine have?

_____

What is the location and size of the page file?

_____

5.   Close the *System Information* window.

Lab 6.4 Using the System Information Tool in Windows 8/10 to View Memory

Objective: To be able to view memory resources currently being used by Windows 7

Parts: A computer with Windows 8 or 10 installed and rights to use the System Information Tool

Procedure: Complete the following procedure and answer the accompanying questions.

1.   Windows 8 and Windows 10 make it harder to get to the System Information Tool than previous operating systems, but you can still use a command to access it. From the search textbox, type **msinfo32** and press Enter.

How much physical RAM is installed?

_____

How much physical RAM is available?

_____

How much total virtual memory does the machine have?

_____

How much available virtual memory does the machine have?

_____

What is the location and size of the page file?

_____

2.   Close the *System Information* window.

Lab 6.5 Using Windows 7 Task Manager to View Memory

Objective: To be able to use the Task Manager tool to view memory resources currently being used by Windows 7

Parts: A computer with Windows 7 installed and rights to use Task Manager

Procedure: Complete the following procedure and answer the accompanying questions.

1.   After logging on to a Windows 7 computer, press the Ctrl + Alt + Delete keys and select the *Start Task Manager* link.

2.   Access the *Performance* tab.

What percentage of the CPU is being used?

_____

What is the significance of the number shown by Threads?

_____

_____

Is the total amount of physical memory RAM, cache memory (virtual memory), or both?

_____

How much RAM is available?

_____

3. Click the *Resource Monitor* button and select the *Overview* tab.

What is the percentage of used physical memory?

_____

4. Expand the *Memory* section.

List three executable (.exe) files running in memory.

_____

5. Open an application such as the Calculator accessory. Locate the application in the *Memory* section.

How many kilobytes are shown for the application in the Commit column?

_____

How many kilobytes are shown for the application in the Working Set column?

_____

How many kilobytes are shown for the application in the Shareable column?

_____

How many kilobytes are shown for the application in the Private column?

_____

6. Select the *Memory* tab.

How much memory is reserved for hardware, if any?

_____

7. Hold the mouse pointer over the colored bar portion of physical memory that represents the amount of memory "In Use." A description of this portion of the bar appears.

What is the exact purpose of the "In Use" section?

_____

8. Hold the mouse pointer over the colored bar that shows how the "Standby" portion of physical memory is being used.

What is the exact purpose of the "Standby" section?

_____

Determine the exact purpose of the "Free" section. Document your findings.

_____

_____

9. Close the *System Resource Monitor* window and the application window you opened to learn about the System Resource Monitor. Close the *Task Manager* window.

Lab 6.6 Using Windows 8/10 Task Manager to View Memory

Objective: To be able to use the Task Manager tool to view memory resources currently being used by Windows 8 or 10

Parts: A computer with Windows 8 or 10 installed and rights to use Task Manager

Procedure: Complete the following procedure and answer the accompanying questions.

1. After logging on to a Windows 8/10 computer, search for and select the *Task Manager* tool.

2. Access the *Performance* tab.

What percentage of the CPU is being used?

_____

CHAPTER 6

Is the total amount of physical memory RAM considered cache memory (virtual memory) or both?

_____

How much RAM is available?

_____

How many RAM slots are used?

_____

What speed of memory modules is used?

_____

3.   Click the *Open Resource Monitor* link and select the *Overview* tab.

      What is the percentage of used physical memory?

_____

4.   Expand the *Memory* section.

      List three executable (.exe) files running in memory.

_____

5.   Open an application such as the Calculator accessory. Locate the application in the *Memory* section.

      How many kilobytes are shown for the application in the Commit column?

_____

      How many kilobytes are shown for the application in the Working Set column?

_____

      How many kilobytes are shown for the application in the *Shareable* column?

_____

      How many kilobytes are shown for the application in the *Private* column?

_____

6.   Select the *Memory* tab.

      How much memory is reserved for hardware, if any?

_____

7.   Hold the mouse pointer over the colored bar portion of physical memory that represents the amount of memory "In Use." A description of this portion of the bar appears.

      What is the exact purpose of the "In Use" section?

_____

8.   Hold the mouse pointer over the colored bar that shows how the "Standby" portion of physical memory is being used.

      What is the exact purpose of the "Standby" section?

_____

      Determine the exact purpose of the "Free" section. Document your findings.

_____

_____

9.   Close the *System Resource Monitor* window. Close the *Task Manager* window.

7 Storage Devices

In this chapter you will learn:

> Basic storage terms

> About PATA, SATA, SSD, and SSHD technologies

> How to install and configure storage devices including RAID

> How to fix storage device problems

> How to keep the hard drive healthy

> How to create and troubleshoot a RAID

> How to create and use Windows Storage Spaces

> Effective phone communication

CompTIA Exam Objectives:

What CompTIA A+ exam objectives are covered in this chapter?

✓ 901-1.1 Given a scenario, configure settings and use BIOS/UEFI tools on a PC.

✓ 901-1.5 Install and configure storage devices and use appropriate media.

✓ 901-1.7 Compare and contrast various PC connection interfaces, their characteristics, and purpose.

✓ 901-1.11 Identify common PC connector types and associated cables.

✓ 901-4.2 Given a scenario, troubleshoot hard drives and RAID arrays with the appropriate tools.

✓ 902-1.2 Given a scenario, install Windows PC operating systems using appropriate methods.

✓ 902-1.3 Given a scenario, apply the appropriate Microsoft command line tools.

✓ 902-1.4 Given a scenario, use appropriate Microsoft operating system features and tools.

✓ 902-1.7 Perform common preventive maintenance procedures using the appropriate Windows OS tools.

✓ 902-3.6 Given a scenario, use appropriate data destruction and disposal methods.

✓ 902-4.1 Given a scenario, troubleshoot PC operating system problems with appropriate tools.

✓ 902-4.2 Given a scenario, troubleshoot common PC security issues with appropriate tools and best practices.

✓ 902-5.4 Demonstrate proper communication techniques and professionalism.

Storage Devices Overview

Storage devices hold the data we are so fond of generating and keeping—photos, PDFs, movies, word processing documents, spreadsheets, and whatever else we can think to save. This data is stored on optical media, flash media, and magnetic media such as hard drives, as shown in Figure 7.1.

FIGURE 7.1 Storage devices

Many folks, especially those who travel frequently, use data storage servers at their company. Data can also be stored "in the cloud." This means that there are storage devices available through the Internet to store data. Some storage is provided by an Internet provider or as a service for a mobile device. Some companies, such as Amazon, Microsoft, Google, SugarSync, Inc., and Dropbox provide cloud storage that may be a limited amount for free with the option to pay for more or they may charge for storage. The services of such a site include backing up the data stored on their drives and having redundant hard drives in their servers. This is known as cloud storage or offsite storage. Microsoft, Google, Apple, and other companies have made it very easy to store data in the cloud or to synchronize data to the cloud. More information on how to do this is covered in Chapter 11 and Chapter 17. Figure 7.2 illustrates this concept, but keep in mind that "in the cloud" is just a ton of hard drives, servers, and other devices in a remote location somewhere.

FIGURE 7.2 Cloud storage

Hard Drive Overview

Hard drives are popular devices for storing data. The drives can be mounted inside the computer case or attached externally to a USB, IEEE 1394 (FireWire), eSATA, or eSATAp port. Hard drives store more data than flash drives and move data faster than tape drives. Today's hard drive capacities extend into the terabytes. Hard drives are frequently upgraded in computers, so it is important for you to understand all the technical issues. These issues include knowing the parts of the hard drive subsystem, how the operating system and the BIOS/UEFI work together with a hard drive, and how to configure and troubleshoot a hard drive.

Hard drives come in different physical sizes (form factors). For desktop and small server models, 5.25-inch (not very popular) and 3.5-inch drives are available. The 2.5-inch form factor is designed for laptops and ultrabooks. A 1.8-inch form factor is available for use and can be found in SSDs, ultrabooks, and ultraportable devices such as MP3 players. Figure 7.3 shows two hard drive sizes.

FIGURE 7.3 Desktop hard drive form factors

A hard drive can also be placed inside an **external enclosure** and attached using a USB, eSATA, eSATAp (USB/SATA) combo port, or IEEE 1394 (FireWire). Figure 7.4 shows a 3.5-inch IDE PATA or SATA to USB or eSATA Sabrent enclosure that includes a cooling fan. Notice that the cooling fan has a filter that protects the fan from dust particles.

FIGURE 7.4 Sabrent external hard drive enclosure

Magnetic Hard Drive Geometry

Traditional mechanical hard drives are magnetic hard drives. These hard drives have multiple hard metal surfaces called platters. Each platter typically holds data on both sides and has two read/write heads, one for the top and one for the bottom. The read/write heads float on a cushion of air without touching the platter surface. Data is written by using electromagnetism. A charge is applied to the read/write head creating a magnetic field. Figure 7.5 shows the major components found inside a mechanical hard drive. The metal hard drive platter has magnetic particles that are affected by the read/write head's magnetic field, allowing 1s and 0s to be "placed" or "induced" onto the drive, as shown in Figure 7.6.

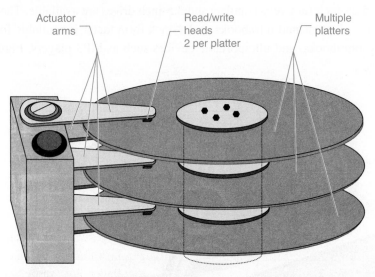

Actuator arms   Read/write heads 2 per platter   Multiple platters

FIGURE 7.5   Hard drive geometry

FIGURE 7.6   Writing to a hard drive

Magnetic hard drives typically have two motors—one to turn the platters and one to move the read/write heads. A hard drive spins at different rotational rates called revolutions per minute (RPMs). Common speeds are 5400, 7200, 10,000, and 15,000 RPM. The faster the drive RPM, the faster the transfer rate and generally an increased cost. A 7200 RPM drive typically transfers data 33 percent faster than 5400 RPM drives.

If a read/write head touches the platter, a **head crash** occurs. This is sometimes called HDI (head-to-disk interference), and it can damage the platters or the read/write head, causing corrupt data. Another important concept is mean time between failures (**MTBF**)—the average number of hours before a drive is likely to fail. Mechanical hard drives do fail and that is why it is so important to back up data. Figure 7.7 shows the inside of a hard drive. You can see the top read/write head and the platters. Keep in mind that you should not remove the cover from a hard drive because you could allow particles into the sealed drive area.

FIGURE 7.7   Hard drive with cover removed

The magnetic hard drive surface is metallic and has concentric circles, each of which is called a track. Tracks are numbered starting with the outermost track, which is called track 0. One corresponding track on all surfaces of a hard drive is a cylinder. For example, cylinder 0 consists of all track 0s; all of the track 1s comprise cylinder 1, and so on. A track is a single circle on one platter. A cylinder is the same track on all platters. Figure 7.8 shows the difference between tracks and cylinders. Notice in Figure 7.8 that a concentric circle makes an individual track. A single track on all the surfaces makes an individual cylinder.

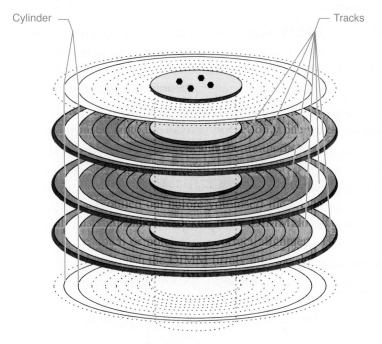

FIGURE 7.8   Cylinders versus tracks

Each track is separated into **sectors**, with the circle divided into smaller pieces. Normally, each sector stores 512 bytes, as shown in Figure 7.9.

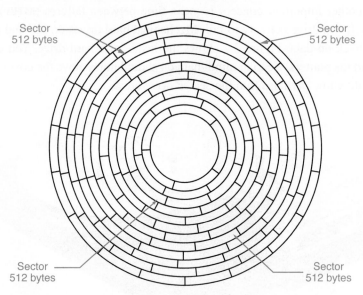

FIGURE 7.9   Hard drive sectors

Solid State Drive (SSD) Overview

SSDs are storage devices that use DRAM (older ones) or nonvolatile flash memory (newer ones) technologies instead of hard drive technologies. SSDs eliminate the number one cause of hard drive failure: moving parts. SSDs typically use flash memory and can therefore be low heat producing, reliable, quiet, secure, long-lasting, and fast. SSDs are installed in laptops and desktop models as internal and external units. SSDs are common in tablets and some mobile devices. They are also used in environments such as temperature extremes or where the drive might be jolted. SSDs can be used in conjunction with mechanical hard drive storage. SSDs are used in the following industries:

> Medical—CRT/MRI image storage, monitoring equipment, portable devices
> IT—Video surveillance, wireless base stations, security appliances
> Industrial—Robotic systems, test equipment, manufacturing devices
> Automotive—Diagnostics, store safety information, store travel statistics

Another difference between mechanical hard drives and SSDs is how data is actually written. Write amplification and wear leveling are two terms used with SSDs that technicians should understand. To write data, an SSD may have to do an erase operation, move data to another location, and then write the information to memory. Still, overall performance is increased. **Write amplification** is the minimum amount of memory storage space affected by a write request. For example, if there is 4KB of information to be written and the SSD has a 128KB erase block, 128KB must be erased before the 4KB of information can be written. Some SSDs clean up data blocks when the SSD is not busy. Writing takes longer than reading with SSDs.

Wear leveling is a technique used to erase and write data using all of the memory blocks instead of the same memory blocks repeatedly. SSD manufacturers use various technologies: (1) software to track usage and direct write operations, (2) a certain amount of reserved memory blocks to use when a memory block fails, and (3) a combination of the two techniques.

SSDs use a NAND structure where a 1 bit indicates that no data is stored in a particular location and a 0 bit indicates the presence of data. **NAND flash memory** retains data even when the device is powered off. Two types of technologies used with SSDs are single-level memory cell (SLC) and multi-level memory cell (MLC). **SLCs** store 1 bit in each memory cell and last longer than MLCs, but they are more expensive. **MLCs** store more than 1 bit in each memory cell and are cheaper to manufacture, but they have slower transfer speeds.

The main drawback to SSDs is cost. SSDs are expensive compared to hard drives. As with flash drives, each memory block of an SSD has a finite number of reads and writes. An SSD that writes data across the entire memory capacity will last longer. Some companies include software with the drive that tracks or estimates end of life. Figure 7.10 shows inside an SSD.

FIGURE 7.10   Solid state drive without a cover

Today, hybrid SSDs are available. A **hybrid SSD** or solid state hybrid drive (**SSHD**) provides a combination of mechanical and flash technologies. The SSHD has some flash memory integrated with a traditional mechanical drive, as seen in Figure 7.11.

The flash memory in an SSHD typically contains the most frequently used data that would be sent to the host interface. Advanced algorithms are used to predict this data. Only if requested data was not in flash memory would data be pulled from the slower mechanical drive. SSHDs provide the best of both worlds—costs are lower per byte because you have a little bit of really fast memory storage and there is a lot of storage space with the traditional mechanical drive. You also do not require a faster RPM traditional drive with an SSHD.

A similar technology is the flash cache modules (**FCM**), which requires software that predicts what data is going to be used and that puts data on an SSD that is separate from the mechanical hard drive. At the time this book was going to press, specific Intel chipsets were required in order to use this technology.

CHAPTER 7

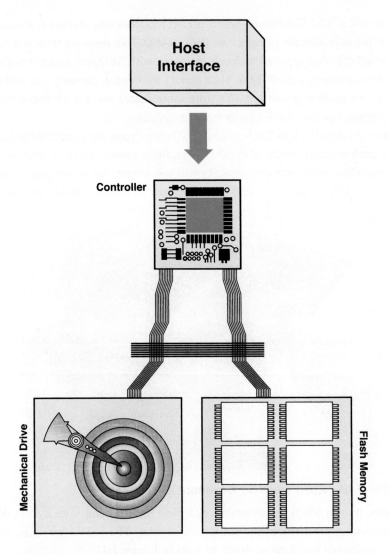

FIGURE 7.11 SSHD operation

Hard Drive Interfaces Overview

A hard drive system must have a set of rules to operate. These rules specify the number of heads on the drive, what commands the drive responds to, the cables used with the drive, the number of devices supported, the number of data bits transferred at one time, and so on. These rules make up a standard called an interface that governs communication with the hard drive. There are two major hard drive interfaces: integrated drive electronics (**IDE**)—also known as the AT Attachment (ATA) or Enhanced IDE (**EIDE**) standard—and Small Computer System Interface (SCSI). IDE is the most common in home and office computers. SCSI is more commonly found in network servers.

Note that there are other interfaces used to attach external storage devices. Most everyone has seen a flash drive or an external hard drive attached to a USB port. Apple has the Thunderbolt interface that can be used to attach external storage and display devices. Chapter 2 introduced the port and Chapter 9 has more information about it. This chapter focuses more on the internal storage interfaces.

Both IDE and SCSI started out as parallel architectures. This means that multiple bits are sent over multiple paths. This architecture requires precise timing as transfer rates increase. With both IDE and SCSI, multiple devices can attach to the same bus. Parallel IDE or Parallel ATA (**PATA**) supports only two devices; parallel SCSI supports more. However, the concept is the same. When multiple devices share the same bus, they have to wait their turn to access the bus and there are configuration issues with which to contend. Figure 7.12 shows the concept of parallel transfer.

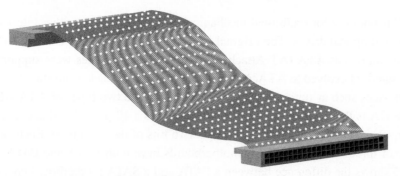

FIGURE 7.12   Parallel transfer

Today, the trend is toward serial architectures. Both the IDE and SCSI standards have a serial architecture available. The ATA serial device is known as a Serial ATA (**SATA**) device, and the SCSI serial device is known as a Serial Attached SCSI (**SAS**) device. A serial architecture is a point-to-point bus where each device has a single connection back to the controller. Bits are sent one at a time over a single link. More devices can attach to this type of architecture because it scales easier and configuration is much easier. Figure 7.13 illustrates the concept of serial data transfer.

FIGURE 7.13   Serial transfer

Figure 7.14 is a photo of a PATA cable and a SATA data cable.

PATA

SATA

FIGURE 7.14   SATA and PATA data cables

SATA in laptops is being replaced by an interface known as M.2. The **M.2** connector allows attaching modules of varying sizes. This serves well for mobile devices and specifically for SSDs. Some desktop motherboards include the M.2 connector. More information and graphics of the M.2 connector are found in Chapter 11.

Integrated Drive Electronics (IDE)

IDE is not only for traditional mechanical hard drives but for other internal devices, such as tape, Zip, and optical drives. The original IDE standard was developed only for hard drives and is officially known as ATA (AT Attachment). Later, other devices were supported by the standard and the standard evolved to ATA/ATAPI (AT Attachment Packet Interface). ATAPI increased support of devices such as optical and tape drives. There are two types of ATA—PATA and SATA.

PATA is the older IDE/EIDE type, which uses a 40-pin cable that connects the hard drive to an adapter or the motherboard and transfers 16 bits of data at a time. Each cable normally has either two or three connectors. Many motherboards have both SATA and PATA IDE connectors. Figure 7.15 shows the difference between a PATA and a SATA motherboard connection.

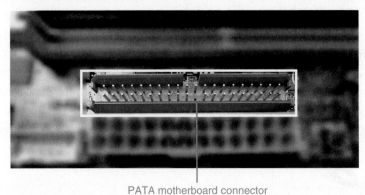
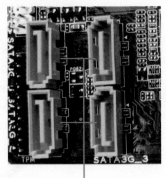

PATA motherboard connector   SATA motherboard connectors

FIGURE 7.15   PATA and SATA motherboard connectors

A motherboard that has two IDE connectors can have up to four PATA devices, two per motherboard connection. Figure 7.16 shows PATA IDE hard drive connectors. Notice the 40-pin connector on the left and the power connector on the right.

FIGURE 7.16   PATA IDE hard drive connectors

The newer ATA standard is SATA (Serial ATA). The original specification transfers data at 1.5Gb/s and is called **SATA 1** or SATA I. The 3Gb/s version is known as **SATA 2** or SATA II, and the latest release is SATA 3 or SATA III, which runs at a maximum of 6Gb/s. These devices are commonly seen marked as SATA 1.5Gb/s, 3Gb/s, 6Gb/s.

SATA is a point-to-point interface, which means that (1) each device connects to the host through a dedicated link (unlike the traditional parallel IDE where two devices share the host link), and (2) each device has the entire interface bandwidth. SATA uses a smaller, 7-pin cable that is more like a network cable than the traditional IDE ribbon cable. SATA supports both internal and external devices. Figure 7.17 shows an internal SATA drive with the cable attached. The data connector is to the left of the power connector.

FIGURE 7.17   SATA hard drive and data cable

An internal SATA device commonly uses a 15-pin SATA power connector rather than a Molex that the older hard drives used. However, some drives do ship with Molex connectors. A Molex-to-SATA converter can be purchased, but the connector can only provide 5 and 12 volts, not 3.3 volts. The good news is that most SATA drives do not use the 3.3V line. Figure 7.18 shows the older Molex power connector compared to the internal SATA power connector.

Molex   Internal SATA

FIGURE 7.18   Hard drive power connectors

Internal SATA data cables are limited to a maximum of 3.3 feet (1 meter). The internal SATA data cable is more likely to be inadvertently unplugged or partially unplugged than the PATA cable. Special cables with locking mechanisms are in an L shape for hard-to-reach places, or low profile form factor cases can be purchased. Figure 7.19 shows these 7-pin internal SATA device cables.

Standard   Locking   L-shaped

FIGURE 7.19   Internal SATA data cables

External SATA (**eSATA**) provides external device connectivity using the SATA standard. It allows shielded cable lengths up to 6.56 feet (2 meters), with faster connections than USB 2.0, 3.0, or most IEEE 1394 types. However, the standard eSATA connection does not provide power to external devices, but an eSATAp combo USB/eSATA port can provide power. Figure 7.20 shows an eSATA cable and eSATA port. An eSATA cable can be rated for 1.5, 3, or 6Gb/s. eSATA cables are limited to 3.3 feet (1 meter) for 1.5Gb/s devices and 6.56 feet (2 meters) for 3 or 6Gb/s transfers. The eSATA connector may be integrated (especially in a laptop) as a combination USB/eSATA port.

SATA port   eSATA cable

FIGURE 7.20   eSATA port and cable

Storage Device Configuration Overview

Drive configuration sometimes includes setting jumpers on the drive and sometimes on the associated adapter to ensure proper termination. Termination is a method used to prevent signals from reflecting back up the cable. Each drive type has a normal configuration method. However, individual drive manufacturers may develop their own configuration steps. Always refer to the documentation included with the drive, adapter, or motherboard for configuration and installation information. The overall steps for installing a storage device are as follows:

Step 1. Keep the drive in the protective anti-static container until you are ready to install.

Step 2. Use proper anti-static handling procedures when installing the drive and handle the drive by the edges; avoid touching the drive electronics and connectors.

Step 3. Turn off and remove the computer power cord when installing the drive.

Step 4. Physically mount and secure the device in the computer and attach the proper cable.

Step 5. Configure the BIOS/UEFI, if necessary.

Step 6. Reconnect the power cord and power on the computer. If a hard drive, prepare the drive for data as described later in the chapter.

PATA Physical Installation

A PATA cable allows two storage devices to connect to a single motherboard connector. Each cable can have a master and a slave device. To distinguish between the devices, the words **master** or **slave** are used. The two settings are simply used to distinguish between the two devices because only one of the two devices (master or slave) can transmit data at a time. Motherboards used to have at least two PATA connectors, but now some may not have any. The first motherboard connector was known as the primary connector. If a second one is installed, it is called the secondary connector. To distinguish between the devices that connect to each cable, the devices are called the primary master and primary slave.

TECH TIP

Attach cable correctly or destroy devices and components

Devices, adapters, controlling circuits, and so on can be damaged if a cable plugs into the connector the wrong way. Some cables are keyed so they insert only one way into the connector.

PATA devices are configured using jumpers. The four options commonly found are single, master, slave, and cable select. The single IDE setting is used when only one device connects to the cable. The master IDE setting is used in conjunction with the slave setting and both are used when two IDE devices connect to the same cable. One device is set to the master setting while the other device uses the slave setting. The **cable select** IDE option replaces the master/slave setting. The device automatically configures itself to either the master setting or the slave setting depending on the specific cable connector to which the device attaches. To use the cable select option, a special 80-conductor, 40-pin cable is needed. Figure 7.21 shows the connections for an 80-conductor cable.

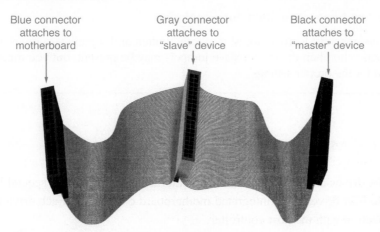

FIGURE 7.21   **PATA cable connections**

There are two methods of configuring PATA IDE devices: (1) configure one device as master and the other device as slave or (2) configure both devices to the cable select option. By doing this, the device that connects to the black connector becomes the "master" and the device that connects to the gray connector becomes the "slave." Figure 7.22 illustrates how multiple PATA devices connect to the motherboard.

Closed means jumpered or enabled

When documentation shows an option as closed, jumpered, or enabled, this means to put a jumper over the two pins to configure the option.

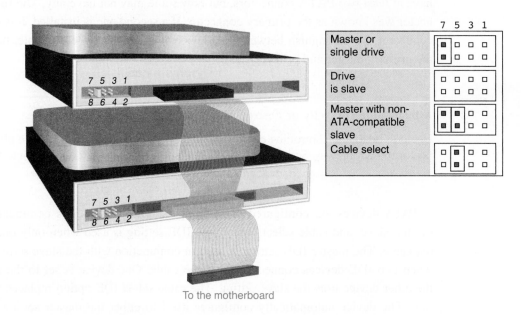

	7	5	3	1

To the motherboard

FIGURE 7.22   Two PATA devices configured with cable select

Adjusting to poorly written documentation

Technicians must learn to adjust to poorly written and sometimes confusing documentation. Jumpers other than the master/slave jumpers may be present, but you must refer to the documentation for the proper settings.

SATA Physical Installation

SATA drives are easy to install. Most internal drives require a special host adapter that supports one to four drives or an integrated motherboard connection. Each drive is seen as a point-to-point connection with the host controller.

SATA drives do not have any master/slave or cable select jumpers/settings. A serial 7-pin data connector attaches from the SATA controller to the internal SATA drive. A 15-pin cable connects power to the drive. The internal SATA power connector is unique, but could possibly be the older Molex connector. A cable converter can be obtained if a Molex connector is the only one available from the power supply. Figure 7.23 shows an internal SATA hard drive with associated cabling. Notice the Molex-to-internal SATA cable converter in the photo.

There are also products available that allow a Serial ATA hard drive to connect to a standard IDE controller. Figure 7.24 shows how the cables connect to the internal SATA drive. Figure 7.25 shows how two SATA drives attach to a motherboard that has two SATA connectors.

FIGURE 7.23   SATA hard drive and cables

FIGURE 7.24   SATA data (left) and power (right) cabling

Figure 7.26 shows a SATA adapter that has two internal ports on the far end and one eSATA port. To install a SATA host adapter, power off the computer and remove the computer power cord. Remove the computer cover and locate an open expansion slot. Some adapters have jumpers for configurable options. Some common options include 16- and 32-bit PCI operations, adapter BIOS enabled/disabled, and Mode 0 enabled/ disabled. Some adapters may provide master/slave emulation options. Most adapters' default settings will work, but always refer to the adapter's documentation for details.

FIGURE 7.25   SATA connectivity

FIGURE 7.26   eSATA connectivity

TECH TIP

Enable SATA port

Some manufacturers require that you enable the motherboard port through the system BIOS/UEFI before any device connected to the port is recognized.

To install an internal SATA hard drive, power off the computer, and remove the computer's power cord. Physically mount the drive into a drive bay. Connect the SATA data cable between the drive and the host controller (usually on the motherboard). Connect the SATA power cable. Figure 7.27 shows an installed internal SATA hard drive.

An external (eSATA) drive normally has no jumpers, terminators, or switches to be configured. However, when installing a faster drive to a slower port—such as when installing a 3.0Gb/s drive to a 1.5Gb/s port—a jumper may need to be configured so the drive is compatible with the port. Always refer to the drive manufacturer's documentation when installing a drive. Attach the power cord to the drive, if applicable, and insert the other end of the power cord into a wall outlet. Attach one end of the eSATA cable to the drive. Plug the other end of the cable into an eSATA port on the computer. eSATA ports are sometimes disabled in BIOS/UEFI. Figure 7.28 shows an external hard drive that supports IEEE 1394 (FireWire), eSATA, and USB as you can see from the ports on the back of the unit.

FIGURE 7.27 Installed SATA hard drive

FIGURE 7.28 External hard drive

Before switching on eSATA drive power, ensure that the drive is positioned where it will stay during operation and that all data and power cords are attached securely. Switch on the drive power. The drive will **mount**. When a drive mounts, a communications channel is opened between the drive and the operating system. Whenever the drive is to be disconnected, it is to be unmounted. Some drive manufacturers provide software for backing up data or configuring the drive in a RAID configuration. Use the Windows *Disk Management* tool to ensure that the drive is recognized. Both RAID and the Disk Management tool are covered later in this chapter.

TECH TIP

Unmounting an eSATA drive

To unmount an eSATA drive, click the *Safely Remove Hardware* icon in the systray area. Select the appropriate drive letter. Remove the drive when prompted by the operating system.

SSD Physical Installation

For a desktop computer, an SSD can be internally mounted (see Figure 7.29) and connected to a SATA/PATA motherboard or an adapter port. An SSD can also attach as an external device to a SATA, USB, or FireWire port. SSDs do not normally require special drivers. Always refer to the SSD mounting directions provided by the manufacturer. The following steps are generic ones:

Step 1. If installing an SSD internally into a desktop computer, power off the computer and locate an empty drive bay, a power connector of the appropriate type (or buy a converter), and an available SATA/PATA port or free PATA connector on a PATA cable.

Step 2. Attach mounting brackets to the SSD. Mounting brackets may have to be purchased separately, be provided with the drive, or be provided as spares that came with the computer.

Step 3. Slide the SSD into the drive bay and secure it, if necessary.

Step 4. Connect the data cable from the motherboard or adapter to the drive.

Step 5. Attach a power cable to the SSD.

Step 6. Re-install the computer cover and power on the computer.

FIGURE 7.29   Internal SSD

TECH TIP

Beware of static electricity

SSDs are flash memory and are susceptible to static electricity. Use proper ESD handling procedures when installing an SSD.

If installing an external SSD, use the following steps:

Step 1. Attach the appropriate USB, SATA, or IEEE 1394 (FireWire) cable from the drive to the computer.

Step 2. Power on the SSD. The system should recognize the new drive.

TECH TIP

Use only one technology

If an external drive supports more than one technology, such as eSATA, FireWire, and USB, attach only one type of cable from the drive to the computer.

System BIOS/UEFI Configuration for Hard Drives

A hard drive is configured through the system BIOS/UEFI Setup program. Setup is accessed through keystrokes during the boot process. In today's computers, the BIOS/UEFI automatically detects the hard drive type. The drive type information is saved in CMOS.

TECH TIP

Configure BIOS/UEFI according to the drive manufacturer's instructions

Drive manufacturers normally include documentation describing how to configure the drive in BIOS/UEFI Setup. Also, they provide software for any system that does not recognize the drive.

Hard drives are normally configured using the Auto-Detect feature included with BIOS/UEFI. The Auto-Detect feature automatically determines the drive type for the system. Table 7.1 shows the most commonly used PATA/SATA hard drive settings. SATA drives can be set in different modes of operation: (1) legacy mode, which is used in a system that does not have SATA drivers natively, (2) Advanced Host Controller Interface (**AHCI**) mode which, when enabled, allows SATA drives to be inserted/removed when power is on and use commands that allow the host circuits to communicate with attached devices to implement advanced SATA features, and (3) RAID mode. RAID is discussed later in this chapter. Note that the BIOS/UEFI is also where you select the drive that will boot the system.

TABLE 7.1   Common hard drive BIOS/UEFI settings

Hard drive type	BIOS/UEFI setting
IDE PATA/SATA/SCSI/SAS	AUTO
SATA	SATA mode: IDE mode (no AHCI or RAID)
SATA	SATA mode: SATA or AHCI (AHCI enabled)
SATA	SATA mode: RAID (AHCI and RAID enabled)

Hard Drive Preparation Overview

Once a hard drive is installed and configured properly and the hard drive type is entered into the Setup program, the drive must be prepared to accept data. The two steps of hard drive preparation are as follows:

Step 1. Partition the drive.

Step 2. High-level format the hard drive.

> **TECH TIP**
>
> **Low-level formatting**
>
> There is such a thing as low-level formatting done at the hard drive factory. Some manufacturers provide software that enables you to low-level format the drive. This should be done only at the direction of the manufacturer.

Partitioning a hard drive allows a drive letter to be assigned to one or more parts of the hard drive. **High-level formatting** prepares the drive for use for a particular file system. This allows the drive to accept data from the operating system. For today's computers, a drive cannot be used until it has been partitioned and high-level formatted; thus, technicians must be very familiar with these steps.

Partitioning

The first step in preparing a hard drive for use is partitioning. Partitioning a hard drive divides the drive so the computer system sees the hard drive as more than one drive. This is like slicing a pie into circular sections instead of triangle sections, but it is still the same pie. The difference is that each section gets a drive letter. Figure 7.30 shows a hard drive platter with some colored sections. Each section between the colored lines can be a volume and receive a different drive letter.

FIGURE 7.30 Visualization of partitioning

Partitioning can be done during the Windows installation process. The Windows **Disk Management** program is used after the operating system is installed to manage disk partitions. Similarly, the `diskpart` utility can be used from the command prompt. Disk Management is normally used to partition additional hard drives and to manage all of them. The first hard drive in the system is normally partitioned as part of the Windows installation process. Additional partitions can be created using Disk Management once the operating system is installed.

Partitioning provides advantages such as the following:

> Dividing a hard drive into separate subunits that are then assigned drive letters, such as `C:` or `D:`, by the operating system
> Organizing the hard drive to separate multiple operating systems, applications, and data
> Providing data security by placing data in a different partition to allow ease of backup as well as protection
> Using the hard drive to its fullest capacity

TECH TIP

How to determine what file system is being used

Right-click any drive in *Windows Explorer* (Vista and 7) or *File Explorer* (Windows 8 and 10) and select *Properties*. The *General* tab shows the type of file system being used.

The original purpose of partitioning was to enable loading multiple operating systems. This is still a good reason today because placing each operating system in its own partition eliminates the crashes and headaches caused by multiple operating systems and multiple applications coexisting in the same partition. The type of partition and how big the partition can be depends on the file system being used. A **file system** defines how data is stored on a drive. The most common Windows file systems are FAT16, FAT32, exFAT, and NTFS. The file system that can be used depends on what operating system is installed, whether the device is an internal device or external, and whether files are to be shared. Table 7.2 lists file systems and explains a little about each one.

TABLE 7.2   File systems

File system type	Description
Compact Disk File System (**CDFS**)	A file system for optical media.
FAT	Also called FAT16. Used with all versions of Windows. 2GB partition limitation with old operating systems. 4GB partition limitation with XP and higher versions of Windows.
FAT32	Supported with all versions of Windows. Commonly used with removable flash drives. Supports drives up to 2TB. Can recognize volumes greater than 32GB, but cannot create them that big.
exFAT	Commonly called FAT64. A file system made for removable media (such as flash drives and SD cards) that extends drive size support up to 64ZB in theory, but 512TB is the recommended max. Made for copying large files such as disk images and media files. Supported by all versions of Windows.
NTFS	Used with Windows Vista, 7, 8, and 10. Supports drives up to 16EB (16 exabytes, which equals 16 billion gigabytes), but in practice is only 16TB. Supports file compression and file security. NTFS allows faster file access and uses hard drive space more efficiently. Supports individual file compression and has the best file security.

File system type	Description
Network File System (**NFS**)	An open source operating system developed by Sun Microsystems found in Linux-based systems. Allows access to remote files over a network.
ext3	Also known as third extended file system. Used in Linux-based operating systems and is a journaling file system (it tracks changes in case the operating system crashes, allowing it to be restarted without reloading).
ext4	An update to ext3 to allow for larger volumes and file sizes within Linux-based operating systems.

An even better reason for partitioning than loading multiple operating systems or separating the operating system from data is to partition the hard drive for more efficient use of space. The operating system sets aside one cluster as a minimum for every file. A **cluster** is the smallest amount of space reserved for one file and is made up of a specific number of sectors. Figure 7.31 illustrates the concept of a cluster. Keep in mind that the number of hard drive sectors per track varies. The outer tracks hold more information (have more sectors) than the inner tracks.

TECH TIP

How to convert partitions

Use the `convert` program in Windows to convert a FAT16, FAT32, or exFAT partition to NTFS without loss of data. Access a command prompt window. Type the following command: `convert x: /fs:ntfs` where *x* is the drive letter of the partition being converted to NTFS.

Press Enter, and then press Y and press Enter. You can add a `/V` switch to the end of the command for a more verbose operation mode.

Any type of partition conversion requires free hard drive space. The amount depends on the size of the partition. Table 7.3 shows that partitioning large drives into one FAT partition wastes drive space. An efficiently partitioned hard drive allows more files to be saved because less space on the hard drive is wasted.

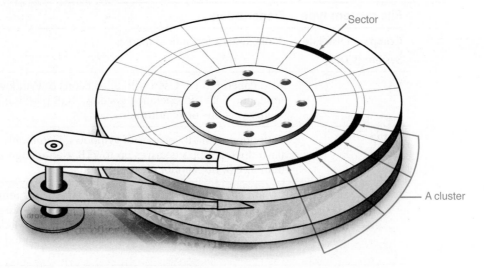

One cluster is the minimum amount of space for a file.

FIGURE 7.31   Cluster

TABLE 7.3 FAT16 partitions and cluster size

Partition size	Number of sectors	Cluster size (bytes)
0–32MB	1	512
32MB–64MB	2	1k
64MB–128MB	4	2k
128MB–256MB	8	4k
256MB–512MB	16	8k
512MB–1GB	32	16k
1GB–2GB	64	32k
2GB–4GB	128	64k

Applications should be in a separate partition from data files. The following are some good reasons for partitioning the hard drive and separating data files from application files:

> Multiple partitions on the same hard drive divide the drive into smaller subunits, which makes it easier and faster to back up the data (which should be backed up more often than applications).
> The data is protected from operating system failures, unstable software applications, and any unusual software problems that occur between the application and the operating system.
> The data is in one location, which makes the files easier and faster to back up, organize, and locate.

FAT32 partitions have been around a long time and are still used. Flash drives are commonly formatted for FAT32 due to the NTFS "lazy write," which prolongs a write and might not release an external drive for some time. The FAT32 file system makes more efficient use of the hard drive than FAT16. The NTFS file system is an efficient one. Table 7.4 lists the default cluster sizes for all versions of Windows Vista and higher.

TABLE 7.4 NTFS partitions and cluster sizes

Partition size	Number of sectors	Cluster size
0–16TB	8	4kB
16TB–32TB	16	8kB
>32TB–64TB	32	16kB
>64TB–128TB	64	32kB
>128TB–256TB	128	64kB

The Windows Setup installation program can be used to create a partition, and the Disk Management tool or `diskpart` utility can be used when the operating system is installed. Use the Disk Management tool to partition and manage any drive that is installed after the first hard drive. The first hard drive is partitioned initially through the Windows installation process. Figure 7.32 shows a screen capture from Windows 7. Notice that the external drives and optical drives also display in the Disk Management window. The file system is shown for each drive, such as the FAT32 file system on an attached flash drive (`G:`).

TECH TIP

Benefits of NTFS

NTFS supports disk quotas, which means that individual users can be limited on the amount of hard drive space. It can also automatically repair disk problems. For example, when a hard drive sector is going bad, the entire cluster is moved to another cluster.

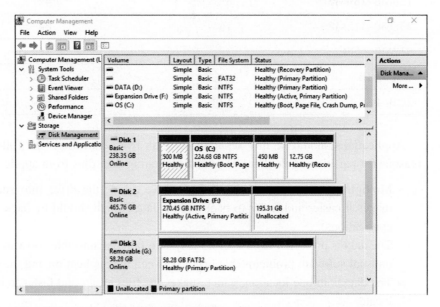

FIGURE 7.32   Windows 7 Disk Management tool

Partitions are defined as primary and extended. If there is only one hard drive installed in a system and the entire hard drive is one partition, it is the **primary partition**. The primary partition on the first detected hard drive is assigned the drive letter C:.

TECH TIP

eSATAs already partitioned

Most eSATA drives are already partitioned and formatted. The drive can be repartitioned and re-formatted as necessary using the *Disk Management* tool.

If the drive is divided, only part of the drive is the primary partition. In older operating systems, the rest of the cylinders can be designated as the **extended partitions**. An extended partition allows a drive to be further divided into **logical drives**. A logical drive is sometimes called a **volume**. A volume is assigned a drive letter and can include a logical drive and removable media such as a CD, DVD, BD, or flash drive. There can be only one extended partition per drive. In operating systems older than Windows Vista, a single hard drive can be divided into a maximum of four primary partitions. Remember that a partition is a contiguous section of storage space that functions as if it is a separate drive. See Figure 7.33 for an illustration of how one hard drive can be divided into partitions.

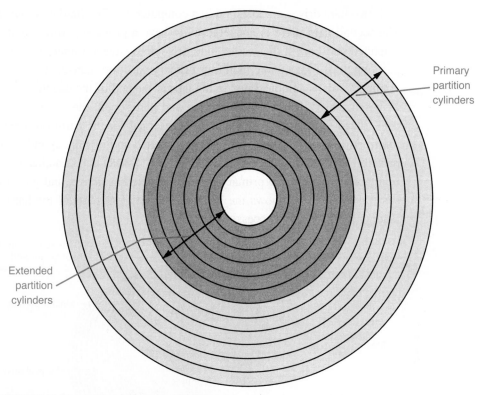

FIGURE 7.33   Hard drive partitioning

The first hard drive in a computer system must have a primary partition, but it does not require an extended partition. If the drive has an extended partition, it can be further subdivided or split into logical drives that appear as separate hard drives to the computer system. Logical drives created in the extended partition are assigned drive letters such as `D:`, `E:`, or others. The only limit for logical drives is the number of drive letters. A second operating system can reside in a logical drive. Figure 7.34 shows an illustration of a hard drive divided into a primary partition and an extended partition further subdivided into two logical drives.

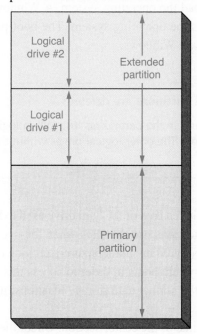

FIGURE 7.34   Two logical drives

If two hard drives are installed in a computer, the first hard drive *must* have a primary partition. The second hard drive is not required to have a primary partition and may simply have a single extended partition. If the second hard drive does have a primary partition, it can have an extended partition, too. Today, more than four primary partitions can exist, so the sections are simply called volumes. This is demonstrated in the labs at the end of the chapter.

When a hard drive is first installed and partitioned, the outermost track on the platter (cylinder 0, head 0, and physical sector 1) is reserved for the partition table. The partition table holds information about the types of partitions created and in what cylinders these partitions reside. The partition table is part of the master boot record (**MBR**) that contains a program that reads the partition table, looks for the primary partition marked as active, and goes to that partition to boot the system. Figure 7.35 shows the location of important parts of the hard drive that allows booting, reading partitions, and accessing files.

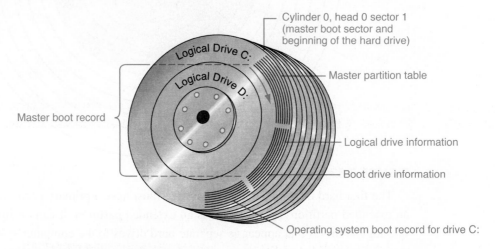

FIGURE 7.35   Hard drive structure

NTFS has two additional terms that you need to be aware of as a technician: system partition and boot partition. A Windows **system partition** is the partition on the hard drive that holds the hardware-specific files needed to load the operating system. A Windows **boot partition** is the partition on the hard drive that contains the operating system. The boot partition and the system partition can be on the same partition with Windows.

TECH TIP

What happens when different types of partitions are deleted?

When a partition is deleted, all information in the partition is lost. When logical drives in an extended partition are deleted, all data is lost. The other logical drives within the extended partition retain their information.

The Host Protected Area (**HPA**) is a hidden area of the hard drive used to hold a copy of the operating system; sometimes installed applications use the HPA when the operating system becomes so corrupt that a re-installation is necessary. Many manufacturers provide a BIOS/UEFI setting or a keystroke that can be used when the system boots in order to access this area. The HPA is commonly found on the hard drive beyond the normal data storage locations; it reduces the amount of storage space available for data.

Look back to Figure 7.32 at the first line of the center section. Under the status you can see that this computer has a recovery partition used to reset the computer to the way it was when it was purchased. Look down to the graphical section in the center and locate Disk 1. The area to the left of OS (`C:`) is an extensible firmware interface (EFI) partition. This type of partition is supported by the UEFI specification and supports the running of specific applications including diagnostics and potentially antivirus software in a graphical environment before the operating system loads. The Disk Management tool also shows external drives such as the FAT32 external flash drive (`G:`).

A partition type that is not shown is GPT, which is available with 64-bit Windows operating systems. GUID, or globally unique identifier, partition table (**GPT**) allows up to 128 partitions and volumes up to 9.4ZB. GPT partitioning is accomplished using the Disk Management tool or using the `diskpart` command-line utility. GPT supports having a backup partition table in case the primary partition becomes corrupt. A GPT disk can also have more than the MBR-based disk limit of four primary partitions.

TECH TIP

You lose data when converting to GPT

MBR-based partitions can be converted to GPT and vice versa, but data is not preserved. This is seen only with systems that have a UEFI BIOS. Back up data if you convert!

Special products can be used that partition the hard drive and allow repartitioning without any data loss. Examples include Acronis's Disk Director, EaseUS's Partition Master, and Avanquest's Partition Commander.

How Drive Letters Are Assigned

An operating system assigns drive letters to hard drives during the partitioning step. The order in which the partitions are assigned drive letters depends on three factors: (1) the number of hard drives, (2) the type of volume on the hard drives (primary or extended), and (3) the operating system.

Note that if a new drive is installed, drive letters for devices, volumes, partitions, or logical drives are added afterward. Drive letters can be changed through the Disk Management tool (right-click on the drive letter) or by using the `diskpart` command-line utility. Be careful, though, because some applications have pointers to specific files on a specific drive letter.

High-Level Formatting

The second step in preparing a hard drive for use is high-level formatting. A high-level format must be performed on all primary partitions, logical drives located within extended partitions, and GPT partitions before data can be written to the hard drive. The high-level format sets up the file system so it can accept data.

NTFS allows support for multiple data streams and support for every character in the world. NTFS also automatically remaps bad clusters to other sections of the hard drive without any additional time or utility. During the installation process, Windows allows for a **quick format** (where you see the word "(quick)" after the option) or a full format (sometimes called a standard format). The **full format** scans for and marks bad sectors. This prevents the operating system from being installed on a sector that may cause operating system issues. The quick format simply prepares the drive for data and takes a lot less time than a full format. Use the full format if you suspect the drive has issues. Figure 7.36 shows the NTFS partition structure once it has been set up and the high-level formatting is completed.

The high-level format creates two file allocation tables (FATs): one primary and one secondary. The formatting process also creates the root directory that renumbers the sectors. The **FAT** keeps track of the hard disk's file locations. It is similar to a table of contents in a book as it lists where the files are located in the partition. Table 7.5 shows the differences between the file systems.

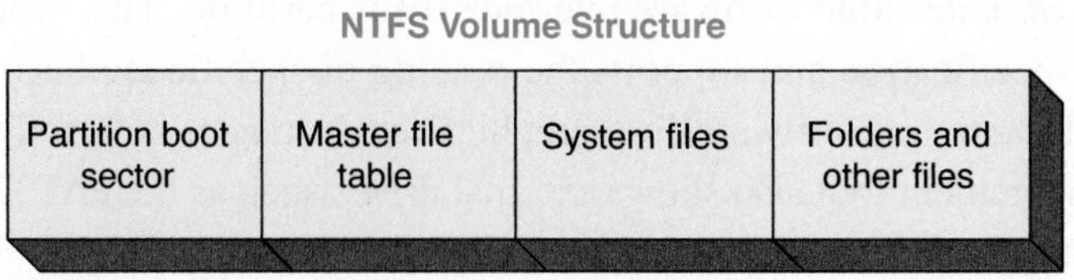

NTFS Volume Structure

| Partition boot sector | Master file table | System files | Folders and other files |

FIGURE 7.36   NTFS volume structure

TABLE 7.5   Comparing file systems

Specification	FAT16	FAT32	NTFS	exFAT
Maximum file size	4GB	4GB	~16TB	~16EB
Maximum volume (partition) size	4GB (2GB, if shared with a really old computer)	32GB (max format)	2TB (or greater)	64ZB (512TB recommended)
Maximum files per volume	~64 thousand	~4 million	~4 billion	Not defined (but 1,000 per directory)

High-level formatting can be performed using the `format` command or by using the Windows Disk Management tool. The area of the disk that contains information about the system files is the DOS boot record (**DBR**) and is located on the hard drive's cylinder 0, head 1, sector 1. The more common term for this today (because DOS is no longer a major operating system) is **boot sector** or volume boot record.

Additional drive partitions and drives installed after the first hard drive partition is created use the Windows Disk Management tool to apply high-level formatting to the drive. The first hard drive partition is normally high-level formatted as part of the operating system installation process. Exercises at the end of the chapter explain how to partition and high-level format a hard drive.

Windows Disk Management

In the Windows environment, storage devices are managed with a snap-in (an installable module) called Disk Management. With Windows, there are two types of storage: basic storage and dynamic storage. The big difference between these two is that you can make partitions and resize changes with a dynamic disk, but not with a basic disk. Table 7.6 explains these and other associated terms.

TECH TIP

Hibernation affects disk space

Whenever you put your computer in hibernate mode, information in RAM is stored temporarily on the hard drive. This requires free hard drive space.

TABLE 7.6   Logical disk management terms

Term	Description
Basic storage	One of the two types of storage. This is what has traditionally been known as a partition. It is the default method because it is used by all operating systems.
Basic disk	Any drive that has been partitioned and set up for writing files. A basic disk has primary partitions, extended partitions, and logical drives contained within the extended partitions.
Dynamic storage	The second type of storage; contrast with basic storage. Allows you to create primary partitions, logical drives, and dynamic volumes on storage devices. More powerful than basic storage in that it allows creation of simple, spanned, or striped volumes using dynamic disks.
Dynamic disk	A disk made up of volumes. A volume can be the entire hard disk, parts of the hard disk combined into one unit, and other specific types of volumes, such as single, spanned, or striped volumes. Cannot be on a removable drive.
Simple volume	Disk space allocated from one hard drive. The space does not have to be contiguous.
Spanned volume	Disk space created from multiple hard drives. Also known as "just a bunch of disks" (**JBOD**). Windows writes data to a spanned volume in such a way that the first hard drive is used until the space is filled. Then, the second hard drive's space is used for writing. This continues until all hard drives in the spanned volume are utilized.
Striped volume	Data is written across 2 to 32 hard drives. It is different from a spanned volume in that each drive is used alternately. Another name for this is striping or RAID 0 (covered in the next section).
System volume	Holds the files needed to boot the operating system.
Boot volume	Holds the remaining operating system files. Can be the same volume as the system volume.
RAW volume	A volume that has never been high-level formatted and does not contain a file system.

   A basic disk, simple volume, or spanned volume can be resized, shrunk, or expanded without affecting data.

TECH TIP

Managing dynamic disks

Use the *Disk Management* tool (found in the *Computer Management* console) to work with dynamic disks or to convert a basic disk to a dynamic one. Once accomplished, the conversion process cannot be reversed. Figure 7.37 shows some of these concepts.

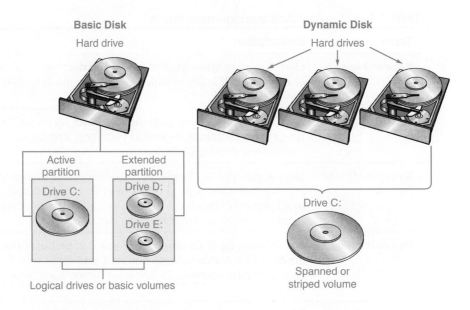

FIGURE 7.37   Disk management concepts

TECH TIP

Determining what type of partition you have

To determine what type of partition is on a computer, use the Disk Management tool.

In order to **extend** (make larger), **split** (break into two sections), or **shrink** (reduce the size of) a partition, use the following steps:

Step 1. Access Windows *Disk Management* tool.

Step 2. Right-click on the drive volume.

Step 3. Select the appropriate option (*Shrink volume* or *Extend volume*).

Figure 7.38 shows a hard drive partition and the steps to shrink it so that another partition can be created.

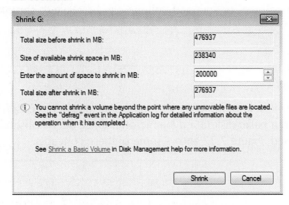

FIGURE 7.38   Resizing a partition

Fault Tolerance

A **drive array** is the use of two or more hard drives configured for speed, redundancy, or both (see Figure 7.39). Redundant array of independent disks (**RAID**) allows reading from and writing to multiple hard drives for larger storage areas, better performance, and fault tolerance. Fault tolerance is the ability to continue functioning after a hardware or software failure. A RAID array can be implemented with hardware or software. Hardware RAID is configured through the BIOS.

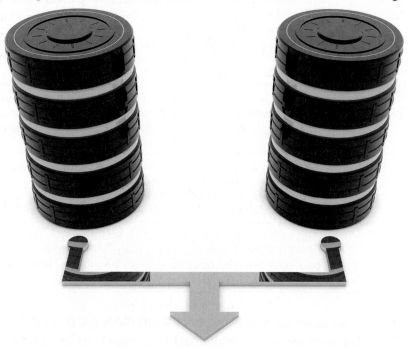

FIGURE 7.39   RAID

Generic hardware RAID steps are as follows:

Step 1. Ensure that the motherboard ports that you want to use are enabled.

Step 2. Ensure that you have RAID drivers for the hard drives used in the RAID.

Step 3. Physically install and cable the hard drives.

Step 4. Enter BIOS/UEFI and enable RAID.

Step 5. Configure RAID in BIOS/UEFI or through a special key sequence to enter the RAID BIOS configuration.

Step 6. Install Windows on a RAID, using the Custom (Advanced) Installation option.

Software RAID is configured through Windows or through software provided by the RAID adapter manufacturer. If you want to be able to control the RAID through Windows and resize the volumes or make adjustments, then use a software RAID. A lab at the end of the chapter demonstrates how to do this.

RAID can also be implemented with flash cache modules (FCMs) and a traditional mechanical hard drive. Intel has specific processors and chipsets that support a RAID configuration. Software on the host device and/or device drivers provides optimization and oversight.

RAID comes in many different levels, but the ones implemented in the Windows environment are 0, 1, and 5. Some motherboards support "nested" RAID, which means RAID levels are combined. This method also increases the complexity of the hard drive setup. Table 7.7 explains these levels.

CHAPTER 7

TABLE 7.7   RAID

RAID level	Description
0	Also called **disk striping** or disk striping without parity. Data is alternately written on two or more hard drives, which increases system performance. These drives are seen by the system as one logical drive. **RAID 0** does not protect data when a hard drive fails. This has the fastest read and write performance.
1	Also called disk mirroring or disk duplexing. **RAID 1** protects against hard drive failure. **Disk mirroring** uses two or more hard drives and one disk controller. The same data is written to two drives. If one drive should fail, the system continues to function. With disk duplexing, a similar concept is used except that two disk controllers are used. Performance is slightly degraded when writing data because it has to be written to two drives.
0+1	A striped set and a mirrored set combined. Four hard drives minimum are required with an even number of disks. It creates a second striped set to mirror a primary striped set of disks. Also called RAID 01. This mode can read from the drive quickly, but a slight degradation when writing.
1+0	A mirrored set and a striped set combined with four hard drives as a minimum. The difference between 1+0 and 0+1 is that 1+0 has a striped set from a set of mirrored drives. Also called **RAID 10**. This mode can read from the drive quickly, but has a slight degradation when writing.
5	Also called disk striping with parity. **RAID 5** writes data to three or more hard drives. Included with the data is parity information. If a drive fails, the data can be rebuilt from the other two drives' information. This level can read and write data quickly.

Figure 7.40 shows the different types of RAID. With RAID 0, blocks of data (B1, B2, B3, etc.) are placed on alternating drives. With RAID 1, the same block of data is written to two drives. RAID 5 has one drive that contains parity information (P) for particular blocks of data such as B1 and B2.

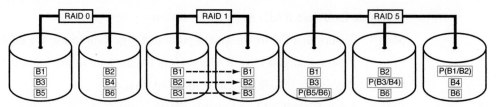

FIGURE 7.40   RAID concepts

Windows Vista Business and higher support simple, spanned, and striped volumes. Refer back to Table 7.6 to reacquaint yourself with these terms. Windows 7/8/10 Professional and higher support simple, spanned, striped, and mirrored volumes. Keep in mind that a spanned volume does not provide redundancy or fault tolerance like most of the RAID levels do.

RAID drives are often **hot swappable**—they can be removed or installed while power is applied to the computer. USB, SATA, and serial-attached SCSI (SAS) all support hot swapping, but RAID is not required to be supported. Always refer to the drive and computer manual before hot swapping any hard drive. RAID rebuilds are time and input/output (I/O) intensive. Be prepared for the system to be out of commission for a while depending on the size of the drive and RAID type.

Hardware RAID for home or business computer used to require a separate RAID adapter and software to perform the RAID. Now many motherboards support RAID as well as the Windows Vista, 7, 8, and 10 operating systems. Many times, you must configure the motherboard BIOS/UEFI for RAID as part of your initial configuration. Table 7.8 shows some common RAID BIOS configuration parameters.

TABLE 7.8 RAID BIOS/UEFI configuration settings

BIOS setting	Description
SATA mode: AHCI Mode	A mode that may mean that hot swapping is supported. A set of commands that can be used to increase storage performance.
SATA mode: RAID Mode or Discrete SATA Mode	Allows you to select a particular RAID level and the drives associated with the RAID.
SATA drives: Detected RAID Volume	Usually an information screen that shows the type of RAID configured, if any.
SATA drives: eSATA Controller Mode	Allows configuration of RAID through the eSATA port.
SATA drives: eSATA Port x Hot Plug Capability	Allows enabling or disabling hot swapping for eSATA ports.

Removable Drive Storage

PATA and SATA interfaces have been used for quite some time to connect hard drives. PATA was used for internal devices. SATA has been used for both internal and external storage devices such as optical drives and tape drives. **Tape drives** can be attached using SATA or can attach to USB, eSATA, eSATAp, or IEEE 1394 ports if they are external devices. External drives might require two USB ports (see Figure 7.41) when an external power source is not attached. Tape drives are installed using similar methods of like devices that use these ports. When tapes are used, the most common types of tapes used for backups are DAT (digital audio tape) and Traven. Tape capacities tend to be lower than optical storage (covered in Chapter 8), which typically has less storage than hard drives. Tape capacities can be anywhere from 12GB to 10TB (but are typically less than this). The most common types of removable storage are optical (CD/DVD/BD), USB flash drives, or hard drive storage devices.

FIGURE 7.41   External hard drive with 2 USB connectors

Windows Storage Spaces

Microsoft Windows 8 and Windows 10 support something called **Windows Storage Spaces**, which combines drives into a flexible data storage option. An administrator first creates a **storage pool**, which is two or more physical disks that can be different types, such as a SATA drive and a USB drive. A **storage space** is a virtual disk created from available space in a storage pool. There are three types of storage spaces:

> Simple—No resiliency provided. Data is striped across physical disks. Provides the highest performance, but there is a loss of data if one disk fails.

> Parity—Stripes data across the physical disks and includes parity information. Slows performance.

> Mirror—Stripes data across multiple disks and copies the same data for the highest level of resiliency.

Unlike RAID, if you add a drive to a storage space, the data will not be rewritten to include the new drive. Instead, new data will use all of the drives. In order to create a storage space, use the following steps:

Step 1. Access the *Storage Spaces* Windows Control Panel link.

Step 2. Select the drives to be used > select *Create pool* (see Figure 7.42).

Step 3. Name the storage space and select the drive letter, file system, resiliency type, and pool size > *Create storage space* (see Figure 7.43).

When created, the storage drive letter appears in File Explorer (see Figure 7.44).

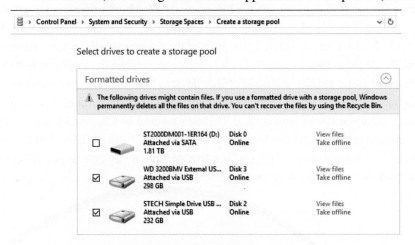

> Control Panel > System and Security > Storage Spaces > Create a storage pool

Select drives to create a storage pool

Formatted drives				⌃

⚠ The following drives might contain files. If you use a formatted drive with a storage pool, Windows permanently deletes all the files on that drive. You can't recover the files by using the Recycle Bin.

☐	ST2000DM001-1ER164 (D:) Attached via SATA 1.81 TB	Disk 0 Online	View files Take offline
☑	WD 3200BMV External US... Attached via USB 298 GB	Disk 3 Online	View files Take offline
☑	STECH Simple Drive USB ... Attached via USB 232 GB	Disk 2 Online	View files Take offline

FIGURE 7.42 Windows Storage Spaces—Creating a storage pool

Enter a name, resiliency type, and size for the storage space

Name and drive letter

Name: Storage space

Drive letter: F: ∨

File system: NTFS ∨

Resiliency

Resiliency type: Two-way mirror ∨

ⓘ A two-way mirror storage space writes two copies of your data, helping to protect you from a single drive failure. A two-way mirror storage space requires at least two drives.

Size

Total pool capacity: 529 GB

Available pool capacity: 529 GB

Size (maximum): 231 GB ∨

Including resiliency: 462 GB

FIGURE 7.43 Windows Storage Spaces—Defining parameters

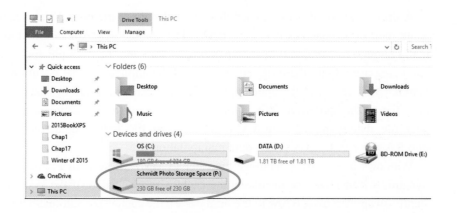

FIGURE 7.44 Windows Storage Spaces, as shown in File Explorer

Disk Caching/Virtual Memory

A hard drive—RAM built into the hard drive—and motherboard RAM (see Figure 7.45) are used as part of any computer's storage system. An easy way to speed up the hard drive is to create a **disk cache**. This puts data into RAM where it can be retrieved much faster than if the data was still on the hard drive. When data is read from the hard drive, the next requested data is frequently located in the adjacent clusters. Disk caching reads more data from the hard drive than requested. Cache on a hard drive controller, sometimes called a data buffer, allows the read/write heads to read more than just one sector at a time. A hard drive can read up to an entire track of information and hold this data until needed without returning to the hard drive for each sector.

FIGURE 7.45 Computer storage system—hard drive and RAM

Both PATA and SATA drives can contain 2MB to 128MB or more of RAM (cache memory). Because many drives are mechanical devices, they take time to reorder write data to the platters. With cache memory installed, information can be prefetched from the computer's system RAM and stored in the hard drive's cache memory. This frees up the system RAM for other tasks and improves the system and hard drive's performance.

A different way of using a hard drive is with virtual memory. Virtual memory is a method of using hard drive space as if it were RAM. The amount of RAM installed in a system is not normally enough to handle all of the operating system and the multiple applications that are opened and being used. Only the program and data of the application that is currently being used is what is in RAM. The rest of the open applications and data are stored in what is called a swap file or a page file on the hard drive. When you click over to a different application that is held in the swap/page file, data is moved from RAM into the swap file and the data you need to look at is moved into RAM for faster access and data manipulation.

Windows uses Virtual memory manager (VMM), as seen in Figure 7.46. The disk cache is dynamic—it increases or decreases the cache size as needed. If the system begins to page (constantly swap data from RAM to the hard drive), the cache size automatically shrinks. In Windows, the virtual memory swap file/page file is called PAGEFILE.SYS. Here is how to adjust it:

> In Windows 7 Windows Explorer, right-click *Computer* > *Properties*. In the left pane, select *Advanced system settings* > *Advanced* tab. In the *Virtual memory* section, click *Change*. Then, to manually configure the settings, clear the *Automatically manage paging file size for all drives* checkbox and adjust the settings as needed.

> In Windows 8, access the *System and Security* Control Panel > *System* > *Advanced system settings* link > *Advanced* tab > the Performance section's *Settings* button > *Advanced* tab > *Change* button. Change the parameters and click the *OK* button twice.

> In Windows 10, access the *Start* button > *Settings*. In the *Find a setting* search textbox, type performance. Select the *Adjust the appearance and performance of Windows* link > *Advanced* tab > *Change* button. Change the parameters and click the *OK* button twice.

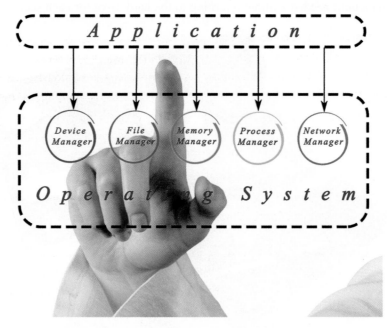

FIGURE 7.46   Windows virtual memory manager

TECH TIP

Where should you keep a swap/page file?

If multiple hard drives are available, a technician might want to move the swap/page file to a different drive. Always put the swap/page file on the fastest hard drive, unless that hard drive lacks space. The swap/page file can reside on multiple hard drives. It is best to keep the swap/page file on a hard drive that does not contain the operating system.

32-bit Windows versions use 32-bit demand-paged virtual memory, and each process gets 4GB of address space divided into two 2-GB sections. One 2-GB section is shared with the rest of the system and the other 2-GB section is reserved for the one application. All the memory space is divided into 4-KB blocks of memory called "pages." The operating system allocates as much available RAM as possible to an application. Then, the operating system swaps or pages the application to and from the temporary swap file as needed. The operating system determines the optimum setting for this swap file; however, the swap file size can be changed.

64-bit Windows can have 2 or 4GB for each 32-bit process. For 64-bit software, 7 or 8TB is the maximum. The operating system kernel gets 8TB maximum. Refer back to Figure 6.16 in Chapter 6 to review this concept.

The page file can get corrupted. If so, boot the system and press F8 while booting. Select the option to repair the computer. If this does not repair it, you may have to make manual adjustments from the command prompt including removing the attributes from the `pagefile.sys` file, and then manually deleting it so it can be rebuilt when Windows boots. Search the Windows website for more details on this harder and more detailed method.

TECH TIP

Adding more physical RAM helps with caching

One of the most effective ways to speed up a computer is to reduce the amount of data that has to be swapped from the hard drive to RAM. This is done by increasing the amount of motherboard RAM.

Troubleshooting Storage Devices Overview

Storage devices are critical to computer users because that is where their data is located. Sadly, users do not back up their data or system frequently. Blackblaze (www.blackblaze.com) did a study of over 25,000 mechanical drives and found that over a four-year period, 78 percent of the drives lasted longer than four years, but 22 percent of them failed during the first four years. Mechanical drives have moving parts and moving parts fail. Expect it!

Tools that a technician needs to troubleshoot storage devices include hardware and software. The list that follows is a good starting point:

> Screwdriver to loosen or remove screws.
> External hard drive enclosure to be able to check a drive from another system or be able to determine whether the problem is the drive or the motherboard port (look back to Figure 7.4 to see one).
> Software such as the `chkdsk`, `format`, or `bootrec` commands, and Windows tools such as Error-checking or Disk Management. `Chkdsk` checks a drive for physical and file structure errors and can attempt to fix them. The `format` command is used to format a disk. The `bootrec` command is used from the System Recovery environment to repair and recover from hard drive issues.
> **File recovery software** is something some companies own and a service they provide. For technicians that do not have this software, they should at least have the name of a company they recommend or use.

The specific hardware or software tool to use depends on the situation and will be covered in the sections that follow. One thing to remember when troubleshooting a storage device is the user. A technician is faced with angry users most when storage devices are involved, especially if it holds their most critical data. Stay calm and do the best you can. Just because a system will not boot from the hard drive does not mean it is bad. There are things you can do as you will soon see.

Slow Performance

Keeping a computer system in a clean and cool operating environment extends the life of the hard drive. The most common hard drive failures are due to moving parts (heads and motors), power fluctuations, and/or failures. Performing preventive maintenance on the entire computer is good for all components found inside the computer, including the hard drive subsystem.

Windows has three great tools to use in hard drive preventive maintenance (see Figure 7.47): Error-checking (*Check now* or *Check* button), Disk Cleanup, and Disk Defragmenter. In Windows, you can use Error-checking/Check now (Vista/7) to locate **lost clusters**, which are clusters disassociated from data files. These clusters occupy disk space. These tools are also good for intermittent read/write errors. Locate the drive in Windows Explorer (Vista/7) or File Explorer (8/10), right-click the drive, and then select *Properties > Tool* tab *> Check now (Vista/7) / Check (8/10)*.

FIGURE 7.47   Disk maintenance

Windows also has a program called **Disk Cleanup** that removes temporary files, removes offline Internet files, empties the Recycle Bin, compresses unused files, removes unused programs, and prompts you before doing any of this. To access Disk Cleanup, follow these steps:

Step 1. Access *Windows Explorer* (Vista/7)/*File Explorer* (8/10).

Step 2. Right-click on the drive letter (commonly c:) and select *Properties*.

Step 3. On the *General* tab, select *Disk Cleanup* button.

Step 4. In the Disk Cleanup window, click in the checkboxes for the options desired and click *OK* (as shown in Figure 7.48). Table 7.9 contains the types of files that can be removed with this tool.

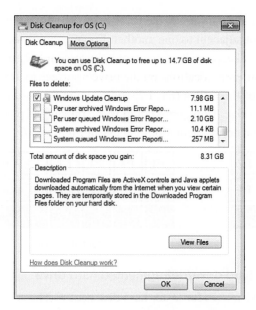

FIGURE 7.48   Disk Cleanup window

TABLE 7.9   Disk Cleanup file removal

File type	Description
Downloaded Program Files	Java applets and ActiveX controls that might be downloaded automatically when a particular website is accessed
Temporary Internet files	Frequently accessed web pages stored on the hard drive for quicker access
Offline web pages	Web pages that can be retrieved from the hard drive even when the computer does not have Internet connectivity
Recycle Bin	Files marked for deletion that are still stored on the hard drive until the Recycle Bin is emptied
Setup log files	Files created by Windows when configuration has changed
System error memory dump files	Data from memory at the time of a blue screen of death (BSOD) crash
Temporary files	Files generated by programs that are usually deleted when the application is closed
Thumbnails	Copies of picture, video, and document thumbnails that display quickly when a folder is opened if thumbnails view is being used
Per user archived/ queued Windows error report	Files used for error reporting and when checking for possible solutions
System archived/queued windows error report	Files used for error reporting and when checking for possible solutions

TECH TIP

Running Disk Cleanup from a command prompt

To run Disk Cleanup from a command prompt, type `cleanmgr` and then press Enter.

Over time, as files are added to a hard drive, the files become fragmented, which means the clusters that make up the file are not adjacent to one another. Fragmentation slows down the hard drive in two ways: (1) the FAT has to keep track of scattered clusters and (2) the hard drive read/write head assembly must move to different locations on the drive's surface to access a single file. Figure 7.49 illustrates fragmentation of three files (F1, F2, and F3) and the results after defragmentation has been executed on the hard drive. **Defragmentation** is the process of placing files in contiguous sectors. Notice the results of the defragmentation process in Figure 7.49.

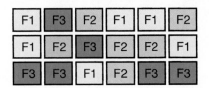

Three fragmented files

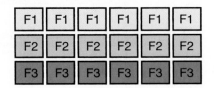

Three contiguous files

FIGURE 7.49   Fragmented hard drive/defragmented hard drive

Defragmenting the hard drive makes for faster hard disk access. These measures also extend the life of the hard drive because the drive's mechanical movements are reduced. The methods used in Windows to defragment are as follows:

> In Windows Vista/7, open *Windows Explorer*, locate a hard drive letter, right-click it, and select *Properties* > *Tools* tab > *Defragment Now* button.

> In Windows 8/10, open *File Explorer*, locate a hard drive letter, right-click it, and select *Properties* > *Tools* tab > *Optimize*.

> From a command prompt, use the `defrag` command.

TECH TIP

SSD defragmentation kills

Do not defragment an SSD as you would a magnetic hard drive. Defragmentation causes more reads and writes, which reduces the life span of the SSD.

You should periodically defragment files on a mechanical PATA or SATA hard drive. Users who delete files often and have large files that are constantly revised should especially make use of the defragmentation tool. You can use the Disk Defragmenter *tool* to check whether a drive partition needs to be defragmented.

TECH TIP

Tool order matters

Use the Error-checking (Check now or Check) and Disk Cleanup tools before running the Disk Defragmenter tool.

Note that Windows 7 automatically schedules your hard drive to be defragmented every Wednesday at 1 a.m. if the computer is powered on. Otherwise, defragmentation runs automatically the next time the computer is powered on. Windows 8 and 10 schedule a weekly hard drive optimization. You can adjust this scheduled time through the Disk Defragmenter tool.

Troubleshooting New Storage Device Installation

Most problems with new drive installation stem from improper configuration of jumpers on PATA drives or problems with cabling. BIOS and the operating system can display a multitude of symptoms including POST error codes, beeps, and messages, such as the following:

> Hard drive not found
> No boot device available
> Hard drive not present
> Inaccessible boot device
> Invalid boot disk

The following tips assist with checking possible problems when the **drive is not recognized** by the system.

> Check the physical settings, if necessary (power cable, jumper settings, secure data cable, data cable pin 1 orientation, and device placement on data cable).
> Check the drive type setting in BIOS Setup and ensure that the ports are enabled (especially SATA ports).
> If after you have configured the drive, installed it, and powered it on, the BIOS shows the drive type as "None," "Not installed," or displays all 0s in the drive parameters even though you set it to automatically detect the drive, then the BIOS is not able to detect it. Check the BIOS/UEFI SATA mode and BIOS/UEFI version. Check all jumper settings, check cable connection(s), and check the power connection. If two PATA drives connect to the same cable, disconnect the slave drive. In Setup, reduce any advanced features to their lowest values or disable them. Increase the amount of time the computer takes to initialize the hard drive by going into Setup and modifying such features as hard drive boot delay or set the boot speed to the lowest value. This gives the hard drive more time to spin up and reach its appropriate RPM before data is read from it. Make sure the motherboard port is enabled.
> Has the drive been partitioned and one partition marked as the active partition? Has the drive been high-level formatted?
> Verify that the mounting screw to hold the drive in the case is not too tight. Loosen the screw and power up the computer. Figure 7.50 shows the mounting screws for a hard drive installed in a tower case.
> If the hard drive does not format to full capacity, (a) your BIOS may not support the larger drive and/or the BIOS must be upgraded, (b) you have selected a file system that does not support larger partitions, or (c) you need an updated driver.
> If during power-on the hard drive does not spin up or the hard drive spins down after a few seconds, check the power connector, the data cable, the drive recognized in BIOS, jumper settings, energy management jumpers or settings in Setup, and any software that came with the drive that enables power management. Disable power management in BIOS and/or the operating system. Try installing the drive in another system.
> If the system locks or you get a blue screen of death (**BSOD**), write down the message or code, if any, and try a warm boot ([Ctrl] + [Alt] + [Delete]). If the drive is recognized after the warm boot, the Setup program may be running too fast for the drive to initialize. Refer to the hard drive documentation to see if the hard drive has a setting to help with this problem.

CHAPTER 7

FIGURE 7.50   Hard drive mounting screws

Troubleshooting Previously Installed Storage Devices

Previously installed boot devices can have all of the symptoms that a newly installed storage device can plus the following additional ones:

> **Loud clicking noise**
> Read/write errors
> Slow to respond
> Blue screen of death (BSOD) or pinwheel of death (Mac OS X)

Because many drives are mechanical devices, they make noises. Sometimes these noises are because the hard drive is being used too much as virtual memory due to a lack of physical RAM. Some noises are normal and some are an indication of problems, as shown in Figure 7.51.

Normal noises

Whining noise on spin up

Periodic clicking or whirling sounds when the drive is being accessed

Clicking sound made by heads parking during power saving modes or when powering off

Abnormal noises

High-pitched whining sound

Repeated clicking or tapping sounds when computer is idle

High-frequency vibration in mounting hardware

Hard drive clicks and/or a POST error

ERROR\\

FIGURE 7.51   Hard drive noises

When a hard drive starts making that loud clicking, tapping sound, back up the drive immediately and go ahead and purchase a replacement drive. The drive is failing!

The following are generic guidelines for hard drives that have worked, but are now having problems or the computer **fails to boot**:

> Run a virus-checking program after booting from virus-free boot media. Many viruses are specifically designed to attack the hard drive. If you have to wipe the hard drive to ensure the

virus is erased before re-installing the operating system, applications, and data, ensure you do a full format and not a quick one as part of the operating system installation process.

> Has there been a recent cleaning of the computer or has someone recently removed the top from the computer? If so, check all cables and verify that they correctly connect pin 1 to pin 1 of the adapter or motherboard. Check the power connection to the hard drive.

TECH TIP

Does your hard drive stick?

Place a hand on top of the drive as you turn on the computer. Does the drive spin at all? If not, the problem is probably a "sticky" drive or a bad drive. A hard drive must spin at a certain RPM before the heads move over the surface of the hard drive. To check to see whether the drive is sticking, remove the drive and try spinning the spindle motor by hand. Otherwise, remove the drive, hold the drive in your hand, and give a quick jerk with your wrist. Another trick that works is to remove the hard drive from the case, place the drive in a plastic bag, and put it in the freezer for a couple of hours. Then, remove the drive and allow it to warm up to room temperature. Then, re-install the drive into the system and try it.

> If the hard drive flashes quickly on bootup, the controller is trying to read the partition table in the master boot record. If this information is not found, various symptoms can be shown, such as the error messages "Invalid boot disk," "Inaccessible boot device," "Invalid partition table," "Error loading operating system," "Missing operating system," or "No operating system found." Use the `diskpart` command from the Windows Recovery Environment (WinRE) to see whether the hard drive partition table is okay. Here are a couple of commands to help within this utility: `list disk`, `list volume`, `list partition`, `detail disk`, `detail volume`, and `detail partition`. Try running `bootrec /fixmbr` or use a hard drive utility to repair the partition table.

> Do you receive a message such as "Disk Boot Failure," "Non-System Disk," or "Disk Error"? These errors may indicate a boot record problem. The solution is to boot from a bootable disc or USB flash drive to see if drive `c:` is available. When doing so, change the BIOS/UEFI boot order settings to boot to your removable media. The operating system may have to be reloaded. Also, verify that the primary partition is marked as active and that there is not nonbootable media such as a disc or USB flash drive inserted into or attached to the system. Check the first boot option setting in BIOS/UEFI and make sure it is set to the appropriate drive.

> If you receive a message "Hard drive not found," "No boot device available," "Fixed disk error," or "Disk boot failure," the BIOS cannot find the hard drive. Check cabling. Place the drive in an external enclosure and attach to a working computer.

> If a self-monitoring, analysis and reporting technology (**S.M.A.R.T.**) error appears, back up data and research the error to take immediate action. S.M.A.R.T. is used to monitor both mechanical hard drives and SSDs. S.M.A.R.T. errors sometimes appear immediately before a failure. Table 7.10 has a few of the S.M.A.R.T. error codes, but remember that drive manufacturers may have their own.

TABLE 7.10　S.M.A.R.T. error codes

Attribute	Description
Reallocated sectors count	The number of sectors that were marked as bad and the data within those sectors had to be moved
Spin retry	The number of times the drive was not up to speed in order to read and write from the drive

Attribute	Description
SATA downshift error count or runtime bad block count	The number of data blocks that contained uncorrectable errors
Reported uncorrectable errors	The number of uncorrectable errors detected
Reallocation event	How many times data had to be remapped
Soft read error rate or TA counter detected	The number of off-track errors

> When Windows has startup problems, the Windows Recovery Environment (WinRE) and *Advanced Options* menu (press F8 on startup) are used. With Windows 8 or 10 devices, the system may boot too fast to access this. Hold down the Shift while restarting the system. Then select *Troubleshoot > Advanced options >* either *Automatic Repair* (in Windows 8)/*Startup Repair* (in Windows 10) or *Command Prompt*. Many times, startup problems are due to a virus. Other utilities that help with MBR, boot sector, and system files are the System File Checker (SFC), and the *Advanced Boot Options* menu. Use bootrec /fixmbr or bootrec /fixboot from the Windows Recovery Environment (WinRE).

TECH TIP

Use System File Checker

You can run the System File Checker program from the command prompt by typing sfc /scannow. The System File Checker is also needed after removing some viruses.

> When Windows has startup problems due to incompatible hardware or software or a corrupted installation process, the *Advanced Boot Options* menu can help.
> If an insufficient disk space error appears or **slow performance** (takes a long time to respond), delete unnecessary files, including .tmp files, from the hard drive, empty the Recycle Bin, and save files to an optical disc, a flash drive, or an external hard drive and remove the moved files from the hard drive. Use the Disk Cleanup and Defragmenter tool. Another option is to add another hard drive and move some (or all) data files to it.
> For eSATA drives, check the power cabling and data cabling. Ensure that the data cable is the correct type for the port and device being used. Partition and format the drive before data is written to it. Ensure that the port is enabled through BIOS. The BIOS may require an update, or a device driver may be required (especially if the drive is listed under "other devices" in Device Manager). BIOS incompatibilities are the most common issue with installations. Note that some operating systems report SATA drives as SCSI drives.
> If the computer reports that the hard drive may have a defective area or if you start getting **read/write failure** notices, right-click on the hard drive volume > *Properties > Tools* tab > *Check now (*Vista/7) */Check* (8/10). The drive may need to be replaced soon.
> If drives fail frequently in a particular computer, check for heat problems, power fluctuations, vibrations, improper mounting screws or hardware that might cause vibrations, and environmental issues such as dust, heat, magnetic fields, smoke, and nearby motors. Consider an SSD if the computer is in a harsh environment.
> If a USB drive is the boot device and the system will not boot, unplug the drive, reattach it, and restart the system.
> If a **proprietary crash screen** appears, note the message and/or code and research from another computer.

> If a **spinning pinwheel**, ball, hourglass, or other application-specific icon appears, a message that an application is not responding (sometimes asking you if you want to wait or kill the application) appears, or a drive takes forever to respond within an application, use the Disk Management tool to view the status of the drive. Note that a colored spinning pinwheel that occurs on a Mac is covered in Chapter 17. Table 7.11 shows some of the normal and problem **drive status** messages seen in the Windows Disk Management tool. These status messages can help with drive management, troubleshooting, and recovery.

TABLE 7.11   Disk Management status states

Disk Management State	Description
Active	The bootable partition, usually on the first hard drive, is ready for use.
Dynamic	An alternative to the basic disk, the dynamic disk has volumes instead of partitions. Types of volumes include simple volumes, volumes that span more than one drive, and RAID volumes.
Failed	The basic disk or dynamic volume cannot be started; the disk or volume could be damaged; the file system could be corrupted; or there may be a problem with the underlying physical disk (turned on, cabled correctly) or with an associated RAID drive. Right-click the disk and select *Reactivate disk*. Right-click the dynamic volume and select *Reactivate volume*.
Foreign	A dynamic disk from another computer has just been installed. Right-click the disk and select *Import Foreign Disks*.
Healthy	The drive is ready to be used.
Not Initialized	A basic disk is not ready to be used. Right-click the disk and select *Initialize Disk*. The **Initialize Disk** option enables a disk so that data may be stored.
Invalid	The operating system cannot access the dynamic disk. Convert the disk to a basic disk (by right-clicking the disk number and selecting *Convert to basic disk*).
Offline	Ensure that the physical disk is turned on and cabled correctly. Right-click it and select *Reactivate Disk* or *Activate*.
Online (errors)	Use the hard drive Error-checking tool. In Windows Explorer/File Explorer, right-click the hard drive partition and then select *Properties*, the *Tools* tab, and *Check now* (Vista/7) /*Check* (8/10) button.
Unallocated	Space on a hard drive has not been partitioned or put into a volume.
Unknown	A new drive has not been initialized properly. Right-click it and select *Initialize disk*. The volume boot sector may be corrupted or infected by a virus.
Unreadable	The drive has not had time to spin up. Restart the computer and rescan the disk (using the *Action* menu item).

RAID Issues

When you add a RAID to a computer, you increase the complexity of the disk management. When two hard drives are configured in a RAID, they are seen as one volume and managed as one volume. Multiply that by the different types of RAID and the number of hard drives involved in the RAID, and you have a real opportunity for some fun issues. Symptoms of RAID problems follow along the same lines of a hard drive failure (read/write failure, slow system performance, loud clicking noise, failure to boot, drive not recognized, operating system not found, or a BSOD). The following issues can help you with RAID configurations:

> If you have done RAID through the BIOS/UEFI, you cannot manage the RAID through Windows (it is grayed out and shows as no fault tolerance). If you want to manage the RAID through Windows, you will have to break the RAID in BIOS/UEFI (remove the RAID) and then re-create the RAID in Windows. Back up your data before doing this.

> Sometimes as part of the RAID configuration, you need driver media for the Windows installation or RAID failure troubleshooting process. Follow the motherboard or RAID adapter's manufacturing directions on how to create this media (usually a USB drive or optical disc, even though the directions on the screen may say floppy disk).

> If Windows won't allow you or give you the option to do a RAID, check the BIOS/UEFI settings and ensure that AHCI has been enabled for the drives.

> If disk mirroring is not an option in Windows Disk Management, check your Windows version. You must have Windows Professional or a higher edition to do the RAID.

> If Windows no longer boots, a BSOD appears, and the Windows boot drive is part of a RAID, re-install Windows if you want to keep the RAID. You may have to get drivers before doing this. If you do not care about the RAID and just want Windows to boot again, remove the hardware RAID. You can also use the BSOD code shown to research the error.

> If a RAID partition suddenly goes missing, check for a virus.

> If you receive a message such as **RAID not found**, check the hardware or software configuration (depending on which type of RAID was configured). A power surge can corrupt a hardware RAID configuration done through BIOS Setup. A system upgrade, application upgrade, or new application can affect a software RAID.

> If the **RAID stops working**, use the Windows Disk Management tool to check the status of the drives. Then check the RAID configuration if the drives are okay.

SSD Issues

The BIOS should recognize an internally installed SSD. If it does not, go into the system BIOS/UEFI Setup and ensure that the connector to which the SSD attaches is enabled. Be especially careful with SATA ports and port numbering. Configure the system to automatically detect the new drive, save the settings, and reboot the system. Here are some things to try, but remember that other hard drive tips still apply, such as those relating to the computer not booting or the operating system not found:

> Restart the PC.
> Try another SATA port or cable.
> Uninstall/re-install the driver.
> Turn off the Wake on LAN BIOS option.

SOFT SKILLS—PHONE SKILLS

Technicians must frequently use the phone in the normal course of business. This includes speaking with customers who call in, those you must call, vendors, and technical support staff. Many technicians' full-time jobs involve communication via the telephone.

Phone communication skills are different from in-person communication because on the phone, you have only your words and voice intonation to convey concepts, professionalism, and technical assistance (see Figure 7.52).

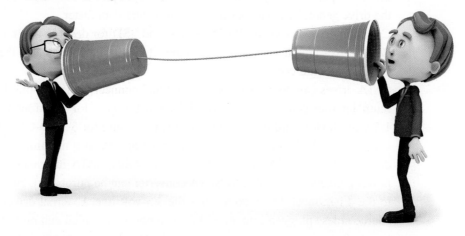

FIGURE 7.52   Telephone communication skills

When dealing with someone in person, you can use some of the following techniques that are not allowed during normal phone conversations:

> Gesture to emphasize points.
> Draw a graphic to illustrate a concept.
> Perform steps needed for troubleshooting faster because you can do them rather than step someone through them.
> Show empathy more easily with your body language, actions, and voice.

When dealing with someone on the phone, the following pointers can help. Some of the tips apply to everyday technical support as well:

> Identify yourself clearly and pleasantly.
> Avoid using a condescending tone.
> Be patient and speak slowly when giving directions.
> Use active listening skills (covered in Chapter 2); avoid doing other tasks when on a call with someone.
> Avoid using acronyms and technical jargon.
> Avoid being accusatory or threatening.
> If the customer is irate, try to calm the customer down and help him or her; however, if the customer continues to be belligerent, turn the call over to your supervisor.
> Escalate the problem if it is beyond your skill level; do not waste the customer's time.
> Do not leave people on hold for extended periods without checking back with them and updating them.
> Speak clearly and loud enough to be heard easily.
> Avoid having a headset microphone pulled away so it is hard to hear you; if you are asked to repeat something, speak louder or adjust the microphone or handset.
> Avoid eating, drinking, or chewing gum when on the phone.

Good interpersonal skills are even more important when on the phone than with face-to-face interactions. Before getting on the phone, take a deep breath and check your attitude. Every customer deserves your best game, no matter what type of day you have had or what type of customer you have previously spoken to.

Chapter Summary

> Hard drive form factors include 5.25-, 3.5-, 2.5-, and 1.8-inch drives. Hard drives come in different speeds: 5400, 7200, 10,000, and 15,000 RPM. The faster the RPM, the more money the drive generally costs, but the drive transfers data faster.

> Common drives today are PATA, SATA, and SSD for desktop and mobile computers.

> PATA drives are internal only and connect to a 40-pin ribbon cable that can have two devices per motherboard connector/cable.

> SATA drives can be internal or external and connect using a 9-pin 3.3-foot (1 meter) maximum internal connector, an external eSATA connector (3.3-foot [1-meter] maximum for 1.5-Gb/s devices and 6.56-foot [2-meter] maximum for 3- or 6-Gb/s devices), or an eSATAp combo eSATA/USB port. SATA 1 (I) drives operate at a maximum of 1.5Gb/s, SATA 2 (II) drives at 3Gb/s, and SATA 3 (III) drives at 6Gb/s. SATA internal drives use a unique SATA power connector. A Molex-to-SATA converter can be purchased, but 3.3 volts is not supplied to the drive; most drives do not use the 3.3-volt line. External drives use an external power source unless plugged into an eSATAp combo port, which can provide power.

> SATA drives require no jumper, and only one device can connect to a SATA motherboard/adapter port.

> SSD drives have become more common in desktops, laptops, and ultrabooks. They are often used in harsh environments, dirty environments, heavy movement environments, and harsh temperature environments. They are extremely fast, but expensive and they connect using PATA, SATA, USB, eSATA, or IEEE 1394 (FireWire) connections.

> SSD drives erase data in blocks instead of by marking available clusters in the FAT with traditional drives. SSD drives should not be defragmented. SSD drives use various technologies to ensure functionality, such as all of the memory being used evenly (wear leveling) and reserved spare memory blocks.

> SSHD is a combination of a mechanical hard drive with flash memory holding the most frequently used data.

> Hard drives must be partitioned and high-level formatted before they can be used to store data.

> Partitioning separates the drive into smaller sections (volumes) that can receive drive letters. The smaller the volume, the smaller the cluster size. A cluster is the smallest space for a single file to reside. A cluster consists of four or more sectors. Each sector contains 512 bytes.

> Partitioning can be done through the Windows installation process or using the Disk Management tool.

> A simple volume is the most common type of partition volume created.

> To create a spanned volume (otherwise known as JBOD), space from two or more hard drives is seen as one drive letter. One drive is filled before any other hard drives are used.

> A striped volume writes data to two or more drives, but does not provide redundancy.
> The system volume holds files needed to boot the operating system (usually C:).
> The boot volume holds the majority of the operating system files (usually C:).
> An HPA or protected partition can be used for system recovery by computer manufacturers.
> Multiple drives can be configured in a hardware or software RAID implementation. Hardware RAID is done using the BIOS/UEFI or a RAID adapter. Software RAID is done using the Windows Disk Management tool.
> RAID 0 or disk striping does not provide fault tolerance, but it does provide fast, efficient use of two or more drives.
> RAID 1 is disk mirroring and this method does provide fault tolerance by having an exact copy of a drive in case one drive fails.
> RAID 5 is disk striping with parity where parity data is kept on one of the three minimum drives. This parity data can be used to rebuild one drive if one of three or more drives fails.
> RAID 10 is a mirrored set and a striped set combined with four hard drives as a minimum. This mode can read from the drive quickly, but a slight degradation when writing.
> Windows Storage Spaces can use a variety of drive types to create a single storage space that can have RAID-like qualities.
> File systems in use are FAT16 (FAT), FAT32, exFAT, NTFS, CDFS, NFS, ext3, and ext4. FAT32 and exFAT are used for external drives, such as flash thumb drives. NTFS is used for internal drives and provides features such as better cluster management, security, compression, and encryption. CDFS is used for optical media. NFS, ext3, and ext4 are used in Linux-based systems.
> Two ways of changing from one file system to another is by using the `convert` command or by formatting the drive. The `convert` command preserves existing data. High-level formatting does not preserve any saved data.
> If a drive fails to be recognized as a new installation, check cabling and BIOS/UEFI settings, especially for a disabled SATA port.
> Normal mechanical drive noises include a clicking when going into sleep mode or being powered down due to self-parking heads.
> Abnormal drive noises include a couple of clicks with a POST beep and/or error, repeated clicking noises, high-frequency vibration due to improper or poor mounting hardware, and a high-pitched, whining sound.
> If a drive fails after operating for a while, check for a virus. See if the BIOS has a virus checker. Try a warm boot to see whether the drive has not spun up to speed yet. Check cabling, especially on SATA. Review any recent changes. Use the Windows Advanced Boot Options menu, Windows Recovery Environment (Windows RE), System File Checker (SFC), and the `bootrec /fixmbr` and `bootrec /fixboot` commands. Boot from an alternate source and check Disk Management for status messages related to the hard drive.
> Hard drive space is used as RAM. Ensure enough storage space is available for the operating system.
> When speaking on the phone to anyone, be clear in your statements, don't use technical jargon, keep your tone professional, and do not do other tasks, including eating or drinking.

CHAPTER 7

A+ CERTIFICATION EXAM TIPS

✓ Know everything about how to configure SATA and SSDs.

✓ Know the purposes of the Error-checking (Check now/Check), Disk Cleanup, and Defragmenter tools.

✓ Use a computer to review the disk tools and how to get to them.

✓ Review all the troubleshooting tips right before taking the exam.

✓ Be familiar with the following Disk Management concepts: drive status and what to do if the status is not in a healthy state, mounting, extending partitions, splitting partitions, assigning drive letters, adding drives, adding arrays.

✓ Know what a normal hard drive sounds like and what sounds a hard drive in trouble makes.

✓ Know the various file systems including exFAT, FAT32, NTFS, CDFS, NFS, ext3, and ext4.

✓ Know the difference between a quick and a full format.

✓ Know the differences between basic and dynamic disks and understand primary, extended, and logical partitions and volumes.

✓ Be able to troubleshoot common symptoms such as read/write failures, slow performance, loud noises, failure to boot, drive not recognized, OS not found, as well as RAID not found or stops working.

✓ Be familiar with BSOD and spinning pinwheel proprietary crash screens.

✓ Know how and when to use Microsoft command-line tools such as `bootrec`, `format`, `diskpart`, `SFC`, and `chkdsk`.

✓ Install a couple of practice drives for the exam. Misconfigure the BIOS and leave a cable unplugged or the power removed so you see the POST errors and symptoms.

✓ Know the common BIOS/UEFI configurations required for storage devices.

✓ Know how and when to configure a RAID and the differences between the various RAID levels.

✓ Be able to configure a drive for Storage Spaces.

✓ Know how to speak professionally.

Key Terms

Review Questions

Consider the following internal hard drive specifications when answering Questions 1–7:

> SATA 6Gb/s transfer rate
> 1TB capacity
> Minimizes noise to levels near the threshold of human hearing
> 3.5-inch 7200 RPM
> 32MB buffer size

1.   Which SATA version is being used?

[1 | 2 | 3 | Cannot be determined from the information given]

2.   Which Windows file system is best to be placed on this drive if encryption will be used?

_____

3.   Which drive preparation steps are *required* to be done if this drive is added as a new drive? (Select all that apply.) [defragmentation | low-level format | high-level format | error checking | RAID | virus checking | partitioning | striping | duplexing]

4.   This drive is meant to be quiet. List two noises that the drive could make that would indicate issues to you. _____

_____

_____

5.   Is this drive internal or external? Explain your reasoning._____

_____

6.   What is this drive's form factor? [6Gb/s | 1TB | 3.5-inch | 7500RPM | 32MB]

7.   How many other devices could be on the same cable that connects this device to the motherboard?

[0 | 1 | 2 | 3 | cannot be determined]

8.   If only two drives are available, which RAID levels can be used? (Select all that apply.)

[0 | 1 | 5 | 10]

9.   A technician has been called to a problem where a S.M.A.R.T. error displays and the user reports the system has been running slow for several months now. Which two tools or actions should the technician use immediately? [chkdsk | partition the drive | high-level format the drive | convert | diskpart | backup the data | attach external drives and configure Storage Spaces]

10. What is the difference between spanning and striping?

   a.   Spanning is done in hardware, and striping is done in software.

   b.   Spanning is done within RAID, and striping is done in Windows or through BIOS.

   c.   Spanning takes two drives, and striping takes three drives.

   d.   Spanning fills one drive before moving to the next drive, whereas striping alternates between the drives.

   e.   Spanning is RAID 0, and striping is RAID 1.

11. A tile and carpet warehouse use several computers for the inventory process. The computers in the warehouse area have a higher hard drive failure rate than those in the office area. Which solution will help this company?

   a.   Replace the hard drives with SSDs.

   b.   Place anti-static mats under the computers and on the floor where people stand or sit to use the computer.

   c.   Install more powerful power supplies.

   d.   Install additional CPU fans.

   e.   Replace the drives with higher-RPM drives.

12. Which of the following can provide the fastest transfer rate for an internal hard drive?

    [PATA | IEEE 1394 | SATA | USB 3.0]

13. Which of the following can provide the fastest transfer rate for an external hard drive?

    [PATA | IEEE 1294 | eSATA | USB 2.0]

14. Which Windows 8/10 feature allows space on an external USB and eSATA hard drive to be seen as one drive letter and provide resiliency? [Storage Spaces | RAID 10 | RAID 5 | Disk Management]

15. What is a drawback of SSDs?

    [installation time | MTBF | maintenance requirements | cost | speed | reliability]

16. You are installing an older PATA optical drive. Which cable connector attaches to the motherboard? [gray | black | white | blue] Which cable connector attaches to the drive if it is the only device on the cable? [gray | black | white | blue]

17. Which tool do most Windows users use to check for lost clusters?

    [Error-checking (Check/Check now) | `diskpart` | Disk Defragmenter | Disk Cleanup]

18. [T | F] By default, Windows 7 automatically defragments all attached hard drives at 1 a.m. on Wednesday or the next time that the computer is powered on after that time.

19. [T | F] If you have enough RAM installed, the hard drive will not be used as cache memory.

20. You are speaking to a customer on the phone who is upset. The customer curses and starts yelling. What should you do?

    a. Hang up on the caller.

    b. Ask the caller if you can put her on hold while she calms down.

    c. Speak to the user using a calm, professional tone.

    d. Stay calm, but raise your voice level a little to show the importance and professionalism of your technical question.

Exercises

Exercise 7.1 Configuring a PATA IDE Hard Drive on Paper

Objective: To be able to configure a PATA IDE hard drive

Procedure: Refer to the following figures and answer the accompanying questions.

Questions: See Figure 7.53 to answer Question 1.

IDE Hard Drive #1
SchmidtMeister 9000
J21 J20 J19 J18 J17

Jumper	Setting	Comments
J17	Cable Select	Open = disabled* Jumpered = enabled
J18	Master/Slave	Open = slave in a dual-drive system Jumpered = master in a dual-drive system Jumpered = master in a single-drive system*
J19	Write Cache	Open = disabled Jumpered = enabled*
J20	Reserved	For factory use
J21	Spare	

* - Default setting

FIGURE 7.53   Exercise 7.1 documentation

1. Using Figure 7.53, circle the jumpers to be enabled (set) to configure IDE Hard Drive #1 as if it is the only drive connected to an IDE port.

2. Now pretend that you have two hard drives that use the same jumpers as in Step 1. Draw the drive jumpers. Circle the jumpers to be enabled (set) to configure IDE Hard Drive #1 as the master drive connected to an IDE port. Keep in mind that IDE Hard Drive #2 shares the same cable with Hard Drive #1.

3. Draw the drive jumpers. Circle the jumpers to be enabled (set) to configure IDE Hard Drive #2 as the slave drive. Keep in mind that IDE Hard Drive #2 shares the same cable with Hard Drive #1.

_____

_____

_____

_____

_____

See Figure 7.54 to answer Questions 4 and 5.

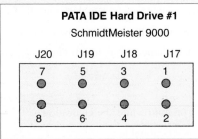

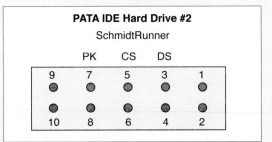

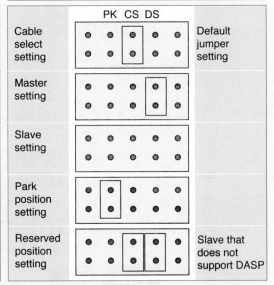

FIGURE 7.54   Exercise 7.1 documentation #2

4. List the jumpers that will be enabled (set) to configure IDE Hard Drive #1 as the master drive connected to a PATA IDE port. Keep in mind that IDE Hard Drive #2 shares the same cable with Hard Drive #1. _____

5.   List the jumpers that will be enabled (set) to configure IDE Hard Drive #2 as the slave drive. Keep in mind that IDE Hard Drive #2 shares the same cable with Hard Drive #1.

_____

_____

Exercise 7.2 Configuring a SATA Hard Drive on Paper

Objective: To be able to configure SATA hard drive jumpers

Parts: Internet access is needed for one question

Procedure: Refer to the following figures and answer the accompanying questions

Questions:

See Figure 7.55 to answer Questions 1–3.

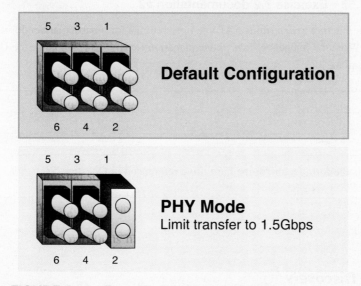

FIGURE 7.55   Exercise 7.2 documentation

1.   Considering the information provided, when would you change the jumpers on this drive?

_____

_____

2.   Considering the information provided, what version of SATA does this drive use natively?

[SATA 1 | SATA 2 | SATA 3]

3.   If this hard drive was to be installed in a desktop model, what form factor would this drive most likely be?

4.   Refer to Figure 7.56. The information provided is from a laptop computer used in a business environment. What do you think would be the effects of installing a jumper on pins 1 and 2 on this drive?

_____

_____

_____

_____

Default configuration
Normal mode

4 3 2 1

Reduced power mode

4 3 2 1

FIGURE 7.56   Exercise 7.2 documentation #2

5. Use the Internet to determine SATA jumper settings for a particular vendor's laptop replacement hard drive. Write the jumper settings and explanation for the jumpers. Write the URL where you found this information.

_____

_____

_____

_____

6. What is the form factor for the hard drive referenced in Question 5?

_____

Activities

Internet Discovery

Objective: To obtain specific information on the Internet regarding a computer or its associated parts

Parts: Computer with Internet access

Questions: Use the Internet to answer the following questions. Write the answers and the URL of the site where you found the information. Assume you have just purchased a Seagate Barracuda 3TB 7200 RPM 6Gb/s hard drive in answering Questions 1–3.

1. What types of cables are needed for this drive? Do they come with the drive? Write the answers and the URL where you found this information.

_____

_____

2. How much cache does this drive have? _____

3. If the computer does not have an available SATA connector, what one recommendation could you make?

_____

_____

4. A customer has a Western Digital WD3200AAKB Caviar Blue PATA hard drive. What are the possible jumper settings for this drive? Write the answer and the URL where you found this information. [Single I Master I Slave I Cable Select I Dual (Master) I Dual (Slave) I Slave Present]

_____

5. Based on the same drive as in Question 4 and information you learned in this chapter, if a customer had a drive already configured to cable select and wanted you to install the Western Digital drive, what setting must be set on the new drive? [Single I Master I Slave I Cable Select I Dual (Master) I Dual (Slave) I Slave Present]

6. Find an eSATA and an internal SATA hard drive that are equal or close to equal in capacity. What is the price difference between the two? Write the answer and the URL where you found this information.

   _____

   _____

   Watch the *How to Fully Use Your 3TB Hard Drive on Windows 7 (MBR to GPT)* YouTube video, found at the following URL to answer Questions 7–10 (if this link does not work, find a video that shows how to install a GPT partition): https://www.youtube.com/watch?v=7KwNaR170mg

7. How many hard disk drives did the presenter have installed as shown in the Disk Management window? _____

8. Even though the Disk 1 drive was originally unpartitioned, before the author did anything to the drive, the drive showed as [1 I 2 I 3] unallocated sections.

9. If the drive has already been partitioned (but doesn't have data on it), what must you do before converting the drive to a GPT disk? _____

10. List one comment that you found interesting and informative. _____

Soft Skills

Objective: To enhance and fine-tune a technician's ability to listen, communicate in both written and oral form, and support people who use computers in a professional manner

Activities:

1. In groups of two, pretend one of you has a hard drive problem. The other student pretends to help you on the phone. Share your phone conversation with two other groups. Select the best group and scenario. _____

2. With two other classmates, come up with 10 additional tips for good phone support that were not listed in the chapter. Share your ideas with the class.

   _____

   _____

   _____

   _____

   _____

   _____

   _____

3. As a team, plan the installation of three storage devices. Two devices are internal SATA drives and an external USB drive. In your plan, detail what drives you are using for the plan, what things you will check for, how you obtain the documentation, and what obstacles could appear as part of the installation process. The user also would like some type of redundancy. What choices might you present to the user? Share your plan with other teams.

CHAPTER 7

Critical Thinking Skills

Objective: To analyze and evaluate information as well as apply learned information to new or different situations

Activities:

1.   List three things that could cause a computer to lock up periodically that relate to the hard drive. What could you do to fix, check, or verify these three things?

_____

_____

_____

2.   A customer wants to either upgrade or replace his hard drive. Go through the steps you would take from start to finish to accomplish this task.

_____

_____

_____

_____

_____

3.   Your team supports a department of 20 workstations. Some people store very important information on their local hard drives. Use the Internet to research redundancy options as well as those presented in the chapter. Develop a list of possible redundancy plans for the department.

Labs

Lab 7.1 Installing a Second PATA Hard Drive and Creating Two Volumes

Objective: To be able to install, configure, and manage a second hard drive using Windows 7, 8, or 10 Disk Management console

Parts: Windows 7, 8, or 10 computer with an available PATA connection on the motherboard, or an available PATA cable connection on an existing PATA connection to the motherboard

                Available power connector

Procedure: Complete the following procedure and answer the accompanying questions.

Notes: Use proper anti-static and gentle handling procedures when dealing with hard drives.

                You must be a user who has administrator rights to configure hard drives.

                If an optical drive is installed, one can be replaced by the new hard drive to perform this lab.

1.   Power on the computer and log in.

2.   There are several ways to get to the window used to manage hard drives. Practice using all methods.

     (a) Click the *Start* button, type **compmgmt.msc** in the Search box, and press Enter.

     (b) In Windows Explorer/File Explorer, right-click *Computer* (Windows 7)/*This PC* (8/10) and select *Manage*.

     (c) Access the *Administrative Tools* Control Panel > *Computer Management*.

3.   In the console tree shown in the left pane, select the *Disk Management* option. Note that the Disk Management tool can also be directly accessed using the **diskmgmt.msc** command. The disks and volumes already installed in the computer display in a graphical manner on the right.

4. Right-click the drive partition labeled C: and select *Properties*.

    Which type of file system is being used? [FAT16 | FAT32 | exFAT | NTFS]

    What is the drive number shown in the right panel? [0 | 1 | 2 | 3]

    What is the amount of free space?_____

5. Shut down the computer and remove the power cord.

6. Access the interior of the computer. Locate an available PATA port on the motherboard or an available PATA cable connector. Determine which port this is by looking at the motherboard's labeling or by using documentation.

    Are you using a PATA port that has nothing attached or an available PATA cable connector that has another device attached?_____

7. If another device is installed on the same cable, remove the drive and determine whether it uses cable select or master/slave jumpers. Handle the drive carefully. If you removed a PATA device to check the drive settings, re-install it into the machine and reconnect the power and data cables.

    If this is the only device that will connect to a motherboard PATA port, connect the PATA cable to the motherboard.

    If another device is present, does the device use the cable select, master, or slave jumper? If you are not using a cable that has another device present, choose not applicable as the answer. [cable select | master | slave | _____ (different setting) | not applicable]

    If a PATA port that has nothing attached is being used, which motherboard PATA port is being used? If you are installing the drive as a second device on the same cable, choose not applicable as the answer. [primary | secondary | tertiary | quaternary | not applicable]

8. On the hard drive given to you by the instructor, configure the drive to the appropriate setting: cable select, master, or slave. Mount the drive, attach the data cable, and attach a power cable.

    Which drive setting did you choose? [cable select | master | slave | _____ (different setting) | not applicable]

9. Re-install the computer power cord and power on the computer.

10. Using previously described procedures, open the *Disk Management* tool. Locate the drive in the bottom section of the window. If you are unsure about which drive is to be partitioned, contact the instructor or lab assistant.

    Note that the drive you were given may have been partitioned already and assigned a drive letter. If the drive was already partitioned and a drive letter has been assigned, locate the drive in the bottom window and right-click the partition. Select *Delete Volume* and click *Yes*. Also note that you may have to delete multiple partitions.

    Note that if the drive shows the status of *Invalid* in the bottom section (left side), right-click the drive in that left section, and select the *Convert to basic disk* option.

    At this point, the drive should show all space as unallocated.

    Was the drive already partitioned? [Yes | No]

    Was the drive already assigned a drive letter? [Yes | No]

11. Right-click the new drive you just installed and select *New Simple volume*. The New Simple Volume Wizard appears. Click *Next*.

    What is the difference between a simple volume and a spanned volume?

    _____

    _____

    What is the minimum number of drives required to create a striped volume?_____

12. Enter a partition size that is less than 32GB and still leaves room on the hard drive. Notice that the partition size is shown in megabytes. Click *Next*.

Which partition size did you choose? _____

13. Select a drive letter (normally, this will be the next drive letter available; take note of your options so you can answer the first question), and then click *Next*.

How many drive letters are available as an option? _____

Which file systems are supported when you use this tool?

_____

Are any file systems supported by Windows that are not shown? If so, what are they?

_____

14. Select the *NTFS* option. Assign the volume label as a couple letters from each lab partner's last name. Note that there is a 32-character maximum for NTFS partitions. Select (enable) the *Perform a quick format* checkbox and click *Next*. Click the *Finish* button.

How can you tell from the information in the Disk Management window whether a partition is NTFS or another file system? _____

15. In the Disk Management window, right-click the free space for the drive you installed. Using the same process, create an NTFS simple volume, add a unique volume label, and perform a quick format. _____

Instructor initials: _____

Lab 7.2 Installing a Second SATA Hard Drive and Creating Two Volumes

Objective: To be able to install, configure, and manage a second hard drive using Windows 7, 8, or 10 Disk Management console

Parts: Windows 7, 8, or 10 computer with an available SATA connection on the motherboard
Available power connector

Procedure: Complete the following procedure and answer the accompanying questions.

Notes: Use proper anti-static and gentle handling procedures when dealing with hard drives.
You must be a user who has administrator rights to configure hard drives.

1. Power on the computer and log in.

2. There are several ways to get to the window used to manage hard drives. Practice using all methods.

   (a) Click the *Start* button, type `compmgmt.msc` in the Search box, and press (Enter).

   (b) In Windows Explorer/File Explorer, right-click *Computer* (Windows 7)/*This PC* (8/10) and select *Manage*.

   (c) Access the *Administrative Tools* Control Panel > *Computer Management*.

3. In the console tree shown in the left pane, select the *Disk Management* option. Note that the *Disk Management* tool can also be directly accessed using the `diskmgmt.msc` command. The disks and volumes already installed in the computer display in a graphical manner on the right.

4. Right-click the drive partition labeled C: and select *Properties*.

   Which type of file system is being used? [FAT16 | FAT32 | exFAT | NTFS]

   What is the drive number shown in the right panel? [0 | 1 | 2 | 3]

   What is the amount of free space? _____

5. Shut down the computer and remove the power cord.

6. Access the interior of the computer. Locate an available SATA port on the motherboard. Determine which port this is by looking at motherboard labeling or by using documentation.

   Which SATA port should you use to install the second hard drive? _____

7. Power off the computer and access System BIOS/UEFI. If you do not know what keystroke is used to access BIOS/UEFI, watch the boot screen. If you still cannot tell, research the computer model on the Internet.

Which keystroke did you use to access BIOS/UEFI?_____

8. Access the section of BIOS that controls the SATA port. The section you must enter varies from computer to computer. Make notes as to where you went to get there in the question below. Ensure the SATA port you located and identified in Step 6 is enabled.

Was the port enabled in BIOS already or did you have to enable it? [already enabled | I had to enable it]

Document the BIOS steps you took to ensure the SATA port was enabled.

_____

_____

9. Save the BIOS/UEFI settings if changes were made.

10. Note that if you power on the computer with nothing attached to the SATA port, you may get an error message. That is okay because the drive has not been installed yet. Power down the computer, remove the power cord, and access the interior of the computer.

11. Mount the SATA hard drive in an available drive bay, attach the SATA data cable, and attach the hard drive power connector to the drive.

12. Re-install the computer power cord and power on the computer.

13. Using previously described procedures, open the *Disk Management* tool. Locate the drive in the bottom section of the window. If you are unsure which drive is to be partitioned, contact the instructor or lab assistant.

Note that the drive you were given may have been partitioned already and assigned a drive letter. If the drive was already partitioned and a drive letter has been assigned, locate the drive in the bottom window and right-click the volume. Select *Delete Volume* and click *Yes*. Also note that you may have to delete multiple volumes.

Note that if the drive shows the status of *Invalid* in the bottom section (left side), right-click the drive in that left section, and select the *Convert to basic disk* option.

At this point, the drive should show all space as unallocated.

Was the drive already partitioned? [Yes | No]

Was the drive already assigned a drive letter? [Yes | No]

14. Right-click the new drive you just installed and select *New Simple Volume*. The New Simple Volume Wizard appears. Click *Next*.

What is the difference between a simple volume and a spanned volume?

_____

_____

What is the minimum number of drives required to create a striped volume?_____

_____

15. Enter a partition size that is less than 32GB and still leaves room on the hard drive. Notice that the partition size is shown in megabytes. Click *Next*.

Which partition size did you choose?_____

CHAPTER 7

16. Select a drive letter (normally the next drive letter available and taking note of your options so you can answer the first question) and click *Next*.

How many drive letters are available as an option?_____

Which file systems are supported when you use this tool?

_____

Are there any file systems supported by Windows that are not shown? If so, what are they?

_____

17. Select the *NTFS* option. Assign the volume label as a couple letters from each lab partner's last name. Note that there is a 32-character maximum for NTFS partitions. Select (enable) the *Perform a quick format* checkbox and click *Next*. Click the *Finish* button.

How can you tell from the information in the Disk Management window whether a partition is NTFS or another file system?_____

18. In the Disk Management window, right-click the free space for the drive you installed. Using the same process, create an NTFS simple volume, add a unique volume label, and perform a quick format.

Instructor initials: _____

Lab 7.3 Installing an External Hard Drive and Creating Two Volumes

Objective: To be able to install, configure, and manage a second hard drive using Windows 7, 8, or 10 Disk Management console

Parts: Windows 7, 8, or 10 computer with an available external connection

Procedure: Complete the following procedure and answer the accompanying questions.

Notes: Use proper anti-static and gentle handling procedures when dealing with hard drives.

                You must be a user who has administrator rights to configure hard drives.

1. Power on the computer and log in.

2. There are several ways to get to the window used to manage hard drives. Practice using all methods.

   (a) Click the *Start* button, type `compmgmt.msc` in the Search box, and press [Enter].

   (b) In Windows Explorer/File Explorer, right-click *Computer* (Windows 7)/*This PC* (8/10) and select *Manage*.

   (c) Access the *Administrative Tools* Control Panel > *Computer Management*.

3. In the console tree shown in the left pane, select the *Disk Management* option. Note that the *Disk Management* tool can also be directly accessed using the `diskmgmt.msc` command. The disks and volumes already installed in the computer display in a graphical manner on the right.

4. Right-click the drive partition labeled C: and select *Properties*.

   What type of file system is being used? [FAT16 | FAT32 | exFAT | NTFS]

   Which is the drive number shown in the right panel? [0 | 1 | 2 | 3]

   What is the amount of free space?_____

5. Locate an available external port that can be used for the hard drive provided.

   Which type of external port did you identify? [USB | eSATA | IEEE 1394 | Other (please identify _____)]

6.   Attach the external drive to the identified external port. Attach external power brick/cord if necessary. Turn on power to the drive if necessary. The system should install the proper drivers and allow the drive to be recognized by the operating system.

7.   Using previously described procedures, open the *Disk Management* tool. Locate the drive in the bottom section of the window. If you are unsure which drive is to be partitioned, contact the instructor or lab assistant.

8.   Note that the drive you were given may have been partitioned already and assigned a drive letter. If the drive was already partitioned and a drive letter assigned, locate the drive in the bottom window and right-click the volume. Select *Delete Volume* and click *Yes*. Also note that you may have to delete multiple volumes.

9.   Note that if the drive shows the status of *Invalid* in the bottom section (left side), right-click the drive in that left section, and select the *Convert to basic disk* option.

At this point, the drive should show all space as unallocated.

Was the drive already partitioned? [Yes | No]

Was the drive already assigned a drive letter? [Yes | No]

10. Right-click the new drive you just installed and select *New Simple volume*. The New Simple Volume Wizard appears. Click *Next*.

What is the difference between a simple volume and a spanned volume?

_____

_____

What is the minimum number of drives required to create a striped volume? _____

11. Enter a partition size that is less than 32GB and still leaves room on the hard drive. Notice that the partition size is shown in megabytes. Click *Next*.

What partition size did you choose? _____

12. Select a drive letter (normally the next drive letter available and taking note of your options so you can answer the first question) and click *Next*.

How many drive letters are available as an option? _____

Which file systems are supported when you use this tool?

_____

Are there any file systems supported by Windows that are not shown? If so, what are they?

_____

13. Select the *NTFS* option. Assign the volume label as a couple letters from each lab partner's last name. Note that there is a 32-character maximum for NTFS partitions. Select (enable) the *Perform a quick format* checkbox and click *Next*. Click the *Finish* button.

How can you tell from the information in the Disk Management window whether a partition is NTFS or another file system? _____

14. In the Disk Management window, right-click the free space for the drive you installed. Using the same process, create an NTFS simple volume, add a unique volume label, and perform a quick format.

Instructor initials: _____

Lab 7.4 Installing a PATA/SATA Hard Drive with the Windows 7/8/10 Disk Management Tool, diskpart, and convert

Objective:	To be able to configure and manage a hard drive using Windows 7, 8, or 10 Disk Management console
Parts:	Windows 7, 8, or 10 computer with an available PATA connection on the motherboard, an available PATA cable connection, motherboard SATA port, USB port, or eSATA port
	Internal or external PATA or SATA hard drive
	Available power connector for an internal hard drive
Procedure:	Complete the following procedure and answer the accompanying questions.
Notes:	Use proper anti-static and gentle handling procedures when dealing with hard drives.
	You must be a user who has administrator rights to configure hard drives.
	If an optical drive is installed, it can be replaced by the new hard drive to perform this lab.

1. Power on the computer and log in.

2. There are several ways to get to the window used to manage hard drives. Practice using all methods.

    (a) Click the *Start* button, type **compmgmt.msc** in the Search box, and press [Enter].

    (b) In Windows Explorer/File Explorer, right-click *Computer* (Windows 7)/*This PC* (8/10) and select *Manage*.

    (c) Access the *Administrative Tools* Control Panel > *Computer Management*.

3. In the console tree shown in the left pane, select the *Disk Management* option. Note that the *Disk Management* tool can also be directly accessed using the **diskmgmt.msc** command. The disks and volumes already installed in the computer display in a graphical manner on the right.

4. Right-click the drive partition labeled C: and select *Properties*.

    What type of file system is being used? [FAT16 I FAT32 I exFAT I NTFS]

    What is the total capacity of the drive? _____

    What is the amount of free space? _____

5. Shut down the computer and remove the power cord.

    Note: Three sections follow. Use the appropriate section depending on whether you are installing an internal PATA, internal SATA, or external drive. Proceed to Step 6 when you are finished with your respective section.

PATA Installation (Only Use This Section if a PATA Drive Is Being Installed)

1. Access the interior of the computer. Locate an available IDE PATA port on the motherboard or an available PATA cable connector. Determine which port this is by looking at motherboard labeling or by using documentation.

2. Determine whether the other device on the same cable (if installed) uses cable select or master/slave jumpers by removing the drive and examining it. Handle the drive carefully. If you removed a PATA device to check the drive settings, re-install it into the machine and reconnect the power and data cables.

    If a PATA drive is being installed, is there a second device on the same cable? [Yes I No]

    If so, does the device use the cable select, master, or slave jumper? _____

3. On the hard drive given to you by the instructor, configure the drive to the appropriate setting: cable select, master, or slave. Mount the drive, attach the data cable, and attach a power cable. Re-install the computer power cord and power on the computer.

SATA Installation (Only Use This Section if a SATA Drive Is Being Installed)

1.   Access the interior of the computer. Locate an available motherboard SATA port. Determine which port this is by looking at motherboard labeling or by using documentation.

If a SATA drive is being installed, which SATA port will be used for the new drive?

_____

2.   Mount the hard drive (provided by the instructor or lab assistant). Attach the data cable and attach a power cable.

3.   Re-install the computer power cord and power on the computer. Enter BIOS/UEFI Setup and ensure that the SATA port is enabled and the drive is recognized.

External Drive Installation (Only Use This Section if an External Hard Drive Is Being Installed)

1.   Locate an available port to be use**d.**_____

2.   Attach the power cord to the drive, if necessary. Attach the drive to the appropriate port. Optionally, power on the drive. If the drive does not have a power switch, it is powered by the port.

Which type of port is being used for the new drive?_____

3.   Power on the computer. Install device drivers if required.

For All Drive Types

6.   Using previously described procedures, open the *Disk Management* tool. Locate the drive in the bottom section of the window. If you are unsure about which drive is to be partitioned, contact the instructor or lab assistant.

Note that the drive you were given may have been partitioned already and assigned a drive letter. If the drive was already partitioned and a drive letter assigned, locate the drive in the bottom window and right-click the partition. Select *Delete Volume* and click *Yes*. Also note that you may have to delete multiple partitions.

Note that if the drive shows the status of *Invalid* in the bottom section (left side), right-click the drive in that left section, and select the *Convert to basic disk* option. At this point, the drive should show all space as unallocated.

Was the drive already partitioned? [Yes | No]

Was the drive already assigned a drive letter? [Yes | No]

7.   Right-click the new drive you just installed and select *New Simple volume*. The New Simple Volume Wizard appears. Click *Next*.

What is the difference between a simple volume and a spanned volume?

_____

_____

What is the minimum number of drives required to create a striped volume?_____

8.   Enter a partition size that is less than 32GB and still leaves room on the hard drive. Notice that the partition size is shown in megabytes. Click *Next*.

What partition size did you choose?_____

9.   Select a drive letter (normally the next drive letter available and taking note of your options so you can answer the first question) and click *Next*.

How many drive letters are available as an option?_____

What file systems are supported when you use this tool?

_____

Are there any file systems supported by Windows that are not shown? If so, what are they?

_____

10. Select the *FAT32* option. Assign the volume label as a couple letters from each lab partner's last name. Note that there is an 11-character maximum for FAT32 partitions and a 32-character maximum for NTFS partitions. Select (enable) the *Perform a quick format* checkbox and click *Next*. Click the *Finish* button.

How can you tell from the information in the Disk Management window whether a partition is FAT32 or NTFS?

_____

11. In the Disk Management window, right-click in the unallocated drive space on the drive you just installed and select *New Simple Volume*. The New Simple Volume Wizard appears. Click *Next*.

12. Select a partition size less than 32GB, but still leave some space on the drive. Click *Next*.

What amount of space did you choose for the logical drive size?_____

13. Accept the drive letter default assignment and click *Next*.

14. Change the file system type to FAT32.

15. Make the volume label a unique name.

Write the volume label chosen._____

16. Select (enable) the *Perform a quick format* checkbox. Click *Next*, review the settings, and click *Finish*.

17. In the Disk Management window, right-click the free space for the drive you installed. Using the same process, create an NTFS simple volume (but still leave some space on the drive), add a unique volume label, and perform a quick format.

Instructor initials: _____

18. You can change a FAT16 or FAT32 partition to the NTFS file system by using the **convert** command at a command prompt. Once a partition is changed, you cannot go back to a previous file system type. Also, data is preserved (but should be backed up before the conversion, just in case of problems). Look to the left of the colored sections to see the disk number assigned (Disk 0, Disk 1, etc.).

In the Disk Management console, which disk number is used for the newly installed drive? [0 | 1 | 2 | 3]

Write the drive letter of the first FAT32 primary partition on the newly installed drive. Note that this drive letter will be used in the coming steps._____

Write the volume label used for the first FAT32 partition. This label is case sensitive, so write it carefully._____

19. Windows 7: Click the *Start* button. Locate the *Command Prompt* menu option. Normally, it is located in Accessories. Right-click the *Command Prompt* menu option and select *Run as administrator*. Click *Yes*.

Windows 8/10: Type **command** in the Search textbox and press (Enter).

20. Type **convert /?** to see a list of options. These options tell you what to type as an option after the convert command.

Which option is used to run convert in verbose mode?_____

Which option is used to convert a volume to the NTFS file system?_____

21. Type **convert x: /fs:ntfs** (where *x:* is the drive letter you wrote in Step 18). For example, if the drive letter written in Step 18 is d:, type **convert d: /fs:ntfs**. Notice the space between the drive letter and /fs:ntfs. /fs:ntfs is used to convert the existing file system (exFAT, FAT16, or FAT32) to NTFS. You are prompted for the volume label for the drive. Enter the volume label you documented in Step 18 and press (Enter). Do not forget that the volume label is case sensitive. The partition is converted and can never be returned to a previous type of file system such as FAT32 unless the drive is reformatted.

22. Use the same process to convert the second FAT32 partition to NTFS. Look up the volume label and the drive letter before starting. Close the command prompt window. Have the Disk Management Window open to verify the file system.

Instructor initials: _____

23. Close the command prompt window. In the *Disk Management* window, right-click the last partition on the newly installed hard drive.

24. Select the *Shrink Volume* option. Reduce the amount of hard drive space and click *Shrink*.

    What was the result in the Disk Management console?

    _____

25. Right-click the second partition on the newly installed drive. Select *Extend Volume*. A wizard appears. Click *Next*. Use the maximum space available on the same drive and click *Next* and then *Finish*.

    What message appears?

    _____

    According to the information in the dialog box, do you think changing this volume to a dynamic disk will matter?

    _____

    _____

26. Click *No* and return to the Disk Management console. Review the disks and determine the disk number and drive letter of the boot volume.

    Write the disk number of the boot volume. [0 | 1 | 2 | 3]

    Write the drive letter of the partition that holds the boot volume. _____

27. Right-click the second partition of the newly installed drive and select *Delete Volume*. Click *Yes*.

28. Partitions can be created from the Disk Management console, and they can also be created using the **diskpart** command utility. Open another command prompt window.

29. At the command prompt, type **diskpart** and press Enter. You may have to click *Yes* to allow access to the tool.

    How does the prompt change? _____

30. Type **help** and press Enter. Use the **help** command to determine which commands are available.

    Which command is used to make a new volume? _____

    Which command can be used to give a drive partition a drive letter? _____

31. Type **create ?** and press Enter.

    Which two options can be used with create? _____

32. Type **create partition ?** and press Enter.

    What types of partitions can be created? _____

33. Press the ↑ key once. The same command appears. Backspace and replace the question mark with the word **primary** so the command reads **create partition primary**. Press Enter.

    What does the feedback say?

    _____

    What command do you think (based on Help) would be used to select a drive?_

34. Type **select disk x** (where *x* is the disk number documented in Step 18) and press Enter. A prompt says the disk is selected.

35. Retype the **create partition primary** command or press the ↑ key until that command appears and press Enter.

36. Look back to the Disk Management console and notice that the part of the drive previously marked as free space is now a partition.

37. At the command prompt, type **detail disk** and press ⟨Enter⟩ to see the partition you just created.

    Based on the command output, what drive letters are currently used?

    _____

38. At the command prompt, type **assign** and press ⟨Enter⟩.

    Look in the Disk Management console window to determine what drive letter was assigned. Write the drive letter._____

    What volume label, if any, was assigned? _____

39. On a Windows 8/10 machine, you will be prompted to high-level format the drive. Click *Cancel* and then *OK*. Skip this step if on a Windows 7 computer.

40. On all versions of Windows computers, at the command prompt type **exit** and press ⟨Enter⟩ to leave the **diskpart** utility.

41. Type **help** at the command prompt and press ⟨Enter⟩ to look for a command to help with the high-level formatting of the drive. The commands scroll too quickly, so type **help | more** and press ⟨Enter⟩. (The ⟨|⟩ keystroke is made by holding down the ⟨Shift⟩ key and pressing the key above the ⟨Enter⟩ key.) One page at a time is shown. Press the Space bar once to see the next page of commands.

42. The next command requires filling in some parameters to perform this step correctly. The parameters are as follows:

    x:—the drive letter documented in Step 38.

    /v:*name*—where name is a unique volume name with up to 32 characters.

    /fs:ntfs—which tells the system to use the NTFS file system. (Other options could be /fs:fat, /fs:fat32, or /fs:exfat, but this lab is using NTFS.)

    /q—which does a quick format.

    Type the command **format *x:* /fs:ntfs /v:*name* /q** and press ⟨Enter⟩. An example of this command is format *x:* /fs:ntfs /v:Goofy /q. Remember that *x* is the drive letter documented in Step 38.

    Note: If you get a message that the arguments are not valid, you did not exit the diskpart utility and did not do Steps 39, 40, and 42. Go back and do them. When asked to proceed, press ⟨Y⟩ and press ⟨Enter⟩.

43. View the results in the Disk Management console. The last partition should be a partition that has a drive letter, a volume name assigned, and uses the NTFS file system.

44. Using whatever method you would like, copy one file to each of the three partitions you have created. Call the instructor over and show the instructor the three files and the Disk Management console. Do not proceed unless you have these parameters done.

Instructor initials: _____

45. Close the command prompt window.

46. Starting with the partition on the far right in the Disk Management console for the newly installed drive, right-click each partition and delete each volume. Call the instructor over when the drive shows as one block (black) of unpartitioned hard drive space.

Instructor initials: _____

47. Shut down the computer. Remove the computer power cord. Remove the data cable from the newly installed hard drive. Remove the power cord from the newly installed hard drive (optional on the external drive). Remove the hard drive. If necessary, re-install the optical drive, data cable, and power cord. Re-install the computer cover and power cord.

48. Boot the computer. Open *Windows Explorer* (Windows 7)/*File Explorer* (Windows 8/10) and select *Computer (Windows 7)/This PC (8/10)*. Ensure that the optical drive is recognized. If it is not, redo Step 47.

49. Show the instructor the optical drive in the Windows Explorer/File Explorer window and give the hard drive and any cable back to the instructor/lab assistant.

Instructor initials: _____

Lab 7.5 Striping and Spanning Using Windows

Objective:	To be able to configure and manage a striped volume or a spanned volume on a hard drive using the Windows Disk Management console
Parts:	Windows computer
	Motherboard or adapter that supports RAID 0
	Two IDE PATA or SATA hard drives
Procedure:	Complete the following procedure and answer the accompanying questions.
Notes:	Use proper anti-static and gentle handling procedures when dealing with hard drives.
	You must be a user who has administrator rights to configure hard drives.
	This lab assumes that you can install and configure two or more SATA or PATA hard drives and have them recognizable in the Disk Management console.

1. Power on the computer and log in. Select the *Disk Management* option from the Computer Management console. The two newly installed hard drives should be visible in the Disk Management console. Initialize the drives, if necessary, by right-clicking them and selecting *Initialize Disk*.

    Which disk numbers are assigned to the newly installed hard drives? _____

2. In the Disk Management console, right-click in the unallocated space of the newly installed drive with the lowest numbered disk. Select *New Spanned Volume*. A wizard appears. Click *Next*.

3. Select the second drive number written as the answer in Step 1 in the Available: pane and click *Add* to move the drive to the Selected: pane. At least two drives should be listed in the Selected: pane. Click *Next*.

4. Select a drive letter to assign to the spanned volume. Click *Next*.

5. Select *NTFS* using the drop-down menu and add a volume label. Select (enable) the *Perform a quick format* checkbox. Click *Next*. Click *Finish*.

6. When a message appears to convert a basic disk to a dynamic disk, click *Yes*. Verify that the spanned volume appears.

    When using the Disk Management tool, how can you tell which two drives are a spanned volume?

    _____

7. Show the instructor the spanned volume.

Instructor initials: _____

_____

8. Use Windows Explorer/File Explorer to view the drive letters assigned and total capacity of each of the two drives.

    What drive letter was assigned to the spanned volume? _____

    What is the total capacity of the spanned volume? _____

    Which RAID level is spanning, if any? _____

9. In the Disk Management console, right-click in the newly created spanned volume space and select *Shrink Volume*. Select a smaller amount of space in the *Enter the amount of space to shrink in MB:* textbox.

How does the Disk Management tool change?

_____

10. Show the instructor the shrunken volume.

Instructor initials: _____

11. In the Disk Management Console, right-click in the spanned volume and select *Delete Volume*. When asked if you are sure, click *Yes*.

12. To create a striped volume from within the Disk Management Console, right-click the lowest-numbered disk of the two newly installed drives and select *New Striped Volume*.

13. In the Available: pane, select the second newly installed disk and click the *Add* button to move the drive to the Selected: pane. Click *Next*.

14. Select a drive letter or leave the default. Click *Next*.

15. Leave the default system as NTFS and select (enable) the *Perform a quick format* checkbox. Click *Next*. Click *Finish*. Click *Yes*.

How do the disks appear differently than the spanned volumes in the Disk Management console?

_____

16. Open Windows Explorer or File Explorer.

How many drive letters are assigned to a RAID 0 configuration?_____

17. Copy a file to the RAID 0 drive. Show the instructor the file and the Disk Management Console.

Instructor initials: _____

18. Right-click in the healthy volume space of either RAID 0 drive.

Can a RAID 0 volume be shrunk? [Yes | No]

19. Select the *Delete Volume* option. Click *Yes*. Show the instructor the unallocated space.

Instructor initials: _____

20. Power down the computer, remove the power cord, and remove the two newly installed drives.

21. Power on the computer and, if necessary, return the BIOS settings to the original configuration. Ensure that the computer boots normally. Show the instructor that the computer boots normally.

Instructor initials: _____

Lab 7.6 Windows Vista Hard Disk Tools

Objective: To be able to use the tools provided with Windows Vista to manage the hard disk drive

Parts: A computer with Windows Vista loaded and administrator rights/password

Procedure: Complete the following procedure and answer the accompanying questions.

Note: The defragmentation and Error-checking (Check now) process can take more than 60 minutes on larger hard drives.

1. Power on the computer and log on using a user ID and password provided by the instructor or lab assistant that has administrator rights.

2. Click the *Start* button, select *All Programs*, select *Accessories*, select *System Tools*, and click *Disk Cleanup*.

3. Select the *My files only* link. The drive selection window appears. Using ▼, select a drive letter and click the *OK* button.

4. The *Disk Cleanup* window appears. Ensure that *only* the following checkboxes are checked (enabled) for lab purposes:

   Temporary Internet files

   Recycle Bin

   Temporary Files

   Click the *OK* button.

5. When prompted, if you are sure, click the *Delete Files* button. Enter the administrator password, if necessary.

   List at least two related topics that are available from the Help and Support Center when getting help on the topic of disk cleanup.

   _____

   _____

   _____

   Instructor initials: _____

6. Click the *Start* button, select *All Programs*, select *Accessories*, select *System Tools*, and click *Disk Defragmenter*.

7. Click on *Select volumes*. Select a particular drive to use.

   What percentage of free space is shown for the drive? _____

8. Select the *How does Disk Defragmenter help?* link.

   What does help say about using the computer during defragmentation?

   _____

9. Click the *Defragment now* button and the *OK* button.

   What would be the determining factor for you in recommending how often a particular computer user should make use of this tool?

   _____

   _____

   List one more recommendation that you would make to a user regarding this tool.

   _____

   _____

10. Click on the *Close* button and close the *Disk Defragmenter* window.

11. Open Windows Explorer. Locate and right-click the hard drive (C:) and select *Properties*. Select the *Tools* tab and the *Check now* button. If the User Account Control window appears, click *Continue*.

12. In the window that appears, select the *Scan for and attempt recovery of bad sectors* checkbox and ensure that the *automatically fix file system errors* checkbox is not checked (not enabled). Click *Start*. Click the *View details* link to answer these questions:

    How many files were processed? _____

    How much space does the system take? _____

13. Call the instructor over when the utility is finished (before you click *OK*). Click *OK* again and close the utility window.

    Instructor initials: _____

CHAPTER 7

Lab 7.7 Windows 7 Hard Disk Tools

Objective: To be able to use the tools provided with Windows 7 to manage the hard disk drive

Parts: Windows 7 computer and administrator rights

Procedure: Complete the following procedure and answer the accompanying questions.

Notes: The defragmentation and Error-checking (Check now) process can take more than 60 minutes on larger hard drives.

1. Power on the computer and log on using a user ID and password that has administrator rights.

2. Click the *Start* button, select *All Programs*, select *Accessories*, select *System Tools*, and click *Disk Cleanup*.

3. The Disk Cleanup window appears. Ensure that *only* the following checkboxes are checked (enabled) for lab purposes:

   Temporary Internet Files

   Recycle Bin

   Temporary Files

   Game Statistics Files (if available)

   Click the *OK* button.

4. When prompted if you are sure, click the *Delete Files* button.

   List at least two related topics that are available from the Help and Support Center when getting help on the topic of disk cleanup.

   _____

   _____

   _____

5. Using Windows Explorer, right-click on the hard disk drive letter to check for errors. Select *Properties*.

6. Click the *Tools* tab. In the Error-checking section, click the *Check now* button.

7. Any files and folders that have problems, you can either select *Automatically fix file system errors* or you can just have the check performed with a generated report at the end. A more thorough disk check can be done using the *Scan for and attempt recovery of bad sectors*. This disk check locates and attempts repair on physical hard disk sections and can take a very long time. The most comprehensive check is to check for both file errors and physical problems on the hard disk surface with the *Automatically fix file system errors* and *Scan for and attempt recovery of bad sectors*.

   For this exercise, just deselect (disable) the *Automatically fix file system errors*. Note that the *Scan for and attempt recovery of bad sectors* checkbox is automatically disabled (not checked). Click *Start*.

   What message appeared when the scan was complete?

   _____

   Instructor initials: _____

8. Click the *Close* button.

9. Either return to the hard drive *Properties* window and select *Defragment now* or click the *Start* button, select *All Programs*, select *Accessories*, select *System Tools*, and click *Disk Defragmenter*.

10. Select a particular drive to use. Select the *Analyze disk* button.

    In the Windows Explorer Properties window General tab, what percentage of free space is shown for the drive?_____

    From the Disk Defragmenter window, select the *Tell me more about Disk Defragmenter* link. What does Windows 7 help say about using the computer during the defragmentation routine?

    _____

11. From the Disk Defragmenter window, click the *Defragment disk* button.

    What would be the determining factor for you in recommending how often a particular computer user should make use of this tool?

    _____

    _____

    List one more recommendation that you would make to a user regarding this tool.

    _____

    _____

12. If class time is an issue, click the *Stop Operation* button. Click the *Close* button. Close the hard drive *Properties* window.

Lab 7.8 Windows 8/10 Hard Disk Tools

Objective: To be able to use the tools provided with Windows 8 or 10 to manage the hard disk drive

Parts: Windows 8 or 10 computer and administrator rights

Procedure: Complete the following procedure and answer the accompanying questions.

Notes: The defragmentation and Error-checking (Check now) process can take more than 60 minutes on larger hard drives.

1. Power on the computer and log on using a user ID and password that has administrator rights.

2. Open *Windows File Explorer*. Locate the *C:* drive in the left pane. You may have to expand *This PC*. Right-click on the *C:* drive and select *Properties*.

   On the General tab, what is the name of the volume?_____

   What is the drive capacity?_____

   What does the option *Allow files on this drive to have contents Indexed in addition to file properties* do?

   _____

   _____

3. Click *Disk Cleanup*. The Disk Cleanup window appears. Ensure that *only* the following checkboxes are checked (enabled) for lab purposes:

   Temporary Internet Files

   Recycle Bin

   Temporary Files

   Game Statistics Files (if available)

   Click the *OK* button. When prompted if you are sure, click the *Delete Files* button.

   What message, if any, was given to you at the end of the process?

   _____

4.   Access the Disk Cleanup window again. Select the *Clean up system files* option. The Disk Cleanup window appears and the related file sections are automatically checked. Click any one of the options that has an enabled (checked) checkbox. Click on the option itself (not the checkbox). Click *View files*.

If no files appear, then (1) you might be viewing an option that takes up no hard drive space. If you think this the case, return to the *View files* window, select another checked option, and click *View Files* again; or (2) enable the viewing of files by clicking on the *View* menu option > *Options* down arrow > *Change folder and search options* > *View* tab > enable (click on) *Show hidden files, folders, and drives* > disable (ensure the option is unchecked) *Hide protected operating system files (Recommended)* > *Yes* (to the warning prompt) > *OK*. The files that are to be deleted appear.

5.   Close the window. Return to the Disk Cleanup window. Click *OK* to delete unused system files. Click *Delete Files*. When finished, access the Disk Cleanup window again by clicking on *Disk Cleanup*.

6.   Select the *More Options* tab. You may have to click on the *Clean up system files* option again to access this tab.

What are the two sections shown in the window that allow for more disk cleanup?

_____

What do you think would be a disadvantage to using the Clean up button for Programs and Features?

_____

_____

7.   Click *Cancel*. Click the *Tools* tab. The Tools tab contains two tools: *Error-checking* and *Optimize and defragment drive*.

8.   Click *Check*. Click *Scan drive*.

What message appeared?

_____

9.   Click *Close*. Click on *Optimize*.

What percentage of the C: drive is fragmented? ____%

Is scheduled optimization turned on or off so that drives are automatically optimized? [on | off]

10.   Click on *Analyze*.

Did the percentage of fragmented drive space change? [yes | no]

_____

11.   Click on *Optimize*. Click on *Close* when the process is done.

In the corporate environment, do you think that any of these processes will be done on a regular basis? Explain your answer.

_____

_____

Lab 7.9 Windows 8/10 Storage Spaces

Objective: To be able to use the tools provided with Windows 8 or 10 to manage the hard disk drive

Parts: Windows 8 or 10 computer and administrator rights

One or more internal, external hard drive, SSD, or SSHD already installed and accessible through Windows Disk Management tool

Procedure: Complete the following procedure and answer the accompanying questions.

1.   Power on the computer and log on using a user ID and password that has administrator rights.

2.   Access the *Storage Spaces* Control Panel.

3.   Select the *Create a new pool and storage space* link > click *Yes* if asked permission to continue.

4.   Enable (click in the checkbox to select) the drive(s) to be used > *Create pool* button.

5.   In the resulting window, name the storage space, optionally select a drive letter and file system, and select the resiliency type.

What resiliency types are available? (Choose all that apply.) [simple | complex | extended | parity | no parity | two-way mirror | three-way mirror]

What resiliency type is the default? [simple | complex | extended | parity | no parity | two-way mirror | three-way mirror]

What file systems are available?

_____

6.   Select the pool size.

7.   Select *Create Storage Space*. The storage space appears in File Explorer.

Which drive letter did you choose?_____

Instructor initials: _____

8.   To remove a storage space, access the *Storage Spaces* Control Panel again.

9.   Locate the Storage Space > *Change settings* > *Delete pool* link located on the right side > *Delete storage space* button.

8

Multimedia Devices

In this chapter you will learn:

> To compare optical drive and disc technologies

> To determine optical drive specifications and features from an advertisement or specification sheet

> To determine the best interfaces and ports used to connect optical drives

> How to install, configure, and troubleshoot optical drives, sound, scanners, camcorders, and digital cameras

> How to use Windows to verify optical drives, audio ports, scanners, and digital camera installations

> How to install and configure other peripheral devices including barcode readers, biometric devices, game pads, joysticks, digitizers, motion sensors, smart card readers, and MIDI-enabled devices

> How to provide support with a positive, proactive attitude

CompTIA Exam Objectives:

What CompTIA A+ exam objectives are covered in this chapter?

✓ 901-1.1 Given a scenario, configure settings and use BIOS/UEFI tools on a PC.

✓ 901-1.4 Install and configure PC expansion cards.

✓ 901-1.5 Install and configure storage devices and use appropriate media.

✓ 901-1.7 Compare and contrast various PC connection interfaces, their characteristics and purpose.

✓ 901-1.12 Install and configure common peripheral devices.

✓ 902-1.5 Given a scenario, use Windows Control Panel utilities.

✓ 902-5.4 Demonstrate proper communication techniques and professionalism.

Multimedia Overview

The term *multimedia* has different meanings for people because there are many types of multimedia devices. This chapter focuses on the most popular areas—optical drive technologies, sound cards, cameras, and speakers. These devices collectively enable you to create and output sound, music, video, and movies. The chapter is not intended to be a buyer's guide for multimedia devices or an electronics "how it works" chapter; instead, it is a guide for technicians with an emphasis on installation and troubleshooting.

Optical Disk Drive Overview

Compact disc (**CD**), digital versatile disc or digital video disc (**DVD**), and **Blu-ray** drives are collectively called optical disk drives (**ODDs**) because they use optical discs that are read from, written to, or both. Optical discs are great to use when creating or playing music CDs or movie DVDs, or for backing up data. CDs are the older technology, but this technology is still in use today in combination with DVD and Blu-ray disc (**BD**) technologies. Blu-ray discs tend to be used for film distribution and for video games. Purchased applications tend to be on CDs or more commonly, DVDs. Applications can also be downloaded from a remote Internet location or remote site or available on a USB drive. Drives can be obtained that can handle CD, DVD, and BD media. Figure 8.1 shows a BenQ CD drive and its various front panel controls.

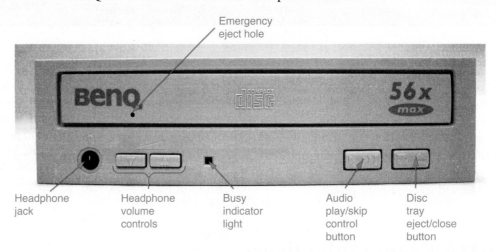

FIGURE 8.1 BenQ CD drive front panel controls

A CD has pits or indentations along the track. Flats, sometimes called lands, separate the pits. Reading information from a CD involves using a laser diode or similar device. The laser beam shines through the protective coating to an aluminum alloy layer, where data is stored. The laser beam reflects back through the optics to a photo diode detector that converts the reflected beam of light into 1s and 0s. The variation of light intensity reflected from the pits and lands is detected as a series of on/off signals that are then converted into binary code. CD and DVD drives use red laser technology, whereas Blu-ray drives use blue-violet laser technology. The blue-violet laser technology has a shorter wavelength, which means that smaller data pit sizes can be used to create higher disc capacities. This translates to more cost, too. Figure 8.2 shows an inside view of a CD drive. The newer technologies operate in a similar fashion.

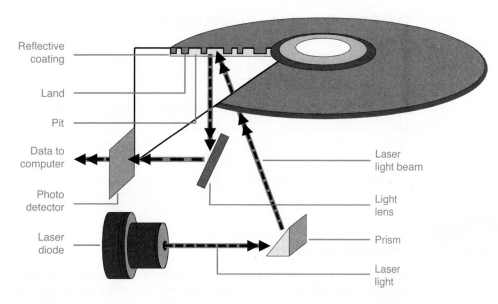

FIGURE 8.2   Inside a CD drive

Optical Drive Features

Optical drives that have an "R" designation can read only from a disk. Drives that have an "RW" or "RE" designation can perform both reads and writes. Drives with a "DL" designation use dual-layer technology where two physical layers are available on the same side of the disc. The laser shines through the first layer to get to the second layer. Table 8.1 lists common media used.

TABLE 8.1   Optical writable media

Media type	Description
CD	650 or 700MB
CD-RW	650 or 700MB
DVD-5/RW	4.7GB single-sided single layer
DVD-9/RW (DVD-9DL)	8.5GB single-sided dual layer
DVD-10/RW	9.4GB double-sided single layer
DVD-18/RW (DVD-18DL)	17.1GB double-sided dual layer
BD/BD-RE	25GB single layer
BD DL/BD-RE DL	50GB dual layer
BD XL	100 or 128GB multi-layer
Mini BD	7.8GB single layer
Mini BD DL	15.6GB dual layer

Optical drives come in a variety of types, classified by the x factor: 1x (single-speed), 2x (double-speed), 32x, 48x, 52x, and higher. Optical drives do not operate at just a single speed, though; the speed varies depending on the type of media being read and whether writing is being done. Table 8.2 shows the generic transfer rates for the different x factors and types of optical drives.

TABLE 8.2 Optical drive transfer speeds

x factor	CD	DVD	BD
1x	150KB/s	1.32MB/s	4.5MB/s
2x	300KB/s	2.64MB/s	9MB/s
12x	1800KB/s	15.85MB/s	54MB/s
22x	N/A	29MB/s	N/A
52x	7800KB/s	N/A	N/A

TECH TIP

How to read the numbers

ODDs are frequently shown with three consecutive factor numbers, such as 52x32x52. The first number is the write speed, the second number the read/write speed, and the third number is the maximum read speed that is used when reading a disc.

A lot of factors can influence how fast a drive transfers data, including how much RAM the computer has, what other applications are running, how much free hard drive space (virtual memory) there is, and the interface used to connect the optical drive; even how much RAM is on the video card can influence an ODD that has video content. Data is stored as one continuous spiral of data on optical discs. This concept is shown in Figure 8.3. Data is, of course, in 1s and 0s, and spaced a lot closer, but the idea of one continuous spiral is important for the write-once technologies. Pits on a DVD are half the size of a CD, and the tracks are closer together so more data can be stored.

FIGURE 8.3 Optical disc

TECH TIP

Some optical drives cannot read Blu-ray discs

Some optical drives cannot read Blu-ray discs because CD/DVD drives use a red laser, and Blu-ray drives use a blue-violet laser. Drives that have both lasers are available.

The steps for copying files to a disc using Windows/File Explorer in Windows follow:

Step 1. Insert an optical disc. From the window that appears, select *Burn files to disc* using Windows Explorer (Vista/7) or File Explorer (8/10).

Step 2. Name the optical disc and select the format type. Click *OK*.

Step 3. Open *Windows/File Explorer* and select any file(s) you want to copy. Drag them to the optical disc drive in the left panel. Continue for any files that may be in other folders.

Step 4. After selecting files, click the optical drive letter in the left panel. All files should be listed in the right panel.

Step 5. Right-click the optical drive letter and select *Close session*.

One way to reduce transfer time when writing data to the drive is by having buffer memory on the drive. When requesting data, the drive looks ahead on the disc for more data than requested and places the data in the buffer memory. **Buffer memory** holds the extra data in the drive and then constantly sends data to the processor instead of the processor waiting for the drive's slow access time. But, buffer memory is not enough. Having little hard drive space or RAM can still slow down or abort the recording process. Microsoft has a free utility called Virtual CD-ROM Control Panel utility for Windows Vista and 7 that is used when someone has an ISO disk image for a specific application or a backup disk image. The utility allows the ISO file to be mounted or seen as a virtual optical disk (and assigned a drive letter). A benefit of using such software is that you do not have to burn the ISO image to a disc. Windows 8 and 10 have this feature built into the operating system. Right-click on an .ISO or .IMG file and select Mount.

TECH TIP

Keep the data coming

One problem with ODDs occurs when data is written to the disc. If the drive does not receive data in a steady stream, a buffer underrun error occurs, and the disc is ruined if it is a –R or +R disc. To avoid this problem, avoid performing other tasks when burning data to disc.

One feature that you might use to compare if two drives have the same x factor is the random access time. The **random access time** is the amount of time the drive requires to find the appropriate place on the disc and retrieve information. Another important comparison point is mean time between failures (MTBF), which is the average number of hours before a device is likely to fail. A closely related term that you might see instead of MTBF is mean cycles between failure (**MCBF**), which is found by dividing the MTBF by the duration time of a cycle (operations per hour). The MCBF is actually a more accurate figure because drives are not used the same amount of time per hour. Keep in mind that for any of these, the lower the number, the better the performance.

Both DVD and BD drives have **region codes**. The world is divided into six regions for the DVD drive and three regions for a BD drive. The drive must be set for the correct region code or the DVDs made for that area will not work. Some drives allow the region code to be changed a specific number of times. When a disc is inserted, the decoder checks which region it is configured for (or, in the case of software decoding, which region the drive is configured for) and then checks for the region code. If the two match, then the movie plays. Table 8.3 shows the region codes for DVD and Blu-ray drives.

TABLE 8.3   DVD/Blu-ray region codes

DVD region code	Geographic area	Blu-ray region code	Geographic area
1	U.S. and Canada	A	North/Central/South America, Southeast Asia, Taiwan, Hong Kong, Macau, and Korea
2	Europe, Near East, Japan, and South Africa	B	Europe, Africa, Southwest Asia, Australia, and New Zealand
3	Southeast Asia	C	Central/South remaining Asian countries, China, and Russia
4	Australia, Middle America, and South America		
5	Africa, Asia, and Eastern Europe		
6	China		

A nice feature to have in a drive is the ability to use the computer to label the disc, such as Hewlett-Packard's LightScribe. The drive and disc must support this technology. Do not use the labels you can attach to the top of the disc. These can come off or not be put on properly and cause vibration and read issues. Write on the non-data side of the disc with a permanent marker as a last resort. Many drive features or capabilities can be determined by looking at the symbols on the front of the drive, as shown in Figure 8.4.

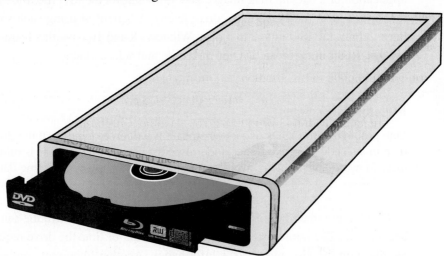

FIGURE 8.4   Optical drive symbols

Optical Drive Interfaces and Connections

An optical drive can be internally mounted and attached to a PATA or SATA interface, or the drive can be externally attached to a USB, IEEE 1394 (FireWire), eSATA, or eSATAp (combo SATA/USB) port. In both desktop and portable computers, the SATA interface is the most common for internal devices and USB for external devices. All-in-one computers, laptops, and ultrabooks tend to have a slot-loaded drive (like a car optical disc player) instead of the tray-loaded desktop models. Figure 8.5 shows a laptop with a slot-loaded drive.

FIGURE 8.5 Slot-loaded optical drive

The following will help you decide which optical drive interface to recommend:

> Is the drive going to be internal or external? If it will be internal, open the case to see if a drive bay is available. Check for a PATA or SATA interface on the motherboard. If PATA is being used, remember that in desktop models, two devices can connect to a single motherboard connector; however, SATA requires one port for each device. Remember that internal devices tend to be cheaper than external.

> If the drive is internal, check that a power connection is available. A Y connector or Molex-to-SATA power converter may have to be purchased.

> If the drive is external, check what eSATA, eSATAp, USB, or IEEE 1394 ports are available. Some USB hard drives take two ports. Ensure the drive comes with cabling or purchase separately.

> Check with the customer about features such as buffer memory and writing labels.

> If the customer wants to upgrade the drive, find out why. Many times, slow access is due to other components in the computer, not the drive.

Optical Drive Installation

One thing to be concerned about with an optical drive is whether the drive is to be installed horizontally or vertically. Not all drives can be installed vertically.

The steps for installing an internal optical drive are almost identical to the steps for installing a hard drive:

Step 1. Download the latest drivers before installation.

Step 2. Install any necessary mounting brackets.

Step 3. Ensure that a proper port/interface is available. Ensure that a power connector is available. Set the appropriate configuration jumpers if necessary. Refer to the drive documentation.

Step 4. Turn off the power. Remove power cords. Remove the laptop battery.

Step 5. Install the drive.

Step 6. Attach the power and data cables.

Step 7. Enter BIOS/UEFI to check drive status. Ensure that the port is enabled. Ensure that the drive is recognized. Note that you may need to reboot the machine once to see this. If the drive is not recognized in BIOS/UEFI (at least that there is a drive attached), re-check settings and cabling.

Step 8. If necessary, install drivers and/or software as part of the installation process. See Figure 8.6. Get the drive functional by using the driver that came with the drive, if possible. Then, upgrade the driver once the drive is recognized by the system.

FIGURE 8.6 Installing software

TECH TIP

PATA connectivity

When connecting an optical drive to a PATA connector that already has a drive attached to one of the PATA cable connectors, you have to know the jumper settings on the already installed drive to correctly install the optical drive. The installed drive settings may have to be adjusted when a second device is added to the cable. The optical drive should be the slave device.

For an external drive, download the latest drivers, ensure that you have the correct port, attach external power to the device as necessary before attaching to the port, attach the cable to the device, and attach the other end of the cable to the computer. Again, you may need a driver upgrade and/or to install some software as part of this process. Remember to check Device Manager to ensure that the device is recognized by the operating system.

TECH TIP

Always test the installation

Test the installation by using the device—play something or write to a disc that you bring along. Ensure that the customer tries the disc and is comfortable with the changes caused by the installation.

Troubleshooting Optical Drive Issues

Windows has troubleshooting tools in the Help and Support Center. Here's how you use them:

Step 1. In Windows Vista/7, click *Start* and select *Help and Support*. In Windows 8 and 10, access the *Search* textbox.

Step 2. In Windows Vista, select *the CDs and DVDs* option.

In Windows 7, 8, or 10, type `troubleshooting` in the Search textbox.

Step 3. In Windows 7, open the *Hardware and Devices troubleshooter* link and progress through the wizard depending on the problem.

In Windows 8, select the first *Troubleshooting* option to be taken to the Troubleshoot computer problems Control Panel > *Hardware and Sound*.

In Windows 10, select the *Troubleshooting* Control Panel > *Hardware and Sound*.

Step 4. Access the appropriate link that relates to the problem that is occurring.

> **TECH TIP**
>
> **Check the easy stuff first**
>
> Verify that the correct type of optical disc is in the drive, is inserted correctly (label side up), and is not dirty or damaged. Test the disc in another drive. Verify that the ODD has a drive letter. Check Device Manager for errors.

The following is a list of problems, along with possible solutions and recommendations:

> If a drive tray cannot be opened, make sure there is power. Use Windows/File Explorer to locate the drive, right-click the drive, and select *Eject*. Some drives have an emergency eject button or a hole you can insert a paperclip into to eject the disc. Refer back to Figure 8.1 to see an example of the eject hole.

> If a drive is not recognized by the operating system, check cables, the power cord, and the configuration (master/slave, cable select, SATA speed, and the port enabled in BIOS/UEFI).

> If a drive busy indicator flashes more slowly than normal, the disc or laser lens may be dirty. Refer to the manufacturer's recommendations for cleaning. See the next section on preventive maintenance for details on how to clean a disc.

> If the drive cannot read a disc, ensure that the drive supports the disc being used. Ensure the disc label is facing up. Ensure that the disc is clean and without scratches. Try the disc in another machine or try a different disc to see if the problem is with the drive or the disc.

> If a drive is not recognized as a recordable device (from Windows Explorer [Vista/7]/File Explorer [8/10], right-click or tap and hold briefly on the drive letter, select *Properties,* look to see if the Recording tab is missing), an updated driver or registry edit is probably needed.

> If a DVD sound track works, but video is missing or distorted, check the cabling. Verify the video drivers. Try changing the display resolution and the number of colors.

> If a message appears about an illegal DVD or BD region error or region code error, change the region if possible. Otherwise, you can't use the disc without using a drive that matches.

> **TECH TIP**
>
> **You can see video but can't hear or vice versa**
>
> Verify that the computer has the hardware and software requirements for DVD playback. Update the optical drive drivers.

CHAPTER 8

> If a drive reads only CDs and not DVDs or Blu-ray discs, update the driver.
> Some optical drive problems are resolved by using DirectX. **DirectX** allows people who write software to not have to write code to access specific hardware directly. DirectX translates generic hardware commands into special commands for the hardware, which speeds up development time for hardware manufacturers and software developers. DirectX may need to be re-installed or upgraded. Access the DirectX Diagnostic Tool in Windows by entering `dxdiag` in the Start/Run or Search dialog box.
> Check to see whether there is a more recent driver for the drive.
> If a drive keeps opening the tray, check for a stuck eject button. Check for a virus. Remove the data cable (but leave the power cable attached) to see whether it is the drive or a signal being sent to the drive to open. If you can hear sound from a DVD, but not a CD, get an updated optical drive driver.
> If you continue to have errors when writing to a disc, clean the laser lens or record at a lower speed. Avoid multitasking when writing.
> If you get a message stating that the DVD decoder is not installed, download a decoder from the DVD drive manufacturer or the computer manufacturer if the drive came with the computer. A **decoder** makes it possible for the disc images to be played/viewed through software on your computer.
> Not to worry if you get a message from an application that requires a disc in a specific drive letter such as the case when you have added more drives. You can change the drive letter using the Windows Disk Management tool. Right-click the drive in the left panel and select *Change Drive Letter and Paths*.
> Blu-ray requirements are much more stringent—ensure all your video drivers, DVD drivers, the display, and video cable are all compliant for playing Blu-ray discs.

Preventive Maintenance for ODDs and Discs

CDs and DVDs have a protective coating over the aluminum alloy-based data layer that helps protect the disc. Blu-ray has a requirement that the BD media be scratch-resistant. They are less likely to need preventive maintenance. However, fingerprints, dust, and dirt can still negatively affect CD and DVD performance.

TECH TIP

Handle discs with care

Always handle a disc by the edges and keep the disc in a sleeve or case to aid in good performance. Never touch a disc's surface, and store discs in a cool location.

When reading information, the optical drive laser beam ignores the protective coating and shines through to the data layer. Even if the disc has dirt on the protective coating, the laser beam can still operate because the beam is directed at the data layer rather than the disc surface. However, if dust or dirt completely blocks the laser beam, the laser beam could be reflected or distorted, causing distortion or data corruption. Special cleaning discs, cloths, and kits are available for cleaning optical discs. A soft lint-free cloth and spit or glass cleaner works, too. Figure 8.7 shows proper handling during the cleaning process.

FIGURE 8.7   Disc cleaning

Mild abrasives or special disc repair kits can be used to repair scratched discs. Examples of mild abrasives include plastic, furniture, or brass polish. When applying the abrasive, do not rub in circles. Instead, use the same technique as cleaning. Start from the innermost portion and rub outward. The abrasive can remove the scratch if it is not too deep. A wax such as furniture or car wax can be used to fill the scratch if it is not removed by the abrasive.

TECH TIP

Cleaning discs

When using a cleaning cloth, wipe the disc from the inside (near the center hole) to the outside of the disc (not in a circular motion) on the side of the disc that has data.

A special component of the optical drive, the **laser lens** (also known as the objective lens) is responsible for reading information from the disc. If the laser lens gets dust, dirt, or moisture on it, the drive may report data or read errors. Some drives have the lens encased in an airtight enclosure and others have a self-cleaning laser lens. If the drive does not have this feature, look for a laser lens cleaning kit. Also, the laser lens can be cleaned with an air blower like ones used on a camera lens. Cleaning the laser lens should be part of a preventive maintenance routine. Some drive manufacturers include a special plate to keep dust away from the internal components. In any case, keep the disc compartment closed to prevent dust and dirt from accumulating on the laser lens and other drive parts.

Introduction to Audio

Video and sound technologies are important today. No multimedia chapter would be complete without mentioning sound (and other devices such as digital cameras covered later). Sound is important to the end user, but sound is also important to the technician such as when the computer does not boot. Motherboards have a small integrated speaker or one that attaches to motherboard pins that allows POST sounds to be heard even if the more advanced sound system is not working. Figure 8.8 shows the motherboard speaker.

FIGURE 8.8 Motherboard speaker

A review of sound ports on the motherboard is good, too, at this point. Ports for speakers and headphones are typically 1/8-inch (3.5mm) connectors that accept TRS (tip ring sleeve) connectors. Figure 8.9 shows common motherboard sound ports.

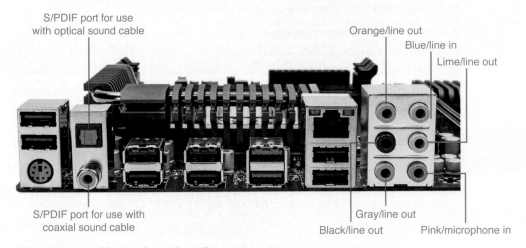

S/PDIF port for use with optical sound cable

S/PDIF port for use with coaxial sound cable

Orange/line out

Blue/line in

Lime/line out

Gray/line out

Black/line out

Pink/microphone in

FIGURE 8.9 Motherboard audio ports

Notice in Figure 8.9 the connection for Sony/Philips Digital Interface Format (S/PDIF). S/PDIF is the newest type of sound port. S/PDIF can be used to carry digital audio signals between audio devices and stereo components or the output of a DVD or BD player in a PC to a home theater or some other external output device. S/PDIF ports can attach using an RCA jack attached to coaxial cable or a TOSLINK connector attached to a fiber-optic cable.

One connection that is not shown in Figure 8.9 is an older 15-pin female MIDI port. Musical instrument digital interface (**MIDI**) is used to create synthesized music. Traditionally, a MIDI device such as a digital piano keyboard would connect using the MIDI interface and the traditional microphone or line out ports. MIDI instruments today typically have a USB connection. If not, a cable converter can be purchased. A MIDI device is considered to be both an input and output device.

Optical drives have the capability to produce sound, usually through a front headphone jack and through a connection to sound through the motherboard or an installed sound adapter. Audio discs can be played on these drives, but the sound does not sound as good through the drive's headphone jack as it does through a stereo system or speakers. Figure 8.10 shows how an audio device connects to a sound card. Figure 8.11 shows typical sound card ports and the types of devices that might connect to these ports. Table 8.4 shows the colors that are normally found on sound ports.

FIGURE 8.10 Audio ports on an adapter and an audio cable

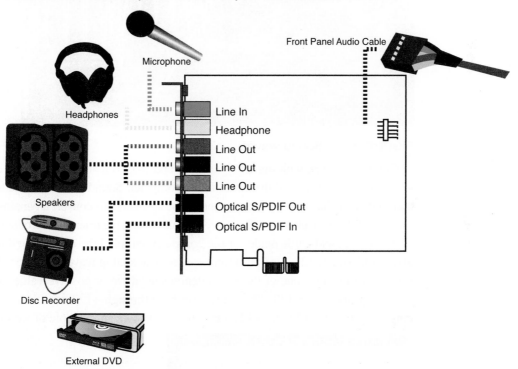

FIGURE 8.11 Sound card port connectivity

TABLE 8.4 Sound port colors

Color	Purpose
Orange/gold	Center speaker or subwoofer
Black	Rear speaker
Light blue	Line in
Lime green	Line out/front channel speakers
Pink	Microphone
Gray	Side speaker

CHAPTER 8

Theory of Sound Card Operation

Sound cards have a variety of options that can include an input from a microphone, an output to a speaker, a MIDI interface, and the ability to generate music. Take the example of bringing sound into the computer through a microphone connected to a sound card. Sound waves are shown as an analog waveform, as shown in Figure 8.12.

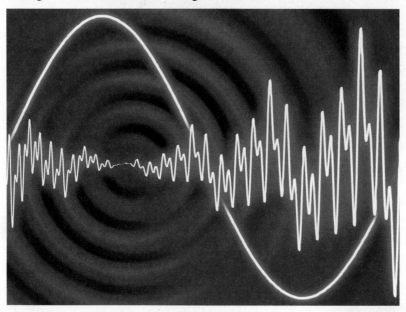

FIGURE 8.12   Sound waves

Computers work with digital signals (1s and 0s), so a sound card must convert an analog signal to a digital format to send the sound into a computer. Sound cards can also take the digital data from optical disc media and output the sound to the speakers. To convert an analog waveform to 1s and 0s, samples of the data are taken. The more samples taken, the truer the reproduction of the original signal.

The first sound cards made for the computer sampled the data using 8 bits. Eight 1s and 0s can give a total of 256 ($2^8 - 256$) different values. The analog waveform goes above and below a center value of 0. Because one of the 8 bits denotes negative or positive value, only 7 bits can represent sampled values. $2^7 = 128$. The values can be 0 through +127 or 0 through −127. (The total value range is between −127 and +127.) Figure 8.13 shows an example of sampling.

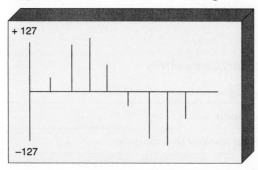

FIGURE 8.13   8-bit sampling

The more samples taken by a sound card, the closer the reproduction is to the original sound signal. The sound card **frequency response** is dependent on the sample rate. This is also known as the sample rate or sample frequency. For a good reproduction of sound, the sound wave is sampled at twice the range desired. For example, a person's hearing is in the 20-Hz to 20-kHz range. Twice that range is approximately 40,000 samples per second. The frequency response for a musical CD is 44,100 samples per second, a good quality sound reproduction for human ears. The first sound cards for computers used eight bits to sample the sound wave and had a frequency response of approximately 22,000 samples per second (22kHz). The sound produced from the original sound cards was better than the beeps and chirps previously heard from the computer. The sound was still grainy, better than an AM radio station, but not as good as an FM radio station or a musical disc.

Next, 16-bit sound cards arrived for computers. The number of possible levels sampled with 16 bits is 65,536 ($2^{16} = 65,536$). When positive and negative levels are sampled, the range is –32,767 to +32,767. The frequency response with 16-bit sound cards is 44kHz, the same resolution as stereo audio CDs. 24-bit sampling results in a 96-kHz sample rate that is sometimes called the audio resolution. The increase in the number of sampling levels and the frequency response allow sound cards to produce quality sound equal to audio discs. See Figure 8.14 for an example of 16-bit sampling. Keep in mind that when more samples are taken, the sound card provides a better frequency response (see Figure 8.15). DVDs require a 48-kHz sampling rate for audio output. Therefore, sound card sampling rates should be a minimum of 48kHz for DVDs and 44.1kHz for CDs.

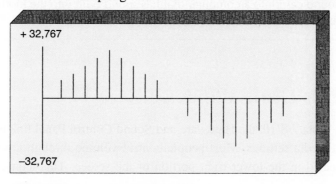

FIGURE 8.14 16-bit sampling

FIGURE 8.15 Digitized sound

Installing Sound Cards

The steps involved in installing a sound card are similar to the steps involved in installing any other adapter. Refer to the manufacturer's instructions when installing devices and adapters.

Step 1. Power off the computer, remove the computer case, and locate an empty expansion slot (making sure it is the appropriate type of slot).

Step 2. Attach appropriate cables, such as the audio cable, from the optical drive to the adapter.

Step 3. Attach external devices, such as speakers. Attach power to the external devices as necessary.

Step 4. Power on the computer. Windows should detect that new hardware has been installed (if Windows does not, use the *Hardware and Sound* Control Panel> *Add a device* link.

Step 5. Load the appropriate device drivers for the sound card.

Once a sound card is installed, there are normally other programs and utilities from the sound card manufacturer that you can install as you would any other application.

TECH TIP

Disable motherboard sound when installing an adapter

If you install a sound card into a computer that has sound built into the motherboard, you must disable the onboard sound before installing the new adapter.

Sound Cards Using Windows

With Windows Vista/7/8/10, the Hardware and Sound Control Panel link is used to change sound and adjust multimedia settings. Most people control volume through a notification area volume control icon located in the lower-right portion of the screen. This icon can be used to mute or adjust sound.

Audio drivers are vastly improved in Windows to accommodate multiple streams of real-time audio and allow a kernel-mode process to handle audio management. This means that the operating system can control all aspects and improve audio performance. Digital audio can be redirected to any available output including USB and IEEE 1394 (FireWire).

TECH TIP

If sound is not coming from the computer

Look for the *Mute* checkbox or icon located in the volume control in the notification area and ensure that the volume is not muted.

Windows also includes a set of Application Programming Interfaces (APIs), which are commands that developers use to communicate with the sound card. DirectX has specific APIs that have commands relating to audio. In DirectX, Microsoft adds such things as DirectSound3D that has more 3-D audio effect commands, supports hardware acceleration, and allows simulation of audio sounds in certain environments, such as a tunnel or underwater. It allows software and game developers to create realistic audio environments such as muffling effects and audio directional effects (that is, the direction a sound comes from).

You can tell whether a device has integrated sound or a sound adapter installed by inspecting the *Sound, video and game controller* category in Device Manager. Figure 8.16 shows a screen capture of Device Manager from a computer that has integrated sound on the motherboard. Note that integrated sound may be located in the *System devices* or *Other devices* categories.

FIGURE 8.16　Integrated sound in Device Manager

Microphones are commonly used in conference calls and Voice over IP (VoIP) calls. VoIP is a technology where phone calls are digitized and transmitted using a data network rather than using a traditional corporate digital voice network or the public switched telephone network (PSTN)—in other words, the traditional phone network. Microphones can be attached to a headset, a separate device, integrated into the computer display, or integrated into the device such as with mobile devices. To see your microphone settings on a Windows device, use the *Hardware and Sound* Control Panel, in the Sound section locate and select *Manage audio devices*, and click the *Recording* tab. Figure 8.17 shows an integrated microphone built into a laptop. Once you select the microphone, you can use the *Properties* button to adjust the microphone settings.

FIGURE 8.17　Integrated display microphone

Speakers

Most people connect speakers to a sound card or integrated sound ports. The quality of sound is personal (see Figure 8.18); sounds that are acceptable to one person are not always acceptable to someone else. Table 8.5 shows some features to look for in speakers.

FIGURE 8.18   Sound quality is personal

TABLE 8.5   Speaker features

Feature	Description
Amplification	Increases the strength of the sound. Sound cards usually have built-in amplification to drive speakers. Amplification output is measured in watts and most sound cards provide up to four watts of amplification (which is not enough for a full-bodied sound). Many speakers have built-in amplifiers to boost the audio signal for a much fuller sound.
Power rating	How loud the volume can go without distorting the sound. This is expressed in watts per channel. Look for the root-mean-square (RMS) power rating: 10 to 15 watts per channel is an adequate rating for most computer users.
Frequency response range	The range of frequency (sounds) that the speaker can reproduce. Humans can hear from 20Hz to 20kHz, and the range varies for each person. Therefore, whether a computer speaker is appropriate depends on the person listening to the speaker. Speaker quality is subjective. Room acoustics and speaker placement also affect sound quality.
Shielding	Cancels out magnetic interference and keeps magnetic interference away from other devices. Speakers usually have a magnet inside them that can cause distortion to a device such as a monitor. These magnets can also cause damage to disks and other storage media. The best optical drive and sound card combination can be downgraded by using inexpensive, poorly shielded speakers.

Most computers come with internal or external speakers. Sometimes the external speakers produce poor quality sound. Also, some of the external speakers are battery- or AC-powered, which might not be desired. One speaker commonly connects to the sound card port, and the other speaker is daisy-chained to the first speaker. Some speakers have an external volume control. Be mindful of this as it is another thing to check for when sound does not occur. Figure 8.19 shows computer speakers that are USB-powered.

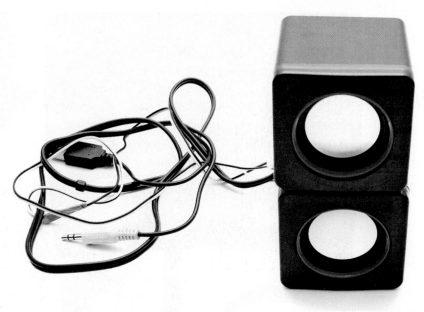

FIGURE 8.19   USB speakers

How to choose speakers

Listen to them without headphones, using an audio (non-software) disc.

USB, IEEE 1394 (FireWire), and wireless solutions can also be used to provide connectivity for speakers. Digital audio is sent over the bus, and an external speaker converts the signal into sound. When audio is converted inside the computer, interference from internal electronic components and external sources (especially if an expansion slot does not have an adapter installed and the case has an opening) can cause audio interference. The drawback to USB is that it puts more work on the CPU. However, in today's multi-core processor environment, this may not be an issue. The following is a list of extras to look for in speakers:

> An external volume control
> Headphone jacks
> Headphone and microphone pass-through connectors (so you do not have to dislodge the computer to reach the jacks)
> AC adapter
> Connectors for the speakers to connect to the sound card
> 7.1 and 5.1 surround sound
> Four- or six-speaker system

Two speakers are normally joined by a cable that may or may not be removable. Figure 8.20 shows the single power cable, a thin cable just right of center that goes to the computer, and the cable on the right that plugs into the second speaker.

When speakers power on, they sometimes emit a popping sound. This is normal, but if the sound continues, the speaker is probably picking up interference from the computer or another device. Try moving the speakers farther away from the computer.

FIGURE 8.20   Speaker connections

Troubleshooting Sound Problems

The best place to start troubleshooting sound problems is to check the easy stuff first. Here are some basic steps to get started:

Step 1. Are speakers plugged into the correct port on the sound card?

Step 2. Is the volume control muted? If so, take it off mute.

Step 3. Is the volume control on the speakers turned up?

Step 4. From within Windows, does the device appear to be playing without sound being heard? In this case, the problem is definitely in the sound system.

Step 5. Do the speakers have power?

The following is a list of common sound problems and solutions:

> If a speaker is emitting unwanted sounds, make sure there are no empty adapter slots in the computer. Next, check the speaker wires for cuts, move the sound card to another expansion slot, and move the speakers farther away from the computer. Finally, move the computer away from the offending device or the offending device away from the computer. If the speakers produce a humming noise and are AC powered, move the speaker power cord to a different wall outlet. Plugging the speakers into the same circuit as the computer is best.

> If sound is a problem or if any solution directs you to update your sound driver, access *Device Manager* and expand the *Sound, video, and game controllers*, *System devices*, or *Other devices* option. Locate and right-click the integrated sound or the sound card and select *Properties*. Select the *Driver* tab and use the *Update driver* button.

> If the sound card is not working, check Device Manager to see whether the sound card is listed twice. If there are two entries for the same sound card, remove both of them by clicking each entry and clicking the *Remove* button. Restart Windows, and the operating system should detect the adapter and either install a device driver or prompt for one. For best results, use the latest device driver from the sound card manufacturer or computer manufacturer in

the case of integrated ports. Note that frequently this is provided through an operating system update.

> In Windows Vista or 7, if you do not see a sound icon in the bottom right corner of the screen, access the *Appearance and Personalization* Control Panel > in the *Taskbar and Start Menu* section, select *Customize icons on the taskbar link* > locate the *Volume* icon. Use the drop-down menu to select the *Show icon and notifications* option.

> In Windows 8 if you do not see a sound icon on the screen, access the *Appearance and Personalization* Control Panel. In the *Taskbar and Navigation* section, select *Customize icons on the taskbar*. Select the *Notification area* tab and locate the *Volume* icon. Use the drop-down menu to select the *Show icon and notifications* option.

> In Windows 10, if you do not see a sound icon on the screen, access *Settings* > *System* > *Notifications & actions* > *Select which icons appear on the taskbar* link > locate the *Volume* icon > select the *On* side.

> If no sound emits from the computer, you can always use the Windows audio troubleshooter. Search Windows Control panels by typing the word `troubleshooting`. In the *Hardware and Sound* section, select the *Troubleshoot audio playback* link.

> If audio is low (see Figure 8.21) no matter what sound is played, the speakers may not be amplified speakers or they may not be connected to the correct sound card port. Also, do not forget to check the computer sound settings through the icon in the notification area. Check Device Manager to see if a yellow question mark is beside the sound card. If so, right-click the sound card, select *Properties*, and then check the Device status section to see the issue. Many issues require driver updates.

FIGURE 8.21   Low or no sound

> If one disc does not output sound, but other discs work fine, the disc may use a later version of DirectX than the one installed. Check the recommended DirectX version for the disc. Also, the disc may have a problem.

> If building a computer, install the sound card after installing the video card, hard drive, and optical drive, but before anything else. Some sound cards are inflexible about system resource changes.

> ⌒ For headphone issues, ensure the cable attaches to the correct line out port. Determine if you want the speakers disabled. Normally, if you plug into the headphones' line out port, the speakers cut off.

> If sound does not come out of the optical drive after the drivers and software load, try the following troubleshooting tips:

> Be sure an audio disc is inserted into the drive.

> If sound no longer comes out of the speakers, check the speaker cables.

> Check the proper installation of the audio cable.

> Ensure that the speakers or headphones connect to the drive or to the sound card or integrated sound port.

> If using speakers, check the insertion of the cable jack into the proper port on the sound card. Verify that the speakers have batteries installed or an AC adapter connected.

> If using headphones, verify that the headphones work on another device before using them to test the drive.

> Get updated drivers from the sound card manufacturer's website.

> If the monitor's image quality decreases after installing a sound card with speakers, move the speakers farther away from the monitor.

Scanners

A **scanner** is a popular input device that allows documents including text and pictures to be brought into the computer and displayed, printed, emailed, pressed to an optical disc, and so on. A scanner is commonly built into a multifunction device (MFD) such as a printer, scanner, copier, and/or fax machine. These are also called all-in-one devices (AIO). The most common types of scanners are listed in Table 8.6. Figure 8.22 shows a flatbed scanner. Figure 8.23 shows a barcode reader. Portable and handheld scanners are being made obsolete due to cameras in mobile devices.

TABLE 8.6   Types of scanners

Scanner type	Comments
Flatbed (sometimes called desktop scanner)	Can scan books, paper, photographs, and so on; takes up a great deal of desk space
Sheetfed	Enables a document to be fed through an automatic document feeder similar to a fax machine; good for scanning multiple documents
Handheld	Slowly moves across the document; user must have patience and a steady hand; portable unit
Film	Scans picture film instead of picture prints
Barcode reader	Handheld device that reads barcodes in checkout lanes and in retail establishments; uploads performed wirelessly or by connecting to a PC

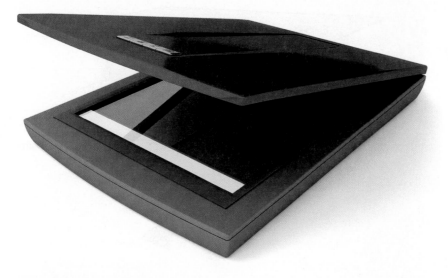

FIGURE 8.22   Flatbed scanner

FIGURE 8.23   Barcode reader

Figure 8.24 outlines how a flatbed scanner works.

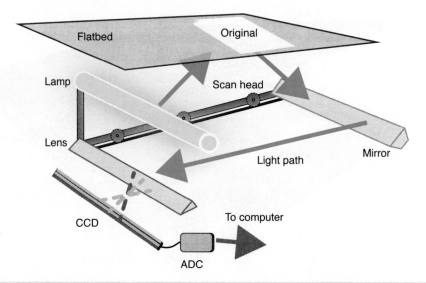

1. A document is placed on the scanner's glass plate. There is a lamp under the glass.

2. The lamp (fluorescent, CCFL [cold cathode fluorescent lamp], or Xenon) turns on.
Light reflects from the document.

3. The scan head is used to capture the reflected light. It moves slowly down the document
by way of a belt. The light reflects through a series of mirrors to the CCD (charge-coupled device) array.

4. The CCD array holds light-sensitive diodes. The diodes convert light into varying
voltage levels. The voltage levels are sent to an ADC (analog to digital converter).

5. The ADC converts the voltage levels to pixels. A pixel is a dot and is the smallest
unit in a picture or document.

6. The pixels are sent through the scanner interface to the computer where the image is
displayed.

FIGURE 8.24   How a flatbed scanner works

Scanners normally attach to a computer using one of the following ports, but USB is the most common connectivity option.

> USB
> IEEE 1394 (FireWire)
> RJ-45 Ethernet
> Wireless

USB devices are easy to install, and USB hubs allow system-integrated USB ports to be turned into multiple USB ports. To install a USB scanner, always follow the manufacturer's directions. The following steps are generic:

Step 1. Install software and drivers.

Step 2. Unpackage and unlock or remove special packaging.

Step 3. Connect the data or network cable as well as the power cable.

Step 4. Power on the scanner. Some scanners have a calibration process that needs to be performed. There may be a special switch or push button that locks/unlocks the scan head.

Step 5. Configure options and default settings.

Step 6. Scan a document to test it.

Step 7. Ensure that the customer is trained and has all scanner documentation.

A scanned image can be saved in several formats. When scanning a document or graphic for web pages, select PNG, PDF, JPEG, or GIF format. The most common graphic file formats are listed in Table 8.7. There are many terms associated with scanning, and Table 8.8 lists the most common of them.

TABLE 8.7   Scanner file formats

File format	Comments
Joint Photographic Experts Group (JPEG)	Small file size; good for web pictures, but not good for master copies. Always compresses the file; the file extension is .jpg.
Graphic Interchange Format (GIF)	Limited to 256 colors, small in size, and good for web pictures; the file extension is .gif.
Tag Image File Format (TIFF)	Good for master copies and large size; the file extension is .tiff or .tif.
Portable Network Graphics (PNG)	Not supported by all applications or older applications; supports 24- and 48-bit color. The file extension is .png.
Portable Document Format (PDF)	Used for web-based forms and scanned words; the file extension is .pdf.

TABLE 8.8   Scanner terms

Scanner term	Comments
Resolution	Measured in DPI (dots per inch); determined by the number of sensors in the CCD array and by the precision of the stepper motor; common resolutions include 300, 600, 1200, 2400, 3200, 4800, 6400, and 9600.
Bit depth	The number of bits used for color; the more bits, the more colors and color depth. Common configurations are 24, 30, 36, and 48 bits.
Interpolation	Software used by the scanner to achieve a greater resolution by filling in the pixels around the scanned pixels.
OCR (Optical Character Recognition)	Software that processes printed or written text characters; not all scanners ship with OCR software.
TWAIN	An application programming interface (API) and communications protocol that is used so that applications can access and acquire images directly from the scanner.

Resolution is an important concept when scanning a document or photo. When scanning something, always think about whether the output is intended for the printer or the monitor. Setting the scanner's resolution to the maximum amount for every scan is not a good idea. Table 8.9 shows some sample resolutions for scanning.

TABLE 8.9   Scanner resolutions

Type of document	Use	Scanner color setting	Recommended resolution (DPI)
Any	Displaying on a monitor	Color, grayscale, or black and white	150
Text	Copying or emailing	Color, grayscale, or black and white	150
Black-and-white photo	Saving, using a website, or email	Grayscale	75–300

Type of document	Use	Scanner color setting	Recommended resolution (DPI)
Color photo	Copying, printing, or creating a document such as a photo or postcard	Color	300
	Using in a website or email	Color	75–150
	Saving	Color	75–300

A scanner's plate glass needs to be cleaned periodically (see Figure 8.25). To test the cleaning, scan a full page without a document loaded onto the scanner. See if the results yield any smudges or streaks. Use these best practices:

> The best cleaning method is to put optical surface cleaning fluid on an anti-static cleaning cloth and then wipe the glass.
> Never spray cleaner directly on the glass.
> Do not use rough paper towels.
> A commercial glass cleaner or water can be used.
> Always remove all cleaner residue from the glass.
> Do not press down on the glass.
> Do not use an abrasive or corrosive solvent.
> Keep the glass dust-free.

TECH TIP

Protect the scanner glass

Be careful with sharp objects such as staples around a scanner. A scratched or damaged glass surface results in permanent marks on scanned images.

FIGURE 8.25   Scanner glass cleaning

Video Recording

Video recording capabilities can be built into a computer or a mobile device, an attachment to a computer, or a standalone digital camera or camcorder used for the purpose of taking photographs or recording movies. A digital camera has a sensor that converts light into electrical charges or digital 1s and 0s. A digital camera resolution is measured in pixels. The resolution is the number of horizontal and vertical pixels the camera can use to display an image. Today, digital camera resolution technology has evolved into megapixels (MP). A camera's photosensors determine how many pixels can be used. Common resolutions for integrated tablet cameras and smartphones are now comparable to digital cameras.

TECH TIP

Caring for a digital camera

Remove disposable (alkaline) batteries from a digital camera when it's not being used for an extended period so they do not leak battery fluids into the camera.

Some cameras store the photographs or movies on flash media (mini-SD, micro-SD, xD, Compact Flash, and so on) or hard drives, usually in the JPEG file format, but some cameras can save in RAW or TIFF formats. Table 8.10 shows camera storage media. Figure 8.26 shows a digital camera with flash storage to the side. Table 8.11 lists common file formats.

TABLE 8.10 Digital camera data storage

Storage type	Comments
Compact Flash (CF)	Introduced by SanDisk; uses flash memory; does not require a battery to store photos once power is removed; includes CF-I and CF-II
SmartMedia	Developed by Toshiba; smaller and lighter than CF; can purchase an adapter card with PC Card/ExpressBus ATA adapter for data transfers
Memory Stick	Created by Sony; small in size; can read/write with the purchase of a Memory Stick reader; includes memory stick (MS), memory stick duo (MSD), memory stick micro (M2)
Secure Digital	Size of a postage stamp; does not require power to retain data; uses flash memory technology; has the ability for cryptographic security; different types include SD, miniSD, microSD, and SDHC
ExpressBus drives	Consumes more power than memory technology
MMC (multimedia card)	A type of flash memory used in many portable devices, including cameras; works in many devices that support SD cards and is less expensive; types include MMC, embedded MMC (eMMC), reduced size MMC (RS-MMC), MMCmicro, dual voltage (DV-MMC), MMCplus (faster MMC), MMCmobile, and MiCard (has two detachable parts—one side for USB and the other side for use with a card reader)

FIGURE 8.26   Digital camera with flash memory

TABLE 8.11   Digital camera file formats

File type	Description
RAW	Outputs raw, unprocessed data; image is not directly usable without further processing
JPEG	Most common type; saves more photos due to compression
TIFF	Larger file size (fewer photos) due to retaining image quality
WAV	Used for voice memos
MOV	Used for movie files

Camcorders are similar to digital cameras in that they store still images and videos, but they are better for creating and storing videos. Camcorders commonly connect to computers or directly to a hard drive so that the videos can be transferred and stored. Digital cameras and camcorders can connect to the computer via USB, mini-USB, IEEE 1394 (FireWire), and mini-FireWire. Attach the cable from the camera to the computer. Power on the camera or camcorder and follow the directions given on the screen. Frequently on a computer, a dialog box appears asking if you want to transfer images/videos. Some camera/camcorder manufacturers provide software that allows you to modify the images or movies.

An alternative is to remove the media storage card and install it into a memory card reader. A memory card reader or multi-card reader is a popular device that many people attach externally or have integrated into a computer or mobile device. A reader has multiple slots that allow different memory media to be read. This device is called many names, and common ones include 15-in-1 reader, 8-in-1 reader, or 5-in-1 reader (depending on how many different slots or types of memory modules it accepts). The reader instantly recognizes inserted memory cards, which can be copied into the computer and manipulated. The media card slots are assigned drive letters that are accessible through Windows/File Explorer. Figure 8.27 shows one of these readers.

TECH TIP

No drive letter

If the media does not appear in Windows/File Explorer, the reader may have been temporarily uninstalled. Use the Safely Remove Hardware and Eject Media tool in the notification area, unplug the cable from the port, and reinsert the cable to ensure the operating system recognizes the reader. If the card reader or ports are still not available or if they are integrated into the computer, restart the computer.

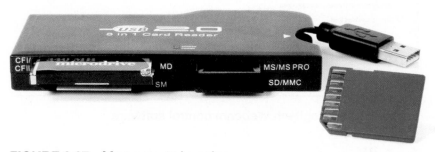

FIGURE 8.27   Memory card reader

Another popular type of digital camera is a **webcam**, which is short for web camera—a digital camera that attaches to a PC for use in transmitting live video or recording video. Web cameras can also attach to VoIP phones and activate when a phone session occurs for instant web conferencing. Some webcams have a small visor that can be flipped over the lens to prevent video when desired. Figure 8.28 shows a wired webcam, but keep in mind that one can connect wirelessly or be integrated into the display or mobile device.

To access an integrated camera in a flat panel display, you normally use a Control Panel or software that comes with the camera, such as the Logitech Webcam Software shown in Figure 8.29. If you ever get a "Bandwidth exceeded" message when you have a camera being used, try lowering the camera's resolution in whatever software is being used.

Regardless of what multimedia device is integrated or connects to a computer, all devices attach and install similarly. When installing a new device for a customer, don't forget to allow the customer to test the device while you are still there. Also, remember to leave all documentation related to the installation with the customer. He paid for the device and is entitled to the documentation.

FIGURE 8.28   Webcam

CHAPTER 8

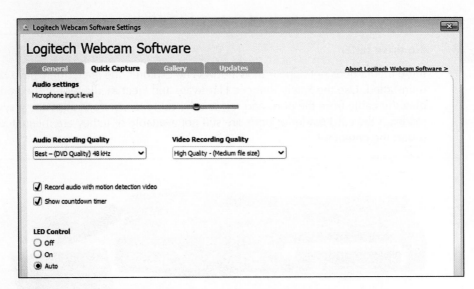

FIGURE 8.29   Logitech Webcam control software

Installing and Configuring Other Peripheral Devices

Other peripheral devices commonly connect to the computer via a USB port. Each device may be configured with software and possible drivers provided by the manufacturer. Many USB devices have drivers provided with the Windows operating system. Let's examine a few that you might see.

Barcode Scanners

A barcode scanner has already been mentioned. These devices commonly connect via USB cable or wirelessly. You might have to reset it by turning off and back on or reattaching to the computer. Some scanners respond to a specific bar code that, when scanned, resets the barcode scanner to defaults, adds the time and date after a barcode scan, omits the first digit, adds four zeros to the beginning of the barcode, and other modifications.

Biometric Devices

A **biometric device** is commonly used to authenticate someone or prove identity such as a retina scanner or **fingerprint reader** (see Figure 8.30). These are discussed more in Chapter 18. To install a fingerprint reader, always follow the manufacturer's instructions. Following are the common steps used:

Step 1.   Install the software provided by the manufacturer.

Step 2.   Attach the fingerprint reader to the computer and ensure the device is recognized by the system. Use Device Manager to verify this if necessary.

Step 3.   Use the fingerprint software to register users who are allowed to access the system.

Step 4.   Verify the configuration by powering off the computer and have each user practice accessing the system.

FIGURE 8.30   Fingerprint reader

Use *Device Manager* to verify that Windows recognizes the biometric device. Device Manager has a category for biometric devices. Sometimes biometric devices are integrated into computers and mobile devices and require the device be enabled through BIOS/UEFI. It is important to use a BIOS/UEFI password so that someone cannot bypass the biometric device by simply disabling it in BIOS/UEFI.

Apple provides Touch ID with its devices. Touch ID allows a fingerprint to be used to unlock the device as well as make online purchases. Touch ID is built into the home button so that the fingerprint can be detected without actually pressing the button.

Microsoft Windows 8.1 provides a fingerprint management application as part of the operating system. This eliminates the need for a fingerprint reader manufacturer from having to provide software. To access the option, access *Settings > Accounts > Sign-in options*. If a fingerprint reader is attached or integrated into the device, the option will be available.

Similarly, Microsoft Windows 10 supports Windows Hello, a biometric device application that supports facial recognition and fingerprint detection. The facial recognition uses iris-scanning technology. To configure Windows Hello, access *Settings > Accounts > Sign-in options*.

Most biometric software requires configuration with the persons who will be allowed access. This requires that the technician either train the computer user how to do this or multiple service calls might have to be made. Sometimes biometric devices require that the software be re-installed. Biometric devices also commonly require preventive maintenance such as wiping the surface of the fingerprint scanner or cleaning the lens of an iris scanner.

Game Pad, Joystick, and Motion Sensors

A **game pad** (see Figure 8.31), **joystick** (see Figure 8.32), and motion sensors are used to interact with games. These devices commonly come with software that if misplaced can usually be downloaded from the manufacturer's website and used to customize the control buttons. Game pads, joysticks, and motion sensors have hardware and software minimum requirements. Game pads and joysticks attach to USB ports and are verified through Device Manager.

FIGURE 8.31   Game pad

FIGURE 8.32   Joystick

Motion sensors are used to detect movement. The motion sensor may be a device that connects to the game console, be integrated into the game console, or be in a hand controller. Usually these devices have an accelerometer that detects and transmits details related to movement, direction, and degree of acceleration. A camera may be part of the system.

Some motion sensors require external power bricks. External motion sensors are normally placed on a stable surface. Those that connect to computers usually do so through a USB port or connect wirelessly. Software is used to calibrate the device.

Digitizers

A **digitizer** (see Figure 8.33) provides input into such documents as architectural drawings, technical plans, and photos. It can also be used to draw electronic pictures.

Digitizers come with a pen that may or may not need a battery. Some pens have replaceable end(s). The digitizer commonly connects through a wired USB connection or it can be wireless. The digitizer tablet comes with software that commonly allows the pen and digitizer tablet buttons to be customized for what the button does and the speed in which some of the buttons react. Some digitizers come with diagnostics that are part of the software.

FIGURE 8.33   Digitizer

Smart Card Readers

A **smart card reader** can attach to a PC or mobile device, connect to a point of sale (PoS) system, be integrated into a keyboard, or be an expansion card that can be inserted into a laptop. Smart card readers are used with credit cards that have a special embedded chip that holds data. The chip is read by the smart card reader. Smart cards can require contact or they can be contactless. Smart card readers are also used with a common access card (CAC) issued to active duty military personnel, government employees, and civilian contractors. Figure 8.34 shows a smart card reader.

FIGURE 8.34   Smart card reader

External smart card readers commonly attach to the USB port but can be a wireless connection. Download the latest driver from the manufacturer's website and install it. The device can be verified in Device Manager. Device Manager has a smart card reader section, but the device may show up under unknown devices when a device driver has not been installed properly. You may have to install a security certificate provided by the employer.

A technology called near field communication (NFC) is related to a smart card reader. With NFC, NFC-enabled devices can be in close proximity to an NFC reader in order to perform financial and ticketing types of transactions. More is covered on NFC in Chapter 11.

CHAPTER 8

SOFT SKILLS—ATTITUDE

A technician's **attitude** (see Figure 8.35) is one of his or her greatest assets. Some consider having a good attitude as simply being positive at work, but this is not the entire picture.

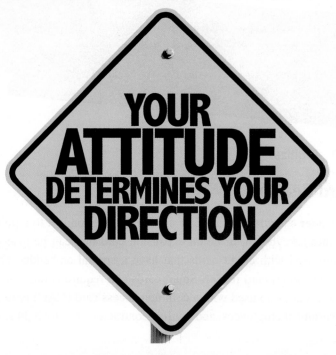

FIGURE 8.35   Your attitude is important

A technician with a good attitude has the following traits:

> **Is proactive, not reactive.** A good technician actively looks for a solution rather than waiting for someone to instruct him or her.

> **Projects confidence.** A technician that lacks confidence is easily spotted by end users. A confident technician isn't arrogant, but instead is secure in the knowledge that a problem can be solved.

> **Seeks solutions instead of providing excuses.** A positive person does not continually apologize or talk in a subservient tone. For example, a positive technician explains issues such as late deliveries in a professional, positive manner.

> **Accepts responsibility for actions taken.** If you forget something or take a misstep, then you should apologize and explain to the customer what happened. Truth goes a long way with customers. A positive technician does not constantly shift blame to other departments or technicians. Even if the other department or technician is responsible, the person with a positive attitude handles the customer and then talks to the other department or technician about the problem.

> **Deals with priority changes professionally.** In the IT field, computer and network problems arise that cause us to reprioritize tasks weekly, daily, and even hourly. These are normal occurrences and a person with a positive attitude understands this.

> **Cooperates and enjoys working with others.** A positive attitude is contagious, and others like being around it.

> **Maintains professionalism even when working with a co-worker who is unethical, un-professional, or uncooperative.** A technician with a good attitude does not let someone else's poor attitude be a negative influence.
> **Embraces problems as challenges to learn and develop skills.** Sometimes, after joining the IT field, a technician becomes complacent and does not seek new skills. The IT field requires that you constantly improve and refine your skills. See a tough problem as a challenge, not a burden. With such an attitude, problems will not frustrate you but will serve as a catalyst for an advancement or make you a better technician.

You should exhibit all these traits consistently to establish a positive mental attitude and make it part of your daily habits.

Chapter Summary

> Install ODDs using the same rules of configuration as for SATA and PATA hard drives.
> Use the appropriate media for the type of drive installed.
> Don't multitask when writing data to an optical disc.
> Optical drives and discs have region codes that must match.
> When purchasing an optical drive, features to look for include ample buffer memory and reduced random access times, MTBFs, and MCBFs.
> For stuck optical discs, use the *Eject* option from Windows/File Explorer or the emergency eject hole.
> Keep the laser lens clean.
> Wipe dirty discs in an inward-to-outward (not circular) motion.
> It's important to ensure that device and video drivers are up-to-date.
> DirectX (`dxdiag`) is used to troubleshoot multimedia issues.
> A decoder must be installed for video to play from a disc correctly.
> A motherboard normally has a small speaker used for POST codes when sound does not work properly.
> If a sound card is installed, disable the motherboard sound ports.
> The higher the sampling rate, the better the audio quality.
> For sound issues, check muting, volume controls, cables, and device conflicts.
> Microphones are used for VoIP and are tested/managed through the *Recording* tab of the Sound window.
> Scan documents at a resolution suited for the final output (print, web, display).
> Do not spray cleaner directly on the scanner glass, but do keep the glass clean.
> Digital cameras commonly have storage media that can be removed and attached directly to a PC or mobile computer using a memory card reader.
> Webcams can be integrated into a display or mobile device or an external unit that is used for conference calls or recording video.
> When installing and configuring common peripheral devices, always follow manufacturer's directions. Commonly software is provided to configure device options.
> A technician should have a positive attitude and project confidence, be proactive, and maintain professionalism when working with others.

A+ CERTIFICATION EXAM TIPS

✓ Review the disc media types and capacities before the exam.

✓ Ensure that you know how to install and configure an optical drive, a sound card, and a scanner.

✓ Know that a digital camera transforms light into 1s and 0s.

✓ Know the various types of flash-based storage media and technology including Compact flash, SD, miniSD, microSD, and eMMC.

✓ Know common sound issues and the easy fixes for them.

✓ Maintaining a positive attitude and projecting confidence are the professionalism and communication skills that are part of the 220-902 exam.

✓ Review the installation tips for other peripherals including barcode reader, biometric devices, game pads, joysticks, digitizer, motion sensor, smart card reader, digital camera, microphone, webcam, camcorder, and MIDI-enabled device.

Key Terms

Review Questions

Consider the following optical drive specifications as you answer Questions 1–7:

> SATA interface half-height internal BD-ROM
> Max. 4X BD-ROM/BD-RE SL and 4X BD-ROM/BD-R/BD-RE DL CAV reading
> Max. 8X DVD-ROM/+R/+RW/+RDL/-R/-RW/-RW DL CAV reading
> Max. 32X CD-ROM/R/RW CAV reading
> Random access times: BD—250ms; DVD—160ms; CD—150ms
> Buffer size 2MB
> System requirements for HD Blu-ray playback: Intel Pentium D 3.0+, 1GB+ of RAM, Vista/ Windows 7, HDCP capable display, or TV for digital output.

1. Which SATA version is being used?

    [1 | 2 | 3 | Cannot be determined from the information given]

2. Can Blu-ray discs be created on this unit? How can you tell? _____

    _____

3. Pretend you are adding this device to a computer. What is the maximum number of devices (if any) that can be on the same cable that connects this drive to the motherboard?

    [None | 1 | 2 | Cannot be determined from the information given]

4. What does the term *random access time* mean? _____

    _____

    _____

5. What is the purpose of buffer memory? _____

    _____

    _____

6. Can a DVD±RW disc be read in this drive? How can you tell? _____

    _____

7. What does BD-RE DL mean? _____

    _____

8. What Apple biometric technology supports fingerprint recognition?
    [Hello world | Touch ID | IT ID | Watch me]

9. Select the non-sound port. [RJ-45 | S/PDIF | TOSLINK | RCA | 1/8-inch TRS]

10. Which optical media has the highest capacity? [DVD | CD | BD]

11. Which drive would have two lasers?

    a. A drive that can handle an 8.5-GB single-sided dual-layer disc

    b. A drive that can handle a double-sided single-layer disc

    c. A drive that can handle a 25-GB dual-layer disc

    d. A drive that can handle a DVD or a Blu-ray disc

12. A PCIe sound card is being installed. Which two steps are most likely going to be done by the technician? (Select two.)

   a. Upgrade the power supply.

   b. Install a driver.

   c. Flash the BIOS/UEFI.

   d. Disable the integrated ports in BIOS/UEFI.

   e. Configure jumpers on the adapter.

   f. Delete the integrated port drivers.

13. Which utility is best used to troubleshoot sound issues?

   [Disk Management | DirectX | BIOS/UEFI diagnostics | Device Manager]

14. Why should a battery be removed from a camera that is not used very often?

   a. in case the battery leaks

   b. in order to preserve the saved files on the memory card

   c. to keep the battery charged

   d. to keep the battery cool

15. A user has attempted a scanner installation to the computer's front USB ports because all the back ports were taken. However, the scanner will not function. What should the technician try next?

   a. Replace the scanner.

   b. Replace the USB port.

   c. Re-attach the USB cable that leads from the front panel to the motherboard.

   d. Add a version 2.0 or higher USB hub to the back USB port.

16. [T | F] Paper towels are okay to use to clean a scanner.

17. [T | F] Part of the installation process for a tablet is to calibrate the camera.

18. Which multimedia device requires calibration as part of the installation process?

   [camera | sound card | scanner | optical disc drive]

19. Which item would more likely be used with a digital camera than with a scanner?

   [flash media | 1.8-inch hard drive | laser lens | optical cleaning cloth]

20. Which scenario is one that most shows a positive attitude?

   a. A technician returns a borrowed disc to a team member after having the disc more than six months.

   b. A technician leaves documentation for a newly installed optical drive with the customer, even though the customer treated the technician poorly during the installation.

   c. A technician eagerly helps reorganize a wiring closet for the company.

   d. A technician smiles when an angry customer is taking out her computer problems on the technician.

Exercise

Exercise 8.1 Multimedia Device Research

Objective: To be able to use the Internet to locate device drivers and technical specifications

Parts: A computer that has Internet access

Procedure: Using the Internet, find the cost, latest device driver, and most important technical specification for the devices found in Table 8.12.

TABLE 8.12   Multimedia Device Information

Device type	Cost	Device driver version	Most important technical specification
Flatbed scanner	_____	_____	_____
Barcode reader	_____	_____	_____
Fingerprint scanner	_____	_____	_____
Game pad	_____	_____	_____
Joystick	_____	_____	_____
Digitizer	_____	_____	_____
Motion sensor	_____	_____	_____
Smart card reader	_____	_____	_____
Digital camera	_____	_____	_____
Webcam	_____	_____	_____
Camcorder	_____	_____	_____
MIDI device	_____	_____	_____
Sound card	_____	_____	_____
Speakers	_____	_____	_____

CHAPTER 8

Activities

Internet Discovery

Objective: To obtain specific information on the Internet regarding a computer or its associated parts

Parts: Computer with access to the Internet

Questions: Use the Internet to answer the following questions.

1. Find a website that sells external optical drives. List the cost of one drive and the website URL.

_____

2. What is the cost of a disc that works in a DVD±RW drive? List the cost and website URL.

_____

3. Find the driver version for a Sound Blaster Audigy Rx PCIe adapter that is going in a 64-bit Windows 8.1 computer. Document the driver download filename and URL where you find this information.

_____

_____

4. An HP G4050 Scanjet scanner attaches to a Windows Vista computer. When the scanning software is accessed, the error "The computer cannot communicate with the scanning device" appears. List the six recommended steps.

_____

_____

_____

_____

5. The president of a company purchased a Canon EOS Rebel T4i digital camera. Which type of memory media does this camera accept? Write the answer and URL where you find the answer.

_____

_____

6. A customer has a Plextor PX-891SAF DVD+/RW drive. How much buffer memory does the drive contain and which interface(s) does it support? Write the answers and website URL where you find the information._____

_____

_____

_____

Soft Skills

Objective: To enhance and fine-tune a technician's ability to listen, communicate in both written and oral form, and support people who use computers in a professional manner

Activities:

1. List some tips for determining whether a computer has an optical drive installed, as if you were stepping through it over the phone with a customer who is not a technician. Using your instructions, practice with a classmate.

2. The class is divided into groups of five. Each group makes a list of three categories that relate to multimedia devices. The five groups share their lists and determine which group works on which category. In 30 minutes, each team comes up with five answers with corresponding questions for their category. The answers are rated from 100 to 500 with 100 being the easiest question. The teams play *Jeopardy!* with the rule that the teams cannot choose their own category.

Critical Thinking Skills

Objective: To analyze and evaluate information, and apply information to new or different situations

Activities:

1. For this activity, you need an advertisement of a sound card, including the technical specifications. Make a list of all terms related to the card that you do not know. Using books, the Internet, or other resources, research these terms and define them.

2. Form teams of two. Several multimedia devices are needed. The devices are numbered. Each team selects a number and installs, configures, and tests the associated device. Each team documents its installation and shares its experience (including lessons learned) with the rest of the class.

Labs

Lab 8.1 Sound and Optical Drives in Windows

Objective: To be able to use the tools provided with Windows to manage sound devices and optical media drives

Parts: A computer with Windows 7, 8, or 10 loaded, has an optical drive installed, and that has Internet access

Procedure: Complete the following procedure and answer the accompanying questions.

Note: Parts of this lab may be different due to the hardware installed and the version of Windows installed.

1. Power on the computer and log in to Windows 7, 8, or 10.

2. Access the *Sound* Control Panel.

    Which tabs are shown in the window?

    _____

    _____

    Which is the default playback device?

    _____

3. With the default playback device selected, click the *Configure* button.

    Which audio channels are available?

    _____

4. Select the *Test* button.

    What was the result?

    _____

5. Click the *Cancel* button and ensure the *Playback* tab is selected. Click *Properties*. The Speakers Properties window opens.

    What jack information displays?

    _____

    _____

6. Click *Properties*.

    What is the device status? _____

7. Select the *Driver* tab.

    What is the driver version?_____

    What is the purpose of the Roll Back Driver button?

    _____

    Can the audio be disabled from this window?_____

8. Click *Cancel*. From the *Speakers Properties* window, click the *Advanced* tab.

    How many bits are used for sampling?_____

    What is the frequency response?_____

9. Click *Cancel*. Select the *Recording* tab.

    What is the default recording device?_____

10. Select the *Sounds* tab. In the *Program* (Windows 7)/*Program events* (8/10) window, select any task that has a speaker icon to the left of it. These sounds are an easy way to check for issues without having to download a sound file. Click *Test*.

    Did sound emit? [Yes | No]

11. Select the *Sound Scheme* drop-down menu.

    Which options are available?

    _____

    What is the checkbox used for in this section?

    _____

12. Click *Cancel*. Close the Control Panel window.

13. Open *Windows Explorer (Windows 7)/File Explorer (8/10)* and select *Computer* (7)/*This PC* (8/10) from the left panel. In the right-panel, right-click the optical drive. Notice the *Eject* option, which can be used to eject a stuck disc.

14. Point to the *Share with* option and select *Advanced Sharing*. The optical drive properties window opens. The *Sharing* tab allows you to share a disc with others.

15. If you closed the last window, go back into the optical drive properties and select the *Hardware* tab. In the *All disk drives:* window, select the optical drive. Select *Properties*.

    What is the device status?_____

16. In the *Properties* window, select the *DVD region* tab if a DVD drive is installed.

    What is the DVD region code? Write *Not applicable* as your answer if a CD drive is installed.

    _____

    _____

17. Select the *Driver* tab.

    Which version of the driver is installed?_____

    What is the date of the driver?_____

18. Use the Internet to determine whether a newer device driver is available. Show this driver to the instructor or lab assistant.

    Instructor initials: _____

19. In the device's properties window, click *Cancel*.

20. In the original optical drive properties window, select the *Customize* tab.

    What types of things can be customized from this tab?

    _____

    _____

21. Click the *Cancel* button. Close the *Windows Explorer* (7)/*File Explorer* (8/10) window.

Lab 8.2 Optical Drive Installation Lab

Objective: To install, configure, and test an optical drive

Parts: A computer with Windows loaded

Anti-static wrist strap or glove

An optical drive with accompanying cable and mounting equipment if necessary

Procedure: Complete the following procedure and answer the accompanying questions.

1. Obtain an optical drive designated by the instructor or student assistant.

    Which type of drive is this? [CD-ROM I CD-R I CD-RW I DVD-R I DVD+R I DVD±RW I DVD-R DL I DVD+R DL I BD-R I BD-RE]

    List the drive manufacturer and model number.

    _____

    If possible, determine whether a driver is available and list the website on which you located this information._____

    Which type of interface does the optical drive use? [PATA IDE I SATA I SCSI I Parallel I USB I FireWire]

2. Power off the computer, remove the power cord, open the computer, and determine whether a cable and interface are available to install the drive. If not, obtain them from the lab supplies, instructor, or lab assistant.

3. Configure the drive as necessary for the type of interface being used.

    Which drive settings did you select, if any?

    _____

4. If appropriate, install the drive into the computer and attach power.

5. If an external device is being installed, a device driver may need to be installed at this point. Always refer to the device installation instructions. Whether the drive is internal or external, attach the correct interface cable to the drive.

6. Power on the computer, load a device driver (if necessary), and ensure that the operating system recognizes the drive. Troubleshoot as necessary until the drive works.

    Which tests did you perform to ensure the drive works?

    _____

    _____

    _____

7. Tell the instructor when the drive is successfully installed.

Instructor initials: _____

8. Remove the drive and reinstall the computer cover. Power on the computer and ensure BIOS/UEFI errors do not appear.

Instructor initials: _____

Lab 8.3 DirectX Diagnostics in Windows 7, 8, or 10

Objective:	To be able to use the DirectX tool provided with Windows 7, 8, or 10
Parts:	A computer with Windows 7, 8, or 10 loaded and with administrator rights and Internet access
Procedure:	Complete the following procedure and answer the accompanying questions.
Note:	This lab may vary due to the equipment installed and the Windows version and service pack.

1. Power on the computer and log in to Windows 7.

2. Click the *Start* button, in the *Search programs and files* textbox, type dxdiag and press [Enter] or select the dxdiag link. The DirectX tool may ask you if you want to check that the drivers are digitally signed and/or to allow an Internet connection for an update. Click *Yes*.

   After the tool is shown and the System tab is displayed, which DirectX version is running? _____

   How much RAM is installed in the computer? _____

   What is the size of the page file? _____

   How much of the page file is currently used? _____

3. Click the *Next Page* button. The next tab displays.

   What notes, if any, appear on the tab?

   _____

4. Ensure you are on the *Display* tab.

   How much RAM is on the video adapter? _____

   Are any DirectX features enabled? If so, which ones?

   _____

   _____

   Research the words *RAM*, *video adapter*, and *DirectX* on the Internet to help with this answer and give a brief description of the features.

   _____

   _____

   _____

   _____

   _____

   _____

5. Ensure the *Sound* tab is selected.

   What is the device type used? _____

   What is WDM? If you do not know, research it on the Internet.

   _____

   _____

   Which driver file is used? _____

   What does WHQL logo mean? If you do not know, research this term on the Internet.

   _____

   _____

6. Click the *Input* tab.

   List any direct input devices displayed.

   _____

7. Expand any USB devices in the Input Related Devices section.

   List any USB devices that are considered to be input devices.

   _____

8. Close the DirectX Diagnostics window.

Lab 8.4 Installing a Sound Card and Speakers in Windows 7, 8, or 10

Objective:　　To install and configure a sound card

Parts:　　A computer with Windows 7, 8, or 10 loaded and an available expansion slot

　　Sound card with drivers or Internet access

　　Optional audio disc

1. Before powering on the computer, determine the current audio capabilities.

   How many sound ports are integrated into the motherboard?_____

   Draw each port and list the purpose of the port. If you do not know, use the Internet to research the computer model._____

2. Connect power to the speakers and attach the speakers to the computer if necessary.

3. Power on the computer and log in to Windows. Access the *Hardware and Sound* Control Panel. Select the *Sound* link.

   On the Playback tab, how many playback devices are listed?_____

4. Right-click the icon that represents the speaker(s) that are enabled and select *Properties*.

   Which name is currently assigned the output device?_____

5. Click in the *General tab* textbox and change the name to something more meaningful.

   List the name assigned._____

   Which output jacks are available for this output device?_____

   What controller is controlling the speakers?_____

6. Click the speaker controller *Properties* button.

   Which driver version is installed?_____

7. Close the Properties window. Back in the Speakers Properties window, select the *Levels* tab.

   Which settings can you control on this tab?_____

   The tabs that are available vary depending on the speakers installed. Which tabs are available for the speakers on your computer?_____

8. Select the *Advanced* tab. Test the quality of the sound output using the *Test* button. Troubleshoot the system if a sound does not emit.

   How many bits are used in converting analog sounds into digital audio?_____

9. Select the *Default Format* drop-down menu. Notice how this is the window where you allow applications to control or change the speaker settings.

   List two other available formats if possible._____

10. Click *Cancel* twice to close the Speaker Properties windows. Power off the computer.

11. Power on the computer and enter the BIOS/UEFI Setup program.

    Which key or process did you use to enter Setup?_____

12. Locate and disable the integrated sound ports. Save the settings and exit BIOS/UEFI Setup.

13. Log in to Windows.

14. Using whichever method you would like ensure that sound does not emit from the speakers. Which method did you use?

_____

15. Shut down the computer and remove the power cord.

16. Access the computer expansion slots and if necessary, remove any slot covers or retention bars.

17. Install the sound adapter into an empty expansion slot and ensure it fits snugly into the slot. Re-install any retention bar as necessary.

18. Attach the power cord and power on the computer. The computer should detect that a new device has been installed. You may be prompted for a device driver and to restart the computer in order to use the new adapter. If you don't have a device driver, go to a computer that has Internet access and download the appropriate driver for the sound card you installed. Note that you may have to power down the computer and look at the sound card (and possibly remove it) in order to get the appropriate model required to download the correct driver.

19. Attach the speakers to the appropriate ports on the newly installed sound card.

20. Using any method, including previously demonstrated methods or by playing an audio disc, test the new sound card.

21. Access *Device Manager* and expand the *Sound, video and game controllers* section.

22. Right-click the newly installed sound card and select *Properties*.

Which I/O address does the adapter use?_____

What is the device status?_____

Instructor initials: _____

23. Power down the computer and remove the power cord.

24. Unplug the speakers from the sound card. Remove the sound card and attach any slot covers.

25. Power on the computer and access BIOS/UEFI Setup.

26. Enable the integrated sound ports and save the settings.

27. Attach the speakers to the motherboard speaker port.

28. Attach the power cord. Boot the computer and log in to Windows again. Test the speakers.

29. Return all parts to the proper location.

Lab 8.5 Installing a USB Scanner

Objective: To be able to install a USB scanner and driver on a Windows-based computer

Parts: USB scanner, USB cable, scanner driver, scanner software/utilities, computer with Windows loaded

Procedure: The procedures outlined below are guidelines. Refer to the scanner's installation instructions for exact procedures.

Installing the Scanner Driver

1. Insert the scanner driver media into the drive. Sometimes you must also select which type of interface connection is going to be used. If this is the case, select *USB*. The software installer sometimes includes additional software programs that can be used to control the scanner and to manipulate scanned images. Many drivers require the computer to be restarted once the installation process is complete.

Connecting the Scanner

2. Some scanners ship with a carriage safety lock. If this is the case, remove the safety lock.

3. With the computer powered on, connect one end of the USB cable to the scanner's USB port and attach the other end to a USB computer port or a USB hub port.

4. If necessary, attach the power cable to the scanner. Attach the other power cable end to an electrical outlet.

5. Power on the scanner.

6. Optionally, if the scanner has a calibrate routine, execute the calibration.

Using the Scanner

7. If the scanner software program(s) did not install during driver installation, install the scanner software programs now.

8. Insert a document to be scanned.

9. Access the scanner software program through the *Start* button and scan the document.

Instructor initials: _____

Lab 8.6 Changing the Drive Letter of an Optical Drive Using the Disk Management and `diskpart` Utility

Objective: To reassign the optical drive letter

Parts: Windows computer with administrator rights

Procedure: Complete the following procedure and answer the accompanying questions.

1. Using Windows/File Explorer, determine the current optical drive letter.

    What drive letter is being used by the ODD drive? _____

2. In Windows 7, from the Start button menu in the Search program and files textbox, type **Disk Management** and press ⎡Enter⎤. In Windows 8/10, use the *Administrative Tools* Control Panel to access and open the *Computer Management* tool. Expand the *Storage* section so that the Disk Management option is available. Select *Disk Management*.

3. Locate the optical drive in the bottom half of the Disk Management window.

4. Right-click or tap and briefly hold the drive icon in the left side of the panel where the drive letter is located and select *Change Drive Letter and Paths*.

5. Select *Change* and use the *Assign the following drive letter:* drop-down menu to select a different drive letter.

    What drive letter did you choose? _____

6. Click *OK* and *Yes* to the notification that some programs might not work properly.

7. At a command prompt, type **diskpart** and press ⎡Enter⎤. Type **list volume** and press ⎡Enter⎤. Look down the Type column for an optical drive and locate the drive to be changed. Ensure that the drive letter in the Ltr column is the same drive letter written down in Step 5.

    Write the volume number that is listed in the same row as the optical drive. _____

8. At a command prompt, type **select volume *x*** (where *x* is the number you wrote in Step 7). A message appears, stating that the volume is selected. If the message does not appear, recheck your steps, starting from the beginning of the lab.

9. Type **assign letter=*x*** (where *x* is the newly assigned drive letter). A message appears, stating that the drive letter assignment was successful. If this message does not appear, redo the exercise.

CHAPTER 8

10. Use *Windows Explorer* (Vista/7)/*File Explorer* (8 or 10) to verify the reassignment, refreshing the screen if necessary. Show the instructor or lab assistant your reassigned drive letter.

Instructor initials: _____

11. In the `diskpart` utility or the Disk Management window, return the drive to the original drive letter. Refer to the answer to the question in Step 1 if you do not remember the original drive letter. Use Windows Explorer/File Explorer to show the instructor or lab assistant that the drive letter has been reassigned.

Instructor initials: _____

9

Video Technologies

In this chapter you will learn:

> To identify the components of the video subsystem

> Various display types

> Basic display terminology

> To install a video card

> Basic video troubleshooting techniques

> To see the problem from the user's prospective

CompTIA Exam Objectives:

What CompTIA A+ exam objectives are covered in this chapter?

✓ 901-1.1 Given a scenario, configure settings and use BIOS/UEFI tools on a PC.

✓ 901-1.4 Install and configure PC expansion cards.

✓ 901-1.7 Compare and contrast various PC connection interfaces, their characteristics and purpose.

✓ 901-1.10 Compare and contrast types of display devices and their features.

✓ 901-1.11 Identify common PC connector types and associated cables.

✓ 901-1.12 Install and configure common peripheral devices.

✓ 901-3.2 Explain the function of components within the display of a laptop.

✓ 901-4.3 Given a scenario, troubleshoot common video, projector and display issues.

✓ 902-1.5 Given a scenario, use Windows Control Panel utilities.

✓ 902-3.2 Compare and contrast common prevention methods.

✓ 902-3.4 Given a scenario, deploy and enforce security best practices to secure a workstation.

Video Overview

Video quality is very important to computer users. A display is one of the most expensive computer components. Users usually derive the most gratification from their display, although sound quality is now becoming as important. Technicians must look at video as a subsystem that consists of the display, the electronic circuits that send the display instructions, and the cable that connects them. The electronic video circuits can be on a separate video adapter or built into the motherboard. Figure 9.1 illustrates a computer video subsystem.

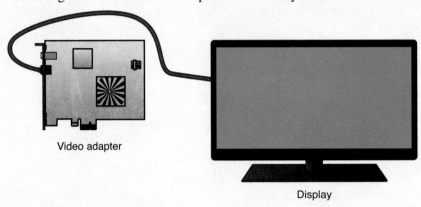

Video adapter

Display

FIGURE 9.1   Video subsystem

Types of Video Output Devices

Video output devices such as displays, projectors, and even TVs are commonly used with desktop and laptop computers. The easiest way to classify video output is by the way in which the output is created—the technology. Table 9.1 lists some of the most popular display output technologies.

TABLE 9.1   Video output technology

Technology	Description
Cathode ray tube (CRT)	Older bulky monitors. A CRT monitor has three color beams (red, green, and blue) directed at a phosphorous dot on the back of the monitor tube The result is a single image on the screen called a **pixel**, or picture element. Pixels are used in other technologies, too. They are just formed differently.
Liquid crystal display (**LCD**)	Technology used in laptops, flat panel monitors, TVs, tablets, smartphones, and projectors. Two glass substrates (see Figure 9.2) have a thin layer of liquid crystal between them. One glass substrate is the color filter, with three main colors—red, green, and blue—that allow millions of colors to be displayed. The other glass substrate is the thin film transistor (TFT) array, which has the technology to direct the liquid crystal to block the light. A **backlight** (that can be a fluorescent lamp or LED technology) extends behind the combined glass assembly, and the light is always on. This is why an LCD monitor appears to sometimes glow even when it's off and why crystals are needed to block some of the light to create the intensities of light. Liquid crystals are sensitive to temperature changes. Laptop displays may appear distorted in cold or hot temperatures due to the liquid crystals.

Technology	Description
Light-emitting diode (**LED**)	A low-power, low-heat, long-lasting electronic device used in many technologies—calculators, home, business, and auto lighting, fiber optics, and displays. LED displays still use liquid crystals; the displays just use an LED backlight instead of cold cathode fluorescent lamp (**CCFL**). LED displays have better color accuracy, are thinner than the LCDs that use CCFLs, and are commonly used for large displays.
Organic LED (**OLED**)	Does not require a backlight like LCDs but has a film of organic compounds placed in rows and columns that can emit light. Is lightweight and has a fast response time, low power usage, and a wide viewing angle.
Digital Light Processing (**DLP**)	A Texas Instrument technology used in projectors and rear projection TVs. DLP has an array of mounted miniature mirrors, one of which is smaller than the width of a human hair and represents one or more pixels. The mirrors are used to create a light or dark pixel on a projection surface by being repositioned to different angles to reflect light. A color wheel or LEDs are used for the primary colors red, green, and blue. Figure 9.3 illustrates the concepts of DLP technology.
plasma	Displays that work similarly to LCDs except that they have plasma gas in little chambers. When electricity is applied inside the chambers, excited electrons hit red, green, and blue phosphorous dots that glow. Many believe that plasma displays require less energy than CRTs. This is not necessarily true. However, LCDs do take less energy than CRTs.
projector	Used to take input from a device such as a computer, laptop, camera, etc., and send that image onto a screen or wall.

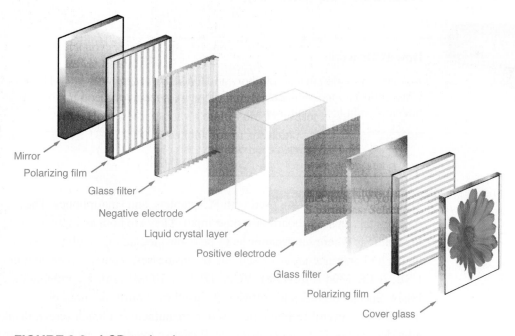

Mirror
Polarizing film
Glass filter
Negative electrode
Liquid crystal layer
Positive electrode
Glass filter
Polarizing film
Cover glass

FIGURE 9.2   LCD technology

Other technologies used in video output include liquid crystal on silicon (LCoS), surface-conduction electron-emitter display (SED), and field-emission display (FED). LCoS is similar to Digital Light Processing (DLP) except that it uses liquid crystals instead of mirrors for higher resolutions. SED and FED technologies are similar: both use electron emitters to energize color phosphor dots to produce an image. The difference is in the electron emitter used.

CHAPTER 9

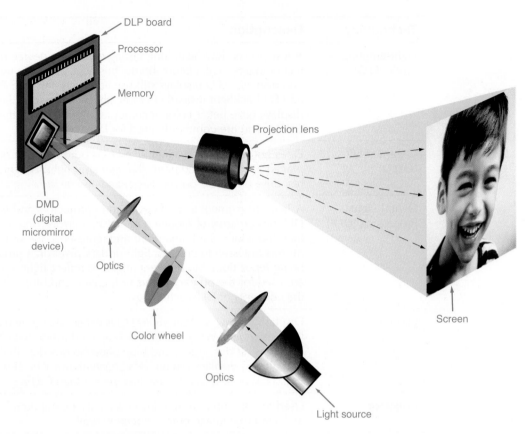

FIGURE 9.3 DLP technology

TECH TIP

How LCDs work

A great short video that shows how an LED-lit LCD works is by Bill Hammack (Engineer Guy video series). One web location at the time of press is http://www.howtogeek.com/92988/how-an-led-lit-lcd-monitor-works-video/.

Touch Screens

Touch screen displays are used with PCs, tablets, and smartphones. They respond to contact on the screen rather than keyboard or mouse input. They are both an input and output device and are used in situations where information is to be controlled and in public areas, such as kiosks at airports, malls, and entrance areas of schools or businesses. Touch screen monitors normally attach to a USB, IEEE 1394 (FireWire), VGA, DVI, or HDMI port, a combination of these ports, or wirelessly. Special drivers and software are used to control the monitor.

There are several technologies used to manufacture a touch screen display. The two most common ones are resistive and capacitive. Resistive touch screens have a flexible membrane stretched over the face of the display. The membrane contains a special metal oxide coating and has spacers that are used to locate the touched spot on the screen. Resistive touch screens are good in manufacturing or in the medical industry where personnel wear gloves. A stylus can also be used with both types of displays.

Capacitive touch screens are more durable than resistive screens. They respond to a touch or multiple touches on the display and easily detect contact. Most touch screens are the capacitive type. Some mobile devices allow you to calibrate the screen or lock the screen orientation using the *Settings* option. The screen orientations of mobile devices have been greatly enhanced due to accelerometers and gyroscopes. An **accelerometer** detects the screen orientation and adapts what is shown on the screen based on that orientation. A **gyroscope** measures and maintains that orientation. Figure 9.4 shows a touch screen. Table 9.2 lists some of the different technologies used with touch screen displays.

FIGURE 9.4   Touch screen display

TABLE 9.2   Touch screen technologies

Technology type	Description
Four-wire resistive	1.7- to 24-inch displays with high resolution. Has a short life span (1 to 2 million touches) and low brightness. Accepts input from fingers, a gloved hand, or a stylus.
Five-wire resistive	10.4- to 24-inch displays with resolution up to 1024×1024. Has a longer life span (30 to 35 million touches) than four-wire resistive and low brightness. Accepts input from fingers, a gloved hand, or a stylus.
Capacitive	12- to 27-inch displays with resolution up to 2560×1440. Has a longer life span than any of the resistive types (100 million touches) and high brightness. Accepts finger input.
Surface wave	10.4- to 30-inch displays with high resolutions. Lasts a long time (50 million touches) and has high brightness. Accepts input from fingers, a gloved hand, or a soft stylus. Tends to have the longest warranties.
Infrared	10.4- to 42-inch displays with high resolutions, long-term reliability (more than 100 million touches), and high brightness. Accepts input from fingers, a gloved hand, and a stylus.

The technologies that enable touch screens allow users to interact with mobile devices and displays of all types with ease. A touch screen has multiple configurations that can be controlled including how swiping is controlled, as shown in Figure 9.5.

CHAPTER 9

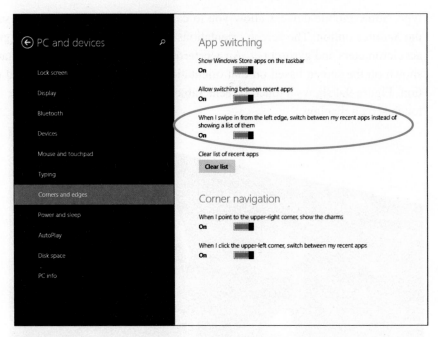

FIGURE 9.5   Sample swipe configuration

In Windows 7, use the *Start* button > *Control Panel* > *Hardware and Sound* > under the *Tablet PC Settings*, select *Calibrate your pen or touch input* > *Display* tab > locate *Display options* and then select *Calibrate*. Follow the instructions on the screen.

In Windows 8, use the *Settings* > *PC and Devices* > *Corners and Edges* as well as the *Calibrate the screen for pen or touch input,* as shown in Figure 9.6. To access this Control Panel in Windows 8 or 10, simply search on the word calibrate and select the *Calibrate the screen for pen or touch input* link in the resulting list. Use the *Setup* button to calibrate the screen for either a pen or for touch.

FIGURE 9.6   Windows touch screen calibration

Video Terminology and Theory

Video has unique terminology associated with it. It is important for a technician to be familiar with video terminology. Let's start with an important term—resolution. A monitor's **resolution** is the maximum number of pixels on the monitor. Figure 9.7 shows this concept.

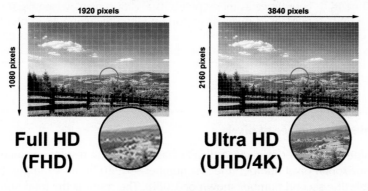

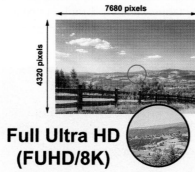

FIGURE 9.7   The concept of display resolution

Two numbers separated by an × (meaning *by*) describe a monitor's resolution, such as 1024×768 (1024 "by" 768). The first number, 1024, is the number of pixels that fit horizontally across the screen. The second number, 768, describes the number of pixels that fit vertically on the screen. The possible monitor resolutions depend on the monitor and the video adapter. Table 9.3 lists other important video features with which technicians need to be familiar.

TABLE 9.3   Video features

Feature	Description
Refresh rate	Measured in hertz (Hz) or milliseconds (ms). How long it takes a screen to be drawn in one second. In LCDs, it is also called temporal resolution. LCDs refresh rates are traditionally 60Hz, but some high-definition TVs (HDTVs) have refresh rates of 120, 240, and even 600Hz.
Frame rate	The equivalent to a refresh rate for motion video. Movies are commonly played at 24 frames per second (fps).
Display size	Display size is typically shown in inches (") that describes how much screen is available from the top left corner to the bottom right corner.
Progressive scaling	Refreshes all of the horizontal lines simultaneously as opposed to the traditional method of interlacing. You can easily tell if a TV (which is sometimes used as a display) uses progressive scaling by the type shown in the advertisement (720p or 1080p).

Feature	Description
Interlaced	The traditional method of scanning where half the horizontal rows of pixels are refreshed and then the other (alternating) rows are refreshed. Displays that use this technology have an i after the type, such as 1080i.
Ultra HD or 4K	Four times as many pixels as a 1080p display (see Figure 9.7). The increased number of pixels is important when receiving 4K content (ultra high definition [UHD] content), which at the time of press is not that common. To handle lower resolution input, the 4K display must do some processing to adjust.

TECH TIP

Determining the number of pixels

To determine the number of pixels a display has, look at the resolution, such as 1920×1080. Multiply the horizontal pixel number (the first number—1,920 in this example) by the vertical number of pixels (the second number shown or 1,080). The result is the total number of pixels, which, in this example, is 2,073,600 (approximately 2 million pixels). See Figure 9.8.

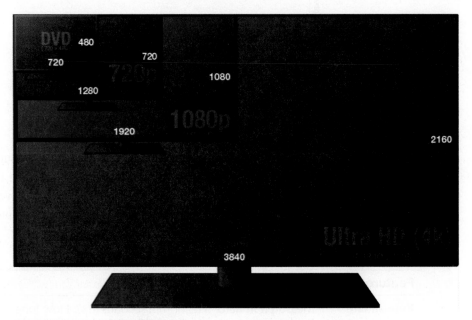

FIGURE 9.8   TV resolutions

To set the resolution in Windows Vista/7/8, access the *Display* Control Panel link > use the *Adjust Resolution* and the *Colors* options to customize the display (see Figure 9.9). To adjust the refresh rate, click the *Advanced Settings* button in the *Screen Resolution* window > *Monitor* tab > and use the *Screen refresh rate* drop-down menu to customize.

In Windows 10, access the *Start* button > *Settings* > *System* > *Display* > *Advanced display settings* link. To adjust the resolution, use the *Resolution* drop-down menu. To adjust colors, use the *Color calibration* link in the *Related settings* section. Note that with some video cards, you might have to use the *Display adapter properties* > *Color Management* tab. To adjust the refresh rate, use the *Display adapter properties* link in the *Related settings* section or use the *Display adapter properties* > *Monitor* tab.

FIGURE 9.9   Display resolutions

TECH TIP

The higher the resolution, the smaller a pixel appears on the screen

Selecting a higher resolution will make the icons in Windows appear smaller. Use the *Display* Control Panel to adjust the icon size.

Displays sometimes have a button that allow a menu to be accessed or have several buttons used to adjust the image quality. You might see this described in documentation or on the CompTIA certification as the on menu display (OSD). Common buttons include the following:

> Power—Powers the monitor on and off
> Input—Available when both analog (VGA and DVI) and digital (DVI, HDMI, or Display-Port) input connectors are on the monitor and used to select between the options
> Auto adjust—Automatically refines the display settings, based on the incoming video signal
> Brightness—Controls the intensity of the image or the luminance of the backlight on an LCD
> Contrast—Adjusts the degree of difference between light and dark
> Position—Moves or adjusts the viewing area by using horizontal and vertical controls
> Reset—Resets the monitor to default settings

See Figure 9.10 to see a sample of the buttons. Note that many flat panel displays are controlled through the *Display* Control Panel or custom software.

FIGURE 9.10 Display controls

LCD

LCD is a video technology used with mobile devices and flat screen displays that are powered by a low-voltage DC power source. They are more reliable and have a longer life span than CRT monitors. The liquid crystals used in these displays are sensitive to temperature changes. That is why they might appear distorted in cold or hot temperatures. Figure 9.11 shows some LCDs.

FIGURE 9.11 LCDs

There are two basic types of LCD: passive matrix and active matrix. The difference between the two lies in how the screen image is created. The cheaper of the two, passive matrix, is made up of rows and columns of conductors. Each pixel is located at the intersection of a row and a column. (This is a similar concept to a cell in a spreadsheet.) Current on the grid determines whether a pixel is turned on or off. Each pixel has three cells in a color monitor: one for red, one for green, and one for blue. Another name for passive matrix is STN (supertwist nematic), which is a technology that twists light rays to improve the display's contrast. Passive matrix displays are not as bright as active matrix displays.

Active matrix displays have a transistor for each pixel. The number of transistors depends on the maximum resolution. A 1280×800 resolution requires 1,024,000 transistors (1280×800 and more are added for color). This technology provides a brighter display (more luminance). Active matrix monitors take more power than passive matrix, but both of them require less power than CRT-based displays. Another name for active matrix monitors is thin film transistor (TFT). TFT displays use three transistors per pixel (one for each color). Table 9.4 describes some common terms and technologies used with LCD/LED displays.

TABLE 9.4   Display characteristics

Characteristic	Description
Viewable size	The diagonal length of the LCD screen surface. Sometimes called viewable image size (VIS).
Native resolution	The optimum setting for an LCD, shown as the number of pixels that go across the screen followed by the number of pixels that go up and down the screen. Examples include 1024×768, 1280×800, and 1920×1080, as seen previously in Figure 9.7.
Response time or synchronization rate	The time it takes to draw one screen (lower number is faster and better) so you don't see blur when there is action on the screen.
Pixel response rate	How fast a pixel can change colors in milliseconds (the lower number is faster).
Viewing angle	At certain angles, the display becomes hard to read. The viewing angle is the maximum angle that you can still see the image on the screen properly. Some displays have different viewing angles for horizontal and vertical perspectives.
Aspect ratio	A ratio of monitor width to height. Common monitor aspect ratios are **4:3** or 5:4, but newer widescreen formats, such as **16:9** or **16:10**, are becoming more prevalent. See Figure 9.12.
Contrast ratio	The difference in light intensity between the brightest white and darkest black, but measured in different ways by manufacturers. A higher contrast ratio such as 800:1 is better than 500:1.
Portrait/landscape mode	Physical turning of a monitor so that the edge of the monitor that is on the left is turned to become the top or bottom of the monitor. Not all monitors have this capability.
Luminance or **brightness**	How much light a monitor can produce, expressed in cd/m^2 (candelas per square meter) or nits. An example of a computer display is 50 to 500 nits. (200 to 250 is acceptable for most users, but 500 is better if video clips or movies are used.)
Lumen	A measure of light output or brightness—how much visible light is coming out of equipment such as lamps, lighting equipment, or projectors. This measure is important when comparing products for a room that has lots of exposure to sunlight, for example.
Twisted nematic (**TN**)	The majority of displays use this technology. It is the cheapest to make and fastest to display. Best viewed from straight on.
Vertical alignment (VA)	Better viewing angles, color, and brightness, but the response time is not too good.
In-plane switching (**IPS**)	A technology that can have a slow response time, but these have really good color and viewing angles important to photo/video editing.
Plane to line switching (PLS)	A Samsung technology that has brighter and clearer images, improved viewing angle, and low production costs.

FIGURE 9.12   Aspect ratio example

LCDs do not have multiple frequency settings, as CRTs do, nor do they flicker (no beam tracing across and down the screen). The number of pixels on a screen is fixed. Manufacturers use image scalers to change resolution. Pixelation is the effect caused by sending a different resolution out to the display than the display design specifications. The LCD monitor must rely on interpolation or scaling of the output rather than having things displayed in the native resolution (the optimum choice).

TECH TIP

Set the flat panel resolution to the native resolution

You can change the resolution through the *Display* Control Panel, but it is best if left to the resolution for which it was designed. Otherwise, the output will not be as sharp as it can be. Use the same Control Panel to change the font size if the icons are too small.

LCDs are found in the desktop and mobile device markets. The desktop monitors that use this technology are called flat panel displays. With flat panel displays, the viewing area is the same as the display measurements (so no trick advertisements).

Either a CCFL or LED backlight bulb is used on many models so images on the screen can be seen. The CCFL type connects to an inverter. The inverter converts low DC voltage to high AC voltage for the backlight bulb. Screens larger than 15.4 inches may need two CCFL backlight bulbs. An LCD with an LED backlight does not need an inverter. An OLED display doesn't need an inverter or a backlight.

TECH TIP

Liquid crystals are poisonous

Be careful with cracked LCDs. If liquid crystals (which are not liquid) get on you, wash with soap and water and seek medical attention.

Video Ports and Cables

Flat panel monitors are digital, but some can work with an older analog adapter that has an analog port, such as an VGA port. This is not a good idea because the digital signal output from flat panel monitors must be converted to analog. The issue of colors with the old monitors is no longer relevant because today's flat panel monitors use transistors to control colors. Some monitors and TVs also provide USB connectivity. Some LCDs have a USB cable from the computer to the monitor. Many monitors act as a USB hub and provide multiple USB ports.

With flat panel monitors, you need an AGP or PCIe adapter that has a digital video/visual interface (DVI) or high-definition multimedia interface (HDMI) port. This would be a good time to review the video ports covered in Chapter 2. Figure 9.13 shows an adapter with three common video ports.

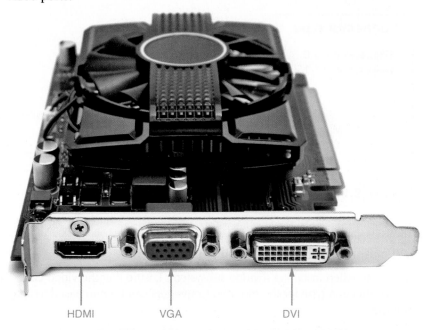

HDMI   VGA   DVI

FIGURE 9.13   Video adapter with HDMI, VGA, and DVI ports

TECH TIP

Use a digital adapter for a flat panel monitor

Using an analog adapter is not recommended for connecting a flat panel display unless the flat panel display accepts analog input. The computer uses digital signals. The digital signals get converted to analog at the video adapter, it is sent to the monitor as analog, and then the monitor has to convert it back to digital for the display output.

With VGA ports, the analog video signals are sent using a VGA cable. The VGA standards did not specify a cable length maximum, but with higher resolutions, a higher quality cable is required. DVI, which uses digital video signals, is a similar situation. The standard does not specify cable lengths, but you sometimes have to install a DVI repeater (booster) for longer distances used with higher resolutions. Note that older DVI ports were not designed to output to some of the newer display formats (no matter what cable you use). With DisplayPorts and HDMI ports, cabling standards do exist, as shown in Figure 9.14.

A type of port you might see on a PCIe card or on an Apple computer is a **Thunderbolt** port. A Thunderbolt port looks like a mini-DisplayPort, but it has a lightning bolt beside it. The Thunderbolt port can provide power to up to seven daisy-chained devices (up to 10.5W). Remember, though, that each device along the chain needs two Thunderbolt ports. The maximum length of a Thunderbolt cable is 10 feet (about 3 meters). Figure 9.15 shows the port. Table 9.5 summarizes video ports for the 901 certification exam. Chapter 2 introduced these ports.

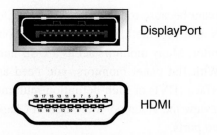

DisplayPort

HDMI

Connector type	Cabling
DisplayPort v 1.0 DisplayPort v 1.1/2	2 meters (~6 feet) max Longer distances with fiber
HDMI	Type A/Category 1 (standard) 720p/1080i Type B/Category 2 (high-speed) 1080p resolutions up to 2560x1600 Type C (mini-connector) Type D (micro-connector) Maximum of 10 meters (~32 feet) with quality/high-speed cabling

FIGURE 9.14   DisplayPort and HDMI cabling

TECH TIP

DVI must match the monitor DVI connection type

Be careful when installing a video subsystem. Ensure that the video card installed matches the DVI connection type for the monitor. Converters can be purchased to adapt to most any type of connector.

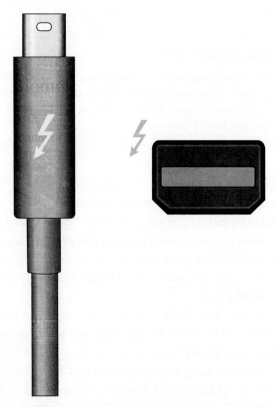

FIGURE 9.15   Thunderbolt connectivity

TECH TIP

Converting DVI to HDMI

A DVI-to-HDMI cable can be used to connect a PC with a DVI port to a device such as a home theater system or flat screen TV that has an HDMI port.

TABLE 9.5   Video connector summary

Port type	Video Analog (A), Digital (D) or both (B)	Transfer speeds	Carries audio	Comments
VGA/DB-15	A		N	
DVI-D	D	Dual-link 7.92Gb/s Single-link 3.96Gb/s	N	16′ (5 meters) maximum cable length
DVI-A	A		N	Rarely used; 16′ (5 meters) maximum cable length
DVI-I	B	Single-link 3.96Gb/s Dual-link 7.92Gb/s	N	16′ (5 meters) maximum cable length
HDMI/ miniHDMI	D	18Gb/s	Y	Up to 16′ for standard cable Up to 49′ for high speed with quality cable and connectors
DisplayPort	D	25.92Gb/s	Y	9.8′ (passive) 108′ (active)
Thunderbolt	D	10Gb/s 20Gb/s (v2) 40Gb/s (v3)	Y	9.8′ copper (passive) 200′ optical
4-pin miniDIN (S-video)	A		N	Can also be 7- or 9-pin; better quality than composite; lower color quality than component video
Composite video	A		N	Uses an RCA or a BNC connector to connect a VCR or DVD to a TV
Component	A		N	Three to five BNC connectors

Note that a **passive cable** is one that does not contain a chip like active cables. **Active cables** have a chip that boosts the signals, thus allowing cables to be thinner and support sending signals further and faster than passive cables. Active and passive cables are found in computer networks and video systems.

Smart TV and Set Top Box Configuration

Once you have a TV cabled, **smart TVs** have some additional configuration to do including putting the TV on the network. Smart TVs are considered smart TVs because they allow the TV to be connected to the network, and thus the Internet. Through the TV, music, photos, and other content can be shared. The TV might even be controlled by voice commands. Figure 9.16 shows a smart TV on the left and an old tube-based TV on the right.

FIGURE 9.16 Smart TV and classic TV

Networks are covered in Chapters 13 and 14, but the basics are that you will probably connect to a wireless network and will need two key pieces of information: the name of the network and the password. From the remote, you can access the menu and normally select a menu option such as *Network, Wi-Fi Connection,* or *Wireless LAN Ready*. You might also like to access utilities such as access to the Internet, apps, or online movies and shows through a product called *Smart Hub* or *Internet Video*.

A set top box (**STB**), set top unit (**STU**), or receiver is an electronic device that you buy or lease from your cable or satellite TV provider. One is shown in Figure 9.17. The device comes with its own remote control. The device connects to the provider network and then you either wire it to your TV or some can be wirelessly paired with the TV. The device can have some of the following features:

> Channel selection
> Volume control
> Parental controls
> Video recording
> Timer
> Favorites
> Number of screens to be shown and what channels are within those screens
> Closed captioning

FIGURE 9.17 Set top box

Multiple Displays

A popular business and home display option is to have two or more displays connected to the same computer. Another option would be to have a laptop with an external monitor attached, and both the laptop display and the external monitor display are active. Figure 9.18 shows an adapter with two DVI connectors that could be used for this purpose. Notice how the card also has an S-video port for a connection to a TV or other video output.

FIGURE 9.18 Dual-display connectivity

To have two monitors connected to a single computer, you have several methods of configuration:

> Use the two video ports on the motherboard (not common).
> Use the integrated motherboard port and buy a video card with one video port. (This is the cheapest solution, but the motherboard might disable the integrated video port automatically.)
> Buy a video card that has two video ports (best option).
> Buy two video cards. (Usually the motherboard has one expansion slot for a video card, and that means using an older and slower technology expansion slot for the second video card.)

Windows must recognize the second monitor as evidenced by two displays appearing in Device Manager or two monitors appearing in the Display Control Panel. In Windows 7/8 use the *Display* Control Panel > select the *Adjust resolution* link > locate the *Multiple displays* drop-down menu to see the desktop options. In Windows 10, use the *Settings > System > Display* link. Figure 9.19 shows how two monitors appear in Windows 8. Figure 9.20 shows how the two monitors appear in Windows 10. You can set individual settings by selecting the number 1 or 2 in the Control Panel and adjusting the settings as needed.

CHAPTER 9

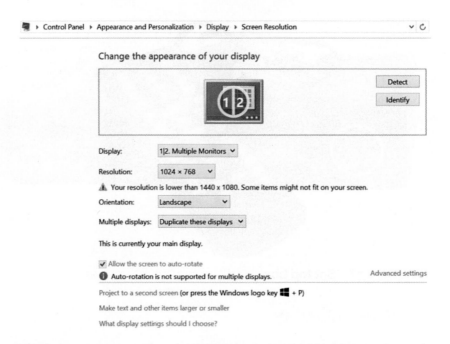

FIGURE 9.19   Windows 8 Display Control Panel with two monitors

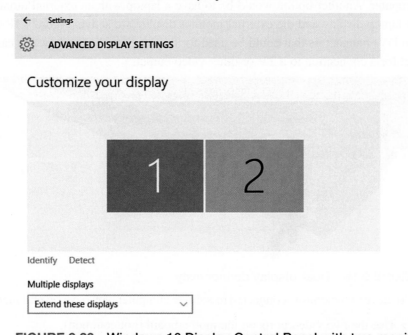

FIGURE 9.20   Windows 10 Display Control Panel with two monitors

Some displays have software that can be used to configure the monitors. Figure 9.21 shows the AMD Catalyst Control Center that is used to configure displays that connect to an ATI graphics card.

You can have what is on one monitor be the same as what is on the other monitor (duplicate the displays) such as what might be needed in retail or a school advisor that is showing someone their academic record. Another option is to extend the display. This allows for the monitors to work as if both of them are the entire desktop such as when an administrative assistant has a PDF open on one screen and a spreadsheet on the other one. An exercise at the end of this chapter demonstrates how to configure multiple monitors.

FIGURE 9.21 AMD Catalyst Control Center

Dual-monitor modes of operation

You can have the same information shown in two monitors, extend your desktop across two monitors, or choose what items are on each desktop.

KVMs

Another variation that some network administrators, technicians, or businesses want is the ability to use the same monitor (and sometimes mouse and keyboard) for two or more different computers. This is best done through a keyboard, video, mouse (**KVM**) switch, which allows at least one mouse, one keyboard, and one video output to be used by two or more computers. Figure 9.22 shows a KVM switch.

FIGURE 9.22 KVM switch

KVM switches usually require no software to use. They are sometimes used with projectors to allow multiple input. Connect the cables to the port and use the dial or push buttons on the front of the KVM switch in order to select which device is used as input or output.

Many people would rather use software to do this function and remotely access the desktop of another computer. Windows calls this built-in software feature Remote Desktop. Remote Desktop is covered in Chapter 16, and a lab at the end of that chapter demonstrates how to use the Remote Desktop utility.

Projectors

Monitors, cameras, TVs, and web cams are not the only peripherals that connect to computer video ports. Projectors have become common devices, and technicians must be familiar with them. A projector allows information displayed on a computer to be projected onto a larger screen. A projector has similar connections to those described for video cards. Cables that convert between the different formats are available. Figure 9.23 shows some of the connectors available on a projector. A projector sometimes connects to other audio and video devices besides computers, such as a document camera, speakers, optical disc players, and smart boards. The VGA in and out ports are two common ports seen on a projector for connecting video. S-video is also quite common. The newer projectors have DVI, DisplayPort, HDMI, and USB ports.

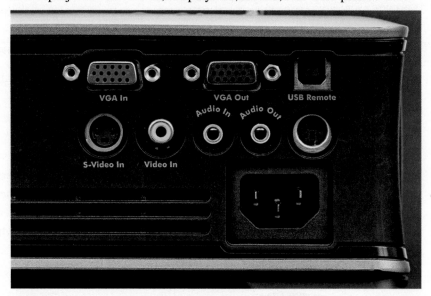

FIGURE 9.23 Projector ports close up

To connect a projector to a PC and a monitor, you need a video distribution (sharing) device, a KVM switch, or two video ports from the PC. A laptop frequently has a video port available for connecting an external monitor or a projector.

Figure 9.24 shows a projector that has a lot of ports. As with video cards, you expect to see VGA, DVI, or HDMI ports, but ports that are often seen on TVs, gaming consoles, optical disc players, or stereos are also available on projectors. Composite video is normally a yellow port (like the one labeled VIDEO in Figure 9.24). The audio RCA ports are normally red and white. **Component/RGB video** analog ports are normally colored red, green, and blue and have the symbols YPrPb above them. (Y is for the luminescence, or brightness, and Pr and Pb are for the color difference signals.) An RJ-45 connector connects the projector to an Ethernet network. Many projectors also have wireless network capabilities.

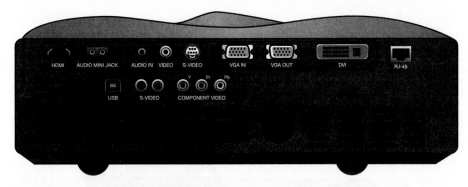

FIGURE 9.24   Projector ports

Treat your projector well. Do not immediately unplug the power to a projector after a presentation; instead, allow the projector to cool down first. You can turn off the projector, but the fan still runs on some models to quickly cool the projector. Keep the filter clean to extend the life of the projector bulb.

Display Preventive Maintenance

It is simple to perform preventive maintenance on a monitor. Static builds up on the face of a monitor, and the screen attracts dust and dirt the way a television does. Anti-static cleaning wipes are available at computer and office supply stores.

LCDs can be cleaned with wipes specifically designed for LCDs. Also, a soft cloth dampened with water or a mixture of isopropyl alcohol and water can be used to wipe an LCD. Do not use glass cleaner to clean LCDs, and never apply liquid directly to a monitor of any type.

Monitor Energy Efficiency

A monitor's life span is normally 40,000 to 60,000 hours. The heat generated inside a display can reduce the life span of the monitor's components. Three things contribute to display power utilization:

> Size—The larger the screen, the more power used.
> Technology—LCDs require less power than plasma displays. LCDs that use LEDs for backlighting require less power than displays that use CCFLs. OLED monitors use even less power.
> Settings—Settings include brightness (brighter settings require more power) and power saver modes.

Some monitors have energy-conservation capabilities. These "green" monitors have software that reduces the power, leaving only enough to allow the monitor to be reactivated to a usable state quickly. The Environmental Protection Agency (EPA) produced ENERGY STAR guidelines to which many monitor manufacturers adhere. According to ENERGY STAR, displays that meet their criteria (http://www.energystar.gov) are 20 percent more efficient than other displays. Figure 9.25 shows the types of conservation that could be implemented in a home, including having energy-efficient displays and TVs.

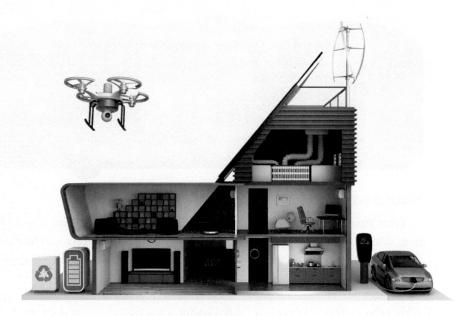

FIGURE 9.25   Energy-efficient home

The following are some best practices for monitor energy efficiency:

> Use the power button/switch to turn off the display when you are finished using it for the day.
> Use the Windows *Power Options* Control Panel to enable a power-saving mode such as sleep mode after a period of inactivity.

To modify the power-saving features, use the *Power Options* (Vista/7) Control Panel, *PC and devices > Power and sleep* setting (Windows 8), or *System > Power and sleep* setting (Windows 10). In Vista/7, select the *Change plan settings* link. In Windows 8 and 10, use the *Sleep* and/or *Screen* drop-down menus.

Privacy

In the past, when monitors did not have fast refresh rates, screen savers were very important. A screen saver changes the image on the monitor constantly to keep any particular image from burning into the screen. With old monitors, if an image stayed on the screen for an extended period of time, an imprint of the image was left on the screen permanently. Today's monitors have high enough refresh rates so that screen savers are not necessary, but now they are an entertainment art form. LCDs use a different technology than CRTs and have never needed screen savers. In Windows Vista, 7, and 8 to configure a screen saver, use the *Personalization* Control Panel > *Screen Saver* link. In Windows 10, search on the word screen saver and select the *Change screen saver* link. The *Blank Screen* option takes the least amount of memory and does not use CPU time. On the *Screen Saver* tab click the *Screen Saver* down arrow to display an options list. Another resource saver is to remove the display's wallpaper option (also found through the *Display* Control Panel). See Figure 9.26.

Screen savers can provide password protection that may be important to some users. With the password screen saver enabled, a user can leave his or her work area, and no one can access the computer without the password. In Windows, use the *Power Options* Control Panel > *Require a password on wakeup* link to configure this option, as shown in Figure 9.27.

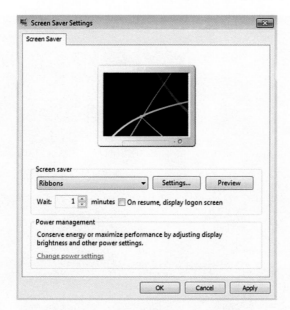

FIGURE 9.26   Windows screen saver

FIGURE 9.27   Windows password protection on wakeup

As a display option, an **anti-glare filter** can be used. An anti-glare filter helps in certain lighting environments and when outside light affects the display. Anti-glare filters are also available for mobile devices and smartphones.

Another display add-on is a privacy screen or privacy filter. A **privacy filter** distorts the display output for anyone except for the person looking directly at the screen. This is good for managers and people who have confidential business matters on their screen when someone might walk up to or by the desk. The screen is a thin plastic shield (see Figure 9.28) that typically fits around the monitor, but some are adjustable for different sizes.

FIGURE 9.28   Privacy filter

Video Adapters

Using millions of colors, motion, sound, and video combined, a computer's video subsystem has made dramatic technological advances. The video adapter controls most of the display output. Video adapters use the AGP or PCIe interface. One of the challenges of interfacing video is finding a good video adapter that uses a high-performance system architecture, such as PCIe.

On the motherboard, the processor and the chipset are responsible for how quickly data travels to and from the video adapter. Such things as upgrading the chipset (motherboard), the processor, or the video adapter to a faster interface speed up video transfer to the monitor. However, special features on the video adapter can also speed up video transfer.

Video adapters have their own processor called the graphics processing unit (**GPU**). Other names include video processor, video coprocessor, or video accelerator. The GPU assists in video communication between the video adapter and the system processor. GPUs are also found in gaming systems, smartphones, tablets, and laptops. Figure 9.29 shows a video adapter with a video processor. GPUs commonly have fans and/or heat sinks attached. Look back to Figure 9.13 for another adapter.

AGP video cards sometimes required extra power and could use a Molex power connector. PCIe cards may require either a 6- or 8-pin connector from the power supply. The 6-pin cable can provide an additional 75 watts of power, while the 8-pin cable can provide an additional 150 watts. A PCIe video card could require multiple power cables as well.

Some video processors are 64- or 128-bit processors. Many users (and technicians) have a hard time understanding how a 128-bit video processor works in a 32-bit or 64-bit expansion slot. The 64 or 128 bits refer to the number of bits the video adapter's accelerator chip accepts at one time. The 64-bit (or higher) video processor controls many video functions on the video adapter otherwise handled by the motherboard processor. Any time information is processed on the adapter rather than the motherboard processor, performance is faster. When signals pass to the motherboard processor through an expansion slot, performance slows. Most video cards today contain a GPU because video is one of the biggest bottlenecks in a computer system.

FIGURE 9.29 Video card with GPU

Specialized Video Cards

A specialized use of video is with TV tuner cards and video capture cards. A **TV tuner card** allows TV signals to be brought into the computer and output to the monitor. Some TV tuner cards have the capability to record video. Figure 9.30 shows a photo of a TV tuner card. Notice the Bayonet Neill Concelman (**BNC**) connector on the far left that allows cable network provider cable to connect directly to the card.

FIGURE 9.30 TV tuner adapter

A **video capture card** usually has specialized software that allows video to be captured from a camera, tape, VCR, DVR, game console, TV channel, optical media, recorder, live audio, or video and manipulated into a presentation, an archived file, or a saved document or streamed onto the Internet. Not all video capture cards support audio. Video surveillance systems sometimes use video capture cards.

CHAPTER 9

A **Thunderbolt card** is simply an adapter that has one or more Thunderbolt ports on it. Another specialized use of video is scalable link interface (SLI) from NVIDIA. SLI links two or more PCIe video cards to share processing on graphics-intensive operations. AMD's CrossFire and CrossFireX perform similarly by allowing multiple GPUs to be used cooperatively in the same computer. Note that the system chipset must be compatible with SLI or CrossFire technologies and you will probably need a power connector from the power supply for each video card.

Video Memory

One of the most important functions of a video processor is to transfer data to and from a video adapter's memory. Memory chips on the video adapter can be regular DRAM chips (including DDR2, DDR3, DDR4, as well as graphics double rate [GDDR] modules, such as GDDR2, GDDR3, GDDR4, and GDDR5).

TECH TIP

How much video memory?

The amount of video adapter memory determines the number of colors available at a specific resolution.

The objective is to get data in and out of the video card memory chips as quickly as possible for a reasonable cost. The adapter must handle a large amount of data due to the increasing number of pixels and colors displayed. Ample, fast memory on a video card allows higher resolutions and more colors to appear on the screen, without the screen appearing to flicker.

Memory on a video card stores screen information as a snapshot of what appears on the screen. The video adapter manufacturer determines the maximum amount of video memory. Many manufacturers make video adapters that are not upgradable. Video memory can be integrated into the card as rectangular chips located around or very close to the GPU (see Figure 9.31). Video memory can also be installed into memory expansion slots on the card similar to the motherboard.

FIGURE 9.31   Video memory close to (along the side and top) the GPU

To determine the amount of video memory an adapter needs, multiply the total number of pixels (the resolution) by the number of bits needed to produce a specific number of colors. Different combinations of 16 1s and 0s create 65,536 (64K) possible combinations as $2^{16} = 65,536$. For example, take a system that needs 65,536 colors at the resolution 1024×768. To determine the minimum video memory necessary, multiply 16 (the number of bits needed for 64K of colors) by 1024 by 768 (the resolution). The result, 12,582,912, is the number of bits needed to handle the combination of 64K colors at 1024×768. Divide the bits by 8 for the number of *bytes* needed. This is the minimum amount of memory needed on the video card: 12,582,912 ÷ 8 = 1,572,864, or 1.5MB. The user needs more video memory if more colors, a higher resolution, or video motion are desired. Table 9.6 lists the number of bits required for various color options.

TABLE 9.6 Bits required for colors

Number of bits	Number of colors
4	16
8	256
16	65,536 (64K)
24	16,277,216 (16M)

Some video cards offer 32-bit color. The extra bits are used for color control and special effects, such as animation and game effects. An exercise at the end of this chapter provides practice for configuring different scenarios. Table 9.7 lists the minimum amounts of video memory needed for specific configurations.

TABLE 9.7 Minimum video memory requirement examples

Total video memory needed (shared and on card)	Color depth	Resolution
1MB	16-bit (65,536 colors)	640×480
2MB	24-bit (16 million colors)	800×600
2MB	16-bit (65,536 colors)	1024×768
4MB	24-bit (16 million colors)	1024×768
6MB	32-bit (true color)	1400×1050
6MB	24-bit (16 million colors)	1600×1200
8MB	32-bit (true color)	1600×1200

If 2-D or 3-D graphics are being used, the calculations shown in Table 9.7 can be used as a starting point, but more memory is needed. For 2-D graphics, multiply the answer by 16 more bits. For 3-D graphics, multiply the final number by 48 bits. Then, divide by 8 to find out how many bytes.

Video RAM is RAM that is used for video exclusively. When this RAM is not enough, motherboard RAM is used. When motherboard RAM is being used in addition to video card RAM, the amount of motherboard RAM being used is known as **shared system memory**, or shared video memory. You see this when you examine the video display properties. Some systems allow customization through system BIOS/UEFI or a special Control Panel provided by the video adapter manufacturer. Common system BIOS options to control shared system memory include AGP Aperture Size and Onboard Video Memory Size. Figure 9.32 shows the properties of a video card that has 512MB of RAM installed (Dedicated Video Memory). The Shared System Memory amount is how much motherboard RAM is allowed to be used by the video card (and the operating system and the applications). For Vista/7/8, use the *Display* Control Panel > *Change display settings* link > *Advanced settings* > *Adapter* tab to see the amount of shared system memory. For Windows 10, use the *Start* button > *Settings* > *System* > *Display* > *Advanced display settings* link > *Display adapter properties* > *Adapter* tab.

FIGURE 9.32   Shared system memory for video

TECH TIP

Checking how much video memory you have

The dxdiag command can be used to examine video properties. Otherwise for Vista/7/8, use the *Display* Control Panel > *Change display settings* link > *Advanced settings* > *Adapter* tab. For Windows 10, use the *Start* button > *Settings* > *System* > *Display* > *Advanced display settings* link > *Display adapter properties* > *Adapter* tab.

Installing a Video Adapter

The first step in installing a video adapter is to do your homework:

> Make sure you have the correct interface type and an available motherboard slot. PCIe and AGP are the most common.
> Gather tools, if needed. Use an anti-static strap or grounding techniques. If a tool is needed, it will be a screwdriver to remove the slot-retaining bracket and to re-insert the screw that holds the adapter.
> Download the latest drivers for the video adapter. Make sure the adapter has a driver for the operating system you are using.
> Ensure that the power supply can supply enough power when the adapter is added. Some high-end video adapters require a PCIe 6- or 8-pin or AGP Molex power connector. Some PCIe cards can use a power cable adapter that converts two Molex power connectors to the PCIe power connector. Other video cards can receive adequate power (up to 75 watts) through the PCIe expansion slot.

Installing a new video adapter

When you install a new video adapter, if it does not work, disable the onboard video port by accessing system BIOS Setup.

Before installing the adapter, power off the computer and unplug it. For best results and to prevent component damage, use an anti-static wrist strap. Access the motherboard and remove any previously installed video adapters (if performing an upgrade). If no video adapters are installed, access the expansion slot.

Sometimes with a tower computer, it is best to lay the computer on its side to insert the video adapter properly. Line up the video adapter's metal connectors with the interface slot. Push the adapter into the expansion slot. Make sure the adapter is flush with the expansion slot. Figure 9.33 shows a video adapter being installed in a tower. Notice that the technician is observing proper ESD procedures. Also notice that a cable from the motherboard S/PDIF out connector attaches to this video card for audio output. Make sure sections of the adapter's gold connectors are not showing and that the card is not skewed. Re-install the retaining screw, if necessary. Connect the monitor to the external video connector. Power on the monitor and computer.

FIGURE 9.33　Video card installation

A video card has a set of drivers or software to enable the adapter to work to its full potential. Individual software drivers from the manufacturer provide system compatibility and performance boosts. The Internet is used to obtain current video drivers from adapter manufacturers. Be sure to use the proper video driver for the operating system. Always follow the adapter manufacturer's instructions for installing drivers.

Troubleshooting Video

As with other troubleshooting, when troubleshooting a video problem, check simple solutions first. Do not assume anything! Verify that the monitor's power light is on. If it is not, check the power cable connectors, surge strip, and wall outlet. Verify that the brightness and contrast settings have not been changed. Check or disable power-saving features while you're troubleshooting. Double-check the monitor cable connected to the video port. Use the built-in diagnostics that some monitors have. Ask the user if any new or upgraded software or hardware has recently been installed, including an operating system automatic update.

> **TECH TIP**
>
> **Keep in mind the video system**
>
> If a piece of video hardware is defective, then it is the display, adapter, motherboard port, or cable. If replacement is necessary, always do the easiest solution first. Replace the display with one that is working.

Many video problems involve a software driver or improperly configured settings. Anything wrong on the display can be a result of a bad video driver, an incompatible driver, an incorrect driver, or an incompatible system BIOS version. The best way to be sure is to download the exact driver for the monitor and the display adapter/port from the Internet or obtain it from the manufacturer. Some troubleshooting tips related to video follow. Remember, these are only suggestions. Research and contact if necessary the monitor, motherboard, or video adapter manufacturer for specific instructions on troubleshooting its equipment.

Common video problems include the following:

> Bent or broken video pins cause **incorrect color patterns** and/or **distorted images**. Carefully examine the monitor's cable ends. The cable may appear to correctly plug into the connector, even when the pins are bent and do not fit properly into the connector. If you find one or more bent pins, carefully use needle-nose pliers to gently straighten the pins.

> If you suspect a video driver problem, use *Device Manager* to locate and expand the *Display adapters* section. Locate the video card and see if there are any visual indications there is an issue. Right-click (or press and momentarily hold) on the video adapter > select *Properties*. From the *General* tab, check the device status section to see whether Windows believes the device to be working properly. Check the video card manufacturer to see whether there is a video driver update for the Windows version being used.

> If you suspect a video driver problem in Windows 7, 8, or 10, boot to Safe Mode, which uses a standard generic video driver to see if the problem is resolved and to determine whether it is a software driver problem.

> If the computer boots in **VGA mode (oversized images and icons)**, the resolution could be set to the wrong setting, but most likely, there is an issue with the video driver.

> Do not use a degausser on an LCD monitor. On LCD monitors, use the vendor-provided software to make adjustments for distortion.

> If a screen has intermittent problems or poor quality, lower the refresh rate or update the video driver.

> **Dead pixels** are the number of pixels that do not light up on an LCD screen due to defective transistors. Dead pixels can be (and usually are) present on LCDs—even new ones. Research the LCD manufacturing standard from a particular vendor for dead pixels before purchasing an LCD. LCD panels with dead pixels can still be used and are common. If there are too many of them, replace the display.

> **Bright spots** occur when a pixel is permanently stuck in the on position. This defect can occur with all LCDs.

> Set the display to the native resolution (the resolution for which the LCD was made).

> If a cursor appears momentarily before the computer boots and then nothing is displayed or a distorted display appears, check for a video driver problem.

> A computer may start normally, but the monitor may not display the Windows startup screen. Sometimes a **dim image** seems to be evident or no image is displayed, but you can hear the hard drive. Reset the display to factory default and then try adjusting brightness and contrast. If that does not help, the inverter most likely needs to be replaced. This is a commonly replaced component in an LCD.

> If a display sometimes **flickers** or appears and then disappears, check the video cable. Horizontal or vertical stripes on the screen are also signs of this problem. Flickering can also be caused by an incorrect refresh rate setting, which can be changed in Windows 7, 8, and 10: *Display* Control Panel > *Change display settings* > *Advanced settings* > *Adapter* tab. Flickering can also be caused by proximity to other radio signals, video devices, speakers, refrigerators, and fluorescent lighting. In such a situation, move the monitor or offending device.

TECH TIP

What to do if a display goes black, red, dim, or pink

Check cabling. The backlight bulb might be faulty. Try swapping monitors.

> If you change the resolution or number of colors and the output is distorted, change the settings back to the original settings, if possible. If not possible, in Windows Vista/7, reboot the computer and use *Advanced Options* and select *Safe Mode* or use the *Last Known Good Configuration* option. If in Windows 8 or 10, *Settings* > *Change PC settings* > *Update and recovery* > *Recovery* > *Restart now* button > after restart select *Troubleshoot* > *Advanced options* > try *Automatic Repair* first and if that does not work, return to *Advanced options* > *Startup Settings* > *Restart* > try *Safe Mode*. If that does not work, use the *Enable low-resolution video* option after the restart.

> If **geometric distortion** occurs (see Figure 9.34) or the screen is not centered correctly, check video cables or reset the display to factory default settings.

TECH TIP

Display is dark

Check to see whether the computer is in sleep mode or won't come out of sleep mode. Check video cable. Hold down the power button and try restarting. Check the power management settings.

> Windows is not supposed to hang during the boot process because of video driver incompatibility. Instead, the operating system loads a default video driver. If video is a problem while working in Windows, boot to *Safe Mode* or use the *Last Known Good Configuration* boot option and then load the correct driver. You could also use the driver rollback option if a new driver has just been installed.

> Check the monitor settings to verify that the monitor detection is accurate. In Vista/7/8, use the *Display* Control Panel > *Display settings* > *Settings* tab. In Windows 10 use the *Settings* > *System* > *Display* link.

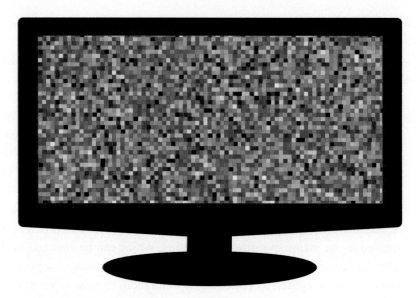

FIGURE 9.34   Geometric distortion

> If a blue screen of death (BSOD) appears, log any error message or code that appears (see Figure 9.35) and try rebooting the computer. You can also boot to Safe Mode and reload a video driver from there.

FIGURE 9.35   BSOD—log the message or error code

TECH TIP

No video?

Check the following: card inserted fully into the slot, cables not properly attached, adapter not supported by the motherboard, auxiliary power not attached to adapter, insufficient power from the power supply, and improper driver installed.

> If horizontal or vertical lines appear, check for loose connections and bent or broken pins. Use built-in diagnostics, if available. Reset to factory default settings.

> If an LCD or plasma display has been left alone for too long, a **burn-in**, image imprint, or ghost image might be seen. Try turning off the display for a few hours. If that does not work, create an all-white image in a graphics program and use it as the screen saver. Turn the display brightness to low and leave on for a few hours.

TECH TIP

See or smell smoke or sparks?

Disconnect the display, if possible, from the power source. Use an appropriate fire extinguisher as necessary. Report the incident.

> Any monitor that won't come out of power saver mode might need one of the following done: (1) update the video driver, (2) flash the system BIOS, (3) check the BIOS/UEFI power settings to ensure that ACPI is enabled so Windows settings can be used, or (4) determine whether the problem is being caused by the monitor or the port. Connect a different monitor. If the video port is built into the motherboard, disable it through BIOS and insert a video card; otherwise, replace the video adapter to see if the port/adapter is causing the problem. Most likely it is a driver or a Windows/BIOS ACPI setting problem.
> If video performance appears to be slow, adjust the monitor to a lower resolution or a lower number of colors (or both). See the exercise at the end of this chapter for step-by-step instructions. Check the video adapter driver to determine whether it matches the installed adapter or whether it is generic. Obtain the specific adapter's latest driver from the Internet.
> If the computer is on for a while, but then the display has issues, check for **overheating** in the computer or on the video adapter. Check for adequate power output from the power supply.
> An **artifact** is something that appears on your screen that should not appear, such as green dotted or vertical lines, colored lines on one side of the screen, tiny glitters, or an unusual pattern. If the display shows an artifact, check for an overheating GPU, insufficient air flow, and a problematic video driver. An integrated video chip may also be going bad.
> If Windows does not show the *Multiple displays* option, then Windows does not recognize the second monitor. Check *Device Manager* for possible driver issues. Check cabling. Check the adapter. Note that if two adapters are used, not all adapters work with one another. If an adapter and a motherboard port are used, the computer may not support such a configuration.
> For projectors, check the correct input using the remote. For the newer version of PowerPoint, the Display Control Panel may need to have the *Duplicate the display* option so that the output can be seen on the screen. Ensure the projector light shows (bulb is good).

TECH TIP

Monitor disposal rules

Many states have specific disposal procedures that must be followed for monitor disposal.

SOFT SKILLS—CHANGE PERSPECTIVE WHEN TROUBLESHOOTING

Troubleshooting is a hard topic to teach. Experience is a great teacher to learn how to tackle device problems including problems with displays. In the classroom, teachers often rely on things going wrong during installation to teach troubleshooting. Also, broken machines can be used to encourage students to jump in and attempt the repair. One troubleshooting technique that is seldom practiced in the classroom, but is great to do is to change your perspective.

When troubleshooting a problem, your perspective is from that of a trained technician—what is going wrong and what do you know about that particular area that can cause the problem? Nothing is wrong with that perspective because that is a normal progression for a technician. But what happens when you are stuck or you are faced with something you have never seen before?

One of the ways you can change your perspective is to put yourself in the mindset of the user. By just a bit of talking with them, you can get an idea of how they think and how they work. Try imagining the problem from their prospective. One, it may give you troubleshooting ideas that you didn't think of before. Two, it will make you more empathetic and a better technician. See Figure 9.36.

FIGURE 9.36   See things from a new perspective

Another way to look at things from a different perspective is imagining a great technician you know. Put yourself in that person's shoes. What would that technician try that you haven't thought of yet? What tricks have you seen tried in the past?

Perspectives shape how we approach problems. By changing our perspective, we change how we troubleshoot problems and how we approach that troubleshooting task. As technicians, we must constantly update and refine our skills because most of our day is spent troubleshooting. See Figure 9.37.

FIGURE 9.37   Changing perspectives

Chapter Summary

> Common video ports for monitors and computing devices include VGA, DVI, DisplayPort, and HDMI. Other types of video ports seen on adapters or projectors include Thunderbolt, S-video (4-pin miniDIN), RCA, BNC, component/RGB, and composite.

> LCD monitors can use CCFL or LEDs for the backlight.

> LCD monitors are designed for a specific resolution, called the native resolution. The display should be configured for this resolution and not changed.

> With an LCD monitor, the viewable size is the true size of the display that can be seen.

> The aspect ratio is a monitor's ratio of width to height.

> The contrast ratio is a value that describes the difference in light intensity between the brightest white and the darkest black. The greater the difference between the two values, the more contrast the monitor can display.

> Never apply liquid directly to a display.

> Video adapters commonly use AGP or PCIe slots and contain a GPU, fans/heat sinks for the GPU, and memory. Some motherboards/chipsets support installing two video adapters that work cooperatively. These adapters commonly require more power and a separate Molex (AGP) or 6-/8-pin (PCIe) power connector from the power supply.

> If you are not using the onboard video port for dual displays, disable the port in BIOS. Note that some adapters will not work when you disable the onboard port and that BIOS may automatically disable the port.

> Video memory can be separate from motherboard RAM, can be shared system memory, or can be a combination of both. The amount of available memory affects the maximum resolution and the number and depth of colors that can be seen.

> A KVM switch can be used to allow multiple computers to use one display, mouse, and keyboard.

> A privacy screen can help protect information on a screen from those passing by the display.

> States commonly have rules about electronic device disposal.

> Pixels on LCD monitors that do not illuminate are called dead pixels. Bright spots are caused by pixels that are always on. Both are normal in LCDs. When too many dead pixels and/or bright spots are shown, replace the monitor.

> When a computer shows a blank screen, check power, display cable, power cable, and the surge protector/UPS. Try rebooting to Safe Mode.

> If an artifact appears, check for heat problems.

> If an LCD or plasma display has burn-in, try turning off the display for a few hours. Create an all-white image in a graphics program and use it as the screen saver. Turn the display brightness to low and leave on for a few hours.

> If geometric distortion occurs or the screen is not centered correctly, check video cables or reset the display to factory default settings.

> If the computer boots in VGA mode, check the video driver.

> If the display image is dim or blank, try adjusting brightness controls and contrast. Reset to factory defaults. Replace the inverter.

> If the display flickers, check the video cable or refresh rate. Check for external radio or other interference sources.

A+ CERTIFICATION EXAM TIPS

✓ Know different types of displays including analog, digital, LCD, plasma, OLED, and a projector. Know that LED and IPS are two technologies that provide wide viewing angles, good color, and consistent backlighting.

✓ Know the difference between using fluorescent or LEDs in an LCD monitor; describe the difference between TN and IPS.

✓ Be able to configure monitor properties including resolution, refresh rate, native resolution, and power settings.

✓ Be able to describe the purpose of an accelerometer and gyroscope. Know that a touch screen might need to be calibrated.

✓ Study the video slots, ports, and cables. Know their particulars. Know that a VGA to DVI or VGA to HDMI adapter converts an analog signal to a digital one.

✓ Know the difference between a video card, Thunderbolt card, TV tuner card, and video capture card.

✓ Know the difference in the following aspect ratios: 16:9, 16:10, and 4:3.

✓ Know the following terms: refresh rate, frame rate, resolution, native resolution, brightness, and lumens.

✓ Know the purpose of privacy/anti-glare filters.

✓ Be able to install and configure multiple monitors.

✓ Know the ports on a projector and how brightness/lumens influence where a projector might be used.

✓ Review all the troubleshooting sections before taking the CompTIA 220-901 exam. Pay particular attention to the bullets that contain key terms.

Key Terms

Review Questions

Consider the following display as you answer Questions 1–6:

> 70,000:1 dynamic contrast ratio
> 16:9 widescreen offers distortion-free images at 1920×1080 (1080p) resolution. Made for multimedia and optimized for HD content
> 1 D-sub input (15 pin), 1 DVI input

1.   What is the purpose of the contrast ratio?

   a. It is a ratio of a monitor's width to height.

   b. It allows a comparison of another monitor in regard to the difference in light intensity between the brightest white and the darkest black.

   c. It allows an expression of how much light the monitor can produce.

   d. The maximum angle that you can stand back and still view the screen and the images on the screen properly.

2.   Which value is the aspect ratio for this monitor?

   a. 70,000:1

   b. 16:9

   c. 1920×1080

   d. 1 D-sub input (15 pin), 1 DVI input

3.   What is the purpose of the aspect ratio?

   a. It is a ratio of a monitor's width to height.

   b. It allows a comparison of another monitor in regards to the difference in light intensity between the brightest white and the darkest black.

   c. It allows an expression of how much light the monitor can produce.

   d. The maximum angle that you can stand back and still view the screen and the images on the screen properly.

4.   What is the native resolution? _____

5.   If someone changed the resolution on the monitor to 1680×1050, what would be the result when viewing the Windows desktop?

   [The icons would be smaller | There would be no discernible difference |
   The icons would be larger]

6.   Which video ports are on this monitor? (Select all that apply.)

   [DVI | HDMI | VGA | DisplayPort | S-video | composite | component]

7.   A projector is turned on and projecting, but the screen is blank and nothing is showing from the PC. What is the first thing to check?

   a. Projector bulb

   b. Windows power options

   c. Available computer video memory

   d. Input source

8.   Which of the following is the newest type of expansion slot used for video cards?

   a. PCIe

   b. AGP

   c. PCIx

   d. PCI

9.   Which video port supports transmission of both audio and video signals?

[VGA | component | HDMI | DVI]

10.   A technician installs a video card because the integrated video port does not work anymore. However, when the technician installs the card into the system, nothing outputs. What is the most likely problem?

   a. The monitor is bad.

   b. The cable is bad.

   c. The onboard port has not been disabled.

   d. The new video card is bad.

11.   How could a technician determine how much shared system memory the video card is using in a Windows 8 computer?

   a. Task Manager

   b. System Control Panel

   c. Display Control Panel

   d. Safe Mode

12.   List two characteristics that make a smart TV "smart."

   _____

   _____

13.   How can a technician easily determine whether Windows detects two displays?

   a. Boot the computer into Safe Mode.

   b. Watch closely for the boot message.

   c. Use Task Manager.

   d. Use the Display Control Panel.

14.   What are the two technologies used by an LCD to display an image on the screen? (Choose two.)
[CCFL | Thunderbolt | AGP | LED | lumen]

15.   Which term describes a pixel that is always on?

[dead | thunderbolt | bright spot | lumen]

16.   [T | F] Dead pixels are normal on a new display.

17.   Which display adjustment is used to adjust the degree of difference between light and dark?
[brightness | position | input | contrast]

18.   How is an OLED better than some of the other display technologies?

   a. Supports viewing from wide angles

   b. Has ozone inside the CCFL

   c. Has more opticals

   d. Does not require a power supply

19.   [T | F] The IPS LCD technology can have a slow response time, but has really good color and viewing angles that are important when editing photographs.

20.   A technician is solving a really difficult problem. One technique that can help is to _____.

   a. Use a working meditative technique.

   b. Look at the problem from a different perspective.

   c. Take a one hour break to ponder the possibilities.

   d. Restate the problem in a different way to the user.

Exercises

Exercise 9.1 Video Memory

Objective: To determine how much memory should be installed on a video adapter, based on customer requirements

Parts: None

Questions: Answer the questions, using the situation given.

1.   What is the minimum memory a video adapter needs if a user wants a 1024×768 resolution with 16 million colors available? [512KB | 1MB | 2MB | 4MB | 8MB]

Use the following specifications to answer questions 2–3.

A video adapter has the following specifications:

> 4GB of 1333-MHz DDR3 RAM

> Up to 2560x1600

> PCI Express x16 2.0 support

> VGA, DVI, HDMI

> 1620-MHz processor

2.   What is the maximum resolution? _____

3.   How many ports does this video card have? _____

4.   A video card is configured for 1920×1080 32-bit true color. What is the minimum amount of video memory this would require? [1MB | 2MB | 4MB | 8MB | >8MB]

5.   A video card has 256MB of memory. The user complains that when watching video clips, the sound and video are sometimes choppy. Upon investigation, the technician determines that the total graphics memory is 1535MB, dedicated memory is 256MB, and shared system memory is 1279MB. What does this mean?

_____

_____

_____

6.   What would you recommend to the customer in question 5 if you were the technician? _____

_____

_____

7.   What is the minimum recommended memory for a video card purchased for a brand new system? Explain your answer.

_____

_____

Activities

Internet Discovery

Objective: To obtain specific information on the Internet regarding a computer or its associated parts

Parts: Computer with access to the Internet

Questions: Use the Internet to answer the following questions.

1.   A customer has a home workstation. Someone gave his teenager the EA Need for Speed Most Wanted game as a present. The customer wants to buy a video card that will allow this game to run. Determine and document the minimum graphics card requirements. Then, locate a video card to fulfill this need. Include the model and basic specifications of the card as part of your documentation.

   _____

   _____

   _____

   _____

   _____

   _____

   _____

2.   What does Samsung state might happen to a 22-inch LED S22B310B monitor if a supersonic humidifier is used near this monitor? Write the answer and the URL where you find this information.

   _____

   _____

   _____

3.   You have a suspect Samsung S22B310B power adapter. Find a replacement part. Write the cost and URL where you find the inverter. _____

4.   A customer has an Acer 21.5" G226HQL monitor. Which submenu item is used to put the monitor in such a mode that it displays scenes in the clearest detail? Where did you find this answer?

   _____

5.   A customer has a BenQ 24" GL2460HM monitor. What does BenQ say about LCD pixels that appear as white, black, green, or red dots and where did you find this information? _____

   _____

   _____

6.   A customer has an HP 23xw 23" IPS monitor that shows a black border around the screen when connecting through the DVI or HDMI port. What can be done for this problem and at what URL was this information found? _____

   _____

   _____

   _____

7.   How do you do a factory reset on a Dell E2414Hr 24" monitor? Write the answer and the URL where you found the solution. _____

   _____

8.   A company has a ViewSonic PJD5155 SVGA DLP projector with a lamp that has just burnt out. What is the replacement lamp part number? _____

Soft Skills

Objective: To enhance and fine-tune a technician's ability to listen, communicate in both written and oral form, and support people who use computers in a professional manner

Activities:

1.   Access a monitor Setup menu. Make a list of some of the settings that would be helpful to a computer user. Include in your list a description of the function. Document this in such a way that it could be given to users as a how-to guide. _____

2.   Write a paragraph describing a problem and how a technician might look at the problem from a different perspective.

Critical Thinking Skills

Objective: To analyze and evaluate information as well as apply learned information to new or different situations

Activities:

1.   A person wants to build a computer and needs help with the video system. Using materials or magazines provided by the instructor or Internet research, recommend the PC video system, keeping in mind that the customer has a motherboard with PCIe slots; uses word processing, spreadsheets, and web browsing; and has a budget of $500 for these components.

2.   A person wants to build a computer and needs help with the video system. Using materials or magazines provided by the instructor or Internet research, recommend the PC video system, keeping in mind that the customer has a motherboard with an AGP slot, plays a lot of computer-based games, and does not have a particular budget for components.

Labs

Lab 9.1 Exploring Video in Windows 7

Objective: To explore video properties using Windows 7

Parts: A computer with Windows 7 installed

Procedure: Complete the following procedure and answer the accompanying questions.

1.   Power on the computer and log in to Windows 7.

2.   Click the *Start* button and select *Control Panel*.

3.   Open the *System and Security* Control Panel.

4.   Access the *Device Manager* link located under the *System* category.

     Assuming that the monitor flickers and redraws the screen incorrectly when a window is moved or resized, what two things would you recommend?_____

     _____

5.   Right-click a specific video adapter and select *Properties*.

     Which bus does the video adapter use?_____

     Can the adapter be disabled using the General tab? [Yes | No]

6.   Click the *Driver* tab.

     Which video driver version is being used?_____

     Can the display adapter be disabled using the *Driver* tab? [Yes | No]

7.   Click the *Driver Details* button.

     List at least two driver files being used, including the full path.

     _____

     _____

8. Click the *OK* button to return to the Properties window.

    List three other things that can be accomplished using the *Driver* tab.

    _____

    _____

9. Click the *Resources* tab.

    List at least two memory address ranges used by the video adapter.

    _____

    Which IRQ does the video adapter use? _____

10. Click the *Cancel* button to return to the Device Manager main screen. Expand the *Monitors* category. Right-click a specific monitor and select *Properties*.

    Which tabs are available in the *Properties* window?

    _____

    Can the monitor refresh rate be changed with the Properties window?

    [Yes | No] If so, what tab is used? If not, what method is used to change the refresh rate?

    _____

    Instructor initials: _____

11. Click the *Cancel* button. Close the *Device Manager* window. Close the *System* Control Panel window.

Lab 9.2 Exploring Video in Windows 8

Objective: To explore video properties using Windows 8

Parts: A computer with Windows 8 installed

Procedure: Complete the following procedure and answer the accompanying questions.

1. Power on the computer and log in to Windows 8.

2. Access *Device Manager*.

    Assuming that the monitor flickers and redraws the screen incorrectly when a window is moved or resized, what two things would you recommend? _____

    _____

3. Expand the *Display Adapters* category.

4. Access a specific display adapter's *Properties* (right-click the specific adapter > *Properties* or double-tap/click on the specific adapter).

    What bus does the video adapter use? _____

    Can the adapter be disabled using the General tab? [Yes | No]

5. Select the *Driver* tab.

    Which video driver version is being used? _____

    Can the display adapter be disabled using the *Driver* tab? [Yes | No]

6. Select the *Driver Details* button.

    List at least two driver files being used, including the full path.

    _____

    _____

7.   Select the *OK* button to return to the Properties window.

List three other things that can be accomplished using the *Driver* tab.

_____

_____

8.   Select the *Resources* tab.

List at least two memory address ranges used by the video adapter.

_____

9.   Select the *Cancel* button to return to the Device Manager main screen. Expand the *Monitors* category. Access a specific monitor's *Properties* (right-click a specific monitor > *Properties* or double tap/click a specific monitor).

Which tabs are available in the Properties window?

_____

Which type of video port is used to connect the display to the computer, if any? [not applicable | PCIe | HDMI | AGP | DisplayPort | PCIx | PCI | VGA | DVI]

_____

Instructor initials: _____

10.   Select the *Cancel* button. Close the *Device Manager* window.

Lab 9.3 Exploring Video in Windows 10

Objective: To explore video properties using Windows 10

Parts: A computer with Windows 10 installed

Procedure: Complete the following procedure and answer the accompanying questions.

1.   Power on the computer and log in to Windows 10.

2.   Access *Device Manager*.

Assuming that the monitor flickers and redraws the screen incorrectly when a window is moved or resized, what two things would you recommend?_____

_____

3.   Expand the *Display adapters* category.

4.   Access a specific display adapter's *Properties* (right-click the specific adapter > *Properties* or double-tap/click on the specific adapter).

Which bus does the video adapter use?_____

Can the adapter be disabled using the General tab? [Yes | No]

5.   Select the *Driver* tab.

Which video driver version is being used?_____

_____

Can the display adapter be disabled using the *Driver* tab? [Yes | No]

6.   Select the *Driver Details* button.

List at least two driver files being used, including the full path.

_____

_____

7. Select the *OK* button to return to the Properties window.

    List three other things that can be accomplished using the *Driver* tab.

    _____

    _____

8. Select the *Resources* tab.

    List at least two memory address ranges used by the video adapter.

    _____

9. Select the *Cancel* button to return to the Device Manager main screen. Expand the *Monitors* category. Access a specific monitor's *Properties* (right-click a specific monitor > *Properties* or double tap/click a specific monitor).

    Which tabs are available in the *Properties* window?

    _____

    Which type of video port is used to connect the display to the computer, if any? [not applicable | PCIe | HDMI | AGP | DisplayPort | PCIx | PCI | VGA | DVI]

    _____

Instructor initials: _____

10. Select the *Cancel* button. Close the *Device Manager* window.

Lab 9.4 Configuring a Second Monitor Attached to a Vista PC

Objective: To connect two monitors and configure Vista

Parts: A computer with Windows Vista loaded

Two video adapters with monitors attached *or* one video adapter that has two video ports with monitors attached

Note: One monitor should be installed, configured, and working before beginning this exercise.

Procedure: Complete the following procedure and answer the accompanying question.

1. Power on the computer and log on using the user ID and password provided by the instructor or lab assistant.

2. Enter *BIOS Setup* and verify whether an option exists to select the order video adapters initialize. Ensure the adapter that is currently installed initializes first. Save the settings.

3. Power off the computer, remove the power cord, and install the second video adapter, if necessary. Attach the second monitor to the video port on either the newly installed video adapter or the second video port on the original video adapter.

4. Power on the computer. If a new video adapter has been installed, Windows will prompt you for the appropriate driver. If this does not occur, manually add the adapter using the *Add Hardware* Control Panel.

5. Right-click an empty space on the desktop and select *Personalization > Display settings* link. Click the *Settings* tab. Two numbered boxes appear in the top section. If you arrange the boxes to be side by side, the monitor output will be spread across the two monitors from left to right. If you vertically arrange the boxes, the desktop will be shown on both screens from top to bottom. Windows supports up to 10 monitors in a single system.

6. Select the *Display* drop-down menu to select the individual monitor. Once selected, the resolution and quality can be adjusted. Ensure the *Extend my Windows desktop onto this monitor* checkbox is enabled. Click *Apply*. For some monitors, Windows may have to be restarted.

    List one instance where you think this technology would be useful.

    _____

    _____

    _____

    _____

Lab 9.5 Configuring a Second Monitor Attached to a Windows 7 PC

Objective: To connect two monitors and configure using Windows 7

Parts: A computer with Windows 7 installed

                 Two video adapters with monitors attached *or* one video adapter with two video ports with monitors attached

Note: One monitor should be installed, configured, and working *before* beginning this exercise.

Procedure: Complete the following procedure and answer the accompanying questions.

1. Power on the computer and log in to Windows 7.

2. Enter *BIOS Setup* and verify whether an option exists to select the order in which video adapters initialize (if two adapters are installed). Ensure that the currently installed adapter initializes first. Save the settings.

3. Boot the computer and access *Device Manager* > Expand the *Display adapters* category.

    Which display adapter is shown?_____

4. Power off the computer, remove the power cord, and if necessary, install the second video adapter.

5. Attach the second monitor to the video port on either the newly installed video adapter or the second video port on the original video adapter.

6. Power on the computer. If a new video adapter has been installed, perform the bulleted steps. If a new video adapter was not needed, proceed to Step 7.

    > Windows will prompt you for the appropriate driver. If this does not occur, manually add the driver using the directions given by the video adapter manufacturer.

    > Verify the second adapter appears in Device Manager and that Windows has installed a driver. Note that not all display adapters are compatible with one another.

7. Access the *Display* Control Panel category found under *Hardware and Sound*. Select the *Change display settings* link. Two numbered boxes appear in the top section when the adapters are recognized by the operating system. (If two displays are not shown, redo Steps 5 and 6.) If you arrange the boxes to be side by side, the monitor output will be spread across the two monitors from left to right. If you vertically arrange the boxes, the desktop will be shown on both screens from top to bottom. If necessary, you can drag the monitor icons so they are arranged in the same way as the monitors are located on the desk.

8. Use the *Identify* button to verify which monitor is the one designated with the number 1 and which monitor is designated with the number 2. The numbers appear on the monitors.

    Do two numbers appear? If not, redo Step 7. [Yes | No]

9. Use the *Multiple displays* drop-down menu to select how the monitors are displayed: (1) *Extend your displays*—the most commonly used option, spreads the desktop across the monitors. (2) *Duplicate your displays*—has the same image on both monitors. This is the default setting and is good when a laptop is being used to project or connect to a large external monitor. (3) *Show your desktop on only one monitor*—sometimes used on a laptop to keep the laptop screen blank while connecting to a large desktop monitor.

    Which option did you choose?_____

10. Select the *Display* drop-down menu to select a particular monitor. Once this is selected, adjust the resolution and quality for that one monitor.

11. Click *Apply*. If needed, restart Windows.

Instructor initials: _____

12. Power down the computer and remove the power cord. If an adapter was installed, removed it, replace the cover plate if possible, and boot the computer. If changes were made to BIOS in the beginning, access BIOS/UEFI, and return the settings to the original condition. Ensure the computer boots without any errors.

List one instance for which you think this technology would be useful.

_____

_____

_____

_____

Lab 9.6 Configuring a Second Monitor Attached to a Windows 8/10 PC

Objective: To connect two monitors and configure using Windows 8 or 10

Parts: A computer with Windows 8 or 10 installed

Two video adapters with monitors attached *or* one video adapter with two video ports with monitors attached

Note: One display should be installed, configured, and working *before* beginning this exercise.

Procedure: Complete the following procedure and answer the accompanying questions.

1. Power on the computer and log in to Windows 8 or 10.

2. Enter BIOS Setup and verify whether an option exists to select the order in which video adapters initialize (if two adapters are installed). Ensure that the currently installed adapter initializes first. Save the settings.

3. Boot the computer and access *Device Manager* > Expand the *Display adapters* category.

What display adapter is shown?_____

4. Power off the computer, remove the power cord, and if necessary, install the second video adapter.

5. Attach the second monitor to the video port on either the newly installed video adapter or the second video port on the original video adapter.

6. Power on the computer. If a new video adapter has been installed, perform the bulleted steps. If a new video adapter was not needed, proceed to Step 7.

   > Windows will prompt you for the appropriate driver. If this does not occur, manually add the driver using the directions given by the video adapter manufacturer.

   > Verify the second adapter appears in Device Manager and that Windows has installed a driver. Note that not all display adapters are compatible with one another.

7. Access the *Display settings* Control Panel. Two numbered boxes appear in the top section when the adapters/monitors are recognized by the operating system. (If two displays are not shown, redo Steps 5 and 6.)

8. Use the *Identify* button to verify which monitor is the one designated with the number 1 and which monitor is designated with the number 2. The numbers appear on the monitors.

Do two numbers appear? If not, redo Step 7. [Yes | No]

CHAPTER 9

9. Use the *Multiple displays* drop-down menu to select how the monitors are displayed: (1) *Extend these displays*—the most commonly used option, which spreads the desktop across the monitors. (2) *Duplicate these displays*—has the same image on both monitors. This is the default setting and is good when a laptop is being used to project or connect to a large external monitor. (3) *Show only on 1* or (4) *Show only on 2*—sometimes used when the second monitor is used for another user and what is on the screen is not to be shown to the second person. Play with these settings. If necessary, you can drag the monitor icons so they are arranged in the same way as the monitors are located on the desk.

Which option did you choose? _____

10. Select the *Multiple displays* drop-down menu to select *Extend these displays*. Select the number 2 monitor in the top window. Adjust the resolution and quality for that one monitor.

11. Click *Apply*. If needed, restart Windows.

Instructor initials: _____

12. Power down the computer and remove the power cord. If an adapter was installed, removed it, replace the cover plate if possible, and boot the computer. If changes were made to BIOS in the beginning, access BIOS/UEFI and return the settings to the original condition. Ensure the computer boots without any errors.

List one instance where you think this technology would be useful.

_____

_____

_____

_____

Lab 9.7 Determining the Minimum Video Memory Installed on a Vista PC

Objective: To understand how to calculate the amount of video memory based on the number of color bits and resolution settings

Parts: Windows Vista computer

Procedure: Complete the following procedure and answer the accompanying questions.

1. Turn on the computer and verify that the operating system loads. Log in using the user ID and password provided by the instructor or lab assistant.

2. Right-click an empty Desktop space and select *Properties > Personalize > Display settings* link. The *Display Properties* window opens. Select the *Settings* tab.

3. Answer the questions that follow. When finished, close any open windows.

   a. In the Colors section, what is the number of bits used for color?

   _____

   b. How many colors can be displayed using the number found in Question 1?

   _____

   c. What is the current resolution setting? (This number is listed as *x* by *x* pixels.)

   _____

   d. Calculate the amount of memory required by multiplying the two numbers that make up the resolution. These numbers are your answer to Question 3. (For example, if the resolution is listed as 1024×768, the calculation would be $1024 \times 768 = 786{,}432$.)

   _____ × _____ = _____

   horizontal bits   vertical bits   TOTAL 1

   _____

e. Take the result of Question 4 (TOTAL 1) and multiply by the number of color bits (the answer to Question 1). The result is the minimum amount of video memory installed *in bits*.

_____ × _____ = _____

TOTAL 1   color bits   TOTAL 2

f. Take the result of Question 5 (TOTAL 2) and divide by eight to determine the minimum amount of video memory installed *in bytes*.

_____ ÷ _____ = _____

TOTAL 2   8   video memory in bytes

Lab 9.8 Exploring Video Memory on a Windows 7, 8, or 10 Computer

Objective: To understand how to calculate and view the amount of video memory

Parts: A computer with Windows 7, 8, or 10 installed

Procedure: Complete the following procedure and answer the accompanying questions.

Note: This process depends on the video adapter manufacturer. You may need to modify the initial steps to find the details for the video memory.

1.   Power on the computer and log in to Windows.

2.   The monitor properties and the video adapter properties are needed to answer the questions. A common way to access both is through Device Manager. Also, the *Display* Control Panel category can be used. You may need to select the *Advanced settings, Change display settings, Display adapter properties*, or another link. Some video adapters have their own Control Panel.

3.   Answer the questions that follow:

a. How many bits are used for color? Note that if 30 or more bits are used, just use 24 bits as your calculation for this exercise. The extra bits are normally for color depth.

_____

b. How many colors can be displayed using the number found in the first question? Refer to the chapter if necessary.

_____

c. What is the current resolution? Note that this number is listed by *x* by *x* pixels.

_____

d. Calculate the amount of video memory required by multiplying the two numbers that make up the resolution. These numbers are the answers found in the second question. For example, if the resolution is listed as 1920×1080, the calculation would be 1920 × 1080 = 2,073,600. Write your total.

_____ × _____ = _____

horizontal bits   vertical bits   TOTAL 1

e. Take the resulting total and multiply by the number of color bits (the total found in the first question).

_____ × _____ = _____

TOTAL 1   color bits   TOTAL 2

f. Take the result of the previous step, TOTAL 2, and divide by eight to determine the minimum amount of video memory needed *in bytes*.

_____ ÷ 8 = _____

TOTAL 2 (video memory in bits)   TOTAL 3 (video memory in bytes)

_____

_____

g. How much total available graphics memory is shown?

_____

h. Is any dedicated video memory used? If so, how much?

_____

i. Is any shared system memory used? If so, how much?

_____

4. When finished, close any open windows.

Lab 9.9 Using DirectX Diagnostics to Explore Video

Objective: To understand how to view video information

Parts: A computer with Windows 7, 8, or 10 installed

Procedure: Complete the following procedure and answer the accompanying questions.

1. Power on the computer and log in to Windows.

2. Using the search function, search for and select DirectX Diagnostics by typing `dxdiag`.

3. Select the *Display* tab and answer the questions.

   a. Who is the video manufacturer? _____

   b. What is the amount of memory shown as "Approx. Total Memory?"

   c. What is the current display mode (resolution, refresh rate, and number of bits used for color)?

   Resolution: _____

   Refresh rate: _____

   Number of bits used for color: _____

   d. Which version of driver is being used? _____

   e. Describe a situation for which you think this information might be relevant. _____

   _____

   _____

4. When finished, close any open windows.

10 Printers

In this chapter you will learn:

> How each type of printer operates

> The steps required to install a printer

> Preventive printer maintenance

> How to control printers from Windows and make printer adjustments

> To solve common printer problems

> Techniques for ethical and professional behavior

CompTIA Exam Objectives:

What CompTIA A+ exam objectives are covered in this chapter?

✓ 901-1.12   Install and configure common peripheral devices.

✓ 901-1.13   Install SOHO multifunction device/printers and configure appropriate settings.

✓ 901-1.14   Compare and contrast differences between the various print technologies and the associated imaging process.

✓ 901-1.15   Given a scenario, perform printer maintenance.

✓ 901-4.6   Given a scenario, troubleshoot printers with appropriate tools.

✓ 902-1.5   Given a scenario, use Windows Control Panel utilities.

✓ 902-2.4   Summarize the properties and purpose of services provided by networked hosts.

✓ 902-5.4   Demonstrate proper communications techniques and professionalism.

Printers Overview

Printers are a common output device. They can be a difficult subject to cover because many different models exist. Of course, that can be said about any peripheral, but the basic principles are the same. The best way to begin is to look at what printers have in common. All printers have three subsystems: (1) the paper transport subsystem, (2) the marking subsystem, and (3) the print engine subsystem. Table 10.1 describes these subsystems.

TABLE 10.1   Printer subsystems

Subsystem	Description
Paper transport	Subsystem that pulls, pushes, or rolls paper through the printer. This can be done using a belt, tractor feed, or rollers. Some printers can even have a duplexer, which is an attachment option that allows printing on both sides of the paper.
Marking	Parts responsible for placing the image on the paper (also called the marking engine). This includes ribbons, ink (print) cartridges, toner cartridges, any moving part that is inside one of these, and anything else needed to print the image.
Print engine	The brains of the operation. It accepts data and commands from the computer and translates these commands into motion. It also redirects feedback to the computer.

Keep the three printer subsystems in mind when setting up a printer and troubleshooting it. Knowing how a specific type of printer places an image on the paper also helps when troubleshooting the printer.

TECH TIP

Dealing with sensitive printed material

If any printouts are on the printer, ask the user to remove and put away. Demonstrate professionalism any time you are exposed to corporate or personal information that might be found on printers, desks, or within documents.

Printer Ports

Printers connect to IEEE 1394 (FireWire), Ethernet, or USB ports. They can also connect wirelessly. Most wired printers attach to a PC by using the USB port and are near the computer. Printers can also be shared using a variety of techniques covered later in the chapter ("Printer Sharing").

With USB printers, the USB host controller (built into the motherboard or on an adapter) powers up and queries all USB devices about the type of data transfer they want to perform. Printers use bulk transfer on the USB, which means data is sent in 64-byte sections Even though a USB port can provide power to smaller devices, a USB printer normally has its own power source.

USB is a good solution for printers because it is fast, and there are usually several USB ports available—or a USB hub can be added to provide more ports. USB uses only one interrupt for the devices connected to the bus. Chapter 4 contains information regarding interrupts.

Categories of Printers

Printers can be categorized according to how they put an image on paper. Printer categories are impact (otherwise known as dot matrix), inkjet, laser, and thermal. There are more types, but these make up the majority of printers used in the workplace and home. Computer users normally choose a printer based on the type of printing they need to do. Table 10.2 describes the five major printer categories.

Each of the five basic printer types is discussed in greater detail in the following sections. The theory of operation for each printer type mainly concerns the marking subsystem.

TABLE 10.2   Printer categories

Type of printer	Description
Impact	Also known as a dot matrix printer. Good for text printing of multiple copies and can produce limited graphics. Uses ribbons, which keeps costs down. It is the only printer that can do multiple-part forms using impact printer paper/forms and supports the 132-column paper needed by some industries.
Inkjet	Much quieter, weighs less, and produces higher-quality graphics than a dot matrix. Uses a print cartridge, sometimes called an ink cartridge, that holds the ink used to produce the text and graphics; the cartridge costs $10 to $60 and can print 100 to 200 pages, depending on the manufacturer, the size of the cartridge, what is printed, and the print quality settings. Color can be done by dot matrix printers, but inkjet printers are best for color printing.
Laser	Produces the highest-quality output at the fastest rate. Toner cartridges can cost $20 to $350. Common in the corporate network environment where users share peripherals and require fast printing often in bulk. Used for graphic design and computer-generated art where high-quality printing is a necessity. Some can produce color output, but at a much higher cost. Some even have stapling capabilities.
Thermal	Uses special thermal paper that is sensitive to heat. An image is created where the heat is applied. Commonly used as ticket printers or receipt printers in retail outlets and gas stations.
3-D	Used to create a 3-D objects using various types of materials including plastics, thermoplastics, clay, alloys, rubber, stainless steel, or metal alloys.

Impact Printers

Impact printers (Figure 10.1) are frequently called dot matrix printers because of the way they create an image on paper. Such a printer has an **impact print head** that holds tiny wires called **print wires**. Figure 10.2 shows an Oki Data Americas, Inc., print head. The print wires are shown on the front of the print head. The print wires can get out of alignment and produce malformed characters.

The wires individually strike a **print ribbon** hard enough to create a dot on the paper. The dots collectively form letters or images. The speed at which the print head can place characters on a page is its characters per second (**cps**) rating. The number of print wires in the print head determines the quality of printing; the more print wires, the better the print quality. The most common print wires are 9, 18, and 24. The 24-pin printers can print near letter quality (NLQ) output.

Each print wire connects to a solenoid coil. When current flows to the print wire, a magnetic field causes the wire to move away from the print head and out a tiny hole. The print wire impacts a ribbon, creating a dot on the paper. Figure 10.3 shows an impact printer print head. To show the individual print wires, the casing that covers the print wires has been removed from the illustration.

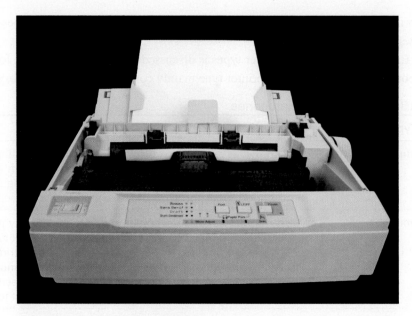

FIGURE 10.1 Impact printer

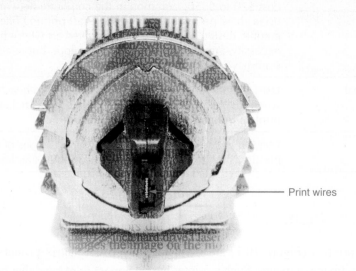

FIGURE 10.2 Impact printer head

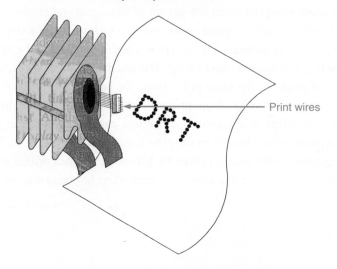

FIGURE 10.3 Impact print head operation

Each wire connects to a spring that pulls the print wire back inside the print head. The images created are nothing more than a series of dots on the page. Dot matrix printers are also called impact printers because the print wire springs out of the print head. The act of the print wire coming out of the print head is called pin firing. The impact of the printer physically striking the ribbon, which in turn touches the paper, causes impact printers to be noisy.

TECH TIP

One direction is not a problem

Most impact printers print bidirectionally. When the print head gets too hot, the printer prints only in the left-to-right direction. This is normal.

Because the print wire impacts the ribbon, one of the most common points of failure with impact printers is the print head. It can be expensive to replace print heads frequently in a high-usage situation; however, refurbished print heads work fine and are available at a reduced price. The companies that refurbish them usually replace the faulty wires and test the print head thoroughly.

Impact printers are the workhorses of printers. One advantage of an impact printer is that it can print multiple-part forms such as invoices, purchase orders, shipping documents, and wide forms. Multiple-part forms print easily on an impact printer because the printer impacts the paper so hard. Special **impact paper** can be purchased so duplicates are made each time a print job is sent. The maximum number of multiple copies each printer handles depends on the printer model. Laser and inkjet printers cannot produce multiple-part forms. They can only make multiple copies of the same document.

TECH TIP

Don't stack

Don't stack things on top of a printer, especially an impact printer. Keep a printer in a cool environment to avoid overheating.

Inkjet Printers

Inkjet printers are much quieter than impact printers and are used to print black and white, gray-scale, and color output. An inkjet printer also has a print head, but the inkjet's print head does not have metal pins that fire out from the print head. Instead, the inkjet's print head has many tiny nozzles that squirt ink onto the paper. Each nozzle is smaller than a strand of human hair. Figure 10.4 shows a photo of an **ink cartridge**. Notice the three rows of nozzles on the cartridge on the left.

One great thing is that the **inkjet print head** includes the nozzles and the reservoir for ink. When the ink runs out, you replace the entire print head. The inkjet printer print head is known as the print, or ink, cartridge. An ink cartridge has up to 6,000 nozzles instead of the 9-, 18-, or 24-pin configuration of the impact printer. This is one reason why the inkjet quality is preferable to an impact printer. Replacing the print head, one of the most frequently used parts, keeps repair costs low, but consumable costs are high. Two alternatives are for the manufacturers to use (1) a combination of a disposable print head that is replaced as needed and a disposable ink tank, or (2) a replaceable print head similar to the impact printer.

FIGURE 10.4   Inkjet print cartridge

Inkjet printers, also called bubble jet printers, use thermal (heat) technology to place the ink on the paper. Each print nozzle attaches to a small ink chamber that attaches to a larger ink reservoir. A small amount of ink inside the chamber heats to a boiling temperature. Once the ink boils, a vapor bubble forms. As the bubble gets hotter, it expands and goes out through the print cartridge's nozzle onto the paper. The size of the ink droplet is approximately two ten-thousandths (.0002) of an inch, smaller than the width of a human hair. As the small ink chamber cools down, suction occurs. The suction pulls more ink into the ink chamber for the production of the next ink droplet.

An alternative for producing the ink dots is to use piezo-electric technology, which uses pressure, not heat, to eject the ink onto the paper. Some companies use this technology to obtain high resolutions. **DPI** is the number of dots per inch a printer outputs. The higher the DPI, the better the quality of inkjet or laser printer output. Figure 10.5 shows the basic principle of how an inkjet printer works. Figure 10.6 shows how paper feeds through the printer and the part associated with that process. Table 10.3 lists the major parts found inside an inkjet printer.

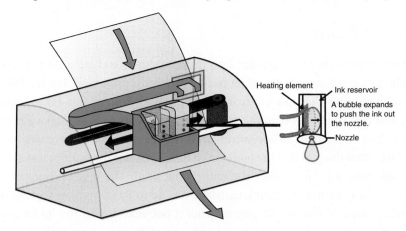

Heating element
Ink reservoir
A bubble expands to push the ink out the nozzle.
Nozzle

FIGURE 10.5   How an inkjet printer works

TABLE 10.3   Inkjet parts

Part	Description
Print head	Contains nozzles used to dispense ink
Print head assembly	Holds the print head and possibly ink cartridge(s)
Ink cartridge	Also known simply as a cartridge; may be one color or have sections for separate colors and may include the print head
Stepper motor	Used to move the print head/ink cartridge from one side of the printer and back as well as move the print head assembly (see Figure 10.6)
Belt	A belt connects to the stepper motor and print head assembly to move the print head and ink cartridge from one side of the printer to the other side (see Figure 10.6)
Stabilizer bar	Guide for the print head assembly for smooth motion
Power supply	Converts wall outlet AC to DC for inside the printer
Carriage	The part of the paper that moves from one side of the printer and back; includes belt, stabilizer bar, print head assembly (print head that may be included with the ink cartridge(s) (see Figure 10.6)
Paper tray and/or paper feeder	Holds paper (see Figure 10.6)
Roller	Moves paper through the printer (see Figure 10.6)

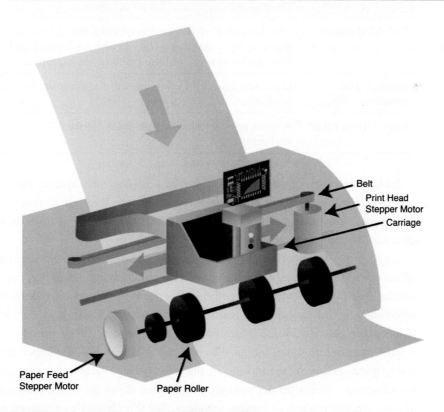

FIGURE 10.6   Major inkjet printer parts

Most inkjet printers have different modes of printing. The draft mode uses the least amount of ink, and the NLQ mode uses the most ink. The quality produced by an inkjet printer is equal to or sometimes higher than that of a laser printer, and inkjet printers print in color, whereas many laser printers print only in monochrome (black and white).

Color inkjet printers usually have a black cartridge for text printing and a separate color cartridge or separate cartridges for colored ink. Buying an inkjet printer that uses a single cartridge for all colors is cheaper on the initial printer purchase but more expensive in the long run. The black ink usually runs out much more quickly than the colored ink. Users should buy an inkjet model with separate cartridges for black ink and colored ink.

There are some alternatives to inkjet technology. Table 10.4 outlines four of them.

TABLE 10.4   Other printer technologies

Type of printer	Description
Solid ink	Sometimes called phase change or hot melt printers; uses colored wax sticks to create vivid color output. The wax stick is melted and sprayed through tiny nozzles onto the paper. The wax is smoothed and pressed as the paper is sent through rollers. The sticks can be installed one at a time as needed. The wax does not melt or bleed onto hands, clothing, or internal printer parts. It can print more colors, is faster, has fewer mechanical parts, and is cheaper than color laser printers but is more expensive than normal inkjet printers.
Dye sublimation	Also known as dye diffusion thermal transfer printers; uses four film ribbons that contain color dyes. The ribbons are heated and applied to the paper. The quality is high, but the printers are expensive.
Thermal wax transfer	Uses wax-based inks like the solid ink printer, but prints in lower resolutions.
Large format inkjet	A wide printer to print large-scale media such as CAD drawings, posters, and artwork.

Inkjet printers can also be integrated with a scanner and operate like a copier as an all-in-one unit. With these units, there are frequently two or even three paper feeds: from the rear paper tray, from a paper tray accessed from the bottom front of the unit, and from the top, which is commonly used for the copying or scanning.

Inkjet printers are perfect for small businesses, home computer users, and individual computer office work. Some models of inkjet printers include faxing, scanning, copying, and printing capabilities. For higher output, a laser printer is more appropriate. A drawback to using ink is that sometimes the ink smears. Ink manufacturers vary greatly in how they respond to this problem. If the paper gets wet, some inkjet output becomes messy. The ink also smears if you touch the printed page before the ink dries. The ink can also soak into the paper and bleed down the paper. Using good-quality paper and ink in the ink cartridge helps with this particular problem. Some manufacturers have a printer operation mode that slows down the printing to give the ink time to dry or a heating process to prevent smudges. See this chapter's section on printer supplies for more information on choosing the correct paper for different printers.

Laser Printers

The term *laser* stands for light amplification by stimulated emission of radiation. A laser printer uses a process similar to a copy machine's electrophotographic process. Before describing how a laser printer works, identifying the major parts inside the printer helps to understand how it works. Figure 10.7 shows a side view of a laser printer with a toner cartridge installed.

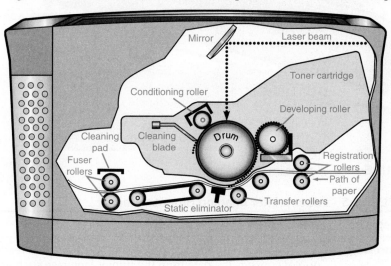

FIGURE 10.7   Inside a laser printer

TECH TIP

Be careful working inside laser printers

Be very careful when working inside a laser printer. There are high voltages and high temperatures in various parts. Turn off the printer and let it cool down before servicing it. Remove power from the printer when possible.

The computer sends 1s and 0s out the port and down the cable to the printer. Because data gets written to a laser drum by placing "dots" close together—similarly to how an inkjet printer squirts dots close together—the data must be prepared before the seven steps of getting the data onto the paper begin. The processing is the preparatory step, where the data is rasterized or converted into dots. Data transmits either through an array of LEDs or through a laser beam. The light beam strikes the photosensitive imaging drum located inside the toner cartridge (see Figure 10.8). Laser toner particles are attracted to the drum. The paper feeds through and the toner transfers to the paper. The toner is then fused or melted onto the paper. Table 10.5 summarizes the seven-step laser printer imaging process.

FIGURE 10.8   Laser imaging drum

TABLE 10.5   Laser printer imaging process steps

Step	Description
Processing	Also known as raster image processing. Gets the data ready to print. The laser printer converts the data from the printer language such as HPPCL (Hewlett-Packard Printer Control Language), Adobe PostScript, or Microsoft OpenXPS (Open XML Paper Specification) into a bitmap image. The laser printed page is made up of very closely spaced dots. Each row of dots is a scan line. The processing step gets the data ready to "write" a scan line.
Charging	Also known as conditioning. Gets the drum ready for use. Before any information goes onto the drum, the entire drum must have the same voltage level. The primary corona (main corona) or **conditioning roller** has up to –6000VDC applied to it. A primary control grid is located behind the corona wire or conditioning roller that controls the amount of voltage applied to the drum's surface (approximately –600 to –1000 volts). The drum gets a uniform electrical charge as a result of this step.
Exposing	Also known as the writing phase. Puts 1s and 0s on the drum surface. Whether the printer uses a laser beam or an LED array, the light reflects to the drum surface in the form of 1s and 0s. Every place the beam touches, the drum's surface voltage reduces to approximately100 volts (from the very high negative voltage level). The image on the drum is nothing more than dots of electrical charges and is invisible at this point.
Developing	Gets toner on the drum (develops the image). A **developing cylinder** (or developing roller) is inside the toner cartridge (right next to the drum) and contains a magnet that runs the length of the cylinder. When the cylinder rotates, toner is attracted to the cylinder because the toner has iron particles in it. The toner receives a negative electrostatic charge. The magnetic charge is a voltage level between –200 and –500 volts. The magnetized toner particles are attracted to the places on the drum where the light beam strikes. A **density control blade** controls the amount of toner allowed through to the drum. The image is no longer transparent on the drum. The image is black on the drum surface.
Transferring	Transfers an image to paper. A **transfer belt** (or an equivalent part such as a **transfer roller, corona,** or **pad**) is located at the bottom of the printer. It places a positive charge on the back of the paper. The positive charge is strong enough to attract the negatively charged toner particles from the drum. The particles leave the drum and go onto the paper. At this point, the image is on the paper, but the particles are held only by their magnetic charge.

Step	Description
Fusing	The **fuser assembly** melts the toner onto the paper. Heat and pressure make the image permanent on the paper. The paper, with the toner particles clinging to it, immediately passes through fusing rollers or a belt that applies pressure to the toner. The top roller applies intense heat (350°F) to the toner and paper that literally squeezes and melts the toner into the paper fibers. Figure 10.9 shows an example of a fuser assembly and the motor used with it.
Cleaning	Wipes off any toner left on the drum. Some books list this as the first step, but the order does not matter because the process is a continuous cycle. During the cleaning stage a wiper blade or brush clears the photosensitive drum of any excess toner. Then an **erase lamp** neutralizes any charges left on the drum so the next printed page begins with a clean drum.

Power supply

Fuser assembly

Fuser motor

Registration
assembly

FIGURE 10.9   Laser printer parts

Laser printers *do* make weird noises

A laser printer frequently makes an unusual noise that is a result of the fusing rollers turning when the printer is not in use. If the rollers didn't turn like this, they would have an indentation on one side. Users not familiar with laser printers sometimes complain about this noise, but it is a normal function of a laser printer.

A mnemonic (where the first letter of a saying helps you remember another word) for the laser printer imaging process is as follows: `People Can't Expect Dummies To Fix Computers.`

Every laser printer that uses the seven-phase imaging process is known as a write-black laser printer. These laser printers produce a black dot everyplace the beam touches the drum. Most laser printers use write-black technology. Write-white laser printers reverse the process, and the toner attracts everywhere the light beam does *not* touch the drum surface. Write-black printers print finer details, but write-white laser printers can produce darker shades of black areas.

To help with this flood of data about laser printers, Table 10.6 lists the major parts of a laser printer and briefly describes the purpose of each part.

TABLE 10.6   Laser printer parts

Part	Purpose
AC power supply	The main power supply for the printer
Cleaning blade	Wipes away excess toner from the drum before printing the next page
Cleaning pad	Applies oil to the fusing roller to prevent sticking; also removes excess toner during the fusing stage
Conditioning roller	Used instead of a primary corona wire to apply a uniform negative charge to the drum's surface
Control panel assembly	The user interface on the printer
Density control blade	Controls the amount of toner allowed on the drum (usually user adjustable)
Developing cylinder	Rotates to magnetize the toner particles before they go on the drum (also called the developing roller)
Drum (photo-sensitive)	Also known as **imaging drum**; accepts light beams (data) from LEDs or a laser; can be permanently damaged if exposed to light; humidity can adversely affect it
ECP (electronic control package)	The main board for a printer that usually holds most of the electronic circuitry, the CPU, and RAM
Erase lamp	Neutralizes any residual charges on the drum before printing the next page
Fuser (fusing) assembly	Holds the fusing roller, conditioning pad, pressure roller, and heating unit
Fusing rollers	Applies pressure and heat to fuse the toner into the paper
High-voltage power supply	Provides a charge to the primary corona or conditioning roller, which puts a charge on the drum
Main motor	Provides the power to drive several smaller motors that drive the gears, rollers, and drum
Pickup rollers (feed rollers)	Rollers used along the paper path to feed the paper through the laser printer
Primary corona (main corona)	Applies a uniform negative charge to the drum's surface
Registration assembly	Holds the majority of the rollers and gears to move paper through the unit
Separate pad (separation pad)	A bar or pad in a laser printer that can have a rubber or cork surface that rubs against the paper as it is picked up
Scanner unit	Includes a laser or an LED array that is used to write the 1s and 0s onto the drum surface
Toner	Powder made of plastic resin particles and organic compounds bonded to iron oxide
Toner cartridge (EP cartridge)	Holds the conditioning roller, cleaning blade, drum, developing cylinder, and toner; always remove before shipping a laser printer
Transfer corona wire (transfer roller or belt)	Applies a positive charge on the back of the paper to pull the toner from the drum onto the paper

Figure 10.10 shows the parts inside the cartridge.

FIGURE 10.10   Inside a laser printer cartridge

TECH TIP

A word about spilled toner

Toner melts when warmed; small toner spills outside the printer can be wiped using a cold, damp cloth. Toner spills in the printer require a special type of vacuum with special bags. Toner on clothing can normally be removed by washing in cold water. Do not put the clothing in a dryer if the toner has not yet been removed. The toner will melt into the clothing making the toner impossible to remove.

Thermal Printers

Thermal printers are used in a lot of retail establishments and at kiosks, gas pumps, trade shows, and basically anywhere someone needs a little printer to print a small document such as a receipt. IT staff commonly have to service thermal printers. A thermal printer uses **special thermal paper** that is sensitive to heat. A print head has closely spaced heating elements that appear as closely spaced dots on the heat-sensitive paper. A **feed assembly** is used to move the thermal paper through the printer. Figure 10.11 shows examples of thermal printers. Figure 10.12 shows an example of how the thermal paper works.

FIGURE 10.11   Thermal printers

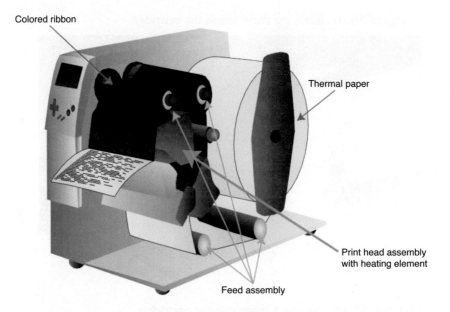

Colored ribbon

Thermal paper

Print head assembly
with heating element

Feed assembly

FIGURE 10.12   Inside a thermal printer

The thermal print head is one of the most important parts of the thermal printer. The print head can be damaged by several factors:

> Residue or material build-up causing uneven printing or missing dots
> Opening the print mechanism while printing
> Poor quality thermal paper
> Dirty environment
> Other objects (stuck labels, staples, paper clip, and debris)
> ESD (Very little voltage can damage the print head. Use self-grounding or an anti-static wrist strap when handling the print head.)
> Excessive moisture such as in high-humidity environments

3-D Printers

3-D printers are used to "print" or create 3-D solid objects out of various types of materials including plastic, ceramics, metals, metal alloys, clay, etc. A 3-D image is scanned into the computer, drawn, or downloaded from the Internet. Software takes the image and slices it into thousands of layers. The printer "prints" each layer until the object is formed. Other 3-D printing methods exist, but the end result is that a solid object is created. Think of the possibilities to be able to print a toy, a cat dish, or that hard-to-get-plastic piece that always breaks on the pool vacuum. Figure 10.13 shows a 3-D printer.

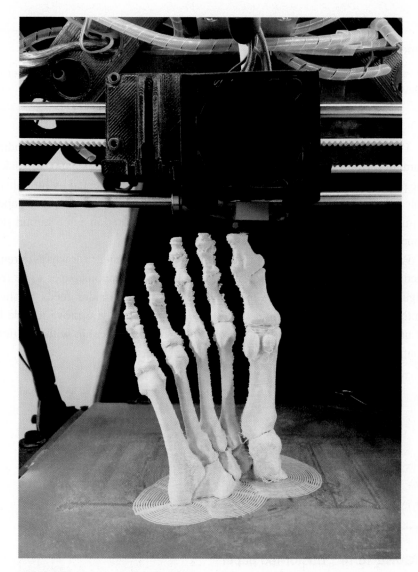

FIGURE 10.13   3-D printing

Paper

The type of paper used in a printer can affect its performance and cause problems. Impact printers are the most forgiving because a mechanism physically impacts the paper. On the other hand, inkjet printers spray ink onto the paper, so the quality of paper determines how well the ink adheres. If the paper absorbs too much of the ink, the printout appears faded. For a laser printer, how well the paper heats and absorbs the toner also affects the printed output. Paper is a big factor in the quality of how long the ink lasts and the quality of print produced.

Erasable-bond paper does not work well in laser printers because the paper does not allow the toner to fuse properly. Many types of paper are available for inkjet and laser printers: transparency paper for overhead projectors, high-gloss paper, water-resistant inkjet paper, fabric paper, greeting cards, labels, recycled paper, and so on. Recycled paper may cause printer jams and can produce lower print quality.

TECH TIP

Paper and pounds

Paper is rated in pounds (abbreviated lb) and shown as 20lb or 20#. A higher number indicates heavier, thicker paper.

The highest-quality paper available does not work well if the surrounding area has too much humidity. Humidity is paper's worst enemy. Humidity causes paper to stick together and reduces the paper's strength, which causes feed problems. Paper affected by humidity is sometimes noticeable because of the lumpy look it gives the paper. If you detect damaged paper, discard and recycle it immediately. For best printing results, keep paper stored in a non-humid storage area and fan the paper before you insert it into the printer's bin.

Paper options also relate to printers. Some impact printers allow you to remove the normal paper feeder and attach a tractor-feed option that allows continuous paper to be fed through the printer. Figure 10.14 shows how the paper with holes on both sides feeds through the impact printer. Both impact and inkjet printers have special feeders or you move a slide bar to feed envelopes or unusual-sized paper through. Laser printers sometimes ship with additional trays and must be configured for this option.

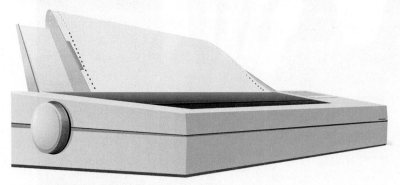

FIGURE 10.14   Tractor-fed paper

Another paper option is a **duplexing assembly** that enables two-sided printing. You may have seen and heard a duplexing assembly in action on a copier. A duplexing assembly is more commonly purchased for a laser printer than any other printer types, but certain inkjet printers also have this optional part. The duplexer is commonly attached to the bottom of a laser printer and the rear of the printer and selected through the *Print* menu of any application. Figure 10.15 shows a duplexing assembly.

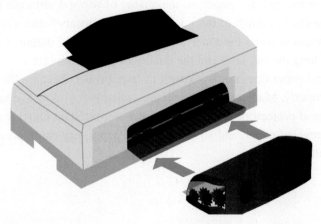

FIGURE 10.15   Duplexing assembly

How to control printer trays and manual feed options

In Windows, the *General* tab on the printer *Properties* tab is commonly used to view the current paper settings. Select the *Preferences* button to configure where you want the printer to look for paper to be used. See Figure 10.16.

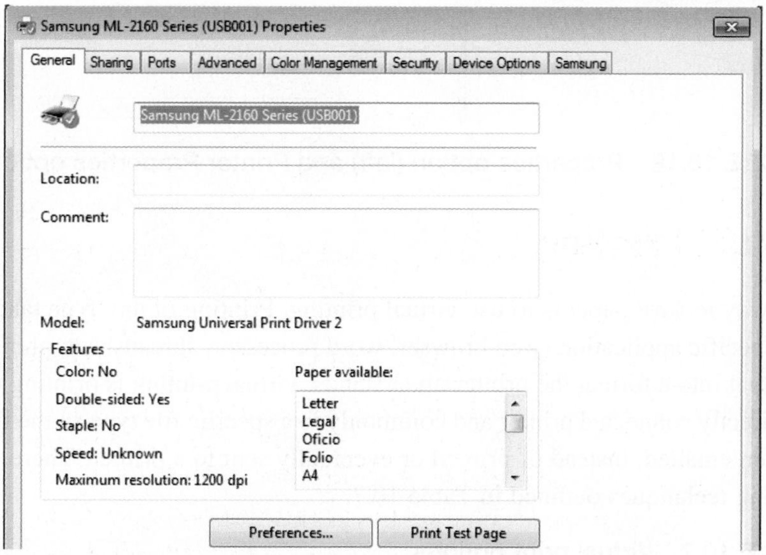

FIGURE 10.16   Paper options for a printer

Most printers also allow the default order in which the printer looks for paper to be configured through either the manufacturer-provider software or the printer *Properties* window. Many printers show both a *Properties* and a *Printer Properties* option (see Figure 10.17). Figure 10.18 shows the difference. You will most likely want the *Printer Properties* option shown on the right.

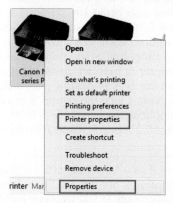

FIGURE 10.17   Right-click menu options for a printer

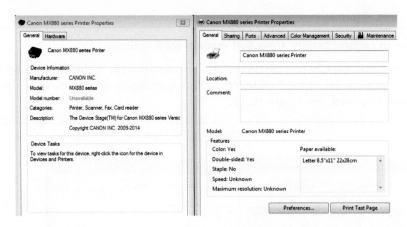

FIGURE 10.18 Properties option (left) and Printer Properties option (right)

Virtual Printing

One way to save paper is to use virtual printing. Printing of any type takes information formatted in a specific application (web browser, word processor, spreadsheet, photo viewer, and so on) and puts that into a format the printer understands. **Virtual printing** is printing to somewhere other than the directly connected printer and commonly to a specific file type so the file can be viewed, saved, or even emailed, instead of printed or eventually sent to a printer. There are four common virtual printing techniques outlined in Table 10.7.

TABLE 10.7 Virtual print options

Virtual print type	Description
Print to file	Takes a print job and saves it as a .prn file to be printed later. Not all printers support this. The file is printer-specific. *File > Print > select Print to file* checkbox (see Figure 10.19) *> OK.*
Print to PDF	Takes a print job and saves it as a Portable Document Format (.pdf) file that can be printed later on to any printer. For Windows Vista/7/8 download free Adobe Systems, Inc. software. Windows 10 includes a native print-to-PDF option. If it is not shown, search for the *Advanced printer setup* Control Panel link *> The printer that I want isn't listed* link *> Add a local printer or network printer with manual settings* radio button *> Next >* from the *Use an existing port* drop-down menu, select *File: (Print to File) > Next.* Once the option is available, in all Windows versions, from any application, select *File > Print >* select *Adobe PDF* (Vista/7/8)(see Figure 10.20) or *Microsoft Print to PDF* (Windows 10)*> OK.*
Print to XPS	Takes a file and saves it as a Microsoft XPS file that allows a document to be printed on any printer, but not modified. From any application, *File > Print >* select *Microsoft XPS Document Writer > Properties > XPS Documents* tab *>* ensure the *Automatically open XPS documents using the XPS viewer* checkbox is enabled (selected). To view the document in the XPS Viewer, browse to the file location and double-click on the file name.
Print to image	When documents cannot print to PDF due to a poor download or damaged content, print to image is a great option. It is also good when you are giving a sample of something, but do not want to give an entire document. Some software allows you to save in a JPEG, TIFF, PNG, or some other image file type. Free software exists to do the same thing.

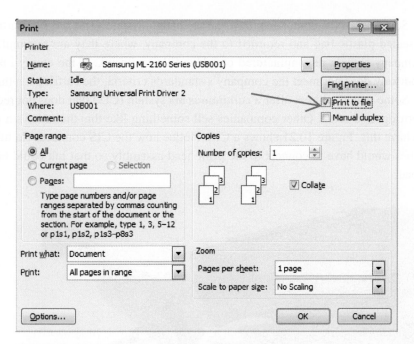

FIGURE 10.19   Print to file checkbox

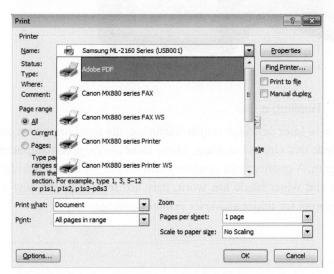

FIGURE 10.20   Print to Adobe PDF option

Refilling Cartridges, Re-inking Ribbons, and Recycling Cartridges

Much controversy exists about re-inking impact printer ribbons, refilling inkjet cartridges, and buying remanufactured laser cartridges. Many people who are concerned about the environment recycle their cartridges. Even if a company or an individual user decides not to purchase remanufactured products, some send empty cartridges to companies that do the remanufacturing or take them to a local office supply company for credit. Refilling ink cartridges significantly lowers printing costs.

If you refill ink cartridges, you should add new ink before an old cartridge runs completely dry. Also, be sure the refill ink emulates the manufacturer's ink. Some ink refill companies use inferior ink that, over time, has a corrosive effect on the cartridge housing. A leaky cartridge or one that bursts, causing ink to get into the printer, is trouble.

Some ink refill companies have an exchange system. The old ink cartridges are placed into a sealed plastic bag and returned to the company, where they are remanufactured. In return, the company ships a remanufactured cartridge filled with ink. If the empty ink cartridge sent to the company does not meet the company's standards criteria, the cartridge is thrown away.

Some manufacturers offer a **continuous ink system** (CIS) that does not require changing out ink cartridges so often. Other companies sell something like this that allows a printer to be modified to have this. Figure 10.21 shows a CIS. Notice how the CIS connects via tubes to the printer. The tubes would have to connect to the print head assembly so that ink could be supplied to the print head.

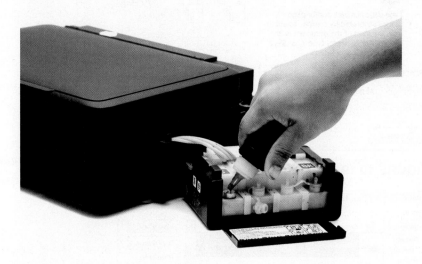

FIGURE 10.21   Refilling a CIS

When it comes to laser cartridge remanufacturing, the most important components are the drum and the wiper blade that cleans the drum. Many laser cartridge remanufacturers use the same parts over and over again. A quality refill company will disassemble the cartridge and inspect each part. When the drum and wiper blade are worn, they are replaced with new parts. Some states have disposal requirements for inkjet and laser printer cartridges.

TECH TIP

Beware of toner cartridges

Toner powder is harmful if inhaled. Wear a mask when refilling. Also, wear disposable gloves when replacing or refilling a toner cartridge to prevent toner from entering your skin pores.

Re-inking an impact printer ribbon is not a good idea. It can cause a mess, and the ink is sometimes an inferior quality that causes deterioration of the print head over time. Because impact printer ribbons are so inexpensive, you should just replace them.

Upgrading Printers

Printers can be upgraded in many ways, and the options available are vendor- and printer-dependent. The most common upgrades include memory and tray/paper feed options. The most commonly upgraded printers are inkjet and laser printers.

The most common upgrade for laser printers is memory. Many laser printer manufacturers use DIMMs and SO-DIMMs now, but some printers have proprietary memory modules. The amount of memory storage available for printers (especially those shared by multiple users) is important because printing errors can occur with too little memory. It is also important to have some means of storage so that the documents can be sent and stored away from the computer that requested the print job. This frees up the computer's memory and hard drive space to do other tasks.

TECH TIP

Printer memory upgrades

Many memory technologies are available for printers, but the common ones are RAM modules, flash memory, and proprietary memory modules. These technologies are installed in the same manner as on a computer. Hard drives can also be attached to some printers for additional storage.

Paper storage trays and feeders are another common upgrade. Laser printers frequently come with various paper storage tray options. When multiple people share a printer, a small-capacity paper tray can be a nuisance. Inkjet printers often have different paper feed options related to photograph printing. Paper designed for printing photographs is available in various sizes. Special paper feed options can be purchased that are mounted onto a printer for rolls or different sizes of paper. With the increased popularity of digital photography, these printer options are quite popular.

Printer Maintenance

Maintenance is important for all types of electronics, but printers have maintenance and preventive maintenance requirements that are a bit different than other devices. For some printers, preventive maintenance kits are available for purchase. Quality printer replacement parts and preventive maintenance kits are important to a technician. Let's examine each printer type and the maintenance procedures associated with each.

Impact Printer Maintenance

Maintenance done on an impact printer commonly involves the following:

> Replacing the ribbon
> Replacing the print head
> Replacing paper
> Clearing and cleaning the paper path

You know it is time to replace the ribbon when the print output is consistently light. The time to replace the print head is when the output shows one or more white horizontal lines. When replacing the printer print head, always follow the manufacturer's instructions. Generic steps to install an impact printer print head are as follows:

Step 1. Power off the printer and allow the print head to cool.

Step 2. Depress the release lever or button that allows the print head to be removed.

Step 3. Insert the replacement print head.

Step 4. Power on the printer and send a sample print job to ensure the print head is firing all pins.

To replace paper, simply insert the paper inside the paper tray. If continuous paper or forms are installed, you may be required to clear and clean the paper path. Ensure the paper aligns properly and evenly to the pins in the continuous (tractor-fed) paper. A sample form may have to be printed to ensure data is placed in the appropriate form fields.

Impact printers usually require cleaning more often than any other type of printer because they are frequently used for continuously fed paper or multiform paper and are often installed in industrial environments. Paper chafe, dust, and dirt cause an insulating layer of heat to form on the printer components, which causes them to fail faster. It is important to vacuum impact printers more often than other printers as a preventive maintenance task.

Inkjet Printer Maintenance

Maintenance done on an inkjet printer commonly involves the following:

> Replacing the cartridge
> Performing calibration/print head alignment
> Clearing paper jams
> Cleaning the print head

You know it is time to replace the ink cartridge when the print output is consistently light, a particular color does not print, or a message appears. The generic steps to install an ink cartridge include:

Step 1. Ensure the printer is powered on.

Step 2. Open the printer cover or door to gain access to the print cartridge assembly. Most printers will move the assembly to a place where access is easiest. Give the printer time to complete this process.

Step 3. Release the old print cartridge. There might be a release lever to access the cartridge. Some cartridges require pressing down to eject or simply pulling out, pulling out and then up, or lifting up. Always refer to the manufacturer's directions. An example print cartridge assembly is shown in Figure 10.22.

Step 4. Remove the protective tape from the new cartridge. Be careful not to touch the ink nozzles and/or the copper contacts that may be on the cartridge.

Step 5. Insert the new cartridge reversing the removal procedure.

Step 6. Replace the printer cover or access door.

Step 7. Print a test page.

FIGURE 10.22   Inkjet ink cartridge assembly

Most inkjet printers have a **calibration** or print head alignment process that must be performed when installing the printer and when replacing the print head to ensure quality output. Each inkjet printer has a different calibration process, but the generic steps are as follows. Note that many inkjet printers come with their own optional software that could be installed to perform this process.

Step 1. Locate the printer in the appropriate Windows Control Panel.

Step 2. Right-click the printer and select Properties or Printer Properties.

Step 3. Locate the calibration function which is commonly found on a Tools, Maintenance, or Advanced tab.

Step 4. Perform the calibration that normally involves printing a page and then selecting specific values through another menu. See Figure 10.23 for an example of the calibration or print head alignment page.

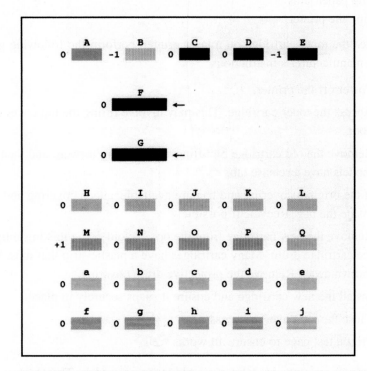

FIGURE 10.23 Sample inkjet print head/calibration output page

A **paper jam** is when the paper gets stuck somewhere along the paper path. The key to clearing or fixing paper jams on any printer is patience. Power off the printer and unplug it. Open the main cover and inspect where the jam occurred. Remove all loose paper from the paper path and paper tray. Sometimes the jam is simply a matter of pulling gently backwards on the paper from the paper tray (however it is always best to try to take the paper through the natural direction of the paper path), fanning through the paper in the paper tray to loosen one piece of paper from the others, or pulling the paper the rest of the way through the paper path. Do not tug; do not tear paper if possible. That will make life more difficult for you.

It may be easier to move the cartridge assembly to the side of the printer. Not all printers allow this. You might also gain access to an area by removing the ink cartridges. Needle-nose pliers and tweezers are great tools for stuck paper. Try to pull in the direction the paper would naturally roll through the printer.

Inkjet printers require little preventive maintenance. Keep the interior and exterior clean of dust and particles. Use a soft brush or nonmetallic vacuum nozzle to remove dust. Do not use any type of lubricants on the print cartridge bar. Use the printer's software or maintenance procedure for aligning the print cartridge each time it is replaced. Some printers have a "clean" maintenance procedure that can be done through the software that ships with the printer.

Some of these processes do not clean the print head well even when using this procedure, and the print heads tend to clog during usage. Remove the print head and clean with a lint-free cloth or with a dampened cotton swab. Allow the cartridge to dry thoroughly and reinstall.

Laser Printer Maintenance

Maintenance done on a laser printer commonly involves the following:

> Replacing a toner cartridge
> Applying a maintenance kit
> Performing calibration
> Clearing paper jams
> Cleaning the printer

To replace the toner cartridge on a laser printer, perform the following generic steps. Always refer to the manufacturer's instructions.

Step 1. Power off the printer.

Step 2. Access the toner cartridge. This may involve lifting the top cover or opening an access door.

Step 3. Remove the old cartridge by lifting up or sliding forward and then lifting up. Some models have a release tab.

Step 4. If the original covering and bag are available, attach covering and insert the cartridge inside the bag. Recycle if possible.

Step 5. Remove the new cartridge from the box. Avoid doing this in sunlight. Avoid touching the cartridge drum. Many cartridges have a plastic strip that must be pulled out and thrown away. Remove the protective drum covering.

Step 6. Install the new cartridge and ensure it snaps securely in place.

Step 7. Close the top cover or access door.

Step 8. Print a test page to ensure all works well.

A **laser printer maintenance kit** is available for some models. The contents of the kit are vendor-specific. A maintenance kit might contain any of the following: separation pad, pickup roller, transfer roller, charge roller, and fuser assembly. Always follow the manufacturer's directions on installing a maintenance kit. The separation pad and pickup rollers commonly require removing an e-clip. An e-clip holds rollers tightly on a bar. They look like the letter C or letter E. See Figure 10.24.

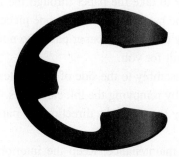

FIGURE 10.24   E-clip

There is actually an e-clip remover tool, but needle-nose pliers and a small flat tip screwdriver can work too. Hold the closed side of the e-clip tightly with the pliers. Use the tip of the screwdriver to gently pry the e-clip off the bar.

A common process done at the end of applying the maintenance kit is to reset the **maintenance counter**. This counter is used to count the number of pages until the next time the message to apply the maintenance kit appears again. Usually this counter is reset through the laser printer menu, but some printers may require a special button sequence.

A laser printer may have software options for cleaning and calibration. The cleaning mode cleans the paper path so that no corner or random specs appear on the output. Calibration is used to help with environmental issues (see the bulleted point on ozone that follows) or print cartridge quality issues. Cleaning mode and calibration are commonly accessed through the printer menu or from manufacturer-specific software on a PC. Some laser printers have an automatic calibration, but still allow it to be done manually.

Laser printers do require some periodic maintenance. The list that follows can help:

> Be careful about using compressed air to clean a laser printer that has loose toner in it. The compressed air could push the toner into hard-to-reach places or into parts that heat up, causing the parts to fail. Be sure to vacuum up laser printer toner before using compressed air inside a laser printer.
> If a transfer corona is used, clean it when replacing the toner cartridge. Some printers include a small cleaning brush for this purpose. Some toner cartridges include a cotton swab. The transfer corona wire is normally in the bottom of the printer, protected by monofilament wires. Be extremely careful not to break the wires or the transfer corona.

TECH TIP

Laser printer preventive maintenance is important

If any toner appears inside a laser printer, do *not* use a normal vacuum cleaner to get it out. The toner particles seep through the vacuum cleaner bag and into the vacuum's motor (where the particles melt). Also, the toner can become electrically charged and ignite a fire. Special high-efficiency particulate air (HEPA) vacuum bags are available for some computer and/or laser printer vacuum cleaners.

> Ozone is a gas produced by laser printers that use a corona wire. Some printers have an ozone filter that removes the ozone gas as well as any toner and paper dust particles. The ozone filter needs to be replaced after a specific number of usage hours. Check the printer documentation for the filter replacement schedule. If you forget to replace the ozone filter, people in the immediate vicinity may develop headaches, sore eyes, dry throat, nausea, irritability, and depression. Most home and small office laser printers do not have ozone filters. When using these printers, the surrounding area must be well ventilated.
> The fuser cleaning pad (sometimes known as the fuser wand) sits above the top fusing roller and is normally replaced at the same time as the toner cartridge. However, the cleaning pad sometimes becomes dirty before it is time to replace the cartridge. In this case, remove the cleaning pad. Hold the pad over a trash can. Use the shaft of a small flat-tipped screwdriver to rub along the felt pad. Replace the cleaning pad and wipe the screwdriver with a cloth.
> The fusing roller sometimes has particles cling to it. When the assembly cools, *gently* scrape the particles from the roller. A small amount of isopropyl alcohol on a soft, lint-free cloth or an alcohol pad can help with stubborn spots.
> If the laser printer uses a laser beam to write data to the photosensitive drum, the laser beam does not directly touch the drum. Instead, at least one mirror is used to redirect the laser beam onto the drum's surface. The mirror(s) need to be cleaned periodically with a lint-free cloth.

Thermal Printer Maintenance

Maintenance done on a thermal printer commonly involves the following:

> Replacing special thermal paper
> Cleaning the printhead/heating elements
> Removing debris
> Checking the feed assembly

Thermal printer preventive maintenance involves cleaning the print head/heating elements and removing debris from the printer and paper path. Isopropyl alcohol or premoistened thermal cleaning swabs can be used to clean the thermal print head and rollers. Compressed air can be used, too. It is recommended that with some thermal printers, you use a cleaning card, cleaning file, cleaning pen, or cleaning swabs. Remember to always use proper ESD procedures and to allow the thermal printer and laser printer to cool before performing preventive maintenance.

Printer Maintenance Conclusion

Printers are critical to some users. Keeping the printer well-maintained and recommending a maintenance routine is part of many technicians' routine. If any type of printer must be sent out for repair, warranty work, or for some other reason, make sure to remind the user or yourself to remove the toner cartridge, platen knobs, and power cords before packing the printer in a box. Check with the receiving company to see if you should send the toner cartridge separately.

TECH TIP

What if you just performed maintenance on a printer, and now the printing looks bad?

After performing preventive maintenance on a printer, the pages may appear smudged or slightly dirty. Run a few print jobs through the printer to allow the dust to settle (so to speak). Never perform any maintenance on any computer part or peripheral without testing the results.

USB Printer Installation

A printer is one of the easiest devices to install. Refer to the printer documentation for exact installation and configuration specifics (see Figure 10.25).

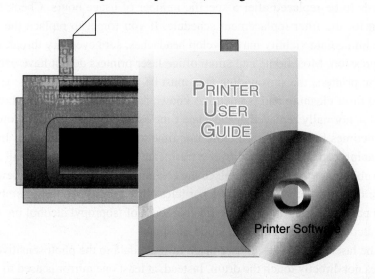

FIGURE 10.25   Printer installation, using software and a manual

The following steps explain how to install a printer that attaches to a USB port:

Step 1. Take the printer out of its box and remove the shipping materials. The number-one reason new printers do not work properly is failure to properly remove all the shipping safeguards.

Step 2. Connect the power cord from the printer to the wall outlet, surge protector, or UPS outlet. Note that most UPS units are not rated high enough for a laser printer to be connected to them.

Step 3. Load paper and the ribbon, ink, and cartridge into the printer, according to the manufacturer's instructions.

Step 4. Turn on the printer and verify that the power light is on.

Step 5. Install the print driver by following the manufacturer's instructions for the particular operating system being used.

Step 6. Attach the USB cable to the printer and to the computer. Note that this cable might not be provided with the printer.

Step 7. Configure options and default settings.

Step 8. Verify the operating system recognizes the printer. Perform a test print to verify communication between the computer and printer. Perform the calibration/print head alignment procedure.

Step 9. Train the user on printer operation and leave all printer documentation with the customer.

TECH TIP

Educate the user on printer functionality and print cartridges

As part of the installation process, ask the user to print something and show him or her any unique features. Inform the user that the cartridge that comes with the printer does not last long and to order a new one as soon as possible.

TECH TIP

For a successful printer installation

The keys to a successful printer installation are to read the printer documentation, use a good cable, load the latest printer drivers (from the manufacturer), and test its operation. Many hours of frustration for the computer user and the technician can be avoided by doing the research before the installation rather than after a problem occurs.

Installing a Local Printer

A local printer is one that connects to a computer. The steps taken depend on how the printer connects to the computer, but the generic steps can be discussed. Always refer to the manufacturer's directions.

Local printers commonly connect through a USB port, a wired or wireless network, or a Bluetooth network. There may be instances where an old 9- or 25-pin serial or 25-pin parallel printer may still be used. As mentioned in the USB section, you may have to install software before attaching the printer cable. Table 10.8 describes some tips for the various installation types.

TABLE 10.8   Printer installation notes per connection type

Type	Notes
USB	If software was installed before attaching the cable, Windows should detect and automatically start the installation process.
Wired network	Use the *Add Printer* wizard. A prompt is available that asks whether the printer is local or networked. A local printer is one that is directly attached to the computer and a networked printer is one attached to another workstation, a print server, or directly connected to the network.
Wireless network	Similar to the wired network except you have to know a few details about the wireless network before installing—wireless network name and security password.
Bluetooth	Bluetooth may have to be enabled first through a switch on the computer or through the Control Panel. Bluetooth must be enabled on the printer to make it discoverable. Note that some Bluetooth devices are always in discovery mode.

If the printer is not discovered, you can use the *Add a printer* link. If the printer does not appear, you can select *The printer that I want isn't listed* link > *Add a Local Printer or Network Printer with Manual Settings* link > *Next* > *Use an Existing Port* > select the appropriate port > Select the manufacturer and printer model from the list or use the *Have Disk* button to browse to the downloaded file.

Printers in the Windows Environment

The operating system plays a big part in controlling a printer. When working in a Windows environment, there are three essential areas for a technician to know (besides knowing how to print): (1) configuration utilities, (2) managing the print driver, and (3) printer settings. Sometimes these areas overlap.

To print in Windows, use one of the following methods:

> Open the file in the appropriate application. Click the *File* menu item and click the *Print* option.
> Drag the file to print to the printer's icon in the *Printers* folder.
> Create a shortcut icon on the desktop for a specific printer and drag the file to this icon.
> Right-click the filename and select the *Print* option.
> From within the application, press the Ctrl + P keys to bring up the *Print* window.
> From within an application, click the printer icon located under the menu bar.

TECH TIP

Using the printer icon in the notification area

When a print job occurs, Windows normally shows an icon of a printer in the notification area (the right side of the taskbar). When the print job is still accessible, you can double-click the printer icon, click the document, and pause or cancel the print job by using the *Documents* menu option.

You can use the *Printers* (Vista)/*Devices and Printers* (7 and higher) Control Panel to add a printer, remove a printer, temporarily halt a print job (pause the printer), and define or change printer settings, such as resolution, paper type, and paper orientation. The Windows *Add a printer* wizard steps you through the installation process. This utility starts automatically when Windows detects a newly connected printer. Once the wizard starts, you must select whether the printer is a local printer (used by only one computer) or a network printer. If the local printer option is selected, you will have to install a print driver. Device sharing and networking printers are covered later in the chapter. For best performance, always use the latest driver from the printer manufacturer for the operating system installed.

A **default printer** is the printer that applications use without any configuration changes. Even if you reply *No* to this prompt, you can change a printer to the default printer at a later date. Right-clicking a specific printer icon also gives you access to the *Printer Properties* window. Through this window, several tabs are available, depending on the printer model. Common tabs include *General, Sharing, Ports*, and *Advanced*. Figure 10.26 shows the *Printer Properties* window. Notice that the *General* tab has a *Print Test Page* button that can be used to test connectivity between the computer and the printer, and the test can be used to ensure that the print driver is working.

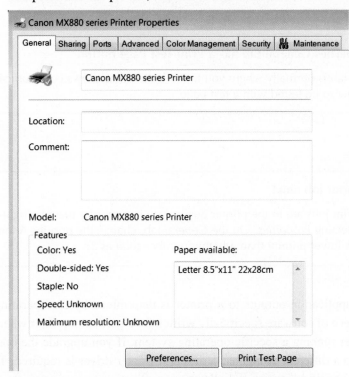

FIGURE 10.26   Printer Properties window

TECH TIP

Setting a printer as the default printer

Locate the printer using the *Devices and Printers* Control Panel. Right-click the appropriate printer > *Set as default printer*. The default printer has a check mark next to the printer icon.

A printer's *Properties* option contains useful tools and settings. Table 10.9 lists the common printer *Properties* window tabs and their general purposes.

TABLE 10.9 Printer Properties tabs overview

Tab	Description
General	Displays the printer name and has a button for printing a test page
Sharing	Shares the printer over a network
Ports	Sets the LPT port number or displays the current port
Advanced	Allows setting of resolution, graphics intensity (darkness), graphics mode, spooling (transmission delay), and defaults
Maintenance	Printer-type dependent; contains links to various maintenance functions including cleaning, calibration, print head alignment, nozzle check, roller cleaning, and quiet mode
Fonts	Displays and installs printer fonts
Device Options	Adjusts print density and quality, displays amount of RAM installed in the printer, and adjusts printer memory tracking

TECH TIP

Printer Properties General tab has a Print Test Page button

The *General* tab is normally where you find a button that allows communication between the PC and the printer to be tested with a test page.

TECH TIP

I want my print job now!

If multiple print jobs are in the printer queue, you can reorder them by right-clicking on a document and selecting *Properties*. On the *General* tab, change the priority. A lower number, such as 1, indicates a lower priority than a higher number such as 3.

How an application outputs to a printer is determined by the operating system used. A **print driver** is a piece of software specifically written for a particular printer when that printer is attached to a computer running a specific operating system. If you upgrade the operating system or move the printer to a different computer, a different printer driver is required. The print driver enables the printer's specific features and allows an application to communicate with the printer via the operating system. Windows applications use one print driver per printer. If you have two printers attached, two print drivers will have to be installed.

TECH TIP

Use the latest print driver

For best results and performance, use the driver provided by the manufacturer designed for the operating system being used.

The print driver and software from the printer manufacturer provide customizable configuration settings for a particular operating system. These settings can be accessed by right-clicking on the printer within the *Devices and Printers* Control Panel window and selecting *Printing Preferences.* Commonly used configuration settings include the following:

> **Orientation** (see Figure 10.27): The way in which the document is presented (portrait like a normal piece of paper or landscape like what a page looks like if you turn the paper sideways).

> **Duplex** (see Figure 10.27): Also known as double-sided printing. Note that in Figure 10.27 that this particular printer does not have a duplexer assembly so printing on two sides would require turning the paper over and sending back through the printer.

> **Collate** (see Figure 10.28): An example of collation would be if you had a 10-page document and wanted three copies of it. With collation enabled, you would get the first copy of the 10-page document, then the second copy, and at last the third copy. Without collation enabled, you would get three copies of the first page, three copies of the second page, and so on.

> **Quality** (see Figure 10.29): A setting that controls the resolution (DPI for example) and amount of ink/toner used.

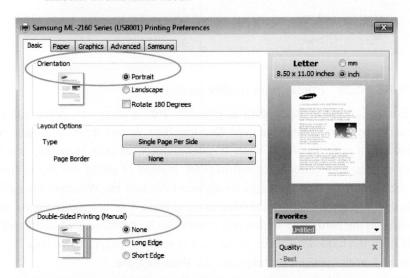

FIGURE 10.27   Printer orientation and duplex settings

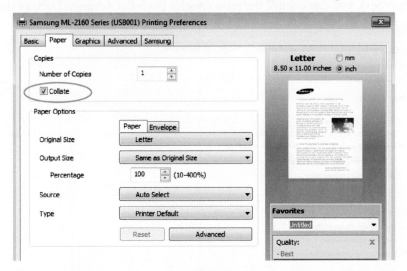

FIGURE 10.28   Printer collate option

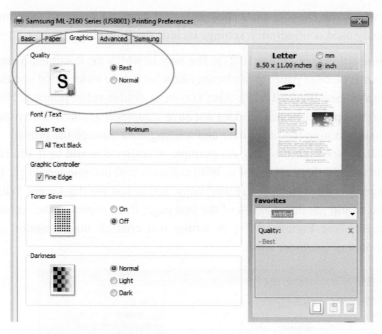

FIGURE 10.29   Printer print quality option

Printers accept as much data as possible from a computer, process that data, output it, communicate to the computer the need for more data, accept more data, and repeat the process. With Windows, a print spooler is used. A **print spooler**, or print manager, is a software program that intercepts an application's request to print. Instead of going directly to the printer, the data goes on the hard drive. The print spooler service built into the Windows operating system controls the data that is going from the hard drive to the printer. A print spooler allows multiple print jobs to be queued on the hard drive so that other work can be performed while the printer prints. The data is sent from the hard drive when the printer is ready to accept more data. Some printers come with their own print manager that replaces the Windows one.

If you right-click a printer and select *Properties* (or sometimes the window is under *Printer properties*), you can control the print spooler from the *Advanced* tab, as shown in Figure 10.30.

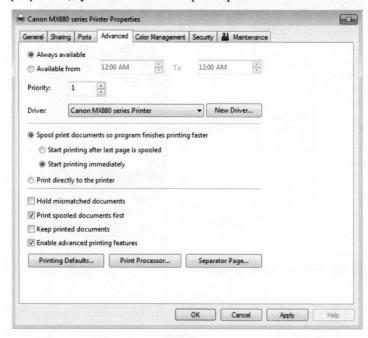

FIGURE 10.30   Spool settings

A print spooler runs as a service in Windows. The print spooler service relies on another service called the Remote Procedure Call (RPC) service and optionally the HTTP service in order to operate. To verify whether the services are running, type `services.msc` at a command prompt, in the *Run* textbox, or in the *Search programs and files* textbox on the *Start* button menu. In the resulting screen, you can see that the Print Spooler and Remote Procedure Call (RPC) services have a status of *Running*, as shown in Figure 10.31.

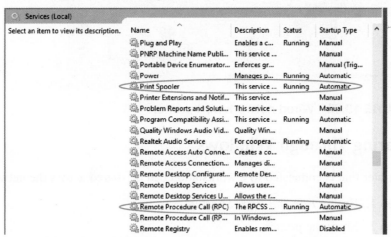

FIGURE 10.31   Print Spooler service

TECH TIP

When not to use spooling

If you have less than 300MB of hard drive space, turn off spooling because the system needs the free drive space to operate. Remove files from the hard drive and clean up if possible or add more storage so spooling can be re-enabled. Note that if a printer is shared, spooling must be enabled.

Printing Device Sharing

Many home users and almost all businesses use printing device sharing (printers that can be used by more than one computer). Printers can be shared using the following methods:

> Connect a printer to a port (USB or the older serial/parallel) on a computer that is connected to the network and share the printer.
> Connect a printer with a wired or wireless NIC directly on the network. Some printers can be upgraded. Some printers can have a wired or wireless network port added to them. Figure 10.32 shows a wired Ethernet port that can be inserted into a printer expansion slot.
> Set up a computer or device that is designated as a print server. Connect the printer to the print server. Connect the print server to the network.
> Use public/shared devices.

A networked printer can reduce costs. Laser printers can be expensive—especially ones that produce high-speed, high-volume, high-quality color output. Buying one printer and allowing users to access it from their individual desktops, laptops, and mobile devices can be cost-effective. It also reduces the amount of office or home space needed. Network printing is a viable alternative to using a computer's USB port. Wired printers can connect to a computer and then be shared or connect to a wired network and everyone on the network can use the printer.

FIGURE 10.32   Wired network port printer

Sharing Through Windows

A printer that is connected to a workstation can be shared across the network by the following:

Step 1. Enable *File and Print Sharing*.

Step 2. Share the printer.

In Windows, to enable *File and Print Sharing*, do the following based on which operating system is installed.

> Windows Vista: *Network and Sharing Center* Control Panel > *Change advanced sharing settings* > expand the current network profile. *Turn on printer sharing > Apply.*

> Windows 7/8/10: *Network and Sharing Center* Control Panel > *Change advanced sharing settings* > expand the current network profile. *Turn on file and printer sharing > Save changes.* See Figure 10.33.

FIGURE 10.33   Enable print sharing

In order to share a directly connected printer so others can access it, right-click on the printer to be shared > *Properties* (might be *Printer properties*) > *Sharing* tab > enable (select) the *Share this printer* option so it is checked > in the *Share name* textbox, type a name for the printer > *OK*. See Figure 10.34.

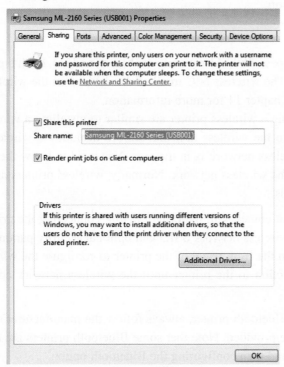

FIGURE 10.34   Printer Sharing tab

Notice in Figure 10.34 that you can install additional drivers for other Windows operating systems so when other computers access this shared printer, they do not have to download and install the driver for this printer.

Wireless Printers

A PC can connect wirelessly to a printer using different methods:

> The printer can have an 802.11 wireless NIC installed or the NIC can attach to a USB port.
> The printer can have integrated Bluetooth capabilities or a Bluetooth adapter attached via a USB port.
> The wireless printer can communicate directly with another wireless device.
> The print server to which the printer connects can have wireless capabilities, and wireless PCs and devices can connect to the printer through the print server (covered in the next section).

Printers with wireless capabilities are common, but the wireless adapter may have to be purchased separately. Refer to Chapters 14 and 15 for more information on wireless networking theory and issues related to installing wireless devices.

The first method is the most common. An 802.11 wireless network is one where an 802.11 access point or combination access point and router coordinates communication between all devices on the wireless network.

TECH TIP

Do your wireless homework

When installing an 802.11 wireless network printer, obtain the SSID and security information before starting the installation.

There are different types of 802.11 networks (a, b, g, n, and ac). Each type has its own frequency and rules of operation. The wireless NIC in all of the devices on the wireless network must be of compatible types. See Chapter 14 for more information.

The steps for installing a wireless printer are similar to installing a wired network printer once the printer is attached to the wireless network. Before installing a wireless printer, you need to ensure a functional wireless network is in the area. You need to know the SSID and any security settings configured on the wireless network. Normally, wireless printers are configured using one of the following methods:

> Install software that comes with the printer *before* connecting the printer. Then use the software to enter the wireless network SSID and optional security parameters.
> Use the controls on the front panel of the printer to configure the wireless settings.
> Use a USB connection to the printer until the wireless network configuration options are entered.

In order to install a Bluetooth printer, always follow the manufacturer's directions, but the following generic steps are provided. Note that some Bluetooth printers are configured by first connecting them via USB and then configuring the Bluetooth option.

Step 1. Install the print driver for the operating system version being used.

Step 2. Ensure Bluetooth is enabled on the computer or mobile device.

Step 3. Ensure Bluetooth is enabled on the printer (usually through a front panel control). Note that you may have to set the visibility option to *Visible to all*.

Step 4. If in Windows, use the Windows printer Control Panel to access the *Add a printer > Add a network, wireless or Bluetooth printer* link. Some manufacturers simply recommend using the Bluetooth icon in the notification area to select *Add a Bluetooth device*. If on a mobile device, something may have to be tapped or a button pushed in order to start pairing with the Bluetooth printer.

Step 5. Ensure the two devices pair properly and that the print function works.

Some wireless printers support **ad hoc wireless printing**, which allows two 802.11 wireless devices to communicate directly without the use of a wireless access point or a wireless router. When a wireless access point or wireless router is used, the alternative mode is known as **infrastructure mode**. To install and configure an ad hoc wireless printer, use the recommended procedures from the printer manufacturer, but the generic steps are provided.

Step 1. Place the printer in ad hoc mode using the front panel controls or software from the printer manufacturer.

Step 2. Place the computer, tablet, or mobile device in ad hoc mode. In Windows, access the Network and Sharing Center Control Panel. The steps taken depend on the operating system as shown in the following:

> Vista: *Set up a connection or network* link > *Set up a wireless ad hoc (computer-to-computer network)* > *Next* > configure the wireless network name and security options.

> 7/8/10: *Set up a new connection or network* link > configure the wireless network name and security options.

Note that you might have to manually configure the wireless NIC IP address and subnet mask. See Chapter 14 for more information on how to do that.

Print Servers

A **print server** connects to a network and allows any computer that is also connected to a network to print to it if the networks are the same or connected to one another. Some print servers can handle both wired and wireless connections. In this case, the print server attaches to a network switch, and a network wireless router or wireless access point attaches to the same switch. Any PCs (wired or wireless) can print to the printer that attaches to the print server. Figure 10.35 illustrates this concept.

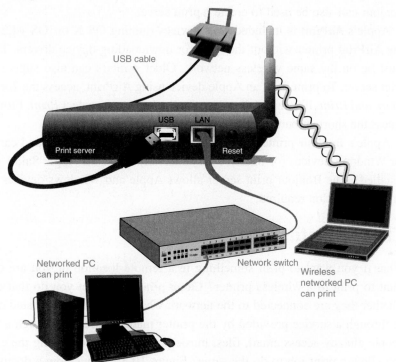

FIGURE 10.35   Wireless and wired print server connectivity

Accessing a Network, Wireless, or Bluetooth Printer

To access a networked printer, use the Windows *Printers* (Vista)/*Devices and Printers* (7 and higher) Control Panel > *Add a printer* > *Add a network, wireless or Bluetooth printer* link. If the printer does not display in the list, select *The printer that I wanted is not listed*. Three options are available (also see Figure 10.36):

> Browse for a network printer
> Type the path to the printer
> Enter the IP address or printer hostname

FIGURE 10.36   Finding a shared printer

See Chapter 14 for more information on configuring network devices.

An older PC can also function as a software print server. The PC can be used for nothing but handling print jobs sent to the printer attached to the PC. Software such as Apple's AirPrint or Bonjour can also be used to create a print server.

Apple's **AirPrint** is included with devices running OS X or iOS v4.2+ can be used to print to any AirPrint printer without the need for downloading device drivers. The printer and the device must be on the same wireless network. Older printers can also support this using a third-party print server. To print from an Apple device using AirPrint, access the *Tools* menu option > *Print* > *Share and Print*. If using Mail, select the *Reply* button > select *Print*. From the Safari web browser, access the shortcut button left of the address bar > *Print*.

Apple's **Bonjour** printer server is available on Apple devices and can be downloaded for free for Windows devices (or installed automatically when the Apple Safari web browser or iTunes is installed). The Bonjour print server allows Apple and Windows devices to share printers without any configuration required.

Cloud Printing

What if you want to print something in a remote location or you are on a wired computer and want to print to a wireless printer? **Cloud printing** can let you do that or print using any device whether they are connected to the network where the printer is located or not. Cloud printing can be through a service provided by the printer manufacturer or through a provider such as Google. People already access email, files, music, and other devices using the cloud, so why couldn't an app allow a print job to do the same? Figure 10.37 shows how a document or a photo could be printed from a cell phone if cloud printing is enabled.

FIGURE 10.37   Cloud printing

Google Cloud Print allows printing from any device to a Google Cloud Print-connected printer. This enables you to print a picture or a document from your phone or mobile device. To determine whether the printer is Google Cloud ready, open a Chrome web browser window. In the address bar, type the following: `chrome://devices` . See any Google Cloud devices or click + (see Figure 10.38). Select whatever printers you would like to add to Google Cloud Print and click the *Add Printer(s)* button (see Figure 10.39). From the resulting screen, click *Manage my printers* to see the options within Google Cloud Printing (see Figure 10.40).

FIGURE 10.38   Viewing Google Cloud–ready devices

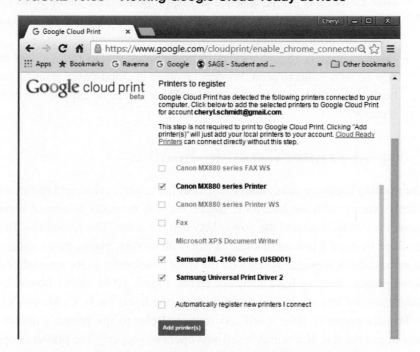

FIGURE 10.39   Viewing Google Cloud printers to register

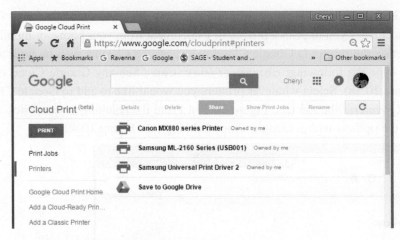

FIGURE 10.40   Google Cloud Print

Once you have printers registered to the cloud, you download an app on your phone or mobile device. Some apps only allow printing from a particular browser. Other apps have you upload a document or photo to the app and then print from there. Finally, you may have to share a photo or document with the app and then print from the app. Many of the printer manufacturers have their own cloud-based print solution and app.

Printing Data Privacy

There are drawbacks to printing to a shared, public, or cloud-based printer that technicians must be aware:

> Printers shared through a PC require that the PC be powered.

> Sharing a printer through a PC means that print jobs are spooled to the PC hard drive (**hard drive caching**). If someone sends an inappropriate print job or prints something that is sensitive corporate information, a technician must realize that the spooled data can be recovered even if the print job completed.

> Privacy: Printers shared wirelessly may require giving the wireless network a password to anyone who wants to print. Printers involved in cloud-based printing require a user to authenticate and register with the app vendor. There can be no expectation of privacy or **data privacy/ security**.

General Printer Troubleshooting

The printing hardware subsystem consists of the printer, cable, and communications port. If something is wrong with the hardware, the problem is normally in one of these three areas. Always check the connections and the power between the areas. The printer has the highest failure rate of the three because it is a mechanical device with motors, plastic gears, rollers, and moving parts. If an **error code** or message appears on the front panel, refer to the manual or online documentation. Some printers beep or have indicator lights. Figure 10.41 shows how one particular printer has indications for low ink in specific cartridges (the lights for B, C, M, and Y).

Printers normally have a self-test routine. Refer to the printer's documentation to determine how to run the test. If a printer's self-test operates properly, the printer is operational. In this case, a remaining print problem has to do with the port, cable, or software.

FIGURE 10.41 Printer indicator lights

Running the self-test from the computer shows that printer connectivity works (the computer can issue a command to the printer and the printer gets it). **No connectivity** is evident if the self-test issued from the computer fails. The self-test is commonly run from the printer's *Properties or Printer properties* option from the *Devices and Printers* Control Panel. Access the *General* tab > *Print Test Page* button. Refer back to Figure 10.32.

> ### TECH TIP
>
> **The paper is not feeding**
>
> If a printer is having trouble with the **paper not feeding**, you should look to see how far the paper went along the paper path before it jammed or could not go any farther. Many paper-feeding problems are due to poor paper quality or the inefficiency of the rubber rollers that move the paper along the paper path. Rubber rollers are normally found in the paper transport system on all printer types, and over time, the rollers become slick from use and do not work properly.

If the **printer will not print**, perform the following generic steps.

Step 1. If the printer attaches to a computer, see if any message appears on the computer.

Step 2. See if any message appears on the printer control panel.

Step 3. Determine whether the correct printer was chosen.

Step 4. Ensure the printer has ink or toner and paper.

> ### TECH TIP
>
> **The paper could be the culprit**
>
> If a printer has trouble feeding paper, ensure that you're using the correct type of paper. One vendor says that 80 percent of all paper jams are due to inferior paper quality, poor paper condition such as damage due to humidity, or an operator-related problem such as the wrong paper size selected in the software program.

If you are **unable to install the printer** using the manufacturer's instructions, then try the following steps:

Step 1. Check cabling and power.

Step 2. Ensure that the manufacturer's directions were followed. Reread them again.

Step 3. Delete the print driver and try the installation again, following the manufacturer's instructions.

Step 4. Download a different print driver and try the installation again.

Step 5. Research the error on the printer manufacturer's website. Documented cases exist where the technician was required to back up the registry, modify the registry, and restart the print spooler in order to repair this issue.

If there is **no image on the printer display**, check that the printer is powered on. Also check the wall outlet by plugging a known working device into the same socket; if applicable, check the power surge strip. The printer power brick may be faulty.

TECH TIP

Mixed-up output

If you see **garbled characters** on the output, check the cable and then the print driver.

If a printer gives a "paper out" message (see Figure 10.42), but the paper is installed in the printer, then check the paper sensor. Sometimes this sensor is an optical sensor, and sometimes it is a plastic piece that flips out. Take the paper out and reinsert it. Ensure that there is no blockage and that the sensor is not sticking (not flipping out properly). Dust and debris can cause both blockage and sensor sticking.

FIGURE 10.42   Printer control panel message

Faded or totally missing print

When the print output is **faded print**, check the ribbon (impact and thermal), ink levels (inkjet), or toner (laser). Check the quality setting. In a thermal printer, reduce the print head energy or print head pressure setting; ensure ribbon and media are compatible. If **printing blank pages**, check the same as the faded print symptom, and ensure the print driver is working properly. You may have to roll the driver back in Device Manager if a Windows Update has just occurred.

If the printer outputs **creased paper**, check the following:

> Ensure the paper guide(s) in the paper tray is set to the correct size and does not push too tightly against the paper.
> Fan the paper before printing.
> Ensure the paper being used meets the manufacturer's specifications.
> Check the paper path for obstructions such as a label, staple, or paper clip.

Some printers have upgradable firmware. Just as a computer's flash BIOS can be upgraded, printers may need a firmware upgrade to correct specific problems. Printer firmware updates can normally be obtained from the printer manufacturer's website.

Another problem could be that the printer is not configured for the correct port. Check that the printer is configured for the proper port. Refer to the printer's documentation for specifics on how to configure the printer for a specific port. To verify which port is currently configured, access the printer manufacturer's software or use Windows *Printer properties* from the Control Panel (right-click on the printer). Access the *Ports* tab. You can also connect a working printer to the port, install the proper print driver, and verify the port works.

What to do with slick printer rollers

Special cleaners such as Rubber Rejuvenator are available for rubber printer rollers that have a hard time picking up paper and sending it through the printer. Some printers have a special cleaning page for cleaning the rollers. Refer to the printer's manual for exact procedures. If a cleaner is unavailable, scrub the rollers with a wire brush or sandpaper to roughen them up a bit, which will enable them to pick up the paper better. If you do not have a wire brush or sandpaper, use the sharp edge of a paper clip to roughen up the rubber part of the roller so it can grip the paper. Vacuum all debris before using the printer.

Another common problem occurs when the printer does not have enough memory. One symptom of this is that when printing, the printer blinks as if it is accepting data. Then the printer quits blinking, and nothing appears or the printer prints only half the page. This could also be caused by insufficient hard drive space when spooling is enabled. Some printers display a **low memory error** message or error code.

What if a printer needs more memory?

Alternatives to adding memory are to send fewer pages of the print job at a time, reduce the printer resolution, reduce the size of the graphics, or standardize the fonts (by not using as many font types, styles, or font sizes). Also ensure that there is ample free hard drive space.

USB-Attached Printer Troubleshooting

If the printer uses a USB port, consult the following list of troubleshooting options:

> If the computer stops responding and the USB device is suspect, power the computer off and then back on again.

> The BIOS/UEFI settings may have to be enabled for USB devices. Different BIOS manufacturers list the USB settings differently. The USB settings may be located under the heading *Enabling onboard USB* or within the PCI section. If you install a USB host adapter and the motherboard also supports USB ports, you may have to disable the motherboard ports through BIOS/UEFI.

> Use Device Manager to check whether USB is listed. Look at the *Universal Serial Bus controllers* section. If USB is not listed, check the BIOS/UEFI settings or update the BIOS. If the USB device is listed, ensure that there are no resource conflicts.

> If there is a USB hub connected to the USB port, disconnect the hub and connect the USB printer directly to the USB port to see if the problem is the hub.

> With the computer's power on, disconnect the USB printer and reconnect it. Go into Device Manager and ensure that there is only one listing for the USB printer.

> Disconnect the USB printer while the computer is powered on. Power down the computer. Then, power on the computer. Insert the USB printer cable into the USB port. The system should automatically detect and install the printer.

> Verify that the USB device works by plugging it into another USB port or another computer's USB port.

> Check that the proper USB cable is being used.

A USB cable can be rated as SuperSpeed, Hi-Speed, or Low-Speed. The SuperSpeed and Hi-Speed cables have more shielding and can support higher speeds. If a SuperSpeed or Hi-Speed USB device attaches to a Low-Speed cable, the device operates at the lower speed. Make sure you have the proper USB cable for a printer that attaches to a USB port.

On the software side, troubleshooting involves narrowing down the problem to the print driver. Because Windows uses one print driver for all applications, check the printing from within several software packages. Use a simple text program such as Notepad to see if simple text will print. Printers need memory to print multiple pages of complex graphics. If a printer prints a couple pages and then stops, or if it prints half a page, ejects the paper, and then prints the other half of the page and ejects the paper, the printer's memory needs to be upgraded. If printing does not occur in all the software packages tested, the problem is most likely the software driver. See the earlier section for specific Windows printer troubleshooting tips.

Windows Printer Troubleshooting

The most common printing test is a test page from an application or from a specific printer's *Properties* or *Printer properties* window, using the *General* tab. Remember that Windows uses a single print driver for all applications. Windows has a Troubleshooter tool. Access the troubleshooting tool based on the Windows version being used.

Windows Vista/7: *Start* button > *Control Panel* > type `troubleshooting` in the Search Control Panel textbox > *Search Windows Help and Support for "troubleshooting"* link > *Troubleshooting* > locate the *Open the Printer troubleshooter* link > *Click to open the Printer troubleshooter* link > follow the directions on the screen.

Windows 8: In the *Search* textbox, type `troubleshooting` > *Hardware and Sound* link > in the *Printing* section, select *Printer* link > follow the directions on the screen.

Windows 10: In the *Search the web and Windows* textbox, type `troubleshooting` > *Troubleshooting* Control Panel > *Hardware and Sound* link > in the *Printing* section, select *Printer* link > follow the directions on the screen.

If the Windows troubleshooter tool does not help, run a self-test on your printer by following the manufacturer's directions. If the self-test works, the printer is usually fine, and the problem lies in the cable, port, software driver, or printer settings.

TECH TIP

Try printing from Notepad

If a printer self-test works, try printing from Notepad. If the file prints, your problem may be a print problem that affects only one application, or the printer does not have enough memory for complex output, such as high-end graphics.

Free hard drive space is important for print spooling. Insufficient free space can cause print jobs to have problems. Even if there appears to be enough hard drive space to spool a printing job, the printer may still need more RAM installed to print a large or complex document.

A print spooler and/or associated services, such as RPC and HTTP, can cause problems and can be stopped or paused. Locate the Print Spooler, RPC, or HTTP service used by the printer (open services by typing `services.msc`). Right-click on the service and select *Properties*. From the window that appears, you can start, stop, pause, or resume a service. Figure 10.43 shows the Print Spooler Properties window. Because the service is started automatically, the only button currently available is Stop.

If the printer works, then the printer, port, and printer cable are all operational, and the problem is in the operating system. To see if the printer driver is the problem, use the *Add Printer Wizard* to install the Generic/Text Only printer driver. See Lab 10.1 at the end of this chapter for more information.

FIGURE 10.43   **Managing the Print Spooler service**

If you reload a printer driver, the old printer driver must be removed first. Some manufacturers have specific instructions for removing their drivers. Always follow their directions. Most of them say to do something similar to the following: Right-click the specific printer icon and click the *Delete* option. Click the *Yes* button when prompted if all the associated printer files are to be deleted. To reinstall the printer, use the Add Printer wizard. The print queue sometimes causes problems. A single document will be in the queue and not print for some reason and cause a **backed-up print queue**. Depending on what rights the user has, sometimes a technician must clear the print queue. The following methods can be used:

> Open the *Printers* (Vista)/*Devices and Printers* (7)/*Printers* (8)/*Printers & scanners* (10) Control Panel. Locate the printer icon, right-click, and select *Open*. Right-click the first document (the one that is causing the problem) and select *Cancel*. To cancel all print jobs, you can select *Cancel all documents* from the *Printer* menu option.

> If the print job has already gone to the printer and is no longer stored on the hard drive, you may not be able to use the first method. In this case, use the *Printer* menu or *Cancel* button to cancel the print job.

> Turn the printer off and back on again.

Note that if you get an access denied message, it means you must be logged on as an administrator to control the print queue. If a user gets the **access denied** message, then the user account must be added to the printer. Access the printer within the *Devices and Printers* Control Panel > right-click on the printer and access *Printer properties* > *Security* tab > add the user account.

Windows also has a few more tools for you. You can use Windows Device Manager to examine system resources and check for problems with the USB controller. If you are having trouble sharing a printer, ensure Windows Firewall is not blocking printer sharing. Take these steps if Windows Firewall is being used (for another vendor's firewall, follow directions from the vendor):

Step 1. Open the Windows Firewall Control Panel.

Step 2. On Windows 7, select the *Allow a program or feature through Windows Firewall* link. On Windows 8/10, select the *Allow an app or a feature through Windows Firewall* link.

Step 3. Locate and check (enable) the *File and Printer Sharing* option. Click *OK*.

TECH TIP

Network printers

If a printer can be seen through the network, but cannot be printed to, verify the printer is up and has no error conditions on the front panel or LEDs. Print a test page using the front panel menu or by using certain buttons if possible. Verify that the network printer has a static IP address and is not configured for DHCP.

Impact Printer Troubleshooting

When technicians state that a print head is not firing, this means that one or more of the print wires are not coming out of the print head to impact the ribbon. A print head that is not firing is evidenced by one or more white lines appearing where the printed dots should be. On a printed page, the white line appears horizontally in the middle of a line. The most likely problem is the print head. However, be aware that the problem could be a bad driver transistor on the main circuit board or a loose cable that attaches to the print head. But because the print head is a mechanical part, it is the most suspect.

If the print is light and then dark, the printer ribbon may not be advancing properly. One of the shafts that insert into each end of the ribbon may not be turning, or the set of gears under the shaft may not mesh properly. Also, there is a motor that handles ribbon movement, and this motor may need replacement. A faulty ribbon can also cause the carriage to seize up. Remove the ribbon and power up the printer. If the carriage moves when the ribbon is removed, but it will not move when the ribbon is installed, replace the ribbon. Some printers have belts that move the print head across the page. A worn, loose, or slipping belt can cause erratic printing.

TECH TIP

Light printing can be caused by several things

Adjust the print head gap to place the print head closer to the ribbon or replace the ribbon. Also, the platen could be misaligned with the bottom paper-feed rollers.

If the printer prints continuously on the same line, be sure the setting for tractor-fed paper or friction-fed paper is correct. Or, the motor that controls paper movement may need replacement. If the printer moves the paper up a small bit after printing, the model may have the Auto Tear Off feature enabled. The Auto Tear Off feature is used with perforated forms needed in many businesses. See the printer's documentation to disable this feature.

Inkjet Printer Troubleshooting

Most inkjet printer troubleshooting involves the print head. Inkjet printers frequently have a built-in print head cleaning routine. Access the routine through the printer's buttons or through software. Most manufacturers recommend cleaning the inkjet cartridge only when there is a problem such as lines or dots missing from the printed output. Otherwise, cleaning the inkjet cartridge with this method wastes ink and shortens the print cartridge's life span.

Usually, inkjet manufacturers include an alignment program to align the dots more precisely. Use the alignment program when vertical lines or characters do not align properly. If the colors do not appear correctly (such as **prints in the wrong color**), check ink levels and run the printer manufacturer-provided color calibration routine. Refer to the printer's documentation for troubleshooting programs, such as the print head cleaning, calibration, and alignment routines.

TECH TIP

Doesn't print in color

Check the printer properties to see if the grayscale option is selected.

Laser Printer Troubleshooting

Laser printers have more mechanical and electronic circuitry than the other printer types, which means there are more things that can go wrong. The following list contains some common symptoms and possible solutions:

> If black **streaks** appear on the paper, the problem causes are the drum, toner cartridge, fusing assembly, or the paper. If the drum cannot hold a charge in a particular place, it can't attract

toner to that area. The drum might have to be replaced. The drum can be part of the toner cartridge or might be a separate unit. The toner cartridge is the easiest thing to replace to see if the streaks stop. Some cartridges have a sliding plastic strip that can be used to remove excess toner from the opening. A dirty or damaged fusing assembly can also cause black streaks. Allow the printer to cool before checking the fuser cleaning pad for toner particles and using a small screwdriver to scrape off the excess particles before reinstalling. Finally, the paper might have a static charge, so fan the paper before reinstalling. This is common on low-humidity days.

> If output appears darker in some spots than others, remove the toner cartridge. Gently rock the toner cartridge back and forth to redistribute the toner. If this does not fix the problem, turn down the toner density by using the *Devices and Printers* Control Panel or software provided by the printer manufacturer. Also, the paper could be too smooth.

> If printing appears light, adjust the darkness setting on the printer or through the printer's operating system settings. The toner cartridge could be low. Damp paper could also cause this symptom. Use fresh paper of the proper weight and finish. If the print appears consistently dark, adjust the darkness setting.

> If a horizontal line appears periodically throughout the printout, the problem is one of the rollers. Check all the rollers to see if one is dirty or gouged and needs to be replaced. The rollers in a laser printer are not all the same size; the distance between the lines is the circumference of the roller. This allows you to easily tell which rollers are definitely not the problem and which ones are likely candidates.

> When white **vertical lines** appear, the corona wires may have paper bits or something else stuck on them. It may also mean that something is caught in the developer unit (located in the cartridge). Replace the cartridge to see if this is the problem.

> Why is the other side of the printed page smudged? The fuser could be faulty, the wrong type of paper could be being used, or the toner may be leaking.

Many laser printer problems involve the toner cartridge, which is a good thing because the cartridge is a part people normally have on hand. Various symptoms can occur because of the toner cartridge: **ghost images**, smearing, **horizontal streaking**, **vertical streaking**, faded printing, one vertical black line, one horizontal black line, a white streak on one side, a wavy image, and so on. One of the easiest things to do is to remove the toner cartridge, hold the cartridge in front of you with both hands, and rock the cartridge away from you and then back toward you. Reinsert the cartridge into the printer and test the printer.

Sometimes, the primary corona wire or the conditioning roller inside the toner cartridge needs to be cleaned. Clean the corona wires with the provided brush or with a cotton swab. Dampen the cotton swab with alcohol, if necessary. Clean the conditioning roller with a lint-free cloth, and dampen the cloth with alcohol, if necessary.

When **toner is not fused** to the paper, you need to determine whether a problem is in the fuser assembly or elsewhere in the printer. Send any output to the printer. When the printer is through with the writing stage and before the toner fuses to the paper, open the laser printer cover and remove the paper. (Determining exactly when to open the cover may take several attempts.) If the paper is error-free, the problem is most likely in the transfer corona (or transfer roller) or fusing assembly.

Experience is the best teacher when it comes to printers. If you work on a couple impact models, a couple inkjet printers, and a couple laser printer models, you will see the majority of problems. Each type of printer has very few circuit boards to replace. Normally, the problems are in the moving parts or are software related.

SOFT SKILLS—WORK ETHICS

Ethics is a set of morals by which you live or work. Employers want employees who possess high ethical standards. This means they want people who are honest, trustworthy, and dependable. IT technicians are exposed to many personal things—passwords, private data, and visited Internet sites, just to name a few. Employers do not want to worry about technicians taking things that belong to others, looking at data that does not relate to the computer problem at hand, and taking or giving away things from the office.

The best ruling factor in ethics is to always be professional. For example, if you are in a situation where someone asks you to share another person's password, ask yourself whether divulging the information is professional. When opening a customer's documents and reading them, ask yourself whether you are being professional. If the answer is no, stop reading. If you are in a customer's office and accidentally see the person's password taped to a CD case, let the person know that you have seen it, suggest that passwords should not be kept in a conspicuous place, and recommend that the passwords be changed right away. One of the biggest assets an IT professional can have is his or her reputation. Being ethical at work goes a long way in establishing a good reputation.

Finally, every IT person can probably remember at least one instance when he or she was asked to do something unethical—charge for more time than was actually spent on a job, provide access to a room or an area where access is normally restricted, or grant privileges that others at the same level do not have. When put in such a situation, there are a few options: (1) Be polite and refuse, (2) adamantly refuse, or (3) report the person to a supervisor. Recommending what to do is difficult, but for most offenses, being polite and refusing is the best course of action and is the most professional. If a request is against corporate policy or could hurt others in the company, you need to report this to a company manager or security. Your own boss may be the best person to inform.

Chapter Summary

> Five types of printers commonly seen in businesses are impact, inkjet, laser, thermal and 3-D printers. Laser and inkjet printers do high-quality printing. A laser printer's supplies cost more than other printers' supplies but last longer and work out to a lower cost per page.

> Printers can be shared using the operating system and a computer connected to a network. A printer can also have its own wired or wireless networking connectivity. With wired networking, the printer has a direct connection to the network. Wireless networking includes 802.11 and Bluetooth technologies. A hardware print server can be attached to a printer to allow sharing, too.

> Impact printers use print wires to impact a ribbon. Inkjet printers use pressure or heat to squirt ink dots onto paper. A laser printer works like a copying machine to produce output.

> The laser printer printing steps include processing and rasterizing the data followed by charging, exposing, developing, transferring, fusing, and cleaning.

> Impact printers can use normal-sized paper and fan-folded paper with pin holes that are fed by a tractor. Laser printers can have extra drawers for paper. A duplexing assembly option can be attached to allow a printer to print on both sides of the paper without intervention. Impact printers use special heat-sensitive paper.

> Print drivers must match the Windows version.

> A printer uses a print spooler or hard drive space that keeps data flowing to the printer in large print jobs. The print spooler can be stopped and started using the Services window (services.msc).

> If a printer doesn't work, check the printer display, the computer for any messages, and that the correct printer was chosen.
> A laser maintenance kit includes parts from a manufacturer that need to be changed after the printer has been used for so many hours. The contents are vendor-specific. The maintenance counter must be reset after a maintenance kit has been applied.
> Printers can be networked by having wired or wireless networking capabilities, connect to a print server, be registered in the cloud, or be shared through the printer to which they attach.
> Virtual printing can be accomplished through the print to file, print to PDF, print to XPS, or print to image option.
> Common printer problems include streaks, light print, ghost images, toner not fusing to the paper, paper path issues, connectivity to the printer, print driver, security settings, and error codes that appear on the printer display.
> A computer technician needs to show ethical work behavior around customers and peers.

A+ CERTIFICATION EXAM TIPS

✓ Know how impact, inkjet, laser, and thermal printers work.

✓ Know the laser printer parts: imaging drum, fuser assembly, transfer belt, transfer roller, pickup rollers, separate pads, and duplexing assembly.

✓ Know the laser imaging process: processing, charging, exposing, developing, transferring, fusing, and cleaning.

✓ Know the inket printer parts: ink cartridge, print head, roller, feeder, duplexing assembly, carriage, and belt.

✓ Know the thermal printer parts: feed assembly, heating element, special thermal paper.

✓ Know the impact printer parts: print head, ribbon, tractor feed, and impact paper.

✓ Know the virtual printing types: print to file, print to PDF, print to XPS, and print to image.

✓ Know the appropriate laser printer maintenance techniques including the following: replacing toner, applying a maintenance kit, calibration, and cleaning.

✓ Know the appropriate thermal printer maintenance techniques including the following: replacing paper, cleaning the heating element, and removing debris.

✓ Know the appropriate thermal printer maintenance techniques including the following: replacing paper, cleaning the heating element, and removing debris.

✓ Know the appropriate impact printer maintenance techniques including the following: replacing the ribbon, replacing the print head, and replacing paper.

✓ Know the appropriate inkjet printer maintenance techniques including the following: cleaning the heads, replacing cartridges, calibration, and clearing jams.

✓ Be able to configure printer options, including paper trays.

✓ Know how to review and control the print driver and print spooler.

✓ Know how to network a printer using a print server, printer sharing, cloud printing, Bonjour, and AirPrint; be aware of data privacy issues including user authentication that may be required, hard drive caching, and seeing corporate/private information that may be printed.

✓ Review all the troubleshooting sections (especially the key term items) before taking the exam.

Key Terms

Review Questions

1. What method does a technician *normally* use to print a test page to prove that connectivity exists between the computer and the printer and to prove that the driver is working properly?

    a. Use a self-test button on the printer.

    b. Use Notepad and print.

    c. Use at least two applications and print.

    d. Use the *Print Test Page* button from the printer properties' *General* tab.

2. Which type of printer would a glass blower who sells art at trade shows most likely use to print receipts? [impact | inkjet | thermal | laser]

3. Which program is used to restart the print spooler in Windows?

    [Device Manager | Services | System Information | DirectX]

4. A Samsung laser printer is showing an error message on the screen that says that the paper is out, but the user shows you that there is plenty of paper in the bin. What should you do?

    a. Turn the printer off and back on again.

    b. Check the paper sensor for debris or dust.

    c. Use the reset sensor to reset the printer paper counter.

    d. Use the Print Test Page button from within Windows to verify connectivity.

5. Which type of printer contains a fuser assembly?

    [impact | inkjet | laser | thermal]

6. [T | F] Use compressed air with a plastic nozzle to remove toner from a laser printer.

7. For what do you use a printer-duplexing assembly?

    a. Two-sided printing

    b. Multiple paper trays

    c. Wired and wireless network connectivity

    d. Rasterization

8. Which component causes ghost images on laser printer output?

    [drum | fusing assembly | LED array/laser | pickup rollers | paper sensor]

9. A college president's administrative assistant calls to report that some pages of the board of trustees' 500-page document are printing only half a page. What is the problem and what can the technician recommend to do to get the document printed?

    a. The print cartridge is defective. Replace the cartridge and reprint.

    b. The print cartridge has toner that is not evenly distribu**ted.** Remove the cartridge, gently shake it back and forth, reinstall the cartridge, and reprint.

    c. The printer does not have enough memory. Ask the user to print a smaller number of pages at a time.

    d. The printer mainboard has issues. Use compressed air to remove dust and debris. Then, try to reprint the pages. Order a replacement mainboard and use another printer if the printing fails again.

10. One of the technicians in your shop frequently swaps parts that do not fix the problem. The parts taken out of customer machines are taken to build private customer computers. This is an example of poor _____. [professionalism | work ethics | relations | troubleshooting skills]

11. Which type of printer can output color documents the fastest? [impact | thermal | laser | inkjet]

12. Which printer option allows multiple copies of a document to be printed in page 1, 2, 3 order instead of all of the page 1s to be printed, then all of the page 2s, and then all of the page 3s? [fusing | collating | duplexing | conditioning]

13. A networked printer is visible through the network, but no one can print to it. What is the first thing the technician should check?

    a. print spooler setting

    b. printer IP address

    c. errors or indicators on the printer

    d. cabling

14. A laser printer outputs streaks on the paper. What is the issue? [drum | roller | ink cartridge | laser]

15. An inkjet printer output appears to have missing elements. What is the first thing that a technician should try if the ink cartridge appears to be full? _____

16. Describe a situation where cloud printing would be beneficial.

    _____

    _____

17. What is the purpose of the belt on an inkjet?

    a. limits the amount of paper fed through the printer to one page

    b. controls the amount of ink allowed onto the paper

    c. moves the paper through the paper path

    d. moves the carriage from one side to the other

18. What would happen if a heating element fails on a thermal printer?

    a. missing printed output

    b. paper doesn't feed through

    c. incorrect colors output

    d. garbled output

19. What is a common method used to perform laser printer calibration?

    a. with a multimeter

    b. with a special tool that is part of the maintenance kit

    c. through the printer menu

    d. with calipers

20. Which option is relevant to virtual printing? [duplexing | PDF | collating | cloud]

Exercises

Exercise10.1 Research a Local Printer

Objective: To use the Internet or a magazine to research information about a printer

Parts: A computer with Internet access

Notes: A printer is not required to be attached to the computer for this lab to be executed.

Procedure: Complete the following procedure and answer the accompanying questions.

A businessman is interested in purchasing two printers. Details for each printer are outlined as follows:

Printer A: A printer to be shared by all employees through the wired Ethernet network. Output should be high-quality black-and-white, grayscale, or color. The printer will not be used for huge print jobs, but to print a proposal for a client or a few handouts for a small number of participants in a presentation. Speed is not an issue.

Printer B: A printer model that will be standard for those that need a printer attached to their workstation. The printer should be able to support wired connectivity to the Ethernet LAN or IEEE 802.11 wireless connectivity. The printer might be shared with computers that do not have a local printer attached. The printer should support quality black-and-white, grayscale, or color. The printer will not be used for a large number of copies. Speed is not an issue. A scanner needs to be part of the printer, too. Concern for the cost of supplies is a concern.

1. Using the Internet, provide the businessman with three suggestions for Printer **A.** List the model number and at least five facts related to the criteri**a.** Find three price quotes for each suggested model and the name of the company for each.

    _____

    _____

2. Using the Internet, provide the businessman with three suggestions for Printer **B.** List the model number and at least five facts related to the criteri**a.** Find three price quotes for each suggested model and the name of the company the price was found.

    _____

    _____

Activities

Internet Discovery

Objective: To obtain specific information on the Internet regarding a computer or its associated parts

Parts: Computer with access to the Internet

Questions: Use the Internet to answer the following questions.

1. A customer has a broken USB inkjet printer that would cost more to repair than to replace. The customer is considering an Epson Expression XP-320 all-in-one printer as a replacement. The customer would also like to have wireless connectivity, cloud printing, and individual color cartridges. Will this printer meet the customer's needs? Explain your answer and write the URL where the information was found.

    _____

    _____

2. What is the latest print driver version for a Cannon PIXMA MG3120 printer if the customer has 64-bit Windows 10 installed? Note that you just want to reload the printer driver. Write the version number and the URL where you found the information.

   _____

   _____

   _____

3. A customer has a Lexmark E460 laser printer connected to a computer that has 32-bit Windows 7. Does Lexmark provide a Windows 7–capable printer driver for this printer? Write the answer and the URL where you found the solution.

   _____

   _____

4. How do you reset the HP LaserJet P2035 to factory default settings? Write the answer and list the URL where you found the answer.

   _____

   _____

   _____

5. You had to replace the drum on a Brother HL-L8250CDN color laser. What process is used to reset the drum unit counter?

   _____

   _____

   _____

   _____

Soft Skills

Objective: To enhance and fine-tune a technician's ability to listen, communicate in both written and oral form, and support people who use computers in a professional manner

Activities:

1. The class is divided into seven groups. Each group is assigned a laser printing process. The group has 20 minutes to research the process. At the end of 20 minutes, each team explains the process to the rest of the class.

2. Pretend you have a job as a computer technician. You just solved a printer problem. Using good written communication skills, document the problem as well as the solution in a professional format. Exchange your problem/solution with a classmate and critique each other's writings. Based on suggestions and your own background, refine your documentation. Share your documentation with the rest of the class.

   _____

   _____

   _____

   _____

   _____

   _____

Critical Thinking Skills

Objective: To analyze and evaluate information as well as apply learned information to new or different situations

Activities:

1.   Two networked PCs and a printer are needed for this activity. Connect a printer to a **PC.** Install the printer, configure the default settings to something different from the current settings, share the printer, and then print from another PC that connects to the same network.

2.   Interview a technician regarding a printing problem. List the steps that technician took and make notes about how he or she might have done the steps differently, based on what you have learned. Share the experience with the class.

Labs

Lab 10.1 Installing a Generic/Text-Only Print Driver on a Windows Vista, 7, 8, or 10 Computer

Objective: To install a generic print driver on a Windows computer and examine printer properties

Parts: Computer with Windows Vista, 7, 8, or 10 installed

Notes: (1) A printer is not required to be attached to the computer for this lab to be executed; (2) in order to install a printer, you must have the specific permission to install a printer and install a device driver.

Procedure: Complete the following procedure and answer the accompanying questions.

1.   Power on the computer and log on using the user ID and password provided by the instructor or lab assistant.

Is a printer attached to the PC? If so, does it attach using wireless or the USB port?

_____

2.   In Windows 7: Click the *Start* button > *Control Panel* > *Hardware and Sound* > *Devices and Printers* > *Add a Printer* link > *Add a local printer* > ensure the *Use an existing port* radio button is selected and the *LPT1: (Printer Port)* option is selected (no matter if a printer attaches to the PC already—you will not be printing from this print driver) > *Next* > in the *Manufacturer* column, select *Generic* > in the *Printers* column, select *Generic/Text Only* > *Next* > in the *Printer name* textbox, type **Class Printer**> *Next* > ensure the *Do not share this printer* radio button is enabled > *Next* > ensure the *Set as the default printer* checkbox is unchecked > *Finish*.

In Windows 8: Search for **printers** and select *Devices and Printers* from the resulting list > *Add a Printer* link > when the system starts searching for printers, select the *Stop* button > *The printer that I want isn't listed* link > enable (select) the radio button for *Add a local printer or network printer with manual settings* > *Next* > ensure the *Use an existing port* radio button is selected and the *LPT1: (Printer Port)* option is selected (no matter if a printer attaches to the PC already—you will not be printing from this print driver) > *Next* > in the *Manufacturer* column, select *Generic* > in the *Printers* column, select *Generic/Text Only* > *Next* > in the *Printer name* textbox, type **Class Printer**> *Next* > ensure the *Set as the default printer* checkbox is unchecked > *Finish*.

In Windows 10: Search for **printers** and select *Devices and Printers* from the resulting list > *Add a Printer* link > when the system starts searching for printers, go ahead and select *The printer that I want isn't listed* link > enable (select) the radio button for *Add a local printer or network printer with manual settings* > *Next* > ensure the *Use an existing port* radio button is selected and the *LPT1: (Printer Port)* option is selected (no matter if a printer attaches to the PC already—you will not be printing from this print driver) > *Next* > in the *Manufacturer* column, select *Generic* > in the *Printers* column, select *Generic/Text Only* > *Next* > in the *Printer name* textbox, type **Class Printer** > *Next* > ensure the *Set as the default printer* checkbox is unchecked > *Finish*.

3. From the *Devices and Printers* Control Panel, locate the *Class Printer icon*, right-click it, and select *Properties*.

   Which tabs are available with the generic print driver?

   _____

4. Click *OK*. Right-click the *Class Printer* icon again and select *Printer properties*.

   Which tabs are available through this option?

   _____

   _____

   Use Table 10.10 to list what is important about each tab or why a technician might use the tab.

   TABLE 10.10   Generic printer Printer properties tabs

Tab	Notes
General	
Sharing	
Ports	
Advanced	
Color Management	
Security	
Device Settings	
Printer Commands	
Font Selection	

   On the Ports tab, what do you think printer pooling is?

   _____

   _____

   Which button on the General tab do you think would be useful to a technician when troubleshooting a printing problem?

   _____

5. Close the window. Right-click on *Class Printer* and select *Printing Preferences*. In the *Orientation* section, select the *Landscape* option.

   How does this change printing?

   _____

6. Select the *Paper/Quality* tab. Click the *Paper Source* drop-down menu.

   Which options are available, even with a generic print driver?

   _____

7. Select the *Advanced* button.

   List three paper size options.

   _____

   _____

   _____

   _____

8. Click *Cancel*; click *Cancel* again. Then, access the *Printer properties* window.

9. Click the *Ports* tab. Notice how LPT1 is checked. If you made a mistake during installation and selected the wrong port, you can change it here. Notice how File: and XPS are options.

10. Access the *Advanced* tab. Select the *Printing Defaults* button. Through this option, you can select the default quality and orientation the printer uses to print. Users must change the settings if they want something other than this. Click *Cancel*. Click the *Separator Page* button.

    What is the purpose of a separator page?

    _____

    _____

11. Click *Cancel*. Click *OK*.

12. To rename the Class Printer driver, right-click on the *Class Printer* within the Control Panel > *Printer properties*. On the *General* tab, change the name of the printer in the first textbox to *IT Printer* > *OK*.

13. To delete the IT Printer, right-click on *IT Printer* > *Remove device* > *Yes*.

Lab 10.2 Installing a Local Printer on a Windows Vista/7/8/10 Computer

Objective: To install a local printer on a Windows Vista, 7, 8, or 10 computer

Parts: A computer with Windows Vista or 7 installed and a printer physically attached to an LPT, COM, or USB port

   Appropriate printer driver for Vista/7

   Internet connectivity or a printer driver

Notes: (1) Always refer to the printer installation guide for installing a new printer. Some printers have their own CD and installation wizard that installs the driver and software; (2) in order to install a printer, you must log on as an Administrator (or use a user ID that belongs to the Administrators group)

Procedure: Complete the following procedure and answer the accompanying questions.

1. Power on the computer and log on using the user ID and password provided by the instructor or lab assistant.

2. Use the Internet to research and download the printer driver based on the printer and operating system version installed. Otherwise, use the driver provided by the instructor or lab assistant.

   Which version of printer driver did you download or do you have?

   _____

3. Attach the printer cable to the correct computer port. Attach the power cord to the printer if necessary and insert the other end into a wall outlet. Power on the printer.

4. Windows normally detects a plug-and-play printer and may complete all the installation steps automatically.

   Does Windows automatically detect and install the printer?

   _____

5. If Windows cannot find the driver, you will be prompted to browse for a printer driver.

6. Once installed, print a test page to ensure communication between the computer and the printer.

    Did the printer print correctly? If not, delete the printer and complete the installation again.

_____

Lab 10.3 Explore a Windows Vista, 7, 8, or 10 Printer

Objective: To explore printer options available through Windows Vista, 7, 8, or 10

Parts: A computer with Windows Vista, 7, 8, or 10 installed and an installed printer

                    Optionally, access to the Internet for researching the latest printer driver

Procedure: Complete the following procedure and answer the accompanying questions.

Note: This process depends on the printer manufacturer. You may need to modify the initial steps to find the details for the specific printer.

1. Power on the computer and log in to Windows.

2. Access the *Devices and Printers* Control Panel. Right-click on the installed printer and select *Printing Preferences*.

    What is the default print quality mode for this printer?

_____

    Is this the most cost-efficient mode available? If not, what is?

_____

3. Using various Control Panel options, answer the following questions.

    a. List one instance in which a technician might use the *Pause Printing* option. If you do not know for sure, research the answer on the Internet.

_____

_____

    b. List the steps necessary to share this printer with other computers.

_____

_____

_____

_____

    c. Which printer option would you use to see how many documents have been sent to the printer?

_____

    d. List information that might be important for business documentation purposes.

_____

_____

_____

    e. What information is provided for troubleshooting printing problems?

_____

    f. To what port does the printer attach?

_____

    g. Which print spooler option is used?

_____

h. Which security options are currently used?

_____

i. If the printer was shared (whether it is or not is irrelevant), does the printer have the option to render print jobs on client computers?

_____

4.   When finished, close any open windows.

11 Mobile Devices

In this chapter you will learn:

> The operating systems mobile devices use

> How to configure mobile devices

> How to back up and secure mobile devices

> How to troubleshoot mobile devices

> The importance of appearance in the IT field

CompTIA Exam Objectives:

What CompTIA A+ exam objectives are covered in this chapter?

✓ 901-1.2 Explain the importance of motherboard components, their purpose, and properties.

✓ 901-1.3 Compare and contrast various RAM types and their features.

✓ 901-1.4 Install and configure PC expansion cards.

✓ 901-1.5 Install and configure storage devices and use appropriate media.

✓ 901-1.12 Install and configure common peripheral devices.

✓ 901-2.7 Compare and contrast Internet connection types, network types and their features.

✓ 901-3.1 Install and configure laptop hardware and components.

✓ 901-3.2 Explain the function of components within the display of a laptop.

✓ 901-3.3 Given a scenario, use appropriate laptop features.

✓ 901-3.4 Explain the characteristics of various types of other mobile devices.

✓ 901-3.5 Compare and contrast accessories & ports of other mobile devices.

✓ 901-4.4 Given a scenario, troubleshoot wired and wireless networks with appropriate tools.

✓ 901-4.5 Given a scenario, troubleshoot and repair common mobile device issues while adhering to the appropriate procedures.

✓ 902-2.5 Identify basic features of mobile operating systems.

✓ 902-2.6 Install and configure basic mobile device network connectivity and email.

✓ 902-2.7 Summarize methods and data related to mobile device synchronization.

✓ 902-3.5 Compare and contrast various methods for securing mobile devices.

✓ 902-3.7 Given a scenario, secure SOHO wireless and wired networks.

✓ 902-4.3 Given a scenario, troubleshoot common mobile OS and application issues with appropriate tools.

✓ 902-4.4 Given a scenario, troubleshoot common mobile OS and application security issues with appropriate tools.

Mobile Device Overview

Mobile devices are an integrated part of today's society. **Wearable devices** such as smart watches, fitness monitors, glasses, and headsets allow us to take our technology wherever we go. Everywhere you look, there are laptops, Android phones, Apple iPhones and iPads, phablets, and new electronics being introduced. Many mobile devices are all-in-one units. Because they have no keyboard, much of the device is devoted to being a touchpad. They are designed to be quick, light, durable, and portable (see Figure 11.1). For some users, they are a second computer—often using these smaller mobile devices while on the go and leaving their desktop model or even their laptop at home. Table 11.1 contains characteristics of various mobile devices.

FIGURE 11.1   Mobile devices

TABLE 11.1   Mobile devices

Mobile device	Description
Tablet	A mobile device that has a touch screen, camera(s), microphone, and possibly one or more ports such as sound, USB, miniDisplayPort, or miniThunderbolt. Tablets connect to the Internet, take, send, receive, and store pictures and video, and are often a good choice for people who travel, people with smaller hands, and young adults. See Figure 11.2.
GPS	Global positioning system or GPS is a series of satellites that provide location, movement, and time information to other devices. A device that supports GPS can be a standalone unit, software that communicates with the satellites, or an app on a mobile device. Figure 11.3 shows a geodesist using GPS at a construction site.
Smartphone	Has the capability to make a call and run apps, play music, track movement using GPS, connect to a wireless network, connect wirelessly to other devices, connect to the Internet through the phone network or wireless network (see Figure 11.4), and take high-resolution pictures and video. Three popular smartphone operating systems are Android, Windows mobile operating system, and Apple iOS.

Mobile device	Description
Phablet	A cross between a smartphone and a tablet. Tend to have a larger screen than a smartphone. Designed more for taking notes or viewing documents easier. May include a stylus, as shown in Figure 11.5.
e-reader	Also known as an e-book. Has an LCD screen designed for reading and storing digital books (see Figure 11.6), magazines, and other online materials. Battery life is extended; some might adapt to the ambient light to better read the text.
Smart camera	Has one or more extra capabilities than a digital camera that are used for such things as facial recognition, measuring, inspection for quality assurance, surveillance, and robot guidance. May include a mobile operating system, have Internet access, and support for wired and wireless networking. To operate an integrated camera on an Apple iOS or Android device, use the Camera option from the home page. Use the Photos application (iOS) or Gallery application (Android) to see the saved images. See Figure 11.7 to see the smart camera attached to a drone.

FIGURE 11.2   Tablet

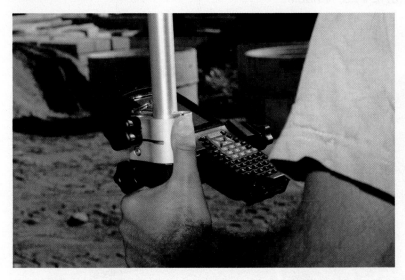

FIGURE 11.3   GPS

FIGURE 11.4   Smartphone

FIGURE 11.5   Phablet

FIGURE 11.6   e-reader

FIGURE 11.7   Smart camera

Mobile Operating System Basics and Features

Mobile devices need an operating system as any computer does. The mobile operating system can be proprietary to a particular vendor, but three common mobile operating systems are Android, iOS, and Windows. **Android** is an open source operating system that is based on the Linux kernel and used for phones and tablets, but is available on laptops and PCs. **Open source** operating systems allow vendors to use the core source code and gives vendors the ability to customize the operating system. Google, Inc. purchased Android in 2005 and it continues to be the most popular mobile operating system (mobile OS) in the world.

Apple's **iOS** is found only on Apple devices. This is an example of a **closed source** or **vendor-specific operating system.** This type of operating system is not allowed to be modified or distributed by anyone other than those designated by the developer such as Apple Inc. Microsoft has several closed source **Windows Mobile** operating systems that relate to mobile devices. Note that some mobile devices support the normal Windows desktop operating system versions. Here are the ones specifically related to mobile devices that are not the full version of Windows:

> Windows Phone: A family of operating systems designed for smartphones.
> Windows 10 Mobile: Successor to Windows Phone that integrates some features common to the Windows desktop and mobile devices into smartphones and small tablets.
> Windows RT: An operating system based on reduced instruction set computing (RISC) architectures, which allows for thinner, lighter, cooler mobile devices and can run longer on battery. Only executes software digitally signed by Microsoft and Windows Store apps.

Mobile Storage

Mobile devices need a place to store data and mobile storage uses the same technology as some PC storage, but of course, the storage media is smaller. Mobile devices do have RAM. Sometimes this RAM is not upgradable in mobile devices such as tablets and smartphones. However, storage in mobile devices is sometimes available using flash memory. **Flash memory** is a type of nonvolatile, solid-state memory that holds data even when the computer power is off. Smartphones, tablets, and other mobile devices use flash memory to store the operating system, apps, and data/video storage. Flash memory for mobile devices includes various types of Secure Digital (**SD**) cards: SD, **miniSD**, **microSD**, SDHC, miniSDHC, microSDHC, SDXC, microSDXC, extreme digital (**xD**), and probably more since this book has been published. On some phones, the micro memory chip is found when removing the back cover and the battery.

Another flash technology used with mobile devices is CompactFlash. **CompactFlash** (CF) has two main standards: CompactFlash and CF+. CompactFlash is a small, 50-pin removable storage device that allows speeds up to 133MB/s. CF cards can store 512GB or more. The CF+ standard allows increased functionality with cards available for Ethernet, fax/modem/wireless, and barcode scanners.

CF cards can be inserted directly into many devices, such as cameras, smartphones, network devices, and tablet PCs. A CF card uses flash memory, which does not require a battery to keep the data saved to it. A CF card can also be installed into a computer with a CF card reader. The CF technology is also used in solid-state drives. Figure 11.8 shows a photo of three flash memory cards (with the CF card on the left and two types of SD cards to the right).

FIGURE 11.8 Flash storage

Flash memory or **storage cards** are found in mobile devices and laptops, but also in desktop computers. Some devices have an SD card slot built into the devices such as the laptop shown in Figure 11.9. Some have an SD tray that pulls out. Insert the flash card into the tray (with the contacts facing down), and then push the tray into the device. Sometimes in order to insert a microSD card into a laptop or tablet, an adapter may have to be purchased so that the microSD card can be used. Figure 11.10 shows how the microSD card inserts into an adapter. That adapter must match the slot size (normally SD) of the mobile device.

FIGURE 11.9 Laptop SD card slot

FIGURE 11.10   Flash media adapter

Flash media is commonly installed in Apple and Android products. When you install flash media into an Android tablet or phone, you can use the *Settings > Storage* option to view the internal memory capacity and any additional memory storage. For an iOS-based device, go to *Settings > General* to see the amount of memory installed.

Some people like to buy a media card reader (also known as a multi-card reader or flash/flash memory card reader) so they can quickly and easily transfer pictures, data, movies, etc. to a PC. Some card readers accept 75 different types of media storage. The card reader attaches to a USB port. Figure 11.11 shows a multi-card reader.

FIGURE 11.11   Multi-card reader

TECH TIP

Don't format CF cards with Windows

If Windows is used to format a CF card, it will place a different file system on the card. Windows can be used to read files from the card or place files on the card, but best practice is to use the formatting option on the device instead of using Windows to format a CF card.

Mobile Wearable Technology Devices

Mobile technology also includes some cool wearable items, such as watches, shoes, and even earrings. Table 11.2 lists some wearable technologies.

TABLE 11.2   Wearable technology

Mobile technology	Description
Smart watch	Like a tiny computer strapped to your wrist (see Figure 11.12). Expensive, but not capable of doing all that your tablet can do. Most smart watches will sync up with a smartphone and support app downloading. Usually must be paired with a phone to make phone calls (some require a nearby microphone). Some can be GPS-enabled so they can be used for tasks such as tracking fitness goals.
Fitness monitor	Detects movement (step counting), calculates distances (some have a GPS feature), counts calories, measures heart rate and pulse, and measures sleep. Some can automatically sync up with a smartphone to keep track of daily/weekly workout activities. Usually water and dust-resistant with a common battery life of a week. Figure 11.13 shows how a smart watch, fitness monitor, and smartphone might all be able to share information.
Glasses	A wearable technology that has a tiny computer display visible to one eye; allows taking photos, videos, making calls; commonly has a processor, RAM, and storage. Could support 3D. See Figure 11.14.
Smart shoes	Allows control of wireless devices such as smartphones and appliances using foot movements.
Earring	Wearable technology that tracks heart rate and calories burned.

FIGURE 11.12   Smart watches

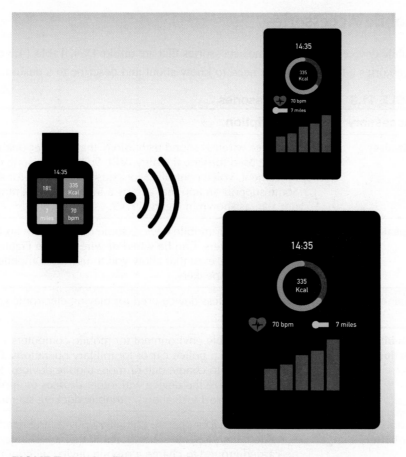

FIGURE 11.13 Fitness monitor

FIGURE 11.14 Wearable technology glasses

Mobile Accessories

Mobile devices also have some accessories that are unlike PCs. Table 11.3 outlines various mobile accessories a technician may need to know about and describe to a customer.

TABLE 11.3 Mobile accessories

Accessory	Description
Headset	Wired or wireless sound technology that fits over one or both ears. Might also be used for virtual reality (VR). Some allow song control by head movement, voice controlled, or pause music play for an incoming call. Some support an app that acts as a trainer or track fitness. May be for only one ear, as shown in Figure 11.15.
Speaker	Built in to your mobile device; some devices have an audio port for external speakers. Can be wired or wireless (see Figure 11.16 for a wireless speaker). Apps exist that allow you to use other mobile devices in the area as additional speakers.
Game pad	Wired or wireless device used for playing electronic games, as shown in Figure 11.17.
Mobile docking station	Provides a stable environment for mobile computers while traveling such as for a laptop in a police car or for military operations. Docking stations are also available to charge one or more mobile devices. Some docking stations also synchronize the device with other devices or applications while charging. Figure 11.18 shows a mobile docking station.
Extra **battery pack** or **battery charger**	All mobile devices operate on battery power and need to be charged. Portable battery chargers are available that are charged and then can be carried around to charge a mobile device without having to attach the mobile device to a wall outlet or PC. Figure 11.19 shows a portable charger.
Protective cover	Because mobile devices are easily dropped, they frequently have either a protective cover for the entire device or a protective cover for just the screen. Figure 11.20 shows the two concepts.
Waterproofing	Waterproofing protects mobile devices from liquids, but there are different levels of protection. Some covers may be waterproof, the device itself might come in a waterproof model, or a waterproof option may be available for the entire device. Waterproof bags are available for mobile devices. There are also treatments that can protect the electronics for accidental immersion. Figure 11.21 shows a waterproof cell phone.
Credit card reader	Credit card readers can be wired or wireless and could attach to a tablet or other mobile device. Some allow printed receipts; others allow an email address to be input instead. Point of sale stands exist that are made specifically for Apple iPads or Android-based tablets. Figure 11.22 shows a credit card reader.
Smart card reader	A device that reads data encrypted on small ID-sized cards. Used in government IDs (with such information as medical/dental records), mobile phones as a subscriber ID module, driver's licenses, some credit cards, and employee badges. Figure 11.23 shows a smart card reader.

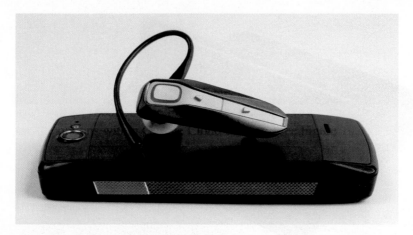

FIGURE 11.15   Wireless headset

FIGURE 11.16   Wireless speaker

FIGURE 11.17   Game pad

FIGURE 11.18   Mobile docking station

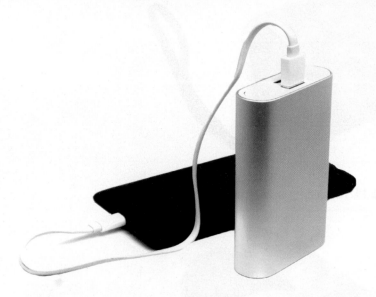

FIGURE 11.19   Portable charger

FIGURE 11.20   Mobile device screen protection

FIGURE 11.21   Waterproof cell phone

FIGURE 11.22   Mobile credit card reader

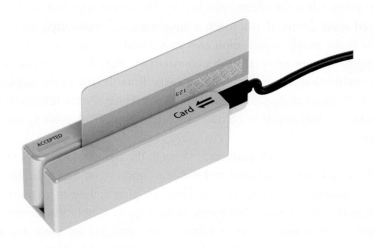

FIGURE 11.23   Smart card reader

Using Mobile Devices

A mobile operating system is different in that, instead of primarily using a mouse or keyboard to interact with the operating system, a finger, stylus, spoken word, or multiple fingers are used. Figure 11.24 shows an ASUS tablet home page that uses Android as the operating system. Figure 11.25 shows an Android-based smartphone. Note that the notification area for a smartphone is usually provided by pulling down a menu from the top of the screen.

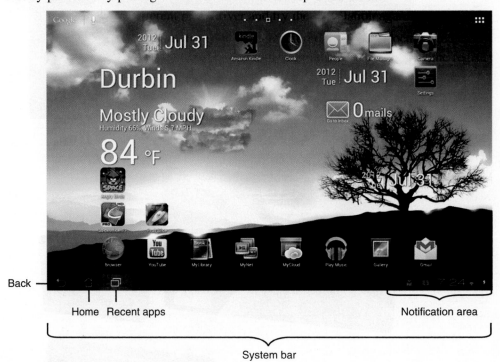

FIGURE 11.24   ASUS tablet home screen

Notice in Figure 11.24 how the **system bar** extends across the bottom of the screen. The back button on the far left is used to return to the previous page. If the keyboard screen is open, the back button will close the keyboard. The home button is used to return to the main home page, but keep in mind that other home pages may be available to the left or right. The third icon from the left on the system bar is the recent apps button. The recent apps button shows thumbnail views of recently used applications. If you touch a thumbnail, the application opens full screen. In the far right corner is the mobile **notification area** that contains icons, such as the battery life, wireless signal strength, time, or external media connectivity. Note that on a smartphone (refer to Figure 11.25), the notification area is commonly a swipe from the top of the display.

Figure 11.26 shows an Apple iOS home page. An Apple iPad or iPhone has a physical home button (not an icon to tap) beside or below the screen. On an iPad, pushing the home button removes the keyboard.

Configuration is commonly performed through the mobile device's *Settings* option, but before getting into any of those, you have to be able to understand touch displays. Touching a display instructs the operating system to do something. Swiping is used to go to the next page of applications or go to the next photo. Multitouch technology is simply the capability to accept multiple touches, such as when two fingers or a finger and a knuckle are used. 3-D touch involves lightly tapping the touch screen to open an application, tapping and holding for a second performs a different function, and still pressing down firmly on the same area performs a third function. This technology is continually evolving.

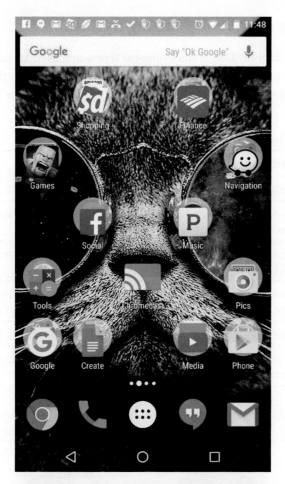

FIGURE 11.25   Android smartphone home screen

FIGURE 11.26   iOS home screen

Interacting with a Mobile Operating System

When interacting with a mobile OS, some common terms are used to control the applications and icons. These terms are described in Table 11.4. As you can see from this list of terms, some interaction requires multitouch. Not all screens support this feature. Refer to Figure 11.27 to see multitouch techniques.

TABLE 11.4   Mobile operating system interaction

Term	Description
Touch or tap	Press an icon or area. Used to open an application.
Double tap	Press an icon or area twice. Used to enlarge an area of a screen or an item such as a picture.
Long touch or touch and hold	Press and hold on an icon or area. Used to move an icon from one home screen to a different home screen or to unlock a tablet.
Swipe or flick	Press and move to the left or right or up and down. Used to move from one home screen to another or to open the notification area on a smartphone.
Scroll	Press and move up or down. Used to quickly go through a list of files or pictures.
Pinch or pinch close	Using two fingers spread apart, bring the fingers closer together. Used to zoom out from an object or area.
Spread or pinch open	Using two fingers close together, move the fingers apart. Used to zoom in on an object or area such as when you want to be able to see a closer view of a map or to read words.

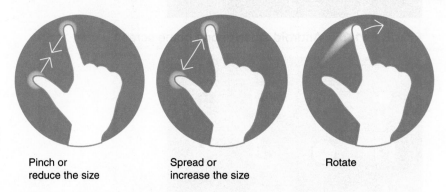

Pinch or
reduce the size

Spread or
increase the size

Rotate

FIGURE 11.27   Multitouch techniques

TECH TIP

What if a device goes to sleep?

Press the power button and optionally enter a pattern, PIN, or passcode. On an Android device, press and drag the lock icon to the unlock icon in the center of the display. Pressing the home button also awakens an iPhone or iPad. Slide the *slide to unlock* bar to the right and optionally enter the passcode.

Cell Phones

Most people are familiar with what a cell phone is, but technicians need to know a little more than the normal user about the phone. Also, some companies issue phones to employees that technicians support. Learning about how phones are identified and when they should be updated is important.

IMEI and IMSI

International mobile equipment identity (IMEI) is a unique number given to a particular cell phone and some satellite phones. It is like a serial number. IMEI numbers are stored in a database or the equipment identity register (EIR). When phones are reported stolen, the database can be updated to mark the number as invalid. When buying a used phone, you might want to check the IMEI number against a mobile blacklist to ensure it has not been lost or stolen.

A company may track IMEIs. The IMEI number is commonly found using one of the following methods:

> Look on the back of the phone.
> Look under the battery. Figure 11.28 shows two smartphones that have the back removed and the battery exposed.
> Use the phone's *Settings > General* or *Settings > About phone* option.
> Dial `*#06#`.
> Look in the SIM card tray for an engraved number or under the SIM card.
> Plug the phone into a PC, and then open *iTunes*. Select the phone from the *Device* menu > *Summary* tab.
> Use Google Dashboard (www.google.com/settings/dashboard) > expand *Android* > locate, and then select *phone*.
> Look on the original box the device came in.
> Use your network provider's website.

Battery

FIGURE 11.28   Cell phones with backs removed

International mobile subscriber identity (**IMSI**) is a unique number that is stored in your smartphone's subscriber identification module (SIM) card. A **SIM** card is used in mobile phones, satellite phones, mobile devices, and laptops. It contains electronics that provide storage of information, such as personal contacts, numbers, phone services, security authentication, and a security personal identification number (PIN). Figure 11.29 shows a SIM card.

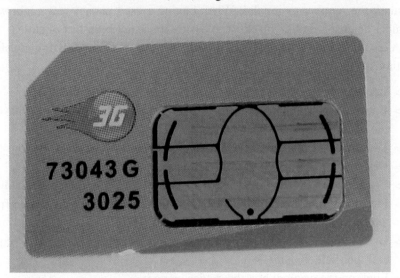

FIGURE 11.29 SIM card

The IMSI has three parts including the country code, the network code (identifies the provider network), and a unique number. The IMSI is used when your phone's network connects to any other network or type of network, such as when you call someone that uses another phone network or call someone's home using your cell phone. The reason this is important is because roaming charges may be assessed on calls that go through or to another network or how many minutes you have on a particular plan.

PRI and PRL Updates

Each phone contains a specific product release instruction (**PRI**) configuration file. This file contains what frequency bands can be used and the default preferred roaming list (**PRL**) to use. The PRL is created by the cell network provider. The information is stored in your phone and used when connecting to a cell tower. The PRL includes service provider IDs and prioritized systems the device may access, such as companies with which a particular company has agreements so that the user may "roam" and still maintain the ability to make/receive calls. PRL updates are automatically pushed out to the latest phones. Most companies have a specific code that can be used to update the latest PRL.

TECH TIP

Why would I want to update the PRL?

Manually update the PRL if the phone is frequently used outside of the "home network" area.

The PRL is what allows a phone to provide a roaming indicator such as when the phone is in its home network (not roaming), when off the home network (roaming), or when roaming is disabled. Phone and data roaming can usually be enabled/disabled through the phone *Settings* option.

Baseband Updates and Radio Firmware

Baseband is a type of signal used in telecommunications networks. A baseband signal is used to send updates to mobile devices such as mobile phones. Actually the **baseband update** is applied to the phone's **radio firmware**, which is low-level software that manages items related to a phone's radio. The radio is what allows a phone to connect to a cellular network, send and receive data, and send and receive phone calls. Firmware is specific to a device and sometimes to a phone network provider.

Some users like replacing the operating system that comes with the phone with another one. The problem is that the phone vendor will send updates to both the operating system and the firmware. When either the operating system or the firmware gets updated without the other (such as when someone loads her own operating system), then problems such as dropped calls, overheating, reduced battery life, reduced time on a single battery charge, poor or no performance on a particular port, high resource utilization, etc. can occur.

To determine the software version and baseband version on a phone, the following generic steps are provided:

> iPhone: *Settings > General > About > Check iPhone firmware version* in the *Version* section for the main operating system version and then *check iPhone Baseband version* in the *Modem Firmware* section for the radio firmware version.
> Android: *Settings > About/About device > Software information.*
> Windows: From *Start,* swipe left to access the *App list > Settings > About > More info.*

See Figure 11.30 for a screenshot from an Android phone.

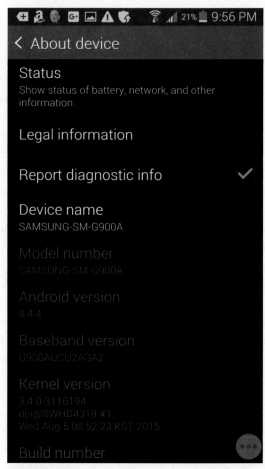

FIGURE 11.30   Cell phone operating system/radio firmware versions

Mobile Apps

Applications, commonly called *apps*, for mobile devices come with the device, can be downloaded free of charge, or can be purchased through the App Store (Apple iOS devices), Google Play (Android devices), or Store (Windows devices). As a result of the mobility features, new apps are being developed constantly, and applications that might not be of much use with a desktop computer are very handy on mobile devices. Table 11.5 shows common mobile apps.

TABLE 11.5   Common mobile apps

Android apps	iOS apps	Windows apps
Gmail	Mail	Mail
Google Maps	Maps	Maps
Gallery/Photos	Photos	Photos
MyLibrary	iBooks	Reader
Chrome	Safari	Edge
Play Music	iTunes	Music
Clock	Calendar	Calendar
Play Store	App Store	Windows Store

Common Apps and Features

One commonly used app is GPS. With GPS, satellites send location information to a receiver on a mobile device. Most mobile devices have GPS capability. Mobile apps provide directions to get to a store or where another person is located, and they show how far you have walked.

Some people disable the GPS capability until they want to use it because of geotracking. **Geotracking** is the ability to track where you are located or, more accurately, where your phone is located. Many applications and social media rely on such data to "publish" your current location or the location of friends you have selected. These are known as **locator apps**. Vendors have pay plans that include the ability to track family members. Companies use geotracking to locate lost and stolen mobile devices. Figure 11.31 shows the concept of geo-tracking.

Gaming on smartphones and tablets has been enhanced through the use of accelerometers and gyroscopes. An **accelerometer** detects the device orientation and adapts what is shown on the screen, based on the device orientation. This is how you can hold a tablet in portrait mode and then move it to a horizontal position to show a landscape picture better. A **gyroscope** measures or maintains orientation.

Because the screen is used to interact with the operating system, screen calibration may need to be performed. Android users use the *Settings* app. Windows users use *Settings > Calibrate the screen for pen and touch input > Calibrate*. You can also download an app to perform screen calibration tasks, such as the following:

> Color calibration
> Sensitivity
> One-hand configuration
> Motion/gestures configuration

FIGURE 11.31   Geotracking in action

Table 11.6 explains some mobile operating system features.

TABLE 11.6   Mobile operating system features

Feature	Description
Internet calling	Use an app such as Skype, Google Hangouts, or WhatsApp to call another person.
Wi-Fi calling	Make a call using a Wi-Fi connection rather than the cell phone network; beneficial when the phone network has a weak signal or to avoid using cell phone network minutes. Some vendors have this as a built-in service, which allows you to use your existing phone contacts.
Virtual assistant	Use voice commands to obtain information such as directions, current sports scores, dictate emails, or text; examples include Apple's Siri, Microsoft's Cortana, Google Now, and SVoice.
Emergency notification	Obtain wireless emergency alerts (WEA); a U.S. method for propagating emergency alerts such as announcements from the national weather service, presidential messages, and emergency operation centers to mobile devices.
Mobile payment service	Pay for services or goods through a mobile device instead of with money or a credit card. Popular in developing countries where banking is not as prevalent as elsewhere. Transactions can be conducted using near field communication (NFC), wireless application protocol (WAP) browser or app, direct mobile billing, or short message service (SMS). See Figure 11.32.
Launcher	Perform administrative tasks such as creating and managing multiple applications using a tool found in the Windows and Apple's versions of the software development kit (SDK). On Android, it is the part of the user interface that allows apps not on the home screen to be managed. A launcher allows manipulation of the graphical user interface (**GUI**) so that multiple apps and/or commands are easily deployed. Some mobile OSes allow creating app groups. See Figure 11.33.

FIGURE 11.32   Mobile wallet

FIGURE 11.33 Application launcher

Obtaining, Installing, and Removing Apps

Mobile device apps are obtained from an outside source such as **Google Play**, Apple's **App Store** (or through iTunes), **Microsoft Store**, Amazon's Appstore for Android, and a host of other content sources. There are other ways to get an app: manually install (side load), use a USB cable (commonly requires a file management app), use your storage media and a media reader, use an app such as Bump to transfer an application (or photos), or use a quick response (QR) code between two devices. An example of a QR code is in Figure 11.32 at the bottom of the cell phone screen. Note that whatever method you use to install an app, you must ensure that the app is from a trusted source or a trusted app developer. Be sure to see what permissions are given when an app is installing. Table 11.7 shows tasks that are commonly done with apps.

TABLE 11.7 Mobile device tasks*

Task	Platform	Description
Delete an app.	Android	Press and hold the app icon and drag it to the trash can.
Delete an app.	iOS	Press and hold the app icon until it jiggles and press the X that appears beside the icon. Press the menu key to stop the jiggling.
Delete an app.	Windows	Press and hold the app icon > tap *Uninstall* > *Yes*.

Task	Platform	Description
Stop an app.	Android	*Settings > Applications > Manage applications >* tap the specific application name > tap *Force stop*.
Force an app to close.	iOS	Press Home button quickly two times > swipe left to locate the offending app > swipe upward on the app preview.
Close an app.	Windows	Swipe down from the top of the screen and drag the app to beyond the bottom of the screen.
Move an app icon.	Android/ iOS	Press and hold the app icon until it jiggles and drag the icon to another location. If the location is another home screen, hold the icon on the edge of the screen until the new location appears.
Create a folder to hold apps.	Android	Press an empty part of the home screen and select folder. To move an item to the folder, press and drag the icon into the folder.
Create a folder to hold apps.	iOS	Press and hold the app icon until it jiggles. Drag the icon onto another app icon. A folder is created that contains both icons. Other icons can now be added.
Create a folder on Start screen for apps.	Windows	From the *Start* screen, tap and drag one tile on top of another.

*Because Android is open source, the exact steps may vary. Also, Apple IOS and Windows for mobile devices are constantly being updated/upgraded.

Two important terms related to Android apps are APK and SDK. An Android application package or **APK** is the file format used to distribute and install Android apps. So if you download an app, it is an APK file. A software development kit (**SDK**) is a set of tools (application programming interfaces [APIs], documentation, programming tools, analytic tools, sample code, etc.) used to develop an app for a specific mobile OS or platform.

Mobile Device Wired Connectivity

Mobile devices have many of the same ports that computers do, but in smaller versions. **Proprietary vendor-specific ports** do exist; these ports are primarily for power connections or as a communication option(s). Let's explore these ports in a little more detail starting with the ports you are most familiar with—USB.

Mobile USB and Lightning Ports

Mobile devices frequently have either a **micro-USB** or a **mini-USB** port. There is even a mini-/micro-AB port that accepts either a mini-/micro-A or a mini-/micro-B cable end. Figure 11.34 shows the standard Type-A USB port found on a PC and the mini-B and micro-B ports found on mobile devices. The micro-USB ports are now a standard interface for smartphones.

Standard Type A   Mini-   Micro-
USB   USB   USB

FIGURE 11.34   USB Type-A, mini, and micro ports

Apple designed the proprietary 30-pin connector for docking Apple mobile devices. Later, Apple released the 8-pin replacement **Lightning port** for its devices. Now Apple is moving to the USB Type-C port. Figure 11.35 shows a Lightning port and connector. Figure 11.36 shows Apple's two connectors on the left followed by the micro-USB, mini-USB, and traditional USB connectors.

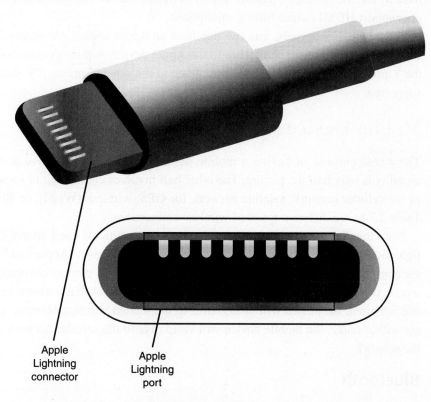

Apple
Lightning
connector

Apple
Lightning
port

FIGURE 11.35   Apple Lightning port and connector

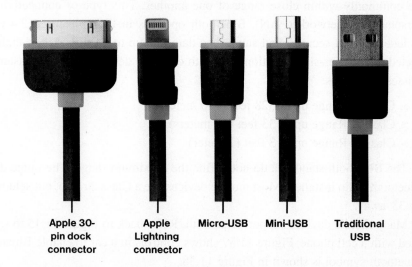

Apple 30-
pin dock
connector

Apple
Lightning
connector

Micro-USB

Mini-USB

Traditional
USB

FIGURE 11.36   Mobile connectors

On devices that don't have a wired RJ-45 network connection but do have a USB port, a **USB-to-RJ-45 dongle** can be used. Wired network connections are faster than wireless and commonly found on laptops, but other mobile devices lack RJ-45 jacks. Refer back to Figure 2.25 for a USB-to-RJ-45 (Ethernet) dongle.

When an HDMI, miniHDMI, or microHDMI connector is on an Android-based device, you connect the correct cable between the Android device and a video output device, such as a monitor or TV. Then, you launch an application such as your photo gallery. Tap the *HDMI Play* control icon. Some applications require no interaction for the HDMI output to work. Note that you might have to use the *Settings > HDMI* option to adjust the resolution. Note that some applications do not support HDMI output from a smartphone.

For Apple iOS devices, you can purchase an Apple Digital AV adapter. This cable is like a Y cable, and the end of the Y attaches to the Apple device. A power connector can connect to one of the Y prongs and an HDMI cable can attach to the other Y prong. TV standards up to 1080p are supported.

Mobile Device Wireless Connectivity

The whole purpose of having a mobile device is being able to move around with it. However, mobility is only half the picture. The other half involves connecting to some type of network such as the cellular network, satellite network for GPS, wireless (Wi-Fi), or Bluetooth. Refer back to Table 2.7 to see different types of wireless connections.

Note that because Android devices are created using an open source operating system, configuration options can be different from one device to another. Apple and Windows have different versions of their mobile OS. By default, when most mobile devices are configured for wireless networks, the device will connect. If you walk out of range of that wireless network and another one is configured, the device will switch over to the second wireless network. If no wireless networks are within range, the mobile device will swap over to the cellular network if you are connected to the network.

Bluetooth

Bluetooth is a radio-based wireless technology used to connect two or more devices together that are commonly within close range of one another. This type of connectivity is called a wireless personal area network (PAN). Bluetooth operates in the unlicensed 2.4-GHz range. Bluetooth includes 128-bit security and supports a data rate up to 24Mb/s. Up to eight devices can be connected in a master-slave relationship (with only one device being the master). Bluetooth has three classes of devices:

> Class 1: Range up to 328 feet (100 meters)
> Class 2: Range up to 33 feet (10 meters)
> Class 3: Range up to 3 feet (1 meter)

The Bluetooth standards do not define the maximum range. The range depends on the type of Bluetooth radio installed. Most mobile devices use a Class 2 radio, but seldom can have connectivity 33' away.

Many mobile devices support Bluetooth. Refer back to Figure 11.15 to see a Bluetooth headset used with a cell phone. Figure 11.37 shows controls in a car to enable Bluetooth connectivity. The Bluetooth symbol is shown in Figure 11.38.

FIGURE 11.37   Enabling Bluetooth connectivity

FIGURE 11.38   Bluetooth symbol

The basic concept behind configuring Bluetooth is that each device must have Bluetooth enabled and "pair" or connect with another Bluetooth-enabled device. Once enabled, Bluetooth broadcasts a wireless signal that other Bluetooth-enabled devices can detect. The basic steps for configuration are as follows:

Step 1. Enable Bluetooth.

Step 2. Ensure pairing is enabled.

Step 3. Pair with another Bluetooth-enabled device.

Step 4. Enter security pin code.

Step 5. Test connectivity.

To enable Bluetooth on an Android phone, you can swipe from the top and tap the Bluetooth icon. On an iPhone, swipe up from the bottom edge of the screen to display the Control Center. Tap the Bluetooth button to enable/disable. On Windows Mobile OS > *Start* > *Settings* > *Connections* > *Bluetooth* > from the menu or *Mode* tab, *Turn On Bluetooth*.

Laptops frequently use a function or Fn key along with a key that has the Bluetooth symbol (F1 – F12) to activate Bluetooth. In Windows, search control panels for `bluetooth` > *Change Bluetooth settings* option > *Options* tab > ensure *Allow Bluetooth devices to find this computer* checkbox is enabled.

Table 11.8 shows basic configuration for the various operating systems once you have ensured the device is powered and ready for pairing.

TABLE 11.8   Bluetooth installation steps

Windows	Apple iOS	Android
Ensure that Bluetooth is enabled. Use the *Add a Bluetooth Device* link > select the device > *Next*. Note that if the device is a Bluetooth printer, use the *Add a Printer* link. You may have to enter a passkey or PIN. Verify connectivity.	Access *Settings* > *General* > *Bluetooth* > ON. In the Devices field, you should see the name of the device. Select the device > *Pair*. You may have to enter a passkey or PIN. Verify connectivity.	Access *Settings* > *Wireless and network* > *Bluetooth settings*. Ensure that Bluetooth is enabled > *Scan devices*. Select the device once it appears > *Accept*. You may have to enter a passkey or PIN. Verify connectivity.

Laptops commonly have Bluetooth installed. To determine whether Bluetooth is installed in Windows 7/8/10, open the *Network and Sharing Center* Control Panel > *Change adapter settings* link. If installed, a Bluetooth adapter displays. Right-click on the adapter to enable or disable the adapter and to pair it with other devices.

If a device does not have Bluetooth capability or if the Bluetooth circuitry fails and the device has a USB port, a **USB-to-Bluetooth** device can be obtained and used. Plug the dongle into a USB port on your laptop. If in the Windows environment, the device will register and the control panel should pop up. In Windows Vista, 7, and 8, look under *Hardware and Sound* > *Add a device* link. In Windows 10, use the *Settings* > *Devices* > *Bluetooth* option. Your Bluetooth device model number displays > select *Next* > follow any additional instructions such as adding a PIN. Always remember to follow manufacturer's directions. Figure 11.39 shows a USB Bluetooth device.

FIGURE 11.39   USB Bluetooth device

IEEE 802.11 Wireless

The 802.11 wireless standard is used to connect the mobile device to a wireless network that operates in the 2.4-GHz and/or 5-GHz range. A wireless access point is used to coordinate and connect multiple wireless devices in the immediate area. Data rates depend on how far away from the access point and what type of walls and materials are between the mobile device and the access point. 802.11 wireless networks are commonly referred to as Wi-Fi. Table 11.9 shows the 802.11 standards related to wireless and the frequency range/speed used with each type.

TABLE 11.9 IEEE 802.11 wireless standards

Standard	Frequency range and speed
802.11a	5GHz–up to 54Mb/s
802.11b	2.4GHz–up to 11Mb/s
802.11g	2.4GHz–up to 54Mb/s
802.11n	2.4 and 5GHz–up to 600Mb/s
802.11ac	5GHz–up to 4.9Gb/s

The reason it is important to know the frequency is so you can determine whether your mobile device can attach to the wireless network. If an 802.11n access point is used, it has the capability to be programmed in both the 2.4- and 5-GHz range, but someone could just configure it to operate in one of these ranges, say 2.4GHz. That would mean your mobile device would have to support the 802.11b, 802.11g, or 802.11n standard. The access point could also be configured to support only 802.11n devices (but this is not common except for maybe within a company). The more devices that connect and transmit/receive data on the wireless network, the worse the performance is. Some access points allow a limited number of wired connections in addition to all of the wireless devices connected to it, as shown in Figure 11.40.

FIGURE 11.40 IEEE 802.11 wireless network

To configure a wireless mobile device for IEEE 802.11 wireless networking, ensure the Wi-Fi option is enabled. Use the same process as outlined for accessing Bluetooth, only select Wi-Fi instead. The basic configuration steps for accessing 802.11 wireless networks are as follows:

Step 1. Enable Wi-Fi through the Device *Settings* option.

Step 2. Select the Wi-Fi wireless network to join.

Step 3. Optionally, enter the security password.

For wireless networks that do not broadcast the SSID (see Chapter 14 for more information on that), the network can be manually configured on a mobile device. To manually add a wireless network on an Android device, use the *Settings > Add network* and manually enter the SSID, security type, and password. Similarly, on an iOS device, use the *Wi-Fi* Settings option and follow the same process.

If the 802.11 Wi-Fi circuitry fails or is unavailable on a mobile device, and the device has a USB port, a **USB-to-Wi-Fi dongle** can be obtained and installed. Figure 11.41 shows one of these.

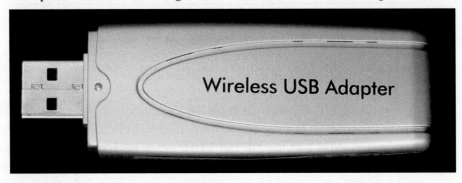

FIGURE 11.41   USB wireless NIC

Airplane Mode

Airplane Mode allows you to disable all wireless communication (Wi-Fi, mobile broadband, Bluetooth, GPS or GNSS, and NFC). In this mode, you could still view a movie or play a game as long as it does not require Internet, cellular, or wireless connectivity. To turn on Airplane Mode, use the *Settings > Airplane Mode* option. Airplane Mode saves on power, secures your mobile device because no wireless communication can occur, and is used when flying (thus the name) and in other communication-sensitive situations.

Table 11.10 has the basic network connectivity configuration options for Android and Apple iOS devices.

TABLE 11.10   Mobile device network configuration options

Connectivity method and device	Path
802.11 wireless—Android	*Settings > Wireless and networks/Wi-Fi*
802.11 wireless—Apple iOS	*Settings > Wi-Fi*
802.11 wireless—Windows mobile	*Settings > Network & wireless > Wi-Fi*
Bluetooth network—Android	*Settings > Wireless and networks > Bluetooth*
Bluetooth network—Apple iOS	*Settings > Bluetooth*
Bluetooth network—Windows mobile	*Settings > Devices > Bluetooth*
Cellular network—Android	*Settings > Wireless and networks/More networks > Mobile networks*
Cellular network—Apple iOS	*Settings > General > Cellular Data*
Cellular network—Windows mobile	*Settings > Cellular*
GPS—Android	*Settings > Location services/Location*
GPS—Apple iOS	*Settings > Location*
GPS—Windows mobile	*Settings > Location*
Airplane Mode—Android	*Settings > Wireless and networks/Flight mode/Airplane Mode*

Connectivity method and device	Path
Airplane Mode—Apple iOS	*Settings > Privacy > Location Services*
Airplane Mode—Windows Mobile	*Settings > Privacy > Location Services*

Hotspot/Tethering

A Wi-Fi **hotspot** is a wireless network that has free Internet access. Hotspots can be found in cities, parks, stores, restaurants, hotels, libraries, government buildings, and schools. Security is a concern with hotspots because no encryption or authentication is commonly required.

Another way of gaining access to the Internet is through tethering. Say you are at a gas station and need to look something up on the Internet on your PC. Your phone has Internet connectivity, but there is no free Wi-Fi. You could have Internet access on the PC through the phone by using tethering. **Tethering** allows sharing an Internet connection with other mobile devices in the nearby area. Tethering might also be considered to be a hotspot. Common methods of using tethering are through Bluetooth, Wi-Fi, or a wired USB connection. Some phone vendors charge for the tethering option. Configure tethering on an Android device using the *Settings > Wireless & Networks* option. Then select whether you are using USB, Wi-Fi, or Bluetooth to tether. On an iPhone, access *Settings >* enable *Personal Hotspot >* the directions for connecting through Wi-Fi, Bluetooth, and USB appear. Figure 11.42 shows wired tethering through USB and the concept of wireless tethering.

FIGURE 11.42   Wireless tethering

Near Field Communication (NFC)

Near field communication (**NFC**) is a radio-based wireless technology similar to radio frequency identification (RFID) that allows two devices to exchange information. There are three modes of NFC operation:

> NFC card emulation: Enables a mobile device to act like a smart card and perform business transactions such as payment-related or ticket purchasing, displaying, inspection, or invalidation
> NFC reader/writer: Allows an NFC device to read information from a tag
> NFC peer-to-peer: Allows two NFC-enabled devices to exchange information

The devices must be within close proximity of one another (4 inches or less). If your phone has the NFC capability and your printer supports NFC, then you can stand next to the printer, tap the *PRINT* option, and send something to the printer. Figure 11.43 shows a man making a payment for purchases using an NFC-enabled smartphone.

NFC can also be used to establish other types of connections such as Bluetooth, Wi-Fi, and data exchange transfers. NFC is being used to allow keyless entry into cars, connect speakers, and provide wireless charging.

FIGURE 11.43   NFC transaction

Infrared

Infrared (**IR**) is a radio-based wireless technology that operates in the 300-GHz to 430-THz range, but many devices use either 2.4GHz or 27MHz. IR is used for very short distances and is cheaper than other wireless technologies. IR requires line of sight; anything from a human to a chair can get in the way and cause lack of connectivity. For that reason, IR is commonly used for short distances to connect wireless devices such as motion detectors, intrusion detectors, TV remotes, hand scanners, a mouse, or a keyboard.

Cellular Data

Two methods for sending data over a cellular network are Short Message Service (SMS) and Multimedia Message Service (MMS). SMS is used for text messages. MMS is used for visual data such as photos or video. Many phone providers charge for these services, so some users like disabling them. On an iOS device, use the *General* Settings option > *Cellular Data*. On an Android device, access the *Wireless and Networks Settings* option > *Mobile Networks* > *Data*. On a Windows mobile device, access *Settings* > *System* > *Messaging* > locate the *SMS/MMS settings* section for the options.

VPN

A virtual private network (**VPN**) is used to connect one device to another device through a public network such as the Internet. Look at Figure 11.44 to see an example of the concept. A salesperson might have a tablet in order to demonstrate a product as well as input customer information. To upload the customer information, the salesperson might need to establish a VPN and a technician might be required to configure this on a phone or other mobile device. Specific network information will be required from the network support staff in order to create this type of connection.

FIGURE 11.44   Concept of a VPN

The general steps to start the VPN configuration are as follows:

> iOS: *Settings > General > VPN*
> Android: *Settings >* select *More* from the *Wireless & networks* section *> VPN > +* (plus sign)
> Windows mobile: *Settings > Network & Wireless > VPN >* select *Add a VPN connection >* configure the VPN settings including the username and password

In order to use the VPN, the user will have to connect using his own username and password.

> iOS: *Settings >* turn *VPN* to on (as seen in Figure 11.45)
> Android: *Settings > General > VPN*
> Windows mobile: *Settings > VPN*

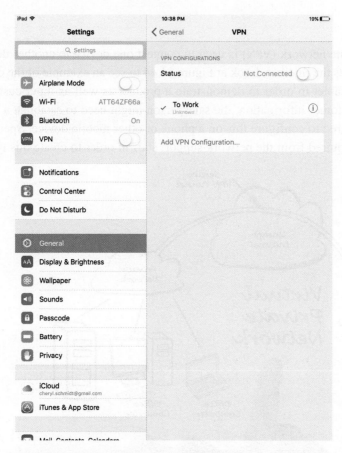

FIGURE 11.45   VPN on an iOS device

Mobile Device Email Configuration

Many people want to check their email on a mobile device. Email can be accessed and delivered using a variety of protocols including the following:

> Post Office Protocol version 3 (POP3): Used to retrieve email using TCP port 110
> Internet Message Access Protocol (IMAP): Used to retrieve email using TCP port 143
> Secure Sockets Layer (SSL): Used to encrypt data between an email client and the email server
> Simple Mail Transfer Protocol (SMTP): An older protocol used to send emails using TCP port 25
> Multipurpose Internet Mail Extensions (MIME) and Secure MIME (S/MIME): Used along with SMTP so that pictures and attachments are supported
> Exchange: Microsoft's application that uses the messaging application programming interface (MAPI) to connect to Microsoft Exchange servers for email, calendar, and contact information

The email server used determines which email client may be used on the mobile device. Several key pieces of information are commonly needed to configure that client and those are identified in Table 11.11. See Chapter 14 to learn more about how protocols work and the purpose of them.

TABLE 11.11   Email configuration parameters

Parameter	Description
Email address	The address used to send you an email such as cheryl.schmidt@gmail.com.
Email protocol	Protocol(s) used to send and receive email.
Server name	The name of the incoming or outgoing mail server (get from the network staff).
Username	The name assigned to you by the company that hosts the email server. This may be the email address.
Password	The password used in conjunction with the username to access the email account.

Most mobile devices include email configuration as part of the mobile OS. Examples include the following:

> Google/Inbox
> Yahoo
> Outlook.com
> iCloud

When you first configure an Android device, you are prompted to either enter your Google account information or create one. The email app that comes with the phone simply opens Gmail. You can add an account by selecting the *Email* Settings option. Use the *Personal (IMAP/POP)* option for configuring Yahoo, Outlook, AOL Mail, and other IMAP/POP type email accounts. Use the *Exchange* option for configuring Microsoft Exchange. Similarly on Apple iOS devices, use the *Mail, Contacts, Calendars* Settings option in order to select *Add Account* > select the particular type of account desired (Exchange, Google, Yahoo, and so on). Figure 11.46 shows this on an iOS device.

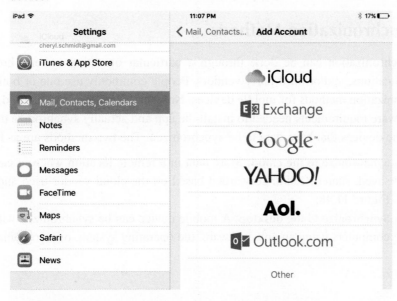

FIGURE 11.46   Email configuration on iOS device

Mobile Device Synchronization and Backup

Synchronization means making the same data available on multiple devices and/or multiple locations. This is sometimes known as a **remote backup**, cloud backup, or cloud storage. The types of data synchronized include personal contacts, programs or applications, email, pictures, music, videos, calendar appointments, browser bookmarks, documents, folders, location data, social media data, and e-books. Synchronization makes life easier so that you do not have to log in to a work computer or bring up a web browser in order to see what is scheduled tomorrow. You can also synchronize your fitness results and maintain them on both your cell phone and mobile fitness device, as shown in Figure 11.47.

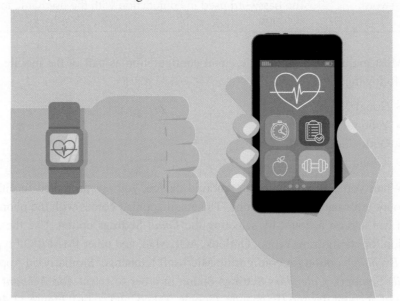

FIGURE 11.47   Fitness app synchronization

Synchronization Methods

Synchronization can be done through a particular operating system, browser, email provider, applications, and/or third-party vendors. People commonly use one or both of the following synchronization methods for mobile devices. Note that whichever type is used, it is important that the software requirements needed to install the app and actually synchronize the data are met on each of the devices that have data to be synchronized. The two methods are as follows:

> **Synchronize to the cloud**: Store data in a remote location where it can be viewed, retrieved, saved, shared, and/or forwarded based on the cloud vendor used and user preferences. See Figure 11.48.

> **Synchronize to the desktop**: A mobile device can be synchronized with one or more desktop computers using an app, software, the operating system, or a combination of these.

FIGURE 11.48   Synchronization to the cloud

Synchronization Connection Types

In order for devices to synchronize data, they have to establish connectivity between devices. Synchronization commonly occurs using one of three types of connections:

> Wired USB connection: The two devices attach to one another using a USB port on each device. An example is an iOS device connected via USB to a computer and using iTunes to synchronize music.

> Wireless connection: The devices attach to one another using any wireless method including a 802.11 Wi-Fi connection and cellular network.

> Wired network connection: Devices attach to a wired network and access the Internet and a cloud-based solution through a web browser.

Figure 11.49 shows synchronization between a mobile phone and a desktop computer.

FIGURE 11.49   Synchronization between mobile phone and PC

Synchronization on Android Devices

Google software is commonly used to synchronize data between an Android device and other devices. Google Drive can be used to store and share documents for free. The Google Chrome browser allows synchronization of bookmarks. Google Photos allows storage and sharing of photos. When you use Google software to synchronize, an Android user can have one authentication in order to access multiple services. This is known as **mutual authentication for multiple services** or single sign on (SSO) and is available through the other mobile operating systems as well. When you use a third-party product to synchronize data, you may be required to install an app on one or more mobile devices and PCs.

The Android device is configured with a Google ID and password using the *Settings* > *Accounts* option and then the three vertical dots in the top-right corner can be tapped to select what to synchronize. Figure 11.50 shows the synchronization settings for email (which is turned on).

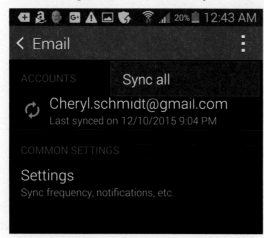

FIGURE 11.50   Android email synchronization

Synchronization on iOS Devices

iOS devices can also use Google Gmail and other apps to synchronize Google contacts and calendar. An individual app may also support synchronization with Google. You can view and add apps by using the *Settings* > *Personal* (which is not used on some Android devices) > *Accounts and sync* or whatever method used by the particular application.

Still iOS users tend to use Apple solutions for synchronization. These include iCloud and iTunes. **iCloud** is used to store, share, and manage data from any device including contacts, calendar, ringtones, photos/videos, and data. Apple has iCloud Photo Library for photos and video and iCloud Drive for document storage. Apple provides free storage (5GB at press time) with the option to pay for more. A Windows device requires a download and installation of iCloud for Windows in order to access data stored there. Figure 11.51 shows the configuration for iCloud on an iOS device and Figure 11.52 shows iCloud Drive configuration.

iTunes can also be used to synchronize Apple devices and to play and manage music, video, books, and lectures. iTunes used to require a USB connection between a mobile device and a PC or Mac but now supports Wi-Fi connectivity. Through iTunes, you can back up personal data (settings, messages, voicemails, and so on) and the Apple device operating system.

iTunes has a 64-bit version for 64-bit Windows operating systems. There is no such application for Android devices. However, you can connect the Apple mobile device to the Android and use the Android *File Transfer* app to transfer files such as the music files (found on the Apple device in the following folder: *Music* > *iTunes* > *iTunes Media*).

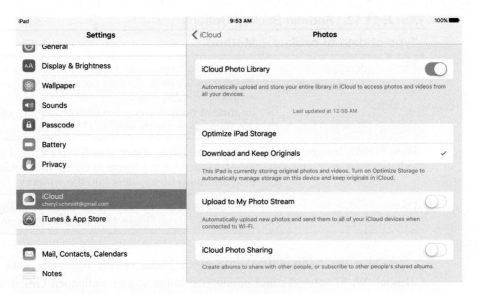

FIGURE 11.51   iCloud configuration screen

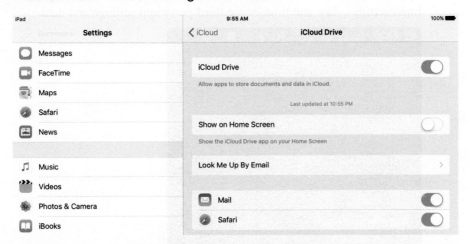

FIGURE 11.52   iCloud Drive configuration screen

To use iTunes, open it from the Apple device or connect the Apple device to a computer or PC. Select the device by choosing the correct device icon in the upper-left corner of the iTunes window. In the left panel *Settings* area are various sections based on what types of items are in your iTunes library (such as Music, Movies, TV Shows, Info, Podcasts, iTunes U, Books, AudioBooks, Tones, and Photos). Each section can be accessed to sync that particular type of content. The Info section is used to sync contacts and calendars. iTunes cannot sync browser email accounts, bookmarks, and other such information.

Back Up and Restore Overview

Synchronization of apps is one way of backing up information, but that doesn't really provide an operating system backup. The mobile device should have the system backed up in case an operating system update fails, a virus infection, or if malware cannot be removed. Apps are available that allow you to remotely back up a mobile device. Backup and restore techniques are just as important in the mobile environment as they are in the desktop arena.

Android-Based Backup and Restore

Android devices have different options based on what type of data you want to back up and/or restore. Table 11.12 lists the major ones.

TABLE 11.12 Android Backup Options

Type of data to backup	Method
Photos/videos	Use Auto Backup. Open Google Photos app > top left, access the menu icon (three horizontal bars) > *Settings* > *Back up & sync* > enable or disable. **Important note:** Turning the backup settings off affects all apps that use Back up & synch such as Google Drive.
Files, folders, images, videos	Use Google Drive. Open a web browser and go to `http://drive.google.com`. Use the menu to create new folders or upload files or drag and drop files/folders into the window.
Data	Use Android Backup Service: *Settings* > *Backup & reset* > enable *Back up my data*. Figure 11.53 shows this screen.

Note that the Android Backup Service backs up the following data and settings: Google Calendar, Wi-Fi networks and passwords, home screen wallpaper, Gmail settings, apps installed through Google Play and backed up using the Play Store app, display settings, language settings, input settings, date and time, some third-party app settings and data.

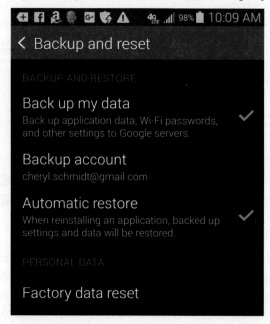

FIGURE 11.53 Android backup and reset screen

Notice in Figure 11.53 how this screen is also where you can perform a factory reset. A **factory reset** is used when a device cannot be repaired using any other method. As the name of the option implies, this option resets the mobile device to the original settings. Android phones keep the OS separate from the apps and data. The OS is read-only. The factory reset resets only the apps and data. That is why you need to back them up. Generic steps to back up an Android-based mobile device are as follows:

Step 1. Boot the device into *Recovery Mode*. Recovery Mode is typically accessed by holding down two or more specific buttons (such as the power, volume, and/or home) while the device boots. See the mobile device manufacturer's website for specific instructions.

Step 2. From the boot menu, select *Backup & Restore* > *Backup*.

Step 3. Once backed up, restart the device and boot normally.

The generic steps for the restore process are the following:

Step 1. Boot the device into *Recovery Mode*.

Step 2. From the boot menu, select *Backup & Restore > Restore*.

Step 3. Once complete, reboot the device to ensure it boots normally.

Note that there are other apps that can be used to back up the operating system and the installed apps.

iOS-Based Backup and Restore Overview

With iOS you can back up your operating system using iCloud or iTunes. If you use iCloud, the backup is stored in the cloud (up to 5GB free at the time of press), encrypted, and can be accomplished using wireless. With iTunes, the backup is stored on a Mac or PC, storage limit is based on storage available on that Mac or PC, and encryption is optional.

iCloud Backup and Restore Overview

iCloud backups do not include data that is already in the cloud, data from other cloud services, Apple Pay information, Touch ID, or content that you got from other vendors (even if available in iTunes or iBooks). In order to make a backup using iCloud, ensure the device connects to a Wi-Fi network > *Settings > iCloud Backup/Storage & Backup >* enable (turn on) iCloud Backup > *Back Up Now.*

You can verify the backup is stored using the following steps: *Settings > iCloud > Storage > Manage Storage >* select the device. The details show the date, time, and backup file size. Backups are automatically made on a daily basis if the device meets the following criteria:

> Connects to a power source
> Connects to a Wi-Fi network
> Locked screen
> Available iCloud storage space

To reset and restore an iOS device using iCloud, do the following generic steps:

Step 1. Boot the device and look for a hello screen. Note that if the device is still functional, you cannot restore from an iCloud backup if the device is configured. Use the *Settings > Erase All Content and Settings option* to wipe the device.

Step 2. Follow the directions on how to set up the device, including the requirement of joining a Wi-Fi network.

Step 3. Select *Restore from an iCloud Backup* and sign in to iCloud.

Step 4. Select a backup. Do not disconnect from the Wi-Fi network. Note that this may take a period of time.

iTunes Backup and Restore Overview

Use the following process to make a backup of an iOS device using iTunes. A lab at the end of the chapter demonstrates the process of backing up to a Mac or PC.

Step 1. Open the iTunes application on the Mac or PC.

Step 2. Connect the iOS device to the Mac or PC using a USB cable. The device icon should display in the top-left corner as shown in Figure 11.54.

Step 3. Make a backup of content downloaded from the iTunes Store or Apple App Store by using the *File* menu option > *Devices* > *Transfer Purchases*. Note that once the file transfer is complete, you might need to use the Ctrl + B.

Step 4. Select whether the backup is to be kept in the cloud (using the *iCloud* radio button) or on the PC or Mac (*This computer* radio button). See Figure 11.54.

Step 5. On a Mac, select *Back Up Now* (as shown in Figure 11.54). On a Windows PC, use the *File* menu option > *Devices* > *Back up*.

Step 6. Once finished, use the iTunes *Summary* option to see the date and time of the backup. In Windows, use *Preferences* > *Devices*. If the file is encrypted, there is a lock icon beside the device name.

A reinstallation of the operating system is known as a **clean install**. To restore a device using iTunes, connect the device to the Mac or PC that has the backup. Cable the device to the Mac or PC. Open iTunes. Use the *File* menu option > *Devices* > *Restore from Backup* option. Select the latest backup and click *Restore*. Note that the file transfer can take some time.

Device icon

Backup stored to cloud or local computer options

FIGURE 11.54   iTunes backup options

OneDrive

Microsoft has a product called **OneDrive** that can be used for synchronization and/or backup and restore operations. At the time this book went to press, new users may use up to 5GB of free storage and share files and folders with others. Office 365 subscribers are entitled to 1TB of storage. Users may place deleted files in a recycle bin and recover them up to three months later without that storage capacity counting. People who use Microsoft Outlook through an Exchange server from any mobile operating system can save files and photos to OneDrive and then access through a web browser or mobile device app. Some mobile Outlook users save their email attachments to OneDrive. Microsoft reserves the rights to monitor any content saved in OneDrive and can remove any files that do not adhere to their strict policy. Figure 11.55 shows a screenshot of OneDrive.

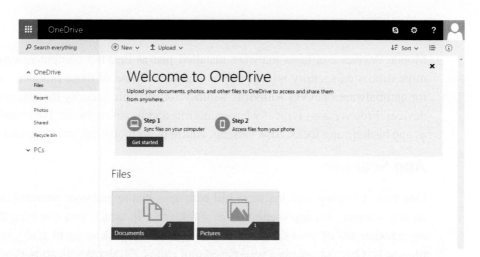

FIGURE 11.55   Microsoft OneDrive

Other Mobile Software Tools

Mobile devices have other tools and sometimes require other tools in order to troubleshoot and manage them. You might also have to download apps to perform specific tasks or to help with troubleshooting. You might consider installing some of these apps as a standard in a business environment.

Mobile Device Management

Mobile device management (**MDM**) is the ability to view and manage multiple mobile devices (see Figure 11.56). In the corporate environment, mobile devices are a challenge to IT staff. Some companies purchase software in order to push updates, track, and remotely wipe data and configurations. The **Apple Configurator** free app is an example of an MDM product. It allows business support staff to configure settings on iOS-based devices before issuing them to users. Using configuration profiles, IT personnel can install specific iOS versions and ensure security policies are applied. Apple Configurator can also be used to wipe the device and provide basic management of deployed devices. Similar products can be purchased that allow more corporate management capabilities.

FIGURE 11.56   Mobile device management

Mobile Antimalware

Mobile devices can have malware installed just as desktop computers can. See Chapter 18 for more details on security issues such as malware. Some of these products, such as Malwarebytes for antimalware or AVG Antivirus security for multiple security threats, are available for mobile devices. Free versions typically have antivirus and/or antimalware. Paid versions add features such as app backup, app locks, SIM locking, antitheft, antiphishing, tracking, and secure web browsing.

App Scanner

One way of helping with malware and with apps that reveal your personal information is to install an app scanner. An **app scanner** is an online tool in which you can type the name of an app to see whether any of your data is at risk and generate a risk score to give you an idea of how risky the app is. One example is a web-based tool called Zscaler Application Profiler (ZAP). Other app scanners are part of a security app such as Sophos Mobile Security. There are also app scanners that manage particular apps and ensure compliance, cloud-based management for specific mobile devices, and enterprise-based mobile device management.

Wi-Fi Analyzer

A **Wi-Fi analyzer** app (sometimes known as a **wireless locator**) is used to identify what wireless networks are in the area, what frequencies (channels) are being used, and to find a less crowded channel for any wireless installations, hotspot, or tethering that may be needed in a particular area. Some give you additional feedback such as a quality rating based on the channel you might select. One optional feature is a signal meter to see the wireless range of a particular wireless network. A Wi-Fi analyzer is particularly useful to a technician to identify potential sources of other wireless interference. See Chapter 14 for more detail on wireless networks and wireless configuration. Figure 11.57 shows a Wi-Fi analyzer (called WiFi Analyzer) designed for Windows 10 devices and available in the Microsoft Store.

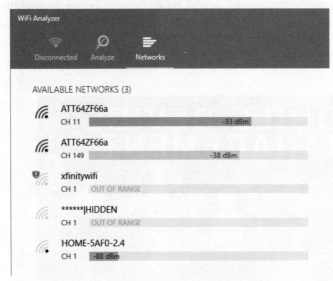

FIGURE 11.57   WiFi Analyzer app screen

Cell Tower Analyzer

A **cell tower analyzer** app (also known as a cell signal analyzer) details information about the cell phone network and possibly wireless networks. The information can include signal strength, data state, data activity, mobile network code (MNC), mobile country code (MCC), IP address, roaming state, phone type, etc. Other apps can show all the cell towers in the area in order to get an idea of cell phone coverage in the areas most used. Figure 11.58 shows a screenshot from a cell tower analyzer app (Network Signal Info).

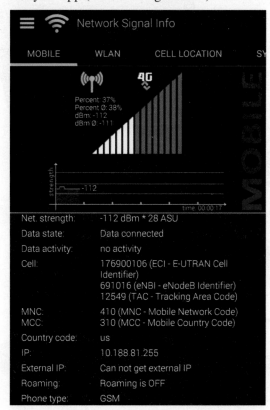

FIGURE 11.58   Network Signal Info cell tower analyzer app

Laptops Overview

Mobile devices are fun to explore, but let's move on to laptops now. Laptops were the first mobile device that technicians had to support. They are an integral part of the IT scene, and IT jobs. Anyone in an IT position is expected to know some technical laptop basics. Technical support staff are expected to know more. Always remember that every laptop is different. Always consult the particular computer manufacturer's website for instructions on replacing anything on your laptop.

Laptop Hardware

A laptop has similar parts and ports as a desktop computer, but some of these components are smaller, naturally. Figure 11.59 shows common laptop parts. Notice in Figure 11.59 how many of the components are built into the laptop motherboard.

Whenever taking anything out of a laptop, one of the major issues is tiny screws. Use a magnetic screwdriver to remove the screws or place the screws on a magnetized tray. Many manufacturers label the type of screws or location for ease of explaining disassembly (see Figure 11.60). Always keep like screws together (in containers or an egg carton) and take notes and photos. All the parts are manufacturer-dependent, but the following explanation and graphics/photos should help.

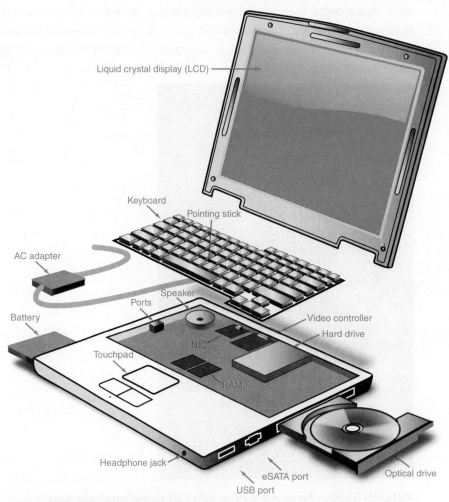

Liquid crystal display (LCD)

Keyboard

Pointing stick

AC adapter

Speaker

Ports

Video controller

Hard drive

Battery

NIC

Touchpad

RAM

Headphone jack

eSATA port

USB port

Optical drive

FIGURE 11.59 Laptop parts

⚠ CAUTION
PC BASE CAN BECOME HOT!
AVOID PROLONGED CONTACT
TO PREVENT HEAT INJURY TO SKIN.

⚠ ATTENTION
LA BASE DU PC PEUT S'ÉCHAUFFER.
ÉVITER LE CONTACT PROLONGÉ
AVEC LA PEAU POUR PRÉVENIR
LES RISQUES DE BRÛLURES.
GM9021049211

WiFi CERTIFIED

FIGURE 11.60 Laptop screws and covers

Some laptop and mobile device compartments require levering the compartment cover away from the case or removing plastic parts such as the cover or frame that fits over a mobile computer keyboard. A plastic **scribe** is the best tool to use for this levering. Figure 11.61 shows a plastic scribe being used to lift the plastic part that is between the keyboard and the laptop screen. Go back to Figure 5.6 to see another photo of a scribe.

FIGURE 11.61   Plastic scribe

External Laptop Devices

Laptops might also have external devices attached. The USB port is the most common port used for external connectivity. For laptops that do not have a USB port, you can use an eSATA port for an external device or add an Express-to-USB card if the laptop has an ExpressCard slot. Note that these USB ports on an ExpressCard (covered in the next section) might not be able to provide the power that a normal integrated USB port could provide. Types of external connectivity include the following:

> External monitor: External monitors attach to a video port. Common video ports on laptops include VGA, HDMI, Thunderbolt, and DisplayPort. HDMI can carry audio and video signals. Thunderbolt can carry not only video, but data and power as well. That is why Thunderbolt can be used for other connections besides video ones. Thunderbolt is also used to connect to docking stations (covered next). Some devices have miniature versions of these ports. Figure 11.62 shows the difference between a DisplayPort and a mini DisplayPort.

> External hard drive: Commonly connects to a USB, IEEE 1394 (FireWire), Thunderbolt, or eSATA port.

> External optical drive (see Figure 11.63): Commonly connects to USB port; useful for tablets and phablets, too.

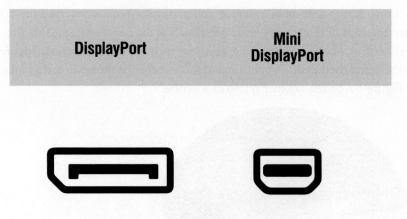

FIGURE 11.62   DisplayPort and mini DisplayPort

FIGURE 11.63   USB optical drive

Some people like having more expandability when in the office than when traveling with the laptop. For these folks, two devices can help—the docking station or port replicator. A **laptop docking station** allows a laptop computer to be more like a desktop system. A docking station can have connections for a full-size monitor, printer, keyboard, mouse, and printer. In addition, a docking station can have expansion slots or cards and storage bays.

Docking stations tend to be vendor proprietary, which means that if you have a particular brand of laptop, you must use the same brand docking station. Typically, to install a laptop into a docking station, close the laptop and slide the laptop into the docking station. Optionally (depending on the model), secure the laptop with locking tabs. Figure 11.64 shows a laptop docking station and the ports that can be found on a docking station.

The **port replicator** is similar to a docking station but does not normally include expansion slots or drive storage bays. A port replicator attaches to a laptop and allows more devices to be connected, such as an external monitor, keyboard, mouse, joystick, and printer, or port replicator. Port replicators can be proprietary or support multiple laptop vendors.

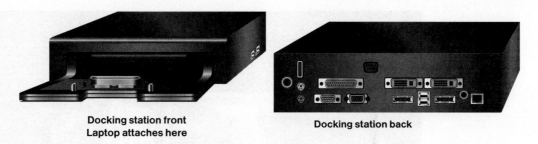

Docking station front
Laptop attaches here

Docking station back

FIGURE 11.64   Laptop docking station

Other Laptop Expansion Options

Laptops can also be expanded by adding expansion cards. The **miniPCI** 32-bit 33-MHz standard was developed to allow PCI upgrades and interface cards to be added to laptops, docking stations, and printers. MiniPCI cards allow USB, IEEE 1394, wireless network, network, sound, modem, and other types of device or memory connectivity. MiniPCI cards have three form factors—Type I, II, and III. Type I and II cards use 100-pin connectors, whereas Type IIIs use a larger 124-pin card.

The **miniPCIe** is the more popular 52-pin little card that fits in the bottom of a laptop or on the motherboard/system board, not a tablet. Three common uses are to install a modem, wireless, or cellular card. A **modem card** is used to allow the PC to connect to a remote modem using an analog phone line. A **wireless card** is used to connect the laptop to an IEEE 802.11 or Bluetooth wireless network. A **cellular card** is used to connect the laptop to the cell phone network. Note that some adapters have the ability of both wireless and cellular built into the same card. Also, these adapters could be attached via a USB port instead of miniPCIe adapter.

To install a miniPCI/PCIe adapter, you may have to disassemble the laptop or remove a screw from the bottom, as shown in Figure 11.65. Or, you may have to lift a lid to access the slot. An expansion slot is shown in Figure 11.66.

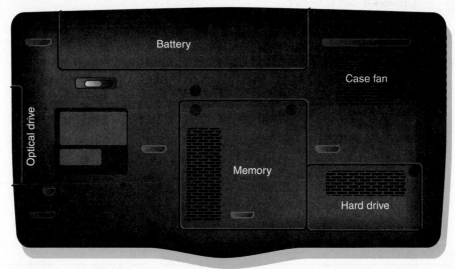

FIGURE 11.65   Laptop underside

An alternative to a miniPCI/PCIe internal adapter is an ExpressCard. **ExpressCard** modules give users the ability to add a wide variety of plug-and-play devices to their computers, including memory, wired and wireless communications, multimedia, security, and networking. The ExpressCard standard supports PCIe, eSATA, IEEE 1394 (FireWire), or USB connectivity through the ExpressCard slot.

FIGURE 11.66 Laptop adapter

Most ExpressCards support hot swapping. Hot swapping allows a card to be inserted into a slot when the laptop is powered on. There are two types of ExpressCards: ExpressCard/34 and ExpressCard/54. The 34 means it is 34mm wide, and the 54 means it is 54mm wide (in an L-type card). Figure 11.67 shows the two ExpressCard form factors.

FIGURE 11.67 ExpressCard types

A type of expansion slot found in both laptops and desktop computers is M.2. The **M.2** expansion slot is quite flexible in that the specification allows different module sizes, including widths of 12, 16, 22, and 30mm, and lengths in sizes of 16, 26, 30, 38, 42, 60, 80, and 110mm. Usually a longer slot will allow the short cards to be installed.

M.2 expansion cards in laptops and desktop computers are used for Wi-Fi, Bluetooth, and cellular network cards as well as SSDs. The support of various card lengths and advanced technology makes M.2 an attractive expansion capability option for solid-state drives and cards in all computer systems and mobile devices. Figure 11.68 shows an M.2 Wi-Fi expansion card and an SSD.

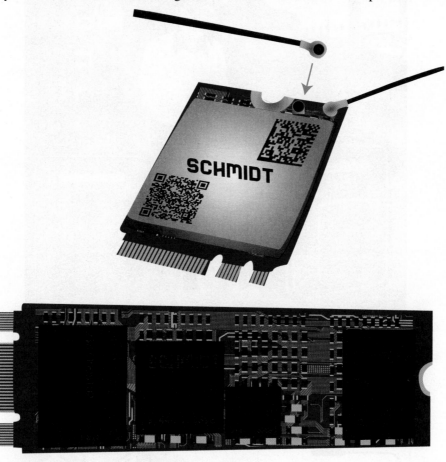

FIGURE 11.68   M.2 wireless card and SSD

Laptop Power

Laptops normally use a battery as their power source, but they can also be powered through an AC wall outlet connection. The AC connection recharges the laptop battery. Figure 11.69 shows the woman in the white shirt working on a laptop that is being charged. A power adapter (sometimes called a wall adapter) converts the AC power from the wall outlet to DC and connects to the rear of the laptop (near to where the battery is located). When a laptop has an AC adapter attached, the battery is being recharged on most models. The port sometimes has a DC voltage symbol below or beside it. This symbol is a solid line with a dashed line below it (▬ ▬ ▬). Figure 11.70 shows an example of a power adapter that would be connected between the laptop and the AC outlet and the power connection on a laptop.

FIGURE 11.69 Laptop powered by AC power

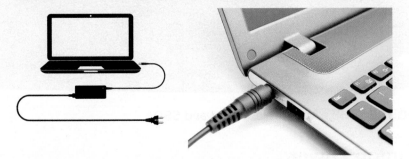

FIGURE 11.70 Laptop power adapter and power connector

When purchasing a new power supply for a laptop or a battery for a mobile device, ensure that it has the same specifications as the one from the manufacturer. Less expensive models might not provide the same quality as approved models. Ensure that the replacement has a power jack that does not wiggle when it is inserted into the device. Ensure that a laptop power brick has the appropriate DC voltage required by the laptop. Current (amperage) should be equal to or more than the original power brick.

TECH TIP

Do not power on after a temperature change

Computers are designed to work within a range of temperatures, but sudden change is not good for them. If a mobile device is in a car all night and the temperature drops, allow the device to return to room temperature before powering it on. Avoid direct sunlight. It is usually 40°F hotter inside the computer case than outside.

Laptop Battery Removal

Laptop batteries fail and have to be replaced. Ensure you disconnect the AC adapter, and power the laptop off before removing the battery. You may have to turn the laptop over to access the battery compartment. Laptop batteries are normally modules that have one or two release latches that are used to remove the module (see Figure 11.71).

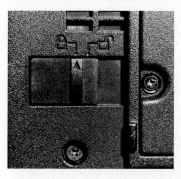

FIGURE 11.71   Release latch for laptop battery removal

Battery technologies have improved in the past few years, probably driven by the development of more devices that need battery power, such as tablets, digital cameras, and portable optical drive players. Laptops use lithium-ion (**Li-ion**) **batteries**, which are very light and can hold a charge longer than any other type. They are also more expensive. Mobile phones, tablets, portable media players, and digital cameras also use Li-ion batteries. These batteries lose their charge over time, even if they are not being used. Use your laptop with battery-provided power. Ensure that a laptop with a Li-ion battery is not plugged into an AC outlet all the time.

> **TECH TIP**
>
> **Keep Li-ion batteries cool**
>
> Li-ion batteries last longer if they are kept cool (not frozen). When you store a Li-ion battery, the battery should be only 40 percent charged and placed in a refrigerator to prolong its life.

Li-ion polymer batteries are similar to Li-ion batteries except that they are packed in pouched cells. This design allows for smaller batteries and a more efficient use of space, which is important in the portable computer and mobile device industries. For environmentalists, the zinc-air battery is the one to watch. AER Energy Resources, Inc., has several patents on a battery that uses oxygen to generate electricity. Air is allowed to flow during battery discharge and is blocked when the battery is not in use. This battery holds a charge for extended periods of time. Another upcoming technology is fuel cells. Fuel cells used for a laptop can provide power for 5 to 10 hours.

Getting the Most from Your Laptop Battery

Mobile devices rely on their batteries to provide mobility. The following tips can help you get more time out of your batteries:

> Most people do not need a spare Li-ion battery. If you are not using a Li-ion battery constantly, it is best not to buy a spare. The longer the spare sits unused, the shorter the life span it will have.

> Buy the battery recommended by the laptop manufacturer.

> For a mobile device or smartphone, use an AC outlet rather than a USB port for faster charging.

> If using a USB port for charging a mobile device or smartphone, unplug all unused USB devices. Note that not all USB ports can provide a charge if the host device is in sleep mode.
> Avoid using an optical player when running on battery power.
> Turn off the wireless adapter if a wireless network is not being used.
> In the power options, configure the mobile device for hibernate rather than standby.
> Save work only when necessary and turn off the autosave feature.
> Reduce the screen brightness.
> Avoid using external USB devices such as flash drives or external hard drives.
> Install more RAM to reduce swapping of information from the hard drive to RAM to CPU or to just be more efficient.
> In mobile devices, keep battery contacts clean with a dab of rubbing alcohol on a lint-free swab once a month.
> Avoid running multiple programs.
> If possible, disable automatic updates.
> Avoid temperature extremes.
> Turn off location services.

Windows *Power Options* Control Panel settings for a laptop include the following links: Require a password on wakeup, Choose what the power button does (as shown in Figure 11.72), Choose what closing the lid does, Create a power plan, Choose when to turn off the display, and Change when the computer sleeps. Laptop power settings affect battery life. Users and technicians should adjust these settings to best fit how the laptop or mobile device is used.

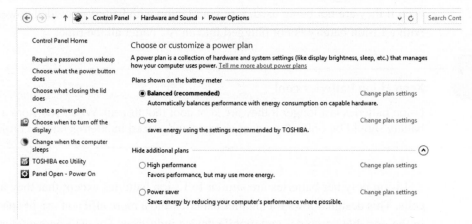

FIGURE 11.72   Laptop Power Options Control Panel

Another way to control the power options setting on a Windows laptop is through the battery meter in the bottom-right corner of the screen on the taskbar. When you hover a pointer over the battery meter, the percentage of battery power remaining is shown. Clicking on the meter allows changing the power option or adjusting the screen brightness. Figure 11.73 shows the screen that displays when the battery meter icon is clicked.

FIGURE 11.73   Laptop battery meter

Laptop Repairs Overview

Laptops are a little more difficult to get parts in order to replace or upgrade them. This is because the parts are smaller and a bit different due to manufacturers keeping the laptops light, portable, and maintaining speeds equal to desktop computers. Laptop repairs require more attention to detail than a desktop model because there are so many screws, much smaller screws, and so little space in which to work. Be patient. The following is a good list of items to remember when disassembling and reconnecting everything in a laptop.

> Use proper anti-static procedures. There are not always good places to attach an anti-static wrist strap. Consider using anti-static gloves (see Figure 11.74). Maintain skin contact when touching parts if no other anti-static tools are used. This is known as self-grounding.

> Organize your parts. Use an egg carton and label individual sections with screws of like length and type and where the screws came from. Otherwise, use tape sticky side up to place like screws on and make notes to go with them.

> Take photos.

> Take notes.

> Use appropriate tools. Scribes are very handy when removing plastic pieces. Very thin needle-nose pliers are great with laptop connectors. A #1 Phillips screwdriver is a must.

> Always refer to the manufacturer's directions when removing and installing parts. Having a tablet or phone where you can pull this document up while you work is fine. Use your resources. No person can know all models of all machines they work on.

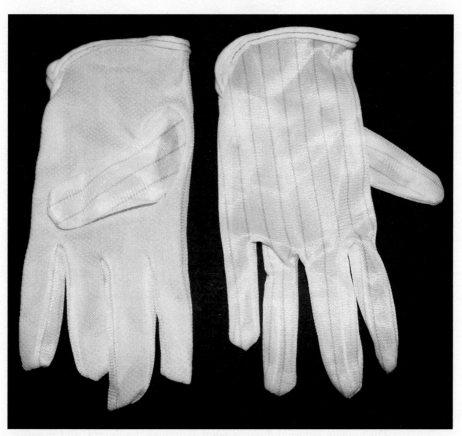

FIGURE 11.74   Anti-static gloves

Laptop System Board/Processor Replacement

Laptop motherboards (**system boards**) are similar to desktop motherboards. A mobile device motherboard holds the majority of the electronics, contains a processor, has memory, and supports having ports attached. However, the processor on a mobile device is normally not as powerful as a desktop model, might have less memory that may not be upgradeable, and has fewer ports. Still some powerful laptops have more power, upgradability, and ports than some low-end desktop models.

In order to get to the system board, at a minimum, screws from the underside of the laptop have to be removed. Sometimes, a hard drive, a drive that inserts on the side, the keyboard, and memory must be removed before you can remove the motherboard. Figure 11.75 shows a laptop system board.

FIGURE 11.75 Laptop system board

Before replacing a motherboard, it is important to do all the following:

> Disconnect AC power connector.
> Remove the battery.
> Disconnect external devices such as mouse, keyboard, and monitor.
> Remove adapters.
> Remove memory from expansion slots.

> Disconnect cables taking care to use any release tabs and not pull on the cables, but on the connector. Needle-nose pliers may be needed.
> Remove the optical drive and hard drive.
> Remove the processor and cooling assembly. Note that this may be done after removing the motherboard. Store the processor in anti-static bag. It will have to be reinstalled and possibly some new thermal paste applied when the new system board is installed.
> Remember that replacement system boards do not come with RAM, a processor, or adapters.
> Make a note or take a photo of the CPU orientation before removing it from the bad/older system board.

Laptop processors are not normally upgraded, but they do sometimes have to be replaced. Always refer to the laptop documentation for motherboard removal procedures. Always power the laptop off. Always remove the laptop battery. Use proper grounding procedures. Many laptop processors have a heat sink and/or fan assembly attached (look back to Figure 11.75). Furthermore, some processor sockets must be loosened or a screw loosened/removed before you lift the processor from the socket, as shown in Figure 11.76. Figure 11.77 shows a processor being removed.

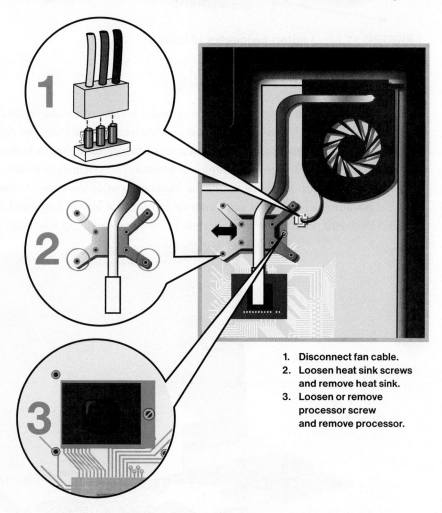

1. Disconnect fan cable.
2. Loosen heat sink screws and remove heat sink.
3. Loosen or remove processor screw and remove processor.

FIGURE 11.76   Laptop processor removal steps

FIGURE 11.77   Laptop processor removed

Laptop Keyboards/Touchpad

Laptops usually have integrated keyboards and a variety of mouse replacement devices, such as a touch stick, touchpad, and/or one or two buttons used for clicking and right-clicking. You should always remove the battery and AC power cord before removing a laptop keyboard or any other internal laptop part. To remove a laptop keyboard, you commonly remove screws from the top or bottom of the laptop and slide or lift the keyboard out of the case. Always refer to the manufacturer's documentation before removing or replacing a laptop keyboard. Figure 11.78 shows the laptop keyboard removal process. Figure 11.79 shows a laptop keyboard that has been removed.

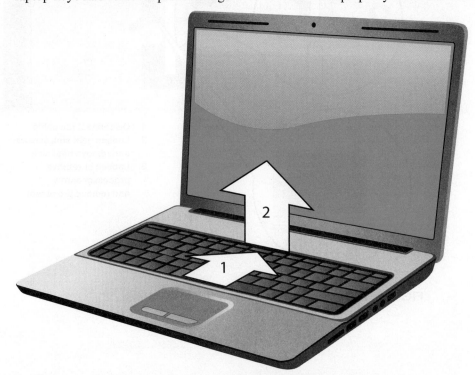

FIGURE 11.78   Laptop keyboard removal process

TECH TIP

These concepts relate to Apple computers, too

Even though this book focuses on PCs, concepts related to CPU, motherboards, expansion slots, cache, and chipsets also apply to Apple computers. Apple computers and PCs have similar CPU and memory requirements.

FIGURE 11.79   Removed laptop keyboard

Replacing the touchpad or mouse-like devices on laptops requires a little more work and disassembly than a keyboard. Sometimes an internal drive, memory, keyboard, wireless network card, and/or the system board must be removed before you can access the screws, connector, and/or cable that hold the touchpad in place. Sometimes the keyboard must be turned upside down to get to the touch stick. Look back to Figure 11.79 and you can see the blue touch stick attached to the keyboard.

Touchpads are also sensitive and may need to be adjusted through the Windows environment during regular use or after a replacement. The touchpad settings in Windows Vista, 7, 8, and 10 are accessed through the *Hardware and Sound* Control Panel > *Mouse*, as shown in Figure 11.80. Notice how this vendor has its own tab. Some vendors have their own touchpad Control Panel.

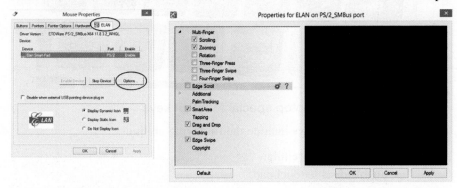

FIGURE 11.80   Touchpad Control Panel

TECH TIP

What to do if the laptop keyboard or touchpad goes bad

You can replace mobile keyboards/pointing devices or use external wired or wireless ones.

Laptops have **special function keys**. These keys are in the uppermost part of your keyboard. They are labeled F1, F2, etc. through F10 or F12. They allow you to quickly control screen brightness, hibernation, turn Wi-Fi on/off, mute the sound, etc. For example, on some laptops when you depress the Fn key (lower left-hand side of keyboard) while simultaneously depressing the F5 key, your screen brightness will increase. Refer to your particular device's user manual or look at the symbols on the keyboard for a clue as to what they can do when combined with the Fn key. Table 11.13 is a sample of one vendor's function keys. Figure 11.81 shows a close-up of some of the laptop function keys. See if you can guess what features they perform.

TABLE 11.13   Sample laptop function keys

Fn key + key listed below	Description
F1	Mute the speaker.
F2	Decrease sound.
F3	Increase sound.
F4	Turn the system off.
F5	Refresh the browser window.
F6	Enable/disable touchpad.
F7	Decrease display brightness.
F8	Increase display brightness.
F9	Switch display output to an external device.
F10	Switch power modes.
F11	Enable/disable Bluetooth.
F12	Enable/disable Wi-Fi.

FIGURE 11.81   Laptop special function keys

Other function keys include the following abilities:

> Enable/disable cellular.
> Enable/disable touchpad.
> Screen orientation.
> Enable/disable GPS.
> Enable/disable Bluetooth.
> Enable/disable Airplane Mode.
> Enable/disable keyboard backlight.

> Video controls (dual displays, external display, laptop display and external display, blank the display). See Figure 11.82 for a couple of examples of video controls that require the use of a function key.

FIGURE 11.82   Laptop video output special function keys

Laptop Memory

The memory chips used with laptops are different from the ones used in desktop or tower computers. Laptops use a special form factor called a small-outline DIMM (**SO-DIMM**). Other types exist (microDIMMs and small-outline RIMMs [SO-RIMMs]), but SO-DIMMs are the most popular, and they come in a 72-pin version for 32-bit transfers and 144-, 200-, 204-, or 260-pin versions for 64-bit transfers. Figure 11.83 shows the difference between DDR, DDR2, and DDR3 SO-DIMMs. A single notch DDR4 SO-DIMM is also available and that module is wider than the others by 2mm. Even though a DDR SO-DIMM appears to have an identical notch as the DDR2 SO-DIMM, they are different by just a fraction and cannot fit in each other's slots. Figure 11.84 shows a photo of a SO-DIMM.

200-pin SO-DIMM DDR

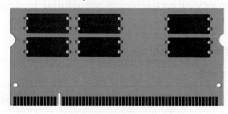

200-pin SO-DIMM DDR 2

204-pin SO-DIMM DDR 3

FIGURE 11.83   SO-DIMM form factors

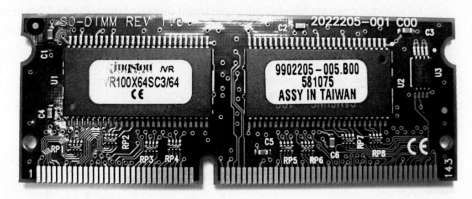

FIGURE 11.84   SO-DIMM photo

Some laptops cannot be upgraded. Many laptops have only one memory slot, so when you upgrade, you must replace the module that is installed. Laptops can also be upgraded with ExpressCards, but this type of upgrade is not as fast as the memory installed on the motherboard. Some smartphones, tablets, and laptops can be upgraded with flash memory cards. Refer back to Figures 11.8, 11.9, and 11.10 to see some examples of flash media.

Planning the Laptop Memory Upgrade

In addition to determining what type of memory chips are going to be used, you must determine what features the memory chip might have. The computer system or motherboard documentation is going to delineate what features are supported. Refer back to Table 6.3 to refresh yourself on memory technologies. Laptop memory advertisements are similar to desktop memory advertisements, as shown in Table 11.14.

TABLE 11.14   Sample SO-DIMM advertisements

Memory	Advertisement
2GB	204-pin SO-DIMM DDR3 1333 Unbuffered 1.35V CAS Latency 9
4GB	204-pin SO-DIMM DDR3 1333 Unbuffered 1.5V CAS Latency 10
8GB kit (2×4GB)	204-pin SO-DIMM DDR3 1600 Unbuffered 1.5V CAS Latency 9

Notice in Table 11.14 that the 2-GB memory module runs at 1.35V and the others run at 1.5V. Some motherboards support **dual-voltage memory**, which means the motherboard supports the memory module that runs at the lower 1.35-V level. 1.35-V memory modules use less power and generate less heat. Note that all memory modules must be 1.35-V modules to operate at 1.35 volts.

Take an example of a user who wanted to upgrade memory for a laptop. First, you would open a web browser and search for the specific model and look for the memory specifications (how many slots and what type of memory the laptop allows). The laptop came with 4GB of RAM, but it has the capacity to hold 8GB. Because the laptop has two memory slots, it currently has two 2-GB SO-DIMMs installed. In order to upgrade, the user will have to purchase two memory modules of 4GB each and replace the modules currently in the laptop.

Laptop Memory Removal/Installation

Many laptops have only one memory slot, so when you upgrade, you must remove the module that is installed. Always refer to the manufacturer's documentation when doing this. Before installing or removing laptop memory, always turn off the laptop, disconnect the AC power cord (if installed), and remove the battery.

When installing memory into a mobile device, refer to the documentation to see whether a retaining screw on the bottom of the unit must be removed or if the keyboard must be removed in order to access the memory slots. Be sure the laptop memory notch fits into the key in the memory slot. Laptop memory is normally installed at a 45-degree angle into the slot. Press down on the module until it locks into the side clips. The trick to installing memory is to push firmly into the slot and then into the side clamps. Figure 11.85 shows how to access the memory module in a laptop and the installation process. Notice that the laptop battery has been removed.

FIGURE 11.85   Accessing and installing a laptop memory module

Laptop Storage

Laptop hard drives come in two major form factors—1.8-inch and 2.5-inch. The **2.5-inch** form factor is designed for laptops. A **1.8-inch** form factor is found in laptops, ultrabooks, and ultraportable devices such as MP3 players. It is also used for SSDs. Figure 11.86 shows a 2.5-inch hard drive installed in a laptop.

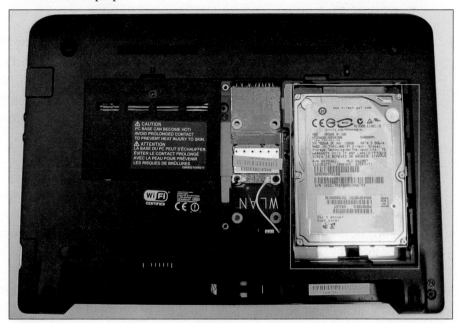

FIGURE 11.86   Installed 2.5-in laptop hard drive

TECH TIP

What to do if you want more storage space for a laptop

Laptops do not normally allow a second hard drive. However, you can add an additional hard drive to the USB, eSATA, combo eSATAp, or IEEE 1394 (FireWire) port.

Hard drives in laptops tend to be one of three types, as described in Table 11.15.

TABLE 11.15   Laptop hard drive types

Type	Description
Mechanical	Traditional drives that require a motor to spin and have read-write heads that float over the hard drive platters.
SSD	Uses flash memory technology to store data. No moving parts and produce less heat than mechanical drives. Very fast, but more expensive than mechanical.
Hybrid	Sometimes known as a solid-state hybrid drive (SSHD). Part of the drive is SSD to store the operating system and the other part is the traditional mechanical drive to hold user data.

Internal Drives

Laptops traditionally had a PATA or SATA hard drive installed, but today they have an SSD instead of or in addition to these hard drive types. Other mobile devices such as ultrabooks and tablets use SSDs as well. A mini PCIe adapter can be used to connect the drive to the system, an M.2 connector, or the drive can be directly attached to the motherboard. Additional storage can be provided by devices that connect to USB, eSATA, eSATAp, or IEEE 1394 ports. ExpressCard hard drives can also be used to provide storage expansion.

External Drives

For external drives, attach the drive to external power if necessary. Some USB devices use external power, some are powered and connect to one USB port, while still others require two USB ports. Some manufacturers may require you to install software before attaching the drive. Once installed, use *Device Manager* to ensure the drive is recognized by the operating system. If the drive is a FireWire device, the drive may appear under the *IEEE 1394 Devices* section of Device Manager.

Hard Drive Replacement

Two methods are used with hard drives installed in portable computers: proprietary or removable. With a proprietary installation, the hard drive is installed in a location where it cannot be changed, configured, or moved very easily. Proprietary cables and connectors are used. With removable hard drives, the laptop has a hard drive bay that allows installation/removal through a single connector that provides power as well as data signaling. Otherwise, the drive could have separate data and power connectors.

To remove a laptop hard drive, always follow the manufacturer's instructions. The following are generic steps for removing/replacing. Always ensure that you are replacing the drive with the correct size and interface before starting this process.

Step 1. Power down the laptop and remove the battery.

Step 2. Turn the computer upside down to locate the panel used to access the hard drive. Note that some laptop models have hard drives that release to the side of the computer.

Step 3. Remove any screws to gain access to the drive. A sliding lock release may also allow access to the drive area. Do not lose these screws. They may not come with the replacement drive.

Step 4. Slide the drive out of the connector and remove it from the unit. Do not force it. Some units have release levers, are mounted on a frame, and/or are mounted on rubber feet. You may need to gently rock the drive back and forth while pulling gently to ease the drive out of the laptop. Remember that this drive has probably never been removed since it was initially installed.

Reverse the process to install a new drive that has the same form factor. Figure 11.87 shows a SATA hard drive being mounted inside a frame before being installed in a laptop.

FIGURE 11.87   Installing a laptop hard drive

Hard Drive Upgrade to SSD

When replacing a laptop hard drive with an SSD, because there is only one drive bay, an external drive enclosure that holds the SSD is needed for the installation process. The enclosure might later be used for the current hard drive to make it an external drive. Also, third-party software that clones your computer and allows you to move selected applications over to the SSD without re-installation of the software is useful. The following are generic steps used to replace a hard drive with an SSD. Remember to have AC power attached during this process. Figure 11.88 shows an SSD drive being installed in a laptop.

Step 1. Delete any unneeded files and folders. Uninstall any unneeded, unwanted, or unused applications.

Step 2. Defragment the hard drive or run Disk Cleanup.

Step 3. Create a system image.

Step 4. Put the SSD in the external enclosure and connect it to the laptop.

Step 5. Ensure Windows recognizes the drive. Use the Disk Management tool to verify. If the drive lists as "Not initialized," right-click on the drive, and select *Initialize disk*. Also ensure that the used space of your current hard drive is less than that of the SSD. Depending on the software you use, you may have to shrink your current hard drive partition that has the operating system installed to less than that of the SSD. If you do, reboot the computer after all operations to ensure the hard drive is still working properly.

Step 6. Use third-party software to clone the current hard drive to the SSD.

Step 7. Power off the laptop. Remove the old hard drive and install the SSD.

Step 8. Power on the laptop and ensure the SSD boots and all applications work.

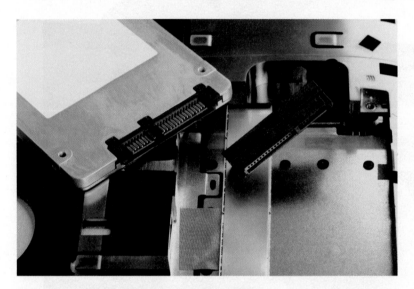

FIGURE 11.88   Installing a laptop SSD

> **TECH TIP**
>
> **Sometimes a noisy hard drive can be a good thing...it is a warning to you**
>
> Mechanical hard drives tend to give indicators that failure is imminent. They make noises, the laptop fails to boot, data blocks are marked as bad, data access might be slow, or error messages appear. SSDs, on the other hand, might fail with no advance warning.

Optical Drive Replacement

Mobile devices that have optical disc drives can be a slot-loaded drive (where you insert the disc into a slot on the side or front of the mobile device) or a mounted drive. Mounted drives commonly require you to turn the laptop over to access the drive. You might even have to remove the keyboard in order to access. Look for the little symbol of the optical disc. Not all manufacturers use this symbol so ensure you research the particular mobile device model. Remove the appropriate screw(s); then pull out the drive. Before replacing an optical drive, try blowing compressed air on the drive to clear out any collected residue. Reinstall and retest. Figure 11.89 shows an internal laptop optical drive.

FIGURE 11.89   Internal laptop optical drive

Laptop Wireless Card Replacement

The laptop wireless card is commonly located under the keyboard or accessible from the underside of the laptop. Refer to the manufacturer's website for the exact procedures. The generic removal steps are as follows. Simply reverse the steps to install the replacement card.

Step 1. Disconnect the AC power and remove the battery.

Step 2. Locate the wireless card. Refer back to Figure 11.86. The WLAN card is to the immediate left of the hard drive and is labeled WLAN (upside down in the photo).

Step 3. Disconnect the one or two wireless antenna cables from the card (see Figure 11.90). Notice in Figure 11.90 that the wires attach to two posts on the wireless NIC. These wires are what connect the antenna to the wireless NIC. A small flat-tipped screwdriver, small needle-nose pliers, or tweezers might be used for this task. Be very careful with this step. Cables are not typically included with the replacement wireless card. Take a picture or make a note about which cable attaches to which connector if multiple cables are used.

Step 4. Ease the wireless card out of the laptop. Note that a lever or tab may be used by the vendor. Make a note or take a photo of how the wireless card inserts into the slot.

TECH TIP

Where is the wireless antenna on a laptop?

For laptops that have integrated wireless NICs, the wireless antenna is usually built into the laptop display for best connectivity. This is because the display is the tallest point of the laptop and therefore closest to the wireless receiving antenna. The quality of these integrated antennas varies.

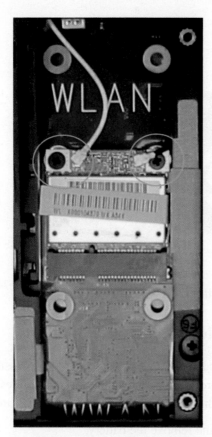

FIGURE 11.90   Laptop wireless NIC

Laptop DC Jack Replacement

Because of the numerous times someone attaches the AC-to-DC power brick, it is no wonder that a laptop power jack needs to be replaced sometimes. You know it is the jack when a new power brick doesn't work, when you physically can see a broken pin or loose pin in the DC jack, or when you use a multimeter to test the DC voltage level coming out of the power brick and it is fine.

The power jack is a DC connector because the power brick takes the AC power from the wall and converts it to DC for input into the laptop. The DC jack comes with a power cable that usually winds through the laptop to attach to the motherboard. It may actually be mounted on a small circuit card. Always refer to the manufacturer's replacement steps.

Figure 11.91 shows how one might connect. Always disconnect the power brick and remove the battery before starting any repair. Note that the cable attached to the DC jack may have retaining clips or be threaded through a very narrow space. Do not damage adjacent parts. Document any parts that you have to remove in order to remove the defective DC jack.

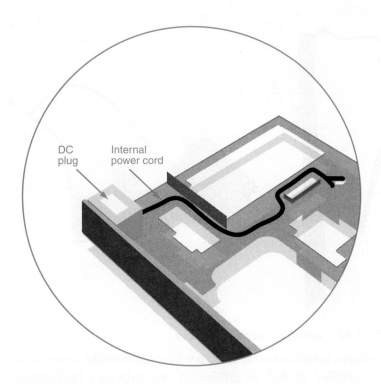

FIGURE 11.91   Laptop DC jack (plug) and power cable

Mobile Device Sound

Laptop speakers are not always of the highest quality. Mobile devices, in general are limited in their sound options compared to desktop computers. A mobile device normally has an integrated microphone, a line out connector for headphones, and sound integrated into the system board.

Laptop devices normally can control sound with buttons above the keypad or by selecting a combination of the [Fn] and another key.

For Android mobile devices, use the *Setting > Sound* option to mute and modify the ringtone. Optionally, you can also select sounds to be played, such as when the screen unlocks or when switching between screens.

For Apple iOS devices, use the *General > Settings > Sounds* option. The speaker volume and sounds heard for email, phone calls, reminders, keyboard clicks, and so on are set on this screen. Both Android and Apple iOS-based mobile devices have volume controls on the sides.

Consider wireless or USB speakers if the laptop speaker fails. Keep in mind that if the sound device is powered by the USB port, this shortens battery life. If the customer insists on laptop speakers being replaced, then they are commonly located in the sides or back corners of the laptop. Figure 11.92 shows two different models of mobile device speakers.

Similar to replacing the DC power jack, when replacing laptop speakers, be careful when tracing and removing the speaker wires. Always refer to the manufacturer's directions. Speaker wires must sometimes be wiggled gently in order to detach. They commonly screw into the motherboard. Inspect the speaker wire path before removing. Other parts may have to be removed in order to remove the faulty speakers.

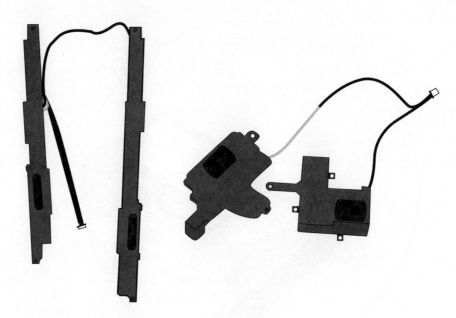

FIGURE 11.92   Internal laptop speakers

Microphones in tablets normally do not have controls like laptops and PCs. Instead, the microphone is controlled through an application that supports a microphone, such as a notepad that allows you to add audio notes or record a lecture or an online conference application. Inside the application, there is normally a little icon of a microphone that you tap to be able to start recording. External microphones can be added using wireless Bluetooth connectivity or an external microphone for those tablets that have a jack. Smartphones, of course, have integrated microphones.

Laptop Display

The laptop display is one of the more complex parts of the laptop. Some mobile devices that serve as laptops have **removable screens**. Some laptops even have **rotating screens** that can be used to show others something on the display, as seen in Figure 11.93. Before diving into the laptop display, return to Chapter 9 and refresh yourself on the following terms: LCD, TTL, IPS, fluorescent and LED backlighting, and OLED.

FIGURE 11.93   Laptop with rotating screen

TECH TIP

Liquid crystals are poisonous

Be careful with cracked LCDs. If liquid crystals (which are not liquid) get on you, wash with soap and water and seek medical attention.

Besides the laptop screen, the display assembly contains other parts and some of them have nothing to do with the screen. Table 11.16 outlines some common components found in a laptop display.

TABLE 11.16   Laptop display components

Memory	Advertisement
Wi-Fi antenna	Attaches to the WLAN card (that is commonly under the computer and/or attached to the system board) in order to receive/transmit wireless signals.
Web cam	A camera used for video conferencing (and as a camera/video recorder in other mobile devices). Some laptops have the ability to use the integrated camera for facial recognition as a security measure. Facial recognition software is used to authenticate a user and allow the user to log on to the computer. However, because the biometric software cannot distinguish between a living face and a digitized image, it is possible to fool the software by using a photograph.
Microphone	A device used to take voice and digitize it into 1s and 0s so that sound may be heard on a conference call or in a recording. Microphones are used for Voice over IP (VoIP) and are tested through the Recording tab of the Sound Control Panel.
Inverter	Converts DC to AC for the CCFL backlight.
Digitizer	Found in a touch screen display; a thin layer of plastic that translates pressure, swipes, or other touch actions into digital signals. Replacement is sometimes difficult and/or expensive.

Laptops use LCDs and have a video cable that connects the LCD to the motherboard. Either a CCFL or LED backlight bulb is used on many models so images on the screen can be seen. The CCFL type connects to an inverter (see Figure 11.94). The inverter converts low DC voltage to high AC voltage for the backlight bulb. Screens larger than 15.4 inches may need two CCFL backlight bulbs. An LCD with an LED backlight does not need an inverter. An OLED display doesn't need an inverter or a backlight.

TECH TIP

Is it worth fixing a laptop display?

Laptop displays might be too expensive to repair, but if the inverter or backlight is the faulty part, the repair cost is negligible.

The lid close detector (displayed in Figure 11.94) can be a physical switch or a magnetic switch located close to the back edge of the keyboard portion of a laptop. The laptop can be configured through power management configuration to go into hibernation, sleep, or standby mode when the laptop is closed.

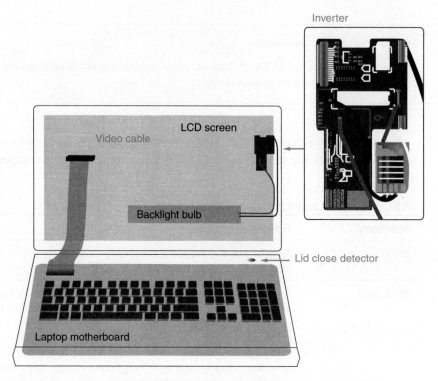

FIGURE 11.94   Laptop video connectivity

The laptop display may need to be replaced as part of a repair. When removing a laptop display, always refer to the directions from the computer manufacturer. The following steps are generic:

Step 1. Use proper anti-static precautions and remove the screws that hold the screen bezel in place.

Step 2. Gently pry the plastic bezel that protects the screen edge from the case.

Step 3. Remove the screen retaining screws.

Step 4. Gently lift the screen from the case. Be very careful with the connectors. Flip the screen so the back of the screen is visible.

Step 5. Notice the ribbon cable that runs up the back of the display. Gently disconnect the cable at the top of the display and the cable that connects to the motherboard. Some are cables you squeeze to release; others have pull tabs or you gently pull from the socket. Figure 11.95 shows the back side of an LCD that uses a CCFL backlight.

TECH TIP

What is the best resolution for a laptop display?

Set a laptop to the native resolution (the resolution for which the LCD was made).

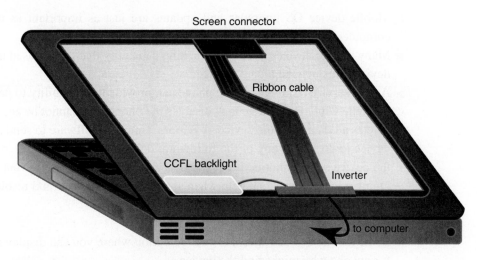

Screen connector

Ribbon cable

CCFL backlight

Inverter

to computer

FIGURE 11.95   Removing an LCD with LED backlight

Mobile Device Security

Laptops have special physical security needs, and locking and tracking devices are available for them. Use a nondescript bag to carry a laptop to reduce the chance of it being stolen. Have an engraved permanent asset tag attached. A **physical laptop lock** or laptop locking station can be purchased and installed on a desk. A user places his laptop into the locking station without worrying about someone coming by if he momentarily steps away from the desk.

Another option is to use the universal security slot (USS) that allows a **cable lock** or laptop alarm to be attached. Special software packages exist that have the laptop automatically contact a tracking center in case of theft. Figure 11.96 shows a USS on a notebook computer.

FIGURE 11.96   Laptop cable lock

Many of the issues for wireless connectivity for laptops also apply to smartphones and tablets. But smartphones and tablets also have issues of their own. Many think that because the devices do not have hard drives, they do not need antivirus or antimalware software. This is a misconception. Install antivirus/antimalware software on mobile devices. Depending on the device, the software may not be able to automatically scan for viruses or even have a set scheduled scan time. Here are some more security suggestions:

> Mobile devices can run each app in a sandbox—a separated space from other apps. This behavior provides a natural security mechanism for applications.

> Mobile device OS upgrades and updates are just as important as updates on a full-sized computer.
> Many mobile devices have GPS tracking capability that can be used to locate a lost or stolen device. This may be a paid service.
> A paid service or an app on the phone can provide the capability to perform a remote lock or a remote wipe. The remote lock disables the phone so it cannot be accessed. The remote wipe deletes all data from the device. A **remote wipe** uses software to send a command to a mobile device to do one or any of the following: delete data, factory reset, remove everything from the device so it cannot be used, and overwrite data storage to prevent forensic data recovery.
> Doing a factory reset can help when some of the app issues and resolutions discussed below do not work.
> Verify phone firmware is the latest version.
> Some mobile devices have a lost mode option where you can display messages on the screen for anyone who might find the device.

Most mobile devices have the ability to do some of the following types of locks or **screen locks**: have a **swipe lock**, PIN, **passcode lock**, security pattern, **facial recognition lock** or unlock, **fingerprint lock**, or password enabled that activates when the device is inactive. **Authenticator apps** can also be downloaded. To configure basic mobile security, perform the following:

> Android: *Settings > Location & Security > Set up screen lock*.
> iOS: *Settings > General > Passcode lock On* option. Use *Settings > Passcode* for more passcode options (see Figure 11.97). You can also configure the *Auto-Lock* time. On an iPad, you can use the *iPad Cover Lock/Unlock On* option.
> Windows mobile: *Settings > Lock screen/lock & wallpaper*.

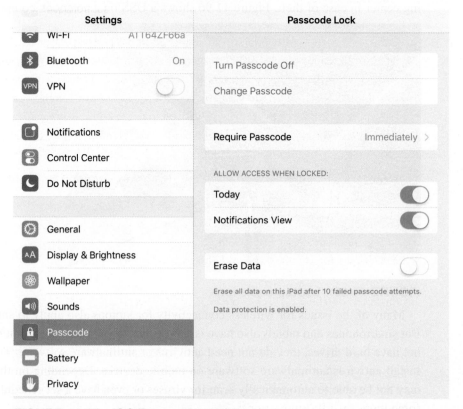

FIGURE 11.97 iOS Passcode settings

Failed Login Attempts or Unauthorized Account Access

Some mobile devices have configuration settings in case the security method fails, such as an incorrectly entered password or **system lockout**. Some devices have a default number of attempts. For an extra security precaution, some devices can be configured for what happens to the device after a set number of failed attempts, such as disabling the device or even erasing the data. Most mobile device users that have this capability enabled have the data backed up to the cloud or onto a machine.

On an Android device, perform a factory reset from the Android system recovery menu. In iOS, you can use the *Passcode Lock* setting (refer back to Figure 11.97) in order to set how long the system waits for the passcode (*Require Passcode* setting*)*. After 6 failed attempts, the iOS mobile device will be disabled for 1 minute; after 7 failed attempts, it will be disabled for 5 minutes; after 9 failed attempts, disabled for an hour. If you enable the *Erase Data* option, the device will be wiped after 11 failed attempts.

So what happens if someone gets your account? Change your password immediately. Change to a different credit card on the account. Notify the vendor (Apple, Microsoft, Google, and so on). If possible, enable two-step verification to prevent future issues. Some email products allow viewing account activity. Many vendors have an option to send you an email when an unusual device was used to access your account.

Unauthorized Location Tracking

Note *that* not all mobile devices have GPS, but they can obtain information from other networks and browsers to provide location services. Apps that use location services also use battery life. To turn location services on, use the following:

> On Android: *Settings > Location*.
> On iOS: *Settings > Privacy > Location services* (Note that you can use the *System Services* option to select which services are allowed to track your location.) Another one is *Settings > Privacy > Advertising >* enable *Limit Ad Tracking* and *Reset Advertising Identifier* so you are prompted for which apps can track. A third one is to change your Safari or other browser settings. For Safari, *Settings > Safari >* enable *Do Not Track*.
> On Windows mobile: *Settings > Location > Location services*. For a particular app, access *Settings > Applications >* locate the particular app > turn off *Use my location*.

Android, iOS, and Windows mobile have apps for dealing with mobile devices that have been lost or stolen, but other free and paid ones are available.

> Android: *Settings > Security > Device Administration*.
> iOS: *Settings > Find My iPhone*.
> Windows mobile: *Settings > Update & security > Find my phone*.

Leaked Personal Files or Data

The way to protect personal files and/or data on a mobile device is to protect the device itself, secure the device, and encrypt your files (see Figure 11.98). Don't enable Bluetooth or GPS unless this is needed. If you think data has already been compromised, change all passwords on all accounts and devices. Watch accounts and notify credit companies, if applicable. You can also factory reset the device.

FIGURE 11.98 Leaked data on a mobile device

Unauthorized Camera/Microphone Activation

As already discussed, some apps intentionally gather information about you using your location and optionally the integrated camera and microphone. One app has the capability of figuring out where you are, who is in the room, the sounds being heard, and correlating the data with others in the same vicinity to create a social network environment. Other apps are used for spying on folks. Research each app that you or the customer installs.

Every Android app is supposed to state what access permissions are required by the app. With Android, you can ensure *Android Device Manager* is enabled (*Settings > Security > Device Administration*). It is enabled by default. See Figure 11.99.

FIGURE 11.99 Android Device Manager

With iOS devices, use *Settings > Privacy > Camera/Microphone* to show what apps have requested access to either the camera or the microphone. Note that not all reported activity has been through an app. So how can you tell if someone has accessed your phone and potentially your camera and microphone as well? Here are some signs:

> Look for strange short message service (SMS) text messages.
> Look for increased phone bills.
> Take notice of any weird activity on your phone (apps locking, opening mysteriously, slow performance).
> Take notice of battery life in case it is losing its charge faster than normal.

Data Transmission Over Limit

Many mobile devices that connect to the cellular network have a specific amount of text, photo, and video allowed in the user's specific rate plan. To view how much data has been used in a specific period or to turn cellular data off, use these steps:

> Android: *Settings > Data usage* (optionally, you can set the mobile data limit)
> iOS: *Settings > Cellular > Cellular Data*
> Windows mobile: *App list > Data Sense* (optionally, you can *Set limit*)

Unauthorized Root Access

A user that has unauthorized root access has access to the mobile device's file system (see Figure 11.100). Through the file system, malicious programs can be installed, files can be downloaded and copied, and private information can be gleaned. **Jailbreaking** (iOS) and **rooting** (Android) are two terms that mean that the operating system has been compromised in such a way that the user has an increased level of privilege on the phone. On Android, this is known as having root access. For iOS devices, users bypass some of the restrictions placed on the device. People do this for several reasons: apps that are pre-installed and unremovable can be removed; features such as tethering that might require an additional charge or are available for free; the device can be made to operate faster; the device is not tied to or monitored by the operating system vendor or the phone vendor; and/or the operating environment can be modified.

Android is an open source operating system, but still vendors are allowed to make modifications and customize it. Both iOS and Android devices have security and operating system releases that are not received by phones that have been rooted or that have been jailbroken. Rooting or jailbreaking a device may void a manufacturer's warranty; makes a device more susceptible to viruses, malware, and security issues; and has an increased possibility of access to the root directory (the starting place for all files). iOS devices that have had the jailbreak performed can be reversed and the original iOS can be restored using iTunes.

FIGURE 11.100   Root access to mobile phone

Mobile Device Travel and Storage

When traveling with a laptop, remove all cards that insert into slots and store them in containers so that their contacts do not become dirty and cause intermittent problems. Remove all media discs such as CDs, DVDs, or BDs. Check that drive doors and devices are securely latched. Ensure that the mobile device is powered off or in hibernate mode (not in sleep/suspend or standby power mode).

Carry the device in a padded case. If you have to place the device on an airport security conveyor belt, ensure that the device is not placed upside down, which can cause damage to the display. Never place objects on top of a mobile device or pick up a laptop by the edges of the display when the laptop is opened. When shipping a mobile device, place it in a properly padded box. The original shipping box is a safe container.

The United States has regulations about lithium batteries on airplanes. If the battery contacts come in contact with metal or other batteries, the battery could short-circuit and cause a fire. For this reason, any lithium batteries are to be kept in original packaging. If original packaging is not available, place electrical tape over the battery terminals or place each battery in an individual bag. Spare lithium batteries are not allowed in checked baggage but can be taken in carry-on bags.

Mobile Device Troubleshooting Overview

Troubleshooting mobile devices is similar to how you go about solving desktop problems. Whether Android, iOS, or Windows is being used as an operating system, you still use *Settings* or various Control Panels in order to make changes to or adjust configuration settings on the device.

The point is that the concept is the same. Hardware is similar. Things that go wrong in a mobile device touch screen are similar to a touch screen on a laptop.

Hard and Soft Resets

Sometimes a simple soft reset is all it takes to fix the problem before delving into some of the other techniques presented. A **soft reset** is simply restarting the mobile device. Some phones have a restart option. Some phones might not restart and the battery has to be removed in order to power off the device. Reasons to do a soft reset include the following abnormal behaviors:

> Unresponsive touch screen
> Slow system response
> Cannot receive, make, send, and/or receive text messages or calls
> Audio issues
> Error code—record before restarting (see Figure 11.101)

FIGURE 11.101   Cell phone error

In contrast, a **hard reset** is another name for a factory reset. This was covered early in the chapter for Android devices. Hard resets are done when no other solution helps with the problem, you have forgotten your password, the screen is unresponsive and a soft reset did not help, or if you installed a software app that you cannot install or it caused erratic behavior that cannot be solved in any other way.

In Android, boot the device into *Recovery Mode* (typically accessed by holding down two or more specific buttons such as the power, volume, and/or home) while the device boots > *wipe data/ factory reset* (press *Power* button to select) > *Yes – erase all user data.*

In iOS, it is *Settings > General > Reset > Erase All Content and Settings > Erase iPhone/iPad.*

In Windows, check the manufacturer. Commonly holding down the power button (or the power button and the increase volume button) for several seconds does it. Sometimes, you might have to disconnect the AC power cord and remove the battery.

Some devices can be fixed by removing the power brick (wall adapter) and the battery and leaving out for about 30 seconds. On some Apple devices, you must hold the power button down for 5 seconds afterward. This is known as a system management controller (SMC) reset. Apple devices also keep configuration settings like volume, date, and time in parameter RAM (PRAM). A small separate battery keeps these settings current. To reset these settings on an Apple laptop, hold the following keys down at the same time while the system is booting: [Cmd] + [Option] + [P] + [R].

Let's go over troubleshooting mobile devices by area of concern. Remember, though, that the Internet has a wealth of technical information available at your fingertips. Research is an important troubleshooting step in order to see how others solved the problem or similar problems.

Mobile Device App Concerns

Since so many apps are free (and even the ones that we pay for), apps do not always play well with one another or with specific operating system versions. In order to troubleshoot apps, sometimes you need to stop the app (perform a **force stop**) or stop other apps because the mobile device is slow to respond due to **high resource utilization** (apps taking all of the memory and processor power). Here's generically how to stop an application, but remember that Android is open source so vendors can implement things differently and iOS and Windows have different versions so the exact steps may be different than those shown.

> Android: *Settings > Apps/Application manager >* locate and select a particular application > *Force stop.*
> iOS: Press *Home* button two times quickly > swipe to find the app to close > swipe up on the app's preview to close it.
> Windows mobile: Swipe down from the top of the screen and drag the app to beyond the bottom of the screen.

You might also be required to uninstall and reinstall the app because the app fails to respond or is not working. There are free app managers that allow you to do this too. The steps below are from within the standard operating system. Note that some apps come with the mobile device and cannot be installed, but can be disabled. Deleting an app deletes the data and settings.

> Android: *Settings > Apps/Application manager >* locate and select a particular app > *Uninstall/ Disable*
> iOS: Press and hold on top of the app icon until all of the icons shake (see Figure 11.102) > tap the *x* in the corner of the icon > *Delete.*
> Windows mobile: Press and hold the app icon > tap *Uninstall > Yes.*

FIGURE 11.102   iOS app deletion

Apps Not Installing

When an app does not install, ensure your hardware/operating system is compatible with the app and has available storage space. Some apps do not run well from an SD card and might need to be installed onto the phone's internal storage. Ensure an antivirus program isn't blocking it. If an app hangs during the installation process, ensure you have a connection to a Wi-Fi or cellular network, restart the device, and start the process again. Try downloading the app from a different Wi-Fi network.

> Android: *Settings > Apps/Application manager > all >* locate and tap on *Market > clear data > clear cache.*
> iOS: Try resetting the network settings: *Settings > General > Reset* and try again. You could reset all settings or take the device to an Apple Store.
> Windows mobile: Close the app and then restart it. Power the device off and back on again. Uninstall and reinstall the app.

Apps Not Loading

When an app does not start, see if the mobile device believes it to be running already. Windows has *Task Manager* and Android has *Settings > Apps/Application manager.* With iOS, you can't really see this, but some apps refresh their content automatically. See these settings with *Settings > General > Background App Refresh.* Windows mobile automatically updates apps. On older versions, Windows mobile allows you to access the *Store > Updates > Update all.* You can always try closing the app and opening it again. Try restarting the mobile device. Try powering down the device and restarting it. Check for operating system updates and if the app has any updates. Lastly, delete the app and reinstall it.

TECH TIP

Email not current on your smartphone?

Check connectivity. If you have Internet/cellular access, restart the phone.

Unable to Decrypt Email

With iOS devices, you can use S/MIME to send and possibly receive encrypted email messages. Use the *Mail, Contacts, Calendar* option > select the appropriate email account > *Account* > depending on the email account type, you can set the S/MIME setting there or go into *Advanced.* Some vendors allow encrypting all messages by default.

Within Android, support for S/MIME is built into email clients and can be accessed through the email app > *Settings* option. Also, web browser add-ons can also be used. Some email apps might require that a security certificate (file) be obtained and copied to the *root directory* (see Chapter 17 for more information on this) or the *Download* folder. Then access your email account > *Settings > Security options > Email certificate >* tap + (plus sign) > select the certificate.

Mobile Device Keyboard/Trackpad Issues

There are symptoms that appear that the solution is not simply to replace the part. The key to some of these issues is to research what others have done when the particular problem has occurred. Software updates sometimes fix some hardware issues.

Keyboard Issues

Not all devices have keyboards. Mobile devices can have wireless keyboards, optional keyboards, and wired keyboards. Three common keyboard issues are Num Lock indicator light, sticking keys, and ghost cursor/pointer drift. Let's start with the Num Lock issue.

The Num Lock key is used to allow keys on the numeric pad to be used as something besides numbers (arrow keys, a home key, page up and page down keys, delete key, insert key, and end key), as shown in Figure 11.103. By pushing the Num Lock key so the **Num Lock indicator light** illuminates on the keyboard, numbers are used. By depressing the Num Lock key so the indicator turns off, then the keys are used for arrow keys and the like. Configure the UEFI/system BIOS for the default action (enabled or not enabled) per the customer's preference.

FIGURE 11.103   Num Lock and numeric key pad

Mobile devices that have keyboards can get dirtier than desktop systems. For a sticky key, do the same process as you would for a desktop keyboard. Shake the dirt out and spray with compressed air as shown back in Figure 1.24. Keys might have to be removed in order to get to the dirt or debris, to clean, or to spray compressed air. Figure 11.104 shows a close-up of a laptop key that has been removed. The key may have to be pushed toward the top of the keyboard and then lifted up in order to remove it. Peek under the key to see how it attaches before prying the key off.

Clear thin, soft polyurethane covers allow the user full function of the keyboard while protecting the keyboard from liquids and debris; it is easy to pop off and wash with dish detergent and water. Laptop backpacks are available that offer good protection against dropping, banging, temperature changes, and liquids. Rugged tablets and laptops offer military-type construction, glove-capable touch instead of bare fingertip, and an outdoor adaptable/readable display. Flexible rubber keyboards are also available.

FIGURE 11.104 Removed laptop key

Trackpad Issues

Another annoying keyboard problem is the illustrious ghost cursor or pointer drift where the pointer moves across the screen even if no one is touching it. This is commonly caused by the improper touchpad sensitivity settings. You might also need to update the touchpad driver installed. Malware or a virus can cause this symptom. In Windows, you can search for `troubleshoot touchpad` and use that guide. Some users disable the touchpad and use a wired mouse.

Mobile Device Display Issues

Displays are critical to mobile devices. They get viewed, touched, and swiped more than any other part. Displays can go out, dim, not respond, flicker, and cause user dissatisfaction. Let's tackle some of the common issues.

Dim Display, No Display, or Flickering Display

A dim display is commonly caused by a lack of interaction, display setting, or low battery. Move the pointer or tap the screen, adjust display settings, and attach AC power to see if it is a battery-related issue. On a laptop, the problem could also be caused by an improperly adjusted backlight or sticky lid actuator switch (the switch that detects you have closed or opened the laptop).

If the device has no display, attach an external display if possible. For a laptop, ensure the appropriate Fn has been used. If showing a presentation, you might have to use the Windows *Change display settings* link to adjust the output to duplicate what is showing on the screen. Check video cabling. Also use the appropriate Fn key, even if an external display is not available.

Check the laptop close switch that is located in the main part of the laptop, close to the back and near to where the display attaches to the laptop. The lid close detector can be a physical switch or a magnetic switch located close to the back edge of the keyboard portion of a laptop. A laptop and some mobile devices can be configured to go into hibernation, sleep, or standby mode when the laptop is closed. Check the power management settings, which can be configured to go into hibernate, sleep, or standby if the laptop is closed. Also check the video cable from the laptop system board to the display.

TECH TIP

What to do if a laptop display goes black, red, dim, or pink

Most likely this is because the backlight bulb is faulty. Otherwise, the problem is the DC-to-AC inverter. Connect an external monitor to the laptop external video port. If the external monitor works, most likely the backlight bulb is the culprit.

For a mobile device, try turning it off and back on. On a laptop or tablet, see if the device appears to boot normally. If the device has recently been exposed to liquid, power off the device, remove the battery, and allow the device to thoroughly dry before trying to power it back on again. A bad LCD backlight or inverter can cause a dim or blank display, too.

A flickering display can be something as simple as adjusting the resolution (should be the native resolution), refresh rate, or tightening the display cable. If you have recently changed the display, check the driver. Move the display to see if the flicker is related to display movement. An inverter and backlight can also cause this problem or show horizontal/vertical lines. Figure 11.105 shows a disassembled phone so you can see how the display attaches.

FIGURE 11.105 Disassembled smartphone

Touch Screen Does Not Respond or Is Inaccurate

The touch screen is a critical part of a mobile device. When it does not respond, users get frustrated. Here are things to try. Note that if the touch screen doesn't respond the way you expect, then all things to try when it doesn't work are good to try for this as well.

> Close some apps to free up memory.
> See if it is app-specific if possible.
> Restart the device. Force the shutdown even if it requires disconnecting the AC power cord and/or removing the battery.
> If the display has had any liquid on it, turn the device off and remove the battery. Allow the device to dry thoroughly before powering on.
> If a screen protector is in place, remove it.

> Shut down the device and remove any memory cards, the SIM card, and the battery for about 60 seconds. Reinstall and power up.
> Some devices have a calibration utility or one could be downloaded to calibrate for touch input. Android: *Settings > Display*. Windows 7/8/10: Search for and use *Calibrate the screen for pen and touch input > Calibrate*.
> Perform a factory restart.

If the touch screen is broken, you should be able to still see what is on the device. When the LCD is damaged, then cracks appear or the screen has dark spots, but the touch screen might still work in places. Screens can be ordered and replaced. There are repair shops that specialize in mobile device displays.

Slow Performance

Slow performance can be a lot of things, but some folks first notice the responsiveness of a touch screen or slowness for data to download. If you suspect the touch screen, troubleshoot that. But if you have ruled out the touch screen, consider the following tips:

> Check battery power level.
> Close apps that aren't being used.
> Close services (Wi-Fi, GPS, location services, Bluetooth, and so on) that are not being used. Put the device in Airplane Mode.
> Attach to a Wi-Fi network.
> Move closer to the wireless access point if attached to Wi-Fi.
> Newer Android devices have an option to reduce the amount of data needed by the Chrome browser using the data saver—use *Settings > (Advanced) Data saver*.

Mobile Device Power Issues

People are not going to use their mobile device if it has power issues. They need that power to be mobile. Power issues can include extreme short battery life, no power, swollen battery, and the battery not charging.

Extremely Short Battery Life

A battery that won't hold a charge for long (or has a power drain) commonly needs to be replaced. However, it could be all of the apps, wireless, location services, GPS, and Bluetooth settings that you have turned on. You should inspect the battery to see if it is swollen. A **swollen battery** is one that bulges and might even leak (see Figure 11.106). Most batteries that won't hold a charge need to be replaced (and replaced immediately if swollen). Also, verify that the battery is actually showing as being charged. Don't just go on the time it has been plugged in. The physical connection to the charger could be a tenuous one. The charger could be faulty too.

FIGURE 11.106   Swollen battery in cell phone

Battery Not Charging

When a battery does not charge properly, the problem could be the battery, the charger, or the connection on the phone. Inspect the connection on the phone first. Do you see any debris, dirt, pins that look like they do not align with the other pins? If so, power off the device, remove the battery, and clean with compressed air or gently try to align pins. Do the same inspection to the charge connector. Take a voltage reading on the charger if possible. See if it is outputting power. See if the same cable and/or charger can charge other devices that require the same voltage and connector type. Try to charge with a different connector such as a car adapter.

No Power or Frozen System

An electronic device that won't power on is useless. Try the following when troubleshooting a mobile device that will not power up.

> Check for power light.
> Ensure the device has not gone into sleep mode. Try waking the device up or power it down and power on again.
> Attach the device to an AC adapter and power up.
> Disconnect the AC power brick, remove the battery, and hold down the power button for a few seconds. Replace the battery and reconnect to AC. Try to power on the laptop again.
> Inspect the power button—has it felt strange lately?
> When you attach the power brick to the mobile device, does the connector attach easily or does it wiggle? Consider replacing the DC power jack if on a laptop.
> Check brightness displays.
> If on a laptop, check the lid close sensor.
> If on a laptop or tablet with keyboard, try closing the display and opening it back up fully (see Figure 11.107).
> Check for malware or virus.

FIGURE 11.107   Close and reopen laptop display

Overheating—Warm/Hot to the Touch

Heat is one of the worst enemies of electronic devices. Leaving mobile devices in hot vehicles and in the sun is bad. If this is the reason for the overheating, power the device down and let it cool. Do not just move it to a cooler spot.

See if you can determine a specific spot that is getting hotter than other places on the device. Determine if that "spot" is where the battery or power is located or another spot on the mobile device. If near the battery, troubleshoot power problems after the device has cooled completely.

Check the battery health icon on the device. Inspect the battery. Replace the battery if you think that is the cause. Close unneeded apps and services. Remove the device from a case, if applicable. Ensure that you are not covering the device's air vents such as laying it on a lap or pillow. Place a laptop on something that elevates it from the desk, such as drink coasters. In addition, pads, trays, and mats can be purchased with fans that are AC powered or USB powered. Research the device vendor to determine if others are having a similar issue.

Mobile Device Sound Issues

Mobile devices have sound issues similar to desktop computers. See Chapter 8 to refresh yourself on issues related to sound. For headphone issues, ensure the cable attaches to the correct line out port. Determine whether you want the speakers disabled. Normally, if you plug into the headphones line out port, the speakers cut off. For Android or iOS devices, check the volume control and whether the device is muted. On tablets or smartphones, check if other applications are using the microphone.

Another common complaint is when headphones are attached, sound still comes through the speakers. Check that the headphones connect securely to the device. Power off the device, remove the battery, and clean the headphone jack.

> Android: Press and hold the power/lock button to change the sound setting to mute everything except the media sound. Close unused apps.
> iOS: Try muting sound and then re-enabling it.
> Windows mobile: Use the *Settings > Sound* option to ensure that the correct volume control was used. Windows has the ability to have different settings for media than ringer.

Mobile Device Network Issues

Chapter 14 goes into more details on networking, but this chapter focuses on basic troubleshooting techniques you can perform on mobile devices that do not require more involved details of how these technologies work. The issues can be broken down into three areas—Wi-Fi, GPS, and Bluetooth.

Wi-Fi Issues

Use the following list to help when troubleshooting Wi-Fi issues on a mobile device.

> Ensure the mobile device is not in Airplane Mode.
> Ensure Wi-Fi is enabled.
> Ensure the correct Wi-Fi network is chosen. If prompted, provide the appropriate security/login credentials.
> Turn Wi-Fi off and then re-enable it again.
> If a laptop always has low signal strength, ensure the wire(s) are attached to the wireless NIC. If the display has been recently replaced, ensure all connectors have been reattached properly and have not been damaged.
> For any device that has low signal strength, move around and try to see if you get more signal bars by moving. The more bars you see, the better the signal strength and speed of transmission. See Figure 11.108.
> With some laptops, you must turn the laptop to a different angle to attach to an access point or have a stronger signal strength (which means faster transfers). Antenna placement is important in a wireless network. Antennas on mobile devices tend to be in the edges or built into the displays.

> If the mobile device connects to a Wi-Fi network unintentionally, turn off Wi-Fi. Some mobile devices have the ability to automatically switch between Wi-Fi and mobile networks in order to keep a solid Internet connection. To disable this in iOS, use *Settings > Wi-Fi >* disable *Auto-Join*. On Android and Windows mobile devices that have Wi-Fi enabled, use *Settings > Wi-Fi >* select and hold on the wireless network that is not wanted > *Forget network* (Android) or *Delete* (Windows mobile).

> Slow or intermittent transmissions can be caused by distance to the access point, other Wi-Fi networks and devices, and the number of devices attached to the same wireless access point that you are.

FIGURE 11.108   Wireless signal strength

GPS Issues

GPS is not provided in all mobile devices. The geographical environment affects GPS reception and can cause intermittent connectivity. If the GPS is installed, but not working, try turning *Location Services* off and back on again. If that fails, restart the device. Some Android devices have assisted GPS which uses GPS satellites, cell towers, and Wi-Fi networks to provide location services. Ensure *Use wireless networks* and *Use GPS satellites* are enabled on an older phone. Some phones have a *High accuracy* setting instead. Windows mobile devices require that the phone radio is turned on and Airplane Mode is not enabled. Another problem is the user might have denied a particular app the right to have access to location services and an app like Google Maps might not be as beneficial as it could be without it. Access the app settings to verify. You could always uninstall and reinstall the app. Turn off any apps that might be using the app that aren't being currently used.

Bluetooth Issues

As with all network connectivity issues (intermittent and lack of), with Bluetooth, turn the device off and back on again. Move the device closer to the other Bluetooth device(s). You could put the device in Airplane Mode and then remove Airplane Mode to toggle all radios off and then re-enable them. Other troubleshooting hints are as follows:

> Check for interference from other devices, including wireless devices on the same frequency. Also look for Windows, Apple iOS, or Android configuration issues.

> If a Bluetooth device is not working in Windows, try the following: Select the Bluetooth icon (🅱) in the notification area on the taskbar and select *Show Bluetooth Devices*. If the device is not listed there, select *Add a device* and try to add it.

> Ensure that the Bluetooth device is charged, powered on, and in the appropriate mode to pair with another Bluetooth device, such as the computing device or car with Bluetooth capability.

> Ensure that other wireless devices, such as wireless networks, automatic lighting and remote controls, cell phones and other portable phones, and microwave ovens, are not interfering with the device.

> Remove unused USB devices.

> If passkeys (PINs) are used, ensure that the keys match.

> If a Bluetooth transceiver is used, move the transceiver to another USB port.

> Remove all other Bluetooth devices to aid in troubleshooting the problematic device.
> In Windows, ensure Bluetooth services are enabled. See Chapter 16 for more information on Windows Services.
> In Windows, ensure that Device Manager shows no issues with the Bluetooth transceiver driver (under the *Bluetooth Radios* section) or the Bluetooth device (sometimes shown under the *Other devices* category). Sometimes, the Bluetooth driver for the host computer must be updated for newer devices.
> You can use similar tricks with Apple iOS and Android devices: (1) Ensure that the device is powered, (2) ensure that Bluetooth is enabled, and (3) ensure that no other wireless networks/devices are nearby (move to another location to see).
> A common method used with Bluetooth devices is to restart the pairing mode on the Bluetooth device or rescan for a device from the iOS/Android computing device.
> If a mobile device unintentionally pairs with another Bluetooth device, turn Bluetooth off (and keep it off unless you are using it). Move the mobile device closer to the Bluetooth device.
> USB-to-RJ-45, USB-to-Bluetooth, and USB-to-Wi-Fi adapters/dongles can be used when one of these network ports fails.

SOFT SKILLS—A WORD ABOUT APPEARANCE

John T. Mallow's 1975 book, *Dress for Success*, heightened some people's awareness of concepts like the power tie, color coordination, and proper wardrobe with the aim of getting ahead in one's professional and personal life. Some of you are simply too young to have read this. Although some of the book's advice may seem a bit quaint today, the fact is, you are nonetheless judged on your personal appearance. This is one soft skill area you cannot afford to ignore at the risk of hindering your chances for advancement, client relationship, or reputation.

Why does appearance matter so much? Research shows that we form opinions about each other within mere seconds of meeting. And some people decide whether or not you are trustworthy in less than a second! Look at Figure 11.109 and imagine each of these people was a technician coming in to fix your computer. What would your impression of that person be just by the attire?

FIGURE 11.109 Professional attire options

So, isn't it logical that you would always strive to project a competent and professional appearance and demeanor to your boss and to your customers? A good rule of thumb is to dress to the level of the client. For example, you would probably dress sharper for a job in a law or doctor's office than you would for a job at Joe the plumber's business. If you knew you were going to be working on laser printers, you probably don't want to wear good clothes or would take a lab coat to protect your clothes.

Be aware of generational bias. In this country, we have four generations who have different values. The Traditionalists, born 1925–1945, value suits, coats and ties for men, and dresses for women. Most of these people are now age 70+ so there are few left in workplaces. The Baby Boomers, 1946–1964, are a little more relaxed about dress codes, but still believe in good appearance—think business casual. Now aged in their 50s to 60s, they are likely to be the bosses and senior management. Next come the GenXers, 1965–1980, who value flexibility and freedom, and are even more relaxed—think casual. Finally comes the GenY, or Millennials, born between 1981 and the present. Millennials value change, diversity, and individual freedom. These are the ones most likely to express themselves with tattoos, piercings, extreme grooming, and so on. To Millennials, dress codes are way less important.

Here are some commonsense guidelines and Table 11.16 has recommendations for attire according to environment:

> Above all, avoid tattered jeans, trainers, and t-shirts, as you could run the risk of looking too scruffy to be taken seriously.

> If your job involves dirty work, for example, pulling optic fiber cables through the overhead or working on laser printers, jeans and chambray shirts are acceptable. Or consider wearing a lab coat. It doesn't hurt to let the client know upon checking in that you are dressed for the dirty job.

> Grooming: Watch your haircuts and (for men) beards. Don't forget your hands and nails, which will be noticed (either consciously or unconsciously) by your boss and customers.

> Cosmetics: Women are more likely to be better liked and trusted if using moderate makeup and little to no perfume.

TABLE 11.17 Attire in specific environments

Environment	Recommended attire
Business dress	Men: Coat and tie. Women: Dress, skirt, pant suit.
Business casual	Men: Dress shirt (tie optional). Woman: Dress, skirt/blouse, pants/shirt
Casual	Men: Collared shirt, polo shirt, nice pants, slacks. Women: Pants, polo shirt

TECH TIP

The colors you wear send subliminal messages

Colors can profoundly affect how other people view you. Here are some of the main ones to bear in mind:

> Black or dark gray: Represents authority and confidence

> Blue: Suggests trust and traditional values

> Green: Portrays empathy and tranquility

> Red: Tells people you are passionate and likely to be an extrovert

> Brown: Says that you are loyal and reliable

It is usually the subconscious mind that notices how others look. So even if you don't consider appearances very important, just remember that, without you realizing it, appearances helped you form an opinion on just about everyone you have ever met. Don't underestimate the importance of dressing appropriately on the job, but don't let your wardrobe impede your ability to do the job.

Chapter Summary

> Mobile devices are used for different purposes and therefore come in a variety of types—laptops, tablets, smartphones, wearable technology, phablets, e-readers, cameras, and GPS.

> Mobile devices have the following common hardware parts: display, flash memory, battery, DC jack, speaker, microphone, speaker, wireless antenna, system board, processor, and expansion options. Other parts that may be more for laptops or tablets include ExpressCards, SO-DIMMs, mechanical, SSD, and hybrid storage, ports and adapters, keyboards, miniPCI/PCIe cards, touchpad, and touch screen.

> Mobile devices have various methods of expansion and connectivity including the following: NFC, proprietary, USB, miniUSB, microUSB, Lightning, IEEE 1394, infrared, tethering, Bluetooth, GPS, cellular, satellite, Wi-Fi, miniPCI/PCIe, docking stations, and port replicators.
> Mobile devices commonly have accessories that need to be installed and/or attached—headsets, speakers, game pads, battery packs/chargers, protective covers, waterproofing, credit card readers, and memory.
> Mobile device operating systems include the open source Android, closed source Apple iOS, and various Microsoft Windows-based mobile operating systems.
> Laptops use [Fn] to control specific functions like Wi-Fi, Bluetooth, speakers, display output, keyboard backlight, and so on.
> Mobile devices need their operating system and data backed up. Two common methods to do this are to back them up to another device or use storage in the cloud.
> Mobile devices need security. Laptops can have locks. All mobile devices need operating system security, personal files and identity security, antimalware, and antivirus. Remote data wiping can be configured if the device is compromised or stolen.
> A plastic scribe helps with prying plastics and covers off. Laptop speakers and DC power plugs frequently have cables that run along the back or sides of the device. Keep screws separated and take notes and photos for any parts removal.
> Conserve mobile device power by adding more RAM, turning off wireless/Bluetooth, turning off unnecessary apps, configuring power options, reducing screen brightness, and avoiding temperature extremes.
> Li-ion batteries are used with mobile devices. If a device must be attached to AC power or a USB port to work, replace the battery with the correct DC power jack, appropriate DC voltage level, and current (amperage) equal to or higher than the original power brick.
> Before removing or installing memory, disconnect the power cord and remove the battery on a mobile device.
> Laptops can sometimes be upgraded with SO-DIMMs. Tablets and smartphones can sometimes be upgraded and have additional storage using flash memory cards.
> AC power goes into the power supply or mobile device power brick. DC power is provided to all internal parts of the computing device.
> Microphones are used for VoIP and are tested/managed in Windows through the *Recording* tab of the *Sound* window.
> Secure a mobile device with a PIN, facial recognition, a password, or a passcode/pattern.
> When replacing a laptop processor, a screw may have to be loosened before you can remove the old processor.
> When replacing a laptop motherboard, additional components may have to be removed.
> Troubleshooting mobile devices commonly includes a soft reset or a restart or a hard reset, which is another name for a factory reset. Android and iOS devices use *Settings* to manage most configurations. Windows uses Control Panels/*Settings*.
> Troubleshooting commonly involves disabling apps, connectivity not being used, and features.
> Troubleshooting sometimes involves removing AC power and the battery.
> Mobile device repairs commonly take different tools including scribes, anti-static gloves, and smaller tools.

CHAPTER 11

✓ Be able to explain the difference between a Windows, Android, and iOS mobile device.

✓ Be able to identify, describe the purpose of, and replace/install the following hardware components: display, flash memory, battery, DC jack, speaker, microphone, wireless antenna, system board, processor, and expansion options. Other parts that may be more for laptops or tablets include ExpressCards, SO-DIMMs, mechanical, SSD, hybrid storage, ports and adapters, keyboards, miniPCI/PCIe cards, touchpads, and touch screens.

✓ Know the difference between a docking station and a port replicator.

✓ Watch a few videos on laptop disassembly.

✓ Be able to describe how to connect an external monitor to a laptop, and make adjustments for various combinations of laptop only, external monitor only, and laptop along with the external monitor. Also know how power options might need to be adjusted.

✓ Review the function of the following: LCD (TN and IPS, fluorescent, LED, OLED, inverter, digitizer), Wi-Fi antenna placement, webcam, and microphone.

✓ Study how to configure and connect NFC, tethering, Bluetooth, GPS, cellular, and Wi-Fi. Right before the exams, use an Android simulator, or ask a friend to lunch and practice on Android, iOS, and Windows device configurations.

✓ A cell phone requires an NFC chip in order to use the mobile pay feature.

✓ Review the types of things you might control with function keys. Know that you might use these to solve problems such as erratic mouse actions (touchpad) and display output.

✓ If a cell phone back won't go back on easily, check for a swollen battery.

✓ Know that Android devices synchronize to the cloud by default. Know that iTunes can be used to backup/restore an iOS device. Know that One Drive is used to access saved attachments from Microsoft Outlook.

✓ Be able to configure security settings on Android, iOS, and Windows devices.

✓ Know that you can physically secure a laptop with a cable.

✓ Know that geotracking is what allows social media apps and tracking apps to locate a phone/person. The location feature might need to be enabled.

✓ Read and reread all the troubleshooting scenarios in the chapter. Troubleshooting mobile devices is a part of both the CompTIA A+ 220-901 and 220-902 exams.

Key Terms

Review Questions

1.   How can you control a laptop keyboard backlight?

_____

2.   Which mobile device feature allows tracking how far someone has walked this week?
     [virtual assistant I accelerometer I gyroscope I pedometer]

3.   In which of the following situations would Bluetooth most likely be used?

     a. To connect to a corporate wireless network

     b. To attach a keyboard to a PC

     c. To connect a PC to a phone line

     d. To connect a flash drive to a camera

4.   Where are miniPCIe cards normally installed?

     a. In tablet computers

     b. In smartphones

     c. On the bottom of a laptop

     d. In a slot adjacent to the processor

5.   List three recommendations for saving power on a laptop.

_____

_____

_____

Consider the following memory advertisements for laptop memory used in Question 6.

a. 2GB (2×1GB) Dual channel kit DDR2 667MHz PC2-5300 desktop DIMM compatible with PC2-5300 (667MHz), PC2-4200 (533MHz), and PC2-3200 (400MHz)

b. 2GB 200-pin DDR2 800MHz PC2-6400 SO-DIMM CL6 1.8V, 256Mx64, non-ECC

c. 2GB (1×2GB) 1333MHz DDR3 desktop unbuffered DIMM

d. 4GB (2×2GB) XMS2 PC2-6400 800MHz 240-pin dual channel DDR2 desktop memory latency of 5-5-5-18

e. 4GB (2×2GB) 240-pin DDR2 PC2-6400 memory kit unbuffered non-ECC, 1.8V, CL6

f. 4GB (2GB×2) 204-pin PC3-8500 SO-DIMM DDR3-1066 memory kit, CL7, unbuffered, non-ECC, 1.5V, 256Mx64

g. 8GB (2×4GB) 1333MHz PC3-1066 204-pin SO-DIMM memory kit, 1333MHz unbuffered CL9

h. 8GB (2×4GB) 240-pin DDR3 1600MHz (PC3 12800) SDRAM, 1.5V, 9-9-9-24

i. 8GB (2×4GB) DDR3 dual channel kit 1600MHz CL9 non-ECC low latency 240-pin

6.   In these advertisements, which memory module(s) would work as an upgrade for a laptop given the following specifications:

     Configured with 1GB DDR2 (works at 667MHz, max 2GB), 1 main memory slot, which is occupied.

_____

_____

_____

_____

7.   List one way that a tablet computer's memory might be upgraded.

_____

_____

8. Which two options are used to backup an iOS device? (Select two.)
   [iBooks | iTunes | Tips | iCloud | iBackup | Backup]

9. Which type of laptop hard drive would provide the best performance?
   [mechanical | SSD | hybrid | stock]

10. What is a drawback of SSDs?

    [Installation time | MTBF | Maintenance requirements | Cost | Speed | Reliability]

11. A technician has been troubleshooting a laptop power issue and now the speakers don't work. What should the technician do first?

    a. Replace the speakers.

    b. Reinstall the original power supply.

    c. Check the speaker cabling.

    d. Replace the power supply with another one.

12. Which icon would be used on a laptop to turn down the volume?

    a.

    b.

    c.

    d.

13. A laptop display is not showing anything, but the technician can hear the hard drive working. The technician connects an external monitor and the monitor works. What should the technician try next?

    a. Replace the laptop display.

    b. Try connecting another external monitor.

    c. Replace the laptop display connector.

    d. Use the appropriate key to retest the output to the display.

14. What is the purpose of a laptop inverter?

    a. To convert DC to AC for the CCFL backlight

    b. To attach the keypad to the keyboard

    c. To allow specific keys to be used as a numeric keypad when enabled

    d. To allow the display to be flipped backward

15. List three recommendations for laptop security.

    _____

    _____

    _____

16. A hybrid drive is:

    a. A mechanical hard drive

    b. An SSD

    c. A combination of an SSD part and an mechanical drive in the same case

    d. An upgraded flash drive

17. Which of the following should be tried first if a mobile device is frozen?

    a. Factory reset

    b. Soft reset

    c. Hard reset

    d. Recovery

18. A user complains that he have slow data speeds on his mobile device. List three things you will check.

    _____

    _____

    _____

    _____

    _____

    _____

    _____

    _____

19. A mobile device continuously attaches to a nearby Bluetooth-enabled computer that is not the computer the user wants to attach. What should be done?

    a. Disconnect the Bluetooth adapter from the nearby computer.

    b. Move the Bluetooth device closer to the desired computer.

    c. Power the nearby computer off.

    d. Put the mobile device in Airplane Mode.

20. [T | F] An accelerometer detects the screen orientation and adapts what is shown on the screen based on that orientation.

Exercises

Exercise 11.1   Identifying Laptop Parts

Objective: To identify various laptop parts correctly

Procedure: Identify each part in Figure 11.110 by matching the component name to the identified part in the photo.

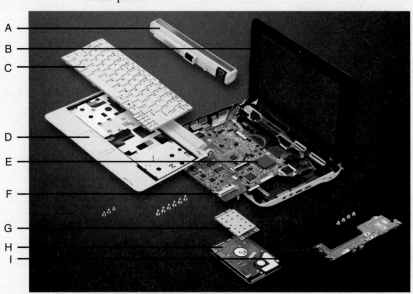

FIGURE 11.110   Laptop part identification photo

Components

LCD	Keyboard
Ports assembly	System board
Mounting bracket for touchpad	Processor
Hard drive	Palm rest assembly
Battery	

A. _____   F. _____

B. _____   G. _____

C. _____   H. _____

D. _____   I. _____

E. _____

Exercise 11.2 Common Laptop Keys

Objective: To identify various keys used on a laptop

Procedure: Match the laptop function key in Figure 11.111 to the description.

FIGURE 11.111 Laptop function key identification photo

a. Increase volume

b. Decrease display brightness

c. Decrease keyboard backlight brightness

d. Pair with Bluetooth Device 1

e. Play/pause

f. Cycle through open apps

g. Mute

h. Increase display brightness

i. Pair with Bluetooth Device 2

j. Increase keyboard backlight brightness

k. Pair with Bluetooth Device 3

l. Enable/disable touchpad

F1 _____

F2 _____

F3 _____

F4 _____

F5 _____

F6 _____

F7 _____

F8 _____

F9 _____

F10 _____

F11 _____

F12 _____

Activities

Internet Discovery

Objective: To obtain specific information from the Internet regarding a computer or its associated parts

Parts: Computer with Internet access

Procedure: Complete the following procedure and answer the accompanying questions.

Questions:

1. Watch the laptop hard drive replacement video at the following URL to answer Questions 1–5 (if this link does not work, find a video that shows a laptop hard drive replacement): https://www.youtube.com/watch?v=wSa3Owia-2k

   List one piece of software mentioned in the video that might be obtained or purchased in order to clone the operating system.

   _____

2. Use the Internet to find an alternative cloning software that could be used. Detail why you think this software would be appropriate and why you chose it.

   _____

   _____

3. What were the two locations for the hard drives in the two laptops and how were they removed?

   _____

   _____

   _____

   _____

4. What power safety procedures were recommended?

_____

5. What power procedure was recommended in the chapter that was not done in this video?

_____

A customer owns a Toshiba Satellite R845-ST6N02 laptop. Use the Toshiba troubleshooting assistant program to help with a battery problem. Use this information to answer questions 6–9.

6. What output values should be on the AC adapter?

_____

7. Assume the values on the AC power brick match those required on the computer. How long should the power button be held down once the external power and battery have been removed from the computer?

_____

8. Which two colors can be used for the power indicator light (if it is working, of course)?

_____

9. Assume you have power and you shut down the computer and removed the AC adapter. What might you do before assuming the battery is dead?

_____

10. A student has an HP ENVY notebook model 15-ae041nr. The screen seems blurry when displaying a browser or even some Windows configuration screens, but other screens appear fine. Use the Internet to find what some people have done. List one or two solutions.

_____

_____

_____

_____

Soft Skills

Objective: To enhance and fine-tune a future technician's ability to listen, communicate in both written and oral forms, and support people who use computers and mobile devices in a professional manner.

Activities:

1. In groups of three, each person finds a video that shows a particular model of laptop being taken apart. Share your findings with the others. Have the team select the best video to share with the class or submit the web link to the teacher.

2. Record yourself describing a mobile device problem and what you did to fix it. Take no longer than 3 minutes. If you have never had a mobile device problem, use the Internet to find someone else's problem that you describe in your own words. No reading aloud. Tell the story.

3. In groups of six, three people must each find a cartoon or story that describes a funny mobile device situation. The other three people should find a cartoon or story that illustrates the need to dress professionally in the IT field. Each person must share findings with the group. Have a category for mobile and a category for appearance. Each person rates each cartoon or story. Summarize your findings in electronic format or verbally.

4. Each group is assigned one of the following laptop parts: (1) processor and heat solution, (2) mechanical, SSD, or hybrid storage device, (3) display, (4) system board, (5) inverter, (6) backlight.

5. Work in teams to outline in words and illustrations how to replace the part and issues related to the replacement. Present the work to the class.

Critical Thinking Skills

Objective: To analyze and evaluate information as well as apply learned information to new or different situations

Procedure:

1. Locate two laptop manuals from two different manufacturers. They cannot just be two models from the same manufacturer. Compare and contrast how the CPU is replaced in each one.

2. Select a laptop that has a mechanical hard drive and pretend it is yours and has been yours for at least a year. Now pretend that you are upgrading to an SSD or a hybrid drive. Select what hardware and software you might need. Price them out. Develop a step-by-step plan of action of how you are going to do this.

3. On a separate piece of paper describe why Wi-Fi networks are so important to cell phone users. Are there any drawbacks to using them?

4. Find a technical job at monster.com, dice.com, or indeed.com. Find at least three graphics or photos showing clothes you think a male or a female would wear to the interview for this job. Find another three graphics or photos that depict what a male or female would wear on a daily basis for the job.

5. Consider Figure 11.112. Identify as many parts of the cell phone as possible. Use Internet resources to help you.

   1. _____   5. _____
   2. _____   6. _____
   3. _____   7. _____
   4. _____   8. _____

FIGURE 11.112   Mobile phone identification photo

Labs

Lab 11.1 Backing Up an iOS Device to a PC or Mac Using iTunes

Objective: To be able to use the iTunes application to back up the operating system and settings on an iOS device

Parts: An iOS-based device

A PC or Mac computer

A USB cable to connect the iOS device to the PC or MAC

An Apple ID and password

Procedure: Complete the following procedure and answer the accompanying questions.

1.   Power on the PC or Mac and the iOS device. Log in as required.

2.   Ensure the PC or Mac has iTunes installed. If the application is not installed, download and install it. Open *iTunes*.

3.   Attach the USB cable from the iOS device to the computer.

4.   On the Mac or PC, the iOS device should display or you can choose it from the top, left where the music notes icon is located. Note that you may have to click *Continue > Get Started* if this is a device that has never been connected before.

What iOS version does iTunes show is on the iOS device?

_____

What is the iOS serial number shown in iTunes?

_____

5.   In the *Backups* section, select the *This computer* radio button.

Looking at the screen, does this Mac or PC where the backup is to be stored have the ability to encrypt the backup file? [Yes | No]

How do you know?

_____

6.   Click the *Back Up Now* button.

What information displays under the *Latest Backup* section?

_____

What option on the screen would you use if you needed to reinstall the iOS operating system?

_____

Lab 11.2 Determining Memory Resources in an iOS-Based Device

Objective: To be able to use the Apple-iOS operating system to determine the amount of memory

Parts: An Apple iPhone or iPad

Procedure: Complete the following procedure and answer the accompanying questions.

1.   Ensure that the Apple device is powered on.

2.   Access the Home screen (by pressing the Home screen button []). Tap on the *Settings* option. Note that you may have to swipe your finger to access the *Settings* option if multiple pages of icons are present.

3. Tap the *General* option. Tap the *About* option. Locate the *Capacity* option, which shows the total amount of memory installed.

   How much memory is available on the device?

   _____

4. Locate the *Available* option, which shows the amount of memory that is not being used.

   How much memory is free?

   _____

5. Return to the Home screen.

Lab 11.3 Determining Memory Resources in an Android-Based Device

Objective: To be able to use the Android operating system to determine the amount of memory

Parts: An Android-based device

Procedure: Complete the following procedure and answer the accompanying questions.

Note: The Android operating system is an open source operating system. Options vary from device to device, but most configuration options are similar.

1. Ensure that the Android device is powered on.

2. Access the Home screen by tapping the Home icon. Tap the *Settings* option. Note that you may have to swipe your finger to access the Settings option if multiple pages of icons are present.

3. Tap the *Storage* option. Locate the total amount of storage.

   How much memory is available on the device?

   _____

4. Locate how much memory is available (not being used).

   How much memory is free?

   _____

   How much memory is being used by applications?

   _____

   Does this device have external storage? If so, how could you tell?

   _____

5. Return to the Home screen.

Lab 11.4 Managing Files on a Mobile Device

Objective: To be able to copy files or send files using an Android or Apple iOS-based device

Parts: Android device or Apple iOS device

Procedure: Complete the following procedure and answer the accompanying questions.

Android

1. If working on an Apple device, please go to Step 16. Power on the Android device.

2. Access the Camera app by touching the *Camera* icon on the Home screen.

3. Normally in the Camera app, there is an icon of a camera or a circle that you touch to take the picture. Frequently, there is a sound effect of a camera shutter. Take a picture.

4. Return to the home screen by touching the home icon. If the home icon is not showing, touch the screen where it normally appears (bottom left, center icon).

5. Locate and access (touch) the *File Manager* app.

6. Unless the settings have been changed, most photos are stored by default on internal storage. Touch the *internal storage* option. The internal storage folders list to the right.

7. Locate and open (touch) the *DCIM* folder.

8. Locate and open the *Camera* folder.

9. To open a picture, touch the filename. Frequently there are options such as rotating or cropping the photo found by touching just outside the photograph.

   What photo options are available?

   _____

10. Return to the file listing by using the *return* button. The return button is the button on the screen that is a return arrow such as the one shown here: ↰ If the return button is not shown, you can touch the bottom left of the screen and the return arrow normally shows.

11. Enable the checkbox by the name of the photograph by touching the checkbox.

12. Options either appear or you can touch an icon normally located in the upper-right or -left corner that allow options to appear. Locate the options that include the copy function.

13. Go to another folder located on your internal storage. Select the *Paste* option.

Instructor initials: _____

14. Delete the original and copied photograph.

Instructor initials: _____

15. Power off the device and return it to the original location.

Apple

16. Power on the Apple device.

17. Access the Camera app by touching the *Camera* icon on the home screen.

18. Tap the icon of the camera to take the picture. Frequently, there is a sound effect of a camera shutter. Take a picture.

19. Notice how a small image of the photograph is available in the lower-left corner. Tap the graphic of the photo. Note that you can also access the photograph using the *Photos* home screen icon.

20. Options are available in the top-right corner. If these options have disappeared, just tap the photo.

    Describe three options available at the top of a photograph.

    Answers may vary a little, but three of the following will be common answers: Edit, Slideshow, a box with an arrow, a trash can, and Done.

21. Select the option that has a box with an arrow in it. Select *Email Photo*.

22. In the *To:* textbox, type a valid email address such as your own by tapping inside the blank space to the right of To:. See the instructor if you don't know of an email address to use.

    What email address did you use?

    _____

23. In the *Subject* textbox, type *Class photo*. Notice how the photo is already attached to the email.

24. Tap the *Send* button in the top-right corner of the email.

25. Take another photograph.

26. Either using the *Camera* app or the *Photos* app, relocate the original photograph.

27. Tap the photo to bring up the options in the right corner if they are not showing. Select the *Slideshow* icon.

28. Select a type of transition by tapping the *Transitions* option.

What transition did you choose?

_____

29. Select *Start Slideshow*. Stop the slideshow by tapping on the screen.

Instructor initials: _____

30. Delete the two photographs.

Instructor initials: _____

31. Power off the device and return it to the original location.

Lab 11.5 Connecting a Mobile Device to a Wi-Fi network

Objective: To be able to connect an Android or Apple iOS-based device to an IEEE 802.11 Wi-Fi network

Parts: Android device or Apple iOS device

Procedure: Complete the following procedure and answer the accompanying questions.

Note: Android is an open source operating system. The operating system may be modified by the vendor. Android simulators are available for free and can be used for the Android portion of this lab.

Android

1. If working on an Apple device, please go to Step 7. Power on the Android device.

2. Access the Home screen by pressing the home button. Locate the *Settings* option by swiping if necessary.

3. Tap the *Settings* option > optionally *Wireless and network* > *Wi-Fi/Wi-Fi settings*.

4. Tap the Wi-Fi network you want to join. Optionally enter the security credentials > *Connect*. Note that if the Wi-Fi network is not shown because the wireless access point is not broadcasting the SSID (see Chapter 14 for more information), then you can tap the *Add Wi-Fi network* option at the bottom of the page and enter the relevant SSID and security credentials.

5. Verify the wireless symbol shows at the top of the mobile device.

6. To disconnect from a network, tap the connected network > *Forget*.

Apple

7. If working on an Android device, please go to Step 1. Power on the Apple device.

8. Access the home screen by pressing the home button. Locate the *Settings* option by swiping if necessary.

9. Tap the *Settings* option > *Wi-Fi*. Ensure Wi-Fi is enabled by tapping the button to the far right of the option to the enabled (right) side.

10. Tap the Wi-Fi network you want to join. Optionally enter the security credentials > *Join*. Note that if the Wi-Fi network is not shown because the wireless access point is not broadcasting the SSID (see Chapter 14 for more information), then you can tap the *Other* option at the bottom of the page and enter the relevant SSID and security credentials.

11. Verify the wireless symbol shows at the top of the mobile device.

12. To disconnect from a network, tap the connected network > *Forget This Network*.

12 Computer Design and Troubleshooting Review

In this chapter you will learn:

> To select computer components based on the customer's needs

> The components best suited for a particular computing environment

> How to design for specific computer subsystems, such as the video or storage subsystem

> How to perform basic trouble-shooting procedures

> How BIOS/UEFI controls the boot sequence and how that helps when troubleshooting

> The purpose of POST error codes

> A list of troubleshooting symptoms that could be on the CompTIA A+ 220-901 exam

> How to deal with difficult customers or situations

CompTIA Exam Objectives:

What CompTIA A+ exam objectives are covered in this chapter?

✓ 901-1.9 Given a scenario, select the appropriate components for a custom PC configuration, to meet customer specifications or needs.

✓ 901-2.9 Given a scenario, use appropriate networking tools.

✓ 901-4.1 Given a scenario, troubleshoot common problems related to motherboards, RAM, CPU and power with appropriate tools.

✓ 901-4.2 Given a scenario, troubleshoot hard drives and RAID arrays with appropriate tools.

✓ 902-5.4 Demonstrate proper communication techniques and professionalism.

✓ 902-5.5 Given a scenario, explain the troubleshooting theory.

Design Overview

Why would employers want technicians to be able to design computers? If you needed a car repaired, wouldn't it be nice to have a person who could design cars to advise you? They would know the best engines, the most fuel-efficient body design, what parts might not work well with other parts, and so on. They would know a lot about all parts of the car. The same is true about those who can design computers: They know a lot about computer parts and how those parts interact with one another.

When you first learn about computers, you learn the language, or lingo. You learn terms such as RAM and processor. Later, when you hear such words, you form images in your mind. You do more than just recognize the words; you actually know what different parts look like. You can explain to someone else what a part does. You continue to grow in a particular area. Designing something is right up there with troubleshooting something well. It involves knowing what you are talking about.

Benjamin Bloom chaired a committee that created a classification of learning objectives that was named Bloom's Taxonomy. Look at Figure 12.1 to see how people normally progress through the learning process from the bottom to the top. Notice that creating is at the top. Of course, employers want people who can design…those are the folks who know all the things that it takes to be able to design.

FIGURE 12.1   Bloom's Taxonomy

This chapter helps you learn how to select components within subsystems, such as video or audio, and the components needed for complete computer builds based on the type of customer and the customer's needs. Even if you are designing just a subset of a computer, such as the video subsystem or an optical drive subsystem, you must know how that subset interacts with other components that might need to be upgraded as well. Be sure to check out the exercises at the end of the chapter that help put all this together. Practice is one of the best teachers.

Computer System Design

Computer users need different types of computer systems. What the user does with the computer dictates the components and peripherals needed. Looking at the computer systems by purpose is a good place to start with design.

Note: The bullets with asterisks are components emphasized on the CompTIA A+ 220-901 exam.

CAD/CAM and Graphics Design Workstations

Computer-aided design (CAD) and computer-aided manufacturing (CAM) systems are used in manufacturing plants by engineers or design engineers to create things. Graphic design personnel also use a similar type of system (see Figure 12.2). A **graphics/CAD/CAM design workstation** would need the following key components:

> *Powerful multi-core processor(s)
> *Maximum system RAM
> *High-end video card(s) with maximum video RAM and graphics processing unit (GPU)
> Large display or dual displays
> Large-capacity hard drive(s) and an SSD
> Possible peripherals include digital tablets, scanners, plotters, and 3D printers
> Quality mouse or input device

FIGURE 12.2　CAD/CAM design workstation

Gaming PCs

Gaming computers are a set of their own. Gamers frequently build their own systems, but some computer manufacturers do make gaming PCs. A **gaming PC** (see Figure 12.3) tends to have the following key components:

> *Powerful multi-core processor(s)
> *High-end video cards (with maximum video RAM and specialized GPU)
> *High-definition sound card and speakers
> *High-end system cooling
> Large amount of RAM
> Large display or dual displays (see Figure 12.3)
> Quality mouse
> Possible gaming console
> Headphones with microphone
> Possible 3D glasses (if supported by the video card and monitor)

FIGURE 12.3 Gaming PC

Audio/Video Editing Workstations

An **audio/video editing workstation** (see Figure 12.4) is used to manipulate sounds (shorten, add, overlay, and so on) or video. This type of system requires a lot of hard drive space and RAM. Here are the most common configuration elements for such a computer:

> *Specialized video card with maximum video RAM and GPU
> *Specialized audio (sound) card and speakers
> *Very fast and large-capacity hard drive
> *Dual monitors
> Powerful multi-core processor(s)
> Large amount of system RAM
> Quality mouse
> Possible digital tablet or scanner

FIGURE 12.4 Audio/video editing workstation

Virtualization Workstations

A **virtualization workstation** can mean two things: (1) a workstation that has at least one operating system, in its own virtual machine that is separate from the host operating system (see Figure 12.5), or (2) a workstation that uses hardware and software virtualization techniques to provide an end user with a controlled workstation environment. Each of these situations requires different hardware and software. In terms of the CompTIA A+ certification, a virtualization workstation is considered to be the first example (a computer that has more than one operating system in a virtual environment). The second example is what is also known as a thin client and it is covered next.

A virtualization workstation would have the following components:

> *Maximum CPU cores
> *Maximum RAM
> Multiple, fast, large-capacity hard drives
> Possible SSDs
> Possible network-attached storage (**NAS**) for increased storage space that can be shared with other devices

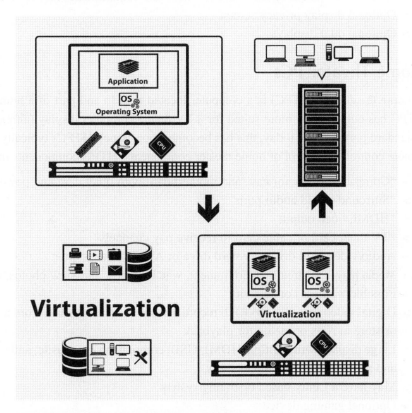

FIGURE 12.5   Virtualization workstation concepts

Thin Client Workstations

A **thin client** workstation is a desktop or laptop that has a display, mouse, keyboard, and network connectivity and runs applications from a server. Thin client computers are less expensive than a normal workstation (but the network infrastructure such as servers, software, storage area network [SAN], and so on to support thin clients costs money). Storage tends to be cloud-based or on remote storage media. Both the hardware (hard drives, number of processors, and so on) and software environment could be virtualized (commonly called desktop virtualization) in order to provide a controlled environment. Corporations use thin clients. Characteristics to look for in a thin client computer include the following:

> *Meets minimum requirements for selected operating system
> *1Gb/s preferred network connectivity
> *Basic applications
> Optional display privacy screen

Thick Client Workstations

In contrast to a thin client workstation, a **thick client** computer is the most common type of desktop or laptop in the work environment. Applications are installed and documents are commonly stored on the local hard drive. An all-in-one computer could be a thick client computer. Computers in small businesses tend to be thick client workstations. A standard thick client computer has the following characteristics:

> *Meets recommended hardware requirements for selected operating system
> *Meets recommended hardware and software requirements for running desktop applications
> Optional display privacy screen
> Optional dual displays

Home Theater PCs

A **home theater PC** (HTPC) is a computer located near to and part of a home theater. As such, an HTPC has output video more suited for a TV than a computer display (although with HDMI being a standard port on a TV today, this has become a non-issue). HTPCs typically have a programmable remote control for control of home theater components. HTPC components include the following:

> *Compact form factor case and motherboard with quiet case and power supply fans
> *Surround-sound audio ports
> *HDMI video output
> *TV tuner card or cable card to receive pay channels
> Audio/video hard drive (**AV hard drive** or AVHD) that is quiet
> **Media player** to stream entertainment, watch videos, and view photos, or listen to music
> Possible wireless connectivity
> Digital video recorder (**DVR**) to record TV shows, transfer data from a camcorder or camera, or store movies or media for playback
> Large display with multiple HDMI, USB, component, composite, and so on audio/video ports and possible wireless connectivity
> May have a Linux-based operating system
> Optional gaming device

Home Servers

A **home server** computer is used to store data, function as a web server, print server, or file server, control media streaming, be accessible from outside the home, control devices, and manage back-ups of other computers. Notice in Figure 12.6, how the home server in the top-right corner physically connects to the wireless router. Servers and networks are discussed in Chapter 14. Typical components found in a home server include the following:

> *Multiple hard drives in a RAID array configuration
> *1Gb/s (1000Mb/s) NIC
> Medium to large case

> Multiple processors or multiple cores in the processor
> Lots of RAM
> Server applications including media streaming, file sharing, and print sharing
> Possible NAS
> Possible KVM switch

FIGURE 12.6 Home server

Industrial Computers

An industrial computer is one used for a specific industry. For example, in a car repair shop, the standard computers used both inside the showroom and in the service and repair center might be in an enclosure (see Figure 12.7) or have keyboard coverings. A kiosk in a mall or school might contain or be controlled by a computer. A kiosk is commonly used to show maps, provide directions, locate personnel, or provide information. Here are some things to consider for an industrial computer:

> Meets recommended hardware requirements based on applications installed
> Optional enclosure for wet, dry, or outdoor environments
> Optional enclosure for a laptop's external keyboard and mouse for unsecure or outdoor environments
> Optional LCD enclosure for harsh, outdoor, public, high-traffic, or industrial environments
> Optional privacy display screen
> Case with air filters that may be removable for cleaning

FIGURE 12.7 Computer in a car repair shop

Mobile Computers

A mobile computer for someone who travels as part of his job also needs special design considerations. Considerations for an "on-the-road" computer design include the following:

> Laptop, ultrabook, or tablet
> Sufficient RAM
> Might need mobile broadband connectivity
> Possible SSD (if jarring or dropping due to handling is a concern or if high speed is needed)
> Compatible smartphone
> Possible projector
> Possible thermal printer for sales-oriented tasks
> Possible portable speakers and headphones with noise cancellation

When you are planning to design an entire computer system, looking at what the user will be doing with the computer is important. Keep in mind that there are many ways to go green and conserve energy in your computer design. The company requesting the design may require green specifications. Cases, motherboards, processors, power supplies, printers, displays, and other computing devices can be designed with energy conservation in mind. The Electronic Product Environmental Assessment Tool (EPEAT) can help with that. The **EPEAT rating system** was designed to work with the EPA in identifying products that have a green (and clean) design. **ENERGY STAR** is another program that has strict energy efficiency standards that a product must meet in order to be ENERGY STAR compliant. Products that earn the ENERGY STAR rating today have low total energy requirements, low power modes, and efficient power supplies.

You can also be conscientious of energy requirements when designing a subsystem. Many times the request for an upgrade will not be for the entire computer, but only for a subsystem. In such a case, the best practice is to look at the subsystem as a unit. The following sections look at the computer subsystems.

Motherboard and Associated Component Design

The motherboard, chipset, and CPU are all directly related to one another and should be designed in conjunction with one another. Using a motherboard that has the Intel Haswell chipset, for example, gives you up to six USB 3.0 ports, a built-in GPU, or a PCIe v3.0 video card expansion slot. You might consider the AMD 990FX chipset to get support for four graphics cards, but you won't get a PCIe v3.0 slot from it (unless there is an upgrade after this book goes to press). Some technicians choose a motherboard based on a specific chipset. Why? Because there might be issues with a specific chipset, but the customer might still need high-end video or USB version 3.0 ports. There might be only one chipset that gives you two PCIe v3.0 slots for bridging video cards or a high number of USB 3.0 ports. In any case, this is something to consider. You also have to remember that things change all the time. Newer technologies such as Skylak, Broadwell, USB 3.1, Thunderbolt, and DDR4 may influence your choices. Refer back to Chapter 2 on ports or Chapter 3 for motherboard and processor information.

Choosing a processor involves selecting Intel or AMD, determining how many processor cores you want, and selecting a specific model. Throughout the years, both manufacturers tend to have had a low-end model for cheaper, less powerful computers, a midrange processor that gives pretty good bang for the buck (price), and very powerful processors. Don't forget CPU cooling either. If you select one of the high-end CPUs, you must have appropriate cooling for it.

When comparing processors, you may also want to consider the nanotechnology used. Processor technology length is measured in **nanometers**. A nanometer is 0.000000001 in length (1×10^{-9}).

Processors and chipsets created using the 14-nm or 22-nm technology can have more transistors in the same amount of space as the processors/chipsets created using the 32-nm or 45-nm technology. Traditionally, the smaller the technology, the lower the heat produced. With lower heat, some components can be made to go faster, but that is not always the case.

Memory ties into processor technology because the type of motherboard/chipset you have will dictate the type of memory supported, the maximum amount of memory the motherboard manufacturer might consider putting on the motherboard, and the maximum memory speed that can be used. Whenever a technician is upgrading or replacing a motherboard, compatibility with existing components is a must.

The most important design consideration for memory is to take advantage of dual-, triple-, and quad-channeling when possible. Ensure that the DIMMs and SO-DIMMS are purchased together and installed according to the recommendations set forth in the motherboard/computer manual. Encourage the end user to buy as much RAM as he or she can initially afford. This area is one of the most influential considerations on the user computing experience. Beef up this subsystem component as much as possible.

When dealing with the motherboard, consider the following:

> Motherboard form factor
> Chipset
> Whether the CPU is included or needs to be purchased separately
> CPU size
> Motherboard socket size
> Nanotechnology used with the processor and/or chipset (14nm, 22nm, 32nm, 45nm, and so on)
> CPU cooling
> RAM
> Number and type of input/output (I/O) ports
> Traditional BIOS or UEFI (replacement for traditional BIOS)

Power Supply and Case Design

When selecting a power supply, it is all about the size (form factor), total wattage for specific voltage levels, number of connectors, and power efficiency. One issue you must consider is how many connectors connect to the same cable. When you have several high-powered devices, you want to be able to connect them with separate power cables, if possible, instead of using two connectors along the same cable. Also, be careful with cables that do not have at least four wires. These are peripheral cables to power 12-volt fans and are normally labeled as fan connectors. Some power supplies have detachable cables that connect between a power supply connector and a device connector. You attach the number and type of cables you need. Buy additional cables of a specific type, as needed. Figure 12.8 shows detachable cables.

When replacing, upgrading, or purchasing a power supply, consider the following:

> Enough power cables for video cards
> Number and type of power cables (SATA, Molex, PCIe, and fan)
> Form factor
> Wattage for the 12-volt line
> Total wattage—use an online power-use calculator
> Quietness
> Mean time between failures (MTBF)
> Overvoltage, overcurrent, undervoltage, and short-circuit protection
> Warranty

FIGURE 12.8   Detachable cables for some power supplies

Keep in mind that the power supply and the case (and the motherboard, too) have to be the same form factor. Some cases accept multiple motherboard form factors. Cases may or may not include the fans that go with the cases. Most cases have at least two locations for fans—one at the front of the case and one at the rear. Fans tend to come in 40-, 60-, 80-, 90-, 92-, 120-, or 140-mm sizes. Look for the following key features in a new case:

> Size (ATX, micro-ATX, BTX, ITX, mini-ITX, and so on), type (desktop, tower, or all-in-one), and physical dimensions
> Number and type of front panel ports
> Number and placement of fans
> Cable management
> Number of expansion slots (need to match or come close to how many are on the motherboard)
> Number and type of accessible drive bays including internal or external
> Outside texture and design (metal, aluminum, plastic, acrylic, see-through)
> Ease of cover removal
> Method of securing expansion cards (screw, plastic tab, and single plastic bar)
> Ability to lock case panels to deter entry

Table 12.1 lists recommendations for cases and power supplies for the different types of users.

TABLE 12.1   Power supply and case design

Use	Design considerations
Graphic/CAD/CAM, gaming PC, home server PC, audio/video editing computer, or virtualization computer	500-W or higher power supply ATX mid- or full-sized tower Two or more case cooling fans
HTPC media center, or thin client	300-W or higher power supply ATX mini- or micro-sized tower
Thick client or normal user	300-W or higher power supply ATX mini-, micro-, or mid-sized tower

Air filters can be cheaply purchased for intake openings (not exhaust) to filter dirt and dust. It is important that you know the direction air is flowing through a system before installing. Some cases come with removable air filters that can be cleaned thoroughly. Some power supplies have air filters installed. Air filters, external storage device enclosures, and special computer and laptop enclosures can help protect against airborne particles that can harm the computer or device.

Figure 12.9 shows a computer case that has removable drives for internal hard drives. Note that even though SATA drives are hot swappable (you can remove them while power is applied), your SATA controller (motherboard) must support this feature, the drive must support it, a SATA power connector must be used, and the drive cannot be in use or used to boot the operating system. For best results, power down the computer before removing an internal SATA drive just to be safe.

FIGURE 12.9   Case with removable internal hard drive trays

Storage Subsystem Design

The storage subsystem consists of magnetic or flash technologies for internal or external hard drives, flash storage (including SSDs), or optical drives.

When adding, replacing, or building a storage subsystem, you must take into account the customer needs, how long the customer plans on storing the data, and how long the customer thinks the storage subsystem will be in use before being upgraded or replaced. Table 12.2 helps with the storage device options.

TABLE 12.2   Storage subsystem design considerations

Feature	Design considerations
Internal connectivity	SATA or M.2.
Internal power	Molex or SATA power connector.
Internal physical size	1.8, 2.5, 3.5, or 5.25 inches and must have an available expansion slot in the case.
External connectivity	USB, IEEE 1394 (FireWire), eSATA, and eSATAp port A NIC may be required for cloud (Internet) storage. May need a media reader for flash media.
External power	Provided by the USB, IEEE 1394, or eSATAp port; otherwise, external power must be used.
Storage technology	Magnetic (hard drive or optical drive); SATA 1.5, 3, or 6Gb/s (SATA1, SATA2, or SATA3), M.2, flash memory (SSD, flash drives, and flash media), or hybrid (magnetic and SSD).
Special storage considerations	RAID requires multiple drives. NAS to share storage with other computers.
Storage device speed	5400, 5900, 7200, 10000, or 15000 RPM for magnetic drives. Transfer rate for SSDs. Input/output operations per second (**IOPS**) for both magnetic drives and SSDs, which is a measurement that takes into account sequential reads/writes as well as random reads/writes.
Optical drive capability	Read-only or read/write.
Optical drive technology	Red-violet and/or blue laser(s).
Drive buffers	Both hard and optical drives can have buffers that can increase data transfer rates.
External considerations	What other devices may share the port. External cages/enclosures can be purchased to turn an internal device into an external device.

Audio Subsystem Design

The audio design consists of the audio ports and speakers. When upgrading or building, let the customer listen to the speakers, if possible. Table 12.3 lists audio design considerations.

TABLE 12.3   Audio subsystem design considerations

Feature	Design considerations
Number of speakers	Two for a casual user or gamer. Three to seven for a music, video, or gaming enthusiast. A 5.1 surround-sound system commonly has a center channel speaker, two front channel speakers for left/right audio, two rear channel speakers for left/right audio, and a subwoofer for low-frequency (bass) sound effects. A 7.1 surround-sound system has the same speakers as 5.1, with two additional center channel speakers for left/right audio.

Feature	Design considerations
Microphone	Integrated into the display, headset, or external. Headset is best for conference calls.
2.0 or 2.1	A 2.0 audio subsystem has two channels (left and right), with the amplifier within one of the two speakers. A 2.1 audio subsystem has two speakers and a subwoofer for the lower-frequency sounds.
Port connectivity	3.5mm mini-plug, S/PDIF TOSLINK, S/PDIF fiber, or wireless.
Sound card	PCI, PCIe, or integrated into the motherboard. Number of type of ports need to match speaker connectivity.
Logistics	Avoid trip hazards. Shelving, wall plates, wall inserts, wall hangers. Speaker location planning.

Figure 12.10 shows the type of audio design you might see in a home theater.

FIGURE 12.10   Home theater audio placement

Display Subsystem Design

Displays are important to the computing experience. With respect to replacing, upgrading, and installing displays, design specifications are important. Table 12.4 shows some design considerations for displays.

TABLE 12.4   Display subsystem design considerations

Feature	Design considerations
Size/aspect ratio	Physical location, space available, and cost are normally the dictating features. Common aspect ratios include 4:3, 16:9, 16:10, and 1.9:1.
Number of displays	Two displays or a single widescreen display is popular in home and work environments.
Type of display	Plasma, LCD with CCFL backlight, LCD with LED backlight (LED), or OLED. Touch screen.
Display conferencing features	Integrated microphone or webcam.
Contrast ratio	A higher number is better (but not all vendors give true numbers).
Video adapter	Slot type. Number and type of ports. Number of cards and support for sharing of resources (scalable link interface [SLI] and CrossFire, for example). RAM. GPU. Power and cooling requirements. Power connectivity requirements.

Mobility Design

Today's computing environment has a lot of mobile devices. Mobile devices are critical to a design solution. Mobile devices will most likely be in addition to more stationary devices such as workstations, printers, and scanners. Laptops and ultrabooks frequently have external peripherals, and few internal parts except for the memory and the SSD can be upgraded. Tablets and smartphones have few or no internal upgradable components. Table 12.5 compares desktop and laptop components. Table 12.6 compares different mobile devices. Keep in mind that these components are constantly being upgraded, and new processors and memory speeds, for example, may be available in different models.

TABLE 12.5   Desktop and laptop component comparison

Component	Desktop	Laptop
Processor	Intel or AMD processors that use the following sockets: Intel LGA 775, 1155, 1156, 1366, and 2011; AMD socket AM3, AM3+, FM1, FM2, and FM2+.	Intel or AMD mobile processors that are either surface mounted or socketed.
Memory	DDR3 DIMMs 1066, 1333, 1600, 1866, 2000, 2133, 2400, 2600, 2666, 2800, 2933, 3000, 3100, or 3200. DDR4 DIMMs 2800, 3000, 3200, 3300, 3333, or 3400.	DDR3 SO-DIMMs 1066, 1333, 1600, 1866, or 2133. DDR4 SO-DIMMs 2133, 2400, 2666, or 2800.
Power supply	ATX, mini-ATX, micro-ATX, ITX, or proprietary.	Proprietary.
Network	10/100 or 10/100/1000Mb/s port.	10/100 or 10/100/1000Mb/s port.
802.11 wireless	May be installed.	Normally included.

Component	Desktop	Laptop
Bluetooth wireless	May be installed.	May be installed.
Optical drive	SATA 3Gb/s or 6Gb/s CD/DVD RW and/or Blu-ray.	SATA 1.5, 3, or 6Gb/s CD/DVD RW and/or Blu-ray.
Hard drive	Internal 2.5- or 3.5-inch SATA 3Gb/s or 6Gb/s running at 5400, 5900, or 7200 RPM, SSD, or hybrid mechanical/SSD.	Internal 1.8 or 2.5-inch SATA 1.5, 3, or 6Gb/s running at 5400, 5900, or 7200 RPM, SSD, or hybrid mechanical/SSD.
Keyboard	Wired or wireless	Integrated
Mouse	Wired or wireless	Integrated touch pad/touch stick

TABLE 12.6   Mobile device design

Mobile device	Common features
Laptop	Requires higher-than-normal RAM and video, if used for gaming Normally has the most powerful processor, RAM, and storage capability of mobile devices Possible touch screen Possible SSD
Ultrabook	No optical drive May not be able to upgrade RAM Low weight Low cost Possible touch screen Possible SSD
Tablet PC	Touch screen Android, Apple iOS, Windows, or Google Chrome, proprietary operating system Little, if any, port connectivity Integrated camera Integrated microphone
Smartphone	Android, Apple iOS, Windows, or proprietary operating system Upgradable flash media Touch screen Integrated camera Integrated microphone

If you can design computer subsystems or an entire computer, you know a lot about the pieces that go into a computer and how they interact. Practicing with different scenarios can help, and there are exercises at the end of the chapter to help you build this skill. You won't believe how much you will learn by looking at component specifications. Investigate component specifications when you shop to increase your knowledge.

Troubleshooting Overview

When a computer does not work properly, technicians must exhibit one essential trait—the will to succeed. The main objective is to return the computer or peripheral to service as quickly and economically as possible. When a computer is down, a business loses revenue and productivity. Therefore, a technician must have a good attitude and a large amount of perseverance and drive to resolve the problem at hand quickly, efficiently, and in a professional, helpful manner.

> **TECH TIP**
>
> **Back up data, if possible**
>
> Before any changes are made to a system, ensure that its data is backed up, if possible.

Technicians must also use all available resources. Resources can be documentation for a particular peripheral, motherboard, or computer; the Internet; your five senses; another technician; corporate documentation; textbooks; experience with similar problems; training materials; previous service history on a particular customer/computer; or an online database provided by a company or partner. Technicians can be stubborn, but they must always remember that time is money, and solving a problem quickly and with the least amount of downtime to the customer is a critical component of a computer support job.

> **TECH TIP**
>
> **Before making changes...**
>
> You must always consider corporate policies, procedures, and impacts before implementing changes.

Evaluating and solving a technology problem is a high-level objective in Bloom's Taxonomy, as shown earlier in the chapter (Figure 12.1). Teaching someone to troubleshoot is challenging. Not every problem can be described in a step-by-step fashion. Troubleshooting is easier if a technician uses reasoning and takes logical steps. Logical troubleshooting can be broken down into the following six simple steps:

Step 1. Identify the problem.

Step 2. Establish a theory of probable cause (question the obvious).

Step 3. Test the theory to determine the cause.

Step 4. Establish a plan of action to resolve the problem and implement the solution.

Step 5. Verify full system functionality and, if applicable, implement preventive measures.

Step 6. Document findings, actions, and outcomes.

Identify the Problem

Computer problems come in all shapes and sizes. Many problems relate to the people who operate computers—the users. Users may fail to choose the correct printer, sometimes push the wrong key for a specific function, or issue an incorrect command.

Have the user demonstrate or re-create the problem. Because the user is often the problem, you can save a great deal of time by taking this step. Do not assume anything! A user may complain that "my hard drive does not work" when, in fact, there is no power to the computer. Often users repeat computer terms they have heard or read, but they do not use them correctly or in the right syntax. By asking a user to re-create a problem, a technician creates a chance to see the problem as the client sees it. Even during a phone consultation, the same rules apply. Whether diagnosing a problem on the phone or in person, be sure to follow these guidelines:

> Do not assume anything; ask the user to re-create the problem step-by-step.

> Question the user. Ask the user if anything has been changed. Do not be threatening; otherwise, the user will not be forthright and honest. Use open-ended questions to get an idea of

what is wrong. Use closed-ended questions (those that require a yes or no answer) to narrow the problem. Refer back to Figure 1.2 to see examples of these techniques.

> Verify obvious conditions, such as power to the monitor or speakers muted through the control panel.

> Do not assume that there is not a problem if the user cannot re-create it. Some problems occur intermittently.

> Back up data, if possible, before making changes.

> Use all your senses. Listen for noises such as from the power supply, case/CPU fans, speaker feedback, hard drive, or optical drive. Power off if you detect a burning smell.

Establish a Theory of Probable Cause

In order to establish a theory of probable cause (and do not forget to question the obvious), you have to have heard or seen the problem as explained by the user. A lot of times, you establish a theory based on analyzing the problem and determining whether the problem is hardware or software related (or both) by using your senses: Sight, hearing, and smell can reveal a great deal. Smell for burning components. Watch the computer boot, look for lights, listen for beeps, and take notes. Use external resources including the Internet to research symptoms. Always question the obvious.

The Boot Process

One thing that might help you establish a theory of probably cause is to examine the boot process. Frequently, a hardware problem is detected during the power-on self-test (POST) executed by the BIOS/UEFI when the computer is first powered on. Remember the traditional BIOS is looking for the boot loader (a small bit of code on a drive). The computer is configured with a specific device boot order. Knowing the steps taken during the boot process helps you troubleshoot an older machine that has the traditional BIOS:

Step 1. The power supply sends a power good signal.

Step 2. The CPU looks in BIOS for software.

Step 3. The CPU executes POST from BIOS. Note that any errors are usually audio or motherboard LEDs or codes at this point.

Step 4. System resources (I/O address, memory addresses, and interrupts) are retrieved from nonvolatile RAM (NVRAM), (which is RAM that can be changed, but data is not lost when power is removed) and assigned to ports, devices, and adapters.

Step 5. Video is initialized, and a cursor appears.

Step 6. POST continues to check hardware and error messages and/or codes can now appear on the display.

Step 7. Based on the boot order configuration in System Setup, the system checks for an operating system from the specified devices.

Step 8. From the first device found that contains an operating system, the operating system loads.

Now on a newer computer that has a UEFI BIOS, things can be a bit different. A UEFI BIOS can optionally have a BIOS compatibility mode where the computer will behave as previously described. However, if the system is natively booting using UEFI, the UEFI standards require a common format for executable code. This allows much more flexibility in the boot process, such as UEFI has to be able to interpret (not just recognize) globally unique identifiers (GUID) partition table (GPT) partitions and the traditional master boot record (MBR). UEFI supports larger drives and partitions.

UEFI has a boot manager. This boot manager can load UEFI drivers and applications and is customizable. These are not operating system drivers. This means that if the operating system has issues, through the UEFI, you can still use your mouse and other devices that have UEFI drivers within the UEFI environment and with UEFI applications that could help with troubleshooting. Refer to Chapter 4 to refresh yourself on the UEFI BIOS. Figure 12.11 shows the boot sequence for a UEFI-based device.

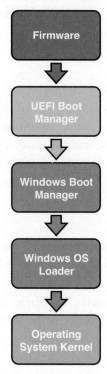

FIGURE 12.11   UEFI boot order

POST Codes

During the firmware phase—whether UEFI or BIOS is used—POST checks out the hardware in a sequential order, and if it finds an error, the BIOS issues a beep and/or displays a numeric error code. Make note of any error codes or beeps. The number or duration of beeps and the numeric error codes that appear are different for different computers.

TECH TIP

Audio POST code: Check video and RAM first

Have you ever been working on a computer and it gives a POST code and you don't want to take the time to look up the code? Audio codes are frequently related to video and memory. Check connections and reset the card or module.

The secret is knowing the BIOS chip manufacturer. The computer or motherboard documentation sometimes contains a list of codes or beeps used for troubleshooting. A single beep is a common tone heard on a successful completion of POST because hardware errors were not detected. Listening is an important part of troubleshooting.

Table 12.7 lists the audio beeps heard on Dell computers. Look at the first line. The 1-1-2 means the computer beeps once, pauses, beeps again, pauses, and then beeps two times. Table 12.8 lists audio beeps for computers that have an AMI BIOS chip installed. Table 12.9 lists the audio beeps heard on a computer with a Phoenix BIOS chip installed.

TABLE 12.7 Dell computer POST audio beeps

Beeps	Description of problem
1-1-2	Processor register failure
1-1-3	NVRAM
1-1-4	BIOS checksum failure
1-3-1 through 2-4-4	Memory modules not identified or used
3-2-4	Keyboard controller test failure
3-3-1	NVRAM power loss
3-3-2	NVRAM configuration
3-3-4	Video memory test failure
3-4-1	Screen initialization failure
4-3-4	Time-of-day clock stopped

TECH TIP

Troubleshoot the first POST code heard or seen

If multiple POST errors occur, troubleshoot the first one heard or seen.

TABLE 12.8 AMI BIOS audio beeps

Beeps	Description of problem
1, 2, or 3	Memory error
4, 5, 6, or 7	Motherboard component
8	Video issue
1 long 3 short	Memory test failure
1 long 8 short	Display test failure
2 short	POST failure

TABLE 12.9 Phoenix audio beep codes

Beeps	Description
1-2-2-3	BIOS ROM (flash the BIOS/motherboard)
1-3-1-1	Memory refresh (RAM contacts/RAM)
1-3-1-3	8742 keyboard controller (keyboard/motherboard)
1-3-4-1	Memory address line error (RAM contacts/RAM/power supply/motherboard)

Beeps	Description
1-3-4-3	Memory error (RAM contacts/RAM/motherboard)
1-4-1-3	CPU bus clock frequency
2-2-3-1	Unexpected interrupt (adapter/motherboard)
2-4-2-3	Keyboard error
3-1-1-1	Onboard I/O port issue

Don't get frustrated at error messages that appear on the screen. Error messages are good things in that they assist you in troubleshooting. Table 12.10 lists the POST error messages sometimes seen on other computers.

TABLE 12.10 Written BIOS POST error messages

Message	Description
BIOS ROM checksum error—System halted	The BIOS has a problem and needs to be replaced.
CMOS battery failed/error	Replace the motherboard battery.
CMOS checksum error—Defaults loaded	CMOS has detected a problem. Check the motherboard battery.
CMOS timer error	The system date/time has not been set. Check/replace the motherboard battery if this is not the first time this computer has been powered on.
Hard disk install failure	The BIOS could not find or initialize the hard drive. Check the hard drive connectivity and power.
Intruder detection error	The computer chassis has been opened.
Keyboard error or no keyboard present	The keyboard could not be found. Check the cabling.
Keyboard is locked out—Unlock the key	Ensure that nothing rests on the keys during the POST.
Memory test fail	A RAM error occurred. Swap the memory modules.
Memory size decrease error	The amount of system RAM has decreased. Check to see whether RAM has been stolen, needs reseating, or needs to be replaced.
Memory optimal error	The amount of memory in channel A is not equal to channel B. For optimal memory performance, they should be equal. See Chapter 6 for more details.
Override enabled—Defaults loaded	The current settings in CMOS could not be loaded, and the BIOS defaults are used. Check the battery and CMOS settings.
Primary master hard disk fail	The PATA hard drive attached to the primary IDE connector and configured as master could not be detected. If it is a new installation, check the cabling, power, and master/slave/cable select settings. See Chapter 7 for more details.
Primary slave hard disk fail	The PATA hard drive attached to the primary IDE connector and configured as slave could not be detected. If it is a new installation, check the cabling, power, and master/slave/cable select settings. See Chapter 7 for more details.

A BIOS can be sold to various computer manufacturers that are then allowed to create their own error codes and messages. The replacement for a BIOS is UEFI, which has a great deal of flexibility in the options and design. Always look in the motherboard/computer manual or on the manufacturer's website for a list of exact error messages.

In addition to hearing audio tones or seeing numeric error codes or written messages, the motherboard might provide additional troubleshooting information such as the following:

> Proprietary crash screen.
> In Windows, you might see a blue screen of death (**BSOD**) with a numeric code and/or a message. You might also see the system display a message saying a particular application is not responding. Use *Task Manager* to stop the application or give the application more time to complete the task. Close other open applications. See Chapter 16 for more Windows troubleshooting.
> On an Apple Mac or other operating systems, you might see a colored **pin wheel** that appears to turn forever. Use *Activity Monitor* to check for processor and RAM performance and free disk space and/or to stop the problem application. See Chapter 17 for more troubleshooting tips on Mac and Linux systems.

When a numeric code appears or certain lights illuminate, you have to use the manual to determine the issue. Some motherboards have a numeric display or colored indicators that display as part of the POST. The meaning of the visual clues can be found in the motherboard or computer manual.

Other Diagnostics

Some technicians carry a POST card as part of their tool kit. A **POST card** is a PCI/PCIe adapter or USB-attached card that performs hardware diagnostics and displays the results as a series of codes on an LED display or LED light(s). These are not as popular today as they once were because many UEFI-based motherboards include powerful diagnostics (see Table 12.11) that can be executed from or downloaded from the computer manufacturer's website. However, they are useful if the system does not boot and no other symptoms appear.

TABLE 12.11   UEFI diagnostic types

Diagnostic	Description
Express, Start, or System test	Similar to POST, checks the main hardware components needed to load the operating system.
Component test	Allows selection of individual parts to test.
Hard drive test	Checks the drive for bad areas and has the capability to mark the area and not use it in the future.
Memory test	Performs multiple reads/writes to memory locations.
Battery test	Checks the battery's power level.

Some motherboard LEDs are used in conjunction with depressible switches to test components. Figure 12.12 shows a motherboard LED, and Figure 12.13 shows some common uses of the motherboard LEDs.

FIGURE 12.12 Motherboard LED

Examples of Motherboard Switches and LEDs

Switch	LED	Explanation
 MemOK!	MemOK	Depress the MemOK switch to determine if the RAM modules are compatible. The MemOK LED illuminates if so.
 EPU	EPU	Enable the EPU switch or enable through BIOS to allow the motherboard to moderate power consumption. When enabled, the EPU LED is lit.
	RAM	The RAM LED illuminates for a memory error.
	Power	The power LED commonly illuminates when power is applied, or if the computer is in either the sleep or soft off power mode.

FIGURE 12.13 Motherboard switches and LED usage

Hardware Errors

Hardware errors might also occur. For example, the display might suddenly go black, the optical drive's access light might not go on when it attempts to access the optical disc, or the printer might repeatedly flash an error code. If you suspect a physical port problem, you can use a loopback plug to test the port. A **loopback plug** sends a signal out one or more electrical pins and allows the signal to come back in on one or more different pins. Loopback plugs are commonly used with the older ports, such as the parallel and serial ports. Today, one of the most common uses for a loopback plug is to test a communication circuit port or an RJ-45 loopback plug to test network port functionality.

TECH TIP

What to do if you smell smoke coming from the computer

Unplug the device if you can. Pull the fire alarm. Call 911. If you see smoke, get a fire extinguisher and PASS (pull the pin, aim at the base of the fire, squeeze the trigger, and sweep slowly side to side).

Hardware errors are usually obvious because of POST error codes or errors that occur when accessing a particular device. Also, some peripherals, such as hard drives and printers, include diagnostics as part of the software that is loaded when the device is installed. These diagnostics are frequently accessed through the device's *Properties* window.

Intermittent Device Failure

Sometimes, none of these hardware troubleshooting actions work. A grounding problem might be the issue. Symptoms of a grounding problem include intermittent or unexplained shutdowns.

Build the computer outside the computer case, on an anti-static mat, if possible. Start with only the power supply, motherboard, and speaker connected. Even though it will normally produce a POST audio error, verify that the power supply fan will turn. Most power supplies issue a click before the audio POST beeps. Next, verify the voltages from the power supply. If the fan turns and the voltages are correct, power down the machine and add a video adapter and monitor to the system. If the machine does not work, put the video adapter in a different expansion slot and try again. If placing the video adapter in a different expansion slot does not work, swap out the video adapter.

If the video adapter works, continue adding devices one by one and checking the voltages. Just as any one device can cause the system not to operate properly, so can any adapter. If one particular adapter causes the system to malfunction, try a different expansion slot before trying a different adapter. If the expansion slot proves to be a problem, check the slot for foreign objects. If none are found, but the problem still occurs, place a note on the expansion slot so that no one will use it.

An **intermittent device failure** is one of the hardest things to troubleshoot. Devices commonly associated with intermittent device failure are the motherboard, RAM, processor, and power supply; however, a failing hard drive can also present itself as an intermittent device failure if the drive is starting to have problems. When considering the motherboard, RAM, processor, and power supply, RAM is the easiest to troubleshoot of these four devices if there are multiple modules installed. Before trying anything else, remove power to the system and push firmly on the memory modules. They can creep up a bit even with the side locking levers in place. Power on and see if the problem reappears. If not, swap the modules to see whether symptoms change (it occurs faster or takes longer for the device to fail) or remove a module. If the system stays stable, reinsert the module and see whether the intermittent failure returns.

For intermittent power issues, first check power output with a power supply tester. Also verify your power supply wattage and ensure it is adequate for the number of installed devices. Inspect power connectors to ensure they have not gotten caught or crimped in the cover.

Determining whether a problem is a motherboard or a processor is tough. The easiest thing to do is check the processor on a different (compatible) motherboard. You might see whether you can use a particular UEFI diagnostic to do an extended test on the motherboard and processor.

Software Errors

Software errors, on the other hand, occur when a computer user accesses a particular application or file or when the system boots. Sometimes, the problem can be resolved with a **warm boot**. Warm booting causes any changes that have been made to take effect without putting as much strain on the computer as a cold boot does. Here are the warm boot (restart) procedures for the different Windows versions:

> Windows Vista or 7: Select the *Start* button > click on the right arrow adjacent to the lock button or Shutdown and select *Restart*.
> Windows 8: Move the mouse to the upper-right corner or swipe from the right edge to access the *Charms* menu > *Settings* > *Power* > *Restart*.
> Windows 10: Select the *Start* button > *Power* > *Restart*.
> In all Windows versions, a warm boot can be performed through Task Manager by holding down the [Ctrl] key, the [Alt] key, and the [Delete] key at the same time > *Task Manager* > *Shut Down* option > select *Restart* from the drop-down menu > *OK*.

TECH TIP

Motherboard manual or website lists the latest error codes

Manufacturers constantly produce BIOS upgrades, and you can use the Internet to verify POST errors that occur and the recommended actions to take.

Files that affect the booting process, such as files in the Startup folder, are dependent on the operating system. If in doubt as to whether a problem is hardware- or software-related, use Windows *Device Manager* to test the hardware to eliminate that possibility. Every software program has problems (bugs). Software manufacturers offer a software **patch** or a **service release** that fixes known problems. Patches or service releases are usually available on the Internet from the software manufacturer. It is important to keep applications and the operating system patched. A **service pack** (in Windows Vista/7) usually contains multiple patches and installs them at the same time rather than in multiple downloads. Chapters 15, 16, 17, and 18 have more information on software-related issues

Test the Theory to Determine Cause

Once you have a theory or suspect a general area, you need to determine the next steps needed to resolve the problem. If you go through the process for what you suspect and the problem is still unresolved, you might have to step back and reevaluate the problem. From there, you can establish a new theory or will need to escalate the problem to a more senior technician.

Divide the problem into logical areas and continue subdividing the problem until it is isolated. For example, if an error appears each time the computer user tries to write data to a CD, then the logical place to look is the optical drive system. The optical drive system includes the user's disc, the optical drive, electronics that tell the drive what to do, a cable that connects the drive to the controlling electronics, and the software program currently being used. Any of these may be the cause of the problem.

Ernie Friend, a technician of many years, advises students to divide a problem in half; then divide it in half again, and then continue to divide it until the problem is manageable. This way of thinking carries a technician a long way. Also, always keep in mind that you will beat the problem at hand! You are smarter than any problem!

TECH TIP

Return original part if it does not fix the problem

Always re-install the original part if the symptoms do not change. Then, continue troubleshooting.

Use Ernie's philosophy with the optical drive problem: Divide the problem in half and determine whether the problem is hardware- or software-related. To determine whether the software application is causing the problem, try accessing the disc from another application. If the second application works, then the problem is in the first application. If both applications have problems, the problem is most likely in the disc or in the drive hardware system. The next easiest thing to eliminate as a suspect is the CD. Try a different disc. If a different disc works, then the first disc was the problem. If neither disc accepts data, the problem is the optical drive, cable, or electronics. Swap parts one at a time until you locate the problem.

If a hardware problem is evident after a POST error or peripheral access/usage error occurs, consider the problem a subunit of the entire computer. For example, if a POST error occurs for the optical drive, the subunit is the optical drive subsystem. The subsystem consists of the drive, the cable, and the controlling circuits that may be on an adapter or the motherboard.

If a problem is software-related, narrow it to a specific area. For example, determine whether the problem is related to printing, saving, or retrieving a file. This may give you a clue about what section of the application is having a problem or may even lead you back to considering other hardware components as the cause of the problem.

TECH TIP

Change or check the easy stuff first

When isolating a problem to a specific area, be practical; change or check the easy stuff first (see Figure 12.14). Time is money—to the company or person whose computer is down and to the company that employs the technician.

"It could be that it's not plugged in, but that would be too easy."

FIGURE 12.14 Check the easy stuff first

When multiple things could cause a problem, make a list of possibilities and eliminate the potential problems one by one. If a display is faulty, swap the display with another before opening the computer and swapping the video adapter.

Also, check with the computer user to see whether anything about the computer has changed recently. For example, ask if anyone installed or removed something from the computer or if new software was loaded before or has been loaded since the problem started. If the problem is hardware-related, you can use the Device Manager and Windows troubleshooting wizards to narrow it down to a subunit.

If you do not hear any unusual audio beeps or see any POST error codes and you suspect a software error, reboot the computer. Before Windows starts, press the F8 key to bring up the *Advanced Boot Options* menu. Select a menu option, such as *Repair your computer, Safe mode*, or *Last Known Good Configuration*. In newer computers, it is not always easy to press the F8 key during startup. Here's how to do this for Windows 8 and 10. Chapter 16 has more information on the Advanced Boot Options menu options.

> In Windows 8, access *Settings* > *Advanced startup options* > locate the *Advanced startup* section and select the *Restart now* button.
> In Windows 10, access *Settings* > *Update & Security* > *Recovery* > locate the *Advanced startup* section and select the *Restart now* button.

Swapping a part, checking hardware settings, and referring to documentation are necessary steps in troubleshooting. Noting error or beep codes is just one element in the diagnostic routine. Determining what the problem is usually takes longer than fixing it. Software problems frequently involve reloading software applications and software drivers or getting software updates and patches from the appropriate vendor. The Internet is an excellent resource for these files and vendor recommendations. Hardware problem resolution simply involves swapping the damaged part. Sometimes, it is necessary to remove or disable unnecessary components and peripherals. This is especially true with notebook computers.

If swapping a part or reloading the software does not solve the problem, go back to logical troubleshooting. Step 2 reminds you to divide the problem into hardware- and software-related issues. Go back to that step if necessary.

Establish a Plan of Action and Implement the Solution

Every repair should involve a plan of action. Having a plan helps you through the problem-resolution process. The plan of action should take you through resolving the problem and implementing the solution. Some repairs take multiple steps. You might have to apply a BIOS update before installing a new adapter. You might have to update the operating system or remove a virus before re-installing or upgrading an application. Having a plan instead of just doing things in a random order saves time, and time is money!

Verify Full System Functionality and Implement Preventive Measures

Never assume that a hardware component or replaced software repairs a computer. The computer can have multiple problems, or one repair may not offer a complete solution. Verify full system functionality and have the user test the computer in normal conditions to prove that the problem is indeed solved. You may need to implement preventive measures, such as cleaning the computer or device or installing a legal copy of antivirus/antimalware software and making sure they have the most recent updates. Preventive measures also include using disk maintenance utilities to clean up the hard drive, cleaning the optical drive laser lens, scheduling disk maintenance, and creating a recovery image.

Document Findings, Actions, and Outcomes and Provide Feedback

Many technicians feel that their work is done once a problem is solved, but it is not. Documenting the steps taken to resolve a problem in a clear, concise manner is important. A lot of times, this documentation is put in a customer's record, or an invoice is generated as a result of the repair. Having easy-to-read and easy-to-understand documentation is important for nontechnical users who see this documentation as well as any follow-up repairs that you or another technician must do. The old adage of the job is not done until the paperwork is done is still true; even though the paperwork is usually electronic documentation, it is still part of the last step.

The best computer technicians are the ones who can repair problems, build trust with users, and explain problems in a way customers can understand. A repair is never finished until the user is informed. Technical training on new equipment or a procedure/process may be necessary. Realize that computer users are intelligent, even if they are not proficient in technical terminology.

A good recommendation is to follow up with the customer one week after the repair to make sure the customer is satisfied and that the problem is solved. If the customer is unhappy, jump at the chance to make good on the repair. The best advertising is good referrals from satisfied customers. Keep in mind that the general rule of thumb is that if the customer is satisfied, he or she will tell 1 or 2 other people about the service. If the customer is dissatisfied, he or she will tell 10 other people about the problem.

Each computer repair is a different scenario because of the plethora of vendors, products, and standards in the marketplace. But this is one thing that makes the job so interesting and challenging. Break down each problem into manageable tasks, isolate the specific issue, and use all available resources, including other technicians, documentation, and the Internet to solve it. Keep a "can do" attitude with intermittent problems—the hardest types of problems there are to solve. Never forget to give feedback.

Sample Troubleshooting Flowcharts

Troubleshooting flowcharts are commonly found in technical documentation. Learning how to read and use them is helpful. Figure 12.15 shows a flowchart that does not have any words in it. The symbols in the sample flowchart are as follows:

> The powder blue rectangle with rounded edges is a terminal block that shows where to start and where to end. Not all flowcharts have that for computer and mobile device repair.
> The lime green parallelogram is used to show input or output. This could be that you generate a report or receive some type of diagnostic data.
> The yellow rectangle is the most common shape you will see in a flowchart. It shows an action to take, task to do, or operation to perform.
> The purple box is a decision box. The direction you go out of the decision box depends on what happens. Notice in Figure 12.15 how there are three results that could be made from the decision box. Pretend these are marked as Yes, No, and Not applicable. So, if whatever you did resulted in the question posed in the purple box to have an answer of yes, the left output from the purple decision box could lead to another action box. If the answer was not applicable and the bottom of the purple decision box was labeled with N/A, then you would terminate and be done (drop to the orange terminal block). If the answer out of the purple decision box was no and the right side of the decision box was labeled with No or N, then you would do the action listed in the right blue action box.

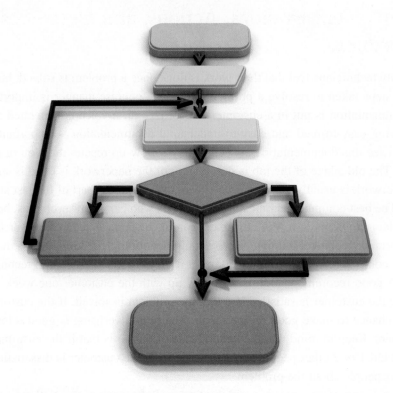

FIGURE 12.15   Sample flowchart

Figure 12.16 shows a simple troubleshooting flowchart. Figure 12.17 has a USB troubleshooting flowchart.

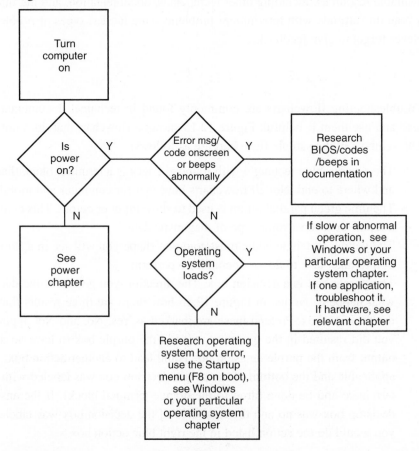

FIGURE 12.16   Basic troubleshooting flowchart

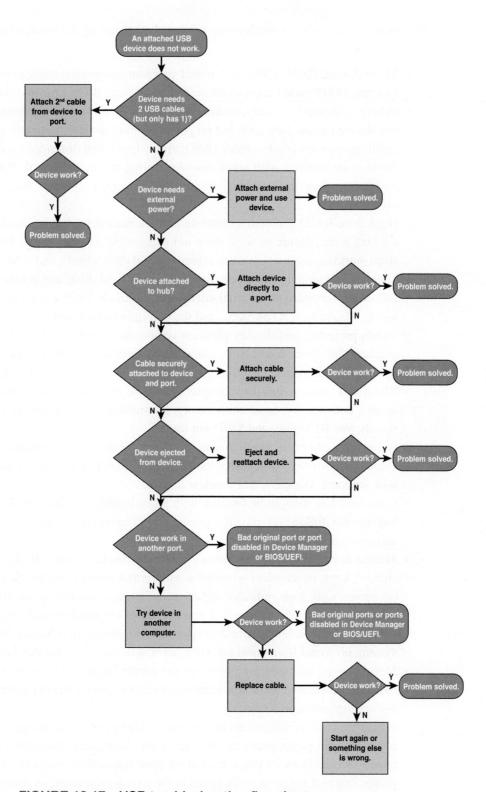

FIGURE 12.17   USB troubleshooting flowchart

Keep in mind that each chapter has one or more troubleshooting sections to help with problems. In addition, the chapters toward the end of this book address problems related to operating systems. Also, the lists that follow include the troubleshooting section of the CompTIA A+ 220-901 certification exam. Chapters 3, 4, 5, 7, 9, 10, and 14 are loaded with suggestions for these symptoms.

Review each chapter's troubleshooting sections before taking the exam with these specific symptoms in mind:

> Motherboard, RAM, CPU, and power problem symptoms: unexpected shutdowns, system lockups, POST code beeps, blank screen on bootup, BIOS time and settings resets, attempts to boot to incorrect devices, continuous reboots, no power, overheating, loud noise, intermittent device failure, fans spin, but no power to other devices, indicator lights, smoke, burning smell, proprietary crash screens (BSOD/pin wheel), and distended capacitors.

> Tools to be familiar with when troubleshooting the motherboard, RAM, CPU, and power problems include the following: multimeter, power supply tester, loopback plugs, and POST card/USB.

> Hard drive/RAID problem symptoms include read/write failure, slow performance, a loud clicking noise, failure to boot, drive not recognized, OS not found, RAID not found, RAID stops working, proprietary crash screens (BSOD/pin wheel), and S.M.A.R.T. errors.

> Tools to be familiar with when troubleshooting hard drive and RAID problems include the following: screwdriver, external enclosures, `chkdsk`, `format`, `file recovery software`, `bootrec`, `diskpart`, and the defragmentation tool.

> Video, projector, and display problem symptoms include VGA mode, no image on screen, overheat shutdown, dead pixels, artifacts, incorrect color patterns, dim images, flickering images, distorted images, distorted geometry, burn-in, and oversized images and icons.

> Wired and wireless problem symptoms include no connectivity, APIPA/link local address, limited connectivity, local connectivity, intermittent connectivity, IP conflict, slow transfer speeds, low RF signal, and SSID not found.

> Hardware tools to be familiar with when troubleshooting wired and wireless problems include the following: cable tester, loopback plug, punch down tools, tone generator and probe, wire strippers, crimpers, and wireless locator.

> Command-line tools to be familiar with when troubleshooting wired and wireless problems include the following: `ping`, `ipconfig/ifconfig`, `tracert`, `netstat`, `nbtstat`, `net`, `netdom`, and `nslookup`.

> Mobile device problem symptoms include no display, a dim display, a flickering display, sticking keys, intermittent wireless, a battery that doesn't charge, ghost cursor/pointer drift, no power, num lock indicator lights, no wireless connectivity, no Bluetooth connectivity, an inability to display to external monitor, a non-responsive touch screen, apps not loading, slow performance, inability to decrypt email, extremely short battery life, overheating, frozen system, no sound from speakers, GPS not functioning, and swollen battery.

> Mobile device disassembly processes for proper re-assembly include the following: document and label cable and screw locations, organize parts, refer to manufacturer resources, and use appropriate hand tools.

> Printer problem symptoms include streaks, faded print, ghost images, toner not fused to the paper, creased paper, paper not feeding, paper jams, no connectivity, garbled characters on paper, vertical lines on page, backed-up print queue, low memory errors, denied access, a printer that will not print, color prints in the wrong print color, an inability to install a printer, error codes, printing blank pages, and no image on the printer display.

> Tools to use with printer problems include the following: maintenance kit, toner vacuum, compressed air, and printer spooler.

SOFT SKILLS—DEALING WITH IRATE CUSTOMERS

One of the most difficult tasks a technician faces is dealing with people who are angry, upset, or frustrated. This is a common issue for those who come to help or try to troubleshoot a problem over the phone. Dealing with irate customers is a skill that you can fine-tune. Listening to peer technicians tell how they have successfully (or unsuccessfully) dealt with a difficult customer can also help. Realize that not only do customers want their computer problems fixed, but they sometimes just need to vent and be heard. Because a technician is the person with the knowledge for at least the start of the resolution and the technician is in front of or on the phone with the person who is not able to do something on the computer, the technician is the common scapegoat and must try to listen to the irritated customer. Some key tips for dealing with customers are shown in Figure 12.18.

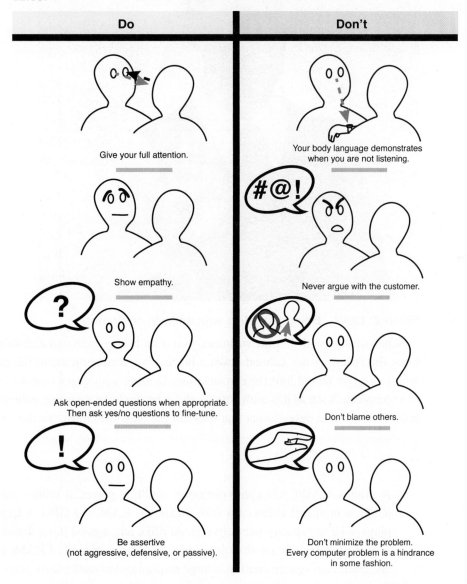

FIGURE 12.18   Dealing with irate customers

The last suggestion in Figure 12.18 about being assertive is one that many people do not understand. Aggression involves dominating a conversation or situation by threatening, bullying, being sarcastic, or showing belittling behavior and/or actions. Some technicians consistently demonstrate aggressive behavior. This reflects poorly on the technician and the company that the technician represents. Passive behavior involves letting others dominate you and expressing yourself apologetically. Technicians who are passive frequently apologize while the customer is trying to explain the problem. Assertive behavior involves being respectful of another person but not allowing him or her to take advantage or dominate the situation. This is the middle ground you want to strive for when dealing with customers. Figure 12.19 shows how a technician might raise his hand in showing a gesture to stop to the customer. This would be an example of assertive behavior to indicate that you want that person to stop what they are doing.

FIGURE 12.19 Being assertive with an irate customer

When dealing with an irate customer, you want to stay calm and maintain your professionalism. Once the customer has calmed down a bit, more information about the problem can be gleaned with less anger mixed into the conversation. Dealing with angry customers is just as much a part of a technician's job as it is with anyone else who works in a service industry. Consider customers' points of view and never forget that they are the ones who must use the devices that you repair.

Chapter Summary

> A graphic/CAD/CAM computer needs multiple powerful multi-core processors, maximum RAM, a high-end video card with maximum RAM and GPU, a large display/multiple displays, a large-capacity hard drive(s), an SSD, and a good input device(s).

> A gaming PC needs a multi-core processor, a large amount of RAM, a sound card and speakers, additional system cooling, a large display and/or multiple displays, and good input/output devices.

> An audio- or video-editing PC needs multiple powerful multi-core processors, maximum RAM, a good video card with maximum RAM and GPU, a sound card, a fast and large-capacity hard drive, dual displays, and a good input device(s).

> A virtualization computer needs multiple powerful multi-core processors, maximum RAM, multiple fast hard drives, an SSD, and a 1Gb/s NIC.

> A standard thick client computer supports desktop applications meets recommended requirements for selected OS.

> A thin client computer supports basic applications meets minimum requirements for selected OS.

> A mobile computer is commonly a laptop with lots of RAM and an SSD, a mobile tablet, a smartphone, and possible devices such as a projector, thermal printer, portable speakers, or headphones with noise cancellation.

> An HTPC has a small form factor with quiet internal devices, a surround-sound card, a TV tuner or cable card, and HDMI video output.

> A home server PC has a medium to large case, multiple powerful multi-core processors, lots of RAM, RAID, server applications such as media streaming, file sharing, print sharing, and a 1Gb/s NIC.

> Processors and chipsets are created using a specific nanotechnology. Common technologies used are 14, 22, 32, and 45nm. The smaller the number, the less space for the same number of transistors.

> When designing a motherboard, the CPU size and motherboard CPU socket must match.

> The power supply, motherboard, and case form factors must match.

> Power supplies must have the correct amount of wattage, wattage for a specific power level, and an appropriate number/type of power cables.

> Air filters and enclosures can help in environments where airborne particles are a concern.

> When designing for internal devices, use SATA or M.2 and have the correct power connector. Ensure that an internal connector is available.

> When designing for external connectivity, ensure that a USB, eSATA, eSATAp, or IEEE 1394 port is available; ensure that enough power is provided to power the device through the port or use an external power supply; and ensure that not too many devices share the same cable, which can affect performance.

> For audio, ensure that the correct number and type of input/output ports are available.

> For common usage, the 2.0 two-channel audio subsystem is used. A 2.1 audio subsystem adds a subwoofer as a third output device for lower frequencies.

> Display design should include physical space consideration, type of display, features that might be integrated into the display such as a microphone or camera, a video port, and memory, GPU, and additional power requirements.

> Mobile designs include all the same major components as a desktop system plus 802.11 and Bluetooth wireless capabilities as well as integrated input devices such as a keyboard and touchpad.

> The six steps of troubleshooting are as follows: (1) Identify the problem, (2) establish a theory, (3) test the theory, (4) establish a plan of action, (5) verify full system functionality and, if applicable, implement preventive measures, and (6) document findings, actions, and outcomes as well as provide feedback.

> BIOS/UEFI controls the boot process. Knowing the following traditional BIOS steps can help with the troubleshooting process. The basic steps that the computer goes through to start up are as follows:

Step 1.   A power good signal is sent from the power supply.

Step 2.   The CPU looks in BIOS for software.

Step 3.   The CPU executes the POST (only audio errors available at this point).

Step 4.   The computer assigns system resources to ports, devices, and adapters.

Step 5. The computer initializes video—a cursor appears.

Step 6. POST continues checking hardware.

Step 7. The computer looks for an operating system from the BIOS-specified boot order devices.

Step 8. The computer loads the operating system or halts with an error.

> UEFI still checks the hardware. The UEFI boot manager can load drivers that allow devices such as the mouse and NIC to be used with UEFI applications. In a Windows environment, the UEFI boot manager turns control over to a Windows boot manager; then the Windows operating system loader controls the loading of the operating system kernel.

> POST error codes are determined by the BIOS/UEFI vendor and the company that makes the motherboard.

> POST codes can be audible beeps, numeric codes, or words.

> The BIOS/UEFI can contain advanced diagnostics.

> The motherboard can contain diagnostic LEDs or a display.

> A POST card can be used to perform diagnostics.

> A loopback plug can be used in conjunction with diagnostics to check older ports, communication ports, or to test network interface ports.

> Re-install parts that do not solve the problem.

> Always document a problem as part of the troubleshooting process. Give users the appropriate documentation. Be professional in your oral and written communication. Provide feedback to the user.

A+ CERTIFICATION EXAM TIPS

✓ The specific types of custom configurations on the exam include the following computer types: (1) graphic/CAD/CAM design, (2) audio/video editing, (3) virtualization, (4) gaming, (5) home theater, (6) standard thick client, (7) thin client, and (8) home server PC. Be able to select the appropriate components and specifications for each configuration.

✓ Be able to explain the purpose of specific components, such as enclosures and air filters, and how they are used as environmental controls.

✓ Review the troubleshooting steps. Even though these steps are logical, when the steps are placed into written questions, they can become tricky. Try to think of the computer problems you solved during the chapter activities. Now relate those steps to the six troubleshooting steps. This will help you remember when you take the 220-902 exam. The six troubleshooting steps could be applied to specific troubleshooting scenarios.

✓ Review the boot process order and procedures listed in this chapter. Knowing this material and the order in which things happen can help you with troubleshooting questions that may appear on the exams.

✓ If you know any technicians, ask them to tell you the problems they solved this week. Another idea is to get them to tell you a problem and you see if you can guess the top things that could cause that problem.

✓ Review the customer support/soft skills section for the best practices in communication skills. The communication questions can sometimes have answers that are very similar. Use the review questions at the end of the chapter to help practice with those types of questions.

✓ The 220-902 exam has very specific criteria for proper communication and professionalism. A specific part of this section is dealing with a difficult customer or situation. Remember to avoid arguing with the customer and/or being defensive. Do not minimize the customer's problem. Avoid being judgmental. Clarify customer statements by asking open-ended questions (which allow the customer to freely explain the situation) to narrow the scope of the problem and by restating the issue or question to verify your understanding. Never disclose work-related experiences via social media outlets.

Key Terms

Review Questions

1. _____ executes POST. [BIOS/UEFI | CMOS | NAS | RAM]

2. Which technology is most likely to be used in a home theater configuration?
   [KVM switch | nanometer | DVR | RAID]

3. List three design recommendations for a home server PC.

   _____

   _____

4. To troubleshoot a variety of possible system startup problems, press the _____ key during the system startup process to bring up the Advanced Boot Options menu.
   [F1 | F2 | F8 | F12]

5. Which of the following would most likely be a design consideration for a gaming PC rather than a computer used for virtualization?

   a. High amount of RAM

   b. NAS

   c. Multiple fast, large-capacity hard drives

   d. Additional system cooling

6. If a computer beeps once during POST, what does this commonly mean to a technician?

   a. There is not a problem.

   b. CPU register test

   c. DRAM refresh

   d. Video initialization error

7. An adapter or USB device that performs diagnostics and displays a code or LEDs is known as a _____. [DIGI card | probe | torx | POST card]

8–10. Group the following computer components into three design subsystems. In other words, group the components that need to be considered together when designing a subsection of a computer. Each group must include at least two components. All components are used.

   power supply   CPU   chipset
   video card   case   CPU cooling
   motherboard   display   RAM

   Group 1 components: _____

   _____

   Group 2 components: _____

   _____

   Group 3 components: _____

   _____

11. A motherboard advertisement lists UEFI as one of the motherboard features. What is UEFI?

    a. A port

    b. A BIOS replacement

    c. An internal interface

    d. A type of storage device

12. Which three design environments would have the largest display needs? (Select three.)

    [CAD | industrial | gaming | home theater | virtualization | thick client | home server]

13. Which type of computer design would be implemented if a workstation ran its applications from a remote server?

    [CAD | industrial | home theater | virtualization | thin client | thick client]

14. When designing, with what computer component would you consider the nanometer measurement?

    [hard drive | motherboard | display | CPU | power supply | air filter]

15. Which two components could have an ITX form factor? (Select two.)

    [hard drive | motherboard | display | CPU | power supply | air filter]

16. Place the six steps of troubleshooting in the order in which they occur.

    _____ First   **a.** Test the theory to determine cause.

    _____ Second   **b.** Establish a theory of probable cause.

    _____ Third   **c.** Document and provide feedback.

    _____ Fourth   **d.** Identify the problem.

    _____ Fifth   **e.** Verify system functionality and, if applicable, implement preventive measures.

    _____ Sixth   **f.** Establish a plan of action to resolve the problem and implement the solution.

17. [T | F] During the *Test the theory troubleshooting* phase, you might be required to escalate the problem to a more experienced technician.

18. A _____ is used to test a communications circuit or RJ-45 port.
    [multimeter | probe | torx | loopback plug]

19. Which computer design environment would have the most need for a laptop enclosure?

    [industrial | gaming | home theater | virtualization | mobile | home server]

20. [T | F] When dealing with an irate customer, it is best to listen to the customer vent.

CHAPTER 12

Exercises

Exercise 12.1 Computer System Design

Objective: To be able to recommend a complete system based on the customer's needs or placement of the system

Parts: Internet access

Procedure: Use the Internet to research specific computers, based on the given scenario.

1. A home-bound elderly person has just had the hard drive fail that was installed in a really old computer. The person has decided to replace the computer rather than fix the broken one. The elderly person uses the computer to shop for family members, check email, play basic computer card games with others online, and view pictures on CDs or DVDs sent by family members. Internet access is through a DSL modem that connects to the USB port and still works. Find a suitable computer on the Internet. The customer would like to keep the cost around $700, including installation, if possible. Write the computer model, basic description, cost, and cost of installation.

    _____

    _____

    _____

    _____

2. A graphic artist would like a second computer as a mobile solution and would like your assistance finding a suitable laptop. The graphic artist does mostly video graphics creation but would like to be able to work some when traveling. Find three possible solutions. Provide the computer model, basic description, and costs of the three laptops.

    _____

    _____

    _____

    _____

    _____

3. A sports complex wants to have a kiosk with a touch screen and that holds a computer that runs specialized software. The software allows folks to search for events and get detailed walking directions to the events and/or a specific sports field. No network connectivity is required. Locate a computer with an HDMI output for connectivity with the touch screen for this outdoor kiosk located in a year-round sports complex. List the model number, basic description, and your fee for installing this system.

    _____

    _____

    _____

    _____

4. A purchasing department is going to a thin-client environment. Select one desktop thin-client computer model and one mobile thin-client model from different manufacturers that can be used in the 10-person department. The models need to support dual displays. Detail any model numbers, basic parts descriptions, and costs.

    _____

    _____

    _____

    _____

_____

_____

_____

_____

_____

5. A small company is expanding and is hiring an administrative assistant for the sales manager. Select a computer, monitor, keyboard, and an inkjet all-in-one printer for this assistant, who will be using Microsoft Office–type applications. The boss has put a $1,200 limit (not counting shipping) on the entire purchase. Provide a detailed list, description, and costs of parts chosen.

_____

_____

_____

_____

_____

_____

_____

6. Select a CAD/CAM manufacturing design computer that uses 64-bit AutoCAD Mechanical 2013 software. Research the AutoCAD Mechanical application's video requirements. Provide a detailed list, description, and cost of parts chosen including the video card and display. Price is no object. (Note that AutoCAD Mechanical requires a 1280×1024 display with true color.)

_____

_____

_____

_____

7. You have an unlimited budget to build the best gaming rig possible. Choose two PC manufacturer sites at which you can select components, monitors, applications, and accessories for your new system.

_____

_____

_____

_____

8. You have an unlimited budget. You need to build two systems from scratch. You will need cases, power supplies, motherboards, CPUs, RAM, hard drives, video cards, and more. List two websites at which you can compare and buy all of the components you need to build your two systems.

_____

_____

_____

Exercise 12.2 Design Components

Objective: To be able to recognize the unique components for a specific computer design scenario

Procedure: Using the list of components, identify which components would be used in the scenarios given. Note that any one component can be used multiple times.

Components

a. Multiple powerful processor cores

b. Maximum RAM

c. Lots of RAM

d. Multiple large-capacity hard drives

e. Large-capacity hard drive

f. RAID

g. Sound card and speakers

h. Powerful video card and RAM on the card

i. Multiple displays

j. Large display

k. DVR

l. TV tuner or cable card

m. 1000Mb/s NIC

n. Computer enclosure

o. KVM switch

Scenario 1

Identify the unique components from the provided list for a computer used for audio and video editing.

_____

_____

Scenario 2

You need to build a computer to test out the Chrome operating system along with your current Windows operating system. You have decided to do this in a virtual environment. Identify the unique components that would be in the computer.

_____

_____

Scenario 3

A customer wants a computer in the den where the TV and surround-sound components are located. Identify the unique components that would be in this computer.

_____

_____

Scenario 4

A tire shop would like to have a computer in the lobby where information about the latest and up-coming sales are displayed. The owner is concerned about theft. What unique component would be needed for this situation?

_____

Scenario 5

A computer programmer works from home but likes to work from several types of computers—a mobile tablet, laptop, and desktop—and to be able to work on any mobile device when traveling. The programmer has decided to create a server to store and access everything from anyplace. The programmer does not want to have to buy another keyboard, mouse, or display for the server but wants to share these components connected to the desktop computer with the server. What unique components would be part of this system?

_____

_____

Exercise 12.3 Subsystem Design Components

Objective: To be able to design a subsystem of a computer, based on design requirements

Parts: Internet access

Procedure: Use the Internet to research specific computers, based on the given scenario.

Scenario 1

You have just ascertained that a customer's older ATX Pentium 4 motherboard in a home computer is bad. The customer wants a motherboard upgrade or replacement. The existing motherboard has a PCI sound card and VGA port that the user would like to continue using. The RAM on the existing motherboard has 512MB of DDR2 memory. The hard drive and optical drive use PATA for connectivity, and the customer would like to continue using these devices and the current operating system. The customer does light computer work but likes listening to broadcasts and music on the computer. Locate suitable replacement upgraded component(s). The budget is $250, including labor. Detail the item, item description, and cost.

_____

_____

_____

_____

_____

_____

Scenario 2

A customer has been given a micro-ATX motherboard, an Intel Core i5 quad-core processor, and RAM. The customer has two 3.5-inch SATA drives and one 5.25-inch optical drive from other computers. The customer would like assistance getting a case and a power supply to handle all these devices. The customer does not have a lot of room but wants a tower case that provides good air flow through the computer. The customer has a budget of $200 for this. Locate a power supply and case for the customer. Detail the items, item descriptions, and costs.

_____

_____

_____

Scenario 3

A retired naval officer has just gotten into classical music and now wants surround-sound in his office. Select an appropriate sound subsystem. The budget is $200. The office system has both PCI and PCIe expansion slots available. List the components, a description of each component, and the cost.

_____

_____

_____

Scenario 4

A college graduate has started her own website design business. She wants a video card that supports two 18- to 20-inch displays. Recommend a video subsystem for her. The budget is $500 maximum. List the components, a description of each component, and the costs.

_____

_____

_____

_____

Scenario 5

Locate a motherboard, power supply, RAM, CPU, and mid-sized case that are compatible with one another for an administrative assistant. The budget is $600. List the components, a description of the components (ensure that you list the type of RAM the motherboard supports), and the costs.

_____

_____

_____

_____

_____

_____

_____

_____

_____

Activities

Internet Discovery

Objective: To become familiar with researching computer items used in designing systems or subsystems

Parts: Internet access

Procedure: Use the Internet to answer the following questions. Write the answers and the URL of the site where you found the information.

1. Locate the Bloom's Taxonomy chart that has been modified by Andrew Churches to include verbs for the digital age. Write at least five verbs that Andrew Churches recommends as being relative to the top level of the taxonomy—the creating level—and the URL where you found the chart.

   _____

   _____

   _____

2. Locate minimum requirements for either a student computer or a staff computer at a particular school. Write the requirements, school name, and the URL where you found this information.

   _____

   _____

   _____

   _____

   _____

   _____

   _____

3. What are the recommended video standards for use when playing Kerbal Space Program on a PC? Write the answer and the URL where you found this information. Then, find a video card that meets those specifications that you would want to play this game. Document the video card and the price.

   _____

   _____

   _____

4. What are the minimum processor, RAM, and display resolution requirements for a client who wants to run AutoCAD 2016 software? Write the answer and the URL where you found the information.

   _____

   _____

   _____

   _____

   _____

CHAPTER 12

5. Find a monitor that supports the minimum display resolution found in Question 4. List the monitor manufacturer, model number, and URL where you found the information.

_____

_____

_____

6. Locate a website that has a troubleshooting flowchart. Write three things the flowchart provides that you find helpful or confusing. Write the URL where the chart was found.

_____

_____

_____

7. Locate one website that lists at least two BIOS/UEFI error codes. Write the URL where this information was found.

_____

8. Find a website that shows at least three recommendations for dealing with irate customers. Write three recommendations and the URL where you found this information.

_____

_____

_____

_____

Soft Skills

Objective: To become familiar with researching computer items used in designing systems or subsystems and to learn how to deal with difficult customers or situations

Activities:

1. Interview or email someone who works in your school to determine the school's minimum hardware requirements for its new computers. Document your findings.

2. In teams of two, find a video that shows how to deal with an irate customer. Document at least three observations from the video and the URL.

_____

_____

_____

_____

3. In teams of two, three, or four, design a computer for a specific purpose. State the purpose and provide all the models, descriptions, and costs. Compete with other teams for the best design.

Critical Thinking Skills

Objective: To become familiar with researching computer items used in designing systems or subsystems

Activities:

1. Refer to Table 12.1, which provides recommendations for hardware components. Find at least one type of computer configuration for which you disagree with the special hardware components; if you agree with them all, then think of one that should be added. List the component and the reason for your disagreement or addition.

    _____

    _____

2. Locate an image that shows Bloom's Taxonomy map, as modified by Andrew Churches. Explain why designing (in the creating stage) is a higher-level skill than the evaluating stage, which includes experimenting, judging, monitoring, and testing.

3. Do you think most technicians are good at designing? Explain your opinion.

Labs

Lab 12.1 Logical Troubleshooting

Objective: To solve a computer problem with logic

Parts: Computer

Procedure: Complete the following procedure and answer the accompanying questions.

1. In teams of two, one person leaves the room while the other person inserts a problem in the machine and powers it down.

2. The person who left the room powers on the computer with the problem and performs troubleshooting. Use the flowchart shown in Figure 12.20 and answer the questions that follow. Once the problem is solved, swap roles.

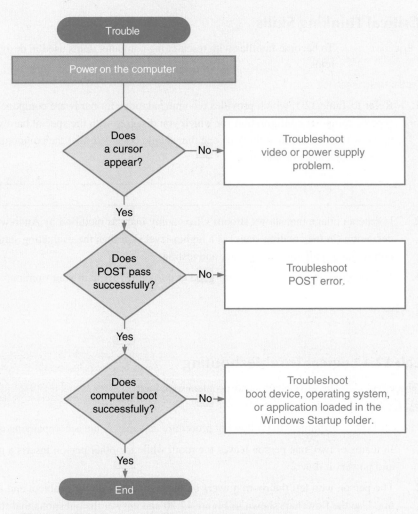

FIGURE 12.20 Lab troubleshooting flowcart

Do you hear any audio clues? If yes, list the symptoms._____

Do any POST errors appear? If so, list them. _____

Are there any startup errors? If so, list them._____

Are there any application-specific problems? If so, list them._____

List any possible techniques to test. Test them one at a time. Document the solution.

_____

_____

_____

13 Internet Connectivity

In this chapter you will learn:

> To configure an internal and external modem

> To explain basic handshaking between a DTE device and a DCE device

> To use Windows tools when working with modems

> To cable and configure a DSL modem and a cable modem

> Other Internet connectivity options, such as satellite, broadband wireless, WiMAX, and wireless modems

> To perform basic modem troubleshooting

> To configure a browser and other basic issues related to a browser

> The benefits of mentoring in the IT field

CompTIA Exam Objectives:

What CompTIA A+ exam objectives are covered in this chapter?

> 901-1.4   Install and configure PC expansion cards.

> 901-2.7   Compare and contrast Internet connection types, network types and their features.

> 901-2.8   Compare and contrast network architecture devices, their functions and features.

> 902-1.4   Given a scenario, use appropriate Microsoft operating system features and tools.

> 902-1.5   Given a scenario, use Windows Control Panel utilities.

> 902-1.6   Given a scenario, install and configure Windows networking on a client/desktop.

> 902-3.1 Identify common security threats and vulnerabilities.

> 902-4.2 Given a scenario, troubleshoot common PC security issues with appropriate tools and best practices.

Internet Connectivity Overview

Connecting to the Internet can be done in a variety of ways: via analog modem, ISDN, cable modem, DSL modem, satellite modem, fiber, wirelessly, power line, or cellular network. These technologies have unique installation and configuration methods, but they all have in common the capability to connect a computer to an outside network. Each technology is a viable option for connectivity in a specific situation. By examining and understanding the technologies, you can offer customers connectivity options. More information about troubleshooting network connectivity is provided in Chapter 14. Let's start with the oldest method: analog modems.

Modems Overview

One of the first devices still in operation that was used to connect to the Internet is the modem. A modem (modulator/demodulator) connects a computer with the outside world through a phone line. This type of technology is frequently called a **dial-up network** because the modem uses the traditional phone line to "dial up," or call, another modem. Modems can be internal or external peripheral devices. An internal modem is an adapter installed in an expansion slot. An external modem attaches to a USB port. A modem converts a signal transmitted over the phone line to digital 1s and 0s to be read by the computer. It also converts the digital 1s and 0s from the computer and modulates them onto the carrier signal and sends the data over the phone line. Modems normally connect to a remote modem through the phone line. Figure 13.1 shows two modems connecting two computers.

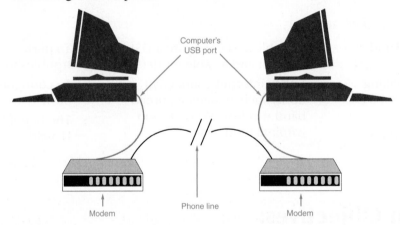

FIGURE 13.1   Sample modem connection

TECH TIP

When connecting a modem to a phone line, be careful with the cabling

Some modems have two jacks on the back. The labeling varies, but one jack is usually labeled PHONE and the other labeled LINE. The LINE jack is for the cable that goes from the modem to the phone wall jack. The modem's PHONE jack is an optional jack that connects a telephone to the modem. Figure 13.2 shows the ports on an internal modem.

FIGURE 13.2   Internal modem ports

Serial Communication Overview

A serial device such as a modem transmits or receives information 1 bit at a time and is traditionally connected to a serial port. With modern computers, a USB-to-serial converter (see Figure 13.3) is used to attach an external serial device such as a modem. An internal modem may be on an adapter. Serial ports are also known as asynchronous ports, COM ports, or RS232 ports. **Asynchronous** transmissions add extra bits to the data to track when each byte starts and ends. Synchronous transmissions rely on an external clock to time the data reception or transmission. Basic terminology associated with asynchronous transmissions is found in Table 13.1.

FIGURE 13.3 USB-to-DB-9 serial converter

TECH TIP

Configuring transmission speeds

When configuring a serial port or using an application, the configured speed is the rate at which the serial port transmits. This is not the speed for an external serial device that connects to the port (such as a modem).

TABLE 13.1 Serial asynchronous transmission terminology

Term	Description
start bit	Used in asynchronous transmissions to signal the start of the data.
stop bit	Used in asynchronous transmissions to signal the end of the data.
RS232C	Standard approved by the Electronics Industries Alliance (EIA) for the serial port used in a computer. Because serial devices use the 9- or 25-pin connector defined by this standard, they are commonly called RS232 serial devices.
bits per second (**bps**)	A measurement used to describe the transmission speed of serial devices and ports. Settings include 110, 300, 1200, 2400, 4800, 9600, 19200, 38400, 57600, and 115200. The application software must match the serial device or serial port's bits per second rate.
baud	The number of times an analog signal changes in 1 second. Some use this term to speak of the modem speed. With today's modulation techniques, modems can send several bits in one cycle, so it is more accurate to specify modem speed in bits per second (bps or b/s).
Universal Asynchronous Receiver/ Transmitter (UART)	A chip on the motherboard for an integrated serial port or on the adapter of an internal modem. It converts a data byte into a serial data stream of single 1s and 0s for transmission. It also receives the bit stream and stores data in its own buffers until the processor can accept the data.

How to Configure Traditional Serial Devices

Serial ports and devices such as internal modems have three important configuration parameters (and others as well, as discussed later): interrupt, input/output (I/O) address, and COM port number. An internal modem has all these parameters; an external modem uses these same parameters, but they are assigned to the serial port to which the external modem connects. Use Device Manager to identify these system resources. Exercises at the end of this chapter show how to view serial device resources.

TECH TIP

Application settings and hardware settings must match

Applications that communicate or control serial devices must have the application settings match the hardware settings; otherwise, communication will not occur.

An understanding of how serial devices operate is essential to a technician's knowledge base if analog modems are in the geographic area. Before installing a serial device and configuring its associated software, a technician must be familiar with the terminology associated with serial device installation. Table 13.2 lists the various serial port settings.

TABLE 13.2   Serial port settings

Setting	Explanation
Data bits	Determines how many bits make up a data word. It is usually 8 bits per data word, but it can be 7 or lower.
Parity	A simple method of checking data accuracy. When parity is used, both computers must be set to the same setting. The choices for parity include none, odd, even, space, and mark. With a space parity setting, both computers always set the parity bit to 0. With the mark parity setting, both computers always set the parity bit to 1. The most common setting is none for modems.
Stop bits	The number of bits sent to indicate the end of the data word. The number of stop bits can be 1, 1.5, or 2. One stop bit is the common choice.
FIFO setting	Used to enable or disable the UART chip's FIFO buffer. This setting gives the processor time to handle other tasks without the serial device losing data. If data is lost, it will have to be retransmitted later, when the microprocessor turns its attention back to the serial device.
Handshaking	The order in which things happen to allow two serial devices to communicate. Knowing this order helps with troubleshooting.
Flow control	Determines how two serial devices communicate. Can be set using software or physical pins on the serial port (hardware). Also called handshaking, which allows a serial device to tell the sending serial device, "Wait, I need a second before you send any more data."

TECH TIP

How does parity work?

Parity can be either even or odd. Take the example of a computer that uses even parity. If the data sent is 10101010, a total of four 1s is sent, plus a 0 for the parity bit. Four is an even number; therefore, the parity bit is set to 0 because the total number of 1s must be an even number when even parity is used. If the data sent is 10101011, a total of five 1s is sent, plus an extra 1 for the parity bit. Because five is an odd number and the system uses even parity, the extra parity bit is set to 1 to make the total number of 1s an even number.

CHAPTER 13

The two common methods for flow control are XON/XOFF (software method) and RTS/CTS (hardware method). **XON/XOFF** handshaking sends special control characters when a serial device needs more time to process data or is ready to receive more data. If one modem needs the remote modem to wait, it will send a certain character (usually [Ctrl] + [S]). Then, when the modem is ready to accept more data, a different control character (usually [Ctrl] + [Q]) is sent.

RTS/CTS (hardware handshaking) uses specific wires on the serial connector to send a signal to the other device to stop or start sending data. The clear to send (CTS) and the request to send (RTS) signals indicate when it is okay to send data. Modem communication normally uses hardware flow control (RTS/CTS) instead of software flow control. Table 13.3 delineates hardware flow control.

TABLE 13.3 Hardware handshaking

Order of execution	Explanation
Both devices (the DTE and the DCE) power on and are functional.	Not applicable
The DTE sends a signal over the data terminal ready (DTR) line.	The DTE says, "I'm ready."
The DCE sends a signal over the data set ready (DSR) line.	The DCE says, "I'm ready, too."
The DTE sends a signal over the request to send (RTS) connector pin.	The DTE (such as the computer) says, "I would like some data."
The DCE sends a signal on the clear to send (CTS) connector pin.	The DCE (such as the modem) says, "Okay, here comes some data."
Data transmits 1 bit at a time over a single line.	Not applicable

The RS232 serial communication standard was developed during a time when mainframes were the norm. A mainframe terminal known as a data terminal equipment (**DTE**) connected to a modem known as a DCE. In today's world, DTE includes computers and printers. On a DTE serial connector, certain pins initiate communication with a DCE device, such as a modem. Table 13.4 shows the common signal names as well as the common abbreviations for the signals used with DTE devices.

TABLE 13.4 DTE signal connections

Signal abbreviations	Signal name
TD	Transmit data
DTR	Data terminal ready
RTS	Request to send

Data circuit-terminating equipment (**DCE**) includes devices such as modems, mice, and digitizers. On the DCE side, the signal names relate more to receiving data. Table 13.5 lists the common signal names used with DCE devices.

TABLE 13.5 DCE signal connections

Signal abbreviation	Signal name
RD	Receive data
DSR	Data set ready
CTS	Clear to send
CD	Carrier detect
RI	Ring indicator

To avoid problems, install the internal modem or attach the serial device and determine which COM port, IRQ, and I/O settings have been assigned to the device.

56Kb/s Modems

Analog modems are one of the slowest type of Internet connectivity. Modems transmit and receive at different speeds. A faster modem means less time on the phone line and less time for processor interaction. However, because modems connect to other modems, the slowest modem determines the fastest connection speed. A slow modem can operate only at the speed for which it was designed. Connecting to a faster modem will not make the slower modem operate any faster. Fortunately, speedy modems can transmit at lower speeds. As a general rule, a modem's speed setting should be set to its maximum throughput.

The phone line limit was once thought to be 28.8Kb/s, then 33.6Kb/s, and finally 56Kb/s. The 56Kb/s data transfer rate is possible only if the transmitted (analog) signal converts to digital one time during the data transmission. Digital phone lines are quieter than their analog counterparts, have less noise on the line, and allow faster data transmissions. For example, consider the scenario of a person dialing into an office network from home that is shown in Figure 13.4.

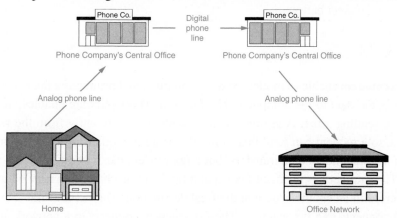

FIGURE 13.4   Normal modem usage

Notice in Figure 13.4 that the signal converts twice. The first time is when the analog signal enters the phone company's central office. Between central offices, the signal stays digital. Then, when the signal leaves the central office to travel to the office building, the signal converts from a digital signal to an analog signal. 56Kb/s transmission speeds do not support two conversions.

If the workplace has a digital line from the phone company or if a person dials into an Internet provider that has a digital phone connection, 56Kb/s throughput on a 56Kb/s modem is achievable. Figure 13.5 shows the difference.

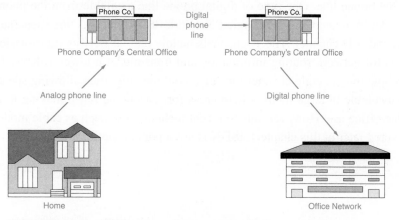

FIGURE 13.5   56Kbps modem connection

In Figure 13.5, only one analog-to-digital conversion exists—the one between the home and the first central office. 56Kb/s speeds, in theory, can exist when only one conversion takes place. However, if the modem cannot run at 56Kb/s, the modem supports lower speeds, such as 33.6Kb/s and 28.8Kb/s.

To configure a dial-up connection using a 56K modem, install the internal modem or connect the external modem to the computer. Ensure the modem connects to a working phone outlet. In Windows, use the following generic procedure, but always check the manufacturer's instructions because some modems have their own installation software.

> Windows Vista/7: Use the *Network and Sharing Center* Control Panel > *Set up a new connection or network* link > *Set up a dialup connection* > *Dial-up* > enter the remote modem phone number, username and password, and name the connection > select *Connect*.

> Windows 8: Access the *Network and Internet* Control Panel > *Dial-up* > enter the remote modem phone number, username and password, and name the connection > select Connect.

> Windows 10: *Access Settings* > *Network & Internet* > *Network and Sharing Center* link > *Set up a new connection or network* link > *Connect to the Internet* > *Next* button > *Dial-up* > enter the remote modem phone number, username and password, and name the connection > *Connect* button.

Fax Modems

A **fax modem** enables a modem to use a computer and printer as a fax machine. The modem portion brings the data to the computer. The facsimile (fax) software enables viewing, printing, replying to, or sending a fax. A regular modem sends data differently from the way a fax machine sends data, so a modem can send faxes only if it is a fax modem. Not all computer-based fax machines can handle modem data transfers, but a fax modem can do both modem and fax transfers.

The Internet has changed fax capabilities. Fax machines can now be used to send a fax that is received in an email account at the final destination. The fax machine can connect to a phone line that connects to a fax gateway. The fax gateway connects to a network and sends the message in email format to the final destination. A fax machine that adheres to the ITU T.37 iFax standard enables a fax machine to be connected to the data network. The fax machine formats the fax into email format for distribution to a person's email account or to the destination fax machine that has its own email address account and connects to a network.

Digital Modems and ISDN

A digital modem connects a computer directly to a digital phone line rather than to a traditional analog phone line. One type of digital phone line available from the phone company is an ISDN line. An Integrated Services Digital Network (**ISDN**) line has three separate channels: two B channels and a D channel. The B channels handle data at 64Kb/s transmission speeds. The D channel is for network routing information and transmits at a lower 16Kb/s. The two B channels can combine into a single channel for video conferencing, thus allowing speeds up to 128Kb/s. They are available in large metropolitan areas for reasonable rates, making it an affordable option for home office use. However, due to recent technologies, such as cable modems and xDSL modems (covered later in this chapter), ISDN is not a popular option today.

VoIP

Traditionally a company had a separate network for voice and data (the network where computers and printers connect). Voice over IP (**VoIP**) uses a corporate data network and/or the Internet for phone traffic rather than using the traditional public switched telephone network (**PSTN**). Free and purchased VoIP software can be used so you can call someone for free using the Internet. Figure 13.6 shows a VoIP phone that cables to a PC and into the corporate data network.

FIGURE 13.6   Corporate VoIP phone

Companies also used a separate network structure for the video network, but that has also now been moved onto the data network. **Convergence** is a term used to describe how these data, voice, and video technologies are now using one network structure instead of multiple ones. Figure 13.7 shows a video conference in the corporate environment where people join using tablets, laptops, corporate conference rooms, and desktop computers.

FIGURE 13.7   Corporate video conference call

Some free software applications and email accounts also support video conferencing using the Internet. Many of you might have experienced this using programs such as Skype, Google Hangout, or FaceTime. Through these applications, the quality may not be as good as with the traditional PSTN. This is because a guaranteed quality of service (**QoS**) is not provided. QoS prioritizes traffic so important traffic like business transaction traffic and VoIP traffic are sure to get through. Figure 13.8 shows this concept.

Bandwidth Use with No QOS

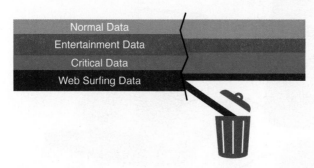

Bandwidth Use with QOS Implemented

FIGURE 13.8   QoS

Technicians must be aware of VoIP for two reasons: (1) A digital phone installed in a corporate office must be connected to the network in a similar fashion to the PC, and (2) a digital phone may be a software application (a soft phone) that has to be installed and configured on a computer.

VoIP has also affected fax capabilities. A VoIP adapter can be installed in the fax machine to connect it to a VoIP gateway. The VoIP gateway connects to a phone line that has a destination fax machine attached. One must realize that once something is converted into 1s and 0s, if that device can be networked, then it is just data to the network and can be transmitted.

One last thing to remember about VoIP in the corporate environment is that no corporate network can do away with the PSTN connection to the traditional phone network. A corporate environment will always need to be able to communicate with the outside world and especially be able to contact emergency services such as the police, fire, and emergency responders.

Cable Modems

One of the most popular items in the modem industry is the **cable modem**, which connects a computer to a cable TV network. Cable modems can be internal or external devices, but commonly are external. If a cable modem is external, two methods commonly exist for connectivity to a PC (1) A NIC built into the motherboard is used or an adapter is installed; a cable attaches between the NIC and the cable modem or (2) the cable modem connects to a USB port on the computer. Figures 13.9 and 13.10 show these two types of connections. Figure 13.11 shows a cable modem that has the coaxial cable on the top for connection to the wall coax connector, both USB and RJ-45 network connectors for connectivity to a PC, and two additional RJ-45 jacks for a printer or additional network devices.

TECH TIP

Cable TV and cable modems

Some cable Internet providers will not provide Internet access through their network unless you have their cable TV service as well.

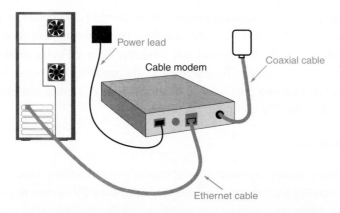

FIGURE 13.9 Cable modem and NIC connectivity

FIGURE 13.10 Cable modem and USB connectivity

FIGURE 13.11 Cable modem ports

Cable modem operation is not hard to understand. Internet data comes in through cable TV coax cable. The coax cable plugs into the cable modem. The cable modem then sends the information out its built-in Ethernet port. A network cable connects from the cable modem's Ethernet port into an Ethernet port on the computer. To send data to the Internet, the reverse happens: The computer sends the data out its Ethernet port into the cable modem. The cable modem sends the data out the coax cable onto the cable TV company's network.

Fiber Networks

A high-speed **fiber network** connection is commonly used to bring bundled technologies to subscribers. These bundles include phone, Internet, and cable TV connectivity. A fiber network has many fiber-optic cables that connect two buildings, multiple companies, and home users. A single fiber carries voice, data, and video using three different optical wavelengths. This same type of connectivity is offered at higher speeds to small businesses. Light flows through a fiber-optic cable (instead of electrical pulses that flow through copper cables). Instead of an electrical pulse being a "1," the light being on is a "1." A zero is the light being turned off. Figure 13.12 shows the basic construction of fiber-optic cable used inside the corporate environment.

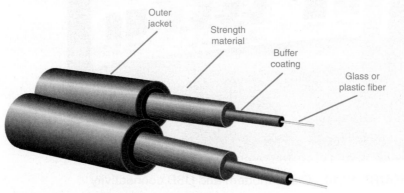

Outer jacket
Strength material
Buffer coating
Glass or plastic fiber

FIGURE 13.12   Fiber-optic cable

Fiber-optic cable has many advantages, including security, long-distance transmission, and bandwidth. Many government agencies use fiber-optic cable because of the high security it offers. Unlike signals from other cable media, light signals that travel down fiber are impossible to detect remotely. Also, because light is used instead of electrical signals, fiber-optic cable is not susceptible to interference from electromagnetic interference (EMI)- or radio-frequency interference (RFI)-producing devices. Fiber-optic cable is the most expensive cable type, but it also handles the most data with the least amount of data loss. Figure 13.13 shows how fiber-optic cable is installed under a city street along with electrical conduits.

FIGURE 13.13   Laying fiber-optic cable

Cable Mode Transmissions

Two terms that are often associated with cable modems are upstream and downstream. **Upstream** refers to data sent from your home to the Internet. **Downstream** refers to the data pulled from the Internet into your computer, as when you download a file or view a web page (see Figure 13.14). With cable modems, downstream transfer rates are faster than upstream transfers. Downstream speeds can be as high as 100+Mb/s for consumers and even higher for businesses. Upstream speeds vary; with an external cable modem, they tend to be between 384Kb/s and 20Mb/s. Even though upstream speeds are slower, cable modems are a huge improvement over analog (dial-up) modems.

Internet Provider

Cable or ADSL Modem

FIGURE 13.14   Upstream and downstream

The speed of a cable modem connection depends on two things: (1) the cable company and (2) how many people in the area share the same cable TV provider. Each cable channel uses 6MHz of the cable's bandwidth. **Bandwidth** is the capacity of the communications channel. Bandwidth is also known as *throughput* or *line speed*. The cable company designates one of the 6MHz channels as Internet access. Several homes can use the same channel, which reduces the amount of bandwidth each house has available. If you have three neighbors who all use the same cable vendor and they are Internet warriors, you will have slower access than if you were the only person in the neighborhood connected.

The minimum amount of hardware needed to have a cable modem depends on the cable company's specifications. Whether you need an internal modem, Ethernet card, and so on, depends on the company from which you receive the cable modem. Some companies include them as part of their rate. Some cable companies install the cable modem and associated software and hardware as part of their package. If you need to install a cable modem, always follow the manufacturer's installation instructions. Chapter 14 includes tips on configuring network adapters.

xDSL Modems

xDSL is another modem technology. The *x* in the term xDSL refers to the various types of digital subscriber line (**DSL**) that are on the market. The most common one is Asymmetrical DSL (**ADSL**), but there are many others. ADSL uses faster downstream speeds than upstream. This performance is fine for most home Internet users. DSL uses the traditional phone line to be able to send and transmit not only voice, but also Internet data. Table 13.6 shows the most common DSL types.

TABLE 13.6 DSL technologies

DSL type	Comments
ADSL	Asymmetrical DSL is the most common with faster downloads than uploads. It has upstream speeds from 0.5 to 3.5Mb/s and downstream speeds from 5 to 150Mb/s. It uses a different frequency level for upstream and downstream communications.
G.SHDSL	Symmetric High-speed DSL is an upgrade to SDSL that supports symmetric data rates up to 4.6Mb/s.
HDSL	High bit-rate DSL is a symmetrical transmission (equal speed for downloads/uploads); it has speeds up to 1.5Mb/s.
PDSL	Power line DSL modulates data speeds from 256K to 2.7Mb/s onto electrical lines and is sometimes called Broadband over Power line (BPL).
RADSL	Rate-Adaptive DSL was developed by Westell; it enables a modem to adapt to phone line conditions. It has speeds up to 2.2Mb/s.
SDSL	Symmetric DSL has the same speed, up to 1.5Mb/s, in both directions.
UDSL	Also known as Uni-DSL or Ultra-high-speed DSL, UDSL has speeds up to 200Mb/s and is backward compatible with ADSL, ADSL2+, VDSL, and VDSL2.
VDSL2	VDSL2 is an upgrade of VDSL that supports voice, video, data, and HDTV, with speeds from 1 to 150Mb/s downstream.

With DSL modems, bandwidth is not shared between people in the same geographic area. The bandwidth paid for is exclusive to the user. DSL is not available in all areas. The DSL Reports' website (http://www.dslreports.com) lists major DSL vendors, other Internet technology vendors, and geographic areas, plus a rating on the service.

An internal or external DSL modem can be used and connected to a regular phone line. The phone line can be used for calls, faxes, and so on at the same time as the modem. An external modem can connect to a USB port or an Ethernet network card. Figure 13.15 shows DSL modem ports, including the DSL connector, which connects to the wall outlet and is labeled ADSL, and the multiple Ethernet LAN connections, which could have connections to one or more computers, printers, external network storage, or other wired network devices.

FIGURE 13.15   DSL modem ports

TECH TIP

Corporate DSL, cable, or fiber

Corporate Internet connectivity can use DSL, cable, or fiber connections. Chapter 14 provides more information on fiber cabling.

A drawback to DSL is that the DSL signal needs to be separated from the normal phone traffic. DSL providers normally ship **phone filters** that must connect to each phone outlet, and a phone, fax machine, or voice recorder attaches to the filter. The connection from the DSL modem to the phone outlet does not have a filter on it.

This chapter does not go into firewalls and network security; they are discussed in later chapters. It is important when installing cable modems and DSL modems to also be familiar with proxy servers, firewalls, port forwarding, file sharing, and so on. When such technologies are improperly implemented or configured, a computer is more prone to attacks, viruses, theft of computer files, and computer takeover. Figure 13.16 shows three different ways to connect a cable or DSL modem. The example on the left is the least secure. File sharing should not be enabled on computers connected in this manner.

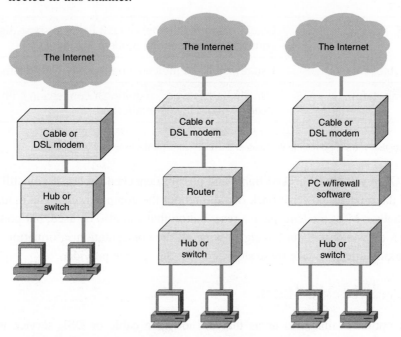

FIGURE 13.16   Cable/DSL modem connectivity

Troubleshooting Cable and DSL Modems

Because most cable and DSL modems are external, the best tools for troubleshooting connectivity problems are the lights on the front of the modem (see Figure 13.17). The lights will vary between vendors, but common ones are listed in Table 13.7.

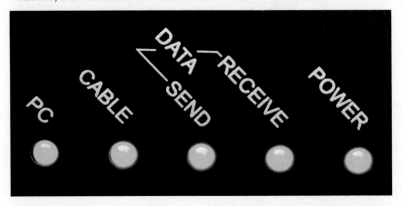

FIGURE 13.17   Cable/DSL modem lights for troubleshooting

TABLE 13.7   Cable/DSL modem lights and troubleshooting*

Light	Explanation
Power	Indicates power to the modem
ENET, E, or Ethernet	Usually indicates connectivity between the PC and the modem; if unlit, ensure that you are using Ethernet (if using USB, this will be unlit), check cabling, and check PC network card settings
USB or U	Usually indicates connectivity between the PC and the modem; if unlit, ensure that you are using USB (if using a NIC, this light will be unlit), check cabling, and check *Device Manager* to see if the modem is recognized
Internet, Ready, or Rdy	Stays lit when the modem has established an Internet connection
PC	Used instead of Ethernet or USB lights to show the status of the connection between the modem and the PC
Cable, data, or D/S	Usually blinks to indicate connectivity with Internet provider
Link status	Usually flashes when acquiring a connection with a provider and is on steady when a link is established

*Note that you should refer to the modem documentation for the exact status of the lights.

Once you have checked lights and possibly checked cables, if you still have a problem, power off the modem, power it back on, and reboot the computer. Give the modem a couple minutes to initialize. Most modems have a reset button that can also be used, but powering off and powering back on works without having to wipe all the configuration information. If a modem is still not working after you take these steps, contact the service provider.

Satellite Modems

An option available to areas that do not have cable or DSL service is satellite connectivity. The satellite relays communication back to receivers on Earth. Satellite connectivity requires a satellite dish and a **satellite modem** at a minimum. It may also require an analog modem and other equipment, depending on the satellite provider. If connected via satellite, the data goes from the computer to the satellite dish mounted outside the home or business (see Figure 13.18) to another satellite dish (and maybe more), up to the satellite orbiting Earth, down to the Internet service provider (**ISP**), and from the ISP to the website requested; the web page returns via the same path it took. Satellite connectivity is not as fast as cable or DSL connectivity, but it can be five to seven times faster than dial-up. The downstream speeds can be from 9Kb/s to 24Mb/s, but they are typically around 500Kb/s. Some providers offer the same upstream speeds.

FIGURE 13.18   Satellite modem and dish

With a satellite modem, TV programs accessed via the satellite can be watched at the same time that web pages are downloaded from the Internet. However, drawbacks to satellite modems are important to mention:

> The initial cost of installing a satellite modem can be high.
> If other people in the area subscribe to the same satellite service, speed is decreased during peak periods.
> Initial connections have a lag time associated with them, so playing multiplayer games is not very practical.
> Virtual private networks (VPNs) are not always supported.
> Weather elements, such as high winds, rain, and snow, affect performance and connectivity.

Modem Preventive Maintenance

The old adage "an ounce of prevention is worth a pound of cure" is especially true in the case of modems. A power surge can come across a phone line just as it can travel over an electrical power line. Most people think and worry about the computer problems that could result from power surges, but they do not stop to think about surges through the phone line. To provide protection for a modem and a computer, purchase a special protection device called a phone line isolator or a modem isolator at a computer or phone store. A power surge through the phone line or cable can take out many components inside a computer, including the motherboard.

Some surge protectors also have modem protection. A cable from the computer plugs into the surge protector. A separate cable connects to another jack on the surge protector, and the other end plugs into the phone or cable company wall jack. The surge protector must, of course, be plugged into a grounded outlet.

Mobile Connectivity

As discussed in Chapter 11, an increasingly popular feature with laptops is **wireless broadband** that has download speeds up to 45Mb/s. This technology is sometimes referred to as wireless or cellular WAN. Cell phone companies and Internet providers offer ExpressCards, USB modems, mobile data cards, or integrated laptop connectivity to have the ability to receive, create, and communicate Internet information within a coverage area. For people who travel a lot, this option gives connectivity in places where data connectivity has not previously been feasible.

Also discussed in Chapter 11 is how some smartphones, computers, and tablets can become **wireless hotspots**. Using a wireless connection, such as a USB port, Bluetooth wireless connectivity, or the cellular network, can provide wireless Internet connectivity to others in the immediate vicinity. Some cell service providers offer this option as part of the cellular plan. The term *wireless hotspot* is also used to refer to an area of wireless connectivity (normally free) such as in a park, coffee shop, or museum. More information on wireless connectivity is provided in Chapters 14 and 18.

WiMAX

Another wireless technology that can be used to connect to the Internet is Worldwide Interoperability for Microwave Access (**WiMAX**). WiMAX is similar to your home or corporate wireless network, but on a much larger scale for a larger coverage area. WiMAX is defined in the IEEE 802.16 standard and can provide Internet access at speeds up to 1Gb/s. WiMAX can also be used for connectivity as part of a cellular network.

WiMAX has two major types of connections: non-line-of-sight and line-of-sight. An example of the non-line-of-sight connection type is a home or portable device can have a WiMAX receiver similar to the wireless broadband receivers. Such a device communicates with a tower that has a WiMAX antenna attached.

The **line-of-sight network** is where the WiMAX antenna mounted on a tower connects wirelessly to another WiMAX antenna mounted on a tower (which might connect to a third WiMAX tower). These connections are also known as line-of-sight backhauls. Eventually, the last WiMAX tower connects via cable to the ISP. Figure 13.19 shows WiMAX connectivity options.

A similar concept to WiMAX is mobile wireless broadband (**WiBro**) or mobile WiMAX, which allows wireless connectivity for moving devices such as from a vehicle or train. Figure 13.20 summarizes WiMAX concepts.

TECH TIP

Laptop wireless WAN connectivity

A laptop that ships with integrated wireless WAN capabilities does not need an additional adapter or antenna. However, the BIOS/UEFI must have the option enabled. Some laptops might have a key combination or a switch to enable the connection. The wireless application software is available through the Start button.

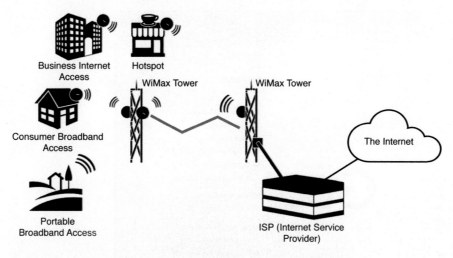

FIGURE 13.19   WiMAX connectivity

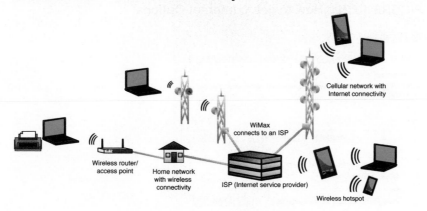

FIGURE 13.20   Wireless Internet connectivity

Web Browsers

A web browser is a graphical interface between a user and the Internet. Common web browsers include Microsoft's Internet Explorer (commonly called IE), Microsoft's Edge (which is the Windows 10 IE replacement), Mozilla's Firefox, and Google's Chrome. Because Internet Explorer ships with Windows, most textbooks use this browser to explain concepts instead of all the rest.

Most browsers are customizable, and many of the settings relate to security, so they are covered in Chapter 18. To get to those settings, click on *Tools* or the Tools icon that looks like a gear in the top-right corner of Internet Explorer (see Figure 13.21). Internet Explorer version 11 has seven main Internet Options tabs (see Figure 13.22).

A user uses these tabs to configure the browser experience. Note that these options can also be reached using the Internet Options Control Panel in all versions of Windows. Table 13.8 explains the main purposes of the main tabs.

FIGURE 13.21   How to get to Internet Options

FIGURE 13.22   Internet Options window

TABLE 13.8   Purposes of the Internet Options tabs

Tab	Purpose
General	Configures the home page (the page that opens every time Internet Explorer opens or the home icon is clicked), deletes or configures how long the browsing history (the websites visited) is kept, configures how tabs are organized and behave, and enables customization of the font, language, and color scheme.
Security	Customizes security options for sites that you trust and ones that you want blocked (see Chapter 18).
Privacy	Configures how your private information is handled, including cookies and pop-ups (see Chapter 18).
Content	Contains Parental Controls, Content Advisor, control security certificates, AutoComplete for ease of completing online forms, and Feeds and Web Slices for providing updated content directly into the browser.

Tab	Purpose
Connections	Configures dial-up (phone line) or VPN (virtual private network) information. VPNs are also covered in Chapters 14 and 18.
Programs	Configures email access, add-ons such as toolbars and extensions, and HTML-editing program options.
Advanced	Shows a list of options that might be set throughout the other tabs, also presented here in one easily configured list of checkboxes.

Internet Options *General* Tab

The *General* tab is one of the most commonly used tabs. Table 13.9 explains the purpose of its main sections.

TABLE 13.9   Internet Explorer General tab sections

Section	Purpose
Home page	Configures the page that opens every time Internet Explorer opens or the home icon is clicked.
Startup	Sets whether to start IE with tabs previously opened or with the home page website.
Tabs	Configures the browsing tabs (not the configuration tabs) and other features, such as warnings and pop-ups (see Figure 13.23).
Browsing history	Deletes or configures how long the browsing history (the websites visited) is kept. If you click on the Settings tab, three tabs are available. The *Temporary Internet Files* tab specifies the maximum amount of space to use (and where that data is stored). See Figure 13.24. The *History* tab sets the number of days to keep a history of your browsing (see Figure 13.25). Use the *Caches and databases* tab to set the amount of cache storage space can be used before displaying a message (see Figure 13.25).
Appearance	Enables you to customize the browser environment, including the colors (see Figure 13.26), language (see Figure 13.26), fonts (see Figure 13.27), and accessibility options (see Figure 13.27).

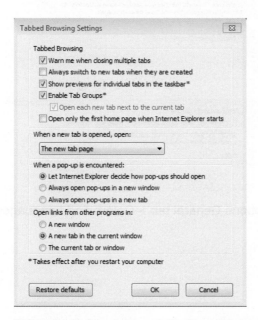

FIGURE 13.23   Internet Options General tab > Tabs button

FIGURE 13.24   Internet Options General tab > Temporary Internet Files tab

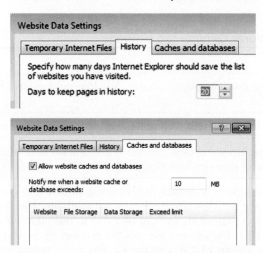

FIGURE 13.25   Internet Options General tab > History and Caches and databases windows

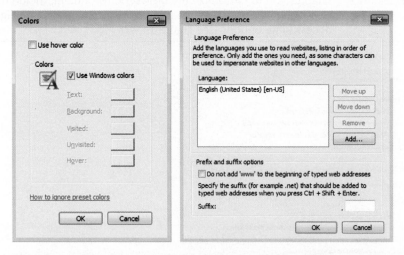

FIGURE 13.26   Internet Options General tab > Colors and Languages windows

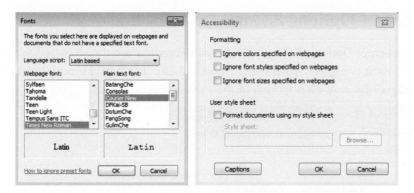

FIGURE 13.27   Internet Options General tab > Fonts and Accessibility windows

Internet Options *Security* Tab

The Internet Options *Security* tab is used to configure security settings related to dangerous or risky online content. Figure 13.28 shows the *Security* tab window. Table 13.10 explains the differences between the four zones.

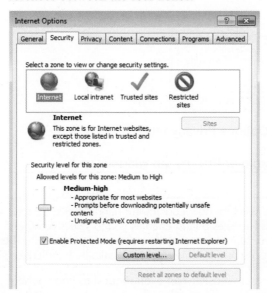

FIGURE 13.28   Internet Options Security tab

TABLE 13.10   Internet Explorer Security tab zones

Zone	Purpose
Internet	Sets the security level related to websites (excluding sites from the other three zones)
Local intranet	Sets the security level related to a private network such as the one found inside a company (as opposed to the Internet, which is the rest of the world)
Trusted sites	Sets the security level related to websites you believe do not have content that will infect the computer
Restricted sites	Sets the security level for websites you definitely do not trust

Internet Options *Privacy* Tab

The Internet Options *Privacy* tab is used to configure settings related to your personal information and how it is used by others (see Figure 13.29). Table 13.11 explains the information that can be configured within each section of the *Privacy* tab window.

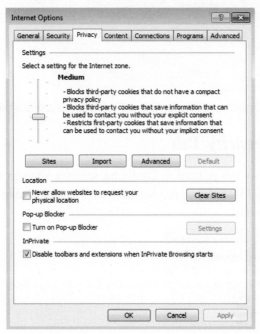

FIGURE 13.29 Internet Options Privacy tab

TABLE 13.11 Internet Explorer Privacy tab window

Section	Purpose
Settings	Sets the security level for how cookies are handled. See Chapter 18 for more information on cookies. The *Sites* button enables you to select whether a site is always allowed or never allowed (blocked) to use cookies (see Figure 13.30). The *Advanced* button enables you to choose how cookies are automatically handled (see Figure 13.30).
Location	Configures whether websites can even request to know where you are located using location services. Even if you allow this, you are prompted whether or not to allow once or always allow the site to know your physical location.
Pop-up Blocker	Controls pop-ups from websites. If you select the option, the *Settings* button is enabled. There, you can select which websites are allowed to produce pop-ups as shown in Figure 13.31.
InPrivate	A configuration that prevents IE/Edge from storing history information and passwords.

FIGURE 13.30 Internet Options Privacy tab > Sites and Advanced Privacy Settings windows

FIGURE 13.31   Internet Options Privacy tab > Pop-up Blocker Settings windows

Private browsing might be important to use in a corporate environment, when using a browser on someone else's computer, going to a website you have never used before, or using a public computer. Here is how to do it in some common browsers:

> Microsoft Internet Explorer: On a desktop, right-click on the *IE/Edge* icon > *Start InPrivate Browsing*. For a mobile device, open *IE* > *Tools* > *Safety* > *InPrivate Browsing*.
> Microsoft Edge: *More actions* (three dots option in top-right corner) > *New InPrivate Window*
> Mozilla Firefox: *Tools* > *Start Private Browsing*
> Google Chrome: Wrench icon > New Incognito window

Internet Options *Content* Tab

The *Content* tab is used to change settings related to what can be seen in the browser window. Figure 13.32 shows the overall screen and Table 13.12 details what each section is for.

FIGURE 13.32   Internet Options Content tab

TABLE 13.12   Internet Explorer Content tab window

Section	Purpose
Family Safety	Links to users and what controls are applied (if any). See Figure 13.33 to see the Parental Controls window and the security warnings that can occur there. Chapter 18 goes into further detail about securing accounts.
Certificates	Used to verify the authenticity of a person, file, or device provided when doing online purchases or sending an encrypted file.
AutoComplete	The *Settings* button allows settings related to filling in information on a web page such as your name, address, and email address (see Figure 13.34 left).
Feeds and Web Slices	Controls settings related to rich site summary (RSS) feeds to receive data, audio, and video information from news sources and the like (see Figure 13.34 right)

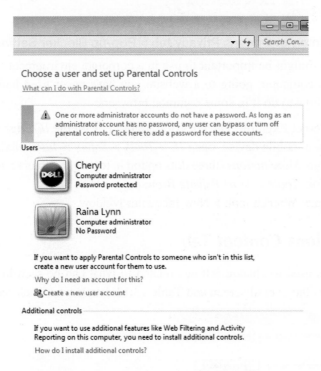

FIGURE 13.33   Internet Options Content tab > Parental Controls window

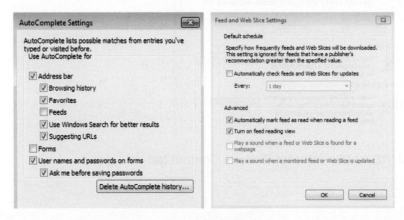

FIGURE 13.34   Internet Options Content tab > AutoComplete Settings window and Feeds and Web Slices Settings window

Internet Options *Connections* Tab

The *Connections* tab (see Figure 13.35) is where you go to configure your Internet connection for a newly installed type (see Figure 13.36), set up a new VPN so that someone can securely access company resources while working from home or away from the office (see Figure 13.37), and connections related to your LAN settings (see Figure 13.38). Chapter 18 details more information about VLANs and proxy servers. For now, concentrate on knowing where you go in Internet Explorer/Edge to configure browser settings.

FIGURE 13.35   Internet Options Connections tab

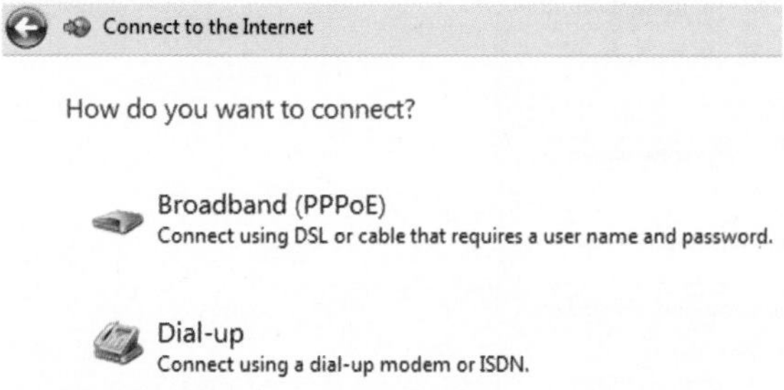

FIGURE 13.36   Internet Options Connections tab > Setup Internet connection window

FIGURE 13.37   Internet Options Connections tab > Add VPN connection window

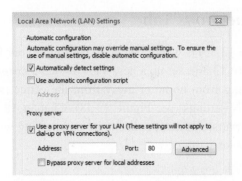

FIGURE 13.38   Internet Options Connections tab > LAN settings window

Internet Options *Programs* Tab

How many times do you think someone downloads a software update of some type and gets the default browser changed to something else? The Programs tab (see Figure 13.39) can help with that and with managing add-ons. **Add-ons** are extensions or plug-ins that provide the browser an additional feature such as a toolbar or the capability to dim everything on the screen except for a running video. Add-ons can also cause security risks. Figure 13.40 shows the Manage Add-ons window.

The HTML editing section has a drop-down menu to select the application used to edit HTML files. Examples include Microsoft Windows, Excel, and Notepad. The last section is used to access the Set Default Programs Control Panel where you can select which application opens a music file, for example. It is similar to choosing your default browser, but for other applications.

FIGURE 13.39   Internet Options Programs tab

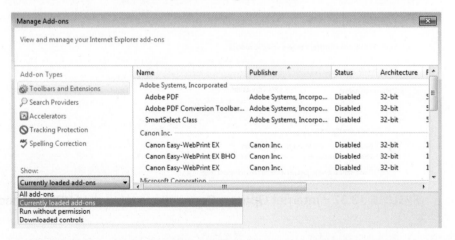

FIGURE 13.40   Internet Options Programs tab > Manage add-ons window

Internet Options *Advanced* Tab

The last tab in *Internet Options* is the *Advanced* tab (see Figure 13.41). This tab is used for all types of options not covered on the other tabs. Table 13.13 outlines just a few examples of the sections.

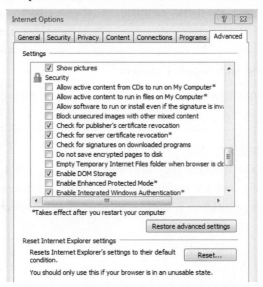

FIGURE 13.41   Internet Options Advanced tab

TABLE 13.13   Internet Explorer Advanced tab window

Section	Purpose
Accelerated graphics	Used to enable software rendering instead of GPU rendering
Accessibility	Used to play system sounds, provide ALT text for images, and reset text sizes
Browsing	Used to set browsing options such as notification of script errors or when a download completes, automatic crash recovery, and loading content in the background to improve performance
HTTP settings	Used to set the HTTP version
International	Used to set settings such as Unicode UTF-8 format, which is a standard way to display characters found in different languages
Multimedia	Used to set whether animations and sounds play
Security	Used to select which version(s) of secure sockets layer (SSL) and transport layer security (TLS) are enabled

Lab 13.3 at the end of this chapter demonstrates the basics of Internet Explorer configuration. Chapter 18 covers a little bit more information regarding the Security Internet Options tab. Chapters 14 and 18 provide more information and labs on networking, network security, and Internet security.

Basic Web Browser Issues

The Internet is commonly accessed through a browser, and configuring the browser is one of the first steps to configuring security. Browsers are commonly upgraded to provide improved security options. Before upgrading an Internet browser, you must determine the current web browser version. With many Windows-based applications, the version is determined by starting the application, clicking *Help > About x* (where *x* is the name of the application), or selecting the question mark menu item. With Internet Explorer (IE), the first two numbers listed are the software version numbers. There is another value called cipher strength that is a bit value for encryption; **encryption** is a protection method used to change data so it cannot be recognized. Encryption algorithms include Data Encryption Standard (DES), Triple DES (3DES), and Advanced Encryption Standard (AES).

> **TECH TIP**
>
> **Why keep your Windows and web browser current?**
>
> Internet hackers frequently target browsers, and constant updates are provided to counter these attacks.

When people connect to the Internet, they normally do so through a web browser. Any web browser can usually be configured for various security options. Because the Microsoft operating systems ship with Internet Explorer, it is covered here. Similar options are available in most browsers.

Hijacked Browser

One issue with browsers is that they can be hijacked (see Figure 13.42). A hijacked browser either replaces the home page with another one or directs whatever web page is being used to a different one. This is called a **browser redirect**. Besides sending you to another web page, a browser redirect can also be used to install a rootkit or install more malware (bad software) that includes keystroke loggers (to record your keystrokes including your ID and password), DNS hijack, or a rogue HOSTS file. A **rootkit** can be used to act as a backdoor to your operating system and may be used to do things that require administrator access. Rootkits can also be downloaded and installed to a flash drive. The HOSTS file is a text file used to manually map a hostname to a particular IP address.

FIGURE 13.42 Web browser redirect

The following recommendations can help with a hijacked browser issue:

> Change the home page URL to your normal home page and not the hijacked page. In any browser, go to the web page you want to be the home page and copy that web address. In Internet Explorer, access the *Tools* (gear) icon > use the *Home page* section on the General tab to type the home page address to use > *Apply* > *OK*. In Microsoft Edge, access the *More* (three dots) option > *Settings* > in the *Open with* section, select the *A specific page or pages* radio button > use the down arrow to select *Custom* > type a web address in the *Enter a web address* textbox.

> If **pop-ups** (unwanted messages, screens, or windows) appear continuously, use Task Manager to stop the `iexplore.exe` process. Re-open Internet Explorer and ensure the pop-up blocker is turned on: *Internet Options* > *Privacy* tab > enable *Turn on Pop-up Blocker*. Otherwise, use an alternative browser, such as Google Chrome or Mozilla Firefox. You can always uninstall and reinstall a browser, too.

> If necessary, start the computer in *Safe Mode with Networking*. If the web browser works properly in this mode, but not when booting as you normally do straight to Windows, a DLL file might have been added to the computer. Run a scan with your antivirus or antispyware application.

> Start the browser with no add-ons to see if one of them is causing the problem. How you do this depends on the browser. In Internet Explorer, perform the following:

> > Windows 7: *Start* > *All Programs* > *Accessories* > *System tools* > *Internet Explorer (No Add-ons)*.

> > Windows 8: Start *Internet Explorer* > *Tools* > *Manage add-ons* > in the *Show* drop-down menu, select *All add-ons* > select the add-on you want to turn off > *Disable* > *Close*.

> If the browser starts working, turn on the add-ons one by one to determine which one caused the problem.

> Determine whether the HOSTS file has been modified and includes some rogue entries. The HOSTS file can be found in the C:\Windows\system32\drivers\etc folder.

Slow Browser

If your browser seems like it is getting slower and slower, but the rest of the machine is running fine, there are a few things you can do.

> Disable unnecessary add-ons.
> Disable all add-ons and re-enable one at a time.
> Disable extensions (in Chrome, these are different than plug-ins).
> Uninstall and reinstall the web browser.
> Use a different web browser.

SOFT SKILLS—MENTORING

Every great technician can tell you that he or she had at least one mentor along the way. When you hear the word *mentor*, it probably conjures up other words and phrases in your head—coach, guidance, teacher, adviser, positive influence, leadership, setting an example, and so on. No technician can attain his or her ultimate level without being mentored and mentoring someone else along his or her career path. Also, no technician can learn everything from a book or from experience. Others helping us along the way enable us to learn faster and more efficiently.

When you enter your first (second, third, or fourth) job in the IT field, you should take a few days to look around the company. Find someone who appears to be very professional and knowledgeable—someone you want to emulate. Talk to that person and explain your goals. Ask if he or she will mentor you and detail what you would like—whether it is help with problems you cannot solve or advice about office politics.

Mentoring is an important part of life. Not only should you consider being mentored, but you should consider mentoring others. Many technicians hoard information from other technicians and computer users. Knowledge is power, and by sharing information with others and helping them along the way, you cement and expand your own knowledge.

Chapter Summary

> Serial devices use either XON/XOFF (software method) or RTS/CTS (hardware method) for flow control.
> Serial devices must be configured for the number of bits, parity, stop bits, FIFO setting, flow control, and handshaking.
> The two sides of the connection must match.
> The speed at which a 56K modem can transmit is limited by the number of analog-to-digital conversions.
> Internet connectivity can be provided by an analog modem, satellite modem, ISDN, cable modem, fiber, DSL modem, or wirelessly through the cell phone network, a wireless hotspot, WiMAX, or a wireless network.
> Cable modem bandwidth is shared by the number of subscribers in an area. A direct fiber connection might be an option.
> A DSL modem uses a phone line. ADSL has a faster downstream than upstream speed.
> WiMAX networks are line-of-sight networks.
> VoIP uses a corporate network and/or the Internet for voice connectivity. Internet-based VoIP does not offer QoS.
> Technicians frequently have to configure Internet browsers. In Internet Explorer, you use the *Internet Options* tabs for configuration. In Edge, use the *More > Settings*.
> Keep a web browser current for security reasons.
> Private browsing prevents the web browser from storing browsing history information and passwords.
> A hijacked browser redirects a browser to a different web page.
> Pop-ups can be managed using the pop-up blocker (in Internet Explorer, it is the *Privacy* tab).
> Disable add-ons to prevent pop-ups and help with a hijacked browser.
> Mentoring is important when you get started as a technician and as you gain experience.

A+ CERTIFICATION EXAM TIPS

✓ The Internet connection types that are on the 220-901 exam are as follows: cable, DSL, dial-up, fiber, satellite, ISDN, cellular (mobile hotspot), and line-of-sight wireless Internet service. Be able to describe these technologies.

✓ Know pros and cons of each Internet connection type. Do and/or review Exercise 13.1 at the end of the chapter.

✓ Know when each Internet connection type would be used.

✓ The 220-902 exam includes the *Internet Options* Control Panel, which includes the tabs that can also be accessed from within Internet Explorer. Be familiar with each tab and why a technician would use the tab. Before the exam, re-examine those options using Internet Explorer.

Key Terms

CHAPTER 13

Review Questions

1. Which of the following are names for a computer's serial port? (Select all that apply.)
    [COM port | asynchronous port | synchronous port | LPT port | RS232 port]

2. Which setting determines how two serial devices establish communication?
    [data bits | stop bits | parity | flow control]

3. Which port is used to connect an external modem if the motherboard did not have a serial port?
    [IEEE 1394 | eSATA | DVI | USB]

4. What is the biggest limitation of a 56Kbps modem transmitting at 56Kbps?

    _____

5. What is VoIP?

    a. A cable modem technology

    b. A method used to wirelessly connect to the Internet

    c. Using a network to carry voice traffic

    d. Communicating faster on the network on downloads than on uploads

6. To connect to the Internet and transmit data and voice using DSL, which component would you need to add to phone jacks that have a phone machine or answering machine attached to them?

    [modem surge protector | phone filter | ISP | RJ-11 connector]

7. [T | F] A cable modem is a good investment for a home network. Explain your answer.

    _____

8. Explain how a NIC is used with a cable modem.

    _____

    _____

    _____

9. List one drawback to a cable modem.

    _____

    _____

10. What does asymmetrical mean in relation to an ADSL modem?

    _____

    _____

11. Can a phone be used at the same time as a DSL modem? Explain why or why not.

    _____

    _____

12. What is the first thing you should check if your Internet connectivity is down and you have a DSL modem installed?

    _____

13. What is wireless broadband?

    _____

    _____

14. Would WiMAX be a good technology for a country that does not have a very strong wired Internet connectivity infrastructure? Why or why not?

_____

_____

_____

15. A new laptop has an integrated wireless LAN. The customer thinks there is a missing wireless antenna. What should you advise the customer?

_____

_____

16. [T | F] A hotspot provides wired network connectivity.

17. What would be the purpose of an Ethernet connection on a cable modem or a DSL modem?

    a. To connect a PC to the phone jack on the wall

    b. To connect a PC to the jack provided by the Internet provider

    c. To connect a PC to the modem

    d. To connect the modem to the jack provided by the Internet provider

18. A customer has a new laptop with wireless WAN capabilities; however, the software does not connect to the Internet. What would you suggest to the customer?

_____

_____

19. What is a phone line isolator?

_____

_____

20. List two ways mentoring can help in the IT field.

_____

_____

_____

Exercises

Exercise 13.1 Exploring Internet Connectivity Options

Objective: To explore different methods of Internet connectivity

Note: This exercise can be done with information found within the chapter or as an Internet research exercise (which would require a device with Internet access).

Procedure: Research and document two advantages and two disadvantages to each of the types of Internet connectivity found in Table 13.14.

TABLE 13.14   Research of Internet connectivity types—answers can vary; possible answers are given.

Type	2 Disadvantages	2 Advantages
56K modem		
ISDN		

Type	2 Disadvantages	2 Advantages
Cable modem		
DSL modem		
Satellite modem		
Wireless broadband		
WiMAX		

Exercise 13.2 Exploring the *Internet Options* tab

Objective: To explore the different tabs found within the Internet Options window

Note: This lab can be done with information found within the chapter, as an Internet research exercise (which would require a device with Internet access), or on a Windows computer.

Procedure: Indicate in Table 13.15 the *Internet Options* tab that would be used to perform the task.

Internet Options tabs: General, Security, Privacy, Content, Connections, Programs, Advanced

TABLE 13.15   Internet Options tab based on specific task

Task	*Internet Options* tab
Enables pop-up blocker	
Maximum amount of disk space for temporary Internet files	
Configures security certificates	
Disables an add-on	
Designates which program opens sound files found in web pages	
Configures a proxy server	
Configures the version of HTTP supported	
Configures a VPN	
Designates URL to be used as the home page	
Configures settings related to inside the corporate network (as opposed to the Internet)	
Sets the default font used for a web page	

Activities

Internet Discovery

Objective: To obtain specific information regarding a computer or its associated parts on the Internet

Parts: Computer with Internet access

Questions: Use the Internet to answer the following questions.

1. Locate a cable modem website that explains how to increase speed on a cable modem. Write the URL where you found the answer as well as the recommendation.

   _____

   _____

   _____

   _____

2. Determine whether cable or DSL modems are supported in your area. If so, determine as many vendors as you can for these products.

   _____

   _____

3. Find one vendor of VDSL in the United States and write down the name of the vendor and the URL where you find the answer.

   _____

   _____

   _____

4. Find a website that describes how modem chat scripts are done and that provides an example of one. Write the URL and your own explanation of chat scripts.

   _____

   _____

5. Determine how much a vendor charges to enable the mobile hotspot option or a phone/device that supports it. Document the amount or phone model number and the URL where you found this information.

   _____

   _____

   _____

   _____

6. Find a vendor in your state that sells wireless broadband for a laptop. What type of technology does it use (USB, ExpressCard, integrated, etc.)? Write the URL, the vendor name, model number, and the cost.

   _____

Soft Skills

Objective: To enhance and fine-tune a future technician's ability to listen, communicate in both written and oral forms, and support people who use computers in a professional manner

Activities:

1. The class is divided into three groups—two groups that will be debating against one another and a third group of judges. The judges have 45 minutes to determine the rules and consequences of how the debate is to be conducted. During the same 45 minutes, the two debating groups will research material and plan a strategy for either cable modems or DSL modems. At the end of 45 minutes, the debate will start, and the judges will mediate with the rules they establish and present to the two teams before the debate begins. The judges, along with the instructor, determine which group proved its point the best.

Using whatever resources are available, research one of the following that has been assigned to you. Share the results with the class.

What is the largest number of IRQs supported by an analog modem that you could find?

What is the fastest DSL, cable, or analog connection within a 60-mile radius of your school?

What is the most common type of Internet connectivity for home users in your area?

What is the most common type of Internet connectivity among businesses in your area?

What is the type and speed of Internet connectivity at your school?

What is the type and speed of Internet connectivity at a college in your state?

Which types of DSL services are available in your state?

Which types of cable modem services are available in your state?

Critical Thinking Skills

Objective: To analyze and evaluate information as well as apply learned information to new or different situations

Activities:

1.   In groups of three, research one of the following issues, as designated by the instructor. Share your findings with the other groups.

> The pros and cons of changing the operating system on a smartphone so that it can be a hotspot. Be prepared to share the group findings.

> What wireless broadband options are available from one of the most popular mobile phone providers in the area? Detail one option, rate plan, and cost. Be prepared to share your findings.

> Determine the best small business class Internet connectivity rates in the area where your school is located. Share at least two competitors' rates if possible. Detail the connectivity speeds and costs per vendor and be prepared to share your findings.

> Find at least three VoIP solutions for home users. Prepare a chart that shows vendors, options, pros and cons of each option, costs, and customer ratings (and comments, if possible). Be prepared to share your findings.

2.   In groups of two, write two analog/cable/DSL modem problems on two separate index cards. Give one problem to another class group and the other problem to a different class group. Your group will receive two index cards from two different groups as well. Solve the problems given to you, using any resource available. Share your group findings with the class.

Labs

Lab 13.1 Exploring Serial Devices in Windows Vista/7

Objective: To explore serial devices and their properties using Windows Vista and Windows 7

Parts: A computer with Windows Vista or Windows 7 installed

              Either a serial port with an external modem attached or an internal modem

Procedure: Complete the following procedure and answer the accompanying questions.

1.   Power on the computer and log on using the user ID and password provided by the instructor or lab assistant.

2.   Click the *Start* button and click *Control Panel*.

3. Click the *System and Maintenance* (Vista) or *System and Security* (7) Control Panel.

4. Click the *Device Manager* link. Note that you may have to scroll down to see this option.

5. Expand the *Ports* option.

6. If *Communications Port (Com1)* is available, right-click and select *Properties*.

   What tabs are available?

   _____

   What is the status of the serial port?

   _____

7. Click the *Port Settings* tab.

   What is the maximum number of bits per second?

   _____

8. Click the *Advanced* button.

   What UART is being used?

   _____

   What COM port is assigned?

   _____

9. Click *Cancel*.

10. Click the *Driver* tab and click the *Driver Details* button.

    List any drivers, including the complete path associated with the serial port.

    _____

11. Click the *OK* button.

    What is the purpose of the *Roll Back Driver* button?

    _____

12. Click the *Resources* tab.

    What IRQ and I/O addresses are assigned?

    _____

Instructor initials: _____

13. Click the *OK* button.

Modems

Note: Skip this section if an internal modem is not installed. If unsure, perform the tasks to see if the steps work.

14. Expand the *Modems* Device Manager category. Right-click a specific modem and select *Properties*. Click the *Modem* tab.

    What COM port does the modem use?

    _____

    What is the maximum port speed?

    _____

    Is the setting for the maximum bits per second on a serial port the speed at which the external modem transmits over the phone line? Explain your answer.

    _____

    _____

Why would you want the speaker volume enabled when first installing a modem?

_____

_____

15.   Click the *Diagnostics* tab and click the *Query Modem* button.

What was the first AT command that was sent to the modem?

_____

16.   Click the *View log* button. Scroll to the bottom of the log.

What communications standard(s) does(do) the modem use?

_____

17.   Close the Notepad log. Click the *Resources* tab.

What IRQ and I/O addresses does the modem use?

_____

Instructor initials: _____

18.   Close the *Modem Properties* window. Close the *Device Manager* window.

19.   Close the *Control Panel* window.

Lab 13.2 Windows 7 Internal or External Modem Installation

Objective: To be able to install an internal modem

Parts: Internal or external modem

Procedure: Complete the following procedure and answer the accompanying questions.

1.   Power on the computer and ensure that it boots properly.

2.   Shut down the computer properly and remove the power cord from the back of the computer. Do Steps 3 and 4 based on the type of modem you have. Then move to Step 5.

Internal Modem Installation

3.   Install the internal modem into an available slot.

4.   Reinstall the computer cover, reinstall the computer power cord, and power on the computer. The *Found New Hardware* wizard appears if this is the first time the computer has had this adapter installed.

External Modem Installation

3.   Attach the external modem to the USB port. Attach power to the external modem, if necessary.

4.   Reinstall the computer power cord and power on the computer. The *Found New Hardware* wizard appears.

Both Modem Installation Types

5.   Install the correct modem driver, using either the one provided with the modem, the one downloaded, or the one provided as part of the operating system.

6.   Access *Device Manager* > expand *Modems* > right-click the internal modem that was just installed > *Properties*.

Under the General tab, what is the device status? It should be that the modem is working properly. If it is not, perform appropriate troubleshooting until it does display that message.

_____

7. Click the *Diagnostics* tab. Click the *Query modem* button.

   List at least two AT commands and the response that is shown in the information window.

   _____

   _____

8. Click the *View log* button.

   What do you think a technician could do with this information?

   _____

9. Close the *Notepad log* window.

10. Click the *Resources* tab.

    What memory range does the adapter use?

    _____

    Which IRQ is the adapter using?

    _____

11. Click the *Advanced* tab.

    When do you think you would use the Extra initialization commands textbox?

    _____

12. Click the *Advanced Port Settings* button.

    Which COM port is used with this adapter?

    _____

    Are FIFO buffers used by default?

    _____

13. Click the *Cancel* button on the next two screens to exit the *Properties* window.

14. If an external modem was installed, power off the modem and disconnect it from the PC. If an internal modem was installed, power down the PC, remove the adapter, and install the slot cover.

15. Power on or reboot the computer and ensure it boots properly.

Lab 13.3 Introduction to Internet Explorer (IE) Configuration

Objective: To become familiar with basic Internet Explorer configuration options

Parts: Windows computer

Note: This lab has been tested on Internet Explorer version 11, but many parts will also be applicable to earlier or later versions.

Procedure: Complete the following procedure and answer the accompanying questions.

1. Power on the computer and ensure that it boots properly.

2. Open Internet Explorer. From the *Tools* (looks like a gear) link, select *About Internet Explorer* to determine the IE version.

   Which version of IE is being used?

   _____

3. Re-access the *Tools* link.

4. Select *Internet Options*.

   What URL is listed as the home page?

   _____

   Is the *Delete browsing history on exit* option enabled or disabled? [enabled | disabled]

   _____

List one corporate scenario for which you think the business security policy would require the *Delete browsing history on exit* option be enabled.

_____

_____

_____

5. Select the *Settings* button in the *Browsing history* section.

How often does the IE browser check to see if there is a newer version of a web page?

_____

What drive partition currently holds temporary Internet files?

_____

If the drive partition that currently holds temporary Internet files is an SSD, would it be better to change this to a different folder? Why or why not?

_____

_____

_____

6. Access the *History* tab from within the *Website Data Settings* window.

What is the number of days the web browsing history is kept?

_____

7. Access the *Caches and databases* tab from within the *Website Data Settings* window.

How much drive space can be used before the user is notified that a website cache or database exceeds that amount?

_____

8. Use the *Cancel* button to close the *Website Data Settings* window. Select the *Tabs* button in the *Tabs* section.

[T | F] To enable tabbed browsing when it has been disabled, you must close all Internet Explorer windows and then reopen Internet Explorer to activate the change.

Based on the configured options, what currently happens when a new tab is opened?

_____

_____

Based on the information in the *Tabbed Browsing Settings* window, what do you think the most secure pop-up setting would be for a corporate environment, and why do you think this?

_____

_____

_____

From the choices provided, what is your favorite way of handling program links provided in a website?

_____

_____

9. Click *Cancel*. Click the *Colors* button.

    Is the *Use Windows colors* option selected (enabled)? [enabled | disabled]

    _____

10. Disable the *Use Windows colors* option. Select the *Use hover color* option.

    Based on what you see as the default settings, which option might you change for a red/green color color-blind person?

    _____

    _____

    _____

    What color is the default hover color?

    _____

11. Click *Cancel*. Click the *Languages* button.

    What two prefix and suffix options are available?

    _____

    _____

12. Click *Cancel*. Select the *Fonts* button.

    What is the current font setting for web pages?

    _____

13. Click *Cancel*. Select the *Accessibility* button.

    List one example of when you might use the formatting options presented in a home computer environment.

    _____

    _____

14. Click *Cancel* twice and close *Internet Explorer*.

14 Networking

In this chapter you will learn:

> To identify common network cables

> About Ethernet networks

> About the OSI and TCP/IP models and different protocols

> To identify MAC, IPv4, and IPv6 addresses

> To set up wired and wireless networks

> Common network troubleshooting tools

> To configure and access a network printer

> To share data using a network

> Basics of cloud computing

> How to be a proactive technician

CompTIA Exam Objectives:

What CompTIA A+ exam objectives are covered in this chapter?

✓ 901-1.4 Install and configure PC expansion cards.

✓ 901-1.7 Compare and contrast various PC connection interfaces, their characteristics, and purpose.

✓ 901-1.13 Install SOHO multifunction device/printers and configure appropriate settings.

✓ 901-2.1 Identify the various types of network cables and connectors.

✓ 901-2.2 Compare and contrast the characteristics of connectors and cabling.

✓ 901-2.3 Explain the properties and characteristics of TCP/IP.

✓ 901-2.4 Explain common TCP and UDP ports, protocols, and their purpose.

✓ 901-2.5 Compare and contrast various Wi-Fi networking standards and encryption types.

✓ 901-2.6 Given a scenario, install and configure a SOHO wireless/wired router and apply appropriate settings.

✓ 901-2.7 Compare and contrast Internet connection types, network types, and their features.

✓ 901-2.8 Compare and contrast network architecture devices, their functions, and features.

✓ 901-2.9 Given a scenario, use appropriate networking tools.

✓ 901-4.4 Given a scenario, troubleshoot wired and wireless networks with appropriate tools.

✓ 902-1.5 Given a scenario, use Windows Control Panel utilities.

✓ 902-1.6 Given a scenario, install and configure Windows networking on a client/desktop.

✓ 902-2.2 Given a scenario, set up and use client-side virtualization.

✓ 902-2.3 Identify basic cloud concepts.

✓ 902-2.4 Summarize the properties and purpose of services provided by networked hosts.

✓ 902-3.7 Given a scenario, secure SOHO wireless and wired networks.

✓ 902-5.1 Given a scenario, use appropriate safety procedures.

Networking Overview

Networks are found all around us. A few examples include the following:

> A network of roads and interstate highways
> A telephone network
> The electrical network that provides electricity to our homes
> The cellular network that allows cell phones/smartphones to connect to one another as well as connectivity between cell phones/smartphones and the wired telephone network and the Internet
> The air traffic control network
> Your network of friends and family

A network as it relates to computers is two or more devices that have the capability to communicate with one another and share resources. A network allows computer users to share files; communicate via email; browse the Internet; share a printer, modem, or scanner; and access applications and files. Networks can be divided into major categories based on the size and type of network. Table 14.1 describes these different networks.

TABLE 14.1   Types of networks

Network type	Description
Personal area network (**PAN**)	Personal devices such as keyboard, mouse, TV, cell phone, laptop, desktop, mobile device, and pocket video games that can communicate in close proximity through a wired or wireless network. Using a Bluetooth keyboard with a PC is an example of a PAN.
Local area network (**LAN**)	A group of devices that can share resources in a single area such as a room, home, or building. The most common type of LAN is Ethernet. A LAN can be wired or wireless. The computers in a networked classroom are an example of a LAN.
Metropolitan area network (**MAN**)	Connectivity between sites within the same city. A MAN connects multiple LANs. MANs can be wireless or use fiber-optic cable. Multiple college campuses connected in a city are an example of a MAN.
Wide area network (**WAN**)	Communication between LANs on a large geographic scale. Two remote locations that have connectivity between them as part of the company network are a WAN.
Wireless LAN (**WLAN**)	A wireless network that consists of an access point and some wireless devices including laptops, tablets, and smartphones. A wireless network can be short range such as when Bluetooth is used or a wider coverage such as a wireless network for a home or business. Wireless bridges might be used to connect devices between two buildings.
Wireless WAN (**WWAN**)	Wireless connectivity for a larger geographic area using a mix of technologies such as cellular or WiMAX.

Today, networks are vital to businesses. They can also be found in many homes. A technician must have a basic understanding of the devices that make up networks and learn how to connect them to existing networks.

Attaching to Different Types of Networks

Computers can attach to different types of networks. A technician must be familiar with attaching computers to three basic types:

> A server-based network
> A workgroup
> A Microsoft HomeGroup

With a **server-based network**, computer users log in to a main computer called a server where they are authenticated (authorized to use the network). The server is a more powerful computer than a normal workstation. The server contains information about who is allowed to connect to the network, and to what network resources (files, printers, and applications) the network user is allowed access. Windows computers in a server-based network are commonly called a **domain**, or a Microsoft Active Directory domain. One or more dedicated servers log and track users and resources. Domains are commonly found in the business environment. Don't worry that you don't know all the components in this picture yet. Those terms are coming.

When working in a corporate environment, technicians commonly have to install new computers, replace computers, or repair computers on the domain. This requires special rights to be assigned to the technician; end users are not normally allowed to add computers to the domain. If a computer ever displays a message that the trust relationship is broken, the computer must be reconnected to the domain.

A Microsoft HomeGroup or a workgroup network does not have a centralized server and has a smaller number of devices. Each computer is its own server, and resources are shared between the workstation computers. This is sometimes known as a client/server relationship. One computer acts as the server and allows information to be obtained by the client or another device. Another name for any network that allows sharing of resources on a small network is peer-to-peer network.

Windows computers in a peer-to-peer network are known as a **workgroup** or Microsoft calls it a HomeGroup in Windows 7, 8, and 10. Two or more computers configured with the same workgroup name can share devices such as printers as well as files and folders. No central server or domain controller is used. Many homes and small businesses use a workgroup environment.

Within the workgroup environment, the computer user sets up passwords to allow others access to the resources through the network. A person uses the network to access remote files, printers, applications, and so forth from his workstation.

A special type of workgroup network is Microsoft's HomeGroup. A **HomeGroup** network is assigned a single password, and other devices within that HomeGroup simply need that password to access resources like files and photos. A HomeGroup is easier to manage because it does not require setting up individual accounts and passwords like a workgroup does. Figure 14.1 shows a workgroup/HomeGroup network. Again, don't worry about knowing the parts shown at this point of the chapter.

Server-based networks are more common in businesses, whereas workgroup and HomeGroup networks are more common in homes and small businesses. A server-based network can consist of 20 or more computers; in contrast, a workgroup network usually has fewer (2 to 20) computers. End-user devices on the different types of networks tend to be the same and configuration of those devices is similar.

CHAPTER 14

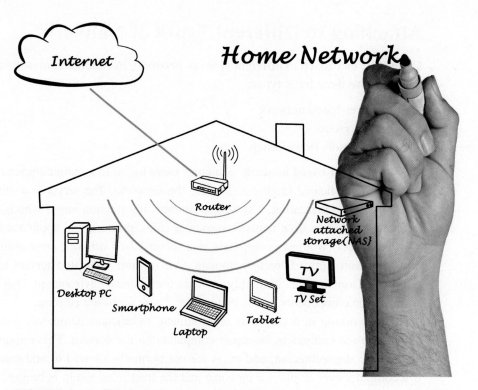

FIGURE 14.1 Workgroup network design

A server-based network is more secure than a peer-to-peer network. This is because the server is normally in a locked network room or wiring closet. Servers have a special operating system loaded on them called a network operating system (NOS), such as Microsoft Windows Server 2012 or Server 2012 R2, Red Hat Enterprise Linux, or Sun Solaris. A network operating system has utilities that allow computer user management (who is allowed onto the network), resource management (what network applications, files, printers, and so on a user can use), and security management (what a user is allowed to do with a resource such as read, write, or read and write). One user ID and password is all a remote user needs to access many network resources located throughout the business organization.

Figure 14.2 shows how a server-based network can be configured. The network has one server in the center, four workstations, and two laser printers. The server has a database of users—CSchmidt, RDevoid, and MElkins—and their associated passwords. The server also has three applications loaded—Microsoft Excel, Microsoft Project, and Microsoft Word. These applications and associated documents are stored on the server. Whether the users can access these applications and documents and what they can do within each document is also stored on the server. In the Permission column of the table located in Figure 14.2 is either R for Read or R/W for Read/Write. This is an indication of what the user can do in a particular application. For example, user CSchmidt has read and write access to Excel, Project, and Word. This means that she can open, look at, and modify documents in any of these three applications. MElkins can read only Excel and Word documents, but she can read and write Microsoft Project documents. CSchmidt can print to either of the laser printers, but RDevoid prints only to the LP1 laser printer.

A workgroup network is not as expensive or as secure as a server-based network. A server is more expensive than a regular workstation, and it requires a network operating system. Because workgroup networks do not use a dedicated server, costs are reduced. Instead of a network operating system, each workstation uses an operating system such as Windows Vista, 7, 8, and/or 10. A workgroup network is not as secure as a server-based network because each computer must be configured with individual user IDs and passwords. Figure 14.3 shows how a workgroup network is configured.

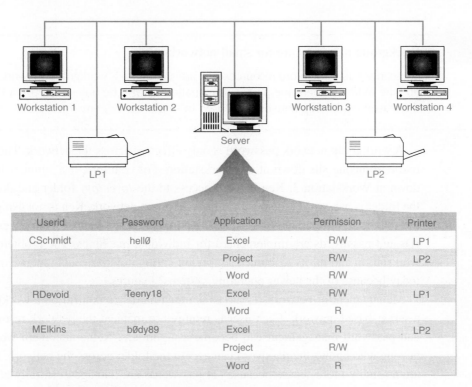

FIGURE 14.2   **Server-based network**

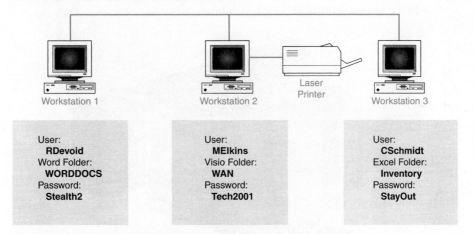

FIGURE 14.3   **Workgroup network**

Figure 14.3 shows three workstations, labeled Workstation 1, Workstation 2, and Workstation 3. Workstation 2 has a shared printer for everyone to use. There are three people in this company: Raina Devoid, Cheryl Schmidt, and Melodie Elkins. RDevoid normally works at Workstation 1 and she has shared a folder on the hard drive called *WORDDOCS* that has a password of Stealth2. CSchmidt and MElkins can access the documents located in *WORDDOCS* from their own workstations as long as they know the password is Stealth2. If RDevoid wants to access MElkins' *WAN* folder, RDevoid must know and remember that the password is Tech2001. If MElkins changes the password on the *WAN* folder, MElkins must remember to tell the new password to anyone who needs access. The password is used only when accessing the WAN folder documents.

Now if someone took this workgroup network and made it a HomeGroup, the HomeGroup would be assigned a single password such as Schm1dt$hare. Any devices accessing the shared resources within the HomeGroup would need the one password. The single password makes it easier to manage the network environment because most things shared at home would not need specialized usernames, passwords, and specified rights.

Workgroup networks are for small networks

You can see that the more resources that are shared on a workgroup network, the more passwords and the more cumbersome password management will be unless you use a HomeGroup. That is the reason workgroup networks are used in small network environments.

A workgroup network password is only effective across the network. The password is not effective if someone sits down at the workstation. For example, if a summer intern, Ken Tinker, sits down at Workstation 3, Ken has full access to the *Inventory* folder and documents. Even though the folder is password protected for the workgroup network, Ken is not using the network to access the folder, so the password is useless. Ken could be prevented from accessing the folder if user IDs and passwords are implemented for individual machines. The problem of having access to a workstation and all its resources simply by sitting down at a computer is not as much of a threat today because of the newer operating systems' features.

Management of network resources is much harder to control on a workgroup network than on a server-based network. Each user is required to manage the network resources on one computer and password management can become a nightmare. Remember with workgroup networks that anyone who knows the password can access the folder across the network. Server-based networks are normally more secure because (1) passwords are managed centrally at the server and (2) the server is normally locked in a wiring closet, server room/network operations center (see Figure 14.4), or at a minimum a locked cabinet.

FIGURE 14.4   Network operations center

When configuring Windows for a network, you are presented with three or four choices: home network, work network, public network, or domain. The option chosen defines, to some extent, the type of network you could configure, as shown in Figure 14.5. Table 14.2 describes each option.

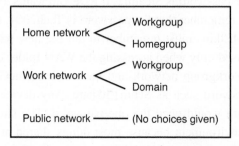

FIGURE 14.5   Windows types of network options

TABLE 14.2   Windows network options

Network option	Description
Home	Used to configure a device participating in a workgroup or a HomeGroup. Network discovery is enabled. Network discovery allows detection by other network devices.
Work	Used to configure a device participating in a workgroup or domain. Network discovery is enabled.
Public	Used to configure a device on a network where the other devices are unknown. Network discovery is disabled.
Domain	Used to configure a device in the enterprise corporate environment where policies are enforced and deployed.

To have a network, the following are required: network adapters (also called NICs), network media (cable or air), and an operating system with network options enabled. The following sections explore these concepts.

Network Topologies

The physical network topology is how the network is wired. Figure 14.6 shows the physical topologies used in networking. Keep in mind that a large business may have combinations of these topologies.

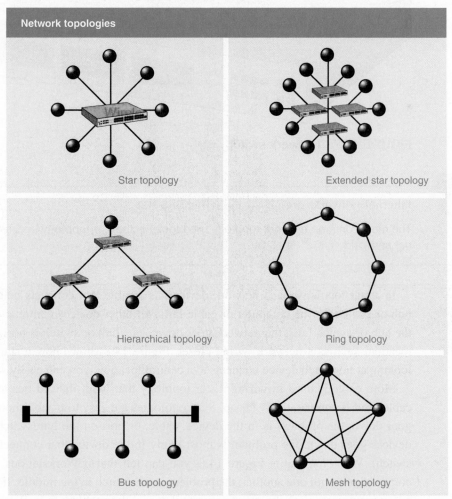

FIGURE 14.6   Network topologies

Ethernet Star Topology

Ethernet is the most common type of LAN. Each network device connects to a central device, normally a hub or a switch. Both the hub and the switch contain two or more RJ-45 network jacks. The hub is not as intelligent as a switch. The switch takes a look at each data frame as it comes through the switch. The hub cannot do this. Figure 14.7 illustrates a switch (although it could be a hub). You sometimes have to look at the model number to tell the difference because they are similar in appearance.

TECH TIP

Why a switch is better than a hub

When a workstation sends data to a hub, the **hub** broadcasts the data out all ports except for the port that originally transmits the data. When a hub is used, collisions can occur. A better solution is a switch. A **switch** keeps a table of addresses. When a switch receives data, the switch looks up the destination MAC address (an address burned into a NIC) in the switch table and forwards the data out the port for which it is destined. A switch also eliminates collisions.

FIGURE 14.7   Network switch

TECH TIP

Ethernet networks are physically wired in a star

The most common network topology used today is the star topology because it is used with Ethernet networks.

In a star topology, each network device has a cable that connects between the device and the hub or switch. If one computer or cable fails, all other devices continue to function. However, if the hub or switch fails, the network goes down. The hub or switch is normally located in a central location, such as a network wiring closet. Figure 14.8 shows how a star topology is cabled. By looking at how each device connects to a central location, you can easily see why it is called a star.

More cable is used in wiring a star topology than with the old bus topology, but the type of cable used is comparatively cheap. Star topologies are easy to troubleshoot. If one network device goes down, the problem is in the device, cable, or port on the hub/switch. If a group of network devices goes down, the problem is most likely in the device that connects them together (hub or switch). When looking at Figure 14.8, you can tell that if Workstations 1, 2, 3, 4, and 5 cannot communicate with one another, the problem is the switch in the middle. If only Workstation 3 cannot communicate with the other network devices, the problem is in Workstation 3, the cable that connects Workstation 3, or port 13 on the switch.

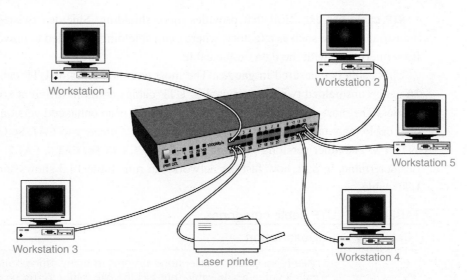

FIGURE 14.8   Star network topology

Network Media Overview

Networks require some type of medium to transmit data. This medium is normally some type of cable or air (wireless). The most common types of cable are twisted pair copper and fiber-optic although some older networks used coax cable. Video networks also use coax. Air is used in wireless networking when data is sent over radio frequencies.

Copper Media

Copper media is the most common cabling used to connect devices to the network. It is also used to connect network devices. Copper media comes in two major types: twisted pair and coaxial.

Twisted Pair Cable Overview

Twisted pair cable comes in two types: shielded and unshielded. The acronyms used with this type of cable are STP (shielded twisted pair) and UTP (unshielded twisted pair). The most common type of copper media used with computer networking and phone cabling is **UTP** cable. Most people are familiar with twisted pair cable because UTP is used in homes for telephone wiring. **Twisted pair cable** is named because each of the four pairs of conductors entwines around each other. Figure 14.9 shows the physical properties of an unshielded twisted pair cable.

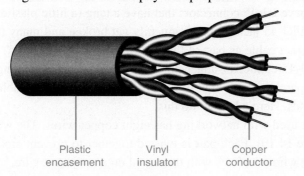

Plastic   Vinyl   Copper
encasement   insulator   conductor

FIGURE 14.9   UTP cable

STP cable has extra foil that provides more shielding. Shielded twisted pair cable is used in industrial settings, such as a factory, where extra shielding is needed to prevent outside interference from interfering with the data on the cable.

UTP cable is measured in gauges. The most common sizes of UTP cable are 22-, 23-, 24-, or 26-gauge unshielded twisted pair cables. UTP cables come in different specifications called categories. The most common are categories 5e (which is an enhanced version of 5), 6, and 7. People (and cable manufacturers) usually shorten the name *Category* to *CAT*, so Category 5 is spoken of as CAT 5. The other versions would be called CAT 3, CAT 5e, CAT 6, CAT 7, and so on. The categories determine, in part, how fast the network can run. Table 14.3 shows some of the categories of UTP cable.

TABLE 14.3   UTP cable categories

Category	Description
3	Mainly installed for telephone systems in many office buildings. Commonly called voice grade cable, but has the capability to run up to the older 10Mb/s Ethernet or 16Mb/s Token Ring topology speeds.
5	No longer a recognized standard; replaced by CAT 5e.
5e	Known as CAT 5 enhanced. Can be used with 10BaseT, 100BaseT, and 1000BaseT (Gigabit) Ethernet networks. Cables are rated to a max of 328 feet (100 meters). However, Ethernet cabling from the end device to the network device normally consists of three runs: (1) the cable from a patch panel to the wall at a maximum of 295 feet (90 meters), (2) the 16-foot (5 meter) maximum patch cable from the wall to a network device, and (3) a 16-foot (5 meter) patch cable from a patch panel to a switch. The total length of cable from device to patch panel is 328 feet (100 meters). Supports frequencies up to 100MHz per pair.
6	Supports Gigabit Ethernet better than CAT 5e but uses larger-gauge (thicker) cable. Supports frequencies up to 250MHz per pair. More stringent specifications to prevent crosstalk (signals from one wire going over into another wire). Commonly used in industry.
6a	Supports 10GBaseT Ethernet and frequencies up to 500MHz.
7	Backward compatible with CAT 5e and 6. Supports 10GBaseT Ethernet and frequencies up to 600MHz.

Terminating Twisted Pair Cable

Twisted pair cables have RJ-45 connectors that have a tang (a little plastic clip) to securely insert the connector into an RJ-45 jack. Tangs frequently get broken and many times a technician must simply make an Ethernet cable as part of the job. So, if a tang breaks off, the RJ-45 connector is cut off and a new RJ-45 connector attached. This is known as terminating a cable. When a new cable is created, you purchase a spool of twisted pair cable, cut off a suitable length, and add RJ-45 connectors to both ends. Here's how to do this.

Twisted pair cable used with networking has eight copper wires. The wires are grouped in colored pairs (see Figure 14.10). Each pair is twisted together to prevent crosstalk. Crosstalk occurs when a signal on one wire interferes with the signal on an adjacent wire.

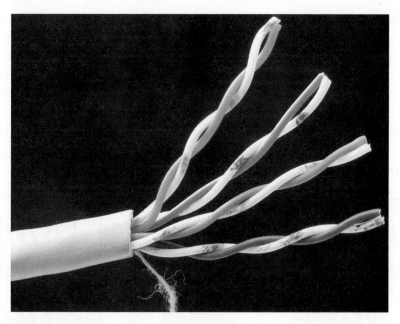

FIGURE 14.10 UTP color pairs

To avoid extra troubleshooting time, most businesses install their network cable according to the ANSI/TIA/EIA-568-A or 568-B (commonly shown as **T568A** and **T568B**) standard. This standard specifies how far the cable can extend, how to label it, what type of connector to use, and so forth. Twisted pair media uses either an **RJ-45** (8 conductor) or **RJ-11** (4 conductor) connector. RJ-45 connectors are used with network cabling. RJ-11 connectors are used with phone cabling. New technicians commonly mistake an RJ-11 phone jack or connector with an RJ-45 network jack or connector. Look inside the connector. An RJ-11 connector has four conductors (wires), and an RJ-45 connector has eight conductors, as shown in Figure 14.11, where the RJ-11 connector is on the left.

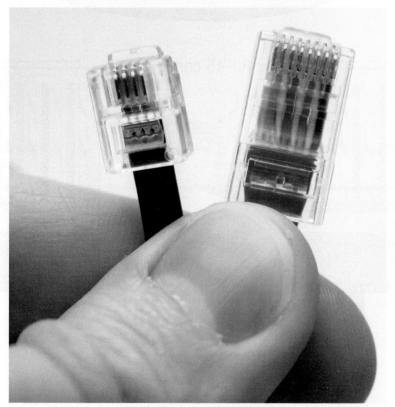

FIGURE 14.11 RJ-11 and RJ-45 connectors

To connect a computer to a switch or network wall outlet, a **straight-through cable** (also known as a patch cable) is used. Both ends of the cable would be wired to the T568A standard, or both ends of the cable would be wired to the T568B standard (more popular method). When connecting two computers together (or two switches), a **crossover cable** is used. A crossover cable has one RJ-45 connector created to the T568A standard and the other end to the T568B standard. Labs 14.1 and 14.2 at the end of this chapter demonstrate how to create these cables. Figure 14.12 shows the color codes associated with the T568A and T568B standards. Figure 14.13 shows the location of pin 1 on an RJ-45 port and connector. Notice in both figures how the tang is pointing down toward the floor.

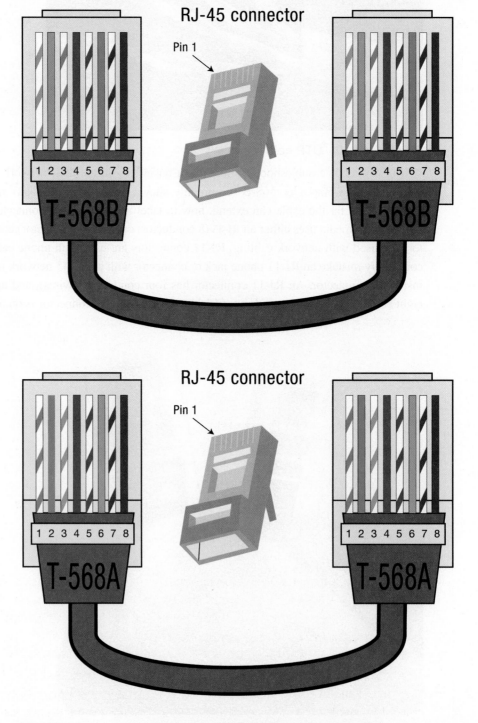

FIGURE 14.12   UTP cabling by color and wiring standards

FIGURE 14.13   Pin 1 on an RJ-45 port and connector

TECH TIP

Network two PCs without a switch or hub

If you have two PCs with Ethernet NICs installed, you can connect them with a crossover cable attached to the RJ-45 jack on each NIC.

To start creating your own cable, the plastic encasement (refer back to Figure 14.9) must be stripped away with a **cable stripper** (also known as a **wire stripper**) to expose approximately 1 inch of the vinyl insulator that covers the copper conductors. Figure 14.14 shows a cable stripper. A **crimper** that is used to secure the cable to the RJ-45 connector sometimes includes a blade and/or a cable stripper (see Figure 14.15). In the first photo, the cable is being stripped of the plastic encasement. Don't cut into the vinyl insulator. The second photo in Figure 14.15 shows the vinyl insulator stripped away.

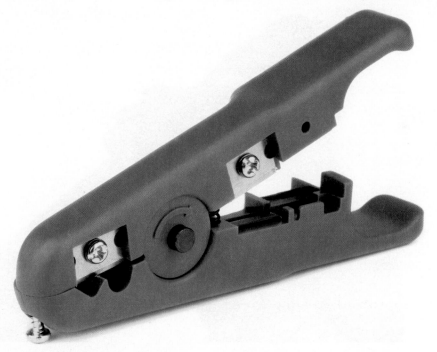

FIGURE 14.14   Cable stripper

After the plastic encasement is removed, the cable pairs are untwisted and placed in the proper color order. Wiggle each cable back and forth to make it more pliable. Cut the cables straight across, leaving 1/2 inch of cable. Insert the cables into the RJ-45 connector in the correct color order. Ensure the tang points toward the floor.

A common mistake when making a cable is not pushing the wires to the end of the RJ-45 connector. Before crimping, look at the end of the RJ-45 connector. You should see each wire jammed against the end of the RJ-45 connector. This is like a set of eight gold eyes staring at you when you turn the connector end toward you to verify that the conductors are pushed far enough into the connector before crimping.

FIGURE 14.15   Crimper used as a wire stripper

Another check to do before crimping is ensure the plastic encasement is inside the RJ-45 connector. You do not want the vinyl insulator outside of the connector or data errors can occur. Notice in Figure 14.16 how the blue plastic encasement is in the wider part of the RJ-45 connector. No unprotected wires are outside the RJ-45 connector.

TECH TIP

Push the cable firmly into the jack

It is important to fully insert the UTP cable into the RJ-45 jack and in the standardized order. A common mistake new technicians make is putting on the RJ-45 connector upside down.

When color order, eight gold connectors pushed to the end, and plastic encasement inside the RJ-45 connector have been verified, you are ready to crimp. Crimping involves carefully inserting the RJ-45 connector into the crimper (while maintaining the wires staying pushed firmly into the connector), and pressing the crimper handles together firmly until it clicks and releases. Figure 14.16 shows a store-bought Ethernet cable that probably had a broken tang. Store-bought Ethernet cables have protective sleeves that go over the RJ-45 connector. The sleeve must be moved back before cutting off the damaged RJ-45 connector and replacing it. The sleeve is slid back over the RJ-45 connector when crimping is complete.

FIGURE 14.16   Crimping an RJ-45 connector

After crimping, you must use a **cable tester** to ensure it is ready for use. Figure 14.17 shows a cable tester. Plug one end of the cable into the RJ-45 jack on the main tester piece (yellow case) and the other end into the RJ-45 cap. Each cable tester is different, so review the instructions if necessary.

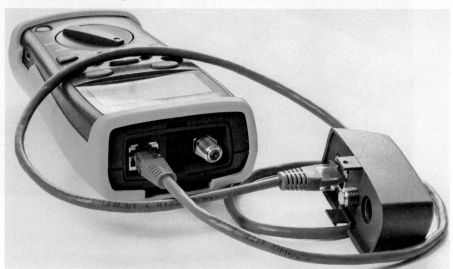

FIGURE 14.17   Cable tester

CHAPTER 14

Twisted Pair Cable in the Corporate Environment

With twisted pair cable, all network devices connect to one central location such as a patch panel, hub, or switch. Refer to Figure 14.8 to see how straight-through cables connect each network device to a switch. In a corporate environment, a patch panel is used. A **patch panel** mounts in a network wiring rack, has network ports on the front of it, and has wiring connected to the back of it to provide network connectivity (see Figure 14.18). The first photo is the front of the patch panel. The second photo is the back.

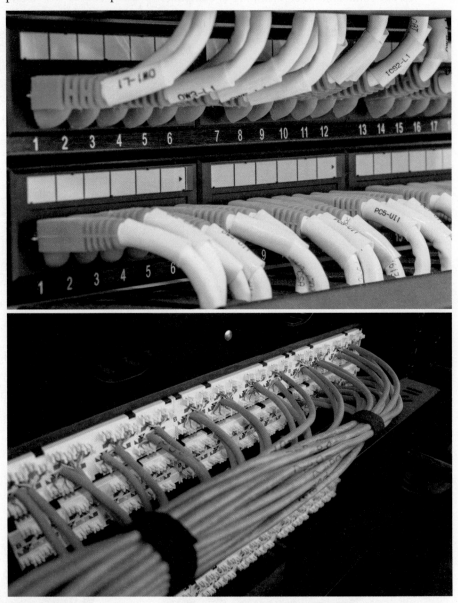

FIGURE 14.18   Front and back of a patch panel

A UTP cable connects from a network device to an RJ-45 wall jack. That wall jack has UTP cabling that goes from the back of the wall jack (see Figures 14.19 and 4.20) to the back of a patch panel. A switch mounts in a wiring rack along with a patch panel. A straight-through UTP patch cable connects from a port on the front of the patch panel to a switch located in the same network rack. Figure 14.20 shows the cabling from PCs to a switch in a corporate environment.

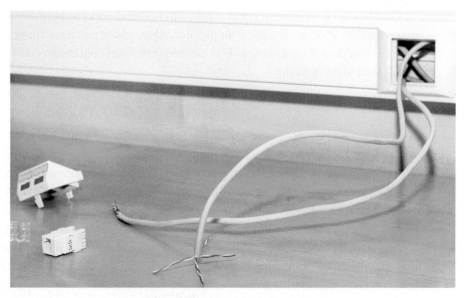

FIGURE 14.19   Network wall jack

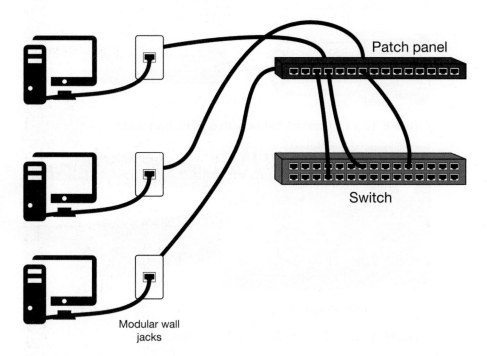

FIGURE 14.20   Corporate network connectivity from PCs to a switch

Label both cable ends

When installing any type of network cable, you should label both ends with a unique identifier that normally includes the building and/or room number.

A special type of UTP or STP cable is plenum cable. Plenum is a building's air circulation space for heating and air conditioning systems. **Plenum cable** is treated with Teflon or alternative fire-retardant materials, so it is less of a fire risk. Plenum cable is less smoke producing and less toxic when burning than regular networking cable.

The alternative to plenum cable is polyvinyl chloride (**PVC**) cable that has a plastic cable insulation or jacket. PVC is cheaper than plenum cable, and it can have flame-retardant added to make it flame-retardant if necessary to become compliant with building codes. PVC is usually easier to install than plenum cable.

Coaxial Cable

Another type of copper cable is **coaxial cable** (usually shortened to *coax*). Coax cable is used in star and bus topologies and is most popularly found in video networks such as those that connect TVs in a school. Most people have seen coax cable in their homes. The cable used for cable TV (CATV) is coax cable, but it is a different type than the cable used with network cabling. Coax cable has a center copper conductor surrounded by insulation. Outside the insulation is a shield of copper braid, a metallic foil, or both, that protects the center conductor from EMI. Figure 14.21 shows the parts of the coax cable and the connector. Figure 14.22 shows two popular coax connectors: Bayonet Neill-Concelman (BNC) and F coaxial connectors. Notice how the **BNC connector** has a notched side to turn and twist onto the receiving connector. The **F connector** simply screws onto the receiving connector. Table 14.4 lists types of coax cables.

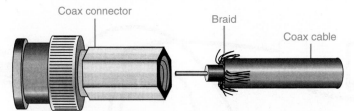

FIGURE 14.21   Coaxial cable with a BNC connector

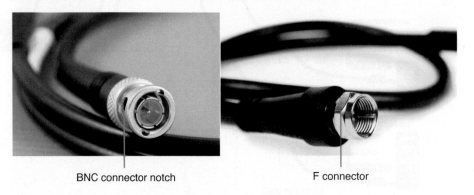

FIGURE 14.22   Coaxial BNC and F connectors

TABLE 14.4   Coax cable types

Coax cable type	Description
RG-6*	This is the type of cable least likely to be used in a network. It is a 75-ohm cable suitable for distributing signals for cable TV, satellite dish, or rooftop antenna. It has better shielding than RG-59, so it is larger in diameter. Typical distances are 1,000' (305m) to 1500' (457m). Can carry frequencies up to 2200MHz.
RG-59	This type of 75-ohm cable is not used in LANs. It is used in video installations. Typical distances are 750' (225m) to 1000' (305m). Can carry frequencies up to 1000MHz.

*RG stands for radio grade.

If a coaxial cable of different impedance attaches to another coaxial cable, signal loss results. Coaxial cable is rated for interior or exterior. Use the appropriate cable type for the installation. Be careful when bending the cable. When there is a problem, the coaxial connector is the most common issue.

Splitter

With both coaxial and twisted pair cabling, a technician might see a splitter. A **splitter** allows two inputs and has one output. Many of you might have seen a phone line splitter installed (see Figure 14.23). An Ethernet splitter looks the same except it has eight conductors in each jack instead of four. An Ethernet splitter is commonly used for two reasons: (1) when only one Ethernet wall jack is in the area and two devices need access (and the technician does not want to install an additional jack) or (2) for monitoring traffic from a specific network device. In this situation a PC goes to one of the two jacks, and a laptop with monitoring software connects to the other jack.

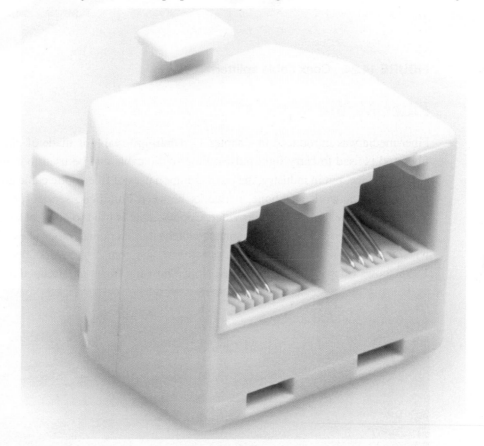

FIGURE 14.23   Phone cable splitter

Coaxial connections can also have a splitter. You might have seen one of these with a cable TV installation (see Figure 14.24). The one connection brings the cable signal into a home. The cable modem and a TV connect to the two outputs. A drawback to using a splitter is degradation of signal quality. Splitters should be avoided when possible.

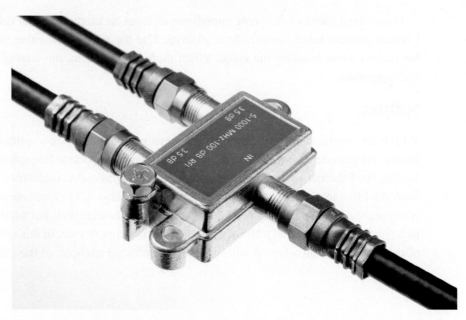

FIGURE 14.24 Coax cable splitter

Fiber Media

Fiber media was introduced in Chapter 13. **Fiber-optic cable** is made of glass or a type of plastic fiber and is used to carry light pulses. Fiber-optic cable can be used to connect a workstation to another device, but in industry, the most common uses of fiber-optic cable are to connect networks forming the network backbone, networks between buildings, service provider high-speed networks, and homes to a service provider. Copper cable is used to connect workstations to a switch. Then fiber cable is used to interconnect switches, interconnect other network devices (especially when the network is located on multiple floors), and connect networks between buildings. Figure 14.25 shows fiber switch connections. Notice how the fibers are grouped in pairs.

FIGURE 14.25 Fiber switch connections

TECH TIP

Two cables are normal with fiber

Each fiber-optic cable can carry signals in one direction, so an installation normally has two strands of fiber-optic cable in separate jackets. Fiber is used in ring and star topologies.

There are many different types of fiber connectors and some of them are proprietary. Four of the most common connectors used with fiber-optic cable are MT-RJ (common in home installations), straight tip (**ST**), subscriber connector (**SC**), and Lucent connector (**LC**). Figure 14.26 shows three of these connectors.

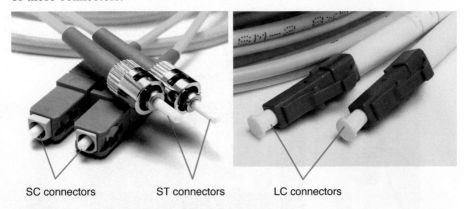

SC connectors   ST connectors   LC connectors

FIGURE 14.26   Fiber-optic connector types

The two major classifications of fiber are single-mode and multi-mode. **Single-mode fiber** optic cable has only one light beam sent down the cable. **Multi-mode fiber** allows multiple light signals to be sent along the same cable. Table 14.5 describes the characteristics of the two types. (Note that fiber's maximum speeds keep increasing as technology keeps changing.)

TABLE 14.5   Fiber-optic cable types

Type	Characteristic
Single-mode	Classified by the size of the fiber core and the cladding. Common sizes include 8/125 to 10/125 microns. The first number represents the size of the core; the second number is the size of the cladding. Single-mode cable allows for distances more than 50 miles (80,000 meters) at speeds more than 100Gb/s.
Multi-mode	Sizes include 50/125 and 62.5/125 microns. Can support distances more than 1 mile (2,000 meters) and speeds up to 10Gb/s. ST connectors are used more with multimode fiber than with single mode.

CHAPTER 14

TECH TIP

Which fiber should I use?

Multi-mode fiber is cheaper and more commonly used than single-mode fiber and is good for shorter-distance applications; however, single-mode fiber can transmit a signal farther than multi-mode and supports the highest bandwidth.

Protecting Your Network and Cable Investment

Quite a bit of money is applied to network cabling. IT professionals are charged with protecting this investment as well as ensuring that cabling does not cause personal safety risks. Network devices should be locked in a secure room or cabinet when possible. Figure 14.27 shows a network cabinet that can have network devices as well as cabling installed inside it.

FIGURE 14.27   Network cabinets

Network cable can be pulled through walls and over ceilings but should be installed in conduit or raceways (mesh racks or ladder racks that keep the cable away from other things) if possible. A professional **cable management system** can help keep network cables organized. Ensure that network cabling is not a trip or other safety hazard in any location. Of course, this increases the cost of the network installation, but it protects the network cabling and people. Figure 14.28 shows a typical network closet for many companies. Figure 14.29 shows a network wiring rack with a cable management system.

FIGURE 14.28   Messy (and dangerous) network wiring rack

FIGURE 14.29   Cable management system

Ladder racks are also a network cable accessory that hold multiple cables going across a room or from one side of the room to a network rack that is located away from the wall. Figure 14.30 shows a network cable ladder rack with bundles of cables.

FIGURE 14.30   Network cable ladder racks

Network Cabling and Troubleshooting Tools

Table 14.6 shows and describes network-related tools used in making cable and troubleshooting cable issues.

TABLE 14.6   Network cabling tools

Tool	Description
Tone generator and probe	A **tone generator** connects to a cable or is inserted into a network jack. The tone generator injects a tone down the cable. The toner **probe** (see Figure 14.32) is touched to the other end of a cable to identify it. The tone generator/toner probe combination identifies cables when they are not labeled or are labeled incorrectly.
Cable stripper	Creates straight-through UTP patch cables or crossover cables. (Refer to Figures 14.14 and 14.15.) Also called a wire stripper.
Punch-down tool (refer to Figure 14.31)	Connects network cables to a patch panel (see Figure 14.32) or phone cables to a punch-down block.

Tool	Description
Cable tester	Checks coaxial and UTP cable (depending on the model). Refer to Figures 14.17 and 14.31.)
Crimper	Permanently attaches an RJ-45 or RJ-11 connector to cable. (Refer to Figures 14.16.)
Multimeter	Takes voltage, resistance, and current readings. (Refer to Figure 5.6.)
Loopback plug	Attaches to a specific port and tests a port or communications circuitry to see if a signal can be sent out and received. If the test succeeds, the port and communication circuits are good.

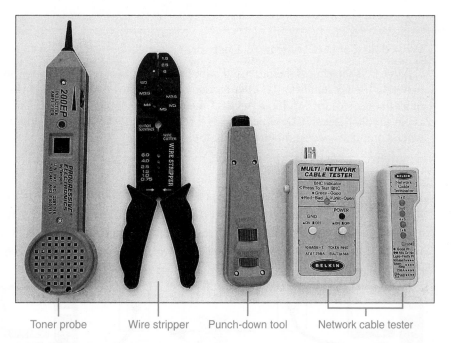

Toner probe   Wire stripper   Punch-down tool   Network cable tester

FIGURE 14.31   Network tools

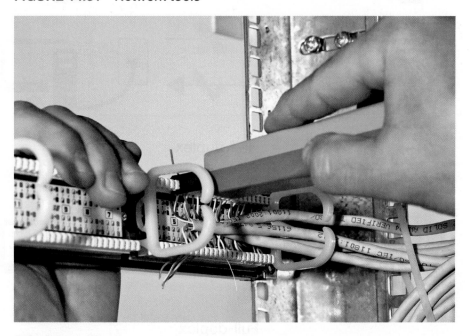

FIGURE 14.32   Punch-down tool

Ethernet Concepts

Ethernet is the most common type of LAN, and more time must be spent on understanding it because technicians constantly add and remove devices from an Ethernet network. Some issues related to Ethernet include full-duplex and half-duplex transmissions, network slowdowns, and increasing bandwidth.

Ethernet networks were originally designed for **half-duplex** (both directions, but only one direction at a time) transmission on a 10Mb/s bus topology. The more workstations on the same network, the more collisions occur and the more the network slows down. In addition, with half-duplex Ethernet, less than 50 percent of the 10Mb/s available bandwidth could be used because of collisions and the time it takes for a network frame to transmit across the wire.

TECH TIP

What does CSMA/CD mean to a network?

CSMA/CD is the access method used with Ethernet networks: the rules for how data gets on the network. The CS stands for "Carrier Sense," which means that the PC checks the network cable for other traffic. MA, for "Multiple Access," means that multiple computers can access the network cable simultaneously. CD, which stands for "Collision Detection," provides rules for what happens when computers access the network at the same time.

Today's Ethernet networks support speeds of 10Mb/s, 100Mb/s, 1000Mb/s (1Gb/s), and 10,000Mb/s (10Gb/s). Most Ethernet NICs are 10/100/1000, which means they can run at either 10, 100, or 1000Mb/s using **full duplex** (transmit/receive simultaneously). Figure 14.33 illustrates the difference between half- and full-duplex operations. Table 14.7 lists the different types of Ethernet networks.

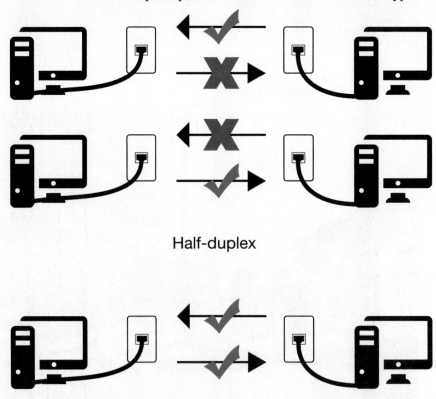

Half-duplex

Full-duplex

FIGURE 14.33   Half-duplex and full-duplex communication

TABLE 14.7   Ethernet standards

Ethernet type	Description
10BaseT	10Mb/s over CAT 3 or 5 UTP cable
100BaseT	100Mb/s over CAT 5 or higher UTP cable
1000BaseT	Also known as Gigabit Ethernet; 1000Mb/s or 1Gb/s over CAT 5 or higher UTP cable
1000BaseSX	1Gb/s using multi-mode fiber
1000BaseLX	1Gb/s using single-mode fiber
10GBaseSR	10Gb/s over multi-mode fiber
10GBaseLX4	10Gb/s over multi-mode and single-mode fiber
10GBaseLR	10Gb/s up to 6.2 miles (10 km) using single-mode fiber
10GBaseER	10Gb/s up to 24.85 miles (40 km) using single-mode fiber
10GBaseT	10Gb/s over UTP (CAT 5e or higher) or STP cable

In the term 100BaseT, the 100 means that the network runs at 100Mb/s. The T at the end of 100BaseT means that the computer uses twisted pair cable. The 1000 in 1000BaseT means that 1000Mb/s is supported. Base means that the network uses baseband technology. Baseband describes data that is sent over a single channel on a single wire. In contrast, broadband is used in cable TV systems, and it allows multiple channels using different frequencies to be covered over a single wire.

TECH TIP

Why full duplex is better than half duplex

With full duplex, collisions are not a problem because full duplex takes advantage of the two cable pairs (one for receiving and one for transmitting). Full-duplex Ethernet creates a direct connection between the transmitting station at one end and the receiving circuits at the other end and allows 100 percent of the available bandwidth to be used in each direction.

Full duplex more than doubles the amount of throughput on a network because of the lack of collisions and transmitting both directions simultaneously. Full duplex is used when a switch is used to connect network devices together. Full-duplex connectivity uses four wires (two pairs). Two of the wires are used for sending data and the other two wires are used for receiving data. This creates a collision-free environment. Using a switch instead of a hub as a central connectivity device speeds up Ethernet transactions because a switch has more intelligence than a hub and creates a collision-free, full-duplex environment. Switches are common devices in today's business network environment.

Ethernet over Power

One way to create an Ethernet network without switches, hubs, or a crossover cable between two PCs is to use electrical outlets. Ethernet over Power (EoP) (also known as powerline communication) sends network data to EoP modules plugged in to power outlets to extend Ethernet networks. Some EoP modules support wireless connectivity as well. To use EoP, you need a minimum of two EoP modules. One module plugs in to a power outlet near the Internet modem. An Ethernet cable attaches from the Internet modem to the EOP module. A second EoP module connects somewhere else in the home or business near a device that has trouble connecting to the Internet due to the absence of Ethernet wiring or weak wireless RF signal. Attach an Ethernet cable between the stranded device and the EoP module, and the device will have Internet access. Figure 14.34 shows this concept.

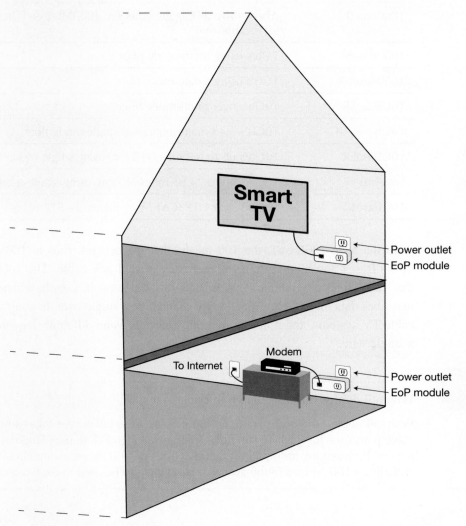

FIGURE 14.34   Ethernet over Power connectivity

The OSI Model

The International Organization for Standardization (ISO) developed a model for network communications known as the OSI (Open Systems Interconnect) model. The **OSI model** is a standard for information transfer across the network. The model sets several guidelines, including (1) how the different transmission media are arranged and interconnected, (2) how network devices that use different languages communicate with one another, (3) how a network device contacts another network device, (4) how and when data gets transmitted across the network, (5) how data is sent to the correct device, and (6) how it is known if the network data was received properly. All these tasks must be handled by a set of rules, and the OSI model provides a structure into which these rules fit.

Can you imagine a generic model for building a car? This model would state that you need some means of steering, a type of fuel to power the car, a place for the driver to sit, safety standards, and so forth. The model would not say what type of steering wheel to put in the car or what type of fuel the car must use but is just a blueprint for making the car. The OSI model is a similar model in networking.

The OSI model divides networking into different layers so that it is easier to understand (and teach). Dividing the network into distinct layers also helps manufacturers. If a particular manufacturer wants to make a network device that works on Layer 3, the manufacturer has to be concerned only with Layer 3. This division helps networking technologies emerge much faster. Having a layered model also helps to teach network concepts. Each layer can be taught as a separate network function.

The layers of the OSI model (starting from the top and working down) are application, presentation, session, transport, network, data link, and physical. Figure 14.35 shows this concept.

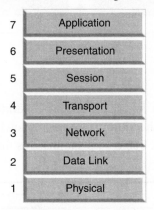

FIGURE 14.35   OSI model layers

Each layer of the OSI model uses the layer below it (except for the physical layer, which is on the bottom). Each layer provides some function to the layer above it. For example, the data link layer cannot be accessed without first going through the physical layer. If communication needs to be performed at Layer 3 (the network layer), then the physical and data link layers must be used first.

TECH TIP

OSI mnemonic

A mnemonic to help remember the OSI layers is `Active People Seldom Take Naps During Parties`. For example, `A` in the phrase is to remind you of the application layer. `P` in People is to remind you of the presentation layer, and so on.

Each layer of the OSI model from the top down (except for the physical layer) adds information to the data being sent across the network. Sometimes, this information is called a *header*. Figure 14.36 shows how a header is added as the packet travels down the OSI model. When the receiving computer receives the data, each layer removes the header information. Information at the physical layer is normally called *bits*. When referring to information at the data link layer, use the term *frame*. When referring to information at the network layer, use the term *packet*.

Each of the seven OSI model layers performs a unique function and interacts with the layers surrounding it. The bottom three layers handle the physical delivery of data across the network. The top four layers handle the ins and outs of providing accurate data delivery between computers and their individual processes, especially in a multitasking operating system environment.

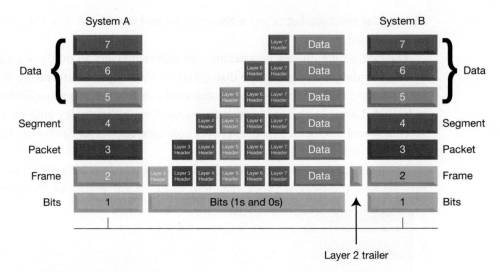

FIGURE 14.36   OSI peer communication

The OSI model can be confusing when you first learn about networking, but it is important. Understanding the model helps when troubleshooting a network. Knowing where the problem occurred narrows the field of possible solutions. Table 14.8 summarizes the OSI model.

TABLE 14.8   OSI model

OSI model layer	Description
Application	Provides network services (file, print, and messaging) to any software application running on the network. **Firewalls** (devices or software that inspect data for security purposes and filter traffic based on network protocols and rules established by a network administrator) operate at this layer.
Presentation	Translates data from one character set to another.
Session	Manages the communication and synchronization between network devices.
Transport	Provides the mechanisms for how data is sent, such as reliability and error correction.
Network	Provides path selection between two networks. **Routers** reside at the network layer and send data toward the destination network. Encapsulated data at this layer is called a packet.
Data link	Encapsulates bits into frames. Can provide error control. MAC address is at this layer. Switches operate at this layer.
Physical	Defines how bits are transferred and received. Defines the network media, connectors, and voltage levels. Data at this level is called bits.

The TCP/IP Model

A **network protocol** is a data communication language. A protocol suite is a group of protocols that are designed to work together. Transmission Control Protocol/Internet Protocol (**TCP/IP**) is the protocol suite used in networks today. It is the most common network protocol and is required when accessing the Internet. Most companies (and homes) use TCP/IP as their standard protocol. The TCP/IP protocol suite consists of many protocols, including Transmission Control Protocol (TCP), Internet Protocol (IP), Dynamic Host Configuration Protocol (DHCP), File Transfer Protocol (FTP), and Hypertext Transfer Protocol (HTTP), to name a few. The TCP/IP model describes how information flows through the computer when TCP/IP-based protocols are used. The TCP/IP model has only four layers, in contrast to the seven layers in the theoretical OSI model. Because there are fewer layers and because the TCP/IP model consists of protocols that are in production, it is easier to study and understand networking from a TCP/IP model prospective. Figure 14.37 shows the TCP/IP model, and Table 14.9 describes the layers.

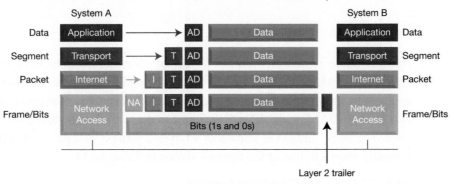

FIGURE 14.37   TCP/IP message formatting

TABLE 14.9   TCP/IP model layers

TCP/IP model layer	Description
Application	TCP/IP-based application layer protocols format data specific for the purpose; equivalent to the application, presentation, and session layers of the OSI model. Protocols include HTTP, Telnet, DNS, HTTPS, FTP, TFTP, TLS, SSL, POP, SNMP, IMAP, NNTP, and SMTP.
Transport	Transport layer protocols add port numbers in the header, so the computer can identify which application sends the data. When data returns, this port number allows the computer to determine into which window on the screen to place the data. Protocols include TCP and UDP.
Internet	Sometimes called the internetwork layer, IP is the most common Internet layer protocol. IP adds a source and destination **IP address** to uniquely identify the source and destination network devices. An IP address is a unique 32- or 128-bit number assigned to a NIC.
Network access	Called link layer in the original RFC (Request for Comment). Defines how to format the data for the type of network used. For example, if Ethernet is used, an Ethernet header, including unique source and destination MAC addresses, will be added here. A **MAC address** is a unique 48-bit hexadecimal number burned into a chip on the NIC. The network access layer would define the type of connector used and put the data onto the network, whether it be voltage levels for 1s and 0s on the copper cable or pulses of light for fiber.

Table 14.10 shows what devices operate at the OSI and TCP/IP model layers. The wireless devices are covered later in the chapter.

TABLE 14.10　Devices and the OSI and TCP/IP models

Network device	OSI layer	TCP/IP layer
Router, wireless router	Network	Internet (internetwork)
Switch, wireless access point, wireless bridge	Data link	Network access
Hub, wireless antenna, cable, connectors	Physical	Network access

Network Addressing

Network adapters normally have two types of addresses assigned to them: a MAC address and an IP address. A MAC address is a 48-bit unique number that is burned into a chip located on a NIC and is represented in hexadecimal. A MAC address is unique for every computer on the network. However, the MAC address has no scheme to it except that the first 24 bits represent the manufacturer. The MAC address is known as a Layer 2 address or a physical address. A MAC address is normally shown in one of the formats shown in Table 14.11.

TABLE 14.11　MAC address formats

Address format	Description
00-11-11-71-41-10	Groups of two hexadecimal digits are separated by hyphens.
01:11:11:71:41:10	Groups of two hexadecimal digits are separated by colons.
0111.1171.4110	Groups of four hexadecimal digits are separated by periods.

The IP address is a much more organized way of addressing a computer and is sometimes known as a Layer 3 address in reference to the OSI network layer. There are two types of IP addresses: IPv4 (IP version 4) and IPv6 (IP version 6). **IPv4** is the most common IP addressing used on LANs. The IPv4 address is a 32-bit number that is entered into a NIC's configuration parameters. This address is used when multiple networks are connected and when accessing the Internet. The IPv4 address is shown using dotted decimal notation, such as 192.168.10.4.

TECH TIP

What is in an IPv4 address?

An IPv4 address is separated into four sections called octets. Each number is separated by periods and represents 8 bits. The numbers that can be represented by 8 bits are 0 to 255.

IPv6 addresses are 128 bits in length and shown in hexadecimal format. IPv6 addresses are used by corporate devices and by some Internet service providers, with more conversions of IPv4 to IPv6 coming soon. Computers today have both an IPv4 address and IPv6 address assigned. An example of an IPv6 address is fe80::13e:4586:5807:95f7. Each set of four digits represents 16 bits. Anywhere there are just three digits, such as 13e, there is a zero in front that has been left off (013e). Anywhere there are double colons (::), a string of zeros has been omitted. Only one set of double colons is allowed in an IPv6 address. Many network cards are assigned IPv6 addresses, even if IPv6 is not used.

One IPv6 address assigned to a NIC is a link-local address. An IPv6 **link-local address** is used to communicate on a particular network. This address cannot be used to communicate with devices on a different network. A link-local address can be manually assigned or more commonly, automatically assigned. Figure 14.38 shows a home computer that has an IPv6 link-local address that has been automatically assigned. You can also see the IPv4 address.

```
Ethernet adapter Local Area Connection:

  Connection-specific DNS Suffix   . : gateway.2wire.net
  Link-local IPv6 Address . . . . . : fe80::13e:4586:5807:95f7%10
  IPv4 Address. . . . . . . . . . . : 192.168.1.64
  Subnet Mask . . . . . . . . . . . : 255.255.255.0
  Default Gateway . . . . . . . . . : 192.168.1.254
```

FIGURE 14.38   IPv4 address and IPv6 link-local address

IPv4 addresses are grouped into five classes: A, B, C, D, and E. Class A, B, and C addresses are used by network devices. Class D addresses are used for multicasting (sending traffic to a group of devices such as in a distributed video or a web conference session), and Class E addresses are used for experimentation. It is easy to tell which type of IP address is used by a device: All you have to look at is the first number shown in the dotted-decimal notation. Table 14.12 shows the common classes of addresses.

TABLE 14.12   Classes of IPv4 addresses

Class	First octet (number) of the IP address
Class A	0 to 127
Class B	128 to 191
Class C	192 to 223

If a computer has the IP address 12.150.172.39, the IP address is a Class A address because the first number is 12. If a computer has the IP address 176.10.100.2, it is a Class B IP address because the first number is 176. A computer with an IP address of 200.1.1.1 uses a Class C address. Addresses are also classified as public addresses and private addresses. A **private IP address** is used inside a home or business. This address is not allowed to be transmitted across the Internet. The service provider or company translates the address to a **public IP address** that is seen on the Internet. Table 14.13 shows the private IP address ranges for each of the IPv4 classes.

TABLE 14.13   IPv4 private IP addresses

Class	First octet (number) of an IP address
Class A	10.x.x.x (where the x represents any number from 0 to 255) or 10.0.0.0 through 10.255.255.255
Class B	172.16.x.x through 172.31.x.x or 172.16.0.0 through 172.31.255.255
Class C	192.168.x.x or 192.168.0.0 through 192.168.255.255

IP Addressing

An IP address is broken into two major parts: the network number and the host number. The **network number** is the portion of an IP address that represents which network the computer is on. All computers on the same network have the same network number. The **host address** (or host portion of the address) represents the specific computer on the network. All computers on the same network have unique host numbers or they could not communicate.

The number of bits that represent the network number and the host number depends on which class of IP address is used. With Class A IP addresses, the first 8 bits (the first number) represent the network portion, and the remaining 24 bits (the last three numbers) represent the host number. With Class B IP addresses, the first 16 bits (the first two numbers) represent the network portion, and the remaining 16 bits (the last two numbers) represent the host number. With Class C IP addresses, the first 24 bits (the first three numbers) represent the network portion, and the remaining 8 bits (the last number) represent the host number. Figure 14.39 illustrates this point.

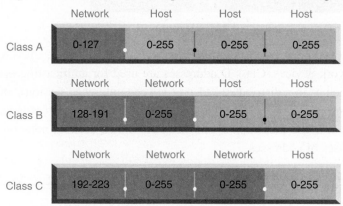

FIGURE 14.39   IP addressing (network and host portions)

To see how IP addressing works, it is best to use an example. Say that a business has two networks connected with a router. On each network, there are computers and printers. Each of the two networks must have a unique network number. For this example, one network has a network number of 193.14.150.0, and the other network has a network number of 193.14.151.0. Notice how these numbers represent a Class C IP address because the first number is 193.

With a Class C IP address, the first three numbers represent the network number. The first network uses the numbers 193.14.150 to represent the network part of the IP address. The second network uses the numbers 193.14.151 in the network part of the address. Remember that each network must have a different network part of the IP address than any other network in the organization. The last part of the IP address (the host portion) will be used to assign to each network device. On the first network, each device will have a number that starts with 193.14.150 because that is the network part of the number and it stays the same for all devices on that network. Each device will then have a different number in the last portion of the IP address—for example, 193.14.150.3, 193.14.150.4, and 193.14.150.5.

On the second network, each device will have a number that starts with 193.14.151 because that is the network part of the IP address. The last number in the IP address changes for each network device—for example, 193.14.151.3, 193.14.151.4, 193.14.151.5, and so on. No device can have a host number of 0 because that number represents the network and no device can have a host number of 255 because that represents something called the broadcast address. A **broadcast address** is the IP address used to communicate with all devices on a particular network.

In this example, no network device can be assigned the IP addresses 193.14.150.0 or 193.14.151.0 because these numbers represent the two networks. Furthermore, no network device can be assigned the IP addresses 193.14.150.255 or 193.14.151.255 because these numbers represent the broadcast address used with each network. An example of a Class B broadcast is 150.10.255.255. An example of a Class A broadcast is 11.255.255.255. Figure 14.40 shows this configuration.

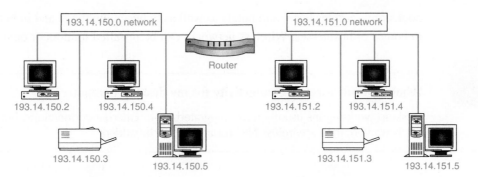

FIGURE 14.40   IP addressing (two networks example)

Notice in Figure 14.44 that each device to the left of the router has an IP address that starts with 193.14.150 (the network number), and each device has a unique last number. The same is true for the devices to the right of the router, except that they are on the 193.14.151.0 network.

Subnet Mask

In addition to assigning a computer an IP address, you must also assign a subnet mask. The **subnet mask** (sometimes shortened to *mask*) is a number that a computer uses to determine which part of the IP address represents the network and which portion represents the host. The default subnet mask for a Class A IP address is 255.0.0.0; the default subnet mask for a Class B IP address is 255.255.0.0; and the default subnet mask for a Class C IP address is 255.255.255.0. Table 14.14 recaps this important information.

TABLE 14.14   IP address information

Class	First number	Network/host number	Subnet mask
A	0–127	N.H.H.H*	255.0.0.0
B	128–191	N.N.H.H*	255.255.0.0
C	192–223	N.N.N.H*	255.255.255.0

*N = network number; H = host number

A subnet mask does not always have to follow classful boundaries. Sometimes, a technician might see a subnet mask that looks like the following examples: 255.255.254.0, 255.255.255.192, 255.255.255.240. These are known as classless inter-domain routing (CIDR) subnet masks. **CIDR** (pronounced cider) is a method of allocating IP addresses based on the number of host addresses needed for a particular network. Because the subnet mask dictates where the network portion ends and where the host portion begins, CIDR subnet masks are those different from the standard 255.0.0.0, 255.255.0,0, and 255.255.255.0 subnet masks.

Wireless Networks Overview

Even though wireless devices have been covered when discussing mice, keyboards, and mobile devices, no network chapter is complete without a thorough knowledge of wireless networking. Wireless networks are networks that transmit data over air using either infrared (1- to 400THz range) or radio frequencies (2.4GHz or 5GHz range). Most wireless networks in homes and businesses use radio frequencies. Wireless networks operate at Layers 1 and 2 of the OSI model.

Wireless networks are popular in home and business computer environments and are great in places that are not conducive to having cabling, such as outdoor centers, convention centers, bookstores, coffee shops, and hotels as well as between buildings and in between nonwired rooms in homes or businesses. Wireless networks can be installed indoors or outdoors.

TECH TIP

What if I want wireless connectivity for my desktop computer?

Desktop workstations usually have integrated RJ-45 Ethernet connections, but if wireless networking is wanted, then a wireless NIC usually has to be added.

Laptops and portable devices are frequently used to connect to wireless networks and have wireless capabilities integrated into them. Laptops also normally have wired network connections. A technician must be familiar with installation, configuration, and troubleshooting of both wired and wireless technologies.

Bluetooth

Bluetooth is a wireless technology for PANs. Bluetooth devices include audio/visual products, automotive accessories, keyboards, mice, phones, printer adapters, cameras, wireless cell phone headsets, sunglasses with radios and wireless speakers, and other small wireless devices. Bluetooth works in the 2.4GHz range, similarly to business wireless networks. It has three classes of devices (1, 2, and 3) that have a range of less than 30 feet (less than 10 meters), 33 feet (10 meters), and 328 feet (100 meters), respectively, and a maximum transfer rate of 24Mb/s. Bluetooth supports both data and voice transmissions. Up to eight Bluetooth devices can be connected in a piconet or PAN (a small network). Bluetooth has always had security features integrated into it, including 128-bit encryption (scrambling of data, as discussed later in this chapter) that uses a modified form of SAFER+ (Secure and Fast Encryption Routine). Bluetooth is a viable network solution for short-range wireless solutions. Figure 14.41 shows a Bluetooth cell phone headset.

FIGURE 14.41   Bluetooth cell phone headset

A Bluetooth network provides computer-to-computer connectivity between Bluetooth devices. Each computer must support a PAN to join the network. Use the *Add a device* (or Add a printer) link from the *Devices and Printers* (Vista/7/8). In Windows 10, use *Settings > Devices > Bluetooth*. Review Chapter 11 for complete installation steps. Chapters 2 and 11 provide more information on how to configure and troubleshoot Bluetooth connectivity.

Missing Bluetooth Control Panel

If the Bluetooth Devices Control Panel does not display or if the Bluetooth icon is not in the notification area on the taskbar, type `bthprops.cpl` at a command prompt.

Wireless Network Components

The most common components of a wireless network are wireless NICs, an access point, a wireless bridge, and a wireless router. Table 14.15 describes the purposes of these parts.

TABLE 14.15 Common wireless devices

Wireless device	Description
Access point (AP)	The central connecting point for a wireless network. Coordinates wireless access for wireless devices. Commonly connects to a wired network.
Wireless NIC	Integrated into a wireless device such as a laptop, smartphone or tablet.
Wireless router	An AP/router device that normally has both wireless capability and a few wired Ethernet ports.
Wireless **bridge**	A physical device or software that connects two or more networks. Could connect a wireless network to a wired network. An example of a wireless bridge is a building where all devices connect wirelessly to the bridge. The bridge connects to the wired network, which eventually connects to the Internet. Many access points or wireless routers can be placed in bridged mode.

Major types of wireless NICs include integrated ports, ExpressCard, USB, PCI, and PCIe. Figure 14.42 shows a wireless USB NIC with a detachable antenna.

FIGURE 14.42   Wireless USB NIC

CHAPTER 14

To determine whether you have a wireless NIC installed on a Windows-based device, perform the following steps:

> Windows Vista/7/8: Access the *Network and Sharing Center* Control Panel > *Change adapter settings* link on the left > Wi-Fi appears in the window, if installed.
> Windows 10: Access *Settings* > *Network & Internet* > *Wi-Fi* appears in the window, if installed.

Figure 14.43 shows a wireless NIC installed in a Windows 8 computer.

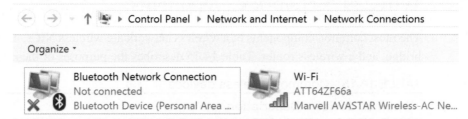

FIGURE 14.43   Wireless NIC in Network Connections window

A **wireless access point** (AP) is a device that receives and transmits data from multiple computers that have wireless NICs installed. The AP can be a standalone unit or can be integrated into an ADSL router, as shown in Figure 14.44. It is the wireless AP part of the router that needs the three antennae shown.

FIGURE 14.44   Access point integrated with an ADSL router

Power over Ethernet (PoE)

Corporate APs are commonly powered through the attached Ethernet cable that goes from the mounted AP to a switch. The switch provides the power through the Ethernet cable using a standard called Power over Ethernet (**PoE**). If the switch does not support PoE, a **power over Ethernet injector** is needed to inject DC voltage power. Figure 14.45 demonstrates these concepts.

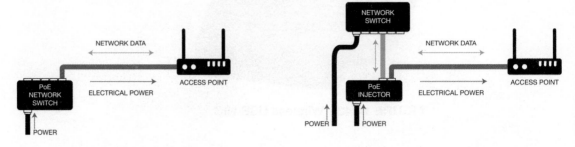

Power Over Ethernet (PoE)   Power Over Ethernet injector

FIGURE 14.45   AP with PoE and PoE injector

Wireless Network Design

The easiest way to describe an access point is to think of it as a network hub, but instead of connecting wired devices and sharing bandwidth, the AP connects wireless devices that share bandwidth. A wireless network or device being in **infrastructure mode** is when an AP is part of the wireless network. The alternative to infrastructure mode is **ad hoc mode** where two wireless devices communicate directly with one another (without an AP). This was discussed in Chapter 10. Figure 14.46 shows a wireless network with an access point and multiple wireless devices.

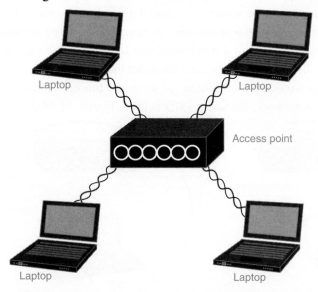

FIGURE 14.46   Infrastructure mode wireless network

Home networks frequently use an integrated services router that allows wireless and wired connectivity. Figure 14.47 shows how a wireless access point connects in this type of environment. Notice how the access point connects to a wired network and gives the wireless devices access to the Internet.

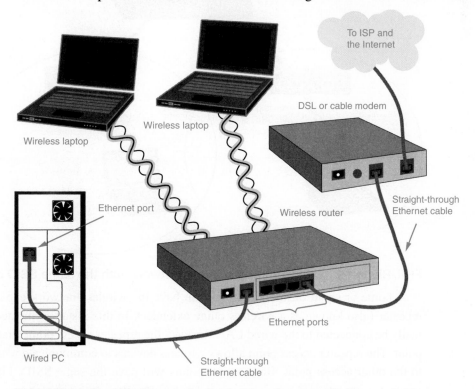

FIGURE 14.47   Wireless and wired network connectivity

Each access point can handle 30 to 200 wireless devices depending on the vendor, wireless network environment, amount of usage, and type of data sent. Each AP is assigned a service set identifier (**SSID**). Many APs have a default SSID that can be changed. An SSID is a set of 32 alphanumeric characters used to differentiate between different wireless networks. An AP broadcasts the SSID, by default. This setting can be changed. When the AP is broadcasting the SSID, wireless NICs can automatically detect a particular wireless network. When the AP is not broadcasting (the SSID cannot be found in the list of wireless networks), the SSID can be manually configured through the AP's configuration window. This is demonstrated in Lab 14.9.

The access point can also be wired or connect wirelessly to another AP, have a wired or wireless connection to a wireless **repeater** (**extender**), or connect to a wired network. The access point can then relay the transmission from a wireless device to another network or to the Internet through the wired network. If two access points are used and they connect two different wireless networks, two different SSIDs would be used. Figure 14.48 shows this concept. If two access points connect to the same wireless network, the same SSID is used. Figure 14.49 shows this concept.

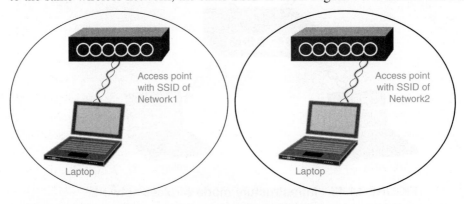

FIGURE 14.48   Two separate wireless networks with two SSIDs

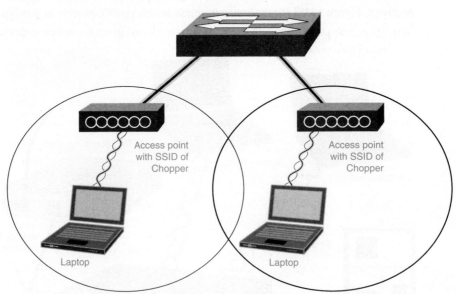

FIGURE 14.49   One extended wireless network with the same SSID on both APs

A home or small business network can have the wireless network expanded using a wireless repeater (also known as a wireless range extender). In this instance, the access point cannot normally be connected to the wired LAN. Instead, the repeater access point attaches to a "root" access point. The repeater access point allows wireless devices to communicate with it and relays the data to the other access point. Both access points will have the same SSID. Figure 14.50 shows this concept.

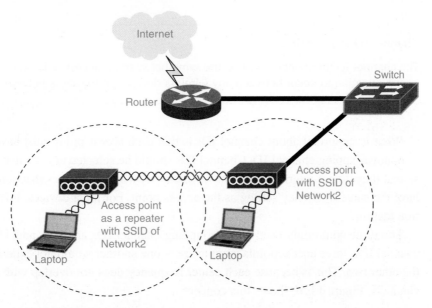

FIGURE 14.50   Access point as a repeater

In addition to SSIDs, an access point can be configured with a password and a channel ID. When an access point is purchased, sometimes a default username and/or password is assigned. Because default passwords are available on the Internet, the password needs to be changed immediately so that unauthorized access is not permitted. Manufacturers recognized this weakness, and as a result many newer devices enable you to create a password during the initial setup. The **channel ID** defines at what frequency the access point operates. With APs that have a 2.4GHz antenna, up to 14 channels are available depending on what part of the world the wireless network is deployed. In the United States, only 11 channels are used, which are listed in Table 14.16.

TABLE 14.16   Wireless frequency channels

Channel ID number	Frequency (in GHz)
1	2.412
2	2.417
3	2.422
4	2.427
5	2.432
6	2.437
7	2.442
8	2.447
9	2.452
10	2.457
11	2.462

The frequencies shown in Table 14.16 are center frequencies. The center frequencies are spaced 5MHz apart. Each channel is actually a range of frequencies. For example, the channel 1 range is 2.401 to 2.423 with the center frequency being 2.412. The channel 2 range is 2.406 to 2.428 with the center frequency being 2.417.

Channel ID must match

The channel ID (frequency) must be the same between an access point and a wireless NIC for communication to occur between any wireless devices on the same network.

What is important about channel IDs is that each access point must have a different frequency or nonoverlapping channel ID. Channel IDs should be selected at least five channel numbers apart so that they do not interfere with one another. The wireless devices that connect to an access point have the same frequency setting as the access point. For most devices, this is an automatic detection feature.

The three commonly used nonoverlapping channel IDs are 1, 6, and 11. By using these three channel IDs, three access points mounted near one another would not experience interference from the other two. This is because each center frequency does not overlap with the adjacent frequency channels. Figure 14.51 shows this concept.

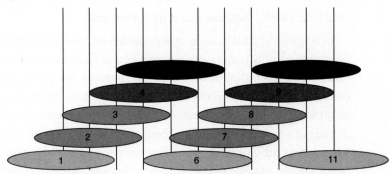

802.11b, g, and n   2.412 2.417 2.422 2.427 2.432 2.437 2.442 2.447 2.452 2.457 2.462
Center Frequencies
(in GHz)

FIGURE 14.51   802.11b/g/n 2.4GHz nonoverlapping channels

Notice in Figure 14.51 that each center frequency is 5MHz from the next center frequency. Also notice that each channel is actually a range of frequencies, shown by the shaded ovals. Channels 1, 6, and 11 clearly do not overlap and do not interfere with each other. Other nonoverlapping channel combinations could be Channels 2 and 7, Channels 3 and 8, Channels 4 and 9, and Channels 5 and 10. The combination of Channels 1, 6, and 11 is preferred because it gives you three channels with which to work. Figure 14.52 shows a different way of looking at how Channels 1, 6, and 11 do not overlap.

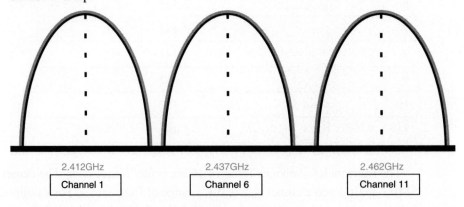

2.412GHz   2.437GHz   2.462GHz

Channel 1   Channel 6   Channel 11

FIGURE 14.52   2.4GHz channel IDs 1, 6, and 11

Figure 14.53 shows how the three nonoverlapping channels can be used to have extended coverage even with multiple access points.

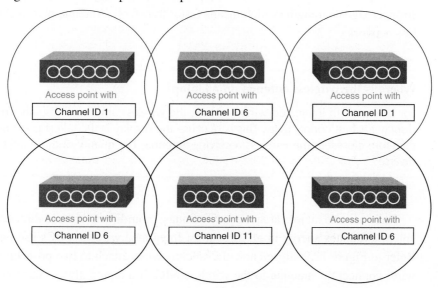

FIGURE 14.53   802.11b/g/n nonoverlapping channel IDs

With 802.11a, 12 20MHz channels are available in the 5GHz range. 802.11n supports 20 and 40MHz channels. 802.11ac supports 20, 40, 80, and 160MHz channels. The 5GHz range has three subranges called Unlicensed National Information Infrastructure (UNII): UNII-1, UNII-2, and UNII-3. Before 2014, UNII-1 was for indoor use only, UNII-2 for both indoor and outdoor use, and UNII-3 for outdoor use only. Now all bands can be used for indoor and outdoor usage. Figure 14.54 shows the 5GHz channels.

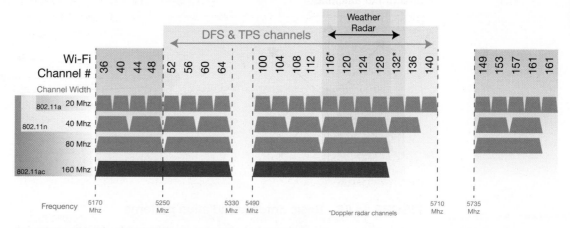

FIGURE 14.54   802.11 a/n/ac 5GHz channel IDs

Devices that work in the UNII-2 frequency ranges must support dynamic frequency selection (**DFS**) and transmit power control (TPC) to avoid interference with military applications. These two terms are most often shortened to simply DFS channels. Channels 120, 124, and 128 are used for terminal Doppler weather radar (TDWR) systems. Channels 116 and 132 may optionally be used for Doppler radar.

Antenna Basics

Wireless cards and access points can have either external or built-in antennas. An antenna radiates or receives radio waves. Some access points also have integrated antennas. Wireless NICs and access points can also have detachable antennas depending on the make and model. With external antennas, you can simply move the antenna to a different angle to obtain a better connection. With some laptops, you must turn the laptop to a different angle to attach to an access point or have a stronger signal strength (which means faster transfers). Antenna placement is important in a wireless network.

TECH TIP

Where is the wireless antenna on a laptop?

For laptops with integrated wireless NICs, the wireless antenna is usually built in to the laptop display for best connectivity. This is because the display is the tallest point of the laptop and therefore closest to the wireless receiving antenna. The quality of these integrated antennas is diverse.

There are two major categories of antennas: omnidirectional and directional. An **omnidirectional antenna** radiates energy in all directions. Integrated wireless NICs use omnidirectional antennas. Refer to Figure 11.90 to see how the antenna wires attach to two posts on the wireless NIC. These wires connect the antenna to the wireless NIC. If a laptop always has low signal strength, ensure these two wires are attached.

A **directional antenna** radiates energy in a specific direction. Directional antennas are frequently used to connect two buildings together or to limit wireless connectivity outside a building. Each antenna has a specific radiation pattern. A radiation pattern (sometimes called a propagation pattern) is the direction(s) the radio frequency is sent or received. It is the coverage area for the antenna that is normally shown in a graphical representation in the antenna manufacturer's specifications. Figure 14.55 shows the difference in radiation patterns between omnidirectional and directional antennas.

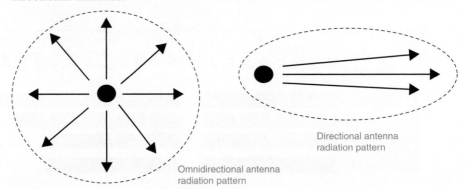

Omnidirectional antenna
radiation pattern

Directional antenna
radiation pattern

FIGURE 14.55   Basic antenna radiation patterns

A wireless network installer must be familiar with an antenna's radiation pattern so that the appropriate type of antenna can be chosen for the installation. As a signal is radiated from an antenna, some of the signal is lost. Attenuation is the amount of signal loss of a radio wave as it travels (is propagated) through air. Attenuation is sometimes called path loss. Attenuation is measured in decibels (dB). The decibel is a value that represents a measure of the ratio between two signal levels.

Things that affect an antenna's path loss are the distance between the transmitting antenna and the receiving antenna, what obstructions are between the two antennas, and how high the antenna is mounted. Another factor that affects wireless transmission is interference, including radio frequencies being transmitted using the same frequency range and external noises. Other wireless devices, wireless networks, cordless phones, and microwave ovens are common sources of interference.

What is the maximum distance of a wireless network?

This depends on the wireless network standard used, the antenna attached to the AP, and the attenuation experienced.

An important concept in relationship to antennas is gain, and to understand gain, an isotropic antenna must be discussed. An isotropic antenna is not real; it is an imaginary antenna that is perfect in that it theoretically transmits an equal amount of power in all directions. The omnidirectional radiation pattern previously shown in Figure 14.55 would be the pattern of an isotropic antenna. A lot of ceiling-mounted APs have omnidirectional antennas. Figure 14.56 shows an AP that could be mounted on the ceiling and have integrated omnidirectional antennas.

FIGURE 14.56   Ceiling-mounted AP

Antenna power levels are described as antenna gain. Gain is measured in dBi, which is a measurement of decibels in relationship to an isotropic antenna. (The *i* is for isotropic.) Some antennas are shown with a measurement of dBd instead of dBi. This measurement is referenced to a dipole antenna. (The *d* at the end is for dipole.) 0 dBd equals 2.14 dBi. More gain means more coverage in a particular direction. Gain is actually logarithmic in nature. A technician must sometimes reduce the transmit power (lower the signal strength) for multiple wireless access points to function in the same building or area.

TECH TIP

What is gain?

Antenna gain is the antenna's output power in a particular direction compared to the output power produced in any direction by an isotropic or dipole antenna.

Imagine a round balloon that is blown up. The balloon represents an isotropic radiation pattern—it extends in all directions. Push down on the top of the balloon, and the balloon extends out more horizontally than it does vertically. Push on the side of the balloon, and the balloon extends more in one horizontal directional than the side being pushed. Now think of the balloon's shape as an antenna's radiation pattern. Antenna designers can change the radiation pattern of an antenna by changing the antenna's length and shape, similarly to how a balloon's looks can be changed by pushing on it in different directions. In this way, different antennas can be created to serve different purposes.

TECH TIP

Understanding gain

A 3dB gain is twice the output power. 10dB is 10 times the power, 13dB is approximately 20 times the power, and 20dB is 100 times the power. Gain that is shown with a negative value means there is a power loss. For example, a −3dB gain means the power is halved.

A **site survey** is an examination of an area to determine the best wireless hardware placement. To take such a survey, temporarily mount an access point. (Or use a telescoping pole to place it at different heights.) With a laptop that has a wireless NIC and site survey software (or a Wi-Fi analyzer/Wi-Fi locator previously mentioned in Chapter 11 and described in a paragraph that follows), walk around the wireless network area to see the coverage range. Some vendors provide site survey software with their wireless NICs.

The site survey can also be conducted by double-clicking the network icon on the taskbar. The signal strength is shown in the window that appears. Move the access point as necessary to avoid attenuation and obtain the largest area coverage. Radio waves are affected by obstructions such as walls, trees, rain, snow, fog, and buildings, so for a larger project, the site survey may need to be done over a period of time. You can see the wireless antenna signal strength in the notification area part of the taskbar. You can also see it from within the wireless NIC properties window. Figure 14.57 shows a laptop wireless antenna signal strength display on a Windows 8.1 laptop.

FIGURE 14.57   Signal strength

The higher the decibel rating, the better the signal

The type of radio antenna and the antenna gain also affect the signal strength. However, no matter how good the antenna, as a wireless device is moved farther away from an access point or another wireless device, the more attenuation occurs. Walls, trees, obstacles, or other radio waves can cause attenuation.

A **Wi-Fi analyzer** or wireless locator can determine whether there are wireless networks or hot spots in the area. Wireless devices can also be attached to pets, people, keys, remotes, and so on. A Wi-Fi analyzer or wireless locator device can locate these devices. A phone or mobile device app can also locate a powered mobile device or locate a person who has a mobile device with this enabled.

Many different types of antennas exist, but four common ones are parabolic, Yagi, patch, and dipole. Parabolic antennas can come in either grid or dish type models and are usually used in outdoor environments. Parabolic dishes provide the greatest distances in a wireless network. Parabolic dish antennas may not come with mounting hardware, so you should research whether additional hardware is needed before purchasing one.

Other antennas include Yagi, patch, MIMO, and dipole. A Yagi antenna can be used indoors or outdoors, depending on the manufacturer. It is used for long-distance communication and normally is not large or difficult to mount. A patch antenna can also be used indoors and outdoors. Patch antennas can be mounted to a variety of surfaces including room columns or walls.

Multiple input/multiple output (**MIMO**) uses multiple 2.4GHz and 5GHz antennas. Figure 14.58 shows an example of MIMO transmissions. Note that each client that attaches to an AP using MIMO can have multiple data streams, the AP still handles one client at a time.

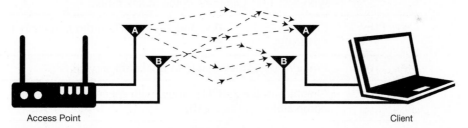

Access Point   Client

FIGURE 14.58   MIMO transmissions

MIMO antennas may be external or built in to the wireless device. By using multiple antennas, greater wireless speeds can be achieved. 802.11n and 802.11ac radios are defined by how many antennas can transmit and receive as well as the number of data streams supported. The documentation is commonly in a number formatted such as 2 x 2:1 or 4 x 4:4 (the maximum for an 802.11n device). The first number is the maximum number of antennas that can transmit. The second number is the number of antennas that can receive data. The last number is the number of data streams supported. 802.11ac uses multi-user MIMO (**MU-MIMO**) and allows up to eight simultaneous streams. MU-MIMO serves multiple devices simultaneously, whereas with pre-802.11ac implementations, APs serve only one user at a time.

A dipole antenna is frequently referred to as a *rubber ducky*. A dipole antenna attaches to wireless NICs and access points and is used in indoor applications. Of all the previously mentioned antenna types, the dipole has the lowest range. Figure 14.59 shows a dipole antenna.

CHAPTER 14

FIGURE 14.59   Dipole (rubber ducky) antenna

Wireless Network Standards

The IEEE 802.11 committees define standards for wireless networks, and they can be quite confusing. Table 14.17 shows the current and proposed wireless network standards.

TABLE 14.17   IEEE 802.11 standards

Standard	Purpose
802.11a	Came after the 802.11b standard. Has speeds up to 54Mb/s but is incompatible with 802.11b. Operates in the 5GHz range.
802.11b	Operates in the 2.4000 and 2.4835GHz radio frequency ranges, with speeds up to 11Mb/s.
802.11e	Provides standards related to quality of service.
802.11g	Operates in the 2.4GHz range, with speeds up to 54Mb/s, and is backward compatible with 802.11b.
802.11i	Relates to wireless network security and includes AES (Advanced Encryption Standard) for protecting data.
802.11n	Operates in the 2.4 and 5GHz ranges and is backward compatible with the older 802.11a, b, and g equipment. Speeds up to 600Mb/s using MIMO antennas. Maximum of 4 simultaneous data streams.
802.11ac	Operates only in the 5GHz range, which makes it backward compatible with 802.11n and 802.11a. Speeds up to 6.93Gb/s. Maximum of 8 simultaneous data streams using MU-MIMO antennas.
802.11ad	Also known as WiGig and works in the 60GHz range. Speeds up to 6.76Gb/s.

802.11-based wireless networks use Carrier Sense Multiple Access/Collision Avoidance (CSMA/CA) as an access method. Network devices listen on the cable for conflicting traffic, as with CSMA/CD; however, with CSMA/CA, a workstation that wants to transmit data sends a jam signal onto the cable. The workstation then waits a small amount of time for all other workstations to hear the jam signal, and then the workstation begins transmission. If a collision occurs, the workstation does the same thing as CSMA/CD; the workstation stops transmitting, waits a designated amount of time, and then retransmits.

Data transfer speed between the wireless NIC and an access point or another wireless device is automatically negotiated for the fastest transfer possible. The farther away from an access point a wireless device is located, the lower the speed. Figure 14.60 shows this concept.

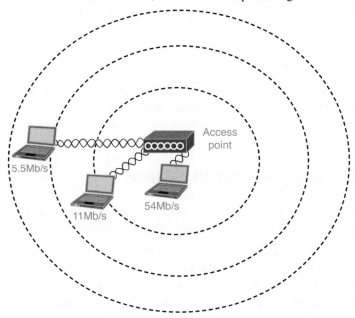

FIGURE 14.60   AP speed ranges

Wired or Wireless NIC Installation

When you install a NIC in a computer, you must take four or more configuration steps before connecting to the network:

Step 1. Determine that an appropriate slot, port, or integrated wireless NIC is available. For example, a NIC can be integrated into the motherboard, require a PCI/PCIe slot, require a mini-PCI/PCIe slot, connect to a USB port, or insert into a laptop slot (ExpressCard or CF NIC—a CompactFlash card that has an RJ-45 NIC port).

Step 2. Optionally, obtain and install the appropriate NIC driver.

Step 3. Give the computer a unique name and optionally join a workgroup or domain.

Step 4. Configure TCP/IP.

Other things could be required, depending on the network environment. For example, if the system is a workgroup network, file and print sharing must be enabled. If a wireless network is configured, the SSID and possibly the security parameters need to be entered. If TCP/IP is configured, some other configuration parameters may be necessary. Lab 14.3 and Lab 14.4 at the end of the chapter demonstrate these concepts.

TECH TIP

How to name a computer

Name a computer using the *System* (Vista/7/8/10) Control Panel. Each device on the same network must be given a unique name.

Configuring an IP Address Overview

When configuring TCP/IP, an IP address and a subnet mask must be assigned to the network device. The IP address is what makes the network device unique and allows it to be reached by other network devices. There are two ways to get an IP address: (1) statically define the IP address and mask or (2) dynamically obtain the address using DHCP.

TECH TIP

My computer's IP address changes

The IP address can change each time the computer boots because with DHCP you can configure the DHCP server to issue an IP address for a specific amount of time.

Statically Configuring an IP Address

When an IP address is statically defined, someone manually enters an IP address and mask into the computer through the *Network and Sharing Center* (Vista/7/8) Control Panel > *Change adapter settings* link; in Windows 10, access *Settings > Network & Internet > Change adapter options* link. Lab 14.3 at the end of this chapter demonstrates this. Most support staff do not statically define IP addresses unless the device is an important network device such as a web server, database server, network server, router, or switch. Instead, DHCP is used. However, in home-wired networks, IP addresses are sometimes statically assigned. Figure 14.61 shows the window that appears when you right-click a particular adapter and select *Properties > Internet Protocol Version 4 (TCP/IPv4) > Properties* button.

FIGURE 14.61 IP address configuration

TECH TIP

What happens if you assign the same IP address?

Entering an IP address that is a duplicate of another network device renders the new network device inoperable on the network and could affect the other device's traffic as well.

Using DHCP

Dynamic host configuration protocol (**DHCP**) is a protocol used to assign IP addresses to network devices. A **DHCP server** (software configured on a network server, router, or multifunction router/AP) contains a pool of IP addresses. When a network device has been configured for DHCP and it boots, the device sends out a DHCP request for an IP address. A DHCP server responds to this request and issues an IP address to the network device. DHCP makes IP addressing easy and keeps network devices from being assigned duplicate IP addresses.

To configure **client-side DHCP** in Windows, access the *Network and Sharing Center* Control Panel > access the *Change adapter settings* link > right-click or tap and briefly hold on the wired and wireless NIC and select *Properties* > double-click or double-tap on the *Internet Protocol Version 4 (TCP/IPv4)* option > ensure the *Obtain an IP address automatically* radio button is enabled. Refer back to Figure 14.61 to see this option.

> **TECH TIP**
>
> **One DHCP server can provide addresses to multiple networks**
>
> A DHCP server can give out IP addresses to network devices on remote networks as well as the network to which the DHCP server is directly connected.

APIPA

Windows computers support automatic private IP addressing (**APIPA**), which assigns an IP address and mask to the computer when a DHCP server is not available. The addresses assigned are 169.254.0.1 to 169.254.255.254. No two computers get the same IP address. APIPA continues to request an IP address from the DHCP server at 5-minute intervals. If you can connect to other computers on your local network but cannot reach the Internet or other networks, it is likely the DHCP server is down and Windows has automatically assigned an APIPA address. To determine if APIPA is configured, open a command prompt window and type `ipconfig /all`. If you see the words *Autoconfiguration Enabled Yes,* APIPA is turned on. If the last word is *No*, APIPA is disabled.

Alternative IP Address

An **alternative configuration** can also be used. An alternative configuration is used when a DHCP could not assign an IP address such as when there are network problems or the DHCP server is down. An **alternative IP address** could also be used on a laptop where at work DHCP is used, but at home the addresses are statically assigned. Figure 14.62 shows the *Alternate Configuration* tab settings. Note this tab appears only if you have the *Obtain an IP address automatically* radio button enabled on the *General* tab of the *Internet Protocol Version 4 (TCP/IPv4) Properties* window.

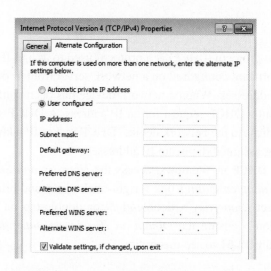

FIGURE 14.62   Alternate Configuration tab

Default Gateway

Another important concept that relates to IP addressing is a default gateway (sometimes called gateway of last resort or simply **gateway**). A **default gateway** is an IP address assigned to a network device that tells the device where to send a packet that is going to a remote network. Default gateway addresses are important for network devices to communicate with network devices on other networks. The default gateway address is the IP address of the router that is directly connected to that immediate network. Keep in mind that the primary job of a router is to find the best path to another network. Routers send traffic from one network to another throughout the Internet. Your router at home might be used to get traffic from your wireless network and your wired network out to the Internet. Consider Figure 14.63 that has a router getting traffic from the network on the left to the network on the right.

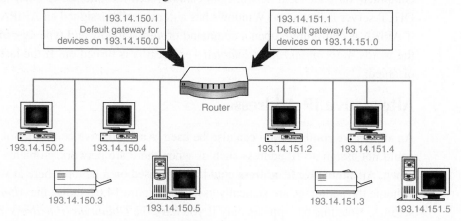

FIGURE 14.63   Default gateway

Network devices on the 193.14.150.0 network use the router IP address 193.14.150.1 as a default gateway address. When a network device on the 193.14.150.0 network wants to send a packet to the other network, the device sends the packet to the default gateway, the router. The router, in turn, looks up the destination address in its routing table and sends the packet out of the other router interface (193.14.151.1) to the device on the 193.14.151.0 network.

The default gateway address for all network devices on the 193.14.151.0 network is 193.14.151.1, the router's IP address on the same network. Any network device on 193.14.151.0 sending information to another network sends the packet to the default gateway address.

TECH TIP

How do I assign a default gateway?

If you are statically assigning an IP address, the default gateway address is configured using the *Network and Sharing Center* Control Panel. Your computer can automatically receive a default gateway through DHCP just like receiving an IP address and mask.

DNS

Other elements of TCP/IP information that may need to be configured or provided through DHCP include DNS server IP addresses. A domain name system (**DNS**) (sometimes called a domain name or **DNS server**) is an application that runs on a network server that provides translation of Internet names into IP addresses. DNS is used on the Internet, so you do not have to remember the IP address of each site to which you connect. For example, DNS would be used to connect to Pearson Education, Inc. by translating the uniform resource locator (URL) of http://www.pearsoned.com into the IP address 159.182.16.65. **Client-side DNS** is configuring a computer to use one or more DNS servers. A computer can be programmed for one or more DNS server IP addresses using DHCP. The DHCP server must be configured for this. Otherwise, a technician can manually configure the system for one or more DNS server IP addresses through the *Network and Sharing Center* Control Panel.

TECH TIP

DNS servers provide name resolution

If a Windows computer is on an Active Directory domain, Active Directory automatically uses DNS to locate other hosts and services using assigned domain names.

If a DNS server does not know a domain name (it does not have the name in its database), the DNS server can contact another DNS server to get the translation information. Common codes used with DNS (three letters used at the end of a domain name) are com (commercial sites), edu (educational sites), gov (government sites), net (network-related sites), and org (miscellaneous sites). Wired and wireless adapters require IP addresses, default gateways, and DNS configuration, but before any wired or wireless adapters are installed or configured, the basic configuration parameters should be determined.

Wireless NIC-Specific Settings

Not all computers in a wireless network need the same type of wireless NIC. With most wireless NICs, the manufacturer's software is normally installed before the NIC is installed or attached to the computer. With all wireless NICs, the latest driver for the particular version of Windows should be downloaded from the manufacturer's website before the card is installed.

After the wireless adapter is installed, SSID and security options can be entered. Specific security options are covered in Chapter 18. Wireless parameters can be configured through a utility provided by the wireless NIC manufacturer or through Windows by selecting the wireless network icon in the notification area, selecting the wireless network shown, and entering the required security information.

If the SSID is not being broadcast, a wireless network can be manually entered using the following procedures for Windows Vista, 7, 8, and 10: *Network and Sharing Center* Control Panel

> *Set up a new connection or network* link > *Manually connect to a wireless network* option (see Figure 14.64).

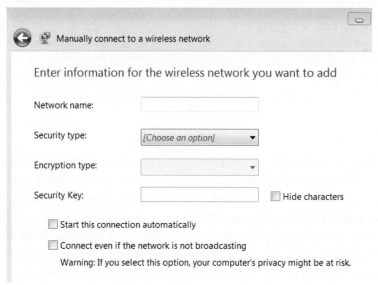

FIGURE 14.64   Windows 7 wireless network configuration window

---

TECH TIP

Disable Windows control of the wireless NIC if other utilities are used

If a vendor provides a method of controlling the wireless NIC with utilities associated with the NIC, use those and not Windows. Otherwise, uninstall the wireless NIC software provided by the vendor.

Another common setting for wireless NICs is the type of encryption used. Encryption is covered in Chapter 18 along with other wireless security measures. The following types of encryption can be chosen and must match what is configured on the wireless AP/router. Note that the list is shown from least secure to most secure. Actually no encryption at all is least secure (see Figure 14.65).

> Wireless encryption protocol (**WEP**): 64- and 128-bit versions
> Temporal key integrity protocol (**TKIP**): May be seen in combination with Wi-Fi protected access (WPA) and/or WPA2
> **WPA:** Might be seen with preshared keys (PSK) meaning a passphrase and/or TKIP
> **WPA2:** Uses the counter mode block chaining message authentication code protocol (CCMP) for added security (might be seen as PSK and/or TKIP)
> WPA2 with advanced encryption standard (**AES**)

FIGURE 14.65   Wireless security options

Wireless NICs are easy to install. The utilities that are provided with the NICs are quite sophisticated but easy to use. Always follow the manufacturer's instructions. All the screens and configuration utilities have the same type of information. Understanding what the configuration parameters mean is important. The hardest part about configuring wireless NICs is obtaining the correct parameters before installation begins. Incorrectly inputting any one of the parameters causes the wireless NIC to not associate with the access point or remote wireless device and to not transmit. Planning is critical for these types of cards.

Advanced NIC Properties

Both wired and wireless NICs have some optional parameters that can be manually configured. These options are shown in Figure 14.66 and discussed in Table 14.18. Access these parameters by right-clicking the NIC from within the *Networking and Sharing Center* Control Panel > *Properties* > *Configure* button > *Advanced* tab.

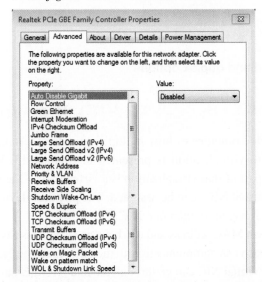

FIGURE 14.66   NIC advanced properties

TABLE 14.18   Network card properties

Configuration property	Description
Speed (NIC property)	Normally automatically configured but manual options include 10Gb/s, 1Gb/s, 100Mb/s, and 10Mb/s.
Duplex	Options include half duplex/full duplex/auto. The default is auto or auto negotiation, to automatically configure full-duplex or half-duplex mode. Duplex might be combined with the Speed configuration option. Speed/Duplex should be manually configured on an important device such as a server. Figure 14.67 shows common speed and duplex options.
Wake-on-LAN	Wake-on-LAN allows the computer to be brought out of a low power mode to have configuration changes or updates made. Usually enabled through the BIOS but also through the NIC properties *Advanced* tab. Other options might include Wake on magic packet or WOL.
Quality of service (**QoS**)	Some NICs have the capability to have QoS features enabled. This allows tagging certain packets for priority transmission. Other similar options might be Priority and VLAN or Tagging.
On-board NIC (BIOS/UEFI)	If the wired or wireless NIC is integrated into the motherboard or mobile device, you might have to access BIOS/UEFI to configure some of the settings related to the NIC.

CHAPTER 14

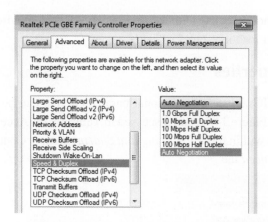

FIGURE 14.67   NIC speed and duplex options

NIC Configuration When Using Virtualization

Virtualization allows a single computer to host multiple operating systems that share hardware resources. An introduction to virtualization is presented in Chapter 15. When you configure a computer for virtualization, part of that virtualization is a virtual NIC. One virtual NIC is standard in a virtual machine. More virtual NICs can be assigned. The physical device has at least one NIC, but if the device is a server, it has more than one NIC.

Each virtual NIC has its own MAC address and can have an IP address assigned. If more than one virtual machine is installed, each can communicate with the other machine based on the NIC settings configured. Furthermore, the virtual NIC can go through the real NIC and have Internet access in the virtual environment. If the virtual machine doesn't have network connectivity, but the host workstation does, verify the virtual NIC settings. Figure 14.68 shows the concept of three virtual machines (one Linux, one Windows 7, and one Microsoft Server 2012, for example) in one physical machine connecting to the one physical NIC even though each virtual machine has its own virtual NIC.

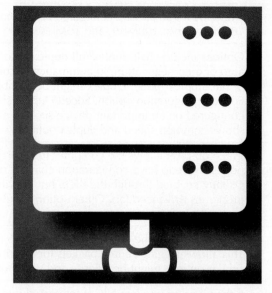

FIGURE 14.68   Virtualized machines connecting to a network

Rather than go into all of different virtualization vendors' products, let's examine VMware Workstation's NIC settings. Other vendors have similar configurations. In VMware Workstation, a NIC can be configured for bridged, network address translation (NAT), host-only, or custom mode. Table 14.19 describes these modes.

TABLE 14.19   Virtualized NIC modes of operation

Mode	Description
Bridged	Usually the default mode. The NIC is normally manually configured and has access to the host machine NIC (which normally is connected to the Internet and provides Internet access to the virtual machine).
NAT (network address translation)	Cannot be seen by other virtual machines but can use the host machine NIC for Internet access. DHCP is also supported.
Host-only	Other virtual machines configured with an IP address on the same network can see and communicate with one another. DHCP is supported.
Custom	Select the VM network that the NIC is assigned to.

Wireless AP/Router Basic Configuration

A wireless AP frequently has the capability to route. This type of device is made for a small office/home office (SOHO) environment. The graphical environment used to configure a SOHO AP varies per vendor, but the process is common. The generic steps follow:

Step 1.   Connect an Ethernet cable between the wireless AP and another device that has a web browser.

Step 2.   Open a web browser and in the address textbox, enter the default IP address of the AP such as http://192.168.1.1.

Step 3.   Enter the default username (if needed) and default password.

Typical menu options are shown in Table 14.20.

TABLE 14.20   Common AP configuration options

Area	Description
Wireless	Used to configure basic wireless settings such as the SSID. Also includes a link to security options such as MAC filtering, authentication, and encryption (covered in Chapter 18).
Security	Used to enable/disable a firewall and configure firewall features such as VPN or allow particular network ports to be opened to allow certain types of traffic through.
Storage	Allows monitoring and control of an attached storage device or even supports a File Transfer Protocol (FTP) server.
Maintenance	Allows viewing the current status of the various components as well as access to any logging that is enabled.
Administration	Allows configuration of the device such as password, IP address assignment, and event logging. Could also include configuration of features such as VoIP or QoS, which allows one type of traffic such as voice, which cannot tolerate delay to take priority over another type of traffic.

Wireless SOHO access points/routers frequently include network functions such as demilitarized zone (DMZ), QoS, DHCP server (sometimes seen as the DHCP on/off setting), router, integrated switch ports, and sometimes include a port to add a hard drive and support network-accessible storage. Note that Chapter 18 has explanations and configuration details related to wireless security, but Table 14.21 introduces some common configuration features.

TABLE 14.21 Common wireless network device configuration settings

Option	Description
SSID	Used to name the wireless network. Cannot contain spaces in the name. Commonly has the SSID broadcast option to enable or disable.
Channel ID	Used to specify a particular 2.4 or 5GHz channel.
DHCP	Used to enable or disable DHCP as well as the specific network number, mask, and range of addresses to use.
demilitarized zone (**DMZ**)	Might be seen as DMZ host. An advanced option that allows a PC or server to be accessed from a remote location.
Port forwarding/port triggering	An alternative to using a DMZ where specific port numbers, ranges of port numbers, and applications are allowed to be used instead of opening all ports. One example of this is when a small company has a web server inside the company and the server needs to be accessed by external users. Port triggering allows data through on a limited basis when a specific/configured situation occurs.
network address translation (**NAT**)/ destination NAT (**DNAT**)	NAT is used to translate from private IP addresses to a public address and enabled by default. DNAT is a public IP address mapped to a specific private IP address used in the home or small business network.
Basic QoS	Used to enable QoS so that traffic such as gaming traffic or voice over IP (VoIP) traffic is prioritized over other data types.
Firmware	Used to update the embedded code within the device. Frequently contains security, performance, and software updates.
Universal Plug and Play (**UPnP**)	An alternative to configure port forwarding that allows peer-to-peer (P2P) gaming applications to function without further configuration. Could be a security risk for other devices on the network.

WWAN Cellular Configuration

Another type of wireless device that you might configure is a wireless broadband device or a WWAN (cellular) connection. A wireless broadband (WWAN cellular) device is normally a USB device, but some mobile devices have this technology integrated into the device. Software is normally installed by either a disc or from the device. The device commonly has a phone number/ account number associated with the broadband card. Figure 14.69 shows the type of information provided for a wireless broadband USB device.

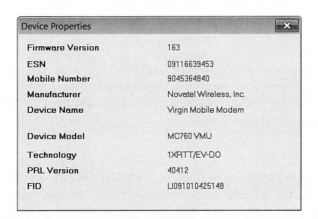

FIGURE 14.69 WWAN cellular properties

Network Troubleshooting

One way to troubleshoot a network is to determine how many devices are affected. For example, if only one computer cannot communicate across a network, it will be handled differently than if several (or all) computers on a network cannot communicate. If a network port is suspect, try another cable or use a loopback plug to test the port. The easiest way to determine how many devices are having trouble is by using a simple test. Because most computers use TCP/IP, one tool that can be used for testing is the `ping` command.

The `ping` Command

The `ping` command can be used to check connectivity around the network (you suspect **no connectivity** or **intermittent connectivity**). Figure 14.70 shows a sample network that is used to explain how `ping` is used to check various network points.

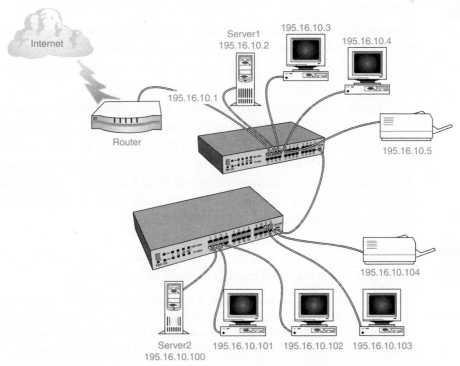

FIGURE 14.70 Sample network troubleshooting scenario

TECH TIP

What does `ping` do?

The `ping` command can be used to determine whether the network path is available, if there are delays along the path, and whether the remote network device is reachable. `Ping` sends a packet to an IP destination (that you determine) and a reply is sent back from the destination device (if everything works fine).

The network shown in Figure 14.70 consists of various network devices, including two servers and two laser printers. The devices connect to one of two switches that are connected using the uplink port. This port allows two similar devices to be connected with a standard Ethernet cable or fiber cable. A router connects to the top switch and the router connects to the Internet.

If the 195.16.10.3 workstation cannot access a file on Server2 (195.16.10.100), the first step in troubleshooting is to ping Server2 from the workstation. If this is successful, the problem is in Server2 or the file located on the server.

If the ping is unsuccessful, there is a problem somewhere between the workstation and the server or on the server. Ping another device that connects to the same switch—from workstation 195.16.10.3, ping Server1 (195.16.10.2). A successful ping tells you the connection between the 195.16.10.3 workstation and the switch is good, the switch is working, the cable connecting to Server1 is fine, and Server1 is functioning.

Pinging devices on the same network is a good check of local connectivity. The term **local connectivity** describes devices on the same network including the default gateway. If a network device can ping other devices on the same network as well as the default gateway, the network device (and all its components and basic settings) is configured correctly.

TECH TIP

Use `ping -t`

`ping x.x.x.x -t` (replace the `x.x.x.x` with an IP address or a URL) issues a continuous `ping` to a remote location. The ping does not stop until the [Ctrl] + [C] keys are pressed.

Now ping workstation 195.16.10.101 (a device other than the server on the remote switch) by typing `ping 195.16.10.101`. If the ping is successful, (1) the uplink cable is operational; (2) the second switch is operational; (3) the cable that connects workstation 195.16.10.101 to the switch is good; and (4) the 195.16.10.101 workstation has been successfully configured for TCP/IP. If the `ping` is unsuccessful, one of these four items is faulty. If the ping is successful, the problems could be the (1) Server2 cable, (2) switch port to which the server connects, (3) server NIC, (4) server configuration, or (5) file on Server2.

TECH TIP

How can I check the TCP/IP protocol stack on my own NIC?

The `ping` command can be used to test a NIC as well as the TCP/IP protocol running on the NIC, with the command `ping 127.0.0.1` (IPv4), `ping ::1` (IPv6), or `ping localhost` The word localhost is a hostname that is translated to an IP address known as a private IP address, or a loopback address, which means it cannot be used by the outside world.

Use the `ping` command followed by the name of the device (or website) being tested, for example, `ping www.pearsoned.com`. A DNS server translates the name to an IP address. If the site can be reached by pinging the IP address, but not the name, there is a problem with the DNS server.

What the `ping localhost` results mean

If a ping is successful (that is, you get a message that a reply was received from 127.0.0.1 or ::1), then the TCP/IP protocol stack works correctly on the NIC. If the ping response is nothing (appears to hang) or a 100% packet loss error, TCP/IP is not properly installed or functioning correctly on that one workstation.

The `ipconfig` Command

To see the current IP configuration on a Windows computer, use the `ipconfig` command from a Windows command prompt. Note that the `ifconfig` command is used in a Linux operating system environment. The `ipconfig /all` command can be used to see both wired and wireless NICs if both are installed, as shown in Figure 14.71. The `ipconfig /all` command also allows you to view MAC addresses.

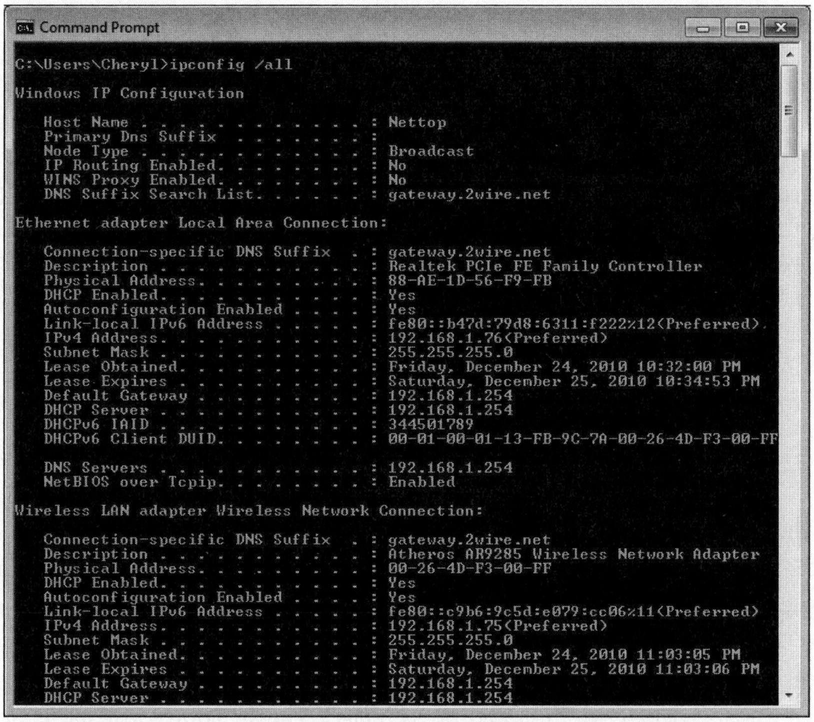

```
Command Prompt

C:\Users\Cheryl>ipconfig /all

Windows IP Configuration

    Host Name . . . . . . . . . . . . : Nettop
    Primary Dns Suffix  . . . . . . . :
    Node Type . . . . . . . . . . . . : Broadcast
    IP Routing Enabled. . . . . . . . : No
    WINS Proxy Enabled. . . . . . . . : No
    DNS Suffix Search List. . . . . . : gateway.2wire.net

Ethernet adapter Local Area Connection:

    Connection-specific DNS Suffix  . : gateway.2wire.net
    Description . . . . . . . . . . . : Realtek PCIe FE Family Controller
    Physical Address. . . . . . . . . : 88-AE-1D-56-F9-FB
    DHCP Enabled. . . . . . . . . . . : Yes
    Autoconfiguration Enabled . . . . : Yes
    Link-local IPv6 Address . . . . . : fe80::b47d:79d8:6311:f222%12(Preferred)
    IPv4 Address. . . . . . . . . . . : 192.168.1.76(Preferred)
    Subnet Mask . . . . . . . . . . . : 255.255.255.0
    Lease Obtained. . . . . . . . . . : Friday, December 24, 2010 10:32:00 PM
    Lease Expires . . . . . . . . . . : Saturday, December 25, 2010 10:34:53 PM
    Default Gateway . . . . . . . . . : 192.168.1.254
    DHCP Server . . . . . . . . . . . : 192.168.1.254
    DHCPv6 IAID . . . . . . . . . . . : 344501789
    DHCPv6 Client DUID. . . . . . . . : 00-01-00-01-13-FB-9C-7A-00-26-4D-F3-00-FF

    DNS Servers . . . . . . . . . . . : 192.168.1.254
    NetBIOS over Tcpip. . . . . . . . : Enabled

Wireless LAN adapter Wireless Network Connection:

    Connection-specific DNS Suffix  . : gateway.2wire.net
    Description . . . . . . . . . . . : Atheros AR9285 Wireless Network Adapter
    Physical Address. . . . . . . . . : 00-26-4D-F3-00-FF
    DHCP Enabled. . . . . . . . . . . : Yes
    Autoconfiguration Enabled . . . . : Yes
    Link-local IPv6 Address . . . . . : fe80::c9b6:9c5d:e079:cc06%11(Preferred)
    IPv4 Address. . . . . . . . . . . : 192.168.1.75(Preferred)
    Subnet Mask . . . . . . . . . . . : 255.255.255.0
    Lease Obtained. . . . . . . . . . : Friday, December 24, 2010 11:03:05 PM
    Lease Expires . . . . . . . . . . : Saturday, December 25, 2010 11:03:06 PM
    Default Gateway . . . . . . . . . : 192.168.1.254
    DHCP Server . . . . . . . . . . . : 192.168.1.254
```

FIGURE 14.71 `ipconfig /all` **command output**

If a network device does not get an IP address properly from the DHCP server, use the `ipconfig /release` command. Then issue the `ipconfig /renew` command. A symptom of this is when the device gets an APIPA (IPv4) or link local (IPv6) address because a DHCP server is unavailable. Also ensure that the device is actually configured for DHCP. A message appears on Windows-based devices when two devices have been manually assigned the same IP address. Note that not all operating systems and/or devices do this. Check any device that has a manually configured IP address for any duplicate IP addresses that are causing an **IP address conflict**. Labs at the end of this chapter guide you through the processes of configuring a NIC and TCP/IP, and sharing network resources.

The `tracert` Command

The `tracert` command is also a commonly used tool in Microsoft, OS X, and Linux environments. The `tracert` command is used to display the path a packet takes through the network. The benefit of using the `tracert` command is that you can see where a fault is occurring in a larger network. You can also see the network latency. Network latency is the delay measured from source to destination and results in **slow transfer speeds**. The `tracert` command is also good to use when you have intermittent connectivity. An example of output from the command is as follows:

```
C:\Users\Cheryl>tracert comptia.org
Tracing route to comptia.org [198.134.5.6] over a maximum of 30 hops:
  1    <1 ms    <1 ms    <1 ms   vankman1 [192.168.1.1]
  2     8 ms     7 ms     8 ms   10.126.208.1
  3    10 ms     8 ms     7 ms   72-31-92-20.net.bhntampa.com [72.31.92.20]
  4    11 ms    14 ms    12 ms   ten0-6-0-11.tamp27-car1.bhn.net [71.44.3.186]
  5    17 ms    16 ms    19 ms   hun0-4-0-3.tamp20-car1.bhn.net [72.31.117.170]
  6    22 ms    19 ms    18 ms   ten0-8-0-0.orld71-CAR1.bhn.net [71.44.1.211]
  7    17 ms    16 ms    19 ms   72-31-217-88.net.bhntampa.com [72.31.217.88]
  8    23 ms    19 ms    14 ms   10.bu-ether15.orldfljo00w-bcr00.tbone.rr.com
     [66.109.6.98]
  9    36 ms    31 ms    31 ms   bu-ether18.atlngamq47w-bcr01.tbone.rr.com
     [66.109.1.72]
 10    23 ms    23 ms    24 ms   0.ae2.pr1.atl20.tbone.rr.com [107.14.17.188]
 11    26 ms    29 ms    23 ms   67.106.215.89.ptr.us.xo.net [67.106.215.89]
 12    50 ms    51 ms    50 ms   207.88.13.54.ptr.us.xo.net [207.88.13.54]
 13    52 ms    56 ms    49 ms   207.88.12.174.ptr.us.xo.net [207.88.12.174]
 14    50 ms    51 ms    51 ms   207.88.12.31.ptr.us.xo.net [207.88.12.31]
 15    49 ms    57 ms    55 ms   ae0d0.mcr1.chicago-il.us.xo.net [216.156.0.162]
 16    54 ms    52 ms    53 ms   216.55.11.62
 17    52 ms    60 ms    52 ms   198.134.5.6
Trace complete.
```

The `nslookup` Command

The `nslookup` command is a program tool that helps with DNS server troubleshooting. Nslookup enables you to see domain names and their associated IP addresses. When an Internet site (server) cannot be contacted by its name but can be contacted using its IP address, there is a DNS problem. The `nslookup` command can make troubleshooting these types of problems easier. To see this tool in action, bring up a command prompt, type `nslookup http://www.pearsonhighered.com` and press (Enter). The IP address of the Pearson web server appears. Type `quit` to return to the command prompt.

The `net` Command

The `net` command is used to manage just about everything on a network from a command prompt. The `net` command is followed by other options and each option has different parameters. Here is the actual command syntax:

```
net [ accounts | computer | config | continue | file | group | help |
helpmsg | localgroup | name | pause | print | send | session | share |
start | statistics | stop | time | use |user | view ]
```

Table 14.22 lists some of the more commonly used `net` command options.

TABLE 14.22 `net` command options and descriptions

Command	Description
net help	Used to get help for the `net` commands. You can also use `net help` followed by the command (`net help computer`) or `net computer /help` or `net computer /?`.
net computer	Used to add or remove a computer from a Microsoft domain.
net config	Used to display information about the Server or Workstation service.
net stop	Used to stop a network service.
net start	Used to start a network service.
net share	Used to create, remove, or view network share resources
net use	Used to map a drive letter to a network resource.
net user	Used to manage user accounts.
net view	Used to view network devices.

The `netdom` command

A similar command is `netdom`, which is used to manage workstations in a domain environment. Use the `netdom /?` command to see all the options. Table 14.23 shows some of the more popular commands.

TABLE 14.23 `netdom` command options and descriptions

Command	Description
netdom add	Used to add a workstation account to the domain
netdom remove	Used to remove a workstation from the domain
netdom reset	Used to reset the connection between a workstation and a network domain controller
netdom resetpwd	Used to reset the computer account password
netdom verify	Used to verify the connection between a workstation and a Microsoft domain controller
netdom join	Used to join a workstation to a domain
netdom renamecomputer	Used to rename a computer and its domain account

NIC Troubleshooting

The following list contains methods that can help with NIC troubleshooting:

> From a command prompt window, use `ping localhost` to test the NIC.
> Ping another device on the same network.
> Ping the default gateway.

> Ping a device on a remote network.
> Use the `tracert` command to see if the fault is inside or outside the company.
> Check the status light(s) on the NIC (see Figure 14.72) to see if the physical connection is good. Different NICs have different colored lights, but the two most common colors used with status lights to indicate a good connection are green and orange. Some status lights indicate the speed at which the NIC is operating (10Mb/s, 100Mb/s, or 1Gb/s).
> Check the status light on the hub or switch (see Figure 14.73) that is used to connect the workstation NIC to the network. Green is a common color for a good connection on these devices.

Status lights

FIGURE 14.72   NIC status lights

> Check cabling. Even though the status lights may indicate that the connection is good, the cabling may still be faulty.
> Update the device driver by obtaining a newer one from the NIC manufacturer website.
> Check the IP addressing used. Use the `ipconfig` command from a prompt to ensure the NIC has an IP address assigned. If you get a duplicate IP address error message, change the IP addressing to DHCP or another statically assigned (not used already) address.

Status lights

FIGURE 14.73   Switch or hub status lights

> If on a mobile device, ensure that wireless is enabled and that the wireless NIC is enabled. Look for a button or a keystroke combination that re-enables the wireless antenna, as well as ensuring the NIC is not disabled in the *Network and Sharing Center* Control Panel.

> If your network connection on the desktop or from within the *Network and Sharing* Control Panel shows **limited connectivity** (see Figure 14.74) or you cannot reach the Internet at all, try rebooting the PC (because of a 169.254.x.x address) or the router (if in a home or small business network). If this is a wireless connection, check security settings, the wireless button that controls the wireless antenna, or a wireless key that toggles the wireless NIC. If wired, the cable could be an issue.

> If the network connection is intermittent or slow on a wireless connection, move closer to the AP, change the position of the wireless device, or add another AP in the area to extend the wireless network. If on a wired connection, check cabling and duplex settings. Replace a hub with a switch.

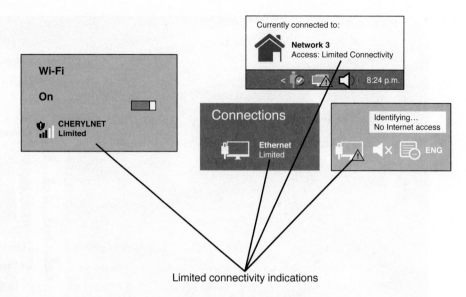

Limited connectivity indications

FIGURE 14.74   Windows limited connectivity network indications

Network Printers

Chapter 10 outlined how to share a printer across a network as well as access a wired or wireless network printer. Now that you know a bit more about networking, it might be easier to understand if you went back and reviewed those processes. **Printer sharing** is commonly done in a home or small business environment. In the corporate environment, a print server is used and printers are published or visible to network users. This printer may or may not be controlled by a printer server, but it will definitely have an IP address assigned. Users can perform **network printer mapping**, which enables network users to add the printer to their computer using the domain printer name or IP address. A print server or printer is assigned an IP address so that other devices on the network can use the printer. This is sometimes called **TCP printing** or TCP/IP printing. To find printers by name in a corporate network domain, do the following:

> Windows Vista/7: Use Windows Explorer to explore the network for printers.
> Windows 8/10: Use File Explorer to explore the network for printers.

You can also use the *Add Printer* Control Panel link > enable the *Select a shared printer by name* radio button and enter the domain name (an example might be the domain name of Schmidtworks in this format: \\Schmidtworks\) and select from the printers that list there. Another option is to add the printer using the printer's IP address. Network printers commonly have a front panel used to access network configuration settings. Printers that connect directly to the network through a wired or wireless connection have a statically configured IP address, mask, and default gateway. Many times technical support staff attach a label to the printer that shows the IP address. You could access the network settings from the printer control panel to view the assigned IP address. Refer to Chapter 10 for how to connect using the printer IP address.

Network Printer Troubleshooting

To begin troubleshooting a network printer, do all the things that are normally done when troubleshooting a local printer. Check the obvious things first. Does the printer have power? Is the printer online? Does the printer have paper? Are the printer's connector(s) secured tightly? Is the correct printer driver loaded? If all these normal troubleshooting steps check out correctly, the following list can help with networked printers:

> Print a test page and see if the printer's IP address outputs or see if the printer is labeled with its IP address. If so, ping the printer's IP address to see if there is network connectivity between the computer and the printer. Use the `tracert` command to see if there is a complete network path to the printer.
> Check the printer's *Properties* page to see if the printer has been paused.
> Cancel any print jobs in the print queue and resubmit the print job.
> Reset the printer by powering it off and back on. If it connects to a print server device, reset it, too.
> If the printer has never worked, try a different version of the print driver.

Network Servers

Servers are an important part of networking and provide different functionality. One server could provide more than one function. For example, a corporate server might serve the role of a web server as well as a DHCP server. Figure 14.75 shows several network servers mounted in a rack. Each physical box could contain several virtualized servers.

FIGURE 14.75   Network servers

Table 14.24 summarizes the most common servers found on a network.

TABLE 14.24   Server types and descriptions

Server type	Description
Web server	Used to provide web-based content that is accessed through a web browser that commonly requests the information through TCP port 80.
File server	Used to store files that can be accessed and managed from a remote location.
Print server	Used to manage one or more network printers. See Chapter 10 for more information.
DHCP server	Used to issue IP-related information including IP address, subnet mask, default gateway, DNS server, and domain name. Commonly has a block of addresses that are in a pool to be assigned to common devices like PCs and IP phones. A few addresses are reserved for statically assigned devices such as routers, switches, APs, and printers.

Server type	Description
DNS server	Used to translate domain names to IP addresses.
Proxy server	Used as a go-between between an application such as a web browser and a real server. Configuration details for how to configure a network device for a proxy server are found in Chapter 18.
Mail server	Also known as an email server. Used to maintain a database of email accounts, store messages (email) sent and received, communicate with other mail servers, and use the DNS protocol to locate other servers.
Authentication server	Used to verify credentials (usually username and password), such as when someone logs in to a domain workstation.

Embedded and Legacy Systems

An **embedded system** is a computer that has a specific function within a larger system. Embedded systems have many of the same components as a desktop or mobile computer: processor, RAM, flash memory, and ports. Embedded systems can be found everywhere including airports, manufacturing plants, medical equipment, electrical systems, mechanical systems, and telecommunication systems. Embedded systems tend to be self-contained, but they commonly attach to a wired or wireless network and may be part of an IT person's responsibility.

A **legacy system** is an outdated computer system or piece of network equipment that needs to be replaced or updated with something new, but is commonly kept because it might cost too much to replace it, it is used with a particular system that can't be replaced, or it provides a functionality that will not be needed too much longer. A legacy system might contain ports that require converters to be attached to the newer equipment, outdated methods used to access it, or proprietary cables that might not be easy to obtain or find. Legacy systems provide a challenge to technicians because of the lack of support and documentation, but still may be part of the job requirements.

Network Terminology

In the networking field, you must be familiar with a great many acronyms and terms. Table 14.25 shows a few of the most common terms.

TABLE 14.25   Common network terms

Term	Description
Address Resolution Protocol (**ARP**)	To send a message using the TCP/IP protocol stack, a computer needs four key addresses: source IP, source MAC, destination IP, and destination MAC. The computer sending the message knows its own source IP and MAC addresses. When the computer does not know the destination MAC address (but knows the destination IP address), ARP is used to discover that destination MAC address.
Backbone	The part of the network that connects multiple buildings, floors, networks, and so on together.
Bandwidth	The width of a communications channel that defines its capacity for data. Examples include up to 56Kb/s for analog modems, 64 to 128Kb/s for ISDN, and up to 100Gb/s for an Ethernet network.
Baseband	The entire cable bandwidth is used to transmit a digital signal. Because LANs use baseband, there must be an access method used to determine when a network device is allowed to transmit such as CSMA/CD.

Term	Description
Broadband	Cable bandwidth is divided into multiple channels. On these channels, simultaneous voice, video, and data can be sent.
Code Division Multiple Access (CDMA)	A protocol used in cellular networks as an alternative to GSM.
Common Internet File System (**CIFS**)	A version of Server Message Block (SMB) used for providing shared network access to files and printers.
FastEthernet	An extension of the original Ethernet standard that permits data transmission of 100Mb/s. FastEthernet uses CSMA/CD just like the original Ethernet standard.
Fiber Distributed Data Interface (FDDI)	A high-speed fiber network that uses the ring topology and the token passing method of access.
Global System for Mobile Communication (GSM)	The most widely used digital technology for cellular networks.
Hypertext Markup Language (HTML)	The programming language used on the Internet for creating web pages.
Internet Control Message Protocol (ICMP)	A Layer 3 protocol used when troubleshooting or evaluating networks. The `ping`, `pathping`, and `tracert` commands use ICMP.
Lightweight Directory Access Protocol (**LDAP**)	Used to access, maintain, and distribute directory/database-type information.
Network Address Translation/Port Address Translation (NAT/PAT)	A method of conserving IP addresses. NAT uses private IP addresses that become translated to public IP addresses. PAT does the same thing except it uses fewer public IP addresses by "overloading" one or more public IP addresses by tracking port numbers.
Point of Presence (POP)	A POP is an Internet access point. Note that POP also means Post Office Protocol, which is covered in the next section.
Simple Network Management Protocol (**SNMP**)	Used to monitor, communicate with, and manage network devices.
Secure Sockets Layer (SSL)	A protocol used to transmit Internet messages securely. This protocol is used with HTTPS and online shopping websites to secure credit card information.
Transmission Control Protocol (**TCP**)	A connection-oriented protocol that ensures reliable communication between two devices. TCP and UDP are the two most common transport layer protocols. TCP is used when a connection needs to be made, and if the data is not received, the data is re-sent. Website connections and some file transfer protocols use TCP.
User Datagram Protocol (**UDP**)	A Layer 4 connectionless protocol that applications use to communicate with a remote device. TCP and UDP are the two most common transport layer protocols. UDP is used when a connection is not that important, low overhead is needed (the UDP header is a lot smaller than a TCP header), or when speed is of the essence. VoIP and DHCP use UDP.

CHAPTER 14

Term	Description
Voice over IP (VoIP)	A method of sending a phone conversation over a data network instead of traditional telephone circuits and wiring. This can include connectivity through the Internet. VoIP can be implemented by installing software on your computer and using speakers or headphones and an integrated or external microphone. Another method can use special network-enabled phones that connect to an RJ-45 jack on your DSL or cable modem the same way your computer connects. In businesses, VoIP phones connect to an RJ-45 data jack that is wired to a PoE network switch. Most VoIP phones have a second RJ-45 port so that a PC can connect directly to the phone instead of having to have a second RJ-45 wall data jack wired to a switch. Corporate VoIP phones commonly use PoE.

The TCP/IP Model in Action

To see the TCP/IP model in action, imagine opening a web browser with two separate windows: http://www.pearsoned.com and http://www.google.com. Two separate packages of data would be formed. For example, because HTTP data is sent, HTTP specifies how the data is to be formatted at the application layer. So, web page 1 gets HTTP data at the application layer and moves down to the transport layer (inside the computer). At the transport layer, TCP is used for HTTP traffic, and TCP adds a source port number 51116 and a destination port number 80 as part of building the transport layer header. All this HTTP and TCP information moves down to the Internet layer, where IP adds a source and destination IP address. Because Pearson Education's web server has the IP address 74.125.47.99, that is the destination IP address. The packet continues moving down the model to the network access layer, and because the LAN is an Ethernet LAN, a source MAC address and destination MAC address are added. The data and all the headers are placed onto the Ethernet cable and sent on their way. The same thing happens with the second web page, except that at the transport layer, TCP adds port number 51117 and destination port number 80.

TECH TIP

Use `netstat` to view current connections

To see current connections and associated port numbers, bring up a command prompt and type `netstat`.

When the Pearson Education web server delivers the web page to the computer, the data is, of course, from the web server, but the TCP port numbers are reversed. The web server places port number 80 as the source port number and port number 51116 as the destination port number. The source and destination IP addresses and MAC addresses are reversed as well. When the original computer gets the message, it knows which browser window generated port number 51116, and it places the Pearson Education information from the web server into the correct browser window. The same is true when the Google request comes back from the Google web server. TCP/IP-based protocols are required to send and receive data through the Internet. Table 14.26 shows some of the most popular protocols, a description, and the TCP/IP port number commonly used. Table 14.27 has some of the common protocols or network standards and the TCP/IP model layer at which they operate.

TABLE 14.26 TCP/IP protocols and port numbers

Protocol	Common port number	Description
Apple Filing Protocol (**AFP**)	548	Provides file services for Mac OS X.
Domain Name System (DNS)	53	Translates Internet names and URLs into IP addresses.
File Transfer Protocol (**FTP**)	21	Sends/receives files from one computer to another network device; actually requires two port numbers: one to issue commands and the other one for data. Port 20 is sometimes used for data but not always.
Hypertext Transfer Protocol (**HTTP**)	80	Provides browser-based Internet communication (see Figure 14.76).
HTTP over SSL (Secure Sockets Layer) (**HTTPS**)	443	Provides encrypted HTTP communication through an SSL session.
IMAP (Internet Message Access Protocol)	143	Supports email retrieval. Allows synchronization from multiple devices.
NetBIOS over TCP/IP (**NetBT**)	137-139	Supports outdated applications that rely on the NetBIOS API to use a TCP/IP-based network. Also known as NBT.
Network Time Protocol (NTP)	123	Synchronizes time between network devices.
Post Office Protocol version 3 (**POP3**)	110	Supports email retrieval and stores email on a single network device (contrast with IMAP).
Remote Desktop Protocol (**RDP**)	3389	Connects one Windows-based computer to a remote Windows computer.
Secure File Transfer Protocol (SFTP)	22	Supports file transfer using the SSH protocol suite.
Service Location Protocol (**SLP**)	427	Announces and discovers services in a LAN.
Server Message Block (**SMB**)/ CIFS (Common Internet File System)	445	Provides access to shared network devices, files, and printers especially in a mixed environment such as a combination of MAC and Windows computers. CIFS is a version of SMB. SMB/CIFS can use TCP port 445, but when used with the NetBIOS API, UDP ports 137 and 138 as well as TCP ports 137 and 139 are used (see NBT).
SMTP (Simple Mail Transfer Protocol)	25	Transmits email and commonly used with MIME (Multipurpose Internet Mail Extensions) to include non-ASCII character sets and other rich media content within the email.
SSH (Secure Shell)	22	Supports secure connectivity to a remote device and allows secure file transfer.
Telnet	23	Supports connecting to a remote network device; is not secure.

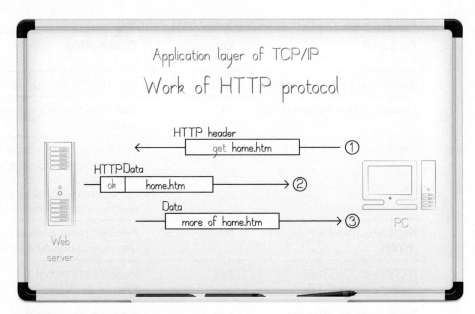

FIGURE 14.76 HTTP in action

TABLE 14.27 TCP/IP layers and associated protocols/standards

Layer	Protocols
Application	HTTP, HTTPS, Telnet, SSH, FTP, SFTP, DNS
Transport	TCP, UDP
Internet (Internetwork)	IP, DHCP, ICMP
Network access	ARP, 802.3 (Ethernet), 802.11a, b, g, n, and ac (wireless)

Using the Network and Sharing Center Control Panel

Even though you can control many things from the notification area or from some of the Settings options on Windows 8 and 10, the bulk of network configuration settings are done through the *Network and Sharing Center* Control Panel. The *Network and Sharing Center* Control Panel has been used both in this chapter and Chapter 13, but knowing the details and purpose of the options is important to IT personnel. Figure 14.77 shows the *Network and Sharing Center* window. Note that the options are the same in Windows 7, 8, and 10.

Notice in the main portion of the screen you see what network is currently being used. You can tell whether the connection is wired or wireless and the name of the network. You can also tell in home or small business networks if the computer can share files with others using the HomeGroup option (which is covered in the next section). This main screen is where you set up a dial-up, VPN, or broadband connection using the *Set up a new connection or network* link. You can also use the *Troubleshoot problems* link to help if issues arise.

Within the left pane are two important links: *Change adapter settings* and *Change advanced sharing s*ettings. The *Change adapter settings* link enables you access to the network adapters installed, as shown in Figure 14.78. If a network adapter is not listed that is installed in the computer, use *Device Manager* to troubleshoot and ensure the device is enabled through UEFI/system BIOS.

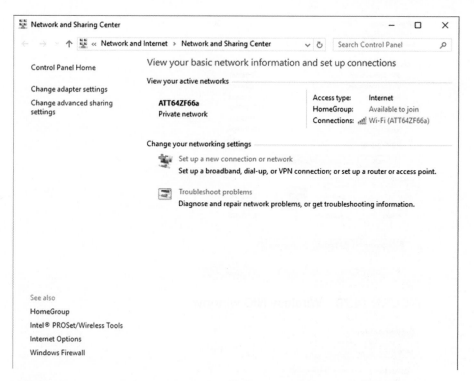

FIGURE 14.77   Windows 10 Network and Sharing Center window

FIGURE 14.78   Windows 10 Network Connections window

The *Network Connections* window is important when configuring an adapter. Here you can perform some of the following tasks:

> Double-click or tap the adapter icon to view device information. A wireless NIC shows wireless connectivity (see Figure 14.79), a wired NIC shows the wired network information (see Figure 14.80), and a Bluetooth adapter shows any Bluetooth pairs. At the bottom of each of the wired and wireless NIC windows, you can see the number of sent and received bytes (refer to Figures 14.79 and 14.80).

> The Details button within the wireless or wired NIC windows (*Wi-Fi Status or Local Area Connection Status*) displays information similar to that provided with the `ipconfig /all` command (see Figure 14.81).

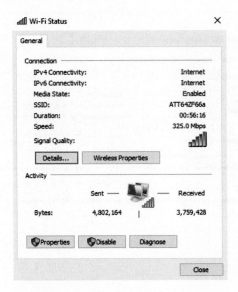

FIGURE 14.79   Wireless NIC window

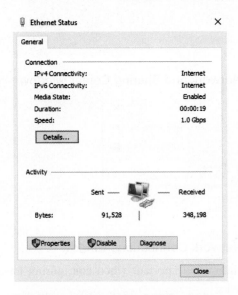

FIGURE 14.80   Wired NIC window

FIGURE 14.81   Wired or Wireless NIC details

> Select the *Wireless Properties* button from within the wireless NIC window (*Wi-Fi Status* window) to view information about the specific type of wireless network. Use the *Security* tab to view the type of security applied.

> Both the wireless and wired NIC windows have the *Properties* button where you can manually configure the NIC properties or modify one of the connections such as the TCP/IPv4 or TCP/IPv6 parameters (see Figure 14.82).

> By double-clicking or tapping the *Internet Protocol Version 4 (TCP/IPv4)* (or *TCP/IPv6*) link, you can configure the adapter for DHCP, statically assign an IP address, or complete an alternative configuration (refer back to Figures 14.61 and 14.62).

> By clicking or tapping the *Configure* button, set wired or wireless NIC-related settings such as speed and duplex (refer back to Figure 14.67).

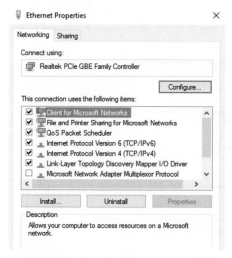

FIGURE 14.82   Wired or Wireless Networking Properties window

> Manually configure the wired or wireless NIC for a specific, nonbroadcasting wireless network (refer back to Figure 14.64).

> Set up a new Bluetooth connection. In Windows 7/8/10, access *Control Panel > View Devices and Printers > Add a device* link. Ensure the Bluetooth device is turned on and visible in the *Add a device* window (see Figure 14.83). Select the device and click *Next*. Sometimes, a PIN or passcode must be verified on both Windows and the device.

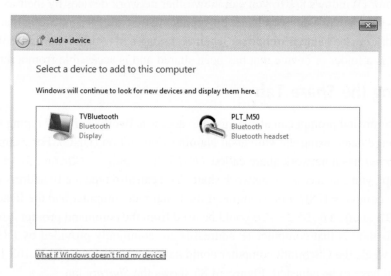

FIGURE 14.83   View Bluetooth devices in the Add a device window

Lastly, from the *Network and Sharing Center* Control Panel, you can select *Change advanced sharing settings*. These settings relate to what we cover next, sharing information across the networks you now are familiar with. Figure 14.84 shows the *Advanced sharing settings* window. Notice in Figure 14.84 there are three distinct and expandable sections: Private, Guest or Public, and All Networks. The Private section has been expanded, so you can see the options. You have seen this before in Chapter 10.

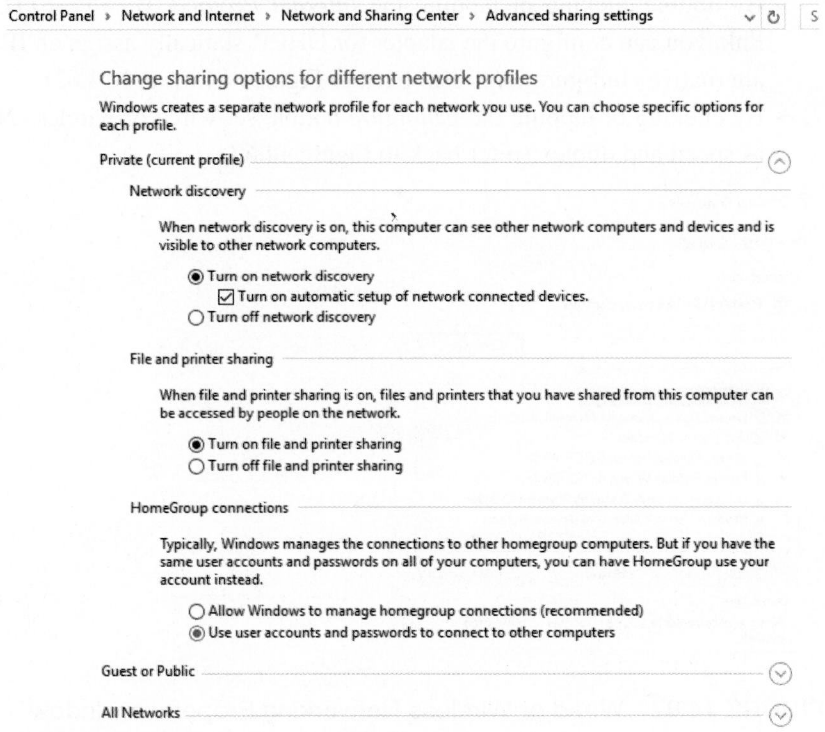

Control Panel > Network and Internet > Network and Sharing Center > Advanced sharing settings

Change sharing options for different network profiles

Windows creates a separate network profile for each network you use. You can choose specific options for each profile.

Private (current profile)

Network discovery

When network discovery is on, this computer can see other network computers and devices and is visible to other network computers.

○ Turn on network discovery
  ☑ Turn on automatic setup of network connected devices.
○ Turn off network discovery

File and printer sharing

When file and printer sharing is on, files and printers that you have shared from this computer can be accessed by people on the network.

○ Turn on file and printer sharing
○ Turn off file and printer sharing

HomeGroup connections

Typically, Windows manages the connections to other homegroup computers. But if you have the same user accounts and passwords on all of your computers, you can have HomeGroup use your account instead.

○ Allow Windows to manage homegroup connections (recommended)
○ Use user accounts and passwords to connect to other computers

Guest or Public

All Networks

FIGURE 14.84 Advanced sharing settings window

Introduction to Shared Folders

When you double-click the *Network* option from within Windows Explorer (Vista/7) or File Explorer (Windows 8/10), you can view other network devices by their assigned names. You can also view network device names by typing `nbtstat -n` at a command prompt. Knowing a network device name is important when accessing a network share across the network. A **network share** is a folder or device that has been shared and is accessible from a remote network device.

Using the *Share* Tab

The command prompt can also be used to access network shares by typing the computer name and the share name using the Universal Naming Convention (UNC). For example, a computer called *CSchmidt* has a network share called *TESTS*. By typing `\\CSchmidt\TESTS` at the command prompt, you can access the network share. You can also type the IP address of the computer instead of the computer UNC. For example, if the CSchmidt computer had the IP address of 192.168.10.5, `\\192.168.10.5\TESTS` could be used from the command prompt instead. The problem with this method is that computer IP addresses are commonly provided by DHCP and could change. Next week, the CSchmidt computer could have the IP address of 192.168.10.77 and the command would have to be adjusted. Figure 14.85 shows the *Sharing* tab.

FIGURE 14.85 Windows 7 Sharing tab

TECH TIP

How to share a folder

To share a folder, use *Windows Explorer/File Explorer*. Locate the folder to be shared and right-click it > *Properties* > *Sharing* tab > *Advanced Sharing* button. In the *Advanced Sharing* > *Share Name* textbox, type a name for the network share. This name appears in Windows Explorer/File Explorer—Network from other computers when accessed across the network.

Mapping to a Share

In a network, it is common to map a drive letter to a frequently used network share. To map a drive letter to a network share in Windows Vista or 7, click the *Start* button > *Computer* > *Map Network Drive* > select a drive letter in the *Drive* box > in the *Folder* textbox, type the UNC for the network share or use the *Browse* button to select the network share. The *Reconnect at Logon* checkbox allows you to connect to the mapped drive every time you log on.

In Windows 8 or 10, use File Explorer to locate and right-click or tap and briefly hold *This PC* > *Map network drive...* > select a drive letter in the *Drive* box > in the *Folder* textbox, type the UNC for the network share or use the *Browse* button to select the network share. The *Reconnect at Logon* checkbox allows you to connect to the mapped drive every time you log on. Figure 14.86 shows the windows to map drive letter Z: to the shared folder on the computer called CHERYL-PC. Expand the CHERYL-PC option to see the shared folders on this computer.

TECH TIP

Mapping from a prompt

A drive can be mapped from a command prompt. Use the net /? command for more help. For example, a computer with the name *TECH01* has a share called *Cheryl*. The following command can be used to attach to it using the drive letter M:

```
net use m: /persistent:yes \\TECH01\Cheryl
```

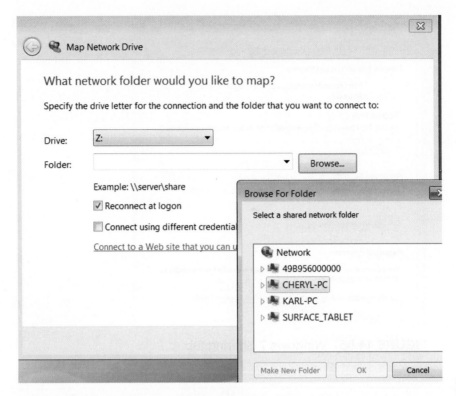

FIGURE 14.86   Windows 7 Map Network Drive window

Computer users commonly have network shares mapped to a drive letter for frequently used network shares. It is faster to access a network share by the drive letter than by searching around for the share through *Network*.

Creating a HomeGroup

Windows 7 and higher makes it easier to create a network at home with the *HomeGroup* option. Here are some pointers to be aware of with Windows HomeGroup:

> Windows 7, 8, and 10 versions can create a HomeGroup.
> Windows Starter and Home Basic versions can join but not create a HomeGroup.
> If Windows XP or Vista computers need to access information from a Windows 7, 8, or 10 computer that is on a HomeGroup network, then access the *User* Control Panel link on the Windows 7 computer to create a new *Standard user* account username and password. Then, from the XP or Vista computer, use Windows Explorer to access the *Network/My Network Places* option in the left panel. Double-click the Windows computer that has the shared documents. Enter the username and password that was created on the Windows computer. Double-click the *Users* share that appears in the window and all files and folders shared on the Windows computer are accessible.
> If a firewall other than the Windows firewall is active, the following ports need to be opened to find other PCs, find network devices, and use a HomeGroup: UDP ports 137, 138, 1900, 3540, 3702, and 5355; TCP ports 139, 445, 2869, 3587, 5357, and 5358.
> Each computer in the HomeGroup needs to have a unique name and belong to the same workgroup. These are changed from within the *System* Control Panel.
> From within the *Network and Sharing Center* window, ensure the network type is set to a home or work network.

To access the HomeGroup Wizard to create or join a network, access the *HomeGroup* Control Panel. Part of the process is to create a password that is used to add other computers to the HomeGroup. Another part of the configuration process is to determine what to share such as pictures, music, videos, documents, and printers. These particular libraries are then made available to other computers on the same network. On another computer, use the *HomeGroup* Control Panel and enter the password to join. Figure 14.87 shows the process for a computer to join a HomeGroup. Select the *Join now* button > select what folders to share > *Next* > enter the password that is on the computer that created the HomeGroup.

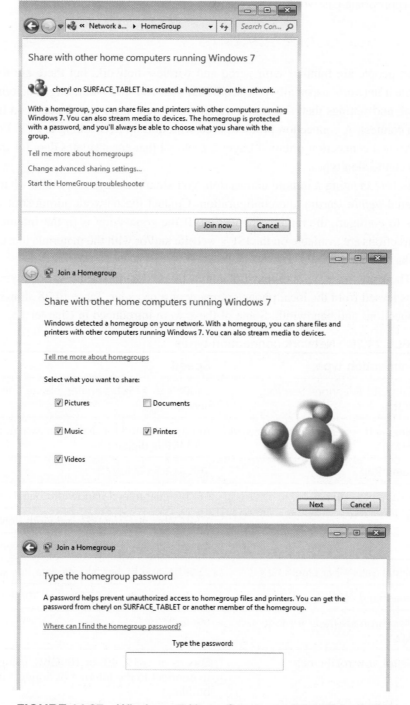

FIGURE 14.87   Windows 7 HomeGroup configuration window

For corporate users, you commonly must use a domain username (a username that has been configured on a centralized server) and a domain password. The rights you have been given determine the network resources you are allowed to access. Common parameters that must be entered when logging in to a domain to access corporate resources are a username and password. Commonly, the domain name must also be specified. If a company domain called GoBig had a user with the username JTech (who had the password 5tay-ouT), Joe Tech might be prompted for a username and password and have to type `GoBig\JTech` for the username because the *Domain_name\Username* format specifies the name of the domain and then the appropriate user ID, followed by the appropriate password in the password textbox.

Network Connectivity

Most people are familiar with wired and wireless network, but there are many methods used to create a network, especially a network that gets you into a building. The type of connection, protocol, and settings that you configure on the remote computer depends on the company to which you connect. A connection protocol used with dial-up networking is PPP. Point-to-Point Protocol (PPP) is a connection-oriented Layer 2 protocol that encapsulates data for transmission over various connection types.

Before creating a remote connection, you should always determine what parameters are to be entered *before* starting the configuration. Contact the network administrator for exact details on how to configure the remote connection. If the connection is to the Internet via an ISP, detailed instructions are available on the ISP's website and/or with the materials that come with the Internet package from the ISP.

There are many types of network connections. Businesses use various types of network connections leased from the local phone company or a provider. Table 14.28 shows the types of network connections and bandwidth. Some of these were introduced in Chapter 13.

TABLE 14.28 Network connection types

Connection type	Speed
Plain Old Telephone Service (POTS)	2400b/s to 115Kb/s analog phone line to perform dial-up networking
Integrated Services Digital Network (ISDN)	Another method for dial-up networking—64Kb/s to 1.544Mb/s digital line
Frame Relay	56K to 1.544Mb/s
56K point to point	56Kb/s guaranteed bandwidth between two points
T1	1.544Mb/s guaranteed bandwidth between two points
T3	44Mb/s guaranteed bandwidth between two points
Digital Subscriber Line (DSL)	256Kb/s and higher; shares data line with voice line
Broadband cable or satellite	56Kb/s (broadband satellite) to 30Mb/s and higher
Asynchronous Transfer Mode (ATM)	Up to 2Gb/s
MetroE (MetroEthernet)	Speeds of 1, 10, 40, or 100Gb/s, using Ethernet technology to connect to the Internet or connect multiple sites/buildings

Cloud Technologies

Cloud technologies were briefly introduced in Chapter 11 to discuss printing to the cloud. Because this is the networking chapter, you should learn a bit more about it because cloud technologies are so prevalent in small, medium, and large businesses alike. So what does something being in the cloud mean? It simply means the network device, application, storage, connectivity, server, and more are not located within the company's physical location. Cloud technologies have been around for years! Think of a small business that doesn't have the resources or manpower to create and maintain a web server. That web server is hosted elsewhere and considered "in the cloud" or out on the Internet somewhere (see Figure 14.88).

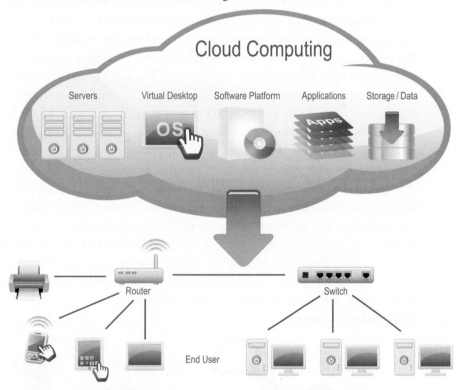

FIGURE 14.88 Concept of "in the cloud"

There are different types of services provided by cloud vendors, which are outlined in Table 14.29.

TABLE 14.29 Cloud service types

Cloud service type	Description
Software as a Service (**SaaS**)	Applications such as a learning management system, enterprise resource planning (ERP), human resources management (HRM), payroll, antivirus, and inventory management that are hosted by another company.
Desktop as a Service (DaaS)	Users access a desktop that is managed by another company or the equipment is located elsewhere. This would simply be the computer in a virtual environment so that the company that uses this service does not have to worry about software licenses, technicians to maintain operating system updates, and backups.

Cloud service type	Description
Platform as a Service (**PaaS**)	Servers, databases, operating system, storage, and development tools provided in an outside environment to relieve the support burden on companies that need an environment to perform high-level programming and develop applications.
Infrastructure as a Service (**IaaS**)	Routers, switches, servers, virtual machines, load balancers, access points, storage, and any other infrastructure device that is provided through the online environment.

Cloud services can be deployed in a combination of ways: private, public, hybrid, and community. A **private cloud** is part of a company's network infrastructure located outside of the business in a remote location, but the company has responsibility for managing the software and/or hardware. For example, a college may purchase licenses for a learning management system (LMS) so that students can view grades and see assignments. The LMS could run on servers that are located in a remote vendor's location, but the college network administrators install, update, and maintain the responsibility for supporting the LMS. Large businesses tend to be the biggest users of a private cloud. With a private cloud deployment, the business doesn't have to worry about providing power, cooling, and space for the equipment and optionally can pay for redundant Internet access and equipment and other features from the cloud provider.

A **public cloud** is an environment operated by a cloud provider. The cloud provider provides services to all business sizes for a cost. Referring to the LMS example, the servers and software for the LMS could be provided by the LMS vendor who has the servers in a service provider's building. In a public cloud, the vendor or cloud provider has the responsibility for managing the software and/or hardware. In a public cloud deployment model, several companies would pay for the services of the public cloud vendor. For an LMS, many colleges would purchase the public cloud option and allow another company to configure, monitor, and maintain the LMS. Figure 14.89 shows this concept.

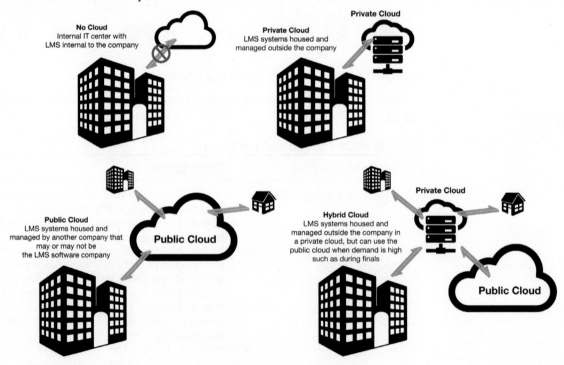

FIGURE 14.89   Cloud deployment models

A **hybrid cloud** is a combination of using a private cloud and a public cloud. The company using cloud services is responsible for the licensing and maintenance of the LMS in the private cloud but might need the services of additional storage or servers during peak times. A hybrid cloud solution could be implemented as a failover solution as well. The private cloud is used, but if a disaster occurs or during planned maintenance periods, the company uses the application in the public cloud instead. Figure 14.89 also includes the hybrid cloud model for the LMS example.

A **community cloud** is when a number of organizations have access to IT resources that are in the community cloud. An example of this might be an IT system that was created by a consortium of colleges in one state that was co-developing the system. The system could be housed in the cloud and tested on systems in the cloud. The cost for the community cloud would be shared by all colleges.

Cloud computing has many benefits to businesses. The costs related to the network operations center have increased due to the use of and reliance on technology. Common network center costs and overhead include power, hardware, hardware redundancy, storage, fire protection system, licensing, cabling/interconnectivity, and backups. Other advantages include the following:

> Corporate focus: Enables a company to focus on core IT services because an outside vendor can focus on its particular strengths (technical expertise on a particular product, staffing levels, quality of service, customer service, and so on).

> 24/7 access: Supports continuous access from anywhere and possibly any device (access is **on demand**).

> **Rapid elasticity**: Facilitates expanding software and/or hardware quickly. For example, if another server or more storage or more of anything was needed, the outside vendor has access to resources that allow expansion on demand. For some companies, if the system were an internal one, these types of expansion might take several months to requisition and obtain.

> **Resource pooling**: By using an outside vendor's services, a company can pool resources with other companies that have the same need. A vendor might have access to hundreds of servers. Company A needs just a few servers right now, but Company B has a high usage rate. The outside vendor can allocate servers to Company B to handle the load right now but later reallocate the additional servers to Company A when its usage increases. The outside vendor can do this easily because of **measured service**: the capability to track (and charge for) cloud consumer usage and apply resources when needed.

CHAPTER 14

SOFT SKILLS—BEING PROACTIVE

A good technician is proactive, which means that the technician thinks of ways to improve a situation, anticipates problems, and fixes them before being told to. A proactive technician follows up after a service call to ensure that a repair fixed the problem rather than waiting for another help desk ticket that states that the problem is unresolved. When something happens or a problem with a customer occurs, a proactive technician provides a list of recommended solutions or procedural changes to the supervisor rather than waiting for the supervisor to delineate what changes must occur.

For example, consider a technician at a college. The technician is responsible for any problems logged by computer users through the help desk. The technician is also responsible for maintaining the computer classrooms used by various departments. Each term, the technician reloads the computers with software updates and changes requested by the teachers. A proactive technician checks each machine and ensures that the computers boot properly and that the load is successful.

Another example involves checking new software. When the computers are reloaded each term, a faculty member is asked to check the load. A proactive technician has a list of "standard" software loaded on the computer such as the operating system, service pack level, and any applications that are standard throughout the college. A separate list would include the changes that were applied to the computer. Then the faculty member can simply look at the list and verify the load. Being proactive actually saves both the technician and the faculty member time.

The opposite of proactive is reactive. A reactive technician responds to situations only when there is a problem reported. The technician is not looking for ways to avoid problems. For example, a proactive technician ensures a computer is configured with automatic updates of virus scanning software. A reactive technician waits until a help desk ticket is created for a computer that exhibits unusual behavior. (It has a virus.)

As a student, practice being proactive. Start an assignment a day before you would normally start it. Talk to your teacher about your grade in advance (before the day preceding the final). Bring something to write with and paper to school. Lastly, take this practice into your IT career. Be proactive as an IT professional and increase the level of service and professionalism to the field.

Chapter Summary

> Networks are created to share data and devices and connect to the Internet. Types of networks include PANs, LANs, MANs, and WANs.
> Networks can be wired or wireless. Wired networks use copper (UTP, STP, and coaxial) or fiber-optic media.
> A workgroup/HomeGroup network is composed of a small number of computers, whereas the client/server type of network is used in companies in a domain environment. A domain environment has a server that provides authentication to resources with a centralized user ID and password. A workgroup network manages the usernames on a computer-by-computer basis, which grows less secure and more difficult to manage as the network grows. A Microsoft HomeGroup network has a single password.
> Ethernet is the most common type of LAN and is wired in a star or extended star topology. A hub or switch is used to connect the devices. Each network connects to a router for communication with other networks. The router's IP address is the default gateway for all network devices on a particular LAN.
> Computers must have IP addresses to participate in a TCP/IP-based network (and gain access to the Internet). IPv4 is the most common addressing used on computers today, but IPv6 addresses are slowly being assigned and used by corporate devices and Internet providers.

> IP addresses are grouped by classes, with a particular subnet mask for each class. Each default mask can be changed to further subdivide a network for more efficient and manageable addressing. DHCP can provide addresses to network devices or a static address can be assigned. Public addresses are routable on the Internet. Private addresses are used within homes and companies. These addresses can be translated using NAT/PAT to public addresses.

> TCP/IP is a suite of protocols that includes the following important ones: FTP, Telnet, SMTP, DNS, HTTP, HTTPS, POP3, IMAP, RDP, DNS, LDAP, SNMP, SSH, SFTP, TCP, UDP, IP, AFP, and ICMP.

> The OSI model is a theoretical model with seven layers: application, presentation, session, transport, network, data link, and physical. The TCP/IP model is a working model and contains four layers: application, transport, Internet (internetwork), and network access. Common application protocols include TFTP, FTP, SFTP, Telnet, SMTP, DNS, HTTP, HTTPS, POP3, LDAP, DNS, SNMP, and SSH. The device and applications that work at Layer 3 (network or Internet layers) include a router, IP, and ICMP. The devices and applications that work at Layer 2 (data link or network access) include a switch, access point, and ARP. Keep in mind that Ethernet has Layer 2 specifications. That is why a MAC address is a Layer 2 address. The devices that work at Layer 1 (physical or network access) are cable, connectors, hubs, and wireless antennas.

> 802.11 and Bluetooth are types of wireless networks. Bluetooth is used in PANs, and 802.11 is used in wireless LANs. 802.11 wireless NICs include 802.11a, b, g, n, and ac. 802.11a, n, and ac work in the 5GHz range; 802.11b, g, and n work in the 2.4GHz range. 802.11 antennas are either directional or omnidirectional.

> The key tools for troubleshooting a networked computer are the `ipconfig`, `ping`, `nslookup`, and `tracert` commands, and a cable tester.

> Sharing can be done by sharing folders or by using a HomeGroup.

> Cloud technology services are classified as SaaS, IaaS, and PaaS. Cloud deployment models include private, public, hybrid, and community.

> A technician should be proactive as opposed to reactive and should prevent problems and situations whenever possible.

CHAPTER 14 (side tab)

A+ CERTIFICATION EXAM TIPS

✓ This chapter provides information related to both the 220-901 and 220-902 exams. The information related to the 902 exam is how to create a HomeGroup, the *Network and Sharing Center* Control Panel, and network installation items (alternative address, dial-up, wireless, wired WWAN [Cellular], NIC properties, network shares, and drive mapping). Review these items before the 902 exam.

✓ Know the difference between a LAN, WAN, PAN, and MAN.

✓ Know the purpose of the network devices: hub, router, access point, bridge, modem, firewall, patch panel, repeaters/extenders, and switch. Review EoP and PoE.

✓ Know the purpose of key network protocols, port numbers used by the protocols, and the difference between TCP and UDP.

✓ Know when to use a particular type of networking tool, whether it is a physical tool or a command.

✓ Know what to do when one or more computers cannot connect to the Internet or when they have an IP address conflict.

✓ Know how to manually configure an IP address on a computer, an AP, a printer, or any other network device.

✓ Know how to configure an alternative configuration on a computer.

✓ Know how to effectively use the following commands: `ipconfig`, `ifconfig`, `tracert`, `netstat`, `nbtstat`, `net`, `netdom`, `nslookup`, and `ping`.

✓ Know the different types of wireless networks and their compatibility with each other.

✓ Understand the need to assign 2.4GHz and 5GHz channels so multiple wireless APs can coexist.

✓ Know the purpose of an IP address, a default gateway, and a subnet mask.

✓ Know the difference between an IPv4 address and an IPv6 address.

✓ Recognize when an address is a private IP address and understand the difference between a public IP address and a private IP address.

✓ Know the different types of network cabling and connectors.

✓ Know the difference between SaaS, PaaS, and IaaS and the four types of cloud deployment.

✓ Know the meaning of the terms rapid elasticity, on-demand, resource pooling, and measured service as it relates to cloud computing.

✓ Know what legacy systems and embedded systems are and that they may have to be supported.

✓ Know port numbers for the following protocols: 21 (FTP), 22 (SSH), 23 (Telnet), 25 (SMTP), 53 (DNS), 80 (HTTP), 110 (POP3), 143 (IMAP), 443 (HTTPS), 3389 (RDP), 137-139 (NetBIOS/NetBT), 445 (SMB/CIFS), 427 (SLP), 548 (AFP).

✓ Know the purpose of the following protocols: DHCP, DNSS, LDAP, SNMP, SMB, CIFS, SSH, AFP, and TCP vs. UDP.

✓ Know the purpose of different servers: web, file, print, DHCP, DNS, proxy, mail, and authentication.

Key Terms

CHAPTER 14

Review Questions

1. Match the network type on the left with the scenario on the right.

   ____ MAN   **a.** Home network of four PCs

   ____ LAN   **b.** City of Schmidtville networks

   ____ PAN   **c.** Hewlett-Packard corporate networks

   ____ WAN   **d.** Bluetooth network of two devices

2. Match the following. Note that even though an answer may be valid for more than one answer, only one answer will allow all answers to be used. No term is used twice.

   a. CAT 3 UTP   ____ Common type of LAN cable

   b. CAT 6 UTP   ____ Delivers TV stations inside a home

   c. Coax   ____ Voice-grade phone network cable

   d. Fiber   ____ Backbone cable

3. When installing UTP, what is the most common mistake technicians make?

   _____

   _____

   _____

4. Match the TCP/IP model layer to the description. Note that a layer can be used more than once.

   a. Application   ____ HTTP   ____ a straight-through cable   ____ a NIC

   b. Transport   ____ a router   ____ UDP   ____ DNS

   c. Internet   ____ a switch   ____ IP   ____ TCP

   d. Network access   ____ ICMP   ____ MAC address   ____ a wireless antenna

5. Explain the difference between half-duplex and full-duplex transmissions.

   _____

   _____

6. What does the *1000* mean in the term 1000BaseT?

   _____

7. Which network device works at Layer 1 and sends received data out all its ports (except the port that received the data)?

   _____

8. What is the most common network protocol suite and the protocol suite required to communicate on the Internet?

   _____

9. Which type of address is 48 bits long?

   _____

10. Which type of address is called a Layer 3 address?

    _____

11. Which type of IP address uses 128 bits? [IPv4 | IPv32 | IPv6 | IPv64]

12. Draw a vertical line between the network number and the host number for each of the following IP addresses (assuming the default subnet mask):

    141.2.195.177

    193.162.183.5

    100.50.70.80

13. What protocol could be used to issue an IP address to network devices?
    [DNS | DHCP | ICMP | ARP]

14. What protocol is used to convert URLs to IP addresses?
    [HTTP | SSH | SSL | UDP | DNS]

15. Two access points connect and extend *the same* wireless network. List the SSIDs for each access point in the following chart.

Access point	SSID
Access Point 1	
Access Point 2	

16. Two access points (AP1 and AP2) operating in the 2.4GHz range have overlapping coverage areas. List the two channel IDs to assign to each access point by filling in the following chart.

Access point	Channel ID
AP1	
AP2	

17. Two 802.11n access points (AP1 and AP2) operating in the 5GHz range have overlapping coverage areas. List the two channel IDs to assign to each access point by filling in the following chart.

Access point	Channel ID
AP1	
AP2	

18. [T | F] When communicating with an access point, a wireless NIC and an access point must be configured to the same frequency.

19. Match the following definitions. Note that not all options on the right are used.

    ____ 802.11a   a. Operates in the 2.4GHz range, with speeds up to 54Mb/s

    ____ 802.11b   b. Operates in the 2.4GHz range, with speeds up to 2Mb/s

    ____ 802.11g   c. Operates in the 2.4GHz range, with speeds up to 11Mb/s

    ____ 802.11i   d. Security specification

    ____ 802.11n   e. Operates in the 5GHz range, with speeds up to 54Mb/s

    ____ 802.11ac   f. Specifies interoperability between access points

                     g. Standard for quality of service

                     h. Standard for wireless interference

                     i. Backward compatible with 802.11a, b, and g

                     j. Allows eight simultaneous data streams

20. Reference Figure 14.90. What IP address is the default gateway for host 203.145.15.2?

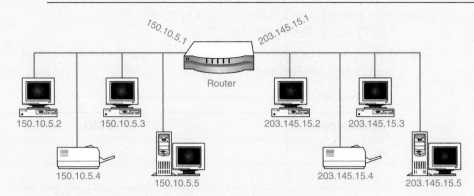

FIGURE 14.90 Review question network scenario

21. Which command determines whether another network device is reachable?

22. A company outsources corporate payroll to a company that provides a cloud-based solution. What type of cloud service is provided? [DaaS | SaaS | PaaS | IaaS]

23. Which type of server issues IP addresses to network hosts? [DHCP | proxy | mail | DNS]

24. What command can be used to see a computer's MAC address?
[netdom | net | netstat | ipconfig /all]

25. A company has its email server in the cloud. The company has a network administrator assigned to maintain and manage the email server. Which cloud deployment model is used? [community | private | public | hybrid]

Exercises

Exercise 14.1 Wireless AP Paper Configuration

Objective: To determine what menu item would be used for specific functions

Procedure: Use the given menu options to determine which one would be used to perform a common configuration task on a wireless AP.

Note: Many times an IT professional must deal with a device or a particular model that is unfamiliar. Many wireless AP menus are similar so practicing which menu option might be the one chosen is a good activity.

Wireless AP Sample menu and submenu options:

A. Setup—Language, Date/Time

B. Wireless—Basic Wireless Settings, Wireless Security, Wireless MAC Filter, Advanced Wireless Settings

C. WAN/LAN—Internet Setup and Network Setup

D. Administration—Management, Access, Security, Factory Defaults, Firmware Upgrade

E. Status—Access Point, Wireless Network, About

Select which menu option would be used to do the following:

_____   1. Change the password used to access the AP menu.

_____   2. Configure for UPnP.

_____   3. Configure to only allow 802.11n 2.4GHz devices to attach (not 802.11b or g).

_____   4. Check connectivity with another device.

_____   5. Change the SSID.

_____   6. Disable SSID broadcasting.

_____   7. Configure the device as a DHCP server for wireless clients.

_____   8. Set the year.

_____   9. Reset the device.

_____   10. Determine how many wireless hosts are currently attached to the AP.

Exercise 14.2 T568B Color Sequence

Objective: To articulate the proper colored order of a T568B straight-through cable

Procedure: Use the given graphic to denote which color of cable goes into the connector from left to right.

Use Figure 14.91 to designate which color of vinyl insulator should go into the connector to make a T568B connector.

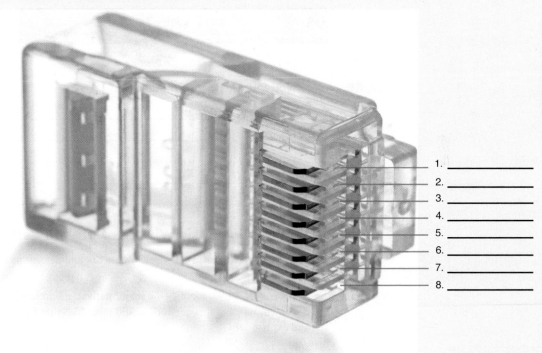

FIGURE 14.91   RJ-45 connector/cabling exercise

1. _____   5. _____

2. _____   6. _____

3. _____   7. _____

4. _____   8. _____

Exercise 14.3 Network Device Recognition

Objective: To recognize a network device on sight

Procedure: Use the given graphics to identify each network device.

Use Figure 14.92 to identify each network device.

Note: Possible answers could include the following. Note that not all devices are used. No device is shown twice.

Possible devices:

Internet router	Termination plate	Switch
Hub	Patch panel	Repeater
Bridge	Wireless router	Firewall

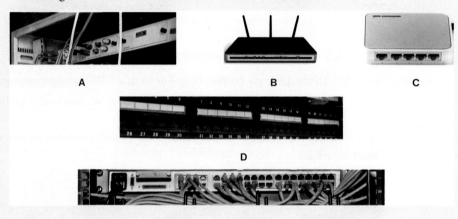

FIGURE 14.92   Network device identification

a._____

b._____

c._____

d._____

e._____

Exercise 14.4 Identifying Basic Wireless Network Parts

Objective: To identify basic parts of a wireless network and determine the type of wireless network used

Procedure: Using Figure 14.93, identify the major parts of a wireless network. For the number 5 blank, document whether this network would most likely be for a home or a corporate network and explain why.

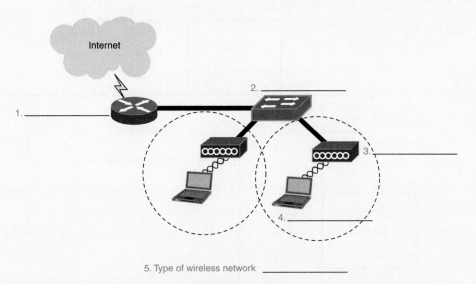

FIGURE 14.93   Wireless network components

1._____

2._____

3._____

4._____

5._____

Exercise 14.5 Wireless Network Case Study

Objective: To design and price a wireless network based on the parameters given

Parts: Computer with Internet access

Note: The instructor or lab assistant can speak on behalf of the faculty members if any design questions arise.

Scenario: A building has just been renovated to include faculty offices and two new classrooms, as shown in Figure 14.94. The only wired networks are in the computer classroom (not shown) and the administrator's office (not shown). The wired network allows access to the Internet. The wired network connections are in the wiring closet shown in the diagram at the intersection of the two hallways. Five faculty members are issued laptop computers. The laptops do not include wireless NICs. The faculty members want to use their laptops in their classrooms and offices. There are also comfortable chairs in the hallways, and faculty would like to use their laptops in the hallways as well. The faculty would like (1) access to the Internet and (2) access to a printer. Currently, there are no printers in the classrooms or the faculty area that they can use.

CHAPTER 14

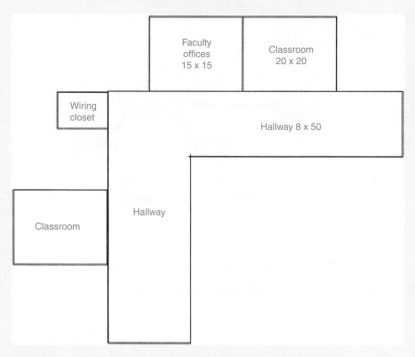

FIGURE 14.94   Building floor plan for wireless design

Tasks:

> Design a wireless network to allow faculty to use their laptops and gain access to the Internet. Provide this drawing in an electronic form to the instructor. This can be done in Word, Visio, PowerPoint, or some other drawing program.

> Provide a detailed list of wireless network parts, part numbers, prices, and a web link where the prices were obtained. This will include the antenna type, a printout of the wireless antenna radiation pattern, and antenna coverage range.

> Provide the instructor with a typewritten list of policies and configuration settings for the wireless network. You are the designer and implementer and what you decide goes.

Exercise 14.6 Network Number and Broadcast Address Practice Lab

Objective: To determine the subnet number, broadcast address, and IP addresses that can be assigned to network devices

Parts: None needed

Procedure: Complete the following procedure and answer the accompanying questions.

1.   Determine the network address for the following IP address assuming that the default subnet mask is used.

   210.141.254.122

   206.240.195.38

   14.130.188.213

   129.89.5.224

   110.113.71.66

2. Determine the broadcast address for the following IP address assuming that the default subnet mask is used.

166.215.207.182

198.94.140.121

97.57.210.192

133.98.227.36

14.89.203.133

Exercise 14.7 CIDR Notation Practice Lab

Objective: To determine the appropriate CIDR notation based on a given subnet mask

Parts: None needed

Procedure: Complete the following procedure and answer the accompanying questions.

Determine the CIDR notation based on the subnet mask given in dotted decimal notation.

255.255.255.0

255.255.255.224

255.255.255.252

255.255.254.0

255.255.0.0

255.255.255.128

255.255.255.192

255.0.0.0

255.255.240.0

255.255.255.240

Activities

Internet Discovery

Objective: To access the Internet to obtain specific information regarding a computer or its associated parts

Parts: Access to the Internet

Procedure: Complete the following procedure and answer the accompanying questions.

1. On an HP Pavilion dm3z laptop, you cannot get the wireless NIC to attach to the wireless network. What are some steps you can take, as recommended by HP, to help in this situation?

Write at least three solutions as well as the URL where you found the solution.

_____

_____

_____

_____

_____

_____

_____

2.   What does the term Wake on Wireless mean and at what URL did you locate the answer?

_____

_____

_____

_____

_____

3.   Locate a type of cloud service that is not SaaS, DaaS, PaaS, or IaaS. Write the cloud service type, its purpose, and the URL where you found this information.

_____

_____

_____

_____

4.   Find an Internet forum that discusses Bluetooth and Windows 7 on Lenovo laptops. Write one key piece of information you found about configuring Bluetooth. Write the URL where you found the information.

_____

_____

5.   Find an Internet site that explains the differences between CAT 5e and CAT 6 UTP cable. Write which standard you would recommend to the CIO and why. List the URL where you found this information.

_____

_____

_____

_____

_____

_____

Soft Skills

Objective: To enhance and fine-tune a technician's ability to listen, communicate in both written and oral form, and support people who use computers in a professional manner

Activities:

1.   Using the Internet, find and access a utility that tests your soft skills. Compare your scores with others in the class and determine how you might improve in specific weak areas.

_____

_____

2.   In groups of two, one person puts a network problem in a computer, while the other person is out of the room. When the other person comes back, they troubleshoot the problem by asking questions of the user (as if they were on the phone helping them). The person performing the troubleshooting cannot touch the computer. Discuss strategies for doing this better before swapping roles.

3.   In groups of two or three, brainstorm three examples of a technician being reactive rather than proactive. List ways the technician could have been more proactive for each example. Share your findings with other teams.

Critical Thinking Skills

Objective: To analyze and evaluate information as well as apply learned information to new or different situations

Activities:

1.   A home user connects to the Internet. The ISP provides hard drive space for the user's web page. Is this a network? Why or why not? Write your answer in a well-written paragraph using good grammar, capitalization, and punctuation.

2.   Use the Internet, magazines, newspapers, or books to find a network installation case study. Make a table of terms they use that were introduced in this chapter. On the left side, list the term and, on the right side, define or describe how the term relates to the network installation. Analyze the installation and discuss with a team. Make a checklist of approved processes and of recommended changes to implemented processes. Share your team findings with the class.

3.   In a team environment, design a wired and wireless network for a small business with 10 computers. Name the business, provide a design and implementation plan, and provide a list of items for which you should do more research. Share your plan with the class.

Labs

Lab 14.1 Creating a Straight-Through CAT 5, 5e, or 6 Network Patch Cable

Objective: To create a functional CAT 5, 5e, or 6 UTP network cable

Parts: UTP cable

              RJ-45 connectors

              Stripper/crimper tool

              UTP cable tester

Note: Standard Ethernet networks are cabled with either UTP cable or RG-58 coaxial cable. In this exercise, you create a standard cable for use with Ethernet networks connected through a central hub or switch.

Procedure: Complete the following procedure and answer the accompanying questions.

1.   Category 5 and higher UTP cable consists of four twisted pairs of wires, color coded for easy identification. The color-coded wires are colored as follows:

     Pair 1: White/orange and orange

     Pair 2: White/blue and blue

     Pair 3: White/green and green

     Pair 4: White/brown and brown

2.   Using the stripper/crimper tool, strip approximately 1/2 inch (1 centimeter) of the protective outer sheath to expose the four twisted pairs of wires. Most strippers have a strip gauge to ensure stripping the proper length. See Figure 14.95.

     Note: To make it easier to sort the wire pairs, the sheathing can be stripped farther than 1/2 inch (1 centimeter), and the wires can be sorted properly and trimmed to the proper length.

CHAPTER 14

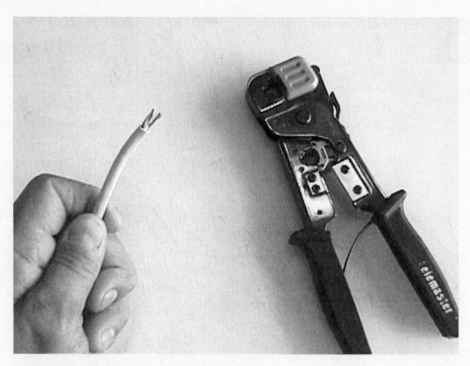

FIGURE 14.95   Strip the cable sheathing

3. Untwist the exposed wire pairs. Be careful that you do not remove more twist than necessary. Sort the wires according to the following:

    Wire 1: White/orange

    Wire 2: Orange

    Wire 3: White/green

    Wire 4: Blue

    Wire 5: White/blue

    Wire 6: Green

    Wire 7: White/brown

    Wire 8: Brown

    Ethernet cable utilizes wires 1, 2, 3, and 6. Using the preceding wiring scheme means that the cable will use the white/orange-orange and white/green-green wire pairs.

    Will both ends of the cable need to follow the same wiring schematic?

    _____

4. Insert the sorted and trimmed cable into an RJ-45 connector. The RJ-45 connector key (tang) should face downward with the open end toward you while you insert the wires. Verify that all eight wires fully insert into the RJ-45 connector and that they are inserted in the proper order. See Figure 14.96.

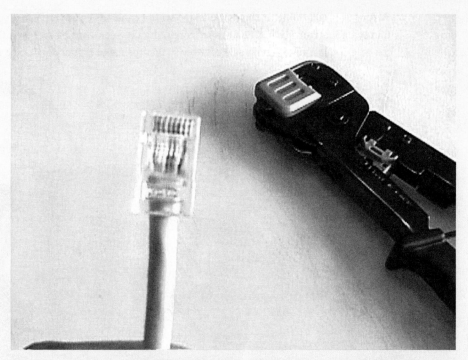

FIGURE 14.96 Push wires firmly into the RJ-45 connector in the correct color order

5. Insert the cable-connector assembly into the stripper/crimper tool and crimp the connector firmly. See Figure 14.97.

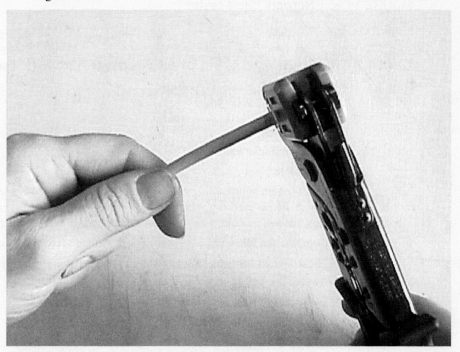

FIGURE 14.97 Crimp the RJ-45 connector firmly

6. Remove the cable/connector assembly from the stripper/crimper tool and verify that the wires fully insert into the connector and that they are in the proper order.

7. Repeat Steps 2 through 6 for the other end of the CAT 5 or higher UTP cable.

    Can the cable be used at this point? [Yes | No]

8. Before using the cable, it should be tested with a cable tester to verify that you have end-to-end continuity on individual wires and proper continuity between wire pairs. Insert the RJ-45 connector into the proper cable tester receptacle and verify that the cable is functional. See Figure 14.98.

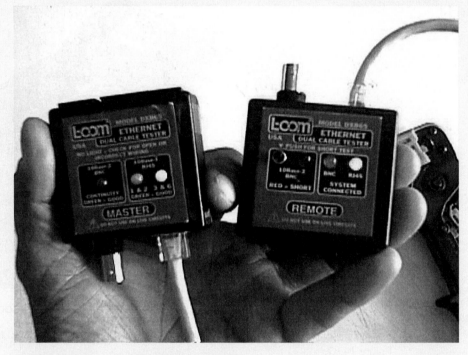

FIGURE 14.98 Network cable tester

Instructor initials: _____

Lab 14.2 Creating a CAT 5, 5e, or 6 Crossover Network Cable

Objective: To create a functional UTP crossover cable

Parts: UTP cable

RJ-45 connectors

Stripper/crimper tool

UTP cable tester

Note: In normal situations, straight-through UTP cable is used to connect to a central hub or switch. In this exercise, you create a crossover cable for use when directly connecting two network devices (computers *without* using a central hub or switch).

Procedure: Complete the following procedure and answer the accompanying questions.

1. Category 5, 5e, 6, and 7 UTP cable consists of four twisted pairs of wires that are color coded for easy identification. The color-coded wires are as follows:

Pair 1: White/orange and orange

Pair 2: White/blue and blue

Pair 3: White/green and green

Pair 4: White/brown and brown

2. Using the stripper/crimper tool, strip approximately 1/2 inch (1 centimeter) of the protective outer sheath to expose the four twisted pairs of wires. Most tools have a strip gauge to ensure stripping the proper length.

   Note: To make it easier to sort the wire pairs, the sheathing can be stripped farther than 1/2 inch (1 centimeter). The wires can then be sorted properly and trimmed to the proper length.

3. Untwist the exposed wire pairs. Be careful that you do not remove more twist than necessary. Sort the wires as follows:

   Wire 1: White/orange

   Wire 2: Orange

   Wire 3: White/green

   Wire 4: Blue

   Wire 5: White/blue

   Wire 6: Green

   Wire 7: White/brown

   Wire 8: Brown

   Ethernet networks utilize wires 1, 2, 3, and 6. Using the above wiring scheme means the cable will use the white/orange-orange and white/green-green wire pairs.

   When making a crossover cable, will both ends of the cable need to follow the same wiring schematic?

   _____

   _____

4. Insert the sorted and trimmed cable into an RJ-45 connector. The RJ-45 connector key (tang) should face downward with the open end toward you while you insert the wires. Verify that all eight wires fully insert into the RJ-45 connector, and that they are inserted in the proper order.

5. Insert the cable-connector assembly into the stripper/crimper tool, and crimp the connector firmly.

6. Remove the cable/connector assembly from the stripper/crimper tool, and verify that the wires are fully inserted into the connector and that they are in the proper order.

7. To create the crossover cable, the wire pairs must be put in a different order. To accomplish this, repeat Steps 2 through 6 on the *opposite* end of the cable, but when sorting the wire pairs, use the following color codes.

Wire 1: White/green	Wire 5: White/blue
Wire 2: Green	Wire 6: Orange
Wire 3: White/orange	Wire 7: White/brown
Wire 4: Blue	Wire 8: Brown

8. Verify both ends of the cables, ensuring that the tang is downward and the colored wires are in the correct order. You can also check the ends of the connectors to see if you see the tip of the copper wire pushed against the end. See Figure 14.99.

   Can the crossover cable be used at this point? [Yes | No]

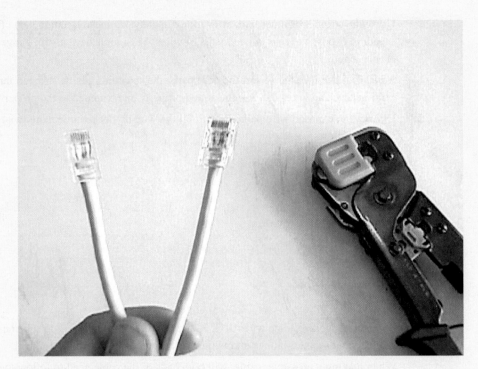

FIGURE 14.99 Verify the color codes on both connectors

9. Before using the crossover cable, it should be tested with a cable tester. This verifies that you have end-to-end continuity on individual wires and proper continuity between wire pairs. Insert the RJ-45 connector into the proper cable tester receptacle and verify that the cable is functional.

   Note: Your cable tester must have the capability to test crossover cables.

Instructor initials: _____

Lab 14.3 Exploring NIC Properties with Windows 7, 8, or 10

Objective: To examine and modify NIC properties including manually setting IP address information

Parts: One computer with Windows 7, 8, or 10 installed

Procedure: Complete the following procedure and answer the accompanying questions.

1. Power on the computer and log on to Windows, if necessary.

2. Access the *Network and Sharing Center* Control Panel.

3. Select the *Change adapter settings* link.

4. Double-click or tap the wired or wireless connection that is currently used to connect the computer to the network.

5. Select the *Details* button. Use Table 14.30 to document key pieces of information assigned to this NIC. Any property that is not shown, simply write *not applicable* for that setting.

TABLE 14.30   NIC lab documentation

Property	Setting
Physical (MAC) address	
DHCP Enabled	[Yes	No]
IPv4 Address	
IPv4 Subnet Mask	
Leased Obtained	
Lease Expires	
IPv4 Default Gateway	
IPv4 DHCP Server	
IPv4 DNS Server	
IPv6 Address	
IPv6 Default Gateway	

6. Close the *Network Connection Details* window. From the *Local Area Connection Status* window, notice that you can disable the NIC from this window. You can also do this if you right-click or tap and briefly hold on the NIC icon. Select the *Disable* button.

   What indication do you have the NIC is actually disabled?

   _____

   _____

7. Right-click or tap and briefly hold on the NIC icon and select *Enable*. Double-click the NIC icon again.

   How many bytes have been sent?

   _____

   How many bytes have been received?

   _____

8. Select the *Properties* button. The *Local Area Connection Properties* window opens. Select the Configure button. The properties for the specific NIC card appear. The tabs at the top of the window are manufacturer-specific, but most manufacturers tend to have the same basic ones.

   Which company manufactured the NIC?

   _____

   Which data bus does the card use? [PCI | PCIe | _____]

   What key information would be important to the tech in the *Device status* window?

   _____

Using the various tabs, determine the following information:

Which driver version is installed?

_____

Are any power management options enabled? If so, which ones?

_____

_____

Which tab can be used to disable the device?

_____

9.   Access the *Advanced* tab. Locate and select the option that allows you to manually set the NIC speed (and optionally the duplex).

What default value is shown?

_____

10. Select the down arrow in the Value menu.

List the available options.

_____

_____

_____

_____

_____

_____

If you were to manually configure this NIC for speed and/or duplex, which option would be best?

_____

_____

In your opinion, why do you think that a 1.0 Gb/s option shows only full duplex?

_____

_____

11. Leave the speed in the original setting and return to looking at the specific properties.

Look through the advanced property options, and list which ones relate to Wake on LAN. Note that you may have to access the option and look at the values to answer this completely.

_____

_____

12. Select *Cancel > Close*.

Lab 14.4 Networking with Windows 7, 8, or 10

Objective: To put two Windows 7, 8, or 10 computers into a network workgroup

Parts: Two computers with Windows 7, 8, or 10 installed

One crossover cable *or* two straight-through cables and a hub or switch

Procedure: Complete the following procedure and answer the accompanying questions.

1.   Power on the first computer and log on to Windows, if necessary. Do one of the following: (1) connect a crossover between the two computer's NICs or (2) connect a straight-through cable from each computer to the hub or switch and power on the switch. Note that the computer may already be on a wired network.

2. In Windows 7, right-click the *Start* button and select *Open Windows Explorer*. Right-click *Computer* in the left pane and select *Properties*. Locate the C*omputer name, domain, and workgroup settings* section.

   In Windows 8/10, open *File Explorer*. Right-click or tap and briefly hold *This PC* in the left pane and select *Properties*. Locate the *Computer name, domain, and workgroup settings* section.

   Document the current settings:

   Original Computer 1 name: _____

   _____

   Original Full computer 1 name: _____

   _____

   Original Computer 1 description, if entered:_____

   _____

   Is Computer 1 on a workgroup or domain? [Workgroup | Domain]

   _____

   Original workgroup/domain name for Computer 1: _____

   _____

3. On the first computer, select the *Change settings* link to the right of the computer name section. Click *Continue*, if necessary.

4. On the first computer, select the *Computer Name* tab. Click the *Change* button. Select the *Workgroup* radio button. Name the workgroup something unique.

   Changed workgroup/domain name: _____

   _____

5. On the first computer, click the *OK* button, and a Computer Name/Domain Changes window appears. Click *OK* and/or *Close* until prompted to *Restart now*.

6. Power on the second computer and log on to Windows, if necessary.

7. In Windows 7, right-click the *Start* button and select *Open Windows Explorer*. Right-click *Computer* in the left pane and select *Properties*. Locate the *Computer name, domain, and workgroup settings* section.

   In Windows 8/10, open *File Explorer*. Right-click or tap and briefly hold *This PC* in the left pane and select *Properties*. Locate the *Computer name, domain, and workgroup settings* section.

   Document the current settings:

   Original Computer 2 name: _____

   _____

   Original Full computer 2 name: _____

   _____

   Original Computer 2 description if entered: _____

   _____

   Is Computer 2 on a workgroup or domain? [Workgroup | Domain]

   Original workgroup/domain name for Computer 2: _____

8. On the second computer, select the *Change settings* link to the right of the computer name section. Click *Continue*, if necessary.

CHAPTER 14

9. Select the *Computer Name* tab. Click the *Change* button. Select the *Workgroup* radio button.

   Name the Workgroup the same workgroup name as used on Computer 1.

   Changed workgroup/domain name: _____

10. Click the *OK* button, and a Computer Name/Domain Changes window appears. Click *OK* and/or *Close* until prompted to *Restart now*.

11. When both computers have rebooted, the IP addresses need to be configured manually.

    On Windows 7 (both computers), click the *Start* button > *All Programs* > *Accessories* > *Command prompt*. In the new window, type `ipconfig /all`.

    On Windows 8/10 (both computers), locate and access the *Command prompt* app. In the new window, type `ipconfig /all`.

    On Computer 1, what is the IPv4 address on the Ethernet adapter?

    _____

    On Computer 1, what is the IPv6 link-local address on the Ethernet adapter?

    _____

    On Computer 1, what is the IPv4 subnet mask?

    _____

    On Computer 1, what is the default gateway?

    _____

    On Computer 1, what is the MAC address?

    _____

    On Computer 2, what is the IPv4 address on the Ethernet adapter?

    _____

    On Computer 2, what is the IPv6 link-local address on the Ethernet adapter?

    _____

    On Computer 2, what is the IPv4 subnet mask?

    _____

    On Computer 2, what is the default gateway?

    _____

    On Computer 2, what is the MAC address?

    _____

    Who is the network adapter manufacturer for Computer 2?

    _____

    How many hexadecimal characters are shown in the Computer 1 IPv6 address?

    _____

    How many bits does this represent?

    _____

12. Complete this step on both computers. Close the Command Prompt window. Access the *Network and Sharing Center* Control Panel > access the *Change advanced sharing settings* link in the left pane.

    Document the current Sharing and Discovery settings for both computers. Note that all options may not be available in Windows Home versions, but the lab still works. You may also have to expand some sections to find them in the particular type of network currently being used.

	Computer 1	Computer 2
Network discovery	_____	_____
File sharing	_____	_____
Printer sharing	_____	_____
Password protected sharing	_____	_____
Media sharing/streaming	_____	_____
Public folder sharing	_____	_____

13. On both computers, select Cancel. From the Network and Sharing Center Control Panel, select the *Change adapter settings* link from the left panel. Right-click or tap and briefly hold *Local Area Connection* or *Ethernet* adapter > *Properties*. In the center window, locate and select *Internet Protocol Version 4 (TCP/IPv4) > Properties* button.

    Document the settings for Computer 1 and Computer 2:

    Computer 1 IP address, mask and default gateway OR obtains an IP address automatically?

    _____

    Computer 1 Preferred and alternate DNS server(s) IP addresses OR obtains DNS server address automatically?

    _____

    Computer 2 IP address, mask and default gateway OR obtains an IP address automatically?

    _____

    Computer 2 Preferred and alternate DNS server(s) IP addresses OR obtains DNS server address automatically?

    _____

14. On Computer 1, select the *Use the following IP address* radio button and type in the following information:

    IP address: `192.168.1.1`

    Subnet mask: `255.255.255.0`

    Default gateway: `192.168.1.254`

    Click the *OK* button. Click the *Close* button at the bottom of the *Local Area Connection Properties* screen.

15. On Computer 2, select the *Use the following IP address* radio button and type in the following information:

    IP address: `192.168.1.2`

    Subnet mask: `255.255.255.0`

    Default gateway: `192.168.1.254`

    Click the *OK* button. Click the *Close* button at the bottom of the *Local Area Connection Properties* screen.

16. On both computers, using previously described procedures, open a command prompt and verify that the IPv4 address has been applied. Note that you may have to scroll up to see the IPv4 address.

    From a Computer 1 command prompt, type `ping 192.168.1.2.`

    What was the response? Note that the default Windows Firewall behavior is to deny pings. When File and Print Sharing is enabled, the firewall automatically enables ICMP messages that include pings.

Sharing and Accessing a Shared Folder

Note: This section can take a little patience due to what type of network the computer uses.

17. On both computers, access the *Network and Sharing Center* Control Panel link > *Change advanced sharing settings* link. Configure the following settings:

    > Network discovery > *Turn on network discovery*

    > File and print sharing > *Turn on file and print sharing*

    Use the *Save changes* button.

18. On Computer 1, using *Windows Explorer* (Windows 7) or *File Explorer* (Windows 8/10), create a text file called *Surprise.txt* in a Documents folder you create called ABC; here is a message to place in the text file:

    `Technology makes it possible for people to gain control over everything, except over technology. -John Tudor`

19. On Computer 1, right-click or tap to select the *ABC* folder > *Share* menu option.

    Now the options you have here depend on the type of network the computer is on. Note that not all options will be available due to the type of network configured. Select the option that best suits your network environment. If necessary, ask the instructor or student assistant what type of network is used.

    > If connected to a HomeGroup, you can select *Homegroup (view)* or (*Homegroup (view and edit)*. If you want to configure a HomeGroup to use this option, see the steps in the chapter.

    > On a domain or workgroup, you can select specific users listed that are available to add or select using the *Add* option to add other users.

    > On Windows 8 and 10, you can also select the *Email* icon and email a link to the share.

    > OneDrive can be used instead of sharing the folder. Drag the folder into OneDrive and share from there.

    An older method of sharing folders is to right-click the folder (or tap and briefly hold) > *Properties* > *Sharing* tab > *Share* button > access the down arrow and choose *Everyone* > *Add* button > *Share* button.

20. On Computer 2, there are several ways to view the share depending on the type of network the computer is on. Note that not all options will be available due to the type of network configured. Select the option that best suits your network environment. If necessary, ask the instructor or student assistant what type of network is used.

    > If on a HomeGroup, use *Windows Explorer/File Explorer* to expand the *Homegroup* option from the left pane. Expand the particular computer to view the shared files.

    > If using OneDrive, access it through *Windows Explorer/File Explorer* or a web browser.

    > If using the older method of folder sharing, use *Windows Explorer/File Explorer* to select the *Network* option from the left pane. In the right pane, double-click the *Computer 1 name*.

Note: If Computer 1 does not appear in the right pane (it can take quite a few minutes to do so), do what many IT personnel do and access the computer using its UNC. From a command prompt or Search textbox, type the following: \\`computername`\`sharename` (where `computername` is the name of Computer 1 and `sharename` is ABC, the name of the share). An example would be \\`Cheryl-PC`\`ABC`.

Note: If no passwords are assigned to the existing user account, a password will have to be applied to the account on both machines.

21. Access the *ABC* folder. Open the *Surprise.txt* document. Try modifying the text inside and saving it on Computer 1.

    Were you successful? [Yes | No]

    _____

    Instructor initials: _____

22. Close the *Surprise.txt* document on both computers.

    Instructor initials: _____

23. Place both computers back in the original workgroup/domain. Refer to Step 7 for the original settings.

24. Configure both computers to the original Sharing and Discovery settings. Refer to Step 12 for the original settings.

25. Place both computers to the original IPv4 IP address, mask, default gateway, and DNS settings. Refer to Step 13 for the original settings.

26. Remove the cable and put the computers back to the original cabling configuration. Ensure that the computer works and has the same access as it had before you began this lab.

Instructor initials: _____

Lab 14.5 Connecting to a Windows Vista/7 Shared or Networked Printer

Objective: To properly share a printer and use a shared or networked printer using Windows Vista/7

Parts: Two networked computers with a printer attached to one and either Windows Vista or 7 installed

Procedure: Complete the following procedure and answer the accompanying questions.

1. Power on the computer that has the printer attached. If necessary, log on to Windows, using the appropriate user ID and password.

2. Click the *Start* button and select *Control Panel*.

3. In Windows Vista/7, access the *Network and Sharing Center* Control Panel. Ensure that *Printer sharing* is enabled through the *Change advanced sharing settings* link.

4. Access the *Devices and Printers* Control Panel. Right-click the printer to be shared and select the *Properties* option.

5. Click the *Sharing* tab. (Note that if the *Sharing* tab is not available, return to the *Devices and Printers* Control Panel, right-click the printer icon > select *Printer properties*.) Select the *Share this printer* radio button/checkbox. (Note that if the option is grayed out, select the *Change sharing options* button [Vista]/*Network and Sharing Center* link [7]. Make changes as necessary. Then continue with the rest of this step.) Ensure the *Render print jobs on client computers* checkbox is enabled.

6. In the *Share name* textbox, type in a unique printer name and limit it to eight characters if possible. It is important that this name is unique.

   What name was assigned to the printer? _____

7. Click the *OK* button.

Printing to a Shared or Networked Printer

8. On the computer that does not have the printer attached, open the *Devices and Printers (7)/Printers (Vista)* Control Panel.

9. Click the *Add a Printer* menu option. The Add Printer Wizard opens. Click the *Next* button.

10. Click the *Add a network, wireless, or Bluetooth printer* option.

11. The printer link should be listed in the window. Click *Next* if the printer is there and then click the *Install driver* button. If the printer is missing, click *The printer that I want isn't listed*. Three methods can be used to find a shared or networked printer:
    > Click the *Browse for a printer radio* button and click *Next*. Double-click the computer icon that has the printer attached. Select the printer and click the *Select* button and click *Next*.
    > Select the *Shared printer by name* radio button. Either type the name of the printer using the format \\`computer_name`\\`printer_share_name` (the computer name that has the printer attached and the printer name set in Step 6) or browse the network for the printer name, click the *Next* button, select the printer, and click *Next*.
    > Select the *Add a printer using a TCP/IP address or hostname* radio button and click *Next*. Type the hostname or IP address. Click *Next*.

12. Select one of these options and locate the shared printer. Print a test page to the shared printer.

    Does the test page print properly? If not, perform appropriate printer troubleshooting.

Lab 14.6 Connecting to a Windows 8 Shared or Networked Printer

Objective: To properly share a printer and use a shared or networked printer using Windows 8

Parts: Two networked computers with a printer attached to one and Windows 8 installed

Procedure: Complete the following procedure and answer the accompanying questions.

1. Power on the computer that has the printer attached. If necessary, log on to Windows, using the appropriate user ID and password/PIN.

2. Access the *Network and Sharing Center* Control Panel. Ensure that *Printer sharing* is enabled through the *Change advanced sharing settings* link.

3. Using *Devices and Printers* Control Panel, locate the *Printers* section. Locate the printer to be shared. Right-click or tap and briefly hold the printer icon > *Properties*.

4. Click the *Sharing* tab. (Note that if the Sharing tab is not available, return to the *Devices and Printers* Control Panel, right-click or tap and briefly hold the printer icon > select *Printer properties*.)

5. Select the *Share this printer* radio button/checkbox. (Note that if the option is grayed out, go back to the *Network and Sharing Center* Control Panel and ensure sharing options are enabled. Make changes as necessary. Then continue with the rest of this step.) Ensure the *Render print jobs on client computers* checkbox is enabled.

6. In the *Share* name textbox, type in a unique printer name and limit it to eight characters if possible. It is very important that this name is unique.

   What name was assigned to the printer? _____

7. Click the *OK* button.

Printing to a Shared or Networked Printer Windows 8

8. On the Windows 8 computer that does not have the printer attached, use *Settings > PC and devices > Devices*.

9. Select the *Add a device* option.

10. The printer should be listed in the window.

    If the printer is missing, click *The printer that I want isn't listed*. Four methods can be used to find a shared or networked printer:

    > Method 1: Select the *My printer is a little older. Help me find it.* link > *Next*.

    > Method 2: Select the Shared printer by name radio button. Either type the name of the printer using the format \\computer_name\printer_share_name or browse the network for the printer name, click the *Next* button, select the printer, and click *Next*. Note that this is sometimes the quickest method for a shared printer as it directly accesses the printer across the network. To locate the computer name, use the *System* Control Panel. The printer share name was issued and documented in Step 7.

    > Method 3: Select the *Add a printer using a TCP/IP address or hostname* radio button and click *Next*. Type the hostname or IP address. Click *Next*.

    > Method 4: Select the *Add a Bluetooth, wireless or network discoverable printer* radio button.

11. Select one of these options and locate the shared printer. Print a test page to the shared printer.

    Does the test page print properly? If not, perform appropriate printer troubleshooting.

Lab 14.7 Connecting to a Windows 10 Shared or Networked Printer

Objective: To properly share a printer and use a shared or networked printer using Windows 10

Parts: Two networked computers with a printer attached to one and Windows 10 installed

Procedure: Complete the following procedure and answer the accompanying questions.

1. Power on the computer that has the printer attached. If necessary, log on to Windows, using the appropriate user ID and password/PIN.

2. Access the *Network and Sharing Center* Control Panel. Ensure that *Printer sharing* is enabled through the *Change advanced sharing settings* link.

4. Using *Devices and Printers* Control Panel, locate the *Printers* section. Locate the printer to be shared. Right-click or tap and briefly hold the printer icon > *Properties*.

5. Click the *Sharing* tab. (Note that if the Sharing tab is not available, return to the *Devices and Printers* Control Panel, right-click, or tap and briefly hold the printer icon > select *Printer properties*.)

6. Select the *Share this printer* radio button/checkbox. (Note that if the option is grayed out, go back to the *Network and Sharing Center* Control Panel and ensure sharing options are enabled. Make changes as necessary. Then continue with the rest of this step.) Ensure the *Render print jobs on client computers* checkbox is enabled.

7. In the *Share* name textbox, type in a unique printer name and limit it to eight characters if possible. It is important that this name is unique.

    What name was assigned to the printer? _____

8. Click the *OK* button.

Printing to a Shared or Networked Printer Windows 10

9. On the Windows 10 computer that does not have the printer attached, use *Settings > Devices > Printers & Scanners*.

10. Select the *Add a Printer* option.

11. The printer should be listed in the window. Click *Next* if the printer is there, and then click the *Install driver* button.

   If the printer is missing, click *The printer that I want isn't listed*. Four methods can be used to find a shared or networked printer:
   > Method 1: Select the *My printer is a little older. Help me find it.* link > *Next*.
   > Method 2: Select the *Shared printer by name* radio button. Either type the name of the printer using the format `\\computer_name\printer_share_name` or browse the network for the printer name, click the *Next* button, select the printer, and click *Next*. Note that this is sometimes the quickest method for a shared as it directly accesses the printer across the network. To locate the computer name, use the *System* Control Panel. The printer share name was issued and documented in Step 7.
   > Method 3: Select the *Add a printer using a TCP/IP address or hostname* radio button and click *Next*. Type the hostname or IP address. Click *Next*.
   > Method 4: Select the *Add a Bluetooth, wireless or network discoverable printer* radio button.

12. Select one of these options and locate the shared printer. Print a test page to the shared printer.

   Does the test page print properly? If not, perform appropriate printer troubleshooting.

Lab 14.8 Installing a Wireless NIC

Objective: To install a wireless NIC into a computer and have it attach to an access point

Parts: A computer with access to the Internet and permission to download files

    A wireless NIC

    An access point that has already been configured by the instructor or lab assistant

Note: To verify that a wireless NIC works once installed, it must have another wireless device such as another computer with a wireless NIC installed or an access point. This lab assumes that an access point is available and allows attachment of wireless devices. The students will need any security information such as WEP key or WPA2 password before they begin. Each student will download the installation instructions and driver for the wireless NIC. Frequently, these files may be in zipped or PDF format. The computer they use may need to have Adobe's Acrobat Reader and/or a decompression software package loaded.

Procedure: Complete the following procedure and answer the accompanying questions.

1. Determine which type of wireless NIC is being installed.

   What type of wireless NIC is being installed? [PCI | USB | PC Card | ExpressCard | PCIe]

   Who is the manufacturer of the wireless NIC?

   _____

   What operating system is used on the computer in which the wireless NIC will be installed?

   _____

2. Using the Internet, determine the latest version of wireless NIC driver for the operating system being used and download the driver.

   What is the latest driver version?

   _____

3. Using the Internet, download the installation instructions for the wireless NIC being used.

   What is the name of the installation document?

   _____

4. Open the document that details how to install the wireless NIC.

5. Follow the directions and install the wireless NIC.

   Does the wireless NIC automatically detect a wireless network?

   _____

   List any specifications given to you by the instructor/lab assistant.

   _____

Lab 14.9 Configuring a Wireless Network

Objective: To configure a wireless AP (access point) or router and attach a wireless client

Parts: One wireless access point or router

    A computer with an integrated wireless NIC or a wireless NIC installed as well as an Ethernet NIC

    One straight-through cable

Procedure: Complete the following procedure and answer the accompanying questions.

1. Obtain the documentation for the wireless AP or router from the instructor or the Internet.

2. Reset the wireless AP or router as directed by the wireless device manufacturer.

   Document the current Ethernet NIC IPv4 settings. [DHCP | Static IP address]

   If a static IP address is assigned, document the IP address, subnet mask, default gateway, and DNS configuration settings.

   _____

3. Attach a straight-through cable from the computer Ethernet NIC to the wireless AP or router.

4. Power on the computer and log on, if necessary.

5. Configure the computer NIC with a static IP address or DHCP, as directed by the wireless device manufacturer.

6. Open a web browser and configure the wireless AP or router with the following parameters:

   Change the default SSID.

   Leave SSID broadcasting enabled for this lab.

   Do not configure wireless security at this time.

   Change the default password used to access the wireless AP/router.

   Document the current settings:

   SSID: _____

   Password for wireless device access: _____

7. Save the wireless AP or router configuration.

8. Disconnect the Ethernet cable.

9. Enable the wireless NIC and configure it for the appropriate SSID.

10. Configure the wireless NIC for a static IP address or DHCP as directed by the wireless AP or router manufacturer.

CHAPTER 14

11. Open a web browser and access the wireless AP or router. If access cannot be obtained, troubleshoot as necessary, or reset the wireless AP or router to default configurations and restart the lab.

What frequency (channel) is used by the wireless AP or router and the wireless NIC for connectivity?

_____

12. Show the instructor the connectivity.

Instructor initials: _____

13. Reset the wireless AP or router to the default configuration settings.

14. Reset the computer(s) to the original configuration settings.

Lab 14.10 FTP Server and Client

Objective: To transfer files from one network device to another, using FTP server and client software

Parts: An application or freeware application that provides the FTP server service

                An application or freeware application that provides the FTP client service

Procedure: Complete the following procedure and answer the accompanying questions.

FTP Server

1. Download, install, and open an FTP server freeware application such as FileZilla. This lab has directions specifically for a Home FTP Server, but the steps for other applications are similar.

2. Start the FTP server. You may need to start the FTP server or the FTP server service. In the Home FTP Server application, click the *FTP Server* tab > *Start Server*.

3. Some FTP server applications allow anonymous users or anyone who connects to the server to download files. Also, some applications allow you to specify what the anonymous user can do such as download, upload, and delete files and directories. To enable anonymous logins within Home FTP Server, click the *FTP Server* tab > enable *Allow anonymous users (allow all active)* checkbox. This same tab can be used to enable specific permissions for creation and deletion of files and directories.

Make a note as to where the default anonymous directory is located.

_____

4. FTP server applications frequently allow web connectivity. To enable the web interface within Home FTP Server, select the *Web interface* tab > enable the *Web interface enabled* checkbox.

What is the default port number used for FTP server?

_____

What is the IP address of the FTP server?

_____

5. Copy some files into the default anonymous directory on the FTP server.

FTP Client

6. Download, install, and open an FTP client freeware application. This lab has directions specifically for the SmartFTP client, but the steps for other applications are similar.

7. Usually, a client requires the following configuration:

(a) Address of the FTP server

(b) User login ID and password *or* anonymous login selected

In the SmartFTP client, type in the FTP server IP address in the *address* textbox > click the *Anonymous* button (option) > click the green arrow to connect. The FTP client displays the files that were copied into the anonymous directory.

Instructor initials: _____

Tightening Security

8. Create a user on the FTP server. In the Home FTP Server, click the *New Member* button > *General* tab > type a name in the *User Name* textbox > type **class999** in the *Password* textbox.

   Make a note of the home directory and permissions for this user.

   _____

9. Click *Apply*. Test the user account from the FTP client application by creating a new entry with the appropriate user ID and password. In SmartFTP, click the *File* menu option > select *disconnect* to disconnect the previous login session. Click the *File* menu option > *New Remote Browser* > in the *Host* textbox, type the FTP server IP address > in the *User Name* textbox, type the *exact* username that was typed in the FTP server application > in the *Password* textbox, type **class999** > in the *Name* textbox, type **FTP with login** > *OK*. The client connects to the FTP server.

   Instructor initials: _____

10. Within the client application, close the FTP session. For the SmartFTP client, use the *Close* button in the upper-right corner of the *FTP with login* tab. Close all tabs and sessions.

11. Delete FTP client entries. From within SmartFTP client, click the *Favorites* menu option > *Edit Favorites Quick Connect* option in the left pane > click once on the FTP server IP address in the right pane > *Edit* menu option > *Delete* > *Yes*. Delete the FTP with login option using the same technique.

   Instructor initials: _____

CHAPTER 14

15 Basic Windows

In this chapter you will learn:

> To identify and use common desktop icons

> To manipulate files and folders in Windows

> How to create a system image in case of emergencies

> About the Windows registry

> How to work from a command prompt

> Techniques to stay current in field

CompTIA Exam Objectives:

What CompTIA A+ exam objectives are covered in this chapter?

✓ **901-4.4** Given a scenario, troubleshoot wired and wireless networks with appropriate tools.

✓ **902-1.1** Compare and contrast various features and requirements of Microsoft Operating Systems (Windows Vista, Windows 7, Windows 8, Windows 8.1).

✓ **902-1.2** Given a scenario, install Windows PC operating systems using appropriate methods.

✓ **902-1.3** Given a scenario, apply appropriate Microsoft command-line tools.

✓ **902-1.4** Given a scenario, use appropriate Microsoft operating system features and tools.

✓ **902-1.5** Given a scenario, use Windows Control Panel utilities.

✓ **902-1.7** Perform common preventive maintenance procedures using the appropriate Windows OS tools.

✓ **902-2.2** Given a scenario, set up and use client-side virtualization.

✓ **902-3.3** Compare and contrast differences of Windows basic OS security.

✓ **902-3.7** Given a scenario, secure SOHO wireless and wired networks.

✓ **902-4.1** Given a scenario, troubleshoot PC operating system problems with appropriate tools.

✓ **902-4.2** Given a scenario, troubleshoot common PC security issues with appropriate tools and best practices.

Basic Operating Systems Overview

Computers require software to operate. An **operating system**, often called an OS, is software that coordinates the interaction between hardware and any software applications, as well as the interaction between a user and the computer. Examples of operating systems include Apple's Mac OS X and iOS; Windows Vista, 7, 8, and 10; and the different types of UNIX/Linux, such as Sun Solaris, Red Hat, SUSE, Google Chrome OS, and Android. One advantage of Linux-based open source operating systems such as Android is that the code that makes up the operating system is open to view and improve upon or change. This sometimes allows for more community-driven features that are not as easily changed in closed source or proprietary software such as Windows or OS X.

An operating system can be a graphical user interface (GUI) or a command-based interface, or it can contain both, which is the most common. An operating system contains commands and functions that both the user and the computer understand. An example is Windows Explorer found in Windows Vista and 7 or File Explorer used by Windows 8 and 10. People sometimes simply say Explorer (which can be confusing because of the Internet Explorer browser, which is now called Edge in Windows 10). **Windows Explorer** and **File Explorer** are used to manage files and folders. The operating system is also responsible for handling file and disk management. That is why the Windows Explorer or File Explorer tools are part of the standard Windows operating system. Figure 15.1 shows Windows Explorer from a Windows 7 computer.

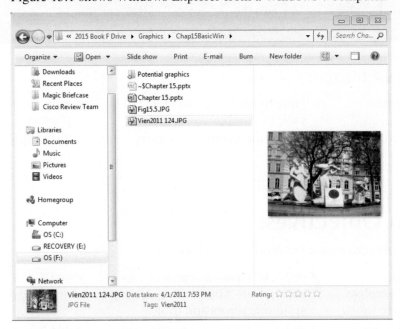

FIGURE 15.1   Windows Explorer

A **file** is an electronic container that holds computer code or data. Another way of looking at a file is to think of it as either a box of bits or an electronic piece of paper with information on it. Look at Figure 15.1 to see Chapter 15.pptx as an example of a file. A **folder** holds files and can also contain other folders. Referring to Figure 15.1, Potential graphics is a folder. With Windows Explorer/File Explorer, you can create, copy, or move files or folders.

An alternative environment used by technicians when there is a problem is the command prompt environment. From a command prompt, you can enter commands that are specific to the operating system. For example, say that you type the word hop from the command prompt. The word "hop" is not a command that the computer understands (has been programmed to understand), so an error message appears because the computer does not know what to do. However, if you type `dir` at a command prompt, the computer recognizes the command and displays a directory: a listing of files.

To access the command prompt from within Windows, use the following steps, but always remember there are several ways of accomplishing almost anything within the Windows environment.

> Windows Vista/7: Access the *Start* button menu > select *All Programs* > locate and click the *Accessories* option, double-click the *Command Prompt* option.

> Windows 8: Access the *Command Prompt* tile located as an option under *Windows System*.

> Windows 10: Type `command` in the *Search the web and Windows* textbox > select *Command Prompt* from the search result.

Some actions performed from the command prompt must be done from an elevated technical status (as an administrator of the machine). To open the command prompt window with these rights, right-click the *Command Prompt* option and select *Run as administrator*. Figure 15.2 shows a command prompt environment.

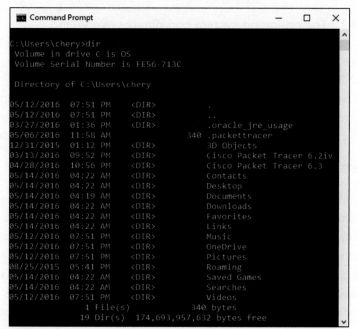

FIGURE 15.2   Windows command prompt

Technicians must be familiar with the GUI environment and function from a command prompt when the only possibility to execute a fix is by typing a command at a command prompt. Not only must technicians be familiar with the tools and environments, they must know multiple operating systems. This makes for a challenging and ever-changing environment. Figure 15.3 shows that the operating system is the An coordinator of all hardware and software. The operating system is the core, or software, that computer device needs to function.

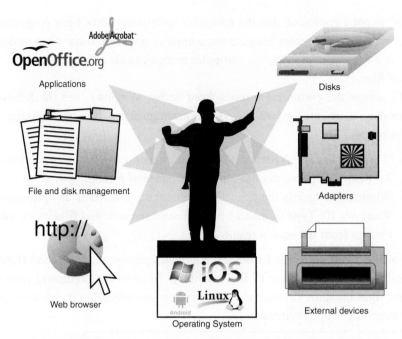

FIGURE 15.3   The operating system coordinates everything

Basic Windows Usage Overview

If you have been using a Windows-based computer your entire life, you might find this first look at the Windows environment a little dry. It's the basics. However, little technical tricks and tips are among these basics and even veteran technicians say, "I didn't know that." So, look for those.

Windows Desktop/Start Screen

Starting on a Windows computer, the user is presented with a logon screen. A user ID and password or PIN is entered as part of the operating system installation process and used thereafter.

When in the Windows environment, the desktop appears. The **desktop** is the area on the screen of a GUI environment in which all work is performed in Windows Vista and 7. It is the interface between the computer user and files, applications, operating system, and installed hardware. The desktop contains **icons**, which are pictures that provide access to various devices, files, applications/apps, or other resources, such as web pages. The desktop can be customized so that the most commonly accessed applications or files are easily accessible. Figure 15.4 shows a Windows 7 desktop.

Windows 8 has a **Start screen**. Windows 8.1 can have a Start screen or the traditional desktop. The Start screen contains tiles instead of icons. These **tiles** provide the same access to files and apps as the traditional icons did. Figure 15.5 shows a Windows 8 Start screen. Notice that tiles are used instead of the traditional Windows icons. A scrollbar at the bottom enables you to see more desktop tiles. The specific tile labeled *Desktop* is used to access a more traditional desktop. You can also configure Windows 8.1 to use the traditional desktop all the time.

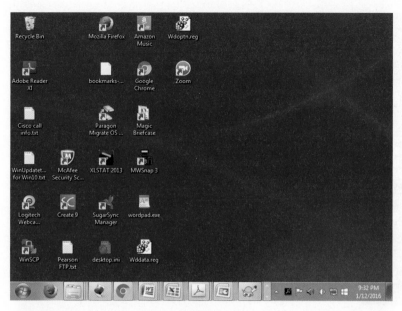

FIGURE 15.4   Windows 7 desktop

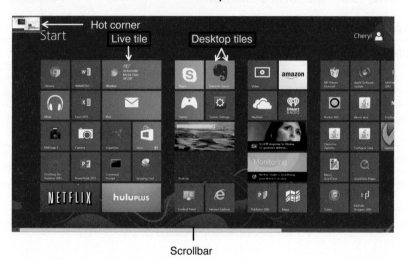

FIGURE 15.5   Windows 8 Start screen

One particular tile of interest is a live tile. A live tile represents an app with content that periodically changes. Weather, news, and photos are common apps that have this feature. You can right-click the live tile to disable the "live" feature.

Windows 8 has hot corners. By moving the pointer to one of the four corners of the screen, you can bring up different options. From the Start screen shown, the top-left corner shows other windows that are open (refer to Figure 15.5).

Click that window area for quick access to that particular application. Point to the right corner and see the charms appear (see Figure 15.6). Charms are a menu to quickly access commonly used Windows features, as outlined in Table 15.1.

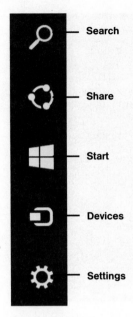

FIGURE 15.6   Windows 8 charms

TABLE 15.1   Purpose of Windows 8 charms

Charm	Purpose
Search	Used to find apps, settings, and files. Some apps allow the Search charm to find content within the app. The shortcut is ▦ + F.
Share	Used to share content with other people using specific apps that support this feature.
Start	Used to open the Start screen.
Devices	Used to send data from the current app to another device such as a printer or external display.
Settings	Used to change settings and access the traditional Control Panels.

TECH TIP

Using the Windows key

The ▦ brings up the Start menu/screen.

Windows 10 enables you to choose the desktop style that you want, which is demonstrated in a lab at the end of the chapter. Figure 15.7 shows a Windows 10 desktop, but you can also choose to show the tiles (tablet mode) similar to Windows 8. The *Search the web and Windows* textbox enables you to search for anything from the desktop. The *Task View* icon enables you to create multiple desktops and switch between them.

TECH TIP

Keeping the desktop organized

Sometimes, the desktop is cluttered with icons the user puts on it. To organize the desktop nicely, right-click an empty desktop space, point to *View* > select *Auto arrange icons*.

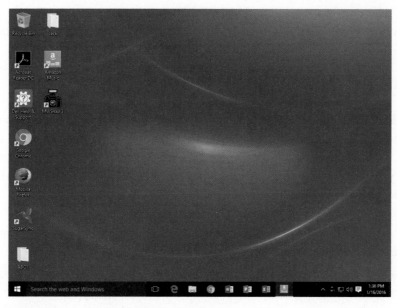

FIGURE 15.7 Windows 10 desktop

One way to modify the desktop is to change the wallpaper scheme. A wallpaper scheme is a background picture, pattern, or color. Other changes to the desktop include altering the color scheme in displaying folders and enabling a screen saver, which is the picture, color, or pattern that displays when the computer is inactive. Labs at the end of the chapter explain how to change these settings.

Shortcuts and Tiles

The Amazon Music icon (refer to Figure 15.7) is a desktop icon called a shortcut. Each of the tiles in the Windows 8/8.1 or 10 tablet mode also represents a shortcut. A **shortcut** represents a **path** (a location on a drive) to a file, folder, or program. It is a link (pointer) to where the file or application resides on a disk. On the traditional desktop, a shortcut has a small arrow in the left corner. When a shortcut icon is double-clicked, Windows knows where to find the specific file the icon represents by the associated path. Users and technicians frequently place shortcuts or tiles on the desktop, so it is important to know how to create, remove, modify, or troubleshoot them.

By default, the Windows Vista/7 desktop displays the Recycle Bin icon only. However, some people like to have Windows icons displayed. Common desktop icons or tiles are listed in Table 15.2.

TABLE 15.2 Common Windows desktop icons or tiles

Icon	Purpose
Documents	Maps to a folder located on the hard drive that is the default storage location for files
Computer/This PC	Accesses hardware, software, and files
Network	Accesses network resources, such as computers, printers, scanners, fax machines, and files
Recycle Bin	Holds files and folders that have been deleted
Internet Explorer/Edge	Starts the Microsoft browser used to access the Internet

To discover the path to the original file used to create a shortcut, right-click the shortcut icon and select *Properties*. Click the *Shortcut* tab and look in the *Target* textbox for the path to the original file. The *Open File Location* (Vista/7) button can be used to locate the original file. If tiles are shown in Windows 8 or 10, right-click the tile and select *Open file location*. Note that you may have to point to the *More* option to access *Open file location*.

Recycle Bin

An important Windows desktop icon is the Recycle Bin, which holds files and folders that the user deletes. When a file or folder is deleted, it is not actually gone. Instead, it goes into the Recycle Bin, which is just a folder on the hard drive. The deleted file or folder can be removed from the Recycle Bin just as a piece of trash can be removed from a real trash can. Deleted files and folders in the Recycle Bin use hard drive space.

> **TECH TIP**
>
> **Need hard drive space? Empty the Recycle Bin**
>
> A technician must remember that some users do not empty the Recycle Bin. Emptying the Recycle Bin frees up space on the hard drive.

The contents of the Recycle Bin take up hard drive space. To change how much space is reserved for the Recycle Bin or the drive on which the deleted files in the Recycle Bin are stored, right-click the *Recycle Bin* and select *Properties*. Labs at the end of the chapter illustrate how to copy, move, and delete files and folders (Labs 15.12 and 15.13) and how to empty the Recycle Bin (Labs 15.1, 15.5, and 15.8).

> **TECH TIP**
>
> **How to delete a file permanently**
>
> If you hold down the [Shift] key when deleting a file, the file is permanently deleted and does not go into the Recycle Bin.

> **TECH TIP**
>
> **Removable media files are permanently deleted**
>
> When deleting a file or folder from an optical disc, a memory card, an MP3 player, a digital camera, a remote computer, or a flash drive, the file or folder is permanently deleted. It does not go into the Recycle Bin, as is the case when a file is deleted from a hard drive.

Windows Vista/7 Desktop Components

The traditional Windows desktop has specific desktop components. Figure 15.8 shows a Windows 7 desktop with the primary components.

The **taskbar** is the bar that commonly runs across the bottom of the traditional desktop. The taskbar holds icons that represent applications or files currently loaded into computer memory. The taskbar also holds icons that allow access to system utilities such as a clock for the date and time and a speaker symbol for access to volume control. Refer to Figure 15.8 to ensure you know the location of the taskbar.

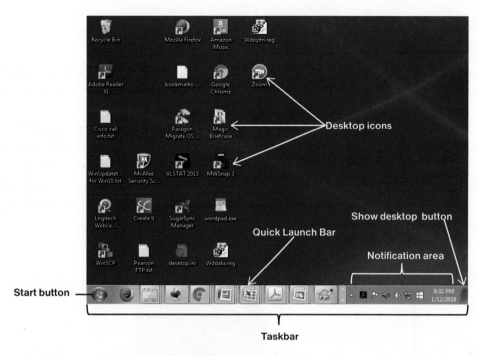

FIGURE 15.8 Windows 7 desktop components

The **Start button** by default is located in the desktop's lower-left corner on the taskbar and is used to launch applications and utilities, search for files and other computers, obtain help, and add/remove hardware and software. Figure 15.9 shows the Windows 7 Start button menu.

FIGURE 15.9 Windows 7 Start button menu

Notice in Figure 15.9 how applications list on the far left. There is a line between the top five applications (Hearts, Google Chrome, Calculator, Snipping Tool, and Printkey) and the rest of the applications. The top five applications are "pinned" to the Start button menu. The bottom part of the applications list contains the most commonly used applications. A lab at the end of the chapter demonstrates how to customize the Start menu.

TECH TIP

Start button missing?

If the Start button is missing, press the ⊞ key or the ⌈Ctrl⌋ + ⌈Esc⌋ key combination.

On the far right of the Start button are commonly used options and the power off option located on the far-right bottom. Click *Shut down* to power the computer off properly. Click the arrow to the right of the *Shut down* option, and you can see other shut-down options (switch user, log off, lock, restart, and sleep) as shown in Figure 15.10. *Standby, Hibernate*, and *Sleep* options are available on computers that support power-saving features and are commonly used with laptops and ultrabooks. If a Windows shield appears to the left of the words *Shut down*, Windows updates are ready and will be installed before the computer is shut down.

FIGURE 15.10 Windows 7 Shut down options

The Windows Vista/7 taskbar has four main areas (see Figure 15.8): (1) the Start button on the far left, (2) icons for commonly used applications or open applications (Quick Launch Bar), (3) the notification area on the right, and (4) the show desktop button on the farthest right. The two closest icons to the right of the Start button (Mozilla Firefox and Windows Explorer) are "pinned" to the taskbar—that is, they are always on the taskbar. The other icons (Hearts, Google Chrome, Microsoft Word, Microsoft Excel, Adobe Acrobat, Microsoft PowerPoint, and Tortoise SVN) are open applications.

TECH TIP

How to modify the buttons shown on the taskbar

Launch the application. Locate the application icon on the taskbar. Right-click and select *Pin this program to taskbar*.

On the far right of the taskbar is the **notification area**, where you can find information about an application or a tool. Referring to Figure 15.8, the icons from left to right are Adobe Acrobat notification of an impending update, Windows Action Center Control Panel, Realtek HD Audio Manager, Windows speaker control (to quickly mute or adjust sound volume), a network icon (where a technician could quickly ascertain whether Internet access were available), a Windows update icon, and the date and time. Other icons are available by clicking the up arrow to the left of the Adobe Acrobat update icon. Notice the space to the far right immediately after the date/time. Click this area to instantly show the desktop area. Click the area again and whatever window you were working within reappears. The *Show Desktop* option is also available by simply right-clicking an empty space on the taskbar. Labs 15.1 through 15.7 demonstrate how to use and control the Windows desktop/Start screen environment.

Windows 8 Desktop/Start Screen Components

The Windows Start screen (the desktop replacement that uses tiles instead of icons) can be used on Windows 8 and 10 desktop computers as well as mobile devices. Figure 15.11 shows a Windows 8.1 desktop with the primary components and Table 15.3 lists the purpose of each one.

TABLE 15.3 Windows 8/10 Start screen components

Component	Purpose
Account settings	Shows the person/account currently logged on. Can be used to change users, change the account picture, lock the screen, or sign out.
Power options	Used to shut down the device, put the device in sleep mode, or restart it (see Figure 15.12).
Search	Same as the Search charm; used to share content with other people using specific apps that support this feature. Notice in Figure 15.13, you can click the down arrow by the word *Everywhere* to select where the search is performed.
Apps arrow	Used to access all the app tiles (see Figure 15.14). Click the up arrow at the bottom of the screen to return to the Start screen.

FIGURE 15.11 Windows 8.1 Start screen components

FIGURE 15.12   Windows 8.1 Power options menu

FIGURE 15.13   Windows 8.1 Search options

FIGURE 15.14   Windows 8.1 all apps screen

Notice in Figure 15.15 that the apps are in alphabetical order. Scroll all the way to the right to see Windows accessories and programs commonly seen from the traditional Start button.

TECH TIP

Adding or removing an app tile to the Start screen

Right-click any tile that does not currently appear on the Start screen, and you can select the *Pin to Start* option to put it there. Select any tile on the Start screen that the user does not want there, and select *Unpin from Start*.

Windows 8.1 also supports the traditional desktop. Press the ▓ key after the Start screen and the traditional desktop appear. Press the same key again, and the Start screen reappears. You can also access the traditional desktop using the *Desktop* tile.

Windows 10 Desktop Components

The Windows 10 desktop can look similar to the Windows 7 desktop but can also use the Windows 8.1 Start screen look or a combination of the two. Figure 15.15 shows a Windows 10 computer with the traditional desktop. The search function is built in to the taskbar and can appear as a search icon, the Cortana search textbox, or the *Search the web and Windows* search textbox. With the Cortana feature you can type or speak a question or statement like, "What's on TV tonight?" or "Show me the latest news."

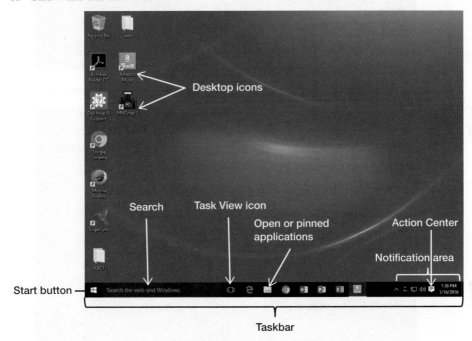

FIGURE 15.15 Windows 10 desktop components

The Windows 10 Start button can be configured to show some tiles (see Figure 15.16) or the Start screen (all tiles), as shown in Figure 15.17. Use the icons on the top and bottom left to re-access the Start button, access the power options, or view the apps in alphabetical order. Scroll down to see the rest of the tiles.

FIGURE 15.16 Windows 10 Start button with some tiles

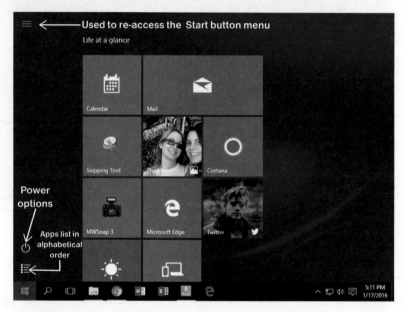

FIGURE 15.17 Windows 10 Start screen view

Windows 10 Task View

The Windows 10 Task View icon (refer to Figure 15.15) is new to Windows. The Task View button enables you to view thumbnails of open apps and easily select which one to access, as shown in Figure 15.18. If you previously used the [Alt] + [Tab] key combination to select an open window, Task View does the same thing but more efficiently. Task View also enables you to create more than one desktop. Select the *New desktop* option in the bottom-right corner to create one. Figure 15.18 shows how two desktops are created. The windows open in Desktop 1 (selected at the bottom) are shown as thumbnails in the top window.

FIGURE 15.18 Windows 10 Task View window

Interactions Within a Window

Whenever anything is double-clicked in Windows, a window appears. A window is a normal part of the Windows environment and common options can appear within a window. Technicians frequently interact with the Windows operating system through a dialog box. A dialog box is used within the operating system and with Windows applications to allow configuration and operating system preferences. The most common features found in a dialog box are a checkbox, a textbox, tabs, a drop-down menu, a Close button, an OK button, a Cancel button, and an Apply button. Figure 15.19 shows a sample dialog box.

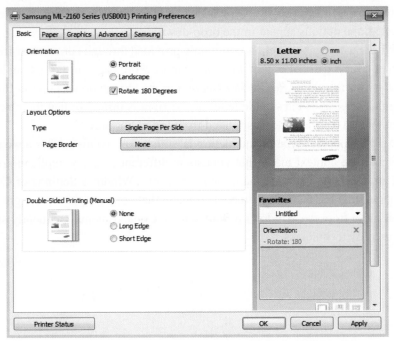

FIGURE 15.19 Samsung printing preferences dialog box

A textbox is an area in which you can type a specific parameter. When the inside of a textbox is clicked, a vertical line appears or the entire default word. Any typed text is placed to the right of the insertion point, or you can just type to replace the highlighted word. Textboxes sometimes have up and down arrows that can be used to select an option or enable a user to type in a new parameter.

Tabs frequently appear across the top of a dialog box. Each tab holds a group of related options. Click the tab once to bring that particular major section to the window's forefront. The tabs in Figure 15.19 are Basic, Paper, Graphics, Advanced, and Samsung.

The **Close button**, which is indicated by an X, closes the dialog box window. When you click the Close button, changes made inside the dialog box are not applied. When you click the **OK button**, all options selected or changed within the dialog box are applied. When you click the **Cancel button**, anything changed within the dialog box is not applied; the options are left in their original state. The **Apply button** makes changes immediately (before clicking the OK button).

TECH TIP

Select *OK* or *Apply* to make it work

To apply a change, inexperienced technicians often make the mistake of clicking the *Close* button (the button with a red X in the top right) instead of the OK or Apply button. When the Close button is used, changes in the dialog box are neither saved nor applied.

When checked, a checkbox option is enabled or turned on. Clicking inside a checkbox option places a check mark inside the checkbox, such as the one for Rotate 180 Degrees (refer to Figure 15.19). If you click again inside the checkbox, the check is removed and the option is not enabled.

A similar dialog box option is a radio button. A **radio button** is a circle that, when enabled, has a solid dot inside it. If a radio button that already has a dot in it is clicked, the dot disappears, and the option is disabled. Referring to Figure 15.19, you see the *Portrait* radio button is enabled and the *Landscape* radio button is disabled.

Drop-down menus are presented when you click a down arrow to see the options. Refer to Figure 15.19 to see two drop-down menus: *Type* and *Page Border*. After a drop-down menu is selected, the options appear in the drop-down menu.

Within a dialog box, help is commonly provided through context-sensitive help. Simply hold the pointer over a particular item and one or more words appear. For example, if you hold the cursor briefly over the words *Rotate 180 Degrees* in the Orientation section in Figure 15.19, the resulting help that appears is the sample letter on the right is turned so that the black circle at the bottom is up at the top (the document is rotated from top to bottom).

Another popular type of interaction is with a **context menu** that appears when you right-click an item. The context menu that appears is different in every application but usually has options that are available from the main menu or from a Windows Settings or Control Panel option. For example, Figure 15.20 shows a context menu that appears when you right-click (or tap and briefly hold) a tile from the Windows 8 Start screen. Context menus frequently save time and commonly are used by technicians.

FIGURE 15.20 Windows 8.1 tile context menu

Managing Windows Files and Folders

Technicians often create, delete, and move files and folders. You need to do these tasks quickly and without error. It is important to think about what file and folder you want to work with, where the files and folders are located now, and where you want the files or folders to be eventually.

Each drive in a computer is represented by a drive letter followed by a colon. For example, the first hard drive partition is represented by `C:`. The optical drive, flash drive, and any external drives are each represented by a drive letter followed by a colon. Windows Explorer (Windows Vista/7) or File Explorer (Windows 8/10) is used to manage files and folders. Figure 15.21 shows drive letters within File Explorer on a Windows 8.1 computer.

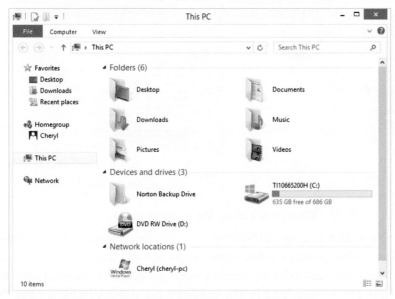

FIGURE 15.21 Windows 8.1 File Explorer drive letters

Discs or drives hold files. A file is kept on some type of media, such as a flash drive, a hard drive, a tape, or an optical disc. Each file is given a name, called a filename. An example of a filename is `WIN8CHAP.DOCX`. Regardless if you use lowercase or uppercase letters, Windows remembers the case; however, it does not require you to remember. Case does not matter when searching for a file or typing a file to open.

TECH TIP

Characters you cannot use in filenames and folder names

Folders and filenames can have all characters, numbers, letters, and spaces *except* the following: / (forward slash), " (quotation mark), \ (backslash), | (vertical bar), ? (question mark), : (colon), and * (asterisk).

Filenames and Extensions

Files are usually kept organized in folders. In older operating systems, a folder was called a directory, and you still see this term today. A folder within a folder is called a subfolder or subdirectory. Windows 7 and higher have automatic groupings, with each one called a **library** for saving files. The Windows 7 libraries include the following: Documents, Music, Pictures, and Videos. By default, applications save files in one of these libraries. You can also create additional libraries as needed.

Every file and folder is given a name and an extension. An **extension** is added to the filename, and the extension can be two or more characters. The filename and the extension are separated by a period. An example of a filename with an extension is `Graphics2016.DOCX`, where `Graphics2016` is the name of the file and `DOCX` is the extension.

Normally with Windows, the application automatically adds an extension to the end of the filename. In most views, Windows does not automatically show the extensions. To view the extensions in Vista/7 Windows Explorer, select the *Organize* drop-down menu > *Folder and search options* > *View* tab > uncheck the *Hide extensions for known file types* checkbox > *OK* (see Figure 15.22).

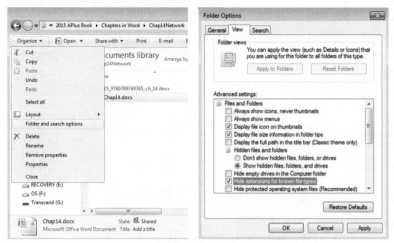

FIGURE 15.22 Windows 7 view file extensions

To view file extensions in Windows 8 or 10 File Explorer, select the *View* tab as shown in Figure 15.23 > enable (select) the *File name extensions* checkbox.

The context-sensitive help appears when the pointer is hovered over the *File name extensions* option (refer to Figure 15.23). The checkbox has a check inside it when the option is enabled.

When Windows recognizes an extension, the operating system associates the extension with a particular application. Filename extensions can tell you a lot about a file, such as what application created the file or what its purpose is. Table 15.4 lists the most common file extensions and their purpose or what application creates the extension.

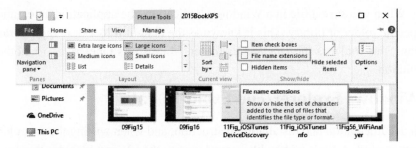

FIGURE 15.23 Windows 10 view file extensions

TABLE 15.4 Common file extensions

Extension	Purpose or application	Extension	Purpose or application
AAX	Audible enhanced audio file	JPG or JPEG	Joint Photographic Experts Group file format—graphics file
AI	Adobe Illustrator or Corel Trace	MPG or MPEG	Movie clip file
BAT	Executes commands from one file and is commonly known as a batch file	ONE	Microsoft OneNote file
BMP	Bitmap file	PCX	Microsoft Paintbrush
CAB	Cabinet file: A compressed file that holds operating system or application files	PDF	Adobe Acrobat—portable document format
COM	Command file: An executable file that opens an application or tool	PNG	Microsoft Paint or Snipping Tool graphics file format
DLL	Dynamic Link Library file: Contains executable code that can be used by more than one application and is called upon from other code already running	PPT or PPTX	Microsoft PowerPoint
DOC or DOCX	Microsoft Word	RTF	Rich text format
DRV	Device driver: A piece of software that enables an operating system to recognize a hardware device	TIF or TIFF	Tag image file format
EPS	Encapsulated postscript file	TXT	Text file
EXE	Executable file: A file that opens an application	VXD	Virtual device driver
GIF	Graphics interchange file	WPS	Microsoft Works text file format
HLP	Windows-based help file	WRI	Microsoft WordPad
INF	Information or setup file	XLS or XLSX	Microsoft Excel
INI	Initialization file: Used in older Windows environments	ZIP	Compressed file

When you save a file in a Windows application, the application automatically saves the file to a specific folder or library. This is known as the default folder or default library. With many applications, this folder is the *Documents* folder, Microsoft's OneDrive, or another cloud-based storage solution.

Windows Explorer/File Explorer Path

In documentation and installation instruction, and when writing the exact location of a file, the full path is used. A file's path is like a road map to the file and includes the drive letter plus all folders and subfolders as well as the filename and extension. For example, if the Chap1.docx file is in the *Documents* folder on the first Windows hard drive partition and the author, Cheryl, is logged on, the full path is as follows:

C:\Users\Cheryl\Documents\Chap1.docx

The first part is the drive letter where the document is stored. The C: represents the first hard drive partition. Computer users have their own folder in the Users folder. The name of the document is always at the end of the path. In the example given, Chap1.docx is the name of the file. Everything in between the drive letter and the filename is the name of one or more folders to get to where the Chap1.docx file is located. The folder in this example is Users. In the Users folder is the Cheryl subfolder. In the Cheryl subfolder is another subfolder called Documents. Finally, within that Documents folder is the Chap1.docx document. Figure 15.24 shows this concept.

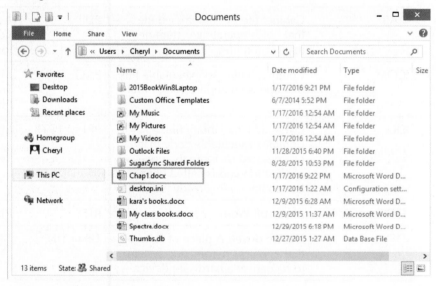

FIGURE 15.24 Windows 8 File Explorer Path

Notice how the path shows at the top of the File Explorer Window and the filename shows within the Documents folder. Note that this was done intentionally to show you the full path. Normally, when you open File Explorer, expand *This PC* on the left and select *Documents*, the Users or Cheryl folder is not shown. The path would simply show as This PC > Documents.

When writing a complete path to a folder, backslashes (the keyboard key above the Enter key) are always used to separate the folder names as well as the drive letter from the first folder name. In Windows 8/10 File Explorer, the greater than sign > is used to separate folders.

In Windows Vista/7, the full path does not show automatically. In Vista/7, from Windows Explorer, click anywhere to the right of the words in the address bar. The full path shows and is highlighted, as shown in Figure 15.25.

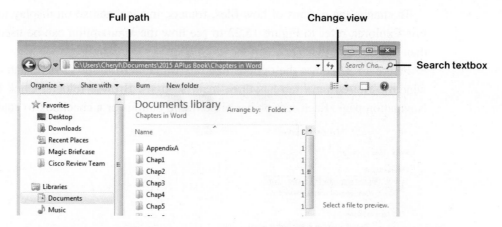

FIGURE 15.25 Windows 7 full path in Windows Explorer address bar

You can also change what information displays or how the information displays in Windows Explorer using the *Change view > More options* down arrow in Vista/7 (refer to the upper-right corner of Figure 15.25). Table 15.5 explains these options.

TABLE 15.5 Windows Explorer display options

Explanation	Windows Vista/7 option
File/folder name shown	List
File/folder shown with size, extension, and modification date	Details
Small graphics with the file or folder name shown under the icon	Small Icons
Reduced size icons with file/folder contents shown	Content
Multiple columns of file/folder icons with name, application, and size shown	Tiles
Varying size file/folder icons	Medium Icons, Large Icons, Extra Large Icons

To display the full path in File Explorer (Windows 8/10), open *File Explorer* > select the *View* menu option > access the *Options* down arrow on the far right > select *Change folder and search options* > select the *View* tab (see Figure 15.26) > enable the *Display the full path in the title bar* option.

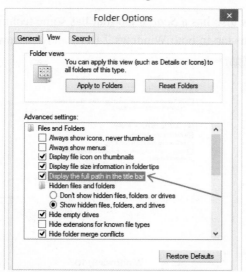

FIGURE 15.26 Windows 10 *Display the full path* option

To change the options of how files, folders, images, and so on display in Windows 8 or 10 in File Explorer, refer to Figure 15.23 to see how the *View* option can be used and is easier to find than in Windows Vista/7.

Figure 15.27 shows the options that are available from the *General* tab of the *Folder Options* window. The *General* tab has three main sections: Browse folders, Click items as follows, and Navigation pane. Each section has either radio buttons or a checkbox to enable each item.

FIGURE 15.27   Windows 8 Folder Options > General tab

Searches and Indexing

You can also use the *Folder Options* Windows Explorer/File Explorer window to help with file searches. You can perform a search from within Windows Explorer/File Explorer (refer back to Figures 15.24 and 15.25) by typing a filename or phrase within the search textbox. You can also start searches from the *Start Search* textbox (Windows Vista) or *Search programs and files* (Windows 7) textbox in the *Start* button menu. In Windows 8, an alternative to File Explorer is to use the *Search* charm. In Windows 10 you can search using the textbox on the taskbar or the Cortana search feature.

The *Folder Options* window also has a *Search* tab that has some technical significance. Figure 15.28 shows the contents of this tab in both Windows 7 (left) and Windows 8/10 (right).

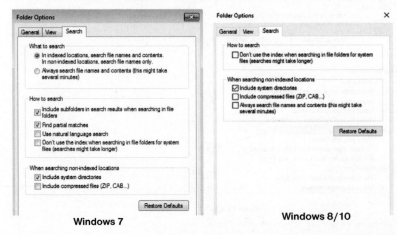

Windows 7   Windows 8/10

FIGURE 15.28   Windows 7 and 8/10 Folder Options > *Search* tab

The first section in Windows 7 is what to search for. Windows 8 and 10 always include file-names and data within the files as well as web searches. The search feature in the operating system deals with searches and is affected by the Windows index feature. **Indexing** is the process used in Windows to quickly search common locations for files and folders, including all libraries, the Start button menu, and Internet Explorer/Edge browsing history. How to modify what is included in the index is covered in the next section.

The *How to search* section in Windows 7 offers several more options than the same section in Windows 8/10. In Windows 7, unchecking the first box in this section means that all the files and folders in the drive, folder, or subfolder will be searched. In Windows 8 and 10, you can see that the index is used by default, but you may enable this option. Files/folders outside the non-indexed locations can be specified in the last section (in the *When searching non-indexed locations* section).

Modifying the Index Locations

To modify what locations get indexed, use a search function and type `indexing` > select *Indexing Options* from the resulting list. Use the *Modify* or *Advanced* buttons to change the settings. Figure 15.29 shows the Indexing Options window as well as the window that appears if you select the *Advanced* button.

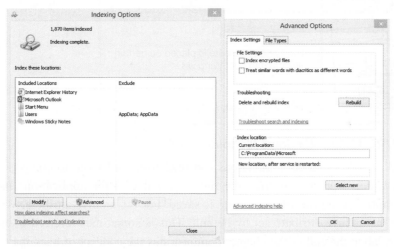

FIGURE 15.29   Windows 8/10 Index Options > Search tab

If you don't want a file to be indexed and easily found, you can right-click the filename, select *Properties* > *Advanced* button > disable (uncheck) the *Allow this file to have contents indexed in addition to file properties* option.

Attributes, Compression, and Encryption

Windows Explorer (Windows Vista/7) or *File Explorer* (Windows 8/10) can be used for setting attributes for a file or folder. The file and folder attributes are read-only, hidden, archive, and system, as shown in Figure 15.30.

TECH TIP

How to change a file or folder's attributes

To change a file or folder's attributes, right-click the filename or folder name > *Properties* > click attribute checkboxes to enable them. (If the file is not a system file, the system attribute is unavailable.) Click *Apply*.

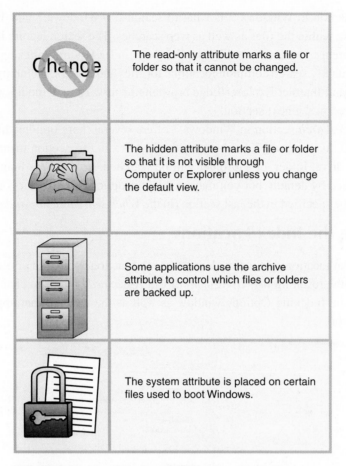

Change	The read-only attribute marks a file or folder so that it cannot be changed.
	The hidden attribute marks a file or folder so that it is not visible through Computer or Explorer unless you change the default view.
	Some applications use the archive attribute to control which files or folders are backed up.
	The system attribute is placed on certain files used to boot Windows.

FIGURE 15.30   Windows file/folder attributes

All Windows-based applications can read from and write to compressed files. The operating system decompresses the file, the file is available to the application, and the operating system recompresses the file when that file is saved. For the archive attribute, Windows files and folders have the archive attribute set by default. This is sometimes referred to as having the archive bit set. A lab at the end of the chapter demonstrates the concept of backups with Windows 7 and 10.

If a hard drive is partitioned for the NTFS file system, files and folders can be compressed or encrypted. Figure 15.31 provides more information on these concepts.

TECH TIP

Compression causes your computer to slow down

When compression is enabled, the computer's performance can degrade because when a compressed file is opened, the file must be uncompressed, and then it must be recompressed to be saved or closed. Degradation can also occur if a compressed file is transferred across a network because the file must be uncompressed before it is transferred.

TECH TIP

What happens when a compressed file is moved or copied?

Moving or copying a compressed file or folder can alter the compression. When moving a compressed file or folder, the file or folder remains compressed. When copying a compressed file or folder, it is compressed only if the destination folder (where you are moving it to) is already compressed. When adding a file to an encrypted folder, the file is automatically encrypted.

Compression involves compacting a file or folder to take less disk space. Right-click on a file/folder to be compressed > *Properties* > *General* tab > *Advanced* > *Compress contents to save disk space* or *Compress* checkbox > OK.

Encryption secures data from unauthorized users using an encryption feature called **EFS** (encrypting file system). Right-click on a file/folder to be encrypted > *Properties* > *General* tab > *Advanced* > *Encrypt contents to secure data* checkbox > OK.

FIGURE 15.31   Windows compression and encryption

Compressed files, system files, and read-only files cannot be encrypted. Windows Vista/7 Starter, Home Basic, and Home Premium versions do not fully support encryption, but the other Windows Vista/7 versions do. In the home Windows versions, the `cipher` command can be used at the command prompt to decrypt files, modify an encrypted file, and copy an encrypted file to the computer. The older Windows versions cannot encrypt.

Similarly, with Windows 8, the basic edition of Windows 8/8.1 (sometimes called Windows 8/8.1 Core in advertisements that target home computers) does not support EFS file encryption. Windows 8 Pro and Enterprise do. Windows 10 Home version does not support file encryption, but Windows 10 Pro, Enterprise, and Education versions do. Again, the `cipher` command can be used to decrypt, modify, and copy an encrypted file obtained from another computer or server that does support it.

When a file or folder is encrypted with EFS, only authorized users can view or change the file. Administrators designated as recovery agents have the ability to recover encrypted files when necessary. Labs 15.15 and 15.19 at the end of the chapter demonstrate how to copy files, move files, and manipulate file attributes, compression, and encryption.

TECH TIP

Copying and moving

When you are copying a file or folder, use the *Copy* and *Paste* functions from the *Edit* Windows Explorer/File Explorer menu option. When you move a file or folder, use the *Cut* and *Paste* functions.

Introduction to Windows Control Panels

Control Panels (also known as Control Panel applets) configure all aspects of Windows and can be accessed from the Start button menu or in Windows 8 from *Settings* charm > select the *Control Panel* link. You have actually been using some of the Windows Control Panels already in this chapter (Indexing Options and Folder Options). Control Panels can be viewed in two different ways: the older view where all Control Panels are shown as icons or the newer method which displays by categories. Actually, the *Settings* option could be considered a third way, but technicians tend to use Control Panels. Figure 15.32 shows Windows 7 Control Panels in icons view (small icons). Figure 15.33 shows Windows 8 Control Panels in category view.

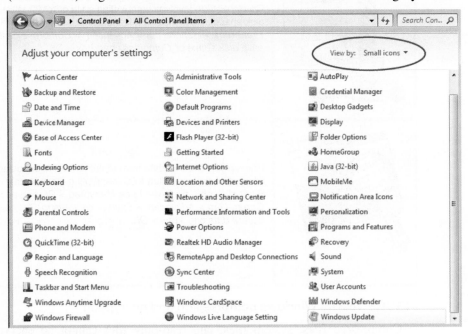

FIGURE 15.32   Windows 7 Control Panels—icon view

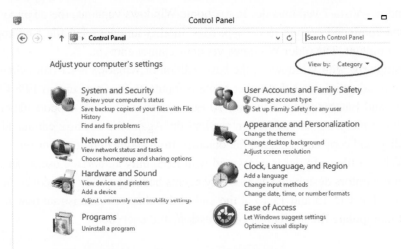

FIGURE 15.33   Windows 8 Control Panels—category view

Table 15.9 in Lab 15.1 shows all the Windows Vista and 7 Control Panel Categories and subcategories. Table 15.14 in Lab 15.5 shows the same thing in Windows 8.1. Table 15.20 in Lab 15.8 shows Windows 10 Control Panels. The major categories are listed in Table 15.6 that follows. Keep in mind that a particular Control Panel might be accessible through two or more Control Panel categories.

TABLE 15.6   Windows Control Panel categories

Category	Description
System and Security	Used to Configure Windows Firewall, power options, storage spaces, Windows Update, join a domain or workgroup, and access Action Center.
Network and Internet	Used to configure wired and wireless NICs, Bluetooth devices, Homegroup, and Internet Explorer/Edge options

Category	Description
Hardware and Sound	Used to view, control, and test devices such as a printer, mouse, keyboard, headset, scanner, sound, and display
Programs	Used to install or remove apps, gadgets, and Windows features
User Accounts/User Accounts and Family Safety	Used to configure user accounts and passwords
Appearance and Personalization	Used to configure desktop options, Start screen, and apply a theme, or change the desktop color
Clock, Language, and Region	Used to set the date and time, modify the language, and configure how numbers, symbols, and currency display
Ease of Access	Used to configure settings for visual, audio, and mobility capabilities

Labs at the end of this chapter and Chapter 16 contains examples of how to use the various Control Panels.

Determining the Windows Version

One Control Panel that is important for technicians is the *System* Control Panel. With this Control Panel you can determine the amount of RAM installed, processor installed, and Windows version. The version of an operating system is important when troubleshooting because it is one more piece of information that can be placed within a search parameter. You can access the same Control Panel by using Windows *Explorer* (Vista/7)/*File Explorer* (8/10) > right-click or tap and briefly hold *Computer* (Vista/7)/*This PC* (8/10) > *Properties*. Figure 15.34 shows the System Control Panel in Windows 10.

FIGURE 15.34   **Windows 10 System Control Panel**

With Windows Vista, 7, 8, and 8.1, upgrades or patches to the operating system are provided by service packs. A **service pack** has multiple fixes to the operating system. Technicians must determine what operating system version is on the computer so that they can research whether a service pack is needed or research a particular problem. Windows 10 provides updates automatically.

Windows Registry

Every software and hardware configuration is stored in a database called the **registry**. The registry contains such things as folder and file property settings, port configuration, application preferences, and user profiles. A **user profile** contains specific configuration settings such as the specific applications to which the user has access, desktop settings, and the user's network configuration for each person who has an account on the computer. The profile is different for each person who has an account on the computer. The registry loads into RAM (memory) during the boot process. When in memory, the registry is updated continuously by changes made to software, hardware, and user preferences.

The registry is divided into five subtrees. Subtrees are also sometimes called branches or hives. The five standard subtrees follow: `Hkey_Local_Machine`, `Hkey_Users`, `Hkey_Current_User`, `Hkey_Current_Config`, and `Hkey_Classes_Root`. Each of these subtrees has keys and subkeys that contain values related to hardware and software settings. Table 15.7 lists the five subtrees and their functions. The registry can contain other subtrees that are user-defined or system-defined, depending on what hardware or software is installed on the computer.

TABLE 15.7 Windows registry subtrees

Registry subtree	Subtree function
`Hkey_Local_Machine`	Holds global hardware configuration. Included in the branch is a list of hardware components installed in the computer, the software drivers that handle each component, and the settings for each device. This information is not user-specific.
`Hkey_Users`	Keeps track of individual users and their preferences.
`Hkey_Current_User`	Holds a specific user's configuration, such as software settings, how the desktop appears, and what folders the user has created.
`Hkey_Current_Config`	Holds information about the hardware profile that is used when the computer first boots.
`Hkey_Classes_Root`	Holds file associations and file links. The information held here is what allows the correct application to start when you double-click a filename in Windows Explorer/File Explorer or My Computer/Computer (provided that the file extension is registered).

Editing the Windows Registry

Most changes to Windows are done through the various Control Panels, but sometimes the only way to make a change is to edit the registry directly. Lab 15.16 at the end of the chapter illustrates this procedure. Depending on the Windows operating system used, one or two registry editors are available from a command prompt: **regedit** and **regedt32**. Figure 15.35 shows the Windows 7 `regedit` utility.

Notice in Figure 15.35 that subtrees appear in the left window, such as `Hkey_Classes_Root` and `Hkey_Current_User`. If you click the arrow beside a subtree, more subkeys appear. After several layers, when you click a folder in the left window, values appear in the right window. These values are the ones you must sometimes change to fix a problem.

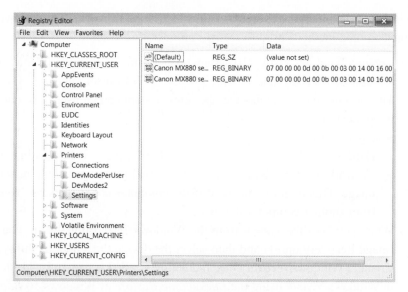

FIGURE 15.35 REGEDIT in Windows 7

Make a backup of the registry before you change it

Before making changes to the registry, you should make a backup of it. This way, if the changes do not work properly, the changes can be easily reversed.

For 64-bit versions of Windows, the registry is divided into 32- and 64-bit keys. The 32-bit keys are kept in a subfolder called *Wow6432Node*, located within the Hkey_Local_Machine key (*Software* folder). On some machines, the vendor may have a subfolder under *Software*; it is this vendor subfolder that contains the *Wow6432Node* folder. Just do a search for *Wow6432Node* to find it. 64-bit software keys are kept in Hkey_Local_Machine\Software subfolders.

Backing Up Data

Having a data backup is important. Many people store their data in a remote location. This is commonly known as cloud storage. Those that have an account with Google (Gmail or another Google product) have access to Google Drive; Microsoft users have OneDrive; Apple users have iCloud; and there are other vendors such as DropBox or SugarSync. Windows Vista, 7, and 10 allow backing up the entire system and files/folders using the Windows 7 *Backup and Restore or the Windows 10 Backup and Restore (Windows 7)* Control Panel. Windows 8 and 10 use *File History*, which saves files that are contained in the libraries (and you can create new libraries), contacts, desktop files, and favorites to external media or a network storage location. *Storage Spaces* (covered in Chapter 7) is another solution for backing up data. Labs at the end of the chapter describe how to use the *Backup and Restore* Control Panel as well as *File History*.

Recovering the Windows OS

When a computer starts performing badly and the operating system tools do not seem to help, you may need to repair, replace, or uninstall/reinstall the operating system. A virus could also cause extensive damage, resulting in the need for an operating system recovery. How you do this depends on what measures have been taken (or not been taken, in some cases) and the type of environment in which the computer is located (home or work). The following list describes some of the common methods used to recover an operating system:

> Create a Windows Vista/7/10 **system image** using the Windows Vista/7 *Backup and Restore or Windows 10 Backup and Restore (Windows 7)* Control Panel > *Create a system image* link. The system image contains the operating system and all user files that can be saved to one of three locations:
  > Optical discs.
  > Hard drive (Do not store on the same hard drive as the operating system.)
  > Network location (Keep in mind that you have to get to the network location to get the image. This might be difficult if the computer is not working. You could burn the image from another computer that works.)
> When you boot the system from the Windows 7/10 original disc, you can select the System Image Recovery option and then select the device that contains the system image.
> Create a Windows **recovery disc** (sometimes called a system repair disc or a recovery drive) in Windows Vista/7 using the *Backup and Restore* or Windows 10 *Backup and Restore (Windows 7)* Control Panel > *Create a system repair disc* link. In Windows 8/10, search for recovery and select *Create a recovery drive*. The system recovery disc can boot the system when you don't have an original Windows disc and then restore the computer from a previously saved system image.
> Use a recovery disc provided by the computer manufacturer to restore the computer to the original "as sold" condition. Caution: None of your data will be restored.
> A recovery partition or section of the hard drive (sometimes called the HPA, or host protected area) is created by the computer manufacturer and commonly accessed through Advanced Boot Options (press F8 while booting. To do the same in Windows 8/10 with an SSD installed or on a mobile device, perform the following:

  > In Windows 8, access *Settings > Advanced startup options >* locate the *Advanced startup* section, and select the *Restart now* button.
  > In Windows 10, access *Settings > Update & Security > Recovery >* locate the *Advanced startup* section, and select the *Restart now* button.

> You can use imaging software. Companies frequently have a standard image stored on a server that can replace a failing operating system or be used on a new computer.
> Backup/restore software may be provided by an external hard drive manufacturer.
> You can use the original operating system discs or image. This method is a risky one because the original discs or image do not contain the latest service packs. Download service packs and copy the service pack to an optical disc *before* re-installing the operating system. Research the service pack requirements before installing. Ensure the computer is disconnected from any network before re-installing the operating system and service packs! Do not connect to the network until the service packs have been installed, or virus infection may result.
> You can select *Safe Mode* from *Advanced Boot Options* (while booting) and use the *System Restore* tool to restore the operating system to a time when it worked.

WinRE

Windows Recovery Environment (**WinRE**) is used when Windows Vista and higher versions do not boot and other tools and startup options do not solve a problem. WinRE has a list of recovery options including a command prompt-only environment. The WinRE environment provides access to tools to troubleshoot the operating system when the tools within the operating system cannot be accessed or don't work properly. The tools are available through a special recovery partition accessed through Advanced Boot Options (F8 while booting) or from the original Windows installation disc. Select *Repair your computer*, and use the *System Recovery Options*. System Recovery Options are covered in detail in Chapter 16. Note that if you are in Windows 8 or 10 and an SSD is installed, you can still get to the Advanced Boot Options using the following process:

> In Windows 8, access *Settings > Advanced startup options >* locate the *Advanced startup* section, and select the *Restart now* button.

> In Windows 10, access *Settings > Update & Security > Recovery >* locate the *Advanced startup* section, and select the *Restart now* button.

Virtualization Basics

An optional technology you might want to implement in any operating system is virtualization. Have you ever seen a TV service that allows you to watch multiple sports channels at once in smaller windows, or a service that allows you to watch a smaller screen of a different channel in the corner of a larger window? That is like virtualization in the computer world. **Virtualization** allows multiple operating systems to be installed on the same computer without affecting each other (or even knowing about the other operating system), share hardware such as CPU, RAM, USB ports, NIC, and hard drive space, and provide a test environment or an operational environment for software that might not be compatible on a specific platform. Virtualization of a PC involves a computer that has a virtual application such as a VMware Workstation, Oracle VirtualBox, Microsoft Hyper-V, or Microsoft Virtual PC that has other instances of one or more operating systems. Figure 15.36 shows the concept of virtualization, and Table 15.8 has some terms commonly used with virtualization.

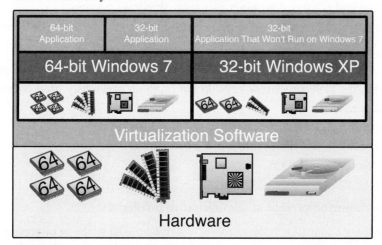

FIGURE 15.36   PC virtualization

TABLE 15.8   Virtualization terms

Term	Description
Host machine	The real computer
Virtual machine	Also called a VM; a separate operating system from the host computer that has specifically chosen hardware components
Hypervisor	Also called virtual machine monitor or virtual machine manager; the software that can create the virtual machine and allocate resources to the virtual machine
Snapshot/ Checkpoint	Similar concept to restore point; a copy or backup of the VM at a particular point in time; the snapshot can revert the VM to that point in time

There are fewer CPUs and less RAM in the VM (virtual machine) on the right than CPUs virtually "installed" in the left VM (refer to Figure 15.37). Within one virtual environment, you should not (and in some instances, cannot) "install" more hardware than is on the host machine (the real machine), even though some virtual software allows you to do so. For example, say that the VM on the left referred to in Figure 15.37 is assigned the full amount of RAM that is on the host machine, 4GB. The VM on the right is assigned 2GB. The total is 6GB, but the host machine has only 4GB. This is allowed and common in the virtual environment. Some virtualization software (but not all) enables you to select 6GB for the VM on the left, but doing so causes degradation in the virtual environment.

Working with VMs makes restoring an operating system (or a VM that holds an operating system) much easier than using the restoration methods previously described. Technicians today are expected to know the basics of working within a virtual environment. Chapter 16 provides more information on installing and configuring VMs.

Command Prompt Overview

Quite a few computer problems are software-related, and many hardware installations have software programs that allow the hardware to work. Running diagnostic software is something a technician also performs from time to time. Even with the advent of newer and more powerful operating systems, a technician still must enter basic commands into the computer while troubleshooting. Functioning from a command prompt is a skill that a technician still must use sometimes. When an operating system does not work, the technician must input commands from a prompt. Also, technicians frequently use commands to bring up a Windows tool rather than remembering where that tool is located within a particular Windows version.

Following are several ways to access a command prompt when the computer is functional:

> Access the *Search* function > type cmd and press [Enter].
> Access the *Search* function > type command and press [Enter]; note that when this option is used, the keyboard arrow keys do not bring up previously used commands as they do when using cmd.
> Access *Accessories* > *Command Prompt* (Vista, 7, and 10).
> Access the *Command Prompt* tile (Windows 8/10).

TECH TIP

Use the command prompt at administrative privileges

When issuing commands from a prompt, you might need to log in or provide credentials that allow you to execute a particular command with administrative privileges. Right-click or tap and briefly hold the *Command Prompt* option > select *Run as administrator*.

When in the command prompt window, you can close the window in several ways:

> Use the Close button in the upper-right corner.
> Click or tap the little black box in the upper-left corner > select *Close*.
> Type the **exit** command.

Command Prompt Basics

Drive letters are assigned to hardware devices when a computer boots. For example, the first hard drive partition gets the drive letter C:. The colon is part of the device drive letter. The devices detected by the operating system can use and be assigned drive letters A: through Z:.

All communication using typed commands begins at the **command prompt**, or simply a prompt. A command prompt might look like F:\> or C:\> or C:\Windows>. Commands are typed using a keyboard or entered through a touch screen. Capitalization does not matter when using a command prompt, but commands *must* be typed in a specific format and in a specific order. Practicing commands from a command prompt is the best way to become proficient at using them.

Files can be organized like chapters in a book; however, on a computer, these file groupings are called a folder (GUI environment) or a **directory** (command prompt environment). The starting point for all directories is the **root directory**. From the root directory, other directories can be created or accessed. The root directory is limited as to how many files it can hold and the quantity depends on the file system used. The root directory is shown with a backslash after the letter: C:\ or E:\. Within the command prompt environment, when you are at the root director, a greater than sign follows the letter and backslash: C:\> and E:\>.

An infinite number of files can exist under each directory. Each filename within a directory must be unique, but other directories can contain the same file. For example, assume that the *Cheryl.txt* file exists in the *Documents* directory. A different *Cheryl.txt* file (or the same one) can exist in the *Lotus* or *Utility* directory (or all three directories for that matter). It could also be the exact same file called *Cheryl.txt* that exists in all three folders. However, a second *Cheryl.txt* file cannot exist in the same folder (directory).

Files are kept in directories (folders) or in the root directory. A **subdirectory** can be created beneath another directory. For example, if a directory (folder) has the name *Book*, below the directory can be subdirectories titled *Chap1*, *Chap2*, *Chap3*, and so on. With the word *root* meaning the start of the directory structure, many people describe the directory structure as a tree. Figure 15.37 illustrates this concept.

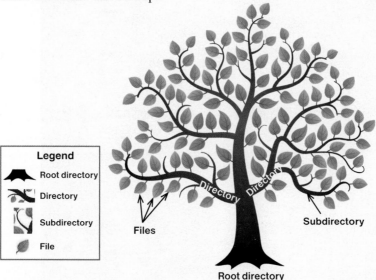

Legend
Root directory
Directory
Subdirectory
File

Files
Subdirectory
Root directory

FIGURE 15.37   Tree structure concepts

Sometimes, it is easier to see some of the file structure concepts from within File Explorer than the command prompt. Figure 15.38 shows the *Documents* directory of the C: drive for the user *Cheryl*. Notice the path is listed at the top of the File Explorer window because that option has been enabled through the *Folder Options* window previously described. Also notice the address bar and how it shows part of the path (<<Users > Cheryl > Documents). Within the window, it shows folders (2015BookWin8Laptop, Custom Office Templates, Outlook Files, and SugarSync Shared Folders). It also shows shortcuts to the My Music, My Pictures, and My Videos folders. Lastly, it shows four files (Chap1.docx, kara's books.docx, My class books.docx, and Spectre.docx) and one hidden file (desktop.ini). As previously mentioned, the settings in Folder Options Control Panel allow the filenames and hidden files to be seen.

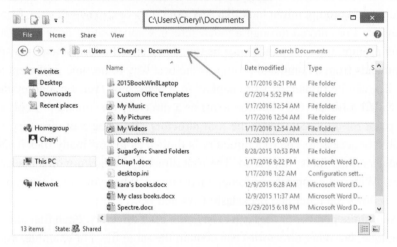

FIGURE 15.38   Sample file structure from File Explorer

Now let's view that same structure from the command prompt using the `tree` command. Note the tree command is not on the CompTIA A+ certification, but it is a handy one to see what directories (and subdirectories) are on the computer. Figure 15.39 shows this prospective from the command prompt.

FIGURE 15.39   Tree structure from a prompt

In Figure 15.39 notice that two commands have actually been given. The first one asks the computer to display a "tree" or the structure starting from C:\Users\Cheryl\Documents. The second command adds an /f so that files are shown.

Every folder along the path is shown, starting with the root directory of C: (C:\). The path tells you exactly how to reach the file. When something goes wrong in a particular application and Microsoft or another vendor posts a solution, Microsoft shows the complete path in the other vendors' directions. It is the only way to clearly tell you where to put a file, delete a file, or replace a file.

Moving Around from a Command Prompt

The most frequently used command for moving around in the cumbersome tree structure is cd (change directory). The cd command enables you to "change" the directory so that the prompt changes to where you are within the directory (tree) structure. For example, say you have a flash drive with a *Test1* directory that has subdirectories called *Sub1*, *Sub2*, and *Sub3*, as shown in Figure 15.40.

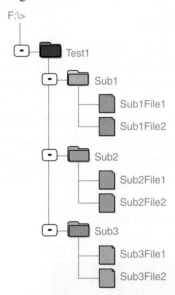

FIGURE 15.40   Sample tree structure

Assume that the prompt is at F:\>. (To get to this prompt, you simply type the drive letter of your flash drive and press (Enter)). To move to the *Sub2* subdirectory (subfolder), type the command cd Test1\Sub2. The prompt changes to F:\Test1\Sub2>. Another command that works is cd F:\Test1\Sub2.

To move to a subdirectory that is on the same level as the *Sub2* directory (such as *Sub1* or *Sub3*), several commands are possible. One way is to type cd.. to move back one level and then type cd Sub1. Notice that there is not a backslash (\) between cd and Sub1. You omit the backslash only when moving one level down the tree structure, as shown in the figure.

From the F:\Test1> prompt, you can type cd Sub1, cd\Test1\Sub1 or cd F:\Test1\Sub1 to get to the *Sub1* subfolder. However, if the prompt shows you are at the root directory (F:\>), either F:\Test1\Sub1 or cd Test1\Sub1 must be used. The other commands given do not operate properly because of the current location within the tree structure. Practice is the best way to master moving around from a prompt. Labs 15.17, 15.18, and 15.19 at the end of the chapter help with this concept.

The `DIR` Command

The `dir` lists all the files and directories from wherever you are at the prompt. Figure 15.41 shows the `dir` command from the root directory of a flash drive (G:\>).

FIGURE 15.41 `dir` command from a prompt

Notice in Figure 15.41 that directories are shown with the indication of `<DIR>`. Files have nothing in that column. Directories in the root directory of `G:` are `Chip`, `Dale`, `cotlong`, `Photos`, and `classes`. Files found in the root directory of the same flash drive are `Dinfo.txt` and `Ninfo.txt`.

Each command commonly has one or more optional **command switches** that change how the command operates. To determine what switches are available with any command, type the command followed by `/?` (*command* `/?` where the *command* is any command). For example, with the `dir` command `dir` `/?` shows all the possible options that can be used with the `dir` command (see Figure 15.42).

FIGURE 15.42 `dir` command switches

Notice in the output of 15.42 how there are optional parameters such as drive: and path. Each optional parameter and switch has brackets ([ ]) around it. Switches are preceded by a / (forward slash). Notice there is no space between the / and the optional switch. For example, with the `dir` command, you could simply type `dir` and press Enter. You could also type `dir` `/p` and display things one page at a time or `dir` `/w` and display the output in a wide format.

Also notice there is an order in listing the switches in the third line from the top. Normally, they are shown in alphabetical order. You can also do multiple switches such as the case with `dir`

/p /w. Also, each switch does not need a space between it, but you do need a space between the command and any of the switches. The command dir /p/w works exactly the same way as dir /p /w. Each command switch is described below all the options. The last thing to notice is that when some commands list more than one page of output, you get a message at the bottom of the screen, as shown in Figure 15.42 (Press any key to continue...).

TECH TIP

Make a command output one page at a time

If a command outputs more than one page at a time, you can use the | more option after the command and make it show only one page at a time. Note that the | (pipe) symbol is created by holding down the [Ctrl] key and pressing the [|] key located directly above the [Enter] key.

TECH TIP

Limited commands in WinRE

Not all command parameters or switches shown may be available when using the Windows Recovery Environment (WinRE), which is discussed in Chapter 16. The WinRE has a limited number of commands. Type the help command to see a list of available commands.

The MD and RD Commands

Sometimes as IT personnel, you might be required to create a directory from a prompt to install software or as part of a repair. The md (make directory) command makes a directory from wherever you are in the directory structure. (And you know this from the prompt.) Consider the following command: F:\>md CTS1133. The *CTS1133* directory would be made in the root directory of the F: drive. Now consider the following set of commands:

```
F:\>
F:\>cd classes
F:\Classes>md CTS1133
F:\Classes>
```

What is different about this set of commands is that before issuing the md CTS1133 command, the cd classes command was issued. The cd classes command changed the prompt to F:\Classes>. Then the md CTS1133 command was issued, thus creating a subdirectory called *CTS1133* under the *Classes* folder.

An alternative way of doing the same thing is to issue the full path with the command, as shown here. Note that the second command would work from any prompt including the C:\> prompt.

```
F:\>md \classes\CTS1133
```

   or

```
F:\>md F:\classes\CTS1133
```

TECH TIP

Full path works from everywhere

If you begin learning the command prompt by typing the full path no matter where you are in the directory structure, you will be better prepared for working in this environment.

The `rd` command removes a directory or subdirectory. Note that if the directory has files in it, an error appears: `The directory is not empty.` The examples here show how to remove a directory from the different prompts. Note that the first one works from any prompt even if it is another drive letter.

```
F:\>rd F:\classes\cts1133
F:\>rd \classes\cts1133
F:\Classes>rd cts1133
```

The DEL Command

Sometimes, a file has to be deleted as part of the repair process. The `del` (delete) command removes a file. It cannot be used to remove a directory. That is an important point to remember. To issue the command simply type the `del` command followed by the name of the file you want to delete. Note that you must be in the correct directory (as shown by the prompt) to use this method. You must include the file extension as part of the filename.

```
F:\>
F:\>cd F:\classes\cts1133
F:\Classes\CTS1133>del homework1.docx
F:\Classes\CTS1133>
```

An alternative method exists that can work from any prompt. This method requires that you type the full path to the file to be deleted, as shown here:

```
F:\>del F:\classes\cts1133\homework1.docx
```

The TYPE Command

Another useful command is the `type` command, which displays text (.txt) or batch (.bat) files on the screen. Many times *Readme.txt* files are included with software applications and utilities. The `type` command allows viewing these files; however, most of the time, these files occupy more than one screen. So, using the `| more` parameter after the `type` command permits viewing the file one screen at a time. After viewing each screen, the (Spacebar) is pressed. For example, `type readme.txt | more` allows viewing the text file called readme.txt one page at a time.

Copying Files

Commands that can copy files are `copy`, `xcopy`, and `robocopy`. The `copy` command is used to make a duplicate of a file. The `xcopy` command is used to copy and back up files and directories. The `robocopy` command enables you to copy a directory, its contents, all its subdirectories (and their subdirectories), as well as each attribute.

We focus on the `copy` command because it is the command you can use in any environment. The `copy` command is an internal command, meaning it cannot be found as an executable file on the hard drive or Windows disc. The operating system can always find an internal command no matter where in the directory structure the command is located. The command enables you to copy a file to a different disk, copy a file from one directory to another, copy a group of files using wildcards, or rename a file as it is being copied. A **wildcard** replaces one or more characters. ? and * are examples of wildcards, where ? represents a single character and * represents any number of characters.

> The `copy` command has three parts, separated by spaces:
>> The command itself (`copy` or `xcopy`)
>> The source (the file being copied)
>> The destination (where the file is being copied to)

In technical documentation, this would be shown as `copy` *source target.*

The destination is optional if the file copies into the current directory. For example, if working from the `E:\>` command prompt and copying a file called *Document.txt* from the hard drive's root directory, then the command could be `copy C:\Document.txt`. The destination is omitted because the file automatically copies to the current drive and directory (which is `E:\`). The same function can be accomplished by typing `copy C:\Document.txt E:\`, which has all three parts: the `copy` command, the *source* (a file called *Document.txt* located on the hard drive or `C:\Document.txt`), and the destination (the root directory of `E:` or `E:\`).

The command requires all three parts if the destination is *not* the current drive and directory. For example, take the situation of being at the `C:\>` command prompt. To copy the `format.com` command from the hard drive (System32 subfolder of the Windows folder) to a disk shown as `E:`, type the following command:

```
copy C:\Windows\System32\format.com  E:\
```

Note that the `copy` command is first. Then the source, location, and name of the file being copied—`C:\Windows\System32\format.com`. Last is the destination, `E:\`, or the root directory of the flash drive where the file is to be placed. If the current directory is the `C:\Windows\System32` hard drive directory, then the source path does not have to be typed. Instead, the command would look like the following:

```
C:\Windows\System32>copy format.com E:\
```

The backslash (`\`) after the `E:` is not necessary if the flash drive does not have directories (folders). The `copy` command does not need the entire path in front of the command because `copy` is an internal command.

TECH TIP

Getting the command straight in your head

Before using any command, consider the following questions:

> What command do you want to issue?
> Where in the directory structure are you currently working? Look at the prompt to see.
> If you are copying a file or moving a file, what is the name of the file, and what is the full path to it? This is the source file.
> If you are copying a file or moving a file, in what directory does the file need to be placed? This is the destination file.

The ATTRIB Command

The `attrib` command sets, removes, or shows the attribute of a file or a directory. Attributes change how a file or directory is displayed on the screen or what can be done with the file or directory. Possible attributes are read-only, archive, system, and hidden:

> The read-only attribute protects files so that they cannot be accidentally changed or deleted.
> The archive attribute marks files that have changed since they were last backed up by a backup program.
> The system attribute designates a file as a system file; files with this attribute do not show in directory listings.
> The hidden attribute allows file hiding and even directory hiding.

Set each attribute using the +*x* switch, where *x* is r for read-only, -a for archive, h for hidden, or s for system. Remove each attribute using the -r, -s, -h, or -a switch with the `attrib` command. One command can set more than one attribute on files or directories. For example, to make the *Cheryl.txt* file hidden and read-only, type `attrib +r +h Cheryl.txt`.

Why Learn Commands?

With many Windows problems, some solutions involve working from a command prompt until a Windows update fixes the problem. Other problems simply involve using a command from a prompt. Commands can also be used in a script. A script is a group of commands in one file that automates a particular task. For example, say that you want to write a script to stop a computer print spooler and delete all spooled files that are in the queue to be printed. The following commands could be written in Notepad and saved to a file called *DeletePrint.cmd*:

```
net stop spooler
del %systemroot%\system32\spool\printers\*.shd
del %systemroot%\system32\spool\printers\*.spl
net start spooler
```

After the file is saved, you could copy this file to a hard drive, type `DeletePrint`, and press [Enter], and the four commands execute.

TECH TIP

Run Device Manager from a prompt

From a command prompt or from the *Search* textbox > type `mmc devmgmt.msc` to start Device Manager. Note that you can access the Microsoft Management Console and still get to Device Manager by simply typing `mmc`.

PowerShell

In today's computing environment, a technician frequently has to do things to hundreds, or even thousands, of computers. Scripts and Windows PowerShell can help. Windows **PowerShell** is a tool to help technicians and network administrators automate support functions through the use of scripts and snippets. Windows 7, 8, and 10 ship with PowerShell as an accessory. Every command that you can type from a command window (and a lot more) can be executed from within PowerShell.

Other Commands You Should Look Over

Before taking your CompTIA A+ certification, a few more commands are discussed in other chapters or are beyond the basics of learning how to function from a command prompt. When you understand how to work from a prompt, any command can be executed fairly easily. In the "Command Format" section that follows, commands shown as key terms (bolded and colored) are objectives for the certification exam. The following list has all the commands and command utilities that a technician should use.

> [command name] /?	> format	> notepad
> bootrec	> gpresult	> nslookup
> cd	> gpupdate	> ping
> chkdsk	> help	> rd
> command	> ipconfig	> regedit
> copy	> md	> regsvr32
> defrag	> mmc	> robocopy
> del	> msconfig	> services.msc
> dir	> msinfo32	> sfc
> diskpart	> mstsc	> shutdown
> dxdiag	> nbtstat	> taskkill
> exit	> net	> tasklist
> expand	> netdom	> tracert
> explorer	> netstat	> xcopy

Command Format

When Windows does not boot, a technician must work from a command prompt. Some of the most frequently used commands are outlined on the following pages. Items enclosed by brackets are optional. Items in italics are command-specific values that you must enter. When the items are separated by a | (bar), one of the items must be typed.

The following section contains a command reference. Some of these commands are used in the labs of this chapter or within chapter text and labs for the chapters that follow. This list is by no means comprehensive. The colored terms are the ones on the CompTIA A+ certification. Visit the microsoft.com website for a complete listing; the TechNet area is a good asset.

TECH TIP

How to get help when working from a prompt

To get help while working from a prompt, type `help command_name` or type `command_name /?`. For example, to get help for the `attrib` command, type `help attrib` **or** `attrib /?`.

ATTRIB

The `attrib` command controls the attribute for a file or folder.

Syntax: `attrib [+|-h] [+|-r] [+|-a]`
                 `[+|-s] [drive:] [path] filename [/S] [/D]`
Explanation: + adds an attribute.
                 - takes away an attribute.
                 h is the hidden attribute.

r is the read-only attribute.

a is the archive file attribute.

s is the system attribute.

[*drive:*] is the drive where the file is located.

[*path*] is the directory/subdirectory where the file is located.

filename is the name of the file.

[/S] includes subfolders.

[/D] includes folders

Example: attrib +h c:\cheryl.bat sets the hidden attribute for a file called *Cheryl.bat* located on the hard drive.

Notes: The dir command (typed without any switches) is used to see what attributes are currently set. You may set more than one attribute at a time.

BCDEDIT

The bcdedit command is used at the command prompt or System Recovery environment to modify and control settings contained in the BCD (boot configuration data) store, which controls how the operating system boots.

Syntax: bcdedit [/createstore] [/copy] [/create] [/delete] [/deletevalue] [/set] [/enum] [/bootsequence] [/default] [/displayorder] [/timeout]

Explanation: [/createstore] creates a new empty BCD store that is not a system store.

[/copy] makes a copy of a specific boot entry contained in the BCD store.

[/create] creates a new entry in the BCD store.

[/delete] deletes an element from a specific entry in the BCD store.

[/deletevalue] deletes a specific element from a boot entry.

[/set] sets a specific entry's option value.

[/enum] lists entries in a store.

[/bootsequence] specifies a display order that is used one time only. The next time the computer boots, the original display order is shown.

[/default] selects the entry used by the boot manager when the timeout expires.

[/displayorder] specifies a display order that is used each time the computer boots.

[/timeout] specifies, in seconds, the amount of time before the boot manager boots using the default entry.

Example: bcdedit / set Default debug on

This command troubleshoots a new operating system installation for the operating system that is the default option that appears in the Boot Manager menu.

Notes: Use the bcdedit /? types command to see a list of data types. Use the bcd /? formats command to see a list of valid data formats. To get detailed information on any of the options, type bcdedit /? followed by the option. For example, to see information on how to export the BCD, type bcd /? export.

BOOTREC

The **bootrec** command is used from the System Recovery environment to repair and recover from hard drive problems.

Syntax: bootrec [/FixMbr] [/FixBoot] [/ScanOs] [/RebuildBcd]

Explanation: [/FixMbr] repairs the hard drive MBR (master boot record) by copying a new MBR to the system partition. The existing partition table is not altered.

[FixBoot] repairs the hard drive boot sector if it has been corrupted and replaces it with a non-Windows Vista or higher boot sector or, if an earlier version of Windows has been installed after Windows Vista, 7, 8/8.1, or 10. [/ScanOs] looks for compatible operating system installations that do not currently appear on the Boot Manager list.

[/RebuildBcd] scans all disks for operating systems compatible with Windows Vista or higher and optionally rebuilds the BCD (boot configuration data). The BCD store provides structured storage for boot settings that is especially helpful in multiple operating system environments. Discovered operating systems can be added to the BCD store.

Example:	bootrec /fixmbr
	This command could be used if a virus has destroyed the master boot record.
Notes:	If you receive an Element not Found error when using the bootrec command, the hard drive partition might not be active. Use the Windows recovery environment command prompt and the diskpart command to select the drive disk number (if you only have one and it has one partition, it will be the command select disk 0, as an example), and then type the command active. Exit the diskpart utility and reboot the computer. Re-access the System Recovery environment and rerun the bootrec command.
	If the system needs a new BCD and rebuilding it did not help, you can export the existing BCD and then delete the current BCD. To export the BCD, type bcdedit /export x:\folder (where x:\folder is the location where you want the BCD store exported). Then type c:, cd boot, attrib bcd -s -h -r, ren c:\boot\bcd bcd.old, bootrec /RebuildBcd to create a backup copy of the BCD store, make it so it is not hidden and can be deleted, and then rebuild it.

CD

The **cd** command is used to navigate through the directory structure.

Syntax:	cd [drive:][path][..]
Explanation:	[drive:] specifies the drive (if a different one than the current drive) to which you want to change.
	[path] is the directory/subdirectory to reach the folder.
	[..] changes to the parent directory (moves you back one directory in the tree structure).
Example:	C:\Windows>cd..
	C:\>
	This command moves you from the *Windows* directory (folder) to the parent directory, which is the root directory (C:\).
	C:\>cd \Windows
	This command moves you from the root directory to the *Windows* directory on the C: drive.

CHKDSK

The **chkdsk** command checks a disk for physical problems, lost clusters, cross-linked files, and directory errors. If necessary, the chkdsk command repairs the disk, marks bad sectors, recovers information, and displays the status of the disk.

Syntax:	chkdsk [drive:] [/r] [/f] [/i] [/b]
Explanation:	[drive:] specifies the drive to check.
	[/r] locates bad sectors and attempts recovery of the sector's information.
	[/f] fixes drive errors.
	[/i] checks only index entries on NTFS volumes.
	[/b] With NTFS, the switch re-evaluates bad clusters.

Example: chkdsk d: This command checks the disk structure on the D: drive.

Notes: This command can be used without switches. For the chkdsk command to work, the file *Autochk.exe* must be loaded in the *System32* folder or used with the correct path and run from the Windows disc. If one or more files are open on the drive being checked, chkdsk prompts you to schedule the disk to be checked the next time the computer is restarted.

CHKNTFS

The chkntfs command can display whether a particular disk volume is scheduled for automatic disk checking the next time the computer is started, or the command can be used to modify automatic disk checking.

Syntax: chkntfs *volume*: [/D] [/X] [/C]

Explanation: *volume*: specifies the drive volume to display or modify.

[/D] places the computer back to default behavior. (All drives are checked at boot time, and chkdsk is run on those that are dirty.)

[/X] excludes a particular volume from the default boot-time check.

[/C] schedules a drive to be checked at boot time. The chkdsk command will be run if the drive is dirty.

Example: chkntfs c: Displays whether the drive is dirty or scheduled to be checked on the next computer reboot.

CIPHER

The cipher command displays or alters file or folder encryption.

Syntax: cipher [/e |/d] [/f] [/q] [/k] [/u [/n]] [*path*|

Explanation: [/e] encrypts the specified folder, including files that are added in the future.

[/d] decrypts the specified folder.

[/f] forces encryption or decryption because, by default, files that have already been encrypted or decrypted are skipped.

[/q] reports essential information about the encryption or decryption.

[/k] creates a new file encryption key.

[/u] updates the encryption key to the current one for all encrypted files if the keys have been changed. /u works only with the /n option.

[/n] finds all encrypted files. It prevents keys from being updated. It is used only with /u.

[*path*] is a pattern, file, or folder.

Example: cipher /e Book\Chap1

This command encrypts a subfolder called *Chap1* that is located in a folder called *Book*.

cipher /e /s:Book

This command encrypts all subfolders in the folder called *Book*.

cipher Book

This command displays whether the *Book* folder is encrypted.

cipher Book\Chap 1*

This command display whether any files in the *Chap1* subfolder of the *Book* folder are encrypted.

Notes: Multiple parameters are separated with spaces. Read-only files and folders cannot be encrypted.

CLS

The `cls` command clears the screen of any previously typed commands.

Example: `C:\Windows>cls`

COMMAND

The **command** command is executed from the *Search* textbox by simply typing command and pressing Enter. A command prompt window appears. Type `exit` to close the window.

Syntax: `command`
Explanation: When `command` is entered, a command prompt window opens.

COPY

The **copy** command is used to copy one or more files to the specified destination.

Syntax: `copy [/a] [/y] [/-y] source [target]`
Explanation: `[/a]` indicates an ASCII text file.
`[/y]` suppresses the prompt to overwrite an existing file.
`[/-y]` prompts to overwrite an existing file.
source is the file that you want to copy, and it includes the drive letter and the path if it is different from your current location.
`[target]` is the location in which you want to put the file and includes the drive letter and path if it is different from your current location.
Example: `copy c:\cheryl.bat f:\`
This command takes a file called *Cheryl.bat* that is located in the root directory of the hard drive and copies it to a flash drive.
Notes: You do not have to put a target if the file is going to the current location specified by the command prompt. If a file already exists, you will be prompted whether to overwrite the file. Compressed files that are copied from the Windows media are automatically uncompressed to the hard drive as they are copied.

DEFRAG

The **defrag** command is used to locate and reorder files so that they are contiguous (not fragmented) and improve system performance.

Syntax: `defrag [drive:] [/a] [/c] [/x]`
Explanation: `[drive:]` is the drive letter where the files are located.
`[/a]` analyzes the drive volume specified.
`[/c]` includes all volumes.
`[/x]` consolidates free space on the specified volume.
Example: `defrag c: d: /a`
This command defragments the `C:` and `D:` drives and analyzes them.
Notes: Multiple switches can be used as long as spaces appear between them.
Multiple drive letters (volumes) can be used with a single command.

DEL

The **del** command is used to delete a file.

Syntax: `del name [/p][/f][/s]`
Explanation: *name* is the file or directory (folder) that you want to delete and it includes the drive letter and the path if it is different from your current location.
`[/p]` prompts for confirmation before deleting.
`[/f]` forces read-only files to be deleted.
`[/s]` deletes files from all subdirectories.

Example: `C:\Windows>del c:\cheryl.bat`
This command deletes a file called *Cheryl.bat* that is located in the *Windows* directory on the hard drive.

DIR

The **dir** command list files and folders and their attributes.

Syntax: `dir [drive:] [path] [filename] [/a:attribute] [/o] [/p] [/s] [/w]`

Explanation: `[drive:]` is the drive letter where the files are located.
`[path]` is the directory/subdirectory to reach the folder.
`[filename]` is the name of a specific file.
`[/a:attribute]` displays files that have specific attributes where the attributes are D, R, H, A, and S. D is for directories; R is for read-only; H is for hidden; A is for archive; and S is for system files.
`[/o]` displays the listing in sorted order. Options you can use after the o are E, D, G, N, and S. E is by alphabetic file extension; D is by date and time, with the oldest listing shown first; G shows the directories listed first; N displays by alphabetic name; and S displays by size from smallest to largest.
`[/p]` displays the information one page at a time.
`[/s]` includes subdirectories in the listing.
`[/w]` shows the listing in wide format.

Example: `dir c:\windows`
This command shows all the files and folders (and their associated attributes) for the *Windows* folder that is located on the `C:` drive.

DISABLE

The `disable` command disables a system service or hardware driver.

Syntax: `disable name`
Explanation: `name` is the name of the service or driver that you want to disable.
Notes: You can use the `listsvc` command to show all services and drivers that are available for you to disable. Make sure that you write down the previous *START_TYPE* before you disable the service in case you need to restart the service.

DISKPART

The **diskpart** command is used to manage and manipulate the hard drive partitions.

Syntax: `diskpart [/add|/delete] [devicename] [drivename | partitionname] [size]`

Explanation: `[/add |/delete]` creates a new partition or deletes an existing partition.
`[devicename]` is the name given to the device when creating a new partition, such as \Device\HardDisk0.
`[drivename]` is the drive letter used when deleting an existing partition such as E:. `[partitionname]` is the name used when deleting an existing partition and can be used instead of the *drivename* option. An example of a *partitionname* is Device\HardDisk0\Partition2.
`[size]` is used when creating a new partition and is the size of the partition in megabytes.

Notes: You can just type the `diskpart` command without any options, and a user interface appears that helps when managing hard drive partitions. Lab 7.4 demonstrates this command.

DXDIAG

The **dxdiag** command is used to perform DirectX diagnostics.

Syntax:	`dxdiag [/dontskip] [whql:on|/whql:off] [/64bit target]` `[/x filename] [/t filename]`
Explanation:	`[/dontskip]` causes all diagnostics to be performed even if a previous crash in `dxdiag` has occurred. `[/whql:on]` checks for WHQL digital signatures. `[/whql:off]` prevents checking for WHQL digital signatures. `[/64bit target]` uses 64-bit DirectX diagnostics. `[/x filename]` saves XML information to the specified filename and quits. `[/t filename]` saves TXT information to the specified filename and quits.
Notes:	When DirectX diagnostics checks for WHQL digital signatures, the Internet may be used.

ENABLE

The `enable` command is used to enable a system service or hardware driver.

Syntax:	`enable name [start-type]`

Explanation:	`name` is the name of the service or driver that you want to disable.
	`[start-type]` is when you want the service or driver scheduled to begin. Valid options are as follows:
	`SERVICE_BOOT_START`
	`SERVICE_SYSTEM_START`
	`SERVICE_AUTO_START`
	`SERVICE_DEMAND_START`

Example:	`enable DHCP client service_auto_start`
Notes:	You can use the `listsvc` command to show all services and drivers that are available for you to enable. Make sure that you write down the previous value before you enable the service in case you need to restart the old service or driver.

EXIT

The **exit** command closes the command prompt environment window.

Example:	`C:\Windows>exit`

EXPAND

The **expand** command uncompresses a file from a CAB file. A CAB file is a shortened name for a cabinet file. A CAB file holds multiple files or drivers that are compressed into a single file. Technicians sometimes copy the CAB files onto the local hard drive so that when hardware and/or software is installed, removed, or re-installed, the application disc does not have to be inserted.

Syntax:	`expand [-i] source [destination]`
Explanation:	`[-i]` renames files but ignores the directory structure. `source` is the name of the file, including the path that you want to uncompress. `[destination]` is the path where you want to place the uncompressed file.
Example:	`expand d:\i386\access.cp_ c:\windows\system32\access.cpl` expands (uncompresses) the compressed file *Access.cp_* and puts it into the *C:\Windows\System32* folder with the name *Access.cpl*.
Notes:	You may not use wildcard characters with the `source` parameter.

CHAPTER 15

EXPLORER

The **explorer** command is used to start Windows Explorer from a command prompt.

Syntax:　　　`explorer`

FORMAT

The **format** command is used to format a disk or drive and can format it for a particular file system.

Syntax:　　　`format [driveletter:] [/q] [/fs:filesystem] [/v:label] [/x]`

Explanation:　`[driveletter:]` is the drive letter for the disk or hard drive volume that you want to format.

`[/q]` is the parameter used if you want to perform a quick format.

`[/fs:filesystem]` is the parameter used if you want to specify a file system. Valid values are as follows: FAT, FAT32, exFAT, and NTFS.

`[/v:label]` The `/v:` must be part of the command followed by the name of the volume assigned.

`[/x]` dismounts the volume first, if necessary.

Example:　　`format c: /fs:ntfs`

Notes:　　　If no `/fs:filesystem` parameter is specified, the NTFS file system is used. FAT is FAT16. FAT16 hard drive volumes cannot be more than 4GB in size.

GPRESULT

The **gpresult** command is used to display group policy settings. A group policy determines how a computer is configured for both system and user (or a group of users) settings.

Syntax:　　　`gpresult [/s computer] [/u domain\user] [/p password] [/user target_user] [ /r] [/v] [/z]`

Explanation:　`[/s computer]` is an optional parameter that specifies a remote computer using the computer name or IP address; otherwise, the local computer is selected by default.

`[/u domain\user]` specifies authentication for the remote computer.

`[/p password]` specifies a password for the remote computer user ID.

`[/user target_user]` specifies to display a user's group policy settings.

`[/v]` outputs data in verbose mode.

`[/z]` displays all available data about the group policy.

Examples:　　`gpresult /r`

`gpresult /s 10.3.207.15 /u pearson\cschmidt /p G#t0Ut0fH3R3`

GPUPDATE

The **gpupdate** command refreshes local- and Active Directory-based group policy settings.

Syntax:　　　`gpupdate [/target:{computer | user}] [/force] [/wait:value] [/logoff] [/boot]`

Explanation:　`[/target:{computer | user}]` is an optional parameter used to specify whether either the *Computer* settings or the current *User* settings are used. When neither is specified, both computer and user settings are processed.

`[/force]` reapplies all settings.

`[/wait:value]` specifies the number of seconds policy processing waits to finish. The default is 600 seconds. A 0 wait value processes immediately. A -1 value places the wait time at indefinitely.

`[/logoff]` forces a logoff after the refresh completes.

`[/boot]` forces the computer to restart after the refresh completes.

Example:　　`gpupdate /force /boot`

HELP

The `help` command displays information about specific commands.

Syntax: `help [command]`

Explanation: `[command]` is the name of the command for which you want help.

Example: `help expand`

Notes: If you do not specify the *command* parameter when using the `help` command, all commands are listed.

IPCONFIG

The `ipconfig` command is used to view and control information related to the network adapter.

Syntax:
```
ipconfig [/allcompartments] [/all|/renew [adapter] |
/release [adapter]|/renew6 [adapter]|/release6 [adapter]|
/flushdns|displaydns|/registerdns|/showclassid [adapter]|
/setclassid adapter [classid]|/showclassid6 [adapter]|
/setclassid6 adapter [classid]]
```

Explanation: `[/allcompartments]` displays information regarding all compartments and, when used with the `/all` option, shows detailed information about all compartments.

`[/all]` displays all configuration information, including IP and MAC addresses.

`[/renew]` renews the IPv4 address optionally for a specific adapter.

`[/release]` releases the IPv4 address optionally for a specific adapter.

`[/renew6]` renews the IPv6 address optionally for a specific adapter.

`[/release6]` releases the IPv6 address optionally for a specific adapter.

`[/flushdns]` removes all entries from the DNS resolver cache.

`[/displaydns]` shows the contents of the DNS resolver cache.

`[/registerdns]` refreshes DHCP leases and re-registers recently used DNS names.

`[/show classid]` displays all configured IPv4 DHCP class IDs allowed optionally for a specific adapter.

`[/setclassid adapter]` configures an adapter for a specific IPv4 DHCP class ID. A class ID is used to have two or more user classes that are configured as different DHCP scopes on a server. One class could be for laptops, whereas a different class could be for desktop computers in an organization.

`[/showclassid6 adapter]` displays all configured IPv6 DHCP class IDs allowed optionally for a specific adapter.

`[/setclassid6 adapter]` configures an adapter for a specific IPv6 DHCP class ID.

Examples:
```
ipconfig /all
ipconfig /release
ipconfig /renew
```

Notes: The three preceding commands are essential to a technician. `ipconfig /all` verifies whether an IP address has been configured or received from a DHCP server. `ipconfig /release` releases a DHCP-sent IP address. `ipconfig /renew` starts the DHCP request process.

MD

The **md** command is used to create a directory (folder).

Syntax: `md [driveletter:][dirname]`

Explanation: `[driveletter:]` is the drive letter for the disk or volume on which you want to create a directory (folder). It can also include the path.

                `[dirname]` is the parameter used to name the directory (folder).

Example: `md c:\test`

Notes: You may not use wildcard characters with this command. The `mkdir` command can also be used to create a directory.

MMC

The **mmc** command is used to open the Microsoft Management Console.

Syntax: `mmc [path\filename.msc][/a] [/64] [/32]`

Explanation: `[path\filename.msc]` is an option to specify where to locate a saved console.

                `[/a]` opens the console in author mode.

                `[/64]` opens the 64-bit console.

                `[/32]` opens the 32-bit console.

Example: `mmc`

Notes: Use the /32 parameter if you are in a 64-bit operating system and want to run 32-bit snap-ins.

MORE

The `more` command is used to display a text file.

Syntax: `more filename`

Explanation: `filename` is the path and name of the text file you want to display on the screen.

Example: `more c:\boot.ini`

Notes: The `Spacebar` enables you to view the next page of a text file. The `Enter` key enables you to scroll through the text file one line at a time. The `Esc` key enables you to quit viewing the text file.

MSCONFIG

The **msconfig** command starts the System Configuration utility from a command prompt instead of a Control Panel. The System Configuration utility is commonly used to troubleshoot boot issues specifically related to software and services. The Startup tab lists software loaded when the computer boots, and a checkbox enables you to disable and enable the particular application. The same concept is used with the Services tab, which contains checkboxes beside services started when the computer boots.

Syntax: `msconfig`

MSINFO32

The **msinfo32** command brings up the System Information window from a command prompt. The System Information window contains details about hardware and hardware configurations as well as software and software drivers.

Syntax: `msinfo32 [/computer computer_name]`

Explanation: `[/computer computer_name]` starts the System Information utility for a remote computer.

Examples: `msinfo`

                `msinfo /computer Cheryl_Dell`

MSTSC

The **mstsc** command starts the Remote Desktop utility.

Syntax: `mstsc [/v:computer[:port]]`

Explanation: `[/v:computer[:port]` specifies the specific remote computer by name or IP address and port number to which you want to connect.

Example: `mstsc /v:Cheryl-PC`

Notes: The default port number for Remote Desktop is 3389, but if a different port has been specified, then you can specify a port using this command.

NBTSTAT

The **nbtstat** command is used to display statistics relevant to current TCP/IP connections on the local computer or a remote computer using NBT (NetBIOS over TCP/IP).

Syntax: `nbtstat [-a remotename] [-A IPaddress] [-c] [-S]`

Explanation: `[-a remotename]` shows the NetBIOS name table for a remote computer designated by `remotename`.

                 `[-A IPaddress]` shows the NetBIOS name table for a remote computer designated by `IPaddress`.

                 `[-c]` shows the NetBIOS name cache, names, and resolved IP addresses.

                 `[-S]` shows NetBIOS client and server sessions.

Examples: `nbtstat -S`

                 `nbtstat -A 10.5.8.133`

NET

The **net** command has many options, and each of those options has specific parameters. A few are given after this one.

Syntax: `net [computer] [group] [localgroup] [print] [session] [share] [use] [user] [view]`

Explanation: `[computer]` adds or removes a computer from the network domain.

                 `[group]` adds, views, or modifies domain groups.

                 `[localgroup]` adds, views, or modifies local groups.

                 `[print]` displays or controls a specific network printer queue.

                 `[share]` manages share resources.

                 `[session]` manages sessions with remote devices.

                 `[use]` attaches to a remote network device.

                 `[user]` adds, modifies, or views a network user account.

                 `[view]` lists resources or computers shared by the computer this is used on.

NET USE

The **net use** command attaches to a remote network device.

Syntax: `net use [drive_letter] [\\server_name\share_name /user:domain_name\user_name [password]]`

Explanation: `drive_letter` is the letter (followed by a colon) that `net use` assigns to the network device connection.

                 `\\server_name` is the name of the network device to which to connect.

                 `share_name` is the name of the share.

                 `domain_name` is the domain used to validate the user.

                 `user_name` is the user to be validated.

                 `[password]` is an optional entry, so the system does not prompt for a password. If this option is not entered, a password prompt appears, and the system automatically assigns a drive letter once a connection is made.

Example: `net use \\ATC227-01\cisco /user:cisco\student`

NETDOM

The **netdom** command manages Active Directory domains and trust relationships. This command has many operations, as shown in the syntax and explanation section.

Syntax: netdom {add | computername | join | move | query |
                  remove | renamecomputer | reset | resetpwd | verify}
                  [<Computer>] [{/d: | /domain:} <Domain>] [<Options>]

Explanation: add adds a workstation to the domain.

                  [computername] manages the primary and alternative names for a domain
                  controller.

                  [join] joins a computer to the domain.

                  [move] moves a computer to a new domain.

                  [query] presents information about the domain membership, trust, and so on.

                  [remove] deletes a computer form the domain.

                  [renamecomputer] renames a domain workstation.

                  [reset] resets the connection between a domain workstation and the domain
                  controller.

                  [resetpwd] resets a computer account password for a domain controller.

                  [verify] verifies the connection between a domain workstation and the
                  domain controller.

NETSTAT

The **netstat** command attaches to a remote network device.

Syntax: netstat [-a] [-e] [-n] [-o] [-p protocol] [-r] [-s]

Explanation: [-a] shows all connections and listening port numbers.

                  [-e] shows Ethernet statistics and can be used with the -s option.

                  [-n] shows addresses and port numbers.

                  [-o] shows active TCP connections.

                  [-p protocol] shows specific connections that use a specific protocol. The
                  protocol parameter can be one of the following: IP, IPv6, ICMP, ICMPv6,
                  TCP, TCPv6, UDP, and UDPv6.

                  [-r] shows the routing table.

                  [-s] shows statistics for a particular protocol.

Examples: netstat
                  netstat -a
                  netstat -p TCP

Note: The parameters used with this command must be preceded by a dash rather
                  than the / (slash) used by most commands.

NOTEPAD

The **notepad** command starts the Windows Notepad accessory.

Syntax: notepad

NSLOOKUP

The **nslookup** command is used to troubleshoot DNS issues.

Syntax: nslookup [-option] [hostname] [server]

Explanation: [-option] is a variety of options that can be used, such as exit, finger,
                  help, ls, lserver, root, server, and set. See Microsoft TechNet for a
                  complete listing.

                  [hostname] is a name of a host, such as the computer name for a specific
                  computer in the organization.

                  [server] is the URL of a specific server, such as www.pearsoned.com.

Examples:	nslookup www.pearsoned.com
	nslookup -querytype=hinfo -timeout=10
Notes:	The second example changes the default query type to a host and the timeout to 10 seconds. You must have at least one DNS server IP address configured on a network adapter (which you can view with the ipconfig /all command) to use the nslookup command. There are two modes of operation: non-interactive and interactive. The non-interactive has more commands than shown in the examples given. The interactive mode is started by simply typing nslookup and pressing Enter.

PING

The ping command tests connectivity to a remote network device.

Syntax:	ping [-t] [-a] [-n *count*] [-l *size*] [-i *ttl*] [-S *source_addr*] [-4] [-6] *target*
Explanation:	[-t] pings the destination until stopped with Ctrl + C keystrokes. To see the statistics and continue, use the Ctrl + Break keys.
	[-a] resolves IP addresses to hostnames.
	[-n *count*] defines how many pings (echo requests) are sent to the destination.
	[-l *size*] defines the buffer size (length of packet).
	[-i *ttl*] defines a Time To Live value from 0 through 255.
	[-S *source_addr*] defines the source IP address to use.
	[-4] forces the use of IPv4.
	[-6] forces the use of IPv6.
	target is the destination IP address.
Examples:	ping -t www.pearsoned.com
	ping -n 2 -l 1450 165.193.130.107
Notes:	The first example pings the Pearson Technology Education website indefinitely until the Ctrl + C keys are used. The second example sends two echo requests (pings) that are 1450 bytes to the Pearson Technology Education website.

RD

The **rd** command is used to remove a directory (folder).

Syntax:	rd [*driveletter*:][*path*] *name*
Explanation:	[*driveletter*:] is the drive letter for the disk or hard drive volume from which you want to remove a directory (folder).
	[*path*] is the optional path and name of the directory (folder) you want to remove.
	name is the name of the folder/directory to remove.
Example:	rd c:\Test\Junkdata removes a directory (folder) called *Junkdata* that is a subdirectory under a directory (folder) called *Test*. This directory is located on the hard drive (c:).
Notes:	You do not have to use the *driveletter*: parameter if the default drive letter is the same as the one that contains the directory to be deleted.

REGEDIT

The **regedit** command accesses the Windows registry editor.

Syntax:	regedit
Explanation:	*All the Windows configuration information is stored in a hierarchical database. The registry editor can modify specific registry keys, back up the registry, or set specific values to the default.*
Notes:	The regedt32 command brings up the same registry editor window.

REGSVR32

The **regsvr32** command registers .dll files in the Windows registry.

Syntax:	regsvr32 [/u] *name*
Explanation:	*name* is the name of the .dll file that will be registered.
	[/u] is an optional switch used to unregister a .dll file.
Example:	Regsvr32 wuapi.dll registers a Windows update DLL file.
Notes:	There is a 64-bit version of this file found in the *SysWow64* folder.

REN

The ren command renames a file or directory (folder).

Syntax:	ren [*driveletter:*][*path*] *name1 name2*
Explanation:	[*driveletter:*] is the drive letter for the disk or hard drive volume where you want to rename a file or a directory (folder).
	[*path*] is the optional path telling the operating system where to find the file or directory (folder) you want to rename.
	name1 is the old name of the file or directory (folder) that you want to rename.
	name2 is the new name of the file or directory (folder).
Example:	ren c:\cheryl.bat c:\newcheryl.bat
Notes:	The renamed file cannot be placed in a new location with this command. Move or copy the file after you rename it if that is what you want to do. The * and ? wildcard characters are not supported.

ROBOCOPY

The **robocopy** command is used to copy files but has a lot more parameters than COPY or XCOPY.

Syntax:	robocopy [*source*] [*destination*] [*file* [*file*]...] [*options*]
Explanation:	[*source*] specifies the source directory in the drive:\ path format or the \\server\share path format.
	[*destination*] specifies the destination directory in the drive:\ path format or the \\server\share path format.
	[*file*] is the files to copy, including wildcards. The default is *.*.
	[*options*] includes various options, such as /s to copy subdirectories (but not empty ones), /e to copy subdirectories (including empty ones), /mov to move files and delete the source, /move to move files and directories and delete the source, /a to copy files with the archive attribute set, and /m to copy files with the archive attribute set and to reset the archive bit.
Examples:	robocopy c:\users\cschmidt\My Documents\Book d:\ /e
	robocopy \\CSchmidt\Book \\RLD\SchmidtBook
Notes:	The first command copies the contents of the *Book* subfolder to the D: drive and includes any empty directories.
	The second command copies all files from the *CSchmidt* computer share called *Book* to the *RLD* computer network share called SchmidtBook.

SERVICES.MMC

The **services.msc** command is used to open the Microsoft Management Console and display the services window.

Syntax:	services.msc
Notes:	The services window shows the applications that run as background applications. Some services are manually started by the user or a technician, some start automatically, some start automatically but delay starting to allow faster booting. This window is commonly used to start a service or to verify a service such as the print service is still started.

SET

The set command is used to display and view different variables.

Syntax:	set [*variable = value*]
Explanation:	*variable* is one of the following:
	AllowWildCards is the variable used to enable wildcard support for the commands that normally do not support wildcards.
	AllowAllPaths is the variable that allows access to all the computer's files and folders.
	AllowRemovableMedia is the variable that allows files to be copied to removable media.
	NoCopyPrompt is the variable that disables prompting when overwriting a file.
	value is the setting associated with the specific variable.
Example:	set allowallpaths = true allows access to all files and folders on all drives.
	set allowremovablemedia = true allows you to use a flash (thumb) drive or floppy.
	set allowwildcards = true allows you to use wildcards at the command prompt.
Notes:	To see all of the current settings, type set without a variable and the current settings display. The set command can be used only if it is enabled using the Group Policy snap-in.

SFC

The **sfc** command starts the System File Checker utility from a command prompt. The System File Checker verifies operating system files.

Syntax:	sfc [/scannow] [/verifyonly] [/scanfile=*file_name*] [/verifyfile=*file_name*] [/offwindir=*windows_directory*] [/offbootdir=*boot_directory*]
Explanation:	[/scannow scans all protected system files and repairs those that are damaged, if possible.
	[/verifyonly] scans all protected system files but does not repair any detected problems.
	[/scanfile=*file_name*] scans the specified file and repairs it if necessary. *file_name* should contain the full path.
	[/verifyfile=*file_name*] verifies the specified file but does not repair it. *file_name* should contain the full path.
	[/offwindir=*windows_directory*] is used for offline repairs for the specified Windows directory.
	[/offbootdir=*boot_directory*] is used for offline repairs for the specified boot directory.
Examples:	sfc /scannow
	sfc /scannow /offwindir=c:\Windows

SHUTDOWN

The **shutdown** command is used to restart or shut down a local or remote computer.

Syntax:	shutdown [-l] [-s] [-r] [-a] [-f] [-m [*computer_name*]] [-t *xx*] [-c "*message*"]
Notes:	If this command is used without any parameters, the command logs off the current user.
	You cannot use the -a parameter except during the timeout period.

Explanation: [/l] logs off the current user.

[-s] shuts down the computer.

[-r] reboots the computer.

[-a] aborts the shutdown process.

[-f] forces active applications to close.

[-m [*computer_name*] specifies a specific computer to shut down.

[/t *xx*] specifies the number of seconds waited before shutting down the computer.

[-c "*message*"] specifies a 127 maximum character message shown in the System Shutdown window.

Examples: shutdown -f -m \\Raina-PC -t 30 -c "Going down in 30 seconds, daughter"

SYSTEMINFO

The systeminfo command displays detailed configuration information about a specific computer.

Syntax: systeminfo [/s *computer*] [/u *domain**user*] [/p *password*] [/fo [table | list | csv]]

Explanation: [/s *computer*] is an optional parameter that designates a specific remote computer using the computer name or IP address; otherwise, the local computer is selected by default.

[/u *domain**user*] specifies authentication for the remote computer.

[/p *password*] specifies a password for the remote computer user ID.

[/fo [table | list | csv]] defines whether the output displays in table format, list format, or csv (comma separated values) format. The default is to display in table format.

Examples: systeminfo

systeminfo /s CSchmidt /u pearson\\cschmidt /p G#T0UT0FH3R#

TASKKILL

The **taskkill** command is used to halt a process or task.

Syntax: taskkill [/s *computer*] [/u *domain**user*] [/p *password*] [/pid *process_id*]

[/im *name*] [/f] [/t]

Explanation: [/s *computer*] is an optional parameter that designates a specific remote computer using the computer name or IP address; otherwise, the local computer is selected by default.

[/u *domain**user*] specifies authentication for the remote computer.

[/p *password*] specifies a password for the remote computer user ID.

[/pid *process_id*] specifies a specific process ID to halt.

[/im *name*] specifies a specific image or application name to halt.

[/f] forcefully terminates the process.

[/t] is a "tree kill" that kills all child processes associated with the process ID.

Examples: taskkill /pid 1230 /pid 1231 /pid 1242

taskkill /im iexplore.exe

TASKLIST

The **tasklist** command is used to list process IDs for active applications and services.

Syntax: tasklist [/s *computer*] [/u *domain**user*] [/p *password*] [/fo {table|list|csv}] [/v]

Notes: This command should be used before the taskkill command.

If no computer is specified, the default is the local computer.

Explanation: [/s *computer*] is an optional parameter that designates a specific remote computer using the computer name or IP address; otherwise, the local computer is selected by default.

[/u *domain\user*] specifies authentication for the remote computer.

[/p *password*] specifies a password for the remote computer user ID.

[/fo {table|list|csv}] specifies the output format (table, which is the default, list, or CSV).

[/v] displays output in a verbose format.

Examples: tasklist /fo csv

TELNET

The telnet command is used to access a remote network device.

Syntax: telnet [*destination*]

Explanation: [*destination*] is the name or IP address of the remote network device.

Notes: The Telnet Client must be enabled through the *Programs and Features > Turn Windows features on or off* Control Panel. SSH is a better tool to use.

TRACERT

The tracert command verifies the path taken by a packet from a source device to a destination.

Syntax: tracert [-d] [*destination*]

Explanation: [-d] does not attempt to resolve intermediate router IP addresses to names and speeds up the tracert process.

[*destination*] is the targeted end device, listed by IP address or name.

Example: tracert -d www.pearsoned.com

TYPE

The type command displays a text file.

Syntax: type *filename*

Explanation: *filename* is the path and name of the text file you want to display on the screen.

Example: type c:\byteme.txt

Notes: The (Spacebar) enables you to view the next page of a text file. The (Enter) key enables you to scroll through the text file one line at a time. The (Esc) key enables you to quit viewing the text file.

WBADMIN

The wbadmin command is used to perform backups and restores.

Syntax: wbadmin [start backup] [stop job] [get versions] [get items]

Notes: Each parameter listed for wbadmin has options (settings) that follow. Use the /? after each parameter to see these options, for example, wbadmin start backup /?.

Explanation: [start backup] begins the backup process.

[stop job] halts the currently running backup.

[get versions] provides a list of available backups from the local computer or from a remote computer.

[get items] provides a list of items included in a particular backup.

Examples: wbadmin start backup

Notes: You cannot recover backups that were made with `ntbackup` using the `wbadmin` command, but you can download the `ntbackup` command/application from Microsoft.

If no parameters are specified after `wbadmin start backup`, the settings within the daily backup schedule are used.

WSCRIPT

`wscript.exe` is the command that brings up a Windows-based script property sheet. This property sheet sets script properties. The command-line version is `cscript.exe`.

XCOPY

The **xcopy** command copies and backs up files and directories.

Syntax: `xcopy source [destination] [/e] [/h]`

Explanation: `source` is the full path from where the files are copied.

[`destination`] is the optional destination path. If the destination is not given, the current directory is used.

[`/e`] copies all directories and subdirectories including empty ones.

[`/h`] copies hidden and system files.

Example: `xcopy c:\users\cheryl\Documents\Chap1\Chap1.docx e:\Book\Chap1`

This command copies a file called *Chap1.docx* (which is located in a folder called *Chap1* that is a subfolder of the *Documents* folder, which is a subfolder of the *cheryl* folder, which is a subfolder of the *users* folder) to the E: drive and places it in the *Chap1* subfolder that is contained in the *Book* folder.

Notes: The `xcopy` command normally resets read-only attributes when copying.

TECH TIP

Operation requires elevation

If a message appears from within the command prompt window that the requested operation requires elevation, close the command prompt window. Relocate the *Command Prompt* Windows Accessory and right-click the option. Select *Run as administrator* and re-execute the command from the prompt.

SOFT SKILLS—STAYING CURRENT

Technicians must stay current in the rapidly changing field of computers. Benefits of staying current include (1) understanding and troubleshooting the latest technologies, (2) recommending upgrades or solutions to customers, (3) saving time troubleshooting (and time is money), and (4) being someone considered for a promotion. Technicians use a variety of methods to stay current, including the following:

> Subscribe to a magazine or an online magazine.
> Subscribe to a news list that gives you an update in your email.
> Join or attend association meetings.
> Register for and attend a seminar.
> Attend an online webinar.
> Take a class.
> Read books.
> Talk to your department peers and supervisor.

Staying current in technology in the past few years has been a challenge for all, but the rapidly changing environment is what draws many to the field.

Chapter Summary

> An operating system can use a GUI or a command-line environment.
> Important Windows components include icons, the taskbar, the notification area, the Start button, desktop shortcuts, and the Recycle Bin.
> Right-click a shortcut or tile and select *Properties* to see the path to the original file.
> Control Panels modify the Windows registry. Technicians commonly use Control Panels to modify how the hardware, software, and operating system environment functions and appears.
> Windows Explorer (Vista/7)/File Explorer (Windows 8/10) is commonly used to manipulate files and folders. Windows libraries (Documents, Music, Pictures, and Videos) are commonly part of the path to stored documents and subfolders.
> Deleted files are stored on the hard drive in a folder called Recycle Bin. The Recycle Bin must be emptied to release hard drive space. This is relevant only to files stored on hard drives.
> Windows supports encryption and compression. Encrypted files that are moved or copied on NTFS volumes remain encrypted. If an encrypted file or folder is moved to a FAT16 or FAT32 volume, the file/folder is decrypted and the person doing the copying must have authorization to perform encryption.
> The Windows registry is a database of everything within the Windows environment. Configuring Control Panel settings modifies the registry. Use `regedit` or `regedt32` to manually modify the registry.
> You can recover the operating system by using a Windows or manufacturer-provided recovery disc, a recovery partition, a previously created image, a reload of the operating system and service packs, and the System Restore tool.
> Commands are used in two environments: (1) a command prompt environment used when the GUI tools do not or cannot correct a problem and (2) when using a scripting environment to deploy the operating system and/or updates to multiple computers. Command switches alter the way the command performs or outputs information. Use `command /?` or `help` to receive help on any particular command.
> Technicians must stay current in the IT field to move up or maintain their current job status. Methods used to stay current include associations, magazines, classes, books, and peers.

**A+
CERTIFICATION
EXAM TIPS**

✓ Go into every Windows Control Panel and ensure that you know common configuration items.

✓ Know the purpose of the WinRE.

✓ Describe the different methods used to repair or replace the OS.

✓ Be familiar with the commands and how to work in the command prompt environment. The following commands are on the 901 certification exam: bootrec, chkdsk, defrag, diskpart, dxdiag, format, ipconfig, nbtstat, net, netdom, netstat, nslookup, ping, and tracert. Practice these commands (and the various switches used with them) the week before taking the 901 exam. Know when to use them. Ask yourself what would be wrong that would force you to use a particular command.

✓ Be familiar with the commands and how to work in the command prompt environment. The following commands are on the 902 certification exam: [*command_name*] /?, bootrec, cd, chkdsk, command, copy, defrag, del, dir, diskpart, dxdiag, exit, expand, explorer, format, gpresult, gpupdate, help, md, mmc, msconfig, msinfo32, mstsc, notepad, rd, regedit, regsvr32, robocopy, services.msc, sfc, shutdown, taskkill, tasklist, and xcopy. Practice these commands (and the various switches used with them) the week before taking the 902 exam. Know when to use them. Ask yourself what would be wrong that would force you to use a particular command.

Key Terms

CHAPTER 15

Review Questions

1. [T | F] Deleted files can be recovered from the Recycle Bin.

2. What Windows option can access various icons or links that can configure the computer?

   _____

3. Describe the most common mistake made when working with dialog boxes.

   _____

   _____

4. In the filename *Opsys_Quiz 4.docx*, what characters represent the extension?

   _____

5. Describe the process to set Windows Explorer or File Explorer so that file extensions are shown.

   _____

   _____

   _____

6. A user is working in Microsoft Word. He saves the document called *Ltr1.docx* to a folder called *Homedocs*. The *Homedocs* folder is a subfolder of the *Work* folder located on the D: hard drive volume. Write the complete path for the *Ltr1.docx* file.

   _____

7. [T | F] File and folder compression can degrade computer performance.

8. What Windows 7 versions do not support encrypting a file with software provided in the operating system? (Select all that apply.) [Starter | Home Basic | Home Premium | Professional | Enterprise | Ultimate]

9. What should a technician create before making changes to the registry?
   [boot disc | backup tape | master disc | registry backup]

10. What command is used to create a directory?
    [CD | MD | DIR | MAD]

11. What Windows Control Panel category adjusts how and when Windows Updates are installed?
    [System and Security | Network and Internet | Hardware and Sound | Programs]

12. List three recovery methods that recover an operating system.

    _____

    _____

    _____

13. List one method of accessing a command prompt when Windows is operational.

    _____

    _____

14. Consider the following directory structure from the F: drive root directory.

    2017_Term (directory)

    CompRepair (subdirectory)

    Opsys (subdirectory)

    Cisco8 (subdirectory)

    VoIP (subdirectory)

If the prompt is `C:\2017_Term>` and you want to move into the *VoIP* subdirectory, what command do you type?

a. `CD VoIP`

b. `CD..`

c. `CD C:\`

d. `CD C:\VoIP`

15. The _____ and _____ file extensions are used with executable files.

16. The Windows database that stores hardware and software configuration information is called the _____.

17. List one registry editor. _____

18. What technology would allow having Windows 7, Windows 10, and Linux on a host computer where each of these operating systems is in a separate "machine."
    [compression | encryption | virtualization | defragmentation]

19. What command would be used on a computer where a specific application has stopped?
    [taskkill | net stop | quit | stop]

20. List two ways that you think you will use to stay current in the IT field.

    _____

    _____

Exercises

Exercise 15.1

Objective: To recognize which command to use for a specific task

Parts: None

Procedure: Match the command to the task by writing the letter of the command beside the task that would use this command. Note that not all commands will be used.

Commands:

a. dir	**e.** gpupdate	**i.** xcopy	**m.** regedit
b. rd	**f.** robocopy	**j.** copy	**n.** tasklist
c. del	**g.** md	**k.** attrib	
d. cd	**h.** gpresult	**l.** sfc	

Task:

_____   A company has deployed a new group policy and the copiers and network scanners recently installed and part of that policy are not accessible from a workstation.

_____   Create a folder.

_____   Remove a file.

_____   Copy a file from one place to another from the Command Prompt option accessed through WinRE.

_____   List all files in a particular directory.

_____   Delete a directory.

_____   Make a file that is read-only editable.

_____   Verifies and optionally repairs operating system files.

_____   Move to a different directory.

Exercise 15.2

Objective: To recognize common Windows Control Panels

Parts: None

Procedure: Match the task to the appropriate Windows Control Panel category. Note that a category can be used more than once.

a. System and Security   **e.** User Accounts/User Accounts and Family Safety

b Network and Internet   **f.** Appearance and Personalization

c. Hardware and Sound   **g.** Clock, Language, and Region

d. Programs   **h.** Ease of Access

Task:

_____   Configure a HomeGroup.

_____   Require a password to be entered when the computer comes out of sleep mode.

_____   Enable screen reading for any text shown on the screen.

_____   Determine whether a computer is on a domain or workgroup.

_____   Access Device Manager.

_____   Customize the Start button menu.

_____   Configure whether hidden files display.

_____   Configure power-saving options.

_____   Disable the showing of Microsoft-provided games.

_____   Back up the system.

_____   Configure the home page for the default Microsoft browser.

_____   Set the proper time zone.

_____   Change the Windows password for a home computer.

_____   Verify a camera shows as attached.

Activities

Internet Discovery

Objective: Access the Internet to obtain specific information regarding a computer or its associated parts

Parts: Access to the Internet

Procedure: Complete the following procedure and answer the accompanying questions.

1. Locate an Internet site that has a tutorial for Windows 8 troubleshooting or usage.

_____

2. What is the latest service pack for Windows 8.1 Pro? Write the service pack number and the URL of the location where you found this information.

_____

3. List three things that you think would be useful from Microsoft's Customizing the Out-of-Box Experience for IT Pros website and explain why you think they would help the technician.

_____

4. Find a web-based article on the differences between Windows 8 and Windows 8 Pro editions. Write the name of the article, three important differences, and the URL.

_____

_____

_____

_____

5. Locate a website that demonstrates how to edit the Windows registry for any version of the Windows 8 operating system. Describe the registry hack using at least one complete sentence. State whether you would deploy such a hack and explain why or why not.

_____

_____

_____

6. Locate a website that describes three things to do if Windows 7 (any version) will not boot. Briefly describe the three things and document the URL.

_____

_____

_____

_____

_____

Soft Skills

Objective: To enhance and fine-tune a technician's ability to listen, communicate in both written and oral form, and support people who use computers in a professional manner

Activities:

1. On a piece of paper or an index card, list two topics you would like to hear about if you were to attend a local association PC users' group meeting. Share this information with your group. Consolidate ideas and present five of the best ideas to the class.

2. In a team environment, select one of the five ideas presented in Activity 1 to research. Every team member presents something about a latest technology to the rest of the class. The class votes on the best presented topic and the most interesting topic.

3. On an index card, document a question that several students have asked the teacher about how to do a particular task. Exchange cards with one classmate. Correct each other's grammar, punctuation, and capitalization. When you have your original card, exchange your card with a different classmate and perform the same task. Rewrite your index card based on the recommendations of your classmates. Keep in mind that all their suggestions are just that—suggestions. You do not have to accept their suggestions. A complaint of industry is that technicians do not write well. Practice helps with this issue.

Critical Thinking Skills

Objective: To analyze and evaluate information and to apply learned information to new or different situations

Activities:

1. Windows Vista will not boot. What will be the first, second, and third thing you try? Explain your reasoning. Answers will vary, but one example is to try System Restore, determine if the problem is hardware, determine if the problem is software, things to try if Windows runs erratically or slowly, and things to try if Windows does not boot at all. This is found at the following URL: http://windows.microsoft.com/en-US/windows-vista/What-to-do-if-Windows-wont-start-correctly

2. In a paragraph, explain why or why you would not use the Command Prompt repair option as a first attempt in a Windows boot failure.

3. Explain a situation of when you would use a Windows boot disc or find one on the Internet. Detail the drawbacks to using it.

4. Find a specific problem on the Internet and what the person did to repair the problem using the command prompt. Share your findings with the class.

Labs

Lab 15.1 Windows Vista/7 Basic Usage

Objective: To work effectively with the Windows Vista/7 desktop, including working with the Start button; managing the display through the Control Panel; changing Start button properties; obtaining help; performing file, folder, and computer searches; and accessing programs

Parts: Computer with Windows Vista or 7 and the Windows Notepad application installed

Procedure: Complete the following procedure and answer the accompanying questions.

1. Power on the computer and log on to Windows if necessary.

Working with the Start Menu

2. Click the *Start* button. The top right of the Start menu on some systems shows who is currently logged on to the computer. Users are created so that the system can be individualized when multiple people use the same computer. If the computers are reimaged every time the computer boots, no programs are "pinned" to the left Start menu.

   What do you think is the difference between the applications listed on the left and those listed on the right side of the Start button menu?

   _____

   _____

   _____

3. You can make changes to the Start button menu by right-clicking the *Start* button > *Properties* > *Start Menu* tab > *Customize* button.

   What is the current setting for the Control Panel option?
   [Display as a link I Display as a menu I Don't display this item]

   What is the current setting for Games?
   [Display as a link I Display as a menu I Don't display this item]

   How many recent programs are currently set to display?

   _____

4. Click *Cancel*. Select the *Taskbar* tab.

   List three options that can be customized through this tab.

   _____

   _____

   _____

5. Select the *How do I customize the taskbar* link. Using the information available, answer the following questions.

   How can you tell if the taskbar is locked or unlocked without moving it?

   _____

   _____

   What toolbars can be added to the taskbar?

   _____

   _____

   _____

   _____

6. Close the Windows Help and Support window.

7. Click the *Notification Area* tab (Vista) or the *Customize* button in the Notification area (7). Click *Cancel* after you answer the question.

   List three system icons.

   _____

   _____

8. Re-access the *Start* menu.

   What are the top four options in the right column of the *Start* menu?

   _____

   _____

9. The *Documents* option represents a folder that is the default storage location for saved files. *Pictures*, *Music*, and *Games* also represent folders. A folder can contain another folder, and this folder is commonly called a subfolder. A file is a document created by an application. Files are stored and organized in folders. Click the *Computer* Start button option. The *Computer* option contains access to drives installed or connected to the computer. Flash drives, hard drives, optical drives, tape drives, and so on are given drive letters such as E: or C:.

   What drive letters are available through the *Computer* option?

   _____

Working with Control Panels

10. Select the *Control Panel* Start button option. *Control Panel* allows access to Control Panel icons or links used to configure the computer. There are two ways to view Control Panels: *Classic* and *Category*. The default view is by category. In Vista, if the words "System and Maintenance" *do not* appear in the right pane, select the *Control Panel Home* link in the left pane. In Windows 7, select *Category* in the View by: drop-down menu.

    List two Control Panel categories shown on the screen.

    _____

    _____

    _____

11. In Windows 7, select *Large icons* or *Small icons* in the View by: drop-down menu. The classic view/ large or small icons is the older method for accessing any particular Control Panel. Return to the *Category* Control Panel view.

    Table 15.9 is to be used as reference material. Note that some systems have special Control Panels due to the hardware installed or type of computer such as a laptop or tablet. Notice how some of the options are found in multiple categories.

Table 15.10 (several pages away) is for you to explore Windows Control Panels and document within Table 15.10 what Control Panel category and subcategory you would use to perform that particular task.

TABLE 15.9 Common Windows Vista or 7 Control Panel categories*

Control Panel category	Subcategory	Function
System and Maintenance (Vista)/System and Security (7)	Welcome Center (Vista)	Used to access basic computer information, information on how to use Windows Vista, and Vista help videos.
	Backup and Restore	Used to save or restore files and folders to or from a different location.
	System	Used to view basic computer properties, such as RAM, processor type, and computer name.
	Windows Update	Used to customize how Vista/7 updates are received and installed.
	Power Options	Used to configure power saving modes.
	Indexing Options*	Used to configure how Vista searches for files and folders more efficiently.
	Problem Reports and Solutions (Vista)	Used to receive help with or view a history of computer problems.
	Performance Information and Tools (Vista)	Used to obtain information about the computer speed and possible solutions related to speed.
	Device Manager (Vista)	Used to view and update hardware settings.
	Administrative Tools	Used to free up hard disk space, manage hard drive partitions, schedule tasks, and view event logs.
	Action Center (7)	Used to view personal information, view a history of computer problems, view performance information, configure backup, troubleshoot problems, and restore the computer to a previous time.
Security (Vista)	Security Center (Vista)	Used to view and modify computer firewall and update settings.
	Windows Firewall	Used to enable and customize security firewall features.
	Windows Update	Used to customize how updates are received and installed.
	Windows Defender*	Used to scan the computer for unwanted software.
	Internet Options (Vista)	Used to customize Internet Explorer.
	Parental Controls (Vista)	Used to change, enable, or disable settings related to family member access.
	BitLocker Drive Encryption (7)	Used to change or use encryption options.

Control Panel category	Subcategory	Function
Network and Internet	Network and Sharing Center	Used to check the status and modify network-related settings as well as share files, folders, and devices on the network.
	Internet Options	Used to customize Internet Explorer.
	People Near Me*	Used to configure the computer for software such as Windows Meeting Place.
	Sync Center*	Used to synchronize mobile devices or network shares.
	HomeGroup (7)	Used to view and change sharing and password options.
Hardware and Sound	Printers (Vista)	Used to add, delete, or customize printer settings.
	Devices and Printers (7)	Used to add/remove a device, scanner, camera, printer, and mouse as well as access Device Manager.
	AutoPlay	Used to change how media is automatically handled when a disc, thumbdrive, or type of file is added or inserted.
	Sound	Used to manage audio devices and change sound schemes.
	Mouse (Vista)	Used to customize mouse and mouse button settings.
	Power Options	Same as in the System and Maintenance (Vista)/System and Security (7) category.
	Personalization (Vista)	Used to customize the desktop, adjusts monitor settings, select a theme, or change the mouse pointer.
	Scanners and Cameras (Vista)	Used to add, delete, or customize settings related to scanners or cameras.
	Keyboard*	Used to customize keyboard settings.
	Device Manager (Vista)	Same as in the System and Maintenance category.
	Phone and Modem Options*	Used to install a modem and control modem and phone dialing properties.
	Game Controllers*	Used to add, remove, and customize USB joysticks, gamepads, and other gaming devices.
	Windows SideShow (Vista)	Used to customize SideShow settings.
	Pen and Input Devices	Used to configure pen options for a tablet PC.

Control Panel category	Subcategory	Function
	Color Management*	Used for advanced color settings on displays, scanners, and printers.
	Tablet PC Settings	Used to configure tablet and screen settings on a tablet PC.
	Display (7)	Used to adjust resolution, configure an external display, or make text larger/smaller.
	Bluetooth Devices	Used to install, configure, and adjust Bluetooth wireless devices.
Programs	Programs and Features	Used to uninstall and change programs as well as enable/disable Windows features such as games, telnet server, telnet client, TFTP client, and print services.
	Windows Defender*	Same as in the Security category.
	Default Programs	Used to remove a startup program, associate a file extension with a particular application, or select the program used with a particular type of file.
	Windows SideShow (Vista)	Same as in the Hardware and Sound category.
	Windows Sidebar Properties (Vista)	Used to add gadgets to the sidebar as well as customize the gadgets displayed on the desktop.
	Desktop Gadgets (7)	Used to add/remove/restore desktop interactive objects.
Mobile PC	Windows Mobility Center	Used on laptops to adjust screen brightness, audio volume, wireless enabling and strength status, presentation settings, and external display control.
	Power Options	Used on laptops and has the same function as in the System and Maintenance category.
	Personalization	Used on laptops and has the same function as in the Hardware and Sound category.
	Tablet PC Settings	Used on laptops and has the same function as in the Programs category.
	Pen and Input Devices	Used on laptops and has the same function as in the Hardware and Sound category.
	Sync Center	Used on laptops and has the same function as in the Network and Internet category.

Control Panel category	Subcategory	Function
User Accounts and Family Safety	User Accounts	Used to add, remove, or modify accounts on the computer.
	Parental Controls	Same as in the Security (Vista)/System and Security (7) .
	Windows CardSpace	Used to manage relationships and information such as a user ID and password for websites and online services. The personal card information is kept encrypted on the local hard drive.
	Credential Manager (7)	Used to store username/password in a vault for easy logon to sites and/or computers.
Appearance and Personalization	Personalization	Same as in the Hardware and Sound category.
	Taskbar and Start menu	Used to customize the Start menu and taskbar by adding or removing icons.
	Fonts	Used to customize available fonts.
	Folder Options	Used to configure how folders are viewed and acted upon, including what files are seen.
Clock, Language, and Region	Date and Time	Used to configure time, date, time zone, clocks for different time zones.
	Region and Language Options	Used to configure the format for date, time, currency, and so on that are region-specific. Also used to customize keyboard settings.
Additional Options		Holds special Control Panels that are system-specific, such as an NVIDIA video display or Java Control Panel.

*Note that in Windows 7, particular options can be found by typing in the subcategory in the *Search Control Panel* textbox.

Fill in Table 15.10 with the correct Control Panel category and subcategory.

TABLE 15.10   Determine the correct Vista/Windows 7 Control Panel

Control Panel category	Control Panel subcategory	Task
		Used to configure the mouse buttons for a left-handed person
		Used to mute the computer speaker sound
		Used to configure the date to be in the format April 15, 201X
		Used to define how fast a character repeats when a specific key is held down

Control Panel category	Control Panel subcategory	Task
		Used to define what page (home page) appears every time Internet Explorer starts
		Used to configure an IP address on a wired or wireless network adapter
		Used to set a printer as the default printer
		Used to verify if Windows recognizes a particular piece of hardware

Working with the Display

12. Ensure you are in the *Category* view. Select the *Hardware and Sound* Control Panel category. In Vista, select the *Personalization* link; select *Display Settings* (Vista). In Windows 7, select *Display*. Note that you may be required to search throughout this area to answer the questions.

What is the current resolution?

_____

How many bits are used for color?

_____

13. Continue working with the *Display* link. Locate and select the *Advanced Settings* button or link. Note: You may have to click *Change Display* or use another Control Panel depending on the manufacturer.

What adapter is used?

_____

How much video memory does the adapter have?

_____

How much total video memory is available? _____

14. Click the *Monitor* tab.

What refresh rate is used?

_____

15. Click *Cancel* on this window and the next window. In Vista, click the *Screen Saver* link. In Windows 7, select the *Personalization* link in the bottom left; select the *Screen Saver* link in the bottom right. Use the *Screen Saver* down arrow to see a list of pre-installed screen savers and click one of the options. Click the *Preview* button. The screen saver appears. Move the mouse to regain control.

Dealing with Power Settings

16. Click the *Change power settings* link. The Power Options Properties window appears. Table 15.11 shows the various power options available in Windows Vista and 7.

What power option would be applied to a laptop being used by a teacher during a 4-hour class?

_____

TABLE 15.11   Windows Vista/7 default power schemes*

Power scheme	Purpose
Balanced (Vista/7)	Default mode; processor adapts to activity being performed; performance provided when the computer is in use; power savings when the computer is inactive. Display powers down after 15 minutes; hard drive powers down after 20 minutes and goes to sleep after 20 minutes.
Power saver (Vista/7)	Provides maximum battery life for laptops. Display and hard drive power down after 20 minutes, and the system goes to sleep after 1 hour.
High performance (Vista/7)	Maximum system performance and responsiveness. Display and hard drive power down after 20 minutes, but the system never sleeps.
Customized (Vista/7)	A scheme created by the user that has different settings than the default three schemes.

*Note that a computer manufacturer may provide additional power schemes.

17. Close all Control Panel windows.

Obtaining Help

18. Click *Help and Support* from the Start button menu. The Help and Support window contains links to online and locally stored help documents.

19. In Vista the standard help links are Windows Basics, Table of Contents, Security and Maintenance, Troubleshooting, Windows Online Help, and What's New.

In Windows 7, the standard three links are How to get started with your computer, Learn about Windows Basics, and Browse Help topics.

In both Vista and 7, the Search Help textbox is used by typing a word or series of words on a specific topic. Note that the Help and Support window may vary depending on the computer manufacturer.

What is the first link listed in the help window?

_____

_____

20. In either Vista or 7, type `monitor quality` in the *Search* textbox and press Enter.

List three settings used to improve display quality.

_____

_____

_____

_____

21. To see a list of troubleshooting topics, type `troubleshooting` in the *Search help* textbox. A list of troubleshooting topics immediately displays. Select the *Offline Help* menu arrow in the bottom-right corner.

What menu options appear?

_____

22. Select *Settings* from the Options menu in Windows 7. Notice how you can customize the type of help you receive by enabling or disabling the online help checkbox.

23. Close any open window.

Searching for Files, Folders, and Computers

24. Click the *Start* button and find the *Start Search* (Vista)/*Search programs and files* (7) textbox, located directly above the Start button. This option is used to hunt for files, other computers on the network, people listed in your address book, and information located on the Internet.

25. In the textbox, type **system configuration**, but do not press Enter. Notice how the program shows in the panel. Always keep in mind that applications are simply a type of file that brings up the specific software. Also, any files that contain the words "System Configuration" appear under the files list. Select the *System Configuration* program from the list. Close the window after the question has been answered.

     List five tabs found in the System Configuration window.

     _____

26. Bring up the search list for system configuration, but don't press Enter again.

> **TECH TIP**
>
> ### Changing UAC (User Access Control) settings
>
> Windows Vista/7 has a UAC dialog box that frequently appears, asking for permission to do something. To change UAC settings, use the *User Accounts* Control Panel > select an account > *Change User Account Control settings*. The UAC settings can also be disabled through the System configuration utility (`msconfig` command) > *Tools* tab > *Disable UAC* (Vista)/*Change UAC Settings* (7) option > *Launch* button > select the appropriate level.

27. In Vista, click the *Search the Internet* option at the bottom of the list.

     In Windows 7, click the *See more results* link and scroll to the bottom of the list; locate and select the *Internet* icon.

     List one URL that the system found.

     _____

     _____

28. Locate the name of the computer, using a Control Panel previously explored. Exchange computer names with a classmate.

     Your computer name _____

     Classmate's computer name _____

29. Return to the computer *Start Search* (Vista)/*Search programs and files* (7) textbox, type in your classmate's computer name, and press Enter. In the resulting window in the Folders panel on the left, select the *Network* option. Note: You may have to change the default settings of the computer: *Start > Control Panel > Network and Internet > Network and Sharing Center > Change Advanced Sharing Settings* > expand *Home* or *Work* as necessary to enable to following: *Turn on network discovery*. Use Windows Explorer to locate a remote network device.

     Does the remote computer name appear? [Yes | No]

     Instructor initials: _____

30. Close the window.

Starting Applications

31. Software applications are accessed through the Start button. Click the *Start* button. The left column contains the most recently used applications. If a program is not listed there and the application is installed, you can access it through the All Programs option. Point to *All Programs*; locate and click the *Accessories* option. Locate and click *Notepad*. The Notepad application opens.

32. Type `Whatever you are be a good one. -Abraham Lincoln`. Click the *File* menu option, *Save*, and then type `quote` in the *File name* textbox. Notice the path for where the document is saved located at the top of the window. The folder and subfolders are separated by arrows. The path is shown at the top of the *Save as* window. An example of the path is *Libraries>Documents*.

   Write the path for where the document will be saved.

   _____

   _____

33. Click the *Save* button. Click the *Close* button (the button with the X) in the right corner. Re-access the *Start* button menu.

   Does the Notepad application now appear in the left column of the Start menu?

   _____

34. In the *Start Search* (Vista)/*Search programs and files* (7) textbox, type `notepad`, but do not press the Enter key. The Notepad application is listed under the Programs section. In the *Start Search* (Vista)/ *Search programs and files* (7) textbox, delete the word *notepad* and type `quote`, but do not press Enter. Your file (and any others that have the word "quote" in the filename or document) will appear under the Files section of the list. Notice the icon beside the filename. Click the *Quote* document. The document opens. Close the document and application.

Recycle Bin

35. Right-click the *Start* button and select the *Explore* (Vista)/*Open Windows Explorer* (7) option. Using the information you wrote down for Step 32, click the first folder you wrote down. It should be located under the Folders (Vista), Desktop (7), or Documents section of the left panel. Double-click the second (and any subsequent) folder you wrote down. Locate the file called *quote*. Do not open the file; just browse until the filename appears in the major window.

36. Right-click the *quote* filename. Notice that there is a Delete option. Do not click this option. Click away from the filename on an empty part of the window and then click once on the *quote* filename to select it. The name is highlighted when it is selected. Press the Delete key. The file is sent to the Recycle Bin and no dialog message appears asking if you are sure. Remember the Recycle Bin is just a folder on the hard drive.

   The Recycle Bin holds deleted files and folders. When a file or folder is deleted, it is not immediately discarded; instead, it goes into the Recycle Bin folder. When a file or folder is in the Recycle Bin, it can be removed. This is similar to a piece of trash being retrieved from an office trash can. A technician must remember that the files and folders in the Recycle Bin take up hard drive space and that users frequently forget to empty these deleted files and folders.

TECH TIP

Files deleted from Recycle Bin cannot be retrieved

When the Recycle Bin has been emptied, the deleted files cannot be recovered without the use of special software.

37. From the window where you located the now-deleted *quote* document, locate the *Recycle Bin* icon in the Folders panel (Vista); for Windows 7, the Recycle Bin icon is commonly located on the desktop—select *Desktop* from the Favorites section. Double-click this icon.

   Does the *quote* text document appear in the Recycle Bin window? [Yes | No]

If not, redo the steps in this section to create and delete the file.

Instructor initials: _____

38. Select the *Empty the Recycle Bin* option from the top menu. A confirmation window appears, asking if you are sure you want to permanently delete the file. Click *Yes*. The name disappears from the Recycle Bin window (as do those of any other files that were located in the Recycle Bin). Close the window.

Pinning an Application to the Start Menu

39. Click *Start* > *All Programs* > *Accessories* and locate the *Notepad* application. Right-click the *Notepad* application and select the *Pin to Start Menu* option.

40. Click the *Start* button. Notice how the Notepad application appears at the top of the Start menu. After the application is pinned, it always appears in that top list.

Instructor initials: _____

41. Right-click the *Notepad* Start button option and select *Unpin from Start Menu*. The application is removed immediately but still resides in All Programs.

Other Windows Vista/7 Differences

42. One of the things that is different in Windows Vista and 7 from Windows XP is the gadgets. Gadgets are mini applications that stay on the desktop. By default, they load to the right, but you can customize where they go. Right-click the desktop and select *Gadgets*.

List three gadgets you would find useful to have on the desktop.

_____

_____

Windows Vista/7 Shutdown Options

43. When you're finished working on the computer for the day, the computer needs to be turned off or shut down properly. All applications and windows should be closed, and then special steps need to be taken for shutting down. Click *Start* and locate the *Start Search* (Vista)/*Search programs and files* (7) textbox you have been using. Immediately to the right of that textbox are two symbols and a right arrow in Windows Vista or a Shutdown button in Windows 7. Refer to Figure 15.10 if necessary.

The shutdown options that commonly appear are listed in Table 15.12, along with the purpose of each one.

TABLE 15.12   Windows Vista/7 shutdown options

Option	Purpose
Switch User	Allows another user to switch to his own environment (desktop, files, and so on).
Log Off	Keeps the computer powered on but logs off the current user.
Lock	Locks the computer, such as when someone goes to lunch. All settings and current applications are left untouched.
Restart	Used when new software or hardware has been installed or when the computer locks.
Sleep	Reduces power consumption but keeps the applications and settings that are currently on the screen.
Shut Down	Powers off the computer.

44. Select the *Shut down* option unless directed otherwise by the instructor or lab assistant.

Lab 15.2 Modifying the Windows Vista/7 Start Button

Objective: To modify the *Start* button menu

Parts: A computer with the Windows Vista or 7 operating system loaded

Procedure: Complete the following procedure and answer the accompanying questions.

Start Menu Icon Size

1. After Windows boots, right-click the *Start* button > *Properties* > *Start Menu* tab > *Customize* button. The radio buttons and checkboxes configure the look of the Start menu. Icon size is controlled by a checkbox at the end of the list.

    What Start menu icon size radio button is currently selected? [Normal | Large]

    _____

2. Set the setting to the opposite (that is, if the box is already checked, uncheck it, and if the box is unchecked, then check it). Click *OK* > *Apply* > *OK*.

3. Click the *Start* button to test the icon size change.

4. Return the icon size to the original setting.

Customizing the Number of Start Menu Programs Shown

5. Right-click the *Start* button > *Properties* > *Start menu* tab > *Customize* button. Locate the *Number of recent programs to display* selectable number option at the bottom of the window. The number of programs shown on the left side (bottom portion) of the *Start* button menu can be modified using the up and down arrows that control the number.

    How many programs are currently set to appear on the *Start* button?

    _____

6. Click the *Cancel* button and, when returned to the previous menu, click *Cancel* again. Click the *Start* button and verify that the number of programs shown is correct. Windows automatically adds the most often utilized programs to the list, but the maximum is set through the window from which you just returned.

7. Right-click the *Start* button > *Properties* > *Customize* button.

    What is the maximum number of recent programs that you can have on the *Start* button?_____

8. Increase the number of programs shown on the *Start* button menu. When finished, click *OK* > *Apply* > *OK*.

9. Click the *Start* button. The number of programs shown on the bottom left of the Start menu should be the number specified. If it is not, access an application not listed on the menu, close the application, and click the *Start* button again.

10. Return the number of *Start* button menu programs to the original setting.

Modifying Vista Default Icon Settings

If Windows 7 is installed, proceed to Step 15.

11. By default, Windows Vista displays web browser and email client icons in the upper section of the left column of the *Start* menu. To change this behavior, right-click *Start* button > *Properties* > *Customize* button. Locate the *Show on Start menu* section.

    Is the Internet link enabled (checked)?

    _____

    Is the E-mail link enabled (checked)?

    _____

12. In Vista, change the two settings in the *Shown on Start menu* section to something different. Click *OK* > *Apply* > *OK*.

13. Select the *Start* button.

Have the changes been implemented? [Yes | No]

14. Return the Start menu to the original settings. Verify by selecting the *Start* button.

Customizing the Start Menu Programs

15. By default, the Start menu has links to Documents, Pictures, Music, Help and Support, and so on in the right column. Click the *Start* button.

What are three items found in the Start button menu right column?

_____

_____

_____

16. Right-click the *Start* button > *Properties* > *Customize* button. Locate the *Computer* section. Some of the options located in this window have three possible selections, similar to the Computer section: (1) Display as a link, (2) Display as a menu, and (3) Don't display this item.

Display as a link means that when the menu option is selected, it opens in a new window. With *Display as a menu*, the option has an arrow to the side allowing you to access all options that windows would normally contain.

What is the current setting for Control Panel?

_____

17. Click the *Cancel* button and, when returned to the previous menu, click *Cancel* again. Click the *Start* button and observe the current *Control Panel* option on the menu.

Does the Control Panel option appear as configured? [Yes | No]

18. Right-click the *Start* button > *Properties* > *Customize* button. Locate the *Control Panel* section. Change the *Control Panel* menu option to one of the other menu settings. Click *OK* > *Apply* > *OK*.

19. Select the *Start* button and select the *Control Panel* menu option.

How is the Control Panel option different?

_____

_____

20. Return the *Control Panel* item to its original setting.

Adding a Program to the Start Menu

21. Click the *Start* button > type `charmap` in the *Start Search* (Vista)/*Search programs and files* (7) text-box. Charmap is the file used to execute the Character Map program. It is commonly found in the *C:\Windows\System32* folder.

Note: If the *Charmap* file is not installed, you can use any program file for this part of the exercise.

22. Locate *charmap* in the resulting *Programs* list. Right-click the *charmap* file, and select the *Pin to Start Menu* option. Click the *Start* button.

Where on the Start button menu is the Character Map application added?

_____

23. To remove a customized application, click the *Start* button, right-click the unwanted item (*charmap* in this case), and select *Unpin from Start Menu*.

Instructor initials: _____

Lab 15.3 Windows 8.1 Basic Usage—Introduction to the Start Screen

Objective: To work effectively with the Windows 8.1 Start screen including working with charms, apps, and tiles

Parts: Computer with Windows 8.1 and administrator privileges

Procedure: Complete the following procedure and answer the accompanying questions.

1.   Power on the computer and log on to Windows 8.1. Note that you may have to swipe up or press a key to access the logon screen.

Working with the *Start* Screen

2.   Access the *Start* screen. This is the screen with all the tiles. If it is not shown, press the ■ key or press the *Windows* icon (looks like four window panes 2×2) in the lower-left corner. The top right of the Start screen shows who is currently logged on to the computer. Users are created so that the system can be individualized when multiple people use the same computer.

3.   The four corners of the Windows 8 computer are hot corners. You can move the pointer to the tip of the corner of the screen (maybe even a little off the screen) to quickly access other tools and screens.

   For example, move the pointer to the top-left corner. A small icon of a recently used app appears (if one has been used). Move the pointer to the bottom-left corner. The Start button icon appears. Selecting the *Start* button toggles between the Start screen and the traditional desktop. Now move the pointer to the top right. Moving the pointer to the top right and bottom right does the same thing: brings up the charms. Note that the pointer needs to hover to the far right.

   What are the five charms?

   _____

4.   Access the *Search* charm. Click the down arrow beside *Everywhere*.

   What are your choices for where you might select to search?

   _____

   _____

5.   The search function is helpful and can be customized. Use the Everywhere option to search and type **internet** into the search textbox. While you are typing, options start appearing below the textbox. Select *Internet Explorer*. The Internet Explorer browser opens. Leave it open.

6.   Re-access *Charms* and select the *Share* charm. The options you have to share with others depend on the apps installed on the computer and the app currently open when you clicked the *Share* charm.

   Which apps can share a web link?

   _____

7.   Move the pointer onto the open Internet Explorer window, click or tap inside the *Internet Explorer* window, and close the window by clicking the *Close button* in the top-right corner (the one with the white X on a red background).

8.   Re-access *Charms* and select the *Start* charm. The Start charm brings up the Start screen, but if you are already on the Start screen, it returns you to the last app you were using.

   What happened when you clicked the Start charm?

   _____

   _____

9.   Re-access *Charms* and select *Devices*. The *Play* option enables you to stream music, a PowerPoint slide show, or videos. The *Print* option enables you to print if the app used supports it. Many of them do, such as Internet Explorer, Microsoft Word, the Camera app (if one is installed on the device), and more. The last option is *Project*, which enables you to send whatever is on the display to a projector, TV, or a second display.

10. Re-access *Charms* and select *Settings*. The *Settings* option contains what most users want to do (but not always what most technicians want to configure or are used to). Note that the *Settings* option can also be launched from the *System Settings* tile. The *Settings* option will be explored in another Windows 8.1 basic usage lab.

    List three Settings options that can be configured from this charm.

    _____

    _____

Manipulating the *Start* Screen

11. Let's explore how to modify tiles. Move your pointer to one of the hot corners to return to the Start screen. See if you can figure out which one will get you there. From the Start screen, tiles that show there can be modified by selecting and dragging them to another location.

    What tile is currently located in the far-left position?

    _____

12. Select and drag the tile located in the far-left position to the last position in the first block of tiles. Then return the tile to the current position.

13. To add an app to the Start screen, access the *Search* charm. Type `command` in the Search textbox. The Command Prompt option appears in the resulting list. Right-click or tap and briefly hold on the *Command Prompt* option in the search list.

    List the options available from the context menu.

    _____

14. Remember from the chapter that the Run as administrator option is sometimes required to use a tool or, in this case, a command prompt. Select the *Pin to Start* option.

15. Move the pointer over and click or tap within the *Start screen*. Use the scrollbar to go to the far right where you see the Command Prompt tile.

    Does the Command Prompt tile appear on the Start screen? If not, redo Steps 13, 14, and 15.

    _____

16. Tap or select the *Command Prompt* tile. The Command Prompt window opens. Close the command prompt window using the *Close button*.

17. Re-access the *Start screen* using whatever method you prefer. Locate the *Command Prompt* tile. Tap and briefly hold or right-click the *Command Prompt* tile to access the context menu.

    List any menu options that were not available from the context menu previously accessed before you pinned the app to the Start screen.

    _____

    _____

18. Hover the pointer over the *Resize* option.

    What choices do you have?

    _____

19. Select a different tile size. Re-access the *Command Prompt* tile context menu again. Select *Open file location*. Windows *File Explorer* opens showing the folder that contains this file (and other files within the same folder). Notice how the Command Prompt option is a shortcut. You can tell because the icon on the left has a bent arrow on it. Also, in the *Type* column, you can see the word *Shortcut*.

20. To see where the original file is located, right-click or tap and hold the *Command Prompt* icon > select *Properties*. Ensure the *Shortcut* tab is selected. The *Target* textbox shows where the file is actually located. The `%windir%` is used to describe the folder where Windows was installed. Commonly, it is `C:\Windows`, but because this might be on another drive letter or installed to a different folder,

Microsoft simply describes it as %windir%. The full path for the command prompt is commonly C:\Windows\Systems32\cmd.exe.

21. Click *Cancel* to return to File Explorer. Close *File Explorer*. Return to the *Start* screen (the one with the tiles).

22. Re-access the *Command Prompt* context menu. Select *Unpin from Start*.

23. To see all the tiles at once, select the minus sign located at the far right of the scrollbar at the bottom of the display. Note that you may have to click or tap at the bottom of the screen to see the scrollbar and to select the minus sign to the far right. All the tiles on the Start screen are shown. Select on any particular tile and the normal tile sizes are shown with that particular tile viewable in the window.

24. Select the minus sign icon again. This time click anywhere that is empty space on the screen; the last view you were on is shown in normal size.

Power Options

25. In the top right of the Start screen is the *Power Options* icon. It is a circle with a vertical line that extends through the top part of the circle. You often see the symbol on power buttons. Click this icon once. Table 15.13 explains the various power options that might be seen.

    What options are available?

    _____

    _____

    What other icon is available to the right of the power options icon? If you do not know what this is, hover the pointer over it to receive context-sensitive help.

    _____

    The shutdown options that commonly appear are listed in Table 15.13, along with the purpose of each one.

TABLE 15.13   Windows 8/8.1 power button shutdown options

Option	Purpose
Lock	Locks the computer, such as when someone goes to lunch. All settings and current applications are left untouched.
Restart	Used when new software or hardware has been installed or when the computer locks.
Sleep	Reduces power consumption but keeps the applications and settings that are currently on the screen.
Hibernate	Reduces power consumption even more so than the sleep mode. Takes longer to resume operations than sleep mode, but not as long as a cold boot.
Shut Down	Powers off the computer.

Apps

26. Select the symbol that is a circle with a down arrow inside it (⊕) located at the bottom of the Start screen. Note that you may have to move the pointer for it to appear.

27. Apps can be shown in different orders. The option at the top tells you how they are sorted.

    What is the current option? [Apps by name I Apps by date installed I Apps by most used I Apps by category]

    _____

28. Use the down arrow by Apps to select *Apps by name*. The app icons are then shown in alphabetical order. Scroll to the right and you may see some apps provided by the device manufacturer. Scroll further to the right and you may see groupings for the Microsoft Office Suite or a particular security software manufacturer. Continue scrolling to the right until you reach the grouping called Windows Accessories.

What three accessories do you think technicians might use the most?

_____

_____

_____

29. The Windows Ease of Access apps are listed next. These are tools to configure the device for those with visual, auditory, or mobility issues. At the far right are the Windows System apps including the Command Prompt. Return to the *Windows Accessories* section. Access the context menu for *Notepad* by right-clicking it or tap and briefly hold. Notice that you can pin an app from the App menu to the Start menu or taskbar. Move the pointer away from the context menu without selecting any option, and click or tap in an empty space.

30. Open both the *Notepad* app and the *Snipping Tool* app.

31. Access and launch any program from the *Start screen* tiles.

32. Return to the *Start screen*. Use the left hot corner button to locate, access, and close the running apps. Locate the app or utility that you launched from a *Start screen* tile. Right-click that thumbnail > select *Close*.

33. Locate the thumbnail for *Desktop*. Windows Accessories run in desktop mode. Click the thumbnail, and you can see Notepad and the Snipping Tool. Close both apps.

Lab 15.4 Windows 8.1 Basic Usage—Introduction to PC Settings

Objective: To be familiar with the Windows 8.1 PC Settings
Parts: Computer with Windows 8.1
               Flash drive
Procedure: Complete the following procedure and answer the accompanying questions.

1. Power on the computer and log on to Windows 8.1. Note that you may have to swipe up or press a key to access the logon screen.

2. Use *Charms* to access the *Settings* charm. Select the *Change PC settings* link.

Working with the PC and Devices Setting

3. Select the *PC and devices* from the *PC settings* list.

Looking over the list, which option are you curious about?

_____

4. Ensure the *Lock screen* option is selected in the left menu. This particular setting enables you to control how the display reacts and possibly the camera as well (if one is installed). The lock screen function is a screen that appears when you have not interacted with the device after a specified amount of time. The lock screen commonly shows such information as time, date, battery status, and network status. Notice that to enable an option, you select one side of a particular option.

What is the current option to play a slide show on the lock screen? [On | Off] Note that if you have trouble telling, the black side of the option points toward one side or the other. The selection chosen is shown as a particular word on the left (either on or off). Change the option by clicking or tapping the side away from the black bar.

5.   Choose the opposite selection for the *Play a slide show on the lock screen* by clicking or tapping the opposite side of the gray box so that the black bar goes to the opposite side. If the answer to Question 4 was *on*, you should turn the option *off*. If the answer to Question 4 was *off*, you should turn the option *on*.

   What visual clue did you have that the option changed?

   _____

   _____

   _____

6.   Return the setting to the original on/off position.

7.   Select the *Display* setting. This setting is commonly used to reset the screen resolution if the user has set it to something less than optimal. You can also use it to connect to a wireless display such as a TV.

   What is the current resolution?

   _____

8.   Select the *Devices* setting. This setting is used to quickly see what devices are attached to the computer. Scroll to the bottom of the option. The last option allows you to configure the saving of videos, music, and photos to a removable drive instead of the local hard drive that may be an SSD.

9.   Attach a flash drive. Notice how the flash drive appears under *Other devices*.

10.   Locate the *Default save locations* section > select the *Set up* button. Notice the types of files you can unselect (because all of them are selected by default). Note that if you have more than one external media attached, the system selects the lowest drive letter by default. This would commonly be an external media that stays attached to the computer.

   What drive letter is assigned to your flash drive where media is now automatically stored?

   _____

11.   Select OK. Notice how the *Default save locations* button changes now to read *Stop saving here*.

12.   Select the *Stop saving here* button. A message appears that music, pictures, and videos will now be saved to this PC. Select *OK*.

13.   Hover the pointer over the flash drive listed in the *Other devices* section and select the drive. Note that flash drives might be seen as a mass storage device. Notice how you can eject the device from here by selecting the *Remove device* link. Select *Remove device*. When asked if you are sure you want to remove the device, select *Yes*. You might have to do this a second time to get this message to appear.

14.   Select the *Mouse and touchpad* option.

   Which mouse button is the primary one? [Left | Right]

   _____

15.   Select the *Typing* option. The two features here are used to spell check, highlight, and automatically fix any spelling errors you make. This might be annoying to you, especially if you have an unusual name or send things to someone with an unusual name.

16.   Select the *Corners and edges* option. This is where you can enable or disable the hot-corner options.

17.   Select the *Power and sleep* option. The options that appear here depend on the type of device that has Windows 8.1 loaded.

   After how much time will the screen dim if there is no activity?

   _____

CHAPTER 15

18. Select the *AutoPlay* option. AutoPlay is sometimes disabled in the corporate environment so that people who have executable files on their removable media can't automatically launch those files. When AutoPlay is disabled (turned off), the user is prompted what to do when digital media is inserted into the computer.

19. Select the *Disk space* option.

    How much free space is on this device?

    _____

    How much free space is taken up by files in the Recycle Bin?

    _____

20. Finally, select the *PC info* option. This information is important to a technician because the type of computer, name of the computer, and amount of RAM, processor, and system type can be used to research problems the machine might be having.

21. Click the left arrow to return to the PC settings screen.

Accounts

22. Rather than taking you through each option, you can answer questions in each section to make sure you are looking at important options. Explore the *Accounts* options to answer the questions.

    What three sign-in options can you use with Windows 8.1?

    _____

    How many digits does a PIN require in Windows 8.1?

    _____

    How would you add an additional account to this machine? Give exact steps.

    _____

    _____

23. Click the left arrow to return to the PC settings screen.

OneDrive

24. Select *OneDrive* from the *PC settings* screen. Explore the different *OneDrive* options to answer the questions.

    What is OneDrive?

    _____

    What is a metered connection?

    _____

    What would be the drawback to allowing upload and download files over metered connections?

    _____

    Would you personally configure the OneDrive uploads and downloads to be on even when the device might be roaming?

    _____

25. Click the left arrow to return to the PC settings screen.

Search and Apps

26. Select *Search and apps* from the *PC settings* screen. Explore the different options to answer the questions.

    List one instance of why someone would want to clear the search history. Describe what you think this does.

    _____

    _____

    What is the default search engine?

    _____

    Can the default search engine be changed? If so, describe how.

    _____

    What app opens .3gpp files by default?

    _____

    What app shows the news by default?

    _____

    How much memory does the *Calculator* app take?

    _____

    What are Quiet hours, and how does that relate to a PC's settings?

    _____

27. Click the left arrow to return to the PC settings screen.

Privacy

28. Select *Privacy* from the *PC settings* screen. Explore the different options to answer the questions.

    Does Windows 8.1 allow you to disable and enable the capability to let apps access the name, picture, and account information found on the computer?

    _____

    What apps, if any, can use the computer's location?

    _____

    Does the device have a webcam? If so, are any devices allowed to use it? Where did you find this information?

    _____

    What apps are allowed to use the computer's microphone?

    _____

29. Click the left arrow to return to the PC settings screen.

Network

30. Select *Network* from the *PC settings* screen. Explore the different options to answer the questions.

    What types of networks are supported?

    _____

    If you turn airplane mode on, what happens to all the settings below it?

    _____

If you worked in a corporate environment in which a proxy server was used and you were required to configure an executive's laptop, what configuration settings would you need to obtain from the network support staff to manually configure the settings?

_____

Which option would you use to join a corporate domain?

[HomeGroup | Domain | Workplace | Connections] Select the *Join* button to add the device to the domain.

Which option would you use to attach the device to the wireless network?

[Connections | Airplane mode | Proxy | Homegroup | Workplace]

31. Click the left arrow to return to the PC settings screen.

Time and Language

32. Select *Time and language* from the *PC settings* screen. Explore the different options to answer the questions.

Can you manually configure the time, or is it automatic with Windows 8.1? [Manual | Automatic]

Does Windows 8.1 support multiple languages to be installed at the same time? [Yes | No]

33. Click the left arrow to return to the PC settings screen.

Ease of Access

34. Select *Ease of Access* from the *PC settings* screen. Explore the different options to answer the questions.

Can the Narrator be turned on and the *Start Narrator automatically* option be turned off at the same time? [Yes | No] What is the purpose of the magnifier?

_____

Does the magnifier have to be on to invert colors? [Yes | No]

In what other way could you adjust color settings for a person who was color blind?

_____

Why do you think someone would want to have the on-screen keyboard enabled?

_____

_____

What is the purpose of the last pointer color option?

_____

_____

35. Click the left arrow to return to the PC settings screen.

Update and Recovery

Note: Be very careful in this section to follow the directions exactly. You can lose all data if you do not.

36. Select *Update and recovery* from the *PC settings* screen. Explore the different options to answer the questions.

When was the last update installed on this computer?

_____

Does Windows 8.1 enable you to choose how updates get installed? [Yes | No]

_____

How does Microsoft handle Windows 8.1 updates when the computer is connected to the Internet on a metered connection?

_____

What is the purpose of the *File History* option?

_____

What three recovery options are available?

_____

_____

Which recovery option would enable you to access advanced options, especially if an SSD is installed in the computer and you cannot press the [F8] key quickly enough to access the options?
[Refresh your PC | Remove everything | Advanced startup]

37. Select the *Restart now* button.

What options are available to you?

_____

_____

_____

38. From the screen shown, select *Troubleshoot*.

What options are available to you?

_____

39. Select *Advanced options*

What options are available to you?

_____

_____

40. Select *Startup Repair*. Note that this provides the same function as pressing the [F8] key during the boot process.

What options are available to you?

_____

41. Select an account and enter the appropriate password > select *Continue*.

42. The system attempts to repair the PC. Select *Advanced options*. You are returned to the same screen as Step 38. Select the *Continue* option.

Lab 15.5 Windows 8.1 Basic Usage—Working with the Traditional Desktop and Control Panels

Objective:	To work effectively with the Windows 8.1 traditional desktop, accessing Control Panels; managing the display through the Control Panel; performing file, folder, and computer searches; and accessing programs
Parts:	Two computers with Windows 8.1 with administrator rights
Note:	This lab could actually be done with one computer, and only Step 37 could not be completed.
Procedure:	Complete the following procedure and answer the accompanying questions.

1. Power on the computer and log on to Windows if necessary.

Working with the Start Menu

2.   Windows 8.1 enables you to work with the Start screen where tiles are located, with the more traditional desktop, or both. Move the pointer to the lower-left corner, and select the Windows icon that appears. The traditional desktop appears.

3.   Notice how the traditional desktop has a Start button (in Windows 8.1 but not Windows 8) that is a little different. The Windows 8.1 desktop also has a taskbar and notification area. Also, the hot-corners options used to access the Start screen, charms, and switch between applications still work.

4.   Right-click or select and briefly hold on an empty space within the *Taskbar* (the bar that runs across the bottom of the display).

List the options available in the context menu.

_____

_____

How can you tell if the taskbar is locked or unlocked without moving it?

_____

_____

What toolbars can be added to the taskbar?

_____

_____

5.   Select the *Customize* link in the Notification area. Note that you may have to select an up arrow to see the link. After you answer the question, select *Cancel*.

List three system icons that can be customized within the notification area.

_____

_____

_____

Working with Control Panels

6.   To access Control Panels in Windows 8.1, access and select the *Settings* charm > select *Change PC Settings* > select *Control Panel* or right-click the *Start* button and select *Control Panel*.

TECH TIP

Different ways to access Control Panels in Windows 8.1

> Use the *Settings* charm > select *PC Settings* > select *Control Panel*.

> Type `control` in *Search* textbox > select *Control Panel*.

> After searching for *Control Panel*, right-click or tap and briefly hold on the icon > select *Pin to Start* so you have a Control Panel tile on the Start screen or select *Pin to Taskbar* so it will be available on the traditional desktop taskbar.

> Use the *Windows key+X* > select *Control Panel*.

> With the Control Panel window open, locate the word *Control Panel* in the address bar > select and drag the words *Control Panel* to the desktop so that a shortcut icon will be created.

> From the *Start Screen*, locate the *Control Panel* App tile.

> From *File Explorer*, select *This PC* in the window to the left > select *Computer* from the menu ribbon (the new term they are calling the menu) > select the *Open Control Panel* icon.

7. *Control Panel* allows access to Control Panel icons or links used to configure the computer. There are two basic ways to view Control Panels: the classic view (small and large icons for each Control Panel) and category view where eight major categories are shown with a few links under each category, but more links are available after you select the link. The default view is by category. To ensure you are in the default view, locate and select the *View by* down arrow on the top right. Ensure *Category* is selected.

   List two Control Panel categories shown on the screen.

   _____

   _____

   _____

8. Select *Large icons* or *Small icons* in the View by: drop-down menu. This view is the older method for accessing any particular Control Panel. Return to the *Category* Control Panel view.

9. Use Table 15.14 as a reference. Note that some systems have special Control Panels because of the type of computer being used. Also, some of the options are found in multiple categories. Use Table 15.15 to explore Windows Control panel, and document which Control Panel category and subcategory you would use to perform that particular task.

TABLE 15.14   Common Windows 8 Control Panel categories*

Control Panel category	Subcategory	Function
System and Security	Action Center	Used to view messages about security and maintenance issues and change security or maintenance-related settings
	Windows Firewall	Used to enable and customize security firewall features
	System	Used to view basic computer properties, such as RAM, processor type, and computer name
	Windows Update	Used to customize how updates are received and installed
	Power Options	Used to configure power-saving modes
	File History	Used to periodically back up files in Documents, Music, Pictures, Videos, and Desktop folders
	BitLocker Drive Encryption	Used to change or use encryption options
	Storage Spaces	Used to create a single storage space from multiple drives (and drive types)
	Work Folders	Used to save files that are accessible from multiple devices that may or may not be connected to the Internet at the time
	Administrative Tools	Used to perform such tasks as freeing up hard disk space, managing hard drive partitions, scheduling tasks, and viewing event logs

CHAPTER 15

Control Panel category	Subcategory	Function
Network and Internet	Network and Sharing Center	Used to check the status and modify network-related settings as well as share files, folders, and devices on the network
	Internet Options	Used to customize Internet Explorer
	HomeGroup	Used to view and change sharing and password options
Hardware and Sound	Devices and Printers	Used to add/remove a device, scanner, camera, printer, and mouse as well as access Device Manager
	AutoPlay	Used to change how media is automatically handled when a disc or type of file is added or inserted
	Sound	Used to manage audio devices and change sound schemes
	Power Options	Same as found in the System and Security category
	Display	Used to adjust resolution, configure an external display, or make text larger/smaller
	Windows Mobility Center	On mobile devices, contains the most commonly used settings such as volume, battery status, wireless network status, and display status
	Pen and Touch	Used to configure pen or touch options for a tablet
	Tablet PC Settings	Used to calibrate the screen, adjust for left- or right-hand-controls, and set the order in which the screen rotates
	Location Settings	Used to control how apps use the device's location
Programs	Programs and Features	Used to uninstall and change programs as well as enable/disable Windows features such as games, telnet server, telnet client, TFTP client, and print services
	Default Programs	Used to remove a startup program, associate a file extension with a particular application, or select the program used with a particular type of file
User Accounts and Family Safety	User Accounts	Used to add, remove, or modify accounts allowed access to the computer
	Family Safety	Used to obtain reports of other users' computer activities, select what can be seen online, and configure time restrictions

Control Panel category	Subcategory	Function
	Credential Manager	Used to store username/password in a vault for easy logon to sites or computers
Appearance and Personalization	Personalization	Used to configure the desktop, background, colors, themes, and screen saver
	Display	Same as in the Hardware and Sound category
	Taskbar and Navigation	Used to customize the Start screen and taskbar
	Ease of Access Center	Used to configure visual, auditory, and mobility options
	Folder Options	Used to configure how folders are viewed and acted upon, including what files are seen
	Fonts	Used to customize available fonts
Clock, Language, and Region	Date and Time	Used to configure time, date, time zone, and clocks for different time zones
	Language	Used to add a language
	Region	Used to configure the formatting of date, time, currency, and more that are region-specific.

*Note that you can find particular options by typing in the subcategory in the *Search Control Panel* textbox.

Fill in Table 15.15 with the correct Control Panel category and subcategory.

TABLE 15.15   Determine the correct Control Panel

Control Panel category	Control Panel subcategory	Task
		Used to configure the mouse buttons for a left-handed person
		Used to mute the computer speaker sound
		Used to configure the date to be in the format April 15, 201X
		Used to define how fast a character repeats when a specific key is held down
		Used to define what page (home page) appears every time Internet Explorer starts
		Used to configure an IP address on a wired or wireless network adapter

Control Panel category	Control Panel subcategory	Task
		Used to set a printer as the default printer
		Used to verify if Windows recognizes a particular piece of hardware

Working with the Display

9. Select the *Hardware and Sound* Control Panel category > select *Display*. Note that you may be required to search throughout this area and select various options to answer the questions.

    What is the current resolution?

    _____

    How many bits are used for color?

    _____

10. Continue working with the *Display* link. Locate and select the *Advanced Settings* link. Note: You may have to select the *Change display settings* link or use another Control Panel depending on the manufacturer.

    What adapter is used?

    _____

    How much video memory does the adapter have?

    _____

    How much total video memory (dedicated video memory) is available?

    _____

11. Select the *Monitor* tab.

    What refresh rate is used?

    _____

12. Click *Cancel* on this window and the next window to return to the *Control Panel* main screen. Select the *Appearance and Personalization* link > select the *Personalization* link > select the *Screen Saver/ Change Screen Saver* link in the bottom right.

    What screen saver, if any, is currently set?

    _____

13. Use the *Screen Saver* down arrow to see a list of pre-installed screen savers and click one of the options. Click the *Preview* button. The screen saver appears. Move the pointer to regain control. Return the screen saver to the original setting (see the answer to Question 12).

Dealing with Power Settings

14. Select the *Change power settings* link. The Power Options window appears. Table 15.16 shows the various power options available in Windows 8.1.

    What power option would a teacher use when using a laptop to teach a 4-hour class?

    _____

TABLE 15.16   Windows 8.1 default power schemes*

Power scheme	Purpose
Balanced	Default mode; processor adapts to activity being performed; performance provided when the computer is in use; power savings when the computer is inactive. Display powers down after 15 minutes; hard drive powers down after 20 minutes and goes to sleep after 20 minutes.
Power saver	Provides maximum battery life for mobile devices. Display and hard drive power down after 20 minutes, and the system goes to sleep after one hour.
High performance	Maximum system performance and responsiveness. Display and hard drive power down after 20 minutes, but the system never sleeps.
Customized	A scheme created by the user that has different settings than the default three schemes.

*Note that a computer manufacturer may provide additional power schemes.

15. Close all Control Panel windows.

Obtaining Help

16. Use the *Search* charm and type **help**. Two main sources of Windows 8.1 help are *Help+Tips* and *Help and Support*. Access the *Help+Tips* link. Notice how this help is more a user-type help feature.

17. Re-access the *Search* charm and access the *Help and Support* link. The standard categories for help are Get started, Internet and networking, and Security, privacy, & accounts. You can use the textbox in the top center to search for specific help topics, or you can access the *Browse help* link.

18. Select the *Browse help* link.

    What is the first link listed in the help window?

    _____

19. Type **monitor quality** in the *Search* textbox and press (Enter) or click the magnifying glass icon to the right of the textbox.

    List three settings used to improve display quality.

    _____

    _____

20. To see a list of troubleshooting topics, type **troubleshooting** in the *Search* textbox. A list of troubleshooting topics immediately displays.

21. Close the *Windows Help and Support* window.

Searching for Files, Folders, Applications, and Computers

22. Folders and files, including executable files, can be located using Windows File Explorer. Open Windows *File Explorer* > locate and select *This PC* > in the *Search This PC* textbox located directly across from the path address box, type **msconfig** and pause a moment before doing anything else.

23. Notice at the top of the ribbon menu that a Search menu option has appeared. Within this option, you can specify whether to include subfolders, the type of file, and advanced options that include searching system files. You can also save the results of a particular search.

    List three kinds of items that could be used in a search.

    _____

24. By now your search should be complete. The `msconfig` command is an important one to technicians because this command launches the System Configuration utility. This utility is covered in more detail in Chapter 16. In the resulting list, locate and launch (double-click or double-tap) the *msconfig* utility (normally the second or third option in the list).

   List the five tabs found in the System Configuration window.

   _____

25. Select *Cancel* to close the System Configuration window. Close *File Explorer*.

26. Another way to locate files is through the Search charm. Type **msconfig** in the Search textbox and select *msconfig.exe* from the resulting list.

27. Select *Cancel* to close the System Configuration window.

28. Using any search method you want, find the *WordPad* application and launch it. Type the following message:

   Your profession is not what brings home your weekly paycheck. Your profession is what you're put here on earth to do with such passion and such intensity that it becomes spiritual in calling. (van Gogh)

29. Select the *Save* icon in the top-left corner (the icon looks like a floppy disk 🖫.)

30. Ensure the address bar shows that the file is saving into *Documents*. If it is not, scroll in the left window to locate and select *Documents*. In the *File name:* textbox, type **Lab4test** and select *Save*.

31. Close WordPad using the *Close* button in the top right corner.

32. Using the *Search* charm, type **lab** in the textbox.

   Did your Lab4test file appear in the resulting search list? If not, redo Steps 28 through 32.

   _____

33. Close the *Search* charm by selecting or clicking somewhere on the desktop.

34. Use the *System* Control Panel to document your computer name.

   Computer name _____

35. To locate other computers on a network from a Windows 8 computer, on your own computer access *File Explorer* > select *Network* from the left. If computers and devices are configured to be seen on the network, then the computers appear in the screen to the right.

36. To configure your computer to be seen through File Explorer, access the *Network and Internet* Control Panel > *Network and Sharing Center* > *Change advanced sharing settings* > expand the section that shows your current profile by selecting or tapping on the down chevron > enable the following: *Turn on network discovery* and *Turn on file and printer sharing* > *Save changes*. Do the same process on the second computer or ask a classmate to do it.

   Document the second computer name _____

37. Use *File Explorer* to locate a remote network device or computer. Do the same on the second Windows 8 or 8.1 computer.

   Does the remote device appear? [Yes | No]

   Does your device appear within File Explorer on the remote device? [Yes | No]

   Instructor initials: _____

TECH TIP

Changing UAC (User Access Control) settings

Windows has a UAC dialog box that appears, asking for permission to do something. To change UAC settings, use the *User Accounts and Family Safety* Control Panel > select an account > *Change User Account Control settings* > move the UAC control bar to have more notifications, less notifications, or no notifications > *OK*.

The UAC settings can also be disabled through the *System Configuration* utility (**msconfig** command) > *Tools* tab > *Change UAC Settings* > *Launch* button > select the appropriate level > *OK*.

38. Close all windows.

Recycle Bin

39. Open *File Explorer* > locate the *Lab4test* document created earlier in the lab. Ensure the file is showing in the right window.

40. Right-click or tab and briefly hold on the *Lab4test* filename. Notice that there is a Delete option. Do not click this option. This is just one way you could use to delete the file, but we are going to use a different way. With the *Lab4test* filename still highlighted (but no context menu showing), press the [Delete] key. The file is sent to the Recycle Bin, which is just a folder on the hard drive. There isn't a message asking if you are sure, like Windows 7 and older operating systems displayed.

The Recycle Bin holds deleted files and folders. When a file or folder is deleted, it is not immediately discarded; instead, it goes into the Recycle Bin folder. When a deleted file or folder is in the Recycle Bin, it can be removed. This is similar to a piece of trash being retrieved from an office trash can. A technician must remember that the files and folders in the Recycle Bin take up hard drive space and that users frequently forget to empty these deleted files and folders.

TECH TIP

Files deleted from Recycle Bin cannot be retrieved

After the Recycle Bin has been emptied, the deleted files cannot be recovered without the use of special software.

41. Locate the *Recycle Bin* icon on the desktop. Note that if the Recycle Bin is not on the desktop, search for the Recycle Bin folder. Double-click or double-tap the *Recycle Bin* icon.

Does the *Lab4test* WordPad document appear in the Recycle Bin window? _____

If not, redo the steps in this section to create and delete the file.

42. Select the *Empty Recycle Bin* from the *Manage* menu ribbon option. A confirmation window appears asking if you are sure you want to permanently delete the file. Select *Yes*. The name disappears from the Recycle Bin window (as do those of any other files that were located in the Recycle Bin). Close the *Recycle Bin* window.

CHAPTER 15

Lab 15.6 Windows 10 Basic Usage—Introduction to the Start Screen

Objective: To work effectively with the Windows 10 Start screen

Parts: Computer with Windows 10 and administrator privileges

Procedure: Complete the following procedure and answer the accompanying questions.

1.   Power on the computer and log on to Windows 10. Note that you may have to swipe up or press a key to access the logon screen.

Working with the *Start* Screen

2.   The *Start* screen displays. The Start screen is customizable so that it can look similar to the traditional desktop, the Windows 8.1 Start screen with all tiles, or a combination of the two.

Which type of Start screen do you see?

A. The traditional Windows Start screen with a Start button in the lower-left corner and a taskbar across the bottom

B. Similar to the default Windows 8 screen where the entire Start screen shows tiles representing apps

C. A combination of the two where some tiles show, but the taskbar still shows across the bottom or appears when the pointer is moved to the bottom of the screen

_____

3.   Let's control the Start Screen so that you can tell what options are available. We need to start by opening *Settings*. How you do this depends on how your Start screen is already configured (and we will place it back that way at the end of this section). Open *Settings* using one of the following methods. Note that all methods may not be available due to the type of device or configuration settings.

> Hold the ■ key down and then press the [I] key.

> Select the *Start* button located in the bottom-left corner. You may have to move the pointer to the bottom of the screen for it to appear. Select *Settings* from the menu.

> Select the *Start* button located in the bottom-left corner. You may have to move the pointer to the bottom of the screen for it to appear. Select the icon that looks like a bulleted list (located below the power icon). Scroll to the S section and select *Settings*.

> Select the icon that has three horizontal lines located in the top-left corner > select *Settings* from the resulting menu.

4.   Select *Personalization* > select *Start*.

Document your current settings so that they may be reinstated at the end of the lab.

Show more tiles [On | Off]

Occasionally show suggestions in Start [On | Off]

Show most used apps [On | Off]

Show recently added apps [On | Off]

Use Start full screen [On | Off]

Show recently opened items in Jump Lists on Start or the taskbar [On | Off]

_____

5.   Turn all options to the *Off* position. Select the *Choose which folders appear on Start* link at the bottom of the right pane.

Document your current settings so that they may be reconfigured at the end of the lab.

File Explorer [On | Off]

Settings [On | Off]

Documents [On | Off]

Downloads [On | Off]

Music [On | Off]

Pictures [On | Off]

Videos [On | Off]

HomeGroup [On | Off]

Network [On | Off]

Personal Folder [On | Off]

---

6.   Configure all the folders to *Off*. Close the *Settings* window to return to the Start screen.

Which Start screen do you now see?

A. The traditional Windows Start screen with a Start button in the lower-left corner and a taskbar across the bottom

B. Similar to the default Windows 8 screen where the entire Start screen shows tiles representing apps

C. A combination of the two previously described Start screens where some tiles show, but the taskbar still shows across the bottom or appears when the pointer is moved to the bottom of the screen

7.   Select the *Start* button from the Start screen.

What menu options appear directly above the Start button?

---

8.   Select the *All apps* option > scroll to the *S* section > select *Settings* > *Personalization* > select the *Start* option. Notice in the preview window how an example of the Windows Start screen and its layout is shown.

9.   Turn the *Show more tiles* option *On*.

How did the preview window change?

If you were to enable the *Occasionally show suggestions in Start* option, how does the preview window change, if at all?

---

10.   Table 15.17 shows the purpose of these options. Figure 15.43 shows where these options would be located on the Start menu. Explore these options to see their effects.

TABLE 15.17   Windows 10 Start screen settings

Setting	Purpose
Show more tiles	Shows one more column of tiles. Note that you can drag the edge of the tiles to make any size you want.
Occasionally show suggestions in Start	Displays ads for suggested apps.
Show most used apps	Dynamically populates with the most commonly used apps.
Show recently added apps	Lists the apps recently installed.
Use Start full screen	Start screen is more like the Windows 8 tiles view full screen. Use the menu icon in the left-top corner to access apps.
Show recently opened items in Jump Lists on Start or the taskbar	Displays as an arrow from the Start menu or on the Start screen. Jump lists are recently used documents, websites, and so on related to a particular app. On the taskbar, right-click an app icon to see the associated jump list.

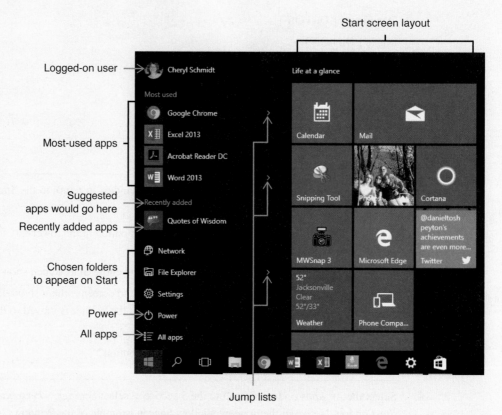

Logged-on user →

Most-used apps →

Suggested
apps would go here →

Recently added apps →

Chosen folders
to appear on Start →

Power →

All apps →

Start screen layout

Jump lists

FIGURE 15.43   Windows 10 Start menu areas

11.   Within the *Start* settings, ensure the *Use Start full screen* option is *Off*. Access the *Chose which fold-ers appear on Start* link at the bottom of the right panel.

12.   Select a couple of these and re-access the Start screen.

List which options you think would be most beneficial for people in a work environment.

_____

_____

_____

13.   Within the *Start* settings, ensure the *Use Start full screen* option is *On*.

14.   Re-access the Start menu by selecting the *Start* icon from the desktop.

Manipulating the *Start* Screen

15.   Let's explore how to modify tiles. Examine the tiles shown in the Start screen.

Which tile is currently located in the far-left position?

_____

16.   Select and drag the tile located in the far-left position to the last position in the first block of tiles. Then return the tile to the current position.

17.   To add a tile that represents an app to the Start screen, access the *All apps* Start menu icon that looks like a bulleted list. Select the *Windows Accessories* menu item > locate, but do not select the *Notepad* application. Right-click or tap and briefly hold on the *Notepad* option. A context menu appears. Move the pointer to the *More* option.

Which additional options are available?

_____

18. Select the *Pin to Start* option. A Notepad tile appears.

    List the options available from the context menu.

    _____

19. Tap or select the *Notepad* tile. The Notepad application window opens. Close the window using the *Close* button.

20. Re-access the *Start* menu using whatever method you prefer. Locate the *Notepad* tile. Tap and briefly hold or right-click the *Notepad* tile to access the context menu.

    List any menu options that were not available from the context menu previously accessed before you pinned the app to the Start screen.

    _____

21. Hover the pointer over the *Resize* option.

    What choices do you have?

    _____

22. Select a different tile size than the one currently used. Re-access the *Notepad* tile context menu again. Select *Open file location*. Windows *File Explorer* opens showing the folder that contains this file (and other files within the same folder). Notice how the Notepad option is a shortcut. You can tell because the icon on the left has a bent arrow on it. Also, in the *Type* column, you can see the word *Shortcut*.

23. To see where the original file is located, right-click or tap and hold on the *Notepad* icon from within File Explorer > select *Properties*. Ensure the *Shortcut* tab is selected. The *Target* textbox shows where the file is actually located. The %windir% is used to describe the folder where Windows was installed. Commonly it is C:\Windows, but because this might be on another drive letter or installed to a different folder, Microsoft simply describes it as %windir%. The full path for the Notepad application is commonly C:\Windows\Systems32\notepad.exe.

24. Click *Cancel* to return to File Explorer. Close *File Explorer*. Return to the *Start* screen (the one with the tiles).

25. Re-access the *Notepad* context menu. Select *Unpin from Start*.

Conducting Searches

26. Searches in Windows 10 are done through the taskbar using the *Search the web and Windows* icon. Note that if you have the Cortana feature turned on, you can speak or type questions or conduct searches through that interface. To ensure that everyone is on the same page, let's get some original configuration stuff documented and possibly changed.

    From the *Start* menu, start typing (note that you do not have to click anywhere) `cor` and select *Cortana & Search Settings* from the resulting list.

    Document the device's current settings related to searching.

    Cortana can give you suggestions, ideas, reminders, alerts and more [On | Off]

    Improve search results for on-device content using my device search history [On | Off]

    Search online and include web results [On | Off]

    Improve web search results using my web search history from signed-In devices [On | Off]

    _____

27. Ensure the *Cortana can give you suggestions, ideas, reminders, alerts and more* option is turned *Off*. Ensure the *Search online and include web results* option is turned *On*.

28. Select the *Search* icon from the taskbar or select inside the *Search the web and Windows* textbox. Type `comm` in the textbox. A list separated by best match, apps, store, Web, and settings appears. Select the *Command Prompt* option. The Command Prompt window appears. Close the Command Prompt window using the *Close* symbol on the top right of the window.

29. Re-access the search function and type **word**. From the resulting list, right-click or tap and briefly hold on the *WordPad* app. Notice how from the search result, you still have access to the context menu that allows you to pin a particular app to the Start menu or taskbar. You also have the option to run an app as an administrator. This is sometimes required with Windows utilities used by technicians (but not needed with WordPad). Click away from the Search list.

30. In the textbox at the bottom of the list, remove *word* and type **trinkets** instead. Notice that because there is nothing within the Windows 10 environment related to trinkets, web links are provided. This is because the *Search online and include web results* option was turned to *On* in a previous step. Select somewhere away from the search list.

Power Options

31. In the Start menu is the *Power Options* icon. It is a circle with a vertical line that extends through the top part of the circle. You often see the symbol on power buttons. Click this icon once. Table 15.18 explains the various power options that might be seen.

TABLE 15.18   Windows 10 power button shut down options

Option	Purpose
Sign out	Allows the current user to log off from the account being used.
Restart	Used when new software or hardware has been installed or when the computer locks.
Sleep	Reduces power consumption but keeps the applications and settings that are currently on the screen.
Hibernate	Reduces power consumption even more so than the sleep mode. Takes longer to resume operations than sleep mode, but not as long as a cold boot.
Shut Down	Powers off the computer.

What options are available?

_____

Controlling the Desktop

32. The desktop is the main screen area that you see when you log in to Windows 10. What is shown on the desktop and default options are customizable like the Start menu.

33. Right-click or tap and briefly hold on an empty space on the desktop. Point to the *View* option.

What options are available in the context menu?

_____

What options are currently enabled?

_____

34. Select the *Show desktop icons* option to disable it (no checkmark beside the option).

What changed?

_____

35. Re-access the *View* context menu and ensure the *Show desktop icons* option is set to the original configuration. See the answer to the question in Step 33.

Task View

36. On the taskbar is the Task View option. Task View allows you to view thumbnails of open apps and easily switch between them.

37. Open the *Notepad*, *Snipping Tool*, and *Command Prompt* apps.

38. Locate and select the *Task View* option on the taskbar. It is located to the right of the search function.

    What happened when you selected the *Task View* option?

39. Locate and select the *Notepad* app. Note that you may have to select a down arrow below the thumbnails to see more thumbnails if you have more apps open than can fit on the screen. Leave these apps open.

40. Task View can also be used to create more than one desktop so that you have one or more specific applications in one desktop and then from another desktop you could have different apps open. Then you can use Task View to easily swap between them. Re-access *Task View* from the taskbar.

41. Select the *New desktop* option from the bottom of the *Task View* window. A numbered desktop appears at the bottom.

42. Access the new desktop just added by clicking that numbered desktop on the far right.

43. On this desktop, open the WordPad app.

44. Now select the *Task View* taskbar option again. The multiple desktops show. Move the pointer to the first desktop, and all open apps appear in the window above. Move the pointer to the desktop you just created, and the WordPad app thumbnail appears.

    One thing to note about the virtual desktops is that they are not totally separated from one another. For example, if you enable the *Use Start full screen* option, it will be enabled across all desktops.

45. Ensure the pointer is pointing toward the last desktop that was just created. Select the X in the upper-right corner to delete that virtual desktop.

46. In the original desktop, ensure any windows you have opened are closed (*Notepad*, *Snipping Tool*, and *Command Prompt).*

Getting the Machine Back in Order

47. Refer to steps 4, 5, and 26 and return all Start settings to their original configuration.

48. Have a classmate verify that the settings are configured properly.

    Are the computer settings back to the original configuration as verified in Steps 4, 5, and 26? [Yes | No]

    Classmate's printed name _____

    Classmate's signature _____

Lab 15.7 Windows 10 Basic Usage—Introduction to Settings

Objective: To be familiar with the Windows 10 Settings

Parts: Computer with Windows 10

                Flash drive

Procedure: Complete the following procedure and answer the accompanying questions.

1. Power on the computer and log on to Windows 10. Note that you may have to swipe up or press a key to access the logon screen.

2. Use the *Start* menu to access *Settings*. The Windows 10 settings has more configurable options than Windows 8/8.1 did without having to use Control Panels.

Working with Windows 10 System Settings

3. Select the *System* option from the *Settings* screen.

Looking over the list, which option are you curious about?

_____

4. Select the *Display* setting. This setting is commonly used to set the size of text and orientation of the display and shows the number of displays detected.

What is the current orientation? [Landscape | Portrait | Landscape (flipped) | Portrait (flipped)]

_____

5. Change the orientation to something else such as *Landscape (flipped)*. Select *Apply*. Select the *Revert* option if you can after you answer the questions that follow. If you cannot select this option, do not worry because without accepting the change, the display changes back to the original setting.

What happened?

_____

_____

6. Select the *Advanced display settings* link at the bottom of the *Display* settings option. This option allows you to reset the screen resolution if the user has set it to something less than optimal. You might also have the *Color Calibration* link.

What is the current resolution?

_____

7. Return to the *System* settings window by selecting the *left arrow* in the top-left corner of the window.

8. Select the *Multitasking* option. The multitasking option has items related to snapping and resizing windows as well as virtual desktop settings that relate to Task View (that was covered in the previous lab).

What is the current setting for showing windows that are open? [Only the desktop I am using | All desktops]

9. Return to the *System* settings window by selecting the *left arrow* in the top-left corner.

10. Select the *Power & sleep* option. This is where you can select a power plan for the system.

At what point will the screen turn off after a period of inactivity?

_____

At what point will the PC go to sleep after a period of inactivity?

_____

Could you configure a Windows 10 computer so that it never went to sleep? [Yes | No]

11. Select the *Advanced power settings* link. Notice how you are taken to the *Power Options* Control Panel.

12. Return to the *System* settings by closing the *Power Options* Control Panel window > in the *System Power & sleep* settings window, select the *left arrow* in the top-left corner.

13. Attach a flash drive to the PC.

14. Select the *Storage* system setting. In the *Storage* section, select the flash drive that has just been attached. Windows categorizes the type of documents found on the drive (system files, apps and games, documents, pictures, music, videos, maps, temporary files, and others) and shows you how much of each type are on the chosen file media.

Return to the *Storage* settings screen and scroll down to the *Save locations* section.

Use Table 15.19 to document current save locations.

TABLE 15.19   Windows 10 save locations

Option	Current setting
New apps will save to:	
New documents will save to:	
New music will save to:	
New pictures will save to:	
New videos will save to:	

Describe a situation in which you think someone might want to change one or more of these settings.

_____

_____

_____

_____

15. On the left menu, select and access the *About* system setting. This screen is chock-full of information important to an IT person.

List five items that you think might be useful to a technical person (and not usually useful to the end user).

_____

_____

Where does the *Additional administrative tools* link take you to?

_____

If you access the *Device Manager* link, does the Device Manager tool open in another window or display within the settings window? [another window | same window]

What information is displayed when the *System information* link is chosen that was not available from the *About* system setting?

_____

_____

16. Return to the *System* settings window by selecting the *left arrow* in the top-left corner of the window.

Devices

17. Select the *Devices* setting. This setting is used to quickly see and configure attached devices. Rather than taking you through each option, answer some questions in each section to make sure you are looking at important options. Explore the different *Devices* options to answer the questions.

Does the Printer & scanners option have any settings related to devices other than printers and scanners? [Yes | No] If yes, explain what is there. _____

_____

Can you configure Bluetooth devices through the *Connected devices* link? [Yes | No]

_____

Does the attached flash drive appear as a connected device? [Yes | No] List two connected devices.

_____

Describe which steps can be taken so the PC can be found by other Bluetooth devices. Note that not all devices have Bluetooth installed. Write not applicable as an answer if this is the case.

_____

_____

Which button is the primary mouse button? [Left | Center | Right]

_____

If the mouse has a scroll wheel, how many lines scroll each time the mouse wheel is rolled?

_____

Can the computer scroll inactive windows when the user hovers the mouse pointer over them? [Yes | No]

Can the Windows operating system be configured to automatically correct misspelled words? [Yes | No]

Can the Windows operating system be configured to recommend alternative words? [Yes | No]

_____

Can you disable AutoPlay through the *AutoPlay Devices* settings? [Yes | No]

_____

What is the default web browser for the machine? How did you find this through settings?

_____

_____

18. Return to the *System* settings window by selecting the *left arrow* in the top-left corner of the window.

Network & Internet

19. Select *Network & Internet* from the *Settings* window. Explore the different options to answer the questions.

What types of networks are supported?

_____

Does Windows 10 allow you to turn airplane mode on? [Yes | No]

_____

_____

If you work in a corporate environment in which a proxy server is used and you are required to configure an executive's laptop, what configuration settings do you need to obtain from the network support staff to manually configure the settings?

_____

Which option would you use to see the MAC address of the Ethernet network card?

_____

Which option would you use to attach the device to the wireless network?
[Wi-Fi | Airplane mode | Proxy | Ethernet | Dial-up]

_____

20. Select the left arrow to return to the *Settings* screen.

Personalization

21. Select *Personalization* from the *Settings* window.

22. Select the *Lock screen* option. This particular setting allows you to control how the display reacts and possibly the camera as well (if one is installed). The lock screen function is a screen that appears when you have not interacted with the device after a specified amount of time. The lock screen commonly shows such information as time, date, battery status, and network status. Notice that to enable an option, you select one side of a particular option.

What is the current option to play a slide show on the lock screen? [On | Off] Note that if you are having trouble telling, a dot points toward one side or the other. The selection chosen is shown as a particular word on the left (either on or off). Change the option by clicking or tapping on the side away from the dot.

_____

23. Choose the opposite selection for the *Show Windows background picture on the sign-in screen* by clicking or tapping the opposite side of the colored oval so that the dot goes to the opposite side. If the answer to Question 22 was *on*, you should turn the option *off*. If the answer to Question 22 was *off*, you should turn the option to *on*.

What visual clue did you have that the option changed?

_____

_____

24. Return the setting to the original on/off position.

25. Access the *Screen saver settings* link at the bottom of the window. An important checkbox for the corporate environment is the *On resume, display logon screen*. You can enable this option and set it for a particular time in case an employee walks away from the computer and is delayed in returning to it. Close the *Screen Saver Settings* window. Select the left arrow at the top of the screen to return to *Settings*.

Accounts

26. Rather than taking you through each option, answer some questions in each section to make sure you are looking at important options. Explore the different *Accounts* options to answer the questions.

What three sign-in options can be used with Windows 10?

_____

How many digits does a PIN require in Windows 10?

_____

How would you add an additional account to this machine? Give exact steps.

_____

_____

What does Synch your options mean?

_____

27. Select the left arrow to return to the *Settings* screen.

CHAPTER 15

Time & Language

28. Select *Time & language* from the *Settings* screen. Explore the different options to answer the questions.

    Can the time be manually configured, or is it automatic with Windows 10? [Manual | Automatic]

    _____

    If the date setting was set to the *dddd, MMMM d, yyyy* option, how would today's date appear?

    _____

    Does Windows 10 support multiple languages to be installed at the same time? [Yes | No]

    _____

    Is any option available that might help with speech recognition for a person from the deep South? If so, what?

    _____

    What is the default voice for apps?

    _____

29. Select the left arrow to return to the *Settings* screen.

Ease of Access

30. Select *Ease of Access* from the *Settings* screen. Explore the different options to answer the questions.

    Can the Narrator be turned on and the *Start Narrator automatically* option be turned off at the same time? [Yes | No]

    What is the purpose of the magnifier?

    _____

    Does the magnifier have to be on to invert colors? [Yes | No]

    In what other way could you adjust color settings for a person who is color blind?

    _____

    Why do you think someone would want to have the on-screen keyboard enabled?

    _____

    What is the purpose of the last pointer color option?

    _____

    _____

    What option would be used to increase the thickness of the cursor?

    _____

    Does Windows 10 support closed captioning? [Yes | Not that I can tell]

31. Select the left arrow to return to the *Settings* screen.

Privacy

32. Select *Privacy* from the *Settings* screen. Explore the different options to answer the questions.

Does Windows 10 allow you to disable and enable the capability to let apps access the name, picture, and account information found on the computer?

_____

What apps, if any, can use the computer's location?

_____

Does the device have a webcam? [Yes | No]

_____

If so, are any devices allowed to use it? Where did you find this information?

_____

Which apps are allowed to use the computer's microphone?

_____

Which apps are allowed to access your call history?

_____

33. Select the left arrow to return to the PC settings screen.

Update & Security

Note: Be very careful in this section to follow the directions exactly. You can lose all data if you do not.

34. Select *Update & Security* from the *Settings* screen. Explore the different options to answer the questions.

When was the last update installed on this computer? How did you find this information? Document your process.

_____

_____

Does Windows 10 allow you to choose how updates get installed? [Yes | No]

What steps would you take to uninstall an update?

_____

_____

What is the purpose of the *File History* option?

_____

What recovery options are available?

_____

Which recovery option would allow you to access advanced options, especially if an SSD is installed in the computer and you cannot press the [F8] key quickly enough to access the options?
[Reset this PC | Remove everything | Advanced startup]

35. Select the *Restart now* button.

What options are available to you?

_____

_____

36. From the screen shown, select *Troubleshoot*.

What options are available to you?

_____

37. Select *Advanced options*.

What options are available to you?

_____

_____

38. Select *Startup Repair*. Note that this provides the same function as pressing the ⎡F8⎤ key during the boot process.

39. Select an account and enter the appropriate password > select *Continue*.

40. The system attempts to repair the PC. Select *Advanced options*. You are returned to the same screen as Step 36. Select the *Continue* option.

Lab 15.8 Windows 10 Basic Usage—Working with Control Panels

Objective: To work effectively with the Windows 8 traditional desktop, accessing Control Panels; managing the display through the Control Panel; performing file, folder, and computer searches; and accessing programs

Parts: Two computers with Windows 10 with administrator rights

Note: This lab could actually be done with one computer and only Step 28 could not be completed.

Procedure: Complete the following procedure and answer the accompanying questions.

1.   Power on the computer and log on to Windows if necessary.

Working with Control Panels

2.   To access Control Panels in 10, access and select the *Settings* charm > select *Change PC Settings* > select *Control Panel*.

TECH TIP

Different ways to access Control Panels in Windows 10

> Right-click or tap and briefly hold the *Start* button > *Control Panel*.

> Type **control** in the *Search* textbox > select *Control Panel*. After searching for *Control Panel*, right-click or tap and briefly hold the icon > select *Pin to Start* so that you have a Control Panel tile on the Start screen or select *Pin to Taskbar* so it displays on the taskbar.

> Use the ⊞ + ⎡X⎤ > select *Control Panel*. With the Control Panel window open, locate the word *Control Panel* in the address bar > select and drag the words *Control Panel* to the desktop so that a shortcut icon is created.

> From the *Start* menu, select the *All Apps* icon > locate and expand the *Windows System* folder > locate and select *Control Panel*.

---

3.   *Control Panel* allows access to Control Panel icons or links used to configure the computer. There are two basic ways to view Control Panels: the classic view (small and large icons for each Control Panel) and category view where eight major categories are shown with a few links under each category, but more links are available after you select the link. The default view is by category. To ensure you are in the default view, locate and select the *View by* down arrow on the top right. Ensure *Category* is selected.

4. List two Control Panel categories shown on the screen.

_____

_____

5. Select *Large icons* or *Small icons* in the View by: drop-down menu. This view is the older method for accessing any particular Control Panel. Return to the *Category* Control Panel view.

Table 15.20 is to be used as a reference. Note that some systems have special Control Panels due to the hardware installed or type of computer such as a laptop or tablet. Notice in Table 15.20 that some of the options are found in multiple categories. Table 15.21 is for you to explore Windows Control Panels and document within the table which Control Panel category and subcategory you would use to perform that particular task.

TABLE 15.20   Common Windows 10 Control Panel categories*

Control Panel category	Subcategory	Function
System and Security	Security and Maintenance	Used to view messages about security and maintenance issues and change security or maintenance-related settings. Similar to the Action Center Control Panel in previous editions.
	Windows Firewall	Used to enable and customize security firewall features
	System	Used to view basic computer properties, such as RAM, processor type, and computer name
	Power Options	Configures power-saving modes
	File History	Used to periodically back up files in Documents, Music, Pictures, Videos, and Desktop folders.
	Backup and Restore (Windows 7)	Used to save or restore files and folders to/from a different location
	BitLocker Drive Encryption	Used to change or use encryption options
	Storage Spaces	Creates a single storage space from multiple drives (and drive types)
	Work Folders	Used to save files that are accessible from multiple devices that may or may not be connected to the Internet at the time
	Administrative Tools	Used for such tasks as freeing up hard disk space, managing hard drive partitions, scheduling tasks, and viewing event logs
Network and Internet	Network and Sharing Center	Used to check the status and modify network-related settings as well as share files, folders, and devices on the network.
	HomeGroup	Used to view and change sharing and password options
	Internet Options	Used to customize Internet Explorer
Hardware and Sound	Devices and Printers	Used to add/remove a device, scanner, camera, printer, and mouse as well as access Device Manager

Control Panel category	Subcategory	Function
	AutoPlay	Used to change how media is automatically handled when a disc or type of file is added or inserted
	Sound	Used to manage audio devices and change sound schemes
	Power Options	Same as found in the System and Security category
	Display	Used to adjust resolution, configure an external display, or make text larger/smaller
Programs	Programs and Features	Used to uninstall and change programs as well as enable/disable Windows features such as games, telnet server, telnet client, TFTP client, and print services
	Default Programs	Used to remove a startup program, associate a file extension with a particular application, or select the program used with a particular type of file
User Accounts	User Accounts	Used to add, remove, or modify accounts allowed access to the computer
	Credential Manager	Used to store username/password in a vault for easy logon to sites or computers
Appearance and Personalization	Personalization	Used to configure the desktop, background, colors, themes, and screen saver.
	Display	Same as in the Hardware and Sound category
	Taskbar and Navigation	Used to customize the Start screen and taskbar
	Ease of Access Center	Used to configure visual, auditory, and mobility options
	File Explorer Options	Used to configure how folders are viewed and acted upon, including which files are seen
	Fonts	Used to customize available fonts
Clock, Language, and Region	Date and Time	Used to configure time, date, time zone, and clocks for different time zones
	Language	Used to add a language
	Region	Used to configure the formatting of date, time, currency, and so on that are region-specific

*Note that particular options can be found by typing in the subcategory in the *Search Control Panel* textbox.

Fill in Table 15.21 with the correct Control Panel category and subcategory.

TABLE 15.21 Determine the correct Control Panel

Control Panel category	Control Panel subcategory	Task
		Used to configure the mouse buttons for a left-handed person.
		Used to mute the computer speaker sound.
		Used to configure the date to be in the format April 15, 201X.
		Used to define how fast a character repeats when a specific key is held down.
		Used to define what page (home page) appears every time Edge starts.
		Used to verify if Windows recognizes a particular piece of hardware.
		Used to configure an IP address on a wired or wireless network adapter.
		Used to set a printer as the default printer.

Working with the Display

4. Select the *Hardware and Sound* Control Panel category > select *Display*. Note that you may be required to search throughout this area and select various options to answer the questions.

    What is the current resolution?

    _____

    How many bits are used for color?

    _____

    _____

    _____

5. Continue working with the *Display* link. Locate and select the *Advanced Settings* link. Note: You may have to select the *Change Display* link or use another Control Panel depending on the manufacturer.

    What adapter is used?

    _____

    How much video memory does the adapter have?

    _____

    How much total video memory (dedicated video memory) is available?

    _____

6. Select the *Monitor* tab.

    What refresh rate is used?

    _____

7. Select *Cancel* on this window and the next window to return to the *Control Panel* main screen. Select the *Appearance and Personalization* link > select the *Personalization* link > select the *Screen Saver/ Change Screen Saver* link in the bottom right.

   What screen saver if any, is currently set?

   _____

8. Use the *Screen Saver* down arrow to see a list of pre-installed screen savers and select one of the options. Select the *Preview* button. The screen saver appears. Move the pointer to regain control. Return the screen saver to the original setting (see the answer to Question 7). Stay on the *Screen Saver Settings* window for the next section.

Dealing with Power Settings

9. Select the *Change power settings* link. The Power Options window appears. Table 15.22 shows the various power options available in Windows 10.

   What power option would a teacher use when using a laptop to teach a 4-hour class?

   _____

TABLE 15.22   Windows 10 default power schemes*

Power scheme	Purpose
Balanced	Default mode; processor adapts to activity being performed; performance provided when the computer is in use; power savings when the computer is inactive. Display powers down after 15 minutes; hard drive powers down after 20 minutes and goes to sleep after 20 minutes.
Power saver	Provides maximum battery life for mobile devices. Display and hard drive power down after 20 minutes, and the system goes to sleep after 1 hour.
High performance	Maximum system performance and responsiveness. Display and hard drive power down after 20 minutes, but the system never sleeps.
Customized	A scheme created by the user that has different settings than the default three schemes

*Note that a computer manufacturer may provide additional power schemes.

10. Close all Control Panel windows.

Obtaining Help

11. Use the *Search* textbox (could be I'm Cortana and you need to go through the dialogs until you select that you are sure you do not want Cortana help, then the *Search the web and Windows* textbox appears) and type `help`. Access the *Show me tips about Windows* link. This takes you directly into the *System* Settings > *Notifications & actions* options which has the capability to automatically display tips about Windows.

12. Windows 10 relies on search results from the Internet more than any prior operating system.

Searching for Files, Folders, Applications, and Computers

13. Folders and files, including executable files, can be located using Windows File Explorer. Open Windows *File Explorer* using any method described in a previous lab. Otherwise, you could right-click or tap and briefly hold the *Start* button and select *File Explorer*. Locate and select *This PC* in the left window > in the *Search This PC* textbox located directly across from the path address box, type `msconfig` and pause a moment before doing anything else.

14. Notice at the top of the ribbon menu that a Search (Search Tools above it) option has appeared. Select the *Search menu* option. Within this option, you can specify whether to include subfolders, the type of file, and advanced options that include searching system files. You can also save the results of a particular search.

    List three *kinds* of items that could be used in a search.

    _____

15. By now your search should be complete. The `msconfig` command is an important one to technicians because this command launches the System Configuration utility. This utility is covered in more detail in Chapter 16. In the resulting list, locate and launch (double-click or double-tap) the `msconfig` utility (normally the second through sixth option in the list).

    List five tabs found in the System Configuration window.

    _____

16. Select Cancel to close the System Configuration window.

17. Another way to locate files is through the Search textbox. Type **msconfig** in the Search textbox and select *System Configuration* from the resulting list.

18. Select *Cancel* to close the System Configuration window.

19. Using any search method you want, find the *WordPad* application and launch it. Type the following message:

    `Your profession is not what brings home your weekly paycheck. Your pro-`
    `fession is what you're put here on earth to do with such passion and`
    `such intensity that it becomes spiritual in calling. —van Gogh`

20. Select the Save icon in the top-left corner (the icon looks like a floppy disk 🖫).

21. Ensure the address bar shows that the file is saving into *Documents*. If it is not, scroll down in the left window to locate and select *Documents*. In the *File name:* textbox, type **Lab4test** and select *Save*.

22. Close WordPad using the *Close* button in the top right.

23. Using the *Search* textbox, type **lab** in the textbox.

    Did your Lab4test file appear in the resulting search list? If not, redo Steps 19 through 23.

    _____

24. Close the *Search* results list by selecting or clicking somewhere on the desktop.

25. Access and use the *System* Control Panel to document your computer name.

    Computer name _____

26. To locate other computers on a network from a Windows 10 computer, on your own computer access *File Explorer* > select *Network* from the left panel. If computers and devices are configured to be seen on the network, then the computers appear in the screen to the right. If your computer is not listed there or a classmate's Windows 10 computer is not listed, proceed to the next step to configure for that.

    Document the second computer name _____

27. To configure your computer to be seen through File Explorer, access the *Network and Internet* Control Panel > *Network and Sharing Center* > *Change advanced sharing settings* > expand the section that shows your current profile (it should be expanded already) by selecting or tapping on the down chevron > enable the following: *Turn on network discovery* > *Save changes*. Do the same process on the second computer or ask a classmate to do it on her computer.

28. Use *File Explorer* to locate a remote network device or computer. Do the same on the second Windows 10 computer.

    Does the remote device appear? [Yes | No]

    Does your device appear within File Explorer on the remote device? [Yes | No]

    Instructor initials: _____

TECH TIP

Changing UAC (User Access Control) settings

Windows has a UAC dialog box that appears asking for permission to do something. To change UAC settings, use the *User Accounts* Control Panel > select an account > *Change User Account Control settings* > move the UAC control bar to have more notifications, less notifications, or no notifications > *OK*.

The UAC settings can also be disabled through the *System Configuration* utility (**msconfig** command) > *Tools* tab > *Change UAC Settings* > *Launch* button > select the appropriate level > *OK*.

---

29. Close all windows.

Recycle Bin

30. Open *File Explorer* > locate the *Lab4test* document created earlier in the lab. Ensure the file is showing in the right window of File Explorer.

31. Right-click or tab and briefly hold on the *Lab4test* filename. Notice that there is a Delete option. (If you do not have this option, you did not actually right-click the *Lab4test* filename.) With the *Lab4test* filename still highlighted (but no context menu showing), press the (Delete) key. The file is sent to the Recycle Bin and no dialog message appears asking if you are sure, like in previous Windows versions. Remember the Recycle Bin is just a folder on the hard drive.

    The Recycle Bin holds deleted files and folders. When a file or folder is deleted, it is not immediately discarded; instead, it goes into the Recycle Bin folder. When a deleted file or folder is in the Recycle Bin, it can be removed. This is similar to a piece of trash being retrieved from an office trash can. A technician must remember that the files and folders in the Recycle Bin take up hard drive space and that users frequently forget to empty these deleted files and folders.

TECH TIP

Files deleted from Recycle Bin cannot be retrieved

Once the Recycle Bin has been emptied, the deleted files cannot be recovered without the use of special software.

---

32. Locate the *Recycle Bin* icon on the desktop. Note that if the Recycle Bin is not on the desktop, search for the Recycle Bin folder. Double-click or double-tap the *Recycle Bin* icon.

    Does the *Lab4test* WordPad document appear in the Recycle Bin window? _____

    If not, redo the steps in this section to create and delete the file.

33. Select the *Empty Recycle Bin* from the *Manage* menu ribbon option. A confirmation window appears asking if you are sure you want to permanently delete the file. Select *Yes*. The name disappears from the Recycle Bin window (as do those of any other files that were located in the Recycle Bin). Close the *Recycle Bin* window.

Lab 15.9 Windows Vista/7 Taskbar Options

Objective: To interact with and customize the Windows taskbar

Parts: Computer with Windows Vista/7 installed

Procedure: Complete the following procedure and answer the accompanying questions.

1. Turn on the computer and verify that the operating system loads. Log on if necessary.

Taskbar Options

2. Locate the taskbar on the bottom of the screen. If it is not showing, move the mouse to the bottom of the screen and the taskbar pops up.

3. To modify or view the taskbar settings, right-click a blank area of the taskbar. A menu appears. (Note that you can also modify the taskbar through the *Taskbar and Navigation* Control Panel.)

4. Select the *Properties* option. The *Taskbar and Start Menu Properties* window appears.

5. Ensure you are on the *Taskbar* tab. The options available on this screen relate to how things are shown on the taskbar. The items with a check in the checkbox to the left are active. To remove a check mark, click in the checkbox that already contains a check in it. To put a check mark in a box, click once in an empty box. Table 15.23 shows the functions of the options.

Document each enabled option._____

_____

What is the current taskbar location? [bottom | right | left | top]

TABLE 15.23   Windows taskbar options and functions

Option	Function
Lock the taskbar (Vista/7)	Prevents the taskbar from being moved
Auto-hide the taskbar (Vista/7)	Hides the taskbar until the pointer is moved to the taskbar area; use the *Keep the taskbar on top of other windows* option with this option to ensure the taskbar is visible when selected
Keep the taskbar on top of other windows (Vista)	Ensures that the taskbar is visible even when a maximized window displays other windows
Group similar taskbar buttons (Vista)	Collapses multiple windows used by the same application buttons into one button
Show Quick Launch (Vista)	Displays the Quick Launch bar on the taskbar
Show window properties (thumbnail) (Vista)	Available on Vista Home Premium and higher; shows a miniature version of open windows
Use small icons (7)	Makes the icons on the taskbar smaller than the default view
Taskbar location on screen (7)	Sets whether the taskbar appears at the bottom (default), or to the left, right, or top
Taskbar buttons (7)	Optionally combines similar labels

Option	Function
Notification area	Customizes the icons and types of notifications that can appear here
Preview desktop with Aero Peek	Enables the desktop to be shown when the pointer is moved to the *Show desktop* button at the far end of the taskbar

6. Ensure the *Auto-hide the taskbar* option is enabled and all other taskbar options are disabled. Select *Apply* and then *OK*. The taskbar disappears from view. If it does not, redo Step 6 (this step) again.

7. Point to the screen where the taskbar is normally located. The taskbar appears. Open the *Notepad* app using any method previously described or one of your own methods. Maximize the screen by clicking the maximize button, which is the center button at the top-right side of the window.

   What happened to the taskbar?

   _____

8. Move the pointer to the screen area where the taskbar is normally located.

   Did the taskbar appear? [Yes | No]

9. Close the *NotePad* window. Bring the taskbar options back up and reset them to their original configuration. Refer to the answer to Question 5 for enabled options. Close the *Taskbar and Start Menu Properties* window.

Instructor initials: _____

10. A sign (<, <<, or ▲) marks the beginning of the Notification area of the taskbar. Three common options are `Clock`, `Volume`, *and* `Network`. The *Clock* option displays the time in the notification area. The *Volume* option is used to change the sound output level. The *Network* option is used to show Internet access status.

11. On the taskbar, click the notification area sign to view hidden icons.

    Did the computer have any inactive icons that displayed? [Yes | No]

    _____

12. Right-click or tap and briefly hold an empty taskbar space and select *Properties*. At the bottom of the *Taskbar* tab is the *Notification area* (7) or the *Notification Area* tab (Vista). The *Customize* button is used to change the settings in Windows 7. Select the *Customize* button. Locate an icon that has the *Show icon and notifications* option enabled and select the down arrow by this option.

    Which two other options did you see?

    _____

    Which option do you personally prefer for the Action Center icon? Explain your reasoning.

    _____

13. Select the *Turn system icons on or off* link. This is where the common icons you most often see are located. It is probably evident as to why on a desktop computer the power system icon defaults to off, but on a laptop or a tablet, the default setting is on. Select *Cancel* two times to return to the Taskbar properties window.

14. Select the *Start Menu* tab.

    The two Vista options shown are *Start menu* and *Classic Start menu*. These determine how the *Start* menu displays. The *Classic Start* menu option displays the *Start* menu like older Windows versions. Windows 7 has a privacy section that determines whether recently opened programs or items display.

    Which *Start* menu option is currently selected on this machine?

    _____

List three things that can be changed through this option.

_____

_____

_____

_____

15. The options can be customized using radio buttons and checkboxes. Scroll through the options to see the selections. Even the size of the Start menu icons can be set in this window. In Vista, stay in this window to answer the next question.

Using the information shown, how many applications currently can display in the *Start* menu's left pane?

_____

16. Use the scrollbar to determine how documents appear on the Start menu. Using the vertical scrollbar, determine whether Help or Help and Support is enabled, meaning that it displays as a Start menu item.

Is Help enabled? [Yes | No]

17. Click the *Cancel* button twice.

Quick Launch Toolbar (Vista) or Taskbar (7)

18. Quick Launch is the taskbar area located to the immediate right of the Start button in Vista. In Windows 7, buttons are simply attached to the taskbar. There are several ways to add an item to the Quick Launch or task bar. The easiest way is demonstrated here. Use the *Start* menu > *Start Search* textbox (Vista) or *Search programs and files* (7). Type `wordpad` in the textbox, but do not press ⏎Enter.

19. In the Search results window, drag the *WORDPAD.EXE* filename to the Quick Launch or taskbar area.

> In Windows Vista, the *Move to Quick Launch* (Vista) message displays when you release the mouse button.

> In Windows 7, the *Pin to taskbar* (7) message displays when you release the mouse button.

20. To access the *WordPad* Quick Launch/taskbar icon, click the double arrows in the *Quick Launch* window or just click the WordPad icon. Any items that have been added to the Quick Launch or taskbar area appear and can be selected. If the *WordPad* option is not available, redo Steps 18 and 19.

21. Click the *WordPad* Quick Launch/taskbar option. The WordPad application displays. Close WordPad.

Instructor initials: _____

22. To remove the *WordPad* icon from the Quick Launch toolbar or taskbar, right-click the Quick Launch area or taskbar *WordPad* option.

In Windows Vista, select the *Delete* option.

In Windows 7, select the *Unpin this program from taskbar* option.

In Vista, a warning message appears that states that the WordPad option will not be available if it is deleted. Click *Yes,* and the WORDPAD.EXE file used in the Quick Launch bar is sent to the Recycle Bin.

23. Use the *Accessories* Start menu option to access the WordPad application.

    Is the WordPad application still available?

    _____

    If so, show the window to the instructor or lab assistant. If WordPad does not start, you did not se-
    lect the *proper* option in Step 18. If this is the case, the WordPad application must be removed from
    the Recycle Bin and placed in its proper folder. The default folder is Program Files\Windows NT\
    Accessories.

    Instructor initials: _____

24. Power off the computer properly.

Lab 15.10 Windows 8/8.1 Taskbar Options

Objective: To interact with and customize the Windows taskbar

Parts: Computer with Windows 8/8.1 installed

Procedure: Complete the following procedure and answer the accompanying questions.

1. Turn on the computer and verify that the operating system loads. Log on if necessary. If the Windows
   Start screen is showing tiles, press the ■ key so the traditional desktop appears. Proceed to Step 2.

Taskbar Options

2. Locate the taskbar on the bottom of the screen. If it is not showing, move the mouse to the bottom of
   the screen and the taskbar pops up.

3. To modify or view the Taskbar settings, right-click a blank area of the taskbar. A menu appears. Select the *Properties* option. The *Taskbar and Navigation properties* window appears. (Note that you
   can also modify the taskbar through the *Taskbar and Navigation* Control Panel.)

4. Ensure you are on the *Taskbar* tab. The options available on this screen relate to how things are
   shown on the taskbar. The items with a check in the checkbox to the left are active. To remove a
   check mark, click in the checkbox that already contains a check in it. To put a check mark in a box,
   click once in an empty box. Table 15.24 shows the functions of the options.

   Document each enabled option.

   _____

   Lock the taskbar [enabled | disabled]

   Auto-hide the taskbar [enabled | disabled]

   Use small taskbar buttons [enabled | disabled]

   Taskbar location on screen [bottom | right | left | top]

   Show Windows Store apps on the taskbar [enabled | disabled]

   Use Peek to preview the desktop when you move your mouse to the Show desktop button at the end
   of the taskbar [enabled | disabled]

TABLE 15.24   Windows taskbar options and functions

Option	Function
Lock the taskbar	Prevents the taskbar from being moved
Auto-hide the taskbar	Hides the taskbar until the pointer is moved to the taskbar area; use the *Keep the taskbar on top of other windows* option with this option to ensure the taskbar is visible when selected
Taskbar location on screen	Sets whether the taskbar appears at the bottom (default), or to the left, right, or top

Option	Function
Taskbar buttons	Optionally combines similar labels
Use small taskbar buttons	Makes icons on taskbar smaller
Show Windows Store apps on the taskbar	Displays downloaded apps
Use Peek to preview the desktop when you move your mouse to the Show desktop button at the end of the taskbar	Hides all open windows when the pointer is moved to the last spot past the date and time at the end of the taskbar

5. Select the Notification area *Customize* button.

   Document the current settings by selecting one of the options.

   Notification area *Customize* button options:

   Action Center [show icon and notifications | hide icon and notifications | only show notifications]

   Network [show icon and notifications | hide icon and notifications | only show notifications]

   Volume [show icon and notifications | hide icon and notifications | only show notifications]

   Windows Explorer [show icon and notifications | hide icon and notifications | only show notifications]

   Any others?

6. Select the *Turn system icons on or off* link.

   Document the current settings.

   Clock [off | on]

   Volume [off | on]

   Network [off | on]

   Power [off | on]

   Action Center [off | on]

   Input Indicator [off | on]

   Any others? _____

7. Return to the *Taskbar and Start Menu Properties* window by selecting *Cancel* two times.

8. Ensure the *Auto-hide the taskbar* option is enabled and all other taskbar options on the *Taskbar* tab are disabled. Select *Apply* and then *OK*. The taskbar disappears from view. If it does not, redo this step.

9. Point to the screen where the taskbar is normally located. The taskbar appears. Open the *Notepad* app using any method previously described or one of your own methods. Maximize the screen by clicking the maximize button, which is the center button at the top-right side of the window.

   What happened to the taskbar?

   _____

10. Move the pointer to the screen area where the taskbar is normally located.

    Did the taskbar appear? [Yes | No]

11. Close the *Notepad* window.

12. Move the pointer so that the taskbar appears. Notice how a sign (▲) marks the beginning of the Notification area of the taskbar. Three common options are *Clock, Volume*, and *Network*. The *Clock* option displays the time in the notification area. The *Volume* option is used to change the sound output level. The *Network* option is used to show Internet access status.

Make the taskbar reappear. On the taskbar, select the notification area sign to show and view hidden icons.

Did the computer have any inactive icons that displayed? [Yes | No]

13. Right-click or tap and briefly hold an empty taskbar space and select *Properties*. Locate the *Notification area* > select the *Customize* button to change the settings. Locate an icon that has the *Show icon and notifications* option enabled and disable it. Verify that the changes were applied.

Which option do you prefer for the Action Center icon? Explain your reasoning.

_____

14. Select the *Turn system icons on or off* link. This is where the common icons you most often see are located. It is probably evident as to why on a desktop computer the power system icon defaults to off, but on a laptop or a tablet, the default setting is on. Select *Cancel* two times to return to the Taskbar properties window.

15. Select the *Navigation* tab. This tab was not in previous versions of Windows because it customizes how corners, charms, desktop, Start screen, and apps are handled. For traditional Windows users, it is important that a technician be familiar with this configuration tab.

Which options are currently enabled?

Corner navigation:

> When I point to the upper-right corner, show the charms [enabled | disabled]

> When I click the upper-left corner, switch between my recent apps [enabled | disabled]

> Replace Command Prompt with Windows PowerShell in the menu when I right-click the lower-left corner or press ⊞ key + X [enabled | disabled]

Start Screen:

> When I sign in or close all apps on a screen, go to the desktop instead of Start [enabled | disabled]

> Show my desktop background on Start [enabled | disabled]

> Show the Apps view automatically when I go to Start [enabled | disabled]

> Search everywhere instead of just my apps when I search from the Apps view [enabled | disabled]

> List desktop apps first in the Apps view when it's sorted by category [enabled | disabled]

16. Select the *Jump Lists* tab. Jump lists allow you to right-click or tap and briefly hold on a taskbar icon and display other items related to that particular icon. For example, if you pinned a browser icon to the taskbar, the jump list for that browser icon would be most often visited websites. For a word processing application, the jump list would contain recently opened files.

What is the default number of items to display in a jump list?

_____

17. Select the *Toolbars* tab. Some of the common Windows toolbars are described in Table 15.25.

TABLE 15.25   Windows 8 taskbar toolbars

Toolbar	Description
Address	Holds commonly used folders, files, and websites
Links	Contains favorite website URLs
Desktop	Displays desktop items in a list format

18. Click *Cancel* to close the *Taskbar and Navigation properties* window.

19. Right-click or tap and briefly hold on an empty space on the taskbar. Notice how toolbars can also be set from the context menu.

20. Bring the taskbar options back up and reset them to their original configuration. Refer to the answer to the questions in Steps 4, 5, 6, and 15 for enabled options.

Instructor initials: _____

Lab 15.11 Windows 10 Taskbar Options

Objective: To interact with and customize the Windows taskbar

Parts: Computer with Windows 10 installed

Procedure: Complete the following procedure and answer the accompanying questions.

1. Turn on the computer and verify that the operating system loads. Log on if necessary.

Taskbar Options

2. Locate the taskbar on the bottom of the screen. If it is not showing, move the mouse to the bottom of the screen and the taskbar pops up.

3. To modify or view the Taskbar settings, right-click a blank area of the taskbar. A menu appears. Select the *Properties* option. The *Taskbar and Start Menu Properties* window appears. (Note that you can also modify the taskbar through the *Taskbar and Navigation* Control Panel.)

4. Ensure you are on the *Taskbar* tab. The options available on this screen relate to how things are shown on the taskbar. The items with a check in the checkbox to the left are active. To remove a check mark (not use an option), click or tap in the checkbox that already contains a check in it. To put a check mark in a box (enable an option), click or tap once in an empty box. Table 15.26 shows the functions of the options.

Document each enabled option.

Lock the taskbar [enabled | disabled]

Auto-hide the taskbar [enabled | disabled]

Use small taskbar buttons [enabled | disabled]

Taskbar location on screen [bottom | right | left | top]

Use Peek to preview the desktop when you move your mouse to the Show desktop button at the end of the taskbar [enabled | disabled]

TABLE 15.26   Windows taskbar options and functions

Option	Function
Lock the taskbar	Prevents the taskbar from being moved
Auto-hide the taskbar	Hides the taskbar until the pointer is moved to the taskbar area; use the *Keep the taskbar on top of other windows* option with this option to ensure the taskbar is visible when selected
Taskbar location on screen	Sets whether the taskbar appears at the bottom (default) or to the left, right, or top
Taskbar buttons	Optionally combines similar labels
Use small taskbar buttons	Makes icons on the taskbar smaller
Use Peek to preview the desktop when you move your mouse to the Show desktop button at the end of the taskbar	Hides all open windows when the pointer is moved to the last spot past the date and time at the end of the taskbar

5. Select the Notification area *Customize* button. You are redirected to the *Settings > System > Notifications & actions* window.

Document the current settings by selecting one of the options.

Show me tips about Windows [off | on]

Show app notifications [off | on]

Show notifications on the lock screen [off | on]

Show alarms, reminders, and incoming VoIP calls on the lock screen [off | on]

Hide notifications while presenting [off | on]

6. Select the *Select which icons appear on the taskbar* link.

Document the current settings.

Always show all icons in the notification area [off | on]

Network [off | on]

Volume [off | on]

Windows Explorer   [off | on]

Microsoft OneDrive [off | on]

Any others? _____

7. Select the back left arrow beside the word *Settings* to return to the *Notifications & actions* window.

8. Select the *Turn system icons on or off* link.

Document the current settings.

Clock [off | on]

Volume [off | on]

Network [off | on]

Power [off | on]

Input Indicator [off | on]

Location [off | on]

Action Center [off | on]

Any others? _____

9. Return to the *Taskbar and Start Menu Properties* window. (It might be easier to close all windows and right-click or tap and briefly hold on an empty taskbar space > select *Properties*.)

10. Ensure the *Auto-hide the taskbar* option is enabled and all other taskbar options on the *Taskbar* tab are disabled. Select *Apply* and then *OK*. The taskbar disappears from view. If it does not, redo this step.

11. Point to the screen where the taskbar is normally located. The taskbar appears. Open the *Notepad* app using any method previously described or one of your own methods. Maximize the screen by clicking the maximize button, which is the center button at the top-right side of the window.

What happened to the taskbar?

_____

12. Move the pointer to the screen area where the taskbar is normally located.

    Did the taskbar appear? [Yes | No]

13. Close the *NotePad* window.

14. Move the pointer to the taskbar area so that the taskbar appears. Notice how a sign (^) marks the beginning of the Notification area of the taskbar. Three common options are *Clock*, *Volume*, and *Network*. The *Clock* option displays the time in the notification area. The *Volume* option is used to change the sound output level. The *Network* option is used to show Internet access status.

15. Make the taskbar reappear. On the taskbar, select the notification area sign to show and view hidden icons.

    Did the computer have any inactive icons that displayed? [Yes | No]

16. Right-click or tap and briefly hold an empty taskbar space and select *Properties*. Locate the *Notification area* > select *Customize* > select *Turn system icons on or off*.

17. Locate an icon that is currently enabled (turned on). Turn that option off.

    Which option do you prefer for the Action Center icon? Explain your reasoning.

    _____

18. Verify that the setting modification is validated by making the taskbar reappear and verifying in the notification area.

19. Close the *Settings* window and re-access the *Taskbar and Start Menu Properties* window.

20. Select the *Navigation* tab. This tab was not in previous versions of Windows because it customizes corner navigation. In Windows 10 it gives you the option to use Windows PowerShell instead of Command Prompt. Windows PowerShell allows commands and scripts to be executed making it more useful than the Command Prompt environment.

    Document your current option:

    Replace Command Prompt with Windows PowerShell in the menu when I right-click the lower-left corner or press Windows key+X [enabled | disabled].

21. Select the *Toolbars* tab. Some of the common Windows toolbars are described in Table 15.27.

TABLE 15.27   Windows 10 taskbar toolbars

Toolbar	Description
Address	Holds commonly used folders, files, and websites
Links	Contains favorite website URLs
Desktop	Displays desktop items in a list format

22. Click *Cancel* to close the Taskbar and Start Menu properties window.

23. Right-click or tap and briefly hold on an empty space on the taskbar. Notice how toolbars can also be set from the context menu.

24. Bring the taskbar options back up and reset them to their original configuration. Refer to the answer to questions in Steps 4, 5, 6, 8, and 20 for option settings.

Instructor initials: _____

CHAPTER 15

Lab 15.12 Windows Vista/7 File and Folder Management

Objective: To create folders, move files, and copy files to new locations

Parts: Computer with Windows Vista/7 installed

A flash drive

Procedure: Complete the following procedure and answer the accompanying questions.

Note: There are multiple ways to do some of the steps in this exercise. Some steps have an alternative method for doing the same procedure. For these steps, you may use either method.

1.   Attach a flash drive. Ensure it is recognizable through *File Explorer* and is assigned a drive letter.

What drive letter is assigned to the flash drive?

_____

2.   Access the *Notepad* Windows accessory or app. Type the following in Notepad:

Develop a passion for learning. If you do, you will never cease to grow. —Anthony J. D'Angelo

3.   Click the *File* menu option and click *Save*.

4.   Select the flash drive letter in the left window. Note that you may have to scroll down to view it in the left window (see Figure 15.44). Notice how the flash drive letter shows in the address bar. In the *File name* textbox, click once and the entire filename of *.txt highlights. Simply start typing to replace the filename by typing **Quote 1**. Notice how the default *Save as type:* option is Text Documents (*.txt). You do not have to add a file extension when you type a name. Quote 1 will be the name of the file and it will have an extension of .txt because of the *Save as* type of document. The full filename will be Quote 1.txt. Select the *Save* button. Note that if you accidentally click somewhere else and *.txt is not highlighted; simply erase all that and type **Quote 1**.

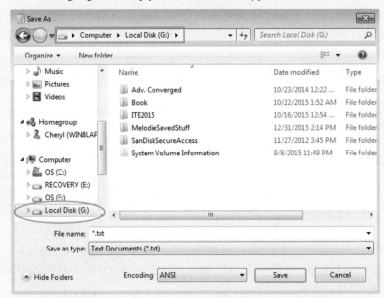

FIGURE 15.44   Windows 7 Saving a Notepad file to a flash drive

5.   In Notepad, click *File > New*. Type the following:

The man who graduates today and stops learning tomorrow is uneducated the day after. —Newton D. Baker

6.   In the *File name* textbox, save the file as *Quote 2* and select *Save*.

7.   Click *File > New*. Type the following:

Don't just learn the tricks of the trade. Learn the trade. —James Bennis

8.   In the *File name* textbox, save the file as *Quote 3* and select *Save*.

9. Click *File > New*. Type the following:

   `Nine-tenths of education is encouragement. —Anatole France`

10. In the *File name* textbox, save the file as *Quote 4* and select *Save*.

11. Click *File > New*. Type the following:

    `Technology is dominated by two types of people—Those who understand`
    `what they do not manage, and those who manage what they do not under-`
    `stand. —Source Unknown`

12. In the *File name* textbox, save the file as *Quote 5* and select *Save*.

13. Close the Notepad application by clicking the *Close* button (which is the button in the upper-right corner with an X).

14. Right-click the *Start* button and select *Open Windows Explorer*. In the left window, use the vertical scrollbar to locate and select the flash drive you are using.

15. In the right window, locate the five files you just created, called *Quote 1*, *Quote 2*, *Quote 3*, *Quote 4*, and *Quote 5*. If the files are not there, redo the lab from the beginning.

Instructor initials: _____

Create a Folder

Note: The following method is preceded by the label *Alternative* is an alternative way to perform the same steps. For these steps, you may use either method. You might consider using one method in one step and then trying it a different way on another step.

16. In the right *Windows Explorer* window, ensure the flash drive is selected in the left panel. Right-click an empty space. Point to the *New* option and click the *Folder* option. A folder appears in the right window with the words *New Folder* highlighted. Type **Learning Quotes** and press Enter.

    Vista alternative: Click the *Organize* down arrow and select *New Folder*. Point to the *New* option and click the *Folder* option.

    7 alternative: Click the *New folder* option from the top line.

    In all versions, a folder appears in the right window with the words *New Folder* highlighted. Type **Learning Quotes** and press Enter.

On Your Own

17. Create another new folder called *General Quotes* using the steps outlined in Step 16.

Instructor initials: _____

Copy a File

18. In the right *Windows Explorer* window, right-click the file named *Quote 1*. A context menu appears. Select the *Copy* option.

    Alternative: In the right Explorer window, click the file named *Quote 1*. Click the *Edit* menu option. In Vista/7, click the *Organize* down arrow.

    Then in all operating system versions, click the *Copy* option from the drop-down menu.

19. In the right window, double-click the *Learning Quotes* folder. The path appears across the top of the window. The right window is empty because the folder does not have any files or subfolders in it yet.

20. In the right window, right-click and a context menu appears. Click *Paste* and the Quote 1 file appears in the right window.

    Alternative: Click the *Organize* down arrow. In both Vista and 7, select *Paste*. The *Quote 1* file appears in the right window.

21. In the left *Windows Explorer* window, click the drive option for the media you are using. The path across the top of the window changes.

On Your Own

22. Copy the files named *Quote 2* and *Quote 3* from the root directory of the flash drive into the *Learning Quotes* folder using the methods outlined in previous steps.

Copy Multiple Files

23. In the left *Windows Explorer* window, click the drive option for the media you are using.

    Alternative: In the address bar, select the left arrow to return to the root directory of the flash drive.

24. Locate the files called *Quote 4* and *Quote 5* in the right window.

25. In the right *Windows Explorer* window, select once on the *Quote 4* filename. The name is highlighted.

26. Hold the Shift key down and select the *Quote 5* filename. Both the *Quote 4* and *Quote 5* filenames are highlighted. *Note:* The Shift key is used to select files that are consecutive in a list (one right after the other). If you want to select files that are not consecutive, use the Ctrl key to select the files.

27. Right-click the files named *Quote 4* and *Quote 5*. A context menu appears. Click the *Copy* option.

    Alternative: Click the *Organize* down arrow and select *Copy*.

28. Double-click the *General Quotes* folder.

    The path across the top changes to $X:\General\ Quotes$ (where $X:$ is the drive media you are using) and the right window is empty because the folder does not have any files or subfolders in it yet.

29. In the right window, right-click an empty space and a context menu appears. Select *Paste*. The *Quote 4* and *Quote 5* files appear in the right window.

    Vista/7 alternative: Click the *Organize* down arrow and select *Paste*. The *Quote 4* and *Quote 5* files appear in the right window.

    How many folders are located in the root directory?

    _____

    How many files are located in the root directory?

    _____

    How many files are located in the *Learning Quotes* folder?

    _____

    How many files are located in the *General Quotes* folder?

    _____

Instructor initials: _____

Copying a File from One Folder to Another

30. In the left window, click the drive option for the media you are using.

31. Open the *Learning Quotes* folder located under the drive option that you are using. The files *Quote 1*, *Quote 2*, and *Quote 3* appear in the right window.

32. In the right window, right-click the *Quote 3* file. From the context menu that appears, select *Copy*.

33. Open the *General Quotes* folder located under the drive media option you are using. The *Quote 4* and *Quote 5* files appear in the right window and the Address textbox shows General Quotes.

34. In the right window, right-click an empty space and a context menu appears. Select *Paste* and the *Quote 3*, *Quote 4*, and *Quote 5* files appear.

35. Using the same procedures previously described, copy the *Quote 1* and *Quote 2* files from the *Learning Quotes* folder into the *General Quotes* folder. At the end of this step you should have three files (*Quote 1*, *Quote 2*, and *Quote 3*) in the *Learning Quotes* folder and five files (*Quote 1*, *Quote 2*, *Quote 3*, *Quote 4*, and *Quote 5*) in the *General Quotes* folder.

Moving a File

36. Create a folder called *My Stuff* in the root directory of the drive you are using. Refer to the steps earlier in the exercise if you need assistance.

37. Open the folder called *General Quotes*. In the right window, all five files appear.

38. In the right window, click once on the *Quote 1* file to highlight it. Hold down the [Ctrl] key and click the *Quote 3* file. Both the *Quote 1* and *Quote 3* filenames are highlighted. *Note*: The [Ctrl] key is used to select nonconsecutive files, whereas the [Shift] key is used to select files that are listed consecutively (one right after another).

TECH TIP

The purpose of Cut and Paste

The Cut and Paste options are used to move a file from one folder to another.

39. Right-click either the *Quote 1* or *Quote 3* filename (with both file names still highlighted). A context menu appears. Select the *Cut* option.

Alternative: Click the *Organize* down arrow and select *Cut*. The *Cut* option moves a file from one folder to another.

40. Open the *My Stuff* folder. The right window is empty because no files have been copied or moved into the *My Stuff* folder yet. In the right window, right-click and select *Paste*. The *Quote 1* and *Quote 3* files appear in the right window.

Alternative: Click the *Organize* down arrow and select *Paste*. The *Quote 1* and *Quote 3* files appear in the right window.

41. Using the procedures just learned, move the *Quote 1* file from the *Learning Quotes* folder into the *General Quotes* folder.

How many files are located in the *Learning Quotes* folder?

_____

How many files are located in the *General Quotes* folder?

_____

How many files are located in the *My Stuff* folder?

_____

Instructor initials: _____

Deleting Files and Folders

42. Open the *My Stuff* folder. The *Quote 1* and *Quote 3* files appear in the right window.

43. In the right window, select the *Quote 1* and the *Quote 3* files. Both the *Quote 1* and *Quote 3* filenames are highlighted.

44. Press the [Delete] key on the keyboard. A message appears on the screen that asks the following: *Are you sure you want to delete these 2 items?* Click *Yes*.

Alternative: Click on the *Organize* down arrow and select *Delete*. A confirmation message appears. Select *Yes*.

TECH TIP

Deleted files on external media are not put in Recycle Bin

When deleting files from an optical disc, a thumb drive, or other external media, the files are not placed in the Recycle Bin—they are deleted. When deleting files from a hard drive, the files get placed in the Recycle Bin.

45. From the flash drive root directory, select the *My Stuff* folder. The *My Stuff* folder is highlighted. Press the [Delete] key on the keyboard. A message appears on the screen asking if you are sure you want to delete the My Stuff folder. Click the *Yes* button.

Alternative: Click the *Organize* down arrow and select *Delete*. A confirmation message appears. Select *Yes*.

Instructor initials: _____

TECH TIP

Skipping the Recycle Bin for deleted hard drive files

If you want to permanently delete a file from a hard drive (the file will not get placed in the Recycle Bin), hold the [Shift] key down while pressing the [Delete] key.

46. Using the previously demonstrated procedures, delete the *Learning Quotes* folder, the *General Quotes* folders, all files contained within each folder, as well as the original *Quote 1, Quote 2, Quote 3, Quote 4,* and *Quote 5* files.

47. Close the *Windows Explorer* window.

Challenge

48. Using Notepad, create three text files and save them to the external media in a folder called *My Files*.

TECH TIP

Retrieving a deleted file

To restore a file that has been accidentally placed in the Recycle Bin, open the Recycle Bin, right-click the file, and click the *Restore* option or click *Restore this item*.

49. On the hard drive or on external media, create a folder called *Computer Text*.

50. Copy the two of the three text files from the *My Files* folder into the folder called *Computer Text*.

51. Move the third text file from the *My Files* folder into the folder called *Computer Text*.

Instructor initials: _____

52. Permanently delete the folder called *Computer Text* and all files within this folder.

Instructor initials: _____

53. Delete the folder called *My Files* and all files within this folder.

Instructor initials: _____

Lab 15.13 Windows 8/10 File and Folder Management

Objective: To create folders, move files, and copy files to new locations

Parts: Computer with Windows 8/10 installed

A flash drive

Procedure: Complete the following procedure and answer the accompanying questions.

Note: There are multiple ways to do some of the steps in this exercise. Some steps have an alternative method for doing the same procedure. For these steps, you may use either method.

1.   Attach a flash drive. Ensure it is recognizable through *File Explorer* and is assigned a drive letter.

What drive letter is assigned to the flash drive?

_____

2.   Access the *Notepad* Windows accessory or app using whatever method you like including using the Search charm/function. Type the following in Notepad:

Develop a passion for learning. If you do, you will never cease to grow. —Anthony J. D'Angelo

3.   Select the *File* menu option and select *Save*.

4.   Select the flash drive letter in the left window. Note that you may have to scroll down to view it in the left window (see Figure 15.45). Notice how the flash drive letter shows in the address bar. Whenever you are at the start of any drive, this is known as the root directory of that drive.

5.   In the *File name* textbox, select once and the entire filename of *.txt highlights. Simply start typing to replace the filename by typing **Quote 1**. Notice how the default *Save as type:* option is Text Documents (*.txt). You do not have to add a file extension when you type a name. Quote 1 will be the name of the file and it will have an extension of .txt because of the *Save as* type of document. The full filename will be Quote 1.txt. Select the *Save* button. Note that if you accidentally selected somewhere else and *.txt is not highlighted, simply erase all that and type **Quote 1**.

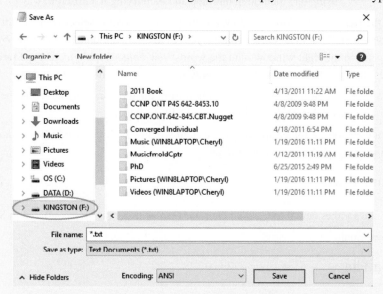

FIGURE 15.45   Windows 10 Notepad flash drive selection

6.   In Notepad, select *File > New*. Type the following:

The man who graduates today and stops learning tomorrow is uneducated the day after. —Newton D. Baker

7.   In the *File name* textbox, save the file as *Quote 2* and select *Save*.

8. Select *File > New*. Type the following:

    ```
    Don't just learn the tricks of the trade. Learn the trade.
    —James Bennis
    ```

9. In the *File name* textbox, save the file as *Quote 3* and select *Save*.

10. Select *File > New*. Type the following:

    ```
    Nine-tenths of education is encouragement. —Anatole France
    ```

11. In the *File name* textbox, save the file as *Quote 4* and select *Save*.

12. Select *File > New*. Type the following:

    ```
    Technology is dominated by two types of people—Those who understand
    what they do not manage, and those who manage what they do not under-
    stand. —Source Unknown
    ```

13. In the *File name* textbox, save the file as *Quote 5* and select *Save*.

14. Close the Notepad application by selecting the *Close* button (which is the button in the upper-right corner with an X).

15. Open *File Explorer*. In the left window, use the vertical scrollbar to locate and select the drive media you are using.

16. In the right window, locate the five files you just created (*Quote 1*, *Quote 2*, *Quote 3*, *Quote 4*, and *Quote 5*). If the files are not there, redo the lab from the beginning.

Instructor initials: _____

Create a Folder

Note: The method shown here that is preceded by the label *Alternative* is an alternative way to perform the same steps. For these steps, you may use either method. You might consider using one method in one step and then trying it a different way on another step.

17. In the right *File Explorer* window, ensure the flash drive is selected in the left panel. Right-click or tap and briefly hold an empty space. Point to the *New* option and select the *Folder* option. A folder appears in the right window with the words *New Folder* highlighted. Type `Learning Quotes` and press `Enter`. The *Learning Quotes* folder now appears in the right window.

    Alternative: Select the *New folder* option from the top corner by hovering the pointer over the top-left corner icons to locate the option that looks like a folder.

    In all versions, a folder appears in the right window with the words *New Folder* highlighted. Type `Learning Quotes` and press `Enter`.

On Your Own

18. Create another new folder called *General Quotes* using the steps outlined in Step 17.

Instructor initials: _____

Copy a File

19. In the right *File Explorer* window, right-click or tap and briefly hold the file named *Quote 1*. A context menu appears. Select the *Copy* option. The file is placed in a Windows utility called the clipboard, which works in the background.

    Alternative: In the right *File Explorer* window, select the file named *Quote 1* > select the *Home* menu option > select *Copy*. The file is copied to the Windows utility called the clipboard, which works in the background.

20. In the right window, double-click or double-tap the *Learning Quotes* folder to open it. Notice how the address bar changes to This PC →] *X:* (name and drive letter of the flash drive) →] Learning Quotes.

    The right window is empty because the folder does not have any files or subfolders in it yet.

21. In the right window, right-click or tap and briefly hold and a context menu appears. Select *Paste* and the Quote 1 file appears in the right window.

    Alternative: In the *File Explorer* window, select the *Home* menu option > select *Paste*. The Quote 1 file appears in the right window.

22. In the left *File Explorer* window, click the option for the flash drive you are using. Note how the path changes in the address bar of File Explorer.

On Your Own

23. Copy the files named *Quote 2* and *Quote 3* from the root directory of the flash drive into the *Learning Quotes* folder using the methods outlined in previous steps.

Copy Multiple Files

24. In the left *File Explorer* window, select the drive option for the media you are using.

    Alternative: In the address bar, select the left arrow to return to the root directory of the flash drive.

25. Locate the files called *Quote 4* and *Quote 5* in the right *File Explorer* window.

26. In the right *File Explorer* window, select once on the *Quote 4* filename. The name is highlighted.

27. Hold the [Shift] key down and select once on the Quote 5 filename. Both the Quote 4 and Quote 5 filenames are highlighted.

    Note: The [Shift] key is used to select files that are consecutive in a list (one right after the other). If you wanted to select files that are not consecutive, use the [Ctrl] key to select the files.

28. Right-click or tap and briefly hold the files named *Quote 4* and *Quote 5*. A context menu appears. Select the *Copy* option.

    Alternative: Select the *Home* menu option > select *Copy*.

29. Double-click or double-tap the *General Quotes* folder.

    The path across the top changes to This PC →] X: (name and drive letter of the flash drive) →] General Quotes. The right window is empty because the folder does not have any files or subfolders in it yet.

30. In the right *File Explorer* window, right-click or tap and briefly hold an empty space and a context menu appears. Select *Paste*. The *Quote 4* and *Quote 5* files appear in the right window.

    Alternative: Select the *Home* menu option > select *Paste*. The *Quote 4* and *Quote 5* files appear in the right window.

    How many folders are located in the flash drive root directory?

    _____

    How many files are located in the root directory?

    _____

    How many files are located in the *Learning Quotes* folder?

    _____

    How many files are located in the *General Quotes* folder?

    _____

Instructor initials: _____

Copying a File from One Folder to Another

31. In the left window, select the flash drive you are using. The flash drive root directory files and folders appear in the right window.

    Alternative: Select the name of the flash drive in the address bar. The flash drive root directory files and folders appear in the right window.

32. Open the *Learning Quotes* folder. The files *Quote 1*, *Quote 2*, and *Quote 3* appear in the right window.

33. In the right *File Explorer* window, right-click or tap and briefly hold the *Quote 3* file. From the context menu that appears, select *Copy*.

34. Open the *General Quotes* folder located under the flash drive option you are using. The *Quote 4* and *Quote 5* files appear in the right *File Explorer* window and the Address bar shows General Quotes.

35. In the right *File Explorer* window, right-click or tap and briefly hold an empty space and a context menu appears. Select *Paste* and the *Quote 3*, *Quote 4*, and *Quote 5* files appear.

On Your Own

36. Using the same procedures previously described, copy the *Quote 1* and *Quote 2* files from the *Learning Quotes* folder into the *General Quotes* folder. At the end of this step you should have three files (*Quote 1*, *Quote 2*, and *Quote 3*) in the *Learning Quotes* folder and five files (*Quote 1*, *Quote 2*, *Quote 3*, *Quote 4*, and *Quote 5*) in the *General Quotes* folder.

37. Create a folder on the flash drive and name it *My Stuff*. Refer to the steps earlier in the exercise if you need assistance.

Moving a File

38. Open the folder called *General Quotes*. In the right window, all five files appear.

39. In the right *File Explorer* window, select the *Quote 1* file to highlight it. Hold down the Ctrl key and select the *Quote 3* file. Both the *Quote 1* and *Quote 3* filenames are highlighted. *Note*: The Ctrl key is used to select nonconsecutive files, whereas the Shift key is used to select files that are listed consecutively (one right after another).

TECH TIP

The purpose of Cut and Paste

The Cut and Paste options move a file from one folder to another.

40. Right-click or tap and briefly hold either the *Quote 1* or *Quote 3* filename (both file names are still highlighted). A context menu appears. Select the *Cut* option. The *Cut* option is used to move a file from one folder to another.

    Alternative: Select the *Home* menu option > select *Cut*. The *Cut* option is used to move a file from one folder to another.

41. Open the *My Stuff* folder. The right *File Explorer* window is empty because no files have been copied or moved into the *My Stuff* folder yet. In the right *File Explorer* window, right-click or tap and briefly hold > from the context menu select *Paste*. The *Quote 1* and *Quote 3* files appear in the right *File Explorer* window.

    Alternative: Select the *Home* menu option > select *Paste*. The *Quote 1* and *Quote 3* files appear in the right *File Explorer* window.

On Your Own

42. Using the procedures just learned, move the *Quote 1* file from the *Learning Quotes* folder into the *General Quotes* folder.

How many files are located in the *General Quotes* folder?

_____

How many files are located in the *Learning Quotes* folder?

_____

49. How many files are located in the *My Stuff* folder?

_____

Instructor initials: _____

Deleting Files and Folders

43. Open the *My Stuff* folder. The *Quote 1* and *Quote 3* files appear in the right window.

44. In the right *File Explorer* window, select the *Quote 1* and the *Quote 3* files. Both the *Quote 1* and *Quote 3* filenames are highlighted.

45. Press the [Delete] key on the keyboard. A message appears on the screen asking the following *Are you sure you want to delete these two items?* if you are on a flash drive. Select *Yes*.

Alternative: Select the *Customize Quick Access Toolbar* down arrow and select *Delete*. Note that the Delete icon may have been added to the top icons and the Customize Quick Access Toolbar option does not have to be used. If deleting from a flash drive, a confirmation message appears. Select *Yes*.

Alternative 2: Select the *Home* menu option > select *Delete*.

> **TECH TIP**
>
> **Deleted files on external media are not put in Recycle Bin**
>
> When deleting files from an optical disc, a flash drive, or other external media, the files are not placed in the Recycle Bin——they are deleted. When deleting files from a hard drive, the files are placed in the Recycle Bin.

46. From the flash drive root directory, select the *My Stuff* folder. The *My Stuff* folder is highlighted. Press the [Delete] key on the keyboard. If working from a flash drive, a message appears on the screen asking, "Are you sure you want to permanently delete this folder?" Select the *Yes* button.

> **TECH TIP**
>
> **Skipping the Recycle Bin for deleted hard drive files**
>
> If you want to permanently delete a file from a hard drive (the file will not get placed in the Recycle Bin), hold the [Shift] key down while pressing the [Delete] key.

Instructor initials: _____

On Your Own

47. Using the previously demonstrated procedures, delete the *Learning Quotes* folder, the *General Quotes* folders, all files contained within each folder, as well as the original *Quote 1, Quote 2, Quote 3, Quote 4,* and *Quote 5* files.

48. Close the *File Explorer* window.

Challenge

49. Using Notepad, create three text files and save them to the external media in a folder called *My Files*.

50. On the flash drive, create a folder called *Computer Text*.

51. Copy two of the three text files from the *My Files* folder into the folder called *Computer Text*.

52. Move the third text file from the *My Files* folder into the folder called *Computer Text*.

Instructor initials: _____

53. Permanently delete the folder called *Computer Text* and all files within this folder.

54. Delete the folder called *My Files* and all files within this folder.

Instructor initials: _____

Lab 15.14 Windows Vista/7 File Extension

Objective: To associate a file extension with a file type

Parts: Computer with Windows Vista/7 installed

Flash drive

Procedure: Complete the following procedure and answer the accompanying questions.

1. Access and launch the *Notepad* Windows accessory/app. Type the following:

`I hear and I forget. I see and I remember. I do and I understand.`
`—Confucius`

2. Select the *File* menu option and choose *Save*.

3. Attach a flash drive. Select the appropriate drive option for the media you are using. In the *File name* textbox, type `Junk`. Click the *Save* button.

4. Close the Notepad application.

5. Right-click the *Start* button and select *Explore* (Vista)/*Open Windows Explorer* (7).

6. Select the *Organize* menu option and select *Folder and Search Options*.

In all operating systems, click the *View* tab. If the *Hide (file) extensions for known file Types* checkbox contains a check mark, click inside the checkbox to remove the check mark. If the checkbox is empty, ignore this step. Click *OK*.

7. In the left *Windows Explorer* window, use the vertical scrollbar to locate and select the disk media you used to save the file. Locate the *Junk.txt* file in the right window and double-click the icon.

What happened?

Did the Notepad application open with the *Junk* file open?

8. Close the Notepad application.

9. In the *Windows Explorer* window, right-click the file called *Junk*. Click the *Rename* option. Ensure the entire filename, *Junk.txt*, is highlighted. Type `junk.abc` and press Enter. *Junk.txt* is renamed to *junk.abc*. A rename warning box appears stating that, "If you change a filename extension, the file may become unusable." It also asks, "Are you sure you want to change it?" Click *Yes*.

What does the *junk.abc* file icon look like now?

10. Double-click the *junk.abc* file icon.

    What happened when you double-clicked on the *junk.abc* file icon?

11. Click the *Select the program from a list of installed programs* radio button and click *OK*. Scroll until you reach the *Notepad* icon. Click the *Notepad* icon and then click *OK*.

    What happened when you clicked the *OK* button?

12. In the Notepad application, select the *File* menu option and choose *New*.

13. Type the following:

    `The only real mistake is the one from which we learn nothing. -John Powell`

14. Select the *File* menu option and click *Save as*. Ensure the disk media option that you are using is the destination. In the *File name* textbox, type **Junk2** and click *Save*.

15. Close the Notepad application.

16. Using Windows Explorer, rename the *Junk2.txt* file to *Junk2.abc*. A rename warning box appears stating that, "If you change a filename extension, the file may become unusable." It also asks, "Are you sure you want to change it?" Select *Yes*. Notice the file icon after the change.

    How is the icon different from before?

17. Double-click the *Junk2.abc* icon.

    What happened when you double-clicked the *Junk2.abc* icon?

    Instructor initials: _____

Lab 15.15 Windows Vista/7/8/10 Attributes, Compression, and Encryption

Objective: To identify and set file and folder attributes, compression, and encryption

Parts: Computer with Windows Vista/7/8/10 installed

Ability to save a file to an NTFS partition

Procedure: Complete the following procedure and answer the accompanying questions.

Note: The compression and encryption portions of this exercise require an NTFS partition.

Managing File Attributes

1. Access and open the *Notepad* Windows accessory/app. Type the following:

   `Aim for success, not perfection. -Dr. David M. Burns`

2. Select the *File* menu option and choose *Save*. In *Windows Explorer/File Explorer* left pane, select a location such as *Documents* or *Desktop*. In the *File name:* textbox, replace the highlighted **.txt* by typing **Attribute File** and select *Save*.

   Document which folder holds the file.

   _____

3. Close the Notepad application.

4. Open *Windows Explorer/File Explorer*.

5. In the left pane, select the option where you stored the file. The *Attribute File* file should be listed in the right pane. If not, redo the previous steps to create the file.

6. Select the *Attribute File* file in the right pane.

7. In Vista/7, select the *Organize* menu option and select *Properties*. The same results can be obtained by right-clicking or tapping and briefly holding on the filename and selecting *Properties*.

In Windows 8/10, select the *Home* menu option > select *Properties*. The same results can be obtained by right-clicking or tapping and briefly holding on the filename and selecting *Properties*.

The file attributes are listed at the bottom. Additional attributes can be viewed for a file stored on an NTFS partition by clicking the *Advanced* button. Note that the *Advanced* button is not available on a flash drive that uses a file system other than NTFS.

What file attributes are listed for the *Attribute File* file?

_____

_____

What file attribute is enabled by default?

_____

8. When the Archive attribute (File is ready for archiving) is enabled, the file is selected for backup by default. Backup applications use this attribute when backing up data. On the main *Attribute file Properties* window, select (enable) the *Read-only attribute* checkbox and select *OK*.

9. Open the *Attribute File* filename. The application opens with the typed text shown. Add the following to the quote:

   Never give up your right to be wrong, because then you will lose the ability to learn new things and move forward with your life. —David M. Burns

10. Select the *File* menu option and select *Save*. With the same name listed (do not change), select the *Save* button.

What happens when the Save option is chosen?

_____

_____

11. Select *Yes* > *OK* > then click *Cancel* to return to the changed document open in Notepad.

12. Select the *Close* button in the Notepad window. When asked if you want to save the changes, select *Don't Save*. The read-only attribute prevented the file from being changed.

13. In the *Windows Explorer/File Explorer* window, right-click or tap and briefly hold the *Attribute File* filename > select *Properties*. Select the *Hidden* file attribute checkbox > select *OK*.

What happened to the *Attribute File* filename in Windows Explorer/File Explorer?

_____

14. In Vista/7 in the *Windows Explorer* window, select the *Organize* (Vista/7) > *Folder and Search Options* (Vista/7) > *View* tab > *Hidden files and folders* > *Show hidden files and folder* (Vista)/*Show hidden files, folders, and drives* (7) radio button. This option is used to see files or folders that have the hidden attribute set or enabled. To make this change applicable to all folders, click the Apply to Folders button. A Folder views dialog box appears stating that the change will occur the next time the folder is opened. Click *Yes* > click *OK*.

15. In Windows 8/10 in the *File Explorer* window, select the *View* menu option > select *Options* > select *Change folder and search options* > *View* tab.

Which one of the two following options is enabled?

[*Don't show hidden files, folders, or drives* | *Show hidden files, folders, and drives*]

_____

16. Select (enable) the *Show hidden files, folders, and drives* radio button or ensure it is enabled. This option is used to see files or folders that have the hidden attribute set or enabled.

    Note: If you want to make this change applicable to all folders, you can select the *Apply to Folders* button, but we will not do this in this lab.

    Does the *Attribute File* appear in the Windows Explorer/File Explorer right pane? [Yes | No]

    If not, press the ⑤ key to refresh the window or select the *Refresh* option from the *View* menu (XP).

    How does the file icon differ from before? Note that you may need to create another text file just to see the difference.

    _____

17. In Windows Vista, click the *Windows Explorer Views* menu option > select *Small Icons*. In Windows 7 *Windows Explorer*, click the *Change your view* icon that contains a down arrow on the right side of the menu bar > select *Small icons*.

18. In Windows 8/10 *File Explorer*, select the *View* menu option > select *Small Icons*.

    How do the icon(s) now appear in the Windows Explorer/File Explorer right pane?

    _____

19. In Windows Vista, under *Views* menu option, select *List*.

    In Windows 7, click the *Change your view* menu option > select *List*.

    In Windows 8/10, select the *View* menu option > select *List*.

    How does the *Attribute File* now appear in the right pane?

    _____

    In Windows Vista, select the *Views* menu option > *Details*.

    In Windows 7, select the *Change your view* menu option > *Details*.

    In Windows 8/10, select the *View* menu option > *Details*.

    Why do you think that a technician would prefer the Details view option over any other option?

    _____

    _____

20. Delete *Attribute File*.

    Did either the hidden or read-only attribute stop the *Attribute File* from being deleted? [Yes |

21. Put the folder options back to the original setting (see Step 13).

Instructor initials: _____

Using Compression

Note: The disk volume must have an NTFS file system on it in order to complete this section. To check the file system, in Windows Explorer/File Explorer open *Computer* (Vista/7)/*This PC* (Windows 8/10). Right-click or tap and briefly hold the hard drive volume that contains Windows and select *Properties*. In the Properties window near the top, the file system is listed.

22. Create a WordPad file called *Compression File* and save it in the *Documents* folder on the hard drive. If necessary, refer to a previous exercise for steps. The text to be placed in the file follows:

```
The most successful career must show a waste of strength that might
have removed mountains, and the most unsuccessful is not that of the
man who is taken unprepared, but of him who has prepared and is never
taken. On a tragedy of that kind, our national morality is duly silent.
-Edward M. Forster
```

23. Copy this text repeatedly in the document until you have four pages of text. You could also copy a picture from the Internet, use the Windows *Snipping Tool* accessory to make screen captures and windows captures that are pasted into the document, and different kinds of fonts and texts to make the document of decent size so this step will work. Note that if you do not make the file size large enough, compression will not occur and you will be back inside the file make it larger.

24. Close the *WordPad* application window. Using Windows Explorer/File Explorer, locate the *Compression File*. Note that you might need to change the view or get the properties of the file to answer the question that follows.

    What is the file size of the *Compression File*?

    _____

25. Right-click or tap and briefly hold on the *Compression File* and select *Properties*. Select the *Advanced* button. In the Advanced Attributes dialog box, locate the *Compress or Encrypt attributes* section.

26. Select (enable) the *Compress contents to save disk space* checkbox. This option is used to compress a file or folder. Select the *OK* button > select *OK* again. Keep in mind that to save disk space efficiently, the file needs to be at least 4K of disk space.

27. Using *Windows Explorer/File Explorer*, locate the file called *Compression File* and open the file's *Properties* window again.

28. On the *General* tab, notice the *Size* and *Size on disk* numbers. If the numbers are the same, you don't have enough information in the file to compress it. Copy more information into it, make sure you use graphics to increase the size, or recopy and paste the information you have to increase the size of the file so it can be compressed. After compression occurs and you can verify through the *General* tab, click *OK* to close the *Compression File Properties* window.

    Document the file size.

    _____

    What visual clue do you have in Windows Explorer/File Explorer that a file is compressed?

    _____

Instructor initials: _____

Enabling Encryption

Note: The disk volume must have an NTFS file system on it to complete this section.

29. Create a file called *Encryption File* using Notepad or WordPad and save it to *Documents*. If necessary, refer to a previous exercise for steps. The text to be placed in the file follows:

    `I do not fear computers. I fear the lack of them. —Isaac Asimov`

30. Close the *Notepad/WordPad* application window. Using *Windows Explorer/File Explorer*, locate the file named *Encryption File*.

    What is the current size of *Encryption File*?

    _____

31. Right-click or tap and briefly hold on the filename (*Encryption File*) > select *Properties* > *Advanced* button. In the Advanced Attributes dialog box, locate the *Compress or Encrypt attributes* section. Select (enable) the *Encrypt contents to secure data* checkbox, the option used to encrypt a file or folder. Note that the checkbox may not be available on some Windows Home versions. See the Tech Tip. Select the *OK* button twice. A dialog box appears asking if you want to encrypt the file and the parent file or encrypt only the file. Select the *Encrypt the file only* radio button > *OK*.

32. The first time that you select to encrypt a file, a prompt appears telling you that you should back up the recovery key. This is EXTREMELY important. If the encryption key used to encrypt your file ever has an issue, you cannot get into your file again. For now, ignore the message and then we will see how to access it and back it up.

   What is the size of the *Encryption File* after encryption?

   _____

   Instructor initials: _____

TECH TIP

Limited encryption support on Home versions

Windows Home versions do not fully support encrypting files. In these versions, the `cipher` command can be used at the command prompt to decrypt files, an encrypted file can be modified, and an encrypted file can be copied to the computer.

Backing Up the File Encryption Certificate and Key

33. In the Control Panel *Search* textbox, type `encrypt` and select the *Manage file encryption certificates link* > *Next* > ensure the *Use this certificate* radio button is selected > *Next* > in the *Back up the certificate and key* window, ensure the *Back up the certificate and key now* radio button is selected (enabled) > use the *Browse* button to specify a backup location that is on some type of removable media and type in a file name so you will know it is your encryption certificate > select *Save*. In the *Password* and *Confirm password* textboxes, issue a password that you won't forget > *Next* > Do not select any files within the *Update your previously encrypted files* window > *Next* > *Close*.

TECH TIP

Recovering EFS-protected files

If your encryption key ever does become corrupted or you move a drive that has encrypted files to another computer, if you have that encryption certificate and key backed up, you can recover it using the following steps:

Step 1. Use the **certmgr.msc** command.

Step 2. In the left window, select *Personal*.

Step 3. From the *Action* menu, select *All Tasks* > *Import* > *Next* > *Browse* > in the drop-down menu to the right of the *File name* textbox, select *Personal Information Exchange (*.pfx; *.p12)* and browse to where the encryption certificate and key are located in the external media and select the file > *Open* button > *Next* > in the *Password* textbox, type the password (that you were never supposed to forget) > select the *Mark this key as exportable. This will allow you to back up or transport your keys at a later time* checkbox > leave the *Include all extended properties* textbox enabled > *Next* > on the certificate store window, just click *Next* > *Finish*. A message appears that it was successful.

---

34. Permanently delete the *Compression File*.
35. Permanently delete the *Encryption File*.

Lab 15.16 Using REGEDIT in Windows Vista/7/8/10

Objective:	To become familiar with the REGEDIT registry-editing utility
Parts:	Computer with Windows Vista/7/8/10 installed and administrator rights
	Flash drive
Procedure:	Complete the following procedure and answer the accompanying questions.
Notes:	REGEDIT is a utility used for editing the Windows registry. With regedit, you can view existing registry settings, modify registry settings values, or create new registry entries to change or enhance the way Windows operates. In this lab, you will use regedit to view the system BIOS and component information on your computer.
Caution:	Editing the registry can cause your computer to run erratically or not run at all! When performing any registry editing, follow *all* directions carefully, including spelling, syntax use, and so on. Failure to do so may cause your computer to fail!

Viewing Registry Information

1. In Vista/7, from the *Start Search* (Vista)/*Search programs and files* (7) textbox, type **regedit** > in the *Programs* section, click *Regedit* > *Continue* (Vista)/*Yes* (7) button, if necessary. The regedit utility opens.

2. In Windows 8/10, search for *regedit* using the Search charm or any search method > open the Windows Registry Editor.

3. In the left Registry Editor window, expand *Hkey_Local_Machine*, *Hardware*, and *Description* by selecting the arrow located to the left of each name. Select the *System* option located under *Description*. In the right window, the system BIOS and component information displays.

   What is the system BIOS version?

   _____

   Who is the manufacturer of the system BIOS?

   _____

   What values are listed in the Component Information option?

   _____

Exporting and Importing a Registry Section

4. Regedit can be used to back up and restore part or all of the registry. To illustrate this point, a portion of the registry will be exported to disk and then imported into the registry. Ensure the following option is still selected in the left Registry Editor window. (Ensure the word System is selected under *Description*.) Here is the full path:

   Hkey_Local_Machine\Hardware\Description\System

5. Select the *File* menu option and choose *Export*. The Export Registry File window opens.

6. Attach a flash drive. Select the down arrow in the *Save in* textbox, and select the appropriate drive option for the flash drive you are using. In the *File name* textbox, type **Registry System Section** and select *Save*. The specific registry key is saved to disk.

7. To restore the registry (or a portion of it as in this exercise), select the *File* menu option and select *Import*. The screen should list the file located on the external disk media, but if it does not, select the appropriate drive letter option for the disk media you are using.

8. Select the *Registry System Section* filename and select the *Open* button. A message appears when the section is successfully inserted into the registry. Show this message to the instructor or lab assistant.

Instructor initials: _____

9. Close the regedit utility.

Lab 15.17 Basic Commands from a Command Prompt

Objective:	To execute basic commands at a command prompt
Parts:	A Windows-based computer with command prompt access
	The ability to save a file to the hard drive *or* access to a flash drive
Procedure:	Complete the following procedure and answer the accompanying questions.
Note:	For each step requiring a typed command, the Enter key must be pressed to execute the command. This instruction will *not* be given with each step.

1. Power on the computer and log on if necessary.

2. Create a file in Notepad called *LadyVOLS.txt* and save the file to the flash drive. Here is some text for your file:

   This is a fine mess you've gotten me into Ollie.

   Go get that Earth creature and bring back the Uranium Pew36 Space Modulator.

   Can you sing "Rocky Top"?

   What drive letter does the flash drive use?

   _____

3. Close Notepad. This file will be used later in the lab.

4. Exit to a command prompt using the directions that follow based on the particular operating system you are using.

   In Windows Vista/7: Use the *Start Search* (Vista)/*Search programs and files* (7) textbox and type **cmd** > press Enter.

   In Windows 8, use the Search charm and type **command** > select the *Command Prompt* option from the resulting list.

   In Windows 10, search for **command** > select the *Command Prompt* option from the resulting list.

   Does a prompt display? If not and you followed every step correctly, contact your instructor.

   _____

   What prompt displays on the screen? This is the folder (directory) from which you are starting.

   _____

5. At the command prompt, type the following: **cd**

   The prompt changes to C:\>. If a message appears stating invalid command or invalid directory, you made a typing error. If you suspect an error, verify the backslash is after cd and that there are no extra spaces. The backslash starts from the left side and goes to the right (\). Other commands use a forward slash, which would be in the opposite direction /.

   cd is the command for change directory, which tells the operating system to go to a different directory in the tree structure. The \ after the **cd** command tells the operating system to go to the root directory. An alternative way of typing this command is **cd** \. Notice the space between the **cd** command and the backslash. There are usually different ways to do every command from a prompt. Note that the **cd** command allows you to return to the root directory at any time.

6. At the command prompt, type **dir**

   A list of files and directories appears. Files are the items that show an extension to the right of the filename, file size, and file creation date. File extensions frequently give clues as to which application created the file. Directories have a <DIR> entry to the right of the name.

List one file including its extension and one directory shown on the screen. Using Table 15.4 or the Internet, try to determine the application that created the file and write that application (if found) beside the filename. Document your findings in Table 15.28.

TABLE 15.28   File and directory

Information displayed	Name	Application
File		
Folder		N/A

7. When the number of files shown exceeds what can display on the screen, the files quickly scroll off the screen until all files finish displaying. The **DIR** command has a switch that controls this scrolling. A command switch begins with a forward slash and enhances or changes the way a command performs. At the command prompt, type **dir /p**.

    After looking at the data on the screen, press Enter again. Continue pressing Enter until the prompt reappears. The /p switch (when used with the dir command, of course) tells the operating system to display the files one page at a time.

8. At the prompt, type the following: **dir /w**

    What is the function of the /w switch?

    _____

    _____

9. At the prompt, type **dir /p**. The information shows one page at a time. If there were more than one page of files and directories, you would press any key to see another page of information.

10. Multiple switches can be used with a command. At the prompt, type the following command:

    dir /w/l

    Using the **dir** command /w and /l switches causes files to display in a wide format and displays the information in lowercase.

11. Different versions of Windows have documentation with online help. To find out the operating system version loaded on the computer, type **ver**.

    Who is the operating system manufacturer, and what version is used on the computer?

    _____

    _____

12. At the prompt, type **dir /? | more**. To create the vertical bar used in the command, hold down the Shift key and, while keeping it held down, press the key directly above the Enter key. It is the same key as a backslash. A short explanation of the command appears followed by the command syntax (instructions or rules for how the command is to be typed). A technician needs to understand command syntax to determine what commands to type when unfamiliar with a command. The | symbol is called the pipe symbol. The | more command tells the operating system to display the output one page at a time. Perform the following activity, and then press any key to continue until you return to a prompt.

    Based on the output, list two switches that can be used with the dir command.

    _____

    _____

Write one switch that can be used with the DIR command along with a short explanation of its purpose. _____

_____

13. Type **cd\XXXXX**, where the **XXXXX** is replaced by the name of the directory you wrote as the answer to the question in Step 6. For example, if I wrote the directory name *Windows*, I would type **cd\ Windows** at the prompt. Note that if you get an *Access is denied* message, simply use the Windows directory. The prompt changes to the name of the directory (folder) such as C:\Windows>.

14. Type the following command: **dir a*.***

   The a*.* is not a switch. This command is directing the operating system to list all files or subdirectories that start with the letter A. The **.*** part means all files. The directory you chose may not have any files or subdirectories that start with the letter A. If this occurs, the operating system displays the message "File not found." The ***** is known as a wildcard. A wildcard substitutes for one or more characters. The first asterisk (*****) is the wildcard for any name of a file. The second asterisk is the wildcard for any extension.

   Does the operating system list any files or subdirectories that start with the letter A? If so, write one of them in the following space. If not, did the operating system let you know this? If so, write the message displayed.

   _____

15. Type the following command: **cd..**

   The **..** tells the operating system to move back (or up if you think about the structure in Windows Explorer/File Explorer) one directory in the directory structure. Because you are one level down (because of typing the **cd\XXXXX** command), this command returns you to the root directory.

   If you want to display a list of all files or directories in the root directory that start with the letter C, what command would you type? Try the command you think is right on the computer to see if it works.

   _____

   Do any commands start with the letter C? If so, write at least one of them down.

   _____

On Your Own

15a. Change to the directory that contains Windows. The directory name is normally *Windows*. If you cannot determine what directory contains Windows, use the **dir** command again. Try repeating the lab until it is easier to do this step.

   Write the command you used to do this.

   _____

   List two Windows files that begin with the letter D.

   _____

   _____

15b. Return to the root directory.

   Write the command you used.

   _____

16. At the prompt, access the flash drive. To do this, you will be typing the drive letter assigned to the flash drive (see the answer to the question in Step 2), followed by a colon, and then pressing the ⌈Enter⌋ key. If a flash drive was assigned the letter G, then the command to type would be `G:` and then press ⌈Enter⌋. Whenever directions are given where the drive letter is not known such as in this lab, then the *X:* (italicized X and then a colon) is used. You always need to substitute your drive letter with the *X:*. Type the following command based on your own drive letter:

    X:

    Notice how the prompt changes to the drive letter of the flash drive. If it does not, you might have forgotten to press ⌈Enter⌋ or you did not replace the *X* with your own drive letter documented in Step 2.

17. From the root directory, use the `TYPE` command to view the text file you just created by using the following command: **type ladyvols.txt**

    What is the result of using the **type** command?

    _____

    Can you edit and change the file using this command? [Yes | No]

    Have a classmate verify your file displays and sign his or her name beside your answer.

    Classmate's printed name _____

    Classmate's signature _____

18. The `DEL` command is used to delete files. From the root directory, delete the file you just created using the following command: `del ladyvols.txt`

    Why do you think you did not have to type `del x:\ladyvols.txt` (the full path) in the last step?

    _____

    _____

Lab 15.18 The `COPY`, `MD`, `DEL`, and `RD` Commands

Objective: To correctly use the COPY, MD, DEL, and RD commands

Parts: A Windows computer with command prompt access

Flash drive

Procedure: Complete the following procedure and answer the accompanying questions.

Notes: For each step requiring a typed command, the ⌈Enter⌋ key must be pressed to execute the command. This instruction will *not* be given with each step.

The directions given in the previous command prompt lab are not repeated. If you have trouble with this lab, it is recommended that you return to and do Lab 15.17 until you are proficient with the concepts, and then do this lab again.

It is critical that you follow directions. For example, if the lab directs you to make a directory called SubFolder1 and use the command `md subfolder1`, a common mistake is for students to type the following: `md subfolder 1`. Notice the difference? A space was added after *subfolder,* and that means that the name of the directory is *subfolder*, not *subfolder1*. When the student has to create *subfolder2* and the command `md subfolder 2` is typed by accident, a message appears that the directory already exists. Why? The `md subfolder 2` command was giving the computer the direction to create a directory called *subfolder* because the space and the 2 in the typed command were ignored.

1. Power on the computer and log on if necessary.

2. Using Notepad, create four text files putting any professional data that you want into the files. Name the files with your first initial and last name plus a number, a dash, and another number. For example, since my name is Cheryl Schmidt, my files would be named *cschmidt1-1*, *cschmidt1-2*, *cschmidt2-1*, and *cschmidt2-2*. Save the files to the root directory of your flash drive.

What drive letter does the flash drive use?

_____

What application did you use to verify what drive letter the flash drive uses?

_____

Have a classmate verify your four files are in the flash drive root directory. Then close Windows Explorer/File Explorer and Notepad.

Printed classmate name _____

3. Access a command prompt. There are multiple methods that can be used. Use a previous lab for instructions.

    At the command prompt, type the command to go to the drive you will be using and press [Enter]. For example, if you are using a flash drive that uses the drive letter G, you would type G: and press [Enter]. The command is as follows: *X:* (where *X* is the drive letter where you are allowed to create files). The prompt changes to the appropriate drive letter such as E:\>.

4. At the command prompt, type the following command: **cd**

    What is the purpose of the cd command?

    _____

    _____

    What is the purpose of the cd\ command?

    _____

5. Create a directory (folder) called *Class*: md class

6. Use the **dir** command to verify the directory creation. If it is not created, redo Step 5.

7. When the directory is created, move into the *Class* directory using the cd command:
    cd class

    If you use the dir command at this point, what two entries are automatically created in a directory?

    _____

8. Within the *Class* directory, create a subdirectory (subfolder) called *SubFolder1*: md subfolder1

9. Move from the *CLASS* folder into the subfolder just created: **cd subfolder1**

    In this step, would the cd *X:*\Class\SubFolder1 (where *X:* represents the flash drive you are using) command have worked as well? Why or why not?

    _____

    _____

    _____

10. From the *SubFolder1* directory, move back one directory: cd..

    What does the prompt look like at this point?

    _____

11. Make another subdirectory called *SubFolder2* that is located under the *Class* directory.

    Have another student verify that both subdirectories have been created by using the **dir** command. Have them sign their name on your answer sheet if the *Class* directory has two subdirectories that have the correct title.

    Classmate's printed name _____

    Classmate's signature _____

12. Return to the root directory of the flash drive. Redo a previous lab if you cannot remember how to do this step.

On Your Own

13a. From the prompt, create two directories on the root directory of the flash drive. Name the directories *Sara and Josh*. Use the **dir** command to verify that the *Sara* and *Josh* directories exist in the root directory of the flash drive.

Have another student verify that two directories are created in the root directory. Ensure that the two names are correct and are readable.

Classmate's printed name _____

13b. Return to the root directory of the *X:* drive (the flash drive root directory).

Draw an image of your directory structure on the flash drive that you have created.

_____

_____

_____

_____

_____

Because you are sitting at the root directory of the flash drive, what do you think would be the results of the following command: COPY C:\WINDOWS\SYSTEM32\ATTRIB.EXE

_____

_____

14. *Note*: This step assumes that Windows has been loaded in a directory (folder) called *Windows*. If it is loaded in a different directory, substitute the name of that directory for *Windows* in the commands. You have to substitute *x:\Class* with a drive letter different from *X:* for the flash drive letter you are using.

From the root directory, type the following command. Notice that the copy command is first. Then the source (the complete path of where the file is located: C:\windows\system32\attrib.exe). Last is the destination: where the file is to be placed (in the class directory found on the flash drive).

copy C:\windows\system32\attrib.exe X:\class

A message appears that one file copied when you did this step correctly. If you did not get such a message, try the command again. Remember that the *X:* is your flash drive letter. You are supposed to type that drive letter rather than the *X*.

To what location do you think the file was copied?

_____

15. From the root directory, verify that the command has been copied by typing the following command: **dir \class**

What is the size of the *attrib.exe* file?

_____

_____

16. To copy the **attrib.exe** command from the *Class* folder into *SubFolder2* (from the root directory), use the following command. Notice the command comes first, and because everything is on the flash drive and the prompt is showing the flash drive, the flash drive letter is omitted from both the source and the destination. The drive letter for the flash drive could precede the backslash (\) before the source and the destination part of the command and it would work just as well (copy X:\class\ attrib.exe X:\class\subfolder1).

copy \class\attrib.exe \class\subfolder2

17. Verify that the file copied correctly using the following command. Notice with the `dir` command, you are instructing the computer to show a directory listing starting from the root drive (because the next part starts with the backslash [\]), then instructing the computer to go into the *Class* directory, and then go into the *subfolder2* directory. You are giving the computer the exact path to take to get to the correct directory to show the listing.

    `dir \class\subfolder2`

    The *attrib.exe* file should be listed. If it is not, redo Step 16.

    Are any other files or folders in the class directory? [Yes | No]

18. Copy the *FLast1-1.txt* text file into the *Subfolder1* directory (which is located under the *Class* directory) using the following command. Remember that *FLast1-1.txt* is your first initial and last name followed by *1-1.txt*. You created this file in the beginning of the lab.

    `copy \flast1-1.txt \class\subfolder1`

    A message should appear that one file copied. If it did not, redo Step 18. Remember that *flast* in the source represents your first initial and last name.

19. Verify that the file copied: **`dir \class\subfolder1`**

    Write the exact command to copy the *FLast1-1* text file from *Subfolder1* into the *Subfolder2* directory. Remember that both *Subfolder1* and *Subfolder2* are subdirectories located under the *Class* directory. The *Class* directory is directly off of the root directory.

    _____

20. Execute the command documented in Step 19. If the message that one file copied did not appear, redo the command or rewrite the command in Step 19. Once the file is copied, verify the copy using the `dir` command.

    What is the full command used to verify the copy in Step 20?

    _____

21. From the flash drive root directory, use the `tree` command to verify your structure. There should be four text files in the root directory with your first name and last name and 1-1, 1-2, 2-1, and 2-2 as part of the filename. There should be directories called *Class*, *Sara*, and *Josh*. Under the *Class* directory, there should be one file and two subfolders. The file is *attrib.exe*. The directories are *Subfolder1* and *Subfolder2*. Under the *Subfolder1* directory is the file *flast1-1.txt*. Under the *Subfolder2* directory is the file *flast1-1.txt*. If any of these are not correct, use *Windows Explorer/File Explorer* to delete any files, directories, and subdirectories you have created and restart the lab.

    `tree /f | more`

On Your Own

21a. From the flash drive root directory prompt, copy the *flast1-2.txt* file from the flash drive root directory into the *Sara* directory. Document the command in the space that follows before attempting to type it.

    Document the command to copy the *flast1-2.txt* file from the root directory of the flash drive into the *Sara* directory.

    _____

21b. From the flash drive root directory prompt, copy the *flast2-1.txt* file into the *Josh* directory. Document the command in the space that follows before attempting to type it.

Document the command to copy the *flast2-1.txt* file from the root directory of the flash drive into the *Josh* directory.

_____

21c. From the flash drive root directory prompt, copy the *flast2-2.txt* file into the *Class* directory. Document the command in the space that follows before attempting to type it.

Document the command to copy the *flast2-2.txt* file from the root directory of the flash drive into the *Class* directory.

_____

Have another student verify that three files are created in the three subdirectories. Ensure that the names are correct and are readable. Windows Explorer/File Explorer can be used to verify, but not correct. A better option would be to use the `dir` and `cd` commands.

Classmate's printed name _____

Classmate's signature _____

21d. Return to the root directory of the *X*: drive (the flash drive root directory). Close all other windows except the command prompt window.

22. A subdirectory can be created within a subdirectory from the root directory. To create a subdirectory called *Fun* within the *SubFolder2* subdirectory (which is under the *Class* directory), use the following command from the root directory. Notice how you must insert the backslashes when you have multiple directories to go through to create the subdirectory.

```
md \class\subfolder2\fun
```

23. Verify the subdirectory creation: `dir \class\subfolder2`. A directory called *Fun* should be listed in the output.

What is the total amount of space the files located within *SubFolder2* occupy?

_____

24. Use the tree command to verify the *Class* folder structure. There should be two subdirectories (*Subfolder1* and *Subfolder2*) and one subdirectory (*Fun*) under *Subfolder2*.

```
tree \class
```

25. To copy all the files located in *SubFolder2* into the newly created *Fun* subdirectory, the following command is used:

```
copy \class\subfolder2 \class\subfolder2\fun
```

A message should appear that two files copied. If you did not receive this message, do not go any further. Try redoing the command. Make sure there is a space between the `copy` command and the first backslash. Make sure there is a space between the first time you type `subfolder2` and the next backslash (between the source and the destination parts).

26. Use the `DIR` command as follows to verify the copy:

```
dir \class\subfolder2\fun
```

27. Wildcards can be used with the `copy` command. To copy all the files that start with the letter A from the *Fun* subdirectory into the *Subfolder1* subdirectory, the following command is used:

```
copy \class\subfolder2\fun\a*.* \class\subfolder1
```

A message should appear stating that one file copied. If you did not receive this message, do not go any further. Try redoing the command. Make sure there is a space between the `copy` command and the first backslash (\). Make sure there is a space between the last asterisk (*) and the next backslash (between the source and the destination parts).

How many files were copied?

_____

Instructor initials: _____

28. The `del` command is used to delete files. Wildcards can also be used with this command. Delete all the files located in the *Fun* subdirectory using the following command. The `*.*` is the wildcard representing all files with any extension.

`del \class\subfolder2\fun\*.*`

When prompted if you are sure, type **Y** and press Enter. Verify the files are deleted with the `dir` command:

`dir \class\subfolder2\fun`

29. The `rd` command removes directories and subdirectories. Note that you can never remove a directory or subdirectory with the `rd` command unless that directory or subdirectory is empty. Remove the *Fun* subdirectory:

`rd \class\subfolder2\fun`

30. Type the command used to remove the *SubFolder2* subdirectory:

`rd \class\subfolder2`

What was the operating system response and what do you think has to be done as a result?

_____

_____

31. Delete the files in the *Subfolder2* subdirectory:

`del \class\subfolder2\*.*`

When prompted if you are sure, type **Y** and press Enter. Verify the files are deleted with the `dir` command:

`dir \class\subfolder2`

32a. Remove the *Subfolder2* subdirectory:

`rd \class\subfolder2`

Verify the results:

`dir \class`

On Your Own

32b. From the command prompt, use the `del`, `rd`, and `dir` commands, delete all files that you have created in the root directory, and verify the deletions.

Write each command you are going to use *before* attempting this part. This is an important part of learning the commands and the prompt is to think about what and how you are going to type something before executing the command.

_____

_____

_____

_____

_____

_____

Write each command used to delete the files in the *Class*, *Subfolder1*, *Sara*, and *Josh* directories and subdirectories.

_____

_____

_____

_____

Write each command used to delete the following directories and subdirectories: *Class*, *Subfolder1*, *Sara*, and *Josh* directories and subdirectories.

_____

_____

_____

_____

Have another student verify your work. Have that student sign and print his or her name to verify that all of the files created during this lab have been deleted.

Classmate's printed name _____

Classmate's signature _____

Lab 15.19 The `ATTRIB` Command and Moving Around in the Directory Structure

Objective: To use the `ATTRIB` command and to work correctly from a prompt when dealing with directories and subdirectories

Parts: A computer with a Windows operating system loaded

Access to modify files on the hard drive or flash drive

Procedure: Complete the following procedure and answer the accompanying questions.

Note: For each step requiring a typed command, the (Enter) key must be pressed to execute the command. This instruction will *not* be given with each step.

1.   Power on the computer and log on if necessary.

2.   Using Notepad, create three files and save them in the root directory of the flash drive. Name the files *Special1.txt*, *Special2.txt*, and *Tickle.txt*.

What drive letter is assigned to the flash drive?

_____

3.   Access a command prompt. Ensure the prompt represents the root directory of the flash drive. Do not use Windows Explorer or File Explorer to verify anything for the rest of the lab. If you need to, you are not where you should be to start this lab. You should practice the previous labs some more.

What does your command prompt look like? Note that it should be the drive letter of the flash drive, a colon, and a greater than sign. If it is not, review the chapter and previous labs for getting to this point before going to Step 4.

4.   From the root directory of the flash drive, type the following command to create a directory called *Junk*: `md junk`

5.   Under the *Junk* directory, make subdirectories called *Sub1*, *Sub2*, and *Sub3*. Use the following commands:

`cd junk`

`md sub1`

`md sub2`

`md sub3`

6. Return to the root directory. Verify by looking at the command prompt after returning to the root directory.

   What command makes the root directory the current directory?

   _____

   Write the command prompt as it appears on your screen.

   _____

7. Make a new directory called *Trash* from the root directory. Within the *Trash* directory, make subdirectories called *Sub1*, *Sub2*, and *Sub3*. Use the following commands:

   `md trash`

   `cd trash`

   `md sub1`

   `md sub2`

   `md sub3`

8. Return to the root directory of the flash drive.

On Your Own

9. Make a new directory called *Garbage* from the root directory. Within the *Garbage* directory, make subdirectories called *Sub1*, *Sub2*, and *Sub3*. Verify the directory and subdirectories were created.

   Write the commands to create a directory called *Garbage* and the three subdirectories.

   _____

   _____

   _____

   _____

   _____

   _____

10. Place the *Special1.txt*, *Special2.txt*, and *Tickle.txt* files in the *Garbage\Sub1* subdirectory.

11. From the root directory, copy all files that begin with the letter *S* from the *Garbage\Sub1* subdirectory and place them in the *Trash\Sub3* subdirectory.

    Write the commands to copy *S* files from the *Garbage\Sub1* subdirectory to the *Trash\Sub3* subdirectory.

    _____

    _____

    How many files copied?

    _____

12. Copy any file that begins with *T* from the *Garbage\Sub1* subdirectory and place it in the *Sub2* subdirectory of the *Junk* directory.

    Write the commands to copy *T* files from one subdirectory to another subdirectory.

    _____

    How many files copied?

    _____

Draw a diagram of how your directory structure that you have created in this exercise including all directories, subdirectories, and files.

_____

_____

_____

_____

_____

_____

_____

_____

_____

_____

_____

_____

_____

Setting/Removing Attributes

13. To make all files in the *Sub3* subdirectory of the *Trash* directory read-only, use the `attrib` command with the +r switch. From the root directory, type the following command:

    `attrib +r \trash\sub3\*.*`

14. To verify the read-only attribute is set, type the following command:

    `attrib \trash\sub3\*.*`

    The *Sub3* subdirectory should list two files. Both have an R beside them indicating that the read-only attribute is set. If the two files do *not* have the read-only attribute set, perform the previous step again.

15. The best way to prove that the files are read-only is to try to delete them. Type the following command:

    `del \trash\sub3\*.*`

16. When asked if you are sure, type **Y** and press (Enter). A message appears on the screen stating, "Access is denied." Then the command prompt appears. If the access denied message does not appear, the files were deleted, which means the read-only attribute was not set. If this is the case, redo this exercise starting with *On Your Own* Step 11 above.

17. Hide the *Junk\Sub2* subdirectory using the following command:

    `attrib +h \junk\sub2`

    No message appears on the screen. The command prompt appears again.

18. To verify that the directory is hidden, type the following command:

    `dir \junk`

    The *Sub2* subdirectory should not appear in the list.

19. Use the `attrib` command to verify that the directory is hidden by typing the following command:

    `attrib \junk\sub2`

    The directory listing appears with an H beside the name.

20. Some operating system files are automatically marked as system files when the operating system is installed. Type the following command to see what files are marked already as system files:

    `attrib c:\*.*`

    List any files that have the system attribute.

    _____

    _____

On Your Own

21. Hide the *Special1.txt* file located in the *Sub1* subdirectory of the *Garbage* directory.

    Write the command you used for this step.

    _____

22. Verify that the Special1.txt file is hidden by using the `dir` and `attrib` commands.

    Write the command you used for this step.

    _____

    _____

    Have a classmate print his name and his signature as well as a statement describing how the person verified that you were in the correct directory.

    Classmate's printed name _____

    Classmate's signature _____

    _____

    _____

    _____

    Instructor initials: _____

23. Remove the hidden attribute from the *Special1.txt* file in the *SUB1* subdirectory of the *Garbage* directory. If necessary, use **Help** to find the switch to remove an attribute.

    Write the command used in this step.

    _____

24. Have a classmate verify that the *Special1.txt* file is no longer hidden.

    Have the classmate write the command he used, his printed name, and his signature.

    Classmate's printed name _____

    Classmate's signature _____

    _____

    _____

    _____

25. Ensure that you are at the root directory.

26. Moving around within subdirectories can be challenging when you are first learning commands. Move to the *Sub3* subdirectory of the *Trash* directory.

    What command did you use to perform Step 15?

    _____

27. To move to the *Sub1* subdirectory from within the *Sub3* subdirectory, type `cd..`; then type `cd sub1` to move into the correct subdirectory.

    What does the command prompt look like now?

    _____

28. A shortcut to move up one directory is to type `cd.` from within the *Sub1* subdirectory. The prompt immediately changes to one level up (the *Trash* directory). Type `cd..`

    The command prompt changes to $X:\Trash>$.

29. Using the `cd..` command again returns one level back in the directory structure to the root directory. Type `cd..` and the command prompt changes appropriately.

On Your Own

30. From the root directory change to the *Sub2* subdirectory of the *Garbage* directory.

    Write the command used in this step.

    _____

    How can one verify that the current directory is *Garbage\Sub2*?

    _____

31. From the *Garbage\Sub2* subdirectory, change the current directory to the *Sub3* subdirectory of the *Trash* directory.

    Write the command you used in this step.

    _____

    Have a classmate print his/her name and his/her signature as well as a statement describing how the person verified that you were in the correct directory.

    Classmate's printed name _____

    Classmate's signature _____

    Classmate name and signature and the following answer:

    _____

32. Using the `cd..` command, move from *Trash\Sub3* to *Trash*.

33. Using the `cd..` command, move from *Trash* to the root directory.

On Your Own

34. Using the `attrib`, `del`, and `rd` commands, delete the *Trash* and *Garbage* directories including all subdirectories underneath them. Write all commands before you attempt this step.

    Write all commands used in this step.

    _____

    _____

    _____

    _____

    _____

    _____

    _____

    _____

    _____

    _____

35. Using the `attrib`, `del`, and `rd` commands, delete the *Junk* directory and all subdirectories. Write all commands before you attempt this step.

    Write all commands used in this step.

    _____

    _____

    _____

    _____

    _____

    _____

Instructor initials: _____

Lab 15.20 Windows 7/10 Backup Software and the Archive Bit

Objective: To explore backup options and how they affect the archive attribute using Windows 7 or 10

Parts: A computer with Windows 7 or 10 installed

   Flash drive

Procedure: Complete the following procedure and answer the accompanying questions.

Note: This lab requires both command prompt and Windows skills.

1. Power on the computer and log in to Windows.

2. Attach the flash drive.

   What drive letter is assigned to the flash drive?

   _____

3. Ensure there are at least three files in the *Documents* folder on the hard drive. You may have to create these three files. This will be the folder that contains the data to be backed up.

   What are the names of your three files?

   _____

4. In Windows 7, from the *Start* menu, access *All Programs > Accessories >* right-click *Command Prompt > Run as administrator > Yes.*

   _____

   _____

5. Use the `CD` command to move into the directory (folder) chosen in Step 2. A hint for you is that you must change the directory into users and the username used to log in to the computer before you can locate the *Documents* folder. For example, the prompt will be as follows (with Cheryl being the username used to log in to the computer): `C:\Users\Cheryl\Documents>`

   Document the command(s) used to accomplish this step.

   _____

   _____

   _____

   _____

   _____

   _____

   _____

CHAPTER 15

6. Use the DIR command to verify that at least three files are in the folder.

   Have another student verify the three files are there.

   Classmate's signature: _____

7. Use the attrib command to determine the attributes set by default on a file saved on a Windows computer. The attribute(s) list to the far left, there is a space, and then the full path to the filename. Leave the command prompt window open.

   Document the attribute(s) found for the three files. The A is for the archive attribute. The R is for the read-only attribute. The H is for the hidden attribute.

   _____

   _____

   _____

8. Search, locate, and select the Windows 7 *Backup and Restore* or Windows 10 *Backup and Restore (Windows 7)* Control Panel.

9. If a backup has been done before, select the *Change settings* link; otherwise, select the *Set up backup* link.

10. Select the appropriate backup destination (flash drive letter as specified in the answer to the question in Step 2) > *Next*.

11. Select the *Let me choose* button > *Next*.

12. Expand folders as necessary by clicking on the arrows and locate and select the folder chosen in Step 2 > *Next*.

13. Click the *Save settings and run backup* button.

14. When the backup finishes, return to the command prompt window and reissue the **attrib** command.

    Did the archive attribute change for the three files? [Yes | No]

    Describe the backup file on the flash drive. In other words, how does the Windows Backup software save the file?

    _____

    _____

15. Using *Windows Explorer/File Explorer,* copy one of the files from the *Documents* folder to the desktop.

16. Using the command prompt window, type **cd** to return to the root directory.

17. Use the cd command to access the *Desktop* directory. A sample command would be cd \users\ Cheryl\desktop if the person who signed onto the computer used the "Cheryl" account.

    Document the exact command you used to access the *Desktop* directory.

    _____

18. Use the attrib command to determine whether a copied file changes the archive bit.

    Document your findings.

    _____

Instructor initials: _____

Cleanup

18. Permanently delete the file copied to the desktop and the three files created in the *Documents* folder.

19. Close all windows.

Lab 15.21 Windows 7 Backup Tool

Objective:	To be able to use the Backup tool provided with Windows 7
Parts:	Windows 7 computer and administrator rights
	Flash drive with 1GB of free space (2GB drive is recommended)
Procedure:	Complete the following procedure and answer the accompanying questions.
Notes:	This lab does not back up the hard drive, but simply illustrates the concept of using the Backup tool.

1. Power on the computer and log on using a user ID and password that has administrator rights.

2. Use the Windows Help and Support tool to answer the following questions. Use the key terms `backup tool` to get started.

    Is shadow copies of shared folders a feature found in Windows 7? [Yes | No]

    What is the purpose of the shadow copies of shared folders?

    _____

    _____

    What command is used to create and manage system image backups for Windows 7–based computers?

    _____

    What are four Windows-based backup tools?

    _____

    _____

    List one recommended location for storing a backup.

    _____

    _____

    _____

    If a flash drive is to be used, what is the minimum amount of free space that must be available on that drive?

    _____

3. Copy at least one file to the Recycle bin.

4. Insert a flash drive. Ensure the drive is visible through Windows Explorer.

5. Using Windows Explorer, create a folder called *Backup* on the flash drive.

6. Locate the *System and Security* Control Panel and select the *Backup and Restore* link.

7. If a backup has not been performed before, you will need to select the *Set up backup* link. If a backup has been performed before, select the *Change settings* link.

    Note: You may need to use the *Refresh* button to be able to see the flash drive. If the flash drive does not appear, ensure it is viewable through Windows AND has OVER 1GB of free space available. Select the appropriate drive letter. Click *Next*.

    Select the *Let me choose* radio button. Click *Next*. If the system is not set up to do the backup on demand, you may have to click the *Change schedule* link to modify it so the backup can be done now. Then, select the *$Recycle Bin* checkbox. Note that you may have to expand the *Computer* option as well as the *C:* drive in order to locate this checkbox. Click *Next*. Select the *Save settings and run backup* button.

8. While the backup is occurring, select the *View Details* button.

Why do you think a technician would use this option?

_____

_____

Were you surprised at the time it took to perform the backup?

_____

Instructor initials: _____

9. When the backup is complete, click the *Close* button, delete the backup from the flash drive, eject the flash drive and give it to the instructor, if necessary, and close all windows.

Lab 15.22 Windows 8.1 File History Utility

Objective: To explore backing up data using the Windows File History utility
Parts: A computer with Windows 8.1 installed
               Flash drive
Procedure: Complete the following procedure and answer the accompanying questions.

1. Power on the computer and log in to Windows.

2. Attach the flash drive to the computer.

Which drive letter is assigned to the flash drive?

_____

3. Search by typing in the words `file history` in the search textbox. Select *File History settings* from the resulting search list.

4. Ensure the *File History* option is turned *On*.

5. If the flash drive is not shown as the drive to back up personal files, use the *Select a drive* or *Select a different drive* link to select the drive.

6. Notice how you cannot select what is backed up. In Windows 8.1, sentences at the top of the screen describe what information is automatically backed up. Also notice how this backup occurs automatically (meaning you would need to leave that drive attached). Select the *Back up now* button.

How much space is the backup going to take?

_____

7. Open *File Explorer* and access the flash drive.

What is the name of the file that contains the backed up data?

_____

8. Return to the *File History Settings* window and turn the option *Off*.

9. Return to *File Explorer* and access the flash drive. Right-click or tap and briefly hold on the *FileHistory* folder > select *Delete* > *Yes*.

Do you think most people will use this option? Why or why not?

_____

_____

Lab 15.23 Windows 10 File History Utility

Objective: To explore backing up data using the Windows File History utility

Parts: A computer with Windows 10 installed

Flash drive

Procedure: Complete the following procedure and answer the accompanying questions.

1. Power on the computer and log in to Windows.

2. Attach the flash drive to the computer.

Which drive letter is assigned to the flash drive?

_____

3. Search by typing in the words `file history` in the search textbox. Select *File History settings* from the resulting search list.

4. Select the + *Add a drive* option. Note that if this option has been used before, you can simply turn the *Automatically backup my files* option on and select the *More options* link to select what files/folders are backed up, how often to back up the files, and how long to keep the backups.

5. After all settings have been configured, select the *Back up now* button.

How much space is the backup going to take?

_____

6. Open *File Explorer* and access the flash drive.

What is the name of the file that contains the backed-up data?

_____

7. Return to the *File History Settings* window and turn the option *Off*.

8. Return to *File Explorer* and access the flash drive. Right-click or tap and briefly hold on the *FileHistory* folder > select *Delete > Yes*.

Do you think most people will use this option? Why or why not?

_____

_____

Lab 15.24 Creating a Windows 7 System Repair Disc

Objective: To create a system repair disc in the Windows 7 environment

Parts: A Windows 7-based computer

1 blank DVD or 8GB+ flash drive

Procedure: Complete the following procedure and answer the accompanying questions.

1. Boot the computer and access the system BIOS. Ensure the system is set to boot first from the drive you are using.

2. Save the settings and exit BIOS. Boot into Windows.

3. Click the *Start* button > *Control Panel* > *System and Security* link > *Backup and Restore* > *Create a system repair disc* link.

4. Ensure the appropriate media is ready (blank DVD or 8GB flash drive). Select the appropriate media > *Next*.

5. Select the *Create disc* button.

How often do you think a home user should create a system repair disc?

_____

_____

When the system repair disc is complete, what is the recommended label for the repair disc?

_____

What is the difference between a system repair disc and a system image disc?

_____

_____

6.   After the disc/drive has been created, click the *Close* button followed by *OK*.

Using the System Repair Disc/Drive

7.   After labeling the system repair disc, re-insert it into the drive or ensure the System Repair drive is attached.

8.   Power down the computer.

9.   Power on the computer using the power button. A prompt may appear that tells you to press any key to start the computer from a CD or DVD. Press any key to boot from the system repair disc.

10.   Select the appropriate language and keyboard settings. Click *Next*.

11.   From this screen, you can either use Windows recovery tools or restore the system from a previously created system image. For this exercise, select the radio button that begins *Use recovery tools*, ensure the correct operating system is highlighted, and click *Next*.

List three options from the resulting menu.

_____

_____

Instructor initials: _____

12.   Select *Shutdown*.

Lab 15.25 Creating a Windows 7 System Image Disc

Objective: To create a system image disc in the Windows 7 environment

Parts: A Windows 7-based computer that has an optical drive installed

1 blank DVD

Procedure: Complete the following procedure and answer the accompanying questions.

1.   Boot the computer and access the system BIOS. Ensure the system is set to boot from the optical drive first.

2.   Save the settings and exit BIOS. Boot into Windows 7.

3.   Click the *Start* button > *Control Panel* > *System and Security* link > *Backup and Restore* > *Create a system image* link.

What three options are available?

_____

4.   Determine from the instructor or lab assistant the appropriate storage medium and select the appropriate radio button. Click *Next*.

5.   Select at least the operating system to back up.

What is the amount of space required to do the system image?

_____

_____

6. Click *Next*. Optionally insert media as directed and select *Start backup*.

   While the image is being created, what option(s) do you have on the screen?

   _____

   Instructor initials: _____

(Optional) Using the System Image Disc

7. To use the system image disc, you can (1) use the Recovery Control Panel, or (2) you can restore starting from a Windows 7 installation disc or system repair disk using the following steps once you boot from the disc: A prompt may appear that tells you to press any key to start the computer from a CD or DVD. Press any key to boot from the system repair disc or Windows 7 installation disc. Select the appropriate language and keyboard settings. Click *Next*. If you booted from a system recovery disc, select the radio button for a system repair disc and click *Next*. If you booted from the Windows installation disc, select *Repair your computer*. (3) Finally, you can do the following if you don't have a Windows 7 installation disc or a system repair disc. Reboot the computer, and as the computer is booting press ⌐F8⌐ to access the Windows Advanced Boot Options screen. Select *Repair your computer*, select the appropriate keyboard, and click *Next*. Select a username, type a password, and click *OK*. Select *Image Recovery* and follow the instructions.

8. For this lab, use the Recovery Control Panel because the computer is working. Click the *Start* button and type **recovery** in the *Search programs and files* textbox.

9. Select *Recovery* from the resulting list.

   Document the path through Control Panels to reach this option.

   _____

10. Select the *Advanced recovery methods* link. Select the *Use a system image you created earlier to recover your computer* option. Follow the instructions on the screen to recovery your computer.

   Instructor initials: _____

Lab 15.26 Creating a Windows 8.1/10 System Recovery Drive

Objective: To create a system recovery drive in the Windows 8.1/10 environment

Parts: A Windows 8.1/10-based computer

   Flash drive or external drive (where the entire contents will be erased)

Procedure: Complete the following procedure and answer the accompanying questions.

1. Boot the computer and log in to Windows.

2. Optionally, attach external media if that is what is being used. Otherwise, a second drive should be available. Note that the amount of space needed on the external media or second hard drive depends on the size of drive (and possibly the size of the recovery partition) of the computer being backed up.

   How much space is used on the drive being backed up?

   _____

3. Use the *Search* function to search on the words recovery drive. Select the *Create a recovery drive* in the resulting search list > *Yes*.

4. Optionally, ensure the *Copy the recovery partition from the PC to the recovery drive* option is selected > *Next*.

5.   Select the appropriate media in the *Available drive(s)* list > *Next* > *Create*.

      While the image is being created, what option(s) do you have on the screen?

      _____

      How long did the backup take to finish?

      _____

Instructor initials: _____

6.   Select *Finish*.

(Optional)

Using the System Recovery Drive in Windows 8.1

7.   To use the system recovery drive, you access the BIOS/UEFI BIOS and ensure the computer is configured to boot from the USB drive.

8.   Attach the USB drive to the computer.

9.   Boot the computer from the USB drive. The *Windows Boot Manager* window appears with the following choices:

      1. Insert your Windows installation disc and restart your computer.

      2. Choose your language settings, and then click *Next*.

      3. Click *Repair your computer*.

Instructor initials: _____

10.   You do not have to go any further because the computer is not broken. Return the system to the original configuration.

16 Windows Vista, 7, 8, and 10

In this chapter you will learn:

> To distinguish between the Windows Vista, 7, 8, and 10 operating systems

> To install, configure, and troubleshoot Windows Vista, 7, 8, and 10

> To install hardware and software in the Windows environment

> To use various tools and features, such as System Restore, driver roll back, and WinRE

> The Windows boot process and how to troubleshoot boot problems

> To use the Computer Management console, Task Manager, and Event Viewer

> How to avoid burnout in the IT field

CompTIA Exam Objectives:

What CompTIA exam objectives are covered in this chapter?

✓ 902-1.1   Compare and contrast various features and requirements of Microsoft Operating Systems (Windows Vista, Windows 7, Windows 8, Windows 8.1).

✓ 902-1.2   Given a scenario, install Windows PC operating systems using appropriate methods.

✓ 902-1.3   Given a scenario, apply appropriate Microsoft command line tools.

✓ 902-1.4   Given a scenario, use appropriate Microsoft operating system features and tools.

✓ 902-1.5   Given a scenario, use Windows Control Panel utilities.

✓ 902-1.6   Given a scenario, install and configure Windows networking on a client/desktop.

✓ 902-1.7   Perform common preventive maintenance procedures using the appropriate Windows OS tools.

✓ 902-2.2   Given a scenario, set up and use client-side virtualization.

✓ 902-3.7   Given a scenario, secure SOHO wireless and wired networks.

✓ 902-4.1   Given a scenario, troubleshoot PC operating system problems with appropriate tools.

✓ 902-4.2   Given a scenario, troubleshoot common PC security issues with appropriate tools and best practices.

Windows Vista/7/8/10 Overview

Windows Vista, 7, 8, and 10 come in 32- and 64-bit versions, each having different tiers available: Starter, Home Basic, Home Premium, Business, Professional, Enterprise, Ultimate, and Education. Depending on the version, enhanced features include

> **Aero**: A Windows Vista/7 graphical environment that introduces rich colors and new features (such as Aero Peek) and enables you to see all open documents by holding a pointer over application icons.
> **Gadgets**: A Windows Vista option where applications such as the calendar and clock are available in a docked sidebar. Windows 7 has a Media Center gadget.
> **Side-by-side apps or windows**: In Windows 7, 8, or 10, drag the top of a window to one side of the screen (until an outline of the window appears). An alternative is to be in an active window and use the ⊞ + ← or → depending on whether you want the active window pinned to the left or right side. Open another window and do the same for the opposite side and the windows or apps are automatically equally sized.
> **Metro UI**: The new tiled look in Windows 8 and Windows 10.
> **Pinning**: The ability to place favorite apps in either the Start button, taskbar, or as a tile on the desktop.
> **OneDrive**: Microsoft's cloud storage that allows files to be synched from multiple devices and accessible from a browser.
> **User Account Control (UAC)**: A method used to notify you of potential security issues before anything is added to or removed from the system.
> **Windows Store**: Where apps are optionally purchased and downloaded.
> **Multi-monitor taskbar**: A Windows 8/10 feature that can be modified by a right-click (or tap and briefly hold on an empty spot) on the taskbar > select *Properties* > locate the *Multiple displays* section > select whether the taskbar shows on all displays and which display buttons should be displayed on.
> **Charms**: A Windows 8 hidden sidebar that, when displayed, provides quick access to search, share content, Start screen, devices, and settings.
> **Windows Recovery Environment (WinRE)**: A place to go when things go wrong.
> **IP version 6 (IPv6)**: Support for the latest protocol for Internet communication.
> **Hyper-V**: A hypervisor for running virtual machines.
> **Cortana**: A Windows 10 virtual assistant.

Windows Vista/7/8/10 Versions

Table 16.1 shows the various versions of Windows that can be purchased with a brief description of each. Each version can be 32- or 64-bit except where noted.

TABLE 16.1   Windows Vista, 7, 8, and 10 editions

Windows editions	Description
Starter: Vista, Windows 7	A 32-bit-only version used with low-cost computers and with tablets.
Home: Windows 10	Designed for home use for PCs and tablets; it is the new equivalent to Windows 7 and Windows Vista home editions.

Windows editions	Description
Home Basic: Vista, Windows 7	Used to surf the Internet and do basic computing. Comes with Internet Explorer, Windows Media Player, Windows Movie Maker, and Windows Mail. CDs can be created, but not DVDs. It does not allow connecting to a network domain (but can join a HomeGroup home network created from a Windows 7 or higher computer); it does not support EFS encryption or provide the full Aero user experience. Windows 7 Home Basic is only sold in certain areas.
Home Premium: Vista, Windows 7	More robust than Home Basic, includes the Aero GUI interface, DVD creation, creating/joining a HomeGroup (7 and higher) home network, and other tools for media creation and editing.
Windows 8	Sometimes known as Windows 8 (Core).
Business: Vista	Designed for computers in the workplace and the domain environment. Aero, encryption, Shadow Copy, and Remote Desktop are supported, but not all the multimedia capabilities are supported.
Professional: Windows 7 and 8	The continuation of the Business edition found in Vista.
Pro: Windows 10	The equivalent of Windows Professional in prior versions.
Enterprise: Windows Vista, 7, 8, and 10	Designed for corporate environments where multimedia editing and creation are used; supports BitLocker drive encryption (covered in Chapter 18) and provides multilingual support. Not sold through retail centers but to corporate and educational institutions using bulk licensing.
Ultimate: Windows Vista and 7	Contains all the Enterprise features, including support for multiple processors, but includes some extras that are downloadable from Microsoft. These include fun utilities and work-related tools, such as the Windows BitLocker Drive Preparation Tool, AppLocker to prevent unwanted corporate applications, and DirectAccess for connecting to the corporate network without a VPN (virtual private network; VPNs are covered in Chapter 18).
Education: Windows 10	Provides everything offered in the Enterprise version of Windows 10, but designed for use by schools and universities.
Windows RT: Windows 8	Installed on advanced RISC machines (ARMs), which are mobile devices. Supports touch-based apps, device encryption, and the ability to manage devices through group policies and the domain environment.
Mobile: Windows 10	Supports mobile device encryption, mobile device management, and side-loading of apps. A mobile operating system that grew from the Windows Phone operating system that works on smartphones, phablets, and tablets.
Mobile Enterprise: Windows 10	Has all the features of Windows Mobile and additionally supports Windows Update for Business and Current Branch for Business features.

32- or 64-Bit OS

Besides having to choose a Windows version, deciding on a 32-bit or 64-bit version is also required. This decision is based on the type of processor installed. Through *Windows Explorer/File Explorer*, right-click or tap and briefly hold on *Computer/This PC* > select *Properties* to see the current version. 64-bit processors have been available for some time, but a 64-bit operating system is a big step. It took over 12 years for a 32-bit operating system (OS) to become the norm in business and home computing environments. Even though Windows XP had a 64-bit version, many consumers have not considered using a 64-bit operating system until Windows Vista or higher. Many books and advertisements refer to a 32-bit processor as an x86 chip, so 32-bit editions might be seen or referred to as an x86 version. 64-bit processors are frequently shown as x64. Table 16.2 lists the differences between 32-bit and 64-bit Windows.

TABLE 16.2   32-bit and 64-bit Windows

32-bit Windows	64-bit Windows
32-bit or 64-bit processor	64-bit processor
4GB RAM limitation	Up to 2048GB RAM supported depending on the version of Windows used
32 bits processed at a time	64 bits processed at a time
32-bit drivers required	64-bit device drivers required, and they must be digitally signed
32-bit applications and some support for older 16-bit applications	32- or 64-bit application support; 16-bit application support using the Program Compatibility Wizard or downloading and using Windows XP Mode in Windows 7
DEP (Data Execution Prevention) prevents a specific type of security attack by using both hardware and software technology	"Always-on" DEP support for 64-bit processes
N/A Better support for multiple processors	Protection for the operating system kernel (the core of the operating system)

Preinstallation of Windows

Windows can be installed from either a central location using a network or locally using an optical disc or external drive. The preinstallation of any operating system is more important than the installation. Technicians who grab a disc or just download and load a new operating system without going through a preparation process are asking for trouble. The operating system is a complex piece of software that is critical to all hardware and other software working.

It is important to follow these steps before installing Windows:

Step 1. Decide whether the installation will be an upgrade or a clean install and which version of the operating system is to be loaded. Take into account software application compatibility.

Step 2. Decide whether the computer will have more than one operating system installed.

Step 3. Plan the partition/volume size and select the file system.

Step 4. Determine whether or not the hardware is compatible.

Step 5. Obtain any drivers, upgrades, or hardware replacements.

Step 6. Back up any data files.

Step 7. Scan for viruses, and then disable the virus protection during the installation process.

Step 8. Temporarily disable any power management or disk management tools.

Upgrade or Clean Install

The first decision to make when planning to install an operating system is whether to upgrade from another operating system or to perform a clean install. An **upgrade** or in-place upgrade is when a computer already has an older operating system on it and a newer operating system is being installed. A **clean install** puts an operating system on a system that does not have one or removes the existing operating system in order to install a new one. There are three reasons to perform a clean install:

> The computer does not already have an operating system installed.
> The current operating system is not upgradable to the desired Windows version.
> The current operating system is upgradable to a specific Windows version, but the existing files and applications are going to be reloaded.

When you decide to upgrade, you must take into account which operating system is installed, which hardware is installed, which applications are being used, and whether or not they are compatible with the new operating system (see Figure 16.1). When Windows is installed as an upgrade, the user's applications and data are preserved if the operating system is installed in the same folder as the original operating system. If Windows is installed in a different folder, then all applications must be reloaded.

FIGURE 16.1   Applications are affected by an OS upgrade

Microsoft describes an **in-place upgrade** as an installation that requires no movement of files. Although an in-place installation can usually be accomplished to upgrade from one version of Windows to another, it isn't always an option. To make sure an upgrade is possible, you will want to consult the documentation for the version of Windows you want to upgrade to. Alternatively, you can use the Windows Upgrade Advisor tool.

Windows Upgrade Advisor

The **Windows Upgrade Advisor** application should always be used before upgrading Windows. Upgrade Advisor, sometimes also referred to as Upgrade Assistant in more recent versions of Windows, can be downloaded, installed, and executed to see whether a Windows Vista, 7, 8, or 10 computer can function well with a higher version of Windows. Upgrade Advisor checks hardware, connected devices, and existing applications, and it makes recommendations before an upgrade. You will want to make sure you have all hardware peripherals that are commonly used with the system connected when you run the advisor tool.

In order to take advantage of Windows reliability, enhancements, and security features, sometimes a clean installation is the best choice. Because a clean installation involves formatting the hard drive, the user's data must be backed up and all applications reinstalled once the Windows installation is complete. Also, all user-defined settings are lost.

TECH TIP

OEM OS cannot go to another computer

An original equipment manufacturer (OEM) version of Windows that is sold as part of a computer sale is not transferable to another computer.

Even when Microsoft states that an in-place upgrade *can* be done, there is no guarantee that all applications and settings will work after the upgrade. In a corporate environment, if custom software is involved, contact the software developer for any known issues or test the software in a test environment before deploying corporate-wide. The information may be posted on the software developer's website. Also, Microsoft has a list of compatible software for many of the popular applications and games on its website.

Easy Transfer and USMT

The **Easy Transfer** program or the User State Migration Tool (USMT) can be used to migrate data when updating Windows when an in-place upgrade is not supported. See Figure 16.2 to see an example of data migration. Windows Easy Transfer (`migwiz.exe`) is free from Microsoft and is used to copy files and operating system settings to another drive, to removable media, over a network, or to another storage location. Once the operating system is installed, the files and settings are reapplied to the upgraded computer. This tool can also be used when a computer is being replaced and a data migration is required, such as when Windows Vista is replacing XP. The Easy Transfer program works only through Windows 8.1, but USMT can be used from XP all the way to 10.

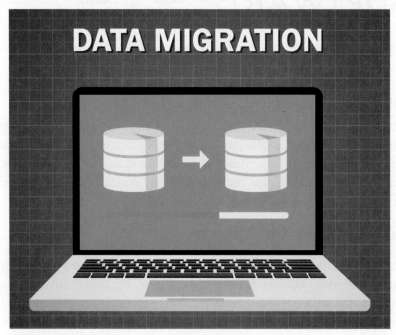

FIGURE 16.2   Local data migration

IT staff use the **USMT** to perform large deployments of Windows. This tool is used from a command line for more control and customized settings, including registry changes. The `scanstate.exe` and `loadstate.exe` commands are used to transfer file and user settings.

Compatibility Mode

Keep in mind while upgrading that not all 16- or 32-bit applications can be used in the 64-bit Windows environment. If a program is proving to be incompatible, try the **compatibility mode** available using the Program Compatibility Wizard: locate the *Programs* Control Panel > use the *Run programs made for previous versions of Windows* link.

Another way of manually assigning a particular application that was made to be compatible with an older (selectable) Windows version is to locate the application in the Start button menu or the executable file on disk. Right-click the application and select *Properties > Compatibility* tab > enable (check) the *Run this program in compatibility mode for* checkbox > use the drop-down menu to select the specific operating system > use the specific video and administrator options available in the *Settings* and *Privilege Level* sections > click *Apply* > click *OK*.

Virtual XP Mode

If the Program Compatibility Wizard does not work, the Virtual XP Mode is an option in Windows 7, but it was discontinued for newer versions of Windows. **Virtual XP Mode** (also known as Windows XP Mode) is an optional program that can be downloaded and used in Windows Vista and in the 7 Professional, Ultimate, and Enterprise editions. Once it is downloaded and installed, access the software by clicking on the *Start* button > *All Programs* > *Windows Virtual PC* > *Virtual Windows XP*. Hardware including optical and USB drives are normally accessible through Windows XP Mode, but not all hardware may work in this environment. Also, Windows XP Mode is not suited for graphic-intensive games or applications.

Windows XP Mode can be customized for a specific Windows version. Right-click the *Windows XP Mode* Start button option and select *Properties > Compatibility* tab. A drop-down compatibility mode menu allows the choice of Windows versions starting with Windows 95. Note that an application installed in Windows XP Mode appears in both the Windows XP Mode application list (in the Windows Virtual PC folder) and in the Windows 7 application list.

Windows XP Mode is not available in Windows 8 or 10 unless you upgrade from Windows 7. If you are supporting a computer that uses Windows XP Mode on a Windows 7 computer that is being upgraded to Windows 8 or 10, you can use two methods to get to data saved in Windows XP Mode:

> Locate and mount the virtual hard disk created for Windows XP Mode (and that contains data from the older application).

> Copy the Windows XP Mode virtual hard disk to another Windows 7 computer and use Windows Virtual PC (that is not supported on Windows 8 or 10) to copy the data from the virtual machine.

Once you have determined whether the software is compatible with Windows, you may have to obtain software patches, upgrades, or buy a new version of the application. This is best done before installing Windows. Be proactive, not reactive—solve any problems you can *before* upgrading or installing any operating system. Such preparation is usually more work than the actual installation process, but any omitted steps will cost you more time in the long run.

CHAPTER 16

TECH TIP

Can't put one copy of an OS on two machines

The retail version of one copy of Windows cannot be installed on two computers at once. However, a retail version of Windows (as opposed to OEM versions) can be uninstalled on one computer and put on a different computer.

More Than One Operating System?

The second preinstallation step is to determine whether to install more than one operating system. This situation is often called a dual-boot or **multiboot** scenario. Both operating systems are best installed on separate drive partitions. Otherwise, you could use virtualization to install and use multiple operating systems (see Figure 16.3). Virtualization is covered later in this chapter.

FIGURE 16.3   Multiboot with virtualization

Planning Drive Space

The third step is to determine how large to make the drive partition (also called volumes) and select the file system to be used. One option is to place the operating system in one partition and data in a separate partition to make it easier to back up the data. Figure 16.4 shows this concept and you might want to review partitions in Chapter 7. Drives can be partitioned during the Windows installation process; otherwise, the entire drive is used by default.

During the installation process, when the partition is created, you are asked whether you want to do a full format or a quick format. A **full format** identifies and marks bad sectors so they will not be used for data storage. A **quick format** skips this analysis. Microsoft recommends doing a quick format if the hard disk has been formatted before and you are sure there are no damaged sectors. A best practice is that if the drive is an older drive, do a full format (but remember this is time-intensive); otherwise, do a quick format. A full format would also be done any time you want to ensure that data is erased, such as installing a hard drive that was removed from another computer.

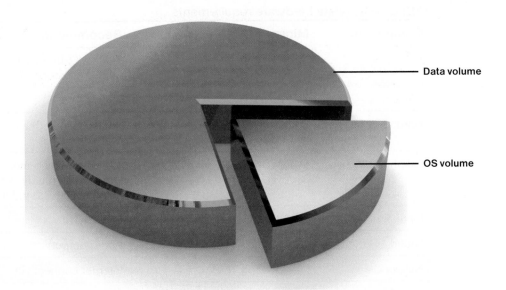

Data volume

OS volume

FIGURE 16.4   Partitioning (dividing) drive space during OS installation concept

The file system should be NTFS for the following reasons:

> Security (individual files can be protected using encryption)
> More efficient use of cluster space
> Supports file compression
> Supports larger hard drive partition sizes
> Includes journaling, which helps to rebuild the file system after a crash or power failure

An issue that is relevant only when upgrading is whether to convert an old FAT16 or FAT32 hard drive partition to NTFS. Once a partition is converted to NTFS, the partition cannot be changed. If you are unsure whether to convert a partition, leave it unchanged and later use the `convert` command to upgrade (without losing any data).

TECH TIP

Using the `convert` command

The `convert` command can be used to change a FAT(16) or FAT32 partition to NTFS and keep the data from the old partition. Use convert `x:` `/fs:ntfs` (where *x:* is the drive to be converted to NTFS). Remember, once you go to a higher file system, you cannot go back.

Hardware

The fourth step when installing Windows is to determine what computer hardware is installed. Table 16.3 lists the minimum and preferred hardware requirements for installing Windows Vista. Table 16.4 lists the requirements for most Windows 7/8/10 installations. One thing that might influence your choice of Windows version is the amount of memory supported by the different flavors.

TABLE 16.3   Vista hardware requirements

Component	Minimum	Recommended
Processor	800MHz, 32-bit or 64-bit multiple core	1GHz, 32-bit or 64-bit multiple core and dual processors
RAM	512MB	1GB
Hard drive space	20GB drive with a minimum of 15GB of available space	40GB drive with a minimum of 15GB of available space
Graphics	SVGA	128MB of video memory and support for DirectX9 or higher with WDDM driver, Pixel Shader 2.0 in hardware, 32-bit color
Optical drive	CD-ROM	DVD-ROM
Sound		Audio output
Network		Internet connectivity

*Note that a tablet PC or touch screen monitor is required to use Windows Tablet and Touch Technology that is available in these versions. The Windows BitLocker encryption tool requires a USB 2.0 flash drive or a TPM version 1.2 or higher motherboard chip.

TABLE 16.4   Windows 7/8/10 hardware requirements

Component	Minimum
Processor	1GHz
RAM	1GB (32-bit)/2GB (64-bit)
Graphics	Support for DirectX9 or higher with 1.0 WDDM driver
Hard drive space	16GB (32-bit)/20GB (64-bit)

Obtain Drivers

Once hardware has been verified, you have to obtain hardware device drivers specific to the operating system from the hardware manufacturer's website as the fifth step. The hardware device may have to be upgraded or replaced. Sometimes, older operating system drivers do work, but many times the older drivers do not work or they do not work properly. This is the cost of going to a more powerful operating system. The customer may also decide at this point not to upgrade, but to buy a computer with the desired version of Windows already installed instead.

The Microsoft Upgrade Advisor tool may have recommended getting updated third-party drivers for specific pieces of hardware. Drivers related to hard drives are especially critical to the installation process: hardware RAID, motherboard AHCI mode, SATA hard drive, and hard drives over 2TB. Obtain any of these hard drive-related drivers *before* the installation or you will not be able to install the operating system to that hard drive.

TECH TIP

If upgrading, ensure Windows updates are current

If upgrading to a new version of Windows, ensure the current version has the latest Windows updates.

Back Up Before an OS Installation

The sixth step is one of the most important: In any upgrade, hardware change, or software change, you must back up the user data. Whether you do a clean install or an upgrade, if the user has data on the computer, it must be backed up before starting the installation process. Also, before backing up the data, remove any unwanted files and/or applications that are no longer needed in order to free up hard drive space. Check and defragment the hard drive.

Once the data is backed up from a Windows system, create a system image backup and system repair disc.

Security Scan

The seventh step in planning for a Windows installation is to scan the system for viruses and malware (see Figure 16.5). Viruses can cause havoc on an upgrade or clean install. The next section provides more information about the most common types of viruses.

FIGURE 16.5   Do a security scan before an OS upgrade

Antivirus software causes issues

Whether doing a clean install or upgrade, disable the antivirus protection until after the installation. If possible, disconnect the computer from the network before disabling the software.

Disable Interfering Software

The last step in the preinstallation checklist is to disable any power- or disk-management tools that are loaded. They can interfere with the new tools provided with Windows and can prevent an operating system from installing. Some security applications including a firewall can interfere with an operating system upgrade as well.

An operating system upgrade or installation can be affected by other software. For example, some antivirus software can be set to load into memory when the computer boots and runs continuously. The antivirus software can prevent the upgrade or patch (service pack) from installing. Other types of software that can prevent an operating system from being upgraded are power management and disk management software/tools. Disable these utilities and applications before attempting an operating system installation or upgrade.

Installation/Upgrade of Windows

After completing all the preinstallation steps, you are ready to install Windows. The installation process is easy if you performed the preinstallation steps. Labs at the end of the chapter guide you through a clean installation (one where no other operating system is on the machine), an upgrade of 7, an installation of 8, and an installation of Windows 10. The number one piece of advice to heed is to do your installation/upgrade research first. The number of possible problems will be greatly reduced.

A simple explanation of the installation covers three phases.

> In the first phase of an installation (sometimes called the Windows Preinstallation Environment or Windows PE), a selection must be made about whether to upgrade or perform a clean installation, the product key must be entered, the time, date, region, and language settings set, and a basic hardware check including available disk space must be accomplished. The computer then restarts.

> After the restart, the second phase begins. During this process, a partition to install Windows can be chosen and setup files are copied to the partition.

> The third phase begins. During this portion, devices are installed, the Administrator password is entered, questions about Windows Updates and such are answered, and the operating system is created. The system restarts a final time and the logon screen is presented.

Part of the installation process is to select the type of network: home, work, or public. Computers on a home network can be a part of a HomeGroup or workgroup. Computers on a company network can see and share information with other work computers but cannot create or join a HomeGroup by default. With a public network, a computer attaches to an unsecure network, as in a restaurant or bookstore. Your computer is not visible to other computers by default when the public network option is chosen. (Table 16.5 shows these types.) Note that you can bypass the network configuration and configure it later. Networking is covered in more depth in Chapter 14.

TABLE 16.5 Network types

Network type	Description
Workgroup	Normally found in a Windows XP home network or small business. You can configure Vista/7 for this type, but file and print sharing are not automatically enabled as they are with a Windows HomeGroup.
HomeGroup	Normally created in a Windows 7, 8, or 10 home or small business environment that automatically turns on file and print sharing. Note that computers with Windows Vista7 Starter or Home Basic can join a HomeGroup but not start one. All Windows 7 and higher operating systems can join the HomeGroup.
Domain	A corporate environment in which users authenticate with a centralized user ID and password. Whatever machine the user goes to, the user ID and password would be the same if the computer has been configured to be on the domain.

Corporate Windows Deployment

Corporate computer installations are much more involved than any other type of deployment. Computers are installed in bulk instead of one at a time, as in a home or small business. The computers are frequently the same model and have the same software installed.

Disk imaging is common in the corporate environment. Disk imaging software makes an exact copy (a binary copy) of the files loaded on the hard drive. The copy is then pressed to an optical disc or an external drive, or put on a network drive to be copied and deployed onto other computers.

Companies need automated installation tools to help with the corporate Windows deployment process. Tools that can help with this are the Windows System Preparation (Sysprep) tool, imaging software such as Symantec Corporation's Ghost program, Microsoft's Setup Manager, Windows System Image Manager (SIM), and Microsoft Deployment Toolkit (SIM). An image can be created and deployed to multiple computers. Table 16.6 describes some of these tools.

TABLE 16.6   Corporate computer deployment tools

Tool	Description
Sysprep	When a prototype computer has Windows, Windows updates, all drivers, and applications installed, Sysprep can remove the security identifier (SID)—a unique number assigned to a computer by a network domain controller as well as other unique information such as the computer name or network domain. The computer is then imaged and the image is deployed to other computers. A third-party utility such as Symantec Ghost Walker or Microsoft's `newsid.exe` can be used to reassign the SIDs after the drive image has been deployed.
SIM (System Image Manager)	Used to create and configure answer files, install applications, apply service packs and updates to an image, and to add device drivers. After the Windows `unattend.xml` answer file is created, you can use the file to answer the installation questions as the files are downloaded from a share or server on the network. SIM is part of the Windows Automated Installation Kit (AIK).
WDS (Windows Deployment Services)	Uses the corporate network(s) to deploy Windows-based operating systems, drivers, updates, and applications using a network-based installation.
MDT (Microsoft Deployment Toolkit)	A GUI shell to make Windows deployment easier. Tools such as USMT, Application Compatibility Toolkit (ACT), Microsoft Assessment and Planning Toolkit (MAP), and the volume licensing application are inside the MDT shell.

When making a Windows image, you have to remove the unique identifiers from the computer before deploying the image to the other computers. This would include a computer name, security identifier (SID), a network domain, and so on. You must also reset or re-arm the Windows activation clock if a single activation key is used. By not doing this, you are prompted for the Windows product key as soon as the computer boots. By re-arming the activation clock, you have a 30-day (Windows 7)/90-day (Windows 8/10) grace period before having to re-enter the product key.

CHAPTER 16

TECH TIP

Three re-arms with Windows

There is no limit to the number of times a computer can be re-imaged, but there is a limit to how many times a computer can be re-armed or have the Windows activation clock reset. You can use the Sysprep tool or the `slmgr -rearm` command to reset the re-arm count. To see how many times the computer has been re-armed, use the `slmgr /dlv` command.

To send corporate computer images across a network, a variety of methods can be used, as shown in Table 16.7

TABLE 16.7   Corporate computer deployment methods

Method	Description
PXE boot (preboot execution environment)	Many computers have a PXE boot option that can be modified to search for the network device that has the computer image. Other programs can be manually configured with the network device information. In either case, the computer finds this network device and obtains an image.
LTI (lite touch installation)	An image can be deployed with little interaction using the MDT. Windows software, drivers, and updates are added to a network share and configuration files are created. Burn the boot images to optical media. Boot the destination computer with the boot image, and the installation files are pulled across the network and installed without further intervention.
Unattended installation or **ZTI** (zero-touch installation)	The MDT is used with Microsoft's Configuration Manager to image a computer without having to touch the remote computer. Other software can also be used.
Remote network installation	A server or network share has the created image that is accessed and deployed to a computer on a remote network. Network bandwidth is affected and this may interfere with normal business operations. For this reason, remote installations are commonly done during light network usage time or during off hours.

When deploying Windows in the enterprise, licensing is handled a bit differently. Larger businesses buy a volume license key (VLK). Two other choices are MAK or KMS. With Multiple Activation Key (**MAK**), the Internet or a phone call must be used to register one or more computers. This method has a limited number of activations, but more licenses can be purchased. The Key Management Service (**KMS**) method is used in companies with 25 or more computers to deploy. Technical support staff can also use a deployment tool that allows automating product key entry and customizing disc installation images, so the computer users are not prompted for a key the first time they use a software package. KMS is a software application installed on a computer. All newly installed computers register with the server that has KMS installed. Every 180 days, the computers are re-activated for the Windows license. Each KMS key can be used on two computers up to 10 times.

TECH TIP

Be responsible

A technician is responsible for ensuring that any computer deployed has an antivirus application installed and that the application is configured to receive virus signature updates. Educate users about viruses and what to do if a computer gets one.

Verifying the Installation

In any upgrade or installation, verification that the upgrade is successful is critical in both home and business environments. After an upgrade has been done, verify that all applications still function. After a new installation has been completed, ensure that all installed hardware is detected by Device Manager (covered in the "Adding Devices" section).

TECH TIP

Reinitialize antivirus software

If the antivirus software were disabled through BIOS/UEFI and through an application, re-enable it after the operating system installation is complete. Verify that all settings are in accordance with the user requirements and departmental/organizational standards.

Troubleshooting a Windows Installation

Installation problems can be caused by a number of factors. The following list shows the most common causes of problems and their solutions:

> **Incompatible BIOS:** Obtain compatible BIOS/UEFI BIOS, replace the motherboard with one that has a compatible BIOS, or do not upgrade or install the higher Windows version.

> **BIOS needs to be upgraded:** Upgrade (flash) the BIOS/UEFI BIOS.

> **Incompatible hardware drivers:** Obtain the appropriate Windows version drivers from the hardware manufacturer (not Microsoft).

> **Incompatible applications:** Obtain upgrades from the software manufacturer, use Windows XP Mode, the Program Compatibility Wizard, a dual-boot environment, and virtualization (covered later in this chapter).

> **Minimum hardware requirements have not been met:** Upgrade the hardware. The most likely things to check are the CPU and RAM.

> **A virus is present:** Run an antivirus program and remove the virus.

> **Antivirus software is installed and active. It is halting the installation/upgrade:** Disable through BIOS/UEFI and through the application. Restart the Windows installation and re-enable when the operating system installation is complete.

> **Preinstallation steps have not been completed:** Go back through the list.

> **The installation disc or download is corrupt (not as likely as the other causes):** Try the disc in another machine and see if you can see the contents. Check if a scratch or dirt is on the disc surface. Clean the disc as necessary. Redownload the operating system.

> **Incorrect registration key:** Type in the correct key to complete the installation. The key is located on the disc or disc case, or in an email.

> **The Windows installation process cannot find a hard drive**: It is most likely due to a SATA drive being used and a driver is not available for the controller. Download the driver, put on a flash drive, or use a software program such as NTLite to create a custom installation disc that includes the downloaded driver.

> **A STOP message occurs when installing a dual-boot system:** Boot from the Windows installation disc rather than the other operating system.

> **The computer locks up during setup and shows a blue screen of death (BSOD):** Check the BIOS/UEFI and hardware compatibility. Also, if an error message appears, research the error on the Internet.

> If you get an **NTLDR is Missing** error on a Windows Vista, 7, 8, or 10 computer during the installation process, try the clean install process over again. The newer operating systems use BOOTMGR, not NTLDR like Windows XP did.

CHAPTER 16

TECH TIP

Installation halts

Try removing any nonessential hardware, such as network cards, modems, and USB devices, and start the installation again. Reinstall the hardware after Windows is properly installed.

> **A message appears during setup that a device driver was unable to load:** Obtain the latest device drivers that are compatible and restart the setup program.

> **After upgrading Windows, the computer freezes**: Boot to Safe Mode and check Device Manager (covered in the "Adding Devices" section) for errors. **Safe Mode** is a boot option that starts the computer with a minimum set of drivers. If no errors are present within Device Manager, disable the following devices if present: video adapter, sound card, network card, USB devices and controller (unless keyboard/mouse is USB), optical drive, modem, and unused ports. Enable each disabled device one at a time until the blue screen appears. When the problem device is known, obtain the appropriate replacement driver.

> **Windows 7 0xC004F061 activation error**: This is caused by a Windows 7 upgrade product key being used on a computer that does not have a version of Windows that can be upgraded to Windows 7. If the drive was formatted *before* starting the installation, the upgrade product key cannot be used. Install Windows 7 with the current Windows running or if you want to format the hard drive and an upgrade version is being used, do so through the Windows 7 installation process: Boot with the upgrade DVD, click *Custom (advanced)*, and select *Drive options (advanced)*.

During the Windows installation there are log files created that can be helpful for resolving installation issues. Table 16.8 outlines important log files for each version of Windows and a brief description of what they contain.

TABLE 16.8 Windows Setup log files

Log file location	Description
X:\Windows\setupapi.log	Device and driver changes, service pack, and hotfix installations
X:\$Windows.~BT\Sources\ Panther\setupact.log	Setup actions performed during the install
X:\$Windows.~BT\Sources\Panther\setuperr.log	Setup installation errors
X:\$Windows.~BT\Sources\ Panther\PreGatherPnPList.log	Initial capture of devices information
X:\$Windows.~BT\Sources\Panther\miglog.xml	User directory structure and SID information
X:\Windows\Inf\setupapi*.log	Plug-and-play devices and driver information
X:\Windows\Inf\setupapi.app.log	Application installation information
X:\Windows\Panther\PostGatherPnPList.log	Device information after the online configuration

Dual-Booting Windows

Sometimes, users like to try a new operating system while keeping the old operating system loaded. A computer that has two operating systems loaded is known as a dual-boot computer. If Windows is installed on an NTFS partition, only a Windows version that supports NTFS can access files in the partition, if required.

TECH TIP

When dual-booting, install the oldest operating system first

When multiple operating systems are installed, use a separate partition/volume for each operating system and install the oldest operating system first.

When installed, the Windows Boot Manager window appears, showing the older version of Windows as Earlier Version of Windows and the newly added Microsoft Windows Vista, Windows 7, or both. From this screen, you can choose the older operating system with the Earlier Version of Windows option or accept the default option. These settings can be changed using the following process: Open *Windows Explorer/File Explorer* > right-click *Computer/This PC* > *Properties* > *Advanced system settings* link > from the Startup and Recovery section, select *Settings* button. The default operating system can be selected from the drop-down menu in the System startup section. The time to display the options in the Windows Boot menu is selectable in seconds as well as via an enable/disable checkbox.

The boot settings can also be changed using the `bcdedit` command: *Start > All Programs > Accessories >* right-click *Command Prompt* and select *Run as administrator >* type `bcdedit /?` to see a list of switches. In Windows 8/10 click the *Start* icon and simply type in CMD; then right-click the *Command Prompt* and select *Run as administrator* and then type `bcdedit /?`.

Table 16.9 lists tips for working with the `bcdedit` command and when error messages occur. Sample error messages follow:

> The Windows Boot Manager (Bootmgr) entry is not present in the Boot Configuration Data (BCD) store.
> The Boot/BCD file on the active partition is damaged or missing.

TABLE 16.9 bcdedit tips

`bcdedit` **command**	**Description**
`bcdedit /export` *`filename`*	Used to export the current BCD registry in case of mistakes.
`bcdedit /import` *`filename`*	Used to restore the BCD from a backup file.
`bcdedit /enum`	Used to view the existing boot menu entries.
`bcdedit /default` *`id`*	Used to configure the default entry. `id` is the identifier for the specific Windows version; for example, if the older version of Windows XP is shown as `{ntldr}`, the command would be `bcdedit /default {ntldr}`.
`bcdedit /timeout` *`seconds`*	Used to change the time the menu displays.

CHAPTER 16

Several options exist when repairing the boot configuration data (BCD) store.

> Use Windows Startup Repair option (covered later in the chapter).
> Rebuild the BCD store using the `bootrec` tool.
> Rebuild the BCD store using multiple `bcdedit` commands. See the Microsoft support website for more details.

Virtualization

As introduced in Chapter 11, PC or client virtualization is the process of running multiple operating systems on a single host machine. PC virtualization allows older software to be executed in a protected environment, new software to be tested in an environment that won't affect the normal operating system, and two operating systems (or more) to be installed that cannot see or interfere with one another.

TECH TIP

You have to buy the OS license

A common misconception about virtualization is that you don't have to buy both operating systems when two operating systems are installed. This is not always true. Depending on the virtual software used, if you want to install Windows Vista in one virtual machine and Windows 7 in another virtual machine, and Windows Server 2012 R2 in a third virtual machine, you would have to purchase all three operating systems.

The hypervisor, as mentioned in Chapter 15, is like an orchestra conductor for virtualization. The hypervisor is responsible for managing and overseeing the operation of the virtual machines (VMs). The hypervisor oversees RAM, hard drive space, and processor(s) that are shared between the VMs. There are two types of hypervisors: Type 1 and Type 2. A **Type 1 hypervisor** is also known as a native hypervisor because the operating system runs on top of the hypervisor. Examples of Type 1 hypervisors include VMware's ESXI and Microsoft's Hyper-V. A **Type 2 hypervisor**, also known as a hosted hypervisor, runs on top of a host operating system such as Windows 7. VMware Player, Oracle VirtualBox, and Windows Virtual PC are examples of Type 2 hypervisors.

TECH TIP

Enable virtualization in the BIOS

You may have to enable virtualization in the BIOS before you can install any type of virtualization software (including Virtual PC/Windows XP Mode) on the computer.

Most Windows versions today have some type of emulation or virtualization included with them. Windows XP Mode is a program downloaded from Microsoft for Windows 7 that uses emulation to run Windows XP applications in a protected environment. Windows Virtual PC allows other Windows operating systems (none older than XP) to run inside Virtual PC as well as one-click access to Windows XP Mode, which is integrated into Virtual PC. Table 16.10 lists the requirements for Virtual PC, which is Microsoft's emulator. An emulator is when you try to make one operating system behave like an older or different one.

TABLE 16.10   Microsoft Virtual PC requirements

Component	Requirement
Processor	1GHz
RAM	2GB
Available hard disk space	15GB per virtual machine

Microsoft provides the Hardware-Assisted Virtualization Detection Tool to quickly determine if your computer can support Windows XP Mode or Virtual PC:

> If the message "There is no hardware-assisted virtualization support in the system" appears, then virtualization is not supported.
> If the message "Hardware-assisted virtualization is disabled" appears, then virtualization has not been enabled in the BIOS.

Windows 8 and 10 Pro and higher versions have replaced Virtual PC with Hyper-V, a virtualization product. See Table 16.11 for the minimum hardware requirements for the Hyper-V client.

TABLE 16.11   Microsoft Client Hyper-V requirements

Component	Requirement
Processor	At least 1 x64 CPU
RAM	4GB

TECH TIP

You can still get a virus

A common misconception about virtualization is that you don't have to worry about security because you are in a "protected" environment. This is not true. The protection is that one operating system is protected from the other operating system, but all virtual machines are susceptible to viruses and security attacks. Install the appropriate protection and see Chapter 18 for more information on security.

Each virtual machine can connect to a network using one of two basic options:

> **Internal network:** The internal network option allows a particular VM access to other virtual machines that (may be on a different computer or another VM on the same computer) connect to the same network.
> **External network:** The external network option allows a particular VM access to a different (external) network from within the VM. In a college environment, for example, if the student computer can access the Internet and that same computer is configured for virtualization, a VM on that student computer can be configured for the external network and have access to the Internet.

To enable Windows Hyper-V, access the *Programs and Features* Control Panel > select *Turn Windows features on or off* > enable the *Hyper-V* checkbox (see Figure 16.6) > *OK*. Labs 16.2 through 16.4 show basic virtualization configuration. Virtualization has been popular with network servers but now applies to desktop operating systems as well. Technicians are expected to be familiar with virtualization because it is found in both home and corporate environments.

CHAPTER 16

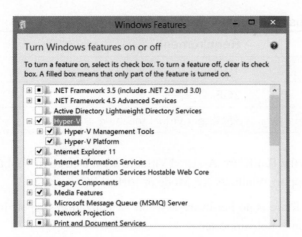

FIGURE 16.6   Enable Hyper-V in Windows 8

Reloading Windows

Sometimes, it's necessary to do a **repair installation** (sometimes called an in-place upgrade or a reinstallation) of Windows, such as when Windows does not start normally or in Safe Mode, or when it has a registry corruption that cannot be solved with System Restore (covered later in the chapter). Hopefully the user has backed up existing data. The installation process should not disturb the data, but there is always a chance that it could.

Windows Resource Protection (WRP) protects operating system files, folders, and important registry keys using access control lists (ACLs). Changes made to a monitored file or folder cannot be changed even by an administrator unless he takes ownership and adds the appropriate access control entities (ACEs). Any file that cannot be repaired by System File Checker (SFC) can be identified with the following administrator command:

```
findstr /C:"[SR] Cannot repair member file" %windir%\logs\cbs\cbs.
log>sfcdetails.txt
```

Use Notepad or the `edit` command to open the file (normally located in the C:\Windows\ System32 folder). From an elevated command prompt, the following commands grant administrators access to the protected files, so they can be replaced:

> `takeown /f filename_including_path` (where `filename_including_path` is the full path and filename of the problem file).
> `icacls filename_including_path`/GRANT ADMINISTRATORS:F
> Then use the `COPY` command to replace the file with a known good one:

> `copy source_filename destination_filename` (where the source and destination are the full path and file).

TECH TIP

Use SFC to solve system file problems

Use the `sfc /scannow` command as an administrator to replace any protected system files that have problems.

Newer Windows versions do not normally have to be reloaded as often as older Windows versions did. Modern Windows computers are more likely to have a computer that allows booting from a flash drive. The operating system image can be copied or downloaded and placed on the flash drive. Change the BIOS/UEFI settings to boot from the flash drive, and the installation process starts. Windows has great tools that help with startup problems, such as a corrupt registry and missing or corrupt boot configuration files. These tools are covered later in this chapter.

> **TECH TIP**
>
> **All existing system restore points are removed when Windows is reinstalled**
>
> After Windows has been installed, no preexisting restore points are kept. You should ensure that the System Restore utility is enabled and back up your data after Windows is installed. You should also apply any service packs and patches after the reinstallation is complete.

Windows Updates

Almost daily, new vulnerabilities are found in every operating system. Windows has a method called Windows Update or Automatic Updates for upgrading the operating system. To configure Windows Vista, 7, and 8 for automatic updates, locate the *System* Control Panel > *Automatic Updates* tab. Windows 10 by default does automatic updates.

> **TECH TIP**
>
> **What is the difference between a patch, a service pack, and a hotfix?**
>
> A **patch** is an update to an operating system. Microsoft releases patches when they are needed for emergency fixes to vulnerabilities and routinely about once a month. A **service pack** is a group of patches; it makes it easier to install one update rather than a large number of separate patches. A **hotfix** has one or more files that fix a particular software problem. Use the systeminfo command to see what hotfixes have been applied.

One way to access Windows Update settings for Vista and 7 is from the *Start* button > *All Programs* > *Windows Update* > *Change Settings*. To access this setting in Windows 8, access the *System and Security* Control Panel > *Windows Update* > *Change Settings*. In Windows 10 the update settings have been moved out of the Control Panel to the new *Settings* menu. To access the update settings in Windows 10, access *Settings* > select *Update and Security*.

From this window in Vista, only two options are available: (1) Use recommended settings and (2) install important updates only. The recommended settings option automatically updates and installs updates classified as Important and Recommended. This setting is a best practice for security reasons. The second setting automatically downloads and installs only updates that are classified as Important by Microsoft. For fine-tuning, technicians should always use the *Windows Update* Control Panel in Vista and 7, which offers more options. Figure 16.7 shows the options available from Windows 7.

> **TECH TIP**
>
> **Windows notification update icon**
>
> In the taskbar notification area, an icon appears when an update has been downloaded and is ready to be installed in Vista/7/8.

CHAPTER 16

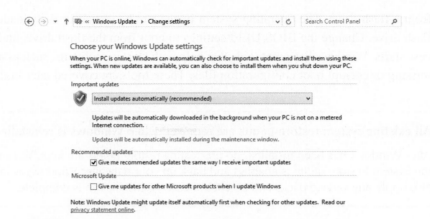

FIGURE 16.7 Windows Update options in Windows 7

The Windows Vista, 7, and 8 Control Panel settings pane has four options:

> Install updates automatically (recommended)
> Download updates but let me choose whether to install them
> Check for updates but let me choose whether to download and install them
> Never check for updates (not recommended)

Windows 10 has removed the options to disable checking and installing updates. In the settings menu you are presented with only the option to allow automatic updates or to be notified when to schedule a restart to install updates. By default (the automatic setting), a Windows 10 device does not restart when the user is using the computer.

TECH TIP

Updates must be installed

Depending on which option is chosen from the System Control Panel in Vista, 7, and 8, updates may be downloaded, but you may have to manually install them. Review the history and try to install the failed updates one update at a time. A system is not protected unless the updates are installed. This is also true for installed applications.

Other options are available such as how to handle recommended options, whether all users on the computer can install updates, and whether to receive updates for other Microsoft products such as Internet Explorer at the same time as receiving operating system updates (see Figure 16.8). If a newly installed service pack causes problems and must be removed, use the `spuninst.exe` command.

TECH TIP

You must be an administrator to change Automatic Update settings

You must be logged in as the Administrator or a user that is a member of the Administrators group to modify Automatic Updates settings.

To customize how the notifications appear in Vista, right-click the *Start* button > *Properties* > *Notification Area* tab > *Customize* button. In Windows 7, right-click the *Start* button > *Properties* > *Taskbar* tab > locate the *Notification area* section > *Customize* button > locate *Windows Update* option under *Icons* column > select the appropriate behavior. In Windows 8 and 10, the system tray notification option for Windows updates has been removed.

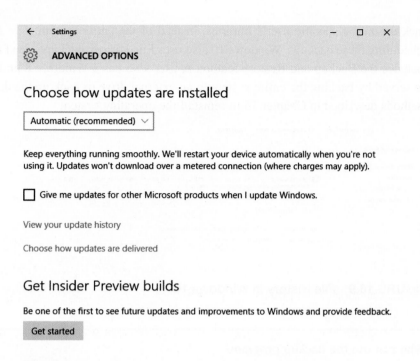

FIGURE 16.8   Windows Update options in Windows 10

Backing Up the Windows Registry and Data

The registry is a database that contains information about the Windows environment including installed hardware, installed software, and users. The registry should be backed up whenever the computer is fully functional and when any software or hardware changes are made.

TECH TIP

Back up the registry

The registry should be backed up and restored on a working computer *before* disaster hits. The time to learn how to restore the registry is not when the computer is down.

The registry can be backed up and restored several different ways:

> Using the `regedit` program
> Using the Backup utility (Vista/7)
> Using the System Restore tool (covered later in this chapter)

The `regedit` program enables you to export the registry to a file that has the extension `.reg`. The file can be imported back into the computer if the computer fails. The `regedit` program and the Backup utility both back up the entire registry.

The Backup utility was introduced in Chapter 15. In Windows Vista/7 the Backup utility is launched by accessing the *System and Security* Control Panel > *Backup and Restore*. The Backup utility is the preferred method for backing up the Windows registry, but in Vista/7 the full version of the Backup tool (the part that can back up the registry) is only available in Windows Vista/7 Business, Professional, Enterprise, and Ultimate versions. The Backup and Restore Control Panel can be used to schedule a backup at a specific type and frequency.

Windows 8 has tried to move away from the Backup and Restore utility in favor of the new File History backup feature, for quicker and smaller spaced backups. File History enables you to back up only a specific user's libraries, instead of the entire system. *File History* also supports scheduling these backups. Windows 10 also uses File History backups (see Figure 16.9), but it still includes the Backup and Restore feature. A user who has a Windows 8 or 10 system would best be served by backing the entire system to an external drive or back up the data and use one of the methods described in Chapter 15 to reinstall the operating system.

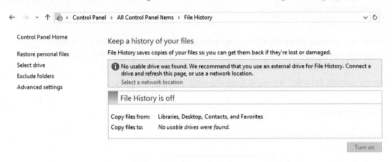

FIGURE 16.9   File History in Windows 10

To correct a problem with the system files, registry, or boot failure, you may also restore from a restore point. Restore points are created by System Restore any time a change happens to the system, such as installing a program or driver. Restore points can be reverted to by opening the System Restore application.

The Windows Vista and 7 Backup and Restore link can also back up the system state. This link can also be used to back up files and an entire disk image. To access this link, click the *Start* button > *Control Panel* > *System and Maintenance* (Vista)/*System and Security* (7) > *Backup and Restore* > *Create a system repair disc*.

Windows 8 will want you to do a File History backup, and if you had to recover the system, you would reinstall it and restore the File History. Windows 10, however, brought back the Backup and Restore feature from past versions of Windows and can be accessed by using the universal search bar on the Start menu and searching Backup and Restore (Windows 7), or by right-clicking the *Start* button > *Control Panel* > *System and Security* > *Backup and Restore (Windows 7)*.

Configuring Windows Overview

One of the most common windows used by technicians is the *Control Panel* window. A Control Panel is a method for configuring various components. Each Control Panel icon represents a Windows utility that customizes a particular part of the Windows environment. The number of Control Panels displayed depends on the type of computer and the components contained within the computer. Control Panels were explored in Chapter 15 and have been discussed throughout the book, but this chapter explores more in-depth tasks with them. Windows has two Control Panel views: *Classic* and *Category*.

With Windows 8, Microsoft tried moving away from Control Panels with the *Settings* option. Once *Settings* has been clicked, the options available from the PC settings window are ones that users would want. This frustrated technicians and users because Control Panels were not easy to find. Microsoft changed this in Windows 8.1 and provided a link within the *PC settings window* to access Control Panel (see Figure 16.10).

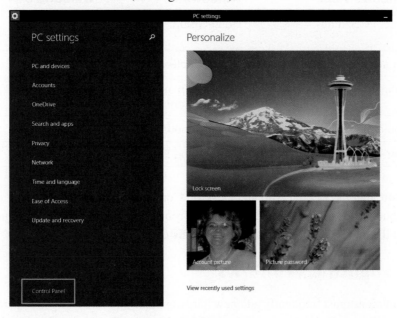

FIGURE 16.10   PC Settings in Windows 8.1

Windows 10 further improves on the *Settings* option but totally redesigned the categories, as shown in Figure 16.11. The options within each category contain much of what is in Control Panels, but it will take a while before technicians move to using these especially because all tools are not within these categories.

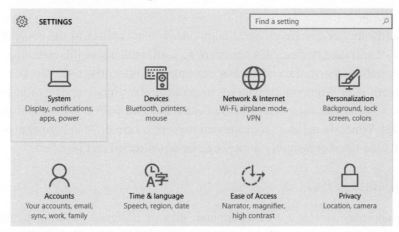

FIGURE 16.11   Settings in Windows 10

Technicians must know which Control Panel category to use for changing a computer's configuration. Review the Control Panels from Chapter 15. This chapter builds upon that knowledge.

Windows has some configuration options that are unique to those particular operating systems. A technician should be familiar with these differences. More labs at the end of this chapter help familiarize you with several Control Panel categories. Table 16.12 shows the unique Control Panels by operating system.

TABLE 16.12   Windows unique Control Panels

Windows Vista	Windows 7	Windows 8	Windows 10
Tablet PC Settings	HomeGroup	Add Features to Windows 8.1	Security and Maintenance
Pen and Input Devices	Action Center	Family Safety	
Offline Files	RemoteApp and Desktop Connections		
Problem Ports and Solutions	Troubleshooting		
Printers	Devices and Printers		

Note that the RemoteApp and Desktop Connections Control Panel link can be used to access a computer such as a workplace computer from a remote place. The configuration requires a URL from the network administrator to make this connection.

Configuring Windows

Technicians must frequently add new hardware and software using the operating system. Windows has specific tools for these functions. Using the correct procedure is essential for success. The following sections highlight tasks a technician commonly performs:

> Adding devices
> Removing hardware components
> Adding a printer
> Installing/removing software

Hardware devices are physical components that connect to the computer. A **device driver** is a piece of software that enables hardware to work with a specific operating system. Device drivers are operating system-dependent. For example, a printer driver that works with Windows Vista may not work with Windows 10. Not all manufacturers provide updates for the newer operating systems. Some device drivers are automatically included with Windows and are updated continuously through Windows updates. A technician must be aware of what hardware is installed into a system so that the latest compatible drivers can be downloaded and installed.

Adding Devices

Plug-and-play devices are hardware and software designed to automatically be recognized by the operating system. These devices include USB, IEEE 1394, ExpressCard, and PCI/PCIe devices. USB, eSATAp, IEEE 1394, and ExpressCard devices can be added or removed with power applied. Adapters are installed and removed with the computer powered off and the power cord removed.

Devices and Printers Control Panel

The Devices and Printers Control Panel is used to view, install, remove, and manage wired and wireless devices such as mice, multimedia devices, printers, and speakers. When a device is added, Windows 8 and 10 now search the Windows Store to see if there is an app from the device manufacturer, whereas Windows Vista and 7 simply defaulted to searching for a driver. If an installed device isn't detected, use the *Add a device* or *Add a printer* link to initiate the process.

Device Manager

Devices recognized or at least sensed by the OS are shown in a **Device Manager** utility (see Figure 16.12). Device Manager is a technician's best friend when it comes to adding devices to a Windows computer.

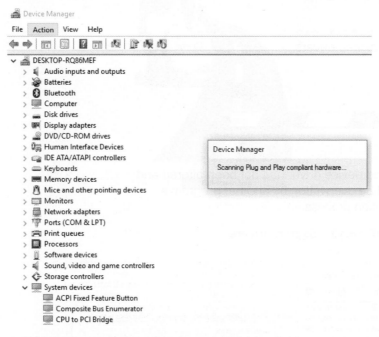

FIGURE 16.12 Device Manager in Windows 10

The keys to a successful device installation follow:

> Possessing the most up-to-date device driver for the specific installed operating system
> Following the directions provided by the device manufacturer

Windows autodetects when a new device is installed or connected and attempts to find the appropriate driver. Windows searches driver packages that are stored in an indexed database. The drivers are stored in the *Windows\System32\DriverStore\FileRepository* folder. All driver files that are not part of the operating system must be imported into this folder before the driver package can be installed. Drivers created for earlier Windows versions may need to be updated.

TECH TIP

Installing a device driver requires Administrator rights

Remember that if the operating system cannot configure a device and prompts for a device driver, you must have Administrator rights to install the driver.

Some Windows device drivers use digital signatures, which is sometimes called driver signing or a signed driver. The digital signature confirms that the device driver for a particular piece of hardware has met certain criteria for WHQL (Windows hardware quality lab) tests and is compatible with Windows. Digital signatures are required for 64-bit kernel mode drivers in Windows. Figure 16.13 shows this concept, and Figure 16.14 shows a signed driver in Device Manager.

Use `verifier.exe` from a prompt to verify installed drivers especially if you have unexplained computer problems.

Use `sigverif.exe` to see signed drivers.

A signed device driver has not been altered and cannot be overwritten by another program's installation process.

FIGURE 16.13   Signed drivers

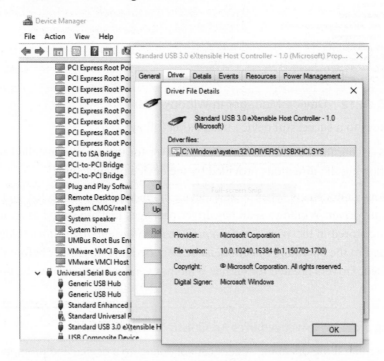

FIGURE 16.14   Signed driver in Device Manager

From the Windows Advanced Boot Options menu (press F8 on startup), select the *Disable Driver Signature Enforcement* option if you suspect that Windows is not booting because of an unsigned driver. The computer boots normally and not in Safe Mode.

To modify how drivers are handled in Windows Vista, access the *System and Maintenance* Control Panel > *System* > *Advanced system settings* link > *Continue* > *Hardware* tab > *Windows Update Driver Settings* button. The three options available follow:

> Check for drivers automatically (recommended)

> Ask me each time I connect a new device before checking for drivers

> Never check for drivers when I connect a device

For Windows 7, 8, and 10 use the *System and Security* Control Panel > *System* > *Advanced system settings* link > *Hardware* tab > *Device Installation Settings* button. The options available in Windows 7, 8, and 10 follow:

> Yes, do this automatically (recommended)
> No, let me choose what to do
> Always install the best driver software from Windows Update
> Install driver software from Windows Update if it is not found on my computer
> Never install driver software from Windows Update

In Windows, most hardware is automatically detected. In Vista, there is no Add Hardware Control Panel, but in Windows 7 there is an *Add a device* link in the Hardware and Sound Control Panel group. This *Add a device* link was moved to the Devices and Printers group in Windows 8 and 10. Lab 16.12 explains how to do this.

Audio Devices

Device Manager can also help when troubleshooting sound. Locate and expand the *Sound, video and game controllers* category. Verify a sound card or integrated sound processor is shown. Right-click or tap and briefly hold on the sound card > select *Properties*. Verify the device status on the *General* tab.

The Sound Control Panel is used to adjust volume output and manage sound-related devices that include speakers, headsets, microphones, and integrated audio devices. From the *Sound* Control Panel, select the *Playback* tab to configure and manage headsets and speakers. Use the *Recording* tab to view the properties of and manage microphones and headset microphones. The *Sounds* tab can be used to select a sound scheme and test particular sounds. The *Communications* tab can be used to filter unwanted sounds. Refer to Chapter 8 for sound troubleshooting tips.

Display/Display Settings

Chapter 9 covered video technologies and configuration, but now take a moment to review tweaking video settings because so much time is spent looking at computer output. The *Display* Control Panel is used to adjust the size of text on the screen (without changing resolution), control and configure multiple monitors, adjust the resolution if someone has set it to a suboptimum setting, and configure the refresh rate. From within the *Display* Control Panel, use the following options to configure video output:

> **Adjust resolution:** Ensure the correct display is chosen if multiple displays are used. Use the *Resolution* drop-down menu to select a resolution and see the recommended resolution. Use the *Orientation* drop-down menu to select whether the display is shown as landscape or portrait. There are also landscape/portrait (flipped) options that are for displays that can be turned upside down for others to view such as in a counselor's or salesperson's office. If a user's screen is upside down, this is where you go to change it.
> **Advanced settings:** Used to view the properties, memory, refresh rate, and color settings (number of bits or depth of the color). Sometimes includes a *Troubleshoot* button or tab.
> **Calibrate color:** Used to configure a display for the best color when set to its best (native) resolution.
> **Change display settings:** Same options as adjust resolution. This screen is also where multiple monitors can be seen and rearranged.
> **Adjust ClearType text:** A series of questions designed to make your text easier to read.
> **Custom DPI:** Adjust the size of text.

Troubleshooting a Device That Does Not Work or Is Not Detected

Use Device Manager to view installed hardware devices, enable or disable devices, troubleshoot a device, view and/or change system resources such as IRQs and I/O addresses, update drivers, and access the driver roll back option. The **driver roll back** option is available in all versions of Windows. This option allows an older driver to be reinstalled when the new driver causes the device to not start, be detected, or not work properly.

> **TECH TIP**
>
> **Driver roll back requires Administrator rights**
>
> You must have Administrator rights to access or use the *driver roll b*ack option in Device Manager.

If the device driver has not been updated, driver roll back is not possible, and a message screen displays stating this fact, and the driver roll back button in Device Manager will be disabled. The troubleshooting tool should be used instead to troubleshoot the device. Lab 16.10 details how to use the driver roll back feature.

Sometimes, Windows installs the wrong driver for an older device or adapter. To uninstall or disable such a driver in Device Manager, right-click or tap and briefly hold the device icon and select *disable*. Sometimes, the computer must reboot, and Windows reinstalls the wrong driver (again). The solution to this is to disable the device and then manually install it. Lab 16.11 illustrates how to disable a device.

To manually install a device:

Step 1. Open the *Device Manager* utility.

Step 2. Expand categories as needed to locate the device for which the driver is to be installed. Note that to display hidden devices in Device Manager, select *Show hidden devices* from the *View* menu option.

Step 3. Right-click the device name and select *Update Driver Software*.

Step 4. Select *Browse my computer for driver software*, select *Let me pick from a list of device drivers on my computer*, and select *Have Disk*. Select the *Browse* button to locate the extracted files. Click the *.inf* file designed to work with the device.

Step 5. Follow the dialogs that continue to update the driver. If you are prompted with a warning about driver compatibility, you can click *No* and continue installing the driver. You can always remove it or roll back the driver if it does not install correctly or if it does not work.

If an `.inf` file cannot be found in a folder from your driver download, look in subfolders or other folders that might hold the file. You could always download the driver again and pay attention to the folder name in which the driver is stored. If there are multiple `.inf` files in the folder, you may have to try them one at a time until you find the one that works with your hardware. Always reboot Windows after a driver installation, even if the system does not prompt for a reboot.

If you cannot install a device driver by its installation program, you can try running the installation program in compatibility mode, using administrative credentials, or manually installing it using Device Manager.

To run the driver installation program in compatibility mode, locate and right-click or tap and briefly hold the executable file for the driver installation program. The same can be done for an application. Select *Properties > Compatibility* tab > enable the *Run this program in compatibility mode for* checkbox > select a version of Windows that it is known to work on (see Figure 16.15) > click *OK*. Double-click or double-tap the executable file icon to start the installation process.

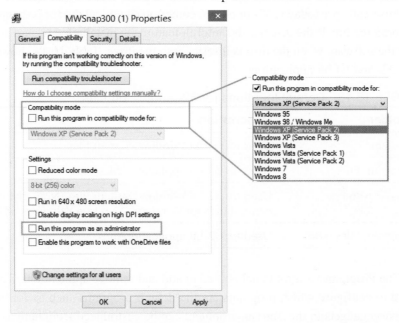

FIGURE 16.15   Installing a driver/application in compatibility mode

To use administrative credentials, locate the executable file used to start the driver installation process. Right-click the filename and select *Run as administrator*, as shown in Figure 16.15. Provide the Administrator password if required. Click *Continue*. Follow the installation instructions as normal.

TECH TIP

Too many tray icons

Many programs and some drivers place icons in the notification area (the area to the right of the taskbar). If they are not used, remove them. In Vista/7, right-click *Start* button > *Properties* > *Notification Area* tab > *Customize* button. In Windows 8, select the up arrow in the notification area > *Customize*. In Windows 8 or 10, right-click or tap and briefly hold on an empty space in the taskbar > *Properties* > *Taskbar* tab > *Notification area: Customize* button.

More Troubleshooting—Using Wizards and Troubleshooting Links

Whenever a yellow warning icon appears next to a device within the Devices and Printers Control Panel, select *Troubleshoot* to open the Windows Troubleshooting Wizard. Windows Vista, 7, and 8 have the Windows *Action Center* Control Panel that can be used to view Windows Update information, maintenance and backup issues, access the *Troubleshooting* link to find and repair issues, and access *Recovery* (which is System Recovery). Windows 10 no longer has the Action Center Control Panel. Use the *Security and Maintenance* Control Panel to locate and use the same tools.

Installing/Removing Software

No computer is fully functional without software. One thing you should know about the newer Windows versions is that they may not support some of the older 16-bit software. Use the Program

Compatibility Wizard or download and use the Windows XP Mode virtual environment for older applications loaded in Windows Vista and Windows 7.

Most software today is 32- or 64-bit, comes on an optical disc or is downloaded, and includes an autorun feature. If the disc has the autorun feature, an installation wizard steps you through installing the software when the disc is inserted into the drive. Table 16.13 shows common locations for the 32- and 64-bit applications.

TABLE 16.13   Default locations for 32- and 64-bit files

Folder	Description
System32	Used for 64-bit Windows system files
Program Files	Used for 64-bit application files
SysWOW64	Used for 32-bit Windows system files (Note that the WOW in the folder name stands for Windows 32-bit on Windows 64-bit.)
Program Files (x86)	Used for 32-bit application files

The Programs Control Panel is used to add and remove applications. This Control Panel is also used to configure which programs are the default programs such as for email or a web browser. Desktop gadgets in the Aero environment can be customized from here as well.

TECH TIP

Launch an application

After an application is installed, launch the application by clicking the *Start* button > *All Programs* (*All apps* in Windows 10) or select the icon for the application (Windows 8) >, locate the application name, and click it.

Programs and Features

The *Programs and Features* Control Panel is the most commonly used subcategory under Programs because it is used to uninstall an application; enable or disable Windows features such as Games, Telnet, TFTP server, or TFTP client; view the version of a particular application; and access the *Program Compatibility* option to execute programs written for older Windows versions. Lab 16.13 illustrates these concepts.

Figure 16.16 shows the *Uninstall a program* link and displays all the currently installed applications. This link can do more than be used to uninstall an application. Select an application and up to three options appear at the top of the column as actions that can be taken: Uninstall, Change, or Repair.

Figure 16.17 shows the *Turn Windows features on or off* window. A check in the checkbox means that feature is enabled. A cleared checkbox means that option is not turned on.

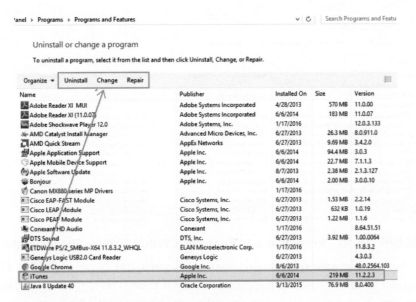

FIGURE 16.16   Programs and Features Control Panel > Uninstall a program window

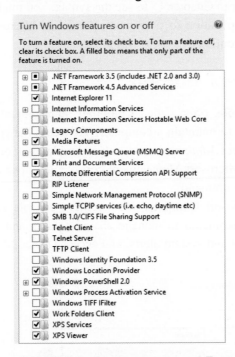

FIGURE 16.17   Programs and Features Control Panel > Turn Windows features on or off window

Figure 16.18 shows the *View installed updates* window. The Adobe Reader and Microsoft Windows updates show; scroll down to see more. Select a particular update and the *Uninstall* option appears at the top. Select *Uninstall* to uninstall a particular update that may be causing issues.

Refer back to Figure 16.15 to see the compatibility options. If an application or executable used to install a device driver displays a message that the software is incompatible with the current operating system, use this tab to make it work.

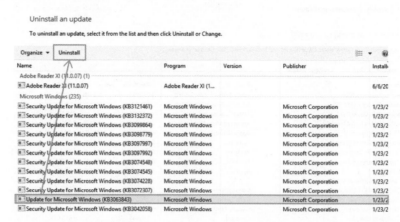

FIGURE 16.18   Programs and Features Control Panel > View installed updates window

Another software-related issue involves dynamic link libraries (DLLs). DLLs are reusable code that can be used by multiple applications. A DLL must be registered with the Windows registry to function. Sometimes, DLL registry links are broken and the DLLs must be reregistered using the `regsvr32.exe` command. Refer to Chapter 15 to see the syntax. You might also have to remove and then reinstall a particular application to fix a particular DLL. Microsoft has a database of DLLs to help with DLL version conflicts.

Microsoft Management Console

The **Microsoft Management console**, often called **Computer Management console**, holds snap-ins, which are tools that are used to maintain a computer. To access the console, use the *System and Security* Control Panel to select *Administrative Tools* > double-click or double-tap *Computer Management*. You can start the Microsoft Management console and open a saved console using the `mmc path\filename.msc` command.

Figure 16.19 shows the Microsoft Computer Management console screen. The Computer Management console allows a technician to manage shared folders and drives, start and stop services, look at performance logs and system alerts, and access Device Manager to troubleshoot hardware problems.

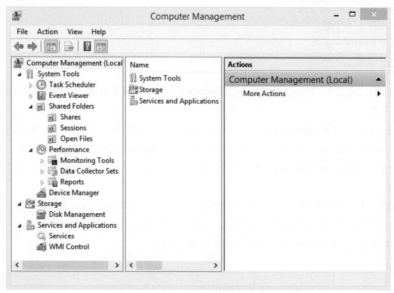

FIGURE 16.19   Computer Management console

Using Component Services?

You can use a particular snap-in called **Component Services** to view, configure, and administer the Component Object Model (COM) components, COM+ applications, and Distribution Transaction Coordinator (DTC). COM applications are a group of components within applications that were designed to work together. When deployed, Component Services can be used to track services and assess performance measures.

Computer Management Console

The Computer Management console is the mother lode of technical tools for the IT technician. The three major tool categories are System Tools, Storage, and Services and Applications. Expand the *System Tools* section to see some of the most technical utilities available to a technician. Expand the *Storage* section to find the Disk Management utility. The expanded *Services and Applications* section shows access to Services and WMI Control.

System Tools

The System Tools section includes Task Scheduler, Event Viewer, Shared Folders, Local Users and Groups, Performance (Windows 7 and higher), and Device Manager. Each of these tools is important when supporting Windows computers. Let's dive into each one.

Task Scheduler

Task Scheduler (`taskschd.msc`) enables you to plan and execute apps, scripts, and utilities on a regular basis. Look at Figure 16.20. Use the actions pane to create a new task, show what tasks are running, and import a task from another machine. If a company has an executable it wants to run at 2 a.m. every week on Wednesday or when a user logs on every time, Task Scheduler is the tool to use.

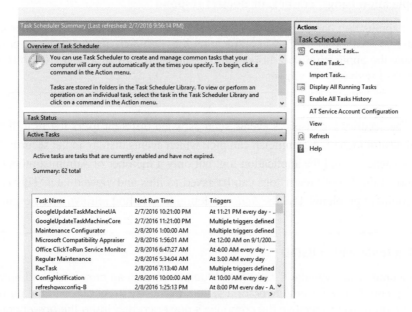

FIGURE 16.20   Task Scheduler

Event Viewer

Logs are created every time something happens within a Windows system, and Event Viewer is what you use to see them (see Figure 16.21). **Event Viewer** is a Windows tool used to monitor various events in your computer such as when a driver or service does not start properly. The Windows Event Log service starts automatically every time a computer boots to Windows. This service is what allows the events to be logged, and then Event Viewer is used to see the log.

FIGURE 16.21   Event Viewer

Access Event Viewer by selecting the *System and Maintenance* (Vista) or *System and Security* (Windows 7, 8, or 10) Control Panel > *Administrative Tools* > *Event Viewer*. The application log displays events associated with a specific program. The programmers who design software decide which events to display in the Event Viewer's application log.

> **TECH TIP**
>
> **Application hangs, crashes, or doesn't respond**
>
> If an application hangs, crashes, or shows a pin wheel and displays a "not responding" message, take a look at the Event Viewer application log. Research any messages or error codes found. Ensure the application does not need to be updated. Any proprietary crash screens should be researched within Event Viewer.

The security log displays events such as when different users log in to the computer (both valid and invalid logins). A technician can pick which events display in the security log. All users can view the system log and the application log, but only a member of Administrators can enable security log information. Event viewer logs can be saved as files and viewed later. This is especially useful with intermittent problems. Use the *Actions* section to save and retrieve saved event viewer log files.

> **TECH TIP**
>
> **What to do with a BSOD**
>
> Sometimes when Windows crashes, a blue screen with an error code and numbers appears on the screen. Check Event Viewer for a system event. Try to reboot with the power button, but it may require you to remove the computer's power cord, reinsert the power cord, and repower on the computer. Once the computer has been restarted, you can research the error message and problem on the Internet.

The most commonly used log is the system log. The system log displays events that deal with various system components such as a driver or service that loads during startup. The type of system log events cannot be changed or deleted.

Figure 16.22 shows the filters applied to see all system events. Figure 16.23 shows the results. Notice in Figure 16.23 how you can select a particular event. The *General* tab shows the gist of the error. Select the *Details* tab for even more details.

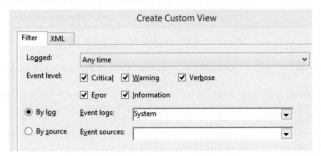

FIGURE 16.22   Event Viewer filter

FIGURE 16.23   Event Viewer filter results

Windows Vista and higher versions improved on Event Viewer by no longer having a 300MB storage limit, as in prior versions, by allowing Event Viewer information to be forwarded to a remote computer, and by allowing the collection of events from multiple remote computers. Windows Event Viewer has two types of logs: (1) Windows logs and (2) Applications and Services logs. Within the Windows Logs section, there are the traditional application, security, and system logs, along with two new ones: setup and forwarded events. Also, there is a new Applications and Services Logs section. Table 16.14 summarizes the types of things you might see in these logs. Event Viewer can display five different types of events. The events and related symbols are shown in Table 16.15.

TABLE 16.14   Windows Event Viewer logs

Major log category	Log	Description
Windows Logs	Application	Contains events logged by software applications. The company that writes the software applications decides what to log.
	Security	Contains events specified by administrators such as valid and invalid logon attempts and network share usage.
	Setup	Contains setup events logged by software applications.
	System	Contains Windows system events such as when a driver or service fails to load or start.
	Forwarded Events	Contains events from remote computers.
Applications and Services Logs	Vendor-specific	Contains logs from a specific application or Windows component. The logs can be one of four types: admin, operational, analytic, and debug. The admin log is for normal users and technical support staff. The operational event is used by technical staff to analyze a problem. The analytic and debug events would more likely be used by the application developer. Both create a large number of entries and should be used for a short period of time only.

TABLE 16.15   Event Viewer symbols

Symbol	Type of event	Description
Lowercase "i"	Information	Normal system operations such as the system being initialized or shut down.
Exclamation mark	Warning	An event that is not critical, but one that you might want to take a look at. The system can still function, but some feature(s) may not be available.
X	Error	A specific event failed such as a service or device that failed to initialize properly.
Yellow key	Success Audit	You can audit a specific event. If successful, this symbol appears.
Yellow lock	Failure Audit	When you specify a specific event to audit and the event fails, the yellow lock appears. An example is when you are auditing a system login and someone tries to log in that does not have a valid username or password, then the system creates a Failure Audit event.

TECH TIP

What to do if the Event Viewer log is full

Start *Event Viewer* > *Action* menu option > *Properties* > *General* tab > *Clear log* button. The *Log Size* option may need to be changed to one of the following: *Overwrite events older than 0 days, Maximum log size,* or *Overwrite events as needed.*

Shared Folders

The Shared Folders tool is used to view shares, sessions, and open files. Shares can be folders that have been shared on the computer, printers, or a network resource such as a scanner. Sessions list network users who are currently connected to the computer as well as the network users' computer names, the network connection type (Windows or Apple Macs, for example), how many resources have been opened by the network user, how long the user has been connected, and whether this user is connected using the Guest user account. Open files are files that are currently open by network users.

In the left Computer Management window pane, expand the *Shared Folders* option and click the *Shares* option. The network shares appear in the right pane. Double-click any of the shares to view the Properties window. From this window, using the *Share Permissions* or *Security* tabs, permissions can be set for shared resources. Permissions are covered later in this chapter and in Chapter 18.

Local Users and Groups

The Local Users and Groups tool is only available in Windows Professional/Pro versions. It is used to create and manage accounts for those who use the computer or computer resources from a remote network computer. These accounts are considered local users or local groups and are managed from the computer being worked on. In contrast, domain or global users and groups are administered by a network administrator on a network server. Permissions are granted or denied to files, folders, and network resources such as a shared printer or scanner. Rights can also be assigned. Rights are computer actions such as performing a backup or shutting down the computer. Open the *Local Users and Groups* option by expanding the *Local Users and Groups* selection in the *Computer Management* window. Double-click or double-tap on the *Users* option and a list of current users displays in the right pane. Figure 16.24 shows an example of local users that have been created for a Windows 8 computer.

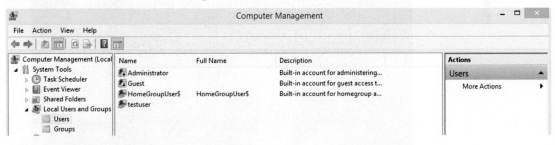

FIGURE 16.24   Local Users and Groups

Notice in Figure 16.24 that the Guest account has a small down arrow in the lower-right corner of its icon. This means the account has been disabled. Double-click the *Guest* icon. Look at the *Account is disabled* checkbox to see if the account is disabled. The box is checked by default, meaning that the Guest account is not available for use. To create a new user, click the *Action* menu option and select *New User*.

TECH TIP

Where are the local user settings?

Windows local user settings are found in the following folder: %*userprofile*%\AppData\Local (for example, C:\Users\Cheryl\AppData\Local). You might have to enable *Show hidden files* in Windows Explorer/File Explorer to see the AppData folder.

Windows has two basic types of user accounts available in the different Windows editions: Standard user and Administrator. The Administrator account has full control over the system, as it always has in Windows. By default, the Standard user cannot install most applications or change system settings. All users on the computer should have a Standard user account that is used for everyday use. Any account designated as an Administrator account should be used only to log on to the system to make system changes and install new software.

In the Windows Professional/Pro and higher versions, there are other types of user accounts that can be used for various security levels. These user groups are covered in Chapter 18, but one user group that should be mentioned here is Power Users. In older Windows versions (Windows XP and lower), users who were in the Power Users group had elevated permissions to perform common configuration tasks such as changing user-related Control Panel settings and changing the time zone. Today, the Standard user group has most of these permissions.

UAC

These two accounts are affected by a feature in Windows called User Account Control (UAC). UAC works with Internet Explorer/Edge, Windows Defender, and Parental Controls to provide a heightened awareness to security issues. A UAC message appears anytime something occurs that normally would require an administrator-level decision to make changes to the system. An application that has a security shield icon overlay is going to display a UAC prompt when executed. If a Standard user is logged in, a message appears stating that the task is prohibited, access denied, or that Administrator credentials must be provided and the Administrator password entered to proceed (see Figure 16.25). This is to protect users from themselves as well as software that is trying to change the system. Even if a person is logged in with an Administrator account, the UAC prompt appears to confirm the action that is about to be performed.

FIGURE 16.25 Administrator credentials required

The following configurations help with UAC:

> To configure a specific application to run in an elevated mode—meaning it has the administrator access token given to it or permission given to it to run—right-click the application and select *Properties > Compatibility* tab > under the Privilege level, select *Run this program as administrator > OK*.

> If a user demands that UAC be disabled, use the System Configuration window (`msconfig`) *Tools* tab. Select the *Disable UAC* option (Vista) or *Change UAC Settings*. Also, an individual account can be changed through the *Change security settings* (Vista)/*Change User Account Control settings* (Windows 7, 8, and 10) link from within the User Accounts Control Panel.

Device Manager

Device Manager was introduced in the "Adding Devices" section earlier in the chapter. Device Manager is used after installing a new hardware device to verify that Windows recognizes the device. Device Manager is also used to change or view hardware configuration settings, view and install device drivers, return (roll back) to a previous device driver version, disable/enable/uninstall devices, and print a summary of all hardware installed.

To verify a device is working properly, expand a Device Manager section. Double-click or double-tap and a device's *Properties* window appears. The *General* tab displays a message whether the device is working according to Windows. The number of tabs a device has depends on the device. Figure 16.26 shows the Device Manager window > *General* tab for a USB mouse as well as the *Driver* tab. The *Driver* tab is used to roll back the driver if an updated driver is installed and does not function properly. It also shows the current driver version. The *Driver* tab can be used to disable the device and uninstall the device driver.

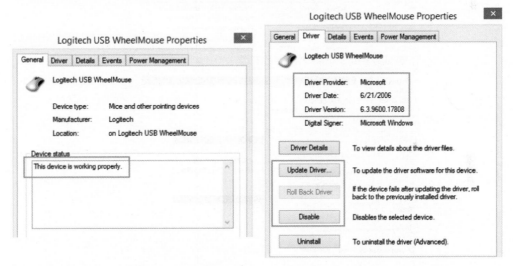

FIGURE 16.26 Device Manager > General and Driver tabs

Managing Storage

The *Storage* Computer Management category includes just the Disk Management tool. The *Disk Management* tool is used to manage hard drives including volumes or partitions. Drives can be initialized; volumes created; volumes formatted for FAT, FAT32, and NTFS; RAID configured; and remote drives managed. Chapter 7 introduced this utility, but let's review the basics again so that you will be prepared for the 220-902 CompTIA A+ certification. Figure 16.27 shows the Disk Management utility. Notice how the drive volumes display in the top window as well as at the bottom. Disks are numbered starting with 0 (Disk 0).

Figure 16.28 shows that you can right-click or tap and briefly hold on a particular drive on the far left and control the drive from there. The menu shown is one for a drive that is already in use and online. If a drive were showing a drive status other than online, actions can be taken from the context menu. See Chapter 7 for a list of conditions that can be seen.

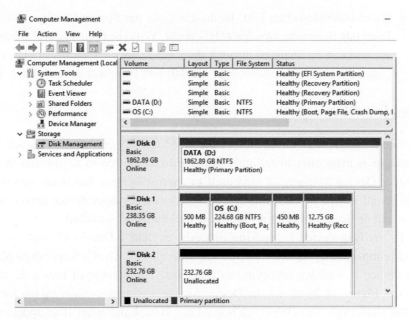

FIGURE 16.27   Disk Management utility

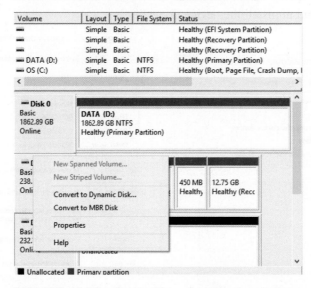

FIGURE 16.28   Controlling a particular disk

Figure 16.29 contains the context menu if you right-click or tap and briefly hold within a disk arrow such as within the slanted lines of the D: drive (Drive 0). Notice how you can delete, extend, or shrink a volume. You can also change the drive letter.

Figure 16.30 shows the commands available if you right-click or tap and briefly hold inside the unallocated space in Disk 2. Because the disk is currently a basic disk, only a simple volume can be created. When you create a volume, you are prompted to select a file system as well as assign a drive letter. See Chapter 7 for more information on volumes and partitions.

TECH TIP

All Windows disk management tools require Administrator rights

You must be a member of the Administrators group to perform any disk management tasks.

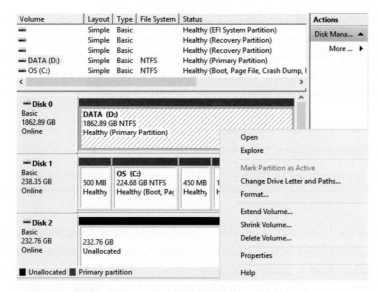

FIGURE 16.29   Managing an existing disk

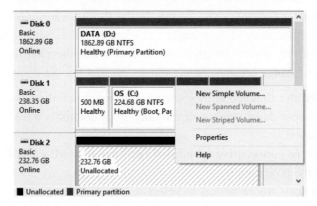

FIGURE 16.30   Managing drive space on a new drive

Disk Maintenance

Disk Management is now done for you automatically in Windows 7, 8, and 10 but not in Windows Vista. Now look at what tools are available to keep mechanical drives running smoothly.

Right-click or tap and briefly hold a drive letter in Windows Explorer/File Explorer > select *Properties*. On the *General* tab, you can access the *Disk Cleanup* tool (`cleanmgr /d drive`), which scans the drive volume to see what files could potentially be deleted. Refer to Chapter 7 for a review of this tool.

The *Tools* tab provides access to two additional tools: Error Checking and Optimize and defragment drive. The Error Checking tool (*Check* button) is extremely important to Windows Vista and Windows 7. The tool checked the drive for file system errors, bad hard drive sectors, and lost clusters. Error Checking is the equivalent of running the `chkdsk` command.

Windows 8 and 10 do not need the drive checked as often because certain disk errors are fixed immediately and do not need a utility executed to make that happen. In Windows 8, Microsoft integrated some of the new features of the Resilient File System (ReFS). **ReFS** is expected to eventually replace NTFS as the file system used on Microsoft Windows systems.

The other tool, *Optimize and defragment drive*, (*Defragment* button or `defrag` command), is used to place files in contiguous clusters on the hard drive. Files and folders become fragmented due to file creation and deletion over a period of time. A defragmented volume has better performance than a volume that has files and folders located throughout the drive. Microsoft automatically runs once a week, but you can always defragment the drive volume manually. You can also use the *Action Center* Control Panel to view the drive status quickly. If a drive status shows as anything but healthy, run a scan or repair the drive status.

> **TECH TIP**
>
> **Defragmentation requires Administrator rights**
> Note that only a member of the Administrators group can defragment a hard drive.

In Windows Vista and Windows 7, you might want to schedule disk cleanup using Task Scheduler. Access Task Scheduler, and from the *Action* menu, select *Create Basic Task* > name the task, and select *Next* >. Then select how often you want disk cleanup to run (the trigger). A good idea is weekly especially if the drive has been used for a while. Depending on the frequency, you have to select other options such as what day of the week you want the task to execute. On the *Action*, select the *Start a program* radio button. In the *Program/script* textbox, type `cleanmgr.exe` or browse to `C:\Windows\System32\cleanmgr.exe`. Select the *Finish* button.

In Windows 8 and 10, search for *Defragment* and select the *Defragment and optimize your drives* option. Select *Change settings*. Select the option that fits the computer user best:

> **Run on a schedule:** Enabled allows selection of how often the drive optimization executes.
> **Frequency:** Choose daily, weekly, or monthly. (The default is weekly and runs during Automatic Maintenance.)
> **Notify me if three consecutive scheduled runs are missed:** Clear this checkbox if the user does not want the notification.
> **Drives:** Select the *Choose* button to select drives. Note that SSDs are not supposed to be defragmented using the drive optimization routine and should be deselected by default.

Managing Services and Applications

The *Services and Applications* section can contain a multitude of options, depending on the computer and what is loaded. Common options include Telephony, WMI Control, Services, and Indexing Service. A frequently used option is *Services*. A service is an application that can be started using this window or configured so that it starts when the computer boots. By clicking the *Services* option, a list of services installed on the computer displays in the right window. Double-click or double-tap any service, and the service *Properties* window appears. From this window on the *General* tab, a service can be started, stopped, paused, resumed, or disabled on the local computer and on remote computers, but you must be logged on as a member of the Administrators group to change a service. Figure 16.31 shows the Computer Management console Services window and some examples of installed services.

If you double-click a service, you can use the *Recovery* tab to determine what happened when a service fails a first time, a second time, and even a third time. For example, if the print service fails the first time, a restart occurs. After the print service fails a second time, the print server can be restarted automatically. The third time the print service fails, a file that pages a technician can be executed.

FIGURE 16.31   Computer Management console—Services window

Data Sources (ODBC)

Open database connectivity (ODBC) is a programming interface that enables applications to access data from a database. Use the **Data Sources (ODBC)** administrative tool to select which particular application drive is associated with a particular type of file. Access the Data Sources (ODBC) Control Panel by searching for the *Administrative Tools* Control Panel > double-click or double-tap on *Data Sources (ODBC)*. Figure 16.32 shows the user data source name (DSN). Figure 16.33 shows the *Tracing* tab that can be used to create logs that help when applications misbehave.

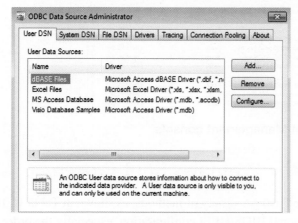

FIGURE 16.32   Data Sources (ODBC) Control Panel

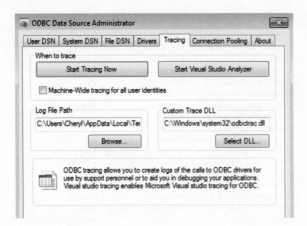

FIGURE 16.33 Data Sources (ODBC) Tracing tab

Print Management Console

The **Print Management** console is used to manage printers on Vista Business and higher versions and Windows 7, 8, and 10 Pro and higher versions. To access the console, use one of the following methods:

> Access the *System and Security* Control Panel > select *Administrative Tools* > double-click or double-tap *Printer Management*.
> Use the `printmanagement.msc` command.

Figure 16.34 shows the Print Management console window. On the left, expand *Custom Filters* to see all the printers, all drivers, the printers that show a not ready status, or printers that currently have print jobs. On the center screen is a list of printers in a home or small business environment. In the corporate environment, this would be more; plus you could use the *Print Servers* option in the left pane. See Chapter 10 for more information on installing and configuring print options.

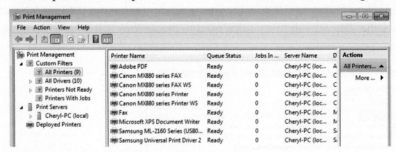

FIGURE 16.34 Print Management console

Overview of the Windows Boot Process

Windows can be booted using a variety of methods, as shown in Table 16.16. Some of these methods may require additional BIOS/UEFI configuration, especially the order in which the computer looks to devices for an operating system (boot order). Some of these options may not be supported.

TABLE 16.16   Windows boot options

Boot option	Description
Internal hard drive partition	Most common method used to boot Windows on a computer.
CD-ROM or DVD optical disc	Requires the Windows disc to be inserted into the drive. Used in troubleshooting scenarios if F8 cannot be pressed to reach the Advanced Boot Options menu.
USB	An operating system must be installed on the USB device, and the computer must support booting from USB; USB is available as a BIOS/UEFI option in the boot order.
External/hot swappable drive	Similar to USB in that it allows the operating system to boot from an external drive attached to the system.
SSD/flash drive	Popular in mobile devices.
Netboot	Enables Apple Mac computers to boot from the network.
PXE (preboot execution environment)	Boots from a computer image housed on a network device. Commonly used for booting a computer over a network.

The **system volume** is the active drive partition that has the files needed to load the operating system. The **boot volume** is the partition or logical drive where the operating system files are located. One thing that people sometimes forget is that the system volume and the boot volume can be on the same partition. These partitions are where certain boot files are located.

Every operating system needs specific files that allow the computer to boot. These files are known as **system files** or startup files. Table 16.17 shows the system files and their specific location on the hard drive.

TABLE 16.17   Windows system files

Startup filename	File location
`bootmgr.exe`	Root directory of system partition
`bootsect.dos` (needed with XP if the computer is a dual- or multi-boot system)	Root directory of system partition
`hal.dll`	`%systemroot%\System32`*
`ntoskrnl.exe`	`%systemroot%\System32`*
`winload.exe`	`%systemroot%\System32`*
`winresume.exe`	Root directory of system partition
`bcd`	`%systemroot%\Boot`
`system` (registry file)	`%systemroot%\System32\Config\System`
`winlogon.exe`	`%systemroot%\System32`
`winresume.exe`	

*%systemroot% is the boot partition and the name of the folder under the folder where Windows is installed (normally `C:\Winnt` or `C:\Windows`)

Reading about Windows files can be confusing because the file locations frequently have the entries *%systemroot%* and *%systemdrive%*. This is because computers can be partitioned differently. If you install Windows onto a drive letter (a partition or logical drive) other than the active partition (normally `C:`), the startup files can be on two different drive letters. Also, you do not have to take the default folder name of *Windows* to install Windows. To account for these different scenarios, Microsoft uses the *%systemroot%* to represent the **boot partition**, the partition and folder that contains the majority of the Windows files. *%systemdrive%* represents the root directory. On a computer with a single operating system, this would be `C:\`.

TECH TIP

Installing Windows with older operating systems

Be careful installing Windows with an older operating system. Windows overwrites the MBR, boot sector, and boot files. That is why few Windows versions are upgradable to Windows 7.

Speeding Up the Windows Boot Process

Windows can seem to take forever to boot (especially if you do not have an SSD), but there are things a technical person can do to help speed up the OS boot process (see Figure 16.35).

FIGURE 16.35   Fine-tune the startup process

The following tips can help reduce the time Windows takes to become operational:

> Configure BIOS/UEFI boot options so that the drive used to boot Windows is listed as the first option.
> Configure BIOS/UEFI for the fast boot option or disable hardware checks.
> If multiple operating systems are installed, use the `msconfig` utility *Boot* tab to reduce the boot menu timeout value.
> Remove unnecessary startup applications using the `msconfig` utility. (This links to Task Manager in Windows 8 and 10.)
> Have available hard disk space and keep the drive defragmented. Note that Windows is automatically configured to defragment the hard drive at 1:00 a.m. on Wednesday. If the computer is powered off, defragmentation occurs when the computer next boots.
> Disable unused or unnecessary hardware using Device Manager.
> Use Windows **ReadyBoost** to cache some startup files to a 256MB+ flash drive, SD card, or CF card. Right-click the device to access the *Properties* option and select the *ReadyBoost* tab.

Note that ReadyBoost does not increase performance on a system that boots from an SSD, so Windows (not Vista) disables ReadyBoost as an option when an SSD is in use.

> Use the *Administrative Tools* Control Panel > access *Services*. Change services that are not needed the moment Windows boots to use the *Automatic (Delayed Start)* option instead of *Automatic*.

Troubleshooting the Windows Boot Process

Troubleshooting the boot process where Windows will not load is sometimes easier than troubleshooting other types of problems that can occur within the operating system. If the computer locks, has a BSOD, or will not start, try the following:

> Remove the power cord and leave the computer powered down 1 to 2 minutes. Then, reinsert the power cord and power the computer on again. Make note of any beeps or error codes. Use these symptoms to start your troubleshooting process.

> Disconnect any unnecessary peripherals from the computer, leaving just the power and monitor connected to see if it starts. If it does, connect peripherals one by one while restarting to see which item is causing a boot to fail.

> Let Windows attempt to repair the computer.

> Determine the last thing that was done before the computer refused to boot. If possible, boot the computer to Safe Mode. Use the System Restore utility to bring the computer back to a date before the issue occurred. The following are some things to try and ascertain from the user:

>> Did a Windows Update just occur?

>> Was an application recently installed?

>> Was any hardware added recently?

>> Did any type of application update just occur?

> If on Windows 8 or 10, use the **Refresh Your PC** tool, which installs a new copy of Windows 8.1 or 10 but keeps the users' data, settings, and Windows 8.1 apps (if there is enough hard drive space to back them up).

> Boot to Safe Mode, and run the System File Checker (**SFC**) to replace missing or corrupt operating system files or load an appropriate graphics driver.

> Use the Last Known Good Configuration option from the Advanced Boot Options menu.

> For information on recovering the Windows OS, see Chapter 15.

> For information on troubleshooting storage devices, see Chapter 7.

Quite a few things can cause Windows to not boot into the graphical interface properly. For example, a nonbootable disk listed as the first boot device or media inserted into an optical drive (and it being listed as a boot device) can cause Windows not to boot. If none of the hard drives contain an active partition or if the hard drive's boot sector information is missing or corrupt (see Chapter 7), any of the following messages or events could appear:

> Invalid partition table

> Error loading operating system

> Missing operating system

> BOOTMGR is missing

> Windows has blocked some startup programs

> The Windows boot configuration data file is missing required information

> Windows could not start because the following file is missing or corrupt

Also note that if you receive a message that you have an invalid boot disk, a disk read error, or an inaccessible boot device, troubleshoot your hard drive and/or BIOS/UEFI settings.

TECH TIP

How to stop programs that automatically load at startup from running

To disable startup programs, hold down the Shift key during the logon process, and keep it held down until the desktop icons appear.

Windows has a plethora of tools and start modes that you can use to troubleshoot the system. If Windows boots but still has a problem, try to solve the problem without booting into one of these special modes. For example, if one piece of hardware is not working properly and the system boots properly, use Device Manager and the troubleshooting wizards to troubleshoot the problem. Another problem can be caused by an application that loads during startup.

If a startup problem appears to occur before the Starting Windows logo appears (**graphical interface fails to load**), the causes are typically missing startup files, corrupt files, or hardware problems. You can use the Windows `bootsect /nt60 all` (or a drive letter instead of `all` if multiple operating systems are installed) to manually repair the boot sector. The `bootsect.exe` file is available from the *Boot* folder of the Windows DVD and can be executed from within the Windows Recovery Environment (WinRE) covered next or from within Windows. If the Windows logo appears but there is a problem before the logon prompt appears, the problem is usually with misconfigured drivers and/or services. If problems occur after the logon window appears, then (1) look to startup applications (hold down the Shift key during startup) or (2) see if the `userinit.exe` file has issues. Use the *Advanced Boot Options* startup menu (press F8 during startup), and from a command prompt, use the `sfc /scannow` command to fix the userinit file.

WinRE

In Windows Vista and higher, the Windows Recovery Environment (**WinRE**) is accessed by booting from a Windows installation DVD > selecting the language parameters > selecting *Repair your computer* > selecting an operating system > selecting *Next*. Some computers have a recovery partition that would contain these tools or it is available through the Advanced Boot Options menu. See the computer documentation for details. The Advanced Options tools are shown in Figure 16.36 and explained in Table 16.18.

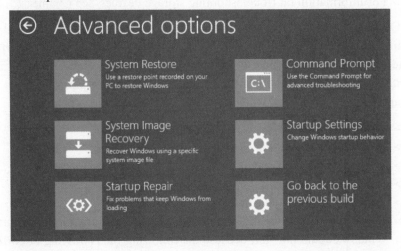

FIGURE 16.36 Windows 10 Advanced Options tools

TABLE 16.18   WinRE tools

Tool	Description
Startup Repair	Analyzes a computer and tries to fix any missing or damaged system files or Boot Configuration Data (BCD) files. This tool can be run multiple times. After a single repair and system reboot, try the tool again (and again). The system could have multiple problems.
System Restore	Works like the System Restore utility in Windows but is used to return the system to an earlier time, such as before a service pack or update was installed and the system stopped booting.
Complete PC Restore (Vista)/ System Image Recovery	Available in Vista Business, Enterprise, and Ultimate and all versions of Windows 7 and higher to restore the contents of the hard drive from some type of backup media, such as another hard drive or DVDs.
Windows Memory Diagnostic Tool	Used to heavily test RAM modules to see if they are causing the system to not boot. Microsoft states that it is unlikely that repeating the test will result in a newly detected error. An extended test is available from the diagnostic menu.
Command Prompt	The Command Prompt option allows execution of any command-line program.
Startup Settings	This option takes you to the *Startup Settings* window, which contains many of the same options available through the *Advanced Boot Options* menu that appears when you press F8 during the boot process (and covered soon in this chapter).
Go back to the previous build (10)	An option to downgrade back to the original operating system that was upgraded to Windows 10. Note that this option is only available for 31 days after the Windows 10 upgrade.

If the computer shows Invalid boot disk, ensure that the BIOS/UEFI boot order settings are correct, no virus is installed, and that the first boot device has a valid operating system installed or on disc. Depending on the installed OS, you can also use `bootrec /fixmbr`, `bootrec /fixboot`. Use other `bootrec` command options if multiple operating systems are installed. Following is a breakdown of the commands you should try after using the Startup Repair option.

> `bootrec /fixmbr`: Used to resolve MBR issues; writes a Windows-compatible MBR to the system partition.
> `bootrec /fixboot`: Used if the boot sector has been replaced with a non-Windows boot sector, if the boot sector has become corrupt, or if an earlier Windows version has been installed *after* Windows was installed and the computer was started with the `ntldr` instead of `bootmgr.exe`.
> `bootrec /scanos`: Used when any Windows operating system has been installed and is not listed on the Boot Manager menu; scans all disks for any and all versions of Windows.

System Restore

Any hardware or software installation can cause a system not to boot or operate correctly. You can use the **System Restore** utility to return the system to an operable state so that you can try the installation again or determine a better method. The System Restore program makes a snapshot image of the registry and backs up certain dynamic system files. The program does not affect your email or personal data files. This program is similar to the *Last Known Good Configuration* Advanced

Boot Options menu item but more powerful. Each snapshot is called a **restore point**, and multiple restore points are created on the computer; you can select which one to use.

In Windows Vista, Windows 7, and Windows 8, restore points are created weekly and whenever a system update occurs. However, you can manually create a restore point at any time especially before performing an important upgrade or installation. A fixed amount of disk space is used for restore points. When new restore points are created, the older ones are removed automatically. System Restore is your number-one tool for solving problems within the operating system and registry. By default, automatic restore points are created only for the system drive (the drive where the OS is installed). In Windows 10, System Restore is disabled by default.

TECH TIP

BSOD after a Windows update

Windows updates include device driver updates. If the computer fails to boot after a Windows update, reboot the computer to WinRE Safe Mode, and use the System Restore tool to restore the registry to an earlier time so that the problem can be researched. If multiple updates were installed, try loading the updates one at a time.

Use System Restore if you suspect that the registry is corrupt. For example, if an application worked fine yesterday but today displays a message that the application cannot be found, you may have a virus, a corrupt application executable file, or a corrupt registry. Run an antivirus check first with updated virus definitions. If free of viruses, use the System Restore utility to roll back the system to yesterday or the day before this problem occurred. Sometimes, System Restore works best if executed from Safe Mode. If System Restore does not fix the problem, reinstall the application.

System Restore requires a file system of NTFS. Windows uses **Shadow Copy** technology, which uses a block-level image instead of monitoring certain files for file changes. Backup media can be optical discs, flash devices, other hard drives, and server storage, but not tape.

Access the window to configure System Restore by searching for the *System* Control Panel > *System Protection* link > *System Protection* tab. Figure 16.37 shows how you can select a specific date during the System Restore process. You can also select the *Show more restore points* checkbox at the bottom of the window to see more of them.

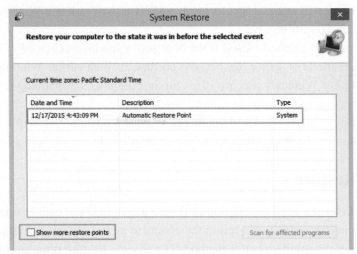

FIGURE 16.37 Windows System Restore

TECH TIP

You can run System Restore from a command prompt

If Windows does not load properly, you can execute System Restore from a command prompt with the command `%systemroot%\system32\rstrui.exe`.

Advanced Boot Options/Startup Settings Menu

When Windows does not boot properly, you can use the Windows **Advanced Boot Options** menu. Tools that troubleshoot Windows boot problems include Last Known Good Configuration, Safe Mode, Windows Recovery Environment, and Startup Repair. Table 16.19 gives a brief description of these options. Note that the options available vary depending on the version of Windows used.

TECH TIP

Press F8 during startup

When Windows is booting, press F8 to access the Windows Advanced Boot Options menu.

TABLE 16.19   Windows Advanced Boot Options window

Boot option	Description
Safe Mode	Uses a minimum set of drivers and services to start Windows; a commonly used option.
Safe Mode with Networking	Same as Safe Mode but includes a NIC driver.
Safe Mode with Command Prompt	Same as Safe Mode except Windows Explorer (GUI mode) is not used, but a command prompt appears instead. This option is not used often.
Enable low resolution video (640x480)	Used when Safe Mode does not work and you suspect the default video driver is not working.
Last Known Good Configuration	A popular option used when a change that was just implemented caused the system to not boot properly.
Debugging Mode	Debugging information can be sent through the serial port to another computer running a debugger program. This option is not used often.
Enable Boot Logging	Enables logging for startup options except for the *Last Known Good Configuration* option. The logging file is called ntbtlog.txt.
Disable automatic restart on system failure)	Prevents Windows from automatically rebooting after a system crash.
Disable driver signature enforcement	Allows drivers that are not properly signed to load during startup.
Start Windows Normally	Restarts Windows and attempts to boot normally.
Repair Your Computer	Used if system recovery tools are installed on the hard disk. Otherwise, these tools are available when booting from the Windows installation DVD.
Reboot	Restarts Windows.
Disable early launch antimalware protection (Windows 8 and higher)	Disables antimalware protection for booting. Sometimes, driver files might be flagged as malware and the system will not boot; disable this feature to boot the system to fix it.

CHAPTER 16

Use Safe Mode when the computer stalls, slows down, or does not work correctly, or problems are caused by improper video, intermittent errors, or new hardware/software installation. Safe Mode can start Windows with minimum device drivers and services. Software that automatically loads during startup is disabled in Safe Mode and user profiles are not loaded.

Safe Mode enables you to access configuration files and make necessary changes, troubleshoot installed software and hardware, disable software and services, and adjust hardware and software settings that may be causing Windows to not start correctly. The bottom line is that Safe Mode puts the computer in a "barebones" mode so that you can troubleshoot problems.

TECH TIP

When to use the Last Known Good Configuration boot option

Whenever the *Last Known Good Configuration* option is used, all configuration changes made since the last successful boot are lost. However, because the changes are the most likely cause of Windows not booting correctly, Last Known Good Configuration is a useful tool when installing new devices and drivers that do not work properly.

If Last Known Good Configuration does not work properly, boot the computer into Safe Mode. If Windows works, but a hardware device does not work and a new driver has been recently loaded, use the *driver roll back* option for the device.

TECH TIP

Accessing *Advanced Boot Options* with an SSD installed

On devices that boot so quickly that pressing F8 is an almost impossible task, Windows 8 and 10 have help. Access *Settings > Change PC Settings > Update and Recovery > Recovery >* under *Advanced startup,* select *Restart now >* after the restart, select *Troubleshoot* from the *Choose an option* window > select *Startup Settings.* (Note that if you do not have a *Startup Settings* option, select *Advanced options* to access it.) Select an option such as *Disable driver signature enforcement.*

System Configuration Utility

The **System Configuration utility** (msconfig command) is used to troubleshoot Windows startup problems by disabling startup programs and services one at a time or several at once. This graphical utility reduces the chances of making typing errors, deleting files, and other misfortunes that occur when technicians work from a command prompt. Only an administrator or a member of the Administrators group can use the System Configuration utility.

To start the System Configuration utility in Windows Vista/7, click *Start > Run* (or press the ⊞ *key plus* R) > type msconfig and press Enter. In Windows 8 and 10, type msconfig in the search textbox. Figure 16.38 shows the System Configuration utility *General* tab.

The first tab is *General.* The *General* tab has three radio buttons: Normal startup, Diagnostic startup, and Selective startup. *Normal startup* is the default option, and all device drivers and services load normally when this radio button is selected.

The *Diagnostic startup* radio button is selected when you want to create a clean environment for troubleshooting. When *Diagnostic startup* is chosen and Windows is restarted, the system boots to Safe Mode and only the most basic device drivers and services are active.

FIGURE 16.38   Windows 8 System Configuration utility: General tab

The *Selective startup* radio button is the most common troubleshooting tab on the General tab. When you choose *Selective startup*, you can pick which startup options load. Use the divide-and-conquer method of troubleshooting to find the startup file that is causing the boot problems. Start with the first checkbox, *Load system services*, and deselect the checkbox > *OK* and restart the computer. When you determine which file is causing the problem (the problem reappears), select the System Configuration tab that corresponds to the problem file and deselect files until the exact problem file is located.

TECH TIP

File fails to open

Check the *System Configuration* utility to verify if *Selective startup* is used and a file has been left unchecked. Otherwise, ensure the application is still installed and other files from this application open properly. Lastly, change folder options so that extensions can be seen, and verify that the file's extension has not been altered.

The *Boot* tab (see Figure 16.39) enables you to control and modify the Windows boot environment. The *Boot* tab functions include selecting the default operating system and the time allotted to wait for the default operating system to load if no other operating system is chosen from the boot menu in a multiple operating system situation. Notice how **Safe boot** and other options are available at the bottom of the window. Table 16.20 describes these options.

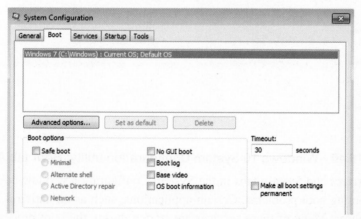

FIGURE 16.39   Windows 7 System Configuration utility: Boot tab

TABLE 16.20 System Configuration Boot Tab > Safe boot Options

Safe boot option	Description
Minimal	Boots in Safe Mode with only critical system services operational (no networking)
Alternate shell	Boots into a command prompt without GUI or networking
Active Directory repair	Boots into Safe Mode running critical system services and Active Directory
Network	Boots in Safe Mode GUI with networking enabled
No GUI	Does not display the Windows welcome screen
Boot log	Stores information about the startup process in the `ntbtlog.txt` file
Base video	Starts in VGA mode
OS boot information	Displays driver names during the boot process
Timeout	Controls how long the boot menu shows before the default boot entry executes

TECH TIP

Computer boots into Safe Mode for no obvious reason

Check the *System Configuration* utility *Boot* tab to see if some form of *Safe boot* is enabled.

Select the *Advanced options* button on the *Boot* tab to define the number of processors and maximum memory used to boot the system if you want less than the maximum (see Figure 16.40). When the *PCI Lock* option is enabled, it prevents Windows from changing I/O and IRQ assignments from those set by the system BIOS/UEFI BIOS.

FIGURE 16.40 Windows 10 System Configuration utility: Boot tab Advanced options

The *Services* and *Startup* tabs in the System Configuration window are also quite useful when troubleshooting boot problems. Certain applications, such as an antivirus program or the printer, run as services. Many of these services are started during the boot process. Use the *Services* tab (see Figure 16.41) to disable and enable these boot services. Enable the *Hide all Microsoft Services* option to view and manipulate third-party (non-Microsoft) services.

FIGURE 16.41 Windows 7 System Configuration utility: Services tab

The *Startup* tab enables you to enable and disable Windows-based startup programs. Figure 16.42 shows a sample Startup tab screen.

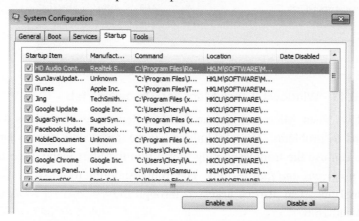

FIGURE 16.42 Windows 7 System Configuration utility: Startup tab

---

TECH TIP

The *Tools* tab is useful

The System Configuration *Tools* tab allows launching such options as Task Manager, Performance Monitor, and Internet Options from Internet Explorer—items that might need to be changed as a result of a startup issue. In Windows Vista and Windows 7 startup options are controlled in the *Startup* tab. However, in Windows 8 and 10, this tab links you to Task Manager (covered next) to manage startup items.

Task Manager

Task Manager is a Windows-based utility that displays applications currently loaded into memory, processes that are currently running, processor usage, and memory details. To activate Task Manager, right-click or tap and briefly hold an empty spot on the taskbar and select *Task Manager*. Task Manager is commonly used to kill (stop) programs that have quit responding. Task Manager is also a great way to get a graphical overview of how the system performs or which programs use a lot of memory. Labs 16.17 and 16.20 at the end of this chapter demonstrate these concepts. Figure 16.43 shows the Task Manager *Processes* tab (which was called *Applications* in Windows Vista and Windows 7), which has the list of applications currently running on a computer.

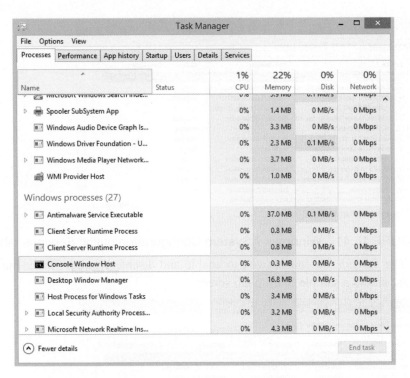

FIGURE 16.43 Windows 8 Task Manager: Processes tab

In Windows Vista, Microsoft has the Problem Reports and Solutions window that helps check for solutions to problems. These solutions can be saved and viewed later. In Windows 7 and higher, you can use the troubleshooting tool. From the Start menu, type `troubleshooting` in the *Search programs and files* textbox. The troubleshooting tool lists first in the output list. These Control Panel links can also be accessed through the `msconfig` *Tools* tab, as demonstrated in Labs 16.14 and 16.6.

TECH TIP

What to do if a system appears to lock up or is slow

Allow the system time to try to respond. If no response, access Task Manager using the Ctrl + Alt + Delete key sequence. Be prepared that it might take a bit of time for Task Manager to open. Access the *Applications* (Vista/7)/*Processes* (Windows 8/10) tab > locate and select the troublesome application > *End Task* button. Normally, if an application is causing a problem, the status shows the application as "not responding." If Task Manager never appears, power down the computer and reboot.

Troubleshooting a Service That Does Not Start

Some Windows services start automatically each time the computer boots. If one of these services has a problem, normally an error message appears during the boot sequence. You can use the System Configuration utility (`msconfig`) previously discussed to enable and disable startup services. You can also use Event Viewer to see if the service loaded properly. Another program that you can use is the Services snap-in used from the Computer Management tool. Or from a command prompt, type `services.msc`, and press Enter. The *Services* tool enables you to view what services have started and stopped and, if desired, enables you to stop a service. Open the Services snap-in (see Figure 16.44). Note the services list in alphabetical order.

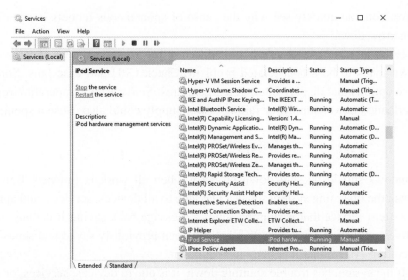

FIGURE 16.44   Windows 10 Services

Note that a similar window shows as a tab within *Task Manager*. The Service window opens, and on the General tab are the *Stop* and *Start* buttons that control the service. Double-click or double-tap any particular service. Figure 16.44 shows the iPod service. Through this window you can control whether the service starts automatically, manually, or is disabled. Notice in Figure 16.45 that because the iPod service is already running, the only action that can be performed is to stop the service.

FIGURE 16.45   Windows 10 controlling a service

Windows Reboots

One of the hardest problems to solve is an intermittent problem, and when Windows reboots spontaneously or shuts down spontaneously, a lot of different things could be the cause. Spontaneous reboots could be caused by a newly installed Windows update, newly installed application, or newly updated driver. A corrupt device driver could also be the culprit, but that is hard to find. An Internet search on your specific hardware device might speed up the troubleshooting process.

A spontaneous reboot can also be caused by a virus or malware. See Chapter 18 for more on those security issues. Other hardware issues could be the RAM, processor, video card, and hard drive. You can quickly see why the cause of spontaneous reboots is one of the hardest problems to narrow down.

However, a spontaneous reboot is different from a spontaneous shutdown. A spontaneous shutdown tends to be a heat-related problem. Check CPU and case fans. Some BIOS/UEFI menus have options that display internal temperatures. Start noting temperature readings. A failing CPU, overloaded power supply, or failing power supply could also cause a spontaneous shutdown.

Shutdown Problems

Windows should be shut down properly when all work is finished. Before Windows can shut down, the operating system sends a message to all devices, services, and applications. Each device or system service that is running sends a message back saying it is okay to shut down now. Any active application saves data that has not been previously saved and sends a message back to the operating system that it is okay to shut down.

If the system has trouble shutting down, it is due to devices, services, or applications. The most common problem is an application that does not respond. When this happens, open Task Manager. Manually stop any applications that show a status of not responding. You may also click any other applications and stop them to see if they are causing the problem. Sometimes, a program does not show a status of not responding until you try to manually stop the application from within Task Manager. If a single application continually prevents Windows from shutting down, contact the software manufacturer to see if there is a fix or check online.

TECH TIP

Try the restart option instead of the shutdown option

If you cannot stop the problem application or determine whether the problem is a service or hardware, try restarting the computer versus shutting down. After the computer restarts, try shutting down again. As a last resort, use the computer power button to power the computer off. Even that sometimes does not work and in laptops the battery might have to be removed.

For problems that deal with Windows services, boot the computer into Safe Mode and then shut down the computer. Notice whether the computer had any problems shutting down. If the process works, use the System Configuration window *General* tab *Selective startup* radio button with the *Services* tab to selectively disable services. Because there are so many services loaded, you might try the divide and conquer method: Disable one-half of the services to narrow the list.

A device does not cause a shutdown problem frequently, so eliminate services and applications first. Then, while working on the computer, notice what devices you are using. Common devices are video, hard drive, optical drive, keyboard, and mouse. Boot to the Advanced Boot Options menu by pressing *F8* during booting or use the *Advanced Options > Startup Settings* in Windows 8 or 10. Select *Enable boot logging*. When the system boots, locate the `ntbtlog.txt` file in the Windows folder. You may have to set folder options within Windows Explorer/File Explorer to list the file and access it. Verify that all your devices have the most up-to-date drivers loaded and that the drivers are compatible with the installed version of Windows.

Sometimes, USB or IEEE 1394 FireWire ports can stop a computer from shutting down or powering off. Check the event logs to see if any device did not enter a suspend state. A feature called USB selective suspend allows the Windows hub driver to suspend a particular USB port and not affect the other USB ports. This is particularly important to laptops, netbooks, and ultrabooks because of power consumption. Suspending USB devices when the device is not in use conserves power. If this is causing the problem, this default behavior can be modified using the *Power options* Control Panel link and accessing the *Advanced power settings*.

Monitoring System Performance

It is important for a technician to understand how a computer is performing and to analyze why a computer might be running slow (see Figure 16.46). To do that, a technician must know what applications are run on the computer and their effects on the computer resources. A technician must also monitor the computer's resource usage when problems occur, change the configuration as needed, and observe the results of the configuration change.

FIGURE 16.46   Slow performance

Utilities commonly used to monitor system performance include Task Manager, Performance Logs and Alerts, Reliability Monitor, and Performance Monitor. Sometimes, a computer seems sluggish. The most common cause of a slowdown is that the computer's resources are insufficient or an application is monopolizing a particular resource such as memory. Other causes of slowdowns include a resource that is not functioning properly or is outdated such as a hard drive; a resource that is not configured for maximum performance and needs to be adjusted; or resources such as hard drive space and memory that are not sharing workloads properly and need adjustment.

Viewing system performance when a problem occurs is good, but it is easier if the normal performance is known. A baseline can help with this. A **baseline** is a snapshot of computer performance during normal operations (before it has problems). Task Manager can give you an idea of what normal performance is. Windows Performance Monitor and Reliability Monitor tools are better suited to capturing and analyzing specific computer resource data.

TECH TIP

When do I need to do with a baseline?

A baseline report is needed before a computer slowdown occurs.

Using Task Manager to Measure Performance

Although Task Manager has been discussed in a previous section, how to use it to monitor computer performance was not discussed. Task Manager is the easiest and quickest way for anyone to quickly and visually see how the computer is performing. Access *Task Manager* and select the *Performance* tab. Task Manager immediately starts gathering CPU and memory usage statistics and displays them in graph form in the window, as shown in Figure 16.47.

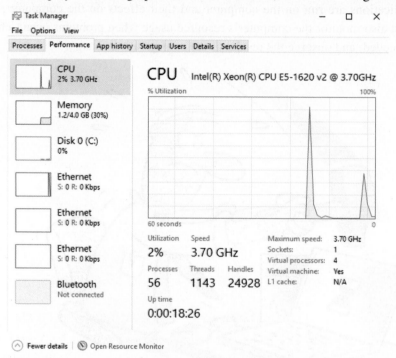

FIGURE 16.47   Task Manager: Performance tab, CPU

TECH TIP

What to do if you think memory is the problem

You can add RAM; create multiple paging files when multiple hard drives are installed in the system; manually set the paging file size; run one application at a time, but don't use Aero (Vista/7); close unnecessary windows; upgrade or add another hard drive; delete unused files; and defragment the hard drive.

CPU Usage shows the processor usage percentage or what percentage of time the processor is working. Actually, the percentage of time the processor is running a thread is a more accurate statement. A thread is a type of Windows object that runs application instructions. The window on the right is a graph of how busy the processor is over a period of time.

In Windows Vista and Windows 7, there was a snapshot of statistics regarding memory at the bottom. In Windows 8 and 10, you must use the *Memory* option on the left to see these statistics. If you think the page file for virtual memory (see Chapters 6 and 7 for more information on using hard drive space as RAM) is too small, you can adjust it with the following steps:

Step 1. In Vista, search for and access the *Performance and Maintenance Control Panel*. In Windows 7, 8, and 10, search for and access the *System* Control Panel > *System Protection* > *Advanced* tab > *Performance* section *Settings* button.

Step 2. Select the *Advanced* tab.

Step 3. In the *Virtual Memory* section, look at the total size of the paging file. Select the *Change* button, deselect the *Automatically manage paging file size for all drives* checkbox, and you can make adjustments, as shown in Figure 16.48.

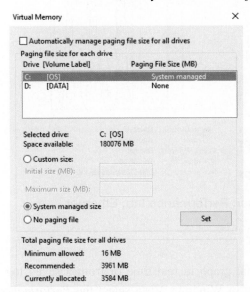

FIGURE 16.48   *Windows 10 manually configure page file (virtual memory) size*

The second window on the left in Windows Vista and Windows 7 displays memory usage at the current moment. The graphic on the right is memory usage over time. To see how much memory an individual process is using, use the *Processes* tab and locate the program executable file. The CPU and memory usage display in separate columns on the *Processes* tab. Windows 8 and 10 offers disk and network columns as well.

Memory is a frequent bottleneck for computer performance issues. You can also use Task Manager to see the total amount of RAM installed and how much RAM is available. Look in the *Physical Memory* information section of the Task Manager *Performance* tab to see this information.

Task Manager also has the *Networking* tab, which displays as a network interface under the Performance tab in Windows 8 and 10 that is useful to technicians. The *Networking* tab shows a graph of network performance for a particular network interface including Bluetooth. Figure 16.49 shows the Task Manager *Performance* option for an Ethernet card.

The Task Manager *Users* tab shows users that are logged on to the computer and the specific performance statistics for CPU memory, disk, and network for that particular user. This is probably one of the least used Task Manager tabs in either the corporate environment or home. However, if multiple people are logged on, one of them might have a particular application or service running that is causing the machine to slow down.

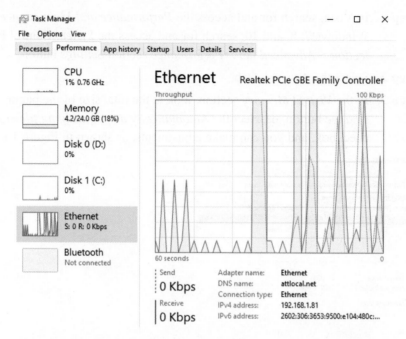

FIGURE 16.49   Task Manager: Performance tab, Ethernet

Performance Monitor

Performance Monitor is a visual graph in real time or from a saved log file providing data on specific computer components. In Windows Vista select the *Performance Monitor* option from the left pane in the *Reliability and Performance* tool. In Windows 7 and higher, use the *System and Security* Control Panel > *Administrative Tools* > double-click *Performance Monitor*. Inside Performance Monitor, counters are used. A **counter** is a specific measurement for an object. Common objects include cache, memory, paging file, physical disk, processor, network interface, system, and thread. Select the + (plus sign) in Performance Monitor to select various counters. At the bottom of the window is a legend for interpreting the graph including what color is used for each of the performance measures and what counter is used. Table 16.21 shows common counters used while within Performance Monitor. Figure 16.50 shows an example of the Performance Monitor.

TABLE 16.21   Performance Monitor counters

Computer component	Object name	Counters
Memory	Memory	Available Bytes and Cache Bytes
Hard Disk	Physical Disk	Disk Reads/sec and Disk Writes/sec
Hard Disk	Logical Disk	% Free Space
Processor	Processor	% Processor Time (All Instances)

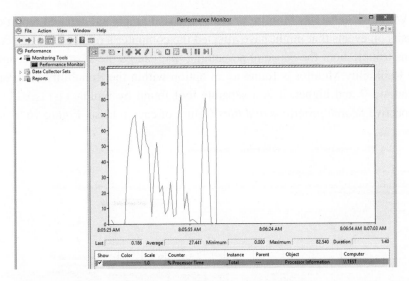

FIGURE 16.50   Windows Performance Monitor

Resource Monitor

The Windows **Resource Monitor** (previously found on the main page of Windows Vista's *Performance Monitor* option) is a nice graphical tool that requires little work but shows the main components of a system. Access the tool by selecting the *Open Resource Monitor* link from within the Performance Monitor window or access the *System and Security* Control Panel > *System* > *Performance Information and Tools* link at the bottom of the left panel > *Advanced tools* > *Open Resource Monitor*. Figure 16.51 shows the Resource Monitor.

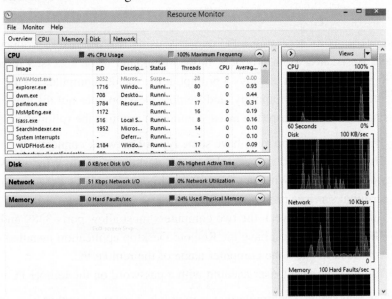

FIGURE 16.51   Windows 8 Resource Monitor

Running any performance monitor tool affects the computer performance, especially when using the Graph view and sampling large amounts of data. The following recommendations help when running any performance monitoring tool:

> Turn off any screen saver.
> Use *Report* view instead of Graph view to save on resources.
> Keep the number of counters monitored to a minimum.
> Sample at longer intervals such as 10 to 15 minutes rather than just a few seconds or minutes.

Windows **Reliability Monitor** provides a visual graph and detailed report of system stability and details on events that might have affected the computer's reliability. The details are to help technicians troubleshoot the cause of something that causes the system to become unreliable. In Vista, the Reliability Monitor is found as an option within the Reliability and Performance Monitor. In Windows 7 and higher, it is a separate tool found by typing `reliability monitor` in the respective *Search programs and files* feature of each release. Figure 16.52 shows this tool.

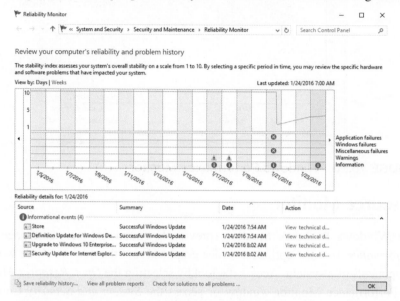

FIGURE 16.52   Windows 10 Reliability Monitor

Supporting Windows Computers Remotely

Windows supports accessing a PC remotely using two Microsoft products: Remote Desktop and Remote Assistance. Both products allow a computer to be accessed remotely. The difference is that Remote Assistance displays a prompt at the remote computer asking permission to allow the computer to be viewed remotely, and Remote Desktop does not display this prompt.

Using Remote Desktop (the **mstsc** command) requires the following elements:

> The remote desktop must have some type of network connectivity.
> The computer used to access the remote desktop must run Windows Vista/Windows 7 Professional or higher, Windows 8/10 Pro or higher, Windows Server, or must have some type of terminal services running.
> Any firewalls between the two computers must allow ports 3389 and 80 to be open.
> The remote PC must have the Remote Desktop application installed.
> You need to know the computer name of the remote PC.
> You need to have a user account with a password on the remote PC.

When you are on a computer that is remotely accessing another computer, there is a bar across the top of the screen that contains the remote computer name. This is how you know that you are on another computer. The user on the remote computer is logged off.

Both Remote Desktop and Remote Assistance are useful for those working at a help desk and for technicians who must support computers located in other locations. With Remote Assistance, one computer user (the Expert) views another computer user's (the Novice) desktop using a secure connection. Remote Assistance (`msra` command) can be initiated using any of the following methods:

> Windows Messenger service
> Email an invitation

> Send an invitation as an email attachment
> Use Easy Connect (Windows 7 or higher)

Remote Desktop is disabled by default in Windows. Open *Windows Explorer/File Explorer* and right-click *Computer* (*This PC* in Windows 8 and 10) > *Properties* > *Remote Settings* link from left panel. In the Windows environment, Remote Assistance now supports computers that use network address translation (NAT); however, you may have to go into the Windows Firewall application and in the left panel select *Allow a program through Windows Firewall*. Select the *Exceptions* tab and locate *Remote Assistance*. You must also set up a password for the guest user and manually send the password to the person invited to take over the computer. To use Windows Remote Assistance, type `remote assistance` in the *Search files and folders* textbox. Click the *Windows Remote Assistance* option. See Figure 16.53 to see the available options.

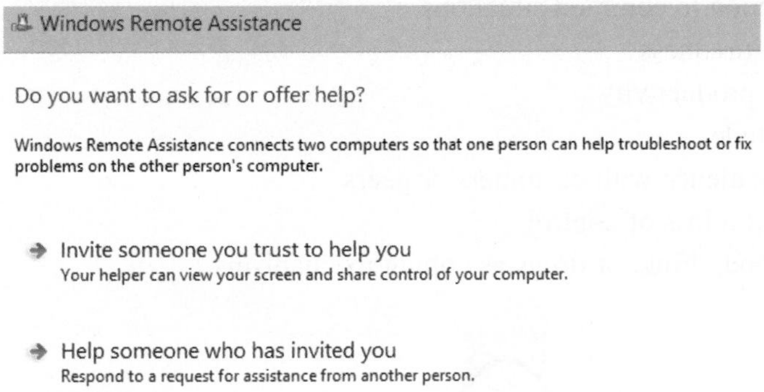

Windows Remote Assistance

Do you want to ask for or offer help?

Windows Remote Assistance connects two computers so that one person can help troubleshoot or fix problems on the other person's computer.

➔ Invite someone you trust to help you
Your helper can view your screen and share control of your computer.

➔ Help someone who has invited you
Respond to a request for assistance from another person.

FIGURE 16.53   Windows Remote Assistance

Preventive Maintenance for Your Operating System

Your operating system is a key component of a working system. Preventive maintenance can help avoid issues and reduce downtime when properly applied. No application or hardware can work without an operating system. It is important that you keep your operating system healthy. The following suggestions can help:

> Always have an antivirus software program that has current virus definitions.
> Make frequent data backups.
> Have a backup of your operating system. Many external hard drives include backup software.
> Ensure that the System Restore utility is enabled.
> Update the operating system with service packs and patches.
> Use the Task Scheduler tool to automate some of the preventive maintenance tasks. You can use the `at` command (type `at /?` from a command prompt to see the options) to create a script file or have an application run at a specific time.

CHAPTER 16

SOFT SKILLS—AVOIDING BURNOUT

Burnout—commonly caused by too much work and stress—is a mental state that can also affect emotional and physical capabilities. Many technicians tire of the fast pace of technology (see Figure 16.54). As a person matures, it seems to take more effort to stay current in the skills required for business. One attraction of technology for many students is that technology is always changing; however, it is this speed of change that provides such a challenge, even to seasoned veterans. A technician may be in the same job for multiple years and burnout is evident. Technicians should monitor their own attitude and mental state constantly and watch for warning signs associated with burnout:

> Overreaction to common situations
> Constant tiredness
> Reduced productivity
> Poor attitude
> Lack of patience with customers or peers
> Feeling of a loss of control
> Use of food, drink, or drugs as coping mechanisms

FIGURE 16.54 Burnout affects your performance

Burnout can be prevented and dealt with if you recognize the symptoms. Working too much, having too many responsibilities, and expecting too much of yourself can lead to burnout. The following list can help you recognize and cope with burnout:

> Take vacations during which you do not stay in contact with work.
> Set reachable goals, even on a daily basis.
> Take a couple breaks during the day to do something nontechnical.
> Learn something new that is not related to technology.
> Have good eating, sleeping, and exercising routines.
> Subscribe to a positive saying or joke of the day.

Chapter Summary

> Windows operating systems can be 32-bit or 64-bit. The 32-bit versions are limited to a maximum of 4GB of RAM; 32-bit operating systems or applications are sometimes referred to as x86 instead of 32bbit.
> Windows operating systems come in different editions that have various features and tools. For example, the Home versions cannot join corporate network domains or encrypt files/folders.
> Windows has Windows Resource Protection (WRP) to protect the key operating system files. The `sfc /scannow` command checks system files.
> There are specific operating system in-place upgrade paths that are permitted. Otherwise, a clean install must be performed. You must activate the Windows license by phone or Internet. A repair installation is performed when Windows has to be reloaded. Use the Upgrade Advisor before upgrading Windows.
> Multiple operating systems may be installed. (Install the oldest one first, and install the operating systems on separate partitions.) Virtualization can also facilitate multiple operating systems installed and make use of the same hardware.
> Compatibility mode, Windows XP Mode, or virtualization can allow older applications to operate properly.
> Corporate Windows deployment involves creating a master image and deploying that image across a network. Deployment methods include PXE boot, unattended installations, LTI, and remote network installation. Network bandwidth is affected by imaging.
> Operating system installation failures are often caused by lack of planning for the installation: insufficient or incompatible hardware, incompatible software, and lack of operating-specific drivers.
> A computer that uses virtualization must have more hardware to run more than a single operating system environment.
> To back up the Windows registry, use regedit, the Backup utility, or the System Restore tool.
> Windows updates include device driver updates. Use the driver roll back feature or System Restore when an update causes the system to not work.
> The Computer Management console can access System tools (Task Scheduler, Event Viewer, Shared Folders, Local Users and Groups, Performance, and Device Manager), Storage, and Services and Applications.
> The Advanced Boot Options menu is commonly used when the tools within Windows cannot be used in the normal boot environment. The most commonly used options are Safe Mode, Safe Mode with Networking, Enable low resolution, Last Known Good Configuration, Disable automatic restart on system failure, Disable driver signature enforcement, and Repair Your Computer.

> The `bootrec` command can detect and repair master boot issues, operating system files, or the boot sector.

> The System Configuration utility (`msconfig`) can control what applications load during the boot process.

> Task Manager can display system performance, stop applications that are not working properly, and view which applications and processes take up memory.

> Event Viewer logs issues with applications and the operating system to provide a historical record and timeline of when things occur.

> Remote Assistance (the `msra` command) and Remote Desktop (the `mstsc` command) are used to control and use a remote computer. Remote Assistance displays a prompt requesting permission.

> Task Scheduler can perform preventive maintenance on a regular basis. Preventive maintenance can reduce downtime and includes keeping the operating system and applications patched, keeping the antivirus definitions current, and keeping the hard drive defragmented and with ample space.

> Technicians can do positive things to avoid burnout including getting good rest, avoiding drugs and alcohol, doing nontechnical things, and having good time-management skills.

A+ CERTIFICATION EXAM TIPS

✓ This chapter and the next chapter cover concepts relating to the 220-902 exam. CompTIA recommends that you have 6 to 12 months of lab or field experience before taking the exam. Students *have* passed this exam right after the course.

✓ Redo all the labs. Ensure that you pay attention to the purpose of the tool and consider why (or in what situation) you would use each Windows tool.

✓ When your own computer momentarily slows down, use some of the tools to examine the cause.

✓ Ensure that you know how to control the boot process and use the Advanced Boot Options menu effectively. Pay attention to Safe Mode. Know the other tools to use before then such as System Restore and Startup Repair.

✓ Set up and use client-side virtualization.

✓ Know the difference between Remote Assistance and Remote Desktop.

✓ Configure a particular monitor if the orientation or alignment is misconfigured using the *Display* Control Panel.

✓ Use all the msconfig tabs including the *Advanced options* button on the *Boot* tab to control Windows startup.

✓ Control, upgrade, and roll back a device driver.

✓ Know the different user accounts and groups and what they can do.

✓ Know the different ways to boot a Windows computer and the different ways to get an operating system onto it.

✓ Be familiar with the following features: Computer Management, print management, Device Manager, local users and groups, Performance Monitor, Services, System Configuration, Task Scheduler, Component Services, Data Sources, Windows Memory Diagnostic Tool, Task Manager (all tabs), Disk Management (know how to install a drive), USMT, Easy Transfer, Upgrade Advisor, System Restore, and Windows Update.

✓ Interact and troubleshoot with the following Windows Control Panels: Display/Display Settings, User accounts, System, Power options, Programs and features, Devices and Printers, Sound, and Troubleshooting.

Key Terms

Review Questions

1. What is the maximum amount of RAM that can be recognized by any version of 32-bit Windows?

    _____

2. A customer has an older 16-bit game as well as some newer 32-bit games. The customer is considering upgrading to 64-bit Windows 10. Will there be any issues with this? If so, what are they and how might they be resolved?

    _____

    _____

3. What `sfc` switch is used to replace a corrupt system file in Windows 7?

    _____

4. List three steps to be taken *before* installing Windows.

    _____

    _____

    _____

    _____

    _____

5. [Yes | No] Is the Upgrade Advisor tool available from the Windows Vista or Windows 7 installation disc?

    _____

6. Which tool can limit the number of applications used to boot the computer? [taskmgr | regedit | msconfig | diskpart]

7. [T | F] Microsoft requires Windows 7 activation within 10 days of installation.

8. Which performance tool would a technician use first to see if the computer has enough hardware resources when a particular application executes?
    [Performance Monitor | Task Manager | Reliability Monitor | Device Manager]

9. How is network bandwidth affected when computer cloning is performed?

    _____

    _____

10. List two solutions for having both Windows 7 and Windows 8 operating systems installed on one computer?

    _____

11. [T | F] Existing restore points are deleted if Windows is reinstalled.

12. [T | F] Device drivers are specific for a particular Windows operating system version.

13. In what way does a Windows Update affect device drivers?

    _____

    _____

14. What user group is allowed to perform the driver roll back?

    _____

15. If a device has to be manually installed in Windows 7, what utility is used and what file extension is required for the driver?

    _____

16. What is the purpose of the System Restore utility?

_____

_____

17. You just installed a new sound card and loaded the driver, but when Windows 7 boots, the computer locks. What boot option should you use to help with this problem?

_____

18. When would a technician use Event Viewer?

_____

_____

19. Detail specifically how Task Manager can monitor computer performance?

_____

_____

20. List three things a student can do to avoid burnout in school.

_____

_____

Exercises

Exercise 16.1 Windows Tools

Objective: To determine which Windows tool to use based on the task

Parts: None

Procedure: Match the task to the best Windows tool to use for the given situation. Note that one tool is used twice.

Tools:

a. Event Viewer

b. System Restore

c. System Repair

d. `msconfig`

e. Device Manager

f. Folder Options

g. System Protection

h. Devices and Printers

i. Disk Management

j. Task Scheduler

k. Services

l. Performance Monitor

m. Task Manager

n. Computer Management console

o. Windows Memory Diagnostics Tool

p. Safe Mode

q. `regsvr32`

r. safe boot

s. Print Management

Scenarios:

_____ 1. Configure two drives in a RAID configuration.

_____ 2. Determine when a user logged in a computer yesterday.

_____ 3. Restart the program that allows the print spooler to function.

_____ 4. You suspect one of the DDR4 modules has an issue.

_____ 5. Quickest way to see the default printer.

_____ 6. Disable a computer vendor app that keeps running every time the computer boots trying to get the user to buy storage space.

_____ 7. Configure a specific number of processes the computer uses to boot the computer.

_____ 8. Run a test of hard drive reads per second and writes per second to see if the drive is causing slowdown issues.

_____ 9. Bring the system back to before a particular Windows update was installed.

_____ 10. Instruct the system to perform disk maintenance twice a week instead of just once.

_____ 11. Have the ability to access Device Manager and the Disk Management tool from one window.

_____ 12. View system files through Windows Explorer/File Explorer.

_____ 13. Testing mode with limited drivers loaded.

_____ 14. Unregister a DLL.

_____ 15. Disable a piece of hardware.

_____ 16. Adjust virtual memory.

_____ 17. View all print servers.

_____ 18. Halt a misbehaving app.

_____ 19. Control the Safe Mode boot type the next time the computer restarts.

_____ 20. Let the OS try to figure out why Windows won't boot.

Activities

Internet Discovery

Objective: To access the Internet to obtain specific information regarding a computer or its associated parts

Parts: Access to the Internet

Procedure: Use the Internet to answer the following questions.

1. Find a website that offers Windows freeware tools. Write the name of the website and the URL where this information was found.

_____

_____

2. What is the latest update available from Microsoft for Windows 8.1? Write the answer and the URL where you found the answer.

_____

_____

3. Find a website that details what to do if a Windows 10 upgrade results in a black screen. Detail what the website recommends and the URL where you found it.

_____

_____

4. Microsoft always has minimum requirements for any of its operating systems. Find a website that tells you what your system should have to run Windows 7 Ultimate efficiently. Write the name of the company that posts the recommendation, the minimum requirements cited, as well as the URL.

_____

_____

_____

5. You get the error code 0x8007232B on a Windows 7 computer. Find a website that describes this error. Write the solution and URL where the answer can be found.

_____

6. Find a certification related to a Microsoft operating system. List the certification and the average salary associated with the certification. List all URLs used to find this information.

_____

_____

_____

Soft Skills

Objective: To enhance and fine-tune a future technician's ability to listen, communicate in both written and oral forms, and professionally support people who use computers

Activities:

1. In groups of two or three students, one student inserts a problem related to Windows on the computer. The other students use the Remote Desktop utility to find the problem and then repair it. Document each problem along with the solution provided. Exchange roles so that each student practices the repair and documentation.

2. Divide into five groups. Five questions about operating systems follow: (1) What should you do *before* installing an operating system? (2) What are alternatives to Vista, Windows 7, 8, or 10 as an operating system, and what are pros and cons of these alternatives? (3) What is the difference between an active partition, a system partition, and a boot partition in regard to Windows (4) What operating systems can be upgraded to Windows Vista, Windows 7, 8, or 10? What is the difference between a clean install and an upgrade, and what determines which one you do? (5) What differences can be seen for a Windows hard drive that has a FAT32 partition and one that has an NTFS partition? Each group is assigned one of these five areas or another set of five questions related to Windows. Each group is allowed 20 minutes (and some whiteboard space or poster-sized paper) to write their ideas. All group member help to present their findings to the class.

3. Find a magazine article related to a Windows solution or feature. Share your findings with the class.

Critical Thinking Skills

Objective: To analyze and evaluate information as well as apply learned information to new or different situations

Activities:

1. Based on the information given in the chapter about Remote Assistance, along with any directions found on the Internet or through Windows help, configure two computers for Remote Assistance and allow a person to take over a computer remotely. Write the steps needed to perform this process. Share the steps with other groups and refine the steps until nontechnical people can use the steps to configure a computer for Remote Assistance.

2. Find a Windows registry hack online, in a book, or from a magazine. Analyze the hack to determine whether it is beneficial to normal users, whether it is beneficial to technicians, whether you would recommend it to a fellow student, and whether you would recommend it to your parents. Write a brief description of your findings including the implications of installing the registry modification.

_____

_____

_____

_____

_____

CHAPTER 16

3. Using any research method and resource, determine the pros and cons of upgrading to Windows 8.1 from Windows 7. Make a list of things to check before upgrading.

_____

_____

_____

_____

_____

_____

Labs

Lab 16.1 Windows 7 Installation

Objective: To install Windows 7 on a hard drive that does not have an existing operating system

Parts: A computer with the minimum hardware requirements for Windows 7

Windows 7 DVD or virtual image of the installation disc

Note: The screens may appear a little differently with different service packs and Windows 7 versions.

Procedure: Complete the following procedure and answer the accompanying questions.

1. Configure the BIOS to boot from the CD/DVD drive.

2. Insert the Windows 7 installation DVD into an optical drive and turn on the computer. The Windows 7 Setup program starts automatically if the BIOS is configured correctly.

3. Select the appropriate regional options and click *Next*.

4. Select *Install Now* to start the Windows 7 installation.

5. Read the EULA (end user licensing agreement). Select the *I accept the License Terms* option and click *Next*.

6. Two options appear for Windows 7: to upgrade or to perform a custom installation. To install Windows 7 as a clean install, click the *Custom (Advanced)* option.

7. When prompted for where to install Windows 7, select the *Drive options (advanced)* option.

8. Delete a partition, create a partition, and format a partition as needed. When finished selecting the partition, click *Next*. If a RAID or SCSI driver is needed, install it at this point.

9. The computer restarts and Windows 7 loads and completes the installation. A username and a computer name are required. The computer name must be unique. Contact the instructor or lab assistant for a unique name if necessary.

10. Contact the instructor for a password for the user account.

Print the exact password to be used with appropriate uppercase and lowercase letters.

_____

11. Enter the password, enter a hint, and then click *Next*.

12. Enter the product key provided. Check with the instructor or lab assistant if you do not have one. Note that you can leave this blank to experiment with the different versions of Windows 7. They all come on the same DVD. You must eventually install a version for which you have a license. Do not experiment with different Windows 7 versions if upgrading from a prior version of Windows as this is not allowed after the old version is upgraded.

13. In the Help Protect Your Computer and Improve Windows Automatically dialog box, select the *Use Recommended Settings* option.

14. In the Review Your Time and Date Settings dialog box, select the appropriate time zone and date options. Click *Finish*.

15. Contact your instructor or lab assistant for the appropriate computer location. If the instructor or assistant is not available, select the *Work* option.

16. Click *Start* and the Windows logon appears.

Instructor initials: _____

Lab 16.2 Installing VMware Workstation

Objective: To install VMware Workstation 12 in preparation for future VMware Workstation labs

Parts: A Windows computer with Administrator rights to install software and

Internet access to download 30-day trial of VMware Workstation

Procedure: Complete the following procedure and answer the accompanying questions.

1. If VMware Workstation 12 is not already downloaded on the computer, go to http://www.vmware.com and download the software.

    Is VMware Workstation already installed on the computer?

    _____

    Is the same version of VMware Workstation downloaded for 32-bit Windows as 64-bit Windows? If you do not know, research this on the Internet.

    _____

2. Start the VMware installer. Accept the end-user agreement. When the Customer Setup window appears, keep the default location selection.

3. Leave the *Check for product updates* option enabled and click *Next*.

4. Either enable or disable the *Help improve VMware Workstation* checkbox.

    Which option did you choose?

    _____

5. Leave the shortcut checkboxes enabled and click *Next*. Click *Continue*.

6. Either enter a license key provided by the instructor or lab assistant or select the *Finish* option. Note that no key is needed for the 30-day trial.

7. When the installation is complete, the VMware Workstation icon appears on the desktop. Note that you may be prompted to restart the computer before using the software.

Instructor initials: _____

Lab 16.3 Installing Windows into a VMware Workstation Virtual Machine

Objective: To install a version of Windows into a VMware Workstation virtual machine

Parts: Windows computer with Administrator rights that has VMware Workstation installed and Windows installation disc or ISO image

Procedure: Complete the following procedure and answer the accompanying questions.

1. Double-click the VMware Workstation icon from the desktop or access the software from the Start button menu. VMware Workstation begins. If this is the first time starting VMware Workstation, you will be prompted to enter in a valid email address to use the 30-day trial. Figure 16.55 shows the VMware Workstation area.

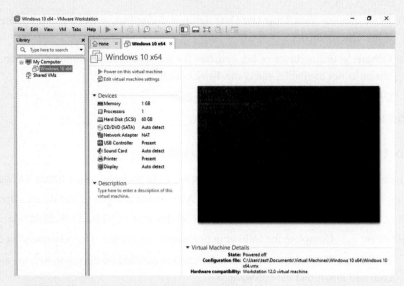

FIGURE 16.55 VMware Workstation

2. Click the Create a New Virtual Machine option.

3. Select the *Typical (recommended)* radio button and click *Next*.

4. If you have a Windows installation disc, insert it now and select the *Installer disc* option. Otherwise, select the *Installer disc image file (iso)* radio button, and browse to the location of the Windows installer ISO file. Click *Next*.

5. Enter the Windows product key as provided by the instructor or lab assistant. Note that the installation can proceed without a key. If Windows 7 or higher is being installed, select the Windows version from the drop-down menu if it is not automatically detected. Optionally, enter a username and password as directed by the instructor or lab assistant. Click *Next*. If a license key was not entered, you will be reminded of that and must click Yes to continue.

   Was a username and password selected as part of this installation process? If so, document the username and password. [Yes | No]

   _____

6. Enter a name for the machine (or leave the default) and select a hard drive location to store the virtual machine file. Click *Next*.

   What name did you install to the virtual machine?

   _____

   Document the path to the folder that contains the virtual machine file.

   _____

7. Keep the default disk size unless instructed to change by the instructor or student assistant, and select the *Store virtual disk as a single file* radio button. Click *Next*.

8. Look over the virtual machine settings.

   What is the default amount of RAM?

   _____

   What type of network adapter is installed?

   _____

   What other devices are automatically installed?

9. The *Power on this virtual machine after creation* checkbox is automatically enabled. Click *Finish*. If you have removable devices attached, you may receive a message. The Windows setup installation process begins if a proper ISO file were found. Answer the installation prompts just as you would a normal Windows installation process.

10. Notice how the virtual machine is within its own tab. Right-click the tab that contains your new virtual machine.

    Document at least four available options that are available from the menu.

    _____

    _____

11. Click away from the tab.

    What message appears at the bottom of the screen that relates to controlling the virtual machine?

    _____

12. Locate the VM in the Library window panel on the left. Right-click the virtual machine you just created.

    Are the options the same as the ones you saw when you right-clicked the virtual machine tab?

    [Yes | No]

13. Select the *View* > *Full Screen* menu options. The virtual machine displays in the full window, looking exactly like a typical Windows screen.

14. Locate and click the VM icon in the top-left corner. Select *Restore* to close full screen mode and return to the VMware Workstation area.

Instructor initials: _____

15. Log in to the Windows environment and continue the installation process if necessary.

16. Shut down the version of Windows used within the virtual environment. It is important to shut down the Windows version inside the virtual machine as it is to shut down Windows properly on an unvirtualized computer.

17. Power off the virtual machine.

Lab 16.4 Working with a VMware Workstation Virtual Machine

Objective: To customize a VMware Workstation virtual machine, create a snapshot, add an icon or software, and revert to a saved snapshot.

Parts: Windows computer with Administrator rights that has VMware Workstation installed and a saved virtual machine

Procedure: Complete the following procedure and answer the accompanying questions.

1. Using whichever method you would like including physical examination, examine the host computer hardware and document the findings.

    How many physical processors are installed in the computer?

    _____

    What method did you use to determine this fact?

    _____

    How many processors are shown within Device Manager?

    _____

    Is this the number of processors installed, or is this how many cores are within the processor?

    _____

    How did you determine this fact?

    _____

CHAPTER 16

If Hyper-Threading is enabled, is the number of Intel processors seen within Task Manager Performance tab affected?

[Yes | No]

Why or why not?

_____

How much RAM is present in the computer?

_____

How many network ports are present in the computer?

_____

How many floppy drives are installed in the computer?

_____

2. Launch VMware Workstation. From the Home tab, select the *Open a Virtual Machine* link. Browse to the location of a previously created virtual machine, and double-click the filename, or click the filename and select *Open*.

How many processors are detected?

_____

Is a printer detected? [Yes | No]

3. Select the *Edit virtual machine settings link*.

What is the maximum amount of memory that can be allocated to this VM?

_____

_____

Is this more than the physical RAM on the host computer?

[Yes | No]

Is this what you expected? [Yes | No] Why or why not?

_____

List one instance in which you might want to use the maximum amount of memory.

_____

_____

4. Click *Processors* in the Device column.

How many processors are currently allocated?

_____

What is the maximum number of processors?

_____

How many cores per processor are currently allocated?

_____

What is the maximum number of cores per processor?

_____

How does this compare to the information you documented about the host computer in Step 1?

_____

_____

5. Select the *Network adapter* option from the Device column.

   How many network adapters are shown?

   _____

   Does this match the number of network ports on the physical host computer? [Yes | No]

6. Select the *Floppy* option.

   How many floppy drives were installed on the physical host computer?

   _____

   Why do you think this would be included in a virtual machine?

   _____

   _____

7. Select the *Sound Card* option.

   What is the device status?

   _____

8. Select the *Options* tab. Select the *General* settings option. From this screen, you can rename the virtual machine and see the guest operating system. You can also set the default directory where snapshots are stored.

   List the working directory where VMs are stored.

   _____

9. Select the *Power* option.

   What power options, if any, are enabled?

   _____

10. Select the *Snapshots* option. Notice how you can take a snapshot every time the computer is powered off. Click *Cancel*.

11. From the main VMware Workstation window, right-click the tab that contains the virtual machine that has already been created.

12. Select *Power > Power on to Firmware*.

    What type of virtual BIOS is used?

    _____

    Is the virtual system time the same as the host machine?

    [Yes | No]

    Does the mouse work in the virtual BIOS window?

    [Yes | No]

13. Using the directions on the screen, select the *Boot* BIOS menu option.

14. Using the directions on the screen, change the boot order so that the hard drive is first and the CD-ROM drive is last.

15. Select the *Main* menu option and access *Keyboard Features*.

16. Change the *NumLock* key to be *On* by default.

17. Press to save and exit the BIOS.

    When do you think a technician would ever enter the virtual BIOS instead of the host computer BIOS?

    _____

    _____

Do you think that changes within the virtual BIOS affect the host computer BIOS? Why or why not?

_____

_____

18. Press F10 to save the changes and boot the virtual machine.

What message, if any appeared?

_____

_____

_____

19. Hold the mouse pointer inside the VMware Workstation window. Do not click. Notice the mouse directions at the bottom of the window.

What keystroke(s) enables you to move outside the VM?

_____

20. Now hold the mouse pointer outside the VMware Workstation window. Notice the mouse directions have changed at the bottom of the VMware Workstation window.

What keystroke(s) enable you to direct input to the VM?

_____

21. From the VM menu option, select *Snapshot > Take Snapshot*. A snapshot is the virtual machine at this point in time. Another way of looking at the snapshot is that it is the operating system as it stands right now. You could make changes to the operating system and then if the changes don't work well, you could revert back to the virtual machine that was the snapshot.

22. Name the snapshot something meaningful such as Windows *X* base load. Click *Take Snapshot*.

What did you name the snapshot?

_____

23. Create a shortcut icon to any application on the virtual machine desktop.

What shortcut did you create?

_____

24. Shut down Windows within the virtual machine.

25. Power off the virtual machine.

26. Open the same virtual machine again, but do not power on the virtual machine.

27. Right-click the virtual machine tab and point to *Snapshot*.

28. Click the name of the snapshot you took in Step 22. Refer to the answer in Step 22 if necessary.

29. Click *Yes* to retain the snapshot.

Is the shortcut icon you created in Step 23 there?

[Yes | No]

Explain why you think this happened.

_____

Instructor initials: _____

30. Shut down Windows in the virtual environment.

31. Power down the virtual machine.

Lab 16.5 Windows Registry Modification

Objective: To modify the Windows registry when given directions to do so

Parts: Computer with Windows Vista, Windows 7, 8, or 10 loaded

Notes: You must be an administrator or a member of the Administrators group to change registry settings. Sometimes, you are given directions by Microsoft to edit the registry to fix a problem. It is important that you follow the directions exactly as directed.

Procedure: Complete the following procedure and answer the accompanying questions.

1.   Power on the computer and verify that Windows loads. Log on to the computer using the user ID and password provided by the instructor or lab assistant.

2.   Open *Windows Explorer (Windows Vista/7) or File Explorer (Windows 8/10)*. Right-click any folder within *Documents*. Note that if no folder exists, create one.

      Which editing options are available for a folder? Select all that apply.

      [Cut | Copy | Paste | Copy To Folder | Move To Folder | Delete | Rename | Send To]

3.   Select the *Start* button (Windows 7/Vista) or right-click the *Start* button (Windows 8/10 > *Run* > type **regedit** and press Enter. Click *Yes*.

4.   Expand the *Hkey_Classes_Root* option by clicking the > (greater than sign) beside the option.

5.   Scroll down to locate and expand *AllFileSystemObjects*. Note that items beginning with a character such as a . (period) are before the alphabetized list of other objects.

6.   Expand the *shellex* object and locate *ContextMenuHandlers*. Shellex is a shell extension key that lets you customize the Windows interface.

7.   Right-click *ContextMenuHandlers* > *New* > *Key*. When the new folder (key) appears, type **Copy To** and press Enter. This registry modification adds a new option to the right-click menu called *Copy To*.

8.   The Copy To object should still be selected in the left window. Double-click the *(Default)* name in the right panel. The Edit String window appears.

9.   In the *Value data* textbox, type the following value exactly as shown (the 0s are zeros):

      {C2FBB630-2971-11D1-A18C-00C04FD75D13}

      Click *OK*.

10.   Verify the change has occurred. Open *Windows Explorer/File Explorer* and right-click any folder.

      Does *Copy To folder* appear as an option?

      _____

      If not, redo the lab.

Instructor initials: _____

11.   Return to the regedit window. Using the same process, create another new key under *ContextMenuHandlers* and name the key *Move To*. The value data for the Move To key is as follows:

      {C2FBB631-2971-11D1-A18C-00C04FD75D13}

12.   Use *Windows Explorer/File Explorer* to create two new folders. Copy a couple of files into each folder. Use the new *Copy To* and *Move To* options you just created.

13.   Delete any folders that you have created.

14.   To delete keys in Registry Editor, select the *Copy To* option in the left panel. From the *Edit* menu option, select *Delete* and select *Yes* when asked to verify. Delete the *Move To* key using the same process.

Instructor initials: _____

15.   Close the *Registry Editor* window.

Lab 16.6 Windows 7 Backup

Objective: To back up files including the operating system if necessary using the Backup and Restore utility

Parts: A computer with Windows 7 installed and Administrator rights

Procedure: Complete the following procedure and answer the accompanying questions.

Note: Even though only three files are backed up using this process, you can use the same process to back up the computer.

1. Create a new folder called *Stuff* under *Documents*.

2. Create three text files of any name and place them in the new *Stuff* folder.

3. Access the *System and Security* Control Panel link > *Backup and Restore* > *Set up backup* link. (Note that if the Backup and Restore link has already been accessed, then the *Change settings* link can be used to complete the lab.) > select a backup destination designated by the instructor or lab assistant > *Next* > select the *Let me choose* radio button > select *Next*.

   Note: You can use the *Let Windows choose* radio button to back up the entire operating system and files.

4. Deselect all enabled checkboxes > expand *OS (C:)* by clicking the arrow beside it > expand *Users* > expand the username used to log in to the computer > expand *Documents* > select the *Stuff* folder to enable it for backup > *Next* > *Save settings and run backup* button.

5. The backup executes. Show the instructor the completed backup.

Instructor initials: _____

6. Delete the *Stuff* folder and the three files contained within it.

Lab 16.7 Windows Update Utility

Objective: To configure a computer for Windows updates.

Parts: Computer with Windows Vista, 7, 8.1, or 10 loaded and Internet access

Note: You must be an administrator or a member of the Administrators group to change Automatic Updates settings.

Procedure: Complete the following procedure and answer the accompanying questions.

1. Power on the computer and verify that Windows loads. Log on to the computer using the user ID and password provided by the instructor or lab assistant.

2. In Vista, select the *System and Maintenance* Control Panel > *Windows Update* link. Click the *Change settings* link.

   In Windows 7, click the *Start* button > *Control Panel* > *System and Security* link > *Windows Update* link.

   In Windows 8.1, right-click the *Start* button (or just search for the Control Panel using the *Search* charm) > *Control Panel* > *System and Security* link > *Windows Update* link.

   In Windows 10, click the *Start* button > *Settings* > *Update & security*.

   What option is currently selected?

   _____

   Which option do you think most large corporations would want as standard and why do you think this?

   _____

3. Close the Windows Update window.

4. Click the *Cancel* button to close the Automatic Updates window.

Lab 16.8 Configuring Windows 7, 8, and 10 for Ease of Access

Objective: To configure Windows 7, 8, or 10 for customers who need a customized environment for visual, auditory, and physical reasons

Parts: Computer with Windows 7, 8/8.1, or 10 installed

Procedure: Complete the following procedure and answer the accompanying questions. Note that not all steps are shown and must explore some settings based on the question asked.

1. To access the Ease of Access Center in Windows 7, click the *Start* button > *Control Panel* > *Ease of Access* link. In Windows 8/10, right-click the *Start* button > *Control Panel* > *Ease of Access* link.

2. Select the *Let Windows suggest settings* link.

    What recommendations does Microsoft make available to someone at the workplace who has trouble seeing images on the screen because of the office lighting? Note that you have to make selections based on the scenario given to obtain this information. You do NOT have to select an option on each of the five screens that presents options. You should only select an option that relates to the scenario given.

    _____

    _____

3. You should be at the *Recommended settings* window after answering the last question. If not, redo Steps 1 and 2 and read the accompanying note with the question. Click *Apply*. Click *OK*.

4. On the *Make your computer easier to use* window, locate the *Explore all settings* section in order to answer the questions.

    What is the purpose of the *Make the mouse easier to use* setting?

    _____

    What is the purpose of the *Make it easier to focus on tasks* setting?

    _____

    Which option do you think might be used on a Microsoft Surface tablet?

    _____

5. Return to the main *Ease of Access* Control Panel and reselect the *Let Windows suggest settings* link. You should be on the *Get recommendations to make your computer easier to use* window. Disable (uncheck) the *Lighting conditions make it difficult to see images on my monitor* checkbox.

6. Select the *Images and text on TV are difficult to see (even when I'm wearing glasses)* checkbox. Click *Next* four times and then click *Done* to view Microsoft's recommendations.

    What options are recommended (checked) by Microsoft for this situation?

    _____

    _____

    _____

7. In the *Change the color and size of mouse pointers* section, select the *Large Inverting* radio button. Select *Apply*.

8. Move the mouse and open *Windows Explorer*.

    Describe your experience.

    _____

    _____

    Would office workers who do not have a visual impairment enjoy this feature?

    _____

9. Change the mouse pointer back to *Regular white*. Ensure that the *Turn on or off High Contrast when left ALT + left SHIFT + PRINT SCREEN* is selected, with all associated checkboxes enabled. Select *Apply*.

CHAPTER 16

10. Hold down the left $\boxed{\text{Alt}}$ key, and while keeping the key held down, press and hold the left $\boxed{\text{Shift}}$ key. While holding down both of these keys, press the $\boxed{\text{Prt Sc}}$ key ($\boxed{\text{Alt}}$ + left $\boxed{\text{Shift}}$ + $\boxed{\text{Prt Sc}}$). Release all three keys.

    What audio signal do you hear?

    _____

    From information in the message, document how to disable the keyboard shortcut if these specific keys are used for another application.

    _____

    _____

11. Click *Yes*.

    Describe the difference in screen appearance.

    _____

    Do you like the high contrast?

    _____

12. Use the same keys again to disable the high-contrast setting. Click *Cancel* in the Recommended settings window.

13. Reselect the *Get recommendations to make your computer easier to use* link. Remove the enabled option checkbox from the *Eyesight* window and click *Next*.

14. In the *Dexterity* window, select the *Pens and pencils are difficult to use* checkbox. Click *Next* or *Done* until you reach Microsoft's recommendations.

    What option(s) are recommended by Microsoft?

    _____

    What are toggle keys?

    _____

    _____

15. Open *Notepad*. Notice the blinking cursor in the top-left corner.

16. Leave Notepad open and return to the *Recommended settings* window, notice the setting for *Set the thickness of the blinking cursor*. Change the thickness of the blinking cursor to 5. Click *Apply*.

17. Return to Notepad and notice the difference in the blinking cursor.

18. Return to the *Recommended Settings* window, and return the thickness to the default setting of *1 and apply the setting*. Close *Notepad*.

19. Return to the *Recommended Settings* window.

    What are Sticky Keys?

    _____

    _____

    Who might benefit from Sticky Keys?

    _____

20. Enable (select) the *Set up Filter Keys* link.

    What are Filter Keys?

    _____

    _____

    What is the default amount of time the *Shift* key has to stay depressed to toggle on Filter Keys?

    _____

By default, do you see a warning message, do you hear a tone, or do you get both a message and a tone when Filter Keys is active? [warning message | tone | both]

What are Bounce Keys?

_____

What is the default time between keystrokes if the Bounce Keys feature is enabled?

_____

Is this setting adjustable? [Yes | No]

21. Click in the *Type text here to test settings* textbox. Type `hello`.

    What happened?

    _____

22. Click the *Set up Repeat Keys and Slow Keys* link.

23. Click in the *Type text here to test settings* textbox. Click and hold the h key down until it appears in the textbox. Finish typing the word `hello` as a message. Note that in a virtualized environment, this option does not work. Simply write the answer virtualization used to the question below if that is the case.

    What indication did you get, in addition to seeing it appear in the textbox, that the letter "took"?

    _____

Instructor initials: _____

24. Click *Cancel* to return to the *Set up Filter Keys* screen.

    What are the other settings this window offers?

    _____

25. Click *Cancel* to return to the *Ease of Access Center*.

26. Return to the *Ease of Access* Control Panel and select the *Let Windows suggest settings* link. Return to the Dexterity window and clear the checkbox for the *Pens and pencils are difficult to use* option. Click *Next*.

27. On the *Hearing* window, select the *Conversations can be difficult to hear (even with a hearing aid)* checkbox. Click *Next* or *Done* until you reach the Microsoft recommendations.

    What options are available?

    _____

28. Enable the *Turn on visual notifications for sounds (Sound Sentry)*. Select the visual warning of *Flash active window*. Click *Apply*. Leave that window open and access the *Hardware and Sound* Control Panel in a separate window. In the *Sound* section, select the *Change system sounds* link. On the *Sounds* tab, select a Windows notification that has a speaker beside it. Click the *Test* button.

    Even if your computer does not have speakers, what visual clue do you get that a sound is being made? Note that this option may not function in a virtual environment.

    _____

29. Close the *Sound* window. Return to the *Recommended Settings* window. Remove the check from the *Turn on visual notifications for sounds (Sound Sentry)*. Click *Apply*. Click *Cancel* to return to the Ease of Access Center.

30. Return to the *Ease of Access* Control Panel and select the *Let Windows suggest settings* link. Return to the Hearing window and disable the *Conversations can be difficult to hear (even with a hearing aid) option*. Click *Next* to advance to the Speech options screen. Enable the *Other people have difficulty understanding me in a conversation (but not due to an accent)* option. Click *Next* or *Done* until you reach Microsoft's recommendations.

    What is Microsoft's recommendation?

    _____

31. Click the *Completing the questionnaire again* link. Return to the *Speech* page and enable the *I have a speech impairment* checkbox.

    Did this change Microsoft's recommendations? If so, what are the recommendations?

    _____

32. Return to the questionnaire and disable all options from the *Speech* page, and click *Next* to advance to the Reasoning window. Select the *I have a learning disability, such as dyslexia* option. Click *Done*.

    What does Microsoft recommend for this type of person?

    _____

    _____

Instructor initials: _____

33. Click *Cancel*. Ensure all Ease of Access options are disabled. Close the *Ease of Access Center* window.

Lab 16.9 Windows System Restore Utility

Objective: To configure and use the System Restore utility

Parts: A computer with Windows 7, 8.1, or 10 installed and Administrator rights

Notes: You must be an administrator to perform System Restore. If System Restore has been disabled, this lab may have to be done over two class periods. One class period would be used to enable it and schedule a restore point and the next class period to perform the system restore. Also note that an antivirus update or a Windows update might have to be reinstalled as a result of the system restore.

Procedure: Complete the following procedure and answer the accompanying questions.

1. Power on the computer and verify that Windows loads. Log on to Windows using the user ID and password provided by the instructor or lab assistant.

2. Hold down the *Windows keyboard key* and press the Ⓡ *key*. In the run box enter in `rstrui` and press *OK*. An alternate way of bringing up System Restore is to type `rstrui` in the *Search* textbox.

3. You should see the System Restore application window.

4. Read the beginning explanation of System Restore.

    What are two reasons that System Restore might be used?

    _____

    [T | F] System Restore does not affect personal data documents.

    [Yes | No] Can a recently installed application be affected by using the System Restore utility?

    [Yes | No] Is the System Restore process reversible?

5. Click the *Next* button. Note that if the Next button is grayed out, you may have to turn system protection on.

    Are any restore points available? If so, list the latest one.

    _____

6. Create a restore point using the *Create* button if one has never been created. Select the newest (one at the top of the list) restore point and click *Next*.

   What does Windows recommend creating if you have recently changed your Windows password?

   _____

7. Click *Finish* to confirm rolling back your system to an earlier time.

   Under what conditions can the System Restore changes not be undone?

   _____

   _____

8. Click *Yes* to the dialog message. The system restarts as part of the System Restore process.

   Instructor initials: _____

9. Log in to Windows and ensure that the system works.

10. After the system has been restored to an earlier time, install any antivirus or Windows updates that have been affected by this system restore.

Lab 16.10 Upgrading a Hardware Driver and Using Driver Roll Back

Objective: To install an updated driver under the Windows operating system

Parts: A computer with Windows Vista, 7, 8, or 10 installed and Internet access

Note: In this lab a new driver is loaded, but then the old driver is reinstalled with the driver roll back feature. The student must be logged in as a user with local Administrator rights to perform this lab.

Procedure: Complete the following procedure and answer the accompanying questions.

1. Turn on the computer and verify that the operating system loads. Log in to Windows using the user ID and password provided by the instructor or lab assistant.

2. Select an installed hardware device and locate an updated driver using the Internet. Printers are a good choice. Download the driver to the hard drive. Note that some drivers may come in a compressed file and must be uncompressed before continuing the procedure.

   What device did you select to upgrade?

   _____

   What location (path, folder, desktop, and so on) was used to download the driver?

   _____

   Instructor initials: _____

Installing the Driver

3. Open Device Manager.

4. Expand the hardware category that contains the device being upgraded by clicking on the arrow beside the category.

5. Right-click the device name and click the *Properties* selection.

6. Select the *Driver* tab.

7. Click the *Update Driver* and select *Search automatically for updated driver software* to look not only on the computer for an updated driver but also search the Internet. Note that if a driver has been downloaded, use the *Browse my computer for driver software* link to locate the downloaded driver.

   Instructor initials: _____

Using Driver Roll Back

8. Use *Device Manager*, right-click the device name again, and select *Properties*.

9. Click the *Driver* tab and click the *Roll Back Driver* button. Click the *Yes* button to roll back the driver. If the device driver has not been updated, driver roll back will not be possible and a message screen displays this fact.

Instructor initials: _____

10. Close all windows and power off the computer properly.

Lab 16.11 Disabling a Hardware Driver

Objective: To disable a driver under the Vista, 7, 8, or 10 operating system

Parts: A computer with Windows Vista, Windows 7, 8, or 10 and a network adapter installed

Note: The student must be logged in as a user with local Administrator rights to perform this lab. In this lab, a driver is disabled and then re-enabled. Sometimes, Windows can install the wrong driver, in which case the driver must be disabled and then manually reinstalled.

Procedure: Complete the following procedure and answer the accompanying questions.

1. Turn on the computer and verify that the operating system loads. Log in to Windows using the user ID and password provided by the instructor or lab assistant.

2. Using *Device Manager*, expand the *Network adapters* category.

    What network adapter is installed in the computer?

    _____

3. Right-click a network adapter and select the *Disable* option.

    What message displays on the screen?

    _____

4. Select the *Yes* button.

    In Device Manager, how is a device that has its driver disabled displayed differently from any other device?

    _____

5. In *Device Manager*, right-click (or tap and briefly hold on) the same network adapter and select the *Enable* option. The device is re-enabled and appears normally in the window.

Instructor initials: _____

6. Close the *Device Manager* window and all other windows.

Lab 16.12 Installing Hardware

Objective: To install a new hardware component under the Vista, Windows 7, 8, or 10 operating system

Parts: A computer with Windows Vista, 7, 8, or 10 installed

                New device to install

                Access to the Internet

Note: The student must be logged in as a user with local Administrator rights to perform this lab. In this lab, the Internet is used to obtain the device's installation instructions and latest device driver, and then the new hardware device is installed.

Procedure: Complete the following procedure and answer the accompanying questions.

1. Log in using the user ID and password provided by your instructor or lab assistant.

2. Using the Internet, locate the manufacturer's instructions for installing the device.

    Who is the device manufacturer?

    _____

3. Using the Internet, locate the latest device driver that is compatible with the version of Windows being used.

Does the device have an appropriate driver for the version of Windows being used?

[Yes | No]

_____

What is the device driver version being downloaded?

_____

4. Connect the device to the computer using the proper installation procedures.

5. Boot the computer. Usually, Windows automatically detects the new hardware and begins the *Found New Hardware* Wizard. If it does not present this wizard, look to see if the hardware device vendor supplied an installation program. If so, use this program to install the device. If no vendor-supplied installation program is available, use *Device Manager* or *Devices and Printers/Add a device* link, as described in the chapter, to install the device. Install the device driver based on the device type and manufacturer's instructions.

Did the Found New Hardware Wizard begin?

_____

6. Test the device installation.

Instructor initials: _____

Lab 16.13 Installing and Removing Windows Components

Objective: To install and remove Windows 7, 8, or 10 components

Parts: A computer with Windows 7, 8, or 10 installed and Administrator rights

Procedure: Complete the following procedure and answer the accompanying questions.

1. Turn on the computer and verify that the operating system loads. Log in to Windows using the user ID and password provided by your instructor or lab assistant. Ensure that the user ID is one that has Administrator rights.

Verifying and Installing Windows Features

2. Open Windows Explorer/File Explorer, right-click (or tap and briefly hold on) *Computer/This PC*), and select *Properties*. Select the *System Protection* link.

3. Create a system restore point by clicking the *Create* button. In the description textbox type class followed by the current date. Select *Create*. A dialog box appears when the restore point has been successfully created. Click *OK*.

4. Click *OK* in the System Properties window.

5. Access the *Programs* Control Panel to select the *Turn Windows features on or off* link from the Programs and features section.

List three enabled Windows features.

_____

_____

_____

_____

List three Windows features that are turned off.

_____

_____

_____

_____

6. Notice how the Games option is controlled through this section if you are using Windows Vista or 7. Expand the *Games* option or another option that can be expanded.

7. Check with your instructor or lab assistant for a specific feature to turn on. One option would be to turn on the TFTP client if it is not enabled.

List the program to be enabled.

_____

8. Select the checkbox for the feature to be enabled and click *OK*. Note that enabling the feature might take a few minutes.

9. Re-access the *Turn Windows features on or off* link to verify that the feature now shows as enabled.

Instructor initials: _____

10. Remove the check from the feature you just enabled and verify that the feature is removed successfully.

11. Access the *Programs* Control Panel. Under the *Default Programs* section, select the *Set your default programs* link.

What can be done from this window?

_____

_____

_____

12. Select *Internet Explorer* from the Programs list. Select the *Choose defaults for this program* link.

List the extensions that are automatically opened by Internet Explorer.

_____

List protocols that are automatically recognized from the address line in Internet Explorer.

_____

13. Click *Cancel* and *OK* to return to the Default Programs window.

14. Select the *Associate a file type or protocol with a program* link.

List one program that does not have a program extension or protocol associated with it (listed as un-known in the *Current Default* column).

_____

15. Leave this window open and create and save a Notepad document called `Superdog.txt`.

Document the location where this document is saved.

_____

16. Open *Windows Explorer (Windows 7)/File Explorer (Windows 8/10)* and locate the *Superdog.txt* file. In Windows 7, select the *Views* drop-down arrow. In Windows 8/10, select the *View* menu option.

What is the current view?

_____

17. Select the *List* view. Reselect the *View* menu option.

    In Windows 7, select the *Organize* menu option > select *Folder and Search Options*. Select the *View* tab.

    In Windows 8/10, select *Options* (located on the far right) > select the *Change folder and search options* link. Select the *View* tab.

    What is the current setting for Hide extensions for known file types? [Enabled | Disabled]

    _____

18. Ensure the *Hide extensions for known file types* option is disabled (unchecked). Select *OK*.

19. Return to Windows Explorer/File Explorer and ensure that the `.txt` extension is visible on the `Superdog.txt` filename. Right-click (or tap and briefly hold on) the *Superdog.txt* filename and select *Rename*. Rename the `.txt` extension to `.cas` (or your own initials, if they are not a common file extension). When the message window appears, select *Yes*.

    How did the appearance of the file change?

    _____

    _____

20. Right-click (or tap and briefly hold on) the *Superdog* filename and select *Properties*.

    What application does Windows assign to open the document?

    _____

21. Click the *Change* button.

    In Windows 7, notice that the *Always use the selected program to open this kind of file* checkbox at the bottom of the window is enabled. Select *Notepad* and *OK*. Click *Apply* and *OK*.

    In Windows 8/10, select the *More options/More apps* link. Select *Notepad* from the list.

22. Locate the *Superdog* file in Windows Explorer/File Explorer and double-click or double-tap the icon.

    Does the file open? If so, in what application?

    _____

23. Close the *Superdog* file. Return to the *Set Associations* window. Scroll down until you see the extension you used when you renamed the *Superdog* filename. Show your instructor or lab assistant the file extension.

Instructor initials: _____

24. Select the file extension in the list, and click the *Change program* button. Use the *Browse* button (Windows 7) or *More options/More apps* link (Windows 8/10) to find the WordPad application. In Windows 7, use the Search feature inside Browse, if necessary. When you find WordPad, select it and click *Open*. Click *OK*.

25. Return to *Windows Explorer/File Explorer*. Locate the *Superdog* file and double-click the icon.

    Does the file open? If so, in what application?

    _____

26. Close the file. Permanently delete the file by holding down the *Shift* key while pressing *Delete*. Click *Yes* to permanently delete the file.

27. On your own, create another file that ends in the same file extension. Try to open it.

    What happens?

    _____

28. Close the file and permanently delete the file.

29. Re-open the System Restore utility.

30. Select the *Choose a different restore point* radio button and click *Next*.

CHAPTER 16

31. Select the *class+date* restore point that was created at the beginning of the lab and click *Next*. Click *Finish*. Read the message that appears and click *Yes*. The system restores the system to the time before this lab was started. The system reboots and a dialog box appears telling you whether the restore point was successful. Click *Close*.

32. Reopen the *Programs* Control Panel and select the *Make a file type always open in a specific program* link.

33. Scroll through the list.

    Is the unique file extension used in this lab located in the list?

    _____

34. Close the *Set Associations* window.

Lab 16.14 Microsoft Management Console

Objective: To access and use the major utilities found in the Microsoft Management Console

Parts: A computer with Windows 7, 8, or 10 installed and Administrator rights

Notes: You must be an administrator to utilize the Microsoft Management Console utilities.

Procedure: Complete the following procedure and answer the accompanying questions.

1. Power on the computer and verify that Windows loads. Log on to Windows using the user ID and password provided by the instructor or lab assistant.

2. To access Microsoft Management Console in Windows 7, click the *Start* button. In Windows 8 or 10, right-click on the *Start* button. In all operating systems select *Control Panel > System and Security* link > *Administrative Tools* > double-click the *Computer Management* option.

   Determine the subcategories for each of the major Computer Management sections. Document the subcategories in Table 16.22.

TABLE 16.22   Windows Computer Management console

Computer Management section	Subcategories
System Tools	
Storage	
Services and Applications	

3. Return to the *Computer Management* window and, if necessary, select the arrow beside *System Tools* to expand the section. If necessary, select the arrow beside *Shared Folders* to expand that section. Click the *Shares* folder. Shares are used when the computer is in a network environment. Other users on different computers can access resources on this computer. When networking is enabled, default administrative shares are created for each hard drive partition. Administrative shares can be easily identified by the $ (dollar sign) after the share name.

   List two default shares located on this machine. If none are available, document the fact.

   _____

4. If necessary, expand *Local Users* and *Groups* and click the *Users* folder.

   List the users shown in the Computer Management window.

   _____

5. To add a new user who will have access to this computer, click the *Action* menu option and select *New User*. Note that you may have to select the *More Actions* link to see this option. The New User window opens. Click the *Question mark* icon located in the upper-right corner of the window. An arrow with an attached question mark appears as a pointer. Move the pointer to inside the *User name* textbox and click. A Help box appears on Windows 7. Windows 8 and 10 launch a web browser to technet.microsoft.com with a KB article on users and groups.

6. In the *User name* textbox, type **Jeff Cansler**. In the *Full name* textbox, type **Jeffrey Wayne Cansler**. In the *Description* textbox, type **Brother**. In the *Password* and the *Confirm password* textboxes, type **test**. Note that if a local policy is applied, you may have to strengthen this password to something like **Test1234%**. Ensure that the *User must change password at next logon* checkbox is disabled (not checked). Select in the *User cannot change password* checkbox to enable this option. Select the *Create* button. Select the *Close* button. The Jeff Cansler user icon appears in the Computer Management window.

   Have a classmate verify the Jeff Cansler user icon. Have the classmate double-click the icon to verify your settings. Are the settings correct?

   _____

   If not, redo the previous step.

   Classmate's signature: _____

7. Log off the computer and log back on using the Jeff Cansler username with a password of *test (or the stronger one of Test1234%).*

   Did the log on process work correctly?

   _____

   If not, log back on using the user ID and password given to you by the lab assistant or instructor for the beginning of the lab and redo Step 6.

8. Log off the computer and log back on using the user ID and password given to you by the lab assistant or instructor (the original user ID and password). Access the *Computer Management* window, and double-click the *Jeff Cansler* user icon. Select the *Member of* tab.

   To what group does the Jeff Cansler user automatically belong?

   _____

9. Select the *Add* button. The Select Groups window opens. In the *Enter the object names to select* textbox, type **Administrators** and select the *Check Names* button. Select the *OK* button. The information shown changes to the user, Jeff Cansler, belonging to both the Users and Administrator groups. Click the *Apply* button and then the *OK* button.

   Instructor initials: _____

10. Re-open the Jeff Cansler user window and select the *Profile* tab.

    The *Profile* tab is used to specify a home directory for the user, run a logon script that sets specific parameters for the user, input a path that specifies where the user stores files by default, or input a shared network directory where the user's data is placed.

    The *Profile path* textbox is where you type the location of the profile using a UNC. An example is \\users\profiles\jcansler.

    The *Logon script* textbox is where you type the name of the logon script file, for example, startup.bat.

    The *Home folder Local path* textbox is where you type the full path for where the user's data is stored by default. An example is C:\users\jcansler. The *Connect* radio button is used to assign a network drive letter and specify the location of a network directory where the user's data is stored. An example is \\users\jcandata. Select the *Cancel* button to return to the Computer Management window. Notice that users that are disabled have a small down arrow on their icon.

    Are any users disabled? [Yes | No]

CHAPTER 16

11. In the Computer Management window, select the *Groups* folder.

List two default groups.

_____

_____

_____

_____

12. Double-click the *Administrators* group icon. The Administrators group has total control of the local machine.

Are any users listed as part of the Administrators group? If so, list them.

_____

_____

Fill in Table 16.23 with the purpose of each group type. Use the *Help* menu item for more information than what is shown in the window.

TABLE 16.23   Windows User Groups

Group	Description
Administrators	
Backup Operators	
Guests	
Users	

13. Exit the help and then click the *Users* folder located in the Computer Management window. Select the *Jeff Cansler* user icon. Click the red *X* icon or click the *Action* menu item, and select *Delete*. A message appears asking if you are sure that you want to delete this user. Select the *Yes* button (twice if necessary).

14. Go into the *Administrators* group and verify that Jeff Cansler no longer appears there.

Have a classmate verify that the Jeff Cansler user icon is deleted. Is the Jeff Cansler user icon deleted? If not, redo the previous step.

_____

Classmate's printed name: _____

Classmate's signature: _____

15. Select the *Device Manager* option located in the Computer Management window. This utility can also be accessed by typing devmgmt.msc in a run box, search textbox, or from a command prompt. Device Manager is used to access and manage hardware devices installed in the computer. It is also used to load new drivers and roll back to an older driver.

16. In the right panel, select the arrow by the computer name if the list is not already expanded. Expand the *Computer* category.

    Is this computer 32- or 64-bit based? [32-bit | 64-bit]

    _____

17. Expand the *Storage* category in the left pane. Select the *Disk Management* subcategory. The right pane displays information about each type of hard disk partition created on the drive. The top window shows information about each disk partition including total capacity, file system, free space percentage, and so forth. The bottom windows show the drives and partitions in graphical form.

18. Right-click the first volume (usually C:) in the upper window and select the *Properties* option. An alternative method is to click the *Action* menu item and select *Properties*. The Disk Properties window opens.

19. On an NTFS partition, the *General* tab contains a *Disk Cleanup* button that can be used to clean up temporary files and delete applications not used, Windows components not used, log files, and old system restores. Select the *Tools* tab.

    What tools are listed on the Tools tab?

    _____

    _____

    Match the following tool to its associated task. Note that Windows 8/10 does not have the Backup tool on the *Tool* tab, but this question should still be able to be answered after reading the chapter.

    _____ Backup   **a.** Scans the disk for damage

    _____ Error-checking   **b.** Used to restore system files that have been saved

    _____ Defragmentation   **c.** Locates file clusters that are not consecutive (contiguous) and
                          places the files in order

21. The Disk Management tool can create disk partitions, delete partitions, convert partitions to NTFS, create logical drives, and convert basic disks to dynamic disks. Select the *Cancel* button.

22. Expand the *Services and Applications* Computer Management category. Select the *Services* subcategory. A service is an application that runs in the background. (You do not see it on the taskbar.) The Services window is used to start, stop, pause, resume, or disable a service. You must be a member of the Administrators group to use this tool.

    List two services that start automatically and two services that require manual starting.

    _____

    _____

    _____

    _____

    _____

    _____

    _____

23. Double-click the *Computer Browser* service. The General tab is used to start, stop, pause, or resume a service (depending on its current state). The buttons in the Service status section are used to control these actions. The *General* tab is also used to set whether the service starts when the computer boots. Select the *Startup type* down arrow to see a menu of startup options.

24. Close the *Service* window without making any changes to the service and close the *Computer Management* window.

Instructor initials: _____

Lab 16.15 Exploring Windows Boot Options

Objective:	To explore Windows 7, 8, or 10 boot options that are used to troubleshoot startup problems
Parts:	A computer with Windows 7, 8, or 10 installed that has the capability to boot from a CD/DVD
	User ID that has Administrator rights
	Windows 7, 8, or 10 DVD or virtual image of the DVD
Note:	In this lab, you boot without startup programs loaded, boot to Safe Mode, boot to Safe Mode with Command Prompt, boot to Enable Boot Logging and examine the `ntbtlog.txt` file, and boot to Recovery Console and examine commands using the command prompt. If the Windows DVD or image of the installation disc is not available, that one section could be skipped.
Procedure:	Complete the following procedure and answer the accompanying questions.

1. Turn on the computer and verify that the operating system loads. Log in to Windows using the user ID and password provided by your instructor or lab assistant.

Using Boot Options

2. On Windows 7 restart the computer and press the ⎡F8⎤ key as the computer boots. If the *Advanced Boot Options* window does not appear, shut down the computer and restart. Press ⎡F8⎤ as the computer boots. The *Advanced Boot Options* menu appears. Select the *Safe Mode* option and press ⎡Enter⎤. Log in with an account that has administrator privileges.

   On Windows 8 or 10, select *Settings > Update and recovery* (Windows 8)/*Update & security* (Windows 10) > select *Recovery* from the left menu > in the Advanced startup section, select the *Restart now button* > select *Troubleshoot > Advanced options > Startup Settings* > select the *Restart* button. After the restart, choose *option 4 (Enable Safe Mode)*.

   When would a technician use the Safe Mode option as opposed to the Safe Mode with Command Prompt option?

   _____

   _____

   _____

   How does the look of the screen in Safe Mode differ from the look of the normal Windows desktop?

   _____

   _____

   What Windows Help and Support topic automatically displays, if any?

   _____

   How can you easily tell you are running in Safe Mode?

   _____

3. Access the *Administrative Tools* Control Panel link. Open *Computer Management*. Expand the *Services and Applications* category. Access the *Services* option.

4. Quite a few services are automatic services that did not start in Safe Mode.

   List two services that did not automatically start because Safe Mode was used.

   _____

   _____

5. Close the *Computer Management* and any Control Panel windows, Restart Windows.

6. Re-access the *Advanced Boot Options (Windows 7)/Startup Settings (Windows 8/10)* menu. Refer to Step 2 if necessary.

   List the boot options available.

   _____

   _____

   _____

   _____

   _____

   Match each of the following definitions to the appropriate boot option:

   _____ Safe Mode

   _____ Safe Mode with Command Prompt

   _____ Enable Boot Logging

   _____ Disable automatic restart on system failure

   a. Starts the system with minimum files and drivers, and only typed commands can be used

   b. Records the boot process into a text file that can later be viewed and used for troubleshooting

   c. Starts the system with minimum files and drivers, including the default video drivers

   d. Allows a technician to have time to document an error that occurs

7. Select the *Enable Boot Logging* option.

   How does the desktop appear when using the Enable Boot Logging option?

   _____

8. Use the *Search* function to locate and access the `ntbtlog.txt` file.

   List two drivers that loaded properly.

   _____

   List two drivers that did not load. Note that you may have to scroll through the list to see these.

   _____

   Instructor initials: _____

9. Close all windows.

Recovery Environment

10. Insert the Windows Installation disc into the optical drive or have the ISO on an external disk and power off the computer. Power on the computer. If prompted, press a key to start Windows from the disc. A menu appears with a default option selected. Press *Enter*. If the computer does not boot from the Windows disc, the BIOS settings probably need to be adjusted.

11. Choose the appropriate language settings and click *Next*.

12. Select *Repair your computer*. In the options window on a Windows 7 computer, select the *Use recovery tools that can help fix problems starting Windows*; enable the *Select an operating system to repair* radio button. On a Windows 8 or 10 computer, select *Troubleshoot*.

13. Ensure that the operating system is selected and click *Next*.

    List the recovery tool options.

    _____

    Which option would be used to repair a system file?

    _____

Which option would be used to check RAM?

_____

Which option do you think would be for advanced technicians?

_____

Which option configures the system to an earlier time such as before a Windows update?

_____

Instructor initials: _____

14. Select the *Memory Diagnostic* link. Select the *Restart now and check for problems (recommended)* link. Do not press a key when the system reboots and asks "Press a key to boot from CD or DVD." List one status message.

_____

_____

_____

15. After the test executes and the computer reboots, as before, do not press any key, even when the message prompts to press a key to boot from a CD or DVD. After Windows reboots, log in again. Open Event Viewer by accessing the following Control Panel links: *System and Security > Administrative tools*. Double-click *Event Viewer* to open the tool.

16. Expand *Windows Logs*. Click the *System* Windows log. Right-click *System* and select *Find*.

17. In the *Find what* textbox, type the following: `MemoryDiagnostics-Results`

    Be careful that you type exactly as shown and click *Find Next*. The corresponding line highlights.

18. Close the *Find* window. Double-click the highlighted line to see the results of the memory diagnostic check. Select the *Details* tab.

    What are the results shown in the friendly view?

    _____

    What Event ID did Windows assign?

    _____

19. Close all windows. Remove the Windows disc and return to the instructor or lab assistant.

Lab 16.16 Windows System Configuration Utility

Objective: To use the System Configuration utility to troubleshoot boot problems

Parts: A computer with Windows installed

    User ID that has Administrator rights

Note: In this lab, create a shortcut to an application and then use the System Configuration utility to prevent it from loading. Explore various options that can be used within the System Configuration utility.

Procedure: Complete the following procedure and answer the accompanying questions.

1. Turn on the computer and verify that the operating system loads. Log in to Windows using the user ID and password provided by the instructor or lab assistant. Ensure that the user ID is one that has Administrator rights.

Creating an Application Shortcut in the Startup Folder

2. Use Windows Explorer/File Explorer to navigate to the following folder: C:\Users*<user name>*\ AppData\Roaming\Microsoft\Windows\Start Menu\Programs\Startup. Note that the *user name* is the name you used to log in to the computer. You may also have to adjust the Windows Explorer/File Explorer view so that hidden items (files and folders) are shown. (In Windows 7, select the *Organize* drop-down arrow > select *Folder and search options* > select the *View* tab > select the *Show hidden files, folders, and drives* radio button > select *OK*. In Windows 8/10, select the *View* menu option > ensure the *Hidden items* option is enabled).

3. In a separate window, use the *Search* feature to locate the original Notepad application (`notepad. exe`). Create a shortcut to the Notepad application and place it in the *Startup* folder located under the *Programs* folder (see Step 2).

   Have a classmate verify your shortcut (especially that it is a shortcut and not a copy of the application or the application itself). Is the icon in the Startup folder a shortcut icon?

   _____

   Classmate's signature: _____

4. Restart the computer and verify that the Notepad program starts automatically when the computer boots. If it does not, redo the lab from the beginning.

   Instructor initials: _____

System Configuration Utility

5. Hold down the *Windows* key and press ⌨R; type **msconfig** and press ⌨Enter. An alternate method is to search for `msconfig`. The System Configuration utility window opens.

   What is the purpose of the System Configuration utility?

   _____

   What tabs are available through the System Configuration utility?

   _____

6. Click the *Diagnostic Startup—Load basic devices and services only* radio button. Click the *Apply* button and then select the *OK* button. A System Configuration message box appears. Select the *Restart* button. When the computer restarts, log in with the same user ID used previously.

   Did the Notepad application automatically start?

   _____

7. Select *OK*. Return to the System Configuration (`msconfig`) utility and select the *Selective Startup* radio button on the *General* tab. Checkboxes are now available so that you can select the startup files that are to be loaded the next time the computer boots. Select the *Load Startup Items* checkbox. Select the *Apply* button and then select *Close*. Select the *Restart* button and the system restarts. Log in using the same user ID and password.

   Did the Notepad application automatically start? Why or why not?

   _____

8. Select *OK* if necessary. Return to the System Configuration utility and select the *Normal Startup— load all device drivers and services* option located on the *General* tab. Note that Windows automatically changes the radio button to the *Selective startup* option.

9. Select the *Startup* tab.

10. In Windows 7, select the *Shortcut to notepad* checkbox to disable it > select *Apply* > select *Close*.

    In Windows 8/10, select the *Open Task Manager* link. In Windows 8/10 Task Manager (*Startup* tab) opens. In Windows 8/10, select *Notepad* and select the *Disable* button.

11. Restart the computer. When the computer restarts, log in using the same user ID and click *OK*.

Did the Notepad application automatically start? Why or why not?

_____

_____

Reopen the System Configuration utility to determine what is different about the General tab. Document your observations.

_____

_____

_____

Match the correct System Configuration utility tab to its characteristic.

_____ General   _____ Boot   _____ Services

_____ Tools   _____ Startup

a. Has an Advanced options button so that you can control the number of processors used to boot the system.

b. Contains applications that begin every time the computer boots

c. Contains a section called [boot loader] that details operating system boot options

d. Has an option to choose which boot files are processed

e. Contains an Application Management option

f. Provides an easy way to launch System Restore and Registry Editor

12. Select the *General* tab and select the *Normal Startup* radio button > select *Apply* > select *Close* > select *Restart*. Log in using the same user ID.

13. After the computer reboots, remove the shortcut to the Notepad application from the *Startup* folder.

Is the Notepad shortcut (and not the original application) deleted?

_____

Instructor initials: _____

Lab 16.17 Halting an Application Using Task Manager

Objective: To use Task Manager to halt an application

Parts: A computer with Windows Vista, 7, 8.1, or 10 installed

Note: At times, it may become necessary to halt an application that is hung or stalled. Windows provides a method to accomplish this through the Task Manager utility.

Procedure: Complete the following procedure and answer the accompanying questions.

1. Turn on the computer and verify that the operating system loads. Log in to Windows using the user ID and password provided by the instructor or lab assistant. Ensure that the user ID is one that has Administrator rights.

2. Open the Notepad utility.

3. Open Task Manager: right-click the taskbar > select *Start Task Manager (Windows 7)/Task Manager (Windows 8.1/10)*.

What type of things can you view from Task Manager?

_____

_____

4. Select the *Applications (Windows 7)/Processes (Windows 8.1/10)* tab.

   What applications, if any, are listed as open? Note that you might need to click the down arrow by the *More details* option in Windows 8.1/10.

   _____

   Instructor initials: _____

5. Select the *Untitled—Notepad (Windows 7)/Notepad (Windows 8.1/10)* option and select the *End Task* button. Notepad closes.

   Could you close the Notepad application from within Task Manager?

   _____

6. Close the *Task Manager* window.

Lab 16.18 Using Event Viewer

Objective:	To use the Event Viewer program to troubleshoot problems
Parts:	A computer with Windows Vista, 7, 8, or 10 installed and a user ID that has Administrator rights
Note:	In this lab, evaluate a computer event to see how to gather information using Event Viewer.
Procedure:	Complete the following procedure and answer the accompanying questions.

1. Turn on the computer and verify that the operating system loads. Log in to Windows using the user ID and password provided by your instructor or lab assistant. Ensure that the user ID is one that has Administrator rights.

2. Event Viewer monitors and logs various events such as when drivers and services load (or fail to load and have problems). Open the *System and Maintenance* (Vista)/*System and Security* (7/8/10) Control Panel > *Administrative Tools* > double-click *Event Viewer*. The Event Viewer window opens to the Overview and Summary window.

   How many total warning administrative events occurred on this computer?

   _____

3. In the left pane, expand the *Windows Logs* section > select *Security*. The most recent events list at the top. You might need to expand the window or reduce the size of the left and right panes in order to see the center pane better. Locate and double-click on the most recent event that shows as *Logon* in the *Task Category column.*

   From the General tab, what was the account name?

   _____

   What time did the logon occur?

   _____

   Was the logon successful? In other words, did Event Viewer show this as an Audit Success or as an Audit Failure?

   _____

4. Close the security event properties window. The Audit Success line in the center pane is still selected. In the right panel, select the *Attach Task to This Event*. Type your first initial and last name as the name of the basic task, for example: cschmidt. Click *Next* on the following two windows.

   What three actions can be taken from this screen?

   _____

5. Select *Cancel*.

6.   In the left panel, select the *Application* option from the *Windows Logs* category.

List the application that caused the first event.

_____

7.   Select the *Windows Logs > Security* subcategory from the left panel.

Scroll through the list of events logged and pay attention to the *Task Category* column. What type of task categories are most common?

_____

Does Windows log an event when a user logs off a Windows computer?

_____

8.   Select the *Windows Logs > System* subcategory from the left panel. Double-click the first event listed. List the source of the first event.

_____

9.   Select the *Copy* button.

10.   Open the *Wordpad* application > access the *Edit* menu item > select *Paste*.

What appeared in Wordpad?

_____

Instructor initials: _____

11.   The event information can be saved as a text file and referenced later, especially when there is a problem. Close *Wordpad* without saving the document. Close the *Event Properties* window.

12.   In Event Viewer, expand *Applications and Services Logs*. Expand the *Microsoft* folder and the *Windows* folder. Expand the *TaskScheduler* to locate and click the *Operational* event log.

What is the first informational TaskScheduler event logged? Note that on a virtualized machine there might not be an event. Just document that you were in a virtual environment as your answer.

_____

13.   Close *Event Viewer*.

Lab 16.19 Using Task Manager to View Performance

Objective: To use the Task Manager program to evaluate basic computer performance

Parts: A computer with Windows Vista, 7, 8.1, or 10 installed and user ID that has Administrator rights

Note: In this lab, evaluate a computer event to see how to gather information using Event Viewer.

Procedure: Complete the following procedure and answer the accompanying questions.

1.   Turn on the computer and verify that the operating system loads. Log in to Windows using the user ID and password provided by the instructor or lab assistant. Ensure that the user ID is one that has Administrator rights.

2.   Open Task Manager: right-click the taskbar > select *Start Task Manager (Windows 7)/Task Manager (Windows 8.1/10)*. Click the *Performance* tab. The Performance tab is used to view CPU and memory usage (Windows 7) and in Windows 8, 8.1, and 10, the performance tab also shows Disk and Ethernet (network) utilization.

3.   Open *Notepad*, access the Internet if possible, open a game if possible, and start other applications.

What happens to the CPU usage as shown in Task Manager as each application is opened?

_____

What is the memory usage?

_____

What is the total physical memory?

_____

How much memory is available?

_____

Instructor initials: _____

4.　Task Manager is a great way to see a snapshot of the status of two of the most important pieces of hardware, the CPU and RAM (even though the Task Manager application increases both the CPU and memory usage). Note that if the CPU and memory utilization stay consistently high, add more RAM first. If the CPU stays consistently level and at a high value, a more powerful processor is in order. Close all windows.

Lab 16.20 Performance and Reliability in Windows 7, 8, and 10

Objective:　　To use Windows 7, 8.1, or 10 tools to verify performance, measure reliability, and trouble-shoot startup problems

Parts:　　Access to Windows 7, 8.1, or 10 with a user ID that has Administrator rights

Procedure:　　Complete the following procedure and answer the accompanying questions.

1.　Turn on the computer and verify that the operating system loads. Log in to Windows using the user ID and password that has full Administrator rights and that is provided by your instructor or lab assistant.

2.　Access the _System and Security Control Panel_ > _Administrative Tools_ > double-click _Performance Monitor_ > select the _Open Resource Monitor_ link. The information shown on the _Overview_ tab is known as the key table. It always contains a complete list of running (active) processes for the system. You can filter the data and look at the information more granularly by using the specific tabs.

3.　Select the _CPU_ tab. Notice the individual programs and processes in the _Processes_ section. Select a particular process by selecting the checkbox by the process name. The top graph shows that particular process in relation to the total CPU usage.

How many CPU threads are used by the Performance Monitor application?

_____

4.　Deselect any individual process(es) in the Processes section. Expand the _Services_ section. Notice the last column: Average CPU. This column shows the average percentage of CPU consumption by a particular service.

What service is taking the most CPU power?

_____

5.　Select the _Memory_ tab. Notice the Commit (KB) column. This column shows the amount of virtual memory reserved by Windows for a particular process.

List two processes and the amount of virtual memory used by the system for each process.

_____

_____

_____

6.　The Working Set column shows the amount of physical memory used by a particular process.

Which process is using the most motherboard RAM?

_____

7. Select the *Disk* tab. Open any file and save it to a different location on the hard drive if possible. Return to the *Disk* tab and notice the disk activity.

8. Select the *Network* tab. Connect to the Internet and return to this tab.

   How many TCP connections are active?

   _____

9. Close the *Resource Monitor* window and return to the *Performance Monitor* window.

10. Ensure that the top object, *Performance*, is selected in the left panel. Notice the *System Summary* section in the center of the right panel.

    What is the available memory in megabytes?

    _____

    Scroll down to see the *PhysicalDisk* component. What is the percentage of idle time?

    _____

    Locate the *Processor Information* section. What is the total percent of processor time?

    _____

11. Expand the *Monitoring Tools* object in the left panel. Select the *Performance Monitor* tool.

    What is the default counter shown?

    _____

12. Select the green plus symbol (+) from the graphical menu at the top of the chart. Scroll through the counters list until you locate and select the *PhysicalDisk* counter down arrow (⊡). Click once on the *Disk Reads/sec* counter. In the *Instances of selected object* window, select the number that corresponds to your primary hard drive partition. Select *Add*. Continue by using the same process to add the following counters.

PhysicalDisk	Disk Writes/sec
LogicalDisk	% Free Space
Memory	Available Bytes
Memory	Cache Bytes
Processor	% Processor Time (All instances)

13. Select *OK*. If a message appears saying that one of the counters is already enabled, select *OK*.

14. Allow the system to run at least 2 minutes. Do things on the computer during this time. Afterward, select the *Freeze Display* menu icon that looks like a pause button on a CD/DVD player.

15. Select the *Change Graph Type* drop-down menu item to *Histogram bar*. This is the third icon from the left on the graphic menu at the top of the graph. Select the *Available bytes* counter.

    What is the average number of available bytes of memory?

    _____

16. Select the *Cache Bytes* counter row.

    What is the maximum number of bytes in cache memory?

    _____

    Look at the bar graph. Which is higher, the number of disk reads per second or the disk writes per second?

    _____

Instructor initials: _____

17. Change the graph type to the *Report* view.

Which one of these views do you think will be most used by a technician?

_____

18. Close the *Performance Monitor* window.

19. In Windows 7, type **reliability** monitor in the *Search* textbox. Select the *View reliability history* link from the resulting list.

In Windows 8/10, search for **view reliability history** and select it from the resulting list.

Describe any event that the system considered important enough to potentially affect the computer reliability.

_____

20. Close all windows.

Lab 16.21 Windows Remote Desktop

Objective: To configure a computer for remote access using the Remote Desktop tool

Parts: Two computers with Windows 7, 8, or 10 loaded

Notes: The Remote Desktop tool is disabled by default and you can connect to (take over) computers running only Windows Professional, Enterprise, or Ultimate, but all Windows 7, 8, and 10 versions can initiate the Remote Desktop connection.

You must have the ability to create users on the remote computer or have a user ID already created that has a password assigned.

Procedure: Complete the following procedure and answer the accompanying questions.

1. On the computer that is to be accessed remotely, power it on and verify that Windows loads. Log in using the user ID and password provided by the instructor or lab assistant.

2. If both computers have a user ID with full Administrator rights and a password, this step can be skipped. Otherwise, access the *User Accounts Control Panel > Manage another account > Create a new account* link > type **tester** in the *New account name* textbox > select the *Administrator* radio button > select the *Create Account* button. Add a password by clicking the *tester* icon > *create a password* link > in the *New password* textbox, type **tester** > in the *Confirm new password* textbox, type **tester** > click the *Create password* button. Close the User Accounts window. Log in using the "tester" account on both computers.

3. On both computers, open *Windows Explorer/File Explorer*. Locate and right-click the *Computer* item (*This PC* on Windows 8 and 10). Select *Properties*.

Document the full computer name for both computers.

Computer 1

_____

Computer 2

_____

4. On both computers, select the *Remote settings* link. The *Remote* tab should be active.

What is the current Remote Desktop setting? [Don't allow remote connections to this computer | Allow remote connections from computers running any version of Remote Desktop (less secure) | Allow connections only from computers running Remote Desktop with Network Level Authentication (more secure (Windows 7)/recommended (Windows 8/10))]

5. On both computers in the Remote Desktop section, select the *Allow [remote] connections from computers running any version of Remote Desktop (less secure)* radio button on Windows 7. On Windows 8 and 10 uncheck the *Allow connections only from computers running Remote Desktop with Network Level Authentication* option.

    What warning appears, if any?

    _____

    _____

6. If necessary, select *OK* on the message. Select *OK*.

7. On computer 1, use the search function to search for the term and access `remote desktop connection`.

8. On computer 1 in the Remote Desktop Connection window, type the other computer's full computer name in the *Computer* textbox. Click *Connect*.

9. Enter a username/password. Click *Yes* on the request for a certification or if a certificate warning appears.

    What happened to the remote computer?

    _____

10. On computer1 (that is controlling computer 2), add a new shortcut to the desktop of the remote computer. When finished, click the close button (X) in the blue Remote Desktop panel located in the top center of the screen. Select *OK*.

11. On the remote computer, log in. Notice the new desktop shortcut.

Instructor initials: _____

(Check for new desktop shortcut.)

12. Delete the newly installed desktop shortcut on the remote computer.

13. From computer 2, do the same procedure: remote into computer 1, create a desktop shortcut on computer 1, release control of computer 1, and verify the desktop shortcut on computer 1.

14. Return all settings back to the original configuration. See Step 4 answer.

15. Remove the *tester* user account from any computer if it was created.

Lab 16.22 Windows Task Scheduler in Windows 7, 8, and 10

Objective: To become familiar with the Task Scheduler tool and the `AT` command

Parts: Computer with Windows 7, 8 or 10 installed and Administrator rights

Procedure: Complete the following procedure and answer the accompanying questions.

Using Task Scheduler

1. Search on `task` in the *Search* textbox and select *Task Scheduler (Windows 7/10)/Schedule a task (Windows 8)* from the resulting list. Task Scheduler opens.

    Based on the information shown in the Overview of Task Scheduler pane, where are tasks stored?

    _____

2. In the *Actions* pane, select *Create Basic Task...* In the *Name* textbox, type your last name > *Next*. Notice the Trigger action is highlighted and Daily is the default task time > select the *One time* radio button > *Next* > set the time to start to be *5 minutes* from the current date and time > *Next*.

    What three actions can you take using this wizard?

    _____

3. Select the *Display a message* radio button and select *Next*. In the Title textbox, give a brief description of this message such as `Scheduled downtime`. In the Message textbox, type a respectable message that a technician might send. An example might be as follows: `Attention students, faculty, and staff. Our scheduled maintenance window will begin in 15 minutes. The server will be down for approximately 2 hours. Thanks for your patience.` Select the *Next* button.

4. Enable the *Open the Properties dialog for this task when I click Finish* checkbox > select the *Finish* button. Note that in Windows 8 or 10, you cannot display a message or send an email any more using Task Manager. If you are on Windows 8 or 10, skip step 5.

5. Only in Windows 7, select the *Run whether user is logged on or not* radio button and click *OK*. Enter the proper credentials with a username and password.

6. Create another scheduled task that runs an application one time at a specific time. Show the instructor this task credentials through the Task Scheduler Library and the task working.

   Document the scheduled task and start time.

   _____

   _____

Instructor initials: _____

Lab 16.23 Windows 8 Upgrade

Objective: To become familiar with upgrading to Windows 8 from Windows 7

Parts: A computer with Windows 7 installed, Internet access, and Administrator rights

Procedure: Complete the following procedure and answer the accompanying questions.

1. On the computer that is to be upgraded, power it on and verify that Windows loads. Log in using the user ID and password provided by the instructor or lab assistant.

2. Download and burn a bootable Windows 8 DVD.

3. Before proceeding it is recommended to back up any important data. If using a virtual machine, it is advised to create a snapshot that can be reverted to if you run into problems.

4. Review the Windows 8 minimum requirements to make sure your computer is compatible.

5. Insert the DVD into the computer and run the `setup.exe` file from the disc. You may be prompted to download updates by the installer; if so, download and install them.

6. When prompted, accept the licensing for the installer.

7. You will be asked if you want to keep files, settings, apps, or nothing. Select *keep files, apps and settings*, then press *Next*.

8. Next review your selections. You should be installing a version of Windows 8 and keeping your personal files. If it looks correct, press *Install*; otherwise, press *Back* and change your selections.

9. The installation will now begin; keep in mind it can take a few hours to complete. During this process the computer may reboot several times.

10. When the installation finishes, you will be at a Windows 8 login screen.

11. When you log back in, you will be given the option to customize or use express settings for the new installation. Choose customize.

12. Pick what settings you prefer.

13. When you finish the customization process, Windows finalizes its installation and brings you to your desktop.

Instructor initials: _____

CHAPTER 16

Lab 16.24 Windows 10 Upgrade

Objective: To become familiar with upgrading to Windows 10 from Windows 8

Parts: A computer with Windows 8 installed, Internet access, and Administrator rights

Procedure: Complete the following procedure and answer the accompanying questions.

1.   On the computer that is to be upgraded, power it on and verify that Windows loads. Log in using the user ID and password provided by the instructor or lab assistant.

2.   Download and burn a bootable Windows 10 DVD.

3.   Before proceeding it is recommended to back up any important data. If using a virtual machine, it is advised to create a snapshot that can be reverted to if you run into problems.

4.   Review the Windows 10 minimum requirements to make sure your computer is compatible.

5.   Insert the DVD into the computer and run the `setup.exe` file off of it. You may be prompted to download updates by the installer; if so, download and install them.

6.   When prompted, accept the licensing for the installer.

7.   You will be asked if you want to keep files, settings, apps, or nothing. Select *Keep files, apps and settings*, and then select *Next*.

8.   Next review your selections. You should be installing a version of Windows 10 and keeping your personal files. If it looks correct select *Install;* otherwise, select *Back* and change your selections.

9.   The installation now begins; keep in mind it can take a few hours to complete. During this process the computer may reboot several times.

10.   When the installation finishes you will be at a Windows 10 login screen.

11.   When you log back in, you will be given the option to customize or use express settings for the new installation. Choose *Customize*.

12.   Pick the settings you prefer.

13.   When you finish the customization process, Windows finalizes its installation and brings you to your desktop.

Instructor initials: _____

17 OS X and Linux Operating Systems

In this chapter you will learn:

> Alternative operating systems to Windows

> How to navigate the user interfaces of OS X and Ubuntu Linux

> How to manipulate files and folders in the graphical and command-line interfaces

> How to create system backups

> How to find UNIX/Linux software

> How to work from a Linux-based command line

> Reasons to be humble in the IT field

CompTIA Exam Objectives:

What CompTIA A+ exam objectives are covered in this chapter?

✓ 902-1.2 Given a scenario, install Windows PC operating systems using appropriate methods.

✓ 902-2.1 Identify common features and functionality of the Mac OS and Linux operating systems.

✓ 902-4.1 Given a scenario, troubleshoot PC operating system problems with appropriate tools.

✓ 902-4.2 Given a scenario, troubleshoot common PC security issues with appropriate tools and best practices.

Introduction to OS X

OS X (pronounced OS ten) is a UNIX-based operating system that was developed by Apple, Inc., for its Macintosh line of computers, called Mac for short. OS X is the second most-used desktop operating system behind Windows and is the most-used type of UNIX/Linux-based desktop operating system.

Like most UNIX/Linux operating systems, OS X utilizes many open source projects to make up the core and functionality of the operating system, along with a touch of Apple's own customization. **Open source** software is software made freely available and is open to outside contribution to improve. Although many parts of OS X are open source, the operating system is not. OS X is unique to Apple-released hardware (see Figure 17.1) because it comes preinstalled only on Macintosh systems and is not sold or distributed to run on other hardware such as Windows and most other UNIX/Linux distributions are.

FIGURE 17.1 Apple computer running OS X

OS X is on its 12th major desktop release, with new releases now planned annually. There was a line of dedicated OS X server operating systems, but that has now been discontinued in favor of a separately purchased add-on from the Apple App Store to provide the same functionality. The desktop OS X releases in the past were called by feline names but are now named after California landmarks. Table 17.1 is a list of OS X distributions by their name and release number.

TABLE 17.1 OS X releases by name and number

Release number	Name (release date)
10.0	Cheetah (March 2001)
10.1	Puma (September 2001)
10.2	Jaguar (August 2002)
10.3	Panther (October 2003)
10.4	Tiger (April 2005)
10.5	Leopard (October 2007)
10.6	Snow Leopard (August 2009)
10.7	Lion (July 2011)

Release number	Name (release date)
10.8	Mountain Lion (July 2012)
10.9	Mavericks (October 2013)
10.10	Yosemite (October 2014)
10.11	El Capitan (September 2015)

OS X is a portable operating system interface (**POSIX**) compliant operating system, meaning it meets the specifications of a standardized operating system outlined by the IEEE Computer Society, containing a Bourne shell and other standard programs and services that are found in all POSIX-compliant operating systems. A **shell** is the user interface used to interact with the operating system. This standardization makes it easier for end users, IT professionals, and developers to use different operating systems that are POSIX-compliant and have the tools available they are familiar with. Because of this standardization, many skills that you learn from OS X can be applied to other operating systems.

Navigating the User Interface

OS X is renowned for its intuitive and easy-to-learn graphical user interface (GUI) that has multiple ways to interact with it, from the standard mouse and keyboard to more advanced trackpad multitouch gestures. The graphical user interface of OS X is called Aqua. Steve Jobs, co-founder of Apple Inc., famously said "One of the design goals was when you saw it you wanted to lick it," referring to the original water-like theme with a heavy use of translucent and reflective design elements within the GUI. Now the GUI is a flatter, toned-down interface that more resembles Apple's mobile operating system iOS than earlier versions of the operating system.

There are four basic elements to the GUI of OS X. The one that sticks out first when looking at the desktop is simply known as the Dock. The **Dock** is the shortcut organizational bar used for launching, switching, and managing applications. You can easily customize the Dock by dragging and dropping applications and folder shortcuts to it. By default, the Dock is at the bottom of the screen but can be changed to be located on the side of the screen.

There is also the **Finder**, which is the file manager included in OS X and is used for navigating and managing files or folders in the file system. The Finder is similar to Microsoft's Windows Explorer/File Explorer. You can open the Finder by clicking the iconic Finder icon known for its smiling face, which is always located on the Dock.

Third, there is the menu bar. The **menu bar** is anchored to the top of the screen and is a dynamically changing bar that presents contextual drop-down menu options on the left side depending on what window is active. On the right side it also provides shortcuts to things such as connecting to a Wi-Fi network or changing volume. It is also informative, displaying information such as battery life on MacBooks and the time.

Lastly, there is the desktop. The desktop can display any mounted drives or disks as well as hold anything the end user wants to save to it such as documents or pictures for quick access. Figure 17.2 shows the four main elements of the OS X operating environment.

Notice in Figure 17.2 the three colored dots on the upper-left corner of the Finder window. The red dot on the far left closes the window. The middle yellow dot minimizes the open window down to the Dock. The green dot (the rightmost one) expands the window to full screen mode. This is universal across all windows in OS X.

Menu bar

Finder window

Finder

Dock

FIGURE 17.2   OS X desktop

TECH TIP

What to do if the Dock is missing

If the dock is not present, try hovering the pointer toward the bottom or sides of the screen. Many OS X users enable the hide dock feature to gain more screen space, making it disappear and only pop up when the pointer is nearby.

On top of the core GUI elements are also a few built-in utilities to make using the GUI easier. OS X supports multiple desktops similar to how Microsoft Windows 10 does with Task View. **Mission Control** is a feature that gives an overview for managing all application windows and virtual desktops. It can be invoked by using the F3 key (F9 on older Mac keyboards) by clicking the Mission Control icon or by swiping up on a trackpad with three or four fingers at once depending on the trackpad settings used. This displays all the running applications (see Figure 17.3), their respective windows grouped together, and any extra virtual desktops. From this view you can create, delete, or rearrange virtual desktops; switch which application windows reside on each virtual desktop; and easily explore all the open application windows.

Although Mission Control is great for managing applications, it cannot launch them. **Launchpad** is an application launcher shortcut. It can be invoked by pressing the F4 key, clicking the Launchpad icon, or doing a thumb + three-finger pinch gesture on a trackpad. From this view (see Figure 17.4) you get a grid-like display of all installed applications that you can click to launch. This grid interface can be searched with the available search bar at the top of the Launchpad interface. Applications can also be sorted into folders and multiple pages in this view for easy organization.

FIGURE 17.3   OS X Mission Control

FIGURE 17.4   OS X Launchpad

Finder is used for navigating the file system, but this can be cumbersome and take a long time to find something, especially if you are not sure where it is located. For searching the system you can use Spotlight. **Spotlight** is a universal search tool that can search every file and directory, but also search things such as contacts, email, music, and even the web. It is invoked by holding down Cmd and pressing the Spacebar, or by clicking the magnifying glass icon on the right side of the menu bar. A large search bar appears in the middle of the screen allowing you to type in your search. The results are then presented to you underneath the search bar.

CHAPTER 17

FIGURE 17.5 OS X Spotlight

You may have noticed that many of these shortcuts have their own dedicated gestures that can be triggered using a trackpad to launch them. Apple first used the idea of finger-based **gestures**, a use of fingers to make a motion to provide input into its mobile operating system iOS. These gestures and functionality were later brought to the MacBook laptops. To easily use these gestures, a user could purchase a Magic Mouse, which is a multitouch mouse sold by Apple, or a Bluetooth trackpad known as the Magic Trackpad. Table 17.2 gives a listing of the most commonly used trackpad gestures and what they trigger. Keep in mind that other gestures can be enabled, and many of them can be changed to a different gesture depending on the user's preference.

TABLE 17.2 Commonly used OS X gestures

Gesture	Action
Swipe left or right with two fingers	Swipe between pages
Swipe left or right with four fingers	Swipe between full screen applications
Swipe up with three or four fingers	Opens Mission Control
Pinch in with the thumb and three fingers	Opens Launchpad
Spread apart the thumb and three fingers	Shows the desktop
Pinch in or out with two fingers	Zooms in or out
Tap with two fingers at the same time	Right clicks
Tap and hold down with three fingers	Takes control of a window allowing you to drag it around the screen

Basic System Usage, Updates, and Backups

When OS X starts, you may be presented with a login screen if the user accounts have passwords enabled. You can log in with a previously created user account, or if enabled, you can use the guest login selection. If you log in as a guest, any changes you make or items you save will be deleted from the system when you log out. Every time the guest user is logged in, you are presented with a fresh desktop experience, as if it had never been used before.

OS X comes bundled with a wide range of software (see Figure 17.6) for general usage as well as system upkeep. Included is an office productivity suite, commonly known as iWork. **iWork** includes a word processor called Pages, a presentation application called Keynote, and a spreadsheet application called Numbers. These are productivity applications that are Apple's answer to the popular Microsoft Office suite. Other useful bundled applications such as Mail, Safari (the default web browser of OS X), Calendar, Contacts, Photos, and so on are available.

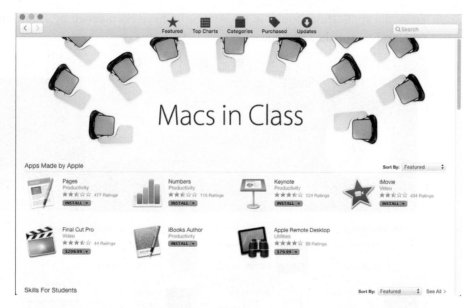

FIGURE 17.6 Apple bundled software

OS X also comes with **iCloud**, a cloud-based service offering storage, application support, and syncing of contacts, photos, email, bookmarks, documents, and more between multiple OS X, iOS, and even Windows devices. On any OS X or iOS device, you can create an iCloud account, either generating a new iCloud domain email or using another email address as your login. When you log in to iCloud on your machine, which can be done inside the *System Preferences* iCloud menu, you can then select which items you want synced between devices. This is a free service for syncing, which includes 5GB of cloud storage with the option to purchase more storage space with a monthly subscription. The whole iCloud service is optional to use but worth looking into for easy syncing to all devices.

One unique feature of iCloud that sets it apart from other cloud services, is it has built-in remote connectivity for OS X. If you log in to iCloud, have Internet access, and enable the **Back to My Mac** feature in the *System Preferences* iCloud menu, you can browse that Mac from another OS X device. The remote Mac appears as a shared device in Finder enabling you to browse the file system. You also see a share screen button to start a remote desktop session.

TECH TIP

iCloud screen sharing requirements

An iCloud screen sharing session needs at least 300Kbps of full-duplex bandwidth. You might need to edit firewall settings to allow the connection to go through.

App Store

Although OS X comes with a wide range of bundled software, it also includes a software marketplace. The **App Store** is a software store where OS X developers can list and sell software through a centralized marketplace (see Figure 17.7). You can find a wide range of software, from simple utilities to advanced 3-D games. The App Store allows for easy management of purchases, as they are tied to a user's Apple ID, so users can install the software on multiple systems or re-download past purchases by logging in with their account. It also allows for easy application updates because developers can push out updates through this centralized repository to end users. This also provides a layer of security. Although you can install software from anywhere, users know the applications found in the App Store have been vetted by Apple and most likely include no harmful or malicious code.

FIGURE 17.7 App Store

Share a Mac Screen

If another user has **screen sharing** turned on, another Mac user can view and even control the display of another Apple computer that is on the network. To do so, open *Finder >* and look for computers that have sharing enabled in the *Shared* section. Hover the pointer over the word *Shared* and select *Show*. Select a particular computer and select *Share Screen*. This is especially helpful to technicians supporting remote users.

System Updates

The App Store is also how Apple releases patches and updates for OS X. It is important to check the Updates tab in the App Store from time to time to get the latest operating system and application updates. You can also have the number of updates available dynamically display on the App Store icon as a reminder that you have updates to perform.

Time Machine

It is easy to recover your previously purchased applications through the App Store, but it is not a backup system. For that you need to set up Time Machine. **Time Machine** is a bundled application in OS X (see Figure 17.8) that enables you to do full and incremental system backups to an external hard drive. It gets its clever naming from the capability to navigate your past backups as if you were traveling through time. Notice in Figure 17.8 how the current Finder is on top. The stacked windows behind it are previous snapshots shown in time order from present to the past.

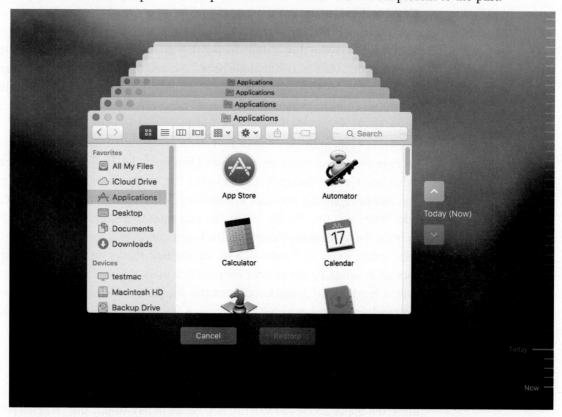

FIGURE 17.8   Time Machine

To use Time Machine, you need to connect an external hard drive to the system, typically through a USB or Thunderbolt connection. You can also do the backups to a disk over your network using a Time Capsule, a remote backup system sold by Apple. When an external drive is connected, you simply go into the Time Machine settings, which are located in the *System Preferences* menu, select the disk you want to use, and turn it on. From there it performs a full system backup and then continues to do a new incremental backup every hour. It retains the past 24 hours of backups, a daily backup for each day in the past month, and a weekly backup for all prior months. It keeps as many of these backups following those rules as it can until you run out of disk space on the drive used. All these backups are done in the background without user intervention after it is set up.

TECH TIP

Requirements for using a disk for backups

When selecting a drive to use for backups, remember that it requires a drive with a partition that is Mac OS Extended formatted, also known as HFS+. By default, OS X cannot write to an NTFS partitioned drive and defaults to using HFS+ partitioning for system partitions. The number of backups possible depends on how big the external drive is. At a minimum you want the drive to at least have as much disk space as your internal Mac hard drive so that you can always fit at least one full backup set on it. The larger the drive, the better. But remember, a single backup is not a reliable way to back up important data. Always have multiple backup options for data that you cannot risk losing. That includes having a local backup such as Time Machine, as well as a remote or cloud backup of important data.

CHAPTER 17

With the Time Machine interface, you can recover deleted files, or even restore older versions of a file, as well as applications that were deleted. If a system failure occurs, you can even take your Time Machine external drive and restore the whole backup from it onto a different Mac, restoring everything as if it were never lost. You would do this by booting the Mac you want to restore to into recovery mode; this is done by holding down the ⌘Cmd key and the letter Ⓡ while the system is starting up. After recovery mode boots, you see the option to select *Restore from a Time machine backup*. Make sure the external Time Machine drive is connected, select this option, and then follow the prompts to restore the backup. If using a networked disk for Time Machine, you have the option to connect to the remote disk for the restore process.

To restore an individual file or find an older version of it, simply select the file or navigate to the location that it was saved to in Finder. Then open the Time Machine application, and it brings up a timeline view of that particular selected file, or the files that have been in the selected location. You can navigate the backups available by scrolling through the timeline presented on the right side. When you find the file or version you want to restore, select it and click the *Restore* button.

If the Time Machine external drive is not connected, local snapshots are automatically created once a day. Refer to Figure 17.8 to see the tick marks on the right bottom. Each tick mark is a backup. Positioning the pointer over the tick mark shows a particular color. For OS X Yosemite or later, a bright red tick mark indicates that the particular backup can be used to restore the system (from a local snapshot or backup drive). A lesser bright tick mark is a backup that can be restored from the backup drive.

Force Quit

OS X is a stable operating system that rarely crashes or requires you to use backups to recover anything, but applications can still run into issues in day-to-day use. When a program stops responding or working properly, it may require the **Force Quit** feature. To access the Force Quit menu, either click the Apple icon on the top left of the screen and then select *Force Quit*, or hold down the ⌘Cmd, Option, and Esc keys at the same time. A menu appears (see Figure 17.9) allowing you to choose which applications to quit.

FIGURE 17.9   Force Quit window

Remote Disc

You may notice that most Macs do not have an optical CD/DVD drive. In fact, no currently released Mac contains an optical drive as Apple is trying to push software distribution through the App Store. However, Apple realizes that users from time to time may need to access a disc. You always have the option to plug in an external USB optical drive, but that isn't always possible. In this instance OS X has a Remote Disc feature. **Remote Disc** is what enables you to remotely use the optical drive of another Mac, or even from a Windows-based PC.

To set up Remote Disc on another Mac, go into the *System Preferences > Sharing* menu. From the first entry you can enable the *DVD or CD Sharing* checkbox to activate it (see Figure 17.10). You have the option to enable approval to be granted on that Mac when another system tries to connect to the optical drive. On the Windows side, install the DVD or CD Sharing Update for Windows. This installs a Control Panel entry so that you can enable remote access to the optical drive. This also includes the ability to require approval before accessing the drive.

FIGURE 17.10 Remote Disc

To access Remote Disc, open *Finder* > select *Remote Disk* link on the left sidebar > choose the remote machine that you want to use. Be aware this requires both machines be on the same local network.

Management and Troubleshooting Tools

OS X comes with a robust set of tools to keep the system running smoothly. But like many things with technology, they eventually break. As an IT professional you need to understand what tools are at your disposal when fixing a system.

The most basic tool is the System Preferences menu (see Figure 17.11). **System Preferences** is the equivalent to the Control Panels in Windows. It contains most of the system settings such as desktop backgrounds and screen savers to more advanced settings such as user accounts and file sharing. Third-party applications can also insert their own preferences menu into the System Preferences menu. The System Preferences shortcut by default is located on the Dock, listed in Launchpad. It can also be opened from within Finder. Select the *Applications* menu on the left side bar and then select the *System Preferences* icon. Table 17.3 lists all the default options in System Preferences as well as a brief description as to what they control.

FIGURE 17.11   System Preferences window

TABLE 17.3   System preferences settings

Option	Description
General	Settings for button, menu, and window colors. Scroll bar behavior. Default web browser choice. Default actions for closing/opening documents and windows. The option to enable handoff. The option to enable LCD font smoothing.
Desktop & Screen Saver	Allows the setting of desktop backgrounds as well as settings for screen savers such as the image to use and when to turn on.
Dock	Controls the size of the dock and how the shortcuts behave.
Mission Control	Controls shortcuts that can be used inside of Mission Control as well as grouping settings.
Language & Region	Allows adding and removing language options as well as setting the local region, calendar used, and date/number formatting.
Security & Privacy	Controls settings for general security such as password requirements to unlock the screen from sleep, disk encryption using FireVault, general Firewall settings, as well as Privacy settings such as using location-based services.
Spotlight	Defines what is and isn't allowed to be searched.
Notifications	Defines what apps can display notifications and how they are displayed.
CDs & DVDs	Allows access to optical discs and control actions for inserted discs.
Displays	Used to manage resolution, brightness, and multiple display settings.
Energy Saver	Controls settings such as when to turn the screen off or put the hard disk to sleep.

Option	Description
Keyboard	Controls function settings as well as shortcuts and auto-correct settings.
Mouse	Sets mouse speed, scroll direction, and primary mouse button side.
Trackpad	Allows users to change multitouch gesture settings.
Printers & Scanners	Where you add and remove printers and scanning devices.
Sound	Controls which audio output/input is used, its volume, and balancing the sound between speakers. Also controls system sounds for alerts.
Ink	Settings controlling handwriting recognition of OS X.
iCloud	Sign-in menu for iCloud and allows enabling of iCloud services.
Internet Accounts	Allows for management for accounts for email, contacts, calendars, and messages.
Extensions	Manages third-party extensions used for customizing OS X.
Network	Contains all network settings.
Bluetooth	Toggles Bluetooth on and off, manages pairing devices such as Bluetooth headsets.
Sharing	Controls all external access settings such as enabling remote login and remote file sharing. Also controls the sharing of devices such as printers. This menu is also used for setting the computer name.
Users & Groups	Menu for creating and deleting user accounts, as well as their settings such as what group they belong in. Also controls what items open automatically when a user logs in.
Parental Controls	Used to manage restrictions for kids' accounts such as restricted websites, time limits for computer usage, and application usage.
App Store	Controls when updates are checked for the operating system and any applications purchased in the Mac App Store, as well as how to update them.
Dictation & Speech	Allows you to enable dictation for typing as well as text to speech to hear written text.
Date & Time	Menu to adjust time zone and the date, and set the clock.
Startup Disk	Menu for selecting a different bootup disk such as an external drive or Boot Camp partition (that allows Windows to be loaded as well).
Time Machine	To toggle Time Machine backups on or off, select which external disk to use, and set how to handle backups.
Accessibility	Controls accessibility options such as colors, zoom, voiceover, captions, and more.

Utilities

For more advanced system management, maintenance, and troubleshooting, use the tools located under the *Utilities* directory. This is found by opening *Finder*, selecting the *Applications* section on the left side of the bar, and going into the *Utilities* folder.

FIGURE 17.12   Utilities window

Activity Monitor

You need to be familiar with a few key utilities to properly troubleshoot an OS X system. **Activity Monitor** is a tool used to see what processes and services are running, plus what system resources are used. It is extremely useful in discovering why a system is running slow (such as when an application appears to be frozen or the system presents a constant spinning **pinwheel**). Look at the *CPU* tab (as shown in Figure 17.13) to see what is consuming most of the CPU processing power. There is also a *Memory* tab to show how much RAM each process is using, as well as a *Disk* tab to show a breakdown of how much disk read/write I/O is occurring. All these statistics are great tools to pinpoint poor system performance due to an errant process or a lack of resources available for what the system is trying to do.

Process Name	% CPU ⌄	CPU Time	Threads	Idle Wake Ups	PID	User
mdworker	9.7	0.51	5	8	677	testuser
Activity Monitor	7.1	0.57	10	3	678	testuser
iconservicesagent	0.6	0.38	6	0	277	testuser
lsd	0.2	0.14	6	0	241	testuser
vmware-tools-daemon	0.2	5.77	4	9	291	testuser
SpotlightNetHelper	0.2	1.67	10	1	320	testuser
Spotlight	0.1	1.03	17	1	308	testuser
Dock	0.1	1.70	6	8	243	testuser
cfprefsd	0.1	0.91	5	0	240	testuser
CoreServicesUIAgent	0.1	0.07	6	0	399	testuser
Finder	0.1	8.57	8	1	641	testuser
fontd	0.0	0.51	3	0	252	testuser
Notification Center	0.0	0.91	5	0	273	testuser
SystemUIServer	0.0	0.38	5	0	244	testuser
swcd	0.0	0.03	4	0	397	testuser
mdworker	0.0	0.05	3	0	350	testuser
distnoted	0.0	0.51	6	0	238	testuser
sharedfilelistd	0.0	0.17	5	0	251	testuser
mdworker	0.0	0.08	4	0	343	testuser
mdworker	0.0	0.05	4	0	344	testuser
Keychain Circle Notification	0.0	0.09	3	0	271	testuser
Photos Agent	0.0	0.42	4	0	302	testuser
storeuid	0.0	0.11	3	0	394	testuser

System:	2.95%	CPU LOAD	Threads	822
User:	6.27%		Processes:	184
Idle:	90.79%			

FIGURE 17.13   Activity Monitor > CPU tab

Console

Console is a centralized place to find system and application logs and messages. OS X and the applications running on it constantly send activity logs to the console. The Console lets you parse these manually or by searching for something specific. This is particularly helpful if you have an application or system service that is not behaving properly, but it is not presenting an error message in the user interface. Most likely, if something has a problem, there will be a log explaining why in the Console. Figure 17.14 shows sample output in the Console.

FIGURE 17.14   Console messages

Kernel Panic

The Console is also good at troubleshooting a **kernel panic**, which is a critical system error that the operating system cannot recover from. When this happens in OS X, the Mac reboots to return to a stable state. Trying to find the cause of a kernel panic can be difficult because a wide array of issues can cause it such as a hardware failure, operating system failure, or a faulty application. If a kernel panic happens only once, it is typically fine to ignore it. But if problems continue to occur, the logs found in the Console utility can be helpful in determining the cause. The kernel panic logs are saved in the /Library/Logs/DiagnosticReports directory, which can be viewed from inside the Console.

System Information

System Information is a utility that provides an overview of the Mac, including basic diagnostic information such as installed hardware, software, and network settings. If you need to find information about what is installed, such as the name of a graphic card, or the firmware version used for the network card, this would be the place to look. It can be accessed from the *Utilities* directory, or by clicking the Apple icon in the upper-left corner on the menu bar, selecting *About This Mac* from the drop-down menu, and then selecting *System Report* from the System Information menu that appears. Figure 17.15 shows sample output for hardware found from the System Information utility.

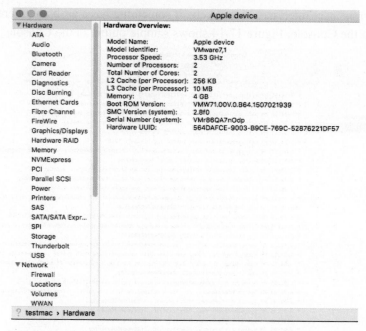

FIGURE 17.15   System Information > Hardware

Keychain Access

Keychain Access is a utility for securely managing saved passwords. Any password saved on the system, whether it be for a Wi-Fi network or a web page login, will be stored in Keychain. These passwords are then encrypted by default with the password for the user account they are saved under. However, a separate password for the keychain can be set up in addition to the password used for the user account.

A common problem occurs when a user updates his password when logging on, and then Keychain asks for his keychain password. This happens if someone uses a network-based account and he updates his account password not using the standard OS X password change feature, or if he uses the reset password feature in the recovery mode of OS X. Not all users are aware what Keychain is or that they even have a keychain password because this happens automatically. To remedy this, open the *Keychain Access* utility, from the menu bar select *Edit* > choose *Change Password for Keychain* > enter the previous password > select *OK*. A window opens to update the password to the new login password.

A useful feature of the Keychain Access utility is the ability to see saved passwords. It is easy to forget passwords. If you were in a situation in which you were already connected to a Wi-Fi network but did not know the password, you could open the *Keychain Access* utility > select *Local Items* > double-click or double-tap the entry for the Wi-Fi network > enable the *Show Password* option. The user will be prompted to authenticate with her keychain password. When authenticated, it displays the saved password unencrypted, as shown in Figure 17.16.

TECH TIP

What to do if users cannot remember their keychain password

If users cannot remember their old keychain password, they need to start a new keychain. This is done in the Keychain Access *Preferences* drop-down menu by selecting *Reset My Default Keychain*. The old keychain can be kept in case users later remember the password, or can be simply deleted.

FIGURE 17.16   Keychain Access

Disk Utility

Disk Utility is an application that handles the management of disks and images in OS X (see Figure 17.17). This utility can be used to rename, reformat, erase, repair, and restore disks. It is a powerful tool and should be approached with caution because the wrong usage could delete all data on the system or on an external disk attached to the system.

FIGURE 17.17   Disk Utility

When a drive is connected to a Mac, it will be mounted and show up on the left side of the Disk Utility window. Selecting the drive gives you a handful of options: first aid, erase, partition, mount, and info. The repair disk option is similar to FSCK or CHKDSK. It checks the file system integrity on a system and repair issues it finds. It is highly advisable not to run this unless you have a system backup and have a reason to run it, such as when a system boots only into safe mode or into recovery mode.

The erase option has the capability to wipe a disk, choose the format for it, and name the partition. You may also perform a secure erase by going into the security options on the menu. The secure erase has a few options, all of which write 0s or random data over the previous data on the disk to make it unrecoverable. You can choose no passes of zeros to quickly wipe out the disk, one pass of zeros, three passes of various types of data that is Department of Energy (DOE)-compliant, or a seven-pass erase that meets the Department of Defense (DOD) standard for safely deleting data. Keep in mind, the more passes you do, the longer it takes to erase the disk.

The *Partition* tab enables you to manage adding and deleting partitions on a disk. An interactive chart shows the physical partition layout. Adjust the chart with your mouse cursor to resize partitions, freeing up space to add new ones, or freeing up space to expand a partition. As with all disk modification, you need to make sure you have any data backed up on a disk that you are repartitioning. Even if done properly, there is always a risk of corruption and data loss.

vBoot Camp

Boot Camp is a boot-loading utility designed to assist with partitioning, installation, and support of running Windows on a Mac. Installation requires a USB flash drive with at least 16GB of space, a Windows installation ISO file or DVD installer, and a minimum 30GB of free space on the hard drive. The Boot Camp application guides you through the process of repartitioning your hard drive to make a partition labeled *BOOTCAMP*. It also takes the Windows ISO or DVD installer and copies it to the USB flash drive and copies the appropriate Mac drivers to it. After Boot Camp sets up the partition and copies everything you need to the flash drive, it reboots the system into the Windows installer allowing you to complete the installation. As always, make sure you back up a system before doing anything involving partitioning. Boot Camp can also be used to remove a Windows partition.

Terminal

Terminal is the terminal emulator for OS X that allows the command-line interface (CLI) access to the operating system. Although the majority of things you do in OS X can be performed in the GUI, there are times where using the CLI is required. You need to know at least a few basic commands and how to use them in case you run into a situation that requires the Terminal to fix. Table 17.4 outlines some of the most basic and commonly used commands. Note that more commands are given later in the chapter.

TABLE 17.4 Commonly used OS X commands

Command	Description
c	Lists the contents of the current working directory
pwd	Shows the current working directory path
cd	Moves between directories
touch	Creates a file
mkdir	Creates a directory
cp	Copies a file
mv	Moves a file

Command	Description
rm	Deletes a file or directory
chown	Changes ownership
chmod	Changes file permissions
sudo	Temporarily gains root privileges
nano	An easy-to-use text editor
less	Shows the contents of a file
grep	Searches output for a specified search term
man	Short for manual, the command man followed by another command brings up a manual for using it

The basic commands in Table 17.4 are enough to navigate the file system, create and remove files and directories, and do some basic troubleshooting. Keep in mind all these commands have extra flags that can be used with them. It is best to reference the man page to discover what a command can do if you are unfamiliar with it. For example, the ls command run by itself shows the contents of the current working directory, but you can also specify a directory that you are not working in to see its contents as shown here.

```
testmac:~ testuser$ ls
Applications   Desktop   Documents   Downloads   Dropbox   Library   Movies
Music    Pictures     Public
testmac:~ testuser$ ls Public
Drop Box
```

As you can see in the preceding command, using ls and specifying another directory (*Public*) allows the contents of the *Public* folder to be seen instead of the user home folder. Example usage of the commands referred to in Table 17.4 is shown here with a brief description.

ls lists the contents inside a directory. These directories are located inside the current path located in the file system.

```
testmac:~ testuser$ ls
Applications   Desktop   Documents   Downloads   Dropbox   Library   Movies
Music       Pictures    Public
```

pwd identifies the current working path you are in.

```
testmac:~ testuser$ pwd
/Users/testuser
```

cd is short for change directory and does exactly as named. Typing cd followed by a directory takes you to that directory. Notice the working path updated on the command line to keep track of current location.

```
testmac:~ testuser$ cd Applications
testmac:Applications testuser$
```

touch creates a blank file with the specified name. This command is not limited to text files. For example, you could make a file with the extension html if you wanted to work on creating a web page. Notice in the following example how the -l is added to the ls command when showing the file created with the touch command. The -l modifier is a flag for what is called long listing. That includes the normal output of the ls command plus add-ins. From left to right the add-ins are as follows: file permission, number of file links, owner name, owner group, file size, time of last modification, and filename. Also specified is the file that the `ls` command was used on. Instead of seeing all contents of the directory, only the file specifics appear.

```
testmac:~ testuser$ touch test.txt
testmac:~ testuser$ ls -l test.txt
-rw-r--r--  1 testuser  Editors  0 Sep 29 13:56 test.txt
```

`cp` is short for copy. The syntax of this command is `cp` followed by the source file and then the destination of the copy. You can also rename the file while copying it.

```
testmac:~ testuser$ cp test.txt testcopy.txt
testmac:~ testuser$ ls
Applications  Documents  Dropbox  Movies  Public
test.txt  Desktop  Downloads  Library  Music  Pictures  testcopy.txt
```

`mv` is short for move. It works similar to `cp`, except it does not keep the original file in place. It actually modifies the file by moving it in the file system. During this process, you have the option to rename the file. In the following example, the testcopy.txt file was moved to testmove.txt. If the files were listed out, testcopy.txt would not exist because it is now named testmove.txt.

```
testmac:~ testuser$ mv testcopy.txt testmove.txt
testmac:~ testuser$ ls
Applications  Documents  Dropbox  Movies  Public
test.txt  Desktop  Downloads  Library  Music  Pictures  testmove.txt
```

`rm` is short for remove. Using the `rm` command designates which files to remove. A single file or multiple files can be designated in this manner.

```
testmac:~ testuser$ rm test.txt testmove.txt
testmac:~ testuser$ ls
Applications  Desktop  Documents  Downloads  Dropbox  Library  Movies
Music  Public
```

`sudo` is a command used to gain superuser (also known as root) privileges. In UNIX/Linux the Administrator account is known as **root**. The root user has absolute power on a system, including within OS X. However, by default, this user account is disabled. It is advised to not log in directly using root because if you were to accidentally run something malicious, the system could be degraded or compromised. However, administrative access is occasionally needed to perform certain tasks such as running a script or installing an application. When you need this access at the command-line level, use the `sudo` command, which invokes a temporary root session to complete the command you are running.

In the following example, the file *importantdocument.txt* was created. When you run `ls -l` for the file, you can see that you are the owner of it. Now pretend that you want to make root the owner of the file, so you attempt to use the command `chown`, which changes file ownership. When `chown` is run, the message "Operation not permitted" displays, meaning you do not have permission to do this. To fix this, add `sudo` to the start of the command. When prompted, enter your account password for verification. The command runs as the root user. Using `ls -l` again you can see the file owner changed from testuser to root.

```
testmac:~ testuser$ touch importantdocument.txt
testmac:~ testuser$ ls -l importantdocument.txt
-rw-r--r--  1 testuser  Editors  0 Sep 30 10:39 importantdocument.txt
testmac:~ testuser$ chown root importantdocument.txt
```

```
chown: importantdocument.txt: Operation not permitted
testmac:~ testuser$ sudo chown root importantdocument.txt
Password:
testmac:~ testuser$ ls -l importantdocument.txt
-rw-r--r--  1 root   Editors   0 Sep 30 10:39 importantdocument.txt
```

To understand how to use the chmod command, you have to understand UNIX/Linux file permissions. There are three types of permissions a user or group can have for a file: read, write, and execute. This is abbreviated with a -rwxrwxrwx syntax, with *r* being read, *w* being write, and *x* being execute. Notice the three sets of rwx entries. The first set starting on the left represents the owner's permissions. The second set represents the group's permissions. The last set represents everyone else, otherwise known as others.

```
testmac:~ testuser$ ls -l importantdocument.txt
-rw-rw-r--  1 root   Editors   0 Sep 30 10:39 importantdocument.txt
```

In the preceding command output, look at the drwxt entries. The root owner of the file can read and write to the file. The users belonging to the Editors group can read and write to the file as well. Everyone else can only read the file and will not be allowed to modify it in any way.

To use chmod to change these permissions, there are various syntax options. The easiest to visualize uses letters. For example, to add a write permissions group to the *importantdocument.txt* file for those known as others, use o+w as the following command shows.

```
testmac:~ testuser$ sudo chmod o+w importantdocument.txt
Password:
testmac:~ testuser$ ls -l importantdocument.txt
-rw-rw-rw-  1 root   Editors   0 Sep 30 10:39 importantdocument.txt
```

This syntax can be used with the letters *u*, *g*, *o*, and *a*. These represent user, group, others, and all. The letters *r*, *w*, and *x* are then used to signify what permissions to either add or subtract for the subject specified. Then specify the file for which permissions are to be changed.

There is a second way of specifying the permissions that involves using numbers to represent the permissions. The syntax for this is a three-digit number string, the first number starting from the left representing owner, the second number representing group, and the final number representing others. The numbers range from 0 to 7. They use binary numbers to represent the permissions value, but the easy thing to do is remember that read permissions equal 4, write permissions equal 2, and execute permissions equal 1. All the permissions you want to assign are added together. For example, if you want to give the root user read (4), write (2), and execute (1) permissions, the group read (4) permissions, and others no (0) permissions, you would end up with 740. You could then use the command chmod followed by this number and then the file that is changed.

```
testmac:~ testuser$ ls -l importantdocument.txt
-rw-rw-rw-  1 root   Editors   0 Sep 30 10:39 importantdocument.txt
testmac:~ testuser$ sudo chmod 740 importantdocument.txt
Password:
testmac:~ testuser$ ls -l importantdocument.txt
-rwxr-----  1 root   Editors   0 Sep 30 10:39 importantdocument.txt
```

nano is a text editor. When using the command line, it is common to need to use a text editor to fix files. Instead of going through the slow process of using a graphical text editor and having to navigate to the file to open it, you can quickly edit a file at the command line.

There are a few command-line text editors available to use in OS X and Linux, vi, emacs, and nano, to name a few. Nano is an easy-to-use command-line text editor. Launch it by typing nano followed by the filename you want to edit. If the file does not exist, nano creates it. Entering the command **q** cancels the editing session. What makes nano so convenient to use is that it is a powerful editor with many options such as search and replace, line numbers, and quick navigation with page up/down. It also has a set of quick controls displayed in its interface, which is helpful for the occasional user who has not memorized all the shortcuts for it.

less is a tool used to quickly view the contents of a file. It presents a window of the contents that can be scrolled through using the [B] key to scroll up and [Spacebar] to scroll down; you can also page to the bottom by holding down [Shift] and pressing the [G] key. less becomes a powerful tool when combined with a search utility known as grep, and using the | (pronounced pipe) function. The [|] key is used for passing output from one command to another. By using less to see the content of a file, you can then pipe it to grep to search for something inside it. As an example, the following text is added to the *importantdocument.txt* file with which we have been working.

```
OS X 10.8       Mountain Lion
OS X 10.9       Mavericks
OS X 10.10      Yosemite
OS X 10.11      El Capitan
```

If you want to find this information contained within a few hundred pages, it would be difficult to find by just reading the document through. Using nano to search could also take a long time because you would have to run the search over and over to find all the multiple entries of it. A better command to use is less to get the output of the file and send it to grep to search for the wanted file.

```
testmac:~ testuser$ less importantdocument.txt | grep Yosemite
OS X 10.10     Yosemite
```

You can see that grep works by taking the input it receives and providing it as a search term. It then outputs every line of the input (*importantdocument.txt*) that contains the search term.

TECH TIP

Use the manual!

You need to know your commands and their options, but it is easy to forget those that you do not use often. For those times where you cannot remember how to use a command, use the command man. man is short for manual and brings up directions on how to use a command as long as it has a manual page entry. The syntax is simply the command man followed by the command you want to know more about.

Introduction to Linux

Linux, released in 1991 by developer Linus Torvalds, is a widely used operating system platform that is similar to trademarked UNIX, a group of operating systems that grew from the AT&T-developed UNIX. It is meant to be a free open source operating system that everyone can use, contribute to, and modify for their needs. Because of this, it is widely used in many different areas of technology such as servers, desktops, embedded systems, smartphones, and so on. It is also mostly POSIX-compliant, so some of the concepts you previously learned in the OS X section of this chapter apply to most Linux systems.

The terminology of Linux can be confusing for someone new to it. The name Linux refers to an operating system kernel. A **kernel** is the heart of an operating system. It acts as the controller and interpreter for nearly everything in a system, so hardware and software can interface and work together. It controls things such as memory management, peripherals, and allocating other system resources to processes.

The Linux kernel is repackaged into different operating system distributions, distros for short. There are hundreds of different distros. See Table 17.5 for a list of the more popular ones and where to find more information about them. All these distros have their differences, but all are Linux operating systems because they use the Linux kernel.

TABLE 17.5   Linux distros

Distro name	Website
Ubuntu	http://www.ubuntu.com
Debian	http://www.debian.org
Mint	http://linuxmint.com
SUSE	https://www.suse.com
Red Hat	http://www.redhat.com/
Fedora	https://getfedora.org
CentOS	https://www.centos.org
Gentoo	https://www.gentoo.org
Arch	https://www.archlinux.org

Anyone going into IT should explore the different types of Linux distros to see the differences and similarities between them. For this chapter we focus on Ubuntu version 15.04, also known as Vivid Vervet, for all examples. Ubuntu is the most widely used home desktop distribution, and it also has a server version. Although you probably will not find Ubuntu in an enterprise environment, you are likely to encounter it in with end users, developers, and simple servers. And a lot of the skills you learn for Ubuntu are usable in other distros.

Ubuntu does not have to be installed onto a computer to experiment with it. Unlike Windows or OS X, you can use a live CD or DVD, which is simply a disc you can boot to. A live CD/DVD runs the operating system as if it were installed on the computer. This makes it much easier to try different distributions without having to dedicate a computer solely to running Linux. If you do this, you need to be careful because you can still modify the local file system on the computer and cause harm to the installed operating system.

TECH TIP

Download Ubuntu

Download Ubuntu's latest release at http://www.ubuntu.com/download/desktop. It will be needed at the end of the chapter to complete the question and lab section.

Navigating the User Interface

There are many types of graphical user interfaces for Linux such as GNOME, KDE, Xfce, and Cinnamon. Each has its own unique interface operation and the tools made available. **Unity** is the name of the graphical user interface in Ubuntu. It has some similarities to the user interface of OS X; though it is drastically different from Windows.

Launcher is the dock-like shortcut bar on the left side of the screen. It is reminiscent of the Dock from OS X; though it doesn't work completely the same. It has the functionality of being an application launcher shortcut as well as having a universal search feature built in to it. By clicking the Ubuntu icon at the top of Launcher, a menu allows a local search on the system, as well as the ability to get results from the Internet. Similar to OS X there is the **Panel**, which is a menu bar at the top of the screen containing contextual information on the left side with static information on the right side. **Nautilus** is the file manager for Ubuntu (see Figure 17.18), and can quickly be accessed by clicking the *Files* icon on the Launcher dock. Even though Nautilus is the default file manager, because Linux is so modular and customizable, this can be replaced with an alternative file manager. Of course, like all other GUI operating systems, there is a standard desktop.

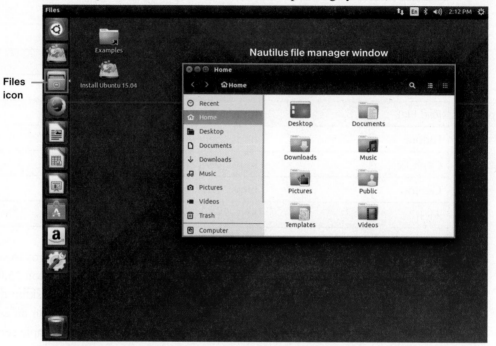

FIGURE 17.18 Nautilus file manager window

Dash is the universal search tool built in to the Launcher bar. It searches local content as well as Internet sources, all of which can be enabled or disabled simply by opening up Dash. There are also subcategories at the bottom of the Dash interface called lenses. By default, there are lenses for universal searching, applications, files and folders, videos, music, and photos, as shown in Figure 17.19.

The Ubuntu user interface is straightforward. You must be aware that a Linux system in an enterprise environment will not be accessed through the GUI. Most of the Linux systems in the corporate environment do not even have a GUI installed. However, a few tools should be mentioned, which are covered next.

FIGURE 17.19   Dash search tool

Basic System Usage, Updates, and Backups

Numerous useful tools come bundled with Ubuntu used for managing the system. Some of these are best used through the GUI. Although everything can be done through the command-line interface, some tools are much easier to use on the desktop.

The best example of this is a tool that is commonly used, GParted. **GParted** is a disk management tool that allows the creation, deletion, and resizing of partitions on a physical disk. GParted has an easy-to-use drag-and-drop interface for partition management that is far easier to visualize and understand than trying to manage partitions from the command line. If you experiment with GParted, be mindful that you can wipe your system if you are unsure of the correct procedures. Figure 17.20 shows the GParted window.

Although Windows uses NTFS and OS X uses the HFS+ file system, there are many more options to choose from on Linux. When installing Linux or partitioning with GParted, be aware of the options. Table 17.6 lists the most common file systems and a brief description. Most distros, including Ubuntu, default to using a file system known as ext4 (fourth extended file system), an improvement on ext3 (third extended file system), which was the most widely used file system for many years.

CHAPTER 17

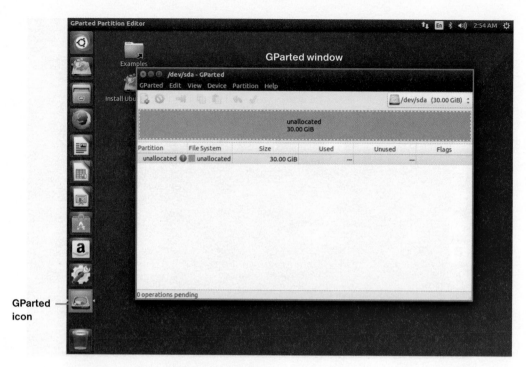

GParted
icon

FIGURE 17.20 GParted window

TABLE 17.6 Linux file systems

File system name	Description
ext3	Third generation of the extended file system that introduced journaling, the capability for a file system to track changes so that the file system can recover from power failures or crashes.
ext4	Fourth generation of the extended file system, contains features such as journaling, volume support up to 1 exibibyte (EiB), and file sizes up to 16 tebibytes (TiB). A common file system choice.
ZFS	File system that focuses on data integrity, can do integrity checks on mounted disks unlike ext4. You would not use ZFS on a machine that is using RAID. It is recommended for use on a single drive or JBOD.
Btrfs	Pronounced "Butter F S," it is a contender to be the successor to ext, adding features such as snapshots, volume spanning, live resizing of file systems, and live adding/removing of disks to live file systems. It can support volumes and file sizes up to 16 exbibytes.

Ubuntu comes with a fair amount of software installed, but one of the great things about using Linux is the amount of open source free software available. It isn't always easy to find software, especially if you are new to Linux and are unfamiliar with the tools that are available. That is where the **Ubuntu Software Center** comes in: a software manager that lets you access software from Ubuntu's repositories. With Ubuntu Software Center (see Figure 17.21) you can install new applications and uninstall existing ones, many of which are available for free. Be aware that although this application is useful for finding new software, you need to use the **Software Updater** tool to update your operating system and applications.

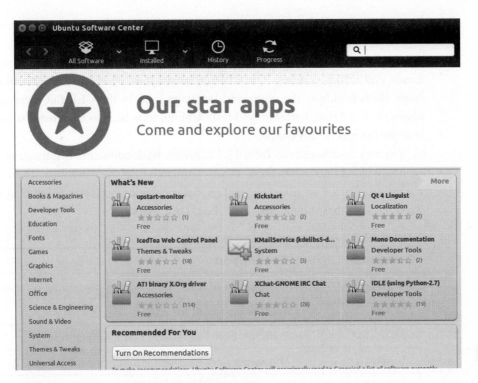

FIGURE 17.21   Ubuntu Software Center

Ubuntu comes bundled with a built-in backup application (see Figure 17.22) that supports local and remote backups, encryption, incremental and full backups, and scheduling, and can run seamlessly in the background. The backup application can be found by searching for backups in Dash. However, there is a wide array of other backup software available for Linux. Many companies have their own backup procedure through custom scripts and use various utilities such as `rsync` to back up to save on resources, instead of doing a full system backup as experienced in most Windows environments.

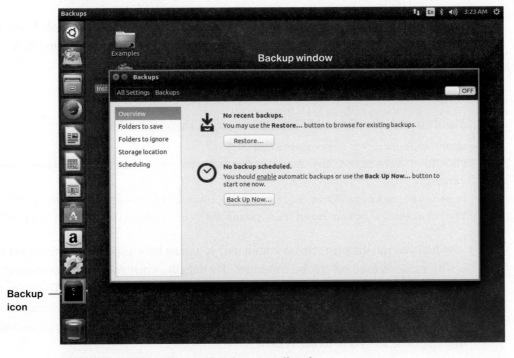

FIGURE 17.22   Ubuntu backup application

Command-Line Interface

The **command-line interface**, abbreviated CLI, is where most system management takes place for Linux and UNIX systems. The CLI for most Linux systems uses a terminal language known as bash. Bash is simply the command language used in the CLI, but there are a few other notable shells such as Dash, fish, zsh, and tcsh. Ubuntu uses bash as do most distros, so we focus on using that for the rest of this chapter.

You may want to refer to Table 17.4 to review basic command-line usage in OS X. Because OS X is UNIX (which Linux is based on), those commands also work in Linux. There are also more advanced commands that we are going to build on that everyone who supports Linux systems should know. See Table 17.7 for these commands and a brief description.

TABLE 17.7   Advanced CLI commands

Command	Description
shutdown	Shuts down or restarts the system depending on options used
passwd	Sets the password for a user
su	Switches from one user account to another
ifconfig	Shows network interface information for Ethernet ports
iwconfig	Shows network interface information for wireless adapters
ps	Show a listing of all current processes
apt-get	CLI utility for managing packages
dd	Copies and converts files
locate	Searches system
updatedb	Updates file database of system for locate command

To use the CLI on Ubuntu, click the *Dash* icon and search for *Terminal*. A few options appear but we use the one specifically labeled *Terminal*. This interface is similar to OS X in that the command line shows the username and computer name.

Shutting Down the System

The shutdown command is straightforward; it shuts down the system.

```
ubuntu@ubuntu:~$ sudo shutdown
Shutdown scheduled for Sun 2016-10-25 16:13:07 UTC, use 'shutdown -c' to
cancel.
Broadcast message from root@ubuntu (Sun 2016-10-25 16:12:07 UTC):
The system is going down for power-off at Sun 2016-10-25 16:13:07 UTC!
```

When you run the shutdown command, you must have superuser permissions to do so, which is why sudo is used before the command. By default, when you run the command, it schedules a shutdown one minute into the future, giving you the option to cancel it. There are also options to schedule it at a different time, have it shut down immediately, or have it restart instead of power off. You can also see that the shutdown was broadcast as a system message to warn anyone else who might be logged in to the system.

`passwd` Versus `pwd`

The `passwd` command, not to be confused with `pwd`, is used to change a user's password. To change the logged-in user, just run the command by itself. A prompt appears to enter the current password and then the new password twice. If you want to change the password of a different user, enter the command followed by the username. Both examples are shown in the following example.

```
ubuntu@ubuntu:~$ passwd
Change password for ubuntu.
(current) UNIX password:
Enter new UNIX password:
Retype new UNIX password:
passwd: password updated successfully
ubuntu@ubuntu:~$ sudo passwd test
Enter new UNIX password:
Retype new UNIX password:
passwd: password updated successfully
```

Notice that you must have superuser permissions to change another user's password. To modify an account, you either need to be logged in to that account or have administrative (root) privileges.

Network Configuration

The command `ifconfig` is an essential Linux command that any Linux administrator or user needs to be familiar with. The basic output shows the current network settings such as IP address, subnet mask, interfaces used, MAC address, and interface statistics.

```
ubuntu@ubuntu:~$ ifconfig
eth0      Link encap:Ethernet  HWaddr b8:27:eb:43:c3:ad
          inet addr:10.0.0.250  Bcast:10.0.0.255  Mask:255.255.255.0
          UP BROADCAST RUNNING MULTICAST  MTU:1500  Metric:1
          RX packets:5633010 errors:0 dropped:6300 overruns:0 frame:0
          TX packets:9370432 errors:0 dropped:0 overruns:0 carrier:0
          collisions:0 txqueuelen:1000
          RX bytes:429577586 (409.6 MiB)  TX bytes:3680672251 (3.4 GiB)
lo        Link encap:Local Loopback
          inet addr:127.0.0.1  Mask:255.0.0.0
          UP LOOPBACK RUNNING  MTU:65536  Metric:1
          RX packets:0 errors:0 dropped:0 overruns:0 frame:0
          TX packets:0 errors:0 dropped:0 overruns:0 carrier:0
          collisions:0 txqueuelen:0
          RX bytes:0 (0.0 B)  TX bytes:0 (0.0 B)

wlan0     Link encap:Ethernet  HWaddr 80:1f:02:bb:ee:fa
          UP BROADCAST MULTICAST  MTU:1500  Metric:1
          RX packets:0 errors:0 dropped:0 overruns:0 frame:0
          TX packets:0 errors:0 dropped:0 overruns:0 carrier:0
          collisions:0 txqueuelen:1000
          RX bytes:0 (0.0 B)  TX bytes:0 (0.0 B)
```

As you can see in the output, we are presented with three different interfaces. `eth0` is an abbreviation of ethernet 0, our wired Ethernet connection. `lo` is an abbreviation of localhost, a loopback interface that is used for testing and routing information inside the operating system. Last is `wlan0`, which represents wireless LAN interface 0. At the moment only `eth0` and `lo` have IP addresses assigned, `wlan0` has yet to be configured.

More advanced usage of `ifconfig` allows you to change interface settings. If we want to set an address for `wlan0`, we would use the syntax of `ifconfig` followed by the interface name `wlan0`, and then the appropriate settings.

```
ubuntu@ubuntu:~$ sudo ifconfig wlan0 10.0.0.200 netmask 255.255.255.0
broadcast 10.0.0.255
ubuntu@ubuntu:~$ ifconfig
eth0      Link encap:Ethernet  HWaddr b8:27:eb:43:c3:ad
          inet addr:10.0.0.250  Bcast:10.0.0.255  Mask:255.255.255.0
          UP BROADCAST RUNNING MULTICAST  MTU:1500  Metric:1
          RX packets:5668535 errors:0 dropped:6327 overruns:0 frame:0
          TX packets:9430245 errors:0 dropped:0 overruns:0 carrier:0
          collisions:0 txqueuelen:1000
          RX bytes:432348412 (412.3 MiB)  TX bytes:3758820467 (3.5 GiB)

lo        Link encap:Local Loopback
          inet addr:127.0.0.1  Mask:255.0.0.0
          UP LOOPBACK RUNNING  MTU:65536  Metric:1
          RX packets:0 errors:0 dropped:0 overruns:0 frame:0
          TX packets:0 errors:0 dropped:0 overruns:0 carrier:0
          collisions:0 txqueuelen:0
          RX bytes:0 (0.0 B)  TX bytes:0 (0.0 B)

wlan0     Link encap:Ethernet  HWaddr 80:1f:02:bb:ee:fa
          inet addr:10.0.0.200  Bcast:10.0.0.255  Mask:255.255.255.0
          UP BROADCAST MULTICAST  MTU:1500  Metric:1
          RX packets:0 errors:0 dropped:0 overruns:0 frame:0
          TX packets:0 errors:0 dropped:0 overruns:0 carrier:0
          collisions:0 txqueuelen:1000
          RX bytes:0 (0.0 B)  TX bytes:0 (0.0 B)
```

Even though an appropriate address has been assigned to `wlan0` for the wireless network, `wlan0` is still not a working wireless interface. Other wireless settings such as the wireless network SSID as well as any authentication settings must still be configured. That is where the command `iwconfig` comes into play. Although `ifconfig` can edit IP settings, it cannot do the wireless specific settings that `iwconfig` provides.

Consider the situation of having a Linux computer connected to a wireless network named Test that uses a WEP encryption key of 1234567890. The following command would be entered:

```
ubuntu@ubuntu:~$ sudo iwconfig wlan0 essid Test key restricted 1234567890
```

TECH TIP

`iwconfig` supports only WEP authentication

It is important to realize that `iwconfig` supports only WEP authentication. For more advanced authentication such as WPA or WPA2, use `wpa_supplicant`. It is recommended not to use WEP if you can use higher-level encryption because WEP is an older standard that is easily cracked.

Viewing Processes

ps is another command to have in your toolbox for administering a Linux system. ps shows all active processes running on a system. This important information tells what is running, how long things have been running, and how many resources they use.

```
ubuntu@ubuntu:~$ ps
  PID TTY          TIME CMD
 4093 pts/0    00:00:01 bash
14766 pts/0    00:00:00 ps
```

By default using ps shows only processes being run by the current user and from the current login session. Generally, ps along with other modifiers is used to get useful information. The most common version of ps used is ps aux. The a modifier lists all processes from other users; u shows the user who is running the process; and x shows processes from all sessions. The ps command effectively shows everything that is running on the system.

```
ubuntu@ubuntu:~$ ps aux
USER       PID %CPU %MEM    VSZ   RSS TTY     STAT START   TIME COMMAND
root         1  0.0  0.1   2148  1348 ?       Ss   Oct23   0:10 init [2]
root         2  0.0  0.0      0     0 ?       S    Oct23   0:00 [kthreadd]
root         3  0.0  0.0      0     0 ?       S    Oct23   0:16 [ksoftirqd/0]
root         5  0.0  0.0      0     0 ?       S<   Oct23   0:00 [kworker/0:0H]
root         7  0.0  0.0      0     0 ?       S    Oct23   1:53 [rcu_preempt]
root         8  0.0  0.0      0     0 ?       S    Oct23   0:00 [rcu_sched]
root         9  0.0  0.0      0     0 ?       S    Oct23   0:00 [rcu_bh]
```

A lesser-known option is to add the f modifier, so the command is ps faux. This shows everything from ps aux as well as organizing the processes in a tree format to see what processes are the parent and child. In the following example, a screen session is running for a script being run by the program supervisor. Some of the command output has been redacted to make it easier to read.

```
root 2316  0.0  0.3   4816  2372 ?       Ss   Oct23   1:02 SCREEN
root 2317  0.0  0.5   5680  4088 pts/1   Ss   Oct23   0:00  \_ /bin/bash
root 2325  0.0  0.3   4592  2660 pts/1   S+   Oct23   0:00       \_ sudo
supervise /etc/init.d/
```

Obtaining Software via the CLI

Earlier in the chapter the Ubuntu Software Center, a utility used to obtain software, was mentioned. apt-get is the command-line interface tool that is the equivalent of Ubuntu Software Center. There is another common command-line package manager named rpm, short for Red Hat Package Manager. Despite its name, it is used on more distros than just Red Hat. There is another lesser-used manager called yum, short for Yellowdog Updater Modified, that builds on rpm.

To use apt-get start by refreshing the list of available software. Systems that use apt-get have a sources list file located at /etc/apt/sources.list, which lists the software repositories that should be checked for available software. It is common to edit this list to add in different sources to get different applications. To update the list of available software from your sources list, you would use the command apt-get followed by the modifier update. Only the first few lines of the example command have been shown here because it can take up a lot of screen space to display the results depending on how many sources you have.

```
ubuntu@ubuntu:~$ sudo apt-get update
Get:1 http://archive.ubuntu.com vivid InRelease [218 kB]
Get:2 http://security.ubuntu.com vivid-security InRelease [64.4 kB]
```

After updating the sources, use the `apt-get` command followed by `install` and then the name of the package to install the software. So if we want to obtain software called *install screen*, a tool used to have multiple screens, from the CLI, execute the following command: `apt-get install screen`.

It is recommended to always simulate a software installation first using the `-s` modifier to make sure the installation will not affect something important on the system.

```
ubuntu@ubuntu:~$ sudo apt-get install screen -s
Reading package lists... Done
Building dependency tree
Reading state information... Done
Suggested packages:
        select screen byobu
The following NEW packages will be installed:
        screen
0 upgraded, 1 newly installed, 0 to remove and 282 not upgraded.
Inst screen (4.2.1.-3 Ubuntu:15.04/vivid [amd64])
Conf screen (4.2.1.-3 Ubuntu:15.04/vivid [amd64])
```

The simulation shows everything as if it installed the screen. Rerun the command without the `-s` modifier and it will install the screen.

TECH TIP

Always download first

When working with systems that need high uptime, it is always advisable to predownload the packages you plan to install ahead of time to avoid downtime waiting for a download to occur. This can be done by running the `apt-get install` command with the `-d` flag to download only.

Copying Data

The command `dd` is a versatile command used to copy and convert data. Some common uses would be copying the contents of a CD to an ISO file, cloning a partition to another one, creating a backup, erasing a disk, and converting a file or its content, and for benchmarking purposes. The general syntax is the command `dd`, followed by the input file, and then the output file. There are many other modifiers such as `conv` for conversions, `bs` for block counts, and `count` for the number of blocks used.

To show off the capabilities of `dd`, see Figure 17.23, which is an environment with two partitions using the application `gparted`. The partitions are equal in size, are virtually empty, and are named /dev/sda1 and /dev/sda2.

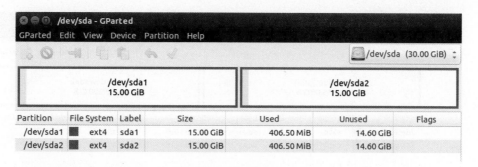

FIGURE 17.23 Disk partitions in GParted

Start by copying the contents of a DVD onto /dev/sda1. The syntax is dd followed by the input file (the DVD), and the output file, which is /dev/sda1.

```
ubuntu@ubuntu:~$ sudo dd if=/dev/sr0 of=/sda1/test.iso
2247744+0 records in
2247744+0 records out
1150844928 bytes (1.2 GB) copied, 23.0764 s, 49.9 MB/s
```

The output shows 1.2GB of data copied, the size of the data on our DVD. It took 23 seconds, and it copied at almost 50MB/s. Look at the partitions with GParted in Figure 17.24. The sda1 file now has more space used, represented by the yellow highlighted space.

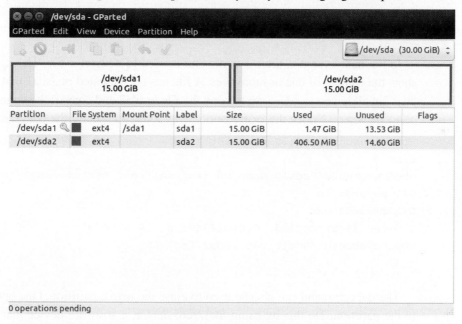

FIGURE 17.24 DVD copied onto sda1 partition

Now use dd to clone sda1 to sda2. The syntax is virtually the same; the only difference is that when you copy one partition to another partition, you use the full device name of the partition (not the folder to which it is mounted). Here's the command and output shown. Figure 17.25 shows the results in GParted.

```
ubuntu@ubuntu:~$ sudo dd if=/dev/sda1 of=/dev/sda2
31455232+0 records in
31455232+0 records out
16105078784 bytes (16 GB) copied, 386.654 s, 41.7 MB/s
```

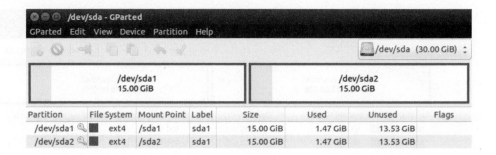

FIGURE 17.25   Cloned partition in GParted

In Figure 17.25, verify in GParted that the `dd` command cloned sda1 to sda2. They are exact clones. Comparing Figure 17.25 to Figure 17.24, notice that even the device label copied over to sda2. And now both partitions use the same amount of disk space. Comparing the mounted partitions, both contain the same file: the ISO previously created.

```
ubuntu@ubuntu:~$ ls -l /sda1
total 1123892
drwx------ 2 root root                16384 Oct 26 02:38 lost+found
-rw-rw-r-- 2 root root           1150844928 Oct 26 02:37 test.iso
ubuntu@ubuntu:~$ ls -l /sda2
total 1123892
drwx------ 2 root root                16384 Oct 26 02:38 lost+found
-rw-rw-r-- 2 root root           1150844928 Oct 26 02:37 test.iso
```

In the next example, the `dd` command is used to convert a file. The `cat` command is used to show the content of one or more files. A file has been created on /sda1 that contains only the word "test" in all lowercase. Use `dd` to copy the file to sda2 and convert the contents of the file to uppercase characters. Notice the `conv` option was added to specify the conversion of uppercase letters.

```
ubuntu@ubuntu:/sda1$ cat test.txt
test
ubuntu@ubuntu:/sda1$ sudo dd if=/sda1/test.txt of=/sda2/test.txt conv=ucase
0+1 records in
0+1 records out
5 bytes (5 B) copied, 0.000263474 s, 19.0 kB/s
ubuntu@ubuntu:/sda1$ cat /sda2/test.txt
TEST
```

The `dd` command can also be used to erase the `sda2` partition. One option is to write all zeros to the partition. Do this by using /dev/zero *device*, a software device that is used specifically for outputting just zeros. It is used as the input file, into the output of sda2, using block sizes of 4k. Doing this is called zeroing out a drive. It is a secure method of erasing data, as the whole drive is filled with zeros until it runs out of space. This makes typical data recovery methods impossible to use and renders the partition useless until it is repartitioned.

```
ubuntu@ubuntu:~$ sudo dd if=/dev/zero of=/dev/sda2 bs=4k
dd: error writing '/dev/sda2': No space left on device
3932161+0 records in
3932160+0 records out
16106127360 bytes (16 GB) copied, 25.5437 s, 631 MB/s
```

Look at Figure 17.26; `sda2` now has an error. That is because Ubuntu cannot find a file system for the device. It has been rendered unusable until it is repartitioned.

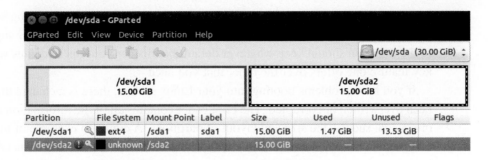

FIGURE 17.26   Unusable partition in GParted

Finding Files

Sometimes, when managing a system at the command line, especially an unfamiliar system, it is difficult to find the location of files. This is where two commands called `updatedb` and `locate` come into use. `updatedb` is a command run to update a local database on the system that contains the full path name of each file. The command `locate` then searches for a file in this database of paths, which is a much quicker way to search for a file than searching the system itself.

There are limitations to this search method. The database of paths has to be updated regularly to be accurate. Usually, this is done by a scheduled task through the cron service. But if you are searching for a file that was recently added, you may need to run the `updatedb` command manually to refresh the database. This is done by just entering `updatedb` and pressing Enter. Because this command looks at the entire file system, run it with superuser permissions to ensure that it can read all file paths.

```
ubuntu@ubuntu:~$ sudo updatedb
ubuntu@ubuntu:~$
```

You can now search the system. If someone left you an important file that you need to retrieve called *testdocument.txt* but gave no indications as to where it is at, we could use `locate` to find the path where the file is.

```
ubuntu@ubuntu:~$ locate testdocument.txt
/home/test/testdocument.txt
```

We can see the testdocument.txt was left in the test user's home directory.

TECH TIP

User forums

Usually, a quick Internet search is enough to find a command to accomplish a task, but some deeper questions might require the advice of those more familiar with using Linux. There are many Linux user forums, but the Ubuntu-specific ones are a good place for a beginner to seek help. They are located at http://ubuntuforums.org.

Missing GRUB/LILO

Linux distros typically install one of two bootloaders, Grand Unified Boot Loader (GRUB) or Linux Loader (LILO). LILO used to be the more predominant bootloader you would find, but things have shifted towards GRUB (the current version which is called GRUB2) being the default because of it supporting more modern features. This has resulted in LILO as being marked as discontinued for now. LILO is an older and more basic bootloader, missing some features such as network boot or having a command-line interface, both of which GRUB supports. The majority of the time you should keep whatever default bootloader your distro comes with unless you find a key feature one offers over the other that you need.

If you have problems booting into your Linux system, there is a change that the bootloader has been overwritten or corrupted. The bootloader contains all of the information about how the disk is organized, such as the size and layout of partitions. A common example of this problem would be a PC technician who has a machine with Linux installed, and decided to install a Windows operating system on the same disk. When the technician does the installation, the Windows installation overwrote the bootloader with its own MBR. Now Linux cannot be loaded because the boot information created by GRUB or LILO no longer exists. To fix this issue, you would need to re-create the bootloader for your system

To fix the broken bootloader in this situation, you would boot to an Ubuntu live CD and run a few commands to fix it. To use LILO to replace the MBR, you would open a command prompt and first install LILO with `sudo apt-get install lilo`. You would then run this command, which references the disk device name of where you installed Linux (or in a more advanced partition setup, where the boot partition is, usually the device containing a /boot partition) `sudo lilo -M /dev/XXX /mbr` replacing XXX with the device name such as sda.

To do the same with GRUB you would install GRUB2 with `sudo apt-get install grub2` and then run the command `sudo grub-install /dev/XXX` replacing XXX with the device name such as sda. All of these scenarios could be slightly different in what needs to be done depending on partition layout and operating systems installed. It is important to read the documentation for either bootloader that you intend to use to make sure you are using a solution that fits the problem.

OS X and Linux Best Practices

As with any operating system, Apple OS X and any flavor of Linux should be maintained using best practices. Key best practices are as follows:

> Perform scheduled backups: Back up the operating system and important data on a regular basis. As an IT staff member, you should gently remind users of this, too.

> Schedule disk maintenance: Drives become fragmented over time. For best system performance, perform disk maintenance on a regular basis.

> System updates: Be sure to install the latest operating system updates for security and performance reasons.

> Driver/firmware updates: Ensure the latest hardware drivers and firmware updates are installed.

> Patch management: Patches are code changes that tend to fix a particular problem in an operating system or application. Patch management is the process of downloading, testing, installing, retesting, and documenting these changes. Patch management helps with security issues too. See Chapter 18 for more information.

> Antivirus/antimalware: Many people believe that Apple computers and Linux-based computers do not need antivirus or antimalware. This is not true. Not only should they be installed, but they also need to receive updates on a regular basis.

SOFT SKILLS—BE HUMBLE

It takes a certain amount of arrogance to be an IT staff member. You have to be confident that you can repair most anything and figure things out. However, that sometimes comes across to others that you are an arrogant person. Anyone who has been in IT knows that you cannot know everything. You might know a little bit about a lot of things. You may know a lot about a specific side of IT. But no one can be an expert in it all. Show a little humility and be humble with your knowledge. Do not lord your knowledge and expertise over those you support. Showing empathy for those people you support and interact with goes a long way. See Figure 17.27.

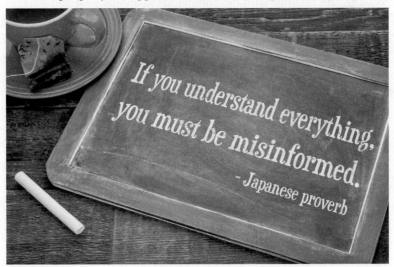

FIGURE 17.27   No technician knows everything

Chapter Summary

> OS X is a UNIX-based operating system developed by Apple.

> Open source software is made freely available and is open for modification.

> OS X can only run on Apple issue hardware; this includes virtual machines.

> The Dock, Finder, and Menu Bar make up the foundation of the OS X user interface known as Aqua.

> Spotlight can be used to quickly search an OS X system to find files, emails, applications, and even web search results.

> iCloud is Apple's online service that provides online storage and syncing.

> To get the most out of using OS X, end users should have an Apple ID to use with iCloud and the Mac App Store.

> Time Machine is the tool used for automated OS X backups.

> Most system settings can be found and managed in the System Preferences menu; it is the equivalent of Control Panels in Windows.

> Boot Camp is the name of an application that comes bundled with OS X; it guides you through installing Windows to a separate partition on a Mac.

> Basic OS X troubleshooting can be done using the Console and Activity Monitor. The Activity Monitor allows you to see what is running on the system, and what resources processes are using. The Console will allow you to see detailed logging of OS X, applications, and services.

> Keychain Access is a utility for storing passwords, but is largely not understood by end users. Be prepared to show users how to update their keychain password when they update their passwords.

> Advanced system administrators will use the Terminal application to access the command-line interface of OS X.

> Linux is an open operating system platform built on top of the principles of UNIX.

> Most Linux administration is going to happen at the command-line level, not in the graphical user interface.

> You must learn the basics of using the command line to properly administer Linux/UNIX systems. Be familiar with the commands in Tables 17.4 and 17.7.

> Be prepared to spend many hours researching to learn how to use Linux/UNIX systems; it can take years to master understanding how they work and how to properly administer them. If you aren't sure about something, use online resources or a colleague to better understand.

A+ CERTIFICATION EXAM TIPS

✓ In the overall scheme of things, this chapter and objectives contained within it are only 12 percent of the exam. That means you will only get a few questions. Spend more time on the Windows troubleshooting section in Chapter 16 and security issues found in Chapter 18.

✓ Know the purpose of the Shell/Terminal and review commands like su/sudo, grep, pwd, passwd, chmod, iwconfig, ifconfig, and apt-get.

✓ Know that the Boot Camp program can be used to install Windows on a Mac.

✓ Know that the Time Machine tool and iCloud can be used to back up/restore Mac images.

✓ Know how to force quit a Mac application.

Key Terms

Review Questions

1. What are the four main parts of the OS X graphical user interface?

   _____

2. [T | F] Ubuntu 15.04 uses the GNOME user interface.

3. What wireless encryption does `iwconfig` support and what is an alternative to using `iwconfig`?

   _____

4. In what ways could you quickly launch an application in OS X?

   _____

5. What type of account do you need to create to purchase software through the Apple App Store?

   _____

6. Write out the steps you would take to create a file with the Terminal application in OS X or Linux.

   _____

7. What `dd` command copies the contents of a partition named /dev/drive1 to another partition called /dev/backup?

   _____

8. What command is used to look for the words *mouse* in a filename? [sudo | apt-get | grep | rd]

9. The _____ command lists the contents inside the current directory.

10. What OS X tool is used to display and modify the main system settings?

    _____

11. How would you create a file from the command-line interface?

    _____

12. What steps would you take in Ubuntu, from the command line, to install a new package named lynx?

    _____

    _____

    _____

13. If an application is not starting properly on OS X, what steps could you take to resolve this?

    _____

14. If a Mac is running slow, what utility could you use to identify the cause of the slowdown?

    _____

15. What is the difference between `passwd` and `pwd`?

    _____

16. How large should a Time Machine backup drive be?

    _____

17. If you wanted to use `chmod` to give a file owner read, write, and execute permissions, which command would you use?

    _____

18. Which command grants temporary superuser permissions?
    [ls | less | root | sudo | app-get]

19. [T | F] The `locate` command searches the Linux file system.

20. How would you find out more information about a Linux command?

_____

Exercises

Exercise 17.1

Objective: To become familiar with Mac OS X tools

Parts: *None*

Procedure: Match the tool to the description.

     a. Time Machine   _____ Stop a non-responsive application

     b. Screen sharing   _____ Configure file sharing

     c. App Store   _____ Get system updates

     d. Force Quit   _____ Use an optical disc on another computer

     e. Remote Disc   _____ Troubleshoot kernel panic

     f. System Preferences   _____ View processes and used system resources

     g. Activity Monitor   _____ View a remote Mac

     h. Console   _____ Create a system backup

Exercise 17.2

Objective: To become familiar with Mac/Linux commands

Parts: *None*

Procedure: Match the command to the description.

     a. `cd`   _____ Delete a file

     b. `rm`   _____ Gain root provilege

     c. `touch`   _____ Move a file

     d. `chown`   _____ Move to a different directory

     e. `mv`   _____ Change the owner of a directory

     f. `grep`   _____ Get help for a particular command

     g. `man`   _____ Create a file

     h. `sudo`   _____ Search output for a specific value

Activities

Internet Discovery

Objective: Access the Internet to obtain specific information regarding a computer or its associated parts

Parts: Access to the Internet

Procedure: Complete the following procedure and answer the accompanying questions.

1.   Search online to find a Linux distro besides Ubuntu.

     Document the website and give a brief description of the distro.

_____

2.   What are some of the common business uses of the distro you found?

_____

3.   Research why Linux servers usually do not have a graphical user interface installed.

Write down the URL of the website you used to help come to your conclusion and explain your reasoning for not installing a GUI.

_____

_____

4.   Linux is a stable platform but still has issues and can crash.

Research what are some log files that are useful in Linux for troubleshooting.

_____

5.   Find a website that describes how to troubleshoot a Linux system that will not boot.

Write the URL and one thing you learned from the site.

_____

_____

Soft Skills

Objective: To enhance and fine-tune a future technician's ability to listen, communicate in oral form, work together in a group atmosphere on technical problems, and support people who use computers in a professional manner.

Activities: Complete the following questions in a group of three and share your opinions.

1.   Write down two things you find confusing about using OS X or Linux and share it with your group. See which areas are the most common problems for everyone.

2.   In your group take the list of the most common confusing items from Step 1 and do more research on them together; try and come to a better understanding of the topic. For the topics that you could not get a better grasp on, create a plan to better understand them. What is your plan?

3.   Working with UNIX or Linux requires the ability to do independent research to discover and understand new technologies in the field. You need to know how to properly search on the Internet to effectively find information, especially when troubleshooting an issue you are unfamiliar with. Have everyone in the group search to find what is the most popular web server application used to run on Linux. Compare answers to see if all got the same results. Also compare what each used to search for the answer. Some searches will be more precise at finding the answer than others. It is important to take a look at how you search to get results as fast as possible.

4.   List the most common answer for the most popular web server to run on Linux, as well as what was the most concise search phrase or term used.

_____

Critical Thinking Skills

Objective: To analyze and evaluate information as well as apply learned information to new or different situations.

Activities: Answer the following questions.

1.   On Ubuntu you have a user who cannot read a file. What would be the first thing you look at to resolve this and why?

2. Write a paragraph explaining why you think businesses prefer to use Linux rather than Windows for server environments.

3. What would the drawbacks be of using Linux rather than Windows for a server?

_____

_____

_____

Labs

Lab 17.1 Using the OS X Graphical User Interface

Objective: To work with the OS X graphical user interface, including the Dock, Finder, Mission Control, and accessing widgets. Also covers basic command-line usage and Time Machine

Parts: Computer with OS X

Procedure: Complete the following procedure and answer the accompanying questions.

1. Start by opening up a *Finder* window.

2. On the left side, you see a sidebar containing shortcuts to different parts of the file system. Right-click the *Applications* shortcut and select *Add to Dock*.

3. You should now have a new shortcut on the right side of the Dock.

    What happens when you click it?

    _____

4. This type of folder shortcut on the Dock isn't limited to just the Applications folder. This can be done with any folder such as Downloads, Documents, and so on. You can drag and drop nearly anything to the Dock to create a shortcut.

    This is a quick way to get access to your applications, but what other ways could you quickly access your applications?

    _____

5. If you want to remove a Dock shortcut, either a folder or application, you simply just drag it off the Dock, hold it with your cursor until it shows the word *remove* above it, and let go of it.

6. Now open the System Preferences menu and go into the Mission Control Panel: *Finder > Applications > System Preferences > Mission Control*.

7. You see a section labeled as Dashboard that by default is set to off. Change the option to *As Space* so that the dashboard appears in a separate space. Close the window.

8. Launch Mission Control (*Finder > Applications > Mission Control*). Notice the window at the top labeled Dashboard. Click this window.

9. The dashboard area is for putting widgets, which are usually shortcuts, mini applications, or reminders.

10. Select the + button at the bottom left and select *Stickies*.

11. A sticky note appears allowing you to save a message.

12. If you click the + button again, you see a *More Widgets* button; click it.

13. A browser window should open allowing you to browse a repository of available widgets. Widgets are slowly being phased out of OS X, but many long-time users still use them.

    Which useful widgets did you find on the Apple widget repository?

    _____

Lab 17.2. Using the OS X Terminal and Time Machine

Objective: To work with the OS X graphical user interface, including the Dock, Finder, Mission Control, and accessing Widgets. Also covers basic command-line usage and Time machine

Parts: Computer with OS X and a Time Machine backup drive

Procedure: Complete the following procedure and answer the accompanying questions.

1. Open the Terminal application by selecting the *Finder > Applications > Utilities > Terminal*.

2. Type in the command pwd, and you will see that you are located in the /Users/YOURUSERNAME directory.

3. Type the command ls to see what folders are in your current directory.

4. Navigate to the *Documents* folder.

   What command did you use to do this?

   _____

5. Create a blank file with the extension .txt. Name the file something unique that does not already exist.

   What command did you use to do this?

   _____

6. Now run a Time Machine backup. If you do not have a Time Machine backup drive set up, you need to connect an external drive to the Mac. You will be prompted when connecting the new drive if you would like to use it for Time Machine; select *yes* and enable backups. After this is enabled, or if you already had backups enabled, you need to trigger a new backup. Open the Time Machine preferences using the following process: *Finder > Applications > System Preferences > Time Machine*.

7. Enable (place a check mark) by +* in the menu bar option.

8. In the right corner of the Menu Bar, click the circular clock icon and select backup now.

9. If this is the first time running a Time Machine backup, it may take awhile to complete. You can check the status of it by clicking the same Time Machine icon in the menu bar. When it shows as completing a backup, return to the Terminal.

10. Make sure you are still in the *Documents* folder. Next delete the file you created in Step 5.

    What command did you use to do this?

    _____

11. Open up a *Finder* window and navigate to the *Applications* folder. There should be a shortcut to it on the left side.

12. Double-click or tap and briefly hold the *Time Machine* icon. This should bring up the Time Machine interface used to recover files.

13. In the Finder window select the *Documents* folder on the left side. Then go back to the most recent Time Machine backup using the timeline on the right side. Select the file you created and deleted earlier, and select *restore*.

    Does the file appear in Finder after clicking restore?

    _____

Lab 17.3 Using Ubuntu Live DVD

Objective: To learn where to get Ubuntu and how to boot into a live DVD environment

Parts: Computer with writeable DVD drive and a blank DVD

Procedure: Complete the following procedure and answer the accompanying questions.

1. To start this exercise, first download an Ubuntu ISO file. The latest ISO can be downloaded from http://www.ubuntu.com/download/desktop. For this exercise and chapter, we use Ubuntu 15.04, but downloading a newer version to follow along with is fine.

2. After you download the image, it must be burnt as a bootable image to your DVD. See the directions that follow for the operating system you are on to create the live DVD.

3. If you are creating a bootable DVD from Windows 7, 8, and 10, insert a blank DVD. Right-click the ISO image you downloaded and choose *Burn disc image*. From the Windows Disc Image Burner window, select the drive for the DVD burner and press *Burn*.

4. If you are creating a bootable DVD and are on OS X, insert a blank DVD. Launch *Disk Utility (Finder > Applications > Utilities > Disk Utility)*. Drag and drop the ISO file to the left pane in Disk Utility. Select the ISO file, and then select *Burn* from the menu above. In the menu that appears, select the DVD drive and then select *Burn*. After burning your DVD, keep the disc inside the optical drive and reboot the system.

5. As the system reboots, access the boot menu. To do this, press a special key as delineated in Table 17.8, which contains keyboard shortcuts for the most common systems. If the keyboard shortcut listed does not work, please research the manufacturer of your system.

TABLE 17.8   Boot menu shortcuts

System manufacturer	Key combination
Dell	F12
Lenovo	F8, F10, or F12
HP	ESC or F9
Asus	ESC or F8
Acer	ESC, F9, or F12
Macintosh	Option

6. When in the boot menu, boot off of the DVD drive. (Make sure the previously created DVD made in a previous step is inserted into the drive.)

TECH TIP

What to do if the system will not boot to the DVD

Make sure the DVD was created as a bootable disc. Boot back into the operating system, browse to the contents of the DVD, and make sure you see different files and folders on it. A common mistake is to burn the ISO file directly to the disc as if it were a regular data DVD. This will not create a bootable disc. The contents of the ISO file must be extracted onto the disc while creating it.

7. After the DVD loads, two options appear: to either Install Ubuntu or to Try Ubuntu. Select the *Try Ubuntu* option to load the live DVD environment.

   Were you able to get boot to the live DVD? If so, show the instructor. Having the live DVD work properly is a requirement to advance to the next lab. If you cannot get it to work, consult with your instructor.

   Instructor's initials _____

Lab 17.4 Ubuntu Command Line

Objective: To learn commands within the Ubuntu environment

Parts: Computer with Ubuntu loaded or an Ubuntu Live CD (see Lab 17.3)

Procedure: Complete the following procedure and answer the accompanying questions.

1. You must have completed the first Ubuntu lab successfully to proceed with this lab.

2. While booted to the live DVD, open the *Terminal*.

   How did you open the Terminal?

   _____

3. What is the current directory your Terminal session started in, and what command did you use to find out?

   _____

4. Notice that the time in the upper-right corner of the screen is likely different than your current local time. To find what time zone the system is set to, find the file named *timezone* and see what is written in it.

   How did you find the timezone file; where was it located? What did it contain?

   _____

   Next you need to install the application screen. List the commands you ran to do this.

   _____

   _____

   _____

   _____

5. Use the man page for apt-get to now uninstall the screen utility.

   What command did you use?

   _____

18 Computer and Network Security

In this chapter you will learn:

> What a company might put in a security policy

> How to perform operating system and data protection

> How to share and protect data

> How to optimize security for Windows

> Methods to use for data destruction and disposal

> How to configure wireless security options

> How to build customer trust

CompTIA Exam Objectives

What CompTIA exam objectives are covered in this chapter?

> 901-1.1 Given a scenario, configure settings and use BIOS/UEFI tools on a PC.

> 902-1.12 Install and configure common peripheral devices.

> 902-1.1 Compare and contrast various features and requirements of Microsoft Operating Systems (Windows Vista, Windows 7, Windows 8, Windows 8.1).

> 902-1.4 Given a scenario, use appropriate Microsoft operating system features and tools.

> 902-1.5 Given a scenario, use Windows Control Panel utilities.

> 902-1.6 Given a scenario, install and configure Windows networking on a client/desktop.

> 902-1.7 Perform common preventive maintenance procedures using the appropriate Windows OS tools.

> 902-2.2 Given a scenario, setup and use client-side virtualization.

> 902-2.4 Summarize the properties and purpose of services provided by networked hosts.

> 902-3.1 Identify common security threats and vulnerabilities.

> 902-3.2 Compare and contrast common prevention methods.

> 902-3.3 Compare and contrast differences of basic Windows OS security settings.

> 902-3.4 Given a scenario, deploy and enforce security best practices to secure a workstation.

> 902-3.5 Compare and contrast various methods for securing mobile devices.

> 902-3.6 Given a scenario, use appropriate data destruction and disposal methods.

> 902-3.7 Given a scenario, secure SOHO wireless and wired networks.

> 902-4.2 Given a scenario, troubleshoot common PC security issues with appropriate tools and best practices.

> 902-5.3 Summarize the process of addressing prohibited content/activity and explain privacy, licensing, and policy concepts.

Security Overview

Computer and network security relates to the hardware, software, and data protection of PCs and mobile devices. Large books are devoted to this topic. This chapter focuses on issues related to a PC technician job and the processes and terminology with which the technician should be familiar. Security should be a concern of everyone in a business or a home. And this, of course, also includes the people who repair and support PCs: the technicians. A technician must implement and explain security concepts. Every technician has the responsibility to promote security consciousness and to train users to be good stewards of equipment and data.

Security Policy

Companies struggle with information technology (IT) security as much as when computers were first used in the corporate environment. Actually, the corporate landscape has become complicated today because people bring their own electronic devices into work. This is commonly called bring your own device, or **BYOD**. Management must define and make clear what is acceptable to put on corporate wired or wireless networks and also what is unacceptable, along with the consequences for doing so.

A **security policy** is one or more documents that provide rules and guidelines related to computer and network security. Every company, no matter its size or number of employees, should have a security policy. Small businesses tend to have general operating procedures that are passed verbally from one employee to another, but it is best to have these processes documented in detail. **Noncompliant systems** or systems that do not meet security policy guidelines are some of the biggest threats to companies today. Some sectors such as education, healthcare, and government require IT security policies.

Common elements of a security policy are shown in Table 18.1.

TABLE 18.1   Security policy elements

Security policy component	Description
Physical access	Describes who is allowed into a building, to what part of the building they have access, and badge/key control. Defines who has keys to the wiring closets and server rooms as well as who is allowed in such places. Delineates what type of security log is kept when a person is allowed access to a space.
Antivirus	States whether antivirus software is required on every system, possibly what product is used, how updates are obtained, and steps taken when a machine is not compliant or if a person refuses to be compliant.
Acceptable use	Also known as acceptable use policy (**AUP**). Defines who has access to, and what level of usage is appropriate for, the company-provided information resources such as email and Internet. Sometimes, it defines what data can be taken from the company or data storage limitations such as no personal data is to be stored on a server or workstation PC. This section normally includes statements about gaming and web surfing during work hours as well as consequences for violations. The details might include defining what web browser and hardware platforms are supported. It might include the process for assigning folder and file rights and what to do if an account has been disabled.

Security policy component	Description
Password	Guidelines for protecting passwords such as not writing them down, a timeline for changing passwords, the number and type of characters required, and processes for forgotten passwords such as whether the new password can be given by phone or by email only.
Email usage	Defines who owns the email because it resides on a company server, how long email is stored, proper usage of email, and when it is backed up. Lawsuits related to this area continue to find for the company regarding email rights because the data is stored on company-owned and provided servers.
Remote access	Contains statements relevant to who is allowed, type(s) of remote access permitted, company resources that can be accessed remotely, the process to obtain desired rights and access, and what type of security level is required.
Emergency procedures	Details what to do when something is missing and the steps to take if a natural disaster such as a hurricane occurs. Stipulates who overrides a security policy and authorizes access to someone.

Many corporate security policies are implemented by user profiles. Within each profile, mandatory requirements such as password length and frequency of password changes are dictated and enforced. The profile also can enforce what network resources a particular user has access to. Even though not every company has a formal security policy, specific points relating to a security policy are referenced throughout this chapter. Whether written or just commonly accepted guidelines, many implementations are based on a particular company's rules for computer and network security.

To ease into the topic of security, the easiest place to start is security prevention methods. Security prevention methods deal with security measures that might prevent a security breach from occurring in the first place. Four methods of security prevention are physical security, digital security, user training, and principle of least privilege.

Physical Security

Typical physical security includes door locks, cipher locks, keys, guards, and fences, but physical security regarding computers can mean much more. For several years, companies have been using electronic key cards for physical access to rooms instead of keys. Electronic key cards (see Figure 18.1) are part of an access control system, which includes the key cards, door readers, and software to control and monitor the system.

Electronic key cards have many benefits, including the following:

> They are easy to program and issue/revoke compared to issuing a key and getting it back from a dismissed employee or one who quits.
> Data is stored in a database instead of on a checkout form.
> Access to information, such as who entered a room and at what time, can be logged and monitored more easily than with a checkout sheet.
> More layers of control can be exercised with key cards. With metal keys, the usual process is to give a key for each room, issue a submaster key for an entire wing, or issue a master key for the entire building.
> When keys are issued and one is lost, the lock must be rekeyed and new keys issued. When an electronic key card is lost, the old card is deactivated, and a new one is issued.

FIGURE 18.1 Electronic key cards

TECH TIP

Watch out for tailgating

Tailgating is the practice of an unauthorized person entering behind an authorized person. Prevention of tailgating (otherwise known as piggybacking) requires training and diligence by all employees.

Other electronic devices and technologies also provide access to computers and rooms. Table 18.2 lists and describes security devices that help with the physical security of computers.

TABLE 18.2 Physical security devices

Device/technology	Description
Smart card	A small ID-sized card that can store data, be encrypted, require authorization for changing, and wiped through a card reader or interact wirelessly with a card reader. Used in government IDs (with such information as medical/dental records) mobile phones as a subscriber ID module, driver's licenses, and employee badges (see Figure 18.2).
Key fob	Used for keyless entry to cars and buildings and interior doors such as a fitness room in an apartment complex.
radio frequency ID (**RFID**)	A technology that allows automatic identification of people, objects, or animals. Uses an RFID tag that is read wirelessly by an RFID reader. Used in libraries, inventory systems, computers, hospital equipment, and in locating lost pets or people. An **RFID badge** can be used to access and track access to a locked area.

Device/technology	Description
Security token	Also called an authentication token, USB token, hardware token, or software token. Because it is in the physical security section, this is a device that authorizes access to something.
Rivest Shamir Adleman (RSA) security token	RSA is a security algorithm method used with a security token, hardware token, DES card, **authentication*** token, or card. May be in a form of a smart token, key fob (see Figure 18.3), small calculator-sized, or USB-attached device. A PIN is frequently required, and a security token (think of it like a password) is generated. Enter the token for network access.
Locked doors	Putting key equipment such as servers, firewalls, switches, and data storage devices behind doors that are locked is an important security measure. Even with a locked room, **disable unused ports** on devices in case the room is compromised.
ID badge	An ID badge, though weak, is still a form of physical security. Some ID badges contain color codes to designate particular groups of employees or include a holographic image that is difficult to reproduce.
Entry control roster	Also known as an access control roster, lists employees who are authorized access to a particular area.
Trusted Platform Module (TPM)	A microcontroller chip on a motherboard used for hardware/software authentication. Stores information such as security certificates, passwords, and encryption keys. **Encryption** is the process of converting data into an unreadable format. It can authenticate hardware devices. Applications can use TPM for file and folder encryption, local passwords, email, VPN/PKI authentication, and wireless authentication.
Computer cage	Physical protection for a computer or laptop in a public location.
Cable lock	Used with devices in common areas such as libraries or lobby areas. Also used to secure laptops. Refer to Figure 11.96.
Mantrap	A method of separating a nonsecure area from a secured area (see Figure 18.4). This could be two doors with a guard, keypad, or some other security means on the second door. Useful in preventing unauthorized access and tailgating.
Privacy filter	Prevents **shoulder surfing** or someone looking over your shoulder to gain information from looking at your screen; allows viewing the screen clearly only if you are sitting directly in front of the monitor to prevent shoulder surfing (see Figure 18.5).
Password security	Do not type or write passwords and keep around the corporate desk. Passwords can be kept digitally in an encrypted file.
Tracking module	Located inside mobile devices and commonly requires a vendor contract. Used to track assets and provide recovery options if the device is lost or stolen. Might include a remote data wiping service.

*Authentication is a term used when describing the process of proving who you are before being allowed onto the computer, to remotely access into a network, or to be allowed access to a network resource such as a printer or shared document.

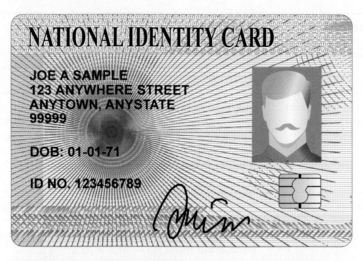

FIGURE 18.2   Smart card

FIGURE 18.3   Electronic key fob

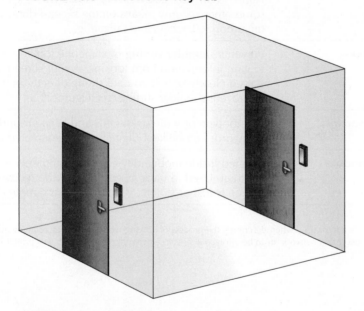

FIGURE 18.4   Mantrap

FIGURE 18.5   Shoulder surfing

Document Security

Some computer data must be printed as part of normal business operations. Some of this printed material must be kept in a locked environment (such as a safe, cabinet, or file cabinet). When others that do not have a "need to know" are in the room, turn the printed material over or, better yet, put it inside a folder. When the material is no longer needed, it can be shredded by a shredding service or using a shredder in the office. Outside companies should provide a **certificate of destruction** or proof of **incineration** (destruction by fire).

Shredders are available for reasonable prices, but they are not the best option in a corporate environment because shredded paper from most models can still be reconstructed (see Figure 18.6). For day-to-day business and personal documents, shredding is still a good practice to keep other people from taking documents out of trash bins (dumpster diving) and using the information for some malicious intent.

FIGURE 18.6 Reconstructing shredded documents

Multifactor Authentication

Smart cards or security tokens are often described as two-factor or **multifactor authentication**. This type of authentication is familiar to most people—you need something you possess, such as your ATM card, your current location, or security token device, and something you know, such as a PIN number, in order to gain access to something (a room, bank account, shared folder, data stored in the cloud, etc.). This is more secure than a password, which is only one factor.

An expanding field related to this is **biometrics**, which is authenticating (proving who someone is) based on one or more physical traits such as a fingerprint, eyeball (retina), or hand. Behavioral traits, such as voice, common web surfing, or purchase habits, can also be used. Voice can actually be both physical and behavioral. A less complex system would just compare voice with a stored voice print. A more complex system compares tone and inflection, too, which is more in the behavioral realm.

Multifactor authentication is when two or more methods are required to gain access to a computer, network room, or other shared media. With computers, one of the two things could be something the users know such as a password or PIN, and the second security measure could be a token, smart card, USB security key device, or a biometric device such as a fingerprint reader or face recognition through a webcam. Biometrics add one more security layer to authentication.

Authenticator apps can be used as part of multifactor authentication. A user preconfigures a particular website for this option. An **authenticator app** provides a one-time password that the user provides to the site in addition to the normal user ID and password.

Biometrics

Biometrics are more secure because a biometric system is more difficult to bypass than a user ID and password. The trait is less likely to be lost than a password. Also, biometrics require that the person being authenticated is present when gaining access. Biometrics are more expensive to implement than a user ID/password scheme. Table 18.3 lists examples of biometric devices used to allow someone to gain access to a room, locker, or device.

TABLE 18.3   Biometric devices

Device	Description
Fingerprint reader/lock	Requires a finger to be placed against a reader and compared against a stored image. Used in the laptop market, with some vendors having these devices already installed. Currently one of the best security measures for touch mobile devices. Can be attached to an existing computer easily via an ExpressCard or USB (see Figure 18.7).
Facial recognition	Integrated laptop webcams can be used. Another system, takes a photo and compares it with an image database (resource-intensive) (see Figure 18.8).
Hand scanner	Requires a palm of the hand to be placed against a reader and is more secure than a fingerprint reader. Higher-end systems can analyze veins in the palm.
Retinal scanner	Sometimes called an eye scanner and closely related to an iris scanner. According to LG Electronics, the human iris is the most distinguishable characteristic.
Voice recognition	A person speaks into a microphone before gaining access to a computer or physical space. Also called speech recognition but not the same as the software used to input data that replaces typing.

FIGURE 18.7   Fingerprint scanner

Applications for biometric devices are not limited to computer/network security. Disney World uses biometrics to ensure that the same person uses a multiday pass. Airports use biometrics for employee-only area access. Police departments use biometrics to gain access to evidence and gun lockers. These devices need to be installed and maintained by the computer and network support staff.

You might be required to use the system/UEFI BIOS Setup program to activate an integrated biometric device. To use the biometric device, optionally download a driver, install, and use a specific application that is available for download, comes with the device or computer, or an application preinstalled on the computer.

FIGURE 18.8 Facial recognition

Digital Security

Digital security deals with protecting the 1s and 0s electronically. All types of devices and techniques can help in this area. The types of digital security prevention methods on the CompTIA A+ certification are briefly outlined here. Some of them are explained in more detail later in the chapter.

> **Antivirus/antimalware**: Software to protect the operating system and applications from small programs that wreak havoc on the system, even causing it not to work at all.

> **Firewall**: Hardware device that protects an organization or software available through the operating system or a third-party vendor designed to protect a particular device. Companies may have more than one firewall depending on their network design (see Figure 18.9).

> User authentication/strong passwords: A method of ensuring the person accessing the device or network is a person who is allowed to do so.

> Multifactor authentication: More than one digital method to verify and identify the person using the device or network resources.

> Directory permissions: When data is shared across a network or stored in one or more folders on a server, permissions can be assigned to differentiate between people that just need to see the data or those that need to change or even delete the data.

> Virtual private network (**VPN**): A method of secure connectivity across an unsecure network such as the Internet to a remote location; an example is a mobile user who must connect to the corporate network to upload data weekly. See the VPN section at the end of the chapter for more information on how to configure a VPN.

> Data loss prevention (**DLP**): Software that protects corporate data from being sent outside the corporate network.

> Disabling ports: In highly sensitive areas, ports such as USB, IEEE 1394 FireWire, eSATA, Thunderbolt, and more are disabled so that an external device cannot be attached and data transferred to that device that may contain corporate or government-sensitive data.

> Access control lists (**ACLs**): Security rules that permit or deny the type of traffic flowing into a device, out of the device, toward a particular network, or specifying the type of traffic such as HTTP or HTTPS packets.

> **Email filtering**: Security rules specific to email that processes incoming messages before putting into specific users' email inbox that searches for and removes suspicious and harmful emails; potentially scans outgoing emails to ensure security or legal compliance (see Figure 18.10). Users are commonly familiar with their spam folder in their email inbox that is evidence of such filtering. Technical staff must sometimes remind them to check there for expected email when sent from an external source.

> **Trusted/untrusted software sources**: Windows users commonly have security software that tells them whether a website or a downloaded file is a trusted or untrusted software source. Linux users have repositories of open source software that has been approved or tested on specific Linux platforms. Linux users should be cautious downloading software from unknown developers that do not make their source code public. All downloads, no matter the operating system, should be aware of untrusted software sources.

FIGURE 18.9   Corporate firewall design

Let's dive in a little deeper into some of these security items and start with the one we all are familiar with: the password. Actually, different types of passwords authenticate users (and devices for that matter). BIOS/UEFI passwords are a great place to start.

FIGURE 18.10   Email filtering

BIOS/UEFI

Most computers have BIOS/UEFI options that prevent others from altering the settings. A BIOS/UEFI password can also be assigned to require a password before the operating system loads. Table 18.4 shows some BIOS/UEFI options related to security.

TABLE 18.4   BIOS/UEFI security options

Option	Description
Supervisor	Unrestricted access to all BIOS options.
User	Enables a limited number of configuration changes such as time and boot sequence.
Trusted Platform Module (TPM)	Allows initialization and seeing a password for the TPM motherboard chip that generates and stores cryptographic keys.
LoJack	Allows locating a mobile device and displaying a message on lost device.
Secure boot	Prevents an unauthorized operating system from loading.
Boot or Power-on password	Required before BIOS/UEFI looks for an operating system. This is not the Windows user password.

In a corporate environment, the supervisor password is commonly configured. Other options that may affect the corporate environment include the following:

> Enabling/disabling device options
> Enabling/disabling ports
> Encrypting a drive
> Enabling TPM
> Enabling Lojack (allows a mobile device to be located, remotely locked, and to display an "if found" message)
> Viewing/changing security levels/passwords
> Restoring security settings to the default values

Laptops, netbooks, and ultrabooks sometimes have an additional password for their internal storage drive. That way, if the device is stolen, the hard drive cannot be inserted into another device and used without knowing the hard drive password. It is a password in addition to the power-on password or Windows password. If this option is available, it is configured through the BIOS/ UEFI.

Operating System Passwords

Passwords authenticate people and should always be required. A great analogy for authentication is the clubhouse that many of us made as children. A secret tap at the door or a special password was the only way to gain access to the private domain. Most people are familiar with the user ID and password method of authentication. Other means could be used including the previously discussed biometric devices. All these provide an additional layer of security beyond the user ID and password method. Windows and other operating systems and applications use the Kerberos protocol to provide authentication. Kerberos uses a key distribution center (KDC) to authenticate users, applications, and services. Password protection is a common method used though, and Table 18.5 lists some password guidelines.

TABLE 18.5   Computer/network password guidelines

Guideline	Description
Reminders	Do not write down your password. Many computer users write down their password and keep it close to the computer. Do not put your password in a document stored on the same computer.
Number of characters/ complexity	Use eight or more characters with uppercase and lowercase letters interspersed with numerals and special characters.
Format	Do not use consecutive letters or numbers on the keyboard, such as *asd* or *123* because they are easy for someone who is watching to guess the password. Do not use passwords that are words such as *children* or *happiness* because password-cracking programs use **dictionary attacks** to hack passwords. These dictionaries even include foreign words and names.
Expiration	On servers, this is known as the minimum password age and the maximum password age. The minimum password age is how long a user must keep a password before changing it. Microsoft recommends 3 to 7 days. The maximum is how long before the user is required to change it. Common values are 30, 60, and 90 days.

Guideline	Description
Reuse	Authentication servers often have a setting that dictates the number of times you have to change to a new password before the old password can be used again. It is best practice to not allow users to reuse passwords and to prevent them from changing the password immediately repeated times to go back to the old password.
Screen saver/lock computer	Use a screen saver or lock the computer with the ■ + Ⓛ option. Configure the screen saver using the *Personalization* Control Panel link to configure the screen saver and require the login credentials to re-access the computer.
Failed attempts	The number of times a person is allowed to try a password that is wrong before being locked out. A common setting is three failed attempts.
Social	People's eyes tend to stray toward movement. If someone is standing near you "shoulder surfing" when you log in, ensure that the person's eyes are averted, or wait until that person moves away to type your password into the system. Obtain a privacy filter.

Windows allows several user ID and password options, including the following:

> Local user ID and password created and maintained on the local PC
> Computer that is part of the workgroup where the user ID and password are created, stored, and maintained on the local computer (similar to the local PC)
> Windows HomeGroup uses the same HomeGroup password on all computers.
> Computer that is part of a domain and the user ID and password are created, stored, and maintained on a centralized network server
> PINs
> Microsoft account password

User Education

Educating users is a great way to prevent security events and issues. Technical staff frequently forget this step because they would rather deal with the machines and the technology than the people who operate and access the devices. Training should start when someone is first hired. New hires should be presented with the acceptable use policy (AUP) previously described. Some companies present this policy every time a user logs in to the network. Users should be reminded that every employee is required to follow corporate end-user policies and apply security best practices with every device used to perform business tasks.

Remind them that everyone is inconvenienced by good security practices that are time-consuming, bothersome, and may sometimes even seem meaningless, until a security event occurs! People tend to take shortcuts. That is why humans are the weakest security link. Users should be reminded that if their computer is remotely accessed by a technician, they should close windows that have corporate or personal information prior to agreeing to the remote connection. Any time that a technician removes a virus or malware from a user device, training should be part of solving the problem. Violations of security best practices are a common security threat and make a company more vulnerable to other security problems. Let's explore some of the common areas that apply to users.

Licensing

One of the hardest ethical problems is when technicians are asked to install software or other content that is not legitimate. Digital rights management (**DRM**) is the technology used to implement controls placed on digital media (software, hardware, songs, videos, and more). Users often request that technicians share with them methods to break copyright laws or copy protection controls. Technicians must maintain their professionalism and ethics to ensure that corporate interests are protected.

In instances like these, it is a great opportunity to talk to users about different software sources:

> Open source: The original software code is provided.
> Freeware: Doesn't cost anything but could include some harmful software.
> Shareware: Might be free at first but may require later payment; may include only part of a particular software package with the option to buy the rest.
> **Commercial license**: Purchased software for a specific number of users and/or machines that may just be one. Even when commercial licensing is obtained, there is an end user licensing agreement (**EULA**) that specifies what can be done with that particular license.
> **Personal license**: Purchased software for a specific number of users and/or machines that may just be one. EULA is part of that. Commonly used for home or small business environments.

In a 2013 Business Software Alliance (BSA) global software piracy study, PC software theft was near 43 percent. **Piracy** (see Figure 18.11) is defined by the BSA in 2016 as the following:
> Copying or distribution of copyrighted software that is not authorized

> Purchasing a copy of a particular application or software and putting it on more than one computer
> Installing, sharing, selling, copying, downloading, or uploading stolen software to another site
> Installing company software on or permitting access to unauthorized devices

FIGURE 18.11   Software pirate

Software companies have different pricing structures for individual or personal licenses and corporate or enterprise licenses. An enterprise license gives a company permission to load the software on unlimited or a maximum number of devices. A personal license is more limiting (usually to one device).

People use software piracy websites to obtain illegal software. These sites are riddled with security threats that are also downloaded. The current penalty in the United States for software piracy is $150,000 per program copied. If prosecuted for copyright infringement, fines can be up to $250,000 and/or up to 5 years in jail. Don't be persuaded to risk your personal life and professional future for software piracy.

Personally Identifiable Information

Personally identifiable information (PII) is information that uniquely identifies someone, such as a Social Security number, employee ID, patient number, passport number, and user ID. It is important to stress to users to not have this lying around, taped somewhere, or available in the work environment except where needed. There are two types of PII: nonsensitive and sensitive. Nonsensitive PII is information that can be found publicly such as a person's name, telephone number, and email address. Nonsensitive information can be transmitted unencrypted (unscrambled and no security) without causing harm to an individual. In contrast, sensitive PII may cause harm and breach someone's privacy if sent non-encrypted. Sensitive PII should be encrypted (scrambled with security algorithms) if sent or is data stored. Sensitive PII should always be in encrypted form.

Security Threats and Vulnerabilities

Several types of security threats and vulnerabilities exist. Many seem to fall in multiple categories because there might be multiple threats. They all do bad and weird things to devices. Malware is a good place to start. **Malware** is software code that is designed to damage a computer system (lockups, slowness, applications crash or won't run or run incorrectly, operating system updates fail, to name a few). In most cases, allowing more BYODs increases the risk of introducing malware into the network. Table 18.6 lists common types of malware.

TABLE 18.6 Types of malware

Type	Description
Spyware	Collects personal information without consent through logging keystrokes, accessing saved documents, and recording Internet browsing. Results in unsolicited pop-ups and identity theft.
Virus	Does something harmful to the computer (display a message, cause it not to boot, make it run slow, changes file or application permissions, or log keystrokes). Commonly attaches itself to an installed program.
Worm	Spreads to other devices and may or may not do anything that causes suspicion.
Trojan	Disguises itself as a legitimate program to gain unauthorized access to a device. Also known as a trojan horse (see Figure 18.12).
Rootkit	Used to gain administrator access (known as root access in Linux) to the operating system.
Ransomware	Restricts access to a device until a user pays money to regain access (see Figure 18.13).

"Sure, bring her in. I've always wanted to work on one of these babies."

FIGURE 18.12 Trojan (disguising itself)

FIGURE 18.13 Ransomware

The following are common symptoms of a virus.

> Computer does not boot.
> Computer hard drive space is reduced.
> Applications will not load.
> An application takes longer to load or function than it used to.

> Hard drive activity increases (especially when no work is being done by the user and the antivirus scan is not running).
> An antivirus software message appears.
> The number of hard drive sectors marked as bad steadily increases.
> Unusual graphics or messages appear on the screen.
> Files are missing (deleted).
> A message appears that the hard drive cannot be detected or recognized.
> Strange sounds come from the computer.

Antivirus applications can be configured to run in manual mode (on demand) or as scheduled scans. When you have an infected computer, you should quarantine it. This means you should disconnect the computer from the network until the computer is virus free. Some antivirus programs can quarantine a computer automatically if the computer has a virus. Many antivirus software programs have the capability to quarantine files—files that appear to the antivirus program as possible virus-infected or suspicious files that might be dangerous. A message normally appears with a list of files that have been quarantined, and each one must be identified as a valid file or to be left in the quarantine (unusable) until a new version of the antivirus signature files has been updated and can identify the file.

Social Engineering

All technicians (and employees) should be aware of social engineering. **Social engineering** is a technique used to trick people into divulging information, including their own personal information or corporate knowledge. Social engineering does not just relate to computers but can be done over the phone, through online surveys, or through mail surveys. No auditing or network security applications and devices can help with such deviousness. Good security awareness helps prevent unintentional disclosures.

Phishing

Closely related to social engineering is the concept is phishing. **Phishing** (pronounced "fishing") is a type of social engineering that attempts to get personal information, and it comes through email from a company that appears legitimate. Phishing emails target ATM/debit or credit card numbers and PINs, Social Security numbers, bank account numbers, Internet banking login IDs and passwords, email addresses, security information such as a mother's maiden name, full name, home address, or phone number. Most browsers include a phishing filter, which proactively warns computer users when they go to a site that is a known phishing site or when a site contains characteristics common to phishing sites.

A variant of phishing is **spear phishing**, which is a targeted method of phishing in which the attacker knows some information about you. The subject line or first part of the message may include your name. The body of the message may reference someone you know or appear to be from a legitimate company with which you do business (see Figure 18.14).

FIGURE 18.14   Spear phishing

Security Attacks

Attacks can come from outside or from within a corporate network. Table 18.7 lists various types of network attacks.

TABLE 18.7   Types of network attacks

Type of attack	Description
Access	Frequently uses multiple dictionaries including foreign ones to gain access to accounts, databases, servers, and/or network devices. Types of attacks include man-in-the-middle, port redirection, buffer overflow, and password.
Backdoor	Also known as trapdoor, a planted program that executes to bypass security and/or authentication.
Botnet	Software that spreads from device to device (see Figure 18.15) that has been hacked and under control of someone else (called zombie computers or zombies).
Brute force	Repeated attempts to check all possible key combinations to gain access to a network device or stored material.
DoS (denial of service)	A string of data/messages sent to overload a particular firewall, router, switch, server, access point, or computer in an attempt to deny service to other network devices.
DDoS (distributed denial of service)	A group of infected computers attack a single network device by flooding the network with traffic.
Man-in-the-middle (MitM)	A technique in which a hacker inserts a device between a sender and a receiver so this device can receive the intended traffic. Access points, DHCP servers, and default gateways are common devices simulated in this type of attack.
Reconnaissance	Attempts to gather information about the network before launching another type of attack. Tools used include port scanners, pings, and packet-sniffing programs.

Type of attack	Description
Replay	A valid network message or certificate is re-sent, usually in an attempt to gain logon procedures.
Smurf	Uses Internet Control Message Protocol (ICMP) to ping a large amount of network traffic at a specific device to deny that device network access, ping a nonexistent device to generate network traffic, or ping all network devices to generate traffic in ICMP replies.
Spoofing	Sending an Ethernet frame with a fake source MAC address to trick other devices to send traffic to a rogue device.
TCP/IP hijacking	A stolen IP address is used to gain access and/or authorization information from the network.
Vulnerability scanner	A software program used to assess network devices to identify weaknesses such as unpatched operating systems, open ports, or missing/outdated virus-scanning software.
Zero day attack	A vulnerability in a particular software application that is found by hackers before it is known/fixed by the software developer.
Zombie	A device that has been hacked and is controlled by someone else or carries out malicious tasks.

FIGURE 18.15   Zombies and botnets

Workgroups and Domains

A workgroup or HomeGroup is a LAN in which each computer maintains its own networked resources, such as whether a file or printer is shared with others. Workgroup networks are more common in small office/home office (SOHO) environments. A domain environment is more common in the business world in which network servers authenticate logins, provide file storage, and provide services such as email and web access. Another name for a domain environment is a server-based network. Figure 18.16 illustrates a workgroup environment; Figure 18.17 shows how a domain environment is different.

Some companies use single sign-on (SSO) for user authentication. **Single sign-on** enables a user to authenticate with a minimum of a user ID and password. With that authentication, the user is allowed access to multiple systems/servers, devices such as printers and copiers, as well as networked-based applications. The alternative is that users are prompted to authenticate or log in each time they access such network connections as the work computer, email, or a shared file server.

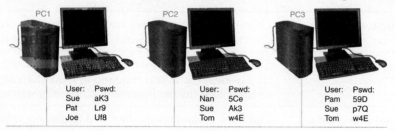

FIGURE 18.16   Windows workgroup model

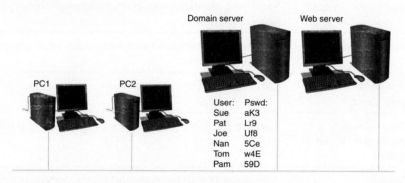

FIGURE 18.17   Windows domain model

Protecting Access to Local and Network Resources

Several techniques exist to protect computer access, and some of them have been considered as part of physical access. Authentication is used to determine what network resources can be used. **Authorization** is the part of the operating system or network controls that grant access to specific resources such as files, folders, printers, video conferencing equipment, scanners, and so on, on a computer system or network.

TECH TIP

Prevent a computer from being seen through the network

Search and access the *Administrative Tools* Control Panel > *Services* > double-click or double-tap *Computer Browser* > from the *Startup type* drop-down menu, select *Disabled* > *Apply* > *OK* > restart the computer.

Users can be added and placed into groups for ease of management. Table 18.8 shows the default local users/groups for Windows Vista, 7, 8, and 10. Note that in Windows Home versions, local groups are not supported.

CHAPTER 18

TABLE 18.8 Windows default users/groups

User or group	Description
Administrator (user)	Has total control of the computer; best practice is to rename the account and password protect it; create another user account that belongs to the administrator group, and has a complex password.
Administrators (group)	A user account that has been created and placed in this group that has total control of the computer.
Guest (user)	A member of the Guest group; disabled by default; no default user rights.
Guests (group)	Used by those that do not have an account on the computer; normally does not require a password; best practice is to disable.
Standard user (user)	Default type of account created when you create a common corporate staff worker; the user is required to request an administrator to make changes to software, hardware, or security settings.
Backup operators (group)	Can back up and restore files and folders regardless of permissions assigned; cannot change security settings; can access the computer from a remote location.
Power users (group)	Same as a Standard user account (change things like time zone or date/time).
Users (group)	Can perform common tasks and create local groups, but cannot share folders or printers.
Remote desktop users (group)	Can log on to the computer from a remote location.
Offer Remote Assistance Helper (group)	Can use the Remote Assistance program to help the computer user.
Network Configuration Operators (group)	Can make TCP/IP changes and release/renew IP addresses.
Performance Log Users (group)	Can manage local or remote performance logs and alerts.

A security best practice in Windows is to create an account that has administrator access and to disable the *Administrator* account (Vista, 7, and 8). Another option in Windows Vista and 7 is to just rename the username to something other than Administrator. The *Guest* account should always be disabled. (It is by default.)

Windows 8 and 10 do not allow disabling the Administrator account, but you can add a user that has administrator access. In Windows 8, access the *User Accounts* Control Panel. Select the *Manage another account* link > select the *Add an account* link. If you don't want to use an email address, you can select the *Sign in without a Microsoft account (not recommended)* link > *Local account button* > enter the information and select *Next* > *Finish*. Select the account just created > *Edit* > change the account type to *Administrator* > *OK*.

In Windows 10, access the *User Accounts* Control Panel. Select the *Manage another account* link > select the *Add a new user in PC settings* link > in the Other users section, select the *Add someone else to the PC* option > if you don't want to use a Microsoft, Skype, Xbox, or other type of email or phone number and account information, select the *I don't have this person's sign-in information* link > select the *Add a user without a Microsoft account* link. Select the newly created user and select the *Change account type* button > change the account type to *Administrator* > *OK*.

The following list contains best practices for securing a workstation in a corporate environment.

> Apply login time restrictions.
> Disable the guest account.
> Enable the feature to lock users out after a specific number of failed login attempts.
> Configure a timeout/screen lock for when users are away from their workstation.
> Implement user permissions and apply the principle of least privilege. Note that this is covered in the next section.

TECH TIP

Use the Lock Computer option

When away from your desk, use the *Lock Computer* option by pressing [Ctrl] + [Alt] + [Delete] and selecting *Lock* or *Lock this Computer*.

Local and Group Policies

Another method of controlling login passwords is through a local- or domain-based group account policy. Policies do more than just define password requirements. They can define the desktop, what applications are available to users, what options are available through the *Start* menu, whether users are allowed to save files to external media, and so on. A domain or **group policy** can be created and applied to every computer on the domain. This practice is common in Microsoft Active Directory (AD) domain networks.

A **local policy** is created on a computer, and it could be used to disable auto-playing of optical discs, prevent users from shutting down or restarting a computer, turn off personalized menus, or keep someone from changing the Internet Explorer or Microsoft Edge home page. A local policy might be implemented in a workgroup setting. A group policy is more common in a corporate environment, and a group policy can overwrite a local policy. If any computer settings on a networked computer in a corporate environment are grayed out, the settings are probably locked out due to the group policy deployed throughout the domain.

TECH TIP

Accessing the local policy and group policy

Access the local policy by typing `gpedit.msc` from a command prompt or from the *Search* textbox. Use the `gpresult` command to display group policy settings. Use the `gpupdate` command to update all domain users with a newly deployed group policy. The `secedit` command is used to configure or analyze the security policy.

Passwords continue to be an issue for everyone. Different requirements, user IDs, and passwords cause stress for many folks. A password manager is an application that is on one computer or a USB drive, mobile app, or web browser plug-in that locally or remotely stores passwords used to access an account. When stored remotely, the passwords and associated data (site, device, and so on) should be encrypted.

Through the defined policy, criteria for auditing can also be set. **Auditing**, sometimes called event logging or just logging, is the process of tracking events that occur on the network such as someone logging in to the network. In the business environment, a server with special auditing software is sometimes devoted to this task because it is so important to security. Labs 18.5 and 18.6 at the end of this chapter detail how to configure a local security policy, log events, and view those audited items. Figure 18.18 shows the Local Group Policy Editor window.

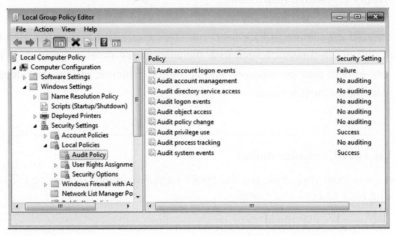

FIGURE 18.18 Local Group Policy Editor window

TECH TIP

Requiring password protection

You can enable or disable password protection through the Network and Sharing Center on a workgroup/HomeGroup computer. If password protection is enabled, the person accessing a shared folder from a remote location must have a user account and password on the computer with the share.

Permissions

Monitoring the users and groups and the devices, data, and applications they have access to is important. Permissions control what can or cannot be done (permit or deny access) to files, folders, and devices from a remote connection. This is similar to file attributes covered in Chapter 15. User-assigned permissions can cause havoc. Network administrators and end users can set permissions on folders, and these permissions may affect another user's access to files and folders. Technicians need to be familiar with permissions.

Two types of permissions can be assigned in Windows: share permissions and NTFS permissions. **Share permissions** provide and/or limit access to data across a network. Share permissions are the only way to secure network resources on FAT16 or FAT32 drives. **NTFS permissions** provide tighter control than shared folder permissions. NTFS permissions can be used only on NTFS drives.

TECH TIP

File permissions change

If you ever notice that file permissions change (you cannot access an application or file that you once could), check for a virus. Note that some viruses that do this may require repartitioning the hard drive and reinstalling the operating system.

Share Permissions

To share a folder other than the Public folder, use *Windows Explorer* (Vista/7)/*File Explorer* (Windows 8/10) > right-click or tap and briefly hold on the folder name > *Share* (Vista)/*Share with* (7, 8, 10). Type the name of the person and click *Add*. You can do one of the following at this point:

> > If the computer is attached to a network domain, select the arrow to the right of the textbox > *Find* > type the name of the person with whom you want to share the folder > *Check Names* > *OK*.

> > If the computer is on a workgroup, click the arrow to the right of the textbox, select the appropriate name, and click *Add*. If the name does not appear, click the arrow to the right of the textbox, and click *Create a new user to create the user account*.

> > If the computer is part of a HomeGroup, you can select *Homegroup (Read)* or *Homegroup (Read/Write)* and the folder will be shared with the appropriate permissions. In Windows Home and Starter editions, you can only join a HomeGroup, not create one.

An alternative method is to locate the folder using *Windows Explorer* (Vista/7)/*File Explorer* (Windows 8/10) > right-click or tap and briefly hold on the folder icon > *Properties* > *Sharing* tab > select the *Share...* button. Figure 18.19 shows this window in Windows 7.

FIGURE 18.19   Sharing a folder; Sharing tab

TECH TIP

Share permissions are only applicable across a network

Notice that shared folder permissions are applicable only across a network. This type of share does not prevent someone sitting at the computer from accessing files and folders. For best protection across a network and at the computer, use NTFS file and folder permissions.

Permissions are set by clicking the *Advanced Sharing* button (see Figure 18.20). Notice how you can limit the number of simultaneous users that can connect to this folder from a remote location. Select the *Permissions* button (see Figure 18.21). Notice how you can select the Allow or Deny checkboxes for the individual permissions.

CHAPTER 18

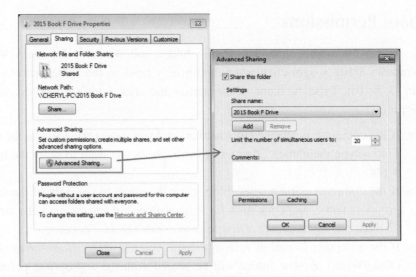

FIGURE 18.20 Folder Sharing tab > Advanced Sharing

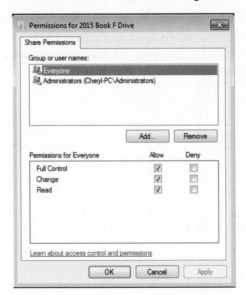

FIGURE 18.21 Folder Sharing tab > Advanced Sharing > Permissions

TECH TIP

What is the maximum number of concurrent users?

A maximum of 20 users can simultaneously use the same shared folder.

Notice in Figure 18.21 how you may select a specific type of permission (Full Control, Change, and Read) on the Allow and Deny columns. Table 18.9 shows the effect of setting one of these permissions.

TABLE 18.9   Share permissions

Permission	Description
Full Control	Users can do everything such as change the file permissions, take ownership of files, and perform everything that can be done with the *Change* permission.
Change	Users can add a new subfolder, add files to a folder, change the data in file, add data to files, change the file attributes, delete folders and files, and do all the tasks that you can do with the *Read* permission.
Read	Users can look at file and folder names and attributes. Also, files and scripts can be executed.

TECH TIP

Principle of least privilege

When sharing access to a folder or to a server room, you should give access to what is needed to the people that need it and no more. Giving people access to an entire drive or building when they just need access to a particular folder or room puts the entire hard drive or company at risk. The principle of least privilege as it relates to computer and network security is that the maximum rights you give people are limited to only the rights they need to do their job.

File and folder security protection is a concern. A subfolder and any files created within that subfolder all inherit security permissions from the parent folder or the folder that contains the subfolder. This feature can be disabled when necessary.

Local and Administrative Shares

Files and folders can be shared in a network workgroup, a HomeGroup, or a domain. A **local share** is something—a printer, folder, or media device—that is shared on a specific computer. **Administrative shares** are shares created by Microsoft for drive volumes and the folder that contains the majority of Window files. An example of an administrative share is a drive volume letter (such as C) followed by the dollar sign ($) symbol (C$). The admin$ administrative share is used to access to the folder that contains the Windows operating system files.

Windows automatically creates these administrative shares, but by default Windows prevents local accounts from accessing administrative shares through the network. If this feature is desired, a registry edit must be made. The `net share share_name$ /delete` command can disable a particular administrative share. However, this is reset when the computer is restarted. A better solution is to make this a policy.

Any local share can be made a **hidden share**, which is a share that is not seen by default through the network. To make a share a hidden share, add the dollar sign ($) symbol to the share name. This might be beneficial to computer users who want to access something from their remote computer without making it visible to other network users.

TECH TIP

Access denied message

If a user or technician ever receives an access denied message on a shared folder or hidden share, ensure the user login is one that has administrative privileges or check assigned permissions on the shared folder.

Public Folder

Windows supports sharing using a newer folder called the Public folder. The default path for the Public folder is C:\Users\Public. You can copy or move any file to the Public folder. This makes it easier to share files with someone, but when files are copied into it, twice as much hard drive space is used because they are in two folders.

If sharing is enabled for the Public folder, anyone with a user account and password on the computer can access the data. In addition, any user on the network can see all files and folders in the Public folder by selecting *Network* from Windows Explorer/File Explorer, accessing the appropriate computer, browsing to the *Users* folder, and opening the *Public* folder. You can set permissions so that the folder is inaccessible or can restrict anyone from changing files or creating new files. However, you cannot pick and choose what files can be seen by individuals.

The Public folder is not shown by default in Windows 7 (but it is in Windows 8 and 10). In Windows 7, you may create a shortcut on the desktop for it. To enable the use of the Public folder, the steps in Windows 7 compared to Windows 8 and 10 are a little different. Do the following based on the operating system being used:

> In Windows 7, access the *Network and Sharing Center* Control Panel > *Change advanced sharing settings* > expand the *Public* section by selecting the down arrow if it is not showing any information below it > locate the *Public folder sharing* area > select the *Turn on sharing so anyone with network access can read and write files in the Public folders* radio button. Note that you must also turn on network discovery and file and print sharing to see shared files across the network. See Figure 18.22.

> In Windows 8/10, access the *Network and Sharing Center* Control Panel > *Change advanced sharing settings* > expand the *All Networks* section by selecting the down arrow if it is not showing any information below it > locate the *Public folder sharing* area > select the *Turn on sharing so anyone with network access can read and write files in the Public folders* radio button. Note that you must also turn on network discovery and file and print sharing to see shared files across the network.

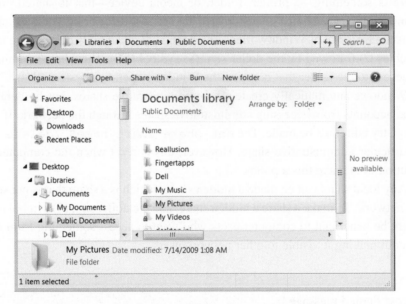

FIGURE 18.22 Windows 7 Public Documents folder

Libraries

Windows uses libraries. A library is similar to a folder, but a library contains files that are automatically indexed for faster searching, viewing, and access. For example, a teacher might store training video clips in a library and share them from a library. This library could contain files from different folders, an external drive, or even a network share.

Windows is configured to have four default libraries: Documents, Music, Pictures, and Videos. Windows Explorer/File Explorer automatically show the libraries. If you right-click the Documents library and select Properties, you can see that both a particular user's Documents folder is shown as well as a public Documents folder. Notice the *Include a folder* button in this window, as shown in Figure 18.23. This button allows more folders to be included in the Documents library. No matter the source of the files, they are all controlled through a single library as if the contents were stored in a single location. Each default library has two default locations configured (My Documents and Public Documents) as shown in Figure 18.30. It may also contain other locations if cloud storage is enabled. The public location is used by any user logged on to the computer. Only one location can be configured as the default save location for files that are moved, copied, or saved to the library.

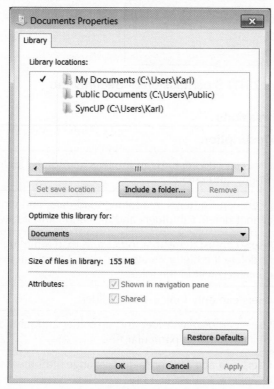

FIGURE 18.23 Windows 7 libraries

NTFS Permissions

On an NTFS partition, additional security protection is available through Windows. To share a folder using NTFS permissions, locate the folder using Windows Explorer (Vista/7) or File Explorer (Windows 8/10). Right-click or tap and briefly hold on the folder name and select *Sharing* (Vista) or *Properties* (7/8/10) > select the *Security* tab. Figure 18.24 shows this window. Notice how more permissions can be administered on an NTFS partition using NTFS permissions rather than share permissions. Table 18.10 defines these permissions.

FIGURE 18.24 Windows 7 NTFS permissions—Security tab

TABLE 18.10 NTFS permissions

Permission	Description
Full Control	Users can do anything in the files and folder, including delete, add, modify, and create.
Modify	Users can list items in a folder, read data, and write data, but they cannot delete subfolders and files and cannot take ownership.
Read & Execute	Users can list items in a folder and read a file, but they cannot change or delete the file or create new files. Users can execute applications contained within the folder.
List Folder Contents	Users can only look inside a folder.
Read	Users can display folder and subfolder attributes and permissions as well as look at a particular file.
Write	Users can add files or folders, change attributes for the folder, and add or append to data in a file.

Inherited permissions are permissions that are propagated from what Microsoft calls a parent object. For example, if a folder is given the Read permission, then all files within that folder cannot be changed (they are read-only). If a subfolder is created, it inherits that permission. If the Allow/Deny checkboxes for any object are selected, the current permissions have been inherited.

There may also be issues when copying or moving is performed on objects that have NTFS permissions set. Here are guidelines for copying and moving:

> When you copy a file/folder on the same or different NTFS drive letter, the copy inherits the destination folder permissions.

> When you move a file/folder on the same NTFS drive letter, the original permissions of the object are retained.

> When you move a file/folder to a different NTFS drive letter, the moved object inherits the destination folder permissions.

> When you copy or move a file/folder to a drive that uses a different file system (like FAT), the object loses all its permissions.

> If you change permissions on a folder that has content, only the new content inherits the changed permissions.

Effective permissions are the final permissions granted to a person for a particular resource. Effective permissions are important when you combine shared folder permissions given to an individual, shared folder permissions given to a group, and individual permissions. The following list outlines some helpful tips when sharing folders and files across a network:

> Folder permissions are cumulative—when you grant folder permissions to a group and then grant an individual permissions to that same folder, the effective permissions for that person is the combination of what the group gets and what the person gets. For example, if the group gets the Write permission and the person gets only the Read permission (and the person is a member of the group that has the Write permission), the person can both read and write files to the folder.

> Deny overrides any allowed permissions that have been set for a user or a group. For example, if a group is denied access to a folder, but a person is specifically allowed access to the folder, the person is not allowed to access the folder.

> When NTFS and shared folder permissions are both used, the most restrictive of the two is the effective permissions.

Windows provides help in determining effective permissions. In Windows 7, right-click a file or folder > *Properties* > *Security* tab > *Advanced* button > *Effective Permissions* tab (see Figure 18.25). In Windows 8 and 10, right-click or tap and hold on a file or folder > *Properties* > *Security* tab > *Advanced* button > *Effective Access*. Note that what is shown is only for NTFS permissions. Share permissions are not part of the Windows calculation for this window. Permissions-related issues are a common problem. A technician must be familiar with the results of misconfiguring them.

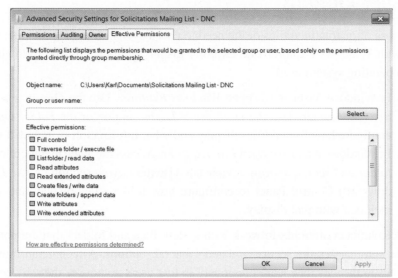

FIGURE 18.25   **Windows 7 effective permissions**

> **TECH TIP**
>
> **All subfolders are shared when a folder is shared**
>
> When you share a folder, all subfolders are automatically shared unless you make the subfolders private.

File Attributes

File attributes were covered in Chapter 15, but need to be reviewed here as well. When a folder is shared across the network, the permissions given specify what a user is allowed to do with a particular folder. By default, all subfolders and files contained within a shared folder or subfolder inherit the same permissions. For example, if you select read-only as the shared folder permission, then someone can open a file, but not modify and save it. If you right-click or tap and briefly hold on the name of a file within a shared folder that has read-only permissions assigned, then select *Properties* in order to access attributes. Notice how the file has the read-only attribute already marked.

Getting the Job Done with the Correct Permissions

When working on a staff member's computers, remember that when logged on as the user, you may not use specific utilities. Commonly used utilities or commands executed from a command prompt may not be available to you unless you operate from the administrator level. Search for `command prompt`. In the resulting list, right-click or tap and briefly hold on the *Command Prompt* option > select *Run as administrator*.

To see some problems, you may need the user to be logged in. Logging in with an account that has administrator access may not show the same issues the user sees. Always ensure users log on and test whatever you fix to ensure it works for their own account and permissions.

Folder Options

Because of quarantined files or the need to check system files, a technician is required to be familiar with Windows Explorer/File Explorer display options. Use the following directions based on the operating system used.

> > In Windows Vista and 7, open *Windows Explorer*. Use the *Organize > Folder and search options > View* tab. Use the *Organize > Layout* option or the *Folder Options* Control Panel to configure how folders/files display and what information is included with that display.
> > In Windows 8 and 10, open *File Explorer*. Access the *View* menu option > *Options > Change folder and search options > View* tab. Use the *Layout* section or *File Explorer Options* (Windows 10) Control Panel to configure how folders/files display and what information is in included with that display.

A technician often has to work with system files and folders that are not seen by default. Table 18.11 summarizes the security-related *View* tab options. A technician must remember to set the settings to the way they were previously so that users do not see them by default. The *View* tab has a *Restore Defaults* button that resets all settings.

TABLE 18.11 Folder Options > View tab

Function	Description
View hidden files	*Hidden files and folders* section > enable *Show hidden files, folders, and drives*
View file extensions	*Files and folders* section > uncheck *Hide extensions for known file types*
View system files	*Files and folders* section > uncheck *Hide protected operating system files (Recommended)*
Sharing menu/options	*Files and folders* section > enable *Use Sharing Wizard (Recommended)*

Protecting the Operating System and Data

Several chapters have contained important security-related tips, steps, and information related to protecting the operating system and data. In this section, let's review some items that pertain specifically to the security of the operating system and data.

> Use the NTFS file system.
> Ensure that operating system and application service packs and updates are applied regularly (good patch management). If a Windows update fails, a message usually appears when the machine reboots. Try the update again; sometimes an update might fail when being installed with other updates. Successfully install as many as you can and then reinstall the failed updates one by one. Note that Windows 8 and 10 come as a package, but they can be uninstalled by update.
> Have an alternative boot source (such as optical disc, flash drive, another hard drive, and operating system discs).
> Install antivirus software with the latest virus definitions.
> Encrypt data that needs to be protected.
> Optionally, place operating system files and data files on separate hard drive partitions.
> Some firmware or driver versions may cause security issues. Keep the versions updated.
> If using virtualization, don't forget that each virtual machine needs the same protection as an individual computer. All concepts in this chapter apply not just to the host machine, but to each virtual machine as well.
> If the computer you use does not need to share files or a printer with others on the network, use the *Network and Sharing Center* Control Panel and disable *file and print sharing*.
> To create a shared folder that is not seen by any others across the network, add a $ (dollar sign) to end of the share name. An example of a hidden shared folder is Book$.
> Use the System Restore program to control restore points before installing new software or hardware. Use the *System* Control Panel > *System Protection* link to access the restore points. See Lab 18.2 for details.
> Disable ports through the system BIOS/UEFI BIOS. Password protect the BIOS to prevent using external devices that might have a virus.

Backups

One hard drive preventive maintenance procedure that is commonly overlooked is performing a backup of the data and operating system. Most people do not realize that the most important part of any computer is the data that resides within it. Data cannot be replaced as hardware can be.

Back up data routinely. Have a routine maintenance plan that you recommend to users. Important data should be backed up daily or frequently, but routine data is usually handled by a monthly backup. The sensitivity and importance of the data determine how frequently backups are performed.

Traditionally, backups have been saved to magnetic tape—quarter-inch cartridge, linear tape-open (LTO) or digital linear tape (DLT) being the most common types—but CDs, DVDs, BDs, thumb drives, external hard drives, and cloud storage are viable alternatives today. Some people use optical discs or thumb drives to back up important data and periodically do a full backup to an external hard drive.

TECH TIP

A second hard drive makes an excellent backup device

Hard drives are inexpensive and easy to install. Install a second one to back up your data.

Backups use the file archive bit. A **full backup** backs up all selected files and sets the archive bit to off. An **incremental backup** backs up all files that have changed since the last backup. The files selected are the ones that have the archive bit set to on. The backup software resets those archive bits to off. A **differential backup** backs up files that have changed since the last full backup (files that have the archive bit set to on), but the backup software does not reset the archive bit like the incremental backup does.

Windows 7 and 10 come with a backup utility, but many external hard drives come with their own software that is easier to use, has more features, and allows easy and selective data backup scheduling. Windows 8 and 10 have the File History utility. No matter what method of backup you use, test your backup for restoration. Install to a different drive if necessary.

TECH TIP

Don't use the same hard drive as a backup device

Backing up data to a different partition on a hard drive is *not* a good idea. Even though there is some chance that your data might be saved, it is more likely the drive will fail. The drive is a physical device that may have moving parts—motor, heads, and so on. Mechanical failure is always a possibility.

Probably the most asked question of those with hard drive failures or failing/failed sectors is regarding file recovery. Windows does not have file recovery software other than locating and repairing lost clusters. However, there are third-party file recovery utilities that you can use. Many times files cannot be recovered unless the file recovery utility was installed prior to the loss. Many companies also provide data recovery services.

TECH TIP

For critical data, keep backups in a different location

Offsite storage for critical data is important even for home users in case of disaster such as flooding, fire, theft, hurricanes, or tornadoes.

Even though much data is stored locally, many companies favor centralized storage, even for individual users. This protects the company's interest, and it also ensures that backups are done on a regular and reliable basis. Another option in business is a thin-client environment in which no hard drives are included with the system. Storage is provided across the network to a central location. This reduces hardware and software costs and PC maintenance staffing costs, and it makes data security easier to manage as well.

BitLocker

BitLocker encrypts an entire disk volume including the operating system, user files, page files (also known as paging or swap files), and hibernation files. It is available on Vista/7 Enterprise and Ultimate, Windows 8 Pro and Enterprise, and Windows 10 Pro, Enterprise, Education, Mobile, and Mobile Enterprise. BitLocker requires two NTFS disk partitions. **BitLocker To Go** is used to encrypt and password protect external drives and removable media that are 128MB and larger. BitLocker can optionally use a trusted platform module (TPM), which is a chip that stores security information such as encryption keys.

Full Device Encryption

Mobile devices support **full device encryption**, which is scrambling or encoding all user data. Once enabled, any new data created is automatically encrypted. Drawbacks to full device encryption are slower performance, and disabling the option might require resetting the option back to factory defaults, thus losing any data and customization. On an Android device, use the *Security* Settings option. Apple iPhones have encryption enabled by default and the option cannot be disabled.

AutoRun and AutoPlay

Disable **AutoRun** to prevent software or programs from automatically starting from an optical disc, flash drive, or external drive. An example of AutoPlay is when you insert a music CD and the music automatically starts playing, or you are prompted for the default action. To change what happens when you insert each type of media device, use the *Hardware and Sound* Control Panel > *Auto Play* link. Use the following steps to disable AutoPlay and AutoRun so that the action will not occur and the user will not be prompted. Note that specific Windows security updates are also required (see http://support.microsoft.com for more details):

Step 1. From a command prompt or the Search textbox, type `gpedit.msc` and press [Enter].

Step 2. Expand *Administrative Templates* > expand *Windows Components*.

Step 3. Select *Autoplay Policies* > double-click or double-tap *Turn off Autoplay* > select *Enabled* > select *All drives* > restart the computer.

Dealing with Mechanical Hard Drives

If donating a computer or replacing a hard drive, data on the drive needs to be removed after the data has been transferred to the new drive or is not needed any longer. Furthermore, the hard drive partitions need to be deleted and re-created. Some hard drive manufacturers have a utility that rewrites (sometimes called **drive overwrite**) the drive with all 1s or all 0s to prevent data remnants from being recovered. Another utility is a **drive wipe**, which may use a number of techniques (not all guaranteed to be 100% effective on highly sensitive data) to remove data from the drive. Some hard drive manufacturers have a **low-level format** utility that is different than the format done through the drive installation/preparation process. You can use the SDelete utility that can be downloaded from Microsoft (http://technet.microsoft.com/en-us/sysinternals/bb897443.aspx).

Another option is to use the `format` and `cipher` commands. Format `x: /p:n` (where *x:* is the drive letter and *n* is the number of passes) to format a disk volume with a zero in every sector. Then use the `cipher /w x:` command, where *x:* is the hard drive volume letter. The `cipher` command writes all unused sectors with 0s, then 1s, and then a random number. Because this command is performed on unused sectors, it is important to remember to use the `format` command first.

A company that has extremely sensitive data stored on a hard drive should destroy the hard drive by (1) secure erasing, which requires special software, (2) degaussing (using electromagnets to change the drives magnetic fields or 1s and 0s, which can be expensive and requires drive disassembly), or (3) drilling through drive platters (see Figure 18.26) and then destroying the pieces with a hammer.

FIGURE 18.26 Drilled hard drive platter

EFS

NTFS volumes can have files, folders, and subfolders encrypted using Encrypting File System (**EFS**). The EFS algorithm originally used Data Encryption Standard (DES), which used 56- or 128-bit encryption, but now the EFS algorithm uses Advanced Encryption Standard (AES), Secure Hash Algorithm (SHA), smart-card-based encryption, and in Windows 7, 8, and 10, Elliptical Curve Cryptography (ECC). **AES** is an encryption standard with key sizes of 128, 192, or 256 bits. AES has been used in wireless government networks for some time and is now common in almost all wireless network implementations that use WPA2 (covered later in the chapter).

When a folder or subfolder is encrypted, all newly created files within the folder or subfolder are automatically encrypted. If any files are copied or moved into an encrypted folder or subfolder, those files are automatically encrypted. System files cannot be encrypted. EFS can use a certificate authority (CA) such as one issued from a server or use a self-signed certificate, as demonstrated in Lab 18.1 at the end of this chapter.

Can you encrypt someone else's files?

The answer is "yes" if you have the write attribute, create files/write data, and list folder/read data permissions for the file.

Data Execution Prevention (DEP)

Data execution prevention (**DEP**) is a security measure implemented in both hardware and software to prevent malicious software from running on a Windows-based computer. DEP is always on and enabled for 64-bit versions of Windows, but the setting can be customized. With hardware-based DEP, the CPU supports enforcing no execute (AMD processors) or **execute disable** (Intel processors). The processor marks memory with an attribute indicating that data inside that memory location should not be executable. (It should just be another type of data or code.) Different processors have different capabilities, but at a minimum, the processor can display a message if code tries to execute from those memory locations marked as no execute or execute disable. This option is simply a bit and is either turned on or off as an option.

With software-enforced DEP, if a program tries to run from a memory location that should not have executable code, the application is closed and a message appears. Software-enforced DEP is available in Windows Vista, 7, 8, and 10. To see this feature, access the *System* Control Panel > *Advanced System Settings* link > select the *Settings* button in the *Performance* area > select the *Data Execution Prevention* tab. Figure 18.27 shows the two options. The Data Execution Prevention tab also shows at the bottom of the window whether the processor is capable of DEP.

FIGURE 18.27   Windows 7 DEP on

Internet Security

Internet security basics were covered in Chapter 13 in the "Basic Web Browser Issues" section. This section goes into more technical detail. First, no system should connect to the Internet without antivirus and antimalware software installed. These applications are your first line of defense for Internet security, but they are not fool-proof.

Second, pay attention to the security alerts provided by antivirus and antimalware software, browser applications, and the operating system! If the message is one you haven't seen before, write it down, take a screen shot of it, and research it. Even if you have seen it before, research and ensure nothing new is the problem.

Money is not an excuse for not having antivirus software. Download Microsoft Security Essentials or another free antivirus program. Ensure that the free antivirus program is from a reputable download site. There are **rogue antivirus** applications that pretend to be software to help you with a computer problem or be provided free to you when in reality, the website has programs that are actually viruses.

For antimalware, Microsoft provides for free the Malicious Software Removal Tool through Windows Vista/7 updates. Other vendors provide free antimalware software, too. It is easier to deal with these issues with security software installed than when it is not.

Microsoft Vista, 7, 8, and 10 come with **Windows Defender**, which works with Internet Explorer/Edge to warn for spyware. The Microsoft Security Baseline Analyzer (MBSA) identifies security misconfigurations on computers. Configure your browser to display a security warning or that you are asked or warned of potential security threats. Windows Defender can be customized as to when updates are downloaded and how often it scans the computer. It shows detailed information about software that is installed on the computer. Labs 18.7 and 18.8 explore some of the Windows Defender options.

Malware Removal

Malware symptoms are numerous; device runs slow, crashes, or locks; applications behave abnormally or not at all; missing files; file attributes have changed; constant storage device activity; constant network activity (more than normal); hijacked email (change the password as soon as you notice); access denied messages; security messages; and renaming, removing, or corrupting system files. Note that access denied messages are sometimes normal if a user account does not have administrative permissions to do a particular task. However, if the problem is malware, the following steps are best practice procedures for malware removal.

Step 1. Identify malware symptoms. Do not take a customer's word that he has a virus or malware. An application could be the culprit, or something else entirely.

Step 2. Quarantine the infected system. Disconnect the system from the network or disable the wireless NIC.

Step 3. For Windows machines, disable *System Restore* by accessing the *System* Control Panel > select *Properties* > in the left pane, select *System protection* > select the appropriate disk > *select* Configure > select *Turn off system protection* (Vista/7) or *Disable system protection* (Windows 8/10) > *OK* > *OK*.

Step 4. Remediate the infected system. You may need to update the antimalware software or have to use another system to research your support options from your antivirus/antimalware software vendor. Rescan the system for security issues using the updated software. Some antivirus software vendors have images that can be downloaded and used to create bootable antivirus discs or flash drives.

   If the system still performs strangely, try booting into Safe Mode and run the virus checker from there. Use the `msconfig` utility to isolate a startup application or service that might be causing the issue. If you purchased an antivirus disc, run the software from the optical disc. Boot from an alternative boot source (flash drive, external hard drive, or operating system disc).

Some worms and trojan horse viruses require that files be manually deleted because they cannot be repaired, but the antivirus software will "quarantine" the file so it cannot be dangerous and affect other files. If it is an executable file, you may have to re-install one or more apps. A hijacked web browser may require browser configuration, different DNS settings, or a new or updated HOSTS file that has been applied after removal. You might be required to use the SFC /scannow command to replace/repair operating system files after removing a virus. Test all applications to ensure that they operate. Then manually delete the file(s) that are quarantined (see Figure 18.28).

Step 5. Schedule antivirus/antimalware scans and run updates.

Step 6. For Windows-based computers, re-enable *System Restore*. Create a new restore point.

Step 7. Educate the user on security best practices.

FIGURE 18.28 Quarantined files

TECH TIP

Manually delete files, if necessary

If the antivirus software or other preventive software applications state that a particular file cannot be deleted, make a note of the file and its location. Windows Explorer/File Explorer *View* options may have to be adjusted before viewing/deletion can occur.

Email Issues

Email has its own section because it is something most people deal with on a daily basis. Avoid checking email on a public computer or an unsecure network. If an email account is hijacked (the user cannot log in using normal procedures, if you get an automated message from an unknown person like it was an automated response to your own email, if people in your contacts send you a note about constant emails or spam from the hijacked account, or if your account has a lot of undeliverable emails), then perform the following steps:

Step 1. Contact the email account company to report the problem.

Step 2. Ensure that Windows, antivirus, and antimalware updates have been applied.

Step 3. Ensure that you have an alternative email account available when you have to register with a site, such as for online shopping.

Step 4. Try logging in to the account from a different computer to see if email settings have been changed. Note: If you can get to the account, change the password.

Step 5. Create rules in your email account to delete files from specific nontrusted sources.

Spam comes in unsolicited email from a company or person previously unknown. People who send this type of email are known as spammers. Most email applications have spam filters that do not catch all spam. Most email applications also enable you to create a rule to block messages from a particular source or subject line. Figure 18.29 demonstrates the concept of a spam filter.

Other problems include email messages sent in clear text. If such an email is intercepted, the message is easy to read. Pretty Good Privacy (PGP) and Secure Multipurpose Internet Mail Extension (S/MIME) are frequently used to provide encryption and authentication for email messages.

FIGURE 18.29 Spam

Digital Security Certificates

A digital certificate authenticates and secures information. The certification authority (CA) is the sender (the device or person who originated the communication). A digital certificate typically contains a public key (a key used with a private key so that messages can be unencrypted), sender information, and the length of time the certificate is to be considered valid. Browsers sometimes present security messages related to certificates. Sample messages are along the following lines depending on the browser:

> The security certificate presented by this website was not issued by a trusted certificate authority.

> www.hacker.com uses an invalid security certificate. The certificate is not trusted because the issuer certificate is unknown.

> www.watchout.com uses an invalid security certificate. The certificate is not trusted because it is self-signed.

If this is a site you should avoid, close the browser. If you want to trust a self-signed certificate, then in Internet Explorer/Edge, use *Tools* (looks like a gear in the upper-right corner) > *Internet options* > *Security* tab > select *Trusted sites* > *Sites* button > ensure the URL is correct > *Add* > *Close* > *OK*. Refresh the web page in Internet Explore/Edge. A message appears. Select *Continue to this website (not recommended)*. Select *Certificate Error* > *View certificates* > *Install Certificate* > *Next* > select *Place all certificates in the following store* > *Browse* > select *Trusted Root Certification Authorities* > *OK* > *Next* > *Finish*. Go back into the *Internet Options Security* tab > *Trusted sites* > *Sites* > remove the URL. Close Internet Explorer/Edge. Reopen the browser and go to the URL. No certificate error appears.

Proxy Server

A company may use a **proxy server** to protect its network. This server acts as an agent (a go-between) between an application such as a web browser and a real server. A proxy server can also cache frequently accessed web pages and provide them when requested from a client instead of accessing the real web server. A symptom that the proxy server configuration is the issue is that the device can reach internal network resources but not external ones (especially if the Internet connection works).

To configure any device or application for a proxy server, obtain the following information:

> IP address of the proxy server
> Port number of the proxy server
> Optionally a username and password, but some organizations use server-based authentication

To configure Internet Explorer/Edge to use a proxy server, use the *Internet Options* from the *Tools* menu bar option > *Connections* tab > *LAN Settings* button > select the *Use a proxy server for your LAN* checkbox > in the *Address* textbox, type the proxy server IP address > type the proxy server port number in the *Port* textbox. This information can be obtained from the company's network administrator or through Web Proxy AutoDiscovery (**WPAD**) protocol. Click the *Advanced* button to set individual IP addresses and port numbers for different protocols. Note that if you don't want the proxy server to be used when accessing resources in the local domain (and speed up this type of access), select the *Bypass proxy server for local addresses* checkbox. Improperly configured proxy settings may cause the computer to be redirected to an invalid website with no Internet connectivity.

Firewall

If a computer connects to the Internet, it should be connected behind a firewall. A firewall protects one or more computers from outside attacks. The concept of a firewall is similar to building a moat with a drawbridge around a castle. The castle is the inside network, the moat with the drawbridge is the firewall, and all outside the castle are "attackers." The drawbridge controls access to and from the castle.

TECH TIP

Antivirus and antispyware applications are needed even when a firewall is installed

A computer protected by a firewall still needs antivirus and antispyware applications for protection. Having a firewall on each computer as well as on a router or modem that connects to the Internet (or a device dedicated to providing firewall services) is common in both home and business environments.

A firewall can be either a software application or hardware, and should be implemented for any computer that connects to another network, especially a computer that connects to the Internet. A firewall keeps hackers from accessing a computer that connects to the Internet. A software firewall is a good solution for individual computers. A hardware firewall is a good solution for home and business networks. Both can be used concurrently. Figure 18.30 shows the concept of a firewall.

FIGURE 18.30   Firewall concept

In a corporate environment, a firewall can create an area called the demilitarized zone (**DMZ**). Servers such as web or application servers can reside in the DMZ. Customers can use that server without having to be let into the part of the network where the sensitive corporate data resides.

A DMZ could also be created by having two firewalls, with one firewall connected to the route, as shown before, and the DMZ connected to that firewall and to a second firewall. The second firewall also connects to the internal corporate network (see Figure 18.31), so the setup looks like this: Internet | Firewall | DMZ | Firewall | Internal corporate network

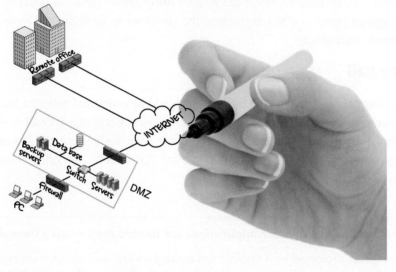

FIGURE 18.31   DMZ

Windows Firewall and Advanced Security

Windows Vista had the Windows Security Center to have a place to oversee the computer security including the Windows Firewall, Windows updates, whether malware protection was enabled, as well as other security settings. Windows 7 did not do things the same way. Windows Vista, 7, and 8 have an Action Center Control Panel that displays messages and warnings related to security and maintenance. Windows 10 has action center alerts, but not the Action Center Control Panel. For Windows 10, to control the types of messages seen, access *Settings > System > Notifications & actions*.

The Windows Firewall application examines packets traveling to and from the computer and filters them (denies or allows them) based on a configured access control list (ACL). Options chosen through the *Action Center* Control Panel affect this ACL. **Port forwarding** is a term used when a packet is allowed through the firewall based on a particular port number/protocol. Port triggering is a similar concept. **Port triggering** allows data into a computer temporarily based on a configured situation.

> **TECH TIP**
>
> **Allowing a program through Windows Firewall**
>
> In Windows 7, open the *Windows Firewall* Control Panel > select the *Allow a program or feature through Windows Firewall* > select *Change settings* > enable the checkbox beside the program you want to allow > *OK*. In Windows 8 or 10, open the *Windows Firewall* Control Panel > select the *Allow an app or feature through Windows Firewall* > *Change settings* > enable the checkbox beside the app you want to allow and select the network types this applies to > *OK*.

To verify whether the Windows Firewall is enabled, access the *Windows Firewall* Control Panel > *Turn Windows Firewall on or off* link. Use the `wf.msc` command to access the *Windows Firewall with Advanced Security* configuration page. To see open firewall ports, use the `netsh firewall show state` command from an elevated command prompt.

Figure 18.32 shows a Windows 7 Firewall Control Panel window. The *Block all incoming connections* checkbox is used in public places like a restaurant or bookstore, so outside users cannot access the computer.

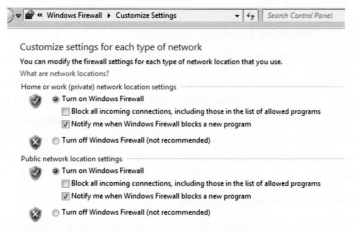

FIGURE 18.32   Windows 7 firewall settings

When Windows Firewall is installed and enabled on a Windows computer and another computer or application tries to connect, Windows Firewall blocks the connection and prompts with a security alert to allow a choice of *unblock*, *keep blocking*, or *ask me later*. Table 18.12 describes these options.

TABLE 18.12   Windows firewall security alerts

Alert	Description
Unblock this program	The program is allowed to execute and the program is automatically added to the Windows Firewall exceptions list.
Keep blocking this program	The program is not allowed to execute or listen. Use whenever you do not know the source of the alert.
Keep blocking this program, but ask me again later	Does not allow the program to execute or listen, but the next time you access the site, the security alert prompts you again.

Windows Vista and 7 have up to three possible network location settings called profiles (depending on the Windows version) that configure the firewall differently. The profile that is active is shown as the current profile. Use the *Network and Sharing Center* Control Panel > *Change advanced sharing settings* link to view this profile. Note that you may have to select a down arrow to view the contents of each profile or select the up arrow to collapse a section (see Figure 18.33 for the sections in Windows 10 that are described after the figure).

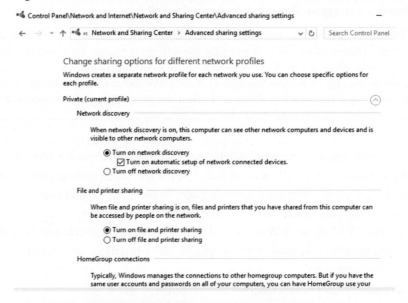

FIGURE 18.33   Windows 10 network profiles

Following are the types of profiles you see in Vista or 7:

> The *Private (Home or Work)* network location setting turns on file sharing and network discovery through the firewall, so communication will be easier at work or in a private home network.
> The *Public* setting configures these settings to be off through the firewall to help protect your computer when on a public network such as when you are in an airport.
> The *Domain* setting is when the computer participates in a Windows Active Directory domain environment.

Windows 8 and 10 have similar options:

> The *Private* network location setting turns on file sharing and network discovery through the firewall, so communication will be easier at work or in a private home network.
> The *Guest or Public* setting protects the computer by turning off file sharing and network discovery and is used when connected to a public network such as in a restaurant or cafe.
> The *All Networks* setting includes private folder sharing, media streaming, file sharing, and password-protected sharing options that can apply to all types of network connections.

TECH TIP

Be sure you work with the correct profile

If you cannot access devices and resources that are normally available through the wireless NIC, ensure the correct location profile is used. Access the *Advanced sharing settings* link from the *Network and Sharing Center* Control Panel. The profile used will have the following words after the profile name: *(current profile)*.

Table 18.13 shows Windows firewall issues and solutions to help with troubleshooting.

TABLE 18.13   Windows firewall and advanced security troubleshooting

Windows firewall issue	Resolutions
The firewall is blocking all connections	Access Windows Firewall and disable the *Block all incoming connections* checkbox.
The firewall is blocking a specific application	If a dialog box appears, select the *Unblock* option to allow it through. If the dialog box does not appear, access Windows Firewall, and use the *Exceptions* tab to create a rule that allows the application through the firewall.
No one can ping a Windows computer	Ensure that *File and Print Sharing* is enabled through the *Network and Sharing Center* Control Panel. Access the *Administrative Tools* link and select *Windows Firewall with Advanced Security*. Select *Inbound rules* in the left pane. Select *New Rule* in the *Actions* column. Select the *Custom* radio button and *Next*. Select the *All programs* radio button and *Next*. Select *ICMPv4* from the *Protocol Type* drop-down box. Select the IP addresses to which this rule will apply and name the rule.
Windows Firewall is turned off every time the computer restarts	Another security firewall is installed.
No one can access local files and/or a shared printer	File and Print Sharing has not been enabled.

Freeware programs are available as well as full security suites such as the ones from McAfee or Symantec that include software firewalls and components to prevent malicious types of software applications from executing.

VPN Configuration

A popular business solution for security is a VPN. A virtual private network (VPN) is a special type of secure network created over the Internet from one network device to another. One example is a home PC that connects to a corporate server and has access to company resources that cannot be accessed any other way except by being on a computer on the inside network. The VPN connection makes it appear as if the home computer is on the inside corporate network. Another example is a branch office network device connecting to a corporate server, VPN concentrator, firewall, or other network device. When connected, the branch office network device connects as if it were directly connected to the network.

Both sides of the VPN tunnel must match

The two devices used to create a VPN tunnel must have identical VPN settings, or the VPN tunnel will not be formed.

To configure a VPN in Windows Vista, 7, 8, or 10, open the *Network and Sharing Center* Control Panel > select the *Set up a new connection or network* link > *Connect to a workplace* > *Next* > *Use my Internet connection (VPN)* > enter the IP address or fully qualified domain name of the network device on the other end of the VPN connection > *Next* > enter the required credentials > click *Connect*. Figure 18.34 illustrates the concept of a VPN.

VPN connection from remote site ISP Server Remote access server Corporate network(s)

FIGURE 18.34   VPN connectivity

Internet Appliances

Other security devices similar to the firewall that an IT staff member should be familiar with include the UTM, IDS, and IPS. A unified threat management (**UTM**) system is a single device that commonly provides multiple security functions such as content filtering, antivirus, antispyware, antimalware, firewall, and intrusion detection and prevention. The device might also have the capability to route, accept VPN connections, and provide network address translation (NAT).

Content filtering uses a device or security software to screen data for specific web addresses, email, or files that are defined as being suspect. This is similar to applying parental controls on a home Windows computer (covered in Chapter 15). Remember from Chapter 14 that NAT translates private addresses used inside a company to public addresses that can be routed over the network. One public address can be used for multiple internal company connections due to port mapping. **Port mapping** allows the combination of one public address and a specific port number to represent one internal company host. The same public address and a different port number represent a second internal company host. Some people also call this concept port forwarding or port address translation (PAT).

An intrusion detection system (**IDS**) can be hardware or software that constantly monitors and scans network traffic for malicious traffic or violations of defined security policies. An IDS is considered to be a passive system; it doesn't take action, it just detects and sends data, reports, and alerts to the network management team (see Figure 18.35). It is like a babysitter whose job is to just tend to the kids (the network data). If there is a fight (a security threat), the babysitter notifies the parents (the network personnel) who deal with the threat.

A similar device is an intrusion prevention system (**IPS**). An IPS is an active system; it constantly monitors and scans network traffic for malicious traffic and violations of security policies as well as takes appropriate action. An IPS can send an alarm, reset connections, block traffic, disable ports, and drop packets. An IPS is like a teacher hall monitor that can issue detention, break up fights, and restore order to the hallway. Sometimes, an IDS and an IPS are both used in a network design with the IDS inspecting the network traffic and reporting the information as well as an IPS taking preventive action.

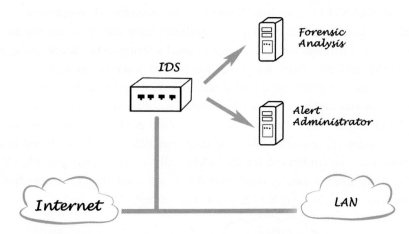

FIGURE 18.35 IDS

Wireless Network Security Overview

Traditionally security has been a concern when installing wireless networks because originally security was disabled by default and there was lack of knowledge about default passwords and misconfigured wireless settings. Wireless LANs are much more secure today and are abundant. Wireless technologies such as Bluetooth are secure because it uses a modified version of Secure and Fast Encryption Routine (SAFER+). However, Wi-Fi LANs may use a security protocol or may be unsecure.

Wireless access points (APs) are an integral part of a wireless LAN and normally mounted in the ceiling or on the wall where they are inconspicuous. Sometimes, they are mounted in or above the ceiling tile in a special enclosure. Networking equipment such as hubs, switches, routers, and servers are locked in a cabinet or behind a locked door in a wiring closet. Customized cabinets can be purchased to secure APs indoors and outdoors.

Data transmitted over air can be in clear text, which means that with special frame capturing software (packet sniffers or analyzers) on a computer with a wireless NIC installed, the data can be captured and viewed. Negotiation between the wireless devices and the AP can be in clear text so that information can be captured. All frames include a source MAC address. Someone with a wireless device and free hacking software can capture the frame to use the MAC address to gain access to other resources (note that the hackers are not this obvious...). (This is known as session hijacking or MAC spoofing.) By default, most APs transmit their SSIDs in clear text. All these issues must be considered when installing a wireless network.

TECH TIP

How a firewall helps a wireless computer

A firewall can protect a computer connected to a wireless network; however, the firewall cannot prevent the outgoing wireless data from being hijacked. The firewall simply protects a hacker from accessing the computer.

Wireless Authentication and Encryption

The original 802.11 standards define two mechanisms for wireless security: authentication and data confidentiality. The two types of authentication are open and shared key. **Open authentication** allows a wireless network device to send a frame to the access point with the sender's identity (MAC address). Open authentication is used when no authentication is required. **Shared key authentication** requires the use of a shared key, which is a group of characters that the wireless network device and access point must have in common. Shared key authentication does not scale well with larger wireless networks because each device must be configured with the shared key authentication (time-consuming), the users must be told of the shared key, and their individual stations must be configured for this. Optionally, a server may provide the shared key automatically. Also, when manually input shared keys are used, the key is not often changed, which leads to security issues. See Figure 18.36 for this concept.

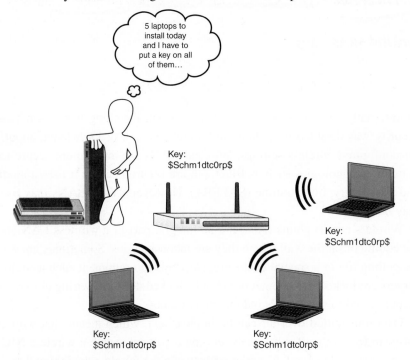

FIGURE 18.36   Wireless security keys

APs that support 802.1x authentication use some form of Extensible Authentication Protocol (EAP). When any type of EAP is used, the user or client to be authenticated is called a *supplicant*. An authentication server holds valid usernames and passwords. The device that is in the middle that takes the client request and passes it on to the server is known as the authenticator. An AP can be an authenticator.

When shared key authentication is used, WEP must be enabled. Wired Equivalent Privacy (**WEP**) encrypts data being transmitted. WEP commonly has two versions: 64-bit and 128-bit. Some vendors may have 256-bit; 64- and 128-bit WEP may also be seen as 40- and 104-bit. This is because each of the two versions uses a 24-bit initialization vector: 40 plus 24 equals 64 and 104 plus 24 equals 128. Sometimes, you might even see that in documentation or website wording, the author mixes the two types of numbers, such as 40-bit and 128-bit, so it can be confusing.

TECH TIP

How many characters do you type with WEP?

If 64-bit WEP is used, five characters are entered (5 times 8 bits—1 for each ASCII character—equals 40 bits) or 10 hexadecimal characters (10 times 4 bits—1 for each hexadecimal character—equals 40 bits). If 128-bit WEP is used and entering the key with ASCII, 13 characters are entered. And if hexadecimal is used with 128-bit WEP, 26 characters are typed.

With WEP enabled, the shared "secret" key is normally entered into the wireless NIC configuration window. Vendors have a variety of ways of inputting this alphanumeric key, but normally it is input in either hexadecimal or ASCII characters.

Some wireless NIC manufacturers allow entering multiple WEP keys; however, only one key is used at a time. The multiple WEP keys are for multiple environments such as a WEP key for the business environment and a WEP key for the home wireless network using the same wireless NIC. Figure 18.37 shows the configuration dialog box for a wireless NIC and where the WEP is enabled on a Windows computer.

FIGURE 18.37   Wireless NIC properties with WEP enabled

To access this configuration in Windows Vista, 7, 8, and 10 use the *Network and Sharing Center* Control Panel > *Change adapter settings* link > select the wireless NIC > *View status of this connection* link > *Wireless properties* button > *Security* tab. Notice in Figure 18.48 there is a drop-down menu for selecting WEP as an encryption type. Most installations require the WEP key be entered manually. This adapter does not enable you to specify the length of the WEP key, so it is the probably the 64-bit version. Some vendors have configuration utilities that allow wireless NIC configuration instead of the normal right-clicking the wireless NIC and selecting *Properties*.

WEP can be hacked. With special software on a laptop that has a wireless NIC installed, WEP can be compromised. Enabling WEP is better than using no encryption whatsoever. However, an improvement on WEP is **Wi-Fi Protected Access (WPA)**. WPA uses Temporal Key Integrity Protocol (**TKIP**) or Advanced Encryption Standard (AES) to improve security. TKIP is an improvement on WEP in that the encryption keys change. Even better than TKIP is AES.

Wi-Fi Protected Access 2 (**WPA2**) is an improvement that includes dynamic negotiation between the AP and the client for authentication and encryption algorithms (see Figure 18.38). WPA2 is

CHAPTER 18

a common choice for securing wireless networks. The 802.11i standard includes Robust Security Network (RSN), which includes some features of WPA2. Third-party products can be used with some vendors' wireless solutions, and some vendors provide extra security with their NIC cards and access points. The drawback to this is that other vendors' products are normally incompatible.

FIGURE 18.38 WPA2

To manually configure wireless settings in Windows Vista/7, use the *Network and Internet* Control Panel link > *Manage Wireless Networks* > *Add* link > *Manually create a network profile* link. The *Security type* drop-down menu has the following options: No authentication (open), WEP, WPA2-Personal, WPA-Personal, WPA2-Enterprise, WPA-Enterprise, and 802.1x. If you select WPA/WPA2, then *TKIP* or *AES* is available from the *Encryption type* drop-down menu.

In Windows 8 and 10, use the *Network and Sharing Center* Control Panel > select the *Set up a new connection or network* link > *Manually connect to a wireless network* > *Next* > type the SSID and appropriate security settings > *Next*. Figure 18.39 shows this window for Windows 10.

> Manually connect to a wireless network

Enter information for the wireless network you want to add

Network name:	ATT64ZF66a
Security type:	WPA2-Personal
Encryption type:	AES
Security Key:	•••••••••••• ☑ Hide characters

☑ Start this connection automatically

☑ Connect even if the network is not broadcasting

   Warning: If you select this option, your computer's privacy might be at risk.

FIGURE 18.39 Windows 10 wireless security window

WPS

Wi-Fi Protected Setup (**WPS**) configures the SSID and WPA2 wireless security key for an AP or a client's devices. It supports 802.11a, b, g, n, and AC devices, including computers, access points, consumer electronics, and phones. The standard allows four ways to configure a wireless network:

> A personal identification number (PIN) is entered. This PIN is sometimes found on a sticker or display on the wireless product.

> A USB device attaches to the AP or wireless device to provide configuration information.
> A button is pushed or clicked. This method is known as push button configuration (PBC).
> The near field communication (NFC) where the wireless device is brought close to the AP (or a device known as the Registrar) and the configuration is applied. RFID tags are suited for this method.

TECH TIP

Avoid WPS

Because of security issues with WPS, disable this mode if possible and do not use it.

MAC Filtering

MAC filtering (also known as MAC address filtering) allows only devices that have been manually entered into the access point onto the wireless network. MAC filtering is used when there is a limited number of wireless devices and those devices' MAC addresses are known by the person who configured the access point. Any new personnel or wireless devices have to be added to the access point manually to use the wireless network.

TECH TIP

Who would use MAC filtering?

Most access points have a limited number of MAC addresses (20 to 50), so this option tends to be used only by small companies wherein they want to have strict control of who gets onto the wireless network.

Default Settings

All wireless networks have security features. A SOHO AP/router can come with a default password and SSID, but many ask you to change it the first time you access the AP/router. Change both of these settings as soon as the access point is powered on. Default passwords are posted on the Internet, and a hacker could lock out access from the access point. Many older APs might be given to someone else or a charity and be a security risk. It is important that you know how to configure basic AP security settings.

TECH TIP

Never leave an access point password set to the default

After powering up an access point and connecting to it, one of the first things to do is change the default password.

Change the access point's default password during installation. Do not leave it set to the default. Make the password a strong one. Use as many characters as feasible. Use uppercase and lowercase letters. Include non-alphanumeric characters, such as #, %, &, or @.

Firmware

Firmware is software that is embedded into a piece of hardware. Firmware can be upgraded in network routers, switches, access points, firewalls, and so on. Companies update this firmware as security issues become known, enhancements become available, or to support new technology. In a corporate environment, it is critical that firmware updates be applied. The process for obtaining and applying firmware updates varies per vendor but is commonly done through a web browser window used to access the network device.

SSID Broadcasting

As mentioned in Chapter 14, the service set identifier (SSID) announces to wireless devices a particular wireless network is in the area. Most access points are configured for SSID broadcasting. **SSID broadcasting** is where the access point periodically sends out a beacon frame that includes the SSID. Wireless NICs can detect this SSID automatically and attach to the access point (see Figure 18.40). This can be disabled as a preventive measure so that the wireless network is not announced in the area.

FIGURE 18.40   SSID broadcasting

TECH TIP

Disable SSID broadcasting

Some companies and home users choose to disable SSID broadcasting and manually enter the SSID into any wireless NIC's configuration. Even though this requires more effort, it keeps the wireless network from being openly advertised.

Wireless AP Installation Checklist

Many wireless access points have the capability to route. The router connects wired network and wireless networks together. A router is also good to have so that DHCP can service both wired and wireless networks and provide a firewall for network security.

Many of the parameters needed for wireless NIC configuration are also needed for access point installation. However, installing an access point is more involved because it is the central device of the wireless network. The following list helps with access point installation. The questions should be answered *before* the access point is installed.

> What SSID is to be used?
> What static IP address will be assigned to the device?
> Is WEP, WPA, WPA-PSK, WPA2-PSK, TKIP, AES, or any other security option enabled?
> What security key lengths, security keys, or passphrases are used?
> Is MAC filtering enabled?
> Is there power available for the access point? Note that some access points can receive power through a PoE switch.
> How will the access point be mounted? Is mounting hardware provided with the access point, or does extra equipment have to be purchased?
> Where should the access point be mounted for best coverage of the wireless network area? Where should the antenna be placed or how should it be angled? Perform a site survey to see best performance. Temporarily mount the access point. With a laptop that has a wireless NIC and site survey software, walk around the wireless network area to see the coverage range. The site survey can also be conducted by double-clicking the network icon on the task bar; the signal strength is shown in the window that appears. Move the access point as necessary to avoid attenuation and obtain the largest area coverage.
> What channel ID will be used?
> Will the access point connect to the wired network and, if so, is there connectivity available where the access point will be mounted?

Wireless networking is an important and popular technology. Technicians today must be familiar with this technology as corporations and home users install these types of products. Because the technology is reasonably priced, many new technicians install their own wireless network for the experience. Enjoy this technology because more wireless technologies are evolving.

Wireless Security Conclusion

Wireless security is an important issue. The following list recaps some of the important issues and provides recommendations along with a few suggestions for a more secure wireless network:

> Change the default SSID and password. Make the password as long as possible and include non-alphanumeric characters.
> Enable encryption on the access point to the highest level possible and still allow wireless NIC access. Use authentication when possible.
> Put the wireless network on its own subnetwork and place it behind a firewall if possible.
> If a small company, consider enabling MAC authentication (MAC filtering) for company devices.
> If supported, authenticate using an authentication server.
> If the SSID is manually configured, periodically change the SSID.
> Assign a static IP address to the access point rather than using DHCP for it.
> Disable remote management on the access point.
> Place the access point in the center of the wireless network and not next to an outside window.
> Use wireless network scanning software to test the network security.

> Require that wireless clients use a virtual private network (VPN) tunnel to access the access point.
> If a rogue access point (an unauthorized AP) is found on the network, disconnect the device and confiscate it. Try to determine who owns the device and report them.

Wireless networks have a strong presence today and will continue to do so in the future. The 802.1x and 802.11 standards are constantly being improved to tighten security for wireless networks so that they rival wired solutions.

Wireless Network Troubleshooting

Troubleshooting wireless networks is sometimes easier than troubleshooting wired networks because of the mobility factor. A laptop with a wireless NIC installed can be used to troubleshoot connectivity, configuration, security, and so on. Most wireless network problems stem from inconsistent configuration. The standards deployed must be for the lowest common denominator. For example, if a wireless NIC supports only 64-bit WEP encryption, then that must be what is used even if 128-bit WEP, WPA, or WPA2 is available on some of the cards.

The following list includes general wireless networking tips designed to steer a technician in the right direction. Most of these tips have been discussed in previous sections, but it is nice to have the following troubleshooting list in one spot:

> Is the SSID correct?
> Is the wireless NIC seen by the operating system? (Use Device Manager to check.) Check the mobile device for a wireless disable button or use a key to disable/enable the wireless NIC.
> Is the correct security level enabled?
> Can any devices attach to the access point? If not, check the access point.
> Is anything causing interference or attenuation? Check antenna placement.
> Is there a channel ID overlap problem?
> A program from the wireless NIC manufacturer can be installed and used instead of using Windows to control the wireless NIC. If the customer wants to use Windows instead of the software provided, access a command prompt with elevated privileges. At the prompt, type `netsh wlan show` settings. From the output, determine whether the Windows automatic wireless configuration is disabled. You may have to disable the wireless NIC and uninstall the vendor software to use Windows to control the NIC.

Security Incident Reporting

Many companies define what to do when a security incident has occurred. However, in some businesses or in an incident that occurs on a home network, people are not always sure what to do. Following are the steps to take:

Step 1. Identify the issue. (See Table 18.14 for issues and best practices.)

Step 2. Report the issue through the proper channels.

Step 3. Preserve the data/device by documenting the incident. Ensure your document includes everything. Any changes or moves, document that as well. Use a chain–of-custody form that travels with the data/device as more people get involved. Chain-of-custody forms commonly have the following information.

> What is the issue (data/device/etc.)?
> How did you get involved with the evidence?

> When did you see the issue?

> What did you do to handle the issue?

> To what person did you turn over the issue, data, device, and so on?

TABLE 18.14   Incident reporting and actions

Type of event	Description
Virus	Disconnect the computer from the Internet and run a full scan. When virus-free, most antivirus software companies have a process for connecting to them automatically to receive a report of the virus scan. You can also notify your Internet provider and file a complaint with the FBI Internet Crime Complaint Center.
Spyware or grayware	Use a freeware or other software application to remove the application. Many of the security suites have a method of reporting found incidents. Submit a report using the FTC Consumer Complaint Form.
Phishing	Notify the agency from which the contact was received. Report the incident to the U.S. Computer Emergency Readiness Team (CERT) at http://www.us-cert.gov/nav/report_phishing.html.
Child exploitation	Use parental control software to prevent this. Log off immediately, and notify your local police department and/or the nearest FBI field office. You can also report the event to the National Center for Exploited and Missing Children.
Software piracy	Report incidents of organized software piracy to the Software and Information Industry Association (SIIA) and the Business Software Alliance (BSA).

If a security incident occurs and you do not know what to do, talk to your supervisor (see Figure 18.41). She should have the experience to guide you or know to whom she should go to resolve the issue. If you feel uncomfortable talking to your supervisor about this, consider the Human Resources department or a higher administrator. The BSA and other organizations allow anonymous reporting. Reporting and documenting security violations is important, especially in the business environment. It is every person's responsibility to be security-aware and responsible.

FIGURE 18.41   Report security violations

A Final Word About Security

Whether a wired or wireless, standalone PC or networked PC, or full desktop computer or smartphone, data and device security are important. Security measures must always be taken. Technicians must be aware of the latest threats, take proactive measures to implement security, and share their knowledge with users so the users can take proactive steps. Security risks and threats cause technicians a lot of work and time. These threats and attacks cost billions in lost data and time to businesses. Because most technicians do not see themselves as a dollar figure on a spreadsheet, they don't realize that if the business loses money as a result of security threats, that the business has to cut costs, and one of those costs could be the technical position. Think about it and be proactive in guarding against security threats.

SOFT SKILLS: BUILDING CUSTOMER TRUST

It is fitting in the security chapter to discuss building a trust relationship with the customer. Trust begins with professionalism. Be professional in your attire, attitude, written communication, and oral communication. Trust also includes being honest with the customer. If you are going to be late, let the customer know that. If you need to do more research, explain the situation. No one can be expected to know all technical information.

Trust also involves being honest if you find confidential material. Do not use or discuss any material you see while in a customer area. If you see confidential material, let the customers know you have seen the material. If the material is a password, let them know and recommend that they change the password immediately.

Do not touch or move things or papers in a customer's area. Always ask the customer to move or put things away to clear the area you need. Do not try to work around a mess. Simply explain that you need space to determine and/or repair the problem.

Trust involves giving customers documentation related to the product just installed or replaced. Trust involves doing what you say you will do. If you say you will call back to check on the situation in the next 24 hours, do so. If you say you will drop off the documentation the following week, do that. Be true to your word.

Trust also involves being honest about billing. Do not overcharge customers. When presenting customers with the invoice or work order, explain details with patience. Do not allow them to argue with you over facts or time. Your time is valuable, too.

You never know where you are going to meet your next boss. Every time you step into a customer's area or talk to a customer, it might lead to a professional reference, a job recommendation, a job lead, or a promotion. Part of building that customer relationship is building trust. Be professional in all that you do.

Chapter Summary

> A security policy guides a company in security matters. The policy defines things such as physical access, antivirus, acceptable usage of devices and data, password policies, email usage guidelines, remote access strategies, and emergency procedures.

> Physical security can include door access, key control, authentication methods including the use of smart cards, key fobs, RFID, biometric devices, physical protection of network devices such as servers, APs, switches, and routers, as well as privacy filters.

> BIOS/UEFI security options include configuring a supervisor/user password, disabling unused ports, disabling USB ports, and disabling device options.

> To protect the operating system, use NTFS, and have a plan for updating the operating system, web browser, antivirus, antimalware, and antispyware. Encrypt files and folders as necessary. Use BitLocker and TPM technologies, implement a firewall, and disable AutoRun.

> If a computer with sensitive data on the hard drive is to be donated, moved, or sold, perform the following: (1) secure erasing, (2) degaussing, and (3) drilling through drive platters and then destroying the pieces with a hammer.

> If virtualization is used, ensure that each virtual machine has adequate protection (firewall, antivirus, antimalware, and antispyware).

> Some virus or malware files are quarantined and must be manually deleted.

> The Windows Guest account should be disabled; the administrator account should be renamed and have a strong password. User accounts provide the amount of administration dictated by what the person requires to do his or her job (principle of least privilege).

> Permissions should be assigned appropriately to remotely accessed files and folders. Use either share permissions or NTFS permissions (for more control), but not both on the same network share. If a file is placed in a folder that has permissions, the file inherits the folder permissions. Effective permissions are the bottom-line permissions someone has when group permissions and individual permissions have been granted.

> A hijacked browser can cause a different home page to appear, a particular web page to be displayed, a rootkit or other malware to be installed, different DNS settings to be applied, or a new or updated HOSTS file applied.

> Email applications now protect against spam, but you can also create rules to block messages from a particular source or subject line.

> On a wireless network, implement encryption and authentication. Change default SSIDs and passwords.

> When a security incident occurs, identify the issue, report it through the proper channels and to the appropriate authorities, and preserve the data by using a chain-of-custody form.

> When dealing with a customer, a co-worker, or your boss, maintain your professionalism and do everything you can to build trust.

A+ CERTIFICATION EXAM TIPS

✓ This chapter has information relating to the CompTIA A+ 220-902 exam and is the most complex chapter because so many security issues need to be experienced to know exactly what things to try. The 902 exam emphasizes security.

✓ Be familiar with wireless security techniques and how to configure them: default usernames, firmware updates, SSID, frequency channel, encryption, SSID broadcasting, MAC filtering, radio power levels, and static IP addressing.

✓ Know the purpose of a TPM, a VPN, an ACL, a firewall, a UTM, an IDS, and an IPS and when to use each of these.

✓ Know what to do if you find prohibited content/data and what PII is.

✓ Review hard drive security including BitLocker and what to do with a hard drive when moving it to another device or simply removing it.

✓ Practice security measures that must be implemented as a technician such as viewing hidden files, using an administrator account/rights, Windows user roles, or adjusting Internet Explorer *Internet Options* tabs.

✓ Practice manually configuring a wireless router/AP with security settings and a wireless NIC.

✓ Review what to do with security problems such as computer slowdowns, lockups, pop-ups, viruses, botnets, zombies, malware, and spam. Know the steps to remove malware.

✓ Know the symptoms of a virus and malware.

Key Terms

Review Questions

1. Match these security policy components with a definition from the following list.

   _____   Physical access

   _____   Acceptable use

   _____   Remote access

   _____   Password

   a. The specific web browser that is allowed to be installed

   b. Defines if you can send the code used to access an account (such as shared network storage) via email

   c. The type of security required for a remote VPN connection

   d. The time, day, and year someone entered a network server room

2. Describe two-factor authentication.

   _____

   _____

3. List two BIOS/UEFI options associated with PC access.

   _____

   _____

4. What wireless security feature would more likely to be used in a small company where the staff are the only ones who use the wireless network?

   a. VPN

   b. IDS

   c. MAC filtering

   d. WPA2

5. List five recommendations for protecting the operating system.

   _____

   _____

   _____

   _____

   _____

   _____

   _____

   _____

6. What is BitLocker?

   _____

   _____

7. [T | F] A new file is created and stored in an encrypted folder. The file must be manually encrypted because it was added after the folder was encrypted.

8. Describe the security rights for a subfolder when the parent folder is shared.

   _____

   _____

9. List three password guidelines you would recommend that a company use.

    _____

    _____

    _____

    _____

10. Where are domain user passwords stored?

    [local database | registry | network server | in the cloud]

11. A network administrator in a large corporation goes to a popular network vendor site to research security settings, but a message appears saying that particular site cannot be accessed and is blocked. What security measure most likely caused this message?

    a. Antivirus software

    b. Antimalware software

    c. Windows Defender

    d. Content filtering

12. Describe the difference between a local policy and a domain policy.

    _____

    _____

    _____

13. What two things are needed to configure a computer for a proxy server?

    [IP address of the proxy server | MAC address of the proxy server | administrator name on the proxy server | IP address of the local computer | MAC address of the local computer | port number on the proxy server | Administrator password on the local computer]

14. What is the purpose of a DMZ?

    _____

    _____

    _____

15. [T | F] A virtual machine should have antispyware installed.

16. What Internet Explorer *Tools* menu option allows active scripting sites to be added for sites you trust?

    [General | Security | Privacy | Content | Connections | Programs]

17. No one can ping a specific Windows 7 computer. What administrative tool can change this default behavior?

    [Windows Firewall | Local Security Policy | Internet Explorer > Internet options | Windows Defender]

18. What type of unsolicited Internet message records the URLs visited and keystrokes used? [virus | grayware | spam | spyware]

19. An unofficial email is sent from your bank, asking you to click a link to verify your account information. What type of social engineering is this?

    [phishing | grayware | spyware | VPN]

20. Match the incident on the left with the action on the right. Even though some of the answers might have multiple answers, the final answers will be such that each answer is used only once.

    _____ virus   **a.** BSA

    _____ child exploitation   **b.** police department

    _____ software piracy   **c.** CERT

    _____ phishing   **d.** FBI Internet crime center

Exercises

Exercise 18.1

Objective: To become familiar with security incident response

Parts: None

Procedure: Answer the following questions.

1. Place the security incident response task in the appropriate order.

    _____ 1st

    _____ 2nd

    _____ 3rd

    a. Report the incident through the proper channels.

    b. Preserve the data/device(s) involved.

    c. Identify the threat.

2. A college requires that all employees use the last four digits of their Social Security number to access the copier. Which type of security threat is this? How would you respond to it?

    a. Malware

    b. Sensitive PII

    c. Security policy

    d. Licensing

    _____

    _____

3. Your neighbor asks if he can borrow your application DVD and code. He promises he will not register the application. How will you respond to this because it is a personal request and not a professional one? To whom would you report this, if anyone?

    _____

    _____

4. You work as an IT support person for a company. The user complains of slowness when opening files. No virus or malware is evident after complete scans have been completed. You open files to test this and find child pornography. What are your next three steps?

    Step 1: _____

    _____

    Step 2: _____

    _____

    Step 3: _____

    _____

Exercise 18.2

Objective:	To become familiar with wireless security options
Parts:	None
Procedure:	Match the scenario to the term. Each answer is only used once.

Scenario:

a. Manually type Layer 2 addresses into a table.

b. Commonly used channels are 1, 6, and 11.

c. Most common corporate wireless security protocol is used.

d. Don't broadcast the name of the network.

e. Nearby companies get a stronger wireless signal than employees.

f. Only has 64- and 128-bit encryption.

g. Someone can get easily into the AP settings.

h. Easy to configure but has security risks.

i. Someone can get into the AP settings using hacking tools.

Task:

_____ WPA2

_____ WEP

_____ MAC filtering

_____ Move AP and/or antenna

_____ 2.4GHz

_____ WPS

_____ Disable SSID broadcasting

_____ Default settings

_____ Update firmware

Activities

Internet Discovery

Objective:	To become familiar with researching computer security concepts using the Internet
Parts:	A computer with Internet access
Questions:	Use the Internet to answer the following questions.

1. Access the Internet Crime Complaint Center to answer the following questions. At the time of writing, the URL is http://www.ic3.gov.

    What are three recommendations for dealing with spam?

    _____

    _____

    _____

    _____

    _____

What is Internet crime, according to this website? Write the answer and the URL at which you found the answer.

_____

_____

_____

_____

_____

2.   Access the U.S. Computer Emergency Readiness Team website and access the technical user link to answer the following questions. At this writing, the URL is http://www.us-cert.gov.

What are the top three high-rated vulnerabilities for the past week?

_____

_____

_____

List three recommendations made by this site for a new computer being connected to a network.

_____

_____

_____

_____

_____

3.   Access the National Institute of Standards and Technology Computer Security Resource Center website to answer the following questions.

Access the glossary of security terms. Windows allows programming of ACLs (access control lists).

What are they and how do they relate to computer security?

_____

_____

_____

Select the CSRC site map link. List one security section that you find interesting, and define one term from that section that is not in this chapter.

_____

_____

_____

4.   Access the Business Software Alliance website to answer the following questions.

According to the website, what percentage of software installed is pirated?

_____

_____

_____

_____

Access the *Anti-Piracy* link.

What is the current maximum fine for each software pirated? In addition, what is the penalty for copyright infringement?

_____

_____

Soft Skills

Objective: To enhance and fine-tune a future technician's ability to listen, communicate in both written and oral form, and support people who use computers in a professional manner

Activities:

1. Prepare a presentation on any topic related to network security. The topic can relate to wired or wireless security. Share your presentation with the class.

2. In small groups, find a security policy on the Internet or use any of your school's computer policies. Critique the policy and make recommendations for how the policy can provide for stronger security.

Critical Thinking Skills

Objective: To analyze and evaluate information as well as apply learned information to new or different situations

Activities:

1. Create a wired workgroup network. Before users are created, determine what security policies will be enforced. Document the security policy. Also determine what activities are logged. Share folders between the computers with security implemented. Document the shares and policies. View and capture activities logged and include with the documentation. Present your design, implementation, and monitoring to the class.

2. In teams, build a wired and wireless network with security in place. Document the security as if you were presenting it to a home network customer who hired you to build and implement it.

Labs

Lab 18.1 Encrypting a File and Folder in Windows

Objective: To provide security for a particular file and folder, enable encryption using Windows Vista, 7, 8, or 10.

Parts: A computer with Windows Vista, 7, 8, or 10 that has at least one NTFS partition.

Note: Two user accounts are needed and possibly created for this exercise: one that encrypts a file and the other account to test the encryption. If two user accounts are not available, most of the lab can still be performed or a second user account can be added. This lab is best demonstrated with two accounts that have local administrator rights.

Procedure: Complete the following procedure and answer the accompanying questions.

1. Power on the computer and log on using the user ID and password provided by the instructor or lab assistant.

2. Access the Computer Management Console using the following directions depending on the operating system used:

In Vista/7, click the *Start* button > *Control Panel* > *System and Maintenance* (Vista)/*System and Security* (7) > *Administrative Tools* > double-click *Computer Management*.

In Windows 8/10, search for and access *Administrative Tools* > double-click or tap and briefly hold on *Computer Management*.

3. Expand the *Storage* option and select *Disk Management*.

How many disk partitions are available?

_____

Do any drive partitions use NTFS?

_____

If so, how many?

_____

Note that if no drive partitions use NTFS, this exercise cannot be completed.

4. Close the *Computer Management* window. Open *Windows Explorer/File Explorer*. Create a text file called *Security Test.txt* and save in the *Documents* folder.

5. Right-click or tap and briefly hold the *Security text.txt* file and select *Properties*. From the *General* tab, select the *Advanced* button.

6. Enable the *Encrypt contents to secure data* option > *OK*. Select the *Apply* button and the warning message, as shown in Figure 18.42, appears.

FIGURE 18.42   Windows encryption warning message

7. The default would be to encrypt the Security text.txt file and to encrypt the *Documents* folder. This may not be what you want to do. Select the *Encrypt the file only* radio button > *OK* > *OK*.

8. In *Windows Explorer/File Explorer*, click an empty spot in the right pane.

Is there any indication the file is encrypted? If so, what is it? Note that you might need to create an unencrypted file to answer this question.

_____

9. In *Windows Explorer/File Explorer*, access the *Properties* window of the *Security text.txt* file again. Select the *Advanced* button. From the *Advanced Attributes* window, select the *Details* button. If this is not available, ensure you are on a file (and not a folder).

What user(s) can access the encrypted file?

_____

10. Notice the certificate thumbprint number to the right of the user. EFS can request a digital certificate from a CA (certificate authority) such as a server. If one is not available, EFS can use a self-signed certificate.

What are the first 16 hexadecimal digits used for the digital certificate?

_____

Compare these digits with a fellow classmate. Are the digital certificates the same? If so, why do you think they are the same? If they are different, why do you think they are different?

_____

11. Select the *Cancel* button on three different windows to exit the *Properties* window.

12. From *Windows Explorer/File Explorer*, open the *Security Test.txt* file, modify it, and save it.

From Windows Explorer/*File Explorer*, does the file appear to still be encrypted?

_____

13. Log off the computer and log on as a different user. If a different user does not exist, create one by using the *User Accounts* Control Panel if possible.

14. Use *Windows Explorer/File Explorer* to locate and open the *Security Test.txt* file located under the other username (commonly found at `C:\users\`*username*`\Documents`). Modify the file and save it, if possible.

Were there any problems opening, modifying, or saving the file?

_____

_____

_____

In one or more complete sentences, explain what happened and why you think it occurred this way.

_____

15. Log off the computer and log on as the original user.

16. Access the *Documents* folder and create a new folder called *Test*. Copy the *Security Test.txt* file into the new *Test* folder.

Is the copied file encrypted in the *Test* folder?

_____

17. Within the *Test* folder, create a new text file called *Security Test2.txt*.

Is the newly created file encrypted?

_____

Instructor initials: _____

18. Encrypt the *Test* folder using the default encryption setting of *Encrypt the file and its parent folder (recommended)*.

Does it change anything within the folder?

_____

If so, what does it change?

_____

19. Within the *Test* folder, create and save a new file called *Security Test3.txt*.

Is the newly created file encrypted?

_____

20. Delete the *Security Test.txt*, *Security Test2.txt*, and *Security Test3.txt* files.

Was there any indication that the files were encrypted when they were deleted?

_____

21. Permanently delete the *Test* folder and any files created in the *Documents* folder.

Lab 18.2 Using Windows 7/8/10 System Protection

Objective: To manually control the settings involved with system restore points using System Protection

Parts: A computer with Windows 7, 8, or 10 loaded with at least one NTFS partition

Note: This lab requires local administrator rights.

Procedure: Complete the following procedure and answer the accompanying questions.

1. Power on the computer and log on using the user ID and password provided by the instructor or lab assistant.

2. Access *Windows Explorer/File Explorer*. Right-click or tap and briefly hold on *Computer (Windows 7)/This PC (Windows 8/10)* > *Properties* > *System Protection* link > *System Protection* tab.

    In the *Protection Settings* section, document the available drives.

    _____

    Document whether protection is currently on or off for each of the available drives.

    _____

3. Select *Configure*.

    What options are available for *Restore Settings*?

    _____

    _____

    Microsoft says, "System Protection can keep copies of system settings and previous versions of files." Do you think this means system files, user data files, or both? Explain your reasoning.

    _____

    Thinking as a technician, which setting is optimum for most users?

    _____

    _____

    Give one situation in which a technician would recommend the *Turn off system protection* option.

    _____

    _____

4. In Windows 7, ensure that the *Restore system settings and previous versions of files* radio button is enabled.

    In Windows 8/10, ensure the *Turn on system protection* radio button is enabled.

    By default, Windows uses a maximum of 10 percent of the hard drive for System Protection. However, the system enables you to adjust this amount in the Disk Space Usage section. Note that if you turn off system protection, you cannot use System Restore.

    What is the current *Max Usage*?

    _____

    Describe a situation in which a technician would want to configure the machine for more than 10 percent of the hard disk space reserved for system protection.

    _____

5. Click *Cancel*.

On Your Own

6. Create a system restore point.

Instructor initials: _____

7. Close all windows.

Lab 18.3 Sharing a Folder in Windows 7

Objective: To share a folder and understand the permissions associated with a network share

Parts: Access to two Windows 7 computers with a user ID that has administrator rights

Procedure: Complete the following procedure and answer the accompanying questions.

1. Turn on both computers and verify that the operating system loads. Log in to Windows 7 using the user ID and password that has full administrator rights and that is provided by your instructor or lab assistant.

2. On the first computer, use Windows Explorer to created two subfolders within the *Documents* folder. Name the folders *READ* and *WRITE*.

3. Within the *READ* folder, create a text document called *readme.txt*. Within the *WRITE* folder, create a text file called *changeme.txt*.

4. On both computers, determine the computer name by accessing the *System* Control Panel. Determine the IP addresses of both computers using the `ipconfig` command.

    Document your findings.

Computer	Computer name	IP address
Computer 1		
Computer 2		

5. On both computers, access the *Network and Sharing Center* Control Panel link to document the current *Advanced Sharing Settings*.

Computer 1	Computer 2
Network discovery [On	Off]	Network discovery [On	Off]
Media streaming [On	Off]	Media streaming [On	Off]
Public folder sharing [On (read only, password required)	On (password required)	Off]	Public folder sharing [On (read only, password required)	On (password required)	Off]
Printer sharing [On	Off]	Printer sharing [On	Off]
File sharing connections [Use 128-bit encryption to help...	Enable file sharing...]	File sharing connections [Use 128-bit encryption to help...	Enable file sharing...]

6. On both computers, enable the following settings.

    > File and Printer Sharing

    > Public Folder Sharing

    > Network Discovery

7. On both computers, use the *Folder Options* Control Panel > *View* tab > in the *Advanced Settings* window, locate the *Use Sharing Wizard (Recommended)* option.

    What is the current setting for the *Use Sharing Wizard* option? [Enabled | Disabled]

8. Ensure the *Use Sharing Wizard* option is enabled. Apply changes as necessary. In Windows Explorer on the first computer, right-click the *READ* folder > *Properties* > *Sharing* tab.

   Document the share network path that appears in the window.

   _____

   _____

9. Select the *Advanced sharing* button > enable the *Share this folder* checkbox > select the *Caching* button.

10. Select the *Configure Offline Availability for a Shared Folder help* link.

    What is the purpose of caching?

    _____

    _____

    [Y | N] Is offline availability enabled by default for a shared folder?

    What command can be used from a command prompt to configure caching options for a shared folder?

    _____

11. Close the help window.

12. In the Offline Settings window, leave the option to the default.

    What is the default setting for offline access?

    _____

13. Select *Cancel*. In the Advanced Sharing window, select the *Permissions* button. Notice how the Everyone group is listed by default.

    Notes: If you want to share with someone who is not listed, use the *User Accounts* Control Panel to create the account; then select that account name in the Permissions window.

    If the local or domain policy requires a password, one should be put on the user account. Best practice is to require passwords on all user accounts.

    If the Everyone user account is selected and password protection is used, a user account is still needed to gain access.

    What permissions are enabled by default for the Everyone group?

    [Full control | Change | Read]

14. Click *OK* on the two windows and then click the *Close* button.

15. Open the *Computer Management* console. Expand *System Tools* and *Shared Folders*. Click *Shares* in the left pane. The READ share lists in the right pane. If the share is missing, redo this lab from the beginning. Close the *Computer Management* window.

16. On the second computer, log on as the user given access in Step 13, or use the user ID and password provided by the instructor or lab assistant.

17. On the second computer, open *Windows Explorer*. Select *Network* in the left pane. In the right pane, locate and double-click the name of the first computer.

    Notes: If the computer does not list, click the *Start* button and in the *Search programs and files* text-box, type \\\\`computer_name` (where `computer_name` is the name of the first computer). Press `Enter`.

18. On the second computer, locate the *READ* share and the *readme.txt* document. Double-click the *readme.txt* file.

    [Y | N] Did the file open?

19. Add a few words to the file. Click the *File > Save* menu option. Leave the filename the same, and click the *Save* button. When asked if you want to replace the file, click *Yes*.

    [Y | N] Did the file save?

20. Close the file and close the window that contains the file.

21. On the second computer inside the *Search programs and files* Start button option, type the share path documented in Step 8 and press [Enter]. If an error occurs, check your typing or redo the steps to get a correct share path document in Step 8.

    What happened?

    _____

22. Close the window. On the second computer, open *Windows Explorer*. Right-click *Computer* in the left pane and select *Map Network Drive*. Use the *Drive* drop-down menu to select a drive letter. In the *Folder* textbox, type the share path for the READ share documented in Step 8. Click *Finish*. The share opens with the drive letter documented in the path at the top of the window. Note that you may have to expand the left pane to see the drive letter.

Instructor initials: _____

23. On the second computer, again access *Windows Explorer* and locate the drive letter that was just mapped to a network drive. Because Windows share paths can be lengthy, a common practice is to use a mapped network drive for the share.

    How can you easily identify mapped drive letters in Windows Explorer (besides a quite high drive letter in some cases)?

    _____

24. Close all windows on the second computer.

25. In Windows Explorer on the first computer, right-click the *WRITE* folder > *Properties* > *Sharing* tab.

    Document the share network path that appears in the window.

    _____

26. Select the *Advanced Sharing* button > enable the *Share this folder* checkbox.

27. Select the *Permissions* button.

28. Select the correct username or group and enable the *Change Allow* checkbox. Click *OK* on two windows and then click the *Close* button.

29. On the second computer, locate the *changeme.txt* document.

30. Modify and save the *changeme.txt* file.

31. On the first computer, open the *changeme.txt* file.

    [Y | N] Was the file changed?

Instructor initials: _____

32. On the second computer, try changing the name of the *changeme.txt* file.

    [Y | N] Could you change the name of the *changeme.txt* file?

33. Verify whether the filename changed on the first computer.

    [Y | N] Did the filename change on the first computer?

    If so, what is the new name?

    _____

34. On the second computer, right-click the *WRITE* folder and select *Always available offline*.

    What indication is given that a folder is available offline?

    _____

    [Y | N] Can a particular file be given this same attribute?

35. Disconnect the second computer from the network by removing the network cable from the network adapter.

36. From a command prompt on the second computer, ping the first computer using the IP address documented in Step 4.

   [Y | N] Did the ping succeed?

37. So with no network access, open the *WRITE* folder and access the *changeme.txt* file. Modify the file and save it.

38. Reconnect the second computer to the network.

39. From the first computer, access the *WRITE* folder.

   [Y | N] Were the document changes made when computer two was disconnected from the network saved on the first computer?

40. On the second computer, again access the *changeme.txt* file and try to permanently delete the file.

   [Y | N] Could you permanently delete the *changeme.txt* file?

41. On the first computer, create a subfolder under the *READ* folder. Name the folder *SUB_READ*. Create a text file in the *SUB_READ* folder called *sub_file.txt*.

42. On the second computer, locate and right-click the *SUB_READ* shared folder. Select *Properties*.

   What attributes does this folder have?

   [Read-only | Hidden | None]

43. On the second computer in *Windows Explorer*, locate the *sub_file.txt* file. Select *Properties*.

   What attributes, if any, are shown as enabled by default?

   [Read-only | Hidden | None]

44. Click *Cancel*. Try to modify the *sub_file.txt* file.

   [Y | N] Could you change the *sub_file.txt* file?

Instructor initials: _____

45. On the second computer, remove the mapped drive (and any drive that you created on your own) by using *Windows Explorer* to locate the mapped drive letter under *Computer* in the left pane. Right-click the mapped drive and select *Disconnect*.

46. On the first computer, permanently delete the *READ* and *WRITE* folders and all files and subfolders contained within them.

47. On the first computer, put the *Advanced sharing settings* options back to the original configuration. Refer to the documentation in Step 5. Put the *Use Sharing Wizard* back to the original setting as documented in Step 7. Show your lab partner the documented settings and the current configuration. Have your lab partner use the following table to document that the computer has been put back to the original configuration.

Computer 1 (permanently deleted folders/sharing settings)
Printed name of lab partner
Signature of lab partner

48. On the second computer, put the *Advanced sharing settings* options back to the original configuration. Refer to the documentation in Step 5. Put the *Use Sharing Wizard* back to the original setting as documented in Step 7. Show your lab partner the documented settings and the current configuration. Have your lab partner use the table that follows to document that the computer has been put back to the original configuration.

Computer 2 (permanently deleted folders/sharing settings)
Printed name of lab partner
Signature of lab partner

49. On both computers, delete any user accounts that have been created. Note that you must be logged in as an administrator to delete user accounts.

Lab 18.4 Sharing a Folder in Windows 8/10

Objective: To share a folder and understand the permissions associated with a network share

Parts: Access to two Windows 8 or 10 computers with a user ID that has administrator rights

Procedure: Complete the following procedure and answer the accompanying questions.

Note: You must have a password assigned to the login account for this lab to work.

1. Turn on both computers and verify that the operating system loads. Log in to Windows 8 or 10 using an account that has full administrator rights and that is provided by your instructor or lab assistant.

2. On the first computer, use *File Explorer* to create two subfolders within the *Documents* folder. Name the folders *READ* and *WRITE*.

3. Within the *READ* folder, create a text document called *readme*. Within the *WRITE* folder, create a text file called *changeme*.

4. On both computers, determine the computer name by accessing the *System* Control Panel. Determine the IP addresses of both computers using the `ipconfig` command.

   Document your findings.

Computer	Computer name	IP address
Computer 1		
Computer 2		

5. On both computers, if the IP address starts with the number 169, use the *Network and Sharing Center* Control Panel > *Change adapter settings* > right-click or tap and briefly hold the Ethernet wired NIC icon > *Properties* > double-click or double-tap *Internet Protocol Version 4 (TCP/IPv4)* > select the *Use the following IP address* radio button. Assign IP addresses as follows:

Computer 1	Computer 2
IP address: **192.168.10.11**	IP address: **192.168.10.12**
Subnet mask: **255.255.255.0**	Subnet mask: **255.255.255.0**

   Apply the changes to the IP address if necessary.

   [Yes | No] Did the address have to be manually assigned on Computer 1?

[Yes | No] Did the address have to be manually assigned on Computer 2?

6. On both computers, access the *Network and Sharing Center* Control Panel link to document the current *Advanced Sharing Settings*. Do this for the current profile as well as the other profiles. You can tell which option is the current profile by looking for the profile that has the words *(current profile)* beside it.

	Computer 1	Computer 2
Private profile		
Network discovery [On | Off]		
Network discovery [On | Off]		
Network discovery *Turn on automatic setup of network connected devices* suboption [Enabled | Disabled]		
Network discovery *Turn on automatic setup of network connected devices* suboption [Enabled | Disabled]		
File and printer sharing [On | Off]		
File and printer sharing [On | Off]		
HomeGroup connections [Allow Windows to manage homegroup connections | Use user accounts and passwords to connect to other computers]		
HomeGroup connections [Allow Windows to manage homegroup connections | Use user accounts and passwords to connect to other computers]		
Guest or Public profile		
Network discovery [On | Off]	Network discovery [On | Off]	
File and printer sharing [On | Off]	File and printer sharing [On | Off]	
All Networks profile		
Public folder sharing [On | Off]		
Public folder sharing [On | Off]		
Media streaming [On | Off]		
Media streaming [On | Off]		
File sharing connections [Use 128-bit encryption to help protect file sharing connections | Enable file sharing for devices that use 40- or 56-bit encryption]		
File sharing connections [Use 128-bit encryption to help protect file sharing connections | Enable file sharing for devices that use 40- or 56-bit encryption]		

	Computer 1	Computer 2
Password protected sharing [On	Off]		
Password protected sharing [On	Off]		

7. On both computers, enable the following settings.

    Private profile:

    Network discovery: **On**

    Network discovery *Turn on automatic setup of network connected devices* suboption: **enabled**

    File and printer sharing: **On**

    HomeGroup connections: *Use user accounts and passwords to connect to other computers:* **enabled**

    Guest or Public profile:

    Network discovery: **On**

    File and printer sharing: **On**

    All Networks profile:

    Public folder sharing: **On**

    Media streaming: **Off**

    File sharing connections: **Use 128-bit encryption**

    Password protected sharing: **Off**

8. After signing off and back on as directed on both computers, both computers should be used to search for and access the *Folder Options* (Windows 8)/*File Explorer Options* (Windows 10) Control Panel > *View* tab > in the *Advanced Settings* window, locate the *Use Sharing Wizard (Recommended)* option.

    What is the current setting for the *Use Sharing Wizard* option? [Enabled | Disabled]

    _____

9. Ensure the *Use Sharing Wizard* option is enabled. Apply changes as necessary. In File Explorer on the first computer, right-click or tap and briefly hold on the *READ* folder > *Properties* > *Sharing* tab.

10. Select the *Advanced sharing* button > enable the *Share this folder* checkbox > select the *Caching* button.

    What is the purpose of caching?

    _____

    _____

    [Y | N] Is offline availability enabled by default for a shared folder?

    What command can be used from a command prompt to configure caching options for a shared folder? Note that you may have to refer to Chapter 15 to answer this question.

    _____

11. In the *Offline Settings* window, leave the option to the default.

    What is the default setting for offline access?

    _____

12. Select *Cancel*. In the *Advanced Sharing* window, select the *Permissions* button. Notice how the Everyone group is listed by default.

    Notes: If you were in the situation in which you wanted to share with someone who is not listed, use the *User Accounts* Control Panel to create the account; then select that account name in the Permissions window.

If the Everyone user account is selected and password protection is used, a user account is still needed to gain access.

What permissions are enabled by default for the Everyone group?

[Full control | Change | Read]

13. Select *OK* on two consecutive windows.

Document the share network path that appears in the window.

_____

14. Select the *Close* option at the bottom. While still working on Computer 1, open the *Computer Management* console. In the left window, expand *System Tools* and *Shared Folders*. Select *Shares* in the left pane. The READ share (along with other shares) list in the right pane.

Is the READ share present? [Yes | No]

If the share is missing, redo this lab from the beginning. Close the *Computer Management* window.

15. On the second computer, open *File Explorer*. Select *Network* in the left pane. In the right pane, locate and double-click or double-tap the name of the first computer.

Notes: If the computer does not show in the list, search for *computer_name* (where computer_name is the name of the first computer). Press (Enter).

16. On the second computer, locate the *readme.txt* document found within the *READ* share. Double-click or double tap the *readme.txt* file to open it.

[Y | N] Did the file open?

17. Add a few words to the file. Select the *File > Save* menu option. Leave the filename the same and select the *Save* button. When asked if you want to replace the file, select *Yes*.

[Y | N] Did the file save?

18. Select *OK*. Close the file and close the window that contains the file. Note that you cannot save it.

19. On the second computer, use the *Search* textbox. Type the share path documented in Step 13 and press (Enter). If an error occurs, check your typing or redo the steps to get a correct share path documents in Step 13.

What happened?

_____

20. Close the window. On the second computer, open *File Explorer*. Right-click or tap and briefly hold on the words *This PC* in the left pane and select *Map Network Drive*. Use the *Drive* drop-down menu to select a drive letter. In the *Folder* textbox, type the share path for the READ share documented in Step 13. Select *Finish*. The share opens with the drive letter documented in the path at the top of the window.

Instructor initials: _____

21. On the second computer, again access *File Explorer* and locate the drive letter in the left pane that was just mapped to a network drive. Note that you may have to expand the left window by moving the pointer over the dividing line between the left and right pane. When the pointer changes to a double arrow, click and move the line to the right. Because Windows share paths can be lengthy, a common practice is to use a mapped network drive for the share.

How can you easily identify mapped drive letters in File Explorer (in addition to a quite high drive letter in some cases)?

_____

22. Close all windows on the second computer.

23. In *File Explorer* on the first computer, locate the *WRITE* subfolder of *Documents*. Right-click or tap and briefly hold on the *WRITE* folder icon > *Properties* > *Sharing* ta**b.**

24. Select the *Advanced Sharing* button > enable the *Share this folder* checkbox.

25. Select the *Permissions* button.

26. Select the correct username or group and enable the *Change Allow* checkbox. Select *OK* on two consecutive windows.

    Document the share network path that appears in the window.

    _____

27. Select the *Close* option at the bottom. On the second computer, using any of the previous techniques demonstrated, locate the *changeme.txt* document located on Computer 1.

28. Modify the text inside the file and save the *changeme.txt* file.

29. On the first computer, open the *changeme.txt* file.

    [Y | N] Was the file changed?

30. On the second computer, try changing the name of the *changeme.txt* file to *changeme2.txt*.

    [Y | N] Could you change the name of the *changeme.txt* file?

31. Verify whether the filename changed on the first computer.

    [Y | N] Did the filename change on the first computer?

    If so, what is the new name?

    _____

Instructor initials: _____

32. On the second computer, right-click or tap and briefly hold on the *WRITE* folder and select *Always available offline*.

    What indication is given that a folder is available offline?

    _____

    [Y | N] Can a particular file be given this same attribute?

33. Disconnect the second computer from the network by removing the network cable from the network adapter or disabling the network card. You may have to research this if you do not remember how to do it.

34. From a command prompt on the second computer, ping the first computer using the IP address documented in Step 4 (or Step 5 if it were manually assigned).

    [Y | N] Did the ping succeed?

35. So with no network access on the second computer, use Computer 2 to open the *WRITE* folder and access the *changeme2.txt* file. Modify the file and save it.

36. Reconnect the second computer to the network or re-enable the NIC.

37. From the first computer, access the *WRITE* folder.

    [Y | N] Were the document changes made when computer 2 was disconnected from the network saved on the first computer?

38. On the second computer, again access the *changeme2.txt* file and try to permanently delete the file.

    Could you permanently delete the *changeme.txt* file?

    [Y | N]

39. On the first computer, create a subfolder under the *READ* folder. Name the folder *SUB_READ*. Create a text file in the *SUB_READ* folder called *sub_file.txt*.

40. On the second computer, locate and right-click or tap and briefly hold on the *SUB_READ* shared folder. Select *Properties*.

    What attributes does this folder have?

    [Read-only | Hidden | Archive | Compress | Encrypt | None]

41. On the second computer in *File Explorer*, locate the *sub_file.txt* file. Select *Properties*.

    What attributes, if any, are shown as enabled by default?

    [Read-only | Hidden | Archive | Compress | Encrypt | None]

42. Select *Cancel*. Try to modify the *sub_file.txt* file.

    Could you change the *sub_file.txt* file?

    [Y | N]

Instructor initials: _____

43. On the second computer, remove the mapped drive (and any drive that you created on your own) by using *File Explorer* to locate the mapped drive letter under *This PC* in the left pane. Right-click the mapped drive and select *Disconnect > Yes*. Close *File Explorer*.

44. On the first computer, permanently delete the *READ* and *WRITE* folders and all files and subfolders contained within them.

45. On the first computer, put the *Advanced sharing settings* options back to the original configuration. Refer to the documentation in Step 6. Put the *Use Sharing Wizard* back to the original setting as documented in Step 8. If you manually configured an IP address in Step 5, return the computer to the *Obtain an IP address automatically* setting. Show your lab partner the documented settings and the current profile configuration. Have your lab partner use the table that follows to document that the computer has been put back to the original configuration.

Computer 1 (permanently deleted folders/sharing settings)

Printed name of lab partner

Signature of lab partner

46. On the second computer, put the *Advanced sharing settings* options back to the original configuration. Refer to the documentation in Step 6. Put the *Use Sharing Wizard* back to the original setting as documented in Step 8. If you manually configured an IP address in Step 5, return the computer to the *Obtain an IP address automatically* setting. Show your lab partner the documented settings and the current configuration. Have your lab partner use the table that follows to document that the computer has been put back to the original configuration.

Computer 2 (permanently deleted folders/sharing settings/IP address)

Printed name of lab partner

Signature of lab partner

Lab 18.5 Creating a Local Security Policy for Passwords

Objective:	To provide additional security by requiring certain password parameters as a local computer security policy
Parts:	A computer with Windows Vista or 7 Professional
Procedure:	Complete the following procedure and answer the accompanying questions.
Notes:	Local administrator rights are required for this lab. The computer should be part of a workgroup, not a domain. However, even though domain policy requirements override local policy, the lab may still work as written.

1. Power on the computer and log on using the user ID and password provided by the instructor or lab assistant.

2. Access the *Local Security Policy Console* using the following steps:

   Start > Administrative Tools Control Panel > double-click *Local Security Policy*.

3. Expand the *Account Policies* option.

   What two options are available?

   _____

4. Select the *Password Policy* subcategory. Table 18.15 details these options.

TABLE 18.15   Windows password policy option descriptions

Option	Description
Enforce password history.	The number of unique and new passwords must be used before an old password can be reused.
Maximum password age.	The number of days a password has to be used before it has to be changed.
Minimum password age.	The fewest number of days a user has to use the same password.
Minimum password length.	The fewest number of characters required for the password. The least the password can be is zero. The more characters required, the better the security. A common setting is 7 or 8; 14 characters is the most you can require in this setting.
Password must meet complexity requirements.	Sets higher standards for the password such as the password cannot be the username, must be six characters or more, requires uppercase and lowercase letters, numerals, and symbols such as # or !.
Store passwords using reversible encryption for all users in the domain.	If enabled, passwords are stored using reversible encryption. Used only if an application uses a protocol that requires knowledge of a user password for authentication purposes.

Use Table 18.16 to document the current settings.

TABLE 18.16   Current password policy settings

Option	Current setting
Enforce password history.	
Maximum password age.	
Minimum password age.	
Store password using reversible encryption for all users in the domain.	

Option	Current setting
Minimum password length.	
Password must meet complexity requirements.	

5.   Change the password policy settings to the options shown in Table 18.17.

TABLE 18.17   New password policy settings

Option	New setting
Enforce password history.	One password remembered
Minimum password length.	Eight characters
Passwords must meet complexity requirements.	Enabled

6.   Create a new user account by using the following directions:

Click the *Start* button > *User Accounts* Control Panel > *Create a new account* link > type Test-student for the new account name and ensure the *Standard user* radio button is selected > *Create Account* button. The Teststudent icon appears in the window. Select the *Teststudent* icon > *Create a password* link > in the *New password* textbox, type student123.

What indication is given that a policy is in place?

_____

7.   Log off as the current user. Log in as *Teststudent*.

What message appeared upon logon?

_____

8.   In the *New Password* and *Confirm New Password* textboxes, type test followed by selecting the right arrow (Vista/7).

What requirements display?

_____

_____

9.   Click *OK*. In the *New Password* and *Confirm New Password* textboxes, type Tester9# and click *OK*.

What message displays?

_____

10. Log off as *Teststudent* and log back in using the original user account.

11. Return to the *Security Policy* console. Expand *Local Policies* and select *Audit Policy*.

What is the current setting for audit account logon events? [No auditing I Success I Failure I Success and Failure]

List three other items that can be audited.

_____

_____

12. Double-click the *Audit account logon events* option. The two options are success and failure and both options can be enabled. Success logs every time someone logs in to the computer. Failure logs every failed logon attempt. Enable both the *Success* and *Failure* checkboxes > *Apply* button > *OK* button.

13. Log off as the current user and log in as *Teststudent* using the password of *Tester?1* (Yes, this is the wrong password.)

    What message appeared?

    _____

14. Click *OK* and this time type the correct password of `Tester9#`. Log off as Teststudent. Log back on as the original computer user.

15. To see events that have been enabled and logged, click the *Start* button > *Administrative Tools* Control Panel > *Event Viewer* > *Security* option in the left pane > expand the *Windows Logs* category on the left and select *Security*. Scroll down to select a line that shows as an *Audit Failure*. Note that you may need to expand the *Keywords* section by moving the pointer over the dividing line between the *Keywords* header and the *Date and Time* column header. When the pointer changes to a bar with two arrows extending from the bar, click and drag the bar to the right to expand the *Keywords* section. Look for a lock graphic instead of a key on the left.

16. Notice that when you select a security event that information about that event shows in the bottom window.

    What event number was the audit failure?

    _____

    [Yes | No] Does the General tab show the computer name for the violation?

17. Close *Event Viewer*. Return to the *Security Policy* console. Set the *Audit account logon* events setting to the original setting. Refer to Step 11 for the original settings.

    Have a classmate verify your setting and print and sign his name on your answer sheet.

    Classmate printed name _____ _____

    Classmate signature _____

18. Configure the *Password Policy* settings to their original configuration. Refer to Step 4 for the original settings.

    Have a classmate verify your setting and print and sign her name on your answer sheet.

    Classmate printed name _____ _____

    Classmate signature _____

19. Expand *Local Policies*. Select the *User Rights Assignment* option. Use Table 18.18 to document the current settings for various options.

TABLE 18.18   Windows user rights assignment settings

Option	Current setting
Access this computer from the network.	
Allow logon through Remote Desktop Services.	
Deny logon locally.	
Force shutdown from a remote system.	
Generate security audits.	
Load and unload device drivers.	
Take ownership of files or other objects.	
Restore files and directories.	

20. Select the *Security* option in the left pane. Use Table 18.19 to document the current settings for various options.

TABLE 18.19   Windows security settings

Option	Current setting
Shut down the system.	
Accounts: Administrator account status.	
Accounts: Guest account status.	
Accounts: Rename administrator account.	
Devices: Allow to format and eject removable media.	
Devices: Prevent users from installing printer drivers.	
Interactive logon: Message text for users attempting to log on.	
Interactive logon: Prompt user to change password before expiration.	
Interactive logon: Require smart card.	
Network access: Let Everyone permissions apply to anonymous users.	
Network access: Shares that can be accessed anonymously.	
Network security: Force logoff when logon hours expire.	
Shutdown: Allow system to be shut down without having to log on.	

21. Close the Security Policy console. Access *User Accounts* and remove the *Teststudent* user account.

Have a classmate verify your setting and print and sign his name on your answer sheet.

Classmate printed name _____ _____

Classmate signature _____

22. Close the *User Accounts* window and reboot the computer.

Lab 18.6 Creating a Local Security Policy for Passwords in Windows 8/10

Objective: To provide additional security by requiring certain password parameters as a local computer security policy

Parts: A computer with Windows 8 Professional or 10 Professional or higher loaded

Procedure: Complete the following procedure and answer the accompanying questions.

Notes: Local administrator rights are required for this lab. The computer should be part of a workgroup, not a domain. However, even though domain policy requirements override local policy, the lab may still work as written.

1. Power on the computer and log on using the user ID and password provided by the instructor or lab assistant.

2. Access the *Local Security Policy Console* by accessing the *Administrative Tools* Control Panel > double-click or double-tap and briefly hold on *Local Security Policy*.

3. Expand the *Account Policies* option in the left pane.

What two options are available?

_____

4. Select the *Password Policy* subcategory. Table 18.20 details these options.

TABLE 18.20   Windows password policy option descriptions

Option	Description
Enforce password history.	The number of unique and new passwords must be used before an old password can be reused.
Maximum password age.	The number of days a password has to be used before it has to be changed.
Minimum password age.	The fewest number of days a user has to use the same password.
Minimum password length.	The fewest number of characters required for the password. The least the password can be is zero. The more characters required, the better the security. A common setting is 7 or 8; 14 characters is the most you can require in this setting.
Password must meet complexity requirements.	Sets higher standards for the password such as the password cannot be the username, must be six characters or more, requires uppercase and lowercase letters, numerals, and symbols such as # or !.
Store passwords using reversible encryption for all users in the domain.	If enabled, passwords are stored using reversible encryption. Used only if an application uses a protocol that requires knowledge of a user password for authentication purposes.

Use Table 18.21 to document the current settings.

TABLE 18.21   Current password policy settings

Option	Current setting
Enforce password history.	
Maximum password age.	
Minimum password age.	
Minimum password length.	
Password must meet complexity requirements.	

Store password using reversible encryption for all users in the domain.

5.   Change the password policy settings to the options shown in Table 18.22.

TABLE 18.22   New password policy settings

Option	New setting
Enforce password history.	One password remembered
Minimum password length.	Eight characters
Passwords must meet complexity requirements.	Enabled

6. Select the *Account Lockout Policy* subcategory. Table 18.23 details these options.

TABLE 18.23   Windows account lockout policy option descriptions

Option	Description
Account lockout duration	The number of minutes someone is locked out if a password is mistyped. A value of 0 requires an administrator to unlock it. Requires the *Account lockout threshold* to be configured.
Account lockout threshold	The number of filed logon attempts that can cause a user account to be locked. A value of 0 will never lock a user out no matter how many times he mistypes his password.
Reset account lockout counter after	*The number of minutes that have to pass before the logon attempt counter is reset to 0 bad logon attempts. Requires the Account lockout threshold option to be configured.*

7. Minimize the local security policy window. Create a new user account by using the following directions based on whether you use Windows 8 or Windows 10:

   Windows 8: Access *Settings > Accounts >* select the *Other accounts* link from the left pane > in the *Manage other accounts* section, select the *Add an account* link > type `Teststudent` for the User name and `Student234%` as the password > type `student 234 percent` in the *Password hint* textbox > select the *Next* button > *Finish*.

   Windows 10: Access *Settings > Accounts >* select the *Family & other users* link from the left pane > in the *Other users* section, select the *Add someone else to this PC* link > type `Teststudent` for the User name and `Student234%` as the password > type `student 234 percent` in the *Password hint* textbox > select the *Next* button.

8. Log off as the current user. Log in as `Teststudent`.

   What message appeared upon logon?

   _____

9. Try to access the *Local Security Policy* Administrative Tools option.

   [Yes | No] Can the Teststudent user change the password policy?

10. Log off as *Teststudent* and log back in using the original user account.

11. Return to the *Local Security Policy* console. Expand *Local Policies* and select *Audit Policy*.

   What is the current setting for audit account logon events? [No auditing | Success | Failure | Success and Failure]

   List three other items that can be audited.

   _____

   _____

12. Double-click or double-tap the *Audit account logon events* option. The two options are success and failure and both options can be enabled. Success logs every time someone logs in to the computer. Failure logs every failed logon attempt.

   What are the current settings?

   Success [Enabled | Disabled]

   Failure [Enabled | Disabled]

13. Enable both the *Success* and *Failure* checkboxes > *Apply* button > *OK* button.

14. Log off as the current user and log in as `Teststudent`, but use the password of `CatchMe123`. (Yes, that is wrong, but do it anyway.)

    What message appeared upon logon? _____

    _____

15. Select *OK*. Log in using `Teststudent` and the correct password of *Student234%*.

16. To see events that have been enabled and logged such as the ones we just set as the local policy, access the *Administrative Tools* Control Panel > *Event Viewer* > expand the *Windows Logs* category on the left and select *Security*.

    [Yes | No] Can the Teststudent user access Even Viewer details that were enabled in the local security policy?

17. Log off as Teststudent. Log back on as the original computer user.

18. Access the *Administrative Tools* Control Panel > *Event Viewer* > *Security* option in the left pane > expand the *Windows Logs* category on the left and select *Security*. Scroll down to select a line that shows as an *Audit Failure*. Note that you may need to expand the *Keywords* section by moving the pointer over the dividing line between the *Keywords* header and the *Date and Time* column header. When the pointer changes to a bar with two arrows extending from the bar, click and drag the bar to the right to expand the *Keywords* section. Look for a lock graphic instead of a key on the left.

19. Notice that when you select a security event that information about that event shows in the bottom window.

    What event number was the audit failure? _____

    _____

    [Yes | No] Does the General tab show the computer name for the violation?

20. Close *Event Viewer*. Return to the *Local Security Policy* console. Set the *Audit account logon events* setting to the original setting. Refer to Step 11 for the original settings.

    Have a classmate verify your setting and print and sign her name on your answer sheet.

    Classmate printed name _____ _____

    Classmate signature _____

21. Configure the *Password Policy* settings to their original configuration. Refer to Step 4 for the original settings.

    Have a classmate verify your password policy settings by printing and signing his name.

    Classmate printed name _____ _____

    Classmate signature _____

22. In the *Local Security Policy* window, expand *Local Policies*. Select the *User Rights Assignment* option. Use Table 18.24 to document the current settings for various options.

TABLE 18.24 Windows user rights assignment settings

Option	Current setting
Access this computer from the network.	
Allow log on through Remote Desktop Services.	
Deny log on locally.	
Force shutdown from a remote system.	
Generate security audits.	
Load and unload device drivers.	
Restore files and directories.	
Shut down the system.	

23. Select the *Security Options* in the left pane. Use Table 18.25 to document the current settings for various options.

TABLE 18.25   Windows security settings

Option	Current setting
Take ownership of files or other objects.	
Accounts: Administrator account status.	
Accounts: Guest account status.	
Accounts: Rename administrator account.	
Devices: Allow to format and eject removable media.	
Devices: Prevent users from installing printer drivers.	
Interactive logon: Message text for users attempting to log on.	
Interactive logon: Prompt user to change password before expiration.	
Interactive logon: Require smart card.	
Network access: Let Everyone permissions apply to anonymous users.	
Network access: Shares that can be accessed anonymously.	
Network security: Force logoff when logon hours expire.	
Shutdown: Allow system to be shut down without having to log on.	

24. Close the Security Policy console. Access *User Accounts* and remove the *Teststudent* user account by selecting the account name > *Delete the account* link > *Delete Files* > *Delete Account*.

    Have a classmate verify your setting and print and sign her name on your answer sheet.

    Classmate printed name _____ _____

    Classmate signature _____

25. Close the *User Accounts* window and reboot the computer.

Lab 18.7 Windows Defender in Windows 7

Objective: To use System Configuration and Windows Defender to troubleshoot boot and spyware problems

Parts: Computer with Windows 7 installed

User logon that has administrator rights

Note: In this lab, you explore various options that can be used within the System Configuration and Windows Defender windows.

If the computer has a third-party security suite such as Norton or McAfee that has antispyware or antimalware, the Windows Defender application may not be enabled.

Procedure: Complete the following procedure and answer the accompanying questions.

1. Turn on the computer and verify that the operating system loads. Log in to Windows.

2. Open *Windows Explorer*. From the *Organize* menu option > *Folder and Search Options* > *View* tab.

    What is the current setting for the Hidden files and folders section? (Do not show hidden files and folders enabled | Show hidden files and folders enabled.)

What is the current setting for the *Hide extensions for known file types* option? [Enabled | Disabled]

What is the current setting for the *Hide protected operating system files (Recommended)* option? [Enabled | Disabled]

3.   Configure the following Windows Explorer settings:

> *Show hidden files, folders, and drives radio button*—enabled (checked)
> *Hide extensions for known file types*—disabled (unchecked)
> *Hide protected operating system files (Recommended)*—disabled (unchecked)

Click *Yes* (if prompted) > *Apply* > *OK*. Close *Windows Explorer*.

4.   Open the *Start* menu and in the *Search Programs and Files* textbox, type defender > click *Windows Defender*. If a note appears that Windows Defender is turned off, select the *click here to turn it on* option. You might have to obtain updates before continuing.

Was Windows Defender disabled? [yes | no]

5.   Select the *Tools* menu option > *Options*.

What actions are defined from this window?

_____

_____

_____

6.   Select the *Tools* menu option > *Quarantined items*.

List any software that Windows Defender has prevented from executing.

_____

7.   Select the *Tools* menu option > *Allowed items*.

List any software that is not monitored by Windows Defender.

_____

What happens if an item is removed from the list and how did you find this information?

_____

_____

_____

8.   Select the *Tools* menu option > *Options* > *Real-time protection* from the left pane.

Is real-time protection enabled? [yes | no]

What options are available besides enabling real-time protection?

_____

9.   Select *Excluded file types* from the left pane.

What file extension is given as an example of a file type to exclude?

_____

10.   Select the *Advanced* option from the left pane.

What type of scanning is enabled? [scan archive files | scan email | scan removable drives | use heuristics | create restore point]

What will a machine do if it uses heuristics?

_____

11. Select *Administrator* from the left pane.

    What two options are configured from here?

    _____

12. Return *Windows Defender* to its original state. See the answers to Step 4.

13. Return Windows Explorer to the original settings. See the settings as the answers found in Step 2.

14. Show the instructor that the settings are re-configured to the original settings.

Instructor initials: _____

15. Close the *Windows Defender* window.

Lab 18.8 Windows Defender in Windows 8/10

Objective: To be able to use System Configuration and Windows Defender to troubleshoot boot and spyware problems

Parts: Computer with Windows 8/10 installed

    User logon that has administrator rights

Note: In this lab, you will explore various options that can be used within the System Configuration and Windows Defender windows.

    If the computer has a third-party security suite such as Norton or McAfee that has antispyware or antimalware, the Windows Defender application may not be enabled.

Procedure: Complete the following procedure and answer the accompanying questions.

1. Turn on the computer and verify that the operating system loads. Log in to Windows.

2. Open *File Explorer* > *View* tab > *Options* > *Change folder and search options* > *View* tab.

    What is the current setting for the Hidden files and folders section? [Do not show hidden files and folders enabled | Show hidden files and folders enabled]

    What is the current setting for the *Hide extensions for known file types* option? [Enabled | Disabled]

    What is the current setting for the *Hide protected operating system files (Recommended)* option? [Enabled | Disabled]

3. Configure the following File Explorer settings:

    > *Show hidden files, folders, and drives radio button*—enabled (checked)
    > *Hide extensions for known file types*—disabled (unchecked)
    > *Hide protected operating system files (Recommended)* —disabled (unchecked)

4. Access the *Windows Defender* Control Panel. Note that if a note appears that Windows Defender is turned off, select the *click here to turn it on* option. You might have to obtain updates before continuing.

    Was Windows Defender disabled? [yes | no]

5. Examine the *Home* tab.

    What actions are defined from this window?

    _____

    _____

6. Select the *History* tab > ensure the *Quarantined items* option is selected.

    List any software that Windows Defender has prevented from executing.

    _____

7.   Select the *History* tab > ensure the *Allowed items* option is selected.

List any software that is not be monitored by Windows Defender.

_____

8.   Select the *Settings* option.

Is real-time protection enabled? [yes | no]

Is cloud protection available? [yes | no]

What options are available besides enabling real-time protection?

_____

_____

_____

9.   In Windows 8, select the *Advanced* option from the left pane. Windows 10 users go to Step 11.

What type of scanning is enabled? [scan archive files | scan email | scan removable drives | use heuristics | create a restore point | allow all users to view the full history results]

10.   In Windows 8, select *MAPS* from the left pane.

What is the purpose of MAPS?

_____

11.   Return *Windows Defender* to its original state. See the answers to Step 4.

12.   Return *File Explorer* to the original settings. See the settings as the answers found in Step 2.

13.   Close all windows.

Lab 18.9 Sharing Files with Windows 8/10 Public Folders

Objective: To be able to access a file from another computer that has been shared through a Windows 8/10 public folder

Parts: Two Windows 8 or 10 computers on a wired or wireless network

Procedure: Complete the following procedure and answer the accompanying questions.

1.   Ensure that both computers have an IP address on the same network. Be able to ping between the computers.

2.   On both computers, make a shortcut on the desktop to the *Public* folder. The public folder is commonly located at `C:\Users\Public`.

3.   On Computer 1, create a text document and put it in the *Public Documents* subfolder.

What did you name the text document?

_____

4.   Ensure both computers are visible from File Explorer by turning on network discovery and file and print sharing. Turn off password-protected sharing.

5.   Ensure both computers can share files using the public folder by enabling the *Turn on sharing so anyone with network access can read and write files in the Public folders* option found in the *All Networks* profile.

6.   From Computer 2, access and change the text document.

[Yes | No] Were you able to change the document across the network. If not, redo the lab.

Instructor initials: _____

Lab 18.10 Configuring a Secure Wireless Network

Objective: To be able to configure a secure wireless AP (access point) or router and attach a wireless client

Parts: One wireless access point or router

A computer with an integrated wireless NIC or a wireless NIC installed as well as an Ethernet NIC

One straight-through cable

Procedure: Complete the following procedure and answer the accompanying questions.

1.   Obtain the documentation for the wireless AP or router from the instructor or Internet.

2.   Reset the wireless AP or router as directed by the wireless device manufacturer.

Document the current Ethernet NIC IPv4 settings. [DHCP | static IP address]

If a static IP address is assigned, document the IP address, subnet mask, default gateway, and DNS configuration settings.

_____

3.   Attach a straight-through cable from the computer's Ethernet NIC to the wireless AP or router.

4.   Power on the computer and log on, if necessary.

5.   Configure the computer with a static IP address or DHCP, as directed by the wireless device manufacturer.

6.   Open a web browser and configure the wireless AP or router with the following parameters:

   > Change the default SSID
   > Disable SSID broadcasting enabled for this lab
   > Configure the most secure encryption and authentication supported by both the wireless NIC client and the wireless AP or router
   > Change the default password used to access the wireless AP or router

Document the settings after you have configured them:

SSID:

_____

SSID broadcasting disabled? [yes | no]

_____

Password for wireless device access:

_____

Type of security used:

_____

7.   Save the wireless AP or router configuration.

8.   Disconnect the Ethernet cable.

9.   Enable the wireless NIC and configure it for the appropriate SSID.

10.   Configure the wireless NIC for a static IP address or DHCP, as directed by the wireless AP/router manufacturer.

11.   Open a web browser and access the wireless AP or router. If access cannot be obtained, troubleshoot as necessary or reset the wireless AP or router to default configurations and restart the lab.

What frequency (channel) is being used by the wireless AP or router and the wireless NIC for connectivity?

_____

12. Show the instructor the connectivity.

Instructor initials: _____

13. Open a command prompt and type `netsh wlan show settings` to see the wireless network settings.

14. Reset the wireless AP or router to the default configuration settings.

15. Reset the computer(s) to the original configuration settings.

Instructor initials: _____

19 Operational Procedures

In this chapter you will learn:

> Proper personal safety precautions and equipment

> Workplace safety precautions, procedures, and equipment

> How to protect computer equipment from airborne pollutants

> How to dispose of waste (computers, mobile devices, batteries, laser printer toner cartridges, monitors)

> A review of troubleshooting procedures

> Proper communication skills

CompTIA Exam Objectives:

What CompTIA A+ exam objectives are covered in this chapter?

✓ 902-5.1 Given a scenario, use appropriate safety procedures.

✓ 902-5.2 Given a scenario with potential environmental impacts, apply the appropriate controls.

✓ 902-5.4 Demonstrate proper communication techniques and professionalism.

✓ 902-5.5 Given a scenario, explain the troubleshooting theory.

Operational Procedures Overview

Being up-to-date on the latest safety precautions and procedures regarding both personal and workplace safety is beneficial to all involved. This chapter reviews the role that federal, state, and local governments play in protecting human health and the environment by operating regulated recycling and disposal sites for electronics. Also covered are the dangers of damaged batteries that leak acid and how to handle those situations. We review why and how:

> Electronics need to be protected from moisture, dust, extreme temperature fluctuations, and weight-bearing loads.
> Toxic fumes can cause degradation of components.
> Electronic waste (computers, mobile devices, batteries, laser printer toner cartridges, and monitors) is considered toxic waste.
> To protect computer equipment with surge (power) suppressors, personal enclosures, and clean rooms.
> Personal protective equipment and personal safety techniques are necessary.
> To properly handle and store electronics using anti-static bags, ESD straps, and ESD mats.
> Equipment grounding, self-grounding, and fire safety knowledge is important.

A review of troubleshooting steps is also included in this chapter. Finally, we discuss why looking, acting, and *thinking* like a professional, along with having good communications skills, is a must in the world we live in.

Workplace Safety Precautions and Procedures

All companies are required to have workplace safety precautions and procedures posted and in effect as mandated by the federal government. Most employers provide education and training of those procedures. Some precautions and procedures are a matter of common sense. Most people will not walk on a slippery floor if a "Wet Floor" sign is posted. As a technician, you will want to keep your work area relatively neat so as not to hamper other workers or potentially cause an accident. You want to make sure to practice good **cable management** where no cables cause a trip hazard (as well as the good network cable management techniques mentioned in Chapter 14). If an accident does occur, do the following:

> Immediately notify medical personnel if needed.
> Report the incident to a supervisor.
> The supervisor must complete an incident report (see Figure 19.1).

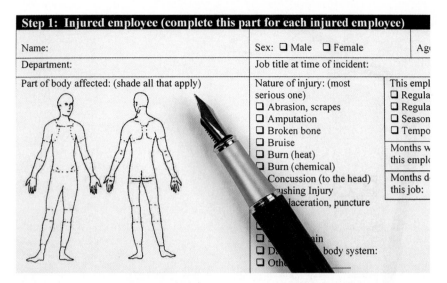

FIGURE 19.1 Incident report

OSHA

Occupational Safety and Health Administration (**OSHA**) is a division of the Federal Department of Labor. OSHA promotes safe and healthy working conditions by enforcing standards and providing workplace safety training. In addition to OSHA, the Environmental Protection Agency (EPA) standards and local government regulations recognize that workplace environments should be free of harmful and/or hazardous chemicals or situations. If harmful or hazardous agents are essential to the manufacturer's productivity, then appropriate precautions should be in place to work with these substances.

An important form required by OSHA is the material safety data sheet (**MSDS**), which outline handling, storage procedures, disposal, and first aid on all potentially harmful or hazardous substances that you may come in contact with while working. Because MSDSs are available to employees, anyone working with these substances should review this important information. A similar form is the safety data sheet (**SDS**) that outlines similar information regarding chemicals.

Fire Safety

It is a rare occurrence when an electrical fire happens in a computer, but one must have **electrical fire safety** knowledge if it does. If a fire occurs inside a computer or peripheral, unplug the equipment if possible, but do not put yourself in harm's way attempting to do this. A **Type C** or a **Type A-B-C fire extinguisher** can be used to put out the fire. Type C fire extinguishers are made specifically for electrical (Type C) fires. Type A-B-C fire extinguishers can be used for Class A, Class B, and Class C fires. Here's some quick information about classes of fires:

> Class A fires involve paper, wood, cloth, or other normal combustibles.
> Class B fires involve flammable liquids and gases.
> Class C fires involve electrical or electronic equipment.

It is a good idea to have a dry chemical 20 pound A-B-C fire extinguisher in homes for the electronics (including computers) located there. Home computer equipment should be listed on the home insurance policy. Figure 19.2 shows a Type A-B-C fire extinguisher.

FIGURE 19.2 Fire extinguisher

When dealing with an electronic device that is on fire, if possible without harming yourself, unplug the device. Remember, though, that with an electrical fire, smoke is a breathing hazard. Burning plastics produce lethal toxic fumes. Always evacuate the people in the building and call the fire department.

In order to use a Type A-B-C or a Type C fire extinguisher, use the following steps:

Step 1. Pull out the fire extinguisher pin (see Figure 19.3).

Step 2. Aim the fire extinguisher nozzle at the base (bottom) of the fire.

Step 3. Squeeze the fire extinguisher handle and move the nozzle back and forth in a slow sweeping motion.

FIGURE 19.3 Pull fire extinguisher pin

A Review of Safety Equipment in the Technical Field Kit

Let us examine three important simple and inexpensive products which should be an essential part of your technical field kit. Your **personal protective equipment** (PPE) should consist of safety goggles or glasses, latex or non-latex (neoprene) or nitrile powder-free gloves, and a dust mask/air filter mask. All of these items can be purchased at most hardware, drug, and grocery stores.

Safety goggles or glasses (see Figure 19.4) protect precious eyes from injury or irritation due to metal chips, wires, sparks, dust, airborne particles, debris, or any type of liquids or contaminants that might be in the working environment. Even though prescription eyeglasses provide some protection, it is wise to have a pair of safety glasses or goggles that will fit over your prescription eyeglasses.

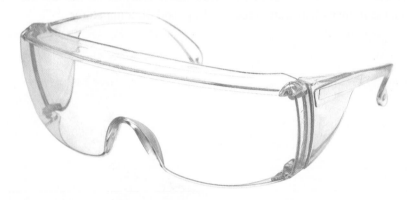

FIGURE 19.4   Safety goggles

Wearing powder-free **gloves** (see Figure 19.5) while working on electronic equipment is recommended for the following reasons:

> Prevents the transference of oils, grime, dirt, and food residue from your hands onto the component parts
> Prevents fingerprints on electronic parts that can hamper connectivity
> Keeps your hands safe from particulates that may come from any task performed
> Presents a professional image in that you care enough about the client's equipment to take precautions

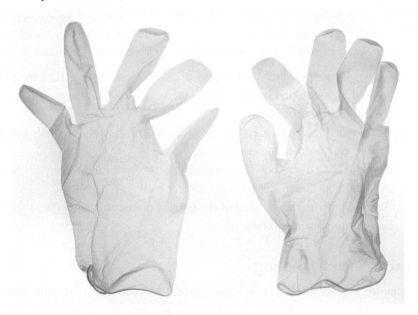

FIGURE 19.5   Gloves

Most technicians wear disposable gloves. Always remember to dispose of the gloves after your task is completed. Some people have a latex allergy or even a skin reaction to latex or to the powder used to coat the inside of the gloves. The common symptoms include itching, dryness, burning, and scaling of the skin. More serious reactions include hives and hay-fever-like symptoms. If in doubt, always wear the powder-free non-latex (neoprene) or nitrile gloves.

Some situations such as working with laser toners require that you wear a **dust mask** or an **air filter mask** to prevent inhalation of harmful airborne particulates, smoke, perfumes, odors, and fumes. When you use **compressed air**, dust and debris are an issue. Simply removing the cover from something that needs vacuuming poses a hazard. Use a vacuum when you can to remove dust and debris, but if in doubt, wear the mask. Dust masks like the one shown in Figure 19.6 are available in many hardware, grocery, drug, and discount stores.

FIGURE 19.6   Dust mask

Personal Safety

Personal and equipment safety is paramount in IT. Having proper personal safety precautions and equipment will facilitate a smoother repair task by getting you into a routine of automatically putting on safety glasses or goggles, vinyl gloves, and a dust mask (when applicable). It will lessen the chance of electrostatic discharge, of forgetting a repair step, or of a careless mishap because your safety procedures will become second nature to you. Other important things to remember follow:

> Remove jewelry, watches, dangling necklaces/earrings, or ID lanyards that could get caught, hooked, or entangled in the equipment.
> Disconnect power cords.
> Be sure that the work area is clear of liquids (coffee, soda, water bottles) and foods that may spill or contaminate the equipment.
> Remember to use good lifting techniques (use your legs, not your back) and be conscious of the 40- to 50-pound weight limit. (Refer back to Chapter 1.)
> Be familiar with the location of the nearest fire extinguisher (see Figure 19.2) with the nearest fire exit in your workplace.

Toxic Waste Handling

Technology is advancing at lightning speed. Mankind is frantically trying to keep up with the latest inventions. The human population is increasing exponentially, our landfills are growing, and our resources are decreasing. Much awareness has been raised in the past few decades about "going green," and the "re-use, recycle, and refill" movement is practiced in many communities. Collectively, as a society, we can make a huge impact. Individually, we can make a difference by being a good steward of our resources. Toxic waste handling does not apply only to oil spills, manufacturing plant chemical spills, pesticides, and other contaminants that pollute our land and waters; it also applies to electronic devices. **Toxic waste handling** is how you deal with things that can harm you and/or the environment. The physical parts, pieces, and batteries of computers, laser printers, and mobile devices must be handled carefully—especially the battery—if the unit suffers damage.

Environmental Impacts

Every state and many cities have specific guidelines about how to dispose of electronics or e-waste (see Figure 19.7). These rules must be followed by technicians who replace broken computer equipment. If you are unsure about how to get rid of any piece of broken electronic equipment, contact your direct supervisor for instructions.

FIGURE 19.7 E-waste

The following list provides alternatives and suggestions for being environmentally conscious about discarding electronics:

> Donate equipment that is operational to schools and charities so that those who do not have access to technology can get some exposure. If the operating system is not transferred to another system, leave the operating system on, and provide proof of purchase along with documentation. Also, do not forget to erase all data stored on the computer before donating it.

> Recycle outdated electronics. If the devices are so outdated that a school or charity cannot use them, consider recycling. Many companies accept old electronics and have determined ways to reuse some of their parts.

> Remove parts that do work and donate or recycle them.

> Buy electronics that are designed to save resources and are easy to upgrade. Extend their usefulness by ensuring they are energy efficient. They will also be more useful if they contain fewer toxins, use recycled materials, and have leasing or recycling programs.

> Check with the computer or component manufacturer to see if it has a recycling program. Most of them do.

Computer Disposal/Recycling

Computers and other electronic devices contain materials such as beryllium, chromium, cadmium, lead, mercury, nickel, and zinc. The levels of these materials increase dramatically every year in landfills and can pose a threat to our environment. Plastics that are part of computers are hard to isolate and recycle, but many electronic parts can be recycled.

Cathode ray tubes (**CRTs**) (see Figure 19.8) are found in older displays, and TVs usually contain enough lead and mercury to be considered hazardous waste. However, the EPA has been successful in obtaining exclusions from the federal hazardous waste standards for unbroken CRTs so that they can be recycled more effectively. In Florida and New York, steps have been taken to increase CRT recycling; however, other states regulate all CRTs as hazardous waste and ban them from being sent to landfills.

FIGURE 19.8 CRT monitor

A **battery** produces DC voltage through a chemical reaction within the battery. Batteries contain acids that can potentially burn or hurt body parts. Batteries can introduce lead and acid into the environment; thus, they need to be recycled (see Figure 19.9). Heavy metals can leach into the ground and water sources. Use proper personal protection equipment such as safety goggles or gloves (see Figure 19.10) when handling batteries.

Lithium-ion (**Li-ion) batteries** found in mobile devices and laptops may need to be replaced in the following cases:

> The device has been subjected to extreme temperature changes.
> The device was dropped, crushed, or flooded with liquid.
> The device has sustained up to 500 cycles of discharge and recharge.

The contents of a Lithium-ion battery are under pressure; thus, Li-ion batteries can explode or catch on fire (see Figure 19.11) if subjected to high temperatures. If you see a bulging Li-ion battery, hear one hiss, or feel one that is overheated, immediately move the device away from anything that might catch on fire. If possible, remove the battery and put it in a safe fireproof place if possible. If it catches on fire, use a foam or an A-B-C fire extinguisher. If on a train or plane, you might see the attendant use water because a Li-ion battery has very little lithium metal that would react with water.

FIGURE 19.9   Battery recycling

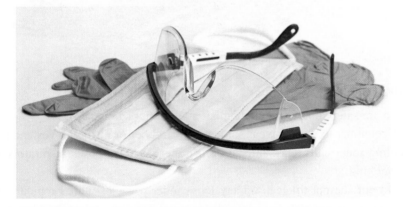

FIGURE 19.10   Personal protection equipment

FIGURE 19.11   Li-ion battery on fire

Recycling all batteries is important. The recommended method of disposal is to recycle the battery at a regulated station. Refer to your local municipality's regulations for recycling and disposing of a Li-ion battery.

Toner Safety and Disposal

Toner found in laser printer toner cartridges is not earth-friendly. According to TonerRecycle.net, it is estimated that more than half of all toner cartridges go into the regular trash; it takes approximately 1,000 years for a print cartridge to fully decompose.

Toner is also not human friendly. If you accidently inhale toner, you could have headaches, eye irritation, itching, and other side effects that are longer lasting. If you accidently come in contact with it, toner can cause itchiness and skin irritation. Figure 19.12 shows some spilled toner.

FIGURE 19.12   Spilled toner

Here are safety pointers to remember about toner safety:

> Remember to always wear some type of rubber or nitrile gloves and a dust mask when handling toner cartridges. Inhalation of toner particles poses respiratory damage equivalent to smoking.

> Do not attempt to clean up any loose toner particles with a regular vacuum sweeper as the toner particles may seep into the vacuum's motor and melt. Always use a high-efficiency particulate air (HEPA) vacuum bag in the vacuum cleaner.

> Allow the printer (and cartridge) to cool before repairing or replacing. The fusing assembly and heated toner can cause severe burns. You should wait after copying or printing before doing any service or removing a toner cartridge.

Proper Component Handling and Storage

Proper handling and storage of electronic parts and equipment will reduce the chance of an electrostatic discharge (ESD). ESD is sneaky. It damages, weakens, and destroys electronic equipment—often without the technician being aware. Atmospheric conditions play a part in ESD in that the potential for ESD is greater when the humidity is low. Anti-static bags for storage, ESD straps and mats for repair jobs, and self-grounding knowledge and techniques are all discussed in Chapter 5. Let's do a brief review.

> Remember to use **anti-static bags** for storing adapters and motherboards when not in use for an extended period of time. Date the bags as a reminder to change them out after a few years as their protective quality diminishes.

> When repairing a computer, wear an anti-static strap, **ESD strap**, and/or heel strap to prevent ESD (see Chapter 5). Caution: The voltages are very high on a CRT monitor (even unplugged) and within a high voltage power supply of a laser printer. Do not attempt to work on either one unless you have special training.

> Place a computer that is being repaired on an **ESD mat**. Some mats have a snap to fasten an anti-static wrist strap to it.

> If an anti-static wrist strap or anti-static heel strap is not available, it is recommended that after removing the external case, you rest your non-dominant arm on an unpainted metal part, leaving your dominant hand free to work the component parts. This **self-grounding** method is an effective way of keeping both the tech and the computer at the same voltage potential. You will have, of course, previously disconnected the power supply to the computer.

Electronic Safety—Equipment Grounding

Equipment grounding is important with any piece of electronic equipment. **Equipment grounding** means that the components in a device such as a computer are at the same voltage potential. This is important to personal safety because a consistent grounding minimizes the potential of voltages being applied to places where it shouldn't be, such as the case. If a piece of equipment is not grounded, someone could receive a shock or electrocution simply by touching it (see Figure 19.13). Review Chapter 5 for more information about power and grounding.

FIGURE 19.13 Electrical shock

Electronic Safety—Power Protection

As mentioned in Chapter 5, power is critical to any equipment working, but it is also hazardous. Two adverse AC power conditions that can damage a computer are overvoltage (a spike or a surge) and undervoltage (a brownout, a sag, or a blackout). Devices such as a surge suppressor (protector), line conditioner, uninterruptible power supply (UPS), and standby power supply (SPS) can help. Here's a recap:

> A **surge suppressor** (protector) is a device that can be connected to a computer to protect against power surges and should be a routine piece of equipment for all computers (see Figure 19.14). The theory behind surge protection is to provide a path of least resistance so that excess electrical surges are directed somewhere beside the devices connected to the surge strip. During a severe thunderstorm, however, even these devices have been fried. The best insurance is always to unplug the main power source to the electronics when they will not be used for an extended period of time or in the event of a storm or power outage. When power is restored, there could be a sharp rise in power that could damage electronics.

FIGURE 19.14   Surge suppressor

> A **line conditioner** (power conditioner) is more expensive than surge suppressors. It protects computers from overvoltages, undervoltages, and electrical line noise by monitoring AC electricity. If the voltage is too low, the line conditioner increases the voltage to the required need. If the voltage is too high, the line conditioner restricts the voltage until the proper level is reached.

> An uninterruptible power supply (**UPS**) or standby power supply (SPS) provides power to a computer or other electronics when there has been a brownout or a power outage. The UPS provides time for the PC to save work and safely power down because power is provided from a battery. Chapter 5 covers more information on this.

Battery Backup

Battery backup provides power to the computer when a brownout or blackout occurs. Many types of standby battery backup products are available, are reasonably priced, and are efficient at saving data in the event of a power failure. Battery backup for a computer is provided by a UPS or an SPS. The amount of time provided depends on the size of the battery and the number and type of devices attached.

Laser printers should not be plugged into a battery backup. Why? It is because the voltages inside the laser printer are usually too high for the UPS to handle (especially the initial surge).

Protecting Equipment from Airborne Pollutants

The EPA's Clean Air Act sets National Ambient Air Quality Standards (NAAQS) for pollutants. **Particulate matter** (PM)—airborne particle pollution—is among these. The EPA works with regional partners in the state and local air quality agencies to ensure that the required safety standards are met. PM can be extremely detrimental to humans causing respiratory problems and to environmental health causing loss of visibility through haze or smog. PM is also detrimental to computer equipment. Humidity, sea-spray, fog, dust, smoke from brushfires, motorized vehicles and machinery, incinerators and various industrial processes are all harmful to sensitive computer equipment.

Some companies utilize an enclosure assembly (**environmental enclosure**) for desktops or laptops to protect parts from PM. These are cases constructed to house the computer while allowing access to operate keyboards, mice, flash drives, etc., without PM contaminating the equipment.

Computer enclosures can also be purchased that protect equipment from drop or weather conditions. Kiosks commonly contain a lockable chamber for the computer contained within. Vendors that supply the military might frequently be required to provide a model that has extra protection for the screen or the entire device. Some vendors target the civilian market with similar "rugged" models or enclosures designed for youngsters. Figure 19.15 shows a computer case designed for a rugged environment.

FIGURE 19.15   Rugged industrial computer enclosure

Other companies may employ an environmental enclosure known as a clean room. A **clean room** (see Figure 19.16) is a specifically constructed, climate-controlled (cool temperature and humidity of 45% to 60%) closed area with special air vents/filters, vacuums, blowers and a circulation system that capture harmful/hazardous particulate matter, scrub and diffuse the PM, and safely eliminate it while allowing the sensitive computer equipment to run.

FIGURE 19.16   Clean room

Temperature and Humidity Control

Computers generate heat; many units together warrant having a cooler ambient room temperature—whether it is in a clean room or in a classroom. High levels of humidity can cause computer equipment to short-circuit because the moisture corrodes the contact points and interrupts connectivity. Dust and debris abrade, plug, and smother connection points and retard or interrupt flow of electricity.

Temperature and humidity are both important in the care and operation of computers and PCs. For example, if a laptop is left outside in a car overnight in the winter and brought inside to a warm area in the morning, condensation will most likely form inside the case. Over time, this would reduce the effectiveness of the connectivity points. It could also cause it not to boot properly when first turned on.

Proper ventilation is important on any electronic device. Check to make sure that the unit's fan is not blocked. Heat generated from an electronic device, if not properly ventilated, can cause overheating and damage to the unit. Refer to Chapter 5 for more information on temperature and humidity control.

Review of Troubleshooting Theory

Troubleshooting is an invaluable skill that you will hone with experience. The old adage "practice makes perfect" applies to your technical skills. By logically processing academic lessons along with practical hands-on work, your thinking processes and physical machinations refine and store procedures and solutions in your "mind bank." You will mentally shift these different thoughts around—like a jigsaw puzzle—to have them fall into place to resolve a problem. Knowing the right questions to ask and how to draw pertinent answers from your customers begins the technical process of pinpointing the problem and positing a solution. Be sure to always back up your customer's data before physically attempting any repairs to their system(s). This is done by copying all data from your customer's hard disk onto another disk or sending it to cloud storage. Always verify with the customer:

> The date of the most recent backup
> Data content and integrity of backup
> The location (physical or virtual) where backup data is stored

If no backup access is available or you are unable to create a backup, it is wise practice to ask your customer to sign a liability release waiver. This will clarify to the customer that permission is being given to work on a device without the safety net of current backup being available, details the work to be done, and releases you (your company) from any liability if their data is corrupted or lost.

Step 1: Identify the Problem—Question the User/Perform Backups

Talk *with* the customer, not to the customer. Listen and allow the customer to explain the problem as the person perceives it to be. Prompt him with open-ended questions such as, "What sounds or lights appear when _____ happens?" Identify how many users are affected. See if you can get the user to show you the problem. Identify any user changes to the computer or device and perform backups before making changes.

Take detailed notes as you are gathering information (see Figure 19.17). This physically documents the problem, creates a log, and helps you mentally process it. In the event that another technician may have to step in, he or she will be able to more readily define a solution because of the good information. And, there will be documentation available to refer back to in the future should other problems arise.

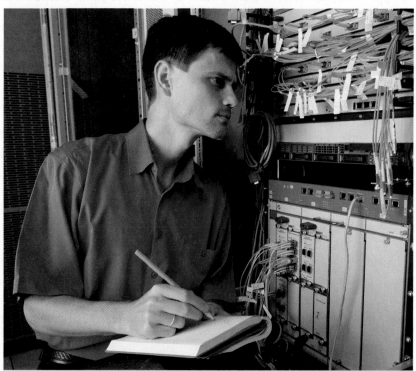

FIGURE 19.17 Take detailed notes when identifying the problem

Step 2: Establish a Theory of Probable Cause (Question the Obvious)

After questioning the user and identifying the problem, such as the computer will not boot, you have to establish one or more theories of what might cause that particular problem. First, rule out the obvious trouble-making causes. You might have to conduct external or internal research. For example, if this is an ongoing problem, ask for any previous documentation to review. You might have to research if others have had the same problem with a particular device model. In this, you might have several theories of what might have caused the problem.

Step 3: Test Your Theory to Determine the Cause

In this step, you need to segment the problem into manageable portions to determine specific causes. Try to prove the theory/theories you developed in Step 2. If the computer wouldn't boot, you might check the power supply, power source, cords, and connectors. Be like Sherlock Holmes and reason out the problem.

Once a theory is confirmed, you determine the next steps to resolve the problem. For example, you find out for sure no DC voltage is coming out of the power supply. You proved your theory that the power supply might be bad.

If one of your theories is not confirmed, you must re-establish a new theory or test one of your other theories. Remember that after all of your theories have been tested, you might need to escalate the problem to a higher level technician. If tier-level support is not in your company, you may have to get help from your supervisor.

Step 4: Establish Your Plan of Action and Implement It

So once you have tested your theory and have that theory confirmed (such as the example that your power supply isn't outputting voltage, but power going into it is good), it is time to establish your plan of action and implement it. In this example, it would mean obtaining a replacement power supply and installing it. Remember that communication is key in this step. Communicate with the user the plan of action and the timeline for the plan. This may require a follow-up email or phone call.

Step 5: Verify Full System Functionality and if Applicable, Implement Preventive Measures

Verifying that the problem has been resolved frequently involves the user trying to do whatever it was that the technician couldn't do before. Sometimes this might mean training the user or putting a new application in place. An example of this is when malware causes some issue on the computer. After removing the malware and possibly restoring data, you might have to install some antimalware software and/or train the user on security. Users get frustrated with technicians closing a problem and saying it is solved without checking with the users to ensure they believe the system is functioning properly or proving to them that it is functioning properly. Make sure that your customer is satisfied with the repair job before you leave.

Step 6: Document Findings, Actions, and Outcomes

All technicians are required to document the issue, the resolution, and even recommendations given to the customer. Historical documentation is important when solving problems especially if another+ technician has to come after you. Chapter 12 has more information on these troubleshooting steps. Return to it for a refresher.

COMMUNICATION SKILLS

Proper communication cannot be stressed enough, no matter where you are or what situation you are in. Good communication skills are priceless. Throughout history, battles have begun because of miscommunication; feuds have been fought because of a careless comment. Many good relationships falter and/or disintegrate because people don't know how to communicate with one another. A poorly worded communication, an off-hand remark, a facial or hand gesture—these may all be misinterpreted by the receiver and the sender is none the wiser that he has just offended someone. Let's explore some areas in which your job as a computer technician will involve good communication skills.

Customer Service

What comes to mind when you hear those two words? A feeling of security and confidence? Or, a rising panic accompanied with a fervent search for antacids and aspirin? On your side? Or, on your customer's? Being of service to others is very rewarding, educational, and fun! Be the best customer service representative that you envision a customer service person to be. You have the skills and training to be tops! Let Figure 19.18 inspire you as a computer technician!

FIGURE 19.18 *Customer service inspiration*

You can set the tone and instill assurance by being the confident, caring professional that you've trained to become. You are the expert. You know more about computer problems than the customers and they are looking to you to solve their problems. You have many avenues of tracking down solutions. Don't be shy about tackling new things. Stretch yourself. Allow new situations to be learning opportunities. Step out of your comfort zone as illustrated in Figure 19.19.

When you have been called in to fix a company's computer, have your ID badge visible. Introduce yourself and state your business. Ask to speak to the person in charge of the device and wait until you are invited or escorted to the work area. Some customers like to hover – out of curiosity, safety concerns, boredom, insecurity, or for any reason. Don't let that bother you. That may be their personal thing. Reassure your customers that you are working diligently on their problem and are taking care of them. Other clients will disappear and you won't have any interaction with them the entire time you're working. As long as you have their contact information, no problem. Focus on the task at hand.

FIGURE 19.19 Comfort zone/opportunity

Use Proper Language

Always address customers by their title: Dr. Schmidt, Mr. Schmidt, Director Durrence, Miss Hannah, Your Honor, Officer Young, Professor Brauda, and so on. Most dictionaries have a section in the back which lists titles and proper forms of address. Mind your manners.

Grooming

Be neat, clean, and well groomed. Wear clean clothes and good shoes. Wear proper-fitting attire because technicians have to get in hard-to-reach places at times (see Figure 19.20). Employ good hygiene. Wash your hands and brush your teeth at least twice daily. Carry breath mints. Do you have dandruff? Do you smoke? Did you just enjoy a spicy lunch? Do a self-check before meeting a customer so as not to offend anyone or embarrass yourself or the customer (see Figure 19.21).

FIGURE 19.20 Dress appropriately

FIGURE 19.21　Bad breath

　　You are your most valuable asset. Take care of your body, mind, and spirit. Your inner self will be reflected outward. Dress like the professional that you are. Always have clean hands when handling someone else's property. Never pick up or handle anything if you've been eating, drinking, or have just applied hand cream. This can leave a residue which might not come off. Go sparingly on colognes, hair sprays, perfumes, and scented lotions as some people have a reaction to the smells—spiking migraines, coughing episodes, and breathing problems. Some cosmetics are also scented and may be the instigator of a discomforting episode.

Be Organized

Be able to flip open your case and pull out exactly what tool or paperwork that you need. Not only does being organized save time, frustration and, ultimately, money, it instills confidence in both your client and you. Rate yourself on organization skills (see Figure 19.22) and make it a goal. Plus, a messy, fumbling technician would not present a very good impression. Before going on a service call or calling a customer, have all of the relevant parts, paperwork, tools, etc., organized and easy to locate.

　　Pick up after yourself and leave the area as clean as or cleaner than it was before you arrived. Reassure your customers that you are working diligently and systematically on their problem. You are taking care of them. Focus on the task at hand. If you like to listen to music while you work, mention to your customer that you are not ignoring him—that is just how you work best.

FIGURE 19.22 Organization measure

Use Proper Language

Use no slang, no profanity, and no jargon. Avoid acronyms (an acronym is a group of words describing something, such as SCUBA = **S**elf **C**ontained **U**nderwater **B**reathing **A**pparatus, or a sentence to help remind you of something specific, such as the laser printer steps = **P**rocessing, **C**harging, **E**xposing, **D**eveloping, **T**ransferring, **F**using and **C**leaning = **P**eople **C**an't **E**xpect **D**ummies **T**o **F**ix **C**omputers). Every profession/industry has its own vernacular so be conscious of using "geek speak" (see Figure 19.23). You want to be careful so as not to confuse or possibly intimidate your customer.

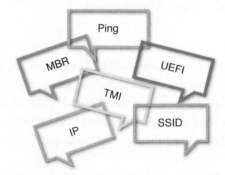

FIGURE 19.23 Avoid "geek speak"

Polish up on your grammar skills. The following is not allowed: "Don't them look good?" or "I seen it doing this." Please use, "Don't they look good?" or "I saw it doing this." Do not use double negative sentences, such as "I don't got no paper with me." Brush up on your spelling and punctuation skills. Understand and properly use words such as too, two, and to; there, they're, and their; lie versus lay; and so on. Write your reports in complete sentences. Type your email in a word processing application to get grammar suggestions. Then, paste the sentences into the email or technical support problem logging application.

Maintain a Positive Attitude—Project Confidence

Walk through the door with a purpose and a smile! Stand up straight, shoulders back with your head held high. Offer your hand in friendship. Emphasize your customer's value with kindness, respect, and gratitude! Project confidence! The customer will be relieved to see you.

In many IT jobs, there is more work than time. Technicians must constantly be juggling to keep up with it all. Make sure you take allowed breaks and do non-technical things. If you are sitting in an office, greet and acknowledge the person as soon as possible. Use a phone or a tablet to keep reminders for the day. If you are going to be late, call the person and let him know (see Figure 19.24). Many customers will rearrange their schedule and tasks to be available when the technician is coming. Courteous promptness will be rewarded.

FIGURE 19.24   I'm waiting

Actively Listen

Listen attentively and maintain good eye contact. The customer will tell you what he or she wants. Take notes. If using an electronic tablet, explain to your customer that you are entering information about the problem to help you speculate on a solution. Be up front and let the customer see what you are doing.

Avoid interrupting the customer. Don't assume anything. Avoid finishing your customer's sentences—it could be perceived that you are rushing your customer (see Figure 19.25). Ask open-ended questions such as "How long has this message been popping up?" or "Have you been to any new/different websites lately?" or "Who else has access to your computer?" After the customer has explained the problem, repeat it back to him or her to make it clear to both of you that you understand the situation. Ask the customer what he or she would like to see happen.

FIGURE 19.25 Hatchet in monitor

Be Culturally Sensitive

Take the time to know your customers. Understand and accept that there will be differences among all people (see Figure 19.26) and it is not your place to judge. Be aware of things that you may do that may be offensive to them. Always try to put yourself in their shoes. If in doubt, ask your customer questions discreetly. Be aware of any facial expressions, hand gestures, or body movements that may be deemed offensive or insulting. If the customer is doing something that you find offensive, you can politely ask her to stop. For example, if someone feels compelled to tell you a joke or anecdote that is degrading, belittling, or humiliating to another person, immediately ask that person to stop. If the behavior continues, you could say, "I'm trying to do a professional job here and I am offended by that."

FIGURE 19.26 Diversity

Be on Time

It is better to be 10 minutes early than 5 minutes late. If something causes you to be late in reaching your next appointment at the agreed time, call that customer as soon as possible. Customers commonly get angry (see Figure 19.27) and calling ahead gives them time to adjust. If you have kept your customer waiting—whether on the phone or in person—apologize, ask if you may go ahead with the work, and thank the customer. Be gracious.

FIGURE 19.27   Lateness can cause angry customers

Time Management

Time management is how much time you budget and then actually spend on doing each task throughout the workday. IT personnel tend to have busy schedules (see Figure 19.28). Be aware of how you might be better at time management and the things that contribute to time management as shown in Figure 19.29.

FIGURE 19.28 Time management

FIGURE 19.29 Time management components

Always remember that you are a paid employee and time is money to the company. If you encounter a chatty person, politely explain that you are on your company's billable hours (see Figure 19.30). Emphasize that you like to stay on schedule for all of your customers and it's best for you to stay on task. Steer the customer towards talking about the problem at hand in a constructive way. For example, if the person is frustrated and is just blowing off steam, politely suggest that perhaps a break or a drink of water might help. This would allow some cooling-off time for the client and alone time for you to work. If the person becomes confrontational, it may be a good time for you to take a break.

FIGURE 19.30   Billable hours

Avoid Distractions

Give your customer your undivided attention. Be in the moment. Here are some best practices:

> Turn off your cell phone or switch to vibrate mode so that you are not interrupted with personal or professional calls.
> Save looking at social media sites and doing any texting until you have finished with your customer.
> Avoid talking to co-workers while interacting with a client.
> Avoid gossiping.
> Avoid personal interruptions.
> Avoid checking your watch, drumming your fingers, yawning, rolling your eyes, sighing, and so on.

Chief complaints from customers are that they feel ignored, not listened to or taken seriously, passed over or put aside, or kept waiting. Do what you can to ensure they don't feel this way. Smile with your eyes as well as your mouth. Be pleasant, but not condescending. Avoid regaling your customers with your own personal life and all its glories and dramas. Remember that the customer is concerned about the immediate problem. This doesn't mean that small talk is off-limits. Just remember to keep it appropriate and professional.

Don't Make Commitments You Can't Keep

Part of your being professional is integrity. Keep the subjects between your customer and you business-like and relevant to the job. Even though the tone is light in Figure 19.31, the point is to be professional and take your job seriously. Do not be flippant.

"The computer repair people
take their job very seriously."

FIGURE 19.31   Be professional

Do not make off-handed promises hoping to appease your client and don't make commitments you can't keep. It is much better to say "I am not sure how long this will take, cost, and so on," or "I am not qualified in that particular area, but I can check on that for you and get back to you." Don't be afraid to call someone else for help. For example, if the problem you see is out of your area of expertise, call up someone more experienced. Many companies have tiers of technical support. There is probably someone senior or a manager that can offer you some advice after you have exhausted the research and resources you have.

Dealing with a Difficult Customer or Situation

When you are faced with an uncomfortable situation, above all remember to breathe deeply and slowly. Not only will this provide your brain with oxygen-enriched blood, it will give you a moment to think and compose yourself before you answer. Here are some suggestions for dealing with difficult customers:

> Let the customer talk.
> Hold good eye contact and give physical affirmation cues, i.e., nodding your head "yes."
> Do not ever tell someone to "calm down." That is akin to scoffing and saying, "You don't have a legitimate complaint." In the end, it is like pouring gasoline on a fire—you add to their madness.
> Do not argue with a customer or be defensive. Remember that the customer has been stewing and fuming about this particular problem and wants to tell you every last detail about it. Again, listen to him or her and don't interrupt or try to finish sentences.
> Remind yourself that you have been trained in this field and are the expert. Don't dismiss the customer's problems. Acknowledge that he is understandably upset, frustrated, angry, and so on, and reassure him in a calm, steady voice that you are there to help.
> Avoid being judgmental.
> Be personable yet professional. Replies such as "I'll do my absolute best to help you" or "I'm sorry that this glitch has been so upsetting to you," or "Let's see what I can do for you." can

go a long way in diffusing the situation. This lets the client know that you, yourself, have a hearty interest in her well-being—you are genuinely concerned with helping.

> Be careful not to giggle or laugh inappropriately—the customer may mistakenly think you are making fun of, belittling, or dismissing the problem.

> Avoid laughing constantly while talking. Some people do this—whether out of nervousness or habit—when engaged in conversation. This would most likely cause the other person to wonder what is so humorous about the situation.

> Always keep in mind what your customers want, need, and/or expect from you (or your company).

> Utilize resources that are available to you from which you can pull answers to solve the problem.

> Don't post work-related frustrations or experiences to social media sites.

> Go over and above the expected service.

> Pay attention to detail.

In order to keep the customer focused on the problem at hand, clarify customer statements by asking open-ended questions to narrow the scope of the problem, restating the issue, or asking questions to verify your understanding of the problem. Gently guide the customer by restating the problem and expanding a bit on the description. After the job is complete, be sure to follow up with the customer— again, thanking him or her for the opportunity to serve, and to allow for any questions. Feedback keeps the lines of communication open and flowing between both of you and nurtures an active work relationship which is so vital to good customer service (see Figure 19.32).

FIGURE 19.32   Feedback

If someone is invading your space (getting too close for comfort), try stepping back one step. If she steps in, raise a palm to give the indication for her to stop (see Figure 19.33).

FIGURE 19.33 Stop what you are doing; stay back

If this does not work, stop what you are doing, look the person in the eyes, and politely ask him or her to give you more room. If someone is verbally abusive to you or maybe even potentially physically abusive, step back, and raise a palm (refer back to Figure 19.33). Give both visual and physical clues to keep the situation from escalating. Keep your voice in an even, professional tone. You can always ask that person to take a short break or you can ask to be excused to give her a moment. You have the right to a safe work environment.

Set and Meet Expectations

A customer usually wants to know when his computer will be fixed. As mentioned previously, if you must give him an estimated repair time—estimate a little longer than you anticipate. That way, if you do finish earlier than you expected, you'll both be happy! Discuss and offer different repair or replacement options, if applicable. Keep your customer informed of your progress. A small morsel of information from time to time helps quell the anxiety about an unknown situation ("Here's where we're at now…" or "Just checking in to let you know that…"). This type of response reassures him that something is actively being done to fix the problem. No one likes wondering or waiting. Think back to when you first encountered problems and frustrations when working with a computer. Treat others as you would like to be treated.

Deal Appropriately with Confidential and Private Materials

Discretion is another integral part of professionalism. Remember to be cognizant of all who may be in the area. Keep information private; hardcopies and faxed materials secured in folders—not spread around on a table for any passerby to read. Speak in a manner such that no one else can hear. Keep your laptop and mobile devices password protected. Keep your own personal information private. You wouldn't want a third party to expose your private information, would you?

When working for a client, if you notice what seems to be sensitive information (for example, passwords taped somewhere, documents left in a printer, employee evaluations, and so on), it is best practice to ask the client to remove that information. Also, it is prudent to notify your client if you may have inadvertently seen sensitive information so that the client may change the password, if so desired. If you spot a bad security practice such as a password taped somewhere, use it as an opportunity to talk about security in today's environment.

Never discuss a customer's business or your professional matters to anyone—while sitting in a restaurant, at a public venue, through social media, or even in off-hand conversation (see Figure 19.34). A 1942 American World War II poster by Designer Seymour R. Goff exclaimed, "Loose lips might sink ships" meaning beware of frivolous or unguarded talk—you never know who may be listening.

FIGURE 19.34   Social network

Provide Documentation

At the end of the service call, provide the proper documentation on the services provided. This could include the following:

> Manuals
> Software or hardware boxes and materials that include proof of purchase, UPC codes, activation codes, registration numbers, and warranty information
> Invoice
> Research or information you used in the repair that might benefit the customer
> Service ticket with details of work performed

Closing Remarks

No IT person is perfect. All that can be done is to strive to be the best professional possible. Try to do the right thing, be professional, be honest, and apologize if you are in the wrong. People will recognize that you are doing the best you can. Keep learning. Even if you are in the same job, there are new technologies and areas that you can improve upon.

Good luck to each of you in your IT profession! It is a wonderful field and there are always opportunities to slide into something new. An inspiring quotation to leave you with comes from Vincent van Gogh, "Your profession is not what brings home your weekly paycheck. Your profession is what you're put here on earth to do with such passion and such intensity that it becomes spiritual in calling."

Chapter Summary

> Three of the most important items in your technician kit should be safety goggles, vinyl or nitrile gloves, and a dust mask/air filter mask. These are your PPE.

> You have the right to expect a safe workplace environment. Federal government agencies such as OSHA and the EPA work hand in hand with state and local governments to regulate, enforce, and promote safe work practices—both for the individual and for the environment.

> A good computer technician knows how to recycle and/or dispose of electronic waste (specifically how to handle computers PCs, batteries, toner cartridges, and CRT monitors), and understands the importance this makes to the health of humans and to the environment.

> The federal government (OSHA, EPA) works in tandem with state municipalities and their local government regulations to monitor environmental impacts of toxic waste. Batteries, mobile devices, computers, and printers all contain toxic heavy metals (cadmium, lead, mercury) that when tossed into landfills can leach out into the surrounding soil and water. Most municipalities have an electronic waste recycling/disposal toxic waste handling site that is county/parish regulated in each state. Never attempt to dispose of any toxic electronic waste by burning (such as in a bonfire or a burning barrel). Never lay heavy items on top of electronic equipment. Never crush or puncture any device that contains a battery as this can cause leakage of heavy metals or chemicals.

> The six steps of troubleshooting are 1) identify the problem, 2) establish a theory, 3) test the theory, 4) establish a plan of action, 5) verify full system functionality and implement preventative measures, and 6) document findings, actions, outcomes, and feedback with the customer.

> Proper communication and positive interaction with customers is a must. Use no profanity, street-talk, or slang. Address customers by their title and surname.

> Attentiveness to customers means good eye-contact, listening actively, not interrupting or finishing the customer's sentences, taking detailed notes.

> Keep personal business and activities out of the work place.

> Hygiene, appearance, manners, and confidence are important traits to possess.

> Look, act, dress, and think like a professional and you will be.

A+ CERTIFICATION EXAM TIPS

✓ The 902 exam has an examination section for operational procedures. Everything in this chapter relates to those objectives except for section 5.3. This information is found in Chapter 18.

✓ Communication techniques and professionalism key areas include the following: use proper language; maintain a positive attitude; project confidence; actively listen; avoid interrupting the customer; be culturally sensitive; use appropriate titles; be on time; avoid distractions, be able to deal with a difficult customer or situation (don't argue or be defensive, don't be dismissive regarding the problem, avoid being judgmental); clarify customer statements with open-ended questions; set and meet expectations/timeline; communicate the status with the customer; provide proper documentation; and deal appropriately with customer's confidential and private information.

✓ Know the six steps of the troubleshooting theory and be able to explain them: (1) Identify the problem. (2) Establish a theory of probable cause (question the obvious). (3) Test the theory to determine the cause. Once confirmed, determine next steps to resolve the problem. If the theory is not confirmed, re-establish the theory or escalate the problem to a higher level of support technician. (4) Establish a plan of action to resolve the problem and implement the solution. (5) Verify full system functionality and, if applicable, implement preventive measures. (6) Document findings, actions, and outcomes.

✓ And last but not least, at this point you've learned every topic that is covered on the CompTIA A+ exams, now take some time to prepare specifically for the certification exams and get the professional credentials you have earned. Refer to the Introduction of this book for details on the two CompTIA A+ exams: 220-901 and 220-902, how to sign up for them, etc. And note that Pearson, the publisher of this book, is offering you an exclusive deep discount on several types of certification exam preparation resources. See the Introduction to this book and the advertisement inserts in the back for more details. Take a look at what they have to offer and figure out which resource(s) would work best for your study style. Good luck!

Key Terms

air filter mask 1246	equipment grounding 1251	SDS 1243
anti-static bag 1251	ESD mat 1251	self-grounding 1251
battery 1248	ESD strap 1251	surge suppressor 1252
battery backup 1252	gloves 1245	time management 1263
cable management 1242	Li-ion battery 1248	toner 1250
clean room 1253	line conditioner 1252	toxic waste handling 1247
compressed air 1246	MSDS 1243	Type A-B-C fire
CRT 1248	OSHA 1243	extinguisher 1243
dust mask 1246	particulate matter 1253	Type C fire
electrical fire safety 1243	personal protection	extinguisher 1243
environmental	equipment 1245	UPS 1252
enclosure 1253	safety goggles 1245	

REVIEW QUESTIONS

1. Professionalism involves:

    [skill | training | integrity | discretion | two of the above | all of these]

2. [T | F] Laughing while your customer is explaining a problem is the best way of developing trust.

3. [T | F] People can glean your personal information and potentially work-related information from your unsecured devices and/or papers left out and about.

4. [T | F] Fixing computers for a living means that you don't have to worry about your appearance or hygiene.

5. A computer technician's repair kit should always include which of the following?

    a. Pen, paper, ID badge

    b. Soap, toothbrush, toothpaste

    c. Surge suppressor, laptop enclosure case, re-sealable anti-static bags

    d. Safety glasses/goggles, gloves, dust mask/air filter mask

6. Which of the following is a good rule to follow when dealing with customers?

    a. Demand payment before the job is started.

    b. Get your parking pass validated.

    c. Treat others as you would like to be treated.

    d. Enjoy frequent coffee breaks with them.

7. A repair job is not complete until

    a. your supervisor signs off on it

    b. you follow up to ensure the problem is solved

    c. the work area is clean and tidy

    d. the invoice is paid

8. What is a safety risk related to old or damaged batteries?

    a. They can leak acid.

    b. They can contain lead.

    c. They can contain water.

    d. All sizes are interchangeable.

9. Equipment grounding means which of the following?

    a. The equipment is tethered to the desk.

    b. The components in a computer are all the same potential.

    c. The technician wears a tether device.

    d. Someone could receive a shock or electrocution from simply touching the case.

10. What is best for cleaning up scattered laser toner particles?

    a. Use a hair dryer to blow away the residue.

    b. Use moist paper towels to wipe up particles.

    c. Use your shirt sleeve to make them disappear.

    d. Use a vacuum cleaner equipped with a HEPA filter while wearing your PPE.

11. In what two situations might a Li-ion battery need to be replaced even if it is new? (Choose two.)

    a. It is subjected to extreme temperature changes.

    b. It is stored in a plastic bin filled with white rice.

    c. It is submerged in water.

    d. It is used near high-voltage equipment.

    e. It is used near an approved regulated waste receptacle.

12. Mobile devices, PCs, monitors, and batteries can be disposed of by

    a. burning them in bonfires

    b. dumping them in landfills

    c. depositing into local municipality approved receptacle

    d. calling 911

13. In the event of an electrical fire, which two fire extinguishers would be best? (Choose two.)

    a. Type A fire extinguisher

    b. Type B fire extinguisher

    c. Type C fire extinguisher

    d. Type D fire extinguisher

    e. Type A-B-C fire extinguisher

14. A device that protects electronic equipment from an increase in power, but not a decrease or outage is a _____. [battery backup | surge suppressor | CRT | UPS]

15. When encountering a difficult or confrontational customer, the best thing to do initially is which of the following?

    a. Step back and breathe deeply a few times before responding.

    b. Call a supervisor.

    c. Suggest a short break.

    d. Reschedule the appointment.

16. [T | F] Federal, state, and local governments do not interact with one another concerning toxic waste issues.

17. Particulate matter (PM), such as airborne pollutants, is

    a. harmful only to humans

    b. common in computer components

    c. easily cleaned up

    d. potentially toxic to humans, animals, and environment

18. Laser toner cartridges

    a. are easily recycled anywhere

    b. can be donated to charities

    c. can be refilled many times

    d. must be disposed of in an approved regulated receptacle

19. If no backup data is available or wanted, it is a wise practice to ask your customer to do which of the following?

    a. Power down the system.

    b. Sign a liability release waiver.

    c. Ask permission to add a new hardware device to the computer.

    d. Remove the hard drive or allow you to do so.

20. What is your most valuable asset? [Your education | Your family | Your money | You]

Exercises

Exercise 19.1 Determine the Troubleshooting Theory Step

Objective: To be able to determine which step of the troubleshooting process is occurring

Parts: No parts are needed for this exercise

Procedure: Match one of the six troubleshooting steps to the situation. Note that a particular step may be the answer for more than one situation.

Troubleshooting steps

a. Identify the problem.

b. Establish a theory of probable cause.

c. Test the theory.

d. Establish a plan of action.

e. Verify full functionality.

f. Document findings.

_____   A USB flash drive is not being recognized in a computer. You move the drive to a different USB slot.

_____   You provide the user with the registration/authentication code for the antivirus software that was installed into the computer after a virus was removed.

_____   You ask open-ended questions.

_____   The user explains what has happened in the past few days that was unusual.

_____   You phone the user to ask if the system appears to be running faster since the new memory module was installed.

_____   You order a new motherboard.

_____   You re-enable automatic Windows updates so they get applied in the future and prevent future issues.

_____   You believe that the problem is either the motherboard or processor.

Activities

Internet Discovery

Objective: To obtain specific information on the Internet regarding a computer or its associated parts

Parts: Computer with access to the Internet

Questions: Use the Internet to answer the following questions.

1. Research how to dress professionally for your job. Write three things that impressed you the most about the advice given and whether you found the website helpful or confusing. Write the URL where the information was found.

    _____

    _____

    _____

2. Locate at least two videos of poor technician interaction/service with customers. Compare with the lessons in this book and write how the techs in the videos could improve their skills.

3. Research at least two local municipalities that have approved regulated sites for recycle and disposal of computer and electronic equipment. List what they advise for their communities. Describe differences in their regulations. List the URL for each municipality.

4. Research electrical fire safety videos. Combine the information from this book with what you learn from the fire safety videos. Document what new things were shown. Describe your confidence level for whether or not you feel that you could extinguish an electrical fire. List the URL where your information was found.

5. Research at least five healthy things to do for yourself every day. Decide which ones you'd like to implement. List the URLs where your information was found.

_____

_____

_____

_____

Soft Skills

Objective: To enhance and fine-tune a future technician's ability to listen, communicate in both written and oral form, and support people who use computers in a professional manner.

Activities:

1. Refine your customer skills by play acting situations with another student. One student plays the technician and the other plays the customer. Instead of asking "Did you do _____?" ask "When did you do _____?" "What happened when you did _____?" or "When did you first notice _____?" Rate each other using positive words. You can give negative feedback, but do it in a positive manner. For example, if the person spoke in a low tone, but the words were good, you might give the following as feedback: Your explanation was very good, but I had a hard time hearing you. You might want to speak up just a bit louder.

2. Hone your job interviewing skills by practicing with another student. Be prepared with questions about the company with which you are seeking employment. Think ahead to what questions a prospective employer might ask you.

_____

_____

_____

3. Put students in groups. Allow each group to inspect the fire extinguisher in the room. Have them research electrical fire safety. Then, the group should create a scenario to demonstrate fire safety. Have them become familiar with fire safety signs and EXIT routes for the classroom. Have the group produce an escape route. Each group enacts the scenario and presents their escape route drawing.

4. Have each student build a virtual wardrobe appropriate for his or her future job. Each student should research websites and record individual garment descriptions and prices in a professionally formatted document. Don't forget accessories such as shoes, hats, purses/briefcases, computer bags, etc. Randomly select students to share and discuss why specific items were chosen. Ask for feedback from other students on choices. Optionally place in presentation format.

Critical Thinking Skills

Objective: To analyze and evaluate information as well as apply learned information to new and different situations.

Activities:

1. Break into groups of three students. Each group is given a box containing a laser toner, a CRT monitor, and a battery. Research local municipality regulations regarding recycling and/or disposal of electronic waste. Present findings to the class. Aggregate all groups' findings in table form. Offer to share with the school.

2. Each student engages a specific number of friends/acquaintances (to be provided by the instructor) in a conversation. Ask about and record specific problems they encounter with their mobile devices and laptops. What problem occurs most? What new problem(s) are presented that were unfamiliar to you? What solutions would you offer clients? Record all data in table form and present to the class.

3. Divide into groups of three or four students. Students are given the following information: a local veteran's home has 100 computers and 10 printers; 96 computers and 8 printers are used by the staff, 4 computers and 2 printers are used by the veterans. The computers and printers used by the veterans experience a high rate of downtime. Think of different reasons as to why the veterans' computers and printers are frequently non-functional. Offer at least three solutions to improve the situation.

    _____

    _____

    _____

    _____

    _____

    _____

    _____

    _____

5. Research on the Internet someone who has a computer problem and what she might have done so far. Outline what she did in each troubleshooting theory step and note which steps might have been skipped.

6. Each student must use the Internet to locate a video that features how the computer user did not have good communication skills. List things that were recommended in this chapter that were not addressed or could've been handled differently.

7. What current news stories feature a safety issue that relates to technology?

A Subnetting Basics

In business, the subnet mask assigned to a device commonly is not the default mask based on the class of IP address being used. For example, at a college, the IP address 10.104.10.88 and subnet mask 255.255.255.0 are assigned to a computer. The 10 in the first octet shows that this is a class A IP address. A Class A IP address has a default mask of 255.0.0.0. The 255 in the subnet mask is made up of eight 1s in binary in the first octet (11111111) followed by all 0s in the remaining octets (00000000.00000000.00000000).

The purpose of the subnet mask is to tell you (and the network devices) which portion of the IP address is the network part. The rest of the address is the host portion of the address. The network part of any IP address is the same 1s and 0s for all computers on the network. The rest of the 1s and 0s can change and be unique addresses for the network devices on the same network. The following important rules relate to subnetting:

- The network number *cannot* be assigned to any device on the network.
- The network number contains all 0s in the host portion of the address. Note that this does not mean that the number will be 0 in decimal. This is explained next.
- The broadcast address (the number used to send a message to all devices on the network) *cannot* be assigned to any device on the network.
- The broadcast address contains all 1s in the host portion of the address. Note that this does not mean that the number will be 255 in decimal.

Consider the IP address and mask used as an example before—10.104.10.88 and 255.255.255.0. Put these numbers in binary, one number on top of the other, to see the effects of the subnet mask:

```
    10              104             10              88
 00001010.01101000.00001010.01011000
 11111111.11111111.11111111.00000000
```

The 1s in the subnet mask show which bits in the top row are the network part of the address. The subnet mask is always a row of consecutive 1s. Where the 1s stop is where the network portion of the address stops. Keep in mind that this does not have to be where an octet stops, as in this example. A good technique is to draw a line where the 1s in the subnet mask stop, as shown in the example that follows:

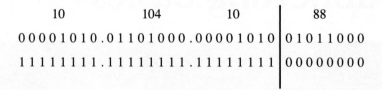

```
       10              104             10    |    88
0 0 0 0 1 0 1 0 . 0 1 1 0 1 0 0 0 . 0 0 0 0 1 0 1 0 | 0 1 0 1 1 0 0 0
1 1 1 1 1 1 1 1 . 1 1 1 1 1 1 1 1 . 1 1 1 1 1 1 1 1 | 0 0 0 0 0 0 0 0
```

At this point, there is no other purpose for the subnet mask. You can get rid of it, as shown in the example that follows:

```
       10              104             10    |    88
0 0 0 0 1 0 1 0 . 0 1 1 0 1 0 0 0 . 0 0 0 0 1 0 1 0 | 0 1 0 1 1 0 0 0
```

All 1s and 0s to the left of the drawn line are the network portion of the IP address. All devices on the same network will have this same combination of 1s and 0s up to the line. All 1s and 0s to the right of the drawn line are in the host portion of the IP address:

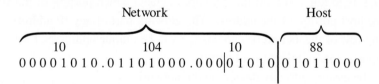

```
              Network                              Host
       10              104             10    |    88
0 0 0 0 1 0 1 0 . 0 1 1 0 1 0 0 0 . 0 0 0|0 1 0 1 0|0 1 0 1 1 0 0 0
```

The network number, the IP address used to represent an entire single network, is found by setting all host bits to 0. The resulting number is the network number:

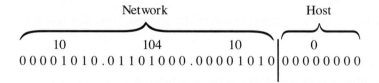

```
              Network                              Host
       10              104             10    |    0
0 0 0 0 1 0 1 0 . 0 1 1 0 1 0 0 0 . 0 0 0 0 1 0 1 0 | 0 0 0 0 0 0 0 0
```

The network number for the network device that has the IP address 10.104.10.88 is 10.104.10.0. To find the broadcast address, the IP address used to send a message to all devices on the 10.104.10.0 network, set all the host bits to 1:

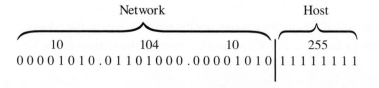

```
              Network                              Host
       10              104             10    |    255
0 0 0 0 1 0 1 0 . 0 1 1 0 1 0 0 0 . 0 0 0 0 1 0 1 0 | 1 1 1 1 1 1 1 1
```

The broadcast IP address is 10.104.10.255 for the 10.104.10.0 network. This means that hosts can be assigned any addresses between the network number 10.104.10.0 and the broadcast address 10.104.10.255. Another way of stating this is that IP addresses 10.104.10.1 through 10.104.10.254 are usable IP addresses on the 10.104.10.0 network.

Consider the IP address 192.168.10.213 and the subnet mask 255.255.255.224 assigned to a computer in a college. What would be the network number and broadcast address for this computer? To find the answer, write 192.168.10.213 in binary octets. Write the subnet mask in binary under the IP address:

```
    192              168             10              213
1 1 0 0 0 0 0 0 . 1 0 1 0 1 0 0 0 . 0 0 0 0 1 0 1 0 . 1 1 0 1 0 1 0 1

1 1 1 1 1 1 1 1 . 1 1 1 1 1 1 1 1 . 1 1 1 1 1 1 1 1 . 1 1 1 0 0 0 0 0
```

Now draw a line where the 1s in the subnet mask stop:

```
    192              168             10              213
1 1 0 0 0 0 0 0 . 1 0 1 0 1 0 0 0 . 0 0 0 0 1 0 1 0 . 1 1 0|1 0 1 0 1

1 1 1 1 1 1 1 1 . 1 1 1 1 1 1 1 1 . 1 1 1 1 1 1 1 1 . 1 1 1|0 0 0 0 0
```

Remove the subnet mask because it is not needed anymore:

```
    192              168             10              213
1 1 0 0 0 0 0 0 . 1 0 1 0 1 0 0 0 . 0 0 0 0 1 0 1 0 . 1 1 0|1 0 1 0 1
```

Set all host bits to 0 to find the network number:

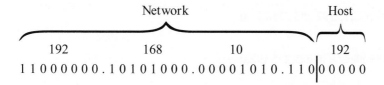

The network number for the network device that has IP address 192.168.10.213 is 192.168.10.192. To find the broadcast address, set all host bits to 1.

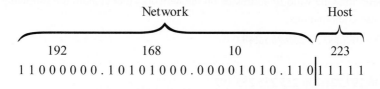

The broadcast address for the network device that has the IP address 192.168.10.213 is 192.168.10.223. Notice how all eight bits are used to calculate the number 223 in the last octet. Valid IP addresses are any numbers between the network number 192.168.10.192 and the broadcast IP address 192.168.10.223. In other words, the range of usable IP addresses is from 192.168.10.193 (one number larger than the network address) through 192.168.10.222 (one number less than the broadcast address). Practice problems in an exercise at the end of this appendix help you explore this concept.

Labs

Lab A.1 Subnet Practice Lab

Objective: To be able to determine the subnet number, broadcast address, and IP addresses that can be assigned to network devices

Parts: None needed

Procedure: Complete the following procedures and answer the accompanying questions.

1.   Determine the network address for the following IP address and subnet mask combinations.

    210.141.254.122 255.255.255.192

    206.240.195.38 255.255.255.224

    104.130.188.213 255.255.192.0

    69.89.5.224 255.240.0.0

    10.113.71.66 255.128.0.0

2.   Determine the broadcast address for the following IP address and subnet mask combinations.

    166.215.207.182 255.255.255.240

    198.94.140.121 255.255.255.224

    97.57.210.192 255.255.224.0

    133.98.227.36 255.255.192.0

    14.89.203.133 255.128.0.0

3.   Determine the valid IP addresses on the networks that contain the following IP address and subnet mask combinations.

    131.107.200.34 255.255.248.0

    146.197.221.238 255.255.255.192

    52.15.111.33 255.255.248.0

    192.168.10.245/30

    209.218.235.117 255.255.255.128

Glossary

Numerals

1.8 inch A storage device form factor.

2.5 inch A storage device form factor.

56Kb/s modem A modem that produces higher transmission speeds and uses traditional phone lines. Actual modem speed is determined by the number of analog to digital conversions that occur through the phone system.

4-PIN 12v Power connector for CPU that is sometimes labeled as AUX.

6-PIN PCIe Power connector for PCIe video adapter.

8-PIN 12v CPU power connector used with an ATX12V v1 power supply.

8-PIN PCIe A video card power connector that is sometimes labeled as a 6 + 2, meaning that the connector can be used with a 6-pin or 8-pin connector.

15-pin SATA power Internal SATA power connector.

20-pin main power Older motherboard power connector.

24-pin main power Main ATX motherboard power connector.

A

AC (alternating current) The type of electrical power from a wall outlet.

AC circuit tester A device that checks a wall outlet's wiring.

accelerometer A technology in mobile devices to detect screen orientation and adapt what is shown on-screen for that viewing mode. A gyroscope measures and maintains that orientation.

access denied Notifies user that user must have specific security rights or be logged on as an Administrator.

access point A component of a wireless network that accepts associations from wireless network cards.

ACL (access control list) A means of providing a security filter where traffic is allowed or denied based on configured parameters.

ACPI (Advanced Configuration and Power Interface) Technology that allows the motherboard and operating system to control the power needs and operation modes of various devices.

active cable A cable with an embedded chip to boost signal strength thus allowing it to be thinner and longer than a passive cable. Used in networks and video systems.

active listening An effective communication technique that ensures what the speaker says is accurately received.

Activity Monitor A troubleshooting tool in an OS X system that sees what processes and services are running, plus what system resources are used.

adapter An electronic circuit card that inserts into an expansion slot. Also called a controller, card, controller card, circuit card, circuit board, and adapter board.

add-ons Extensions or plug-ins that provide a browser additional features such as a toolbar or the capability to dim everything on the screen except for a running video. Add-ons can also cause security risks.

ad hoc wireless printing Enables two 802.11 wireless devices to communicate directly without the use of a wireless access point or a wireless router.

administrative share A share created by Microsoft for drive volumes and the folder that contains the majority of Windows files. An administrative share has a dollar sign at the end of its name.

ADSL (Asymmetrical DSL) A type of digital subscriber line (DSL) that provides speeds up to 150Mb/s; it provides faster downloads than uploads.

Advanced Boot Options A Windows boot menu used to access tools used for troubleshooting. Press `F8` when the computer is booting (and before Windows loads) to access the Advanced Boot Options menu.

Aero   A look and feel for the computing environment in Windows Vista and higher that includes transparent icons, animations, and customized desktop gadgets.

AES (Advanced Encryption Standard)   Used in wireless networks and offers encryption with 128-bit, 192-bit, and 256-bit encryption keys.

AGP (accelerated graphics port)   An extension of the PCI bus (a port) that provides a dedicated communication path between the expansion slot and the processor. AGP is used for video adapters.

AHCI (Advanced Host Controller Interface)   One mode of operation for SATA drives, which enables SATA devices to be inserted or removed when power is applied and communication exists between the host controller and attached SATA devices.

air filter mask   An item that should be included in a technician's toolkit as personal protection equipment. That air filter or mask should be used whenever dust, airborne particles, or debris could cause personal issues.

Airplane Mode   Enables users to disable all wireless communication but still view a movie or play a game that does not require Internet connectivity.

AirPrint   An Apple print server.

alternative configuration   A method of configuring IPv4 parameters that will be used if the main IPv4 parameters (such as DHCP) cannot be used or are impractical to use. A good use of an alternative configuration is when a laptop is used both at work and at home. At work, DHCP could be configured, but at home, the alternative configuration might contain a statically assigned IP address.

alternative IP address   A method of assigning an IP address used when the DHCP server is down or the server could not assign an IP address such as when there are network problems.

ALU (arithmetic logic unit)   The part of a processor that does mathematical manipulations.

AMD (Advanced Micro Devices)   A company that makes processors, graphics processors, and chipsets. AMD is the largest rival of Intel for PC processors.

amp   Short for ampere, a measurement of electrical current.

amplification   Increasing the strength of a sound. Amplification output is measured in watts. Sound cards usually have built-in amplification to drive the speakers. Many speakers have built-in amplifiers to boost the audio signal for a fuller sound.

analog signal   Used mainly by older video ports, modems, and sound devices; its signal strength varies in amplitude.

Android   A mobile device operating system.

antenna   A component that attaches to wireless devices or is integrated into them. An antenna radiates or receives radio waves.

anti-glare filter   Helps in certain lighting environments and when outside light affects the display.

antimalware   Software used to protect the operating system and applications.

anti-static bag   A plastic enclosure that protects electronic gear from being affected by static charges if the equipment were left exposed.

anti-static wrist strap   A strap that connects a technician to a computer that equalizes the voltage potential between the two to prevent electrostatic discharge (ESD).

antivirus   Software that protects the operating system and applications from malware.

AP (access point)   See *wireless access point*.

APIPA (automatic private IP addressing)   A Windows option that enables a computer to automatically receive an IP address from the range 169.254.0.1 to 169.254.255.254.

APK   This is the file format that can be used to distribute and install Android apps.

Apple Configurator   A free mobile device management tool (MDM) that enables you to view and manage multiple mobile devices. Can also wipe the device.

application layer (OSI)   Layer 7 of the OSI model, which defines how applications and the computer interact with a network.

application layer (TCP/IP)   The top layer of the TCP/IP model. It formats data specific for a particular application. It is equivalent to the OSI model's application, presentation, and session layers. Common application layer protocols include Telnet, HTTP, HTML, DNS, POP, IMAP, and FTP.

Apply button   A button located in the bottom-right corner of a dialog box; clicking the Apply button saves any changes the user has applied to the window.

App scanner   An online tool in which you can type the name of an app to see if any of your data is at risk and the seriousness of any risk.

App Store   An Apple tool that enables a user to shop for various applications to download on a device.

apt-get   The LINUX command-line interface tool that is the equivalent of Ubuntu Software Center; a utility to manage software.

APU (accelerated processing unit)   A processor that combines the central processing unit (CPU) with a graphics processor unit (GPU).

archive attribute   A designation that can be attached to a file that marks whether the file has changed since it was last backed up by a software program.

ARP (Address Resolution Protocol)   A protocol that can discover the destination MAC address when the destination IP address is known.

artifact   An unusual pattern or distortion that appears on a screen, such as green dotted or vertical lines, colored lines on one side of the screen, or tiny glitters, which could indicate problems such as an overheated GPU or insufficient air flow, or with a video driver.

aspect ratio   An LCD characteristic that describes a ratio of monitor width compared to height. Common monitor aspect ratios are 4:3, 5:4, 16:9, or 16:10.

asynchronous   Transmissions that do not require a clock signal but instead use extra bits to track the beginning and end of the data.

ATAPI (AT Attachment Packet Interface)   The hardware side of the IDE specification that supports devices such as optical drives and tape drives.

ATA standard (AT Attachment standard)   The original IDE interface that supported two drives. Now in two types: PATA and SATA.

attrib   A command that designates a file as hidden, archived, read-only, or a system file.

attitude   A person's behavior and/or mindset towards another person or a thing.

ATX (Advanced Technology Extended)   A form factor for motherboards, cases, and power supplies.

ATX power supply form factor   The shape and size of a power supply that is designed to fit and function with an ATX motherboard and ATX case.

audio/video editing workstation   A computer used to create and modify sound or video files. The computer commonly has multiple powerful multicore processors, maximum system RAM, specialized video and audio cards, one or more fast and large-capacity hard drives, good speakers, quality mouse, dual displays, and possibly a digital tablet and scanner.

auditing   Tracking network events such as logging onto the network domain. Auditing is sometimes called event logging or simply logging.

AUP (acceptable use policy)   Defines rules regarding using a company network, data, and a specific application.

authentication   The process of determining whether a network device or person has permission to access a network.

authenticator app   Can be downloaded and, if a site is configured to use, provides an additional level of security for mobile devices.

authorization   Controls what network resources such as file, folders, printers, video conferencing equipment, fax machines, scanners, and so on can be accessed and used by a legitimate network user or device.

AutoRun   A setting that dictates whether software or programs start automatically from discs or drives.

auto-switching   A type of power supply that monitors the incoming voltage from the wall outlet and automatically switches itself accordingly. Auto-switching power supplies accept voltages from 100VAC to 240VAC at 50Hz to 60Hz. They are popular in desktops, laptops, and mobile device power adapters.

B

backlight   A fluorescent lamp or LEDs that are always on for an LCD.

back side bus   Connections between a CPU and the L2 cache.

backed up print queue   One or more documents that have been queued up for print and the printer does not execute the print command causing a log-jam effect.

Back To My Mac   A feature in the *System Preferences* iCloud menu that enables you to browse that Mac from another OS X device. The remote Mac appears as a shared device in Finder, enabling you to browse the file system.

bandwidth   The communications channel width that defines its capacity for carrying data.

barcode reader   Handheld device that reads barcodes in checkout lanes and in retail establishments.

baseband   A networking technology where the entire cable bandwidth transmits a digital signal.

baseband update   Applied to a phone's radio firmware (a low-level software that manages items related to the phone's radio).

baseline   A snapshot of a computer's performance (memory, CPU usage, and so on) during normal operations (before a problem or slowdown is apparent).

basic disk   A Windows term for a drive that has been partitioned and formatted.

basic storage   A Windows term for a partition. Contrast with *dynamic storage*.

battery   Small self-contained unit used to power a device without using an AC outlet.

battery backup   Provides power to the computer when a brownout or a blackout occurs.

battery charger   A portable battery pack that can be charged and carried to charge a mobile device in lieu of plugging the mobile device into an outlet.

battery pack   A portable battery device that can be charged and carried to charge a mobile device in lieu of plugging that device into an outlet.

baud   The number of times an analog signal changes in 1 second. If a signal is sent that changes 600 times in 1 second, the device communicates at 600 baud. Today's signaling methods (modulation techniques, to be technically accurate) allow modems to send several bits in one cycle, so it is more accurate to talk in bits per second rather than baud.

bcdedit   A command that can modify the Windows boot settings.

BD (Blu-ray disc)   An optical media with a higher data capacity than a CD or DVD.

belt   In an inkjet printer, the belt connects to the stepper motor and print head assembly to move the print head and ink cartridge from one side of the printer to the other side.

biometric device   A device used to authenticate someone based on one or more physical traits such as a fingerprint, an eyeball (retina), or a hand, or a behavioral trait such as voice or signature.

biometrics   The use of one or more devices that can authenticate someone based on one or more physical traits such as a fingerprint, an eyeball (retina), or a hand, or a behavioral trait such as voice or signature.

BIOS (basic input/output system)   A chip that contains computer software that locates the operating system, POST, and important hardware configuration parameters. Also called ROM BIOS, Flash BIOS, or system BIOS. Replaced with UEFI BIOS.

bit   An electrically charged 1 or 0.

BitLocker   A Microsoft utility that encrypts an entire disk volume, including operating system files, user files, and swap files. The utility requires two disk partitions at a minimum.

BitLocker To Go   A Microsoft application that can encrypt and password protect external drives and removable media that are 128MB or larger.

blackout   A total loss of AC power.

Bluetooth   A wireless technology for personal area networks (PAN).

Blu-ray   A type of optical disk technology that uses a blue laser instead of a red laser (like the kind used in CD/DVD drives) to achieve the higher disc capacities.

BNC connector (Bayonet Neill–Concelman)   A connector used on coaxial cable.

BonJour   An Apple printer server that enables Apple and Windows devices to share printers without any configuration required.

boot   Describes the process of a computer coming to a usable condition.

Boot Camp   A boot loading utility designed to assist with partitioning, installation, and support of running Windows on a Mac.

boot partition   A type of partition found in Windows that contains the operating system. The boot partition can be in the same partition as the system partition, which is the part of the hard drive that holds hardware-specific files.

bootrec   Windows command used to repair and recover from hard drive problems.

boot sector   Previously called DBR or DOS boot record, this section of a disk contains information about the system files (the files used to boot the operating system).

boot sector virus   A virus program placed in a computer's boot sector code, which can then load into memory. When in RAM, the virus takes control of computer operations. The virus can spread to installed drives and drives located on a network.

boot sequence   In the BIOS configuration settings, boot sequence prioritizes devices in the order the computer looks for boot files. Also known as boot drive order.

boot volume   Holds the majority of the Windows operating system files. Can be the same volume as the system volume (which holds the Windows boot files.

botnet   A security attack in which software spreads from device to device. This is because a hacker has control of computers called zombies.

b/s (bits per second)   The number of 1s and 0s transmitted per second.

bridge   A physical network device or software that connects two or more networks. Could connect a wireless network to a wired network. Bridges are part of the data link layer of the OSI model and part of the network access layer in the TCIP/IP model.

brightness   A measure of light output coming out of video equipment.

bright spot   Caused by pixels that are always on.

broadband   A networking technology where the cable bandwidth is divided into multiple channels; thus, the cable can carry simultaneous voice, video, and data.

broadcast   See *broadcast address*.

broadcast address   IP address that communicates with all devices on a particular network.

brownout   A loss of AC power due to overloaded electrical circuits.

browser   A program that views web pages across the Internet. Common web browsers are Internet Explorer, Microsoft Edge, Firefox, Chrome, Safari, Opera, and NeoPlanet.

browser redirect   An instance in which a hijacked browser sends a browser to a different web page. A browser redirect can also be malware or install a rootkit that can act as a backdoor to your operating system.

brute force   A type of attack in which repeated attempts try to gain access to a network device or stored material.

BSOD (blue screen of death)   The monitor screen displays all blue and the computer locks or is nonfunctional.

BTX (balanced technology extended)   A form factor for motherboards.

buffer memory   Memory installed in optical drives and hard drives that reduces transfer time when writing data to the drive by securing more data than requested and placing the data in the buffer. It holds the extra data in the drive and constantly sends data to the processor instead of waiting on the drive.

buffered memory   A type of memory in which the modules have extra chips (registers) that delay data transfers to ensure accuracy.

built-in diagnostics   In BIOS configuration settings, used to access diagnostic tests for hard drive, memory, battery, power, processor, and other hardware diagnostic tests.

burn-in   An image imprint, or ghost image seen on a display screen when an LCD or plasma display has been left on for too long.

bus   Electronic lines that enable 1s and 0s to move from one place to another.

bus-powered hub   A device with no external power supply that enables other USB devices to be connected and powered by the bus. Contrast with a self-powered hub.

bus speed   The rate at which a computer pathway used for transmitting 1s and 0s operates.

bus speed (BIOS)   Shown in the traditional BIOS; usually monitored and displayed in a UEFI environment.

BYOD (bring your own device)   Describes mobile devices that are brought to the work environment and used on the wired or wireless network.

byte   8 bits grouped together as a basic unit.

C

cable lock   A security device to prevent theft of a laptop.

cable management system   Helps keep network cables neat and organized. Ladder racks are a type of a cable management system.

cable modem   A modem that connects to the cable TV network.

cable select   A setting used on PATA IDE devices when a special cable determines which device is the master and which one is the slave.

cable stripper   A tool used to cut away the sheathing over a cable's copper wire. Also called a wire stripper.

cable tester   Checks coaxial and UTP cable ends (depending on the model) to determine if cable terminals are suitable for use.

cache memory   Fast memory designed to increase processor operations.

calibration   A print head alignment process that must be performed when installing the printer and when replacing the print head.

Cancel button   Located in the bottom-right corner of the window; clicking it ignores any changes the user has made and restores parameters to their original state.

capacitor   An electronic component that can hold a charge.

carriage   An internal inkjet printer part that carries the printhead.

CCFL (cold cathode fluorescent lamp)   The older flat-panel backlight technology used before LED backlights were used.

CD (compact disc)   A storage medium that holds up to 700MB of data, such as audio, video, and software applications.

cd   Also known as the CHDIR command in Windows. Used from a Windows or a Linux/OS X command prompt to change into a different directory.

CDFS (Compact Disc File System)   A file system for optical media.

CD-RW (compact disc rewritable)   A CD drive that can write data multiple times to a particular disc.

cellular card   Used to connect a laptop to a cell phone network.

certificate of destruction   A security measure that provides proof that printed material or stored data has been destroyed.

Certified W-USB   A type of USB that supports high-speed, secure wireless connectivity between a USB device and a PC.

channel ID   Used in wireless networks to define the frequency used to transmit and receive.

charging   A laser printing process that can also be known as conditioning. This process gets the drum read for use by applying a uniform voltage on the drum surface using a primary/main corona or a conditioning roller.

charging USB port   A port that can provide power to charge and run an unpowered attached device such as a flash drive.

check box   Provides the user the ability to enable an option. Clicking in the check box places a check mark that enables the option. Clicking again removes the check mark and disables the option.

chipset   One or more motherboard chips that work with the processor to allow certain computer features, such as motherboard memory and capacity.

chkdsk   A program that locates clusters that are disassociated from the appropriate data file.

chmod   OS X command that gives file owner read, write, and execute permissions.

chown   OS X command that changes ownership.

CIDR (classless interdomain routing)   A type of subnet mask that does not have a classful boundary. CIDR is a method of allocating IP addresses based on the number of host addresses needed for a particular network.

CIFS   A version of Server Message Block (SMB) that can provide access to shared network devices, files, and printers, especially in a mixed work environment of MAC and Windows computers.

CL rating (column address strobe [CAS] latency)   The amount of time (clock cycles) that passes before the processor moves on to the next memory address. Chips with lower access times (CL rating) are faster than those with higher access times (larger numbers).

clamping speed   The time that elapses from an overvoltage condition to when surge protection begins.

clamping voltage   The voltage level at which a surge protector begins to protect a computer.

cleaning   A laser printing process that describes removing residual toner from the drum by using a wiper blade or brush.

clean install   Loading of an operating system on a computer that does not already have one installed.

clean room   A specifically constructed, climate-controlled (cool temperature and humidity of 45% to 60%) closed area with special air vents/filters, vacuums, blowers, and a circulation system that captures harmful/hazardous particulate matter, scrubs and diffuses the PM, and safely eliminates it while allowing the sensitive computer equipment to run.

client-side DNS   When individuals or businesses configure their computer to use one or more domain name system (DNS) servers to translate Uniform Resource Locator addresses (URLs) into IP addresses.

clock   An electronic component that provides timing signals to all motherboard components. A PC's clock is normally measured in MHz.

clock speed   The rate at which timing signals are sent to motherboard components (normally measured in MHz).

clock speed (BIOS)   Shown in the traditional BIOS; usually monitored and displayed in a UEFI environment.

Close button   Located in the upper-right corner of a dialog box with an X, a button that closes the dialog box.

closed source   A vendor-specific operating system, that is, Apple OS for Apple devices only.

cloud printing   Enables users to print in a remote location or from a wireless printer.

cluster   The minimum amount of space that one saved file occupies.

CMOS (complementary metal oxide semiconductor)   A special type of memory on a motherboard in which Setup configuration is saved.

CMOS battery   Small, coin-shaped lithium battery that provides power to CMOS memory.

coaxial   A type of cabling used in video connections. Has a copper core surrounded by insulation and shielding from EMI.

cold boot   Executes when the computer is turned on with the power switch. Executes POST.

collate   In printing, complete copies of documents in numerical order one set at a time.

command   A command issued from the Run utility in Windows to bring up a command prompt window.

command-line interface   An operating environment that is not graphical and only typed commands are available.

command prompt   Otherwise known as a prompt, a text-based environment in which commands are entered.

command switch   An option used when working from a command prompt that allows a command to be controlled or operated on differently.

commercial license   Software purchased for a specific number or users and machines.

CompactFlash (CF)   A type of removable flash memory storage that can be inserted into many devices, such as disk drives, cameras, PDAs, mobile phones, and tablet PCs.

Compatibility Mode   A Microsoft Windows tool used to emulate older operating systems so that older applications or hardware can be used on a newer operating system.

component/RGB video   Three RCA jacks commonly found on TVs, DVD players, and projectors. The three connections are for luminescence or brightness and two jacks for color difference signals.

Component Services   A Microsoft Management Console snap-in that can configure and administer Component Object Model (COM) components, COM+ applications, and the Distributed Transaction Coordinator (DTC).

composite video   A yellow RCA port normally found on projectors, TVs, gaming consoles, stereos, and optical disc players.

compressed air   A can that when the top is depressed, emits high-powered air that removes dust from hard-to-reach places such as under keys, under motherboards, and inside power supplies and devices.

compression   Compaction of a file or folder to take up less disk space.

computer cage   Physical protection for a computer or laptop.

Computer Management console   A Windows tool that displays a large group of tools on one screen.

COMx   Designation for a communications port, where the x represents a COM port number, such as COM1 or COM2.

conditioning roller   Used in a laser printer to generate a large uniform negative voltage to be applied to the drum.

Console   In OS X, a centralized place to find system and application logs and messages. It allows parsing manually or by searching for something specific.

content filtering   A device or software that screens data for suspect security risks.

context menu   A menu of options usually available from the main menu that is brought up by right-clicking an item.

continuity   An electrical resistance measurement to see if a wire is good or broken.

contrast ratio   An LCD characteristic that describes the difference in light intensity between the brightest white and the darkest black. A higher contrast ratio is a better characteristic.

Control Panel   A Windows icon that allows computer configuration such as adding or removing software, adding or removing hardware, configuring a screen saver, adjusting a monitor, configuring a mouse, installing networking components, and so on.

convert   A command issued from a command prompt that changes an older file system into NTFS.

cookie   A program that collects information that is stored on a hard drive. This information could include your preferences when visiting a website, banner ads that change, or what websites you have visited lately.

COPY   A command used from a command prompt to transfer one or more files from one place to another.

counter   A specific measurement for an object in the Windows System Monitor tool.

cp   An OS X command to copy a file. Short for copy.

cps (characters per second)   The number of characters a printer prints in 1 second.

CPU   See *processor*.

CPU speed   The rate at which the CPU operates. It is the speed of the front side bus multiplied by the multiplier. Normally measured in GHz.

CPU throttling   Reducing the clock frequency to reduce power consumption.

CRC (cyclic redundancy check)   An advanced method of data error checking.

creased paper   Paper that does not feed properly through a printer; check paper size, fit, and manufacturer's specifications.

credit card reader   A small wired or wireless device that attaches to a mobile device to record point of sales; some allow printed receipts, others allow an email input instead.

crimper   Tool that permanently attaches an RJ-45 or RJ-11 connector to a copper core cable.

crossover cable   Cabling that connects two like devices (for example, two computers, two switches, or two routers).

crosstalk   A type of EMI where signals from one wire interfere with the data on an adjacent wire.

CRT (cathode ray tube)   The main part of a monitor, the picture tube.

CSMA/CA (Carrier Sense Multiple Access/Collision Avoidance)   A common access method (set of communication rules governing networked devices) used in wireless and older Apple networks.

CSMA/CD (Carrier Sense Multiple Access/Collision Detection)   A common access method (set of communication rules governing all network devices) used by Ethernet.

CTS (clear to send)   Part of the RTS/CTS hardware handshaking communication method. Specific wires on the serial connector are used to send a signal to the other device to stop or start sending data. The CTS and RTS (request to send) signals indicate when it is okay to send data.

current   Describes how many electrons are going through a circuit and measured in amps.

cylinder   On a stack of hard drive platters, the same numbered concentric tracks of all platters.

D

dash   The universal search tool built in the OS X Launcher bar. It searches local content as well as Internet sources, all of which can be enabled or disabled simply by opening up dash.

data bits   A serial device setting for how many bits make up a data word.

data collector set   Data collected through Performance Monitor in Windows Vista and higher operating systems.

data link layer   Layer 2 of the OSI model, which accurately transfers bits across the network by encapsulating (grouping) them into frames (usable sections).

data privacy   A security concern whether measures are implemented that protect data being transmitted or stored.

Data Sources (ODBC) (open database connectivity)   A programming interface that allows applications to access data from a database.

date/time (BIOS option)   A manual setting in BIOS/UEFI Setup that dictates the current time and date to the computer.

DB-15   Male plug on the end of a VGA cable, which was designed for analog output to a CRT monitor. A DB-15 connector fits into a female DE-15 connector.

DBR (DOS boot record)   An area of a disk that contains system files.

DC (direct current)   The type of power a computer needs to operate.

DCE (data circuit terminating equipment)   Refers to serial devices such as modems, mice, and digitizers.

dd   In OS X, an advanced command-line interface command that copies and converts files.

DDoS (Distributed Denial of Service)   A type of security attack in which several computer systems are used to attack a network or device with the intent of preventing access such as to a web server.

DDR (double data rate)   Data is transmitted on both sides of the clock signal and uses 184 pins. Sometimes called DDR SDRAM or DDR RAM.

DDR2 (double data rate 2)   An upgrade to the DDR SDRAM standard and sometimes is called DDR2 RAM. It includes the following modules: DDR2-400, DDR2-533, DDR2-667, DDR2-800, and DDR2-1000. DDR2 uses 240-pin DIMMs and is not compatible with DDR; however, the higher-end (faster) DDR2 modules are backward compatible with the slower DDR2 modules.

DDR3 (double data rate 3)   An upgrade from DDR2 for speeds up to 1600MHz that better supports dual-core and quad-core processor-based systems.

DDR3L   A DDR3 module that runs at a lower voltage (1.35V) than the 1.5V or higher DDR/DDR2/DDR3 modules. Less voltages means less heat and less power consumed.

DDR4   Operates at a lower voltage and faster speeds than DDR3 and lower modules.

DDR4L   Operates at a lower voltage (1.05V) than a standard DDR4 module.

DDR RAM See *DDR*.

DDR SDRAM See *DDR*.

DE-15   A type of female connector that receives the DB-15 male connector of a VGA cable.

dead pixel   A pixel on an LCD monitor that does not illuminate.

decoder   In DVD drives, hardware or software that converts the MPEG-2 video to readable images.

default gateway   The IP address of a Layer 3 device, such as a router, that is directly connected to its immediate network. It tells a device on its network where to send a packet destined for a remote network.

default printer   When a computer can use multiple printers, the one printer that all applications use by default. A computer user can change the printer to a different one through the Print dialog window. To mark a printer as default, right-click the printer icon and click the Set as default option.

defrag   The command that starts the defragmentation process of reordering and placing files in contiguous sectors.

defragmentation   A process of reordering and placing files in contiguous sectors.

degausser   A device that demagnetizes monitors. Also called a degaussing coil.

DEL   A command issued from a command prompt that deletes a file or folder.

density control blade   A part inside a laser printer's toner cartridge that controls the amount of toner released to the drum.

DEP (data execution prevention)   Software-based and hardware-based security measures to prevent malicious software from executing in specific memory locations.

desktop   The interface between the user and the applications, files, and hardware, which is part of the graphical user interface environment. It is the area in which all work is performed.

developing   Describes a laser printer process in which toner is attracted to the laser printer drum.

developing cylinder   A component inside a laser printer's toner cartridge that applies a static charge to the toner so that it will be attracted to the drum. Sometimes called a developing roller.

device driver   Special software that allows an operating system to access a piece of hardware.

Device Manager   A Windows program that views and configures hardware.

DFS (Distributed File System)   A Microsoft-provided set of network services that allow easy access to network shares.

DHCP (Dynamic Host Configuration Protocol)   A method to automatically assign IP addresses to network devices from a pool of IP addresses.

DHCP server   Software configured on a network server or router that issues IP addresses from its pool of numbers upon request to a network device.

dial-up network   A network formed by using a modem that connects to the traditional phone network. The modem connects to a remote network device.

dialog box   A window used by the operating system that allows user interaction to set preferences on various software parameters.

DIB (dual independent bus)   Using two buses (a back side and front side bus) to relieve the bottleneck when the CPU communicates with RAM, L2 cache, chipset, PCI bus, and so on.

dictionary attack   A method that determines a password to gain access to data.

differential backup   Backs up files that have changed since the last full backup (files that have the archive bit set to on), but the backup software does not reset the archive bit like the incremental backup does.

digital modem   A modem that transmits directly on digital phone lines.

digital signal   A signal using 1s and 0s to represent data.

digital signature   Confirms that the hardware or updated driver being installed is compatible with Windows; sometimes called driver signing.

digitizer   Provides input into such documents as architectural drawings, technical plans, and photos. It can also be used to draw electronic pictures.

dim image   A video condition when little to no image displays on a laptop, but you can hear the hard drive. Reset the display to factory default. May require replacing the inverter.

DIMM (dual inline memory module)   A style of 168-pin, 184-pin, 240-pin, or 288-pin memory chip normally used for RAM chips on Pentium and higher motherboards.

DIN connector   A round connector with small holes, normally keyed with a metal piece or notch so that the cable inserts only one way. Examples include keyboard and mouse connectors.

DIR   A command used from a command prompt that displays the contents of a directory.

directional antenna   A type of antenna that radiates energy in a specific direction.

directory   In older operating systems, an electronic container that holds files and even other directories. Today's operating systems use the term *folder*.

DirectX   A Microsoft technology that integrates multimedia drivers, application code, and 3-D support for audio and video.

disable execute bit   When enabled in BIOS/UEFI, prevents executable code such as those found in viruses or other malware loading into memory locations in which operating system code resides.

disable unused ports   A security measure performed on network devices to protect ports in case the room where the device is located is compromised.

disc   Describes CDs, DVDs, and BDs.

disk   Media used to store data.

Disk Administrator   A Windows program that allows testing, configuration, and preventive maintenance on hard disks.

disk cache   A portion of RAM set aside for hard drive data that speeds up hard drive operations. A cache on a hard drive controller is also known as a data buffer.

Disk Cleanup   A Windows utility that helps free up hard drive space by emptying the Recycle Bin, removing temporary files, removing temporary Internet files, removing offline files, and so on.

disk duplexing   A technique that uses two disk controllers and allows the system to continue functioning if one hard drive fails. Data is written to both sets of hard drive systems through the two controllers. Disk duplexing is considered to be RAID level 1.

Disk Management   A Windows tool that can partition and manage hard drives.

disk mirroring   A process that protects against hard drive failure by using two or more hard drives and one disk controller. The same data is written to both drives. If one hard drive fails, the other hard drive continues to function. Disk mirroring is considered to be RAID level 1.

disk striping   Another name for RAID 0 where data is alternately written on two or more hard drives, thus providing increased system performance.

Disk Utility   A powerful application that manages disks and images in OS X. The utility can rename, reformat, erase, repair, and restore disks. It should be approached with caution because the wrong usage could delete all data on the system, or on an attached external disk.

diskpart   A command-based utility used in preparing hard disk partitions and volumes for use.

display   A device that shows computer output. Also called a monitor.

DisplayPort   A port, developed by Video Electronics Standards Association (VESA), that can send and receive audio and video signals. Used primarily for display devices and can connect to a single link DVI or HDMI port with the use of a converter.

display size   A measurement of how much video screen can be seen from the top-left corner to the bottom-right corner (and shown in inches).

distended capacitor   Bulging end or top of these small components indicate it's time to change them or the component in which they are on including the motherboard.

distorted image   Caused by broken or bent video pins on a monitor cable.

DLP (data loss prevention)   Software that protects corporate data from being sent outside the corporate network.

DLP (Digital Light Processing)   A technology used in projectors and rear-projection TVs that is an array of miniature mirrors that create pixels on a projection surface.

DMZ (demilitarized zone)   A network area that is separate from the corporate network but contains servers that are accessible to outside devices.

DNAT (destination network address translation)   A method of mapping a public IP address to a specific private IP address used in a home or small business network.

DNS (Domain Name System)   Translates Internet names into IP addresses. Also known as domain name server or DNS server.

DNS server (Domain Name System server)   Application on network server that translates Internet names into IP addresses.

Dock   The shortcut organizational bar used for launching, switching, and managing applications on the OS X graphical user interface (usually the bar at bottom of screen).

docking station   A part that has connections for a monitor, printer, keyboard, and mouse that allows a laptop computer to be more like a desktop system.

Documents   The default library grouping used by Window 7 applications when saving files.

domain   A term used in Windows server-based networks where users are required to have logins, and file storage, email, and web-based services are commonly provided.

DoS (denial of service)   A type of security attack in which the intent is to make a machine or a network unusable.

dot matrix printer   See *impact printer*.

double-sided memory   A single memory module that contains two memory modules in one container (two banks). Data is still sent to the CPU 64 bits at a time. Some use the terms single-sided and double-sided to describe memory modules that have chips on one side (single-sided) or both sides (double-sided). Another name is double-ranked memory.

downstream   Describes information pulled from the Internet such as when viewing web pages or downloading a file.

downstream port   A USB port that connects a USB hub or USB device.

DPI (dots per inch)   A printer measurement used with inkjet and laser printers that refers to how many dots are produced in an inch.

DRAM (dynamic random-access memory)   One of two major RAM types that is less expensive but also slower than SRAM. DRAM requires periodic refreshing of the electrical charges holding the 1s and 0s.

drive array   The use of two or more hard drives configured for speed, redundancy, or both.

drive encryption (BIOS)   A BIOS/UEFI setting that scrambles all the data on the hard drive as a security measure.

drive not recognized   A storage device error condition that indicates something is wrong with the physical settings, BIOS/UEFI settings, cabling, or lack of power.

drive overwrite   A utility that rewrites the drive with all 1s or all 0s to prevent data from being recovered.

driver   See *device driver*.

driver rollback   A feature in Windows that allows an older driver to be re-installed when a new driver causes problems.

driver signing   A technology that verifies whether a driver has been digitally signed and approved to work with the specific Windows operating system environment.

drive status   A storage device state that can be viewed within Windows Disk Management.

drive wipe   A technique that can eradicate personal or corporate data from a hard drive before donating or reusing a computer.

DRM (digital rights management)   Intel's specification covering high-bandwidth digital content protection (HDCP), which protects copyrighted material, such as movies.

drop-down menu   An option box with a down arrow; clicking the arrow reveals additional choices for the option.

D-shell connector   A connector with more pins or holes on the top side than the bottom so that a cable inserts in only one direction. Examples include older parallel, serial, and video ports.

DSL (digital subscriber line)   A type of Internet connection that uses the traditional phone line. A filter is needed on each phone outlet that has a normal analog device attached to separate the analog sound from the Internet data.

DTE (data terminating equipment)   Refers to computers and printers.

dual-boot   Capability to boot from one of two installed operating systems.

dual-channel   A system in which the motherboard memory controller chip handles processing of memory requests more efficiently by handling two memory paths simultaneously.

dual-core   A type of processor that combines two CPUs in a single unit. Note there are now tri-core, quad-core, hexa-core, and even octa-core processors.

dual-link   A type of digital visual interface connector from the computer port to the display.

dual-rail power supply   Describes two +12-volt lines available in a power supply.

dual-voltage   A type of power supply that can be used with 120- or 240-volt electrical systems.

dual-voltage memory   Motherboard memory modules that use less power and produce less heat if the motherboard supports this feature. Not all installed modules must support the lower voltage for the system to take advantage of the modules that do support the lower voltage.

duplex   An assembly option that allows a printer to print on both sides of a paper without intervention.

dust mask   An air filter mask. A covering designed to protect the nose and mouth from harmful particulate matter (PM) or fumes.

DVD (digital versatile disc or digital video disc)   A newer media technology than CDs but having less capacity than a Blu-ray disc.

DVD drive   A drive that supports CDs as well as music and video DVDs.

DVD-R   WORM technology used with DVD drives that is similar to CD-R drives. DVD-R discs can use one or two sides and are available in 3.95GB, 4.7GB, and 9.4GB. DVD-R discs are sometimes shown as two different types, DVD-R(A) and DVD-R(G). DVD-R(A) targets the "authoring" business for professional development of DVDs. DVD-R(G) is more for home users and lay people. Both can be read by most DVD players and drives, but DVD-R(G) drives usually cannot write to DVD-R(A) media.

DVD+R   A type of read/write DVD supported by the DVD+RW Alliance that can record (one time per disc) up to 4.7GB on single-sided DVD+R discs.

DVD-RAM   A type of drive that uses a laser to heat the disc and to magnetically charge it. Data can be written to the disc.

DVD-R DL (DVD-R dual layer)   Similar to DVD-R in that it can record one time. Uses double-layered discs to store up to 8.5GB and supported by the DVD Forum.

DVD+R DL (DVD+R dual layer)   Similar to DVD+R in that it can record one time. Uses double-layered discs to store up to 8.5GB and supported by the DVD+RW Alliance.

DVD-ROM   A technology that produces discs with superior audio and video performance and increased storage capacity.

DVD-RW (DVD-rewritable)   A type of read/write DVD format supported by the DVD Forum. Similar to DVD-R except you can erase and rewrite data. Uses 4.7GB discs, and most DVD-ROM drives and DVD-Video players support this format. Sometimes known as DVD-R/W or DVD-ER.

DVD+RW (DVD read and write)   A drive that can be read from and written to and that holds 3GB.

DVD±RW (DVD-rewritable)   A type of read/write DVD format that is supported by both the DVD Forum and the DVD+RW Alliance. These drives read most CD, DVD, and DVD+R DL discs and write to CD-R, CD-RW, DVD+R, DVD-R, DVD-RW, and DVD+RW discs.

DVI (Digital Visual Interface)   A port on a digital video adapter that connects flat panel monitors to the computer.

DVI-A   A type of dual-link connector that is less common than DVI-D or DVI-I. It can carry a DVI signal to an analog display, most commonly a CRT monitor.

DVI-D   A type of video connector used with digital monitors.

DVI-I   The most common type of DVI video connector that is used with both analog and digital monitors.

DVI port (digital video/visual interface)   A port on a video adapter that connects flat panel monitors to the computer.

DVI to HDMI converter   Video connector with a DVI connector on one end and an HDMI connector on the other.

DVI to VGA converter   Video connector with a DVI connector on one end and a VGA connector on the other.

DVR (digital video recorder)   A special hardware component to a home theater configuration to record TV shows, transfer data from a camcorder or camera, or store movies or media for playback.

DXDIAG   A Windows command to access DirectX software that helps resolve DirectX display and sound driver problems.

dynamic disk   A Windows term for volumes that can be resized and managed without rebooting.

dynamic storage   A disk that has been configured for the Windows operating system. The unit can be resized and managed without rebooting and contains primary partitions, extended partitions, logical drives, and dynamic volumes.

E

e-reader   Also known as an e-book.

Easy Transfer   A free application from Microsoft that copies files and operating system settings to another drive, removable media, over a network, or to another storage location.

ECC (error correcting code)   Uses a mathematical algorithm to verify data accuracy. ECC is more expensive than parity, and the motherboard or memory controllers must also have additional circuitry to process ECC.

ECHO OFF   A command used from a command prompt that prevents characters from displaying on the screen.

Edge   Windows 10 browser that is the replacement for Internet Explorer.

EDIT   A command that brings up a text editor. A text editor enables file creation and modification.

EEPROM (electrically erasable programmable read-only memory)   A nonvolatile memory technology that can store a small amount of data. EEPROMs were previously used for the computer BIOS. Flash memory is used today.

effective permissions   The final permissions granted for a particular resource. Folder permissions are cumulative; the combination of the group and the person's permissions. The deny permission overrides any allowed permission set for a user or a group. When NTFS and shared folder permissions are both used, the more restrictive of the two becomes the effective permissions.

EFS (Encrypting File System)   A Windows encryption feature in which only the authorized user may view or change a file encrypted with EFS.

EIDE (Enhanced Integrated Drive Electronics)   Signifies two IDE connectors (four devices) and support of the ATAPI standard.

electrical fire safety   Knowledge of how to extinguish an electrical fire using fire extinguisher Type A-B-C or fire extinguisher Type C.

electronic key card   An alternative to a key for room or building access.

email filtering   Security rules specific to email that processes incoming messages before forwarding on to a specific user.

embedded system   A computer that has a specific function within a larger system such as in medical, manufacturing, or airport industries.

emergency notification   Wireless emergency alert (WEA); a U.S. method of propagating an emergency announcement such as an Amber Alert, Presidential Announcement, and weather alert.

EMI (electromagnetic interference)   Electronic noise generated by electrical devices.

enabling/disabling devices (BIOS)   A BIOS/UEFI option that enables configuration of motherboard-controlled deices.

encryption   A method of securing data from unauthorized users. Data is converted into an unreadable format.

energy absorption/dissipation   A surge protector feature that describes that the greater number of joules that can be dissipated, the more effective and durable a surge protector is.

ENERGY STAR   A set of energy efficiency standards including those relating to total energy requirements and low power mode(s), and an efficiency standard that a product must meet to achieve this standard.

entry control roster   A list of employees who are authorized in a particular area. Also called an access control roster.

environmental enclosure   A housing assembly that encloses a desktop or a laptop computer to protect it from particulate matter (PM) while allowing user access to a keyboard, a mouse, and other components.

EPEAT rating system   A rating system that works with the Environmental Protection Agency (EPA) to identify products that have a green (and clean) design.

equipment grounding   The components in a device such as a computer that are at the same voltage potential. This is important to personal safety because consistent grounding minimizes the potential of voltages being applied to places in which it shouldn't be, such as the case. If a piece of equipment is not grounded, someone could receive a shock or electrocution simply by touching it.

erase lamp   A component inside a laser printer that neutralizes any charges left on the drum so that the next printed page receives no residuals from the previous page.

error code   May be displayed when a printer has inadequate memory or when the computer has a problem.

eSATA (external serial ATA)   A port used to connect external SATA devices to a computer.

eSATA port   A nonpowered port used to connect external storage devices at a maximum of two meters.

eSATAp port   A port that accepts both eSATA and USB connectors, which can provide power when necessary. Also known as eSATA/USB or power over eSATA.

ESCD (extended system configuration data)   Data that provides the BIOS and operating system a means for communicating with plug and play devices. As the computer boots, the BIOS records legacy device configuration information. Plug and play devices use this information to configure themselves and avoid conflicts. When an adapter has resources assigned and the resources are saved in ESCD, the resources do not have to be recalculated unless a new device is added to the computer.

ESD (electrostatic discharge)   Occurs when stored-up static electricity is discharged in an instantaneous surge of voltage. Cumulative effects of ESD weaken or destroy electronic components.

ESD mat   A pad that is placed on a surface to prevent electrostatic discharge events. It commonly has a place to attach an anti-static wrist strap.

ESD strap   An item that fits around a technician's wrist and connects to an electronic component so that the technician and the component are at the same voltage potential, thus preventing an electrostatic discharge event, which can cause damage to electronic components.

Ethernet   A network system that carries computer data along with audio and video information. Ethernet adapters are the most common network cards.

Ethernet over Power (EoP)   Also called powerline communication. Sends network data to EoP modules that are plugged into power outlets to extend Ethernet networks.

Ethernet port   An RJ-45 port that connects a device to the wired network.

EULA   (end user license agreement) Legal language that specifies what can and cannot be done with a particular software application or operating system.

Event Viewer   A Windows tool that monitors various events in the computer.

exabyte (EB)   1 billion times 1 billion bytes, or 2^{60} (1,152,921,504,606,800 bytes).

executable file   A file with a *BAT*, *EXE*, or *COM* extension that starts an application, a utility, or a command. A file on which the operating system can take action.

execute disable An Intel feature that prevents malicious software from executing in specific memory locations.

exFAT   A file system type that improves upon FAT32 by having a theoretical maximum file size of 16EB, maximum volume size of 64ZB (but 512TB is current limit), smaller cluster sizes than FAT32, and an increased number of files allowed in a directory. Created for external storage media such as Flash drives and hard drives for saving images/video.

exit   This command closes the command prompt environment window.

expand   Command used to uncompress a file from a CAB file.

expansion slot   A motherboard socket into which adapters are connected.

Explorer   A Windows-based application that details certain information for all folders and files on each drive. It is used most commonly to copy or move files and folders. Sometimes called Windows Explorer. Now called File Explorer.

exposing   A laser printer process that has also been called the writing phase. Light is directed toward the drum to put 1s and 0s on the drum surface. Everywhere the light hits the drum changes the drum surface voltage.

ExpressCard   A replacement for PC Card technology that supports advanced serial technologies PCI-Express or USB connectivity through the ExpressCard slot and is used in laptop computers.

ext3 (third extended file system)   A file system type used in Linux-based operating systems that introduced journaling.

ext4 (fourth extended file system)   A file system type used in Linux-based operating systems that supports larger volumes and file sizes than ext3.

extender   Another name for a wireless repeater that increases the size of the wireless network.

extended partition   A hard drive division.

extension   In operating systems, the three or more characters following the filename and a period (.). The extension associates the file with a particular application that executes the file.

external command   A command located on a disk that the operating system must locate before the command can execute.

external data bus   The electronic lines that allow the processor to communicate with external devices. Also known as external data path or external data lines. See also *bus*.

external data lines   See *external data bus*.

external enclosure   A container for internal storage devices so that they may be attached as external devices.

F

F connector   A type of coaxial cable terminal end. It simply screws into the receiving connector.

facial recognition lock   A type of security lock on a mobile device or computer that uses the integrated camera and stored data to determine whether someone is granted access to the computer.

factory reset   Option to reset a computing device back to original settings.

faded print   A condition that arises due to inadequate ribbon, ink level, or toner. Check quality setting. In a thermal printer, reduce print head energy or print head pressure setting.

fail to boot   An error condition that occurs when the storage device is not responding.

fan   Mechanical cooling device attached to or beside the processor, or in the case.

fan speed   A BIOS/UEFI setting or monitoring capability that shows the speed in which the CPU and/or case fans operate.

FAT (file allocation table)   A method of organizing a computer's file system.

FAT (file system type)   A file system type also known as FAT16.

FAT12   An old file system that was originally designed for floppy disks.

FAT16   A file system supported by DOS and all Windows versions since DOS. DOS and Windows 9x have a 2GB limit. Newer Windows operating systems have a 4GB limit.

FAT32   A file system that supports hard drives up to 2TB in size.

fault tolerance   The capability to continue functioning after a hardware or software failure. An example of fault tolerance with hard drives is RAID configurations.

FCM (flash cache modules)   Predicts what data is used and puts that data on an SSC that is separate from the mechanical hard drive.

FDDI (Fiber Distributed Data Interface)   A high-speed fiber network that uses the ring topology and token passing access method.

feed assembly   The part of a computer responsible for taking the paper through the printer.

feeder   On a paper try, device that rolls the paper through the paper tray.

female port   A type of connector on a motherboard or a separate adapter with recessed portions (or holes) that accept a male cable's pins.

fiber network   High-speed, high-capacity computer network composed of optic fiber cables.

fiber-optic cable   An expensive network cabling made of plastic or glass fibers that carry data in the form of light pulses. Handles the greatest amount of data with least amount of data loss. Comes in single-mode and multi-mode.

FIFO setting   A serial device setting that enables or disables the UART's buffer.

file   An electronic container holding data or computer code that serves as a basic unit of storage.

File Explorer   A Windows-based application that details certain information for all folders and files on each drive. It is used most commonly to copy or move files and folders. Sometimes called Windows Explorer.

filename   Describes the name of a file. In older operating systems, the filename was limited to 8 characters plus a three-character extension. Today's operating systems allow filenames up to 255 characters.

file recovery software   An application used to recover data from a storage device.

file server   A computer configured to store files that can be accessed and managed from a remote location.

file system   Defines how data is stored on a drive. Examples of file systems include FAT16, FAT32, exFAT, and NTFS.

Finder   One of the four basic elements of OS X graphic user interface, the file manager is used for navigating and managing files or folders in the file system. It is similar to Microsoft's Windows Explorer.

fingerprint lock   A type of security lock on mobile devices and computers that requires a valid and stored fingerprint to be matched with whomever tries to gain access.

fingerprint reader   A biometric device used for user identification.

firewall   Software or a hardware device that protects one or more computers from being electronically attacked. It inspects data for security purposes and filters traffic based on network protocols and rules established by a network administrator. Firewalls operate at the OSI model application layer.

FireWire   See *IEEE 1394*.

FireWire 400   An IEEE 1394 standard that transfers data at 400Mb/s.

FireWire 800   An IEEE 1394 standard that transfers data at 800Mb/s.

FireWire port   A serial technology developed by Apple. See also *IEEE 1394*.

firmware   Combines hardware and software attributes. An example is a BIOS chip that has instructions (software) written into it.

fitness monitor   A wearable mobile device.

flash BIOS   A type of motherboard memory that allows updates by disk or by downloading Internet files.

flash memory   A type of nonvolatile memory that holds data when the power is off.

flickers   Display has something on it that appears and then disappears. Check video cable.

flow control   A serial device setting that determines the communication method.

[Fn]   A function key that when used with another key provides a specific function such as turning up speakers, connecting to an external monitor, or turning on the wireless adapter. This key is commonly found in laptops.

folder   In Windows-based operating systems, an electronic container that holds files as well as other folders. Folders were previously called directories in older operating systems.

Force Quit   An OS X feature that closes a MAC application that has stopped responding.

force stop   Allows a user to kill an app immediately.

form factor   The shape and size (height, width, and depth) of motherboards, adapters, memory chips, power supplies, and so on. Before building or upgrading, make sure the device's form factor fits the computer case.

format   A command that prepares a disk for use.

formatted (disk)   A disk that has been prepared to accept data.

fragmentation   Occurs over time as files are saved on the hard drive in clusters not adjacent to each other, which slows hard disk access time.

frame   The encapsulated data found at Layer 2 of the OSI model.

frequency response   The number of samples taken by a sound card.

frequency response range   The range of sounds a speaker can reproduce.

FRU (field replaceable unit)   Describes a computer part that can be replaced without having to send the entire computer to the manufacturer.

FSB (front side bus)   Part of the dual independent bus that connects the CPU to the motherboard components.

FTP (File Transfer Protocol)   A standard used when transferring files from one computer to another across a network.

full backup   A method of backing up a hard drive where the archive attribute is used. The backup software backs up all selected files and sets the archive bit to off.

full device encryption   A security measure found on mobile devices that supports encoding or scrambling all user data.

full-duplex   A serial device setting that allows the sending and receiving device to send data simultaneously. On a cable, the capability to transmit data in both directions simultaneously.

full format   During an installation process to partition a hard drive, this option identifies and marks bad sectors on the drive so they will not be used for data storage.

fully buffered memory   A technology used in network server memory that requires a special memory controller sometimes advertised as FBDIMMs.

fuser assembly   Found in a laser printer; melts the toner onto the paper.

fuser cleaning pad   The pad located above the laser printer's fuser roller that lightly coats it with silicon to prevent the paper sticking to the roller.

fusing   A laser printing process in which toner is melted into the paper.

fusing roller   A laser printer part responsible for heating the toner and melting it into the paper.

G

gadget   A Windows Vista option where applications such as the calendar and clock are available in a docked sidebar. Windows 7 has Media Center gadgets.

game pad   A device that attaches to a USB port and interacts with games.

gaming PC   A computer design that includes a powerful processor, high-end video or specialized GPU, a good sound card, and high-end cooling due to the demands placed on hardware when playing computer-based games.

gateway   An IP address assigned to a network device that tells the device where to send a packet that is going to a remote network. Also known as a default gateway, or a gateway of last resort.

Gb   An abbreviation for gigabit.

GB   See *gigabyte*.

geo-tracking   The ability to track where a GPS-capable mobile device, such as a cell phone, is located. Companies can also use it to locate lost or stolen mobile devices.

geometric distortion   A video issue in which the screen looks unusual and is not centered correctly. Check video cables or set the display to factory defaults.

gestures   On a touch device, using finger motions (swipe, pinch, tap, spread, and so on) to manipulate applications or features.

ghost image   A burn-in; an image seen on a display screen when an LCD or a plasma display has been left on for too long.

gigabyte   Approximately 1 billion bytes of information (exactly 1,073,741,824 bytes); abbreviated GB.

gigahertz   1 billion cycles per second (1GHz). Expresses the speed of a processor.

glasses   Wearable mobile device.

gloves   Latex, nonlatex, neoprine, or vinyl protection for hands when working on electronic equipment.

Google Play   A feature on Android devices that enables users to purchase applications.

GParted   Bundled with Ubuntu, a disk management tool that allows the creation, deletion, and resizing of partitions on a physical disk.

gpresult   Command that displays group policy settings. A group policy determines how a computer is configured for both system and user (or a group of users) settings.

GPS (Global Positioning System)   A satellite-based navigation system that transmits location information to receivers in mobile devices. Most mobile devices have GPS capability.

GPT (GUID, or globally unique identifier, partition table)   A type of partition table available in 64-bit Windows editions. GPTs can have up to 128 partitions and volumes up to 18EB.

GPU (graphics processing unit)   A video adapter processor that assists in video communication between the video adapter and the system processor. Also known as video processor, video coprocessor, or video accelerator.

gpupdate   Command used to refresh local and active directory-based group policy settings.

graphical interface fails to load   A Windows startup problem in which startup files are missing or corrupt or there are hardware problems.

graphics/CAD/CAM design workstation   A powerful computer system utilized by design engineers or graphic designers. It usually has multicore processors, high-end video cards with maximum GPU and video RAM, large displays, large-capacity hard drive and SSD, and maximum system RAM. Output devices such as scanner, plotter, or 3-D printer.

grayware   A generic term for applications or files that affect computer performance and cause unexpected and unsolicited events to occur. Can come from downloading shareware or freeware, infected emails, selecting an advertisement shown in a pop-up window, or through a Trojan virus. Spyware, adware, and malware are all types of grayware.

grep   A common OS X utility, it searches output for a specified term.

group policy   A type of security policy applied in a network domain environment. The policy dictates what a set of users can do.

grounding   Also called grounding out. Occurs when the motherboard or adapter is not installed properly and has a trace touching the computer frame.

GRUB (Grand Unified Boot Loader)   A Linux bootloader that generally replaces the earlier LILO bootloader. It contains all information about how a disk is organized, such as the size and layout of partitions. The latest version is called GRUB2.

GUI (graphical user interface)   In operating systems, an interface in which the user selects files, programs, and commands by clicking pictorial representations (icons) rather than typing commands at a command prompt.

gyroscope   A technology used in mobile devices that measures and maintains screen orientation. Used with an accelerometer so that a mobile device can be turned and the screen orientation also turns.

H

half-duplex   A serial device setting that enables either the sending or the receiving device to send data, one device at a time. On a cable, the capability to transmit in both directions but not at the same time.

handshaking   The method by which two serial devices negotiate communications.

hard drive   A sealed data storage medium on which information is stored. Also called a hard disk.

hard drive caching   Data sent to and stored on a PC's hard drive.

hard reset   Describes turning a device off and back on or a factory reset of a mobile device.

hardware   A tangible, physical item, such as the keyboard or monitor.

HAV (hardware assisted virtualization)   A required feature of Microsoft's Windows Virtual PC. This feature is available on some computers and can be enabled or disabled through the system BIOS.

HD-15   The female VGA port that has three rows of holes. Also known as DE-15 port.

HDCP (high-bandwidth digital content)   Intel's feature to prevent video piracy on the DVI, DisplayPort, or HDMI port. For example, you could not see a movie broadcast by an HDCP-enabled computer unless the external display were also HDCP-capable.

HDD (hard disk drive)   A mechanical drive with metal platters used to store data.

HDMI (high-definition multimedia interface)   An upgraded digital interface that carries audio and video over the same cable.

HDMI-to-VGA converter   Video connector with an HDMI connector on one side and a VGA port on the other.

hdwwiz.exe   The command that can open the Add Hardware Wizard.

head crash   Occurs when a read/write head touches a platter, causing damage to the heads or the platter.

headset   A mobile wearable device.

heap   Memory allocated to Windows core files that records every Windows action, such as each mouse click, each resizing of a window, and so on.

heat sink   A metal device for cooling the processor by conducting heat to its fins or bars. Convection then transfers the heat away by flowing air through the case.

heat spreader   Aluminum or copper fittings on memory modules used to dissipate heat.

Help button   A question mark button located in the upper-right corner of a dialog box. Clicking it allows access to information on various topics.

hertz   A measurement of electrical frequency equal to one cycle per second. Abbreviated Hz.

hexa-core   A six-core processor.

hibernate mode   A low-power state used in computing devices that saves information in RAM to nonvolatile memory such as a hard drive or flash media.

hidden attribute   A designation that keeps a file from being seen in directory listings. However, with today's operating systems, this attribute does not help because the operating system makes it easy to see hidden files.

hidden share   A share that has a dollar sign ($) added to the share name so that the share is not shown to a remote networked computer.

high-level format   A process that sets up the file system for use by the computer. It is the third and last step in preparing a hard drive for use.

high resource utilization   When the mobile device is slow to respond due to applications taking all the memory and processor power.

HomeGroup   A Windows 7 and higher feature to make home networking easier to configure and join.

home screen   The starting place for any mobile device running either iOS or Android and is where application icons are found. This is also the GUI interface for input to the operating system.

home server   A server commonly used to be a web server, print server, control home devices, manage backups, and be accessed from outside the home. A home server commonly includes the capability to stream sound or video, share files, have a Gigabit NIC, or have a RAID hard drive array.

home theater PC (HTPC)   A computer, part of a home theater. HTPC typically has a programmable remote control for control of all home theater components. Components include a compact form factor case and motherboard with quiet fans and quiet power supply fan, surround-sound audio ports, HDMI video output, TV tuner card or cable card to receive pay channels, audio/video hard drive (AV hard drive or AVHD) that is quiet; media player to stream entertainment, watch videos, view photos, or listen to music; digital video recorder (DVR) to record TV shows, transfer data from a camcorder or camera, or store movies or media for playback; and large display with multiple HDMI, USB, component, composite, and audio/video ports and possible wireless connectivity.

horizontal streaking   Occurs in a laser printer; may be due to insufficient toner levels in the cartridge.

host   Another name for a network device. It also represents a part of an IP address. An IP address has a network portion and a host portion.

host address   A portion of an IP address that represents the specific network device.

host machine   In a virtualization environment, the real computer.

hot fix   Software that has one or more files that fix a particular software problem. Contrast this to a patch or a service pack.

hotspot   A wireless network that has free Internet access. Security is a concern because no encryption or authentication is commonly required.

hot swappable   Describes hardware that can be installed with power applied.

hot swapping   Allows adapters to be inserted into a slot or devices to be attached or unattached while the computer is powered.

hot spot   See *wireless hot spot.*

HPA (Host Protected Area)   A hidden part of the hard drive that is used to reinstall the operating system. It sometimes contains applications that are installed when the computer was sold. Using an HPA reduces the amount of hard drive space available to the operating system.

HPPCL (Hewlett-Packard printer control language)   A popular print software that translates between the printer and the computer.

HT   See *Hyper-Threading.*

HTML (Hypertext Markup Language)   A programming language used to create Internet web pages.

HTPC (home theater PC)   A special hardware component to a home theater configuration, which has a compact form factor case and motherboard with quiet fans and quiet power supply fan.

HTTP (Hypertext Transfer Protocol)   A standard for Internet data communication.

HTTPS (HTTP over SSL)   Encrypted HTTP communication through an SSL session. Web pages are encrypted and decrypted.

hub   A device used with the universal serial bus or in a star network topology that allows multiple device connections. A network hub cannot look at each data frame coming through its ports like a switch does.

hybrid cloud   A type of cloud technology in which the company has some cloud services maintained by internal staff (private cloud) and some cloud services that are outsourced (public cloud).

hybrid SSD   A drive that has two parts: a mechanical hard drive as well as flash memory used as an SSD.

Hyper-Threading   A technology created by Intel that is an alternative to using two processors. HT allows a single processor to handle two separate sets of instructions simultaneously.

HyperTransport   AMD's I/O architecture in which a serial-link design allows devices to communicate in daisy-chain fashion without interfering with any other communication. Thus, I/O bottleneck is mitigated.

hypervisor   In a virtualization environment, the software that creates the virtual machine and allocates resources to the virtual machine. Also called virtual machine monitor or virtual machine manager.

I

I/O address (input/output address)   A port address that allows an external device to communicate with the microprocessor. It is analogous to a mailbox number.

I/O shield   A part that allows for optimum air flow and grounding for the motherboard ports.

IaaS (Infrastructure as a Service)   A type of cloud technology service. It describes routers, switches, servers, virtual machines, load balancers, access points, storage, and any other infrastructure device that is provided through the online environment.

ICH (I/O controller hub)   A part of the chipset that controls such motherboard components as SATA ports, PCI and PCIe slots, USB ports, audio ports, and integrated network cards. Also known as the south bridge.

iCloud (offsite data storage)   An Apple cloud-based service that comes with OS X offering storage, application support, and syncing of contacts, photos, email, bookmarks, documents, and more between multiple OS X, iOS, and even Windows devices.

ICMP (Internet Control Message Protocol)   A Layer 3 protocol used for troubleshooting network connectivity. Commands that use ICMP include `ping`, `pathping`, and `tracert`.

icon   An operating system graphic that represents a file, an application, hardware, and shared network resources.

ID badge (identification badge)   A physical security measure to identify a person as an authorized person.

IDE (Integrated Drive Electronics)   An interface that evolved into the ATA (now PATA) standard that supports internal storage devices.

IDS (intrusion detection system)   Software or hardware that is designed to detect potential security issues that could be or allow an illegal entry to the computer or network. The IDS could log the incident, contact someone, and perform security measures to prevent invasion.

IEEE (Institute of Electrical and Electronics Engineers)   An organization that provides a framework for defining standards relating to computers and networks.

IEEE 1394   A port that uses the IEEE 1394 standard for high-speed audio and video device data transfers known as FireWire. A single port supports the connectivity of up to 63 devices.

ifconfig   In Linux/UNIX environment, a command that shows network interface information for Ethernet ports.

IGP (integrated graphics processor)   Sometimes called an iGPU. Speeds up video processing.

iGPU (integrated graphics processing unit)   Speeds up video processing with reduced power consumption.

imaging drum   Photosensitive drum located inside a toner cartridge; attracts laser toner particles.

IMAP (Internet Mail Access Protocol)   A protocol used to receive email through the Internet.

IMEI (International Mobile Equipment Identity)   A unique number given to a cell phone and to some satellite phones. A serial number.

impact paper   Special paper designed to withstand the pressure of image struck upon it.

impact printer   Sometimes called a dot matrix printer. A type of printer that physically impacts a ribbon that places an image on the paper.

impact print head   Holds tiny wires called print wires; found in dot matrix printers.

IMSI (International Mobile Subscriber Identity)   A unique number that is stored in your smartphone's Subscriber Identification Module (SIM) card.

in-place upgrade   A method of upgrading Windows when an older Windows version is already installed.

incineration   Destruction by fire.

incorrect color pattern   Caused by bent or broken video pins on a monitor's cable ends.

incremental backup   A method used with a full backup. The incremental backup goes faster because it backs up only files that have changed since the last backup.

indexing   A Microsoft Windows configurable feature that allows quick searches for files and folders.

infrared   A technology utilizing infrared light that allows devices to communicate across a wireless network. Examples are laptop computers, printers, and handheld computing devices.

infrastructure mode   A type of wireless network that contains an access point for wireless devices to be connected together.

inherited permissions   Windows NTFS permission type that is propagated from what Microsoft calls a parent object. For example, if a folder is given the permission of Read, then all files within that folder inherit the read-only attribute.

initialize disk   A disk option available through the Windows Disk Management tool that enables a disk so that data may be stored on it.

ink cartridge   A container that holds the ink and the nozzles for the inkjet printer. Also known as a print cartridge.

inkjet printer   A type of printer that squirts ink through tiny nozzles to produce print. Inkjet printers produce high-quality, high-resolution, color output.

inkjet print head   Holds the ink reservoir and the spray nozzles; easily replaced.

input device   Used to enter data into a computer. Some examples are keyboard, mouse, joystick, touch screen, trackball, camera, game console, scanner, and digital pen.

Intel Corporation The largest processor manufacturer in the world. Intel also makes chipsets, motherboards, network cards, microcontrollers, and other electronic chips and components.

interlacing A scanning method used with monitors in which only the odd-numbered pixel rows are scanned, followed by the even-numbered pixel rows.

intermittent connectivity A symptom of poor or faulty connections with devices on the same network. Use the ping command to check connections all around the network.

intermittent device failure A symptom of a faulty device when sporadic or irregular problems occur with that device.

internal command A command that is part of the command interpreter that the operating system does not have to locate to execute. An example of an internal command is DIR.

internal data bus The electronic lines inside a processor. See also *bus*.

Internet appliance Describe any device that can connect to the Internet through a wired or wireless network.

Internet Explorer An application used to access the Internet through a network or dial-up access. Now called Microsoft Edge.

interrupt See *IRQ*.

intrusion detection/notification Also known as chassis intrusion, this option provides notification when the computer cover is removed. It is enabled/disabled through BOS/UEFI.

inverter Converts low DC voltage to high AV voltage for the backlight bulb in an LED display.

IOPS (input/output operations per second) A measurement of hard drive speed for both magnetic drives and SSDs that takes into account sequential reads/writes as well as random reads/writes.

IP (Internet Protocol) A Layer 3 protocol that is part of the TCP/IP protocol suite.

IP address A type of network adapter address used when multiple networks are linked. Known as a Layer 3 address, in IPv4 it is a 32-bit binary number with groups of 8 bits separated by a dot. This numbering scheme is also known as dotted-decimal notation. Each 8-bit group represents numbers from 0 to 255. An IPv4 IP address example is 113.19.12.102. Also see IPv4 and IPv6.

IP address conflict When two devices have been manually assigned the same IP address. Check any device that has a manually configured IP address for any duplicate IP address.

ipconfig A command used from a command prompt in Windows to view the current IP settings.

IPP (Internet Printing Protocol) A protocol used for network-connected printers that can include remote print job management and print configuration such as media size or print resolution.

IPS (intrusion prevention system) A security device that actively monitors and scans network traffic for malicious traffic and violations of security policies as well as takes appropriate action.

IPsec (Internet Protocol Security) A suite of protocols for securing a communication session such as a VPN tunnel.

IPv4 (Internet Protocol version 4) A type of IP address that uses 32 bits (four groups of 8 bits each) shown as decimal numbers in dotted-decimal format. An example of an IPv4 address is 192.168.10.1.

IPv6 (Internet Protocol version 6) A type of IP address that uses 128 bits represented by hexadecimal numbers. An example of an IPv6 IP address is fe80::13e:4586:5807:95f7. Each set of four digits represents 16 bits.

IR (infrared) A technology used for wireless input/output, but useful over only short distances.

IRQ (interrupt request) A microprocessor priority system that assigns a number to each expansion adapter or port to facilitate orderly communication.

ISDN (Integrated Services Digital Network) A digital phone line that has three separate channels, two B channels, and a D channel. The B channel allows 64Kb/s transmission speeds. The D channel allows 16Kb/s transmissions.

ISO (Industry Standards Organization or International Organization for Standardization) An international group that provides technical specifications related to computers, networks, and telecommunication.

isotropic antenna A type of antenna used as a reference for other antennas. It is not a real antenna. An isotropic antenna theoretically transmits an equal amount of power in all directions.

ISP (Internet service provider) A vendor that provides a connection to the Internet.

iTunes   An Apple program that allows users to play and manage music, books, movies, and lectures.

ITX   A motherboard form factor size that is smaller than ATX, the most common form factor. Comes in mini-ITX, nano-ITX, and pico-ITX sizes.

`iwconfig`   In Linux/UNIX systems, a command that shows network interface information for wireless adapters.

iWork   An OS X office productivity suite containing a word processor, a spreadsheet, and presentation applications.

J

JBOD (just a bunch of disks or just a bunch of drives)   A term given to combining more than one drive that is recognized as a single drive letter or a single virtual disk. This is similar in concept to RAID but is not one of the RAID levels.

joule dissipation capacity   A measure of a surge protector's capability to absorb overvoltage power surges. The higher the capacity, the better the protection.

joystick   A device that attaches to a USB port and is used to interact with games.

jumper   A plastic cover for two metal pins on a jumper block.

K

Kb   Abbreviation for kilobit.

KB   See *kilobyte*.

kernel   The heart of an operating system. It acts as the controller and interpreter for nearly everything in a system so that hardware and software can interface and work together. It controls memory management, peripherals, and allocating other system resources to processes.

kernel panic   A critical system error that the operating system cannot recover from. When this happens in OS X, the Mac reboots to return to a stable state.

keyboard   Allows users to provide input into the computer.

keyboard port   DIN connector on the motherboard into which only the keyboard cable must connect.

Keychain Access   An OS X utility for managing saved passwords securely.

keyed   A connector or cable that has an extra metal piece that allows correct connections.

key fob   Used for keyless entry.

kibibyte   A binary prefix term that is used to describe 2^{10} or 1,024 and is abbreviated KiB. Instead of saying that it is 1 kilobyte, which people tend to think of as approximately 1,000 bytes, the term kibibyte is used.

kilobyte   Approximately 1,000 bytes of information (exactly 1,024 bytes).

KMS (Key Management Service)   A service used in companies that have 25 or more Windows computers to deploy. KMS is a software application installed on a computer. All newly installed computers register with the computer that has KMS installed. Every 180 days, the computer is re-activated for the license. Each KMS key can be used on two computers up to 10 times. Contrast with *MAK*.

KVM switch (keyboard, video, mouse switch)   A component that allows multiple computers to be connected to a single keyboard, monitor, and mouse.

L

L1 cache   Fast memory located inside the processor.

L2 cache   Fast memory located inside the processor housing, but not inside the processor.

L3 cache   Any fast cache memory installed on the motherboard when both L1 and L2 cache are on the processor. Could also be located inside the processor housing.

LAN (local area network)   A group of devices sharing resources in a single area such as a room or a building.

laser lens   A component of the optical drive that reads the data from the optical disc; susceptible to dust accumulation. Also known as an objective lens.

laser printer   A type of printer that produces output using a process similar to a copier. Laser printers are the most expensive type of printer.

laser printer maintenance kit   Vendor-specific. May include a separation pad, pickup roller, transfer roller, charge roller, and fuser assembly.

Last Known Good Configuration   Used when the Windows configuration has been changed by adding hardware or software that is incompatible with the operating system or when an important service has been accidentally disabled.

latency   In networking, the amount of delay experienced as a packet travels from source to destination.

launcher A dock-like shortcut bar that allows manipulation of the graphical user interface (GUI) so that multiple apps and/or commands are easily deployed. It has the functionality of being an application launcher shortcut as well as having a universal search feature built-in to it.

Launchpad An OS X application launcher shortcut.

LCD (liquid crystal display) A video technology used with laptops and flat screen monitors. The two basic types of LCD are passive matrix and active matrix.

LC fiber connector A common connector used with fiber-optic cable, manufactured by Lucent.

LDAP (Lightweight Directory Access Protocol) A common network term. It is used to access, maintain, and distribute directory and database-type information.

LED (light-emitting diode) A video output technology that is a low-power, low-heat, long-lasting electronic device using liquid crystals.

legacy system An outdated computer system or piece of network equipment that needs to be replaced or updated.

less A common OS X command that shows the contents of a file.

library Windows 7 storage that is similar to a folder but that is automatically indexed for faster searching.

Lightning port An Apple port/cable used to connect displays and external drives.

Li-ion battery A lithium battery, which is light and can hold a charge for a long period of time; found in cell phones and portable devices such as cameras.

LILO (LInux LOader) A Linux bootloader now largely replaced by GRUB/GRUB2. LILO is older and more basic, without features like network boot or command-line interface.

limited connectivity An error condition when Internet connectivity is lost.

line conditioner A device that protects a computer from overvoltage and undervoltage conditions as well as adverse noise conditions. Also known as a power conditioner.

line-of-sight network In WiMAX wireless networks, the between-towers connection that travels from WiMAX tower to WiMAX tower. Also called line-of-sight backhauls.

link-local address A type of IPv6 address assigned to a NIC. It is used to communicate on a particular network and cannot be used to communicate with devices on a different network.

Linux Released in 1991 by developer Linus Torvalds, is a widely used operating system platform that is similar to UNIX. It is a free open-source operating system that anyone can use, contribute to, and modify for their needs. It is widely used in many different areas of technology such as servers, desktops, embedded systems, and smartphones.

liquid cooling An alternative to a fan or sink for processor cooling. Liquid is circulated through the system. Heat from the processor is transferred to the cooler liquid.

local administrator A user account that has full power over a Windows-based computer. A local administrator can install hardware and software; uses all the administrative tools; creates and deletes hard drive partitions or volumes; and creates, deletes, and manages local user accounts.

local connectivity Describes devices on the same network including the default gateway. Pinging devices on the same network is a good check of local connectivity.

local policy Security rules that can be applied to a computer.

local share Something such as a printer, folder, or disc that has been made available across a network.

locate An OS X command that searches for a file in a database of paths. Commonly used subsequent to **updated**, which is a command used to update a local database on the system that contains the full pathname of each file.

locked doors Where network equipment should be stored behind as a security measure.

logical drive A division of an extended partition into separate units, which appear as separate drive letters.

LoJack (BIOS option) A BIOS setting option that controls locating the device, remote locking the device, remote data deletion, and displaying an "if lost" message.

loopback address A private IP address of 127.0.0.1 or ::1 that can test a NIC's basic network setup and the TCP/IP stack.

loopback plug A troubleshooting device that allows port testing.

lost cluster A sector on a disk that the file allocation table cannot associate with any file or directory.

loud clicking noise A symptom that a mechanical hard drive is failing.

low-level format   A utility that formats a drive; note that this is different than the high-level format done on a newly installed drive or during an operating system installation.

low memory error   Caused by a printer not having enough memory or by insufficient hard drive space.

ls   An OS X command to list the contents of a currently working directory.

lumen   A measure of light output or brightness; how much visible light is coming out of equipment such as lamps, lighting equipment, or projectors.

M

M.2   A type of connector that allows attaching modules of varying size. First found in mobile devices and used for SSDs but now found on desktop motherboards.

MAC address (Media Access Control address)   One of two types of addresses assigned to network adapters, used when two devices on the same network communicate. Known as a Layer 2 address.

MAC filtering   A security feature on an access point that allows MAC addresses to be entered to limit the number of wireless devices allowed on the wireless network.

mail server   Also known as an email server. Used to maintain a database of email accounts, store email that has been sent and received, and communicate with other mail servers.

maintenance counter   Reset through the laser printer menu to count the number of pages until the message to apply the maintenance kit appears again.

maintenance kit   A collection of items commonly used with technical support. Includes a portable vacuum, toner vacuum, compressed air, swaps, monitor wipes, lint-free cloths, general-purpose cloths, general-purpose cleanser, denatured alcohol, anti-static brush, optical drive cleaning kit, gold contact cleaner, safety goggles, and an air filter or mask.

MAK (Multiple Activation Key)   A method in which the Internet or a phone call must be made to register one or more Windows computers. This method has a limited number of activations.

male port   A connector on a motherboard or adapter with protruding pins that accepts a cable with a female connector.

malware   Software code designed to damage an electronic device (cause lockups, slowness, crash an app, cause the device to not run or boot, and more).

MAN (metropolitan area network)   In a networking environment, describes networks that span a city or town.

man   As an OS X command, short for manual. The command **man** followed by another command brings up an instruction manual for using the other command.

man-in-the-middle (MitM)   A security attack in which a hacker inserts a device between a sender and a receiver so that this device can receive the intended traffic. APs, DHCP servers, and default gateways (routers or Layer 3 devices) are common devices simulated.

mantrap   A method of separating a nonsecure area from a secure area to prevent unauthorized access and tailgating.

MAP (Microsoft Assessment and Planning Toolkit)   Used for planning a Windows deployment in a corporate environment.

MAPI (Messaging Application Programming Interface)   A Microsoft-proprietary protocol used with email.

marking   The part of the printer that places the image on the paper. Also called the marking engine or marking subsystem.

mask   An article of personal protective equipment that is to be used to prevent inhalation of harmful airborne particulates and fumes when working in dusty environments such as when working on a computer or laser printer or inside a network wiring closet.

master   A jumper setting used to configure a PATA IDE device; the controlling device on the interface.

Mb   An abbreviation for megabit.

MB   See *megabyte*.

MBR (master boot record)   A program that reads the partition table to find the primary partition used to boot the system.

MBSA (Microsoft Baseline Security Analyzer)   A tool that can identify security misconfigurations.

MCBF (mean cycles between failures)   A performance comparison measurement which is found by dividing the mean time between failures (MTBF) by the duration time of a cycle (operations per hour). The lower the number, the better the performance.

MCH (memory controller hub)   A part of a chipset that connects directly to the processor. The MCH controls RAM and video expansion slots. It is also called the north bridge.

MD   A command issued from a command prompt that creates a directory (folder) or subdirectory.

MDM (mobile device management) The capability to view and manage multiple mobile devices.

measured service The capability to track cloud consumer usage and apply resources as needed based on usage.

mebibyte A binary prefix value that describes a value of 220 or 1,048,576 and abbreviated MiB.

media player A special hardware component to a home theater configuration that allows streaming entertainment, watching your videos and photos, or listening to your music and possible wireless connectivity.

megabyte Approximately 1 million bytes of data (exactly 1,048,576 bytes). Abbreviated as MB.

memory The part of a computer that temporarily stores applications, user documents, and system operating information.

memory address A unique address for memory chips.

Memory Diagnostic Tool A tool accessed by booting from Advanced Boot Options menu in Windows to thoroughly test RAM.

menu bar A component of OS X GUI, it is anchored to the top of a screen and is a dynamically changing bar that presents contextual drop-down menu options on the left side depending on which window is active. On the right side, it provides shortcuts such as connecting to a Wi-Fi network or changing volume. It is also informative, displaying information such as battery life on MacBooks and the time.

metro UI A Windows graphical user interface where tiles are used on the desktop.

MFD (multifunction device) A device such as an all-in-one printer that includes a printer, scanner, copier, and fax machine. The term might also describe a network device that commonly includes a router, access point, and switch.

MFP (multifunction product, printer, or peripheral) Also known as an all-in-one printer. See also *MFD*.

micro-ATX A smaller version of a standard ATX-sized motherboard form factor.

micro-ATX power supply form factor A smaller version of a standard ATX-sized power supply.

microphone An audio input device that can be integrated into the mobile device or can be added externally as with a wireless Bluetooth device; controlled with an app.

microprocessor See *processor*.

microSD A storage device with nonvolatile flash memory used for mobile devices.

Microsoft Management Console Holds snap-ins or tools used to maintain the computer. Also known as the Computer Management console.

Microsoft Security Essentials A free antivirus program for Windows Vista and 7 (but not Windows 8 or 10 because it is integrated into Windows Defender).

Microsoft Store Mobile device apps can be obtained through this source.

micro-USB A standard interface port on mobile devices and smartphones.

MIDI (Musical Instrument Digital Interface) An interface built in to a sound card to create synthesized music.

MIME (Multipurpose Internet Mail Extension) When used with SNMP, allows non-ASCII character sets and other rich media content to be included with email.

MIMO (multiple input/multiple output) Describes 802.11n wireless technology in which multiple antennas operate cooperatively to increase throughput on a wireless network.

mini-ATX A smaller version of a standard ATX-sized motherboard form factor.

mini-DIN A motherboard connector sometimes called a PS/2 connector that connects keyboards and mice.

mini-DIN-6 connector A connector that is round with six small holes keyed to prevent incorrect cable insertion. Mouse and keyboard connectors are examples of this type of connector.

miniHDMI An upgrade to DVI, these connectors are used with mobile devices. Carries audio and video over the same cable.

mini-ITX A smaller version of the ITX motherboard form factor size.

mini PCI A 32-bit 33MHz standard used in laptops, docking stations, and printers.

mini PCIe A 52-bit expansion slot or card used in mobile devices.

miniSD A storage device with nonvolatile flash memory used for mobile devices.

mini-USB Port found on mobile device.

Mission Control An OS X utility that gives an overview for managing all application windows and virtual desktops.

MLC (multi-level cell)   A cell that stores more than 1 bit in a memory cell that is used in a SSD (solid state drive). Contrast with *SLC*.

MMC (Microsoft Management Console)   Also known as the Computer Management Console. Holds tools such as Device Manager, Disk Management, Local Users and Groups, Event Viewer, Task Scheduler, Performance, Shared Folders, and Services.

mobile docking   Recharging station that provides a stable environment for mobile devices. Some mobile docking stations can charge more than one device at a time.

mobile payment service   The ability to pay for goods or services through a mobile device instead of with cash or a credit card.

modem (modulator/demodulator)   A device that connects a computer to a phone line, or connects computers and mobile devices to broadband, wireless, Wi-Fi, Bluetooth, or satellite networks.

modem card   Allows PC to connect to a remote modem using an analog phone line.

modem isolator   See *phone line isolator*.

Molex   A type of power connector that extends from the computer's power supply to various devices.

monitor   Displays information from the computer to the user.

motherboard   The main circuit board of a computer. Also known as the mainboard, planar, or system board.

motion sensor   A device used to detect movement.

mount   To make a drive available and recognizable to the operating system.

mouse   A data input device that moves the cursor or selects menus and options.

mouse port   A DIN connector on the motherboard that should accept only a mouse cable.

MOV (metal oxide varistor)   An electronic component built in to some surge protectors to absorb overvoltage spikes or surges.

msconfig   A system configuration utility command that allows an Administrator to enable or disable services, access control panel links, and control applications.

MSDS (material safety data sheet)   A document that contains information about a product, its toxicity, storage, and disposal.

MSI (message signaled interrupt)   A type of interrupt method that delivers up to 32 interrupts to the CPU using software and memory space on behalf of a single device. A PCIe card is required to support MSI.

msinfo32   A command used to bring up the System Information window from a command prompt. The System Information window contains details about hardware and hardware configurations as well as software and software drivers.

MSI-X (message signaled interrupt)   A type of interrupt method that allows a device to allocate up to 2,048 interrupts. Note that most devices do not use this many. A PCIe card is required to support MSI-X.

mstsc   A command used to control and use a remote computer; brings up the Remote Desktop utility.

MTBF (mean time between failures)   The average number of hours before a device fails.

multiboot   A situation in which a computer can boot from two or more operating systems.

multifactor authentication   Using two or more factors to provide access. Can be something you possess such as a card, current location, security token provided code, PIN number, fingerprint, facial recognition, palm print, or a password.

multi-mode fiber   A type of fiber-optic cabling that allows multiple light signals to be sent along the same cable.

multi-monitor taskbar   A Windows option in which the taskbar can display on all displays or across them.

multimeter   A tool used to take voltage, current, resistance, and continuity.

multiplier   A motherboard setting used to determine CPU speed. (Multiplier times bus speed equals CPU speed.)

multitouch   A technology used on mobile devices to use a finger or knuckle to interface with the operating system by pinching, spreading, rotating, or swiping.

MU-MIMO (multi-user multiple input/multiple output)   A wireless technology used with the 802.11ac that allows up to eight simultaneous streams from multiple devices.

mv   An OS X command that moves a file.

N

NAND flash memory   An SSD storage technique in which data is retained even when the device is not powered.

nanometer   A measurement of processor technology length equal to .000000001 meter (1 times $10-9$). For example, chipsets created using 22nm technology have more transistors in the same amount of space as chipsets created using 32nm or 45nm technology.

nanosecond One-billionth of a second.

NAS (network-attached storage) A special hardware component of virtualization to increase storage space that can be shared with other devices.

NAT (network address translation) A method of conserving public IP addresses. NAT uses private IP addresses that become translated to public IP addresses.

native resolution The number of pixels going across and down a flat panel monitor. This resolution is the specification for which the monitor was made and is the optimum resolution.

Nautilus The default file manager in Linux systems.

NBT (NetBIOS over TCP/IP) Uses TCP ports 137–139 to support outdated applications that rely on the NetBIOS API to use a TCP/IP-based network. Also known as NetBT.

nbtstat A command to view other network devices by their assigned names and display statistics relevant to current TCP/IP connections on the local computer or a remote computer using NBT.

net From a prompt, the **net** command manages almost everything on a network. It is followed by other options and each option has different parameters.

NetBEUI A nonroutable network protocol commonly found on peer-to-peer networks. Can work only on simple networks, not on linked networks.

NetBIOS (Network Basic Input/Output System) An older method of providing name resolution and connectivity methods for both connectionless and connection-oriented communication sessions.

NetBT (NetBIOS over TCP/IP) Uses TCP ports 137–139 to support outdated applications that rely on the NetBIOS API to use a TCP/IP-based network. Also known as NBT.

netdom From a prompt, a command that can manage workstations in a domain environment.

netstat A command that can view current network connections and the local routing table for a PC.

net use The **net** command controls and monitors network devices. Many subcommands are used with the **net** command; for example, the **net use** command attaches to a remote network device.

network Two or more devices that can communicate and share resources between them.

network layer Layer 3 of the OSI model that coordinates data movement between two devices on separate networks.

network number The portion of an IP address that represents which network the computer is on.

network port A port that connects a computer to a wired network.

network printer mapping Enables network users to add the printer to their computer using the domain printer name or IP address.

network protocol A data communication language.

network share A folder or network device that has been shared and is accessible from a remote computer.

NFC (near field communication) A technology that connects nearby devices without a cord.

NFS (Network File System) An open standard protocol used for sharing files across a network.

NIC (network interface card) An adapter used to connect a device to a network.

NLX (New Low Profile Extended) A motherboard form factor.

NNTP (Network News Transfer Protocol) A protocol used to deliver news to network clients. Uses TCP port 119. If TLS (Transport Layer Security) is used, then the port number is commonly 563.

no connectivity An error condition that exists if the self-test issued from a computer fails.

no image on the printer display Check that the printer is powered on; check the power outlet; and check the power brick.

non-ECC A type of memory that does not do error correction. Most workstation memory is non-ECC memory.

noncompliant system A system that does not meet security policy guidelines and could be a potential security threat.

nonparity A less expensive type of memory chip but does not perform error checking.

nonvolatile memory Memory that remains even when the computer is powered off. ROM and flash memory are examples of nonvolatile memory.

north bridge Describes the connection from the CPU to RAM, the video expansion slot, and to the PCI/PCIe bus.

notification area (mobile) A place on mobile devices that contains information such as battery life, wireless signal strength, time, or external media connectivity. Usually in the lower-right corner on a tablet and at the top of the display on a smartphone.

notification area (Windows) The far right area of the taskbar, which contains information about an application or tool, such as security, network access, speaker control, or date and time.

notepad An accessory program on Windows.

nslookup A Windows troubleshooting command that displays network domain names and their associated IP addresses.

NTFS (New Technology File System) File system used with operating systems today (starting with Windows NT).

NTFS permissions A security measure that can dictate what a specific user or group can do with a file or folder.

NTLDR (new technology loader) A file used during the Windows XP boot process. In Windows Vista and higher, this function is performed by the Windows Boot Manager that calls the `winload.exe` executable file to handle the boot process.

NTLDR is missing A Windows boot error condition in which the operating system needs to be reinstalled.

NTP (Network Time Protocol) A protocol that synchronizes time between network devices.

Num Lock indicator light The light above the Num Lock key that glows when the key is depressed and the function is activated.

O

OCR (optical character recognition) A technology used to convert an image into text. Commonly used application with scanners.

octa-core An eight-core processor.

ODD (optical disk drive) A collective term for CD, DVD, and BD because they use optical discs that are read from, written to, or both.

OEM (original equipment manufacturer) The original producer of a product. That product is bought by a company that rebrands or sells the part or computer under its own name.

ohm A measurement of electrical resistance.

OK button A button located in the bottom-right side of a dialog box that can be clicked to save any changes applied and close the window.

OLED (organic LED) Does not require a backlight like LCDs but has a film of organic compounds placed in rows and columns that can emit light. Is lightweight and has a fast response time, low power usage, and a wide viewing angle.

omnidirectional antenna A type of antenna that has a radiation pattern in all directions.

on demand 24/7 access from anywhere and possibly any device.

on-board NIC (BIOS/UEFI) A BIOS/UEFI setting where you can enable or disable an RJ-45 port built in to the motherboard.

on-die cache L2 cache when housed in the processor packaging.

One Drive Microsoft's cloud storage solution.

open authentication Used in wireless networks; allows a wireless device to send a frame to the access point with the sender's identity (MAC address).

open source Operating system that allow vendors to use the core source code and the ability to customize the operating system, for example, Google Android or Linux.

operating system (OS) A piece of software that loads a computer and makes it operational.

optical drive A storage device that accepts optical discs such as CDs, DVDs, or BDs that have data, music, video, or software applications.

optical mouse A mouse that has optical sensors used to move the pointer.

orientation The way in which a document or screen is presented: portrait versus landscape.

OS See *operating system*.

OSHA (Occupational Safety and Health Administration) A division of the Federal Department of Labor that promotes safe and healthy working conditions by enforcing standards and providing workplace safety training.

OSI model (Open Systems Interconnect Model) A standard for information transfer across a network that was developed by the International Standards Organization. The model has seven layers; each layer uses the layer below it, and each layer provides some function to the one above it.

OS X A UNIX-based operating system that was developed by Apple, Inc., for its Macintosh line of computers, called Mac for short. OS X is the second most-used desktop operating system behind Windows and is the most-used type of UNIX/Linux-based desktop operating systems.

output device A piece of computer hardware that receives (not sends to) data from a computer. An example of an output device is a monitor.

overclocking Manually changing the front side bus speed and/or multiplier to increase CPU and system speed, but at a cost of increasing the CPU operating temperature.

overheating   Causes artifacts on display screen. Check GPU or video adapter for overheating. Check power supply for adequate power output.

oversized images   May be an issue with the video driver or the resolutions could be incorrectly set.

overvoltage   A condition when the AC voltage is over the rated amount of voltage.

ozone filter   A part of a laser printer that filters out the ozone produced by the printer.

P

PaaS (Platform as a Service)   One of three types of cloud services. It describes servers, databases, operating system, storage, and development tools provided in an outside environment to relieve the support burden on companies that need an environment to perform high-level programming and develop applications.

packet   Encapsulated data found at Layer 3 of the OSI model.

PAE (physical address extension)   A feature provided by Intel that allows up to 64GB of physical memory to be used for motherboards that support it.

page   In Windows disk caching, a 4KB block of memory space. The operating system swaps or pages the application to and from the temporary swap file as needed if RAM is not large enough to handle the application.

page file   A single block of memory space, 4KB in size, used to store files and may also retrieve a file located on a disk.

PAN (personal area network)   A network of personal devices such as PDAs, cell phones, laptop computers, and pocket video games that can communicate in close proximity through a wired network or wirelessly. A Bluetooth wireless keyboard and mouse is a PAN.

Panel   A part of a Linux GUI and similar to OS X, Panel is a menu bar at the top of the screen containing contextual information on the left side with static information on the right side.

paper jam   When paper gets stuck along the printer paper pathway.

paper not feeding   May be due to poor paper quality or to the inefficiency of the rubber rollers that move the paper.

paper transport   The part of a printer that moves paper through the printer.

Parallel ATA   See *PATA*.

parity   A method of checking data accuracy.

particulate matter (PM)   Airborne particle pollution.

partition   A process that can divide a hard drive so that the computer sees more than one drive.

partition table   A table that holds information about the types and locations of partitions created. Occupies the outermost track on the platter (Cylinder 0, Head 0, Sector 1) and is part of the master boot record.

passcode lock   Security configuration on a mobile device.

passive cable   A cable without an embedded chip to boost signal strength. Shorter and thicker than an active cable.

passive cooling   A method of processor heat reduction that does not involve fans but does involve a heat sink.

passwd   A Linux/UNIX command to set or change a user password.

password (BIOS)   BIOS/UEFI settings that provide protection of the BIOS menu option by configuring one or more passwords to access the Setup program.

password security   The act of being conscientious about where passwords are written and stored.

PATA (parallel ATA)   A technology used with IDE devices that allows two devices per channel.

patch   A piece of software that fixes a specific problem in an application or operating system.

patch panel   Used with twisted-pair cable as a central location to which network cables terminate. It mounts in a network wiring rack, has network ports on the front, and has wiring connected to the back to provide network connectivity.

path   A reference that tells where a file is located among drives and folders (directories).

PC (personal computer)   A common name for a computer, derived from the IBM PC brand.

PCI (Peripheral Component Interconnect)   An older 32-bit and 64-bit, 66MHz local bus standard found in computers.

PCI bus speed   Speed at which data is delivered when PCI main bus is used on the motherboard. Commonly operates at 33mHz and 66mHz.

PCIe   A point-to-point serial bus used for motherboard adapters. Each bit can travel over a lane, and each lane allows transfers up to 250MB/s with a maximum of 32 lanes (which gives a total of 8GB/s transfer rate).

PCIe bus speed (Peripheral Component Interconnect Express)   The main high-speed serial motherboard bus, designed to replace the PCI, PCI-X, and AGP bus standards.

PCI-X   A parallel PCI bus that can operate at 66, 133, 266, 533, and 1066MHz and is backward compatible with the previous versions of the bus but allows for faster speeds.

Performance Monitor   A Windows tool that monitors resources such as memory and CPU usage, and allows creation of graphs, bar charts, and text reports.

Performance utility   A utility that monitors memory and other hardware parameters usage aspects.

personal protection equipment   Also known as PPE; part of a computer technician's work kit: safety glasses/goggles, latex or nonlatex/vinyl gloves, and an air filter/dust mask.

personally identifiable information (PII)   Information that uniquely identifies someone such as an employee ID, Social Security number, patient number, passport number, or driver's license number.

petabyte (PB)   1 thousand terabytes, or 2^{50} (1,125,899,906,842,600 bytes).

PGA (pin grid array)   A type of processor housing.

PGA2 (pin grid array 2)   A type of processor housing used in mobile devices.

phablet   A small mobile device that is a combination of a phone and a tablet.

phishing (pronounced "fishing")   A type of social engineering that attempts to get personal information through email from a company that appears legitimate. Targets obtaining ATM/debit or credit card numbers and PINs, Social Security numbers, bank account numbers, an Internet banking login ID and password, an email address, security information such as a mother's maiden name, full name, home address, or phone number.

phone filter   A part used with DSL Internet connectivity that must be attached to every phone outlet. The traditional analog device connects to this part. The filter allows the DSL signal to be separated from the normal analog traffic.

phone line isolator   A surge protector for the modem, protecting against power fluctuations in a phone line. Also known as a modem isolator.

physical laptop lock   Also called a laptop locking station. A security measure to attach a laptop to a location such as a desk.

physical layer   Layer 1 of the OSI model, which defines how bits are sent and received across the network without regard to their structure.

pickup rollers   Feed rollers.

picosecond   One-trillionth of a second.

PII (personally identifiable information)   A method of identifying, locating, or contacting a particular person.

PIN (personal identification number)   A unique identifier used to access an account or device such as a mobile tablet.

pin 1   A designated pin on every cable and connector that must be mated when attaching the two. Usually designated by a stenciled or etched number, a color stripe, and so on.

pin firing   The act of a print wire coming out of a dot matrix printer's print head and impacting the paper.

`ping`   A network troubleshooting command used to test TCP/IP communications and determine whether a network path is available, whether any delays exist along the path, and if a remote network device is reachable. Use `ping` with the private IP address 127.0.0.1 or ::1 to test a NIC's basic network setup.

pinning   The act of placing favorite applications in either the Start button, taskbar, or on a tile on the Windows desktop.

pin wheel   A spinning wheel generated by the operating system to indicate possible problems such as a nonresponsive application.

pipeline   Separate internal data buses that operate simultaneously inside the processor.

pipe symbol   A character (|) used at the command prompt that allows control of where or how the output of the command is processed. For example, a command can be "piped" to display only one screen at a time.

piracy   The act of copying or distributing copyrighted software.

pixel   Short for picture element, the smallest displayable unit on a monitor.

PKI (Public Key Infrastructure)   A method of managing digital security certificates.

plasma   A display that has little chambers containing plasma gas. When electricity is applied inside the chambers, excited electrons hit red, green, and blue phosphorous dots that glow.

platter   A metal disk of a hard drive on which binary data is recorded.

plenum cable   A type of cable that is treated with fire-retardant materials so that it is less of a fire risk.

PnP (plug and play)   A bus specification that allows automatic configuration of an adapter.

PoE (power over Ethernet)   A method of powering a remote device through a switch or patch panel.

POP (Point of Presence)   An Internet access point.

POP3 (Post Office Protocol)   Used to retrieve email from a mail server.

pop-ups Small windows that appear (pop up) to display messages, warnings, or advice. They often are a nuisance but can be managed through the browser's pop-up blocker feature.

port   A connector located on the motherboard or on a separate adapter.

port forwarding   The process of sending data through a firewall based on a particular port number or protocol.

port mapping   The combination of one public address and a port number that represents one internal company host; also called port address translation (PAT).

port replicator   A part that is similar to a docking station. It attaches to the laptop computer and allows more devices such as a monitor, keyboard, and mouse to be connected.

port triggering   Temporarily sending data through a firewall based on a preconfigured condition.

POSIX (Portable Operating System Interface) A designation that meets the specifications of a standardized operating system outlined by the IEEE Computer Society, containing a Bourne shell and other standard programs and services that are found in all POSIX-compliant operating systems. OS X is POSIX-compliant.

POST (power-on self-test)   Startup software contained in the BIOS/UEFI that tests individual hardware components.

POST card   PCI/PCIe adapter or a USB attached card that performs hardware diagnostics and displays the results as a series of codes on an LED display or LED lights.

POTS (plain old telephone service)   The traditional analog phone network used to connect homes and small businesses.

power   A measurement expressed in watts that represents how much work is being done.

power good signal   A signal sent to the motherboard from the power supply during POST that signifies that power is acceptable.

power over Ethernet injector   A method of providing power to a remote device using an injector when a PoE switch or patch panel is not available.

power rating   A measurement expressed in watts-per-channel that represents how loud the speaker volume can go up without distorting the sound.

PowerShell A Windows technology to help technicians and network administrators automate support functions through the use of scripts and snippets.

power supply   A device that converts AC voltage into DC voltage that the computer can use to power all internal and some external devices.

power supply tester   A tool that checks DC voltages sourced from the power supply.

PPP (Point-to-Point Protocol)   A connection-oriented Layer 2 protocol that encapsulates data for transmission over remote networks.

PPTP (Point-to-Point Tunneling Protocol)   A method/protocol used to create a VPN.

preemptive multitasking   A type of multitasking in Windows that allows the operating system to determine which application gets the processor's attention and for how long.

prefix notation   A method used to describe a subnet mask. It includes a forward slash followed by a number such as /24. The number is how many consecutive bits are set in the subnet mask.

presentation layer   Layer 6 of the OSI model that defines how data is formatted, encoded, converted, and presented from the sender to the receiver, even though a different computer language is used.

preventive maintenance   Something that is done to prolong the life of a device.

PRI (Primary Rate Interface)   24 64K channels used with ISDN.

primary corona   A wire in the laser printer responsible for generating a large negative voltage to be applied uniformly to the laser's drum.

primary partition   The first detected drive on a hard drive.

print cartridge   A container that holds the ink and the nozzles for the inkjet printer. Also known as an ink cartridge.

print driver   A piece of software that coordinates between the operating system and the printer.

print engine   The part of a printer that translates commands from the computer and provides feedback when necessary. The print engine is the brains of the printer operation.

printer sharing Commonly used in a home or small business environment allowing multiple users on the same printer. Contrast with a printer server used in corporate environments.

printer will not print   A variety of reasons: paper not inserted correctly, power cord dislodged or not plugged in, printer not reading computer command.

print head   The part of the dot matrix printer that holds the print wires and impacts the ribbon.

printing blank pages   Ensure the print driver is working properly; check the ribbon (impact and thermal), ink levels (inkjet), or toner (laser). Check quality setting.

Print Management   A Windows console used to manage printers.

print ribbon Struck by the print head to leave images on paper.

print server   A device (computer or separate device) that connects to a printer used by multiple people through a network.

prints in wrong color   Check ink levels. Check computer `printer` command.

print spooler   Also known as a print manager, a software program that intercepts the request to print and sends print information to the hard drive where it is sent to the printer whenever the microprocessor is not busy with other tasks. A print spooler allows multiple print jobs to be queued inside the computer so that other work can be performed.

print to file   Takes a print job and saves it as a .pm file to be printed later.

print to image   Virtual printing; printing to a location other than to the directly connected printer and to a specific file so that the information can be viewed, saved, or emailed.

print to PDF   A print job that is saved to Portable Document Format (.pdf) file and can be printed later on any printer.

print to XPS   A Microsoft file that allows a document to be printed on any printer but not modified.

printwire   A component of a dot matrix printer's print head that is a single wire that connects to a spring and impacts a ribbon to make a single dot on the paper.

privacy filter   A physical filter added to a monitor to distort the display output for anyone except for the person looking directly at the screen. Also known as a privacy screen.

private cloud   Part of a company's network infrastructure located outside the business in a remote location, but the company has responsibility for managing the software and hardware.

private IP address   Used inside a home or business. This address is not allowed to be transmitted across the Internet. Contrast to a public IP address.

PRL   The default preferred roaming list (PRL) created by the cell network provider.

probe   Used with a tone generator to identify cables when they are not labeled or incorrectly labeled.

processing   A laser printing process in which the data is converted from the printer language into a bitmap image. This process is also known as raster image processing.

processor   The central 32-bit or 64-bit electronic chip that determines the processing power of a computer. Also known as microprocessor or central processing unit (CPU).

Program Compatibility Wizard   A program that can check for software application compatibility with a newer Windows version.

progressive scaling   Refreshes all the horizontal lines simultaneously instead of the traditional method of interlacing.

projector   Takes input from a device such as a computer, laptop, camera, and so on and sends that image to a screen or wall.

PROMPT   A command that changes how the command prompt appears. See also *command prompt*.

proprietary crash screen   An error condition on a particular computer or application.

proprietary vendor-specific ports   Ports primarily for power connections or as a communication option(s).

protective cover   On mobile devices, protection for either the screen or for the entire whole unit.

proxy server   A server that acts as a go-between for an application and another server.

ps   A Linux/UNIX command that lists all current processes.

PS/2 port   Common name for keyboard and mouse connectors, which are examples of miniDIN-6 connectors.

PS/2 to USB converter   Connector with a PS/2 connector on one end and an USB connector on the other.

PSTN (Public Switched Telephone Network)   Describes the traditional phone network including satellite, cellular, wired, and wireless worldwide connectivity.

PSU (power supply unit)   See *power supply*.

public cloud   A service or environment operated by an external vendor such as to provide a service or application to a company.

public IP address   A service provider or company translates a private IP address to a public IP address that is seen on the Internet.

punch down tool   An implement that terminates cable on a patch panel.

PVC (polyvinyl chloride)   Cable that has a plastic insulation or jacket that is cheaper and easier to install than plenum cable. It can have flame-retardant added.

pwd   In the Linux environment, identifies the current working path you are in.

PXE boot (preboot execution environment)   An option some computers have that can be modified to search for the network device that holds the computer image.

Q

q   An OS X/Linux command to quit or cancel an editing session.

QoS (quality of service)   A collection of techniques that ensure that the most important corporate data, voice, and/or video is sent before other noncritical data that may get dropped as a result.

QPI (Quick Path Interconnect)   An Intel technology used as an alternative to the front side bus (FSB) in which a point-to-point connection is made between the processor and a motherboard component.

quad-core   Four processors on a single motherboard by having either two dual-core CPUs installed on the same motherboard or two dual-core CPUs installed in a single socket.

quadruple-channel   A memory type in which a motherboard can access four memory modules simultaneously.

quality   A printing option that dictates how much ink/toner/DPI is used.

quick format   During an installation process, a function used to prepare a hard drive partition but does not identify and mark bad sectors so that they will not be used for data storage. A full format, in contrast, does evaluate the drive for bad sectors but takes quite a bit longer to prepare the partition for use.

Quick Launch bar   Located immediately to the right of the *Start* button on the taskbar, a section of the taskbar that contains icons used for opening applications.

R

radiation pattern   Sometimes called a propagation pattern, the direction(s) a radio frequency is sent or received.

radio   A wireless input/output technology. Has a longer range than infrared.

radio button   Similar to a check box, a round space on a dialog box that allows the user to enable a single option by clicking it. A solid dot in the button means the option is enabled; an absence of the dot means a disabled option.

radio firmware   A low-level software that manages a cell phone's radio connection to a network. A baseband signal sends updates to both the phone's operating system and its radio firmware. Without the same updates, the cell phone experiences problems.

RAID (redundant array of independent disks)   Allows writing to multiple hard drives for larger storage areas, better performance, and fault tolerance.

RAID 0   Also called disk striping without parity, enables data to be alternatively written on two or more hard drives but be seen by the system as one logical drive. RAID level 0 does not protect data if a hard drive fails; it increases only system performance.

RAID 1   Also called disk mirroring or disk duplexing, it protects against hard drive failure. See also *disk mirroring* and *disk duplexing*. Requires two drives at a minimum.

RAID 5   Describes putting data on three or more hard drives, with one of the three drives used for parity. See also *RAID*.

RAID 10   A RAID condition in which a mirrored set and a striped set are combined. Takes four hard drives as a minimum.

RAID not found   An error condition that sometimes occurs with a power failure or surge, system upgrade, application upgrade, or new application installation.

RAID stops working An error condition that requires using the Windows Disk Management tool to verify the status of the drives used in the RAID.

RAM (random-access memory) A volatile type of memory that loses its data when power to the computer is shut off.

RAM drive A virtual hard disk created from RAM.

random-access time A performance comparison measurement; it is the amount of time a drive requires to find the appropriate place on the disc and retrieve information.

ransomware A security situation in which a hacker has restricted access to a device until the user pays money to regain access.

rapid elasticity The ability for a provider to expand software and hardware quickly in response to a customer's needs.

RAW volume A part of a hard drive that has been set aside as a volume but has never been high-level formatted and does not contain a specific type of file system.

RCA A type of connector used with coaxial cable.

RD A Windows command used to remove a directory (folder).

RDP (Remote Desktop Protocol) A Microsoft protocol used for accessing and controlling networked computers and mobile devices.

read-only attribute A designation that can be applied to a file so that the file is not accidentally erased.

read/write failure An error condition that indicates a hard drive has a defective area.

read/write head The part of a floppy or hard drive that electronically writes binary data on disks.

ReadyBoost A utility that can speed up the Windows boot process by caching some startup files to a 256MB+ Flash drive, SD card, or CF card.

recovery disc A disc used to boot a system when you don't have an original operating system disc and then restore the computer from a previously saved system image. Sometimes called a system repair disc.

Recycle Bin A location in Windows-based operating systems in which user-deleted files and folders are held. This data is not discarded from the computer. The user must empty the Recycle Bin to erase the data completely.

refresh (process) A rewrite of the information inside memory chips.

refresh rate The maximum time a monitor's screen is scanned in 1 second.

Refresh your PC A Windows 8/10 tool that reinstalls the operating system but keeps user data and settings.

ReFS (resilient file system) The Microsoft replacement file system for NTFS.

REGEDIT A Windows utility that can modify and back up the registry.

REGEDT32 One of two Windows registry editors. See also *registry* and *REGEDIT*.

region code A setting on a DVD or Blu-ray drive or disc that specifies a geographic region. The drive's region code must match the disc's region code to play.

registered memory Memory modules that have extra chips (registers) near the bottom of the module that delay all data transfers by one clock tick to ensure accuracy.

registry A central Windows database file that holds hardware and software configuration information.

regsvr32.exe A command used to register .dll files in the Windows registry.

Reliability Monitor A tool that provides a visual graph in Windows Vista or 7 of how stable the system is and details on events that might have affected the system reliability.

remote wipe Uses software to send a command to a mobile device to delete data, perform a factory reset, remove everything from the device so that it cannot be used, and overwrite data storage to prevent forensic data recovery.

removable screen Some devices that serve as a laptop have screens that can be detached.

repair installation Used when you have to reload the Windows operating system. Sometimes called an in-place upgrade or a re-installation.

repeater A network device that boosts the network signal. Network switches are repeaters. Wireless repeaters boost the wireless signal to extend the wireless network.

resistance A measurement in ohms of how much opposition is applied to an electrical circuit.

resolution The number of pixels shown on a monitor or the output of a printer.

Resource Monitor A graphic tool that shows performance for the main system components.

resource pooling By using an outside vendor, a company can pool resources (servers, storage space, and more) with other companies.

restore point A snapshot image of the registry and some of the dynamic system files that have been saved previously by the System Restore utility. This is used when the Windows computer has a problem.

return The center (round) AC outlet plug. Other terms used are common or neutral.

RFI (radio frequency interference) A specific type of EMI noise that occurs in the radio frequency range. Often results from operation of nearby electrical appliances or devices.

RFID (radio frequency identification) A technology that allows automatic identification of people, objects, or animals.

RFID badge (radio frequency identification badge) A card that can be used to access to a locked area and a record of that entry logged.

RG-59 A type of coax cable used in video networks.

RG-6 A type of coax cable that can connect cable TV, satellite disk, or a rooftop antenna.

RGB/component video Red, green, and blue RCA jacks for connecting a scanner or camera.

RIMM A trademark of Rambus, Inc., that is a type of memory module used on video adapters and that may be used on future motherboards.

RIS (remote installation service) A service that allows PXE-enabled devices to execute specific variables used to remotely control and even reload a remote device.

RISC (reduced instruction set computer) A type of computing device that uses a small set of instructions to operate. Contrast with CISC devices. Common RISC devices include smartphones and tablets.

riser board A board that connects to the motherboard that holds adapters.

RJ-11 A type of connector used with analog modems and traditional phone jacks.

RJ-45 A type of connector used on Ethernet network cards and ports. Used to connect a device to the wired network.

rm Short for remove, an OS X command that deletes a file or directory.

RMA (return materials authorization) A number used to track and return defective parts (normally under warranty).

robocopy A command used to copy files. It has more parameters than COPY or XCOPY.

rogue antivirus A downloaded application that appears to help someone with a problem, but in reality, the downloaded application is a virus.

roller Pickup roller/feeder roller that can move paper through a printer.

root In UNIX/Linux, the administrator account. The root user has absolute power on a system, including within OS X.

root directory The starting place for all files on a disk. A hard drive is limited to 512 entries. The designation for a hard drive's root directory is C:\.

rootkit Malicious software that hackers install to gain administrator access to an operating system. It can also be downloaded and installed to a flash drive.

rotating screen Display screen on certain laptops with the capability to turn 306 degrees.

router A network device that determines the best path to send a packet. Works at OSI model Layer 3.

RSA security token (Rivest Shamir Adleman) A security algorithm used with a security token, hardware token, DES card, and authentication card serial interface standard.

RTC (real-time clock) The computer clock that keeps track of the current time.

RTS (request to send) Part of the RTS/CTS hardware handshaking communication method. Specific wires on the serial connector send a signal to the other device to stop or start sending data. The CTS (clear to send) and RTS signals indicate when it is okay to send data.

RTS/CTS (request to send/clear to send) A method of serial device handshaking that uses signals on specific pins of the connector to signal the other device when to stop or send data.

S

S/PDIF (Sony/Phillips digital interface format) Defines how audio signals are carried between audio devices and stereo components. It can also be used to connect the output of a DVD player in a PC to a home theater or some other external device.

S-video port A composite video port, coded yellow, that uses a 7-pin mini-DIN connector.

SaaS (Software as a Service)   One of three cloud service types. It describes applications such as a learning management system, enterprise resource planning (ERP), human resources management (HRM), payroll, antivirus, and inventory management that are hosted by another company and accessible from anywhere.

Safe boot   A Windows System Configuration Option found on the Boot tab.

Safe Mode   A Windows option used when the computer stalls, slows down, does not work properly, has improper video settings or intermittent errors, or when a new hardware/software installation causes problems. In Safe Mode, Windows starts with minimum device drivers and services.

safety goggles   A personal protection device that should be worn when working on equipment to protect the eyes from debris, chemicals, and liquids.

sag   A momentary undervoltage condition that occurs when the wall outlet AC voltage drops.

SAN (storage area network)   A collection of storage media that is centrally managed and available to a multitude of network devices such as servers, network-based applications, virtual machines, and users.

SAS (serial-attached SCSI)   SAS devices connect in a point-to-point bus. Used in the enterprise environment in which high reliability and high mean time between failures is important.

SATA (Serial ATA)   A point-to-point architecture for IDE devices that provides faster access for attached devices.

SATA 1 (Serial ATA 1)   A SATA device that has a maximum transfer rate of 1.5Gb/s.

SATA 2 (serial ATA 2)   A SATA device that has a maximum transfer rate of 3Gb/s.

SATA 3 (serial ATA 3)   A SATA device that has a maximum transfer rate of 6Gb/s.

SATA-PM (Serial ATA Port Multiplier)   A device that connects multiple eSATA devices to a single eSATA port.

satellite modem   A type of modem that can provide Internet access at speeds faster than an analog modem but slower than cable or DSL access.

scanner   An input device that allows printed documents to be brought into the computer and from there digitally displayed, printed, saved, or emailed.

SC fiber connector   (subscriber connector) An older type of fiber-optic connector.

SCP (Secure Copy Protocol)   A means of using SSH to securely transfer one or more files across a network.

screen sharing   An OSX feature that allows one user to view and even control the display of another Apple computer that is on the network.

screwdriver   A tool that removes screws. Common types of screwdrivers used in IT support are flat-tipped and Phillips.

scribe   A plastic tool that helps with prying plastics parts or covers off laptop and mobile devices.

SD (Secure Digital)   A storage device with nonvolatile flash memory used for mobile devices.

SDK (Software Development Kit)   Contains a set of tools, such as application programming interfaces, programming tools, analytic tools, and sample code that develop an app for a specific mobile OS or platform.

SDRAM (synchronous DRAM)   Provides fast burst memory access by placing new memory addresses on the address bus before prior memory address retrieval and execution completes. SDRAM synchronizes its operation with the CPU clock signal to speed up memory access.

SDS (safety data sheet)   A document that describes a product including its toxicity, storage, and disposal procedures. Also contains information regarding health or safety concerns.

sector   The smallest amount of storage space on a disk or platter, holding 512 bytes of data.

secure boot   A BIOS/UEFI setting option that prevents unauthorized software from loading during the boot process.

Secure Sockets Layer   See *SSL*.

security policy   One or more documents that provide rules and guidelines related to computer and network security.

security token   A device used for security access; also called an authentication token, USB token, hardware token, or software token.

self-grounding   The act of placing a part of your body in contact with an electronic device to prevent an electrostatic discharge (ESD) event.

self-powered hub   A type of hub power mode in which an external power supply is attached.

separate pad   A bar or pad in a laser printer that can have a rubber or cork surface that rubs against the paper as it is picked up.

Serial ATA   See *SATA*.

server-based network   A basic type of LAN in which users log in to a controlling computer, called a server, that knows who is authorized to connect to the LAN and what resources the user is authorized to access. Usually found in businesses that have 10 or more computers.

service   A Windows process that provides a specific function to the computer.

service pack   An upgrade or a patch provided by a manufacturer for an operating system.

service release   Software available from a manufacturer to fix a known problem (bug) in its applications program.

services.msc   A command that brings up the Services snap-in Computer Management tool so that you can start and stop services.

session layer   Layer 5 of the OSI model, which manages communication and administrative functions between two network devices.

Setup   Software that tells a computer about itself and the hardware it supports, such as how much RAM memory, type of hard drive installed, current date and time, and so on.

sfc   A command used to start the System File Checker utility. The System File Checker verifies operating system files.

sfc /scannow   The most common SFC option used that checks and replaces any Windows files and .dll files that might have issues. This is especially important after removing some viruses.

SFF (small form factor)   A smaller motherboard form factor that is likened to storage boxes, such as a shoe box or a small storage bin.

SFX12V   A type of power supply used with Micro-ATX and FlexATX motherboards.

Shadow Copy   A Windows technology used with the System Restore program that uses a block-level image instead of monitoring certain files for file changes.

shared key authentication   A method of authentication used in wireless networks that uses a group of characters that both the wireless device and the access point have in common.

shared system memory   The amount of motherboard RAM used for video because the amount of video memory on the video adapter or built in to the motherboard is not enough for the applications used.

share permissions   A security measure that can dictate what a specific user or group can do with a file or folder that can be accessed across a network.

shell   A standardized user interface to interact with the operating system.

shielding   Cancels out and keeps magnetic interference from devices.

shortcut   An icon with a bent arrow in lower-left corner. It is a link to a file, a folder, or a program on a disk. If the file is a document, it opens the application used to create the document.

shoulder surfing   Someone behind you looking at what you type or what is on the screen to glean unauthorized information.

Show Desktop   An icon you can click to reduce all open windows on the screen and show the desktop. Click it again, and the original document reappears.

shrink (partition)   The act of making a hard drive section smaller.

shutdown   A Linux/UNIX command to shut down or restart the system, depending on options used.

SID (security identifier)   A unique number assigned to a Microsoft-based computer.

sidebar   A feature in Windows Vista and 7 that is a collection of customizable desktop gadgets.

side by side apps   A feature in Windows 7 and higher where you can drag a window to one side of the screen and another window to the other side and then snap in equal distance from the sides of the screen.

sigverif.exe   A command used to view signed device drivers.

SIM (System Image Manager)   Used in Windows to deploy an image of one computer to multiple computers.

simple volume   A Windows term for the storage 0-pin or 72-pin unit that contains the files needed to load the operating system. The system volume and the boot volume can be the same unit.

single link   A type of DVI video connection that allows resolutions up to 1920×1080.

single-mode fiber   A type of fiber-optic cabling that sends one light beam down the cable.

single-sided memory   A memory module that the CPU accesses at one time. The module has one "bank" of memory and 64 bits are transferred out of the memory module to the CPU. More appropriately called single-banked memory. Note that the memory module may or may not have all its "chips" on one side.

single sign-on   An authentication technique that allows a user to authenticate to multiple systems, servers, printers, and other network devices with a minimum of a user ID and password.

site survey   Used in wireless network design to determine the best wireless hardware placement for the optimum coverage area.

slave   An IDE setting for the second device added to the cable. The device should be a slower device than the master.

SLC (single-level memory cell)   A cell that stores 1 bit in a memory cell and is more expensive and longer lasting than an MLC.

sleep-and-charge USB port   A computer port that provides power to an attached device (power to charge the device) even when the computer is powered off.

sleep mode   A low power state that allows a device to be "woken up" and resumed faster than a cold start.

SLI (Scalable Link Interface)   An NVIDIA technology that connects two or more video cards so that they may share resources from each card to provide better computer graphics.

slow performance   An indication that a computer system is operating in a less than efficient manner. Could be caused by lack of hard drive space, not enough memory, a poorly performing application, malware, or insufficient CPU cores/speed.

slow transfer speed   The results of network latency, the time measured to transmit data from source to destination.

SLP (Service Location Protocol)   A TCP/IP protocol that announces and discovers services in a LAN.

S.M.A.R.T. (Self-Monitoring, Analysis, and Reporting Technology)   A feature that allows a storage device to send messages about possible failures or data loss.

smart camera   More capable than a digital camera, may have features such as facial recognition, measuring, inspection for quality assurance, surveillance, and robot guidance. May include a mobile operating system, have Internet access, and support for wired and wireless networking.

smart card   A small ID-sided card that can store data, be encrypted, and swiped through and/or interact wirelessly with a smart card reader. Examples of a smart card are identification, medical, credit, and access.

smart card reader   A device used to read the embedded chip in smart cards.

SmartMedia   A card, smaller than a credit card, used to hold audio and video files.

smartphone   Has more capabilities than a cell phone, such as Internet connectivity, GPS tracking, runs apps, takes pictures, plays music, or connects wirelessly to other devices.

smart TV   A TV that connects to a wired or wireless network, and thus the Internet. Through the TV, music, photos, and other content can be shared. The TV might even be controlled by voice commands.

smart watch   Wrist watch capable of limited functions, such as synching with a smartphone, downloading apps, or GPS tracking.

SMB (server message block)   A means of providing access to shared network devices and files.

SMTP (Simple Mail Transfer Protocol)   A standard used for email or for transferring messages across a network from one device to another.

snapshot   In a virtualization environment, a copy or backup of the VM at a particular point in time used to revert the VM to that point in time. It is similar in concept to a restore point.

SNMP (Simple Network Management Protocol)   A standard that supports network monitoring and management.

social engineering   A technique used to trick people into divulging information including their own personal information or corporate knowledge.

SO-DIMM (small-outline DIMM)   A special small DIMM used in laptop computers.

soft reset   Simply restarting a device. Contrast this to a hard reset, which is also called a factory reset.

software   An application consisting of a set of instructions that makes the hardware work.

Software updater   An Ubuntu tool used to update Linux operating systems and applications.

SOHO (small office/home office)   A description given to a small network that might consist of wired and wireless devices, Internet connectivity, VoIP, and even a VPN connection into the corporate network.

solder joint   A solder connection on the back of a motherboard or an adapter.

sound card   An adapter also known as an audio card that has several ports that convert digital signals to audible sound, and also the reverse. Common devices that connect to the ports include microphones, speakers, and joysticks.

south bridge   A connection from the processor to parts of the motherboard including the PCI/PCIe (non-video) slots, ports, and other motherboard components. Also called the front side bus.

spam   Email that is unsolicited and comes from unknown people or businesses.

spanned volume   A Windows term that describes hard drive space created from multiple hard drives.

SPD (serial presence detect)   An extra EEPROM feature that allows the system BIOS to read the EEPROM (which contains memory information such as capacity, voltage, error detection, refresh rates, and data width) and adjusts motherboard timings for best CPU to RAM performance.

speaker   Mechanical device that produces acoustic sound. May be internal or external to a computer or mobile device.

spear phishing   A targeted type of social engineering in which the attackers know some information about someone that lulls them into thinking an email or other electronic message is safe.

SPGA (staggered pin grid array)   A processor package type used by Intel.

special function key   Uppermost keys on a keyboard, activates a specific function with one touch of that key. Labeled F1, F2, and so on, controls things like sound on/off, screen brightness dimmer/brighter, and more.

special thermal paper   Paper sensitive to heat; used in retail establishments.

speed (NIC property)   A network card configuration property. It is normally configured automatically, but manual options include 10Gb/s, 1Gb/s, 100Mb/s, and 10Mb/s.

spike   An overvoltage condition of short duration and intensity.

spinning pinwheel   An error indication that can indicate a lack of response from the hard drive and/or a particular application.

split (partition)   The act of dividing a particular space on a storage device.

splitter   A convenient device used with twisted-pair and coaxial cables that allows two inputs and one output. Splitters result in signal quality degradation so should be avoided if possible.

spoofing   Sending an Ethernet frame with a fake source MAC address to trick other devices to send traffic to a rogue device.

Spotlight   An OS X universal search tool that can locate every file and directory and also search email, contacts, music, and even the web.

SPS (standby power supply)   A device that provides power to the computer only after it first detects an AC voltage power-out condition.

spyware   Software that collects information without consent using keystroke logging, gaining access to saved documents, and recording Internet activity. Results in unsolicited pop-ups and identity theft.

SRAM (static random-access memory)   Memory that is faster but more expensive than DRAM. SRAM is also known as cache memory, or L2 cache.

SSD (solid state drive)   A drive that uses nonvolatile flash memory and no moving parts to store data. It is faster but more expensive than a hard drive.

SSH (secure shell)   A means of secure data communication including remote connectivity of devices and file transfers.

SSHD (solid state hybrid drive)   A drive that contains both a mechanical hard drive and flash memory used as an SSD.

SSID (service set identifier)   A set of up to 32 alphanumeric characters used in wireless networks to differentiate between different networks.

SSID broadcasting   Used with wireless network access points to periodically send out a beacon frame that includes the SSID. Wireless devices can automatically detect the SSID from this beacon.

SSL (Secure Sockets Layer)   A protocol used to transmit Internet messages securely.

standby mode   A low power Windows power option mode that allows a computer to be used again faster than if it were powered on as a cold start.

standby power   Power that is always provided, even when a computer is powered off. It is why you have to unplug a computer when working inside it.

standoff   A plastic connector on the bottom side of a motherboard.

star topology   The most common Ethernet network topology, in which each device connects to a central hub or switch. If an individual device or cable fails, the rest of the network keeps working. But if the hub or switch fails, the entire network goes down.

start bit   A bit used in asynchronous communications that signals the beginning of each data byte.

GLOSSARY

Start button   Located in the lower-left corner of the Windows desktop, a button that is used to access and launch applications, files, utilities, and help, as well as to add/remove hardware and software.

Start screen   On Windows 8/10, the initial screen that has tiles instead of the traditional desktop icons.

STB (set top box)   Set top unit (STU), or receiver that is bought or leased from a cable/satellite TV show provider.

ST fiber connector   A (straight tip) common type of fiber-optic connector.

stop bit   A bit used in asynchronous communications that signals the end of each data byte.

storage card   Removable data storage device frequently used in mobile devices and laptops. Also known as flash memory card.

storage pool   A Microsoft Windows 8/10 technology that allows the creation of a storage area that is made from two or more physical drives that can be different types such as an internal SATA drive and external USB drive.

storage space   A Microsoft Windows 8/10 technology that allows creation of a virtual disk from a storage pool.

STP (shielded twisted pair)   Network cable with extra foil to prevent outside noise from interfering with data on the cable.

straight-through cable   A network cable that uses twisted-pair copper wires and RJ-45 connectors at each end. The cable uses the same pinout and is also known as a patch cable.

streak   Paper issue caused by the drum, toner cartridge, dirty or damage fusing assembly, or the paper.

striped volume   A Windows term describing how data is written across 2 to 32 hard drives. It is different from a spanned volume in that each drive is used alternately instead of filling the first hard drive before going to the second hard drive. Other names include striping or RAID 0.

STU (set top unit)   A set top box (STB) or receiver bought or leased from a cable/satellite TV show provider.

su   An OS X command that switches from one user account to another.

subdirectory   A directory contained within another directory. Today's subdirectories are called subfolders.

subnet   A portion of a network number that has been subdivided so that multiple networks can use separate parts of a single network number. Subnets allow more

efficient use of IP addresses. Also called subnetwork or subnetwork number.

subnet mask   A number the computer uses to determine which part of an IP address represents the network and which portion represents the host.

sudo   An OS X command that allows a user temporary root privileges.

surge   An overvoltage condition that is like a spike but with a longer duration.

surge suppressor/protector   A device that helps protect power supplies from overvoltage conditions. Also known as surge strip.

swap file   A temporary file in hard disk space used by Windows that varies in size depending on the amount of RAM installed, available hard drive space, and the amount of memory needed to run the application.

swipe lock   Ability to lock out a mobile device or its screen with a finger sweep movement.

switch   In star networks, a Layer 2 central controlling device. Looks at each data frame as it comes through each port.

swollen battery   A bulging battery requires immediate replacement as it may not hold a charge and could soon leak.

synchronize to the cloud   When storing data in a remote location in which it can be viewed, retrieved, saved, shared, and/or forwarded based on the cloud vendor used and user preferences.

synchronize to the desktop   When a mobile device exchanges and stores data with one or more desktop computers using an app, software, the operating system, or a combination of these.

synchronous   Describing transmissions that require the use of a clock signal.

system attribute   A file designation to mark a file as a system file. By default, files with this attribute set do not show in directory listings.

system bar   On a mobile tablet, the bottom area, containing a back button, home button, recent applications opened, and the notification area.

systemboard   Synonymous with motherboard. In a computer, holds the majority of the electronics, contains a processor, has memory, and supports having ports attached.

System Configuration utility   A Windows utility that allows boot files and settings to be enabled/disabled for troubleshooting purposes. The command that brings this utility up is `msconfig.exe`.

system file   A file that is needed to allow a computer to boot. A file type that is also known as a startup file.

system image   Contains a saved copy of the operating system and all user files that can be used to restore a damaged or corrupted computer.

System Information   An OS X utility that provides an overview of the Mac, including basic diagnostic information such as installed hardware, software, and network settings.

system lockout   A configuration setting to prevent unauthorized access when a security method is not successful. For example, incorrectly entering a password three times.

System Monitor   A Windows utility that monitors specific computer components and allows creation of graphs, bar charts, and text reports.

system partition   A type of active hard drive partition that contains the hardware-specific files needed to load the operating system.

System Preferences   An OS X basic management and troubleshooting tool, equivalent to Control Panels in Windows. It contains most of the system settings such as desktop backgrounds and screen savers to more advanced settings such as user accounts and file sharing. Third-party applications can also insert their own preferences menu into the System Preferences menu.

system resources   The collective set of interrupt, I/O address, and DMA configuration parameters.

System Restore   A utility that makes a snapshot of the registry and backs up certain dynamic system files. When a problem occurs, use this utility to take your system back to a time before the error started.

system volume   A Windows term describing the storage space that holds Windows operating system files used to boot the computer.

T

T568A   An ANSI/TIA/EIA Ethernet network cabling standard.

T568B   An ANSI/TIA/EIA Ethernet network cabling standard.

tablet   A mobile device with touch screen, camera(s), microphone, and possibly one or more ports such as sound, USB, miniDisplayPort, or miniThunderbolt. Tablets connect to the Internet; take, send, receive, and store pictures and video; and are often a good choice for people who travel.

tailgating   A breach of physical security that occurs when an unauthorized person enters a secure space behind an authorized person. Training and diligence by all employees is the only way to stop tailgating.

tape drive   A means of backup used with servers.

taskbar   On a Windows program, the bar that runs across the bottom of the desktop. It holds buttons that represent files and applications currently loaded into RAM. It also holds icons representing direct access to system tools.

TASKKILL   A command used to halt a process or task.

TASKLIST   A command used to list process IDs for active applications and services. Note this command should be used before the TASKKILL command.

Task Manager   A Windows-based utility that displays memory and processor usage data, and displays currently loaded applications as well as currently running processes.

Task Scheduler   A Windows-based utility that allows applications or tasks to be executed periodically or at a specific date and time. This can include a system-wide message.

Task View   This icon allows the user to create multiple desktops and switch between them.

TCP (Transmission Control Protocol)   An OSI model Layer 4 standard that ensures reliable communication between two devices.

TCP/IP (Transmission Control Protocol/Internet Protocol)   The most widely used network protocol stack for connecting to the Internet. Developed by the Defense Advanced Research Projects Agency in the 1970s, it is the basis of the Internet.

TCP printing   Also known as TCP/IP printing. The ability to connect to and print to a printer that has been assigned an IP address.

TDR (time domain reflectometer)   A device used to check fiber connectivity.

teamwork   The ability to work with others toward a common goal.

Telnet   An application that allows connection to a remote network device.

temperature monitoring   A BIOS/UEFI setting and output that shows key temperature readings for the CPU and case interior.

terabyte (TB)   Approximately 1 trillion bytes of information, or 2^{40} (1,099,511,627,776 bytes).

terminal   The terminal emulator for OS X that allows the command-line interface (CLI) access to the operating system. Certain tasks or functions are not GUI-friendly so a CLI command is required.

tethering   Allows sharing of Internet connectivity among mobile devices in the area. It is a form of hotspot.

textbox   An area with a dialog box where the user may type preferred parameters applied to the software in use.

TFT (thin film transistor)   A type of array used in LCDs to direct the liquid crystal to block the light from the backlight.

TFTP (Trivial File Transfer Protocol)   A nonsecure means of quickly transferring files from one device to another device.

TFX12V   A type of power supply used with Micro-ATX and FlexATX motherboards.

thermal pad   A cushion that sits on top of the processor to provide uniform heat dispersal.

thermal paste   Applies between the processor and its heat sink to provide a thermal pad that disperses heat more evenly.

thermal printer   A printer commonly used in retail that uses heat and special thermal paper to create the printed image.

thermal sensor   A feature found on memory modules that is used by the BIOS/UEFI to read and adjust settings for optimum performance.

thermal wax transfer   A type of printer that uses wax-based inks similar to the solid ink printer, but it prints in lower resolutions.

thick client   A business computer that has applications loaded on the local hard drive. Contrast with thin client.

thin client   A type of computer that does not have all the ports and components (such as a hard drive) of a traditional PC.

This PC   A Windows desktop icon or tile that accesses hardware, software, and files.

thread   A unit of programming code that receives a slice of time from Windows, so it can run concurrently with other units of code or threads.

throttle management   The ability to control processor speed by slowing the processor down when it is not used heavily or is running too hot.

Thunderbolt card   An adapter that allows adding a Thunderbolt port to a computer that does not have one. A Thunderbolt port is an updated port that uses some of the DisplayPort technology that was developed by Intel and Apple.

Thunderbolt port   A type of video port on PCIe adapters or on Apple computers.

Thunderbolt-to-DVI converter   Connector cable with a Thunderbolt plug and a DVI.

tile   A square block on a Windows 8/10 Start screen with a picture of the function it performs when activated.

Time Machine   A bundled application in OS X that performs full and incremental system backups to an external hard drive. It gets its clever naming from the capability to navigate past backups as if traveling backward through time.

time management   How much time you budget and then actually spend on doing each task throughout the workday.

TKIP (Temporal Key Integrity Protocol)   A method of encryption that is an improvement over WEP because the encryption keys periodically change.

TN (twisted nematic)   The majority of displays that use LCD technology. It is the cheapest to make and fastest to display. Best viewed from straight on.

tone generator   A tool used with a toner probe to identify cables when they are not labeled or incorrectly labeled.

toner   The combined particles in a laser toner cartridge that produce an image when fused onto paper. Harmful if inhaled. Messy if spilled.

toner is not fused   Determine if the problem is in the fuser assembly or elsewhere in the printer; send output to the printer. When printer finishes the writing stage and before the toner fuses to the paper, open the laser cover and remove the paper. If the paper is error free, then the problem is most likely in the transfer corona or fusing assembly.

toner vacuum   A vacuum used inside a laser printer that will not damage the vacuum as a result.

TOSLINK   A type of fiber S/PDIF connection.

touch screen   An alternative way to input a device into a computer. Used in kiosks.

TouchFlo   A multitouch technology for mobile devices developed by the HTC Corporation that distinguishes between a finger and a stylus and responds appropriately.

tower   A computer model with a motherboard that mounts perpendicular to the floor.

toxic waste handling   The regulated removal and disposal of anything harmful to you and the environment. Some physical parts, pieces, and batteries of computers, laser printers, and mobile devices are considered toxic e-waste because of the heavy metals and chemicals contained inside of them.

TPM (BIOS)   The trusted platform module (TPM) is a BIOS/UEF option that allows initialization and setting a password for the TPM motherboard chip that generates and stores cryptographic keys.

TPM (Trusted Platform Module)   A motherboard chip used for hardware and software authentication. The TPM can authenticate hardware devices. Applications can use the TPM for file and folder encryption, local passwords, email, VPN/PKI authentication, and wireless authentication.

tracert   A network troubleshooting command that displays the path a data packet takes through a network, thus allowing one to see where a fault occurs in larger networks.

transfer belt   Located at the bottom of the printer.

transfer corona   A wire inside the laser printer that applies a positive charge to the back of the paper so that the toner is attracted to the paper as it moves through the printer.

transferring   A laser printer process where the toner (image) moves from the drum to the paper.

transfer roller   A roller inside the laser printer that replaces the transfer corona. The roller applies a positive charge to the back of the paper so that the toner is attracted to the paper as it moves through the printer.

transport layer   Layer 4 of the OSI model, which determines the details on how the data is sent, supervises the validity of the transmission, and defines the protocol for structuring messages.

triple-channel   A type of memory execution in which motherboards access three memory modules simultaneously.

trojan   A virus program that appears to be a normal application but when executed changes something. It does not replicate but could gather information that can later be used to hack into one's computer.

Trusted/untrusted software source   A security measure that is built in to some browsers and security software that tells them whether a website or downloaded file is a trusted or untrusted software source.

TVS rating (transient voltage suppressor)   A measure of a surge protector's capability to guard against overvoltage conditions. The lower the TVS rating, the better.

TV tuner card   An adapter that allows a computer to receive and display television-based video on a computer monitor.

twisted-pair cable   Network cable made of eight copper wires twisted into four pairs. Can be shielded or unshielded.

type   A command that displays a file's contents on the screen.

Type 1 hypervisor   Hypervisors manage and oversee the operation of virtual machines. A Type 1 hypervisor has the operating system running on top of the hypervisor. Also known as a native hypervisor.

Type 2 hypervisor   In a virtualization environment, a hypervisor that runs on top of a host operating system to manage and oversee the virtual machine. Also known as a hosted hypervisor.

Type A-B-C fire extinguisher   A fire extinguisher that can be used on either Type A, Type B, or Type C fires.

Type C fire extinguisher   A fire extinguisher that can be used only on electrical fires.

U

UAC (User Access Control)   A Windows dialog box that appears and asks permission to do something that might be harmful or change the operating system environment. Some changes require an administrator password to continue.

UART (universal asynchronous receiver/transmitter)   A chip that coordinates the serial port or device activity.

Ubuntu Software Center   A software manager to access Ubuntu's repositories of open source software. It can install new applications and uninstall existing ones, many of which are available for free.

UDP (User Datagram Protocol)   A Layer 4 connectionless standard that applications use to communicate with a remote device.

UEFI (Unified Extensible Firmware Interface)   The replacement for the traditional BIOS that has a boot manager instead of the BIOS controlling the boot processor. The UEFI environment allows for a graphic interface, the use of a mouse, antivirus software to be used before the operating system loads, and Internet access.

UL 1449 VPR   A voltage protection rating standard developed by Underwriters Laboratories to measure the maximum amount of voltage a surge protector allows through to attached devices.

ultra HD   A display technology that is also known as 4K. It has four times as many pixels as a 1080p display.

unable to install printer   Check cabling and power; follow the manufacturer's instructions; delete the print driver and try installation again; download a different print driver and try installation again; research error on manufacturer's website and document.

unattended installation   A method of installing Windows where the remote computer does not have to be touched. Use Microsoft Deployment Toolkit with Configuration Manager.

unbuffered memory   Memory that does not delay all data transfers by one clock tick to ensure accuracy as registered memory does. Used in low- to medium-powered computers.

unbuffered SDRAM   A type of memory used frequently in low- to medium-priced home computers.

UNC (universal naming convention)   Used at the command prompt to obtain network shares.

undervoltage   A condition that occurs when AC power drops below 100 volts, which may cause the computer's power supply to draw too much current and overheat.

unity   The graphical user interface in Ubuntu. It has some similarities to the user interface of OS X; though, it is drastically different from Windows.

upgrade   Installing a newer or more powerful operating system where one already exists. An upgrade can also be installing newer hardware.

UPnP (universal plug and play)   An alternative to port forwarding that allows peer-to-peer (P2P) gaming applications to function without further configuration.

UPS (uninterruptible power supply)   A device that provides power for a limited time to a computer or device during a power outage.

upstream   Describes information that is sent to the Internet, such as transmitting email or uploading a file to a server.

upstream port   A USB port that connects a computer to another computer or another hub.

URL (uniform resource locator)   A method of accessing Internet resources.

usable host numbers   The number of host bits (and associated IP addresses) that can be used by network devices residing in a subnetwork.

usable subnets   The number of subnetworks that can be used when an IP network number is subdivided to allow more efficient use of IP addresses.

USB (universal serial bus)   A bus that allows 127 devices to be connected to a single computer port.

USB A-to-USB B converter   Connector cable with a USB A plug and a USB B plug.

USB flash drive   Sometimes called a flash drive or a memory stick, a drive that allows storage via a USB port.

USB OTG (USB on the go)   Allows two USB devices to communicate without the use of a PC or a hub that is backward compatible with the USB 2.0 standard.

USB port   A port on a motherboard or on an adapter that allows the connection of up to 127 devices.

USB to Bluetooth   An adapter that connects Bluetooth to a laptop or mobile device that has a USB port.

USB-to-Ethernet converter   Connector cable with a USB plug and an Ethernet end.

USB to RJ-45 dongle   An adapter that connects Bluetooth to a laptop or mobile device that has a USB port.

USB to Wi-Fi dongle   An adapter that connects Bluetooth to a laptop or mobile device that has a USB port.

USB Type-A   An upstream male connector on a USB cable that connects to an upstream Type-A port on a host computer or other hub.

USB Type-B   A downstream male connector on a USB cable that connects to a Type-B connector on the downstream device.

USB Type-C   A reversible plug connector for USB devices and hosts, and which will eventually replace USB Type-A/Type-B plugs.

user profile   All settings associated with a specific user, including desktop settings, network configurations, and applications that the user has access to. It is part of the registry.

USMT (User State Migration Tool)   A Windows tool used when deploying a large number of Windows computers.

UTM (unified threat management)   A security device that provides multiple functions such as content filtering, antivirus, antispyware, antimalware, firewall, and intrusion detection and prevention.

UTP (unshielded twisted pair)   The most common network cable. Comes in different categories for different uses. See also *twisted-pair cable*.

V

vertical lines   May be caused by debris on the corona wires or in the developer unit in the cartridge. Replace cartridge.

vertical streaking   Can occur because of toner cartridge. Remove toner cartridge, hold toner cartridge in front of you with both hands and rock it gently back and forth, re-insert cartridge into printer and test printer.

VGA (video graphics array)   A type of monitor that displays at least a 640×480 resolution or greater and connects to a 15-pin D-shell connector.

VGA mode   Oversized images or icons on the display screen.

VGA port   A type of 15-pin three-row video port that normally has a CRT monitor attached.

vi   A command-line text editor used by OS X and Linux.

video capture card   An adapter that allows video to be taken from a camera, DVD, recorder, or live video, edited if necessary, and saved.

viewable size   The diagonal length of an LCD screen.

virtual assistant   A mobile operating feature that uses voice commands to obtain information such as directions and current sports scores, and dictate emails or text.

virtualization   A process that allows a computer to run multiple operating systems without affecting each other, share hardware, and provide a test environment for software that may not be compatible on a specific platform.

virtualization support   A BIOS/UEFI option to enable or disable the capability of the computer to be used in a virtualization environment where more than one operating system can share the same hardware resources.

virtualization workstation   A computer that has multiple operating systems in a virtual environment in which one operating system has no interaction with the other operating system; they are independent of one another. A virtualization PC has multiple powerful multicore processors, maximum RAM, multiple fast large-capacity hard drives, 1Gb/s network connection, virtualization software, and a possible NAS.

virtual machine   A way for an operating system to appear as a separate computer to each application. One computer that has two or more operating systems installed that are unaware of each other due to virtualization software.

virtual memory   A method of simulating extra memory by using the hard disk space as if it were RAM.

virtual printing   Printing to somewhere other than to the directly connected printer and to a specific file so that the information can be viewed, saved, emailed, or sent to another printer.

virtual XP mode   A Windows Vista/7 tool that was previously known as Windows XP Mode that can be downloaded and used in Windows Vista/7 Professional and higher versions to allow older applications to run.

virus   A program designed to change the way a computer originally operated.

VIS (viewable image size)   The actual area of a monitor seen by a user.

VoIP (Voice over IP)   A way of sending phone calls over the Internet or over networks that traditionally transmitted only data.

volatile memory   Memory that does not remain when power is removed.

volt   The measurement for voltage.

voltage   An electronic measurement of the pressure pushing electrons through a circuit. Voltage is measured in volts.

voltage (BIOS)   A BIOS/UEFI option used in overclocking.

volume   A section of a storage device that receives a drive letter and data can be written to it.

VPN (virtual private network)   A remote computer connecting to a remote network by "tunneling" over an intermediate network, such as the Internet or a LAN.

W

Wake on LAN   A BIOS and adapter feature that allows a network administrator to remotely control power to a workstation and allows a computer to come out of the sleep mode.

Wake on Ring   A BIOS and adapter feature that allows a computer to come out of sleep mode when the telephone rings, so the computer can accept fax, email, and so on, when the user is absent.

WAN (wide area network)   Two or more LANs communicating, often across large distances. The most famous WAN is the Internet.

warm boot   Restarting a computer by pressing Ctrl + Alt + Delete or by clicking the Windows Restart option. Puts less strain on a computer than a cold boot.

waterproofing   A mobile device accessory that protects against liquid damage. Waterproofing options come in different levels of protection.

watt   The electrical measure in which computer power supplies are rated.

wearable devices   Mobile devices worn on one's person, such as smart watches, fitness monitors, headsets, and even glasses.

wear leveling   The process of writing and erasing data in different memory blocks of SSDs (solid state drives) to prolong the life of the drive.

web cam   Short for web camera, a small camera used for communicating via video across the Internet.

web server   A computer configured to provide web-based content that is accessed through a web browser.

WEP (Wired Equivalent Privacy)   A type of encryption that is sometimes used in wireless networks.

WiBro (mobile Wireless Broadband)   Also known as mobile WiMAX, it allows wireless connectivity for moving devices, such as those on a bus or train.

Wi-Fi analyzer   Used to identify what wireless networks are in the area, what frequencies (channels) are used, and to find a less crowded channel for any wireless installations, hotspot, or tethering that may be needed in a particular area. Also known as a wireless locator.

Wi-Fi antenna   Attaches to a WLAN card to receive or transmit wireless signals.

Wi-Fi calling   A common mobile device app used to make phone calls using a Wi-Fi connection rather than a cell phone network.

wildcard   A special character used at the command prompt when typing commands. The **?** character is used to designate "any" for a single character place, whereas the * character denotes any characters from that place forward.

WiMAX   A wireless technology that could be used to connect the Internet with a large-scale coverage area and access speeds up to 1Gb/s. Also used for connectivity as part of a cellular network.

Windows Aero   See *Aero*.

Windows Defender   A Windows application that detects spyware.

Windows Explorer   See *Explorer*.

Windows Memory Diagnostic Tool   A tool used to thoroughly test RAM.

Windows Mobile   Microsoft-developed closed source operating systems for mobile devices.

Windows Storage Spaces   A Windows 8/10 technology that allows combining different types of storage devices into one writable space.

Windows Store   A Microsoft site where apps can be purchased and downloaded.

Windows Upgrade Advisor   A Microsoft tool that can be downloaded and executed to determine if a computer can function well with a higher version of Windows installed.

Windows XP mode   See *virtual XP mode*.

WinRE (Windows Recovery Environment)   An alternative to Console Recovery found on the Windows Vista and 7 installation disc that includes multiple tools used to troubleshoot Windows when it does not work properly.

wireless access point   A device that receives and transmits data from multiple computers that have wireless NICs installed. The access point can be a stand-alone unit or it can be integrated into an ADSL router.

wireless broadband   A feature available from service providers that allows PC Cards, USB modems, mobile data cards, or integrated laptop connectivity to have the capability to receive, create, and communicate Internet information within a specific coverage area.

wireless card   Also known as a wireless NIC. Electronic device that allows wireless network connectivity.

wireless hotspot   A place where wireless Internet connectivity is available.

wireless network   A type of network that uses air as the media to connect devices.

wire stripper   A tool used when adding a connector onto a network cable.

WLAN (Wireless LAN)   A wireless network that consists of an access point and some wireless devices including laptops, tablets, and smartphones.

workgroup   A term given to a peer-to-peer Windows network. A workgroup does not use a server to authenticate users during the login process.

worm   A virus program that replicates from one drive to another. The most common worm virus today is an email message that, when opened, sends the virus to every address in the user's address book.

WPA (Wi-Fi Protected Access)   A data encryption program that uses Temporal Key Integrity Protocol (TKIP) or Advanced Encryption Standard (AES) to improve security.

WPA2   An improvement over WPA that includes dynamic negotiation between the AP and the client for authentication and encryption algorithms. It is a common choice for securing wireless networks.

WPAD (Web Proxy Autodiscovery)   A method of discovering the proxy server IP address and port number.

WPS (Wi-Fi Protected Settings)   A method used to easily configure a wireless device for the SSID and WPA2 security.

write amplification   The minimum amount of storage space affected by a request to write data on a solid state drive. For example, if the SSD has a 128KB erase block with a 4KB file to be saved, 128KB of memory is erased before the 4KB file is written.

WRP (Windows Resource Protection)   A tool that protects system files and registry keys in Windows.

WWAN (wireless wide area network)   A wireless network that extends across more than one county such as when WiMAX is used.

X-Y

XCOPY   An external command that transfers files from one place to another in the command prompt environment.

xD (extreme digital)   A storage device with nonvolatile flash memory used for mobile devices.

xDSL   Used to describe the various types of digital subscriber lines (DSLs) available for connecting to the Internet. Examples include ADSL, CDSL, DSL Lite, HDSL, RADSL, SDSL, VDSL, and x2/DSL.

XON/XOFF   A method of handshaking that uses special control characters to coordinate data transmissions.

XMP (extreme memory profile)   A type of memory module that allows the BIOS/UEFI to configure voltage and timing settings.

Z

zero day attack   A vulnerability in a particular software application that is found by hackers before it is known or fixed by the developer of the application.

ZIF socket (zero insertion force socket)   A common CPU socket that has a lever that provides easy access for CPU removal.

ZIP (zigzag inline package)   A type of chip packaging that had offset pins. Similar to DIP but not as wide.

zombie   A device that has been hacked and is controlled by someone else or that carries out malicious tasks.

ZTI (zero-touch installation)   A method of imaging a computer without having to physically touch the computer. Commonly used in a corporate environment.

GLOSSARY

Index

INDEX

INDEX

D

INDEX

INDEX

INDEX

INDEX

INDEX

INDEX

INDEX